Marriages *and* Obituaries *from* The Macon Messenger

1818-1865

Compiled by:
Willard Rocker

Southern Historical Press
Greenville, South Carolina

Copyright 1988
By: The Rev. Silas Emmett Lucas, Jr.

All rights reserved. No part of this publication may be reproduced, stored in a retrieval system, transmitted in any form, posted on to the web in any form or by any means without the prior written permission of the publisher.

Please direct all correspondence and orders to:

www.southernhistoricalpress.com
or
**SOUTHERN HISTORICAL PRESS, Inc.
PO BOX 1267
375 West Broad Street
Greenville, SC   29601
southernhistoricalpress@gmail.com**

ISBN #0-89308-340-2

Printed in the United States of America

INTRODUCTION

The marriage and death notices contained in this volume have been abstracted from the newspaper holdings of the Genealogy Department of the Washington Memorial Library in Macon, Georgia. These particular abstracts are taken from the *Georgia Messinger* (in publication at Macon, Georgia, 1825-April 8, 1847) and the *Georgia Journal and Messenger* (in publication at Macon, Georgia, April 15, 1847, through November 13, 1869). Both were weekly publications. The time span covered by these abstracts represents the inclusive publications dates.

Willard L. Rocker

FROM THE GEORGIA MESSENGER (MACON, GEORGIA)

May 19, 1823

Horrid Murder! On the 14th inst. Mr. JOHN M. WILLIAMS of Jones County, near Clinton, after inhumanly beating and stabbing, cut his wife, throat - or rather, cut her head almost off - leaving a space of but an inch or inch and a half on the back part of her neck that was not cut. Our informant says, the remainder appeared to be cut to the bone. After having completed this horrid act, he turned the edge of his razor (the instrument used) upon his own throat, and while in this act a neighbour rode up and took the razor from him. He is yet alive, but so bad is his wound, that his life is nearly despaired of. He has left four small children - one only ten days old.

May 19, 1823

MR. JAMES S. RICHARDSON was killed in Sparta on Tuesday evening last by a fall from the window of his apartment, in the second story of the Eagle Tavern. He was not discovered until a late hour in the evening - when found, the vital spark was extinct. He was a native of England and a teacher of music. (Patriot)

June 9, 1823

Died in Louisville, on the first inst. in the 16th year of her age, MRS. JANE ANN GRANBERRY, consort of George Granberry, Esq. Mrs. Granberry was the only daughter of a fond parent, and the wife of an affectionate husband, who a little more than five months ago led her to the altar (with eulogy).

June 9, 1823

Yesterday a man by the name of JAMES BROWN was found drowned in Walnut Creek near the bridge, on the road leading to Milledgeville, about a mile from this place. The verdict of an inquest held over him, that he "came to his death by violence."

June 23, 1823

Died in this county on the 31st of May, MR. GEORGE WILSON, about 40 years of age.

July 28, 1823

Died on the 21st inst. MISS ANNE L. RUTHERFORD, in the 25th year of her age - daughter of James and Elizabeth Rutherford, of Scriven county, dec'd.

Aug. 11, 1823

Died, at Richmond, Va. on the 2d inst. MR. MARCUS LEVI, for thirty years well known in that city. He was of the Hebrew congregation and considered an expert in most of the rituals of that people.

Aug. 18, 1823

Died in Marion, on the 5th inst. SUSAN, daughter of EDWIN HART, ESQ. aged 16 years (with eulogy).

Aug. 18, 1823

JOSHUA BARTON, ESQ. attorney of the U.S. for the District of Missouri, was killed in a duel at St. Louis, on the 30th ult. which grew out of a publication in one of the newspapers, touching the proceedings at the last session of Congress, concerning the Surveyor General's accounts.

Aug. 25, 1823

WILLIAM TEMPLE FRANKLIN, grandson of Dr. Franklin, and editor of his works, died on the 15th of May last, at Paris. The Paris Constitutional of the 18th of June contains an obituary notice of the deceased.

Sep. 8, 1823

Drowned on the 18th ult. off Cape Look Out, MR. RICHARD POWELL, (while on his passage on board the sloop Express, from Baltimore to Charleston), a native of Louisville, Ge. aged 35. He was taken with a fit and fell overboard.

Sep. 8, 1823

Died in Clinton, Jones Co. on the 30th ult. after a short sickness, COLIN MURCHISON, aged 26 years; a native of North Carolina. He was a member of the Volunteer Company of this place, commanded by Capt. Davis, and was interred with military honors by said company, on the 31st.

Sep. 22, 1823

Notice of the death of HON. ELIJAH BOARDMAN, Senator of the United States from the State of Connecticut.

Sep. 22, 1823

The REV. WM. WARD, an active and zealous Baptist Missionary, died at Serampore, (East Indies,) of the cholera morbus, after an illness of one day, on the 7th of March last.

Sep. 29, 1823

DANIEL STURGES, Esq. Surveyor General of this State, died in Milledgeville on the 17th inst. Benjamin H. Sturges, his son, had been appointed, to that office by the Executive.

Oct. 8, 1823

Died in Virginia, on the 15th ult. JOHN W. EPPES, Esq. formerly a distinguished member of Congress from that state.

Oct. 8, 1823

Died in Fort Hawkins, on Friday morning, the 3rd inst. of intermittent, MRS. FRANCES BIDDLE WOOD, consort of Mr. Samuel Wood, and granddaughter of the late Judge Biddle of Pennsylvania and niece of Marks John Biddle Esq. of the same state, in the 33rd year of her age (with eulogy).

Oct. 15, 1823

Died at Philadelphia, on Sunday the 14th ult. GEN. HENRY LALLEMAND, one of Bonaparte's brave and intelligent officers. He had resided in the United States a considerable time, and was much esteemed by those who knew him. His Treatise on Artillery has been translated by Professor Renwick of N.Y. and adopted by the war department, as the manual of the American Artillery Corps.

Oct. 15, 1823

Died in Somerset county, Md. MRS. MARY PARKS, aged 115 years and five months.

Oct. 15, 1823

Died at Philadelphia, com. JOHN SHAW, of the U.S. Navy, aged 50.

Oct. 15, 1823

   Died in Hartford, Pulaski County, on the 3d inst. MR. ROBERT L. CHURCH, a native of R. Island, aged about 26.

Oct. 22, 1823

   Died in Macon on the 19th inst. after a painful illness of 19 days, MR. ISSACHAR BATES, age 29 years, late of Thompson Conn. His remains were committed to the ground with Masonic honors in Fort Hawkins on the 21st.

Oct. 22, 1823

   Died in Columbia county, on the 5th inst. the wife of Dr. Lewis French, (formerly JULIA ANN NEWTON of New Haven, Conn.) aged 27.

Oct. 29, 1823

   Died at the residence of Dr. Collins, in Twiggs County on the 19th inst. THOMAS I. PACE, age 13 years, son of Major Thomas Pace of Washington Co.

Nov. 5, 1823

   Died in Macon on the 1st inst., MR. CHAUNCEY CLARK, age 23, a native of Wethersfield, Conn. His funeral was attended with the honors of Masonry.

Nov. 5, 1823

   Died in Macon on the 4th inst. MRS. ROXANA K. BATES, aged 25, widow of Mr. Isachar Bates, (whose death was noticed in the Messenger two weeks since), and a native of Woodstock, Conn. She has left an orphan son aged 15 months. She had long been a member of the Presbyterian Church.

Nov. 5, 1823

   Departed this transitory life on the 24th ult. in Jones county, ROBERT MATHEWS, son of Collin W. Alexander, Esq. aged 21 months.

Nov. 12, 1823

   On Friday the 7th instant, agreeably to sentence, JOHN M. WILLIAMS was executed in Clinton for the murder of his wife. (with detailed story).

Nov. 26, 1823

   Died in Milledgeville on Sunday night last, after a short illness, WILLIAM ROBERTSON, ESQ. late Secratary of the Senate, which office he filled with credit for about 30 years.

Jan. 7, 1824

   RUFUS PUTNAM, brigadier general by brevet at the close of the Revolutionary War, and one of the first if not the first settler in Ohio, lately died in Marietta, aged 90 years.

Mar. 17, 1824

   Died in Beaufort District, S.C. after a lingering illness, MRS. SUSAN G. FRIARSON, wife of James S. Friarson, Esq. of Fort Hawkins.

June 9, 1824

   Died in Baltimore on 24th May, GEN. WM. H. WINDER, aged 49.

June 9, 1824

Died in Marietta, (Ohio,) GEN. RUFUS PUTNAM, aged 86. He engaged in the old French and Indian War at the age of sixteen, and was an active officer in the war of revolution. In 1788 he raised a company of forty adventurers and formed the settlement in Ohio, at the mouth of the Muskingum. He afterwards held the appointments of Judge of the Supreme court of the Northwest Territory, and Surveyor General of the U. States.

June 23, 1824

Died on board the U.S. frigate Constitution, at New York, on the 2d inst. CAPTAIN EVANS, of the U.S. Navy, Commander of the New York Station. While ascending the side of the Consitution, in perfect health he ruptured a blood vessel and died in twenty minutes afterwards.

June 30, 1824

Died in this town on the 28th inst., MR. SAMUEL KNAPP, aged 21 years. He was on his way from Mobile to Connecticut (His native state) and was taken sick immediately on arriving here, and survived but six days.

July 21, 1824

Died in New Haven, Conn. LIEUT. TIMOTHY MIX, aged 85; he served in the campaign against Canada in the year 1775 as surgeon's mate. At the taking of Stoney Point by the English during the revolutionary war was, whilst in the act of firing his piece, his right hand was shot off, when he instantly seized the match with his left hand, and fired the piece, in consequence of which, 40 of the enemy fell. The number of his descendants amounted to 100...9 children, 63 grandchildren, and 28 great-grandchildren.

Aug. 4, 1824

Died in Houston County, THOMAS MACKEY - a person well known in this vicinity.

Aug. 11, 1824

Died on the 3rd inst., at his residence in Lexington, STEPHEN UPSON, ESQ. He had been for several years an active member of the Legislature. In him Georgia has lost a grate, a useful, and an honest man. (Newspaper of August 18th contains a long obituary on him-states he was a native of Conn., attended Yale, came to Georgia in 1807, is survived by a widow and five children).

Sept. 8, 1824

Died on Monday, the 16th Aug. in Lower Marion Township, Montgomery County, Penn., the venerable CHARLES THOMPSON, ESQ. in the 95th year of his age. He was one of the most vertuous, stedfast, energetic, and useful patriots of the Revolution. He enjoyed as sole Secretary of the Revolutionary Congress, the highest confidence of that body.

Sept. 8, 1824

Died in Franklin county, Missouri, on the 6th ult. JOSEPH JONES MONROE, ESQ., brother of the President of the United States.

Sept. 8, 1824

The National Intelligencer of 24th Aug. announces the death of JOHN TAYLOR of Caroline, Virginia, a Senator of the United States.

Sept. 29, 1824

COL. NICHOLAS WARE, one of the Senators to Congress from this state, died in New York where he had been for some weeks confined with a disease which, before he left this place, had excited strenuous apprehensions as to its consequences; left wife and several children (Aug. Chronicle).

Oct. 27, 1824

Died in New York harbor, on the 8th inst. on board U.S. Store ship Decoy, just arrived from the West Indies, LT. GAMBLE of the U.S. Navy.

Oct. 27, 1824

Murder! On Saturday last, MR. JOSEPH WHITE and a lady, who resided in the fork of the Coosa and Talapoosa rivers, about half a mile from the Indian line, in this county were inhumanly murdered, it is supposed by the Indians. It appears that about ten o'clock on Saturday night last, a number of Indians or other persons, yet uncertain, entered the house of Mr. W. and inflicted on him ten or twelve wounds, apparently with a tomahawk; and after murdering him they set fire to the house, in which a lady who had been acting as house-keeper for Mr. White perished. On making their excape, they fired a rifle ball into the house of a Mr. Spragins, a neighbour of Mr. White, and shot him in the mouth. (Montgomery Republican)

Dec. 1, 1824

Murdered! HENRY HILL who was employed as a ferryman at Macon was killed Sunday morning by Joseph S. Loring in an altercation; he sustained several heavy blows from a heavy stick in Loring's hands, dying the next day (Monday) of his injuries.

Feb. 2, 1825

Died at Baltimore, on the 14th instant, the HON. ROBERT GOODLOE HARPER, a distinguished citizen of that place - an eminent lawyer and formerly a member of Congress.

Feb. 2, 1825

Died at New Haven, Conn. on the 8th instant, ELI WHITNEY ESQ. aged 59; inventor of the cotton gin (long obituary with eulogy).

May 18, 1825

Died in Augusta, on the 6th inst. of a pulmonary complaint with which he had been long visited, ROBERT WALKER, ESQ. late Judge of the Superior Courts of the Middle Circuit of this state, in the 51st year of his age.

May 25, 1825

Drowned! A person named THOMAS SMITH was drowned in this place, near the Ferry, on Sunday last. While crossing the river, with three others, in a batteau, it was purposly upset near the bank, and all got on shore without difficulty...

June 8, 1825

Drowned - On Wednesday last, the body of a young man named DANIEL McKAY was found in the Ocmulgee, in this town. He is supposed to have fallen into the river on Tuesday night while in a state of intoxication. We understand that he was recently from Richmond county, N. Carolina, where his relations reside.

June 29, 1925

    Died at his residence in Staten Island on 11th inst., DANIEL D. TOMPKINS, ESQ., late Vice-President of the United States, in his 51st year.

Sep. 28, 1825

    Died at his residence in Baldwin County, on Thursday, 22 Sept. JOHN MILES ESQ. in the 67th year of his age - In his death society has lost another veteran of 76 - the Baptist church (of which he was a member for 35 years) one among its brightest ornaments - the orphan and the widow a generous friend. He has left a wife and nine children to mourn his loss.

Sept. 28, 1825

    Died in Twiggs County, on the 24th inst. the REV. VINCENT A THARP, aged about 60 years. He had been for many years one exemplary and zealous preacher of the Baptist denomination.

Nov. 9, 1825

    Died on Saturday the 8th inst. at Mifflintown, Pa. HENRY BRACKBILL, SEN. aged 99 years and 7 months. This interesting old man was born in Philadelphia in 1726, in March, and served in the British army at the taking of Havenna, 1754... (extensive biographical data in the obituary).

Dec. 21, 1825

    Died in Milledgeville, on Sunday morning last, after a short illness of the pleurisy, JOHN ABERCROMBIE, ESQ. a member of the House of Representatives from Hancock county - He has been an active member of that branch of the Legislature for several years, and last year filled the Speaker's chair.

Feb. 15, 1826

    Died at Camp Morgan, Marshal's Ferry, on Flint River, on the 2d inst. of the pleurisy, DAVID COX, a traveller, supposed to belong in Georgia - and to be aged about 23.

Mar. 15, 1826

    Died at Washington, a few days since, the HON. JOHN GAILLARD, a member of the Senate of the U.S. from South Carolina. He has for several sessions been President pro tem of that branch of Congress.

Mar. 22, 1826

    Died in this town, on the 16th inst. MRS. JUDITH S. COLEMAN, wife of Robert Coleman, Esq. in the 40th year of her age. (with eulogy.)

Apr. 19, 1826

    Died at his residence in Bibb county, on the 15th inst. of the influenza, JOHN DAVIS ESQ. He had served as a Justice of the Inferior Court of Burke County many years ago, then moved to Twiggs County where he held the same office there; and on the organization of Bibb County was elected to same office there.

May 3, 1826

    Murdered! MAJ. JOSEPH MORGAN was shot in the head and killed in his bed while asleep by HUGH GALLAGHER, a drunken Irish employee, who had been quite disorderly and unruly and who Maj. Morgan made go to bed for the night. Arising later in the night, Gallagher took a gun and went to Maj. Morgan's bed and shot him. He escaped but was found and arrested the nest day. Maj. Morgan lived on the

(May 3, 1826, cont'd.)   road to Marion and was Cashier of the Branch here of the Bank of Darien, and previously held the same office at Marion.

June 21, 1826

Died in this town on the 18th instant of the consumption, MRS. MARTHA B. DAWSON, wife of the late Wm. W. Dawson, and formerly of Northampton county, North Carolina.

June 28, 1826

Died, in New-Haven, Conn. on the 9th inst. REV. JEDIDIAH MORSE, D.D. LL.D. aged 65. Dr. M. had been well known as a laborious Minister of the Gospel, and the author of several works of merit.

July 5, 1826

Died in Savannah, on the 24th ult. MR. HUGH McNIEL, a Merchant of this place, aged about 27 years. Mr. McNiel had for several months been in ill health. He left here for its benefit, a short time previous to his death, intending to visit his relations in Scotland of which country he was a native. Soon after arriving in Savannah, his illness increased, so that he was unable to embark, and he survived but a few days. By his death, Macon has lost an upright and worthy citizen.

July 11, 1826

Died in this town on the 6th inst. ISABELLA CATHERINE, only child of MR. RALPH KING, aged one year and eight months (with poem of death).

July 18, 1826

Obituary of President THOMAS JEFFERSON.

July 25, 1826

Obituary of President JOHN ADAMS.

Aug. 1, 1826

Died in this place on Friday the 28th ult. MR. JOSEPH CLARK, in the 37th year of his age, after a long and lingering illness of 9 weeks, which he bore with christian fortitude. He has left an affectionate wife and children to lament their irreparable loss. He was a native of New-York, but a resident of this place.

Aug. 8, 1826

Died at Sparta, on Saturday the 22d inst. SOPHOS STAPLES, ESQ. Attorney at law, formerly of Connecticut.

Aug. 8, 1826

Murdered! A MR. WOODWARD of Twiggs County was recently murdered by two of his slaves while he was asleep.

Aug. 15, 1826

Departed this life on the 30th July last, at his residence in Upson county, after a severe illness, which he bore with christian fortitude, the REV. THOMAS LEVERETT, in the 50th year of his age. He was a pious, orderly member of the Baptist Church, and three years a Minister of the Gospel.

Aug. 29, 1826

Died in this place, on Wednesday last, MR. GEORGE DANE, Silversmith, a native of London, aged about 29 years.

Aug. 29, 1826

Died at Sarasota Springs, on the 17th ult. HENRY HARTFORD ESQ. of Darien, in the 51st year of his age.

Aug. 29, 1826

Died suddenly, at Sarasota Springs, on the 2d inst. HUGH TAYLOR, ESQ. an old and respectable inhabitant of Sparta, Georgia.

Sep. 19, 1826

Died in this county on the 10th inst. JOHN ARCHER, son of DAVID G. WORSHAM, aged five years eleven months, & one day.

Sep. 26, 1826

Died on Thursday last, at Camp Hope, about two miles from this place, MR. THOMAS STEWARD, a citizen of Augusta, and a native of Dumfries, Scotland, aged about 50 years. He has been a resident of Augusta about 25 years, where he acquired considerable reputation as an architect. Being in a very infirm state of health, he visited the Indian Springs, but failing to receive the expected benefit from them, he commenced his journey for home. While on his way, at the place above named, accompanied by a young man, a relative, he suddenly expired in his gig.

Oct. 3, 1826

Died on the 9th inst. of the prevailing fever, at the house of DR. DRURY SPAIN, in the Creek Nation, while on his way from Montgomery, Alabama, to New York, MR. HENRY FINCH, merchant, aged 30 years, a native of Connecticut.

Oct. 17, 1826

Died at his seat near Baltimore, on the 26th ult. CAPT. ROBERT TRAIL SPENCE, a distinguished officer of the U.S. Navy, and who, we have understood, had recently been appointed to the command of our squadron in the West Indies.

Oct. 17, 1826

Died at Lebanon Springs, N.Y. WILLIAM CRAFTS, ESQ. editor of the Charleston Courier, a scholar and a fine writer.

Oct. 24, 1826

Died in this place, on Sunday, the 22d inst. after a long and distressing illness, MR. JOHN GUYTON, in the 43d year of his age - a citizen of Dublin, Georgia. He was yesterday buried with Masonic Honors by Macon Lodge No. 34.

Oct. 31, 1826

Died at his residence in Forsyth, Monroe County, on the 21st inst. after a lingering and distressing illness of fourteen days, MR. EBER TOMPKINS, Merchant, formerly of Plymouth Litchfield Co. Conn. aged about 28 years. His remains were interred with masonic honors by the Brethren of Monroe Lodge, of which he was a member. (with eulogy).

Nov. 14, 1826

Died recently in Philadelphia, SELLECK OSBORN ESQ. a Poet of considerable eminence, and formerly a Republican Editor of several newspapers - particularly one in Connecticut, where in the heat of party times, he was imprisoned twelve months, for what the then ascendant party deemed libelious publications in his paper.

Nov. 14, 1826

    Died in this county, on the 6th inst. at the residence of Thomas Lundy, Esq. MR. PLEASANT N. WEST, aged about 23 years. From his individual papers, it appears that he was a native of North-Carolina, but the particular section is not designated. He had resided in Liberty County in this state, as an Overseer, and had been one of the Guard at the Penitentiary in Milledgeville. His friends are informed that he left a small sum of money, a watch and clothing, which his relatives may procure by application to Mr. Lundy.

Nov. 14, 1826

    Died in this town, on the 13th inst. MAJOR JOHN HUMPHRIES, aged about 50.

Nov. 14, 1826

    Died in Clinton, on the 7th inst. after a short indisposition, MR. JOHN HAMILTON, an esteemed and worthy young man.

Nov. 14, 1826

    Died in Milledgeville, on the 9th inst. MR. ORRIN SHAW, merchant of that place.

Nov. 21, 1826

    Died in this county, on the 14th inst. MR. ZACHARIAH WILLIAMSON, aged 74. He was a soldier through the war of our revolution, and fought in many battles.

Nov. 28, 1826

    Died on Saturday the 12th inst. Fair Hope, M'Intosh County, MAJ. GENERAL JOHN M'INTOSH, in his 72d year. This Gentleman at 20 years of age became an officer of the Revolutionary Army, and served during the whole period of the revolution with equal zeal and intrepidity (with eulogy.)

Dec. 12, 1826

    Died in this place, on the 10th inst., MR. CHESTER RIGGS, aged 50 years - a native of Middlebury, Conn.

Jan. 2, 1827

    Died after a lingering illness, at his residence in Covington, Newton county, on Sunday the 24th ultimo, JOEL FLANAGAN, ESQ. a Justice of the Inferior Court of Newton county (with eulogy).

Jan. 2, 1827

    Died at his father's residence in Twiggs county a few days ago, NATHANIEL PACE, son of Major Thomas Pace, aged 15 years.

Jan. 9, 1827

    Died at Lexington on the 19th ultimo, DOCTOR JOEL ABBOTT. His devotedness to Georgia, whose interests he assisted in promoting for several years as a member of Congress (Constitutionalist)

Jan. 23, 1827

    Died in this county, suddenly, on the 14th inst. MRS. MARTHA GAULDING; wife of John Gaulding; aged about 39 years; left bereaved husband and children; member of Methodist Church.

Apr. 10, 1827

Died in Warren county, North-Carolina, on the 16th ult. GEN. ROBERT R. JOHNSON, aged 49, He has left a wife (known in the vicinity as formerly the wife of Gov. Hawkins, dec.) and 7 children to deplore their loss.

Apr. 24, 1827

Died in Culpepper co. Va., MAJ. GABRIEL LONG, aged 76. He was the last surviving officer who commanded a company in Col. Morgan's celebrated Rifle Regiment, and was engaged in no less than eighteen actions. He left the advance at Saratoga, and commenced the battle with his own hand. In one of the engagements with Burgoyne, he saved the life of Lieut. White, now Judge White, of Virginia. Gen. Lafayette honoured him with the command of a large partisan corpse in his division, and he closed his military career at the capture of Lord Cornwallis.

May 15, 1827

Died at his residence in N York on the 29th ult. the HON. RUFUS KING, in the 73d year of his age.

May 29, 1827

Died at Rowley, Mass. on the 7th inst. after many months of extreme suffering, MR. ROBERT S. COFFIN well known throughout this country as the Boston Bard.

May 29, 1827

Died in Twiggs county, THEOPHILUS M. CHAMBERLAIN, Esq. a native of Halifax, N.B. but for several years a resident of that county.

June 19, 1827

Died in Clinton, on the 16th inst. MR. PETER PEASE, aged about 30.

July 17, 1827

Died in this place, on the 12th inst. of the cholera morbus, MR. CASWELL LESTER, aged probably, about 28, a resident of Lowndes County.

July 24, 1827

Died in this place, on Sunday the 15th inst. JUDITH HARRIET, daughter of MR. GEO. JEWETT, aged one year and 5 months.

Aug. 7, 1827

Died in this place on the 1st inst. ANDREW D. DOUGLAS, about 17 years, the only son of Mr. D-vid Douglas of this place.

Aug. 14, 1827

Died in Twiggs county, on the 7th inst. the REV. THEOPHILUS PEARCE, aged about 60 years, an exemplary christian and preacher of the Baptist denomination.

Aug. 21, 1827

Died in this place a few weeks ago, MAJOR HENRY TERRELL, about 70 years of age; he was formerly from Fauquier county, Virginia, but for many years had resided in different villages in Georgia. Major Terrell was one of the patriots of the revolution, in which, and the Indian wars, he was an active, daring and perservering soldier; was at the surrender of Lord Cornwallis at Yorktown, in many other battles, and in several Indian skirmishes. This veteran in years and perils, retained active bodily and mental energies,

(Aug. 21, 1827 cont'd.) all within a few days of his death; having, as late as the evening of his life, partaken of the enjoyment of a deer chase.

Aug. 21, 1827

Died on Thursday morning the 9th inst., the HON. JOHN ELLIOTT, late a Senator in the Congress of the U.S. from the State of Georgia. (with eulogy)

Sep. 4, 1827

Died at Covington, Newton county, on Friday the 24th of August, after an illness of five days, REBECCA FRANCES RHEA, daughter of Andrew Rhea, of Fayetteville, Geo. and sister to the junior editor of this paper (with eulogy).

Sep. 4, 1827

Died in Jones county on Saturday morning, the 24th ult. after a short but severe illness, in the 13th year of her age, MISS SARAH, eldest daughter of MR. JOHN DORSEY. Also, in the same county, a few days ago, CADWELL MITCHELL, ESQ. a respectable planter of Jones county.

Sep. 4, 1827

Died in Hancock county, on the 22d ult. GEN. EPPES BROWN, aged about 60. Gen. B. was for many years a senator in the legislature, and uniformly a co-worker with the Republicans.

Sep. 11, 1827

Died on the 15th August, at his residence in Beaufort, S. Carolina, MR. CARLOS TRACY, a native of Conn. and for many years a resident of Georgia.

Sep. 18, 1827

Died in Macon on the 17th inst. in the twenty second year of her age, MRS. LUCY V. POWLEDGE, consort of Mr. Philip Powledge, and daughter of F.H. Godfrey, Esq. Mrs. Powledge lingered for eighteen months under a deep consumption, which eventually severed her from the things of this world.

Sep. 18, 1827

Died on the 15th inst. MARY HENRIETTA, infant daughter of Mr. JOHN T. ROWLAND, aged about 4 months.

Sep. 18, 1827

Died in Caswell county, N.C. on the 15th ult. in the 88th year of his age, GEN. ARCHIMEDES DONOHO, of bilious fever, of six days duration. The deceased was an officer in the U. States' army during the late war, and served with fidelity and credit and in the south. At the close of that contest he resigned his commission, returned home, and settled in Milton, N.C. devoting his attention chiefly to agricultural pursuits.

Sep. 18, 1827

Died at his residence in Laurens county, on the 9th inst. WILLIAM FULLWOOD, ESQ. in the 28th year of his age.

Sep. 25, 1827

Died in Monroe county on the 31st day of July, MR. CHARLES M. POTTER (?), a native of the state of New York. He died of the cholera morbus.

Sep. 25, 1827

Died in this place, on the 20th inst. JOEL RUSHIN, ESQ. for several years a resident of this place.

Sep. 25, 1827

The public are already apprised of the death of CAPT. MATTHEW TALBOT. He died at his seat in Wilkes county on Tuesday morning the 18th inst. after three days illness of billious fever; member of state constitution of 1798, as one of the delagates from Wilkes; member of the State Senate, President of that body for five years (with eulogy).

Oct. 2, 1827

Died in Augusta, on the 23d ult. after a protracted illness, FREEMAN WALKER, ESQ.

Oct. 23, 1827

Died in this vicinity, on the 21st inst. of a lingering consumption, CAPT. PETER LEQUEX, in the 41st year of his age. Captain L. was formerly a captain in the U.S. army, but for the last two years, resided in this place (with eulogy).

Oct. 30, 1827

Died in Covington, Newton county, on the 14th inst. MRS. NAOMI J. STEWART, after a short and severe affliction of two days (with eulogy)

Oct. 30, 1827

Died in this place on the 18th inst. WILLIAM F. son of ALEXANDER D. and EMILY C. BROWN, aged one year and ten months (with poem).

Nov. 13, 1827

Died at Fort Hawkins, yesterday evening, MR. NATH'L CORNWELL, of the firm Cutter-Cornwell-an illustrious and enterprising merchant and worthy citizen.

Nov. 20, 1827

Died in this place, on the 15th instant, MR. JOSEPH WILSON, about 65 years of age; he was formerly from Petersburg, Va.

Nov. 20, 1827

Died near Fort Hawkins, on the 18th instant, MR. MURPHEY CHAMPION.

Nov. 20, 1827

Died at his residence near Clinton, a few days ago, RICHARD HARRIS, Esquire, a wealthy and respectable planter of Jones county.

Nov. 27, 1827

Died in Jones county on the 16th inst. MRS. LOUISA MEASLES, wife of Mr. Wm. Measles.

Dec. 4, 1827

Died in Raleigh on Friday night last, after a short and distressing illness, MRS. ALTONA H. FORSTER, aged 30, relict of the late Rev. Anthony Forster, of Charleston, S.C. and daughter of Joseph Gales, Esq. (with eulogy).

Dec. 4, 1827

>Died also, on Sunday morning, in the 73d year of his age, JOHN HAYWOOD, ESQ. Public Treasurer of the State, which office he has filled for the long term of 41 years (with eulogy-<u>Raleigh Register</u>).

Dec. 4, 1827

>Died in New York, on Wednesday evening, the 14th inst. THOMAS ADAM (?) EMMET, ESQ. He was seized about two o'clock, on that day with an alarming attack of appoplexy whilst engaged in the Circuit Court of the United States, as one of the counsel in the cause of the Sailor's Snug Harbor. (Also quotes notice from the <u>New York Statesman</u> of the 15th inst.).

Jan. 1, 1828

>Died in Laurens county, on 1st inst. MRS. ELIZA TUCKER, consort of Dr. Nathan Tucker. She was a most amiable woman, in every respect, and her loss will long be deplored by a bereaved husband and child, and numerous relatives and friends.

Jan. 21, 1828

>Died in this place, on Saturday morning, after a short illness, THOMAS A BILLUPS, ESQ. - formerly of Greene county, but for sometime past a resident of Macon. He was interred on Sunday morning by Macon Lodge, with the honors of masonry.

Feb. 11, 1828

>Died in this town, on the 4th inst. MRS. ANNA D. BATES, wife of Thomas G. Bates, Esq.

Mar. 3, 1828

>Obituary of GOVERNOR DE WITT CLINTON - died 11th inst. very suddenly, either from an apolectic fit or by the rupture of a blood vessel near the heart.

Mar. 10, 1828

>Died at Washington, on the 24th ult. after a short illness, MAJOR GENERAL JACOB BROWN, Commander in chief of the army of the United States.

April 7, 1828

>Died in Monticello on the 4th inst., COL. NATHAN WARNER.

Apr. 7, 1828

>A newspaper account of the testimony given at the trial of The State vs. WM. FIELDS for the murder of JAMES O. ABBOTT.

Apr. 21, 1828

>Died at Washington, Wilkes county, on the 5th inst. JOHN K.M. CHARLTON, ESQ. formerly one of the Editors of the Augusta Chronicle, and recently Editor of the Washington News.

May 17, 1828

>Died in this town, on Tuesday last, CAPT. ANDREW JETER, aged 75, a soldier of the Revolution. On Wednesday his body was interred with Masonic and Military honors, by the Macon Lodge and Capt. Danelly's Company of Macon Volumteers.

May 17, 1828

Died in Washington city, on the 2d inst. the HON. THOMAS TUDOR TUCKER, Treasurer of the United States, in the 84th year of his age. He had been confined to his bed, by the malady which terminated his life, for thirteen weeks, and died in the entire possession of his faculties, and in the most resigned and pious frame of mind. Was Representative from the State of South-Carolina in the Congress of the United States (National Intel.)

May 31, 1828

Died in Jones county, on the 24th inst. JOHN JENKINS, ESQ.

May 31, 1828

Died in Macon, MR. CHARLES P. CLEMENCE, aged about 24 - formerly of Stirbridge, Mass.

June 14, 1828

Died in this place, on Sunday last, DAVID WASHINGTON, son of MR. JEREMIAH SMITH, aged 9 months and 10 days.

Aug. 9, 1828

Died near Clinton, Jones county, on the 31st ult. MRS. SARAH MORTON, aged 58 years. She was an esteemed member of the Baptist church.

Aug. 9, 1828

DUNCAN G. CAMPBELL is dead. Left widow and orphan.

Aug. 9, 1828

Died at the residence of his son-in-law, Mr. Chrystie (Clarystie?), of Fishkill, New York in his 81st year. He was born in Maryland in 1748 and moved to Ga., before the Revolution. In 1776 he was a delegate to the state's first Constitutional Convention, then served as a legislator and member of the Executive Council; Served in campaigns against the Indians on the western frontier during the war, and was promoted to Lieut. Col.; delegate to Continental Congress, 1780-83, and to the Constitutional Convention in 1788-89 which adopted the U.S. Constitution; was U.S. Senator from Georgia, 1789-1793; having married in New York City he moved there and spent his last 30 years there. There he was a member of the New York legislature, and was appointed by President Jefferson as Commissioner of Loans serving until the office was abolished. For the last ten years he was a state inspector of Prisons.

Sep. 27, 1828

Died in New York, on the 6th inst. the venerable THEODORUS BAILEY, for many years Past Master of that City. Gen. Bailey was a patriot of the Revolution.

Sep. 27, 1828

Died in Washington City, on the 11th inst. very suddenly, after an illness of some weeks, DON PABLO OBREGON, Minister from the Republic of Mexico to the United States. (Later accounts state that he committed suicide while in a state of mental derangement).

Oct. 4, 1828

Died in Sutton, Mass. on the 14th of Sept. MRS. MARY BROWN, wife of Mr. Owen Brown, merchant, in this town.

Oct. 4, 1828

> Died at his residence in Twiggs county on the 13th Sept. after a tedious and severe indisposition, THOMAS ARRINGTON, ESQ. in the 35th year of his age. At the perios of his death he was Clerk of the Superior Court of Twiggs county. As a husband, father, citizen and friend, his greatest value was known (with eulogy).

Oct. 11, 1828

> Died on Wednesday morning, 8th inst. MARTHA-ANN, youngest daughter of JACK (?) D. CLARKE, ESQ. of this county, aged 6 years and 4 months.

Oct. 18, 1828

> Died in Milledgeville, on Thursday last, of the cholera morbus, DR. CHARLES WILLIAMSON - one of the candidates for member of Congress at the recent election.

Oct. 25, 1828

> Died in Henry county, Alabama, on the 17th ult. after a protracted and violent attack of billious fever, COL. WILLIAM C. WATSON, a native of North Carolina, and formerly a citizen of Baldwin county.

Oct. 25, 1828

> Died at Sullivan's Island, South Carolina on the 6th inst. COMMODORE ROBERT HENLEY, of the United States navy. He was interred at Charleston.

Oct. 25, 1828

> Died at Greenbush, Rensselaer county, state of New York, about the last of September, GENERAL JOHN J. VAN RENSSALEAR, a native of that county.

Nov. 1, 1828

> Died at New London, Conn. JOHN G.C. BRAINARD, Esq. late Editor of the Connecticut Mirror, aged 32 (with eulogy).

Nov. 8, 1828

> Died in Washington City, on the 12th Oct. the celebrated Vocalist, MRS. FRENCH, in the 88th year of her age.

Nov. 15, 1828

> Died in Charleston on the 2d inst. in the 76th year of his age, MAJOR GEN. THOS. PINCKNEY, a distinguished officer of the Revolution, and President General of the Cincinnati of the United States.

Nov. 15, 1828

> Died on the 30th ult. in the ?1st year of her age, after a severe and protracted illness, MRS. CAROLINE A PHILIPS, consort of Col. M. Philips, of Monticello.

Dec. 6, 1828

> Died in Clinton, on the 28th ult. MISS ELIZA JUSTICE, in the 17th year of her age, daughter of Mr. Dempsey Justice, formerly of Baldwin county.

Dec. 6, 1828

> Died in Monroe County on the first instant, MR. JOHN CHAPPEL in the 63d year of his age. For upwards of forty years he was a zealous member of the Methodist Episcopal Church (with eulogy).

Dec. 13, 1828

    Died at Eatonton, Putnam county, on the 2d inst. MR. RILEY ROCKWELL, aged 33, formerly of Danbury, Conn.

Dec. 13, 1828

    One of our ablest physicians and best men - DR. SETH WARD died at his residence in Kingston, Morgan county, in thirty two hours after an attack of congestive fever. He was born in Amelia county, Virginia, but had been for the last nine years a successful practitioneer of medicine in Georgia (Recorder) (Dr. Ward was a few years since, a resident of Macon).

Dec. 13, 1828

    Died in Monroe county, on the 4th inst. MRS. MARGARET BAXTER, aged 86 years. She enjoyed good health till within a few moments before her death. She had been many years an exemplary member of the Baptist Church.

Dec. 13, 1828

    Died at Milledgeville on the 15th ult. MR. WILLIAM T. WILLIAMS, formerly of Franklin county, N.C.

Jan. 17, 1829

    Died at the Hermitage, near Nashville, Tenn. on the 22d Dec. MR. RACHEL JACKSON consort of Gen. Jackson, President elect of the U.S.

Jan. 24, 1829

    Died on the 6th inst. MAJOR GENERAL JOHN A HEARD, of Elbert county, in the 35th year of his age.

Jan. 24, 1829

    Died in Montgomery, Ala. on Tuesday morning last, of a lingering illness, MR. JAMES LESLIE, a citizen of Clinton, Geo.

Jan. 31, 1829

    Died in Louisville, on the 18th instant, after a short illness, MISS MARY M. FLEMING, aged 11 years and six months - daughter of the late Robert Fleming, Esquire.

Feb. 7, 1829

    Died in this place, on Sunday the 25th ult. MR. BALDWIN FLUKER.

Feb. 14, 1829

    Died in New Haven, Conn. on the morning of the 26th inst. NATHAN SMITH, M.D. Professor of the Theory and Practice of Physic and Surgery, in the Medical Institution of Yale College, aged 66.

Feb. 14, 1829

    Died in Salem, Mass. on the 29th of January, the honorable and venerable TIMOTHY PICKERING, aged 84 years - most of the incidents of whose life were connected with the Revolution, Independence, measures and politics of our beloved county. He was colonel of one of the first patriotic regiments in this State; afterwards an Aid to General Washington, and subsequently Secretary of State, a National Senator, &c. (Conn. Journal).

Mar. 7, 1829

Died in Macon on the 20th ult. MR. WM. F. BROWN, aged 58, formerly of Connecticut, but for several years a resident of Clinton and this place.

Mar. 7, 1829

Died in Clinton on 6th instant MR. SOLOMON HOGE, innkeeper in that place.

Mar. 7, 1829

Died at Montpelier, Vt. at the residence of James Madison, on Wednesday Feb. 11th ELEANOR MADISON, the venerated parent of out ex-President - aged 98 years.

Mar. 7, 1829

Died at the Navy Yard in Washington on the 23d ult., aged 79 years, COMMODORE THOMAS TINGEY, Commandant of that Yard, and for twenty eight years a resident of this city in that capacity.

Apr. 4, 1829

Died on the Apalachicola river, on his pasage from New-Orleans to Fort Gaines, on the 11th inst. DR. A.M. WATSON, of the latter place (Columbus Enquirer).

Apr. 18, 1829

The Boston papers announce the death of the venerable DR. EDWARD QUGUSTUS HOLYOKE, of Salem, on Tuesday evening 31st ult. about six o'clock, in the hundred and first year of his age.

Apr. 18, 1829

JOSEPH WILLIAMS was executed in Marion, Twiggs County, Friday of last week for murder of Nimrod Phillips.

Apr. 25, 1829

Died on Tuesday the 7th inst. near Greenville, Meriwether county, of a pulmonary complaint, MRS. ELIZA B. MERRILL, wife of Lemuel Merrill, Esq. aged 29 years (with eulogy).

May 2, 1829

Died in Muscogee county on the 25th of April last, MRS. LYDIA CHAPMAN of Monroe co. in the seventy second year of her age (with eulogy).

May 9, 1829

Died in Savannah, a few days ago, the HON. WILLIAM DAVIES, Judge of the Superior Courts in the Eastern Circuit.

May 9, 1829

Died in Darien, on the 18th ult. CAPTAIN CHARLES F. GRANDISON, late Editor of the Darien Gazette. He was a man of singular abilities, much eccentricity, and great general information acquired by extensive travelling in almost every quarter of the world. He had followed several pursuits - chiefly, that of a seaman and encountered and escaped many perils. His genealogy is wrapped in complete mystery, and from where he "hailed," or who are his relatives, is entirely unknown.

May 9, 1829

   Died in Jones county, on Saturday the 26th inst. JAMES BILLINGSLEA,
   ESQ. a respected citizen, and one of the richest planters in the
   county.

May 30, 1829

   Died in this place, on Saturday night the 23d inst. MRS. ELIZABETH
   WRIGHT, wife of Maj. Edward W. Wright - and daughter of Luke J.
   Morgan, Esq. aged about 20 years; member of Presbyterian Church.

May 30, 1829

   Died in Augusta, on the 21st inst. DR. B.D. THOMPSON, an eminent
   physician of that place.

June 6, 1829

   Died in Twiggs County, on the 30th of May, MR. GABRIEL PARKER.

June 6, 1829

   Another of the heroic race has passed from the scene; JOHN JAY,
   the companion and friend of Washington, the co-adjutor of Hamilton
   and Madison, learned Judge, able Foreign Minister, distinguished
   Chief Magistrate, Senator, Scholar (NOTE: paper was torn and other
   data hard to read).

June 13, 1829

   GENERAL DANIEL STEWART, a Patriot of 1776, died at his residence
   in Liberty County, on the 27th ult. aged 69 years. Joined the
   standard of his country at age 16 and was frequently in battle under
   Generals Sumpter, Marion, and Col. Wm. Harden at Pocotaligo, was
   taken prisoner near Charleston, and put on board the English Prison
   Ship in that horbor: and probably no man suffered more or went
   through more perils and hardships during the whole war and the
   different Indian depradations afterward, on the Georgia frontier
   (Georgian).

June 13, 1829

   Died in Middletown, Conn. on 10th May, of pulmonary Consumption,
   WILLIAM HENRY PAINE, aged 20, son of Edward Paine, Esq. of this
   state.

June 13, 1829

   Another patriot of the Revolution gone! CAPT. ALLEN M'LANE,
   collector of the port of Wilmington and the honest father to our
   minister to England died at Wilmington about sunset on Friday,
   the 22d May, in the 83d year of his age.

June 20, 1829

   Died in Hamilton, Butler county, Ohio, on Thursday, the 19th ultimo,
   CAPTAIN JOHN CLEVES SYMMES, extensively known as the author of the
   theory of Open and Concentric Spheres. Capt. Symmes was a native
   of New-Jersey, but emigrated at an early age to the Western country.
   He was attached to the army of the United States for a number of
   years, and during the late war distinguished himself on the Northern
   frontiers by his coolness and intrepidity (Gazette).

June 27, 1829

   Died in Augusta, on the 16th inst. in the 32d year of his age,
   JOHN D. WALKER, originally of Richmond county, but for the last
   two years a resident of Macon.

June 27, 1829

Died in Edgefield village, South Carolina on Tuesday, the 17th ult. TOM a negro man belonging to Mrs BACON, at the great age of one hundred and thirty years. He himself rated his age at a few years higher; and from the reach of memory, there is little doubt but that he was as old as had been stated.

June 27, 1829

Died at Roxbury, Mass. on the 4th inst. GEN. HENRY DEARBORN, aged 80 years - an officer of the Revolution.

Aug. 15, 1829

Died in this place, on the 11th inst. MARGARET JANE, daughter of E. CALHOUN (?), aged about 8 months.

Aug. 29, 1829

Died in Athens, on Sunday the 22d inst. AUGUSTIN SMITH CLAYTON, JR. second son of the Hon. A.S. CLAYTON. He left Athens on Thursday morning in his usual health, to attend the Court sitting for this county at Watkinsville, sickened with a bilious cholic in the evening, was brought home on Friday, and on Saturday evening, at aobut nine o'clock, breathed his last.

Aug. 29, 1829

Died at the Indian Springs, on Monday morning last, MR. ARTHUR DEAN, aged about 24, a merchant of Milledgeville. He was a native of New-York, where his parents now live. His disease was a violent attack of billious fever.

Aug. 29, 1829

Died of a billious fever at the residence of Doctor A.B. POPE, in Jackson, Butts county, on the evening of the 18th inst., MR. WALTER T. KNIGHT, attorney at law, after a protracted and painful illness of fifteen days. About an hour previous to this melancholy event, MRS. ELIZA R. KNIGHT, wife of the deceased, who a few days before had been attacked by the same disease, also expired.

Aug. 29, 1829

Died in this town, on the 28th inst. MARY, daughter of MR. DAVID F. WILSON, aged about 14 months.

Sep. 5, 1829

Died at Milledgeville, on the 22d August, after a protracted illness of the Typhus fever, the REV. GEORGE HULL. He was a Presiding Elder of the Methodist Church, and stationed preacher in Milledgeville.

Sep. 5, 1829

Died on the 24th inst. in Marion, Twiggs county, after seven days illness, in the 31st year of his age, DR. OWEN C. FORT.

Sep. 12, 1829

Died in this place, on Thursday night last, CAPT. CHARLES BULLOCK, aged about 45 years. Previous to the commencement of the town of Macon he was Post Master and Inn Keeper at Fort Hawkins, and since that time, one of the proprietors of the Mansion House. He was the first Senator elected in this county, to the State Legislature, and has since filled various public and responsible stations.

Sep. 12, 1829

Died at his residence, in Charlotte, N.C. on the 28th ult. JOSEPH WILSON ESQ. after an illness of only three or four days. Mr. Wilson occupied an elevated stand as a lawyer - was for many years Solicitor of the 5th Circuit - and as a prosecuting Officer, was perhaps unrivalled.

Sep. 12, 1829

Died in Monroe county on the 10th instant MRS. SUSANNAH CLAYTON, wife of Mr. D. Clayton of Hartford.

Sep. 19, 1829

Died in Twiggs County, on the night of the 26th August of a severe and lingering illness, MRS. MARY R. TARVER, in the twentieth year of her age, consort of Dr. Tarver, and the youngest of the two remaining daughters of old Mrs. Slappey. In death has gone to join friends gone before, and her only child, an infant son, JOHN RANDOLPH, who dies a few months previous (with eulogy).
(NOTE: Papers of Columbia, S.C. and Tuscaloosa, Ala. are requested to publish the above, for the information of the friends and acquaintances of the deceased).

Sep. 19, 1829

The funeral sermon of CAPT. CHARLES BULLOCK, will be preached at the Methodist Church on Sunday morning, 27th inst.

Oct. 10, 1829

Died at the residence of James N. Bliss, in Hartford, on the 1st Oct. DR. AUSTIN JANES, recently of this place, and a native of Massachusetts.

Oct. 24, 1829

Died in Perry County, Ala. MR. SAMUEL C. BRAME, recently a resident of this place.

Nov. 6, 1829

JAMES FLEWELLEN, a most estimable and worthy citizen, was killed in a fight with JAMES COHORN at Warrior Plantation in the western part of the county, receiving three knife stabs from which he died two hours later. Cohorn was severely wounded by knife cuts made by his antagonist. The Inquest jury found that it was a case of murder and Cohorn was arrested and is now in jail here.

Jan. 9, 1830

Eulogy on ISAAC WELCH which was to accompany notice of his death in last weeks paper. (NOTE: That issue of the paper is missing - eulogy states he was a soldier, leaves a wife, and was a philanthropist).

Feb. 13, 1830

Died in Monroe County, a few days since WILLIAM CULLODEN, ESQ. Post Master at the Office known as Culloden's Store. Mr. Culloden was a native of Ireland but had spent much of his early life in the East Indies.

Feb. 13, 1830

Died at his residence near Buffalo, the noted Seneca Chief SA-GU-YU-WHA-HAH, (KEEPER AWAKE) so long known to the whites by the appellation of RED JACKET, aged 80 years.

Mar. 20, 1830

   Died in Clinton, on Tuesday night last, MRS. CAROLINE IVERSON,
   wife of Maj. Alfred Iverson (with eulogy).

Mar. 20, 1830

   Died in Milledgeville, on the night of the 6th inst. MRS. SARAH W.
   McCOMBS, wife of Robert McCombs, Esq.

Mar. 27, 1830

   Died at his residence in Monroe county, on Friday the 19th inst.
   after an illness of ten days, MR. JOSEPH COTTEN, in the 56th year
   of age. By his death, a disconsolate widow and five tender orphans,
   are left to mourn their irretrievable loss (with eulogy).

Aug. 7, 1830

   Died in this place on the 1st inst. HENRY G., infant son of ISAAC
   G. SEYMOUR, ESQ. aged 10 months.

Aug. 14, 1830

   Died in this county, on the 6th inst. AUGUSTUS FRANKLIN, aged six
   months, infant son of D.G. WORSHAM, ESQ.

Aug. 21, 1830

   Died in this vicinity on the 8th instant, SAMUEL GILLESPIE, ESQ.
   formerly a Merchant of this place, aged 23 years.

Aug. 21, 1830

   Died in Milledgeville on the morning of the 5th inst. COL. ROBERT
   R. RUFFIN, aged 42 years. His disease, the dropsey of the heart
   and lungs, was lingering, and excruciating beyond description.
   His death was sudden, though unexpected.

Aug. 21, 1830

   Died in Twiggs county, on Monday the 10th inst. after a short
   illness, CAPT. CHARLES CARDIN. At the time of his death, Capt. C.
   was Receiver of Tax Returns.

Sep. 4, 1830

   Died near Macon, on the 30th ult. WILLIAM MORRISS, infant son of
   NANCY and FRANCIS H. GODFREY.

Sep. 11, 1830

   Died in Houston county, on Saturday last MR. GEORGE WALKER, aged
   about 60 years. He was formerly a resident of Twiggs county, where
   his remains were interred on Sunday.

Sep. 11, 1830

   Died at Blount Springs, on the 20th of July, DOCT. WILLIAM AUGUSTUS
   KING, Professor of Chemistry in the University of Alabama; aged
   about 27 years.

Sep. 11, 1830

   Departed this life in Columbus, on the 20th inst. MRS. TABITHA B.
   LAMAR, consort of Mirabeau B. Lamar, Esq. in the 21st year of her
   age. She has left a fond husband and two children (One an infant).
   (Enquirer)

Sep. 11, 1830

New York, Aug. 23 - The venerable COL. MARINUS WILLETT is no more. He died last evening at his house, Cedar Grove, in the 91st year of his age. Col. Willett distinguished himself by his bravery and good conduct in the war of the revolution. His courage, prowess and presence of mind were particularly displayed in conflicts with the Indians who took part with Great Britain.

Sep. 18, 1830

Died in this place, on the 15th inst. MR. OLIVER A. STORRE, aged about 65 - a native of Vermont.

Sep. 18, 1830

Died in this place on Saturday last, JOHN HENRY TALLY, youngest son of JOHN R. & SUSAN P. TALLY - aged 15 months and 18 days.

Oct. 16, 1830

Died in Macon, on the 30th ult. WILLIAM MORRIS, infant son of FRANCIS H. and NANCY GODFREY (with eulogy).

Oct. 23, 1830

Died in Augusta, on Monday last, JAMES R. GOULD, son of JUDGE GOULD of Litchfield, (Conn.). Mr Gould was a member of the Bar of this State.

Oct. 23, 1830

Died in Columbia County, on the 18th inst. PETER CRAWFORD, ESQ. Mr. C. at the time of his death, was senator elect of that county and for many years a member of the state legislature. In that body he held a prominent place.

Oct. 30, 1830

Died in this place, on the 24th inst. THOMAS KETLER ECKLEY, aged 21 months and 9 days - son of MR. LEVI ECKLEY.

Nov. 13, 1830

Died in Forsyth, on the 10th inst. ELIZA JACKSON, daughter of WILLIAM F. JACKSON, Esq.

Nov. 27, 1830

Died in this place, on Tuesday evening last, MR. JAMES RUST, aged about 30 years; formerly of Poughkeepsie, New York.

Dec. 18, 1830

Died in this place, on Friday, the 10th inst. MR. EDWIN CONE, aged about 25, formerly of New Haven, Connecticut.

Dec. 18, 1830

Died in Forsyth, on the 9th instant, ZENO ALVORENO JONES, son of Wm. C. JONES, aged 3 months and 23 days.

Jan. 22, 1831

Died at the residence of DR. JAS. THWEATT, of Monroe county, on Friday morning last, MR. JAMES TWEATT, formerly of Clinton.

Mar. 5, 1831

Died in this county, on Thursday of last week, THOMAS LUNDY ESQ. formerly of Hancock county.

Mar. 12, 1831

>Died suddenly in this place on the 10th inst. MARCELLUS STOVALL BIRDSONG, age 3 years 7 months and 19 days, eldest son of ROBERT BIRDSONG.

Mar. 12, 1831

>Died on Monday night last, at his plantation near Milledgeville, MR. WYATT FOARD, for many years a respected and estimable citizen of that place.

Apr. 16, 1831

>Died at his residence, in Harris county, Ga. on the 28th of March last, MRS. SARAH S. GRANBERRY, wife of Maj. George Granberry, in the 22nd year of her age, leaving an afflicted husband and two small children.

Apr. 23, 1831

>Died in Worcester (Mass.) on Monday, the 4th inst. ISAIAH THOMAS, ESQ. L.L.D. aged 82 years. The deceased was connected with the history of the typographic art in this county; established newspaper The Massachusetts Spy in Boston more than sixty years since.

Apr. 30, 1831

>Died in this place, on the 29th. inst. MRS. _____ HILL, wife of Henry B. Hill, Esq. (NOTE: The above blank also appeared in the notice).

June 4, 1831

>Died on Friday the 27th ult. MRS. CLARISSA REDDING, consort of Robert G. Redding of Monroe county, Ga. aged 20 years and 7 days (with eulogy).

July 2, 1831

>Died in this place, on Monday morning 27th ult. CAPT. WM. J. DANELLY, aged 30 years. His death was sudden and unexpected. He was seized with an inflammation of the brain, which terminated his life in a few hours. At the time of his death, he was commander of the Macon Volunteers - had represented the county in the Legislature, been Intendant of Macon, and a Justice of the Inferior Court. He was, on Tuesday, buried with Masonic and Military honors.

July 9, 1831

>Died in this place, on Wednesday the 6th inst. MRS. LOUISA C. SMITH, wife of Mr. John P. Smith, aged about 28 years (with eulogy).

July 16, 1831

>Death of PRESIDENT JAMES MONROE announced.

July 16, 1831

>Died in East Macon, on the 13th inst. MRS. MARTHA BAKER, aged about 17 years, wife of BENJ. H. BAKER of this place (with eulogy).

July 23, 1831

>Died on the 5th inst. MRS. ELIZABETH B. DEAN, Consort of James Dean, Esq. of Houston county.

July 30, 1831

>Died in Twiggs county, on the 24th instant, MR. JAMES GUERRY.

July 31, 1831

    Died in this place, on the 25th inst. OLIVER F., infant son of MR. OLIVER SAGE, aged 16 months.

Sep. 3, 1831

    Died in this place on the 27th ult. after a short, painful illness, MISS MARGARET McCALLUM, aged 16 years (with eulogy).

Sep. 10, 1831

    Died at Woodville, Ala. on the 25th July in the 24th year of her age, MRS. TERESA MARGARET BOOTH, consort of Maj. John P. Booth, of Apalachicola. She left a husband and three small children to lament her untimely death.

Sep. 17, 1831

    Died at his residence in Twiggs county, Georgia, on Friday the 9th inst. MR. ALLEN DORMON (?) a native of North Carolina, but for many years a resident of Georgia, in his Seventy-third year. He was a plain honest farmer, and has left a large number of relations and friends to regret his death (Alabama papers requested to copy).

Oct. 8, 1831

    Died in this county, on the 29th ult. MRS. ELIZABETH FITZPATRICK, wife of Rene Fitzpatrick, Esq.

Oct. 8, 1831

    Died near Knoxville, Tennessee, (where she had gone for the benefit of her health) on the 15th September, MRS. ELIZA A. BULLOCK, in the 37th year of her age, widow of the late Capt. Charles Bullock of this place.

Oct. 8, 1831

    Died on the 17th ult. in Bibb county, MRS. SUSANNA ALLEN, aged 35 years - Wife of B. Allen. In the death of Mrs. Allen, the Methodist Episcopal Church has lost a devoted member - her bereaved husband an affectionate wife - her children, a fond mother.

Oct. 29, 1831

    Died in this place, on the 22d inst. MR. JAS. S. WEEKS, aged 33 years.

Nov. 5, 1831

    Died in Crawford county, on the 27th ult. MRS. SARAH HOLLOMAN, wife of Eaton Holloman, and also her infant daughter. She was in the 38th year of her age, and had been an acceptable member of the Methodist Episcopal Church for the last four years. She has left a husband and four children to lament her death - being sensible of her death, she called her family around her bed, and announced to them her assurance of an everlasting happiness.

Nov. 12, 1831

    Died in this place, on the 8th inst. MR. BAILEY GODDARD, aged 33 years - formerly of Athol, Mass. but for some years a resident of this place. He left a wife and child to mourn his untimely exit.

Nov. 12, 1831

    Died in Milledgeville, on Monday last, MRS. LUCINDA BETTON, wife of Capt. Solomon Betton, and sister of the Hon. Charles Fenton Mercer, of Virginia. She was for many years a member of the Methodist Church.

Nov. 19, 1831

 FREDERICK S. FELL, senior editor of this paper departed this left on Thursday evening, after a protracted illness. (Savannah Republican)

Jan. 7, 1832

 Died in this place, on Wednesday the 4th inst. REUBEN TURNER, ESQ. aged 33 years - formerly of Burke county; and for several years past a respectable and esteemed citizen of Macon.

Jan. 14, 1832

 Died on the 2d instant, at her residence in Twiggs county, MRS. SARAH A. THARP, widow of the late Rev. Vincent A. Tharp, in the 66th year of her age - member of the Baptist Church for many years.

Mar. 24, 1832

 Died at the residence of his son, DANIEL W. SHINE, in Twiggs county, on Sunday, 11th March, after an illness of ten days, MR. JOHN SHINE, in the 73d year of his age. The deceased was born in Jones county, North Carolina, in 1759, and devoted a part of his youth to the service of his country in the revolutionary war, under the command of General Caswell, and was at the battle near Camden, S.C. in 1780. Leaves children, grandchildren and great-grandchildren (with eulogy).

Apr. 7, 1832

 Died in Clinton on the 24th ult. MR. HARVEY H. SQUIRE, aged 23 years.

Apr. 28, 1832

 Died at Newnan, Coweta county, on the morning of the 31st March, of a pulmonary disease, COL. ZACHARIAH PHILLIPS, in the 45th year of his age.

Apr. 28, 1832

 Died on the 18th inst. after a long and protracted illness, the REV. THOMAS DARLEY, in the 64th year of his age, and 32d of his ministry, leaving a wife and 16 children to deplore his loss.

May 5, 1832

 About a week since, an individual by the name of JOHN RENFROE, formerly of Jones County, during the night threw himself from a window of the second story of Mr. Riley's Hotel, and fractured his skull so severely, that he died in a few hours. He is supposed to have been delirious at that time.

June 2, 1832

 Died in Houston county on Saturday the 26th inst. GEORGE H., youngest son of HENRY & NANCY WIMBERLY, aged six years.

June 21, 1832

 Died on Monday the 11th inst. REBECCA MARINDA, infant daughter of JUDGE and MRS. STRONG of this place.

June 21, 1832

 Died in Monroe county, on the 13th inst. MR. ISAAC JONES, after a lingering illness of 18 months, aged about 56 years.

July 5, 1832

 Died at the Montpelier Springs in Monroe County, on the wd inst. MRS. NANCY COOK, consort of Maj. Philip Cook, of Twiggs County,

(July 5, 1832, cont'd)   after a distressing illness of more than ten months, in the 38th year of her age.

July 5, 1832

Died at Fortville, Jones County, on the 2d inst. MARY DRUSILLA, daughter of MR. WM. DANIEL, of this place, aged 15 months.

July 26, 1832

Died on Friday, the 20th inst. in the 35th year of his age MORTIMER R. WALLIS. Mr. W. was one of the first citizens of Macon, and held the office of Post Master ever since an office was established in this place.

Aug. 30, 1832

Died in Taliaferro county, on the 20th inst. in the 10th year of her age, MISS MARIA JANE SMITH, daughter of Mr. JOHN SMITH, of this place. Her death was occasioned by the upsetting of a carriage, the injury received from which she did not survive more than an hour.

Aug. 30, 1832

Died in Jefferson, Jackson county on the 19th inst. COL. THOMAS W. MURRAY, of Lincoln county - Col. M. is well known to the people of Georgia, as a member of our Legislature, and at the time of his death, as a candidate for Representative in Congress.

Sep. 6, 1832

Died in Macon, on Sunday morning last, the 2d inst. MRS. ELIZABETH EVANS, formerly of Boston, Mass. in the 63d year of her age. She had been for twenty-three years a member of the Methodist Episcopal Church.

Sep. 20, 1832

Died in this place, on Saturday evening last, HENRY ST. GEORGE, infant son of DR. AMBROSE and MRS. MARY BABER, aged 16 months and 29 days (with eulogy).

Sep. 20, 1832

Died on Sunday morning last, at the house of Capt. L. Newcomb, after an illness of nine days, of the Billious fever, MR. THOMAS M. DRISCOLL, aged 28 years, a native of Savannah and at the time of his death an inhabitant of that city. Dr. Driscoll was on a summer visit to the up country, and no doubt contracted the disease which terminated his life, from exposure in travelling. Being an old and respectable member of the Savannah guards, the Macon Volunteers paid to his memory the last tribute of respect, by an observance of all the military honor bestowed upon a member of its own corps.

Sep. 20, 1832

Died at Lumpkin, Stewart county, on the 8th inst. JAMES WOOD, ESQ. attorney at law of that place.

Sep. 27, 1832

Died in this place, on Saturday last, MR. EDWARD GRIFFIN. Also, ELIZABETH, the daughter of MR. DAVID F. WILSON, in the 6th year of her age.

Sep. 27, 1832

Died in Milledgeville, on the 12th inst. MRS. ELIZABETH MICKLEJOHN, consort of Mr. George Micklejohn of this place, in the 51st year of her age.

Sep. 27, 1832

Died in Milledgeville, on Sunday night last, CAPT. SOLOMON BETTON, aged 72 years, an old and highly respectable citizen of that place.

Sep. 27, 1832

Died in Milledgeville, on the 6th inst. after a painful and protracted illness, MRS. SUSAN P. KNOX, wife of Mr. H. Knox, in the 27th year of her age.

Sep. 27, 1832

Died on the 4th inst. in M'Intosh county, LT. COL. WM. P. HOPKINS, late a representative in the State Legislature; from that county, in the 24th year of his age.

Sep. 27, 1832

The Washington Intelligencer states that COMMODORE CHARLES B. THOMPSON died a few days ago at the Hot Springs, in Virginia. He had been in ill health for a long time, having brought his disease with him, several months ago, from the Pacific, where he was in command of the United States squadron for two or three years.

Oct. 11, 1832

Died in this place, on the 8th inst. MRS. NANCY LAMAR, wife of Dr. Thos. R. Lamar (with eulogy).

Oct. 11, 1832

Died in this place, on the 9th inst. JOHN N. BACON, a native of South Carolina, aged 31 years. He left a bereaved widow to deplore the loss of an affectionate husband.

Oct. 25, 1832

Died lately at his residence in Columbia county, Ga. CAPTAIN THOMAS COBB, at the advanced age of one hundred and ten years. He was a native of Buckingham county, Virginia. His patriotism induced him to take part with the country in the struggle for independence of these states, and was often associated in the counsels of the chiefs of those startling times. He held offices under the Commonwealth, after it had obtained self government, and removed to Georgia about the year 1783. He was an agriculturalist, and the efficient manager of his plantation for eighty or ninety years (Constitutionalist).

Oct. 25, 1832

Died in Hancock county, on the 28th ult. CAPTAIN JEFFREY BARKSDALE, at an advanced age: he was a Revolutionary Soldier.

Nov. 8, 1832

Died in this place, on 31st Oct. MR. REUBEN BURROUGHS, aged about 49 years. His death was occasioned by bruises received from the fall of a piece of scantling from a building on which he was at work, which he survived a few days.

Jan. 24, 1833

Died in this place, on the 21st instant, MRS. _____ ERWIN, wife of Leander A. Erwin. (NOTE: The "blank" appears in the notice).

Mar. 7, 1833

Died at his residence, near Waynesboro, Ga. on the 23d ult. DR. SOUTHWORTH HARLOW, aged 53 years, a native of Plymouth, Mass. but a citizen of Georgia 23 years.

Mar. 7, 1833

Departed this life, on Sunday night, 24th ult. in Glynn County, DR. WILLIAM B. ROGERS, of this place, aged about 33 years. Dr. R. had been to the low country, to try the benefits of a milder climate upon a diseased constitution; but receiving no relief, he was on his way home, to breathe his last in the arms of this friends, when his strength failed him, and he sunk into everlasting sleep. Dr. R. had been a resident of this county for several years, elected to Senate of the State, and at the time of his death was President of the Branch of the Darien Bank established here (Telegraph).

Mar. 14, 1833

Died in this place, on Sunday, the 10th inst. VIRGINIA CAROLINE, daughter of MR. S. ROSE - aged about 20 months.

Apr. 4, 1833

Died in Forsyth, on the 28th ult. WILLIAM P. HENRY, ESQ. Clerk of the Superior Court of Monroe County - a kind and indulgent father, an affectionate husband (with eulogy).

Apr. 18, 1833

Died in Forsyth, on the 9th inst. BENJAMIN VIRGINIUS, only son of DR. JOHN S.B. LAW, aged 5 years and 6 months.

May 9, 1833

Died in Warren County, on the 1st May, MAJ. ROBERT A BEALL, SENR. in the 68th year of his age.

May 16, 1833

JAMES STAFFORD of Camden County, a convict in the State Penitentiary, in attempting to escape last Monday, was shot dead by a guard.

June 27, 1833

Died on the 21st of May, near Talbotton, MR. JAMES BLANTON, of Columbus, formerly a resident of Macon. His disease was consumption, with which he had been sometime afflicted. His health having improved, he commenced travelling for its benefit, but suffered a relapse, which soon brought him to the grave. A wife and child mourn an untimely bereavement, and the Methodist Church (of which he had been many years a member) a zealous and exemplary brother.

June 27, 1833

Died near this place on Sunday last, DR. BENJAMIN F. OWENS, a useful and enterprising citizen. About a year since he put in operation a steam mill, the first erected in the upper section of the state. While absent for the purchase of his machinery, by exposure, he contracted a malady by which he gradually wasted till the time of his decease. A wife and three children mourn his loss. On Monday he was buried with Masonic honors by Macon Lodge, of which he was a Past Master.

July 4, 1833

Died near this place on Friday last, CHARLES LEVI, son of LEVI ECKLEY, ESQ. aged about 2 years.

July 11, 1833

Died in this city on the morning of the 4th, OGLETHORPE, only child of MYRON BARTLETT, ESQ. aged about ten months.

July 25, 1833

    Died at the house of William Barnes in Talbot co. on Friday the 12th inst. of the Billious Fever, on the tenth day of his sickness, WILLIAM (WILSON?) HOGAN, in the 27th year of his age. Mr. Hogan was a native of North Carolina, but a resident of Georgia for several of the last years of his life. He has left an affectionate wife and child to mourn their irreparable loss, a kind father and mother, and numerous relatives and friends.

July 25, 1833

    Died on the 30th June, ISABELLA L., infant daughter of MATTHEW and PENELOPE McCULLERS, aged two months and three days (with eulogy).

July 25, 1833

    Died in this city, on the 18th instant, of an inflammatory billious attack, MR. JAS. P. CAMPBELL, son of James A. Campbell, of Pike county, in the 19th year of his age. He had belonged to the Methodist Church for two years past (with eulogy).

Aug. 1, 1833

    Died in Vineville, (near Macon,) on the 29th ult. instant and only daughter of EDWARD R. and MARY ANN S. BALLARD, aged six weeks.

Aug. 1, 1833

    Died in Oglethorpe County, on the 21st inst. MARY ANNA ELIZABETH, daughter of ROBERT and MARY H. BIRDSONG, aged 1 year and 17 days.

Aug. 8, 1833

    Died in this place, on the 5th inst. of a fit of apoplexy, MR. PETER P. ROCKWELL, in the 31st year of his age - a native of Danbury, Connecticut.

Aug. 29, 1833

    Died in this place, on the 28th inst. at Erwin's Hotel, of the billious fever, MR. JAMES S. DICKSON, of Woodville, Miss. He was on his way to Charleston and arrived here about a week since, under the influence of the fever of which he died.

Sep. 5, 1833

    Died in Roanoke, Stewart County, Ga. of inflammatory fever, on Wednesday, the 14th ult. the REV. MOSES MATHEWS, formerly of Monroe County, in this State, in the 60th year of his age. He has left a widow, several children, and numerour friends to deplore their irreparable loss. He had been a member of the Methodist Episcopal Church from his youth, and a minister of the gospel for nearly forty-one years (with eulogy).

Sep. 12, 1833

    Died at the Montpelier Springs, on the 1st inst. JAMES EDMOND (EDWARD?), son of MR. JAMES GODDARD, aged 6 (?) months.

Sep. 12, 1833

    Died on the 3d inst. ROXANA KENDALL, aged 7 years 9 months and 26 days, only daughter of THOMAS G. BATES, ESQ. (with eulogy).

Sep. 19, 1833

    Died in this county, a few days since, CAPT. REDDIN RUTLAND. He was one of the earliest settlers of this vicinity.

Sep. 19, 1833

Died at Montpelier Springs, on the 7th inst. CHARLES AUGUSTUS, aged 2 years, 7 months and 14 days - and on the 10th, LEONORA VALEREA, aged 4 years, 1 month and 7 days - children of PHILIP A. and ELIZABETH A. CLAYTON.

Sep. 26, 1833

Died on the 15th instant, after a short illness, in the sixth year of his age, THOMAS SYDENHAM, son of DR. THOMAS HAMILTON, of Troup county.

Sep. 26, 1833

Died in Milledgeville, on the 17th inst. ELENORA, daughter of MR. RANDOLPH L. MOTT, of this place, aged 2 years and 6 months.

Oct. 3, 1833

Died in this place, on the 1st ins. JOHN M. SHELMAN, ESQ. aged 36 years - His death was occasioned by his being thrown from a gig on the 29th ult. He received a severe injury on the head, and never recovered his reason after the fall. He left a wife and seven children to lament his loss. He was buried on the 2d by the Macon Volunteers, with military honors. (As a tribute to Lieut. John M. Shelman, members of Macon Volumteers to wear crape on the left arm for thirty days).

Oct. 10, 1833

Died at his residence in Houston county, on the 24th September, of an organic disease, MR. WILLIAM RIGGINS, in the 25th year of his age. Member of Methodist Episcopal Church.

Oct. 10, 1833

Died in this place on the 6th instant, ELIZA MILDRED, aged 13 months and 14 days, daughter of PHILIP A. and ELIZABETH ANN CLAYTON.

Oct. 10, 1833

Died in Savannah on the 30th Sept. HENRIETTA PHILLIPS aged 6 years and 4 months, youngest daughter of BENJAMIN J. and MARIA PHILLIPS of Macon.

Oct. 17, 1833

Died at his residence in Harris county, on the 31st day of August last, ISAAC HILL, in the 33d year of his age; he had been a member of the Baptist Church about seven years - he left a wife and five children.

Oct. 24, 1833

Died at Vineville on Monday evening, after a painful and protracted illness, JOSEPH A., aged 8 years, third son of A.R. FREEMAN of this city.

Oct. 24, 1833

Died in this place, on the 22d inst. CAROLINA GEORGIA, daughter of MR. S. ROSE, aged 6 months and 18 days.

Nov. 14, 1833

Died on the 7th inst. ISAAC HARVEY, JUN. son of Isaac Harvey, senr. aged 8 years, of this city.

Nov. 14, 1833

Died in this place on the 17th ult. MR. JOHN DALTON, aged 88 years - a soldier who shared in the dangers of many hard fought battles of our revolution.

Nov. 21, 1833

Died in Marion, Twiggs County, on Sunday morning 17th inst. JAMES OLIVER, ESQ. in the 40th year of his age.

Jan. 16, 1834

Died in Forsyth, on Thursday, the 9th instant, MR. JAMES L. ANDERSON, (son of WM. R. ANDERSON, of Monroe County,) aged 24 years. On Monday, the 6th inst. the deceased, in company with his neighbors, came to town for the purpose of voting at the election for County officials. While there, in attempting to secure a dirk knife from one Lewis, a drunken wretch, who was in the altitude of stabbing a Mr. Wood, his foot slid and he fell, when Lewis jumped upon him and stabbed him in three places, before he could be taken off. Two of the stabs entered the body, one a little above the centre of the shoulder blades, the other grazing the second rib of the right side, and entering near the kidnies. He left a small family and numerous friends, to mourn his fate.

Jan. 23, 1834

Died on the evening of the 11th instant, at his residence in Houston County, CAPT. GEORGE TARVIN, in his 75th year. He was a soldier in the revolution, and was retained after peace, as an officer, for many years.

Jan. 30, 1834

Died in this city, on Thursday, the 16th inst. CAROLINA CALHOUN, youngest daughter of GABRIEL and ANN S. CAPERS, aged 4 months and 10 days (with poetic eulogy).

Feb. 13, 1834

Died in Twiggs county, on the 11th day January last, of the nervous fever, HARDY BROWN, ESQ. in the 40th year of his age. The deceased was a native of Jones county, North Carolina, from whence he removed in the latter part of 1824, and became a citizen of Georgia.

Feb. 20, 1834

Died in Clinton, on the 17th instant, at the residence of Mr. Thomas B. Slade, MRS. ELIZABETH BLOUNT, aged 47 years and 4 months. She was the widow of James Blount, Esq. and daughter of P.G. ROULHAC, a native of France, who came to this country during our revolutionary contest. She was a native of North Carolina, and removed to this State with her husband, in 1815. Not a member of any church, until within the four or five last years, when she attached herself to the Baptist denomination; had endured the loss of her husband and eldest son, soon after her removal to this State (with eulogy).

Feb. 20, 1834

Died in Georgetown, D.C. on the 3d instant, LORENZO DOW, a well known itinerant preacher. Native of Coventry, Connecticut; traveled extensively in England and Ireland, and repeatedly visited almost every portion of the United States. He had been a public preacher for more than thirty years, and it is probable that more persons have heard the gospel from his lips, than from those of any other individual since the days of Whitfield. He wrote several books, particularly a history of his own life; a Methodist.

Feb. 27, 1834

Died in Houston County, on the 13th inst. of Scarlet Fever, after an illness of ten days, MARY JANE, daughter of AUGUSTUS HOWARD, aged 2 years, 3 months and 26 days.

Mar. 6, 1834

Died in East Macon, on Saturday the 1st inst. AMANDA LOUISA, infant daughter of GEORGE B. and MARITA WARDLAW, aged 1 year, 1 month and 20 days.

Mar. 6, 1834

Died in Savannah, on the 14th ult. in the 32d year of her age, MRS. MARTHA DANIELL, daughter of the late Major John Screven, and wife of Dr. W.C. Daniell, of that place.

Mar. 6, 1834

Death of MR. JOHN HARRISON, formerly of New Haven, Conn. - who died in this place on the 27th ultimo, aged 32 (with eulogistic poem).

Mar. 13, 1834

Died in East Macon on the 5th inst. JAMES STILES, infant son of JOHN and NANCY OLIVER, aged 4 years and 5 months.

Mar. 13, 1834

Died in Augusta, on the 6th inst. the venerable THOMAS CUMMING. In respect of his memory, the Banks of the city were closed til after the funeral.

Mar. 20, 1834

Died on Thursday evening last, ANN GILMAN, eldest child and only daughter of ISAAC H. and JANE SMITH, in the 7th year of her gae.

Mar. 20, 1834

Died in Houston county, on the 15th inst. MARY WIMBERLY, daughter of ELIJAH E. CROCKER, aged 4 yrs. 8 months and 22 days.

Apr. 17, 1834

Died in this city, on the 9th instant, MR. CHARLES A. JONES, formerly of New-Haven, Conn. aged 27 years; member of the Macon Debating Society (Newspaper contains a resolution adopted by that body as tribute of respect to him).

Apr. 17, 1834

Died in Perry, Houston County, on Sunday morning the 6th inst. the REV. ROBERT FLOURNOY, aged 37 years; member of Methodist Episcopal Church (with eulogy).

Apr. 24, 1834

Died on Sunday last, after a long and painful illness, MRS. HARRIET E. COLLINS, wife of Dr. Robert Collins, of this place (with eulogy).

May 8, 1834

Died in this city on the 28th April, THOMAS CAMPBELL, ESQ. aged about 35 years - formerly of New York, but for the last ten years, a citizen of this place.

May 22, 1834

Died in this place on the 16th inst. MRS. NANCY B. GREEN, aged 27 years; wife of Mr. WM. A. GREEN - also her infant child, WM. GREEN.

June 5, 1834

Died in this place, of a disease of the liver, MRS. LUCY G. MOORE, wife of Mr. SAMUEL MOORE, aged 30 years - also, her infant son, aged 13(?) days.

June 19, 1834

Died on the 2d inst. in the 54th year of his age, in the city of Savannah, JOHN H. MOREL, ESQ. late Marshal of the District of Georgia.

June 26, 1834

Departed this life on the 20th inst. MRS. HARRIET COLLINS, of Macon; consort of Mr. CHARLES COLLINS, and daughter of the REV. ANTHONY G. SMITH, aged 21 years, 2 months and 3 days (with eulogy).

June 26, 1834

Died in Augusta on the 11th inst. MR. CHARLES WILLIAMSON, formerly of this place, aged 59 years 2 months and 26 days.

July 17, 1834

Resolutions of Respect to the memory of JUDGE L.Q.C. LAMAR, recently deceased Judge Superior Court of the Ocmulgee Circuit. Resolutions adopted by the Macon Bar. (NOTE: No obituary was located).

July 17, 1834

On Saturday July 5th, MRS. MARIA L. BROWN, consort of MR. ISRAEL F. BROWN of Clinton, in her 19th year: died in childbirth, the child dying two days later; member of the Methodist Church.

July 17, 1834

Died on the 9th inst., at Vineville, MR. L. BURNAP(?), for many years a merchant of Eatonton and Macon.

July 17, 1834

Died in Macon on the 12th inst., GEORGE SUMMERFIELD PARKER, infant son of WILLIAM C. PARKER, ESQ., age 3 months 2 days.

July 17, 1834

On Friday night last, a respectable man named HUFF, formerly an overseer in this neighborhood but recently an inhabitant of Chatham County, died suddenly, in East Macon. He went to rest in apparent health, but was found dead in the bed next morning, without having alarmed any of the family, although a child slept with him. Coroner's award, visitation of God. In his possission was found a will appointing Judge Nicoll of Savannah his executor; but although he rode a good horse and was on a long journey, only five cents in money.

July 17, 1834

About ten miles from Macon on the same night, a woman called LUCY HODGE, after having done a hard day's washing ans eaten a hearty supper, went to bed with a child; but was found dead in the bed next morning. Verdict, visitation of God. (Macon Telegraph).

July 24, 1834

    REV. JOHN M. GRAY of Harris County died in Alabama on the 14th inst.; formerly a resident of Twiggs Co. He was spending the night at the home of a "steam-doctor" who was to operate on him. He took a dose of lobelia and died that night about 11 o'clock. "Thus one of the most useful men in the western part of Ga. has fallen a victim to the system of steam quackery." Was a Baptist minister.

July 24, 1834

    Died at the residence of his son-in-law, the REV. W.C. HILL, in Monroe county, on Sunday morning, the 20th inst., the REV. ISAAC SMITH, in the 76th year of his age. He was a soldier in the revolution, under Washington, and was present at most of the principal actions which were fought by his distinguished leaders and although his term of service expired before the close of the war, yet he was present, as a volunteer, at the capturing of Cornwallis, at Yorktown; after which he retired from military life. After laboring for many years in the itinerant field, he located and settled in the town of Camden, S.C. and remained for a period of nearly thirty years; preached to inhabitants of North and South Carolina, Georgia, Alabama, Mississippi and Louisiana; a missionary to the Creek Indians.

July 24, 1834

    Died in this city on the 22d inst. JULIA ELEANOR VIRGINIA, daughter of LEVI ECKLEY, ESQ. Aged 9 months and 2 days.

July 31, 1834

    Died in Macon on the 25th inst. JACKSON PARKER, aged 20 years.

Aug. 7, 1834

    Died in this place, on the 5th inst. of the billious cholic, CAPT. RICHARD MARCELLIN, a native of the vicinity of Bordeaux, (France,) aged about 45 years.

Aug. 7, 1834

    Died on the 2d inst., CAROLINE EULALIA, daughter of ISAAC C. SEYMOUR, ESQ. aged 17 months.

Aug. 14, 1834

    Died in Fayette county, on the 25th July, SERGEANT JAMES TRIFLE, a member of the Fayette Blues. He was buried on the 26th with military honors, and in testimony of respect to his memory, the corps resolved to wear a badge of mourning for fifteen days; member of the Baptist Church; left a wife and two children.

Aug. 14, 1834

    Died suddenly in this city, on the 11th inst. AMANDA SYMMANTHA, daughter of WILLIAM C. PARKER, ESQ. aged 7 years 8 months and 6 days.

Aug. 21, 1834

    Report of deaths in Macon for week of Aug. 19th: Aug. 11th, AMANDA S. PARKER, age 7 years, of fever; Aug. 13th, BRIDGET DUGAN, age 36, of inflammatory fever; Aug. 18th, ANDREW J. HOLLINGSWORTH, age 8 months, of inflammation; Aug. 17th, ROBERT RHODES, age 16 years, of exposure and fever.

Aug. 28, 1834

    Died on the 20th inst. and in the 31st year of his age, GEORGE W. DILLINGHAM, ESQ. formerly of Lee, Berkshire Co. Mass. but for several years past, merchant of this city (with eulogy).

Aug. 28, 1834

Deaths in Macon, for week ending 26th inst. published by order of the Board of Health: GEO. A. EVANS, measles, age 1 year 10 mo.; ELLEN THOMPSON (colored), billious fever, 38 years; SARAH (colored), comsumption, 35 years.

Sept. 11, 1834

Sexton's Report of deaths in Macon up to the 11th of September, 1834, CATHERINE B. GODDARD, died 3d Sept. 1834, native of Middlesex, Connecticut, age 26 years; Infant slave of J.L. MASTIAN, died 5th Sept. 1834; Infant slave of WM. SOLOMONS, died 6th September, 1834.

Sept. 18, 1834

Died in this city, on the 14th inst. MRS. SUSAN C. TRACY, age 26 years, wife of EW'D D. TRACY, Esq.

Sept. 18, 1834

Sexton's Report of deaths for week ending September 16: 11th, Coloured man, 65 years old by rupture of blood vessel; 11th, 1 Coloured child 3 months; 14th, MRS. TRACY, age 26, of fever.

Sept. 25, 1834

Died in Jones county, at the residence of her brother, Wm. JOHNSON, MRS. CATHARINE MARTIN, of this city, aged about 55 years, of fever; member of Baptist church.

Sep. 25, 1834

Sexton's Report of deaths for week ending 23d inst: LUCINDA H., daughter of LARKIN GRIFFIN, aged 3 months.

Sep. 25, 1834

(Lexington, Sept. 15th, 1834) - Death of JUDGE WILLIAM H. CRAWFORD - he breathed his last at 3 o'clock this morning very suddenly of disease of the heart.

Oct. 2, 1834

Died on the 24th Inst. in the Town of Perry, Houston county of Typhus Fever, MRS. MATILDA R. OWENS, consort of JAMES N. OWENS, in the 21st year of her age.

Oct. 2, 1834

Sexton's Report of deaths for week ending October 1: Sept. 24 - LOUISA VIRGINIA, daughter of ROBERT W. FORT, aged 4 months; Sept. 25 - Coloured child, age 2 months; Sept. 29 - WM. G. GAMBLE, aged 4 years and 7 months, of bowel complaint.

Oct. 16, 1834

Died in Houston county, on the 26th ult. MR. ROBERT DANIEL SMITH, of the firm of Smith & Alford, aged 24. His remains were brought to this place for interment.

Oct. 16, 1834

Died in this City, GEORGE W. ALFORD (of the above firm), son of COLLIN ALFORD, of Fayetteville. He came to this place a few days before in ill health, and died on the 13th inst. His age was about 22 years; member of Methodist Episcopal Church.

Oct. 16, 1834

    Sexton's Report of deaths in Macon for week ending Oct. 8th: Oct. 4th, ELIZABETH ALLEN, age 30 years; Oct. 6th, SARAH ISAAC, age 22; Oct. 7th, negro child, age 4 years.
    Report for week ending Oct. 15th: Oct. 9th, negro woman age 22 years; Oct. 13th, GEORGE W. ALFORD, age 22, of Houston Co., of bilious fever.

Oct. 23, 1834

    Died in this City on Tuesday night the 21st inst. CAPT. LEMUEL NEWCOMB, aged about 33 years. His remains were carried to the grave on yesterday, under the Military escort of the Macon Volunteers, whose Commander he formerly was; - accompanied also by the Brethren of Macon Lodge (of which he was Sen. Warden).

Oct. 30, 1834

    The HON. THOMAS S. GRIMKE of South Carolina, died a short time since in Columbus Ohio, of the Cholera.

Oct. 30, 1834

    Sexton's Report of deaths in Macon for week ending October 29th: Oct. 11 - POLLY HOLLY, aged 40, consumption; Oct. 14 - STEPHEN BALLARD (BULLARD?), aged 52, of fever; Oct. 20 - negro child 3 years old; Oct. 24 - HANNAH (colored) age 30 years; Oct. 23 - CAPT. L. NEWCOMB age 35 years, of fever; Oct. 26 - JANE HODGKINS, 3 years, fever.

Nov. 6, 1834

    Died in Clinton, on the 28th inst. MISS HELEN L. LORD, daughter of JOSEPH L. LORD, Esq. Taunton, Massachusetts. This interesting young lady visited Georgia about twelve months past in company with a sister hoping that the mildness of a southern climate might restore her health, which had been impaired by a consumptive habit. Shortley after her arrival, she received an invitation to give Musical Instruction in Mr. T.B. Slade's School at Clinton, which she accepted. In June last her health suddenly declined, and she was constrained to abandon the idea of giving instructions any longer (with eulogy).

Nov. 6, 1834

    Died in Milledgeville on the 29th ult. COL. ZACHARIAH LAMAR, aged 65 years.

Nov. 6, 1834

    Died on Tuesday the 28th inst. AURELIUS JOHN BENJAMIN HOWARD, aged six months and sixteen days, son of THOMAS and HENRIETTA HOWARD, Bibb county.

Nov. 13, 1834

    Died on the 20th October, at the residence of WM. P. CARLES, in Shrewsbury, New Jersey, MR. GUY CHAMPLAIN, late of this city.

Nov. 20, 1834

    The Macon Volunteers published tribute of respect to SERGEANT GUY (GAY) CHAMPLAIN, member of that company. (this obituary appeared in issue of November 13, 1834).

Nov. 27, 1834

    Died in this place on the 14th inst. MR. HENRY YONGE, recently from McIntosh County.

Nov. 27, 1834

   Died on the 23d inst. aged 4 years MARTHA ANN CAMILLA, daughter of
   MR. HENRY CHAMPION.

Dec. 25, 1834

   Died of pulmonary consumption on the 21st inst. at the residence
   of his widowed mother in this city, DOCTOR LOUIS JEFFERSON WILLIAMSON
   KEATZ.

Jan. 1, 1835

   DENNIS N. OWENS, convicted of the murder of JOHN MANSON, was
   executed in the neighborhood of this city on Friday last.

Feb. 12, 1835

   Died in Columbia, S.C. on the 4th inst. GENERAL WADE HAMPTON, in
   the 81st year of his age.

Feb. 12, 1835

   Died in this city, on the 11th inst., of the Pleurisy, MR. THOMAS
   TOOMEY, a native of Ireland.

Feb. 19, 1835

   Died in this City, on the 17th inst. MR. MARTIN SIMMONS, Clerk of
   the Inferior Court of this county.

Feb. 19, 1835

   Died in Monroe county, on the 10th instant, after an illness of
   several days, MRS. SUSANNAH, consort of WM. G. FITZPATRICK.

Apr. 2, 1835

   Died at Forsyth, Monroe county, Ga., on the 4th ult., MR. ISAAC P.
   EVANS, aged 23 years.

Apr. 9, 1835

   Died in Greensboro, on the 16th inst. COL. JAMES FAUCHE, in the
   81st year of his age.

Apr. 9, 1835

   Died in Milledgeville, on the 2d inst. HENRY W. MALONE, ESQ.,
   recently Cashier of the Central Bank.

Apr. 9, 1835

   Died in Tennessee, on the 5th March, BISHOP McKENDREE, of the
   Methodist Church, aged nearly 78 years.

Apr. 23, 1835

   Departed this life on the evening of the 16th inst. WILLIAM
   THOMAS CLAYTON, aged 21 months and 9 days - son of ROWLAND and
   NANCY BIVINS of Bi-b County.

May 7, 1835

   (From Columbus Sentinel) - We have been informed by some gentlemen
   of the first respectability, direct from Texas, that MR. ELLIS of
   the State of Georgia, was murdered by his companion, a MR. JAMES
   JENKINS, on the Colorado river in Austin's Colony, on the 27th of
   March last.

May 7, 1835

   (From Georgia Journal) - Announce the decease of MR. JOHN R.W. CLARK
   last Saturday evening, of Small Pox. He was the youngest of the
   two surviving sons of the late Governor Clark, and being not more
   we think than 19 or 20 years of age.

May 14, 1835

   Died in New York, on the 29th ult. MR. OLIVER SAGE, aged 33 years -
   formerly a resident of Macon.

May 28, 1835

   Died in this county on the 24th inst., JOHN BULLOCK S-------(dim),
   the 15-year old son of FREDERICK and SUSAN S----- (dim).

July 2, 1835

   Died at his residence in Twiggs county, near Marion, on the night
   of 22d instant, MAJ. WILLIAM CROCEER, in the 58th year of his age;
   member of State Legislature; left bereaved family.

July 2, 1835

   Died in Henry county, on the 29th ult. SAMUEL JOHNSON, ESQ.

July 16, 1835

   (Philadelphia Advertiser, July 7th) - announces death of JOHN
   MARSHALL, the Chief Justice of the United States. He departed this
   life, in this city, at twenty minutes after six o'clock, on Monday
   evening, the sixth instant.

July 16, 1835

   Died in Monroe county, on the 6th inst., MRS. MARY GIBSON, consort
   of Col. Churchill Gibson, in the 45th year of her age; member of
   Baptist Church; left bereaved family.

July 16, 1835

   Died in this city on the 13th inst. ED. MITCHELL SIMS, son of
   ZACHARIAH SIMS, aged 13 years.

July 23, 1835

   Died on the 8th instant, at the residence of A.R. STEPHENS, near
   this city, EDWARD J. HARRISS, son of WILLIAM and LUCY S. HARRISS,
   aged 13 months and 20 days.

July 23, 1835

   Died of the inflammatory fever, in the 44th year of his age, in
   the city of New York, on the 11th April, MALCOM FERGUSON, ESQ.
   a merchant of Thomasville, Thomas County, Georgia. He left an
   affectionate wife and three small children.

Aug. 13, 1835

   Died in this place on Friday 31st ult. MRS. NOAH STEPHENS, a native
   of Windsor, New York.

Aug. 27, 1835

   Died in East Macon on the 19th instant, ANN ELIZABETH, only child
   of BENNETT and ELIZABETH ADAMS, aged 1 year and 10 months.

Sep. 10, 1835

Died at his residence, in Clinton, of billious fever, on Monday evening, 31st August, GEN. WILLIAM FLEWELLEN, in the 48th year of his age. For the last 23 years of his life, a member of the Methodist Episcopal Church; left wife and children (with eulogy).

Sep. 10, 1835

Died 20th August of _____ (dim), MR. MILES KING, aged 26 years, native of _____, S.C. (dim).

Oct. 1, 1835

Died on Saturday, the 26th inst., in the 27th year of his age, MR. JOHN HOLMES, Teller of the Branch of the Bank of Darien, in this place. Left wife and two young children (with eulogy).

Oct. 8, 1835

Died in this place on Sunday morning the 4th inst. MARY JOSEPHINE, infant daughter of NATHAN C. and TABITHA E. MUNROE, aged fifteen months.

Oct. 22, 1835

Died in this city, on the 13th inst., MR. JOHN H. WATSON, aged about 27 years, a native of Mecklenburg county, Va., but for several years a resident of this place. He was buried with military honors by the Macon Volunteers, of which corps he had been a member for several years.

Oct. 22, 1835

Died in Tennessee, a short time since, traveling for the benefit of his health, FRANCIS H. GODFREY, ESQ. an old inhabitant, and much respected citizen of this county.

Oct. 22, 1835

Died in Augusta, the 15th inst. ROBERT H. MUSGROVE, ESQ. in the 47th year of his age.

Oct. 22, 1835

Letters received from England, which arrived yesterday, containing intelligence of the death of the HON. WM. T. BARRY, our Minister to Spain, and late Post-Master General. His death occurred in England.

Oct. 29, 1835

Died in Havannah, of cholera, MR. NOEL CLARK, of Boston, aged about 26, son of the late JOSEPH HILL CLARK.

Oct. 29, 1835

Died at the residence of Mrs. Franklin, in Athens, on Saturday the 10th inst., MRS. ANN McDONALD, consort of the HON. CHAS. J. McDONALD, of Macon, and daughter of the late COL. ABEDNEGO FRANKLIN.

Nov. 5, 1835

Died at his residence in DeKalb county, on the 21st of October, DANIEL B. WORSHAM, in the 43d year of his age, after a protracted and severe affliction of the dropsy of the chest; left a wife to mourn his loss.

Nov. 5, 1835

   Died at the residence of his father in Vineville Sunday, the 1st inst., MR. JAMES C. OLDERSHAW, age 29 years, native of New York City but for last five years a resident here.

Nov. 5, 1835

   Died in Wilcox County, Ala., on the 7th inst., HON CHARLES TAIT in his 63rd (65?) year, a native of Louisa Co., Va., but moved many years ago to Georgia where he was one of the most distinguished men of his time. He was Judge Superior Court and U.S. Senator.

Nov. 22, 1835

   Died on the 20th inst. after a brief illness of eight days, MRS. MARY LAMAR, consort of JAMES LAMAR, of Bibb county.

Nov. 22, 1835

   Died in this City on the 16th ult. after a lingering illness, MR. JOHN WESLEY HAMILTON, in the 26th year of his age.

Dec. 10, 1835

   Departed this life, on Sabbath morning last, MRS. MARY E. RUSSELL, wife of MR. EDMUND RUSSEL of this city, and daughter of COLONEL DAVID WILSON(?) of Deerfield, Mass. The deceased was in the prime of life, just closing her twentieth year (with eulogy).

Dec. 10, 1835

   Died in this city on the 2d inst. with consumption, MRS. MARY DANIEL, in the 66th year of her age. She was a member of the Baptist Church for the last 15 or 20 years - a native of North Carolina, but a resident in Macon the last two years.

Dec. 17, 1835

   Contains a eulogistic poem to the memory of MRS. MARY E. RUSSELL who departed this life Dec. 6, 1835.

FROM "THE GEORGIA MESSENGER"
(Published weekly at Macon, Ga.)

Jan. 7, 1836

   Died on Saturday last, CHARLES CEKLEY, infant son of BENJAMIN and ELIZA TRAPP, and aged 11 months and 21 days.

Jan. 7, 1836

   Died at Savannah, on Saturday the 29th ult. HON. T.U.P. CHARLTON, distinguished citizen of the state of Georgia.

Jan. 7, 1836

   Died on the 13th ult. at his residence in Oglethorpe county, REV. BENJ. POPE, of the M.E. Church.

Jan. 7, 1836

   Died in Milledgeville, on Sunday the 20th ult. MAJ. WM. W. CARNES, late Comptroller General.

Jan. 7, 1836

   Died on the 5th ult. at his late residence in Montgomery county,
   Alabama COL. BENJ. B. LAMAR, formerly of this state.

Jan. 21, 1836

   Departed this life on the 11th inst., at the residence of her father,
   (THOS. SWIFE, ESQ.) in Morgan county, MRS. HARRIETT T. FURLOW,
   consort of JAMES W. FURLOW, of Monroe county, in the 19th year of
   her age.

Feb. 4, 1836

   Died on Saturday last, in the 61st year of his age, MR. ZACHARIAH
   SIMS, an old inhabitant of this city, and an industrious and most
   ingenious mechanic.

Feb. 11, 1836

   Died in this city, on the 4th inst., AUGUSTUS BEALL, son of MR. S.
   ROSE, aged about eighteen months.

Feb. 11, 1836

   Died on Wednesday evening, the 3d inst. GEORGE G., eldest son of
   DR. G.G. SMITH, formerly of this place, aged two years and seven
   months.

Feb. 11, 1836

   Died in this city, on the 4th instant, COL. ARCHIBALD DARRAGH,
   aged about 48 years, a native of Pennsylvania, but for many years
   a resident of this vicinity.

Mar. 3, 1836

   Died in this city on the 1st inst. WELLINGTON SUMNER, son of CAPT.
   HENRY S. CUTTER, aged 3 yaers and 9 months.

Mar. 17, 1836

   Died in this city, on the 5th inst., MRS. ANNA V., wife of DAVID
   RALSTON, ESQ. aged about 48 years.

Mar. 17, 1836

   Died in Monroe county, on the 15th inst. MR. JEPTHA BRANTLEY, aged
   about 48 years.

Mar. 24, 1836

   Died on Sunday 13th inst. AURELIA PENICE, infant daughter of
   GEORGE P. and LOUISA B. WAGNON, aged 8 months.

Mar. 31, 1836

   Died in this city, on the 29th inst. MR. BEVERLY REW, aged about
   50 years - a native of North Carolina.

Apr. 7, 1836

   Died on the 7th February, on the Seneca Reservation, in Pennsylvania,
   the celebrated CHIEF GAR-YAN-WAH-GAH, or CORNPLANTER, aged about
   100 years. This noble Indian, at an early period of the Revolutionary War, took an active part on the side of the Americans in that
   glorious struggle. When solicited by Washington to send some of
   his young men to Philadelphia for the purpose of be educated, he
   sent at the head of the band his son, Henry O'Bail. He, with his
   associate, RED JACKET, was, for many years, the councellor and

(Apr. 7, 1836, cont'd.)   protector of the interests of his nation.

May 12, 1836

   Died in this city, on the 10th instant, ROLLIN LEONIDAS, son of R.E. and M.N. CHURCH, aged 1 year and 7 months.

June 2, 1836

   Died in this County, on the 27th ultimo, MR. ELIJAH COTTON, aged 56 years.

June 9, 1836

   Died in this place, on Thursday last, MR. B.W. ALLMOND, a soldier in the late Florida campaign. He was for some time previous to his return laboring under a pulmonary affliction, occasioned by exposure.

Jul. 7, 1836

   Died, at his residence in Bibb County, on the 11th ultimo, MR. ROBERT DIXON, aged 77 years. Mr. Dixon served three years and three months in the Revolutionary struggle.

Jul. 7, 1836

   Died at his residence in Houston County on the 20th inst. PETER B. GREENE, in the forty-second year of his age' member of Methodist Episcopal Church.

Jul. 14, 1836

   Died in Knoxville (Georgia), on the 25th ultimo, MRS. BALSORA TROUTMAN, aged 32 years, 7 months and 16 days. (Obituary notice deferred to next week).

*Jul. 21, 1836

   Obituary notice of MRS. BALSORA TROUTMAN, deferred from previous week's issue.

Jul. 21, 1836

   Died in Marion county, on the 13th inst. MARY LOUISA, infant daughter of JEREMIAH and ELIZABETH VIRGINIA WYCHE - aged two years and five months.

Aug. 11, 1836

   Died on the 3d inst. at the house of Mr. John Worsham, near Thomaston, after a short confinement, MR. DAVID MELTON of Putnam county. He was acting wagon master of a detachment of wagons in public service; left an affectionate family to deplore his loss.

Aug. 18, 1836

   Died in Perry, Houston County, on the 20th ultimo, MISS ELIZA GUERRY, eldest daughter of THEODORE GUERRY, aged 17 years. She had been afflicted some time with the billous fever, which gradually underminded her constitution and finally terminated her existence.

Aug. 25, 1836

   Died on Monday the 22d inst., at 10 o'clock, in this place, the REV. JOHN HOWARD, of the M.E. Church, in the 45th year of his age. He was recovering from an attack of Bilious Fever, when an attack of Cholera Morbus terminated his existence.

Aug. 25, 1836

　　Died in Hawkinsville, on the 7th inst. MR. DAVID THOMPSON, of Laurens county, aged about eighteen years.

Sep. 15, 1836

　　Died in this city, on the 10th instant, MR. JONATHAN C. PHELPS, aged 22 years - a native of Farmington, (Connecticut).

Oct. 6, 1836

　　Died on the 23d ult. at his residence in Talfair Co. GEN. JOHN COFFEE, for many years, a prominent citizen, and at this time, one of our Representatives in Congress.

*Jul. 21, 1836

　　Died, in this city, on the morning of the 16th inst., GEN. ROBERT AUGUSTUS BEALL, aged aobut 32 years.

Oct. 6, 1836

　　Died at the residence of Welcome Parks, Esq. in Jasper County, on Saturday the 24th ultimo, VOLUMNIA JEMISON, daughter of THOMAS and SARAH (E.?) HARDIMAN, of this place, aged five years.

Oct. 13, 1836

　　Departed this life in Twiggs County Oct. 6, 1836, after a painful illness of two weeks, MRS. CATHERINE ANDERSON, aged -2 years, consort of CAPT. THO. W. ANDERSON, formerly of S. Carolina. She has left a bereaved husband and six children. (NOTE: Page torn and proper age illegible).

Oct. 13, 1836

　　Died in Monroe County, at the house of Mr. Joseph Howard on the 14th September, MRS. JERUSHA ANN (HOWARD) PARHAM, wife of MR. STITH PARHAM, of Upson County, in her 20th year.

Oct. 13, 1836

　　And on the 16th, SAMUEL S. HOWARD, in the 19th year of his age. They were the daughter and son of JOSEPH and ELEANOR HOWARD, both from a relapse of Measels; members of Methodist Episcopal Church.

Oct. 20, 1836

　　Died in Augusta on the 14th inst. MR. JAMES R. SINCLAIR. He was a native of England, and had been a teacher of Martial music in this city for two years past. He was a member of the Macon Volunteers; and was wounded at Fort Cooper, in their recent Florida Campaign.

Oct. 20, 1836

　　Died in Barnesville on the 15th inst. JOHN CRAWFORD in the 79th year of his age; member of Presbyterian Church for last five years; left an aged wife and number of children, relatives and friends.

Nov. 17, 1836

　　Died in this city, November 15, JOHN HASELTON, aged 33, formerly of Boston, Mass.

Nov. 24, 1836

　　Died on 21st inst. in East Macon, JOHN THOMAS GROCE, only child of MR. LEWIS GROCE, aged one year and eight months.

Dec. 1, 1836

    Departed this life, at the house of Mr. George W. Thompson, Line Creek, Ala., in the 29th year of her age, MRS. M.P. BOREN, of Macon, Geo. on the 24th inst. Left an affectionate husband and two small children.

Dec. 8, 1836

    Died in this county on the 3d instant, MRS. ELIZA A. LOWE, aged about 20 years - wife of MR. THOMAS LOWE.

Jan. 5, 1837

    Died in Irwinton, Ala. on the 22d inst. MRS. HETTY MOORE, in the 23rd year of her age - wife of CAPT. JOHN M. MOORE, and late of Houston county, Ga.

Jan. 19, 1837

    Died in this county, on the 12th inst. THOMAS P. STUBBS, SENR. aged about 50 years.

Jan. 19, 1837

    Died on the 17th inst. JOSEPH SEPTIMUS THOMPSON aged 20 years 2 months and 27 days. The deceased came to his death by a gun shot wound in the leg, occasioned by the accidental discharge of a gun by one of his juvenile associates.

Feb. 16, 1837

    Died in Savannah on the 9th inst. of inflammation, MR. JEREMY STONE, aged about 40 years. He was one of the earliest settlers of this place, and for a few years past had resided in Savannah.

Feb. 16, 1837

    Died in Monroe county on the 4th inst. of the Pleurisy JOHN SHOCKLEY ESQ. in the 51st year of his age.

Mar. 23, 1837

    Died on the 18th inst. at the residence of her husband, in Crawford county, Ga. in the 36th year of her age, MRS. SARAH WORSHAM, wife of DAVID B. WORSHAM, ESQ. after an illness of six months. Left husband and four children; for last two years of her life, a member of the Presbyterian Church.

Mar. 30, 1837

    Died in Richmond county at the residence of GEN. VALENTINE WALKER, in the 22 year of her age MRS. ELIZABETH L. REA, wife of DANIEL T. REA of this place, after an illness of ten months.

Apr. 20, 1837

    Died in Cassville on Tuesday morning 21st of March last, of a disease consequent upon a severe attack of bilious fever enduced in Jones county last fall JOSEPH J. HAMILTON ESQ., in the thirty fifth year of his age; has left a wife and three children.

Apr. 20, 1837

    Departed this life on the 15th inst. in the 60th year of his age, MAJOR SOLOMON GROCE, an old and highly respectable citizen of Bibb county.

Apr. 20, 1837

    Died on Saturday the 15th inst. in Baldwin County, MRS. JANE M. TORRANCE, in the 34th year of her age, the wife of WILLIAM H. TORRANCE, Esq. and daughter of the late PETER CRAWFORD, of Columbia county.

Apr. 27, 1837

    Died in Hawkinsville, on the 18th instant, DELAMAR CLAYTON, ESQ. A victim of despair from repeated domestic afflictions, this estimable man fell in the prime of life by his own hand (Fed. Union)

Apr. 27, 1837

    Died in Milledgeville, on the 23d instant, GENERAL D,B. MITCHELL. An emigrant from Scotland in his early youth, he has been a conspicuous man in Georgia, and twice elected to fill the Executive Chair. (Fed. Union.)

May 11, 1837

    Died in this city on the 1st inst. DANIEL R. CLEVELAND, formerly of Salem, Washington Co., N.Y. aged 56 years.

May 25, 1837

    Died at his residence in Dooly county, on the 13th inst. DR. JOHN L. SHELBY, in the 26th year of his age; highly respected and successful practitioner of Medicine; he had spent the last winter in Philadelphia, with a view to improvement in his profession. Has left a bereaved wife and orphan son.

Jun. 1, 1837

    Died on the 23d ult. in the 24th year of her age, MRS. CINDERILLA GAINER, wife of MR. JOSEPH GAINER, of this city.

Jun. 1, 1837

    Departed this life on Tuesday, the 23 ult. at his residence near Milledgeville, WILLIAM H. TORRANCE, ESQ., lawyer of high legal attainments.

Jun. 8, 1837

    Died in this place, on the 2d inst. MRS. ELDOCIA R. TRAVIS, consort of JOHN S. TRAVIS, in the 21st year of her age.

Jun. 22, 1837

    Died in Meriwether county, Ga. on Sabbath, 4th inst. DR. H.H. TIGNER, aged 45 years, after a protracted illness of seven months; member of Methodist Episcopal Church. (To the above obituary from the Columbus Inquirer, we would add, that Dr. Tigner was our first subscriber in Monroe county).

Jun. 22, 1837

    Died on the 18th inst. at the residence of her father, ROGER MACARTHY ESQ. MRS. MARY ANN LIPPITT, aged 31 years. of Consumption. In all the relations of Daughter, Sister, Mother and Wife, she was faithful, affectionate, and beloved. In 1834 she made a public profession of her faith in Christ, as a member of the Protestant Episcopal Church in this City.

Jul. 6, 1837

    Died in this city on the 4th inst. MRS. LUCIA R. HART, consort of MR. TRUMAN HART, aged about 21 years. She was a native of New

(Jul. 6,, cont'd.) - England, who relinquished her parental home, soon after her marriage, for a residence in Georgia.

Jul. 13, 1837

Died in Warren County, N.C. on the 29th June, the HONORABLE NATHANIEL MACON, aged 83 years. He was a private soldier in the Revolution; and for more than fifty years filled various offices of high respectability in his State.

Jul. 13, 1837

Died in Laurens county on the 4th July, GEN. DAVID BLACKSHEAR, in the 74th year of his age. He was born in North Carolina and at 16 years of age took up arms in the Revolution, and continued his service to his country until the close of the war. During the late war eith England, he served as a Brigadier General on our sea-board.

Jul. 13, 1837

Died in Savannah on the 29th ult. after a protracted illness, MRS. MARY ANN WASHBURN, wife of MR. JOSEPH WASHBURN and recently of this City. On the 8th ult., at Covington, their son AUSTIN F. aged 3 years.

July 13, 1837

Died in this city on the 29th ult. LOUISA PLEASANT, daughter of ROBERT and MARY BIRDSONG, aged 17 months.

Jul. 20, 1837

Died in Monroe county on the 3d inst. of congestive fever, MR. GEORGE W. CALDWELL, eldest son of CHARLES Y. and MARY CALDWELL, in the 29th year of his age. He was for last four years of his life a member of the Methodist Episcopal Church.

Aug. 3, 1837

Died at the residence of MR. STEPHEN MENARD, near this city, on the 31st July, in the 44th year of his age, MR. JOHN ALEXANDER CHOTARD, a native of the city of Niort, in the Department of Deux-Sevres, France. He had been in the U. States about five years, and for the last two, a resident of this city. He was attached to the Imperial Guard under Lafayette, from whom he brought letters of introduction to this country. His remains were interred with military honors by the Macon Volunteers.

Aug. 3, 1837

Died in this city on the 29th July, MR. JOEL B. BENNETT, aged 21 years. He was a native of Fall River, Mass. Although he had resided among us but a few months, his amiable and upright conduct had won the esteem of all who knew him.

Aug. 24, 1837

Departed this life, on the 14th of August, MRS. ELIZABETH SANDERS, wife of MR. WILLIAM SANDERS, of Bibb county, both formerly of Hancock county, in the 45th year of her age, leaving a husband and eight children with a number of relatives throughout Georgia and Alabama to mourn her loss.

Aug. 31, 1837

Died in Pontotoc, Miss. on the 2d inst. MR. JAMES A BLANTON, aged about 35 years - formerly one of our most respected and enterprising citizens.

Sep. 7, 1837

Died at Vineville, on the 29th ult. in her twelfth year, VIRGINIA WOODSON STRONG, third daughter of CHRISTOPHER B. STRONG, Esq.

Sep. 7, 1837

Died at Clarksville, Habersham county, on the 28th Aug. of consumption, MRS. MARTHA ELLIS, aged twenty-one years, a native of New-York, wife of MR. WILLIAM S. ELLIS of this city.

Sep. 14, 1837

Died at McDonough, Ga. on the 30th ult. VICTORIA, infant daughter of NATHAN C. and TABITHA E. MONROE of this city, aged one month and twelve daus.

Sep. 21, 1837

Died in Houston county, on Monday the 11th inst. SARAH DUBOIS, only child of DR. ISAAC D. and MRS. LOUISA B. NEWTON, aged about two years.

Sep. 21, 1837

Died on the 19th inst. at the residence of COL. H.G. LAMAR, BENJAMIN, eldest son of JAMES LAMAR, in his 18th year.

Sep. 28, 1837

Died on the 8th inst. at his residence near Wetumpka, Ala. BENJAMIN T. CHAPPELL, aged 30 years, formerly of Hancock county in this state.

Oct. 12, 1837

Died on Sunday the 8th inst. at the residence of his Father, near the city of Macon, JOSEPH PALMER CUTTER, eldest son of CAPT. HENRY S. and ANNA CUTTER, aged about 12 years, and 6 months.

Oct. 12, 1837

Died in East Macon on Wednesday the 4th ult. CASSANDRA OLIVIA HOGE, youngest daughter of the late Solomon Hoge Esq. of Clinton Jones county, aged 8 years 1 month and 4 days.

Oct. 19, 1837

Died in this city, on the 9th instant, MR. HARDY HARRELL, aged 66 years.

Oct. 19, 1837

Died in Philadelphia, on the 21st ultimo, MR. CHALKLEY B. COLLINS, in the 29th year of his age. He was a native of Pennsylvania, and for several years past a resident of this city.

Oct. 19, 1837

Died in this city on the 5th inst. MAJ. J. LOVING, aged 66 years, a native of Virginia, and a resident of Macon, since its earliest settlement.

Oct. 19, 1837

Died in this city on the 9th inst. MR. LUCIUS ARMS, aged 49 years - a native of Massachusetts, but for several years past a resident of this place.

Oct. 26, 1837

Perished, by the wreck of the steam packet "Home," on her voyage from New York to Charleston, on the night of the 9th inst. OLIVER H. PRINCE, ESQ., and his wife, MARY R. PRINCE, the former a native of Connecticut, and the latter of Georgia. Mr. Prince left Athens (the place of his residence) in May last for Boston to superintend the printing of a Digest of the Laws of Georgia which he had recently compiled by authority of the Legislature; and having completed his work, embarked, in company with his wife, on board the above packet. Mr. Prince for more than twenty-five years was a practioner of Law in this State. Mr. P. was one of the earliest settlers of Macon. He was one of the five commissioners who laid out the town, and superintended the sale of lots. In 1832 he abondoned the practice of the Law, and became the Editor of the Georgia Journal. Mrs. Prince had been for more than ten years a consistent member of the Presbyterian Church.

Oct. 26, 1837

Died in this city, on Tuesday morning, 24th inst. JOHN E. CARTER, son of MR. JOHN H. CARTER, of Boston, Mass., in the 21st year of his age. He had resided in Macon less than a year.

Oct. 26, 1837

Died in this City, on the 25th inst. MT. JAMES T. LEWELLEN, aged 25 years. He was a native of Lynchburg, Va. but for several years past a resident of this city. He was a soldier in the Macon Volunteers in the Florida expedition, and was wounded in a skirmish with the Indians, near the Withlacoochy.

Oct. 26, 1837

Died in Forsyth on the 4th inst. MRS. JULIET McKAY consort of DANIEL McKAY Esq.

Nov. 2, 1837

Died in this city on the 26th ult. CAPT. JOHN ELLSWORTH aged about 40 years. He was born in Dover, England, but came to N. York, at an early period of his childhood, where he resided many years. In 1836 he was in the service of his country - as an officer in the company of the Macon Volunteers during a campaign in Florida; was buried with military honors.

Nov. 16, 1837

Died in this city on the 14th instant after a short illness DR. HARRIS LOOMIS, aged about 37 years. He removed from Fayetteville, N.C. to this city about two years since. He was a man of considerable acquirements as a Botanist.

Nov. 16, 1837

Died in this city on Saturday the 11th inst. MRS. ANN ELLSWORTH, widow of CAPT. JOHN ELLSWORTH, aged about 55 years.

Nov. 16, 1837

Died in this city on the 14th (11th?) inst. ROBERT JENNINGS, aged 21 years, a native of Nottaway County, Virginia, for the last three years a resident of this place.

Nov. 16, 1837

Died in Troup county, Ga. at 12 o'clock on Saturday night Oct. 28th, MRS. SELINA C. FELTON, consort of RICHARD FELTON, and daughter of WILLIAM BATTLE, Sen., formerly of Taliaferro county, in the 31st year of her age; member of Baptist Church; left husband and two orphan sons.

Dec. 7, 1837

  Died in Vineville, on the 27th ult. MR. JOHN R. GAHAGIN, aged about 30 years.

Dec. 21, 1837

  Died in this City on the 9th inst., GEORGE AUGUSTUS, son of JOHN D. and MARY W. WINN.

Dec. 28, 1837

  DR. PHILIP SYNG Physic, eminent surgeon and physician, and celebrated lecturer, died in Philadelphia, on Friday, after a lingering illness; had retired from his professorship in the Medical School of the University of Pennsylvania. (Aug. Chronicle)

Dec. 28, 1837

  MR. PAUL ALISON, engineer of the locomotive Washington (Charleston and Hamburg Rail-Road), died in a train mishap, (NOTE" Article gives details of the train wreck)

Jan. 4, 1838

  Died at his residence in Houston County, on the 22d Dec. MR. STIMPSON CHANGE, aged about 90 years. Mr. C. was a soldier in the Revolution, and in our border warfare when the Oconee was our Western Boundary.

Jan. 4, 1838

  Died in Monroe Co. on the evening of the 25th inst. MISS REBECCA A. daughter of WARREN and MARY BARROW, aged 16 years.

Jan. 18, 1838

  Died in this city on the 11th inst. MRS. MARTHA wife of PETER SOLOMON ESQ., in the 25th year of her age. She has left a husband and two small children.

Jan. 18, 1838

  Died in this City on the 4th inst. MRS. JANE FLINT, aged 73 years and 6 months.

Jan. 25, 1838

  Died on Saturday the 15th inst. the REV. KITTRELL WARREN of Houston county, in the 54th year of his age. He had been to Dooly county attending one of his appointments as a Minister of the Gospel of Christ, when on his return home, he was thrown from his Mule, and before assistance reached him he was speechless, and soon after expired.

Feb. 1, 1838

  Departed on the 22d of this month, in 37th year of her age, MRS. MARY TISSEROT, consort of MR. B. TISSEROT: member of Presbyterian Church.

Feb. 22, 1838

  Died on Monday, Feb. 19, MRS. NANCY LOVING, widow of MAJ. JOHN LOVING, aged 44 years and 25 days.

Mar. 1, 1838

  Died on the 25th inst. MRS. CATHERINE CAMPBELL, wife of JEHU CAMPBELL ESQ., aged forty-three years. For the last seven years of her life, she was a member of the Presbyterian Church.

Mar. 1, 1838

   Died in Macon on the twenty-fourth inst. CHARLES COTTON, aged
   four years and seven months, son of CHARLES & ELIZABETH W. COTTON.

Mar. 8, 1838

   Died in Sumpter county, on the 29th February, MR. WM. M. TERVIN,
   aged about 24 years, formerly of Houston Co.

Mar. 15, 1838

   Died in this City on Thursday the 8th inst., after a protracted
   illness, MR. WILLIAM D. MANGHAM, in the 22d year of his age.

Apr. 5, 1838

   Died at his residence, in Monroe county, on the 12th ult. MR. LEVI
   STROUD, aged 51 years, after a protracted and painful illness.

Apr. 5, 1838

   Departed this life on the 27th, of March, at her father's in Talbot
   County, MRS. NANCY BALL, wife of the REV. JAMES M. BALL of Houston,
   and daughter of MOSES and TABITHA BOYNTON, formerly of Baldwin,
   now Talbot county, aged 27 years and 3 months, leaving an afflicted
   husband and five small children, and an infant 3 months old; member
   of Methodist Episcopal Church.

Apr. 12, 1838

   Died in Pike County near Zebulon on the 3d inst. MRS. JANE CAMPBELL,
   in the 54th year of her age; member of Methodist Episcopal Church.

May 3, 1838

   Departed this life, at Thomaston, Upson county, Ga., on Wednesday
   the 25th of April, MR. JULIUS CLARK. His last illness, an inflammation of the lungs, was painfully protracted to the seventh week.
   Mr. Clark was a native of Windham county, Connecticut; resided in
   Thomaston for ten years.

May 3, 1838

   Died of inflammatory rheumatism, at his residence in Monroe County,
   on the night of the 28th April, MR. ELI W. BOZEMAN, in the 42d year
   of his age, leaving a widow and four children.

May 17, 1838

   Died in this city on the 15th inst. after a lingering illness,
   MAJ. EVANS MYRICK, aged about 55 years; member of the Methodist
   Church.

May 24, 1838

   Died on the 16th inst. MRS. MARY SMITH, consort of MR. JOSEPH
   SMITH, of this city.

May 31, 1838

   Died near this city on the 310th inst. MR. _____ CROW, aged
   24 years; a native of North Canton, Hartford county, Connecticut.
   (NOTE: First name is not shown in newspaper)

May 31, 1838

   Died on the 28th of May 1818, at his residence in Wilkinson county,
   CHARLES WHITEHURST in the 66th year of his age. A native of North
   Carolina, but had been a citizen of said county more than twenty

June 14, 1838

   Died in this place on the 8th inst. after a protracted illness of
   27 days, MR. WM. F.J. HUEY, aged about 22 years.

June 14, 1838

   Died in Irwinton, Ala. on Wednesday morning, the 30th ult. of
   Hermorrhage of the lungs, COLONEL DAVID S. BOOTH, in the 61st year
   of his age. (Col. B. was one of the first settlers of Macon.)

June 21, 1838

   Died in this city, after a protracted illness, on the 16th inst.,
   MRS. ANN RYLANDER, wife of MR.E. RYLANDER, aged about 30 years.

June 21, 1838

   Died on Saturday last, the 9th instant, THOMAS B. MULFORD, ESQ.,
   aged 41 years, 9 months and 18 days. (He removed a few years since
   to Irwinton, from Monroe Co., Geo.)

June 21, 1838

   Died on Sunday, the 17th inst. of the Cholera Morbus, MORRIS
   MATTHEWS, the enterprising proprietor of the Indian Spring Hotel,
   aged 47 years.

July 12, 1838

   Died in this City, on the 5th inst. MR. WILLIS T. SAGE, aged about
   39 years. He was a resident of Greenfield Mass. but for the last
   eleven years, a resident of this place. He was bred to the Printing
   business, and for the first years of his residence here, was Foreman of this office. He was buried with military honors by the Bibb
   Cavalry, of which corps he was a member.

July 12, 1838

   Died on the 10th inst. CHARLES, only son of CHARLES and MARY DAY,
   of this city, aged 4 years, 2 months and 20 days.

July 19, 1838

   Died on Sunday night, the 15th inst., ELIZA ELLEN, daughter of
   JOHN M. & ELIZA SIMS, of this city, aged two years and nearly two
   months.

July 26, 1838

   Died in this county, on the 19th inst. MRS. CHARLOTTE MARY FURLOW,
   wife of DR. TIMOTHY M. FURLOW, and daughter of the late SAMUEL
   LOWTHER, ESQ. of Clinton, aged about 23 years.

Aug. 2, 1838

   Died on the 20th ult., the REV. DANIEL DUFFEY, a native of Ireland,
   in the 76th year of his age, at his residence in Crawford County;
   member of Methodist Episcopal Church 36 years, and a Local Preacher
   most of that time.

Aug. 2, 1838

   Died in Monroe County on the 24th (?) ult. MRS. NANCY PICKARD, wife
   of HENRY H. PICKARD, in the 75th year of her age.

Aug. 9, 1838

   Died on the 8th inst. SARAH ANN R.C. RUSSELL, daughter of A. & F.

(Aug. 9, cont'd.) - RUSSELL, (recently from Monroe County.) Aged 2 years 4 months and 24 days.

Aug. 9, 1838

Died in Carrollton, Miss. on the 28th July, of the billious fever, MR. JOSEPH GALES JOHNSON, a native of Virginia, aged about 22 years.

Aug. 9, 1838

MR. EMANUEL DE LA MOTTA, senior editor of the Savannah Republican, who left that city a short time since for the North, for the benefit of his health, died on his passage from Philadelphia to New York, on the 25th ult., at which latter city he was interred.

Aug. 23, 1838

Died at his residence in Monroe county, on the 14th inst. MARINER CULPEPPER ESQ. in the forty-sixth year of his age. Although the deceased had not united in public profession with any church, his sentiments were with the regular Baptists.

Aug. 23, 1838

Died, in New York, on the 11th inst., MR. HENRY J. CHAPMAN, merchant of this city, in the 27th year of his age, son of AMBROSE CHAPMAN ESQ., of Monroe county.

Aug. 30, 1838

Died in East Macon, on Sunday evening the 26th inst. SARAH ELIZABETH, youngest daughter of THOMAS L. and MARTHA ROSS, aged just nine months.

Sep. 13, 1838

Died in this City, on the evening of the 9th instant, MR. WILLIAM SUTTON WADE, aged 29 years; for last three years, a member of the Baptist Church.

Sep. 13, 1838

Died in the town of Rome, Floyd county, on the 1st inst. MRS. MARTHA ANTOINETTE LUMPKIN consort of COL. JOHN HENRY LUMPKIN, in the eighteenth year of her age.

Sep. 20, 1838

Died at Montpelier Spring, Monroe county, on the 19th inst., MR. JOSEPH D. WEED, of this city, aged about 26 years. His funeral will take place at the ringing of the bell, from the Presbyterian Church this day.

Sep. 20, 1838

Died on the 9th inst. of the Yellow Fever, while on his passage from Charleston to Bridgport, MR. BENJ. W. PLATT, of this city, formerly of Bridgport, Connecticut, aged about 27 years.

Sep. 27, 1838

Died at Wetumpke, Ala. on the 16th inst. of billious fever, ISAAC HARVEY ESQ. formerly a citizen of this place, aged about 52.

Sep. 27, 1838

Sexton's Report of Deaths: There were 47 deaths in the city of Macon from the 3d of July to the 23d of September inst. inclusive, as reported by the Sexton, viz. 24 whites, and 23 persons of color. July 3d, MR. MORGAN's child; 4th, ELIZA JACOBS; 6th, WILLIS T. SAGE:

(Sep. 27, cont'd) - 10th, CHARLES DAY's son; 30th, WM. CUMMINGS'
child; August 6th, JORDAN ODOM's child; 22d, MRS. BUTLER's child;
23d, MR. STARKS; 27th, THOS. ROSS' child; 23d, COL. CAMPBELL's child;
28th, MR. ROBERTSON and son; JORDAN ODOM's daughter; 31st, MR.
McKEE's son; September 1st, MRS. COLLIN's child; 3d, FREDERICK
BEALL's child; 6th, MR. GRIFFIN's child; MR. WEED's child; 7th,
THOMAS S. WADE: 17th, MRS. OWEN's son; 20th, JOSEPH D. WEED: 22d,
WM. HIGHTOWER's son; Owners names of the blacks - July 13th, S.S.
VIRGIN's; E.D. BLAKE'S; 14th, ALEXANDER RUSSELL's; 24th, DR. WILEY's;
25th, DR. FRANKLIN's; 30th, MISS CAMPBELL's; Aug. 3d, J. WAINRIGHT's;
4th, MR. HAY's; 7th, WM. B. PARKER's; T.T. NAPIER's; 9th, CHAS.
COLLIN's; A.R. RALSTON's; 12th, LOUISA WILLIAMS'; 14th, J. HOLLEMON"s;
15th, LEVI ECKLEY's; 20th, JOS. WILSON's; 23, MR. MOORE's; 29th,
MR. SINCLAIR's; 31st, LEVI ECKLEY's; Sept. 1st, JOHN HOLLINGSWORTH's;
14th, MR. NETHERLAND's; 20th, JOHN ROSS'.

Oct. 4, 1838

Died on Sunday afternoon, after a short but severe illness, MAJOR
THOMAS NAPIER, one of the oldest citizens of Macon, aged 71.

Oct. 4, 1838

Died in Tuscaloosa, Alabama, of fever, on the 21st inst. the REV.
CHARLES HARDY, Pastor of the Methodist Episcopal Church in that city.

Oct. 11, 1838

Died in Athens, Ga., on the 2d instant, WILLIAM R. DAWSON, son of
the HON. WILLIAM C. DAWSON, in the 19th year of his age.

Oct. 18, 1838

Died in Clinton on Saturday the 13th inst. CHARLOTTE MARY LOWTHER,
infant daughter of T.M. FURLOW, of this county, aged two months and
twenty seven days.

Oct. 18, 1838

Died in Houston county on the 14th ult. WILLIAM HENRY, infant son of
MAJOR H.B. HATHAWAY, aged 1 year and 8 months.

Oct. 25, 1838

Died in this city on the 21st inst. JAMES RANDOLPH, son of MR.
ISAAC HOLMES, aged about one year.

Nov. 1, 1838

Departed this life on Thursday evening, the 18th ult., in the 25th
year of her age, MRS. REBECCA A. LAMAR, consort of JEFFERSON J.
LAMAR, of Lumpkin, Ga., member of Methodist Episcopal Church.

Nov. 8, 1838

Died in this county on the 26th ult. WILLIAM JOHNSTON ESQ., aged
87 years. Mr. Johnston was among the earliest settlers in this
vicinity; He was an officer in the war of the Revolution, and
fought under Col. William Washington and Gen. Morgan.

Nov. 15, 1838

Died at Travellers' Rest, Dooly County, on the 26th ult. MRS. MARY
JONES, consort of DAVID JONES, ESQ., in the fifty-fourth year of
her age; member of Methodist Church.

Nov. 15, 1838

Died on the 3d inst. MRS. SUSAN CARROLL, consort of THOS. W. CARROLL,
of Monroe county, in her fifty-seventh year; member of Baptist
Church for eleven years.

Nov. 15, 1838

Died in Athens on the 27th ult., DAVID THOMAS, (of Camden county), aged fifteen years, a member of the Freshman Class, of Franklin College.

Nov. 15, 1838

Died in Twiggs county, MAJ. GEO. W. WELCH, a highly esteemed citizen.

Nov. 15, 1838

Died on the 28th ult. at Greensboro Ga. after an illness of nearly six weeks, JAMES RONALDSON BINNEY, formerly of Philadelphia, and recently engaged as an assistant in the Engineering department Georgia Railroad.

Nov. 15, 1838

Died in Camden county, on the 1st inst. MAJ. JOHN HARDEE, in his 71st year.

Nov. 15, 1838

Died in Darien, on the 31st ult. - MR. CHARLES S. DODGE, in his 38th year.

Nov. 22, 1838

Died, at his residence in Monroe county, on the evening of the 14th inst. COL. CHURCHILL GIBSON, in the 57th year of his age. He was a good neighbor, an affectionate husband, a kind father, generous and humane master.

Dec. 20, 1838

Died on the 17th inst. after a very short illness, MRS. ELIZABETH C. wife of MR. GEORGE W. PRICE, of this City; member of Protestant Episcopal Church; left afflicted husband and two motherless infants.

Jan. 3, 1839

Died in Madison Morgan county, on the 29th Dec. MARY ELIZABETH, infant daughter of COL. JOHN G. RIVES, aged two months and eight days.

Jan. 10, 1839

Died in this City on the 16th inst. MRS. CATHERINE PARMELEE, in the 27th year of her age, (wife of MR. A.C. PARMELEE.)

Jan. 17, 1839

Died in Marion, Twiggs county, on Tuesday the 8th inst. MR. JOHN FLEMING, in the 63d year of his age.

Jan. 24, 1839

Died in this city, on Friday morning last, MR. JAMES HOUSE, a native of Columbia S.C., aged about forty years.

Feb. 14, 1839

Died in Montgomery county, Ala. on the 29th Jan'y last, MRS. MARTHA E., wife of FRANCIS HAYNIE, ESQ. in the forty second year of her age. (with eulogy).

Feb. 14, 1839

Died in Milledgeville, on the 31st ult., MRS. JEAN MONCURE ORME, wife of RICHARD M. ORME, one of the editors of the Southern Recorder.

Feb. 21, 1839

Another Revolutionary soldier gone! Departed this life, on the 20th ult. MAJ. RICHARD RESPESS, a native of Newbern, N.C. in the 90th year of his age; member of the Baptist Church for more than fifty years. (with eulogy).

Mar. 21, 1839

Died at his father's residence in this city, on the morning of the 14th inst. ADAM ORSAMUS, eldest son of PLEASANT and ELIZABETH HEATH, aged 21 years and 19 days. (with eulogy).

Apr. 4, 1839

Died in this city, on the 2d instant, MRS. _____ NAPIER widow of MAJ. THOS. NAPIER. (NOTE: The "blank" appears in the announcement).

Apr. 18, 1839

Departed this life on the 25th of last month after a short but painful illness, JAMES McCOWN TILFORD, ESQ., twenty-five years of age; represented Macon county last year in the Legislature as Senator. (with eulogy - from Standard of Union)

Apr. 25, 1839

Died with the Croup, on the 20th inst. LAURA BEATRICE, the younger daughter of JOHN J. & ELIZA R. DUFOUE of St. Marys Ga., being 2 years 6 months and 16 days old.

May 9, 1839

Died in this city, on Thursday evening last very sudeenly, MRS. ELIZA, wife of MR. GEORGE JEWETT, aged 35 years; left husband and children; member of Church of Christ.

May 16, 1839

Died in Wetumpka, Ala. on the 6th inst. in the 39th year of her age, MRS. LUCINDA KELTON, consort of MR. ROBERT KELTON, formerly of this place, a native of Franklin County, North Carolina.

May 16, 1839

Died on Saturday morning last THOMAS (E?) son of SAMUEL S. VIRGIN, aged 11 months and 10 days. Also MUNROE, son of MYRON BARTLETT ESQ. aged 7 months.

May 23, 1839

Died in this City, on the 21st inst. MRS. SARAH WOODWARD, consort of MR. JOHN L. WOODWARD, of Monroe county, aged 31 years; for the last ten years a member of the Methodist Episcopal Church (with eulogy).

June 6, 1839

Died in this place, of Cancer, on Friday last, MRS. ANN SIMMONS, in the 63 year of her age. She was for sixteen years a member of the Baptist Church.

June 6, 1839

   Died in Harris county, MR. THOS. G. BATES of this city, aged about
   43 years. While travelling, he was attacked by brain fever, which
   terminated his life in a few hours. He was a native of Connecticut,
   but had been a resident of this city since its settlement; a member
   of the Baptist Church.

June 6, 1839

   Died at the Indian Spring, on the 1st inst. of the Consumption,
   DR. JAMES PATRICK aged 37 years - a resident of this city, and a
   native of Rockingham county, N.C.

June 6, 1839

   Died in Hancock county, GEN. HENRY MITCHEL aged 79 years.

June 6, 1839

   Died in this city on the 29th ult. JOHN GIBSON, son of WILEY J.
   GIBSON of Ala., in his 16th year.

June 20, 1839

   Died on the 12th inst., at the residence of THOMAS B. SLADE, in
   Vineville, his niece MISS SARAH HENDERSON, aged 16 years - daughter
   of the late DR. WM. HENDERSON and MARY ANN HENDERSON of Martin Co.,
   N.C. (with eulogy)

June 20, 1839

   Died in Vineville, on the 14th inst. MR. EDWARD R. BALLARD, aged
   about 37 years.

June 20, 1839

   Died near Blountsville, Jones county, on Monday the 10th inst.,
   MR. JOHN TICKNER.

June 20, 1839

   Also, on Wednesday the 12th inst., of a protracted illness, MAJ.
   JOHN CURETON, in the 43d year of his age.

June 27, 1839

   Died in Harris county, on the 10th inst., MAJOR HARDY CRAWFORD, in
   the 40th year of his age, leaving a disconsolate widow and six
   children.

July 4, 1839

   Died at his residence in this place on Friday night the 21st ult.
   the HON. AUGUSTINE C. CLAYTON. Judge Clayton wss born in the State
   of Virginia on the 27th Nov. 1783. He completed his education at
   the University of Georgia in 1804; pursued the study of Law under
   the late Judge Carnes; chosen a representative in the lower, and
   subsequently in the higher branch of the Legislature; thrice
   elected Judge of the Supreme Court of the Western Circuit; in 1832
   was elected a representative in Congress, for the State of Georgia;
   a Trustee of the University of Georgia (South.Whig)

July 4, 1839

   Departed this life, on 18th ult. after a painful and protracted
   illness of some years, EMILY MILLEDGE, consort of MILLER W. McCRAW,
   of Monroe county, in the 31st year of her age; left husband and
   three little children; member of Methodist Episco;al Church during
   the last nine years of her life (with eulogy).

July 4, 1839

Died in Sumpter County, on the 14th ult. COL. JOHN McCARTER, for many years known in Georgia as a Military Officer of the first talent; member of Methodist Episcopal Church.

July 11, 1839

Departed this life in the city of Macon, on the 6th inst., ROBERT W. FORT. He was born in Brunswick county Virginia, in the year 1802, removed to Georgia in the spring of 1818, and settled in Putnam county. He has leved successively in Powelton, Milledgeville, Macon and Charleston. In 1824 he joined the Methodist Episcopal Church (with long eulogy).

July 11, 1839

Died on the 8th inst., JOHN JOSEPH SIMS, son of JOHN H. and ELIZA SIMS, of this city, aged 1 year 4 months and 24 days.

Aug. 1, 1839

Died at the residence of his mother in Monroe county, on the 23d July, WM. S.C. REID, ESQ. in the 47th year of his age. He was born in Hancock county, and received his education in the University at Mount Zion. He completed his study of the Law at New Haven, Conn. and was admitted to the bar in Augusta in 1826, when he located in Clinton, and afterwards moved to this city where resided till his death.

Aug. 1, 1839

Died at his residence in Monroe county, on the 21st of June last, PITT MILNER, in the 71st year of his age; Deacon of Baptist Church for forty-seven years. (with eulogy).

Aug. 8, 1839

Died in Macon, on Thursday the 1st instant after an illness of seven or eight days, JOHN WILLIAMS ESQ. He contracted his disease in the lower counties, and finding himself very ill, he hastened to Macon, where he arrived exhausted with fatigue and disease, and survived only one week. He was born on the 10th April 1782 in Bertie county, North Carolina, from which State his father emigrated to Georgia when his son was an infant. He was for many years a citizen of Baldwin county, which county he twice represented in the Senate of the State, and subsequently was placed by the Legislature at the head of the Treasury Department. He has left a numerous family of children and grandchildren to mourn his loss.

Aug. 8, 1839

Died on Friday 26th July, of croup, MARGARET GORHAM aged 1½ years, youngest child of MR. JOHN PHILLIPS, of this city.

Aug. 15, 1839

Died at his residence in Talbot county, on the 8th inst., MR. DAVID HIGHTOWER, in the 21st year of his age, (son of JAMES HIGHTOWER, of Upson county); member of Methodist Church about two years).

Aug. 22, 1839

Died on the 26th ult., at the country residence of His Excellency GENERAL M.B. LAMAR, MRS. REBECCA LAMAR, in the 65th year of her age. Mrs. Lamar, the mother of our respected President, arrived in the Republic a few months since, on a visit to her son. (From the Texas National Intelligencer)

Aug. 29, 1839

Died on the 22d inst. in this place, of the billous fever, MR. JAMES E. RODGERS, second Engineer of the Steam-boat Sam Jones, a native of Pittsburgh, Pa.

Aug. 29, 1839

Departed this life at Forsyth, on the night of the 24th August, after a painful illness of nineteen days, AUGUSTA ADELAIDE, eldest daughter of WILLIAM S. and MARTHA NORMAN, aged 9 years, 11 months and 23 days. (with eulogy).

Aug. 29, 1839

Died in this city, on Wednesday evening last, after a short illness, MARY TABITHA, eldest daughter of GEORGE JEWETT, in the 11th year of her age.

Aug. 29, 1839

Died in this city, on the 19th inst. JOHN RANDOLPH, son of MR. J. COWLES, aged about two years and eight months.

Aug. 29, 1839

Died in Irwinton, Ala. on the 23d August, THOMAS HOWARD ESQ., in the 53d year of his age. His disease was an apparent affection of the Liver, and dropsey, with which he was confined about six weeks at the time of his decease. He removed from here in January last for the purpose of settling in Alabama.

Sep. 5, 1839

Died at his residence in Monroe county on the 23d Aug. of the congestive fever W.W. BLACK in the 55th year of his age.

Sep. 5, 1839

Died in Thomaston on the 27th of August, MISS ELIZA ANN THWEATT, in the 12th year of her age; member of Methodist Church. She has left a kind and indigent father, an affectionate mother, and several brothers and sisters (with eulogy).

Sep. 12, 1839

Died in this city on the 6th inst. MARY GARDNER, only daughter of NATHANIEL BARKER, ESQ. of this city, aged 3 years 5 months and 4 days (with eulogy).

Sep. 12, 1839

Died in East Macon on Saturday morning 8th inst., MRS. ELIZABETH ANN COOK, wife of HENRY L. COOK, aged 21 years, a native of Connecticut.

Sep. 12, 1839

We learn from the Frankfort Commonwealth of Tuesday last that JAMES CLARKE ESQ., Governor of Kentucky, died that morning about 8 o'clock. (Charleston Courier)

Sep. 12, 1839

SEXTON'S REPORT OF DEATHS: Aug. 1, JOHN WILLIAMS, native of Georgia, resident of Macon, age 57 years, bilious fever contracted in the low country; Aug. 3, ELIZABETH JERMAINE, resident of Macon, age 28 years, child bed; Aug. 7, JOHN LONG, native N.C., resident of

(Sep. 12, cont'd.) - Macon, age 20 years, brain fever, boat hand;
Aug. 13, SARAH E. JERMANY, native of Macon, resident of Macon, age
2 months, bowel complaint; Aug. 19, ELIZABETH COLEMAN, resident of
Macon, age 82 years, 6 months, old age; Aug. 22, MARY T. JEWETT,
native and resident of Macon, 11 years, inflammation of the bowels;
Aug. 23, JAS. G. ROGERS, native of Pennsylvania, Steam-boat engineer,
age 23 years, bilious fever; Aug. 24, JOHN TAYLOR, resident of Macon,
20 yrs., brain fever, river craft; Aug. 25, infant of MRS. W.,
stillborn; Aug. 27, _____ DODD, native of Kentucky, resident of
Macon, age 25 years, bilious fever; Aug. 30, JOHN FRILL, native of
Ireland, resident of Macon, age 23 years, bilious fever, boat hand;
Sept. 7, MARY G. BARKER, native and resident of Macon, age 3 years.
Same day ELIZABETH COOK, native of Connecticut, resident of East
Macon, age 21 years, bilious fever; Sept. 8, BENJAMIN PHILLIPS,
resident of East Macon, age 45 years, liver complaint; Sept. 9,
THOS. FINERON, native of Ireland, resident of Macon, age 23 years,
bilious fever, railroad; Sept. 10, MRS. HEATH, native of N.C.,
resident of East Macon, age 45 years, consumption. During the same
time, 7 negroes - 4 grown 3 children.

Sep. 12, 1839

We regret to announce that our esteemed fellow citizen, Commodore
DANIEL T. PATTERSON, of the United States Navy, and Commandant of
the Navy Yard and station in this city, expired on the morning
of Sunday 25th instant, at a quarter past 8 o'clock, at his residence in the said yard, after a short but severe illness of about
30 hours. (National Intelligencer)

Sep. 19, 1839

Died at the residence of Col. Seaborn Jones, near this City, MISS
SARAH AMANDA BENNING, in the seventeenth year of her age. (with
eulogy - Enquirer)

Sep. 19, 1839

Died in Warrenton, on the 25th August, ELLEN LOUISA, infant daughter
of EDWARD B. and ANN F. YOUNG, aged one year and thirteen days.

Sep. 19, 1839

Died in Henry county, on Thursday the 12th inst. PEYTON SMITH,
infant son of WILLIAM L. and ORRY COX TUGGLE, aged 1 year, 1 month,
and 20 days.

Sep. 19, 1839

Died at Laurensville, S.C. on the 29th ult., SAMUEL BENTON TAYLOR,
ESQ. Attorney at Law of Hawkinsville Geo. Mr. Taylor was in the
25th year of his age and had been a resident of Georgia for the
last five years. He was on his way to the place of nativity in
North Carolina, on a visit to his parents.

Oct. 3, 1839

Notice of the death of GEN. ROBERT Y. HAYNE, the President of the
Rail Road Company and one of South Carolina's favorite and most
gifted sons. He died on Tuesday last of fever, after an illness
of about a week, having been attacked a few days after his arrival
at Ashville from Charleston. (Pendleton Messenger)

Oct. 10, 1839

Death of the esteemed philanthropist MATTHEW CAREY, ESQ. He died
on Monday evening, between eleven and 12 o'clock, at his residence
in Walnut Street. (long obituary - from Philadelphia U.S. Gazette).

Oct. 10, 1839

Died in Mooresville, Alabama, on the 24th ult. MRS. ANN D. HARRIS, consort of MR. WM. T. HARRIS, formerly of Macon, after a short illness.

Oct. 17, 1839

Died on the 13th inst. after a lingering illness of a pulmonary character, MRS. MATILDA E. WOOD, aged 29 years - wife of MR. THOS. WOOD of this city.

Oct. 17, 1839

Died on the 20th ult., near the Oneida Castle, ONDAYKA, head chief of the Onadagas, aged about 96 (Oneida Whig).

Oct. 31, 1839

Died on Friday, 24th inst. after a protracted illness, MARIA N., wife of R.E. CHURCH, of this city, aged 31 years.

Oct. 31, 1839

Died on the 29th inst. ELIZABETH ANN, Infant daughter of H.L. COOK, aged three months and 13 days.

Nov. 7, 1839

Died at his residence in Jones county, on the 30th October, MR. JAMES WADSWORTH, near 75 years of age. He was a citizen of North Carolina during the Revolutionary war; he was actively engaged with the Whigs in the struggle for Independence, subsequently removed to Hancock county, Ga., from there to his late residence.

Nov. 14, 1839

Died at her residence in Bibb county, on the 7th inst. MRS. PENELOPE THOMPSON, in the 76th year of her age, after a protracted illness of nine months. She was left a widow, with a large family of children, which she raised and lived to see all married except two.

Nov. 14, 1839

Died on the 6th inst. in this county, MRS. JUDY COLLINS, wife of MR. THOS. COLLINS, aged nearly 70 years; for the last 35 or 40 years a member of the Baptist Church.

Nov. 21, 1839

Died in Houston County Ga. Oct. 17, 1839, MRS. SARAH A. RUMPH, wife of MR. JACOB RUMPH, and daughter of MR. JOHN and MRS. A.B. McCANTS. She had been married three years, and for six years had sustained an orderly and acceptable connection with the M.E. Church. Mrs. Rumph was near the completion of her 22d year and has left one son about 17 months old. (with eulogy)

Dec. 26, 1839

Died on Sunday evening last, THEODRICK L. SMITH, aged 40 years, a native of Virginia but for many years a highly respected inhabitant of this city. He was interred Monday evening with the usual honors by the masonic fraternity.

Jan. 2, 1840

Died in Sumpter county on the 26th Dec. MRS. MARTHA HANSON, (late MARTHA TERVIN) wife of MR. F.T. HANSON. They had been married only two days previous, and she expired very suddenly.

Jan. 23, 1840

Died on the 19th December, in Sumter County, ELIZABETH FORT TOMLINSON, wife of DR. JARED TOMLINSON, aged 23 years (with eulogy).

Feb. 6, 1840

Died in Tallahassee, Florida, on the 27th ult. FELIX McKENNE HOBBY, aged 2 years and 10 months, son of ALFRED M. and ANN E. HOBBY.

Feb. 6, 1840

Died in Athens, on Monday, the 27th ult., ZACHARIAH LAMAR, eldest son of HOWELL and MARY ANN COBB, aged three years and 27 days.

Feb. 13, 1840

Died in this City, on the night of the 10th inst. of the consumption, MR. RODMAN E. CHURCH, aged 32 years. He was formerly of Durham, in the state of Connecticut, but had resided here since the early settlement of the place; for eight years had been a member of the Presbyterian Church. He was buried on the 11th by the Macon Volunteers of which company, he had for many years, been a good and prompt soldier; and it is believed that the seeds of the disease of which he died, were contracted during the hardships and exposure of the Florida Campaign in 1836.

Mar. 12, 1840

Died in this city of consumption, MR. J.H. MOORE, a native of New Hampshire, for the last 10 or 12 years a resident of New York. He has for many years, been a professor of the religion of Christ.

Mar. 26, 1840

Died in this City on Friday night last, MRS. CATHARINE B. GRESHAM, wife of J.J. GRESHAM, Esq., and daughter of DR. A.H. FLEWELLEN of Columbus, Ga. Mrs. Gresham had not yet reached the nineteenth year of her age, and had been married but a few months previously; member of the Methodist Episcopal Church (with eulogy).

Mar. 26, 1840

Died in this city on the 21st inst. CHARLES WARREN, aged 11 years and 22 days, eldest son of JAMES and SOPHRONIA GODDARD.

Mar. 26, 1840

Died in this City, on Wednesday, the 25th inst., BENJAMIN F., youngest son of D.F. GRIFFIN.

Apr. 9, 1840

Departed this life in Macon county, Ga. on the first day of April, 1840, REV. ELIAS JORDAN, aged 36 years. Mr. Jordan was a local preacher of the Methodist Episcopal Church; left a large family, consisting of a wife and children.

Apr. 16, 1840

Departed this life, yesterday morning, after a painful indisposition, MRS. MARTHA ANN SHINHOLSTER, aged 32 years, consort of THOS. J. SHINHOLSTER, of this city, leaving an affectionate husband and four children; for more than twelve years a member of the Methodist Episcopal Church.

Apr. 16, 1840

Died at his residence in Macon county, on the 13th inst., JOHN STAPLER, in the 51st year of his age - leaving a wife, and numerous

(Apr. 16, cont'd.) - relatives and friends to mourn their loss. (with eulogy).

May 7, 1840

Died in Vineville, on the 5th inst. COL. WM. NIXON, aged about 67 years. He was formerly from Camden South Carolina.

May 21, 1840

Died in this city, on the 7th inst., MR. ISAAC C. COLLIER, in the 18th year of his age; a member of the M.E. Church (with eulogy).

May 21, 1840

Died in Athens, Ga. on the 11th inst., GEN. BURWELL POPE, in the 50th year of his age.

May 21, 1840

Died in this city on the 13th inst., JAMES WILLIAM youngest child of MR. and MRS. R.B. WASHINGTON, aged about six months.

May 28, 1840

Died in this county, on the evening of the 26th inst. after a lingering illness, MAJ. TARPLEY HOLT, aged about 63 years; member of Methodist Church.

May 28, 1840

Died on Monday morning last, JOSEPH, infant son of GEO. P. and ELLEN C. COOPER, aged ten months and 15 days.

May 28, 1840

Died in Houston county, at the residence of J.W. Williams, on the 23rd May, MR. THOMAS REDD, aged about 48 years - formerly a resident of Macon.

June 11, 1840

Departed this life in this city, on the 6th inst., after a long and protracted illness, MR. THOMAS J. HOLLINGSWORTH, in the twenty-second year of his age - son of JAMES and ELIZABETH HOLLINGSWORTH.

June 18, 1840

Died in Culloden, on the 2d June, (inst.) ELIZA C., wife of AMOS M. HAMMOND, in the 29th year of her age.

June 25, 1840

Died in this city, on the 20th inst. MISS URANIA PORTER, formerly of Hartford, Conn. The deceased came to reside in this city two or three years since.

July 2, 1840

Died at his residence, in Carroll county on the 14th ult. the HON. WILLIAM G. SPRINGER, in the 51st year of his age.

July 2, 1840

Died at his residence in Starkville Lee County, on the morning of the 19th ult., DR. LEONARD WEEKS, from an attack of inflammation of the lungs which put a period to his existance in thirty hours; has left a bereaved widow.

July 9, 1840

   Died in San Augustine, Texas on the 2d day of April, after a painful illness of four weeks, COL. JOHN THOMAS, formerly of Laurens county, Ga.

July 9, 1840

   Died in this City on the 3d ult. JAMES HAMILTON COWLES, son of JERRY COWLES, aged 2 years and 23 days.

July 9, 1840

   Died on the 28th ult., REMEMBRANCE CHAMBERLAIN SAUNDERS, a native of Vermont, aged about 28 years.

July 9, 1840

   Died in East Macon on the 8th inst., JAMES S. FRIERSON, ESQ. of Early county, formerly a resident of this City.

July 30, 1840

   Died near Columbus, on the 14th inst. MR. TANDY W. KEY, aged 55 years, a highly respectable citizen of Henry county. His death was occasioned by being thrown from his horse, which he survived but a few hours.

July 30, 1840

   Died in this City, on Sunday night last 26th inst. after a lingering illness, WILLIAM HENRY, infant son of DANIEL T. & FRANCES DRIGGERS, aged 1 year 4 months and 15 days.

Aug. 13, 1840

   Died in Forsyth, on Friday last, JOSEPHINE, daughter of GEO. P. and ELLEN C. COOPER, of this City, aged 2 years, 3 months and three days.

Aug. 13, 1840

   Died at Montpelier Springs on Friday, the 7th inst. HORACE KELLOGG, only child of HORACE and HARRIET FITCH, of this City, aged 1 year, 5 months and 25 days.

Aug. 20, 1840

   Died in Athens, on the 21st ult. MOSES WADDEL, D.D. late president of Franklin College, aged 70.

Aug. 20, 1840

   Died in Auburn, (Ala.) DRURY Y. MINS, aged 24 years, formerly of Monroe county, Ga.

Aug. 27, 1840

   Died in Vineville on the 25th inst. WILLIAM PETTIBONE, youngest son of GEORGE JEWETT, aged 4 years and 5 months.

Sep. 3, 1840

   Died suddenly in Perry of Croup, on the morning of the 21st ult., WILLIAM, infant son of GEORGE and MARY PATTEN.

Sep. 3, 1840

Died in Sumter county, on Sunday afternoon, the 16th ult., at the residence of his Step Father, MR. ROBERT LOUDON - MR. JAMES H. RONALDSON, a merchant of Haynesville, Houston county. Mr. Ronaldson had been thrown from his horse three months age, and had been complaining previous to his leaving Houston for his Mother's residence, where he was attacked with fever - a relapse took place which resulted in inflammation of the brain.

Sep. 17, 1840

Died in this city, on the 12th inst. MRS. ELIZABETH WADE, consort of MR. ZACHARIAH WADE, aged about 57 years; a member of the Baptist Church.

Sep. 24, 1840

Died on the 13th of August, of congestive fever, at the residence of Mr. Blackshear Bryan of Pulaski, MRS. ELIZABETH JARVIS, consort of MR. GEORGE JARVIS, in the 36th year of her age.

Sep. 24, 1840

Departed this life in Houston County, on Thursday morning, 17th inst., at the residence of her grand-father, MR. HEZEKIAH THOMSON - after a short illness of congestive fever, MARY EMMA THOMSON aged 11 years, two months and 9 days (with eulogy).

Oct. 8, 1840

Died at Matogorda, Texas, on the 26th August - EDWARD L. HOLMES, ESQ., aged 26 years; former resident of this city; devoted to profession of Law (with eulogy).

Oct. 15, 1840

Died in Columbus Ga. on the 2d inst., MRS. CATHARINE GARDNER, in the 27th year of her age, consort of BENJAMIN GARDNER.

Oct. 15, 1840

Died in this city on the 11th inst. ELLEN CORRINNA, infant daughter of JAMES and SOPRONIA GODDARD, aged sixteen months.

Oct. 22, 1840

On the 18th inst. at the house of his Brother-in-law THOS. HARDEMAN ESQ. Departed this life, BENJAMIN W. SPARKS, youngest son of THOS. SPARKS, late of Putnam county, Geo., in the 21st year of his age, deprived in early life of the fostering guardianship of his parents, an orphan boy; placed at the Georgia Manual Labor School; continued his studies until 1836, when he bid a reluctant adieu to the home of his sister, for a residence with a brother in Louisiana, after a stay of about 3 years, he was laid prostrate by an attack of the congestive fever; he survived but never fully recovered his health (with eulogy).

Oct. 22, 1840

Died in Houston county, on the 17th inst., FREDERICK D. WIMBERLEY, ESQ., aged about 30 years.

Oct. 29, 1840

Died at his residence in Houston County, on the 17th inst., of congestive fever, FREDERICK D. WIMBERLY, aged thirty-one; an alumnus of Franklin College; left wife and children (with long eulogy).

Oct. 29, 1840

   Died in Perry, on the 27th instant, LEWIS J. JORDAN, ESQ., recently Clerk of the Superior Court of Houston County.

Oct. 29, 1840

   Died in Macon County on the 17th instant, MR. ISIAH LAW, in the 57th year of his age.

Nov. 12, 1840

   Died in Upson County, on the 29th October, MRS. SARAH BURK GIBSON, consort of OBADIAH C. GIBSON, ESQ: had been suffering for six months past with a pulmonary affection; was 25 years and six months old; left husband and five little children; member of Methodist Episcopal Church about ten years past (with eulogy).

Nov. 12, 1840

   Died on the morning of the 3d inst. MRS. ELIZABETH E. GRIFFIN, daughter of APPLETON ROSSETER, of Florida, in the 25th year of her age (with eulogy).

Nov. 12, 1840

   Died in Houston county, on Monday the 2d inst. of dropsy of the heart, MISS MARGARET CORNELIA, eldest daughter of MAJ. H.B. HATHAWAY, in the 16th year of her age.

Nov. 12, 1840

   Died in Forsyth, on the 28th ult. ROBERT COLEMAN, ESQ. aged 56 years. He was one of the earliest settlers of the city, and still resided in the vicinity.

Nov. 12, 1840

   Died in this city on the 4th inst. MR. CHESTER HILLS, formerly of Hartford, Conn.

Nov. 12, 1840

   Died in Milledgeville, on the 27th ult. MR. GEO. R. CLAYTON, aged 61 years.

Nov. 19, 1840

   Died at her father's residence in Wetumpka, Ala., of nervous fever, after an illness of twenty-six days, MISS LOUISA JANE, daughter of HENRY VAN BIBBER, aged 15 years, 7 months and 26 days.

Nov. 26, 1840

   Died in this city, on the 23d inst. MRS. REBECCA C. WIMBERLY, wife of COL. JAMES WIMBERLY, in the 51st year of her age; left husband, children, brother and sisters; member of Methodist Church (with eulogy).

Nov. 26, 1840

   Died in Hamburg, S.C. on the 10th inst. after seven hours illness, MRS. ELLEN M. WOODS, in the 23d year of her age, formerly of Milledgeville.

Nov. 26, 1840

   Died in Monroe county, on the 7th inst., MR. PATRICK McCALLUM, about 55 years old.

Dec. 3, 1840

Died at her residence in Wetumpka, Alabama, on the 14th of November, MRS. JANE LEAK, consort of the late REV. SAMUEL LEAK, of Pike county, Ga., in the 59th year of her age. She was an acceptable member of the Church upwards of 25 years.

Dec. 3, 1840

Died at his residence in Hamilton county, Florida, on Monday the 2d November instant, after an illness of three weeks APPLETON ROSSETER, ESQ. in the 69th year of his age.

Dec. 17, 1840

Died at Hawkinsville, on the 9th December, S. TOURTELOTT, formerly of Mass. aged 29 years.

Dec. 24, 1840

JEFFERSON J. LAMAR, ESQ. died on the 15th instant at his residence in Stewart county, in consequence of the wound he received at the hands of John Reynolds, about the first of October last. (Southern Recorder)

(Spring Hill, Stewart co. Dec. 15, 1840) - Mr. Lamar died this morning about 10 o'clock, of the wound he received on the evening preceding the election in October last. Mr. Lamar was in the prime of life and usefulness (being 38 years of age).

Dec. 24, 1840

Died very suddenly in this place, on the 19th inst. of apoplexy, CEPHAS SMITH, about forty years of age, a native of Rutland, Vermont; member of the Mutual Aid and Benevolent Association, the Macon Volunteers, and the Macon Lodge.

Jan. 7, 1841

Died on the 20th Nov. MRS. FRANCES ADAMS, wife of MR. JAMES ADAMS of Jasper county, aged 38 years, 11 months and 15 days.

Jan. 7, 1841

Died on the 5th inst. in Scottsboro, REBECCA MARSHALL, youngest daughter of ELIZABETH and JOEL T. TUCKER, aged one year five months and twenty-one days.

Jan. 7, 1841

Died in Pulaski county, 1st October last, MR. SIMEON GREY, formerly of Warren county, aged 37 years.

Jan. 21, 1841

Died near Milledgeville, on the 16th instant, WILLIAM D. JARRATT, ESQ., in the 64th year of his age. He was among the early settlers of that place, and has been one of its most prominent and respectable citizens.

Jan. 28, 1841

Died in this City on the morning of the 26th inst. EMMA CORNELIA, infant daughter of WM. B. and ADILADE WATTS, aged about 5 months.

Jan. 28, 1841

Died in this City, on the 26th inst. MISS JANE SHACKLEFORD, aged about 14 years, daughter of FR. R. SHACKLEFORD ESQ. of Darien. She was a student at the Female College, and while sitting in her

(Jan. 28, cont'd) - rroom alone, on Wednesday of last week, her clothes took fire. She lingered in great pain for about six days before she expired.

Feb. 4, 1841

Died in Columbus, Ga. MRS. APHIA COLQUITT, consort of the HON. WALTER T. COLQUITT. We understand that Mrs. C. had been married only about one month previous to her death.

Feb. 4, 1841

Died in New-Orleans, of Consumption, on the 13th instant, MRS. MARY S., consort of MR. GEORGE C. McNEILL, of this city, aged 24 years.

Feb. 4, 1841

Another Revolutionary soldier gone! Departed this life at his residence in Monroe county, on the 4th inst. BENJAMIN HAYGOOD, SR. in the 83d year of his age. He was a native of North Caroline, where, in the 17th year of his age, he volunteered in the cause of liberty; and after the expiration of his first term of service, he was found twice again in the field as a volunteer; was married in his 20th year to MARY STEWART, and they for 62 years enjoyed each other's society; member of Baptist Church; removed to Georgia in 1791.

Feb. 11, 1841

Died in this City on the 9th inst. CHARLES L. BOWERS of New Haven Conn. aged 25 years.

Feb. 18, 1841

Died on the 10th inst. in Upson county, MR. CHAUNCY BEACH, about 38 years of age, a native of Northford, Connecticut; for nearly two years an orderly and pious member of the Methodist Church.

Mar. 11, 1841

Died in this City on Saturday the 6th inst. MR. JOHN H. OGLESBY, (Printer) aged 37 years. He was a native of Lynchburg, Virginia.

Mar. 25, 1841

Died on Monday the 22d inst. of Inflamatory Rheumatism, MR. ADDISON PRATT of this city, late of Fayetteville Onondaga County New York, aged 26 years. The deceased has left a disconsolate wife and child, affectionate Parents, a loving Brother and Sisters.

Mar. 25, 1841

Departed this life on the 20th inst. at his residence near Forsyth, Ga. ISAIAH CHAPMAN, ESQ. in the 59th year of his age. He had long been afflicted with a tumour on his breast, which finally terminated his earthly career; member of the Methodist Episcopal Church.

Apr. 22, 1841

Died in this county, on Tuesday the 14th inst. LUKE J. MORGAN, ESQ. aged about 60 years; one of the earliest settlers of the county.

May 6, 1841

Died at the poor house in this city, on the 2d inst. GILAM WATKINS, aged 72 years.

May 27, 1841

Died in this city, on Friday night the 21st inst. MRS. MARGARET GAINER, wife of MR. JOSEPH GAINER, in her twenty-second year (with eulogy)

May 27, 1841

    Died on Sunday evening, MRS. SARAH ANN CASSELS, wife of REV. S.J. CASSELS.

June 17, 1841

    PHILIP THURMAN departed this life on the 9th inst. in the 77th year of his age. He was a revolutionary soldier - was present at the surrender of Cornwallis; professed religion in August, 1837, and joined the Methodist Episcopal Church in November of the same year. (with eulogy)

June 17, 1841

    Departed this life, on the 20th of April, at the residence of Capt. Ralph Smith, of Spartanburg Districk, S.C. MISS ARAMINTA JANE CLENDINEN, of LaGrange, Ga. aged 21 years; a member of the M.E. Church; has left a mother and an only brother. (with eulogy).

June 24, 1841

    Died in this county, on Saturday the 19th inst. MRS. MARY DIXON, wife of MR. JOSIAH DIXON, aged about 56 years; a member of the Methodist Church upwards of thirty years (with eulogy).

June 24, 1841

    Died on the 18th inst. at the residence of Dr. H.L. Battle in Crawford county, MISS EMILY JANE, daughter of CAPT. JOSIAH HORTON of Monroe County, in the 19th year of her age (with eulogy).

June 24, 1841

    Died in Monroe county, on the 8th inst. MRS. MARY W. BILLINGSLEY, daughter of the REV. DAVIS SMITH, in the 19th year of her age, after a few days illness. She was interred in the same grave as her infant child, which died the day previous.

June 24, 1841

    Died in this city on the 18th inst. RACHEL, infant daughter of J.S. and M.M. WINN.

July 15, 1841

    Died in this city, on the 29th ult. JULIA EMILY, infant daughter of MR. S. and MRS. M.J. HART, aged twenty-five days.

Aug. 5, 1841

    Died in this City on the 23d ult. THOMAS J. SAULBURY, ESQ., Clerk of the Inf. and Court of Ordinary of this county, aged about 31 years. On the 24th ult. he was interred by Macon Lodge, and the Macon Volunteers, with Masonic and Military honors.

Aug. 5, 1841

    Died on Wednesday the 28th July, ELLA AMANDA, infant daughter of HON. E.A. NISBET, aged 14 months.

Aug. 5, 1841

    Died in this City on the 28th July, SARAH MASON, daughter of JAMES and CATHARINE WILLIAMS, aged nineteen months.

Aug. 12, 1841

    Died in this city, on Thursday night the 5th instant, COL. SIMON BATEMAN, of Houston county, probably about 46 or 47 years of age.

(Aug. 12, cont'd.) - He was taken severely ill while travelling to Milledgville and Putnam county. He arrived here on the 2d, and was confined to his bed until his death. He had filled the offices of justice of the inferior court and sheriff of his county.

Aug. 12, 1841

Died at Rotherwood, Carroll county, at the residence of her late brother, WM. G. SPRINGER, MRS. CATHARINE ALEXANDER, daughter of the late JOHN SPRINGER, of Wilkes county, Geo.

Aug. 12, 1841

Died at his residence near Milledgeville on Wednesday the 4th inst., COL. SAMUEL ROCKWELL: for many years a leading member of the bar; was buried with Masonic and Military honors.

Aug. 12, 1841

Died on the 8th inst. in Culloden, SAMUEL BIVENS ESQ. aged about 36 years.

Aug. 26, 1841

Died on the 25th inst. of bilious fever, ELBRIDGE GREENE, eldest son of GREENE and M.E. HILL, aged twelve years and nearly eight months.

Aug. 26, 1841

Died at his residence in Dooly county, on the 15th inst. of congestive fever MR. EDWARD G. BROWN, formerly of Houston county, in the 58th year of his age. He was a native of Sumter District, S.C. and removed from thence to Houston county, where he resided until last winter, and then moved to Dooly county.

Aug. 26, 1841

Died on the 17th inst. in Monroe county COL. NEEDHAM R. BRYAN in the 35th year of his age, leaving a wife and four children; a member of the Methodist Episcopal Church. (with eulogy)

Sep. 2, 1841

Died on the 22d ult. at the residence of her father, JOHN POWERS, ESQ. in the county of Monroe, MRS. NARCISSA GRIFFIN, wife of DANIEL GRIFFIN, ESQ. principal Engineer of the Monroe Rail Road Company, in the 32d year of her age (with eulogy)

Sep. 2, 1841

Died in Montgomery county, on Saturday the 14th inst. COL. CHARLES RICHARD HAYNIE, aged 24 years.

Sep. 2, 1841

Died in Washington, on the 24th ult., JOSEPH GALES, SR., aged about 81 years, father of one of the Editors of the National Intelligencer, and for many years Editor of the Raleigh Register.

Sep. 2, 1841

Died in Milledgeville on the ____ ult., the HON. CHS. EATON HAYNES aged 58 years.

Sep. 9, 1841

Died on the 22d ult. at the residence of her father, JOHN POWERS, ESQ. in the county of Monroe, MRS. NARCISSA GRIFFIN, wife of DANIEL GRIFFIN, ESQ. principal Engineer of the Monroe Rail Road Company,

(Sep. 9, cont'd.) - in the twenty-third year of her age. (We republish the above notice for the purpose of correcting an error which occurred in its publication last week).

Sep. 9, 1841

Died near this city, on Sunday last, MR. ANGUS McCALLUM, aged about fifty-five years, formerly of Robertson county, N.C.

Sep. 16, 1841

Died in Apalachicola, 21st ult. MR. MARTIN SNYDER, a native of New York, educated at Washington, D.C.

Sep. 16, 1841

Died in Apalachicola, on the 24th ult. COL. J.B. WEBB of the Florida Journal, formerly of Columbus.

Sep. 23, 1841

Died in Butts county, a few days since, the REV. JESSE MERCER of Wilkes county - one of the oldest and most distinguished preachers of the Baptist Church in Georgia.

Sep. 30, 1841

Died on the 24th ult. at her residence in this city MRS. LURACY LUNDY aged 56 years, 2 months and 22 days.

Sep. 30, 1841

Died at his residence in Houston county, on the 12th inst. MR. STERLING C. WILLIAMSON, in the 75th year of his age, formerly of South Carolina. (The Columbia (S.C.) Chrinicle will please copy the above).

Sep. 30, 1841

Died in Houston county, on the 20th inst. MR. FRANCIS ALLEN, aged about 68 years, formerly of Camden, S.C.

Oct. 14, 1841

Died in this county on the 1st October, MAJ. WM. WADSWORTH aged 91 years and 6 months. His death was occasioned by being thrown from his horse the day previous.

Oct. 14, 1841

Died at his residence in Twiggs county, on the (25th?) ult. MR. WILLIAM A. THARP, aged 53 years, after a short illness of three days; a member of the Inferior Court. In his death his family has lost a kind father, his wife an affectionate husband (with eulogy).

Oct. 14, 1841

Died at Tarversville, Twiggs county, on the 29th August, after a lingering illness, MRS. JOANNA R. TARVER, wife of WM. M. TARVER, aged 40 years.

Oct. 21, 1841

Departed this life on the 4th inst., in Jones county in the 75th year of her age, MRS. FRANCIS LAMAR, consort of JOHN LAMAR, SENR., left children and grandchildren.

Nov. 4, 1841

    Departed this life on the 31st ult., MRS. LUCY ANN STRONG, wife of the HON. C.B. STRONG of Vineville, near this city, and daughter of the late MILLER WOODSON of Virginia. (An obituary notice accompanying the above notice will be published next week).

Nov. 4, 1841

    Departed this life on the 19th ult., in Stewart county, Ga. DR. JOHN BAILEY, a native of Brattleboro Vermont; a physician of much skill; left wife and two children.

Nov. 4, 1841

    Died in this county, on the morning of the 16th ult. of the Typhus Congestive Fever, MRS. MARY JOHNSON, consort of JACOB JOHNSON, in the 57th year of her age.

Nov. 11, 1841

    Obituary and notice (eulogy) to MRS. LUCY ANN STRONG. (NOTE: The notice minus the eulogy appeared in issue of Nov. 4, 1841).

Nov. 11, 1841

    Died in Hawkinsville on the 17th ult. MR. DAVID I. HOLT, aged about 43 years, formerly of Clinton, Ga. but more recently a resident of Texas. He left the United States for Texas, with the battalion of Col. Wm. Ward, and served in it till after the desperate battle of "The Refugio", when he separated from the corps in search of water, and escaped the capture and massacre of his associates, which followed. After several hairbreadth escapes, and putting in requisition his talents for "tall walking," he escaped from the Mexicans, and arrived among his friends. He was appointed an Alcaide by the Government of Texas, which office he continued to hold after his visit to the United States.

Nov. 18, 1841

    Departed this life at his residence in Twiggs county, MAJOR PHILLIP COOK, in the 66th year of his age; a sheriff of Baldwin county in 1809; elected to captaincy of a militia corps of cavalry, and later promoted to the command of a squadron of cavalry; captaincy and later Major in U.S. service during War of 1812; assigned to post at Fort Hawkins; after the war became principal keeper of the Penitentiary of Georgia (with eulogy).

Nov. 25, 1841

    Died at the residence of his father, in the vicinity of this city, on Monday the 22d inst. JOHN PATTERSON SMITH, ESQ., only son of MR. JOSEPH SMITH, in the 22d year of his age.

Dec. 2, 1841

    Died on the 22d ult. near this city, JOHN PATTERSON SMITH, ESQ. in the 22d year of his age (with eulogy).

Dec. 9, 1841

    Died in this city on the 7th inst. MR. GEORGE BARLOW aged about thirty years, a native of Laurens county, but more recently a resident of Macon county.

Dec. 9, 1841

    Died in this city on the 5th inst. LOUISIANA SUSAN, daughter of PIETY and GEO. W. ALDEN, aged three years and eight months.

Dec. 9, 1841

Died at his residence in Tazewell, Marion county, Ga. on the 19th inst. ARTHUR WASHINGTON BATTLE, ESQ. son of JOSEPH and RHODA BATTLE, in the 26th year of his age, leaving a wife and three children. (with eulogy)

Dec. 9, 1841

Died at the residence of her father, in Walker county, Ala. on the 5th ult. MRS. HARRIET J. BULKLEY, wife of MR. EDWARD C. BULKLEY, of this city, aged 24 years.

Dec. 16, 1841

Died near Livingston, Ala. on the 28th ult. in the 32d year of her age, MRS. JANE M. WARD, formerly of this city.

Dec. 23, 1841

Died in Washington City, on Sunday last, COL. JOHN W. HUNTER, Door-keeper of the House of Representatives, aged about 76 years. Col. H. served in the Revolutionary war with fidelity and bravery, and was in the battle of Eutaw and other hard fought fields. He was a native of Virginia, but for a long time a citizen of Georgia prior to his removal to this city. (Constitutionalist).

Jan. 13, 1842

Died in Crawford County on the 5th inst. JACOB FUDGE, a native of Pennsylvaina, aged 84 years. He was a revolutionary soldier.

Jan. 13, 1842

Died in Monroe county, on the 7th inst. MRS. MERCY, consort of the REV. DANIEL KELSEY, formerly of West Poultney, (Vt.); member of Methodist Episcopal Church about sixteen years; left a husband and infant child.

Jan. 20, 1842

Died at his residence in Talbot county, on the 15th day of January, instant, RODERICK LEONARD, ESQ. in the 56th year of his age. He was for many years a member of the Legislature from the county of Morgan - and represented that county in the Senate and House of Representatives; member of Methodist Episcopal Church.

Jan. 20, 1842

Suicide! A gentleman direct from Marietta brings the melancholy information that about 4 o'clock last Friday evening in Mr. B. Roberts Tavern at that place, MR. O. CONE, attached to the Corps of Engineers belonging to the State Rail Road, terminated his life by shooting himself through the head with a small pocket pistol. He is said to have been a young man of promise, about 23 years of age.

Jan. 27, 1842

Died in Monroe county, on the 19th inst. MARTHA FISK, aged six months and one day, infant daughter of DR. JOHN W. STROTHER.

Jan. 27, 1842

Died in this county on the 24th inst. ELBERT CALHOUN, ESQ. aged about 60 years.

Feb. 10, 1842

Died on the 5th instant, in the 47th year of her age, MRS. SARAH

(Feb. 10, cont'd.) - W. STILES, wife of JOSEPH G. STILES, ESQ. of Jones County; member of Methodist Episcopal Church; left husband and children to mourn their loss. (with eulogy)

Feb. 10, 1842

Died in this city, on Sunday the 30th ult. MRS. ELIZABETH CHAPMAN, in the forty-fourth year of her age, wife of AMBROSE CHAPMAN; member of the Baptist Church.

Mar. 10, 1842

Departed this life, in Anson county, N.C. on the 20th of December 1841, after a short but severe illness, the REV. ELIJAH SINCLAIR, of the Methodist Episcopal Church, and a member of the Georgia Conference, but recently a merchant of Savannah.

Mar. 24, 1842

Died on the 20th ultimo, at his residence in Macon county, after an illness of only a few hours, WILLIAM HOLLINSHEAD, aged 70 years, 7 months and 22 days; member of Baptist Church; an affectionate father, kind husband, good master.

Mar. 24, 1842

Died in this city, on the 16th inst. FRANCIS QUIGLEY, aged about 40 years, a native or Ireland.

Mar. 24, 1842

Died in this city, on the 23d inst. VIRGINIA, youngest child of J.E. and C.C. WELLS, aged 16 months and 25 days.

Mar. 24, 1842

....learn from the Savannah papers the death of WM. W. GORDON ESQ., who died in Savannah on the 20th inst. of billious pleurisy, after a very brief illness; left wife and children (with eulogy).

Mar. 24, 1842

Last night about 9 o'clock a fatal affray took place in this city, on Bridge Street. A young man by the name of MELTIAH HEBBARD was shot in the left breast and died almost instantly.

Mar. 31, 1842

Died in this county, on the 12th inst. MR. THOMAS COLLINS, SEN. in the 69th year of his age.

Mar. 31, 1842

Died in Marion, Twiggs county, on the 7th inst. JAMES SOLOMON, ESQ., in the 42d year of his age.

Mar. 31, 1842

Died in the city of New York, on the 16th inst. MR. B.C. HOUGH, of Hawkinsville, Ga., in the 32d year of his age, a native of Connecticut, but for many years a successful and enterprising merchant of his adopted state.

Apr. 7, 1842

Died in Columbus, on the 1st inst. MR. GEO. R. HURLBUT, a native of Litchfield county, (Conn.) and recently a resident of this city. He fell victim to his exertions in aiding to extinguish the recent fire in that city. He was badly injured in one of his legs, (in blowing up a building,) which was amputated the day before his

(Apr. 7, cont'd) - decease. By profession he was a Teacher of Music.

Apr. 7, 1842

Died in this city on Thursday last, MR. CHAS. G. ADKINS, aged about 22 years.

Apr. 14, 1842

Died in this city on the night of the 8th inst., in the twentieth year of her age, MRS. MANFREDONIA, wife of MAJOR WILLIAM L. MAXWELL of Tennessee, and youngest daughter of THOS. T. NAPIER of the former place - leaving behind a husband and infant son. (with eulogy)

Apr. 14, 1842

Died in this city, on sunday night last after a sudden and severe illness, aged 52 years, MR. JOHN MARTIN, native of Rockingham county, North Carolina, but for the last twenty years a resident of this State, and for seven years a highly respected inhabitant of this city; a kind master and affectionate father.

Apr. 14, 1842

Died in this city on the 5th inst. WILLIAM S., infant son of ELIZABETH and Z.B. WADE, in his seventh month.

Apr. 14, 1842

Died in this city on the 8th inst. MRS. ELIZABETH WADE, wife of Z.B. WADE, aged 30 years.

Apr. 14, 1842

Died in Twiggs county, on the 2d inst. MRS. SARAH G. EZELL, wife of LEVI EZELL, of Houston county, aged about 25 years. The death of this estimable lady was both sudden and singular. While travelling in a carriage with her husband, near the residence of Dr. Slappy, from some unknown cause, she expired instantly without uttering a groan or word.

Apr. 21, 1842

Died in this county on the 11th inst. MRS. MARGARET CASON, wife of MR. SAMUEL CASON, aged about 60 years.

Apr. 21, 1842

Died in this city on the 5th inst. MRS. WINNIFRED HAMILTON, wife of MR. G. ZIMMERMAN, in the 19th year of her age.

Apr. 28, 1842

Died at the Warrior in this county, on the 11th inst. of Billious Pleurisy, MRS. MARGARET CASON, consort of MR. SETH CASON, in the 58th year of her age. She had been for 21 years a consistent member of the Presbyterian Church. She has left behind a husband and four children to mourn their loss.

Apr. 28, 1842

Died in Lanier, Macon county on Friday the 8th inst., of Pulmonary consumption, MR. GERSHAM BUTLER, aged about 34 years, formerly of Wethersfield, (Rocky Hill Village) Connecticut, but for the last five years a citizen of this State.

May 12, 1842

Died on the 30th ult. PHILIP THURMOND, youngest son of DR. A.F.

(May 12, cont'd) - and ELIZA HOLT, aged one year, eight months and ten days.

May 12, 1842

Died in this city, on Sunday evening last, MRS. ADELINE M. FORT, aged 43 years, relict of the late MR. ROBERT W. FORT, of this city.

May 12, 1842

Died in this City, on Saturday last, MR. JOHN OLIVER, aged about 40 years - one of the first settlers of Macon. He was buried with military honors the following day, by the Macon Volunteers, of which corps he was an old member.

May 12, 1842

Died in this city, on Sunday morning last, of a pulmonary affection to which he had been for several years subject, MR. HAMILTON ATCHISON, of Lexington, Kentucky, aged about 40 years.

May 19, 1842

Died in Russell county, Ala. (near Columbus), on the 7th inst. HINES HOLT, SEN. in the 72d year of his age.

May 19, 1842

Died in this city, on the 2d inst. WILLIAM T. KENNEDY, infant son of WM. C. and ELLEN B. KENNEDY, aged nine months and 11 days.

June 2, 1842

Died in this city on the 29th inst. MRS. MARY BEALL, wife of GEN. ELIAS BEALL, aged about 60 years.

June 16, 1842

Died in Thomas county on the 30th ult. GEORGE HAMILTON, infant son of DUKE and SARAH HAYS, aged one year 8 months and 16 days.

June 30, 1842

Died in Forsyth, on Wednesday the 22d inst. after a long and painful illness, ALFRED BROOKS, in the 41st year of his age. (with eulogy)

July 7, 1842

Departed this life after a painful and protracted illness of 47 days duration, on the 30th June, in the town of Zebulon, Pike county, Ga. in the 37th year of his age, RICHARD S. WALKER, ESQ. Mr. Walker was a native of James City county, (Va.) born on the 15th August, 1805, and emigrated to Georgia, it is believed, in 1820, where he has constantly resided since.

July 14, 1842

Died in Savannah, on Saturday the 2d inst. (at the residence of his brother, G.B. LAMAR) JOHN T. LAMAR, ESQ. of this city. He died of paralysis, with which he had been attacked a few days previous. He was among the early settlers of our city. His funeral was attended by the Savannah Guards, Capt. Bowen, in complement to the Macon Volunteers, of which he was an honorary member.

July 28, 1842

Departed this life on the 25th inst. in the 22d year of his age, EDMUND BOOKER WRIGHT, a member of the Episcopal Church. He languished upon a bed of sickness and pain for eighteen days. (with eulogy)

July 28, 1842

    Departed this life on Tuesday morning the 12th inst. at half past 5 o'clock in the morning, at the residence of Mr. M.E. Evans, near Columbus, Ga. MRS. MARTHA HOWARD, wife of MR. AUGUSTUS HOWARD, in the 27th year of her age (with eulogy).

Aug. 11, 1842

    Died in Bibb County, on the 27th July, MRS. ANN B. HARDEN, widow of JAMES HARDEN, aged nearly 67 years.

Aug. 11, 1842

    Died in this city on the 9th inst. GURDON I., son of ISAAC G. SEYMOUR ESQ., aged ten weeks

Aug. 18, 1842

    Died in Jones county, on the 29th July, WARD WILDER, aged about 48 years.

Aug. 18, 1842

    Died in this city on the 16th inst. in the 27th year of his age, THOMAS A BARNARD, ESQ. a native of Poughkepsie, New York, but for the last three years a resident of this city. Mr. B. was graduated from Yale College in 1837 and after preparing himself for the bar, emigrated to this State.

Aug. 25, 1842

    Died on the 13th inst. at the residence of Col. William O. Baldwin, in Montgomery county, Ala. MR. FRANCIS H. BULKLEY, a native of Hartford, Conn. in the 24th year of his age, for many years a resident of the city of Montgomery.

Aug. 25, 1842

    Died on the 2d inst. after a short but severe illness, JOSEPH T. WILLIAMS, of Georgia, while on a tour thro' the country West of the Mississippi, in the 35th year of his age.

Sep. 8, 1842

    Died on the 30th August, EDWARD HENRY, only son of D.F. and ELOISA CLARK, aged five years and one month.

Sep. 15, 1842

    Died in Russell county, Ala. on the 25th August, MR. WM. PERRY, aged 75 years, formerly a resident of Twiggs county, Ga.

Sep. 15, 1842

    Died in Monroe county on the 31st August, BENJAMIN BRANTLEY, ESQ. aged about 55 years; a member of the Baptist Church.

Oct. 6, 1842

    Died at Mount Pleasant, near this city, on Sunday the 25th inst. MRS. ISABELLA CLARKE, in the 56th year of her age, a native of Kelso, (Scotland,) and formerly a resident of Charleston and Savannah.

Oct. 20, 1842

    Died in Decatur, DeKalb county, on the 16th inst. DAVID B. BUTLER, ESQ., of this city, aged about 38 years, of bilious fever. He was among the early settlers of our city, a member and Elder of the Presbyterian Church of this city for several years; member of the Macon Volunteers.

Oct. 20, 1842

    Died in this city on the 5th inst. at the residence of J.B. Andrews, MRS. ELIZABETH ANDREWS, daughter of MRS. ELIZABETH SHORT, of Brunswick county, (Va.) in the 55th year of her age.

Oct. 20, 1842

    Died in Andover, Mass. on the 22d inst. at the residence of the late Hon. John Phillips, MRS. SARAH ANN, wife of JOHN PHILLIPS, EDQ., late a resident of this city, and daughter of late JONA. DORR, ESQ., of Roxbury, Mass., aged 31 years.

Oct. 20, 1842

    Departed this life on Sunday 25th September last, at her residence near Macon, MRS. ISABELLA CLARK, in the 57th year of her age; a native of Scotland, but for many years a resident of Macon and its vicinity. She was left a widow when most of her children were in the helpless years of infancy; a member of the Presbyterian Church at Macon; has left five children to mourn (with eulogy).

Oct. 20, 1842

    Died in Claborn Parish, Lou., on the 12th May last, of the Consumption, MRS. SARAH FULLER, wife of MR. JOHN M. FULLER, formerly of Houston county, Geo., and daughter of the late GEO. WALKER SEN., in the 32nd year of her age. She united herself with the Methodist Church in 1835. Left husband and children (with eulogy).

Oct. 20, 1842

    On the 11th inst. an inquest was held by Wm. Robertson, Coroner, for the county of Bibb upon the body of WILLIAM POWELL. He died very suddenly, as was supposed by strangulation, by attempting to swallow a piece of beef. He was a man somewhat advanced in years and had been a resident of this vicinity for some time. He died at the house of Mrs. Edwards near Walnut Creek Bridge.

Oct. 20, 1842

    Also on the 15th an inquest was held on the body of a German, found in the Ocmulgee River between two and three miles above this city. His name was GOTLIP ZIMMERMAN, a native of Baden, and aged about 25 years. Verdict of the Jury, that he came to his death while in a state of Mental derangement. He had resided here for about three years past - but loosing his wife and child a few months since, seemed unceasingly to prey upon his spirits, and at times he appeared to be partially deranged, and would often visit the grave of his wife about four miles distant, in the night, and at other times. He left here on Sunday night previous, as was supposed for that purpose, and probably getting bewildered, he wandered to the River in the night and was drowned.

Oct. 27, 1842

    Another Revolutionary hero has bade us farewell. Died, at his residence in Jones county, on the 18th of October 1840, the venerable citizen and patriot - JOHN LAMAR, ESQ. in the 81st year of his age. Very shortly after entering the Army, he was deputed with others to the performance of a perilous duty, in which he was deserted by his companions, and left to execute the order alone. For this act of intrepidity and fidelity, the Government tendered him a Lieutenant's Commission in the Regular forces, which, however, he modestly declined, on the ground that he was too young and inexperienced, he being at the time only in his seventeenth year. He served under Gen'ls Marion and Pickens, attached generally to the Battalion of the latter, was at the battle of the Eutaw, Cowpens, Siege of Augusta, and in several other engagements - once taken a prisoner, but made his escape from the camp of Lord Cornwallis, rescueing at the

(Oct. 27, cont'd.) - the same time one of his cousins - was twice wounded during the war by the British, and once by the Indians after his removal to this State. He was a descendant of the Huguenots - was born in South Carolina, and emigrated to the State of Georgia, at the close of the Revolution. A member of the Baptist denomination for nearly fifty years (with eulogy).

Nov. 10, 1842

Died in Vineville, on the 12th October, MRS. TEMPERANCE BRYAN, wife of MR. BLACKSHEAR BRYAN, aged 31 years - and daughter of GEN. MATHEW EXUM.

Nov. 10, 1842

Died in Bibb County, on the 4th Nov'r of conjestive fever, MR. THOMAS GATES, aged about 41 years.

Nov. 10, 1842

Died in Troup county, on the 10th October, DR. ROBERT C. BROWN, aged about 40 years.

Nov. 24, 1842

Died at his residence in Houston county, (Ga.) on the night of the 12th inst. MR. MOSES ROUNTREE, in the 48th year of his age. Mr. R. was from Sumter District, (S.C.) but resided in this State for the last seven years.

Dec. 1, 1842

Died on the 24th inst. in the 33d year of her age, MRS. FRANCES ALEXANDER McKENZIE ROWLAND, wife of COL. ISAAC B. ROWLAND, of this city.

Dec. 1, 1842

Died in this city, on the 24th inst. MR. JOHN JEPSON, aged about 40 years, a native of Greene county, Ga.

Dec. 1, 1842

Died in this city, on Saturday night last, MR. DAVID RALSTON, a native of Aberville District, S.C., a citizen of Ga. since 1809, aged 48 years - one of the original founders of Macon.

Dec. 8, 1842

Died in this city, on the 5th inst. MARY JANE daughter of JAMES and CATHARINE WILLIAMS, aged nine years, nine months and twenty-four days.

Dec. 15, 1842

Announce death of HON. R.W. HABERSHAM (Athens Banner).

Dec. 22, 1842

Died on Saturday last, the REV. DR. JAMES GRAHAM, pastor of the Roman Catholic Church of this City, aged about 33 years.

Dec. 22, 1842

Died in this county on the 7th inst., MR. WM. A THRAP, aged about 30 years.

Dec. 22, 1842

Died in Monroe county, MAJ. JAMES W. TINSLEY, aged about 50 years.

Dec. 22, 1842

>   Died in this city on the 21st inst. JOHN M. SALFNER, aged three years and three months.

Dec. 22, 1842

>   Died in this City on the 17th inst. MR. MARTIN L. HARDEN, aged about 33 years.

Jan. 5, 1843

>   Died in this city, on the 26th Dec. MR. JOHN C. RYLANDER, aged about 72 years, formerly a resident of Effingham county.

Jan. 5, 1843

>   Died on the 17th Dec. last in this city, the REV. JAMES GRAHAM Pastor of the Roman Catholic Church, aged 34 years (with eulogy).

Jan. 26, 1843

>   Died lately in Baltimore, FRANCIS S. KEY, ESQ., of Washington City, a distinguished member of the bar, and author of the national song, "The Star Spangled Banner."

Feb. 9, 1843

>   Died at the house of Dr. R.A. Nash, in Twiggs county, on the first of January, WM. ST. LEGER MUSGROVE. He died of bilious pleurisy. He was born and raised in Liverpool, (Eng.) and has taught school in various parts of this State for the last twenty years.

Feb. 23, 1843

>   Died at his residence in Twiggs county, Ga. January 11, 1843, MR. EDMUND HODGES, aged about 79 years. About two years before his death, he became a member of the Methodist Episcopal Church.

Mar. 9, 1843

>   Another Revolutionary Soldier Gone! Died at his residence in Monroe county, on the 9th inst. ANDERSON REDDING, in the 80th year of his age. Born of a very respectable family in the State of Virginia; He was present, a soldier, at the surrender of Lord Cornwallis at Yorktown; removed to Georgia in 1782; worthy member of Methodist Episcopal Church (with eulogy).

Mar. 16, 1843

>   Died at his residence in Macon county, Ga. 25th February last, MR. JOHN RUSHIN, aged 69 years, lacking a few days. Native of North Carolina, and at 21 years of age removed with his wife to Washington county, afterwards to Warren, then to Jones, and from thence to Macon county, where his wife RACHAEL RUSHIN died 12th June, 1833, in the 67th year of her age - having reared a family of eleven children, seven of whom still survive. About six years since, he was united with the Baptist Church at Travelers' Rest. He has left behind him a second wife, his children, grandchildren, and great grandchildren.

Mar. 23, 1843

>   Died in Monroe county, on the 19th February, MR. SIMEON BROOKS, aged 28 years; left wife and two children.

Apr. 6, 1843

(CORRECTION) In announcing the death of JOHN RUSHIN, of Macon county three weeks since, an error was committed with regard to his age. He was 79 years old, lacking a few days (instead of 69, as heretofore published).

Apr. 13, 1843

Died in Lowndes Co. Mississippi on the 31st March of apoplexy, after an illness of eight hours, MRS. ELIZABETH GRIFFIN, wife of GEN. L.L. GRIFFIN.

Apr. 20, 1843

Died at Mount Meigs, Ala. on Friday last, GEN. JAS. C. WATSON of Columbus. His remains were brought to Columbus and interred on Sunday.

May 11, 1843

Died at his residence in Twiggs county, Ga. on the 5th inst. GEN. EZEKIEL WIMBERLY, in the 69th year of his age. He was a Colonel in the army during the late war with Great Britain, and served two campaigns in that capacity, and was afterwards elected by the legislature to the office of Major General, which he filled until his declining years occasioned his resignation. He represented the county of Twiggs in the State Legislature for a number of years, both in the House of Representatives and in the Senate, and he was twice chosen by the people of the State as an Elector of President and Vice President of the United States. (The Georgia Journal, Southern Recorder and Columbus Enquirer, will please copy).

May 18, 1843

Died in this county on the evening of the 11th inst. MARTHA ELIZA, only daughter of T.M. and MARGARET E. FURLOW, aged two years and seven months.

June 8, 1843

Died at the residence of Robert Beasly, Esq. in this city, on the 3d inst. MR. STERLING P. LYNN, aged 27 years, (formerly of Thomaston) son of MR. ASA LYNN, of Meriwether county, Ga.

June 15, 1843

Died in this city on the 1st inst. MRS. LOUISA LONG, aged 72 years, widow of MAJ. EVANS LONG, of Baldwin county; a consistent member of the Baptist Church for the last twenty years.

June 22, 1843

On Monday last, MR. ASHBEL L. STOCKING was drowned about twelve miles below this City, in the Ocmulgee River. He was buried yesterday at 3 o'clock P.M. Mr. Stocking was about 22 years of age, a native of Chatham, (Conn.) where he has parents living. He also has a brother living in New York, by the name of HARVEY STOCKING. He has resided in this city for two years past with MR. J.P. GAVIN, Auctioneer.

June 29, 1843

Died this morning, at a quarter of 6 o'clock, at the house of a friend - George Ticknor, Esq. in Park Street - HON. HUGH S. LEGARE, Attorney General of the U. States and Acting Secretary of State. Mr. Legare died of indigestion, or stoppage in the bowels, and has been very unwell since his arrival here on Friday last. Mr. Legare was a resident of Charleston, South Carolina; (Boston Times).

June 29, 1843

    Died in Forsyth, on the 22d inst. of the scarlet fever, HELEN, daughter of H.H. LUMPKIN, ESQ. aged one year and one day.

June 29, 1843

    Died in Milledgeville, on the 22d inst., MR. GEO. STEELE, (Printer,) aged about 31 years.

July 6, 1843

    Died on the 28th June, at Rollin's Chalybeale Springs Meriwether County, MRS. MARTHA LOVETT, wife of NAPOLEON B. LOVETT, in the 30th year of her age. She was a native of Screven County, but had resided in Meriwether for the last 12 years. She had been affected with a nervous disease for several years, which finally terminated her life with spasms; has left husband and four children.

July 6, 1843

    Died in East-Macon on the 4th inst. ZENOBIA PALMYRA, daughter of THOS. A. and ELIZA ANN BROWN, aged about 18 months.

July 13, 1843

    Died in Vineville, near this city, on the 4th inst. in the 29th year of her age, MRS. ELIZA SIMS, daughter of MR. JOSEPH SMITH, and wife of MR. JOHN H. SIMS. As a daughter, sister, wife and mother, she will be remembered by her surviving friends.

July 13, 1843

    Died in Vineville, on Sunday evening the 9th inst. at the residence of Mrs. Nixon, ELIZA VIRGINIA, infant daughter of S.M. STRONG, ESQ.

July 20, 1843

    Died in this city, on the 12th inst. HAMILTON STEPHEN, son of MR. and MRS. CHARLES COLLINS, aged fourteen months and six days.

July 20, 1843

    Died in Jones county, on the 1st inst. MR. H.F. WILLIAMS, aged 40 years.

July 20, 1843

    Died in Monroe county on the 17th inst. CHARLES TURNER, son of JAMES and SARAH C. CONNALLY, aged 5 years and three months.

July 20, 1843

    Died at Pindertown, Dooly county, on the 18th ult. WM. J. FOARD, ESQ. aged 32 years.

July 27, 1843

    Died in this city, on Sunday evening last, MISS INDIANA HARDAWAY, daughter of MAJ. JAMES H. HARDAWAY, aged 18 years.

July 27, 1843

    Died in this city on Monday last, THOMAS CAPERS, infant son of MR. BENJAMIN R. WARNER, aged seven months.

July 27, 1843

    Died in East Macon, on Sunday night last, MARIETTA, daughter of MR. JOSEPH WILLETT, aged about one year.

Aug. 3, 1843

Died in this City, on Saturday evening 29th ult. in her sixteenth year, MISS REBECCA ANN LAMAR, daughter, and only child of GENERAL MIRABEAU B. LAMAR, late President of the Republic of Texas (with eulogy).

Aug. 10, 1843

An inquest was held on the 4th inst. on the body of a man named JOHN McLURE, who had died suddenly the night previous. The verdict of the Jury was, that he came to his death by an Apoplectic fit. He was apparently about 35 years of age, and had for several years been in the employ of Mr. James R. Butts of this City, and was reputed an honest, sober and industrious man. Several hundred dollars in money and evidences of debt, money deposited, etc. were found among his papers, but no clue to the place of his nativity. Some letters were found from a brother living in New York, and a sister in Massachusetts.

Aug. 10, 1843

Died in Sumpter county on the 12th ult. MR. JOSEPH DOUGLASS, in the 75th year of his age. He was a native of Mecklinburg county, N.C., and among the first settlers of Monroe county. He was the owner of the land on which the flourishing village of Culloden is situated, and erected the first cabin on the spot. The next settler of the village was WM. CULLODEN, an Irishman by birth, who had spent the prime of his life in India. He erected a small store house there, in the fall of 1823 - and with these individuals, the rise and history of the place is closely identified.

Aug. 10, 1843

Died in Jones county, on the 2d ult. MISS MARTHA TOOL, in the 21st year of her age.

Aug. 24, 1843

Died at LaGrange, Ga. on the 13th inst. at the age of 21 months and six days, PLEASANT WIMBERLY, infant son of the REV. C.W. and ELIZABETH KEY.

Aug. 24, 1843

Died in this city, on the 19th inst. PAULINE MARY ELIZABETH daughter of J.H. DAMOUR, aged about 19 months.

Sep. 14, 1843

Died in Dooly county on the 3d inst. of the conjestive measles, ARTHUR A. MORGAN, ESQ. aged 42 years, late Judge of the Southern Circuit.

Sep. 14, 1843

Died in Thomaston, Upson county, on the 10th instant, GEORGE CARY, ESQ. - a member of Congress; distinguished Jurist.

Sep. 14, 1843

Died in Macon County on the 29th Aug. JOHN HANNON ESQ. aged about 60 years.

Sep. 21, 1843

Died in Jones county, Sept. 17th, MARY FRANCES, eldest daughter of JOHN LAMAR, ESQ. of this city, aged five years and ten months. (with eulogy)

Sep. 21, 1843

Died at Lanier, Macon county, on the 10th instant, DOCT. JOHN J. MILLER.

Sep. 28, 1843

Another Rev. Soldier Gone! Departed this life on the 18th instant, at the residence of his son, James Horsley Esq., VALENTINE HORSLEY, aged 85 years and 8 months. He was born in the State of Maryland, and at the age of 15, he moved to the State of Virginia; entered service of his country in Rev. War and was at the surrender of Lord Cornwallis at Yorktown; afterwards moved to York District South Carolina; member of Baptist Church.

Sep. 28, 1843

Died in this City on the 9th inst. GEORGE, infant son of EDMUND and ELIZA JANE RICHARDSON, of Albany, Baker county, aged six weeks.

Oct. 5, 1843

Died on Saturday morning, 30th inst. after a short illness, ALLEN L. LUCE, a native of New Bedford, (Mass.) and for several years a resident of this city.

Oct, 5, 1843

Died in this city, on the 1st inst. MRS. ELIZABETH WASHINGTON, wife of MR. GEORGE H. WASHINGTON.

Oct. 5, 1843

Died in Jones county, on the 27th ult. MR. THOMAS LOWE, aged 48 years; recently represented the county in the Legislature.

Oct. 5, 1843

Died in Russell county, Ala. on the 13th ult. JONATHAN A. HUDSON EDQ. aged about 42 years. He was formerly a resident of this city, and the first Sheriff elected in Bibb county.

Oct. 5, 1843

Died in this county, at the residence of his brother (Lewis Beddingfield), of remittent fever, ROBERT BEDDINGFIELD of Lowndes county, Miss. aged about 50 years - formerly a merchant of Twiggs county, Ga.

Oct. 5, 1843

Died on the 30th ult., in the vicinity of this place, at the residence of John Anderson, MISS MARY B. WILLIAMS, aged 20 years; daughter of JOHN L. WILLIAMS formerly of this place.

Oct. 5, 1843

Died at his residence near Monticello, (Fla.) on the 2nd ult. C.I. JOHN A. CUTHBERT, in 54th year of his age.

Oct. 19, 1843

Died in this city, on the 26th Sept. after a painful illness of three days, LOUISA J. HIGHTOWER, aged 8 years and 23 days.

Oct. 19, 1843

Died in this city, on the 16th ult. JULIA LAURA, aged 5 weeks, daughter of A. HOLDER.

Oct. 19, 1843

    Died in this city, on the 17th inst. WM. HENRY HARRISON, son of GEO. P. WAGNON, aged 1 year and 2 months.

Oct. 19, 1843

    Died in Monroe county, of congestive fever, on the 14th inst. MR. JAMES LUCKEY - a promising young man in the bloom of youth - the only son of MR. JOHN LUCKEY.

Oct. 19, 1843

    Died in Albany, Baker county, on the 11th inst. THOMAS HARDIN, infant son of MR. and MRS. P.A. LAWSON of that place. (The Southern Recorder and Christian Index will please copy)

Oct. 26, 1843

    Died in this city, on the 20th of October, after an illness of thirty days, MRS. LOUISA B. WAGNON, consort of GEO. P. WAGNON. She has left an aged mother, husband and four children; member of Methodist Episcopal Church. Three days before her death her babe died.

Oct. 26, 1843

    Died in Vineville, on the 19th inst. MRS. MILLY SMITH, wife of JEREMIAH SMITH, aged about 37 years.

Nov. 2, 1843

    Died at the residence of Turner Hunt, in _____ county, on the 10th ult. JENKINS HUNT, aged 6 years and 11 months, youngest son of TURNER and DELLA HUNT, after a severe illness of three days.

Nov. 9, 1843

    Died in Macon county, on the 21st October last, of a severe and varied affliction, MISS ETHAMEA MILLER, aged 16, daughter of ROBERT and R_____.

Nov. 9, 1843

    Died on 23d October, HENRY JEFFERSON, son of WILLIAM W. and CAROLINE M. CHAPMAN, aged one year six months and eleven days.

Nov. 9, 1843

    Died in this city, on the 6th inst., MR. JAMES M. PHELPS, of Phelps & Experience, aged 35 years.

Nov. 9, 1843

    Died in this city, on the 5th inst., LEWIS H. (ACHORO?), aged 5 years.

Nov. 9, 1843

    Died in this city, on the 2d inst., MR. HENRY FLANDERS, a native of Connecticut, but for many years a resident of _____, aged 38 years.

Nov. 9, 1843

    Died in this city, on the 7th inst., CATHARINE ARNETT, daughter of JAMES and CATHARINE WILLIAMS, aged _____ and twenty days.

Nov. 23, 1843

   Died in this City on Tuesday the 21st inst., CATHERINE VIRGINIA, daughter of MR. and MRS. STEPHEN MENARD, aged 2 years and 2 months.

Nov. 23, 1843

   Died in Bibb County on the 20th inst. JAMES GATES, in the 76th year of his age, a good citizen, and for many years a member of the Baptist Church.

Nov. 30, 1843

   Died at Travellers Rest Dooly County on the 28th ult. WARREN ABEL, infant son of RACHEL JANE and ABEL HOLTON of that place.

Dec. 28, 1843

   Died in Monroe county, at the residence of Col. Josiah G. Jordan, on the 22d November last, ARON JORDAN, ESQ., aged 82 years - a Revolutionary soldier, and for the past 20 years a consistent member of the Methodist Episcopal Church.

Jan. 4, 1844

   Died in this City on the 30th ult. MARY ELIZABETH, daughter of MR. F. WRIGLY, aged eleven weeks.

Jan. 11, 1844

   Died at Vineville, near Macon, Ga. on the 8th inst. MISS JANE M. JEWETT; member of Protestant Episcopal Church (with eulogy).

Jan. 25, 1844

   Died at his plantation near Waynesborough, Burke county, on the 17th inst. JOHN A. PARSONS ESQ., after a protracted illness of 18 days.

Feb. 1, 1844

   Died at Hawkinsville, on the 27th ult. MR. JOHN RAWLS, aged 56 years.

Feb. 1, 1844

   Died near this city, on Saturday last, MR. ALEXANDER E. PATTON, aged 37 years.

Feb. 8, 1844

   Died in Oxford, Newton county, on the 28th January, of a few days illness with scarlatina, ISAAC NEWTON, infant son of DR. G.G. SMITH, aged eight months and ten days.

Feb. 8, 1844

   A Coroner's Inquest was held on Tuesday the 6th inst. in this City, on the body of WILLIAM LEFEVER, from North Carolina. Verdict of the Jury - Death from "Intemperance." It is believed that he arrived here about a week previous to his death, and from his conversation, it was understood that he was on his way to Alabama, to see his Mother, who resides there.

Feb. 15, 1844

   Died in Jamaica (Long Island) suddenly of Scarlet Fever CAROLINE EULALIA, daughter of MR. HENRY K. CARTER, formerly of this place - aged 5 years.

Mar. 7, 1844

The Philadelphia papers of Wednesday last announce the death of NICHOLAS BIDDLE ESQ. He died at his country residence, Andalusia, on the 27th ult. He was about fifty-eight years of age.

Mar. 7, 1844

GOV. THOMAS REYNOLDS of Missouri, committed suicide at Jefferson city on the 9th inst. by shooting himself through the head with a pistol. The St. Louis Republican of the 12th last says the Governor had been in bad health for some time past.

Mar. 7, 1844

Died on the 22nd of February, at the house of Mr. Wm. Gray, near this city, MRS. ELIZA MARIA GNECH, in the 63d year of her age.

Mar. 7, 1844

Died in this city, on the 5th instant, of liver complaint, JOSHUA G. MOORE, ESQ. aged about 45 years. (He was buried yesterday by the Macon Volunteers, with Military honors.)

Mar. 7, 1844

Died of asthma, in Hamburg, Macon county, on the evening of Wednesday, the 28th ultimo, DR. WILLIAM BROWN, aged 53 years. Dr. Brown was a native of Massachusetts, but for the last fifteen years a citizen of this State. Up to the time when he became an invalid, which was about four years since, from the disease of which he ultimately died, he was a man of extensive business pursuits (with eulogy).

Mar. 14, 1844

Horrible murder! On the night of the 20th ultimo, on Shoebooty Creek, in Clark county, Mississippi, the dwelling of G.W. GARDNER was burned, and in it, JULIAN GARDNER, (wife of the said G.W. Gardner) her infant daughter, and JAMES GARDNER brother of G.W. Gardner, aged about 13 years. (NOTE: Mrs. G. and the young lad were first killed with an axe. Then the infant's throat was cut with a razor blade. Then the house was set on fire).

Mar. 21, 1844

Died in this city, on the 12th instant, of the Scarlet Fever, aged two years and seven days, VIRGINIA, infant daughter of COL. HENRY G. and MARY ANN LAMAR.

Mar. 21, 1844

Died in this city on the 20th inst. KER BOYCE, infant son of JOHN D. and MARY M. WINN, aged four months and one day.

Mar. 28, 1844

Died of scarlet fever, at the residence of her father, in Houston county, on the 14th inst. SARAH ELIZA LOUISA, only daughter of GEO. P. WAGNON, aged three years and six months.

Apr. 4, 1844

Died on the 13th ult. MARIA ANNETTE, daughter of MR. and MRS. CHARLES COTTON, of this city - aged about six months.

Apr. 18, 1844

Died on the 11th inst. EDWARD AUGUSTUS, aged seven years two months and eight days. On the 17th inst. LOUISA JONES, aged two years

(Apr. 18, cont'd.) - and seven months, children of MR. and MRS. GEO. A. KIMBERLY, of this city.

Apr. 18, 1844

Died in this city, on the 17th inst. WILLIAM CUMMING, ESQ. aged about 43 years. He was one among the earliest settlers of our city.

Apr. 18, 1844

Died on Saturday night last, an infant son of MR. CURTIS LEWIS, aged about eight months.

Apr. 18, 1844

Died in Eatonton, on the 8th inst. JOSEE DUNN, ESQ. of Forsyth, Monroe county, aged 53 (58?) years. He was among the earliest settlers of that county, and one of its most respected and influential citizens.

Apr. 18, 1844

Ex-Governor WILLIAM CARROLL died at his residence in Nashville, Tennessee, on the 22d ult. in the 56th year of his age. At the celebrated conflict at New Orleans, Gen. Carroll was a chief actor, and only second to Gen. Jackson himself.

Apr. 25, 1844

Death of another venerable and distinguished patriot of the Revolution, MAJOR GENERAL MORGAN LEWIS, President General of the Society of the Cincinnati of the United States. He died on Sunday the 7th instant, in the 90th year of his age. He was a son of FRANCIS LEWIS, one of the signers of the Declaration of Independence, and was born in this city on the 16th Oct. 1754. (NOTE: Obituary contains extensive biographical data).

Apr. 25, 1844

Died in this city on the 18th inst. of scarlet fever, LOUISA ANN, aged five years and eight months, daughter of MR. J.H. DAMOUR.

May 2, 1844

The HON. HENRY BALDWIN, one of the Judges of the Supreme Court of the United States, died at his lodgings at the Merchants' Hotel, in Philadelphia on Sunday evening, 21st ult., at a quarter past nine o'clock.

May 2, 1844

Died in this city, on the 18th ult., HENRY HILL, aged 8 years 10 months and 6 days. On the 30th ult. ROBERT GRESHAM, aged 1 year 1 month and 18 days - children of EDWARD C. BULKLEY.

May 2, 1844

Died in this city, on the 27th ult., of inflammation of the bowels, FRANCIS J., infant son of MR. and MRS. W.C. and E.B. KENNEDY.

May 2, 1844

Died in this city, on the 22d ult. GEORGE McDUFFIE, youngest son of GEORGE P. WAGNON, aged 5 years.

May 16, 1844

Died of malignant scarlet fever, at the residence of Mr. Calvin W. Battles, in Monroe county, on the 27th April last, MARY JANE, daughter of JOHN G. and MARY S. RAINES, of Upson county, in the eleventh year of her age.

May 23, 1844

    Died in this city, on Sunday last, MRS. MARY F. CLEVELAND, relict of HON. JESSE F. CLEVELAND, and daughter of MAJOR JAMES SMITH, aged about 28 years.

June 6, 1844

    Died in this city, on the 2d inst. ANNA C. LEWIS, aged 2 years, daughter of JOHN L. LEWIS, of Columbus, Geo.

June 6, 1844

    Died in this city on the 24th ult. MARY ELLA, aged two years, daughter of T.P. and REBECCA STUBBS.

June 6, 1844

    Died in this city, on the 1st inst. ELAM ALEXANDER SUBERS, aged ten years three months and 27 days.

June 20, 1844

    Died in this City, on 15th inst. JAMES DICKSON, infant son of ISAAC H. MORELAND, aged 1 year 4 days.

June 20, 1844

    Died in this City, on the 18th inst. MRS. LUCY CLARY ANN EVANS, wife of MR. RUFUS K. EVANS, aged about 34 years.

June 27, 1844

    Died in Marietta, Cobb County, on the 15th instant, MISS JULIA S., daughter of MAJOR WM. Y. HANSELL, aged about 16 years.

July 4, 1844

    A man named THURSTON committed suicide in the Charleston prison on Thursday last, by swallowing a large quantity of Morphine. He had been recently pardoned by the Governor of Georgia, for some crime committed in that State, and was brought to South Carolina to stand a trial for forgery committed on the Planter's and Mechanic's Bank. (Columbia Chronicle)

July 11, 1844

    Died in this city on the 6th inst. after a short illness, G.W. HURT, aged 22 years and 11 months, son of WM. O. HURT, of this city, formerly of Virginia.

July 18, 1844

    Died in this city, at the Floyd House, on the 15th inst. MR. JAMES H. WILSON, supposed to be about 35 years of age. He arrived here from Savannah, on the 11th, apparently in bad health. He was not known to any person in the city, nor has any thing relating to him been ascertained, except from a paper he had, which was dated in Savannah, July 10th, signed Andrew Folliard recommending him to the attention of Wm. H. Crawford, Esq. of Americus.

July 18, 1844

    Died in this city very suddenly on the 16th inst. MR. JONATHAN B. MORRELL, (book binder) formerly of New Haven, Conn., aged about 40 years.

July 25, 1844

    On the 11th inst., DR. B.L. FRANKLIN, aged about 26 years, and

(July 25, cont'd.) - formerly a resident of our city, was instantaneously killed at a mining establishment, in Cherokee county, Ga., by the machinery and employed in the works.

Aug. 1, 1844

Died in the city of Savannah, on the 20th ult. MRS. MARTHA ANN WHITE, wife of MR. JOSEPH A. WHITE, of this city, in the twenty-fourth year of her age. An orphan in early life; as a sister, wife, mother and christian, she will be remembered and lamented.

Aug. 15, 1844

Died in this city, on 23d July, JAMES MONROE, youngest and only son of WILLIAM D. HURT, aged 13 years.

Aug. 22, 1844

Died in Twiggs county on Thursday, the 15th inst. of congestive fever, MICHAEL DEGNAN, aged 28 years. A native of Oxford, Mayo county, Ireland - a citizen of the United States for the last seven years.

Aug. 29, 1844

On the evening of the Democratic Convention in this city, about 7 o'clock, MR. THOMAS SWEENEY was stabbed, and died between three and four o'clock the next morning. Mr. Sweeney was an Irishman, of industrious habits, and has left a wife and child. The report of the Coroner's Inquest was, that he came to his death by a stab wound in the left side with a knife, either by a person of the name of Barnes or Vaughn, of Washington county.

Aug. 29, 1844

Died near this city, of congestive fever, on the 28th inst. MR. LUCAS McCALL, aged about 37 years. He was a native of Lebanon, (Conn.) but for several years a resident of this vicinity. His funeral will be attended this morning at 8 o'clock, from the academy in East Macon, by the Franklin Lodge I.O.O.F. and the Macon Volunteers, of which he was a member.

Aug. 29, 1844

Died in Culloden, Monroe county, on the 18th inst. of billious congestive fever, after an illness of seven days, MAJ. HENRY S. CUTTER, in the 25th year of his age (obituary notice next week)

Sep. 5, 1844

Died in Macon county, of congestive fever, on the 29th ult. DR. MILES K. HARMAN, aged about 36 years, (son of ZACHARIAH HARMAN, ESQ., of Monroe county) (with eulogy).

Sep. 5, 1844

Died on the 29th ult. in Crawford county, ZEPHENIAH EDMUND, aged about fourteen months, first and only child of SAMUEL R. and MARY ADALINE BLAKE of this city.

Sep. 12, 1844

Died in Culloden, Monroe county, on the 18th inst. of billious congestive fever, after an illness of seven days, MAJ. HENRY S. CUTTER, in the 25th year of his age. Has left wife, and infant child, mother, four sisters, an only brother; member of Baptist Church (with eulogy)

Sep. 19, 1844

Died in this city on the 15th inst. SPEIGHT, son of J.A. and MARTHA A. WHITE, aged one year and 15 days.

Sep. 26, 1844

Died in this county, on the 10th inst., LUKE ROSS, in the 69th year of his age. He was a native of North Carolina, and one of the earliest settlers of this vicinity.

Sep. 26, 1844

Died on the 12th inst. MR. ROGER McCALL, aged about 55 years. He was among, if not the very earliest settler of this city.

Sep. 26, 1844

Died, on the 10th ultimo, at his residence, three miles from Macon, of billious inflammatory fever, MR. ANDERSON RICE, in the 60th year of his age. Mr. Rice embraced the christian religion thirty-five years since, at the Sparta camp-meeting in Hancock county, and attached himself to the Methodist Episcopal Church. He left a much afflicted wife on the border of the "spirit" world... (Macon, Sept. 15, 1844 J.B.P.).

Oct. 3, 1844

Died in this City, 29th September, MRS. ANN L. ROSS, consort of MR. JOHN B. ROSS, in the 28th year of her age. For fifteen years she lived an exemplary member of the Methodist Episcopal Church She has left a husband with five children (with eulogy).

Oct. 10, 1844

Died in this city, of consumption, MR. THOS. H. GRIFFITH, aged about 22 years - a native of Maryland.

Oct. 10, 1844

Died in Monroe county, on the 24th ult. of congestive billious fever, at the residence of his father, ARCHIBALD PERKINS, in the 22d year of his age. (with eulogy)

Oct. 17, 1844

Died on the 11th inst. in this county, ABNER A. LUNDY, a native of Hancock county, Ga. in the 31st year of his age.

Oct. 17, 1844

Died on the 16th inst. after a severe and protracted illness, WILLIAM THOMAS, only son of SABERD ODUM, aged one year 11 months and 3 days.

Oct. 31, 1844

Died in this city on the 13th inst. MRS. TABITHA L. KNIGHT, in the 29th (?) year of her age - wife of MR. JAMES A. KNIGHT. (Augusta and Columbus papers are requested to copy).

Oct. 31, 1844

Died at the residence of Mr. Wm. Gray, on the 23d instant, JOHN D., infant son of J.D. and A.A. GRAY, aged 8 months.

Nov. 7, 1844

Died at his residence in Hancock county, on the 25th ult. HAMILTON BONNER, in the 72d year of his age. He was a native of Prince

(Nov. 7, cont'd.) - George county, Virginia, settled in Warrenton, N.C. 1791, married 1800, and emigrated to Georgia in the year 1802 (with eulogy).

Nov. 14, 1844

Died in this city, November 11th, MR. JAMES WOOD, in the 96th year of his age. Was born in Salem, New Jersey, where, in early manhood, he took a vigorous part in the revolutionary struggle of that period. After passing a number of years in Europe, devoted equally to commercial enterprise and scientific research, he established himself in Charleston, of which place he has been a respected resident for the last fifty years, until the strong desire of dying among those he best loved, drew him to our city (with eulogy).

Nov. 28, 1844

Died in this city on the 21st inst. MR. AUGUSTUS B. HIGGS, aged 35 years, recently a resident of Houston county.

Dec. 5, 1844

Died in Monroe County on the 11th ult. MRS. CAROLINE SUSAN TYLER, wife of WM. P. TYLER, and daughter of DOLPHIN FLOYD, ESQ.

Jan. 9, 1845

Died on the 23d inst. DAWSON PHILLIPS, ESQ. aged 60 years, and old and much respected citizen of Jones county.

Jan. 9, 1845

Died in East Macon on the 2d inst. MRS. MARY J. MORELAND, in the 23d year of her age, wife of ISAAC H. MORELAND.

Jan. 16, 1845

Died in this city on the 10th inst. MARGARET CORINNE, infant daughter of EDWARD D. and CAROLINE TRACY.

Jan. 16, 1845

Died in this city, on the 7th inst., ELIZABETH REA, aged three years and y months; and on the 11th inst. CHARLES, aged 5 years and 2 months - children of CHARLES & ELIZABETH W. COATES.

Jan. 23, 1845

Died in this city on the morning of the 9th inst. of scarlet fever, MARY ELIZABETH FELYN (?), only child of GEO. B. & M.A. ROBERTS, aged nearly 2 years.

Jan. 23, 1845

Murder! ROBERT P. BALDWIN was found dead on Friday morning last, in Monroe County, about two and a half miles from Forsyth. He was murdered by being beaten on the head by some person or persons yet unknown.

Jan. 30, 1845

Died in the county of Crawford on the 10th inst. MRS. MARGARET CAMPBELL, wife of MR. WM. CAMPBELL; member of the Presbyterian Church.

Jan. 30, 1845

Died, in East Macon, on the 4th inst. of a short but severe illness, JOSEPHINE, the only daughter of MR. & MRS. LIGHTFOOT, aged 7 years.

Jan. 30, 1845

    Died in Jones county, on the 24th inst. MR. JOHN B. DAME, aged 36 years.

Feb. 6, 1845

    Died in East Macon, on the 25th ult., JOSEPH MORGAN BROWN, son of THOS. A. & E.A. BROWN, aged 5 years 1 month and 7 days.

Feb. 20, 1845

    Departed this life at Greenhill, the residence of her father, on Tuesday the 11th inst., at eight minutes past 11:00 A.M., ANNA W. FIELD, wife of MR. SAMUEL FIELD, and only daughter and child of MR. ISHAM H. & MRS. PATIENCE SAFFOLD, after an illness of four or five days. Her infant son had passed away a few hours before her.

Feb. 27, 1845

    Died in this county, on the 20th inst. MR. SOLOMON GROCE, aged about 38 years.

Mar. 20, 1845

    Suicide! On the afternoon of Tuesday last, a young man aged about 20 years by the name of LAFAYETTE EDWARDS shot himself in the body with a Pistol, of which he died five or six hours afterwards.

Mar. 27, 1845

    Died in this city on the morning of the 23d inst. (?) MRS. MARY HALL, wife of MARTIN HALL, ESQ., aged 43 years (?). The ced'd whose maiden name was MARY McCOOK was born in Hancock county; resided for many years in this city; in the spring of 1843 she united with the Baptist Church in this place.

Mar. 27, 1845

    Died in this city on the 20th inst., MRS. SALINA P. HALL, aged 73 years.

Apr. 17, 1845

    Died in this city, on the 15th inst., THOMAS MOORE, aged about 15 years - son of the late JOSHUA G. MOORE dec'd.

Apr. 24, 1845

    Died in this city on the 17th inst. LEONARD A. ADAMS, (Tinner), aged about 40 years, native of Hartford co. (CT.) and for many years a resident of this city.

Apr. 24, 1845

    Died in East Macon, on the 20th inst. ENGERTON DURRETT, aged about 4 months - son of MR. H.L. COOK.

May 1, 1845

    Died after a few days illness at the residence of her son GEO. PATTEN, in this city, on Wednesday the 23d inst. at 1 o'clock P.M., MRS. ELECTA PATTEN, aged 76, relict of COL. JONATHAN PATTEN, formerly of Stockbridge, Mass., and three years a resident of this state; member of the Presbyterian Church.

May 1, 1845

    Died in Columbus on the 17th ult., MRS. ANN E. COOPER, aged 19 years wife of ALEXANDER A. COOPER, ESQ., and daughter of MRS. E.A. BILLUPS, formerly a resident of this place.

May 1, 1845

    Died in this city on the 27th ult. after a short and painful illness, MR. JOHN S. LEONARD, aged 27 years - a native of Maryland.

May 8, 1845

    Died in this city on the 1st inst. ALEXANDER, only child of ALEXANDER & MARGARET SCOTT; aged 16 months.

May 8, 1845

    Died in this city on the 6th inst. THOMAS, youngest son of DR. R.H. RANDOLPH, aged two years and eight months.

May 22, 1845

    Died on the 13th inst. MARSHALL M. RUNNELLS, a son-in-law of BENJAMIN ALLEN, of this county, aged 36 years.

May 29, 1845

    Died on the 21st inst. in Jones county, MARY ANN ROBERTS, in the 17th year of her age, consort of GREEN ROBERTS, and daughter of GEORGE & RACHEL BROACH.

June 5, 1845

    Died on the 29th instant, at the house of FREDERICK SIMS, in this place, MRS. MARY BULLOCK, in the 88th year of her age; member of Methodist Episcopal Church for the last 66 years of her life; the widow of DANIEL BULLOCK, who bore his full share in the Revolutionary War, and was the mother of MRS. CHARLES BULLOCK, the first Senator in the state legislature from this county. (Mississippi and Texas papers please copy).

June 5, 1845

    Died on the 12th inst. in Monroe county, MR. JOHN REDDING, aged about 54 years. He was among the earliest settlers of that county; member of the Methodist Church.

June 19, 1845

    Died in Albany, (Geo.) on the 11th inst. of inflammation of the brain COL. JOHN JONES, Editor of the "Courier" of that city.

June 19, 1845

    Died in this city on the 9th instant HENRY COSSETT, infant son of HENRY L. and MARTHA J. JEWETT, aged 5 months and 15 days.

June 19, 1845

    Died on the morning of the 14th inst. after a short illness at his residence in this city JOHN LAMAR, ESQ., in the 36th year of his age.

June 19, 1845

    Died in Vineville on the 5th inst. of Croup, MARCUS A. FRANKLIN, only son of SAMUEL and SARAH ANN VIRGIN, aged 3 years 5 months and 25 days.

June 26, 1845

    Died in Jones county on the 7th inst. MR. CHARLES R. EATON, aged about 48 years; a native of Virginia but for many years past had resided in Georgia. (North Carolina papers will please copy).

June 26, 1845

    Died in this city, on the 24th inst. of a pulmonary affection JOHN P. BALLARD, ESQ., aged about 54 years. He was, we believe, a native of New York, where he has many relatives living, and had resided in Darien and this city for upwards of twenty years past; interred by Macon Lodge No. 6 with usual ceremonies of the Craft.

July 3, 1845

    Homicide! A young man (DR. A.J. TRIPP) was killed in Eatonton on Monday the 23d ult. by a stab received from MR. A.B. HOXEY. The assault grew out of a quarrel which had occurred on Saturday previous.

July 17, 1845

    Died in this city on the 15th inst. of congestion of the brain MR. GEORGE CLARK, aged 28 years, a native of Farmington, (Conn.) but for several years a resident of this city.

July 24, 1845

    Died in this city, on the 13th inst. MR. AUGUSTUS C. BRUCE, formerly of South Carolina but for sometime a resident of this city, aged 23 years; his remains were buried by the Order of Odd Fellows of which he was a member.

July 24, 1845

    Died in this city on the 17th inst. MR. HENRY A. CANDLER, in the 45th year of his age, for many years a resident of this city.

July 24, 1845

    Died in this city on the 22d inst. JAMES S. SMITH, ESQ. aged about 22 years.

Aug. 7, 1845

    Murder! A negro woman was murdered by the overseer of COL. H.G. LAMAR at his plantation in this county on Monday evening last. The act was committed from a very slight cause. The woman was stabbed severely with a knife in the left breast, and her skull fractured by a blow with a rock of which she died immediately. The name of the overseer is THOMAS FREEMAN, who has been arrested and is now in jail in this city.

Aug. 7, 1845

    Died in this city, on the 2d inst. ELLA LANE, daughter of A.F. & E. HOLT, aged eight months and 17 days.

Aug. 7, 1845

    Died in Henry county, on the 1st inst. MR. JAMES R. PERRY, aged 48 years; native of North Carolina, but in early life removed to this state, and for several years resided near this city.

Aug. 7, 1845

    Died in DeSoto county (Miss.) on the 19th July HENRY CLAY, son of C.F. and MARY E. WIMBERLY, aged 3 years and 9 months.

Aug. 21, 1845

    Died in this city on the 16th inst. SAMUEL T. ROWLAND, aged about 33 years - a native of Dutchess county New York but for several years a resident of this city.

Aug. 21, 1845

> Died in this city on Friday, the 15th inst. CHARLES HENRY SHERMAN, aged about 19 years; native of Wayland, Mass. - for the last several years a resident of this place.

Aug. 28, 1845

> Died in this county on the 22d inst. ZACHARIAH COWART, ESQ. aged about 60 years.

Aug. 28, 1845

> Died in this city after a lingering illness MR. YOUNG JOHNSTON, ESQ. aged about 50 years.

Aug. 28, 1845

> Died in this place at the residence of COL. H.G. LAMAR, on the morning of the 22d inst. HENRY GANAWAY, aged 4 months and 23 days, infant son of DR. ALBERT and MRS. S.S. REES, of Americus, Sumpter county.

Aug. 28, 1845

> Died in this city, on the 26th inst. MRS. ELLEN INGRAHAM, wife of MR. JOHN S. INGRAHAM, in the 25th year of her age; born in Twiggs county where her parents, MR. JOHN and MRS. MARTHA FLEMING formerly resided; her widowed mother will survive her in this place; about three years ago she united with the Baptist Church in this city.

Sep. 4, 1845

> Died in this city, on the 23d ult. PHILIP BETHEA, eldest son of WM. D. and REBECCA T. RAINY, aged 3 years 2 months and 18 days.

Sep. 4, 1845

> Died in Jones county, on the 26th August, WILLIAM MATTHEWS, second son of JAMES W. and LOUISA FURLOW, aged 2 years 6 months and 18 days.

Sep. 18, 1845

> Died in Athens on the evening of the 9th inst. JAMES A.S. RUTHERFORD, aged 16 years and 3 months, son of WILLIAM RUTHERFORD, ESQ. of Monroe county, - a member of the University of Georgia.

Sep. 18, 1845

> Died at Woodville, Baldwin county, on the 9th inst. MRS. CATHERINE M., wife of the HON. SEATON GRANTLAND and daughter of the late CAPT. GEORGE DABNEY, of Hanover county Virginia.

Sep. 18, 1845

> Trial for murder! On Wednesday of last week the trial of JAMES HUDGINS, for the murder of JOHN ANDERSON commenced in Monroe Superior Court, Judge Tracy presiding.

Oct. 2, 1845

> Died in Houston county on the 17th ult. from constipation of the bowels, MARY, wife of JAMES HOLMES, ESQ., in the 60th year of her age.

Oct. 16, 1845

> Died in this city on the 13th inst. after a severe and painful illness, SARAH ELIZABETH, infant child of MR. S. ODOM - aged 16 months and 11 days.

Oct. 16, 1845

Died in this city on the 13th inst. THOMAS R. GARDNER, aged about 35 years, a native of Rhode Island.

Oct. 16, 1845

Died in Vineville, on the evening of the 12th inst., GEORGE FREDERICK, youngest son of GEORGE JEWITT, in the 12th year of his age.

Oct. 16, 1845

Died on the 6th inst. in Houston county, after a painful illness of 11 months, MRS. ELIZABETH D. EUBANKS, 32 years and 8 months old, consort of EDWARD EUBANKS: member of the Methodist Church from the early age of 14; has left a husband and five small children.

Oct. 23, 1845

Died in Covington, on the 10th Sept. MRS. LORENA WILLIAMSON, aged 42 years, wife of GEN. J.N. WILLIAMSON.

Oct. 23, 1845

Died in Marietta, on the 12th inst. COL. JEREMIAH LEAKE, aged about 25 years; formerly a resident of this city and more recently of Zebulon; recently Master of Montgomery Lodge of Zebulon, and was buried by Kennesaw Lodge with the honors of Masonry.

Nov. 13, 1845

Died in Macon, on the 29th Oct. in the 58th year of his age, after an illness of six weeks, DR. JOHN H. WRIGHT, formerly of Milledgville; for many years a member of the Methodist Episcopal Church.

Nov. 27, 1845

Died on the 21st inst. in Macon county, after a short, but severe illness of only a few days, MRS. LOUISA JANE HENRIETTA CROCKER, consort of DR. WILLIAM N.L. CROCKER, and eldest daughter of JOHN and POLLY VIRGINIA STAPLER, aged 32 years 5 months and 14 days.

Nov. 27, 1845

Died in this city, on Saturday night the 22d inst. MAJOR GEORGE W. MOORE, aged 71 years; formerly a resident of Oglethorpe, but resided in this county almost from its settlement.

Nov. 27, 1845

Died in this city on the 25th inst. WILLIAM ALBERT, infant son of COL. R.A.L. and MRS. ELIZA A. ATKINSON, aged 6 months and 13 days.

Dec. 11, 1845

Died in Athens, on Friday evening the 28th ult., after a protracted illness, REV. IGNATIUS A. FEW, LL. D. - his remains were taken to Oxford, there to be interred.

Dec. 18, 1845

Died in Macon on Saturday, 13th inst. MARY GRIMES ROSS, relict of the late LUKE ROSS, aged 61 years.

Dec. 18, 1845

Died in this city, on Saturday the 13th inst. after an illness of a few days GEORGE ROBERT, eldest son of WASHINGTON and SALINA S. POE, aged 11 years 9 months and 6 days.

Jan. 1, 1846

Died in Starkville, on the 21st inst. of nervous fever, MISS MARIA W. MACON, in the 15th year of her age, daughter of WM. G. MACON, ESQ. (long obituary).

Jan. 15, 1846

Died in this city, on the 7th instant, MRS. LOUISA M. WEED, wife of MR. E.B. WEED, in the 36th year of her age; died of consumption; a Presbyterian; left husband and children (long obituary).

Jan. 15, 1846

Died, at Midway, near Milledgeville, on the 23d of December, of scarlet fever, JOHN CLARENCE, infant son of GEORGE W. and MARTHA E. FISH, aged 15 months and 8 days.

Jan. 22, 1846

Died, in this city, on the 12th inst., MR. CHARLES G. ST. JOHNS, formerly a resident in Macon, and lately in New York.

Feb. 5, 1846

Died, in this city, on the 22d of January last, MRS. SARAH JANE, consort of MR. RICHARD L. HUNTER, and daughter of THOS. H. and MATILDA A. FLINT, in the 24th year of her age, after a short but pianful illness; member of Methodist Episcopal Church. (long obituary).

Feb. 5, 1846

Died in Twiggs county, on the 1st inst., MRS. CAROLINE E. DAVIS, wife of BENJAMIN DAVIS, and daughter of LARKIN GRIFFIN, on this city.

Feb. 12, 1846

Murder will out - the REV. DANIEL SIMMONS, of the Baptist Church, was arrested yesterday and brought before ROBERT D. WIGGINS, ESQ., upon complaint of MR. ARCHIBALD LEWIS, as being a fugitive from justice, charged with having committed homicide, by killing H. DAVIS, in the year 1822, or 1823, in the county of Tatnall, State of Georgia...(Mobile Herald & Tribune).

Feb. 19, 1846

Died in this city on the 14th inst. MR. DAVID SHERMAN FAIRCHILD, aged about 28 years. Mr. F. was a native of Indiana, where he has parents living.

Mar. 5, 1846

Died near Nantucket, Feb. 15, JAMES BOLIVAR ALEXANDER, native of Hamilton county, Ohio, resident of Macon, Georgia, of inflammation of the brain.

Mar. 19, 1846

Died in Georgetown, S.C. on the 12th ult. the REV'D ELIJAH SINCLAIR, of the Methodist Church - his complaint was consumption. He was formerly a resident of Macon, Ga.

Mar. 19, 1846

Died in Washington, Ga. on the 19th ult., MR. J. KAPPEL, SR., Printer, in the 54th year of his age.

Apr. 23, 1846

Died suddenly in this city, on Monday, 13th inst. MRS. MARY M. WINN, wife of JOHN D. WINN, in the 46th year of her age; for last twenty-five years in communion with the Presbyterian Church; leaves husband, six children, numerous relatives and friends. (Watchman & Observer please copy).

Apr. 23, 1846

Died in Pulaski County, on the 11th inst. MR. BLACKSHEAR BRYAN, aged about 46 years. Mr. Bryan was a resident of Vineville, near this city, but while at his plantation, he waa attacked with the Measles, from which he partially recovered, but taking a relapse, his life was soon terminated; left a wife and only son.

May 28, 1846

Died in Hillsboro, on the evening of the 11th inst., in full assurance of a blissful immortality, MRS. LUCINDA R. MORRIS, wife of MR. JOHN G. MORRIS, in the 36th year of her age.

June 4, 1846

Died in this city, on the 20th ult. JAMES HERBERT, only child of JAMES H. and LAURA A. BISHOP, aged two years two months and 26 days.

June 11, 1846

Died in this city, on the 9th inst. MR. HENRY ALLEN, aged about 26 years, late of Granby, Conn.

June 11, 1846

Died in this city, on Tuesday evening, 9th inst. after a short and severe illness of five days, MRS. MARGARET, wife of ALEXANDER SCOTT, ESQ. and daughter of the late DRURY WILLIAMS, of Florida.

June 18, 1846

Died in this city, on the 12th inst., MRS. ELIZA W. BIVINS, wife of MR. WILLIAM BIVINS, in the 58th year of her age; member of the Protestant Episcopal Church. (long obituary).

June 18, 1846

Died on the 15th inst. PHILIP ANN BETHEA, only daughter of WM. D. and REBECCA T. RAINEY, aged one year and three days.

June 18, 1846

Died in this city, on the 27th of May, MR. CHARLES F. HAWLEY, (of the late firm of Messrs. Grummon & Co.) aged about 27 years, late of Bridgeport, Conn.

June 25, 1846

Murder in Sumter County - A murder was committed in this county yesterday on the person of THOMAS M. MANN, by a man named JOHN GRISWOLD. Mann was shot through the chest with buck shot, at the distance of about five feet. Griswold has escaped: he is about five feet seven inches high black hair and eyes, and fair skin. He is a carpenter by trade, about thirty years old, and is a northern man. I understand the widow offers a large reward for the apprehension of Griswold.

June 25, 1846

Departed this life in the city of Macon, on the 18th inst. CLEMENTIUS DAVIS, infant son of COL. H.G. and MRS. M.A. LAMAR, aged three months and 18 (?) days.

June 25, 1846

   Died in this city on the 21st inst. MARY SINGLETARY, infant daughter of BENJAMIN R. and MARY M. WARNER, aged three months and eleven days.

June 25, 1846

   Died in this city on the 22d instant, JAMES HENRY, infant son of MR. & MRS. GRANVILLE WOOD, aged 18 months.

July 2, 1846

   COL. JOHN CROWELL died very suddenly at his residence at Fort Mitchell, Russell county, Ala., on the 25th ult. Col. C. is well known to the people of Georgia as the late United States Agent of Indian Affairs in this State.

July 2, 1846

   Died in this city, on the 25th ult., DR. WM. GREEN, aged about 79 years; resided in this city for several years past, and is well known to the people of Georgia as a man of high literary attainments, and an able political writer; born in the city of Dublin, where he received his education in Trinity College; emigrated to America in 1800, in consequence of the unfortunate struggles of his countrymen in the cause of political freedom, and to which cause he was ever ardently attached.

July 9, 1846

   Died in this city, on the morning of the 4th inst. EDMUND JONES, infant son of JOHN J. and MARY E. GRESHAM, aged seven months and 25 days.

July 23, 1846

   Died in Vineville, on the 16th inst., MALONE SOLOMON, only son of MR. PETER and LOUISA SOLOMON, aged one year 9 months and 4 days.

July 30, 1846

   CALEB J. McNULTY, former Clerk of the House of Representatives, a private in one of the Ohio companies of volunteers, died on board of the steam-boat, on his way to Texas, on the 10th inst.

Aug. 6, 1846

   Died in Monroe county, on the 25th ult. ZACHARIAH HARMAN, SEN. ESQ. aged about 65 years; native of North Carolina.

Aug. 6, 1846

   Died in Harris county, on the 28th ult., in the 42d year of her age, MRS. MARY W. SUTTON, consort of MR. JAMES N. SUTTON.

Aug. 13, 1846

   Died on the 10th inst. at the residence of his father, JOSEPH N. EVANS, M.D., second son of MR. JOHN P. EVANS, of this city (Macon, Ga.) aged 23 years. He had just prepared to enter upon the duties of his profession, when he was attacked by disease, and hurried to the grave.

Sep. 3, 1846

   ...death of COL. ALEX. M'DONALD at his residence in Eufala, Ala.; formerly from Jasper county, in this State, and President of the State Agricultural Society of Alabama.

Sep. 17, 1846

    Died in this city on the 14th inst. after a lingering illness JOHN TEAT, aged about 16 years. (Columbus papers will please copy).

Sep. 24, 1846

    Died in Upson County, on the 10th inst. CAPT. JOSEPH WHEATON, at an advanced age. He was a native of Providence, R.I., but for many years a resident of that county.

Sep. 24, 1846

    Died in Pulaski County, on the 8th inst. THOMAS WHALEY, aged about 20 years, only son of JOHN and REBECCA WHALEY.

Sep. 24, 1846

    JOSIAH HUDGENS was tried for the murder of his overseer, JOHN ANDERSON, in Monroe county, last week, Judge Floyd, presiding. The murder was committed in June 1845...

Oct. 1, 1846

    GEN. WM. G. SMITH, late Post Master of this city, died of congestive fever on the 24th inst. after a short but severe illness, in the thirtieth year of his age; a native of Jones county, in this State, but had resided in this city for the last eight years. The remains of the deceased were interred at Rose Hill Cemetery, on Friday evening, with Military and Odd Fellowship honors (Telegraph).

Oct. 1, 1846

    Died on the 17th Sept. in Houston county, Geo., at the residence of MR. JOSEPH TOOKE, MRS. ELIZABETH C. LOPER, wife of MR. M.J. LOPER, and daughter of MR. CHAMPION and MRS. LOUISA BUTLER, of East-Macon, Ga., aged about sixteen years (long obituary).

Oct. 8, 1846

    Died at his residence in Houston county, on the 1st inst. after a protracted illness of four or five weeks, MALCOLM T. GILBERT, in the 28th year of hi age; left a widow and two orphans.

Oct. 15, 1846

    Died at his residence, in Monroe county, on the 2d inst. MR. ROGER MACARTHY, at the venerable age of 88 years; a native of Ireland, but had resided in this State for the last fifty years.

Oct. 15, 1846

    Died in this city, on the 12th inst. CAROLINA CAPERS, daughter of BENJAMIN R. and MARY S. WARNER, aged two years.

Oct. 15, 1846

    Died at Bridgeport, Conn. on the 1st inst. MR. FORDYCE WRIGLEY, aged 43 years, a native of Spencer, Mass., resident of this city for the last fifteen years. (NOTE: a memorial tribute to him was published in same issue by Franklin Lodge No. 2, I.O.O.F., Macon, Ga.)

Oct. 22, 1846

    Died in this city on Monday the 19th inst. MR. ANDREW RAINEY, aged forty-eight years.

Oct. 29, 1846

Announce the death of JAMES GODDARD ESQ. - died at Greenfield Massachusetts, on the 19th inst. Mr. Goddard left here for the North late in the season, in the prosecution of his business...

Oct. 29, 1846

Died in this city, on Sunday the 25th inst., in the 47th year of his age, ABRAHAM P. PATRICK, ESQ., a native of North Carolina, but for the last eighteen years a resident of this town; known as one of our most successful and prominent merchants, first as a member of the House, Patrick & Martin, and Patrick & Logan of this city, and subsequently as a member of the extensive and respectable house of North, Manning & Patrick, New York. (long obituary).

Oct. 29, 1846

Died in this city on the 24th inst., MR. JOHN ROSE, aged about sixty-six years - formerly a resident of Jones county.

Oct. 29, 1846

Died in Jones county, on the 12th inst. ISAAC T. MORELAND, after an illness of 5 days, with the congestive fever - aged 62 years, 1 month and 26 days. In his death, the county has lost one of her most valuable citizens, his children a kind father, his companion an affectionate husband, he was a humane master. We trust that he is reaping his reward.

Oct. 29, 1846

Died at the residence of Judge Pearce, in Upson county, on the morning of the 26th last, MR. GEORGE W. MADDOX, in his 25th year.

Nov. 5, 1846

Died in this county, on the 29th ult. ELIZABETH McDONALD - aged 2 years, 1 month, and 3 days, daughter of DANIEL WADSWORTH ESQ. On the 29th ult., his wife MRS. ELIZABETH WADSWORTH - aged 44 years, and 3 days - leaving three small children, and a bereaved husband.

Dec. 3, 1846

Died in Thomas county, on the 13th ult. MR. JOHN R. HAYES, aged about 32 years, formerly a resident of this city, and one of the Mercantile firm of Hamilton, Hayes & Co.

Dec. 3, 1846

Died on Sunday last, at Milledgeville, CAPT. WILLIAM F. SCOTT, an old and highly respected citizen.

Dec. 17, 1846

Died in Columbus, on the 25th ult. MR. JOHN HUNTER, aged about 65 years - formerly a resident of this city, and of Savannah.

Dec. 17, 1846

Died in Clark county, on the 27th ult. MAJ. JACOB WOOD, aged 78 years - well known as President of our State Senate for many years, and a prominent member of the Legislature.

Dec. 17, 1846

Died in Macon county, Ala. ISAAC T. CUSHING, aged 69 years - formerly of Milledgeville.

Dec. 17, 1846

Died in Leon county, Florida, MAJ. JOHN HARDIN, aged 75 years - formerly a resident of Twiggs county, Ga.

Dec. 17, 1846

Died in Savannah, on the 5th inst. MR. JOSEPH CUMMING, - one of the oldest and most respected merchants of that city.

Dec. 24, 1846

Died in this city, on the 21st inst. MR. JOHN BARR, a native of England, aged about 50 years.

Dec. 31, 1846

Died in this city, on the 24th inst. COL. JOHN S.M. BALDWIN, aged 37 years and 4 months.

Dec. 31, 1846

Died in this city, on the morning of the 29th inst. DR. JAMES WOOD, aged about 44 years. Dr. Wood was a native of Charleston S.C., but formerly practiced in his profession ofr several years in New York and Boston, and removed to this city a few years since for the benefit of his health; member of Independent Order of Odd Fellows in this city, and was by them, together with the Floyd Rifles, of which he was an honorary member, yesterday consigned to the tomb. Dr. Wood died very suddenly, having been indisposed only for a day or two, but not supposed to be seriously ill. On the morning of the 24th he was found dead in his bed; supposed he expired by rupture of blood vessel.

Jan. 7, 1847

Departed this life, on Monday, 22d ult., at his residence in Houston county, MR. JAMES A BRYAN, in the 46th year of his age.

Died in this city, on the 25th ult., in the 22d year of her age, after a brief but severe illness, MRS. ELIZA, consort of MR. GREEN J. BLAKE, of this city.

Jan. 14, 1847

Late arrivals from Mexico bring intelligence of the death of CAPT. ISAAC HOLMES, Captain of the "Macon Guards" of the Georgia Regiment ...remains of Capt. Holmes, under the sacred charge of Mr. George Robinson, the devoted friend of the deceased, are on their way to the U. States. They will pass through our city, where arrangements are already made to pay suitable honors to the memory of the gallant dead. (Columbus Times)

Jan. 21, 1847

Died at his residence in Twiggs county, on the 16th inst. HENRY SOLOMON, ESQ. aged 54 years.

Notice of the death of COL. EVERARD HAMILTON. (Savannah Republican 13th inst.).

Masonic tribute to death of CAPT. ISAAC HOLMES. Obsequies of Capt. Holmes: mortal remains, under the charge of his faithful friend, Mr. Geo. Robinson (who has had the care of them from Monterey), his relative, Mr. Randolph L. Mott, a military detachment from the Columbus Light Guards, Masonic committees from Columbian and Oglethorpe Lodges, Columbus, from Muscogee Lodge of Odd Fellows, Columbus, and a committee of our own citizens, reached the Railroad Depot on Monday last, and were escorted by the Macon Volunteers, Floyd Rifles, and the detachment of Columbus

(Jan. 21, cont'd) - Light Guards, to the residence of the deceased, where they remained until Tuesday...then taken in charge by the Volunteers, and under a military escort, conveyed to the Twon Hall. ...will remain in Town Hall until 12 o'clock, today, when it will be removed to its final resting place in Rose Hill Cemetery.

Jan. 28, 1847

Remains of CAPT. ISAAC HOLMES, of the "Macon Guards," who died at Camp, near Monterey, on the 6th ultimo, reached our city, in charge of Mr. Geo. Robinson, on Friday morning last....(Muscogee Democrat).

Died in Vineville, on the 22d inst., MRS. MARTHA W. BAILEY, wife of COL. SAMUEL T. BAILEY, and eldest daughter of the HON. CHRISTOPHER B. STRONG.

Died in this city on the 24th inst., AUGUSTUS MITCHELL MENARD, aged 19 years, son of MR. STEPHEN MENARD.

Died in Burke county, Ga., on the 20th inst., BENJAMIN C.H. EVANS, M.D., son of MR. JOHN P. EVANS, of this city, formerly of Rochester, N.H., aged 26 years.

Feb. 4, 1847

Died in this city, on the 2d inst. MR. FENNER BROWN, native of Rhode Island, but for several years a merchant in East Macon.

Feb. 18, 1847

Died in this city on Tuesday, 9th inst., MRS. EMILY O. HINES, wife of RICHARD K. HINES, ESQ., and daughter of the late DR. JAMES NISBET, in the 41st year of her age.

Died at her plantation in Chatham county, on Saturday, 30th ult., MRS. MARY HARRISON, consort of the late COL. WM. HARRISON, in the 61st year of her age.

Feb. 25, 1847

Died in this city, on the 20th instant, in her 23d year, MRS. MARY ADALINE BLAKE, wife of SAMUEL R. BLAKE, ESQ. (with eulogy).

Mar. 4, 1847

Remains of MR. JAMES GODDARD, who died last summer in Massachusetts, have been brought to this city, and will be deposited in the Presbyterian Church until 3 o'clock, P.M. this day, when they will be removed to Rose Hill Cemetery.

Mar. 11, 1847

Died in Wetumpka, DR. REUBEN FITZGERALD, aged 58 years, native of Pittsylvania county, Va., and formerly of Twiggs county, Ga.

Mar. 25, 1847

Died in this city, on the 24th inst., of the Consumption, MR. CHAS. WINSLOW, aged about 29 years.

Apr. 29, 1847

Died at the residence of her parents, near this city, on the 19th instant, MRS. SARAH A.R. BLOUNT, aged 27 years and 11 months. She was the wife of THOMAS H. BLOUNT and the daughter of MARK D. and NANCY M. CLARK (with eulogy). (Christian Index will please copy.)

May 19, 1847

Died in this place on the 11th inst. MRS. ELIZABETH JAMESON, consort of DR. DAVID JAMESON, aged 48 years (with eulogy) (Alabama papers will please copy).

May 26, 1847

Died in this city, on the 19th inst., JONATHAN HUGHES, infant son of WM. B. and C.A. HARRISON, aged two months and 14 days.

Died in this city, on the 23d inst., ELLA JANE, daughter of DR. H.K. and MRS. THEODOSIA GREEN, aged two years and two months.

Died in this vicinity on the 22d inst. CHARLES JOSEPH, son of B.F. and SARAH L. GRIFFIN, aged 2 months and 3 days.

Departed this life on the 11th instant, at her residence, in Houston county, MRS. GATSEY ANN PRINGLE, wife of JAMES ADGER PRINGLE, and youngest child of JOEL and NANCY LOFTIN, in the 23d year of her age; left behind her one child...

Died in Taylor county, Mississippi on the 7th inst. MR. JAMES HOLLINGSWORTH, in the fifty-fifth year of his age; for many years a resident of this city, but for the last two or three years a resident of the above county and State.

June 2, 1847

Died in Culloden, Ga., on the 23d ult., in the 21st year of her age, MRS. E.C. MATHER, consort of MR. J.C. MATHER, both natives of Connecticut. Having been a mother for four months only, her only source of regret was to leave her child so young.

Died on the 24th ult., at the residence of her father in Lee county, MARY ANN, eldest daughter of COL. WM. A. and ELIZABETH F. MAXWELL, aged 5 years, 7 months and 10 days.

23 June 1847

Died in this city, on Tuesday, June 15th, NARCISSA GRIFFIN, only child of LEWIS N. and SARAH M. WHITTLE, aged three years, eight months and twenty-two days.

Died in Pulaski county, on the 29th ult., the REV. WILEY F.D. HOLDER, (of the Methodist Church,) in the 47th year of his age.

The Southern Recorder announces the death of JAS. CAMAK, ESQ., of Athens. "long and widely known as the Editor of the Georgia Journal, as first President of the Central Bank, and of late as Editor of the Southern Cultivator, and for his practical efforts promotive of agriculture."

June 30, 1847

Died at his residence in Jasper county, on Monday, the 21st inst., MR. MOSES B. HAIRSTON, in the 31st year of his age - leaving a disconsolate widow, an infant son and many relatives...

July 7, 1847

Died at the residence of her father, in Cass county, Geo. on Friday, the 18th ult., CAMILLA, daughter of HON. MARK A. COOPER, aged 17 years.

Died at his residence in DeKalb Co., on the 22d ult., of a spinal affection, ALSTON H. GREEN, aged 59 years.

July 14, 1847

Died in this city, very suddenly, on the 7th instant, of an apoplectic fit, (as is supposed) MR. GEORGE WOOD, aged about 40 years - a native of New York.

July 21, 1847

Died in Bibb county, on the 6th inst., very suddenly, DR. WM. STEWARD, aged about 27 years.

Died at his residence in Putnam County, on the 7th inst. RICHARD H. SEYMORE, at an advanced age; an active Whig in the war of the revolution and did good service in the patriot army; consistent member of Methodist Episcopal Church.

July 28, 1847

Died in Athens, on Thursday July 15th, after a short and painful illness, MRS. MARIA T. BOARDMAN, aged 32 years (eulogy).

Died at his residence in this city, on the 22d inst. DR. RICHARD HENRY RANDOLPH, in the fifty second year of his age (with eulogy).

Died in Pike county, near Barnesville, on the 20th inst., MR. JOHN JENKINS, aged 87 years, 6 months and 3 days; a worthy soldier of the Revolution, and for some time one of General Washington's life-guard, and was present at the capture of Lord Cornwallis at Yorktown; the last of the survivors of the Revolution in his county.

Died in this city, on the 23d inst. MR. JOSEPH BARKER, aged about 33 years - son of CAPT. DAVID BARKER, of Branford, Conn.; member of I.O. of Odd Fellows; buried in Rose Hill Cemetery.

Died in New York, on the 5th inst. at the residence of Major John Pettus, MRS. HARRIET HELEN, wife of WILLIAM RICHARD PETTUS, ESQ. of St. Marks, Florida, and only daughter of the late WILLIAM J. DANNELLY, of Macon, Georgia, aged 18 years. Also on the 6th inst. her infant daughter.

Drowned. On the 19th inst. MR. WM. HIGHTOWER, of this city, and his son, about 9 years old, went down the Ocmulgee river about three miles, for the purpose of fishing. The batteau in which they were, was discovered upset on the evening of that day, and their bodies were found on the 21st instant, and a coroner's inquest held over them. The batteau was probably upset accidentally, and both drownded. Over $70 in gold and silver was found on the body of Mr. H., and $34 in paper money.

Aug. 4, 1847

Died in Monroe county, on the 27th ult., WM. O. PRATT, ESQ., aged 46 years - formerly sheriff of said county.

Died at the residence of her husband, B.H. RUTHERFORD, in Houston county, on the 27th inst., H.T.V. RUTHERFORD, daughter of COL. THOMAS MOUGHON, in the 42nd year of her age (with eulogy).

EX-GOVERNOR EDWARDS died at his residence in New-Haven, on Thursday evening, in the 68th year of his age; Governor of the State of Connecticut, Speaker of the State Legislature, Member of Congress, and of the United States Senate.

Aug. 11, 1847

Died in Houston county on Wednesday the 4th inst. VIRGINIA, daughter of DANIEL GUNN, aged 14 years (with eulogy).

Aug. 25, 1847

The Savannah Georgian of the 16th reports the death of SHEFTALL SHEFTALL, ESQ. - a Revolutionary soldier gone; distinguished by his "Knee-Breeches" and his "Cocked Hat"; born in Savannah 85 years ago; at the siege of Savannah; in the surrender of this city he was taken prisoner, by the British, and confined for six months upon the prison-ship at this port and at Charleston... from Charleston taken to West Indies where he was permitted to return to Philadelphia of his parole of honor; sent to Charleston, with a flag of truce, to take money for the relief of American prisoners there; held appointment of Assistant Commissary in the Army; admitted to the Bar, in Camden county shortly after the War, and was the oldest lawyer in the State.

Sep. 8, 1847

Death of SILAS WRIGHT. Expired on morning of 27th ult. of apoplexy, at his residence in Canton, St. Lawrence county, New York; born in 1795; entered profession of law; in 1838 elected to US Senate, where he remained until his resignation in 1844; in 1823 elected to State Senate of NY; in 1829 chosen State Comptroller.

Sep. 22, 1847

Death of RICHARD HENRY WHITE. This distinguished orator, poet, and politician died of Yellow Fever, in New Orleans on the 10th inst., a native of Dublin, Ireland, but migrated to this country in early life and settled in Augusta, where he was a store companion with Mr. McDuffie.

Sep. 29, 1847

Died in Houston county, on the 26th inst. GAZAWAY BASIL, second son of ZACHARIAH and MARTHA A. LAMAR, aged three years four months and twenty seven days.

Oct. 13, 1847

Died at his residence in Crawford county on the 22nd August of congestive fever, O.M. COLBERT in the 38th year of his age; member of Jackson Lodge No. 48; his remains were attended in procession to the house of his father, followed by 4 or 500 mourning friends and there buried with Masonic honors; has left a wife and six children; funeral services will take place at Pleasant Grove on 2d Sabbath in October.

Died at Stanforville, Putnam county, on the 22d ult., CLARK BLANFORD, ESQ. aged about 58 years - member of Baptist Church.

Died at her residence in Macon County, after a painful illness of a few days, MRS. POLLY N. STAPLER, in the 53d year of her age.

Oct. 20, 1847

Died at his residence in Clinton, Jones county, Ga., on the 7th instant, in the 47th year of his age, MR. STEPHEN CLOWER, eldest son of PETER CLOWER, ESQ.; deceased has left behind him aged parents, brothers and sisters.

Died at Culloden, on Saturday morning the 9th instant, of Puerpal Convulsions, SARAH W., consort of ASA W. CHAPMAN, and daughter of the late DR. CULLEN LOCKET, aged 18 years, 5 months and 18 days.

Died of Typhus Fever on the 24th September, at the residence of Thomas S. Chappel in Twiggs county, MRS. MARY M. GIBSON, wife of THOMAS GIBSON, and daughter of SAMUEL and SARAH L. BRAGG, of Wilkinson county, aged 18 years, 9 months and 2 days (with eulogy).

Oct. 20, 1847

    Death notice of CHANCELLOR HARPER. The South Carolina papers announce the death of this distinguished Judicial Officer. He expired at his residence in Fairfield District on the 10th inst.

    Death of COL. McINTOSH. This oft' distinguished officer has at last fallen, in the front of his regiment and on the field of victorious battle...Mr. Kendall in his letter of the 26th says: "this brave officer died last night, and is to be buried to-morrow with all military honors. He fell pierced by two balls while gallantly leading his men to attack the Casa Mata on the 8th September"...

Oct. 27, 1847

    The examination before the Bench of Magistrates in the case of the state versus PETER SHANNON charged with killing ALONZO BROWN on Friday last in this city resulted in the commitment of the accused to the county jail to await his trial at the next Bibb Superior Court.

Nov. 3, 1847

    Died in Forsyth MR. JOHN CANDLER, aged about 30 years. He was a volunteer in Mexico, under Capt. Holmes, and died of disease contracted in the service.

Nov. 10, 1847

    Died in this city on the 7th inst., MR. CYRUS K. WENTWORTH, aged 31 years; for several years a resident of Milledgeville; on Saturday he was attacked by Cholera Morbus, and as a remedy, took Morphine and some other preparations of Opium...it is supposed the medicine proved too powerful...expired on Sunday morning about 9 o'clock; member of Macon Lodge No. 6, and of Franklin Lodge I.O.O.F.. by whom he was buried with their usual honors, on Monday evening, in the Masonic burial lot, at Rose Hill Cemetery.

    Died in this city on the 7th inst., MR. E.N. WOOD, aged about 25 years; one of Capt. Holmes' company of volunteers in Mexico, and died from disease contracted in that service; formerly member of Floyd Rifles by whom he was buried with military honors, on Monday last.

    Died in Burke county, on the 23d ultimo, HENRY P. son of DR. T.A. and MRS. M.V. PARSONS, aged three years and eight months.

    Shocking murder at Sharpsburg, Kentucky. Murder of MR. J.C. ROBINSON, principal teacher of the academy at that place...

Nov. 17, 1847

    Died at the residence of his mother in Upson county, on Sunday morning the 14th inst. MR. REUBEN H. WHITE, merchant of this city, in the 30th year of his age; native of Elbert county, Ga., but when quite young moved to Upson county, where he resided until spring of '43, since which time he has been a resident of Macon, engaged in Mercantile business, the junior partner of the firm of A.J. WHITE & CO.; remains consigned to grave at Antioch Church in Upson County, with Masonic honors by Morning Star Lodge of Thomaston and a delegation from Macon Lodge No. 6, of which latter he was a worthy member.

Dec. 1, 1847

    Died, in Monroe county, on the 20th ult. of the congestive fever, after an illness of thirteen days, MRS. SOPHIAH BENTON, wife of JOHN BENTON, ESQ. in the 56th year of her age.

Dec. 1, 1847

Died in this city on the morning of the 27th inst. MRS. TABITHA N. BARTLETT, wife of DR. MYRON BARTLETT, in the 32d year of her age.

Dec. 15, 1847

Died, at the residence of Thomas Dyson, Esq. in this county, on Sunday morning the 28th ult., MATTHEW A. HUBERT, in the 23d year of his age; gallant Georgian who served in Regiment of Col. Jackson in Mexico, where he contracted a disease which brought him to a premature grave; returning home from Mississippi, on his arrival at Columbus he found the Georgia Regiment preparing to march to Mexico...(with eulogy).

Dec. 22, 1847

Died at his residence in Monroe county, Ga., on the 22d day of November last, after an illness of nearly five weeks, MR. JAMES CONNALLY, in the 44th year of his age; born in Jackson county, Ga. 29 December 1803, and early in life emigrated to Alabama, where he remained until about the year 1825, when he removed to Georgia again, and settled permanently; in 1839 connected with the Methodist Episcopal Church; left wife...(with eulogy).

Died in Burke county, on the 14th inst., JULIA VIRGINIA, only daughter of DR. T.A. and MRS. M.V. PARSONS, aged eight years and two months.

Dec. 29, 1847

Died in Twiggs county, on the 14th instant, MRS. CYNTHIA SOLOMON, wife of HARDY SOLOMON, ESQ.

Died in Twiggs county, on the 19th inst. MR. JOHN FINCH, aged about 19 years.

Died at her residence in Lanier, Macon county, on Sunday evening, the 19th instant, MRS. REBECCA, consort of ROBERT BROWN, deceased, in the 41st year of her age; leaves five children to mourn their loss.

Died on the 3d inst., of the croup, THOMAS ERASTUS, son of THOMAS and R.A. WOOD, aged four years 8 months.

Death of HON. ROGER L. GAMBLE - expired at his place in Jefferson County on the 20th inst. of apoplexy.

Jan. 5, 1848

Died in this City, on the 3d inst., MR. FERDINAND HORN, aged about 31 years - formerly of Pulaski county. He was yesterday buried by Macon Lodge No. 6, of which he was a member; left wife and child.

SENATOR FAIRFIELD of Maine died suddenly at Washington City, on the 26th ult., under the effects of a surgical operation for dropsy in the knee joint; commenced life as a sailor boy, rose gradually to the command of a vessel, became lawyer and reporter of the Supreme Court decisions of his State, member of Maine Legislature, Governor of the State, member of Congress, finally U.S. Senator.

Jan. 12, 1848

Died in this city, on the 5th inst., JAMES McCOUN TILFORD, ESQ. a native of the State of Tennessee; resided for several years, and practiced Law, in Lanier, Macon, Houston county, and was once Senator from that county. From his papers, it appears his parents

(Jan. 12, cont'd) - reside at Hickory Creek, Warren county, Tennessee.

Melancholy death - death of MR. HARVEY SHOTWELL, one of our oldest and most esteemed citizens, from a pulmonary affection; native of New Jersey, of Quaker descent; engaged in drug business which has, since the decline of his health, carried on under the firm name of Shotwell and Gilbert.

Jan. 19, 1848

Died in Clinton, Jones county, at the residence of Peter Clower, Esq. MRS. NANCY REDDING, in the 55th year of her age, after a protracted illness of twelve months; a brother and sister are left to mourn the loss.

Notice of death of JOHN M. PATTEN, formerly of Cass County, but more recently Private Secretary to His Excellency Governor Towns.

Feb. 9, 1848

Death, in this city, on yesterday morning, of DOCTOR MYRON BARTLETT, former Proprietor and Editor of this paper, in his 50th year; native of Concord, New-Hampshire, but a citizen of Georgia for last 25 years (with eulogy).

The Richmond Whig announces the death of HON. JOHN WINSTON JONES of Va., late Speaker of US House of Representatives.

Died on the 29th ult. at his residence in Dooly county, near Traveller's Rest, DR. WADE H. POWELL, aged 29 years; left wife and one child; was a Botanic Physician; consigned to grave with Masonic honors by his brethren of Traveller's Rest Lodge, No. 65.

Feb. 16, 1848

Died in Albany, Baker county, WM. G. MACON, ESQ. formerly a resident of this city.

Mar. 1, 1848

Died in Columbus, on the 24th ult. MR. HENRY L. COOK, of East Macon, aged 36 years.

Died in this city, on the 27th inst. MRS. L.B. DURRETT, widow of DR. RICE DURRETT, aged 53 years.

Fatal railroad accident. JOSEPH H. STOKES, ESQ., an Attorney at Law, of Dalton, was killed instantly at Kingston, on the Western & Atlantic Railroad, on Saturday evening last, the 19th inst. by attempting to enter the passenger train while it was in motion... (Augusta Sentinel).

Mar. 8, 1848

Died in this City on Wednesday the 23d inst. HARRY aged 3 years and 4 months, and on Saturday the 26th inst. GRACE aged 1 year and 5 months children of GEORGE and MARY L. PATTEN (with eulogy).

Mar. 22, 1848

Died in Houston county, on the 16th inst., in the 36th year of her age, MRS. PARRISADE REDDING, wife of ROBERT G. REDDING of said county. (Columbus Enquirer and Montgomery, Al. papers please copy).

Remains of veteran McINTOSH, which were escorted from this City to Savannah on Thursday last, by detachments from Macon Volunteers and Floyd Rifles, under command of Capt. Conner, were received in Savannah, by Savannah Volunteer Guards, and interred on Saturday, with Civic and Military honors.

Mar. 22, 1848

Northern papers announce the death of HON. AMBROSE SPENCER - a State Senator of New York, Judge of the Supreme Court, member of Congress; died at his residence, in Lyons, Wayne county, on Monday, at age of about 85 - was President of the Baltimore Convention of May, 1844, which nominated Clay and Frelinghuysen.

HENRY WHEATON the diplomatist and author died recently at Boston; had been appointed Professor of International Law in Harvard University...

Mar. 29, 1848

Died in this city, on Thursday the 23d inst., MRS. HENRIETTA G. - wife of EDWIN GRAVES, aged 30 (with eulogy).

Died in Culloden, Ga., on the 24th March, JANE HENRIETTA, infant daughter of H.E. and E.M. MORROW, aged 11 months and 4 days.

The Savannah Republican of Monday last reports the death of FRANCIS WINTER, who departed this life on Saturday evening last, in 34th year of his age; native of Maine, but for last 13 years a resident of Savannah; one of the proprietors of Savannah Republican.

Apr. 5, 1848

Died in Twiggs county, Feb. 26th, after a long and painful illness, in the 36th year of her age, MRS. SARAH McALLUM, daughter of MARY and JAMES WARE, and consort of ARCHIBALD McALLUM; member of Baptist Church (with eulogy).
(Christian Index will please copy)

Died in Perry, Houston, Ga. on 9th inst. at her son's residence, Col. J.D. Havis, MRS. MARY HAVIS, aged nearly 84 years. (Columbia, S.C. papers please copy).

Apr. 19, 1848

Died in this city on the 14th instant, after a short illness, FRANCIS, infant son of MARTHA M. and JAMES W. DENTON, aged six months and seven days.

Departed this life in Butts county, on the 7th inst. after a protracted illness of several months, MRS. ADALINE McMICHAEL, daughter of JAMES A. and MRS. R.J. McCUNE, and wife of JOHN B. McMICHAEL, aged 22 years and 3 months (with eulogy).

JAMES IRVIN, JR. son of JAMES IRVIN, ESQ. of New Orleans, and grandson of Henry Clay, shot himself through the head, in his chamber at the St. Charles Hotel, about 6 o'clock, A.M. on Monday, the 3d inst.

Apr. 26, 1848

Notice of the death of CAPT. KENDALL, gallant officer of the Georgia Mounted men (Muscogee Democrat).

Tribute of respect by Houston Lodge, No. 35, held on Friday night, April 7, 1848 - on death of JOHN B. HOLMES.

May 3, 1848

The Columbia, S.C. papers announce the death of DR. JAMES DAVIS, in that place, on Saturday evening last; was Surgeon of the Palmetto Regiment, and died of a lingering illness, contracted while in discharge of his official duties; was brother-in-law to HON. WM. C. PRESTON.

May 3, 1848

Alabama Journal reports death of DR. SAMUEL C. OLIVER - for many years a Senator from this county.

May 10, 1848

Died at his residence in Houston county, on the 30th ult. MR. HEZEKIAH FINNEY in the 47th year of his age. (Columbus papers will please copy).

Died near Jackson, in Butts county, Geo. April 26th MRS. MARTHA HARKNESS, wife of JAMES W. HARKNESS and daughter of RICHARD and LUCY BOYDE of Ala. aged 27 years; member of Baptist Church (with eulogy).

Tribute of respect - departed this life on the 21st ult. E.B.J. ADAMS, aged 18 years, 10 months and 9 days, son of DANIEL and ELIZABETH ADAMS.

Notice of the death of HON. SENATOR CHESTER ASHLEY - died at Washington City on first day of the month; funeral took place on ensuing day in Hall of House of Representatives; was U.S. Senator from Arkansas - died at 2 o'clock P.M. on Saturday (Baltimore Sun).

May 17, 1848

Died at his plantation, near Columbus, on the 29th ult., DR. SAMUEL BOYKIN, aged 61 years.

Died in Baldwin county, on the 30th of April, MR. BENJAMIN L. LESTER; has left a widow and three small children.

New York papers announce the death of CORNELIUS HEENEY, ESQ., at Brooklyn, on Wednesday, at advanced age of 94; native of Ireland; connected with John Jacob Astor in fur trade.

May 24, 1848

Died on the 17th inst. at the residence of S.P. Bond, Esq. in Drayton, Dooly county, Georgia, MR. CONSTANTINE H. LAND, a comparative youth. (Savannah and Jacksonville papers copy).

May 31, 1848

Death of the venerable REV. ASHBEL GREEN, of Philadelphia, the oldest Presbyterian minister in U.S.; occurred in that city on Friday morning.

June 7, 1848

Died in this City, on the 24th ult., at the house of Major Hardaway, MR. CORBIN L. HUNTON, of Montgomery, Ala. in the 21st year of his age (with eulogy).

June 14, 1848

Died in Jones county, Ga. on the 7th instant, at the residence of Capt. John Towles, in the 39th year of his age, after lingering several months, MR. PHILO Z. ROSE, native of Connecticut, but for last 15 (illegible) or 20 years a citizen of this state; has left an only child a little daughter 11 or 12 years of age (Conn. papers please copy)

June 21, 1848

Died at the house of Major Hardaway on the 11th inst. GEORGIA LOGAN, infant daughter of SAMUEL G. HARDAWAY of Montgomery, Ala., aged 16 months. (Montgomery papers copy).

June 21, 1848

Departed this life on 4th June, in the city of Macon, in the 21st year of her age, MRS. MARTHA M. DENTON, wife of JAMES W. DENTON; born in Camden, S.C., "born again" in this place (with eulogy)
(Telegraph and Milledgville papers please copy).

June 28, 1848

Died in Hillsboro, Jasper county, on Sunday the 18th instant, MR. JOHN G. MORRIS, aged 35 years.

Muscogee Democrat of Thursday the 22nd: sudden death last night of REV. THOMAS GOULDING, D.D., venerable Pastor of Presbyterian Church of this city; was 62 years of age on 14th of March last, nearly two-thirds of his life having been passed in work of Ministry; has left an aged wife and eight children.

July 5, 1848

Died at his residence, in the village of Fort Valley, in Houston county, on Friday morning the 23d ult., MR. JAMES A EVERETT, in the 61st year of his age (eulogy).

Died in this city, on the 29th ult. JOHN E. JEFFERS, ESQ., had been Clerk of Inferior Court for several years; buried on 30th with honors of Masonry by Macon Lodge No. 6, and the Macon Volunteers.

July 12, 1848

Died on the 22d June last in Crawford co. after a long and painful illness, WILLIAM C. SLATTER ESQ. in the 40th year of his age (Telegraph please copy).

Aug. 23, 1848

Died on the 10th inst. at the residence of Mr. George Walker, of Pulaski county, HENRY E. WIMBERLY, the youngest son of the late GEN. EZEKIEL WIMBERLY, of Twiggs county, aged 22 years (with long eulogy).

Aug. 30, 1848

Died in Perry Houston county, on Sunday the 20th inst. after an illness of only seven hours, ROBERT S. son of JOHN G. and LUCINDA WHITE, aged 2 years 4 months and 29 days.

Sep. 6, 1848

Died in Houston County, on the 20th ult. LOUIS WILLIAMSON, son of PAUL S. and MARTHA E. DINKINS, aged 2 years and 3 months.

FREDERICK SIMS, ESQ., one of our oldest and most respected citizens, met with a most melancholy and painful death on the 29th ult. Mr. S. was acting temporarily as conductor of the passenger cars upon the Macon and Western Railroad, and at the time of his death, had charge of the down train. About 15 miles above Macon and while passing through a plantation, the whistle gave warning of some obstruction. Mr. S. anxious to discover the cause leaned as far as possible out of the car which brought his head suddenly in contact with a post, breaking his skull and killing him almost instantly; was member of Georgia Legislature, Post Master and Mayor of city of Macon; a Mason.

Sep. 13, 1848

Died on the 19th ult., at his residence in Gwinnett County, ABSALOM MARTIN, in the 4th (newspaper error - left out first digit) year of his age; for last 30 years a resident of same place; left wife and five small children (with eulogy).

Sep. 20, 1848

Died on the 20th of August, near Macon, MRS. LUCY H. DOZIER, wife of A.F. DOZIER, aged 30 years and 6 months; left husband and an only child.

Died in Macon county, on the 7th inst. JOHN J. HAUOABOOK, ESQ. aged about 45 years - formerly of South Carolina.

Died at the Indian Springs, Ga. on 12th August MR. TIMOTHY CURLISS, a volunteer of the Massachusetts Regiment, and recently from Mexico; died of Chronic diarrhea.

Sep. 27, 1848

Died at her mother's residence, near Mossy creek, Houston county, on Monday the 18th of September, SARAH ELIZABETH PAGE, second daughter of MAJ. THOMAS PACE, aged 10 years, 5 months and 20 days; died of inflammation of the bowels, after a short illness of 3 days; has left an affectionate mother (with eulogy).

Died at Rotherwood, Carrol Co., Ga., on the 12th inst. MRS. ELIZA B. NAPIER, wife of THOMAS T. NAPIER, ESQ., within a few days of the 39th year of her age; funeral discourse preached by Rev. J.Y. Alexander; buried in family cemetery at Rotherwood (with eulogy).

Oct. 18, 1848

Died at the house of Lewis Beddingfield, Esq., near this City. MR. SAMUEL TOMPKINS, of Albany, Baker county, aged about 55 years. Mr. Tompkins had been to this place on business, and was taken sick on Sunday last, and expired on Friday the 13th inst.

Oct. 25, 1848

Died in this City on the 20th inst. after a severe illness of three days, MISS MARY J. COLEMAN, aged 19 years (with eulogy).

Died in Lumpkin, Stewart county, Ga., on Sunday the 8th inst., after a long and painful illness, BENJAMIN, the only son of JOHN A. and ANNA M. TUCKER, aged 18 months. (The Spartan and Greenville Mountaineer, S.C. please copy).

Died at Monticello, Geo. on the 13th instant, after a lingering illness, MR. WILLIAM TOLEFREE, in the 47th year of his age; from age of 14 years was connected with public press in New York, and known as member of Fire Department in that city.

Nov. 1, 1848

Died on the 18th ult. at the house of her grandmother, MRS. SARAH TOUNSLEY, IRENE C. CHAIN, aged about 9 years, daughter of MRS. ELIZABETH KELSEY (formerly ELIZABETH CHAIN) consort of the REV. DANIEL KELSTY.

Died in Knoxville on the 19th inst. CAPT. DAVID M. CAUSEY, aged 32 years. Capt. Causey rode out on horse-back late in the evening of 17th inst. and on his return in this village, his horse became frightened and reared up and fell backwards and crushed him in such a manner that he survived the accident but 42 hours; has left wife to mourn; also there is a tribute to him from Union Lodge No. 14 I.O.O.F.

Tribute of respect by Macon Lodge No. 6 (Masonic) to memory of DR. ABNER F. HOLT, late Worshipful Master of the Lodge.

Nov. 8, 1848

Died at the residence of his father in Pulaski county, on the 15th inst. JOHN M. BOOTH, eldest son of THEOPHILUS D. BOOTHE, aged 20 years, 10 months and 15 days.

Nov. 8, 1848

The corpse of EX-GOVERNOR McNUTT of Mississippi, says the Memphis Enquirer of the 24th morning, arrived in this city last night, we presume on its passage to his residence at Jackson, Miss. He died on Sunday night, at Cockrum's Cross Roads, after a short illness of an inflammatory character.

Nov. 22, 1848

Died in this city, on the 16th instant, CAPT. A.D. POWELL, aged about 35 years - on the 18th, his daughter, MARY ELIZABETH, aged about 4 years.

Died on the 17th, MR. ARNOLD JOHNSON, aged about 55 years.

Cincinnati papers report the death of GENERAL JAMES TAYLOR - born in 1769, in Caroline county, Va.; emigrated to Kentucky in 1792; died at his residence at Newport, Ky. on Tuesday, the 7th instant...

Dec. 6, 1848

Died on the 15th Nov. MRS. SARAH A.F. WILLIFORD, wife of WILLIAM S. WILLIFORD, of City of Macon, and daughter of JOSEPH FELT, ESQ. of the City of Savannah, aged about 27 years (with eulogy).

Died in Macon on the 18th ult., MISS EMILY CARTER; such was the nature of the disease with which she was seized that in two short hours she was rendered insensible, and so continued till her death (with eulogy).

Dec. 13, 1848

Died in the vicinity of this place, on Saturday evening, the 2d instant, after a lingering and painful illness, MRS. MARY DUKE, in the 68th year of her age; member of Baptist Church 35 years (LaGrange paper please copy).

Jan. 3, 1849

Died at the residence of her father in Houston county Ga. on the 23d inst. VELINDA R. daughter of FARIBA and HUGH ALLEN in the 30th year of her age (with eulogy).

Died in Crawford county on the 26th ult. MR. JOHN CURTIS, aged 52 years (with eulogy).

Jan. 24, 1849

Died after a short but painful illness on the night of the 14th inst., at the residence of Mrs. Wm. G. Smith, in this city, in the 16th year of her age, MISS MARGARET ANDERSON, daughter of the late CAPT. THOS. W. ANDERSON, formerly of Twiggs county (with eulogy)

Died in Fort Valley, on the 17th inst., MRS. MARTHA ANN WALKER, consort of GEORGE T. WALKER, in the 21st year of her age...resided ther three years previous to her death; left behind a fond husband and an aged father (with eulogy).

Died in this city, on the 19th inst., ALBERTA, daughter of HON. E.D. and MRS. CAROLINE W. TRACY, aged 20 months.

Died in Savannah, on the 17th inst., after a short illness, MR. HUGO THOMPSON, in the 34th year of his age; was from Baker county, and was taken ill while on a visit to the city on business.

Jan. 31, 1849

Died at Tuskegee, Ala. on Monday, the 15th day of January, A.D. 1849, MRS. MARY D. HOLT, widow of HINES HOLD, SEN., in the 75th year of her age.

Died in this city, on the 24th inst. WILLIAM DEVEAUX, formerly of Wilkes county, but for last eight years a resident of this city, aged 60 years. Mr. D. was for some time employed at this office, and among the oldest printers in this State.

Savannah papers announce the death of MAJOR CHARLES STEPHENS a worthy and meritorious citizen who served faithfully in war of 1812 and also in Florida campaign of 1836; had been for 17 years captain of the Chatham Artillery.

Information wanted. By application to the Post Master of this City information can be had, that may be of benefit to the mother or other near relatives of ELIAS D. FIELDS, who recently died in the army. He belonged to Company A, Capt. A.K. Blyth, of 2d Regt Mississippi Rifles. His mother is supposed to reside in vicinity of Macon, and to have married a second time.

Feb. 21, 1849

Died in this City, on the 4th inst., EMELINE L.C. GODDARD, daughter of the late BAILEY and CATHERINE R. GODDARD, in the 17th year of her age.

Death of HON. EDW. D. TRACY, which took place at his residence in this city yesterday morning. Judge Tracy was a native of Conn., but has resided in this city for nearly a quarter of a century.

Notice of death of JAMES S. BULLOCK, ESQ. of Roswell, Cobb county. He expired of an organic affection of the heart, suddenly while sitting in his pew at church.

Feb. 28, 1849

Died in this city, on the 22d inst., ALICE, daughter of MR. JOHN D. GRAY, aged 7 months.

Died at his residence in Twiggs· county, Ga., on the 22d ult., MR. STEPHEN JONES, in the 63rd year of his age; his disease was Ischuria notha; born in North Carolina; emigrated at an early age to this state; not in affiliation with any church at time of his death but expected to receive his initiation into the church at Woods Meeting House; has left a fond and aged companion, affectionate daughter, two devotedly dutiful sons.

Mar. 7, 1849

Died in this city, on the 15th inst., in the 47th year of her age, MRS. SARAH ROSS, consort of HENRY G. ROSS; a resident of Macon from its infancy; mother of large family; for 20 years a member of Methodist Episcopal Church (with eulogy).

Mar. 28, 1849

Died on the evening of the 14th inst., in Vineville, MR. GEORGE JEWETT, in the 50th year of his age; a native of Granby, Conn., but had been for last 27 years a resident of this place; interred by Brethren of Macon Lodge No. 6, of which he was one of the first officers and founders.

Apr. 4, 1849

Died in Harrison county, Texas, on the 14th of January last, of cholera, MAJOR JAMES E. SLATTER, formerly of Crawford county, Ga.

Apr. 25, 1849

Died at Woodville, Monroe County, on Sunday night the 15th inst., MRS. MICHAL POWERS, wife of JOHN POWERS, ESQ., aged 64 years.

May 30, 1849

Died in this city, on the 27th instant, MARIE HELEN COOK, daughter of J.W. KNOTT, ESQ., aged about 13 months.

Died in this city on the 28th instant, MRS. SARAH A.E., wife of WILLIAM H. BRAY, and daughter of the late FREDERICK SIMS, aged 21 years.

Died in Columbus, on the morning of the 21st instant, of scarlet fever, EVA, infant daughter of COL. HINES and MRS. SARAH A.C. HOLT - aged 9 months and 17 days. And on the evening of the same day, HINES, son of same parents, aged 2 years 9 months and 13 days.

Learn from the Louisville Journal that MRS. S. HOWE died in that city on the 9th...a poetess of more than ordinary genius.

June 20, 1849

Died, in Twiggs county, May 17th, MR. JOEL DENSON, aged 66 years. Mr. D. was a native of North Carolina; moved to Twiggs county in 1808, and is buried on the spot he first settled; exemplary member of Baptist Church...his death bed scene was rendered more impressive by the presence of his aged mother and father, bending under the weight of near a century...(with eulogy).

Died, at the residence of his parents of inflammation of the bowels, on the 6th instant, JAMES C., aged 1 year, 5 months and 24 days, youngest child of JAMES C. and NANCY RAY (with eulogy).

Died, in Perry, on the 24th ult., MRS. SOPHIA C. HAVIS, (wife of COL. J.D. HAVIS), aged 38 years. She had been in feeble health for some time...left husband and children; for 18 years a consistent member of the church of Christ. (with eulogy).

Died at St. Mark's, Florida, on the 7th inst., ALFRED M. HOBBY, ESQ. aged 53 years; a native of Augusta; resided in this city several years previous to his removal to Florida.

Died, at his residence in Dooly county, on the 29th May last, JOHN A. LEARY, aged 47 years 3 months and 13 days, after a short but most virulent attack of Pneumonia; a native of North Carolina, and removed to this State about 20 years ago; leaves wife and four children.

A Telegraphic dispatch received from Atlanta on Monday last stated that "Passengers by the morning's train from Chattanooga, state that JAMES K. POLK died on last Friday evening, at his residence in Columbia, Tennessee."

Tribute of respect by Hampden Lodge, No. 19, I.O.O.F. (Perry, Georgia) dated June 2, 1849 - on occasion of the death of MR. CORDY D. STOKES, late a member of said Lodge (with eulogy).

June 27, 1849

Died, at Jeffersonville, Twiggs county, Geo., on the 26th ult., JOHN PENDLETON LONG, eldest son of ELIAS and MARIAH L. LONG, aged six years (with eulogy).

Died in Memphis, Tenn., on 8th April last, of cholera GEO. F. CROCKER, aged 29 years - formerly resident of Macon.

June 27, 1849

    Departed this life, at the residence of his son, in Crawford county, Ga., on the 13th instant, REV. JAMES HUDSON. His disease was Phthisis Pulmonalis; an aged Minister of the Gospel; member of Methodist Episcopal Church (with eulogy).
    (Milledgeville Recorder please copy)

    From a letter of Memphis Eagle, bearing date at Galveston, June 3, we learn that COL. JACK HAYS died of cholera, at San Antonio, a few days previous.

July 4, 1849

    Died at Bluntsville, Jones county, on the 26th ult., FRANCIS TUFTS, ESQ. aged about 60 years.

    Died in Monroe county, on the 28th ult., very suddenly (while at work in his field) MR. JOHN BENTON, SR., aged about 55 years.

    Notice of death of AMORY SIBLEY, ESQ., who departed this life about 3 o'clock on Saturday morning, after a brief illness; native of Grafton, Mass., but a resident of Augusta for about 30 years; engaged in mercantile pursuits; in 1834 elected President of Mechanics Bank; at time of his death was President of Iron Steamboat Company.
    (Aug. Constitutionalist)

July 11, 1849

    Died at Barnesville, Pike county, on the 23rd ult., CAPT. JOEL S. WILLIS, aged about 28 years; interred with honors of Masonry, by "Pinta Lodge," of which he was the principal founder, and Master at time of his death.

July 18, 1849

    Died on the 4th inst., in this city, CAROLINE ELIZABETH, wife of DR. J.W. BENSON, in her 24th year (with eulogy).

    Died on the 5th inst., JOSEPH WESLEY, son of CAROLINE ELIZABETH and DR. J.W. BENSON, aged 5 days (with eulogy).

    The Washington Union of the 13th reports the death of MRS. D. MADISON, relict of JAMES MADISON, once the President of the United States.

July 25, 1849

    Died in Upson County, on the 13th July, MRS. ELIZABETH GOOCH, consort of WM. D. GOOCH, in the 21st year of her age; member of Methodist Church.

    Died on Friday morning, the 13th inst., of congestion of the brain, at the residence of David Clopton, Esq. in Paulding county, ALBERT HENRY, only child of EDWARD R. and MARTHA E. PEASE, of this city, aged 2 years, 5 months and 10 days.

Aug. 1, 1849

    Died in Troy, New York, MR. NATHANIEL EELLS, aged about 50 years; for 25 years a resident of Georgia, most of which time he lived in this city.

    Died in Bibb county, on 2d July, MARTHA LOUISA HOLLEMAN, aged 9 years and 4 months, daughter of ZACHARIAH and ANNE HOLLEMAN, formerly of South Carolina.

Aug. 1, 1849

Died on Monday morning, the 23rd inst., MARY ELIZABETH, only daughter of A.C. and REBECCA L. MOREHOUSE, aged 2 years, 5 months and 16 days.

MRS. ELOISE, wife of THOS. B. GOULDING and daughter of the HON. JNO. A. and MRS. LOUISA CUTHBERT of Mobile, departed this life in this city on the 11th inst. (with eulogy)
(Columbus Enquirer)

Aug. 8, 1849

Died on the 29th and the other on the 30th ult. the twin babes (girls) aged 9 months, children of THOMAS and ALLEY CRAWFORD, of Henry county.

Died in East Macon, on the 23d ult., MRS. THOMAS LIGHTFOOT, SR., aged about 83 years.

A telegraphic dispatch to the N.Y. Herald, dated at New Orleans the 28th ult. mentions that MAJ. GATES of the 8th Infantry died of Cholera, at Fredericksburg, Texas, on 28th of June. LIEUT. BROOKS of the same regiment was accidentally killed a few weeks since, by being thrown from his horse.

Aug. 15, 1849

On Sunday last, in Eastern part of this county, a man of the name ISHAM HICKS, was shot by his wife and killed. We understand that the family had a drunken carousal on Saturday night, in which the children and the man and his wife participated, and that Hicks, while still drunk on Sunday, commenced beating his wife, when the latter seized a loaded rifle and discharged its contents into his abdomen, of which wound he died on Monday about noon (Columbus Democrat).

Aug. 22, 1849

Died in Lumpkin, Stewart county, on the 3d inst. BENJ. W. CLARK, ESQ., son of the late JEREMIAH CLARK of Savannah.

Another Revolutionary soldier gone! Died, at his residence in Jasper county, on the 10th instant, MR. RICHARD CARTER in his 84th year; born in Halifax, Virginia, and was a soldier in the Revolutionary War; removed to Georgia more than sixty years since, and was one of the first settlers of Jasper county, having resided in this county about forty-two years; has left a widow with whom he had lived more than sixty years (Souther Recorder please copy)

Notice of the death of HON. ALBERT GALLATIN - occurred at Astoria, near New York, on the 12th inst., age about 89 years (long biographical sketch - in encyclopedia so didn't copy).

Aug. 29, 1849

Died at Richland, Twiggs county, Ga., on the 18th of August, MR. JACON BURBANK, aged 29 years;; from Marion, in the State of New York, a son of REV. J. BURBANK of that place, came to Georgia about five years ago, and engaged in the duties of a Teacher (short eulogy).

Sep. 5, 1849

Died, at the Gordon Springs, Walker county, on the morning of the 29th ult., OLIVER PROCTOR FELT, only son of JOSEPH FELT, ESQ. of Savannah, aged 29 years; interred with military honors by Chatham Artillery, Grand Lodge of the State, Magnolia Encampment No. 1, and DeKalb Lodge, No. 9 I.O.O.F.; the German Friendly Society also attended the corpse to the grave.

Sep. 5, 1849

A correspondent at Thomston, Upson county, informs us that HENRY PLATT was killed on the 27th ult. about 6 miles South of that village; resided at Philadelphia and was engaged in collecting for the Union and Intelligencer at Washington city, the New Orleans Picayune and various Northern periodicals. He was travelling in a Buggy, when a tree fell, instantly killing both Mr. P. and his horse, and crushing the vehicle.

Sep. 12, 1849

Died in Auburn county, N.Y., on Sunday evening, Sept. 2nd, MRS. JANE L. WENTWORTH, formerly of Macon, surviving but a few days the loss of her only child, CHARLES EDGAR WENTWORTH, who was drowned on the 24th ult., aged about three and a half years.

Died in Coweta county, Ga., on Tuesday, the 4th of Sept., BENJAMIN B., youngest son of REV. P.A. and SARAH J. STROBEL of this city, aged three months and eight days.

Died, on the 16th of August last, in Wilkinson county, MR. JOHN M. GRAN, in his 34th year; native of Mississippi; a tender husband..

Death of MISS MARY PAYNE, of Lexington, Kentucky, who fell victim to the dreadful epidemic, which has visited that country, on August 25th, 1849...torn from the embrace of kind parents... (with eulogy).

ELISHA REESE, convicted of the murder of MRS. ELLEN PRATT, was executed near this city on Friday, in the presence of some five thousand persons...

Death of HON. EDWARD J. BLACK, of Scriven county, for several years a Representative in Congress from the State of Georgia; died on Saturday. 1st inst., in Barnwell District, South Carolina at the residence of Mr. George Robertson, the grandfather of Mrs. Black. Mr. B. had been in declining health for several years.

Tribute of respect by St. Patrick's Lodge, No. 32 (Danville, Sumter Co., Sept. 6th, 1849) - on death of A.J.C. HORNE fallen by death on morning of 4th inst.; left widow and an orphan child...

Sep. 19, 1849

Died on the 5th inst., in Lee County, Virginia, HATWELL, daughter of ZADOK and MARY A. JACKSON, aged 4 years 2 months and 6 days.

Died in Monroe County, on the 13th inst., MR. SIMON HOLT, in the 69th year of his age.

Died in Bibb County, on the 14th inst., MR. JEREMIAH BURNETT, aged 63 years.

Died in Twiggs county, on Wednesday, the 5th of September, at 7 o'clock, P.M., in the 16th year of her age, MISS MARY ANN BURNS, eldest child of MR. and MRS. JAMES C. BURNS: member of Baptist Church...on the morning of the 6th, just ten hours after the death of MARY, died CORNELIA, their infant child, aged 6 months (with eulogy).

The Richmond Enquirer, of Saturday, had the following telegraphic dispatch, dated Wheeling, September 8, 1849 - "HON. A. NEWMAN, of Virginia, member of Congress, (from this district,) died at Pittsburg today, of cholera, at 2 P.M."

Sep. 26, 1849

Departed this life, at his residence in Monroe county, on the 13th instant, SIMON HOLT, ESQ., in the 69th year of his age; from

(Sep. 26th, cont'd.) - State of Virginia, but one of the first settlers of Putnam county in this State, and represented that county for many years in the House and in the Senatorial branch of the State Legislature; devoted member of Methodist Episcopal Church between forty and fifty years; for the last five years has been confined to his bed and house, laboring under a chronic disease...

Oct. 3, 1849

Died in this city, on the 24th ultimo, CORINNE, youngest daughter of E.A. and A.M.F. NISBET, aged 1 year and 8 months.

Oct. 10, 1849

Died in Culloden, Georgia, on Friday, the 29th ult., MRS. VICTORIA J. consort of JOHN F. TROUTMAN, and daughter of COL. JAMES P. HOLMES, of Early; a devoted wife and affectionate mother.

Died suddenly, at her residence in Jones county, on the 27th ult., MRS. MARY E. ZACHRY, aged 57 years.

The Augusta Constitutionalist, of Saturday, announces the death of P.C. GUIEU, former editor of the Constitutionalist. He died last evening, at the residence of his brother, in this city; connected with the press of this State for last thirty or forty years; a native of St. Domingo, and came to this country when a young man.

Oct. 17, 1849

The Baltimore Sun of the 18th announces the death of poet EDGAR A. POE...

Oct. 24, 1849

Died very suddenly, on the 22d inst., MARK DONALD, son of THOMAS H. and SARAH R. BLOUNT, aged 6 years 2 months and 2 days.

Nov. 21, 1849

Died in this city, on the 18th inst., MRS. REBECCA LYON, widow of JOHN LYON, aged about 55 years - late of St. Augustine, Florida.

Died of Consumption, on the 8th inst., at the residence of Col. Hallowes, near St. Mary's Ga., FRANCIS EDWARD NICOLL, Merchant of this city.

A barbarous murder was committed at a Wagon Yard in the outskirts of our city on Wednesday night last, between nine and ten o'clock. The murderer is by the name of BURGE, who came here from Marion county, with a load of cotton. The person murdered is RICHARD ALTMAN of Crawford county, who came for the purpose of hauling Goods...

Nov. 28, 1849

Died at Dalton, Ga., on the 21st inst., E. CLIFTON BLAKE, ESQ., formerly of this city; left wife and number of relatives.

Tribute of respect by St. Thomas Lodge (Masonic), No. 49 (Thomasville, Ga., Nov. 17th, 1849) on death of JOHN G. PONDER - died on the night of the 21st ult. in Pulaski county.

Dec. 5, 1849

Died in Hawkinsville, on the 25th ult., in the 24th year of her age, MRS. GEORGIA V. FRAZIER, wife of DR. WIM. M. FRAZIER, and daughter of DR. CHARLES J. PAYNE of Milledgeville (with eulogy).

Dec. 5, 1849

Tribute of respect by Holcomb Lodge, No. 30, I.O.O.F. (Fort Valley, Ga., Nov. 23d, 1849) - on death of EILLIAM E. BEALL, who died suddenly on the morning of the 18th instant, in the 27th year of his age.

Dec. 12, 1849

Died in this city, on the 7th inst., MR. JOHN EXPERIENCE, aged about 40 years - native of Canada, and a resident of this city for several years past.

The Columbus Enquirer announces the death of GEORGE W. HARDWICK, one of the editors and proprietors of that paper; a graduate of Oglethorpe University; member of the legal profession; died of consumption in the 31st year of his age.

Tribute of respect by Houston Lodge, No. 35 (Perry, Ga., Dec. 1st, 1849) - on death of BRO. THOMAS B. ALDRIDGE.

Dec. 26, 1849

Died in California, a short time since, ELLSWORTH FOSTER PARK, ESQ., late of Hawkinsville, Ga., and son of COL. JOHN G. PARK.

Died at her residence in this city, on Tuesday the 18th inst., MRS. ELIZA M. RANDOLPH, relict of the late DR. R.H. RANDOLPH, in the 40th year of her age; member of the Presbyterian Church; left children.

Died, on the 20th inst., at his residence in Houston county, after a very brief illness of an affection of the heart or cramp cholic, DANIEL GUNN, ESQ., in the 54th year of his age; born in Halifax county, Virginia, but resided most of his life in the State of Georgia (with eulogy).

Jan. 2, 1850

From a notice in the Boston Atlas, we learn that WILLIAM MILLER, who took the lead, some years ago, in the "advent" movement, died on the 20th instant, at the age of 68.

Tribute of respect by Eureka Lodge, No. 95 (Starkville, Dec. 15th, 1849) - on the death of BROTHER ENOCH JORDAN.

Jan. 9, 1850

Died in this county, on the 3d inst., DANIEL WADSWORTH, ESQ., (One of the earliest settlers of this vicinity) aged about 75 years.

Died at San Francisco, California, in October last, JOHN THEODORE HARBAUM, aged about 45 years; native of Prussia, and for several years a resident of this city.

Jan. 16, 1850

Died in Upson county, on the 6th inst. ROBERT COLLIER, ESQ., aged about 70 years. Mr. C. was one of the earliest settlers of that county...in the Legislature, and as one of the Judges of the Inferior Court, he served it for several years; member of the Methodist Church.

Announce the death of DR. ABNER H. FLEWELLEN, formerly of Jones county, but for last eight or ten years a resident of this place... on Tuesday morning he was taken suddenly with a disease resembling in its effect Cramp Cholic; it continued its attacks until Thursday evening, and on this (Friday) morning he breathed his last, in the 50th year of his age; member of Methodist Episcopal Church (with eulogy) - (dated Columbus Dec. 28, 1849)

Jan. 23, 1850

Died in this city, on the 14th inst., MR. ENOCH LUNSFORD, aged 74 years.

Died in Milledgeville, on the 6th inst. CHARLES H. RICE, ESQ. Secretary to the Executive.

Departed this life of the 5th inst. in Bibb county, at the residence of his father, ROLIN BIVINS, ESQ., JAMES S. BIVINS, in the 22nd year of his age; died of inflammatory rheumatism; had just finished his colllediate course in Oglethorpe University; some four years ago he joined the Methodist Church (eulogy)
(The Southern Presbyterian will please copy)

Jan. 30, 1850

Died January 20th, 1850, at the residence of Nathan S. Tucker in this city, MRS. ELIZABETH MORRIS, aged 71 years. She was born in Nottoway county, Virginia, in the year 1779, but resided in Georgia for the last 40 years.

Died in this city, on the 12th inst., JAMES M. BLAKE, aged 26 years and 1 month.

Feb. 6, 1850

Died in Lee county, on the 13th January, MR. THOMAS BUTLER - aged about 65 years.

Died in Griffin, on the 5th instant, MISS ROWENA, eldest daughter of N.C. MUNROE, ESQ. of Vineville.

Announce the death of WILLIAM H. ANDERSON, ESQ., of this city, which occurred at Orange Spring, East Florida, on the 28th ult. Mr. A. was a native of Virginia, and was educated for the Bar, and occupied a seat in the House of Delegates in that State. He removed to this city a little over a year ago and entered upon the practice of his profession...while in attendance upon the Supreme Court in Decatur, last summer, he contracted a slight cold which settled upon his lungs and caused his speedy dissolution...was in the 28th year of his age.

A fire took place on the 27th ult. at Peoria, Illinois, which destroyed the offices of the Daily Champion and Weekly Register, and JOHN KIRKPATRICK and J. PICKETT, editors of the respective papers, perished in the flames.

Feb. 13, 1850

Death of COL. JOHN W. CAMPBELL, formerly of Georgia, occurred suddenly on 23d day of January at his residence in DeSoto Parish, Louisiana.

Feb. 20, 1850

Died on the 6th inst., at the residence of his father, in Hayneville, Houston county, WILLIS M. WATSON, son of JACOB WATSON, aged 26 years 1 month 7 days, leaving a wife and an infant son, four months old, a father, mother, brothers and sisters to mourn the loss.

Tribute of respect by Fort Valley Lodge, No. 110 - to memory of REV. JOHN FULWOOD, who departed this life on the 1st of February, in the 63d year of his age, at his residence in Houston county.

Feb. 27, 1850

A correspondent from Ware county, (Geo.) writes: On the 21st inst., the House of JAMES ASPINWALL Ware county, was struck by

(Feb. 27, cont'd.) - lightning. Aspinwall was instantly killed - his wife bad wounded, and the two others (men) present stunned for some time...

Apr. 3, 1850

Notice of the death of HON. JOHN C. CALHOUN...

Apr. 17, 1850

Died at his residence near Culloden, on the 27th ultimo, JOHN KING, ESQ., aged 87 years. He was a Scotchman by birth, but came to the United States, then Colonies, in the 12th year of his age. For the last sixty years, he was a citizen of Georgia, residing in the counties of Elbert, Jones and Monroe. For near 70 years, he was a member of the Presbyterian Church; having become a member in his 18th year (with eulogy).

Died in Milledgeville, of inflammation of bowels, on the 8th inst., five minutes after 6 o'clock, P.M., MRS. ELIZABETH BETHUNE, consort of B.T. BETHUNE, ESQ., in the 28th year of her age.

Died at Washington City on Sunday April 7th, MRS. DAWSON, wife of HON. W.C. DAWSON, Senator in Congress from Georgia.

The Albany Patriot states that JOHN SMALLEN was shot in the neck on the night of the 7th inst., in Albany, by a man named HIRAM WOODALL, and died of the wound in a few minutes.

May 1, 1850

Died in Wynnton, on Sabbath morning the 21st of April, after a protracted illness, CHANDLER HOLT, son of CAPT. JAMES and MRS. MARGARET D. SHAW.

MAJOR O'BRIEN of the United States Army, who died recently of Cholera at Indianola, Texas, was a native of Pennsylvania. At age 14 he entered Military Academy at West Point, where he graduated with high honor, and was, subsequently, tendered the Professorship of Mathematics in that Institution. Preferring active service, he was attached to 4th Artillery, then in service in Florida, and immediately joined the regiment. In July 1846, he left Carlisle Barracks with Col. Worthington's battery, for service in Mexico, and participated in several battles there...

Another Revolutionary soldier gone. The Marietta Helicon of the 25th ult. announces the death in Cobb county, Georgia, near Powder Springs, on the 4th day of March 1850, aged 106 years and 6 months of JOHN COMBS, native of Virginia, but for last fifty years, or more, a citizen of Georgia. Was buried with the honors of War. Had lived a Pensioner, as a Revolutionary soldier, since 4th March, 1831.

May 8, 1850

Died in this city, on the 26th ult., of tubercular consumption, MRS. LOUISA E., consort of DR. J.T. COXE, of Forsyth - aged 25 years and 26 days.

May 15, 1850

Died in Jasper, on 7th April, ANNE MATTHEWS, youngest daughter of HENRY S. and ANNA S. GLOVER, and granddaughter of the late MRS. MARY G. REESE (Southern Presbyterian please copy)

June 5, 1850

Died in this city, on the 15th inst., SARAH L., infant daughter of Z.O. and CASSANDRA WHITEHEAD, aged 9 months and 4 days.

June 5, 1850

Notice of the death of FRANKLIN H. ELMORE, the successor to Mr. Calhoun in the United States Senate; expired on the 29th ult. and was interred in the Congressional Cemetery on the 31st.

REV. ISAAC BORING, of the Georgia Conference, died of Cholera in St. Louis, while attending the General Conference of the Methodist Episcopal Church South.

June 12, 1850

Died at his residence in Telfair county, on the first of June, JOHN McDUFFIE, in the 74th year of his age, after an illness of three years and eight months. Mr. McDuffie's disease was dropsey.

Departed this life, on the 5th inst., TELLULAH, (aged seven years,) daughter of CHARLES B. and SUSANNAH B. PATTERSON (with eulogy).

Announce the death in this city, on Friday night last, of SCOTT CARY, ESQ.; native of North Carolina; but resided in Georgia for last forty, and in this city for last 24 years; interred in Rose Hill Cemetery, on Sunday morning last - in 69th year of his age.

Tribute of respect by Lafayette Division, No. 43 Sons of Temperance, held at Perry (Georgia), June 6th, 1850 - on death of JOHN W. COOPER.

June 26, 1850

Died in Vineville, on the 24th instant, MISS MARY ANN JAPPIE, aged about 50 years.

On Tuesday night last, about 11 o'clock, a wood car coming down the Macon and Western Railroad, on arriving near the Depot, passed over the body of a man who was lying on the rails, by which he was instantly killed. His name was STEPHEN DAVIS. He lived in this county, a few miles from this city. He was probably drunk at the time.

July 3, 1850

Died in Dahlonega, Georgia, on the 21st ult., at 6 o'clock P.M., MRS. SUSAN R., wife of COL. A.W. REDDING, Supt. of the U.S.B. Mint, and daughter of the late DRURY JACKSON. Mrs. R. lived 42 years lacking one day, thirty of which were spent in communion with the M.E. Church.

July 17, 1850

Died in Milledgeville, on the 9th inst., MRS. ELIZA M. JARRATT, wife of DR. W.A. JARRATT, aged 24 years. About seven years ago, she was baptized by Rev. J.R. Kendrick, and united with the Macon Baptist Church (with eulogy)

Notice of the death of President ZACHARY TAYLOR.

Communication from Washington Lodge, No. 46 (Pondtown, Ga., July 6th, 1850) - on death of SAMUEL ELKINS.

July 24, 1850

Died at his residence at Etowa, Cass county, on the 7th inst., after a short illness JOHN S. RANDLE, recently of Stewart county, in his 45th year; buried in Rose Hill Cemetery.

July 31, 1850

Died in this city, on the 29th inst. MRS. ELIZA B. HOLZENDORF, aged about 41 years - wife of MR. JOHN HOLZENDORF.

Aug. 7, 1850

Died in this city, on the 3d inst. MRS. S.F. BURNEY, aged 20 years, daughter of JAMES KIRKSEY, ESQ., of Tallahassee, Fla.

Died at the residence of MAJOR JAMES PEARSON, in Twiggs county, on the 4th instant, BENJAMIN SMITH, in the 56th year of his age.

Melancholy suicide - a young lady named KEAN, residing in Covington, Ky. drownded herself in the Ohio river on Sunday week...

Aug. 14, 1850

Died at his step-father's, (Col. William Rutherford, in Culloden,) THOMAS GREENE BARRON, on the 5th of August, 1850, in the 19th year of his age. Tho' young, he had married a few months since... has left a mother and wife to mourn.

Died in Houston county, on the morning of the 26th of July, at his residence near Fort Valley, STERLING TOOKE, aged about 57 years. He was violently attacked with bilious colic, which proved fatal in less than twenty-four hours.

Died on Thursday, the 1st inst., at the residence of his parents, in Thomas county, RICHARD, son of DR. THOS. B. and MRS. ELIZABETH WINN - aged 8 years and a few days (eulogy).

Died at the Pulaski House, Savannah, on the night of the 9th inst., NELSON McLESTER, ESQ., late of Columbus, Ga.

Died on the 6th inst., in New York city, after a long illness, SAMUEL D. CORBITT, late of Savannah, Ga., in the 47th year of his age.

A rencounter occurred at Fenn's Bridge, Jefferson county, on the 29th ult., in which EZEKIEL FINNEY was stabbed by COL. JOHN J. LONG of Washington county, and expired immediately of the wound...

Brevet GENERAL R.B. MASON died suddenly in St. Louis, of cholera, on the 26th ult.; succeeded Gen. Kearney as Governor of California.

Aug. 21, 1850

Departed this life, on the 11th inst., MICHAEL LEWIS, in the 26th year of his age, after a short but severe illness; native of Poland.

Died at the residence of Davis Gammage, Horsehead, Macon county, Ga., on Sunday evening, 11th instant, his oldest daughter, SARAH FRANCES GAMMAGE, after an illness of two months, of disease of the heart, in the 9th year of her age.

Aug. 28, 1850

Died in this city, on the 24th instant, SARAH SIMS, only child of WILLIAM H. BRAY, aged 15 months.

Died in this city, on the 24th inst., WM. BIVINS, ESQ., aged about 64 years.

Nashville, Tennessee paper announces the death of DR. GERARD TROOST, who died in that city on the 15th inst. Mr. T. had been Professor of Chemistry, Geology, and Mineralogy, in the Nashville University, for past twenty years, and, for the greater part of that time, Geologist of the State of Tennessee.

Sep. 4, 1850

Died in Upson county, on the 26th of August, 1850, EDWARD HOLLOWAY, who was born in Edgefield District, South Carolina, on 22d February 1787. Capt. Holloway, during the last war with Great Britain,

(Sep. 4, cont'd.) - served his country as an officer in the U.S. Army. After the war, he left the army, and in the winter of 1816-17, came to Putnam county, in this State, where, on the 16th day of April, 1818, he was married to MISS NANCY BRYAN, a stepdaughter of BENJAMIN WHITFIELD, Senior, dec'd. At the close of 1822, Capt. Holloway settled in Pike, now Upson county, on his plantation seven miles east from Thomaston, where he continued to live till his death. He was the principal officer of the Upson Light Dragoons for many years, from its organization in 1825; repeatedly represented Upson county in the Senate of the State Legislature, and had been Senator from counties of Upson and Crawford.

Oct. 2, 1850

Died on the 19th of September, by a fall from a building at his mills, MR. JOSEPH WILLET, of East Macon; born in Norwich, Conn., and removed to Georgia in his 18th year; died in his 53rd year - has resided for last 35 years in Macon - and was, it is believed, the very first inhabitant of the city; felled the first tree (with eulogy).

Oct. 9, 1850

Died on the morning of the 30th ult., at her residence in Bibb county, MRS. AMY G., consort of EDMUND GILBERT, in the 67th year of her age; has left an affectionate husband and a numerous offspring...member of Baptist Church for 21 years (with eulogy).

Oct. 16, 1850

Died in Chattanooga, on the 4th inst., JOSEPH THOMAS, son of J.A.R. and MARY A. BENNETT, aged 10 months and 2 days.

Died in this county, on the 13th inst., MR. ABRAM MASSEY, aged about 60 years - a native of North Carolina, but for about 20 years, of Jones county, Ga.

Oct. 23, 1850

Died in Crawford county on the 15th ult., REV. JAMES MATTHEWS, after an affliction of sixteen months; caused by the upsetting of his carriage; born in Warren county in this State in 1790; member of the Baptist Church for 21 years; beloved wife and several children are left to mourn the loss.

Oct. 30, 1850

Departed this life, on Wednesday, 23d instant, in the 65th year of his age, MARK D. CLARKE, ESQ., a native of Savannah, but for many years a citizen of Bibb county (with eulogy).

Nov. 6, 1850

Died in Culloden, on the night of the 21st inst., JOHN SNEAD, aged 77 years 4 months and 17 days. Followed by tribute of respect from Salem Lodge dated Wed. evening Sep. 23d, 1850.

Died in this city, on the 29th Oct., ANNA MARIA, only daughter of JNO. R. and ELIZABETH HARMAN, aged 4 years 6 months and 12 days.

Died at the residence of his son in this city, on the 30th Oct., MR. THOS. SPRINGER, aged about 90 years; born in Union District, South Carolina; member of the Baptist Church.

Died Oct. 27th, in Roswell, Cobb county, BAYARD HAND, son of DR. C.T. QUINTARD, aged 14 months.

Nov. 6, 1850

We regret to learn that a fatal affray o-curred at Calhoun, in Gordon county, on Saturday last, during a political meeting. The difficulty occurred between CAPT. CHARLES HAMILTON and his brother and two young men by the name of Johnson - sons of Col. Johnson of Cass county. Both the Hamiltons and one of the Johnsons were wounded. Charles Hamilton received three wounds - two in the back and one in the hand - which it is supposed he cannot survive. Jefferson Johnson and the younger Hamilton were also severely wounded, but is supposed will recover.

Nov. 13, 1850

Died at Wynton, on the 11th of October, COSAM EMIR BARTLETT, in the 57th year of his age; native of New Hampshire, but has long resided in the south, and was extensively known in Florida and Georgia, as a conductor of the Press.

Nov. 27, 1850

Died in Laurens county, on the 19th inst., after a protracted illness, SARAH, consort of JAMES WRIGHT, in the 56th year of her age.

Died at the residence of his father, in this city, on the 21st inst., THEODORE H. GRAY, son of MR. WM. GRAY, in the 16th year of his age; died suddenly.

Notice of the death of COL. RICHARD M. JOHNSON, of Kentucky. Was Vice President of United States in term of Mr. Van Buren.

Dec. 4, 1850

Died on the 15th inst., in Orangeburg, South-Carolina, MRS. ELIZABETH C. RUMPH, in the 46th year of her age, consort of CHARLES E. RUMPH of Macon co. Ga.

Dec. 11, 1850

Died in Vineville, on the 5th inst., GARTEN SPARKS, son of JANE and THOMAS HARDEMAN, JR., aged 15 months. (Columbus papers please copy).

Dec. 18, 1850

Died on Saturday morning the 7th of December, at her residence near Pondtown, MRS. SARAH J. BLACK, wife of DR. ROBERT C. BLACK, aged 27 years and 10 months; has left a husband and three small children (with eulogy).

Died in Culloden, on the 30th ult., after an illness of 21 days, of Typhoid Pneumonia, MISS H.A. HODGES, in the 15th year of her age, second daughter of DEBORA and JOSIAH HODGES of Houston county.

Jan. 1, 1851

Card from ELIZABETH RUMPH (wife of CHARLES E. RUMPH) dated December 27th, 1850 - As I have recently been informed that my death had been published in a Georgia paper some few weeks since, this will show that it is a base falsehood, fabricated without doubt to carry out some evil design. I can scarcely believe that MR. CHARLES E. RUMPH could have had it done, as strange as his conduct has been for some time past...

Jan. 8, 1851

Died November 5th, 1850, at Dry Creek, near Coloma, California, JAMES M. TANNER, of Butts county, Ga., aged 26 years (Griffin papers please copy)

Jan. 8, 1851

Savannah papers report the death of REV. EDWARD NEUFVILLE, D.D., Rector of Christ's Chrucy. He expired on the 1st inst., after a residence in Savannah of nearly a quarter of a century.

Jan. 15, 1851

The Savannah Republican of the 8th inst. announces the death of the HON. THOMAS SPALDING. Died on the 4th inst. at the house of his son, CHARLES SPALDING, ESQ.

Jan. 22, 1851

Died in Monticello, Georgia, on the 7th inst. REBECCA M. GLOVER, wife of ELI S. GLOVER in the 24th year of her age; left husband and two children (with eulogy).

Died on Monday, Dec. 30th, MRS. LUCY VIGAL, aged 51 years, at the residence of her husband, near East Macon.

Died at the residence of his mother, MRS. ELVIRA FLEWELLEM, in Wynnton, near Columbus, on Saturday morning, the 4th inst. ALEXANDER HOLLOWAY FLEWELLEN, only son of the late DR. ABNER H. FLEWELLEN, aged 7 years 7 months and 6 days.

Died at Shell Point, Florida, on the 10th inst., MRS. CAROLINE, wife of J.B. SHORES, ESQ., aged 45 years, a native of Burke county, Ga.

Died at Perry, Houston county, on Sunday the 5th inst., CHARLES WEST, oldest son of MRS. CLIFFORD S. and J.H. POWERS, ESQ., aged 2 years and 3 months.

Jan. 29, 1851

Died at Tallahassee, Florida, on the 9th inst. of consumption, MR. CHARLES INGRAM, a native of Bibb county, Ga., aged 49.

Died at his residence, in Putnam county, on the 7th inst., PEYTON HOLT, ESQ., in the 77th year of his age.

Feb. 5, 1851

Died in this city, on the 3d inst. MRS. ELIZA W. LAMAR, wife of DR. THOMAS R. LAMAR.

BRINKLY BISHOP, who was convicted during the recent session of Bibb Superior Court, of the murder of TURNER SMITH, was on Friday last brought before Judge Stark and sentenced to be hung on the 28th day of March.

Death of MR. WILLIAM T. ATKINS, of this city, aged 27 years - he expired of Chronic Diarrhea, at San Jose, California, on the 2d of December last...

Feb. 12, 1851

Died of Pulmonary Consumption, at Dublin, on the 31st ult. MRS. MARGARET S. YOPP, consort of JEREMISH H. YOPP, ESQ., in the 44th year of her age; left husband and children (eulogy).

Died in Macon, on the 8th inst., MRS. ANN ELIZA CARVER, wife of ROBERT CARVER, and daughter of MAJOR JAMES H. HARDAWAY, in the 37th year of her age; for 18 years a member of the Presbyterian Church (with eulogy).

The HON. B.W. CROWNINGSHIELD, of Salem, ex-Secretary of the Navy under President Madison, fell dead in a store in Boston on the 3rd inst. The cause was disease of the heart; was nearly 80 years old.

Feb. 19, 1851

Died at his residence in Monroe county, of the Palsy, on the 6th inst., AMOS PONDER, ESQ., in the 66th year of his age; member of the Baptist Church.

HERR RYNINGER, the celebrated wire-walker, who has recently been performing through the Southern cities attempted on the 4th inst., to walk from the top of the State House in Baton Rouge to the Market House. When he was about midway he fell, and was so much injured that he expired about 6 o'clock the same evening.

The Columbus Times announces the death of HON. ROBERT R. ALEXANDER, who expired at his residence in that city on the 14th inst...but 39 years of age; born in Putnam county, educated at University of Georgia, read his profession with the late Wm. H. Torrance, Esq., and was a citizen of Columbus for last 15 years; Judge of Superior Court of the Chattahoochee Circuit.

Feb. 26, 1851

Died in East Macon on the 11th inst., GEORGE VIGAL, ESQ., in the 62d year of his age; left six children.

Died in Knoxville, Ga. of Typhoid Fever, on the 20th inst., SIMEON ARTEMUS, infant son of GEORGE T. and ANN WALKER, aged 9 months and 11 days.

Died on the 24th inst., at the residence of her father, near Macon, MRS. MARY E.S. HARTSCN, aged 25 years; daughter of WM. SHIVERS, JR.

Death on the 23rd inst., of WILLIAM SCOTT, ESQ., of Vineville. His disease was consumption; one of the earliest settlers of the county, and by his industry and economy, had accumulated a handsome property...just entered upon his 50th year.

Mar. 5, 1851

Died on Saturday morning, the 8th ult., at his residence in Lowndes county, PHILIP McRAE, at the advanced age of 95 years, believed to be, at the time of his death, the oldest man of his county. He emigrated with his parents from his native place, Ross-Shire, Scotland, to North Carolina, at the age of 10, and removed to Georgia about 1812; for last 60 years of his life a member of the Presbyterian Church, and for 35 years Ruling Elder; has left a widow and number of children, grand-children and great-grand-children, in this State and Florida.

Died on the night of the 23rd ult., at the residence of her son, Henry W. Tindall, MRS. ELIZABETH HUNT, in the 74th year of her age, after a short but severe illness, of Palsy; member of Methodist Episcopal Church about 35 years.

Died in Sumter county, on Wednesday, 26th ult., ALVA, eldest son of E.W. and M.A. ALLEN, aged 3 years 1 month and 21 days.

Died in Savannah, on the 20th inst., MRS. ELIZABETH HOPKINS, aged 78 years 10 months and 10 days, wife of BENJAMIN B. HOPKINS, for many years a resident of this city.

Died in this county, on the 22d ultimo, of Consumption, MR. JAMES H. AMASON, aged about 32 years...recollected by many of our subscribers as out travelling Agent a few years past.

Died in Oglethorpe county, Ga., on the 19th ult., in the 24th year of her age, MRS. NAOMI LANDRUM, wife of REV. SYLVANUS LANDRUM and daughter of the late REV. JACK LUMPKIN.

Mar. 5, 1851

Tribute of respect by Pleasant Ridge Lodge, No. 103 (Masonic) dated February 18, 1851 - on death of I.M.H. CARLETON - died on the 6th inst., in the 24th year of his age, at the home of Mr. Wm. D. Stewart, in Macon county, Ga. He was making an active preparation for trip to California, and while out on business was attacked with typhoid fever.

Mar. 19, 1851

Died in this city, on the 14th inst., MR. WM. W. BALDWIN, aged about 38 years.

Died in Upson county, on the 12th inst., MR. MARTIN GAVIN, a native of Queens county, Ireland, and formerly a resident of this city.

The Columbia, South Carolina Telegraph reports that GENERAL GEORGE McDUFFIE expired at 9 o'clock A.M. yesterday, at the residence of Richard Singleton, Esq., in Sumter.

Mar. 26, 1851

Died on the evening of the 14th inst., of Inflammatory Rheumatism, after a painful illness of some days, CHARLES, the fourth son of MR. and MRS. GREEN HILL of Houston county, aged 9 years 10 months and 28 days.

Departed this life, at the residence of her husband, at 2 o'clock, P.M., on Monday the 10th inst., after a painful illness of one week, MRS. MARTHA HOLMES, consort of MAJ. JAMES P. HOLMES, of Fort Gaines; native of this State; a member of the Methodist Episcopal Church; left husband and three children.

Apr. 9, 1851

Died in California, on Monday night, 20th of January 1851, or erysipelas, after an illness of ten days, FRANCIS M. MEANS, youngest son of JAMES and MARY ANN MEANS, of Upson county, Ga., aged 23 years 10 months and 1 day.

Died of Typhoid fever, at the residence of his relative, Mr. C.M. Lucas, in Crawford county, on the 19th March, MR. JOHN L. DUGGER, in the 36th year of his age.

Died in this city on the 1st of April, after an illness of 13 days, of Scarlet Fever, RYLAND JUDSON, son of LEWIS J. and MARGARET GROCE, aged 3 years 1 month and 2 days (Telegraph copy).

Tribute of respect by members of the U.S. and Mexican Boundary Commission, held at San Elizario, Texas, on 9th day of February, 1851 - on death of EDWARD C. CLARK, of Rhode Island.

Apr. 16, 1851

Departed this life in Crawford county, on Sunday the 6th inst., after a painful and protracted illness of eleven weeks and three days, MRS. SARAH M. ANDREWS, wife of A.G. ANDREWS, and second daughter of E. SIMONTON, in the 27th year of her age; has left a husband and four small children (with eulogy).

Apr. 23, 1851

Died, on the 1st inst., in Talbotton, of Acute Dysentery, MRS. ANN CASTENS, consort of JAMES W. CASTENS, aged 27 years; member of M.E. Church; left husband, sister, brothers and children (with eulogy).

Apr. 30, 1851

Departed this life, on the night of the 21st of April, at her father's residence in Crawford county, Ga. MISS LOUISA C. eldest daughter of SAMUEL P. and CAROLINE M. CORBIN, aged 21 years; member of ME Church; died of Typhoid Fever (with long eulogy).

Died in the city of Augusta, on the 10th of April, 1851, MRS. LOUISA, consort of DR. PAUL F. EVE, and daughter of MAJOR and MRS. GEORGE L. TWIGGS.

Died on the 12th inst., at the residence of Wright Knowles, in Wilkinson county, of inflammation of the brain, after a brief illness of six days, JOHN STOKES, aged 21 years; left a disconsolate mother and sister.

The Norfolk papers announce the death, in that city, on Monday the 22d inst., of COM. JAMES BARRON, senior officer of the US Navy, in the 83rd year of his age; entered the service 9th of March, 1798, and his commission bears date of May 22d, 1799...

The Richmond Republican reports that Most Reverend ARCHBISHOP SAMUEL ECCLESTON, who has been lying sick at his residence at the convent, in Georgetown, for several weeks, died last evening, at twenty five minutes past six o'clock; was born in June 1801 in Kent county, Md., near Chestertown, where his father was a wealthy farmer; was brought up in the Presbyterian faith and has a brother a Presbyterian minister; had filled the Archaeopiscopal See in the Roman Catholic Church since September 1834; funeral to take place in Baltimore on Saturday.

May 7, 1851

Died in this city on the 3rd inst., MRS. BOON, consort of DR. J.R. B_ON.

HON. CHRISTOPHER B. STRONG died in Perry, on Thursday night last; known in Georgia as a lawyer of distinction; buried in Rose Hill Cemetery in Macon, Georgia.

May 21, 1851

Died in this city, on the 12th inst., in her 25th year, MRS. MARY, wife of JACKSON BARNES.

Death of WAID L., youngest son of FREDERIC L. and PHOEBE CROWDER, who departed this life in Monroe county, on Monday morning, the 5th inst., in the 26th year of his age (with long eulogy).

May 28, 1851

WILLIAM AUGUSTINE, son of COL. and MRS. PATTERSON, died at Oakly Grove, Houston county, the residence of his grandparents, MR. and MRS. EDGEWORTH, on the 24th of April, aged 2 years and 5 months (with eulogy).

Died in this city, on the 24th inst., MRS. CATHARINE A. consort of ROBT. A. SMITH, ESQ.

Died on Monday, May 19th, LEWIS NEALE, infant son of MR. and MRS. L.N. WHITTLE, aged 7 months and 1 day.

June 4, 1851

Died in this city, on the 1st inst., of the Scarlet Fever, LEMLE DUNCAN, infant son of ROB'T NISBET of Louisville, aged 1 year 6 months and 14 days.

June 4, 1851

Died in Pulaski county, in the vicinity of Hawkinsville, on Monday the 26th ult., MRS. MARIDLEY ANDERSON, wife of JOHN S. ANDERSON, ESQ., after a painful and protracted illness, in the 42d year of her age (with eulogy)

Tribute of respect by Union Lodge, No. 14 I.O.O.F. - on death of G.B. FELTS who departed this life the 30th inst.

June 11, 1851

Died in Crawford county, on the 28th of May, of Typhoid Fever, MR. DAVID S. SAYLOR, second son of MR. ESAIAS SAYLOR, in the 22d year of his age; leaves a father, brothers and sisters to mourn the loss (South Carolinian and Southern Christian Advocate please copy).

June 18, 1851

Died at her but recently occupied home in Decatur Co., on Monday, the 9th inst., MRS. LOUISA WILKIN, (formerly Louisa King) consort of DR. ANDREW A. WILKIN, in the 24th year of her age; member of Presbyterian Church.

Died in Macon county, on the evening of the 11th inst., CHARITY ANN DELILAH, eldest daughter of MR. and MRS. DAVIS GRAMMAGE, aged 7 years 8 months and 29 days (with eulogy).

Died in Vineville, on the 14th inst., BENJAMIN JONES, infant son of COL. H.J. and V.B. LAMAR, aged 4 months (Columbus papers please copy).

Died at the residence of his father, in Houston county, on the 27th day of June, of Consumption, JACOB V. RUMPH, eldest son of MR. LEWIS RUMPH, in the 37th year of his age.

SARAH H. HARBUCK, wife of JAMES HARBUCK, ESQ., departed this life at her residence in Crawford county, Ga., on the 17th ultimo; daughter of WILLIAM and ANN HURMONDS of Jackson county, Ga., born on the 17th of May, 1814; married the 13th December 1831; joined the Methodist E. Church 1843; leaves a husband and four children.

Tribute of respect by Houston Lodge, No. 35 (Perry, June 14th, 1851) - on death of JAMES E. DUNCAN, who departed this life on the 12th inst.

June 25, 1851

Died at the Indian Springs, Butts county, on the 7th inst., MRS. VALINDA, wife of DR. H. BRANHAM, of Eatonton, Putnam county.

Died in Jones county, on the 11th inst., MR. REUBEN ROBERTS, in the 61st year of his age.

Died in the city of Macon, on the 21st inst., MRS. MARY E., wife of JAS. VAN VALKENBURGH, in the 41st year of her age; eldest daughter of NATHAN CHURCH, ESQ., of Troy, NY, and born in 1810; her parents were Baptists; and both died before she was age 15; she then became the ward of ISRAEL SEYMORE, ESQ., her uncle, whose guardianship was every way parental; married JAS. VAN VALKENBURGH 1827; in 1833 joined Church under pastoral care of Rev. D. Dunbar, of New York City, and of which church her husband was a member; subsequently the family changed its membership to 16th St. Baptist Church, where her membership remained until her death; in 1847 removed to Macon, Ga...illness was Dysentery (with eulogy).

July 23, 1851

> Died in Houston county, on the 8th inst., at the residence of his son, (ROB'T C. REDDING), REV. ARTHUR REDDING, of Harris county, in the 82nd year of his age; for 52 years he officiated as a local preacher, and was the second oldest preacher belonging to the Methodist connection South...for two years his health had been failing...(long eulogy).

July 30, 1851

> Died in the city of London, on the 5th ult., EDWARD A. BRODDUS, M.D. of Monticello, Jasper county, Georgia, in the 50th year of his age (with eulogy).

> Departed this life, in the city of Macon, on the 14th of July, JOHN W.W. WHITTINGTON, son of E.O. and MARTHA E. WHITTINGTON, aged 7 years and 10 months (with eulogy).

Aug. 6, 1851

> Died on the 13th of July, MRS. SARAH FOLSOM, consort of RANDAL FOLSOM, ESQ., of Lownds Co. Ga. in the 53rd year of her age.

Aug. 13, 1851

> Tribute of respect by Union Lodge, I.O.O.F. No. 14 (Knoxville, June 1851) - on death of RICHARDSON FEAGAN.

Aug. 20, 1851

> Died in this city, on the 17th inst., JOHN, only son of J.W. and HARRIET A. BABCOCK, aged 7 months and 22 days.

Sep. 3, 1851

> Died on the 23d inst., at the house of Rev. Mr. Reid, in Sumter District, South Carolina, MR. JOHN C. GOULDING, youngest son of REV. DR. GOULDING late of Columbus, Ga.; victim of disease incurred in war with Mexico, in which he served a campaign (Athens and Columbus papers please copy).

> Died in this county, on the 21st ult., MR. ADAM ROBERTSON, aged about 80 years; one of the earliest settlers of this vicinity.

Sep. 10, 1851

> Died at Monticello, August 29th CHARLES EUGENIUS, infant son of GEO. T. and VIRGINIA L. BARTLETT, aged 11 months and 11 days.

Sep. 17, 1851

> Died at his residence in Sumter county on the 2d inst., MR. JAMES WHITE in the 6ed year of his age; native of Warren county, North Carolina but removed to Georgia, when quite a young man, and subsequently resided in the counties of Greene and Monroe; settled in Sumter in 1842.

> Died in Zebulon, on the 4th inst. after a short illness MRS. CATHERINE W. STOW aged 27 years - wife of MR. JOHN B. STOW, and daughter of the late FREDERICK SIMS, ESQ.

Sep. 24, 1851

> Died in Dekalb county, on the 3d inst. LOUISA E., daughter of STEPHEN and LOUIS COLLINS, of this city, aged 9 months and 14 days.

> Died in Macon, at the residence of her son, Dr. W.H. Banks, on the 21st inst., MRS. HARRIET W. BANKS, relict of the late JAS. BANKS of Murfreesborough, NC, in her 67th year.

Sep. 24, 1851

Died in this city, on the 19th inst., MR. SIMEON BUFORD, formerly of Sandersville, and more recently the keeper at the Floyd House, in this city.

Oct. 8, 1851

Died in Houston county, Ga., Sept. 15th MR. EZEKIEL MURRAY, aged 50 years.

Died on the 25th September, at the residence of Charles Walker, in Pulaski county, CHARLES HUNTER, in the 79th year of his age.

Died of Typhoid fever, in this county, on the 23rd of September, JAMES M. McFARLIN; his illness was protracted about 17 days.

Died in this city, on the 30th ult., BAZIL LAMAR, son of GEORGE J. LUNSFORD, aged 11 years 2 months and 14 days.

Died in Clinton, Georgia, on the 3rd inst., MR. PETER CLOWER, in the 77th year of his age; born in Warren county, Georgia; for last 43 years a resident of Jones county; a member of the Methodist Episcopal Church.

Died in Crawford county, MR. W.B. CORBIN, (son-in-law of T.A. BREWER, ESQ.); member of the Baptist Church.

Oct. 15, 1851

Died in Twiggs county, Sept. 10th, of typhoid fever, in the 22nd year of her age, MRS. AMELIA HENRY, wife of WM. J. HENRY, and daughter of MRS. ELIZABETH and MR. JOHN H. DENSON (eulogy) (Columbus Enquirer please copy)

Died in this city on the 3rd inst., MRS. SUSAN SIMS, relict of the late FREDERICK SIMS, in the 51st year of her age.

Died in Vineville, on the 13th inst., JOSEPH A. OUSLEY, infant son of ROBERT F. and E.C. OUSLEY, aged 17 months and 7 days.

Oct. 22, 1851

Died at his residence in Haynesville, Houston county, on the 3rd inst., WILLIAM S. COALSON, ESQ., in the 46th year of his age; left wife and six daughters (Recorder copy)

Died of Cholera Infantum, in Starkeville, Lee county, Ga., on the 10th inst., JOHN WYCHE, infant son of COL. Z. and MRS. MARY A. JACKSON, aged 10 months and 15 days (Christian Index please copy)

Oct. 29, 1851

Died at his residence, in Wilkinson county, on the 3d inst., MR. DANIEL BURKE, in the 73d year of his age.

Nov. 12, 1851

Died on the morning of the 19th ult., at his residence in Macon Co., Ga., the REV. JOHN McKENZIE, in the 71st year of his age; native of North Carolina but resident of this State more than 60 years; shortly after his marriage in 1804, he settled in Jones Co.; about 1827 moved to that portion of Houston co., now Macon; was baptized by Rev. Jesse Mercer; ordained as a Baptist Minister.

Died in Vicksburg, Miss., on the 8th ult., of congestive chills, MRS. MELVINA JONES, consort of MR. G.W. JONES, and daughter of MR. JAMES HOLLINGSWORTH, for many years a citizen of this city.

Nov. 19, 1851

   Died in this city, on the 15th inst., after a brief illness, MR. JOHN EANES, a native of Virginia, but for last 14 years a resident of Macon, in the 62d year of his age (with eulogy)

   Died in this city on the 15th inst., in the 36th year of his age, DANIEL D. McNEILL, a native of Person county, North Carolina, but for last 13 years a resident of this city.

Nov. 26, 1851

   Died of Typhoid Fever, at Americus, at 9½ o'clock A.M. on Friday, 21st inst., LEANDER M. HUDSON, in the 29th year of his age.

Dec. 10, 1851

   Died at the residence of her father, FR. E.E. JONES, in Madison, on Wednesday, 3rd instant, MRS. VIRGINIA E. NISBET, wife of CHARLES E. NISBET, ESQ.

Dec. 17, 1851

   Died at his residence in Sumter county, Ga., on the 27th Nov., HENRY H. LUMPKIN, JR., ESQ., in the 30th year of his age; (with long eulogy)

Dec. 31, 1851

   Died in Pulaski county, on Thursday, the 25th inst., of Typhoid Fever, MRS. MARY ANN BURCH, wife of EDWARD A. BURCH, and daughter of ULYSSES CRUTCHFIELD, in the 28th year of her age; left husband and three small children.

Jan. 7, 1852

   Died near Hawkinsville, on 5th of December, 1851, after a short and painful illness, MRS. MARTHA G. BAGBY, wife of A.G. BAGBY, in the 47th year of her age; a devoted wife and affectionate mother; for upwards of twenty years a member of the Baptist Church.

   MR. CHOICE KINNEY, of Cassville, who was so seriously injured by the running off of the Western & Atlantic train, near Cartersville, on the 23rd ult., has since died of his wounds.

Jan. 14, 1852

   The Savannah News reports that the steamer Magnolia, which plies between that city and Florida, was blown up on Friday last, while taking in cotton at the plantation of James Hamilton Couper, at St. Simons Island. CAPT. McNELTY, and ten or twelve of the crew were lost or killed...

Jan. 21, 1852

   Died at his residence in Laurens county, MR. EASON ALLEN, in the 65th year of his age; left an aged widow and daughter (with eulogy)

   Atrocious murder and robbery. On Sunday night, about 11 o'clock, two persons came to the house of MR. HERRING, in Columbia county, on the Washington road, nine miles above Augusta, and called him to the front door, and requested to be allowed to stay all night. He asked them in. They told him to come out, as they had a horse and buggy with them. As soon as he got outside the door, he was shot down. Mrs. Herring then barred the door and prevented the entrance of the murderers. About an hour afterwards, they returned and fired through an auger hole in the door and killed her... Mr. and Mrs. Herring were an elderly couple, aged about 60 years each, and were living by themselves, there being no other persons, white or black, living on the premises. (Augusta Constitutionalist, Jan. 13)

Jan. 21, 1852

Dreadful accident. On Saturday, the 10th inst., MARION FRANKLIN STEWART, son of THOMAS W. STEWART, deceased, and POLLY H. STEWART, (widow,) a resident of Jones county, came to his death in a hunting accident while hunting rabbits with his brother, HENRY JASPER STEWART...his age was 17 years 1 month and 22 days. His mother, at the time of the accident, was at her plantation in Twiggs county, some 30 miles off (details of accident given in the story)

Jan. 28, 1852

Died at the Stone Mountain, in DeKalb county, on the 4th inst., PAUL A. HARALSON, ESQ.

Died on the 4th instant, in Pulaski county, at the residence of John F. McLeod, MRS. SUSAN T. MONK, in the 66th year of her age, after a painful illness of 51 days.

Feb. 4, 1852

Died on the evening of 28th January, RICHARD KENNON HINES, aged 46 years 3 months and 13 days. The parents of Mr. Hines emigrated from Virginia to Pittsboro, North Carolina, where his father died, and where he was born 15 Oct. 1805. His mother removed from thence, whilst he was still a child, to Morgan county, Ga., and subsequently to Putnam county. He was graduated at Franklin College in 1824, with the highest honor of his class, and having studied law in the office of Judge L.Q.C. Lamar, and opened an office in city of Milledgeville, he was married on 18 Jan. 1824 to a daughter of DR. JAMES NISBET, of Athens...represented the county of Baldwin in the General Assembly (with eulogy) (Telegraph please copy)

Feb. 11, 1852

Savannah Republican of 6th inst. announces the death in that city, at 4 o'clock that afternoon, of DR. COSMO P. RICHARDSONE, in the 48th year of his age. Dr. R. was born in Edinburgh, Scotland, and came to Savannah when but three years old. At the time of his death, he was a member of the Board of Aldermen, and the commanding officer of the Savannah Volunteer Guards - the oldest infantry company in the city or State (with eulogy).

Feb. 18, 1852

Died in this city, on Monday morning, the 16th inst., after a short, but painful illness, MR. DANIEL HEIDT, a native of Savannah, aged 43 years.

Died in Oglethorpe, on the morning of the 10th inst., MR. ROBERT P. ROBINSON, formerly, and for many years, a merchant of this city.

Died on the morning of the 6th inst., in Americus, Sumter county, while on a visit to her friends at that place, MRS. MARY BEAUFORT MATHEWS, in the 29th year of her age, consort of DR. W.A. MATHEWS, of Fort Valley, Houston County.

Feb. 28, 1852

Died on Wednesday evening last, MRS. MALINDA SHELTON, wife of MR. E.L. SHELTON of this city, in the 28th year of her age.

Died in this city, on the night of the 23d inst., after a short but severe illness, MR. JAMES A. DUDLEY, Printer, aged about 27 years, native of Utica, New York. Mr. D. has resided in this city only about two months, and during the greater part of that time filled the situation of Foreman of the Telegraph Office. He was known to the Craft in the cities of N.Y., Washington, Richmond, and Charleston, having spent time in each of those places.

Feb. 28, 1852

Died on the 6th ult., at his residence in Wilkinson county, in the 48th year of his age, SAMUEL BRAGG, ESQ.; left wife and children.

Tribute of respect by members of the Bar of the Southwestern Circuit (Starkville, Lee Co., Feb. 5th, 1852) on death of RICHARD K. HINES.

Mar. 3, 1852

Died of Bronchitis, in Lowndes county, Ga., DR. RICHARD A. TRIPPE, son of JUDGE TURNER H. and MARY A. TRIPPE, of Cass county, Ga., in the 27th year of his age...

Died in Zebulon, at the residence of her parents, on the 22nd ult., in the 26th year of her age, MRS. MARY ARNOLD, eldest daughter of JAMES and MARGARET STEWART.

Died in Houston county, on the 21st inst., DAVID HOWARD, son of LEWIS and MARIA RUMPH, aged 2 months and 12 days.

Mar. 10, 1852

Died suddenly, of apoplexy, on the 31st of December last, in Washington county, Texas, RICHARD M. HOLT, ESQ., a native of Georgia, in the 40th year of his age.

Died on Sunday morning, 7th inst. of congestion of the brain, after an illness of three days, CONWAY FORTESCUE, only son of MR. and MRS. L.N. WHITTLE, aged 4 years 5 months and 23 days.

Died very suddenly, at Birdsville, Burke county, on the 4th inst., SYMAN HALL, infant son of HENRY W. JONES, aged 10 months.

Died on the 2d inst., in Chambers county, Ala., HENRY CHAPPELL, aged 47 years.

The Savannah Republican of the 6th inst. announces the death in that city of the HON. WILLIAM B. BULLOCH, in his 77th year; youngest son of ARCHIBALD BULLOCH; entered the law office of Judge Stephens when quite a young man, and became a prominent member of the bar as early as 1800...during War of 1812 he mustered into the service of the United States the heavy Artillery of this city; member of US Senate in 1813; in 1816 was elected President of the Bank of the State of Georgia, of which he was one of the founders, continued in this office for 27 years; was subsequently collector of this port; Mayor oa the city in 1809; at age of 27 was chosen Vestryman of Christ Church...

Mar. 17, 1852

Died in this city, on Wednesday night last, JOHN HENRY MORGAN, aged about 38 years; buried with Masonic honors on Thursday.

Died on Thursday last, MRS. SARAH A. USHER, a highly respectable widow of this city, aged 74 years.

Died in this city, on the 27th ult., CAROLINE PLANT WRIGLEY, aged 13 years; one of the twin daughters of the late FORDYCE WRIGLEY.

Died in this city, on the 9th inst., MR. MIDAS L. GRAYBILL, in the 42d year of his age, after a protracted and severe illness of many months; a resident of Macon for more than 20 years.

Mar. 24, 1852

Died in Rome, Floyd county, on the 11th inst., MRS. MARY A., wife of T.J. PERRY, and daughter of LEROY PATILLO, ESQ., of Monroe, Walton county.

COL. W.S. KING, aged 51 years, one of the Associate Editors and Proprietors of the Charleston Courier, died, of pneumonia, on Friday last.

From the Savannah Republican of the 19th inst. - By the late arrival last night of the steamship Isabel from Havana, we learn that BENJAMIN SNIDER, of this place, died in that city on Thursday, the 11th inst., in the 51st year of his age...had gone to Havana on account of his precarious health...was accompanied by his son... his wife, hearing of his critical condition, took passage on the Isabel on her last trip hence, but unfortunately arrived about an hour after his death...twice elected Alderman and twice represented the county in the State Senate...at time of his death he was the senior partner and founder of the house of Snider, Lathrop & Nevitte, one of the largest Dry Goods establishments in Savannah; was President of the German Friendly Society, and first Vice President of the Port Society; member of Methodist Episcopal Church for 30 years.

Mar. 31, 1852

Died at Buena Vista, Marion county, Ga., on the 20th March, 1852, MRS. JULIA, wife of MR. GEORGE BROWN, and daughter of COL. NATHANIEL H. and MRS. REBECCA W. RAINES, of Talbotton, Ga. She had attained 22nd year of her age on the 24th of January last. Puerperal fever, assuming at length the typhoid type, bore her away from earthly life (with eulogy).

Died in Albany, Baker county, of a dropsical affection, after a long and very serious attack of Scarlatina, on the morning of the 3rd ult., at half-past 4 o'clock, MARTHA ANNA W., youngest daughter of CAPT. CALEB W. and JANE G. REMBERT, formerly of South Carolina, in her 7th year.

Also, at the same place, on the morning of the 26th inst., at 7 o'clock, of Phthisis Pulmonalis, after an affliction of nearly two years, MRS. ELIZABETH M. SCOTT, consort of DR. HENRY A. SCOTT, and oldest daughter of CAPT. CALEB W. and JANE G. ERMBERT, in her 20th year (with eulogy). (Citizen please copy)

Died in this city, on Tuesday, 23d inst., ROBERT FYFE, aged 18 months and 23 days, son of HUGH McLEAN.

Departed this life on Tuesday, 16th inst., after a few days painful illness, in Macon county, Ga., MRS. LAVINIA A. COOK, consort of DR. JOHN R. COOK, in the 36th year of her age; leaves husband and five little children; member of Methodist Episcopal Church.

Died in Eatonton, on the 25th inst., EMMA C., eldest daughter of DR. J.G. and MARTHA GIBSON, aged 2 years 8 months and 21 days. (South Carolinian, Columbia, please copy).

MR. CHARLES COTTON died in this city on the 25th inst. in the 59th year of his age; a native of New York, but had resided in Macon since 1825, and for the greater part of that time, was a partner in the mercantile firm of Rea & Cotton.

Apr. 7, 1852

Died in this city, at the Floyd House, on Saturday night last, DR. G.W. BISHOP, aged about 26 years, of Patrick county, Va., but for many years a resident of Charlottesville, in the same State. Dr. B. came to this city in November last, laboring under

(Apr. 7, cont'd) - a severe attack of Bronchitis, which terminated his life; interred in Rose Hill Cemetery on Sunday afternoon.

Died in Thomaston, Upson county, on the 28th ult., SAMUEL HICKS, aged about 60 years; a native of Augusta, Ga., for many years a resident of Columbia and Upson counties.

Died in LaGrange, on the evening of the 27th ultimo, in the 20th year of her age, MRS. MARY HAWKINS MORGAN, wife of MR. ROBERT J. MORGAN, and daughter of the late DR. ANDREW and MRS. CAROLINE M. BATTLE.

Apr. 14, 1852

Died in this city, on the 9th inst., of consumption, at the residence of her uncle, Col. J.D. Watkins, MISS ANGELINA G. PRENTISS, daughter of WILLIAM and ANGELINA PRENTISS, of the city of New York, aged 13 years 11 months.

Died on the 30th ult., at the residence of his father, in Houston county, SAMUEL L. RUMPH, of Consumption, aged 33 years.

Apr. 21, 1852

Died in Glennville, Ala., April 10th, 1852, MRS. MARY ANN BLOUNT, in the 23rd year of her age. She was born in Gadsden county, Florida, and taised in Decatur county, Georgia; leaves a husband and three children and numerous friends in Gadsden county, Florida, Decatur, Georgia, Leon county, Texas, and Barbour, Ala. (Florida papers please copy).

Died at his residence, near Hawkinsville, on the 30th ult., DR. WILLIAM MARTIN FRASER, aged 34 years; native of Liberty county, Ga., but having lost his parents at a very early age, he was sent to Scotland, where he received a most thorough education; graduate of Queen's College, at Aberdeen, and of the Medical College, and of the Royal College of Surgeons, at Edinburgh; commenced the practice of his profession at Hawkinsville in 1844.

A gentleman from Eatonton has brought us the melancholy intelligence of the death of HON. JAMES A MERIWETHER, at his residence in that place, on Sunday morning, the 18th inst., of Typhoid Fever.

Apr. 28, 1852

Died in Jones county, on the 16th inst., of inflammation of the brain, ROBERT HARDEMAN, youngest child of WILEY and DELILAH FRANKS, aged 8 years and 10 months (with eulogy) Columbus papers please copy)

Tribute of respect by Weston Lodge, No. 80 (Stewart County, April 15, 1852) - on death of FRANCIS SCOTT.

May 5, 1852

Died at his residence in Columbus, on the 13th inst., MR. JAMES T. RIVES, aged 37 years 3 months and 13 days.

Died in Lee county, Ga., on the 16th ult., MRS. MARY A. JACKSON, consort of COL. ZADOC JACKSON, and daughter of JOHN JOHNSTON, formerly of Troup county.

May 12, 1852

Died in this city, on the 5th inst., MAJ. JAMES SMITH, aged about 66 years, formerly a resident of Clinton - but for several years past of this city.

May 19, 1852

Died in this city, on Monday, the 10th inst., MRS. ANN McDOWN, a native of the county of Cavan, Ireland, but for many years a resident of this place, aged 58 years.

Died at his residence in Louisville, Jefferson county, Ga. May 5th, ROBERT NESBITT, ESQ., aged 35 years and 5 days, after a protracted illness of 8 weeks; member of Odd Fellows (with eulogy) (Savannah Republican and Augusta Constitutionalist will copy)

Died, on the 8th inst., at the Brownwood Institute, BENJAMIN W. BRYAN, son of NANCY and BENJAMIN BRYAN, of Houston county, Ga., in the 17th year of his age (with eulogy and tribute)

May 26, 1852

Died at the residence of her father, PETER RANDLE, ESQ. near Forsyth, on the 17th of May, MARY ANGELINA, wife of JAMES EGBERT THOMPSON, in the 22nd year of her age; member of the Baptist Church; married about six years (with eulogy)

Died in Pulaski county, on the 12th inst., MARY EDITH, youngest daughter of EDWARD A. BURCH, aged 1 year 4 months.

June 2, 1852

Died in Columbus, on Tuesday, 18th ult., LAURA WINSHIP, second daughter of JOHN R. and ELIZA J. STURGIS, aged 5 years 4 months 28 days.

Died in this city, on the 28th ult., MR. MICHAEL CUNNIAN.

June 9, 1852

Tribute of respect by St. Patrick's Lodge, No. 52 (May 21st, 1852) - on death of ROBERT NESBIT.

Died in Talbot county, Ga., on the 5th of February, 1852, MR. JAMES B. HOLCOMBE, after a lingering bronchial affection of three years; had resided for a number of years in Monroe county, and had only been in Talbot about one year before his death...interred with Masonic honors by Olive Lodge in Talbotton...about 5 months before his death, he connected with the Methodist Episcopal Church (with eulogy)

June 16, 1852

Died in this city, on Monday the 14th inst., of Typhoid Fever, MR. WILLIAM M. CHERRY, in the 23rd year of his age; native of Mecklenburg county, North Carolina.

Died in Lee county, on Tuesday, the 8th inst., MR. PEYTON T. SMITH, formerly of Putnam county, leaving a wife and two children. (Recorder and Federal Union will copy)

Tribute of respect by Wornam Lodge No. 116 (Clinton, Jones county, Ga., June 12, 1852) - on death of HENRY M. TODD.

June 30, 1852

Died in Jones county, on the morning of the 9th inst., HENRY M. TODD, in the 25th year of his age. He was interred by the brethren of Wornam Lodge, of which he was a member, on the 10th inst., with Masonic Honors.

Died in Jasper county, on the 24th inst., after a protracted illness of several months, MRS. ANN T. KEENE, aged about 44 years.

June 30, 1852

Died in East Macon, on the 27th inst., MR. LESLIE L. COATES, aged 25 years. (Milledgeville papers please copy)

Died in Laurens county, on the 20th inst., MRS. MARY JANE BLACKSHEAR, wife of the HON. EDWARD JEFFERSON BLACKSHEAR, in the 27th year of her age; was daughter of COL. JAS. J. and MARTHA PITMAN, of Marianna, Fla., and was married in Dec. 1846; leaves behind a husband and four little children, father and mother, brothers and sisters (with eulogy)

The RIGHT REVEREND CHRISTOPHER EDWARDS GADSDEN, D.D. of the Protestant Episcopal Church and Bishop of the Diocese of South Carolina, died at his residence in this city, yesterday morning, at age 68; native of this city and grandson of GEN. CHRISTOPHER GADSDEN, a distinguished worthy of the revolution; graduate of Yale College; ordained Deacon of July 25, 1807, by Bishop Moore of New York; and Priest in April 1810, by Bishop Madison, of Virginia; in Jan. 1808 he was elected Rector of Biggin Church, in Parish of St. John's, Berkley, and resigned 2 Feb. 1810 to enter duties of Assistant Minister of St. Phillips Church, in this city, to which office he was chosen 21 Dec. 1809; on 17 July 1814 was chosen Rector of St. Phillips, as the successor of Rev. James Dewar Simons, and continued to officiate there until his death; in 1840 was elected Bishop of this Diocese, as successor of Rt. Rev. Nathaniel Bowen, D.D. and was consecrated in Trinity Church, Boston, on Sunday, June 21, 1840. (Charleston Courier, 25 inst)

Learn from the New York Courier of Tuesday, that on Friday evening last, at Stamford, Connecticut, MRS. NATHANIEL B. WEED, wishing to have a tooth extracted, requested that chloroform be administered. The dentist complied with her desire, but she had hardly commenced initiating the fumes, when she sank back upon the sofa and expired. Mr. Weed is a wealthy merchant of New York, the brother and partner of H.D. Weed of Savannah, and the brother of E.B. Weed of Macon.

July 7, 1852

Died at Fort Valley, on Tuesday, the 26th ult., MARY ANGELINA, youngest daughter of JUDSON A. and ELIZA A. KENDRICK, aged 7 months.

Notice of the death of HENRY CLAY in Washington City, on Tuesday the 28th ult., at 11¼ o'clock, A.M.

July 14, 1852

Died in Starkville, Lee Co., on the 3rd inst. GEORGE C. TICKNOR, formerly of Jones Co.

Died at his residence, in Bladen county, North Carolina, after a short but painful illness, on the 8th day of June last, MR. JOHN D. SALTAR; leaves two brothers in the State of Georgia. (Georgia papers copy).

Died in Dublin, Laurens county, on the 21st ult., JEREMIAH H. YOPP, ESQ. He was for more than 30 years a citizen of Dublin.

Died in the same village, on the 29th ult., MR. JOHN LOWTHER. He was raised in this place and spent his life in the mercantile business; leaves a widow and several children.

July 21, 1852

Died of Congestive Fever, on Saturday, June 26th, at her residence in Crawford county, MRS. NANCY CLEVELAND, consort of the REV. W.C. CLEVELAND, aged 49 years 3 months and 29 days.

July 21, 1852

Died in Howard, Steuben Co., NY, on the 6th ult., REV. LEVI ROSE, aged about 49 years.

Washington, July 16, ROGER JONES, Adjutant General of the US Army, died last evening in this city. He was appointed Second Lieutenant of Marines, Jan. 26, 1809; Colonel, March 7, 1825; and Major General by Brevet, May 30, 1848. Gen. Jones was a native of Virginia.

July 28, 1852

Died in New Haven, Conn., July 13th, of Typhoid Fever, MRS. LOUISA G. FITCH, wife of LEWIS FITCH, formerly, for many years a resident of this city. (with eulogy)

Died, at the residence of his father, in Crawford county, on Saturday, the 3d inst., of Typhoid Fever, DAMUEL CORBIN, JR., in the 18th year of his age (with eulogy)

JOHN McKINLEY, one of the Associate Justices of the Supreme Court of the United States, died on the 19th inst., at his residence in Louisville, Kentucky, of apoplexy; a native of Virginia.

Letter signed by J. McKinstry, Brevet Major, U.S.A. - and headed San Diego (California) June 18, 1852 - The body of your lamented friend, COL. CRAIG, has been found, and interred at the "Almo Mucho" on the desert lying between Vallencia and the Colorado river. His effects will be sent to my care, subject to the order of his family. His murderers, Corporal Hays and Private Condon, of D Company, Indiana Infantry, were apprehended by the Indians at Temacula on Sunday last, and are now in confinement, heavily ironed, at the mission of San Diego...Colonel Craig, on the morning of the 16th instant, when about one third of the way across the desert from this side, met two deserters from Camp Yuma, trying to make their way into the settlements...Colonel Craig was fired upon within a few feet of the deserters; received the shot in the front and lower part of his body; did not speak and expired in about ten minutes. He was buried on the desert at a place called the "Alamo Wells".

Aug. 4, 1852

Died of Consumption, on the 24th ult., at her residence in Upson county, Ga., M S. MATILDA T. PERRIMAN, aged 45 years and 3 months; member of Baptist Church for 24 years; leaves six children (with eulogy)

Died on Sunday morning, July 25th, in Scottsboro, at the residence of Mrs. Catherine Fitzgerald, MISS SYSIGAMBIS MANGUM, aged 18 years; was a resident of Glynn county, but since January had been a pupil in Chalmers Institute; member of Methodist Church.

The Savannah Republican of 28th ult. reports the sudden death in that city, yesterday, of GEO. GLEN, ESQ. He underwent great fatigue at the beginning of the last week in removing his books, records &c., from his former office in the Court House, to the new Custom House, and went home with a chill and fever yesterday week, since which time he has been confined to his house. At time of his death, he was Clerk of the Supreme Court of US; was 70 years and 4 months old at death.

Aug. 11, 1852

The HON. ROBERT RANTOUL, Representative from Massachusetts, died to-day in Washington, of erysipelas (dateline Baltimore, Aug. 8)

Aug. 18, 1852

Died at his residence in Marion county, on Saturday the 3d ult., WILLIAM POWELL, in the 75th year of his age; represented the county in the State Legislature several times.

Died at his residence in Talbot county, on the 31st July last, CHARLES ALLEN, in the 73rd year of his age; member of the Methodist Episcopal Church, South.

Died in this city on the 11th inst., MR. THOMAS F. NEWTON, a native of the State of Maryland, but for last 16 years a resident of this city.

Died at the residence of Alexander Melrose, on the 9th inst., ISABELLA, only daughter of GENL. H. and R.J. McLEOD, aged 1 year and 8 months.

Died in Barnesville, on the 6th inst., of Typhoid Fever, MRS. EMILY C., wife of CHS. A NUTTING, and daughter of JORDAN COMPTON, ESQ., of Jasper County, aged 26 years.

Died near Milledgeville, on the 9th inst., MRS. FRANCES HUSON, aged 82 years. Known as a Hotelkeeper in Milledgeville, for many years past.

The widow of GENERAL TAYLOR died on the 14th inst., at East Pascagoula, Mississippi.

Sep. 1, 1852

Died at Brothersville, Richmond county, on the 23d inst., MRS. ELIZA J. BARNES, consort of WM. E. BARNES, formerly of this place.

DR. JOSEPH M. BOGGS, a young physician of Savannah, committed suicide in that city, on the evening of the 24th inst., by taking prussic acid.

Sep. 8, 1852

Bloody retribution - MARK SULLIVAN, who murdered MR. JORDAN in Washington county, Alabama, a few years ago, for which he was sentenced to the penitentiary, returned home a short time since, and was shot, one day last week, by a son of Jordan, a lad of 12 or 15 years of age. Sullivan died the nest day; before he was buried one of his sons was thrown from his horse and instantly killed. We understand that Sullivan attempted to shoot young Jordan first, but his gun missed fire, and before he could make the second attempt, Jordan shot him (Sav. News).

Death of Georgians in California - Among the deaths in Sacramento Valley, we note the following: Died suddenly on the 22d July, at Hawkins' bar, Toulomne River, COL. THOMAS MYERS, late of Macon county, Ga. Among the interments at San Francisco, we notice the name of MR. L.D. BEEL, of Georgia, aged 30 years, buried July 11th, and the name of JESSE WALTHINGHAM, of Georgia, aged 38 years, buried July 13th.

Sep. 15, 1852

Died at his residence, in Macon county, on the 9th inst., MR. URIAH SLAPPEY, aged 57 years.

Died in New York, a few days since, MR. LAIRD H. WILEY, a resident of Houston, and formerly of Bibb county.

Died on the 13th inst. MRS. MARY H., wife of WILLIAM C. BANDY, and daughter of PLINEY SHEFFIELD, ESQ., of Thomas county, aged 23 years; leaves a husband and a helpless infant.
(Savannah Republican and Georgian will please copy)

Sep. 15, 1852

   HON. EDWARD GILBERT, ex-member of Congress from California, recently
   killed in a duel at Sacremento, by GEN. DENVERS, was the senior
   editor of the Alta California, and a native of New York; formerly
   an officer in Col. Stevenson's regiment. The duel grew out of
   a political discussion.

Sep. 22, 1852

   Died in this city, on the 16th inst., MISS MARTHA T. WILLIAMS,
   eldest daughter of REUBEN WILLIAMS, ESQ. of Lee County, Georgia,
   in the 19th year of her age. Just two months previously, Miss
   W. had graduated at the Wesleyan Female College. (with short eulogy)

   Tribute of respect by Twiggs Lodge, No. 164 of Free and Accepted
   Masons (Sept. 17, 1852) - on death of DR. T.J. JOHNSON, who came
   to his death by being accidentally thrown from his horse.

Sep. 29, 1852

   Died in Brooklyn, NY, on the 2d inst., at the residence of Mr.
   William Prentiss, her son-in-law, MRS. VIRGINIA HUNT, aged 60
   years; for last two years a resident of Macon.

   Died at the residence of Mr. Robert A. Allen, near Augusta, on
   Sunday 26th inst., MR. BENJAMIN B. HOPKINS, aged 76 years, formerly
   a citizen of Macon (obituary next week).

   Died at Marietta, on Friday the 24th inst., FREDERICK R. TARVER,
   ESQ. of Twiggs county, on the 24th year of his age.

   Died, on the morning of the first September, Surgeon DANIEL C.
   McLEOD, of the US Navy, who had been in charge of the Naval
   Hospital on this Station, since 1st of May last; born in New York
   and entered the US Navy in 1832 having been appointed from the
   State of Georgia, in which he then resided; received commission
   as Surgeon in 1841; interred in Burial Ground attached to US
   Naval Hospital (dated US Navy Yard, Pensacola, Sep. 2, 1852) -
   (with long eulogy)

   The Palmetto State Banner reports the death of COL. JOHN SINGLETON -
   had returned home a few days since, leaving his family in Virginia,
   when he was attacked suddenly with congestive fever, which terminated his useful life yesterday.

   Tribute of respect by Mount Hope Lodge, No. 9 (Sep. 9, 1852) -
   on death of HENRY TILLMAN.

Oct. 6, 1852

   Died at Buena Vista, Ga., on 18th September, ANN ELIZA, aged 16
   months, daughter of GEORGE W. and SARAH ANN McDUFFIE.

   Columbus Times of 29th ult. reports the death of GENERAL S.
   ARMSTRONG BAILEY. He died suddenly at his residence in the vicinity of this city, on Sunday, the 26th inst., at half past eleven
   o'clock; for many years a resident of this city; member of the bar;
   Agent of the Bank of Charleston in this city, and general superintendent of its interests in the surrounding country - in Georgia
   and Alabama; leaves a large family.

Oct. 13, 1852

   Died in Forsyth, on Tuesday evening, the 5th inst., MARY OLIVIA,
   aged 10 months and 15 days - only daughter of MR. and MRS. O. MORSE.

   HON. E.O. HANNEGAN, who killed his brother-in-law, the gallant CAPT.
   DUNCAN, in a drunken brawl some time since, is now claer from all
   legal proceedings. His case was brought before the Fountain (Ind.)
   Circuit Court, but the Grand Jury failed to find an indictment.

Oct. 20, 1852

　　Tribute of respect by Burns Lodge, No. 56 F.A.M. (Lanier, Ga., Oct. 9th, 1852) - on death of WILLIAM ANSLEY, who departed this life at the residence of his brother, in Upson county, on the 5th inst.; a member of this Lodge since its formation in 1847.

Oct. 27, 1852

　　Died at Starkville, Lee county, Ga., on the 19th inst., DR. JOHN C. CALHOUN, in the 25th year of his age; the eldest son of DR. E.N. and MRS. LUCY B. CALHOUN of Decatur, Gal; victim of Typhoid Fever.

　　Tribute of respect by Union Lodge, No. 27 (Thomaston, Ga., Oct. 9, 1852) - on death of JOHN W. LOWE, who departed this life on the 8th inst., aged 23 years and 10 days.

Nov. 10, 1852

　　Died in this city, on the 9th inst., MR. ALFRED C. MOREHOUSE, aged 35 years, a native of Syracuse, NY, but for last 12 years a resident of this city; at time of death was a Representative from county of Bibb in the Georgia Legislature.

　　Died in Gordon, on the 6th inst., MR. JAMES M. FOLSOM, aged about 41 years; his remains brought to this city and interred with honors of Masonry, by Macon Lodge No. 5, and a portion of Camel Lodge No. 140, (to which he belonged) in the Masonic burial lot in Rose Hill Cemetery; a native of New Hampshire, but for several years a resident of Savannah, and formerly Master of Solomon's Lodge, No. 1 of that city, and Senior Warden of the Grand Lodge of Georgia.

　　Died in Athens, on the 12th ult., LAURA ROOTES, youngest child of GOV. and MRS. HOWELL COBB, aged 10 months and 11 days.

　　Died in Oglethorpe, on the 8th inst., MR. TIMOTHY DICKINSON, formerly a resident of this city.

Nov. 17, 1852

　　Died in Thomaston, Upson county, on Thursday, 28th October, MRS. EPHATA C., wife of WILLIAM D. WOODSON, and daughter of the late SAMUEL BOWDRE, of Columbia county, Ga.; member of Methodist Episcopal Church (with eulogy).

　　Died on Sunday, 7th inst., at Springfield, Mass., MR. LEWIS W. BABCOCK, aged 28 years, for several years a resident of this city.

Nov. 24, 1852

　　Tribute of respect by Carmel Lodge, No. 150 (Irwinton, Wilkinson county, Ga. Nov. 16th, 1852) - on death of JAMES M. FOLSOM.

　　The HON. DAVID HENSHAW, formerly Secretary of the Navy, died at his residence at Leicester, Mass., on Thursday.

Dec. 1, 1852

　　Died in Crawford county, on the 14th inst., MAJ. RICHARD W. ELLIS, aged nearly 70 years. Maj. Ellis removed from Baldwin to this city soon after its settlement, where he resided until within a few years past; held office of Magistrate, County Surveyor. (with short eulogy)

Dec. 8, 1852

　　Died in Houston county, on the 21st November, at a quarter past 1 o'clock, MR. JAS. GATES. Mr. G. was born in Newbury District, South Carolina 15 Dec. 1804; moved to this State and was a resident

(Dec. 8, cont'd) - of Jones county for a number of years, when he removed to Bibb county, where after a few years residence, he was elected Tax Collector, and subsequently Sheriff of the county, finally removed to Houston county; member of Missionary Baptist Church for 8 years and a Deacon for several years (with eulogy)

Died on Saturday afternoon, Nov. 20th, at the residence of his uncle, Benj. Bryan, in Houston co., JOSEPH M. BRYAN, son of BLACKSHEAR and TEMPERANCE BRYAN, deceased, in the 25th year of his age (with long eulogy)

Died, in Houston county, on the 29th ult., MRS. MARY JOINER, consort of Capt. MEREDITH JOINER, in the 69th year of her age; native of NC, and her husband was among the pioneer settlers of this county, having moved to the place where she died in 1818; consostent member of church for 54 years (with eulogy).

The HON. JOHN W. CROCKET died at Memphis, Tenn., of pneumonia, on the night of the 24th inst.

Dec. 15, 1852

Died in Dooly county, on the 27th November, JAMES WILLIAM, infant son of JAMES M. and ARTEMESIA E. JONES, aged 16 months and 17 days.

Died in Jones county, Ga., on the 9th Dec. 1852, MRS. MARY CARD, in the 71st year of her age, of protracted illness, which she bore for four years preceding her death; exemplary member of Baptist Church for nearly 40 years; leaves an aged husband, four children, and number of grand-children.

Died at his residence in Augusta, on the 2d inst., after a short illness of four days, CAPT. L.N. MITCHELL, formerly of Savannah.

Died on Saturday, the 12th inst., in Vineville, MARTHA, wife of O.B. RICE, in the 31st year of her age.

Died on Saturday night, about 5231ve o'clock, JOHN O'KEEFE who was killed in front of the Washington Hall, by JOHN T. BOYD, a journeyman saddler in the employ of Wm. T. Mix & Co.; a native of Ireland; a school teacher.

Tribute of respect by members of First Class of US Corps of Cadets, held on evening of Nov. 24th, 1852 - on death of HENRY T. LATHAM, who departed this life at his home in Campbelltown, on the 14th inst.

Dec. 22, 1852

Died at Pilatka, Florida, on the 7th inst., of Consumption, MR. PETER C. MITCHELL, (son of LEWIS MITCHELL) of this city, aged about 33 years and 5 months; body will be received and be buried with Masonic honors by Macon Lodge, No. 5, on Thursday.

Dec. 29, 1852

The death of HORATIO GREENOUGH, the sculptor, occurred on Saturday, after a long and painful attack of brain fever; born in Boston 1805 and graduated at Harvard University, at Cambridge, in 1825; his principal productions include the collossal statue of Washington in the Capitol, the Chanting Cherubs, executed in 1828 for Mr. Fenemore Cooper, the Medora finished in 1831 for Mr. Gilmore of Baltimore, the Rescue and busts of John Quincy Adams and Josiah Quincy.

Jan. 5, 1853

HON. WILLIAM TAYLOR, Judge of the Superior Courts of the South-Western Circuit, died on the 24th ult., at the residence of his brother-in-law, Maj. L.S. Brookin, about sixteen miles West of

(Jan. 5, cont'd) - Newton, in Baker county, and that MAJ. BROOKIN died on the following day. Their deaths are attributed to diseased Oysters, which they partook at Newton.

Jan. 12, 1853

Died in this city, on the 2d inst., GEN. JOSEPH BENNETT, aged about 58 years; native of New York, and one of the first settlers of this city.

Died in this city, on the 7th instant, FRANCIS ALEXANDER MENARD, aged 52 years, a native of France, but for many years a resident of Macon.

Tribute of respect by members of the Bar at Cuthbert Dec. 28, 1852- on death of HON. WILLIAM TAYLOR, presiding Judge of the South- Western Circuit; attacked by Cholera Morbus, of which he died on the evening of the 24th inst., in the 42d year of his age.

Death of SAMUEL RAY, ESQ. occurred in this city on Thursday morning, the 6th inst.; native of North Carolina but a resident of this city for many years; suffered severely from hemmorage of the lungs; for last seven years was connected with the Georgia Telegraph, as Editor and Proprietor; a zealous Democrat and a Southern Rights man (with long eulogy).

COM. CHARLES W. MORGAN died at Washington on Wednesday, where he had lately assumed command of the Navy Yard, succeeding Commodore Ballard; his age was not far from 60 years; was twice married; first wife was a MISS REED, of South Carolina; the second he married abroad, and she survives him; he died on the day following that on which the resolution was offered by Mr. Hale, of New Hampshire, in the US Senate, to enquire into his conduct, in certain particulars, as Commodore of the Mediterranean squadron.

The Boston papers of Jan. 1 contain communications of the death of their excellent citizen, AMOS LAWRENCE, ESQ.; born in Groton, Mass. in 1776; engaged in business in Boston since 1806; of late years was senior partner of the firm A. & A. Lawrence & Co.

Jan. 19, 1853

Died in Wilkinson county, on the 2d inst. KELLY GLOVER, ESQ., aged about 61 years. Also, his wife, ELIZABETH GLOVER, on the 1st inst., aged about 65 years.

The HON. CHARLES H. ATHERTON, father of SENATOR ATHERTON, died at Amherst on Saturday.

EX-GOVERNOR CABELL, of Virginia, father of the HON. E.C. CABELL, of Florida, died at Richmond, Jan. 13, 1853.

Jan. 26, 1853

Died in Athens, on the 24th inst., of Pneumonia, THOMAS B. LAMAR, son of MRS. B.B. LAMAR, of Vineville, in the 20th year of his age. The funeral will take place this morning, at 10 o'clock, at the residence of Mrs. Lamar.

Feb. 2, 1853

Died in Monroe county, on the 19th January, MRS. PHEBE, consort of FREDERICK CROWDER, in the 58th year of her age, after a painful and protracted illness of nearly two years; member of Baptist Church for 34 years; leaves husband and children.

Died in Jones county, on the 8th of January, of Paralysis, ALEXANDER J. HUNT, aged about 46 years.

Feb. 2, 1853

Died in this city, on the 12th of January, in her 48th year, MRS. NARCISSA ARNOLD, wife of PETER ARNOLD; member of the Baptist Church; leaves husband and children.

Feb. 9, 1853

Died, in Twiggs county, on the 1st inst., RICHARD DESHAZO, in the 52d year of his age.

HON. NATHAN C. SAYRE died at his residence in Sparta, on Saturday last, of disease of the heart; for several years a member of the Legislature, and for one term, Judge of the Superior Courts of the Northwestern Circuit.

Tribute of respect at Demosthenian Hall, Athens, Jan. 24, 1853 - on death of THOMAS B.J. LAMAR.

Feb. 16, 1853

Died on Wednesday the 9th inst., in this city, MR. WILEY V. WAGNON, in the 42d year of his age; a resident of Macon for 16 years.

Died, in Hawkinsville, Ga., on the 8th of February, GEORGE McMULLIN, of Typhoid Pneumonia.

Died in Savannah, on the morning of the 10th inst., KATE SEYMOUR, only daughter of COL. ISAAC G. and MRS. C.E. SEYMOUR, aged 18 years.

Feb. 23, 1853

Died in the vicinity of Macon, on the 20th inst., of Pleurisy, ELEAZAR McCALL, aged about 56 years. He was located at Fort Hawkins before the city of Macon was laid out, and has been a resident of the city or vicinity since 1820; first Judtice of the Peace elected in East Macon District, when the county was organised; interred on 21st at the Burial Ground on Ft. Hill, by Macon Lodge, No. 5 of which he was Senior Warden when it was organised in 1824, and its Master in 1828.

March 2, 1853

Died on the 5th ult., in Jones county, (at the residence of her son, THOMAS S. HUMPHRIES) NANCY HUMPHRIES, in the 81st year of her age. (City, Milledgeville and Montgomery papers copy).

Mar. 9, 1853

Died in Houston county, on the 26th inst., of Inflammation of the Tongue, MR. THOMAS HARDISON, aged about 22 years.

Mar. 16, 1853

Died in Hawkinsville, on the 28th of February last, of Typhoid Pneumonia, JAMES AUGUSTUS HOBBS, son of REV. BERRY HOBBS, in the 20th year of his age (with eulogy).

Tribute of respect by Morning Star Lodge, No. 27, A.F.M. (Thomaston, Ga., March 4th, 1853) - on death of SAMUEL CARRAWAY.

Mar. 23, 1853

Died in this city, on the evening of the 15th inst., WILLIAM MONTGOMERY, youngest child of DR. JAMES M. GREEN, aged 19 months.

Died in Dale county, Ala., of the Typhoid Pneumonia, on the 3d inst., MR. ANTHONY M. THOMPSON, late of Houston county, Ga. (Columbus and Augusta papers please copy).

Mar. 23, 1853

WILLARD B. BOYNTON, second son of WILLARD and ROBY BOYNTON, died at their residence in Lumpkin, Stewart county, Ga., on the 8th inst., in the 22d year of his age; suffered for last two years from a wasting pulmonary disease (long eulogy).

Augusta Chronicle & Sentinel, 15th inst. reports that a murder was committed about 1 o'clock yesterday, near the Quaker Springs in this county, on the Washington road, about seven miles above the city, by FRANCIS TOMPKINS on the person of GAMIL FLANEGAN. Tompkins rode up to the door with his gun, alighted and shot him through the head, then made his escape.

Philadelphia papers report the death of DR. WM. E. HORNER, Professor of Anatomy in the University of Pennsylvania; a native of Virginia; for more than thirty years connected with the chair of Anatomy at University of Pennsylvania.

Mar. 30, 1853

Died in this city, on the 12th inst., PHILO EMMA, first and only child of JNO. S. and ELIZABETH ANN LIVINGSTON, aged 6 months and 12 days.

Died at Naples, on the 11th of February last, in the 16th year of her age, ANNE ELIZABETH, the youngest daughter of the HON. GEORGE W. CRAWFORD, of Bel-Air, Ga.

Apr. 6, 1853

Distressing railroad accident and loss of life - dateline Cumberland March 28 - an accident on the Baltimore and Ohio railroad yesterday. Following were killed: DANIEL HOLT, of the firm of Holt & Maltby, Baltimore; AURELIUS SALIE supposed to be from South Carolina; LEWIS DELINE, a French emigrant returning home from California; RICHARD CLAYTON, of Wellsville, Virginia; a small step-son of ROBERT MURRAY; a child of MR. GIESE, of St. Louis. (story gives details of the railroad accident)

Tribute of respect by Georgia Military Institute March 28, 1853 - on death of Cadet F.B. HELVENSTEIN, who departed this life on the 26th inst.

Apr. 13, 1853

Notice of the death of MRS. FILLMORE, wife of ex-PRESIDENT.

From the Detroit Advertiser comes a notice of the death of MRS. CASS, daughter of DR. JOSEPH SPENCER, of Conn., who removed to Lausingburg, NY, in 1786, at which place she was born Sept. 27, 1788; five years afterwards removed to Wood County, Virginia, where she resided until she was married to GENERAL CASS in 1806; after a residence of about 8 years in Muskingum county, Ohio, she came to reside in Michigan, then a territory, over which Gen. Cass had been appointed Governor in 1815; from then until 1832 resided there, when she left to make her residence in Washington with her husband, who had been appointed Secretary of War, under Gen. Jackson; in 1836 she accompanied Gen. Cass to Paris, where he served as Minister to France, returning to this city in advance of him in 1841; Gen. Cass' family now occupies three daughters and one son, Lewis Cass, Jr., US Charge at Rome. Two of the daughters are married and reside at Detroit.

Apr. 20, 1853

Died in Greensboro, NC on Sunday morning, the 3d inst., GENERAL JOHN M. LOGAN, aged about 54 years; native of Raphoe, county Donegal, Ireland, and emigrated to this country about thirty years ago, during which time he resided in county of Guilford; for last

(Apr. 20, cont'd) - 16 years was clerk of the county court; predisposed to dropsy of the chest, with an attack of which he lingered some two months before his decease; buried Monday afternoon with Masonic honors (from the <u>Patriot</u>) a brother of our fellow-citizen, GEO. M. LOGAN, ESQ.

Apr. 27, 1853

Died in California, on 29th January last, BENJAMIN H. WARNER, grandson of the late B.B. HOPKINS, ESQ.

May 4, 1853

Tribute of respect by Thomaston Chapter, No. 29, R.A.M., 19th of April, 1853 - on death of SAMUEL CARRAWAY.

May 11, 1853

Died in Vineville, on the 30th ult., MRS. ELIZA F. BAILEY, wife of SAMUEL T. BAILEY, ESQ.

May 18, 1853

Died on Tuesday evening last, of apoplexy, CHARLES ROONEY, ESQ., of this city, in the 45th year of his age; leaves wife and five young children; his remains were yesterday followed to the grave by the largest concourse of citizens we have seen assembled in Marysville for a similar occasion; native of Georgia, and had resided in Macon and Columbus.
(From Marysville, Cal. Express)

Died in this city on the 13th inst., MR. WILLIAM SKELTON KING, aged about 35 years; native of Richmond, Va., but resided for several years in Charleston, SC, previous to his removal to this city in Feb. 1849; a Foreman of this office; printer; buried with military honors by Macon Volunteers, of which he was a member, on 14th instant. (Richmond paper please copy).

WILEY HOFFMAN, of Emanual county, was shot by his wife on Sunday evening, the 1st inst. (details in story).

May 25, 1853

MAJOR GEORGE L. TWIGGS, a prominent citizen of Augusta, Ga. (second son of GEN. JOHN TWIGGS, of Revolutionary memory, and brother of MAJOR GENERAL DAVID TWIGGS, of US Army) died at his summer residence, nine miles below that city, on the 16th inst., in the 64th year of his age.

From Savannah Republican comes notice of the death of P.B. CONNELLY, ESQ., who died very suddenly at his residence in Jefferson county, Ga., on the 17th inst., in the 51st year of his age (with eulogy).

June 1, 1853

Died at Griswoldville, Jones county, on the 21st inst., of the Measles, MR. JAMES SHELL, aged 35 years; known to the planters of Georgia as a travelling agent for the Cotton Gin Factory of S. Griswold, Esq.; buried in Clinton, with Masonic honors, by Wornam Lodge, No. 116, on 22d inst.

Died in Thomaston, Ga., on the 12th instant, MRS. SARAH, wife of SIMEON ROGERS, ESQ.

June 8, 1853

Died of Cholera Infantum, May 31, in New York city, at the residence of Mr. W.C. Richards, BLANCHE, only child of J.J. and S.M.H. RICHARDS, of this city, aged 3 years and 21 days.

June 8, 1853

Died in New York, on the 1st inst., CAPT. ALEXANDER SCOTT, aged about 40 years; native of Maryland, and had resided in this city for last 15 years; was appointed a Captain in the late war with Mexico, but was, by ill health, prevented from fulfilling the duties of that office; at the time of his death he was one of the proprietors of the Lanier House.

Wednesday morning early, the 1st inst., on the road to Marion, about two miles from this city, MARK SWEENY was murdered by negro runaway named John or Jack and belonging to Chas. E. Taylor, of Pulaski county (details in story).

The Savannah Reputlican announces the death of WILLIAM DEARING, ESQ., yesterday morning in that city, in the 68th year of his age; in feeble health for sometime, having been attacked with paralysis, and had removed to Savannah the past winter; highly esteemed in Athens, Augusta and Charleston; among the first, if not the first man in the State, to start a Cotton Factory; leaves a wife and several children, among the latter the Hon. Wm. E. Dearing, Mayor of Augusta; remains to be taken to Athens, Ga. for interment.

The Charleston Courier of the 12th reports a fatal railroad accident in which the Engineer ISAAC WINTERS and fireman SAMUEL WILLIS were killed. Another fireman W.F. SNEAD was severely injured and not anticipated to live...

The Griffin Union reports that a young lady, daughter of MR. BURTON WHITAKER, of Henry county, died suddenly, one day last week, from eating what she supposed to be "Angelica" and her sister by merely tasting it was so much affected that she did not recover for several days.

June 15, 1853

Died in Americus, (Ga.,) on Sunday evening, June 5th, ARTHUR DAVIS, infant son of ELIZA M. and REV. P.A. STROBEL, aged 13 days.

Notice of the death of C.E. TEFT, third and only surviving son of J.I. TEFT, of Savannah, in the 29th year of his age; his parents survive him.

June 22, 1853

Died in Eatonton, on the 3d inst., GEN. ROBERT BLEDSOE, in the 71st year of his age.

Died in Wilkinson county, on the 15th inst., MRS. SARAH P., consort of DR. JAS. HUMPHREYS, in the 23d year of her age.
(Savannah News please copy).

The Savannah Georgian of the 19th reports the death of REV. S.J. CASSELS, the Principal of Chatham Academy; a native of Liberty county in this State; graduated with high honor at Franklin College; soon after entered ministry of Presbyterian Church, having studied Theology under Dr. Waddell, President of Franklin College; a few years ago was compelled to give up preaching, by bronchitis, became a citizen of Savannah, and opened a school for the instruction of youth.

June 29, 1853

Died at Griswold, on the 25th inst., WALTER BONNER, infant son of R.W. and E.L. BONNER, aged 9 months and 16 days.

Death of THOMAS CATER JOHNSON, aged 11 years, son of FRANCIS S. and LUCIA JOHNSON, who died yesterday, from an accidental discharge of his own gun...(Clinton, June 26, 1853)

June 29, 1853

Murder - T. CUYLER, ESQ., was killed at Adairsville, Gordon county, on Saturday night last, by some person or persons, who are, as yet unknown. His death, it seems was caused by severe blows upon his head with stones, by which it was shockingly mangled; was an engineer upon several Georgia railroads; has left a wife (the daughter of DR. THOMAS HAMILTON, of Cass) and several children.

COL. A.C. CLEVELAND, formerly of Crawford, but for several years past a citizen of Marion county, was murdered at Poindexter on Wednesday last, by a man by name of JACOB MARTIN...(Oglethorpe Dem. June 4)

July 6, 1853

Died at Griswoldville, on Saturday the 25th inst., WALTER, infant son, and only child of R.W. and E.L. BONNER, aged 9 months and 16 days.

Tribute of respect by Fort Valley Lodge, No. 110 F.A.M., June 8th, 1853 - on death of THOMAS A. DODGE, who died on 28th May, 1853, in the 24th year of his age.

July 13, 1853

Died at Jeffersonville, June 23d, of Typhoid Fever, MISS SARAH T. DUPREE, daughter of DR. IRA E. DUPREE, aged 15.

Died in this city, on Saturday, the 2d inst., MRS. JULIA A. MOULTON, wife of THOS. MOULTON, formerly of New Haven, Conn.

Died in this city, July 2d, DR. ELLIOT I. SMITH, son of the late MAJ. JAMES SMITH, aged 27.

Died in Crawford county, MARY N.J. OSLIN, only child of DR. J.W. OSLIN, of Ft. Valley, Ga., aged 12 months and 2 days.

The National Intelligencer reports the death of DR. NATHANIEL CHAPMAN, eminent physician of Philadelphia, and for many years connected with the University of Pennsylvania - departed this life on Friday afternoon, about six o'clock, at his residence in Philadelphia; we believe in his 75th year.

July 20, 1853

The Savannah Republican a-nounces the death of MRS. HENRY R. JACKSON of that city on Saturday morning last, about 4 o'clock; leaves husband, four small children, a mother, and several brothers (with eulogy)

July 27, 1853

Died in Sumpter county, on the 23d June, MR. EZEKIEL SMITH, aged 53; for more than 20 years a resident of this city.

Died also on the 17th inst., in East Macon, JOHN S. SMITH, son of the above, aged 18 years.

Died near this city, on the 24th inst., MRS. SARAH HUGHES, aged 65 years.

Aug. 3, 1853

MR. RICHARD HENRY LEE, editor of the Cincinnati Daily Commercial, died at Cincinnati on Thursday the 21st inst. He was the direct descendant of his namesake, who signed the Declaration of Independence.

Aug. 10, 1853

Died at the Floyd House, in the city of Macon, on the evening of the 6th inst., N.G. SLAUGHTER, ESQ., of Marion county, Ga. He was taken with Diarrhea, on a visit to Brunswick, and had got this far on his return home, when he became so feeble as to be forced to stop. He lingered here ten days...

Died in Bienville Parish, near Minden, La., on the morning of the 9th ult., after a painful illness of six days, MRS. HEPSEY LEARY, wife of MAJ. CALVIN LEARY; born in Lenoir county, North Carolina on 20 Feb. 1811, where she was raised and married, and with her husband moved to Houston county, Ga., in early part of 1833, where they resided until winter of '49 and '50, when they removed to this Parish; left husband and seven children, viz.: four sons and three daughters, besides her aged parents.
(Bienville Parish, La., July 12, 1853)

Died at the residence of his father, in Randolph county, Ga., of Typhoid Dysentery, WILLIAM R.D. SMITH, son of JOEL E.J. and MARY J. SMITH, aged 1 year 9 months and 25 days.

MRS. CAROLINE M. CORBIN, consort of MR. SAMUEL P. CORBIN, departed this life July 23d, in the 52d year of her age; was born in Lexington District, South Carolina in 1801; for many years prior to death a resident of Crawford county, Ga.; member of Methodist Episcopal Church (with eulogy)
(Southern C. Advocate please copy)

Dreadful railroad accident. Philadelphia, August 3 - Last evening a train of ten platform cars on the Delaware and Belvilere Railroad, containing 200 workmen, returning from repairs on the Delaware Canal, ran off the track, about nine miles above Lambertville, killing ten men, and badly wounding twelve or fifteen others. The names of the killed are: MATTHEW MALONE, MICHAEL CAVENRY, JOHN IRVIN, PATRICK COFFIN, JEREMIAH LEARY, JOHN DIRGHAM, MICHAEL McGETRICK, THOMAS MORAN, BARTHOLOMEW SHEHAN, MICHAEL DALTON. The accident was caused by a cow jumping in front of the train, and five of the cars were carried down a steep embankment.

New Orleans, August 5 - COL. BLISS, son-in-law to GEN. TAYLOR, died this day at Pascagoula, of yellow fever. The deaths of this disease in this city in the last 24 hours 123.

Aug. 17, 1853

Died at Oglethorpe, on the 27th ult., DR. JAS. M. FOKES, about aged 31 years, formerly a resident of Jefferson County.

Died in Twiggs County, on the 27th inst., MRS. MARTHA H. MILLER, wife of SETH S. MILLER, in the 21st year of her age - eldest daughter of E.E. CROCKER, ESQ.

Died in Houston county, (at the residence of her husband, COL. E.A. WIMBERLY,) on 18th of July, MRS. ANN E. WIMBERLY, in the 29th year of her age; youngest daughter of the late JOEL DENSON, ESQ., of Twiggs county; leaves a husband and four little daughters (with eulogy)

Aug. 24, 1853

N.O. Daily Crescent announces the death of COL. BLISS, of the US Army, the son-in-law of late PRESIDENT ZACHARY TAYLOR; died of yellow fever, at East Pascagoula; was Assistant Adjutant General of U.S.A. during Mexican war and went with the army of occupation under General Taylor; participated in battles of Palo Alto, Resacca de la Palma Monterey and Buena Vista...(with eulogy)

Died in this city, on the 18th inst., MR. SAMUEL SMITH, aged 39 years - son of the late GEO. A. SMITH.

Aug. 24, 1853

Died on Sunday morning, August 14th, in Madison, Ga., of Cancerous affection of the throat, COL. STEWART FLOYD; a prominent member of the Georgia Legislature for many years; a lawyer; member of Methodist Episcopal Church; died in the 51st year of his age.

Accident on the State Road - A locomotive exploded at Moon's Station, about eight miles above Marietta, on the 18th inst., by which two firemen and the cunductor (MR. P.G. GREESON) were killed. The persons killed belonged to the Highwassee road...

Aug. 31, 1853

Died in Starksville, on Wednesday the 10th inst., DANIEL TILLMAN, in the 40th year of his age. The deceased from being a pennyless orphan boy amassed wealth...
(Savannah Republican will please copy)

Died in Sandersville, Ga. after a protracted illness of 29 days, of typhoid fever, MISS E.M. WARTHEN, aged 18 years 1 month and 22 days.

Died in Pulaski County, on the 24th inst., JAMES JARVIS, in the 42d year of his age.

Died at Barnesville, on the 29th inst., MR. DANIEL HIGHTOWER, a worthy and highly respectable citizen of Pike County.

Sep. 7, 1853

Died in East Macon, on the 1st inst., WILLIAM H.B. NELSON, infant son of J.B. and MARY J. NELSON, aged 9 months and 3 days.

Died in this city, on the 30th ult., BENJAMIN FORT, in the 50th year of his age.

Died in Eatonton, on the morning of 2d inst., MRS. DENNIS, wife of M. DENNIS, ESQ.

Sep. 14, 1853

Died in Stewart county, Sept. 4th, 1853, at the residence of Col. D. Stone, (her step-father,) MISS CEPHELONIA COVINGTON BROOKS, aged 14 years, daughter of the late COVINGTON BROOKS, deceased; had been a pupil in Masonic Female College, at Lumpkin (with long eulogy)

Died in Jackson county, Florida, on the 2d instant, CORA ELIZA, infant daughter of BENJAMIN G. and SUSAN E. LIDDON - aged 14 months and 24 days.

MRS. HARRIET R. DENNIS, consort of MICHAEL DENNIS, died in Eatonton, of billious inflammatory fever, on Friday, 2d September, at about two o'clock, A.M., in the 34th year of her age (with long eulogy)

The Washington Star relays a telegraphic dispatch from New York on Saturday from Pensacola, saying that COMMODORE JOSIAH TATNALL (the commander of the yard there) was dead; a native Georgian, son of JOSIAH TATNALL, formerly Governor of this State, and was at time of his death, about 55 or 60 years of age; was at the repulse of the British at Craney Island in 1812; and afterwards at battle of Bladensburgh; during late war with Mexico he was commander of "Musquito Fleet," under the walls of Vera Cruz...presume his remains will be brought to this city, and will find their lasting place in the family vault of the Tatnalls, at Bonaventure, four miles south of this city (Savannah Republican, 10th inst.)

21 Sep. 1853

Died in this city, on Sunday evening, the 18th instant, after a long and severe illness, MRS. WM. C. BURNHAM, aged 22 years and 2½ months.

Died at his residence in Americus, Sumter county, Ga., on the 13th inst., J. ANSON HOGUE, in the 12st year of his age.

Died in Columbus, on the 8th inst., MRS. LOUISA H. LAWTON, wife of ALBERT S. LAWTON.

Died in Mobile, of Yellow Fever, HOPE A. SLAUGHTER, formerly a resident of Jones and Crawford counties, Geo.

HON. ANGUS M. KING died at Americus, on the 5th inst., after a lingering illness, of consumption; for several years was Judge of the Superior Courts of the Flint Circuit.

Death of a GREAT man. The last Home Gazette publishes an Obituary notice of STERN SIMMONS, who died at Goshen, Lincoln county, Geo. It says, "that he was probably the largest man in the United States - a week before his death, he weighed 645 pounds...

HANSELL DILLARD, a colored man, well known as the keeper of the Confectionary on Jackson Street for many years, was killed in an engagement with a boy named Dock, belonging to MRS. GOULDING of this place, on Monday morning last...
(Athens Banner, 8th inst.)

Sep. 28, 1853

Died in this city, on the 24th inst., MR. JACOB I. TODD, aged about 75 years.

Died near this city, MRS. LYDIA RICHARDSON, wife of MR. JAMES RICHARDSON, aged about 53 years.

HON. GEORGE POINDEXTER, formerly US Senator from Mississippi, died in Jackson, in that State, on the 5th inst. He was the first delegate to Congress from Mississippi, and on her admission to the Union was immediately chosen as US Senator; likewise at one time Governor of the State; in early life he was a supporter of Gen. Jackson, but in later years acted with the Whigs.

Oct. 5, 1853

Among the victims from the epidemic in New Orleans are CHAS. D. MOREHEAD, brother of Ex-Gov. MOREHEAD, of Kentucky, his wife, son and daughter.

Died in Milledgeville, on the 20th inst., after a few days illness, MR. NICHOLAS W. SMITH, aged about 45 years.

Died in Meriwether Co., on 28th Sept., CHARLES Y. CALDWELL, ESQ. aged about 64 years; native of North Carolina; resided for several years in Monroe County - afterwards in Houston, and recently had taken up residence in Meriwether.

Macon Superior Court Sept. Term 1853 - offers tribute of respect on death of HON. ANGUS M. KING; a native of Georgia; of Scottish descent; in his 19th year he volunteered in the Creek War of 1814, and served a campaign under Gen. Flody; on his return, being poor, he taught a school, and in the meantime pursued a course of legal studies; when called to the Bar, he located at Clinton, and afterwards in Forsyth; in 1826 was candidate for Congress; was elected Judge of the Superior Courts of the Flint Circuit for two full Terms...

Oct. 12, 1853

Died in this city, on the evening of Sunday, the 9th inst., in the 29th year of his age, MR. LEWIS B. WOOD of the firm of E.L. Strohecker & Co.; druggist - a native of Fredericksburg, Va., but for three years and six months a resident of Macon (with eulogy)

Died in Houston county, at the house of Col. Phillip Lamar, on the 15th September, of bowel disease and teething, MARTHA VIRGINIA, aged 1 year 13 days, only daughter and child of SAMUEL D. and SARAH JANE FULLER.

COL. HENRY P. JONES died at one of his plantations in Laurens county, on Sunday morning last, of inflammation of the bowels, aged 65 years; born and reared in Burke county; his father was a sterling Whig of the Revolutnion, and Col. Jones was one of the wealthiest men in Georgia; leaves his large estate to six children
(Sav. Republican)

Oct. 19, 1853

Died of yellow fever, in Shieldsborough, Miss., Sept. 7th, 1853, in the 25th year of his age, DR. IRA E. DUPREE, JR., son of DR. IRA E. DUPREE, of Jeffersonville, Ga.

Oct. 26, 1853

Died in this city on the morning of the 25th inst., at 7 o'clock, MRS. LIZZIE MASON, wife of M.M. MASON, aged 28 years. The friends and acquaintances of Mr. Mason, and those of Col. R.A.L. Atkinson and family, are invited to attend the funeral of Mrs. Mason, this morning at 10 o'clock, at the M.E. Church.

Died in this city, on the 14th inst., MR. HENRY H. PARK, aged 33 years; native of South Deerfield, Mass., and had recently settled in this city.

Died in this city, on the 12th inst., ROBERT, son of DR. ROBERT COLLINS, aged 6 years and 5 months.

Died on Saturday, the 22d instant, of Congestion of the Brain, at the residence of his uncle, Garrett Smith, Houston county, WM. A. REDDING, aged 2 years 1 month 1 week, eldest son of ABNER F. and A.E. REDDING.

Died of Typhoid fever, in Americus, Ga., 10th Oct., in the 20th year of his age, MR. JOHN T. HODGES, eldest son of MR. WILLIAM J. RONALSON.

On 16th October, MRS. TERRINDA F. HAWKINS, consort of WILLIS A. HAWKINS, departed this life, at her residence in Americus, Ga. Had been confined to her bed 16 days with Puerperal fever; was born 15 Aug. 1827 and was 26 years 3 months and 1 day at her death; in 1840, (being only 14 years of age,) she made a public profession of religion (with eulogy)
(Americus, Oct. 19th)

Nov. 2, 1853

Died near Twiggsville, Twiggs county, Ga., Sept. 30th, of Billious fever, MARY JANE, only child of JAMES and ELIZABETH THOMPSON, aged 6 years 24 days.

Tribute of respect by Patrick Henry Lodge, No. 173 (Drayton, Dooly County) - on death of ABNER TYSON, Worthy Master who departed this life, at his residence in this county, on the 18th ult.

Nov. 9, 1853

Died in Dooly county, on the 18th ult., after a protracted illness, DONALD B. JONES, ESQ., aged about 62 years; a native of South Carolina, but for several years past a resident of Houston and Dooly counties.

Died at Monticello, Jasper county, Ga., on 9th Sept. 1853, the venerable ANTHONY DYER, in the 89th year of his age.

Died on the 20th ult., after a protracted illness, on the Colorado, Texas, MRS. MARTHA C. GORDON, consort of GEN. JOHN W. GORDON, formerly of Jones county, in this State.

Died in Talbotton, on the 1st October, JULIA REBECCA, daughter of LEWIS WIMBERLY, ESQ., aged 15 years 1 month 23 days (with eulogy)

Thomaston, Oct. 7th, 1853 - Obituary of CAROLINE A.D. RICHARDSON, consort of COL. M. RICHARDSON, of Thomaston, Upson county, Ga., her death occurred on 30th Sept.; a member of M.E. Church. (with long eulogy)

Nov. 16, 1853

Tribute of respect by Jackson Lodge, No. 48 Oct. 22, 1853 - on death of Worshipful Master, D.G. WORSHAM on Thursday 20th Oct.

Nov. 23, 1853

Died in Dooly county, on the 14th inst., GEORGE C., son of IRWIN BULLOCK, in the 23rd year of his age.

Died in Dooly county, on 13th of September, MARTHA C., youngest daughter of ISAAC J. NEWBERRY, in the 7th year of her age.

Died in Tuskegee, Alabama, on the 21st of October, JAMES B. DENSE, coach painter, aged 55 years; a native of Schenectady, NY, but for last 34 years a resident of the South.
(Milledgeville, Augusta and Charleston papers please copy)

The HON. C.J. ATHERTON died Tuesday, Nov. 15 at Manchester, N.H.

Superior Court of Greene County - The Christian Index of the 12th says - an adjourned session of the Superior Court of Greene County was held in Greensboro last week. The case of the State against BENJ. F. WILLET, charged with the murder of FELIX W. JANES, was brought up on Wednesday morning...

Nov. 30, 1853

Died at Dalton, on the 13th inst., after a lingering case of typhoid fever, COL. JOHN HAMILTON, aged about 50 years.

Died in this County, on the 22d inst., MR. THOMAS KING, sen., aged 65 years.

Died at Midway, near Milledgeville, on Monday morning, Nov. 7th, 1853, MR. WM. T. BRYAN, aged 19 years 6 months 2 days - fourth son of DAVID and CATHERINE BRYAN, Bellvue, Ga.; was a student at Oglethorpe College; and had he lived, would have graduated at the next Commencement; member of the Presbyterian Church (with long eulogy)

Obituary of MRS. M.M. MASON. Some six years since she embraced religion, attached herself to the Methodist Church; a member of the "Female Tract Society"; (with long eulogy).

Regret to announce the death of WILLIAM W. ARNOLD, ESQ., a Member of the House of Representatives, from county of Pike. He died at his residence in Zebulon, on Sunday the 27th inst.; a member of the Bar.

Nov. 30, 1853

A young man by the name of COWAN, from Twiggs county, was run over by one of the cars of the South Western Railroad, at Fort Valley. He was on the back platform of the Passenger car as it was backing. He fell, raised himself up, and was in the act of crossing the east rail, when run over by two of the wheels. His body was dreadfully mashed and mangled - both the ancle and thigh on one side was broken. He died in a few minutes. (Oglethorpe Democrat, 23d inst.)

Dec. 7, 1853

Athens, Ga., Nov. 26th, 1853 - In letter to the Editors of the Chronicle & Sentinel - announces the death of Judge CHARLES DOUGHERTY. He was on his return from a hunt, in company with two friends. When about four miles from town, in the vicinity of "Wilson's Mill," on climbing a fence he fell backwards and expired in a few minutes. It is supposed to have been occasioned by an apoplectic fit.
(Very long obituary given in another column)

The HON. ANSON G. PHELPS, President of the New York Colonization Society, is dead.

Dec. 28, 1853

Died on the 5th inst., at his residence in Houston Co., after an illness of eight days, NATHAN G. LEWIS, ESQ., in the 42d year of his age; a native of South Carolina, but in 1830 removed to Georgia in company with his father, and settled in Houston county, where he has ever since lived until his death; at age 18 united with the Methodist Church; leaves a wife, four helpless orphans, an aged mother, and several brothers and sisters...(with long eulogy)

Died in this city, on the morning of the 23d inst., MRS. WM. O. HURT, after a long and protracted illness, aged 49 years; a member of the Baptist Church for last 21 years.

Died in Baker County, on 22d Nov., MRS. WM. H. ELLISON, (formerly a resident of the vicinity of Macon) aged about 80 years.

Jan. 4, 1854

Died in Crawford county, on the 11th of December 1853, GEORGE H.D. STROTHER, eldest son of DR. JOHN W. and HARRIETT A. STROTHER, in his 14th year. (with eulogy)

Died at his residence in Houston county, on the morning of the 27th inst., MR. ZACHARIAH LAMAR, of Pneumonia, after a distressing illness of 17 days; in his 46th year and a resident of this county for fourteen or fifteen years; leaves a wife and six children. (Savannah, Charleston and N.Y. City papers please copy)

Died in Columbus, on Saturday, the 24th ult., MRS. ANN.J. MANGHAM, consort of CAPT. JOHN C. MANGHAM, of Griffin, Ga., in the 51st year of her age.

Died on the 28th December, at the residence of Irwin Bullock, of Dooly Co., Ga., of Congestion of the Brain, URIAH B. BULLOCK, aged 12 years 7 months, son of IRWIN BULLOCK.

EDWIN B. WEED, one of the oldest citizens of this place, died at his residence in this city, on the 1st inst., at 5 o'clock, P.M.; had been suffering for some time from a pulmonary complaint; a native of Connecticut, but in early life emigrated to Savannah, from whence he removed to this place, where for more than twenty years he has been an active, successful and prominent merchant; in his 47th year.

Jan. 11, 1854

Died in this city, on the 5th inst., MR. JOHN W. TUCKER, aged about 31 years and 4 months.

Died at the Georgia Academy for the Blind, after a brief illness, of pneumonia, ANDREW J. ADDISON, in his 19th year; a native of Habersham county, Ga.; from early infancy he had suffered the loss of sight...

Died in this city, on the 8th inst.; COL. ORRAMEL H. THROOP, aged about 54 years; native of Kinderhook, New York and had resided in this city about two years; lived in Massachusetts, Louisiana and Florida, in each of which he held Military Commissions; in Florida, he received commissions of Captain, Major and Colonel, and held that rank under General Taylor in the Seminole war; was a skilful artist as an Engraver, which profession he followed during his residence here; he was interred on the 9th inst., by Macon Lodge, No. 5, and the Fire Companies of this city, in the Masonic lot in Rose Hill Cemetery with usual honors of Masonry.

Jan. 18, 1854

Died on 25th day of December, at the residence of Duke H. Hays, Esq., in Decatur county, DR. R.H. McGOLDRICK, in the 46th year of his age; was born in Baltimore, Maryland, and for twenty years an eminent physician in the city of Macon; leaves a wife and two children.

Died on the 5th instant, near Thomaston, MRS. JANE COBB, wife of MAJ. WM. A. COBB; a member of the Methodist Church.

Died in Savannah, on the 14th inst., MR. LOYAL SCRANTON, aged 56 years; a merchant of that city; buried on 15th by the Phoenix Riflemen and Masonic Fraternity.

Died at Chattanooga, Tenn., on the 5th inst., COL. BENJAMIN R. MONTGOMERY, a well known and highly respected citizen of that place.

Died in Sandersville, on the 10th inst., SAMUEL B. CRAFTON, ESQ., Editor of the Central Georgian, aged about 26 years.

Homicide in Sumter. Parties concerned were WILLIAMS, JOHNSON, and ENGRAM. Their given names have not been furnished. Williams and Johnson had a grudg against Engram, and had threatened personal violence. On the 7th inst., they met at a mill, and a son of Engram being present, heard a conversation between them, in which they threatened to whip or kill his father. This he communicated to him. Williams and Johnson left the mill, and some time after Engram took the same road, armed with a double-barrel shot gun. He came up with them, and in attempting to pass, Williams stepped from behind a tree, and caught the bridle of Engram's horse, and made some remark. Johnson was standing in the road. Both were armed with rifles. Engram immediately fired at Williams, and shot him in the breast. Johnson advanced, when Engram also shot him in the breast, and both died immediately.

Jan. 25, 1854

Died near Hawkinsville, Pulaski county, Ga., on the 10th inst., of Typhoid fever, MR. BARTLETT BRIDGER, aged 59 years.

Died on the 16th inst., MRS. ELIZABETH W. MITCHELL, aged 19 years, wife of HUGH N. MITCHELL, ESQ. of Athens, and daughter of LORENZO D. McMILLAN, of Macon county.

Died at Starkville, Lee county, on the 11th inst., WILLIAM M. GILMORE, in the 39th year of his age; for many years Sheriff, once a Representative in the Legislature, and at the recent elections, called to the Clerkship of Superior Court.

Jan. 25, 1854

    Sav. Georgian of 19th inst. announces the death of HON. ROBERT M. CHARLTON who died at his residence in that city, after a somewhat protracted illness, at an early hour yesterday morning; we believe he was a native of this city; at age 28 eas elected Judge of Superior Court of the Eastern Circuit; subsequently Mayor of Savannah; frequently a member of the Georgia Legislature; and recently a Senator in Congress. appointed by Gov. Cobb to fill the vacancy occasioned by the resignation of Judge Berrien.(long eulogy)

Feb. 1, 1854

    Died at Newark, N.J., on 24th January, MRS. CORNELIA J.T. ROFF, wife of MR. A.A. ROFF, of this city.

Feb. 8, 1854

    Died at her residence in Lowndes county, very suddenly, on Sunday, the 29th ult., at 11 o'clock, A.M., MRS. MARY GRAHAM, relict of the late ALEXANDER GRAHAM, of Talfair county, Ga., aged 67 years 1 month; she brought up a large family of twelve children to maturity.

    Died on 5th January 1854, at his father's residence in Houston county, JOHN DEMPSEY BROWN, in the 21st year of his age (with eulogy).

    Died in Savannah, on the 2d inst., COL. WM. ROBERTSON, aged about 54 years; for several years Editor and proprietor of the Savannah Georgian, and a member of the Legislature from Chatham county.

    Died at Terversville, Twiggs county, of Cengestive Fever, on 24th September 1843, MADISON ABANATHY, son of SIGNAL RAINEY, in the 4th year of his age. (EDITOR'S COMMENT: WAS THIS AN ERROR ON THE PART OF THE NEWSPAPER?)

    Died at the same place, of Inflammation of the Brain, on the 11th January 1854, JAMES SIGNAL, son of SIGNAL RAINEY, in the 19th year of his age.

    Died at the same place, of Typhus Fever, on 16th January 1853, SIGNAL RAINEY, in the 53d year of his age; member of the Baptist Church; leaves wife and four children. (EDITOR'S NOTE: WAS THIS DATE MEANT TO BE 1854?)

    Died at his residence in Lee county, on the 25th ult., MR. JAMES COX, in the 52d year of his age; for last ten years a consistent member of the Methodist Episcopal Church.

Feb. 15, 1854

    Died in this city, on the 9th inst., of Pneumonia, CATHERINE REBECCA, youngest daughter of HEZEKIAH and ELIZABETH McGRAW, aged 14 months 23 days.

    Died in the vicinity of Cool Springs, Wilkinson county, Ga., on Tuesday, the 3d ult. MARY E. ALLEN, aged 40 years, leaving her husband and many relatives and friends to mourn.

Feb. 22, 1854

    Died in this city, on the 13th inst., GEORGE R. CLAYTON, ESQ. Agent of the South-Western Railroad at Oglethorpe.

    Died in this city, on the 18th inst., after a lingering illness, REV. SIMEON L. STEPHENS, a minister of the Methodist Episcopal Church, aged about 50 years.

Feb. 22, 1854

    Died in Milledgeville, on the 8th inst., MRS. MARY A. MOTT, widow of WM. A. MOTT, ESQ.

    Died near Louina, Ala., on the 14th inst., MR. SOLOMON STEPHENS, aged 77 years.

    Died in Philadelphia, on the 8th inst., WILLIAM S. GREINER, late merchant of Augusta, in the 51st year of his age.

Mar. 1, 1854

    Died in this city on the 25th inst., MRS. FRANCES DRIGGERS, wife of DANIEL T. DRIGGERS, aged 38 years.

    Died, at his residence in Fayetteville, NC, on Saturday, 19th February, 1854, HON. ROBERT STRANGE, in the 59th year of his age; for many years a judge of the superior courts of law and equity, and from 1836 to 1840 a senator in Congress; at time of his death he was a solicitor of the fifth judicial circuit of North Carolina; an affectionate husband and kind father.

    Tribute of respect by the Macon Volunteers February 22, 1854 - on death of MAJOR GEORGE TAYLOR, U.S.A... The Federal Union has lost a gallant, skillful officer of her Army, and Georgia has lost a noble son...we tender to his father MR. JAMES TAYLOR and his family, of this city, our sentiments of condolence and sympathy.

Mar. 8, 1854

    A.A. HUNT, of Lee county, who killed WILLIAM RALSTON, of this place, during the session of the Legislature in Milledgville, was tried during the term of Baldwin Superior Court...the negro boy TOBE, who attempted to kill his master, MR. HAWKINS, in May last, was also tried during the term and sentenced to be whipped and branded.

    The death of GENERAL ARMSTRONG, of the Washington <u>Union</u> has created the necessity for the election of a Printer of the House of Representatives...

    DR. GARDNER, whose trial at Washington City has attracted so much attention, was on the 3d inst., found guilty, and sentenced to twelve years imprisonment in the Penitentiary. On the 4th inst., he committed suicide, by taking Strychnine.

    On Sunday night, the 26th ult., the galleries of the Orleans Theater, in New Orleans, fell during the performance, killing two persons, and seriously infuring many others...killed was FLORIAN MALUS, a young man, for many years deputy of Lucien Hermann and John Claiboine...FERGUS TOLEDANO, a youth of 15, son of CHRISTOVAL TOLEDANO, who lives on the other side of the river, was also killed instantly...(long story with details)

    The Columbus <u>Times</u> announces that ALEXANDER MARK ROBINSON, was on the 27th inst., shot down in the streets of Columbus while in the discharge of his duty as Deputy Sheriff of the county of Muscogee On the night preceeding, DAVID WRIGHT of this city and a man named JACK BOYD, of Macon, had committed a misdemeanor, and warrants were issued for their arrest...(long story with details)

Mar. 15, 1854

    The funeral of DR. GARDNER took place on Saturday and was attended by only a few of his personal friends. His brother, CHARLES GARDINER, was present and will be examined before the Coroner's Jury on Friday next.

Mar. 15, 1854

LUCIUS L. WITTICH for many years a prominent Lawyer in Madison, Morgan county, and one of the able ministers of the Methodist Conference of this State, died at his residence in Madison on the 8th inst., a native of Wilkes county, but at an early age his father removed to this place, where he was raised, and continued to reside, with the exception of one year, until his death; educated at the University of Georgia, graduating with high honors of his class, and soon after studied law and entered upon that profession in Madison; a local preacher in the Methodist Episcopal Church; his last years were spent in teaching - several of which as Rector of the Madison Female Academy - one as Professor of Mathematics, at Emory College, and lastly as President of the Madison Female College; he died in the 50th year of his age. (from Family Visitor of 11th inst.)

The Mobile Register reports that GEN. THOMAS D. KING died in that place, on Friday night last, the 24th ult. He was en elder brother, we believe, of our late distinguished citizen, HON. WILLIAM R. KING, Vice-President of the United States, and resided in Alabama since the establishment of the State Government - in 1836 he was one of the Democratic Electors.

Mar. 22, 1854

Died at his residence in Talbot county, Ga., on the 27th of February, MR. BENJ. T. EMANUEL, in the 49th year of his age, after a short but painful illness, of Typhoid Pneumonia. (with short eulogy)

Mar. 29, 1854

Died in Milledgeville, on the 14th inst., PETER J. WILLIAMS, ESQ., in the 66th year of his age; had long been a resident of Milledgeville; had been a member of the Legislature, and held several offices of responsibility and trust under our State government.

Died in Milledgeville, on the 19th inst., COL. CHARLES R. HUSON, in the 44th year of his age.

Died at his residence in Jasper county, on the 9th inst., COL. JOHN C. WATTERS, in the 66th year of his age.

GOV. DUVAL, for many years Governor of the Territory of Florida, died in Washington, where he had gone upon professional business, on the 19th inst., in the 70th year of his age. At the time of his death he was a citizen of Texas, having removed with his family to that State in 1848.

The Christian Index announces the death of REV. B.M. SAUNDERS, formerly President of Mercer University and for many years an infulential Clergyman of the Baptist denomination of Georgia.

Apr. 5, 1854

Died in Macon, on the 30th ult., after a painful illness of nearly three weeks, MR. HEZEKIAH McGRAW, aged 36 years 3 months and 5 days; left wife and little daughter.

Apr. 12, 1854

Died in Milledgeville, on the 2d inst., MR. THOMAS WARE, aged about 45 years.

Died in Palatka, Fla., March 13th, MARIETTA, eldest daughter of NATHAN PECK, JR., of New-Haven.

Apr. 26, 1854

Died at his residence, in Bibb county, on Friday morning the 14th inst., in the 58th year of his age, MR. PETER STUBBS, ESQ.

Died at his residence in Madison, on Sunday, the 16th inst., after a protracted illness, CHARLES WHITING, in the 54th year of his age.

The HON. JOSEPH STURGIS, of Columbus, formerly Judge of the Superior Courts of the Chattahoochee Circuit, and a member of the last Legislature of this State, died at Washington City, on the 17th inst. His remains were brought to Georgia for interment.

DR. JOSEPH J. SINGLETON, late Senator in the Georgia Legislature from Lumpkin county, died of apoplexy at his residence in Dahlonega, Ga., on the 10th inst.

May 10, 1854

Died in this city, on the 2d inst., MR. WM. B. THOMAS, aged about 55 years; a native of New Haven, Conn.; had been a resident of McIntosh county for more than twenty years; and recently settled a few miles from this city.

Died suddenly, in Columbia county, Georgia, on the evening of 21st April, in the 25th year of his age, DR. OCTAVIUS LAFAYETTE BARNES, son of JOHN BARNES and HARRIET BOWDRE DARSEY.

Died on the morning of the 18th ult., in Panola county, Miss., COL. URIAH IRWIN BULLOCK, in the 47th year of his age; a native of Georgia and at one time a member of her State Legislature; was in Texas during her struggle for liberty, and battled side by side with the brave Burleson; emigrated to Panola county about eight years ago; was violently attacked by an affection of the brain on the evening of the 16th ult., and on the morning of the 18th was a corpse; leaves a wife and five children.

May 17, 1854

Died in this city, on the 9th inst., MR. WILLIAM CRAFT, aged about 49 years.

Died in Macon, Geo., May 2d, MR. WILLIAM B. THOMAS, aged 55 years; a native of Connecticut; for more than thirty years a consistent member of the Protestant Episcopal Church. (with eulogy)

Died on the morning of the 30th ult., at the residence of her parents, MRS. CHARTER CAMPBELL, of Madison, Ga., eldest daughter of HARPER C. BRYSON, ESQ., of Augusta, a-ter a painful and lingering illness of seven weeks, aged 23 years.

May 24, 1854

Died at Key West, on the 24th ult., at the residence of the HON. S.J. DOUGLASS, of inflammatory billious fever, MISS DORA TRIPLETT, aged about 22 years; a native of Wilkes county, Geo...obituary notice in Tallahassee Sentinel gives eulogy.

Died in Thomas County, Ga., May 5th, in the 27th year of her age, MRS. ELIZABETH WADE, wife of ELIJAH WADE, JR.; leaves a husband and three children.

Died at Barnesville, on the 15th inst., THOMAS W. HARRIS, aged 38 years.

Died in this city, on Monday, the 15th inst., MRS. M.A. CAREY, aged about 65 years.

May 31, 1854

Died at the residence of Peter Solomon, Esq., in Vineville, on the evening of the 25th inst., MR. LARKIN GRIFFIN, for many years a worthy and highly esteemed citizen of Macon, aged 55 years.

June 7, 1854

Died on the 21st of May, in Early county, of Bronchetis, MR. JOSHUA McDONALD.

LUKE WEST, for many years, well known in this city, and throughout the country, as the principal performer in the original Campbell Minstrels, died in Boston, on the 28th ult., in the 29th year of his age. His real name was WILLIAM SHEPHERD. He has left a very handsome fortune to his widow and child.

MR. T.F. MEAGHER, soon after his arrival at New York, recently, from California and the South, received the intelligence of the death of his wife who was upon a visit to his relatives in Waterford, Ireland.

The Augusta Constitutionalist learns that on Saturday night 27th ult., a quarrel ensued at Appling, Columbia county, between THOMAS SEAY and DR. O'FERRELL, which resulted in the latter being killed...

Melancholy accident in Jacksonville. On Monday last, the 22d ult., about breakfast time, a fire broke out in the country residence belonging to COL. HART...one of his daughters perished in the devouring element. (Savannah News)

June 14, 1854

Died in this city, on the 12th inst., of Pneumonia, MISS KATY MURDOCH.

Died in Perry, Ga., on Tuesday, May the 9th, MR. WASHINGTON SPIER, in the 56th year of his age.

Died of Congestive Fever, in Bossier Parish, La., on the 22d inst., MRS. MARY B. HODGES, wife of GEN. JOHN L. HODGES, in the 36th year of her age; leaves husband and seven children; member of Baptist Church since 1846 (with short eulogy)

The Southern Recorder of the 13th inst. announces the unexpected demise of two of our worthy citizens. J.T. McNEIL, ESQ., and his lady visited Tennessee...were attacked by cholera...Mrs. McNeil arrived here on Friday last and died on Tuesday morning. Mr. McNeil died of same disease on the Thursday morning following. The colored nurse also died on Wednesday night.

June 21, 1854

Died in Montgomery, Ala., on Saturday the 20th ult., MR. PEYTON B. COBB, in the 25th year of his age, formerly of Thomaston, Ga., and son of MAJ. WM. A. COBB, of the latter place.

June 28, 1854

Died at the residence of JAS. P. ALLEN, June 13th, MRS. ANNA V. ALLEN, in the 20th year of her age; was wife of RUFUS ALLEN, and daughter of ROBERT C. REDDING, of Muscogee County; only five months before was she married...(with eulogy)

PATRICK HENRY'S youngest son NATHANIEL, died recently, destitute and alone, at an inn in Floyd County, Va.; died of dropsy of the chest; his last occupation was teaching.

July 5, 1854

Died in this city, on the 1st inst., LEWIS CHARLES, infant son of DR. E.L. STROHECKER, aged 8 months and 20 days.

Died in this city, on the 2d inst., the REV. M.M. MASON, aged about 46 years; a native of South Craftsburg, Vt., and for several years a resident of this city; an efficient teacher, and author and publisher of the first edition of "Southern class Book"; at time of his death, and for several years previous, he was a Justice of the Inferior Court of Bibb County.

A man by the name of JOHN SIMMONS was found dead, sitting in a chair, on the 28th inst., in a house on Fourth Street. He was an Englishman by birth, aged from 45 to 50 years, and had worked on the Central Railroad. A Coroner's Inquest rendered a verdict that he died of intemperance.

Cincinnati, June 27 - Last evening a box was sent to the Marine Hospital, corner of Longworth and Western Row, and deposited in the room of the steward of the institution, J.H. ALLISON. About 10 o'clock the steward and his wife, being alone in the room, opened the box. When in the act of doing so, it exploded with tremendous force...Mr. and Mrs. Allison are both dead.

July 12, 1854

Died at the residence of Leroy Napier, Esq., near this city on Saturday, the 8th inst., his daughter CAROLINE MATILDA, aged 24 years, wife of MAJOR JAMES T. WELSMAN, of Charleston, SC; as daughter, sister, wife, mother and christian, those towards whom she stood in the several relations...

Died in Twiggs County, on the morning of the 4th of July, in the 21st year of her age, MRS. GEORGIA ANN, consort of CHARLES P. REYNOLDS.

Died in Houston County, near Wellborn's Mills, MAJ. OLIVER H.P. WELLBORN, (of Consumption,) on the 1st inst., aged 32 years. On the same day, MALISSA BARKER, of Congestive Fever, aged 13 years - daughter of JOSEPH and MARY BARKER. On the 5th inst., MARY, daughter of DR. B.Q. SMITH, aged 3 years and 6 months.

Died in Houston county, about three weeks since, MR. EZEKIEL EVANS, aged 65 years. On the 29th June, ROBERT EVANS, aged about 40 years. On the 9th inst., MR. NEEDHAM SMITH, aged about 50 years.

Died in Charles county, Maryland, in the 35th year of her age, FLORA, wife of EDMUND J. JOHNSON of this city, and daughter of WALTER L. CAMPBELL, late of Macon county.

A correspondent at Wellborn's Mills, Houston county, informs us that during a thunder storm on the 6th inst., two children of JESSE AMMONS were killed by a stroke of lightning.

The Augusta Constitutionalist announces that on Saturday, July 2d, about 2 o'clock, P.M., at the residence of Mr. J.W. Swain, in Newton county, Georgia, DR. J.W. HITCH, WILLIAM WILSON and ISAAC CHRISTIAN, JR., were instantly killed by a stroke of lightning. Dr. Hitch and Mr. Wilson were single men, but Mr. Christian leaves an affectionate wife and three children. Dr. Hitch was formerly of South Carolina, but other two were from Georgia.

Notice of the death of ROBERT A. WHYTE, junior editor of the Georgia Home Gazette, who departed this life in Augusta, on the morning of the 4th of July, in the 26th year of his age; a native of North Carolina, where an aged mother survives; leaves several married sisters in other States; funeral obsequies at the Presbyterian Church, whither the remains were escorted by the Clinch Rifles, of which Maj. Whyte was a member; buried in City Cemetery with military honors. (Aug. Constitutionalist, 5th inst.)

July 12, 1854

The venerable THOMAS RITCHIE expired in Washington City, at noon on the 3d inst.; editor of the Richmond Enquirer...recent death of his younger son THOMAS RITCHIE, JR....and other son was married only a few weeks ago (with long eulogy)

July 19, 1854

Died suddenly, on the 6th of July, at Middleville, Charles county, Maryland, (the residence of her brother, JOHN G. CAMPBELL,) FLORA A. JOHNSTON, the beloved wife of E.J. JOHNSTON, of Macon, in the 26th year of her age; the deceased had recently gone on a visit (with her idolized little children) to spend the summer months in the society of her brothers and sisters...(with eulogy).

Died in Monroe county, on the 15th inst., JOHN POWERS, ESQ., in the 75th year of his age; native of Halifax Co., NC, and removed to Greene Co., Ga., where he lived several years; then removed to Monroe, and was one of its earliest settlers. Being in feeble health at this time, he started for the Indian Springs by the Railroad, on the morning of the 15th. On arriving at Forsyth, he deemed himself too unwell to proceed, and started to return home in a buggy. About six miles from Forsyth, he stopped at the house of Roland Redding, and remained there several hours, apparently in usual health when he lay down on a couch, and suddenly expired. He was brought to this city, and interred in Rose Hill Cemetery on the 16th inst.

Died at the Stone Mountain, on the 7th inst., MR. KENNETH McKENZIE, a native of Scotland, and for many years a citizen of Columbus.

Died at the Indian Springs on the 1st inst., MRS. C.A. VASON, consort of COL. DAVID A. VASON of Albany, Ga. and daughter of COL. HENRY and URANIA POPE, formerly of Wilkes county, Ga., in the 36th year of her age; leaves a husband and three children.

Died in Meriwether county, on the 24th ult., MRS. P.A. COX, wife of ANDREW COX, aged 33 years.

Died in this county, on the 15th inst., MR. SEABORN J. SAUNDERS, aged 42 years.

Died in this county, on the 18th inst., of paralysis, the HON. JOHN BAILY, in the 64th year of his age; was elected to the Legislature and for many years was a Judge of the Inferior Court of this County.

Died in Vineville, on the 16th inst., DR. CHAS. THOMPSON, in the 47th year of his age; formerly of Richlan Dist. SC; died about two hours previous, his daughter MARY C. THOMPSON, aged 13 years.

Mortality in Macon from 15th June to 19th July: M.M. MASON, aged 46 years, disease general debility; THO. MILLER, (late of Mobile,) about 45, consumption; Infant son of DR. E.L. STROHECKER, 8 months; GOV. TOWNS, 53 years, paralysis of long standing; CHAS. U. WEEKS, 7 years, whooping cough; child of MRS. GOLD, age & c. unknown; MRS. CONNELLY, (Irish woman,) murdered by her husband.

Others interred in our Cemetery during the last month: MRS. WELLSMAN, of Charleston, died in Vineville; JOHN POWERS, of Monroe co., disease apoplexy; DR. CHAS. THOMPSON, 46 yrs., Vineville, consumption; MISS MARY C. THOMPSON, 13 yrs., Vineville, diarrhea; _____ COFFEE, Irishman, died in Oglethorpe.

July 26, 1854

Died in this city, on the 20th inst., of consumption, MR. N.B. COPE, about 34 years, formerly of Savannah.

July 26, 1854

Died in Louisville, Ga., on the 23d of June, after an illness of 44 days, MRS. MARY H. WRIGHT, in the 29th year of her age; at age of 14 she became a member of the Baptist church, during a season of great religious fervor in Augusta, and continued therein seven years; at the expiration of which time, and as the only inducement of her beloved husband's connection with the church, she then became a Methodist. (with long eulogy)

Died in Pulaski county, on the 16th inst., MRS. SARAH P. LESTER, aged 55 years.

JOSEPH HENRY LUMPKIN, JR., eldest son of Judge Lumpkin, of the Supreme Court, died at Lexington on the 12th inst., in the 27th year of his age.

Aug. 2, 1854

Died, on the 19th ult., at his residence in Macon co., JOSEPH JOHNSON, ESQ., in the 43d year of his age; a resident of this community for more than twenty years; member of M.E. Church; leaves a wife, two daughters and one son (with short eulogy)

The only daughter of EX-PRESIDENT FILLMORE died at Aurora, New York, on the 26th ult., of cholera.

National Intelligencer of last Friday announced the death, from paralysis, of GEN. NATHAN TOWSON, Paymaster General of the Army; associated with action upon the Niagara frontier during the War of 1812-15; especially distinguished in the battles of Chippewa and Bridgwater, and in the sortie from Fort Erie; a native of Maryland, and at death was age 71.

REV. JACKSON P. TURNER, eminent and useful minister of the Methodist Episcopal Church, South, died with Typhoid Pneumonia in Talbotton, Ga., Monday, July 24th, 1854; was appointed at the last Georgia Conference Presiding Elder of the Columbus District. (Columbus Times).

Aug. 9, 1854

Died in this county (Ruthland's District,) on the 7th inst., MR. JOHN T. CHAPMAN, aged about 44 years, leaving widow and two children; member of Methodist Church, which he joined in May last.

Died at the Indian Springs, on the 3d inst., of inflammation of the bowels, ISAAC P., infant son of MR. and MRS. ISAAC WINSHIP.

The Buffalo Commerical Advertiser of Saturday reports the death of MR. CHAS. FILLMORE, brother of EX-PRESIDENT FILLMORE. He died Thursday at St. Paul, Minnesota.

Aug. 16, 1854

Died near Chapel Hill, Texas, on the 12th July, at the residence of her husband, MRS. CAROLINE ELIZABETH, consort of DR. ROBERT T. FLEWELLEN, and daughter of the late JAMES BIVINS, of Culloden, aged 23 years and 25 days. (City papers copy)

A long tribute to the memory of MRS. JAMES T. WELSMAN. Written by Mary Bates, Dudley, July 26, 1854.

Aug. 23, 1854

Died after a protracted illness of chronic Diarrhea SARAH VICTORIA, daughter of G.W. and MARTHA FACKLER of Meriwether Co., aged 15 months 13 days.

Aug. 23, 1854

Horrible tragedy in Missouri...Smithville, Clay county, Mo. It appears a fracas occurred, in which JOHN W. DOUGLASS was killed, WILLIAM ROSS and JOHN ROSS, father and son, were dangerously, and IRA TRITT severely stabbed by SAMUEL and WILLIAM SHACKLEFORD and JOHN W. CALLOWAY...eventual hanging of the offenders...Calloway was a mere boy, and the two Shacklefords were quite young men (details from the Parkville Luminary of the 8th inst.)

The HON. S.U. DOWNS, Ex-Senator of Louisiana, and Collector of the port of New Orleans, died at Crab Orchard Springs, Kentucky, on Monday the 14th inst.; a native of the State in which he died, but in early life emigrated to Louisiana and became a successful practitioner at the bar, and a prominent politician of New Orleans; his senatorial career embraced the struggle upon the Compromise of 1850.

ROBERT M. GRAHAM, indicted for the murder of COL. CHARLES LORING, of New Orleans, at the St. Nicholas Hotel in New York, on the 3d inst., was on Monday arraigned at the Court of General Sessions and pleaded not guilty.

Letter headed Fort Union, (New Mexico,) July 2d, 1854 - ...War between troops in this territory and the Tacarela Apaches...in battle on the 30th ult. J.E. MAXWELL, son of Mrs. Maxwell, of Athens, Ga. was killed; Lieut. Maxwell was graduated from the military Academy in 1850, and served honorably as a Brevet and 2d Lieutenant in the 3d regiment of infantry ever since...Lieut. Maxwell was buried at his post, with military honors (details of battle given in the story)

Aug. 30, 1854

Died in Savannah, on the 23 inst., MR. BLAKE B. STRONG, aged 18 years, son of the late JUDGE STRONG of Macon, Ga.

Died in Marion Co., on the 17th inst., of Croup, after an illness of only 24 hours, ROSELLE, daughter of JOHN C. and EMELINE C. MATHER, aged 2 years.

Died in this county, on the 25th inst., MR. WM. SAUNDERS, aged about 64 years; one of the earliest settlers of this county, where he had resided more than thirty years; had taken this paper since May, 1823, paid for it punctually every year, for 32 years, and generally in advance - and is now in advance to April, 1855.

Died at Catoosa Springs, Ga. on the 22d inst., of typhoid fever, MR. JOHN W. PEARSON, of Macon, aged 37 years, son of MAJ. JAS. PEARSON, of Twiggs county.

Died at Helicon, Lowndes Co., Ala., on the 19th August, 1854, JAMES W. PATTILO, in the 26th year of his age, an Engineer of the Girard and Mobile Railroad; a native of Virginia, but in early youth removed with his parents to Georgia, and until he attained man's estate, resided in Houston county; graduated with honor in Class of 1851 at Western Military Institute; his death was caused by exposure on the Western Division of the Mobile and Girard Railroad, in the vicinity of Mobile, during the excessive hot weather of last June and first of July past (with eulogy) (Mobile and Columbus, Ga. papers copy)

HON. DANIEL E. HUGHER died at Sullivan's Island, opposite Charleston, on Monday, aged 75 years; distinguished citizen of South Carolina; had been member of both branches of the legislature, a judge, and finally Senator of US in 1842.

Sep. 6, 1854

Died in Savannah, on the 2d inst., of the yellow fever, MR. JACOB DEMMING, in the 21st year of his age; for several years served as an apprentice in this office...(with eulogy)

Died on the 28th August, JOHN WILLIAM, aged 1 year 9 months, only child of DR. WM. S. LIGHTFOOT of this city.

Died in Americus, on the 31st ult., COL. FELIX GIBSON, of Florida, aged about 58 years, formerly of Wilkes Co., Ga.

Died in Philadelphia, Tennessee, on the 16th ult., MRS. JULIA, wife of COL. A.W. COZART, and daughter of the late CHARLES Y. CALDWELL; born in Monroe Co., Ga., where she grew up and married... about a year and a half ago she removed with her husband to their present home...(with eulogy)

The National Intelligencer of the 30th ult. says: We learn with much satisfaction that the report of the death of EX-SENATOR DOWNS, Collector of New Orleans, is premature. The error, we understand, arose by confounding him with Commodore Downes, of the Navy, recently deceased...

Sep. 13, 1854

Died at the residence of his father, on the 5th inst., of typhoid fever, THOMAS G., son of W.F. and AGNES WILLIAMS, of Pike county, Ga., in the 23d year of his age; leaves a father, a mother, a wife and child. (Telegraph and Federal Union please copy)

Died at her residence in Jones county, Ga., of typhoid fever, on the 10th inst., MRS. LOUISA J. RIDLEY, consort of DR. J.B. RIDLEY, and daughter of COL. MARTIN W. and LUCRETIA STAMPER, in the 27th year of her age.

Died at Midway, on Wednesday last, of typhoid fever, MISS MARY M. TUCKER, daughter of the late HARPER TUCKER, ESQ., aged 19 years in April last. (with short eulogy)

Died on the 28th ult., in Cuthbert, of Typhoid Fever, WILLIAM JANES, in his 47th year (with short eulogy).

Health of Macon - On the books of the Sexton, there is record of the burial on the 5th inst. of CHARLES JUNG, a native of Germany and resident of Charleston, who died on the morning of that day, at the Lanier House in this city. After his interment, it was rumored that he had died of yellow fever.

DR. P.H. WILDMAN and the two DRS. SCHLEY, MR. JOSEPH and MR. BENGAMIN BOROUGHS, and WALTER R. FLEMING, (lately a citizen of this place, where many of his relatives yet reside) are among the victims of Yellow Fever whose deaths have been recently reported from Savannah. The brothers Schley and the brothers Boroughs, all died at Bath in Richmond Co., where they had gone with the disease upon them.

The Milledgeville Recorder says that GIDEON COPENHAVER, a convict in the Penitentiary, was found hung and dead in his cell on Saturday morning last. He was about 30 years of age, and has respectable connections in Kentucky. He was one of the associates of the celebrated Dr. Roberts, who robbed John Jackson, of Monroe, and was tried and convicted in that county a year or two since.

The Savannah Republican of the 8th says: learn from dispatch received here yesterday morning from Augusta announcing the death at Richmond Hill, near that place, of DR. FREEMAN SCHLEY, of Savannah. The deceased was seized by the prevailing epidemic some days ago, and just after his elder brother, DR. J.M. SCHLEY, was attacked, and both of them were taken to Richmond Hill, the family seat...

Sep. 10, 1854.

Died in this city, on the 11th inst., of yellow fever, MR. WALTER R. FLEMING, of Macon, aged 30 years; had been but a few years resident of our city. (Savannah Republican) (with eulogy)

MRS. ELIZABETH BENTON, wife of COL. THOS. H. BENTON, died in Washington City, on Sunday evening, the 10th inst., in the 60th year of her age, and was buried on Tuesday, the 12th inst.

MR. REESE, conductor on the Georgia Rail Road, was shot in Augusta on Monday morning the 11th inst., between 3 and 4 o'clock, and died shortly afterwards.

From the Nashville Banner - Death of HON. EPHRIAM H. FOSTER, which took place on Wednesday night at 11 o'clock, at the residence, in this vicinity, of his brother-in-law William Nichol.

Savannah Repub. Sept. 14 - announces that BISHOP BARRON, of the Catholic Church, died in this city yesterday morning, of pneumonia. Bishop B. was advanced in years, and had returned from the coast of Africa some time since, on account of ill health, having been appointed a missionary to that country.

Sep. 27, 1854

Died in this city on the 21st inst., of yellow fever, MR. McGILBERT McSWAIN, a conductor on the Central Railroad. He was a member of Hamilton Lodge, No. 16, Sandersville, and was interred by members of the Macon Lodge No. 6, in their burial lot in Rose Hill Cemetery.

Health of Macon. Interments for week, ending Saturday last (werd inst.):
MR. JACOB MASTICK, yellow fever, native of Germany and resident of
    Savannah (18th)
_____ DOYLE, Yellow fever, native of Ireland, recently from
    Charleston and Augusta (21st)
FANNIE W. WALLON, 2 years old, inflammation of brain, from
    Savannah (21st)

Savannah Republican, Sept. 20 - The Right REV. FRANCIS XAVIER GARTLAND, Roman Catholic Bishop of the Diocese of Georgia, died at the residence of Mr. Prendergast, in this city, yesterday morning at half-past 11 o'clock, of yellow fever; was born in Dublin, and his parents came with him to this country while he was yet an infant; educated at Mount St. Mary's College; entered priesthood at Philadelphia; was consecrated Bishop of the Diocese of Georgia in 1850; arrived in this city in November of that year; has relatives now living in Philadelphia.

Augusta Chronicle & Sentinel reports an accident on the Georgia Railroad on Thursday night, below Camak, between the up passenger train and a down freight train, by which the engineer on the up train, ROBERT SPENCER, and a fireman named CHAS. MARSH were instantly killed, and that HARRY DORSEY, Engineer, and THOS. GIBSON, fireman, on the down train were seriously injured. JOHN BALDWIN, machinist, was badly scalded. The accident is said to have been caused by the freight train being out of time; the name of the conductor of which train is FRANCIS GOLDING.

Oct. 4, 1854

Died in Columbus, on Friday, the 22d inst., at the residence of James Vernoy, MR. SHERROD A. LAWRENCE, of Disease of the lungs, in the 34th year of his age.

Died in this city on the 25th ult., ARTHUR J. PIGOTT, aged about 35 years - a native of Philadelphia, and late an Engineer on the Central Railroad. (Philadelphia papers copy)

Oct. 4, 1854

HON. HUGH A. HARALSON died at his residence in LaGrange on the 25th ult.

Health of Augusta. The Chronicle & Sentinel of 27th ult. lists interments in that city for week ending at 3 o'clock, PM on 25th September:

    P. SIMON, yellow fever
    MISS LINTEPOWDER, yellow fever
    MRS. JACKSON, yellow fever
    JOHN ROBERTSON, Scotland, 25 years, yellow fever, contracted disease in Savannah
    LEOPOLD COHN, Germany, 30 years, yellow fever
    ADELIA FORCE
    MARGARET CONNOR, Ireland, 21 years, yellow fever
    J.W. WILCOX, Connecticut, 21 years, yellow fever
    child of P. SIMON, Augusta, aged 4 years, yellow fever
    PAT HALLAGHAM, Ireland, 55 years, yellow fever
    JAMES KENNEDY, aged 19 years, yellow fever, contracted disease in Charleston
    JACOB HOBER, Germany, 28 years, yellow fever
    W.H. HOLLMAN, S.C., 59 years, yellow fever
    OLIVER FIFIELD, Connecticut, 31 years, yellow fever
    THOS. CALHOUN, Augusta, 12 years, yellow fever
    JANE M. ROBERTS, England, 20 years, yellow fever
    J.C. GRISWOLD, North Carolina, 24 years, yellow fever
    MICHAEL MAHER, Ireland, yellow fever
    MARGARET SHOVERLAND, Ireland, 18 years, yellow fever
    W. SHAW, England, 45 years, yellow fever
    C.W. MARCH, New Jersey, 24 years, accident
    VIRGINIA DOSWELL, Virginia, 28 years, yellow fever contracted in Charleston
    _____ McKINNIE, Ireland, 22 years, yellow fever
    BENJAMIN LESSES, came from Blackville on the cars
    JAS. H. RHIND, residence Sand Hills, 45 years, yellow fever
    MRS. J.T. GARDINER, Augusta, 28 years, yellow fever
    JOSEPH LEECH, Ireland, 32 years, yellow fever
    OTTO LENTZ, Germany, 31 years, yellow fever
    MRS. HUBER, Germany

Savannah Georgian of 29th ult. reports that HON. JOSEPH W. JACKSON, late member of Congress from this District, died of yellow fever at his residence in Savannah, about -- o'clock yesterday; commenced his political life under auspices of Gov. Troup; frequent member of city council, Mayor of Savannah, and served repeatedly in one or the other branch of the Georgia Legislature; in Feb. 1850 he was elected to Congress of the United States, to fill the vacancy caused by resignation of Hon. Thomas Butler King (with eulogy)

Augusta Chronicle & Sentinel, 27th ult. - Reports death of JAMES G. GOULD, ESQ., which occurred at Marietta, on Thursday last. To escape the ravages of pestilence in the city, he left with wife and infant child for Marietta; a graduate of Yale; had begun to prepare himself in his father's (JUDGE W.T. GOULD'S) office for the profession of the Law; leaves a father, mother, brother, sister, and wife.

Augusta Constitutionalist - JAMES RHIND, ESQ., Cashier of the Branch of State Bank in this city, expired at his residence on the Sand Hills, on Monday morning; comparatively a young man.

Sav. Georgian, 26th inst. - ISAAC P. WHITEHEAD, of the firm of Rabun & Whitehead, died last night.

HARMAN BLENNERHASSETT, the second son of HARMAN BLENNERHASSETT, of the Island in the Ohio river, which bears that name, died in New York on the 17th ultimo, after a protracted illness. He was an artist of very considerable eminence. The only surviving member of the family, Jos. L. Blennerhassett, now lives in Troy, Missouri.

Oct. 11, 1854

Report contradicted. It gives us sincere pleasure to contradict, upon the authority of the Savannah News, the report of the death of MRS. ALETHIA BURROUGHS, wife of BERRIEN BURROUGHS and daughter of the HON. WM. LAW. The News says: "We have seen a letter stating that she had so far recovered as to have commenced her journey from Athens to Clarksville, the residence of her father, with other members of her family, on Monday the 2d inst."

REV. JEHIEL TALMAGE, formerly Pastor of the Presbyterian Church at Knowlton, Warren Co., N.J., died at the residence of his son, REV. P.S. TALMAGE, at Bloomfield, N.J. on the 26th ult., in the 70th year of his age. The Southern Recorder of yesterday says the deceased was a brother of Rev. Dr. Talmage of Oglethorpe University, and uncle to three other clergymen of same name, one of whom - Rev. J.V.N. Talmage - is an able Missionary in China, in the service of the American Board of Foreign Missions.

Oct. 18, 1854

In the last severe storm at Matagorda, Texas, MRS. RUTHERFORD, the mother of GENERAL GORDON, and formerly a resident of Milledgville, received some severe injuries from which it is feared she cannot recover.

Southern Recorder of yesterday - In a rencontre at the house of Mr. B. Brake, of this county, we learn that a young man by name of THOMAS MOULTRIE, of Washington county, was accidentally shot with his own pistol, on Thursday, the 12th inst. The young man was the second son of B.H. MOULTRIE, ESQ., who removed from this city to Jefferson county, a year of two ago.

WILLIAM DARBY, the statistician and geographer, died at his residence in Washington city, on Monday morning, in the 80th year of his age.

The coroner's jury have found MR. GEORGE W. GREEN, a wealthy citizen of Chicago, guilty of poisoning his wife with strychnine.

MR. W.C. BEMAN, who has been for some months in custody, on the charge of robbing the mails, died in the jail at Savannah on the 5th inst., of yellow fever., He was to have been tried at the November term of the US District Court of Georgia.

Oct. 25, 1854

Died at Independence, Jackson Co., Missouri, of Consumption, MR. ALEXANDER E. HAMMERSLEY, formerly a resident of this city and Forsyth. His relations can obtain further information by writing to Chas. A. Brown, at the above named place.

Died in Atlanta, Ga., on Thursday 19th inst., MR. JOHN L. BARRINGER, of the firm Barringer & Brothers, of this city.
(Columbus Times)

Died at his residence, in Putnam county, on the 13th inst., WM. DENNIS, JR., in the 37th year of his age.

Nov. 1, 1854

Died on the morning of the 28th ult., near Pond Town, ALICE, infant daughter of WM. A. and JANE E. BLACK, aged 2 years and 28 days.

Among the number of deaths from Yellow Fever at Beaufort, So. Carolina, we notice that of MRS. SARAH E. HABERSHAM, aged 65; native of Beaufort, and widow of the late HON. R.W. HABERSHAM, formerly a Representative in Congress from this State.

Nov. 1, 1854

The HON. HUGH A. GARLAND, a distinguished son of Virginia, died at St. Louis on the 15th inst.

Jacksonville Republican publishes list of names of persons, who died of Yellow Fever in St. Marys, Ga., up to 21st of last month: H. CALDWELL, ELKINS, COAL, J. FLOYD, MEREDITH, WEBB, ROBERT DOWNES, BACON JR., HAMBLETON, STILES COOPER, MAGILLIS, McDONALD SR., PREVAT, MRS. BRIGGS and daughter, MRS. HOLZENDORF and her two children, MISS PROCTOR, MRS. VALENTINE, MRS. SMITH and daughter, MRS. M.C. GILLIS, MISS ARNOW.

Nov. 8, 1854

Died on the evening of Friday, October 20th, 1854, at his residence, near the town of Hawkinsville, MR. JOHN V. MITCHELL, aged 48 years 6 months; buried with Masonic honors on a part of his plantation; has filled offices of Clerk of the Superior, and Inferior Courts for the county, consecutively for 18 years, which office has become vacant by his death; he also held office of the Judge of the Court of Ordinary; profession of Dentistry; member of Mount Hope Lodge of F.A.M., No. 9, ever since its organization in this place - about 23 years, and held the highest in the gift of Lodge.

University of Georgia, Demosthenian Hall, October 11th, 1854 - tribute of respect on death of classmate and college friend FRANCIS M. BOWEN.

Nov. 15, 1854

Died in this city, on the 10th inst., MR. WM. MELROSE, aged about 54 years; a native of Scotland, and one of the early settlers of our county, and one of its most active merchants, and enterprising business men.

Died in this city on the 10th inst., FRANCIS WRIGHT DeLOACHE, aged 3 years 6 months 7 days. On the 11th, RYLAND KENDRICK DeLOACHE, aged 5 years 7 months 21 days - sons of MR. JACKSON DeLOACHE.

Augusta Chronicle & Sentinel announces that ROBERT F. POE died at his residence on the Sand Hills Monday afternoon; a native of Augusta, where he has ever lived; Cashier and President of Bank of Augusta.

The remains of GOV. BURT arrived in Columbia, South Carolina on Wednesday last. They were to have been taken to Pendleton the next day for interment.

Nov. 22, 1854

Died on the 18th inst., THERESE, eldest daughter of J.M. BOARDMAN, aged 3 years 3 months 18 days.

Died in this city on the 15th inst., MRS. MARY BORIN, in the 71st year of her age; for 27 years an exemplary member of the Presbyterian Church.

Died in this city, on the morning of the 5th inst., GEORGE WILCOXSON DeLOACHE, aged 1 year 5 months 26 days - son of MR. JACKSON DeLOACHE. This is the third and only remaining child of his parents, who has died within a week. (with eulogy)

Died in Marietta, on the 10th inst., COL. THOMAS ROBINSON HUSON, aged about 45 years. He had been suffering under an excruciating malady, which the best physicians could never define; his body was conveyed to Milledgeville, and interred in the family burial place.

Died at Midway, on Thursday afternoon, Nov. 2d, VAN LEONARD, infant son of SAMUEL E. and HENRIETTA WHITAKER, aged 10 months and 9 days.

Nov. 22, 1854

Died in Vineville, at the residence of Major Benjamin Bryan, on the 19th of September, HINTON B., third son of WILLARD and ROBA BOYNTON, of Lumpkin, Stewart county, in the 18th year of his age.

MRS. MARTHA ALLEN, consort of the late CHARLES ALLEN, of Pleasant Hill, Talbot Co., Ga., died of congestive chills at her residence on the 2d inst.; member of Methodist Episcopal Church; leaves seven children (short eulogy).

The Augusta papers announce the death in that city from Yellow Fever, of DR. JAMES D. MACKIE, an accomplished physician, formerly of Sparta, and brother-in-law to REV. DR. MYERS, late President of the Wesleyan Female College.

CHARLES W. STEWART, an officer of the House of Representatives, committed suicide in Washington on Sunday night in the Speaker's Room at the Capitol by taking poison.

Savannah Republican of Nov. 15 reports that CAPT. JOHN HUNTER expired at his residence in this city last evening about five o'clock, after a somewhat lingering illness, aged 87 years; born at South Shields, England, and for some time a seaman in the British Navy; resided about thirty years in Darien and Savannah; a Mason - for several years regularly elected Deputy Grand Master of the Grand Lodge of Georgia; has lived 44 years with present wife, whom he now leaves with two granddaughters.

MRS. ELIZABETH HAMILTON, relict of GEN. ALEXANDER HAMILTON, and daughter of GEN. PHILIP S. SCHUYLER, of revolutionary fame, died in Washington city on Thursday; married then LIEUTENANT COLONEL ALEXANDER HAMILTON on 7 Dec. 1780, there being not quite a year's difference in their ages...lived to age 97 years 3 months; member of Episcopal Church.

Nov. 29, 1854

Died in Macon County, on the 18th inst., MRS. MATILDA SLAPPY, wife of REUBEN H. SLAPPY, ESQ.

Died in Crawford County, on the 10th ult., the REV. DOLPHIN DAVIS, aged 63.

Died on 10th October, at Bellevue, Camden county, Ga., (the residence of his grandmother,) RICHARD WILLIAM HAMILTON, aged 21 years 11 months, son of the late COL. EVERARD HAMILTON, formerly of Savannah, Ga.

Died of fever, on night of 18th October, at the residence of his father, SEATON GRANTLAND, ESQ., DR. FLEMING TINSLEY GRANTLAND, in the 36th year of his age (short eulogy).

Dec. 6, 1854

Died in Vineville, on the morning of the 23d ult., REV. MICAJAH THOMAS, in the 66th year of his age.

Died on the 18th ult., MARIA THERESE, eldest daughter of J.M. BOARDMAN, ESQ. aged 3 years 3 months 18 days; and on the 28th ult., MILLIE PIERPONT, infant daughter of the same.

With regret we announce the deaths in this city, on Monday last, of P.M. JUDSON, ESQ., the Cashier of the Manufacturers Bank of Macon, and of ROBERT P. HALL, ESQ., a member of the Macon Bar. Mr. Juson died early in the morning on Monday, and was buried on Tuesday afternoon, in Rose Hill Cemetery, by Franklin Lodge, No. 3, of the IOOF, of which he was a member. Mr. Hall died at 9 o'clock the evening of the same day, and his remains were carried, after a funeral service at the Episcopal Church, to Crawford county for interment.

Dec. 6, 1854

A father convicted of the murder of his daughter. ALFRED ARTIS, of Shelby county, Ohio, was tried last week and convicted of murder in the first degree. Another daughter older than the deceased, was witness against him.

Dec. 13, 1854

THOMAS J. SIMS, a youth of this city, of 17 or 18 years of age, while hunting in the vicinity on the 11th inst., was killed by the accidental discharge of his gun whilst loading it.

The Tallahassee Journal, of Saturday, announces the death of GEN. JOHN SCOTT BROOME, of Madison county, brother of GOV. BROOME of Florida. He died on Wednesday evening, after an illness of about a week.

Dec. 20, 1854

Died in Houston County, on the 13th inst., MR. DAVID M. HOLMES, a much esteemed and valued citizen.

Augusta Constitutionalist states that a young man named THOMAS SMITH, aged about 23 years, a Conductor on a freight train of the Georgia Railroad, was almost instantly killed at Madison on Wednesday last. He was coupling two cars together...the two came together, crushing him between them. He lived but a few hours after the accident; member of Odd Fellows; remains conveyed to Rome where his family reside.

Madison Family Visitor - The little girl, and only child of MR. W.G. GREEN, of this place, caught fire from some coal left on the hearth, by which the child was left during the absence of the mother, who had stepped out for a few minutes, and was so severely burned that she died the next morning.

Dec. 27, 1854

Died in Vineville, on the afternoon of the 24th inst., of pneumonia, WILLIAM A. DEAN, in the 30th year of his age.

Fatal affray - A difficulty occurred in Henry county on Thursday night of last week, between JAMES HILSMAN and WM. WYATT, which resulted in the death of the former. It appears that Wyatt had eloped and married Hilsman's daughter, on the day previous... (Griffin Union, 23d inst.)

Fatal accident - MICHAEL HUGHES, one of the train hands employed on the Central Rail Road, in passing from one car to the other, whilst the train was in motion, yesterday morning, near the thirty-seven mile post, fell under the cars, and was dreadfully mangled, by the wheels passing over him. His body was brought to the city last evening. (Savannah News, 21st)

Jan. 3, 1855

Died in Madison, Morgan county, Ga., on the 29th ult., of pneumonia, BESSIE, only child of C.E. NISBET, ESQ., of Cuthbert, Ga., aged 4 years 3 months 26 days. (with eulogy)

Died on the 24th ult., near Columbus, MANSFIELD TORRANCE, ESQ., a well known and much esteemed citizen.

Account of death of two men named MILLER and NASH, by the hand of MR. GUNTER, in Fannin County...(Dahlonega Signal, Dec. 23)

Jan. 10, 1855

On the 1st inst., says the Albany Courier, THOMAS HATCHER, of this city, shot and, it is feared, fatally wounded STEPHEN SAUCER, a well known former resident of this city, now living east of the river.

The N.Y. Evening Post announces the death of THOMAS W. DORR of Rhode Island after a long and painful illness.

CHARLES SIGOURNEY, ESQ., one of the oldest and most highly respected merchants of Hartford, Ct., died very suddenly on Saturday afternoon. He was the husband of MRS. SIGOURNEY, the poetess.

Jan. 17, 1855

Died on 29th December last, at the house of his son, DR. WM. P. BEASLEY, in Troup county, Ga., MAJ. JARREL BEASLEY, in the 76th year of his age (with eulogy)

CAPTAIN SAMUEL PHILBROOK, a native of New Hampshire, but for thirty five years a resident of Savannah, died in that city on Saturday last, in 63d year of his age.

HON. MR. NORRIS, member of the Senate from New Hampshire, died suddenly in Washington City on Thursday night the 11th inst., of disease of the heart.

The Columbus Enquirer of 13th inst. says the trial of DAVID WRIGHT, for the murder of Deputy Sheriff ROBERTSON, of this county...returned verdict guilty.

Jan. 31, 1855

Among the deaths at San Francisco, we find the name of MRS. JULIA STANLY, wife of HON. EDWARD STANLY, formerly of North Carolina.

A dispatch to the Columbus Times, dated 25th inst., from Charlotte, N.C., says: REV. CYRUS JOHNSON, D.D., of this town, died very suddenly of apoplexy this morning, in an omnibus whilst going to the railroad depot. He was on his way to Fort Mills for the purpose of marrying a gentleman and lady this evening. He was the second clergyman engaged to perform the ceremony. The REV. A.S. WATTS, who had been engaged for the same purpose, died on the day appointed for the wedding, and was buried yesterday. Dr. Johnson will be buried to-morrow.

From New York Herald, Jan. 8 - MADAME SILVIE deGRASSE, ALEXANDRINE DE PAU died on the 5th inst., in the 82d year of her age, at her residence, No. 2 De Pau row; funeral ceremonies celebrated in St. Anne's Church, Eighth-street, by Rev. Dr. Forbes; a Catholic; born in Paris 1772 - youngest of six daughters of Count De Grasse; during Revolution of 1789, fled to Boston; then went to Charleston, where she married Mr. De Pau; leaves four daughters and one son, another having died last July, in Philadelphia, in 55th year of his age; names of surviving children are MRS. T.O. FOWLER, MRS. SAMUEL W. FOX, MRS. H.W. LIVINGSTON, MRS. MORTIMER LIVINGSTON, MRS. WASHINGTON COSTOR, and MR. DE PAU.

Feb. 7, 1855

Died at his residence, in this city, on the 26th inst., DR. THOMAS B. GORMAN, in the 60th year of his age; a native of South Carolina; when about six months old, his father died...became instructor of youth at Milledgeville, Ga.; here he studied Medicine and then attended Lectures in Philadelphia; settled in practice of Medicine in Monroe county, Ga.; about 16 years ago he removed to this city, where he resided up to time of his death; member of Methodist Episcopal Church; leaves widow and children (long eulogy)

Feb. 7, 1855

Died in Clinton, on 16th January, MRS. FRANCES GIBSON; for nearly thirty years known as hostess of hotel in that place.

Departed this life, on Thursday, the 1st inst., at the residence of Rev. Wm. J. Harley in Sparta, Hancock Co., Ga., MRS. BETHIA BATTLE, relict of the late R.T. BATTLE, in the 67th year of her age; member of Baptist Church (with short eulogy)

Tribute of respect by South-Western Lodge, No. 143, Oglethorpe, Ga. Jan. 29, 1855 - on death of AUGUSTUS B. CHAPMAN who died at his father's residence in Crawford county on the 16th inst.

Tribute of respect by Morning Star Lodge, No. 27, Thomaston Jan. 20, 1855 - on death of HENRY GARLAND.

Charleston Courier of 30th ult. announces that DR. WILLIAM CAPERS, one of the Bishops of the Methodist Episcopal Church, died at his residence at Anderson, C.H., on Monday morning, in the 66th year of his age; born in St. Thomas Parish 26 Jan. 1790; received M.A. degree from South Carolina College; received as travelling Minister in 1808; in 1838 was sent to England as representative of American Methodist Episcopal Church to the British Conference, and for several years he was one of the general Missionary Secretaries; in 1846 was elected Bishop.

STEPHEN PLEASONTON, for fifty years, Fifth Auditor of the Treasury, died in Washington City on the 1st inst., JOHN W. MAURY, prominent citizen of Washington, formerly Mayor of the city, and at time of his death, President of the Bank of the Metropolis, also died on 2d inst.

Wife shot by her husband. A man living in Russell county, Ala. went to the house of MR. GEORGE MOORE, who lives about three miles west of Girard, and while there, a serious altercation ensued between the parties, during which Mr. Moore took down his gun and was in the act of shooting his antagonist, when MRS. MOORE ran between them... the gun was discharged, wounding her so seriously, that her life is despaired of. (Columbus Enquirer)

Feb. 14, 1855

Died on the 24th ult., at Jeffersonville, Twiggs county, MARY JANE, eldest daughter of ELLIS and MARIA L. LONG, in the 17th year of her age (with eulogy)

GREEN H. JORDAN, ESQ. died at his residence, Jackson Hall, Baldwin county, near Milledgeville, on Tuesday the 6th inst., in the 66th year of his age.

The Marshall (Texas) Republican reports particulars of a bloody and fatal affray which occurred at a drinking house at Sugar Hill, in Panola county, on the evening of the 24th ult. The affray commenced by a quarrel between a man named CRAIN and one JOHN GLASS, the latter shooting an old man named YEARY dead for interfering; while Yeary's son was stooping over his father he was stabbed in the back by SIMEON GLASS, John's brother; young Yeary then rose and rushed upon the murderer of his father, wrenched the pistol from his grasp, pursued him through the house into the yard, and killed him with a bowie knife. While this was taking place, Simeon Glass was shot dead by several of the crowd whom he had attacked with his knife. Man named HAYWOOD probably fired the fatal shot.

A.C. DEVEREAUX of Hancock County, lately a citizen of this place, was killed by OBADIAH ARNOLD, at his liquor shop in the county aforesaid on Tuesday last. Arnold and Devereaux were cousins. (Fed. Union, 6th inst.)

Feb. 14, 1855

HON. HARMAN KNICKERBACKER died yesterday at his residence in
Schaghticoke, aged 75 years. The death of his wife occurred only
a few weeks since; was immortalized by Washington Irving, who made
him the original of his Diedrich; held for a time the office of
County Judge, and in 1810-13 represented this district in Congress;
as a politician, he was a federalist in early life; after the
inauguration of Jackson, he classed himself as a Democrat.
(Troy Budget)

Feb. 21, 1855

Died in East Macon on the 13th inst., MRS. MARY J. NELSON, aged
about 23 years, wife of JAMES B. NELSON. (Papers in Americus will
please copy)

The Charleston Courier of 15th inst. announces the death of COL.
FRANCIS KINLOCH HUGER, who expired at his residence in that city;
in 82d year of his age, at 1 o'clock yesterday afternoon; son of
COL. BENJAMIN HUGER, of the revolution; when a young man, he joined
Dr. Eric Bollman, of Philadelphia, in his attempt to liberate
LaFayette from the dungeons of Olmutz...appointed a Captain in
US Army in 1798; resigned and retured soon afterwards, but on
breaking out of war in 1812, was recalled and soon received command
of a regiment of artillery attached to the Southern Division;
served his native State in both branches of the Legislature.

Feb. 28, 1855

Died at Hudson, N.Y., on the 17th inst., of dropsy of the brain,
EDITH MANNERS, infant daughter of WM. C. and CORNELIA H.B. RICHARDS,
of N. York, aged 13 months.

We regret to learn that MR. JAMES HERRING, of Troup county, who was
in our city a few days ago, died very suddenly on Saturday last,
at LaGrange, a few hours after he reached his home.

Mar. 14, 1855

Died in Washington, Ga., on Wednesday, the 28th February, SARAH H.,
the beloved wife of ADAM L. ALEXANDER and daughter of the late
FELIX H. GILBERT, aged 49 years.

Died also, in the same place, on Sabbath day, 4th March, her
daughter-in-law, MARY LOUISA, the beloved wife of WM. F. ALEXANDER,
and daughter of the HON. ROBERT TOOMBS.

Charleston Mercury - announces death of RT. REV. IGNATIUS ALOYSIUS
REYNOLDS, Bishop of Charleston. He expired yesterday morning, at
quarter past six, in the 57th year of his age; born near Bardstown,
Kentucky 22 August 1798; came of an old Maryland family, who were
among the early settlers of the then wild country of Kentucky;
educated at St. Mary's College, Baltimore; long-time Vicar-General
to Bishop Flaget; Rector of St. Joseph's College, near Bardstown,
and President of Nazareth Female Institute of Kentucky; was consecrated Bishop of Charleston at Cincinnati, in March 1844, and
entered upon the episcopal duties in April following (with eulogy)

Mar. 21, 1855

Died in Sumter County, on the 12th inst., COL. GEORGE L. DOUGLASS,
aged 55 years. On the 13th MISS MARTHA JANE, daughter of J.V.
PRICE, ESQ., in the 14th year of her age.

Died on the 9th inst., CHARLES STEWART, ESQ. aged about 59 years -
formerly of Monroe county, but for several years past a highly
respected citizen of Macon and Sumter counties.

Mar. 28, 1855

Lee Superior Court - The case of the State vs. JOHN M. BERTINE for the murder of WILLIAM SPENCE, in August 1854, was tried, and resulted in conviction. The Sumter Republican states he was sentenced to be hung on the 27th of April, whilst the Albany Courier of a later date states that a new trial was granted him.

COL. McCLUNG, the noted duellist and distinguished officer of the Mississippi rifle regiment in the Mexican war, committed suicide in Jackson, Miss., on Saturday last.

Terrific explosion. Five white men, two white boys, and thirty colored men were killed by an explosion in the Midlothian coal pits in Chesterfield county, Va., on Monday evening last. The names of the white sufferers are as follows: SAMUEL GOULDIN, manager of bands; JOHN LESTER, J. EVANS, JOSEPH HOWE, and the two boys, JONATHAN JEWETT and WM. WRIGHT.

LADY SUFFOLK died at Edgar's Hill, Bridgeport, Vt., on the 7th inst.

Apr. 4, 1855

MRS. ELIZABETH McNIEL, widow of the late GEN. JOHN McNEIL, and sister of the President of the United States, died in Concord, New Hampshire, on Wednesday the 28th ult., in the 68th year of her age.

Apr. 11, 1855

Died in Athens, on the 31st ult., at the residence of his father, PROF. JAMES P. WADDELL, MR. MOSES WADDELL, in the 20th year of his age, after a tedious illness of five months.

Apr. 18, 1855

Died in this City, on Monday evening last, WM. T. MIX, ESQ., in the 35th year of his age; a native of Connecticut, but had lived many years in Newark, New Jersey, before coming South.

Died in this city on the 15th inst., MR. JOSEPH SMITH, aged about 78 years.

Died on Tuesday evening last, MR. JOHN DACY, of this city.

Tribute of respect by Traveller's Rest Lodge, No. 65, March 24th, 1855 - on death of DANIEL SYKES.

Three men were killed in a quarrel in Emanuel county...On second day of April, MATHEW and SAMUEL WILLIAMSON and some others went to MR. L. WILKIES, where there was a party of men, and called them to come out. MR. J. MOSELY went out to them, when he was knocked down with a gun, having his jaw broken, and as his brother ROGER MOSELY stooped down to pick him up, he was stabbed through and died instantly. Then both parties began to fire, in which MATHEW WILLIAMSON was killed and SAMUEL WILLIAMSON wounded - he has since died.

The Savannah Republican of the 11th inst. announces the death in that city, at 1 o'clock yesterday afternoon, from erysipelas, of BENJ. E. STILES, aged 54; at one time engaged in the mercantile business, as member of the firm Stiles and Fannin...

Apr. 25, 1855

MR. DANIEL DOUGHERTY, an old and esteemed citizen of this place, in a personal rencontre with a man named JAMES MARTIN, who inflicted three wounds upon the former with a large case knife...Mr. Dougherty expired immediately upon the spot...(Atlanta Examiner, 18th inst.)

Apr. 25, 1855

DAVID NEWMAN, who died lately in Granville county, N.C., was cabin boy of Paul Jones, a cannonier for Rogers at Tunis, an actor in the scenes at Tripoli, and at Sandy Fork a corporal in the Philadelphia regiment.

Died in this city, on the 18th inst., MR. JOHN M. KUNZE, aged about 88 years; of German descent and native of Strasburg, in France, and had arrived in this country since 1798; a merchant and bank officer; acting Secretary of the Grand Lodge of Georgia for several years; had resided in Philadelphia, Augusta, Savannah, Brunswick, and this city; was a soldier in the army of Napoleon, in Italy, which he left, through the influence of his mother, at the Black Forest, in the year 1796, at the time of the celebrated retreat by Jourdan and Moreau, shortly before embarking for this country; in emigrating, he was the associate of John Jacob Astor, of N. York; his body was carried to Augusta for interment, where he has relatives residing.

Died in Baker county, on the 18th inst., of consumption, MRS. DOLLY COLQUITT, wife of the HON. A.H. COLQUITT, and daughter of the late GEN. H.H. TARVER, of Twiggs county. Her body was brought to this city, and interred in Rose Hill Cemetery on the 20th inst.

Died in Columbus, on the 13th inst., of scarlet fever, ROBERT BREWER, eldest son of MR. ROBERT C. FORSYTH, aged 3 years and 3 months.

May 2, 1855

Died at the residence of his son, NATHAN C. MUNROE, in Vineville, on the 24th ultimo, NATHAN MUNROE, at the advanced age of 82 years; a native of New York, where he was a merchant for many years.

CAPT. D. DILL, who served with honorable distinction in the Seminole campaign in Florida, in 1836, and also as Captain of the Augusta Blues in Col. Jackson's Georgia regiment of volunteers, in Mexico, in 1846-7, died at Memphis, Tenn., on Friday of last week.

May 9, 1855

HON. WALTER T. COLQUITT died yesterday at the house of Wm. Ross, Esq., in this city, after a long and very painful illness; had been Judge of the Superior Court, Representative in Congress, Senator in the US Congress. (Telegraph of yesterday)

May 16, 1855

Died in Perry, on the 18th ult., DR. FOWLER HOLT, in the 50th year of his age.

Died in this city, on the 6th of May, at the Georgia Academy for the Blind, AMANDA R. HALL, in her 13th year; daughter of JOHN HALL of Whitfield Co.; became a pupil in the Academy for the Blind Oct. 1, 1853 (with short eulogy)

Departed this life, on Thursday the 3d day of May, at his residence in Pulaski county, MR. J.A.L. COLEY, in the 48th year of his age. (with eulogy)

May 23, 1855

Died on the 8th of April, at her residence in Americus, in the 58th year of her age, MRS. CHARITY D. MACON, relict of WM. G. MACON, formerly of Macon.

May 30, 1855

D.J. McCORD, ESQ., prominent citizen of Columbia (S.C.) and a

(May 30, cont'd) - son-in-law, we believe, of the venerable JUDGE
CHEVES, died on Saturday last. He was one of the co-editors of
Nott & McCord's Reports, so well known to lawyers.

June 6, 1855

Died in Summerville, near Augusta, Ga., of Pulmonary Consumption,
on the 20th ult., MRS. ELIZABETH D. BROWN, widow of WM. SPENCER
BROWN, and daughter of JUDGE BARNES, of Philadelphia.

Died at Madison, on Sunday the 13th ult., MISS REBECCA, daughter
of REV. C.W. KEY, in the 15th year of her age.

June 13, 1855

Died in this city, on the 6th inst., of consumption, MR. PATRICK
CUNNINGHAM, aged 52 years.

Died at Fort Valley, on the 4th inst., very suddenly, while on his
way to Macon, MR. MATHEW B. McCOMB, a merchant of Hawkinsville,
aged about 48 years.

Died in Twiggs county, on the 6th inst., MR. WM. MARTIN, aged about
36 years; a Mason - member of Twiggs Lodge, No. 164, by which he
was buried on the 8th inst.

Died on the 2d inst., MRS. MARIA FOISSIN OSBORNE, wife of JOHN H.
OSBORNE, of this city; a native of Charleston, So. Ca. but had
resided for many years in this State, at St. Mark's and at this
city. (Charleston papers please copy)

June 20, 1855

Died at the residence of his father, near Glennville, Ala., May
30th, 1855, JAS. AUG. BASS, in the 27th year of his age; a native
of Putnam county, Ga.

June 27, 1855

Died on the 22d inst., CARRIE ALIDA, daughter of A.A. and C.E.
MANARD, aged 13 months and 5 days.

Died at the residence of Dr. J.C. Harvey, near Knoxville, Crawford
county, on the 2d inst., DR. RICHARD HARVEY, in the 58th year of
his age; a native of Hancock county, but removed to Crawford county
soon after its settlement.

Died at his residence in Crawford county, on the 11th inst., in
the 56th year of his age, WILLIAM ZEIGLER; born in Edgefield District
S.C., whence he removed to Crawford co., Ga. In 1827, where he
remained engaged in agriculture to death; his remains now rest in
a temporary vault in Rose Hill Cemetery, in Macon, Ga., where they
will remain until a permanent vault shall be completed according
to his directions. (with eulogy) (Southern Recorder please copy)

July 4, 1855

Died in this city, on the 2d inst., CHS. E.S. BRANTLY, aged 2
years 11 months 25 days - son of WM. S. and SUSAN A. BRANTLY.

Died, at Griswoldville, on Thursday, the 28th inst., ELIZABETH H.,
daughter of THOMAS and SARAH HARDEMAN, and wife of E.C. GRISWOLD,
in the 32d year of her age; leaves a husband and three children -
one of whom is a prattling little boy of 20 months (with short
eulogy)

Tribute of respect by Twiggs Lodge, No. 164 (Marion, Twiggs Co.,
June 1855*) - on death of WM. J. MARTIN, who died on the evening
of the 6th inst., at his residence in this county, in the 35th
year of his age.

July 11, 1855

Died at Indian Springs, Butts county, on the 3d inst., of dropsy, WILLIAM KING, in the 39th year of his age; a native of New York, but for 16 years a resident of this city.

MARTHA J. SLAPPEY, daughter of R.R. SLAPPEY, of Twiggs county, died in Vineville at the residence of her uncle, Benjamin Bryan, on the 26th of June, aged 16 (with very long eulogy)

HON. OWEN H. KENAN died recently at his residence in Whitfield county.

DR. WILLIAM TERRELL expired at his residence in Sparta, Hancock county, on the morning of the 4th inst.; believed to be a native of Wilkes county, and removed to Hancock in early youth; represented the county in the Legislature, and subsequently in the Federal Congress; devoted to agriculture and endowed the Professorship of Agriculture in the University of Georgia. (Savannah Georgian)

The widow of DE WITT CLINTON died at the residence of her daughter, in Poughkeepsie, on Monday - in the 72d year of her age.

July 18, 1855

EDWARD E. POWERS, of Columbus, Ga., died suddenly at Chicago, Illinois, on the 13th ult., aged 62; a native of Bernardstown, Massachusetts; gave $10,000 to the Female Orphan Asylum at Columbus, Ga.

Homicide - WILLIAM BARWICK, a resident of this county, was killed in a street rencontre on Friday afternoon last by AUGUSTUA SWAIN and GREEN W. JACKSON. The wounds were inflicted with a bowie knife and club...(Thomasville Watchman, 11th inst.)

The Marietta Prohibitionist of the 11th inst. announces the death of two worthy citizens, ROBERT and CC. BOSTWICK, who lost their lives on the steamer Lexington, recently blown up on the Ohio river near Rome, Ind. The deceased were brothers, merchants of our city, and were on their way to market for fresh supplies.

July 25, 1855

Died in this city, on the morning of the 24th inst., after an illness of a few hours, MISS ELIZA W. COTTON, eldest daughter of the late CHARLES COTTON, aged 27 years 6 months.

Died at Lumber City, Telfair Co., at the residence of her son-in-law, CHARLES H. STEWART, on the morning of the 6th ult., MRS. MARGARET McLAUGHLIN, age 75.

Died at his residence in Abbeville District, S.C., on the 20th ult., JOSHUA HILL, ESQ., aged 92 years 20 days; a Rev. soldier and patriot; member of Baptist Church for upwards of 60 years (with short eulogy)

Homicide in Jones County. SYLVESTER S. LORD, a young man about 28 years of age, was killed on Tuesday evening the 17th inst., a few miles west of Clinton, by JOHN TOWLES. It appears that the parties had met at Dames Ferry, eighteen miles above this city on the Ocmulgee river, where they had a violent altercation about political matters...

CAPT. E.P. POWELL, of Resaca, was killed in that place, Saturday, the 7th inst., by MATHEW COPELAND. (Cassville Standard)

$200 reward. Stop the murdered!! The above reward will be paid for the arrest and delivery to the Sheriff of Jones county, Ga., of JOHN TOWLES, who killed SYLVESTER S. LORD, of said county, on Tuesday, the 17th inst., by shooting him with one of Colt's repeat-

(July 25, cont'd) - ing pistols. Said Towles is about 22 years of age, 5 feet 6 or 8 inches high, rather darkish complexion and hair, nose inclined to be Roman, weighing about 145. On his neck is a circular spot, of a yellowish hue, and projecting from the surface. He is fond of spirits, especially Peach Brandy...

Aug. 1, 1855

Died in Vineville, on the 24th ult., of paralysis, MRS. ANN BYRON, aged about 75 years - (formerly MISS JAPPIE, a native of New York City).

Died in Clinton, Jones county, on Sunday evening, July 28th, MOSES R. DRAPER, in the 37th year of his age, son of the late JOSHUA DRAPER, of Warren county, and brother of JAMES M. DRAPER, of this city.

Died at Barnesville, Pike Co., Ga., on the 23d ult., of Scarlet Fever, JOHN LATHROP, infant son of MR. JOHN A. and MRS. ELIZABETH FRYER, aged 10 months.

A telegraphic dispatch was received in this city on Monday morning, announcing that the body of J.J. ORR, (one of our most estimable and successful business men who has been for some time engaged upon a large contract on the Savannah and Gulf Railroad) had been found about eight miles from Hinesville, Liberty county, and with marks upon it which showed that he had been most brutally murdered..

Aug. 8, 1855

Died near Macon, on the morning of the 24th ult., THOMAS CLARENCE, son of JAMES N. and SARAH ANN KING, aged 17 months 11 days.

The Columbia Times reports that DR. JOHN C. CALHOUN, third son of the late HON. JOHN C. CALHOUN, died Tuesday morning last, at the residence of Maj. J.H. Rion, in Winnsboro, where he had recently arrived from Florida, afflicted with Consumption. His remains arrived in this city yesterday by the Charlotte Road, destined to the final resting place, Fort Hills, S.C.

Aug. 15, 1855

Died in this city, on the 8th inst., SOLOMON HUMPHRIES, a free man of color, aged about 54 years. He was a resident of this place at the earliest settlement, and since that time has been well known - first as a small trader, and afterwards, for many years, as a merchant and cotton dealer. His uprightness and strict integrity in business, and quiet and gentlemanly demeaner, always secured for him the respect and friendship of all who knew him.

L.O. REYNOLDS, ESQ., one of our most prominent and estimable citizens, and since its first organization, the popular and efficient President of the South-Western Railroad Company, died in the 55th year of his age, on Tuesday of last week, at the Warm Springs in Virginia, whither he had gone several months ago in very feeble health; a native of East Hartford, Conn.; came to Savannah in 1816, and engaged in mercantile pursuits until 1826, when he was employed as an engineer on the Savannah and Ogeechee Canal; subsequently engaged at Fort Pulaski, while that fortification was being built, and also in several preliminary surveys for railroads - among others upon the Central Road in this State, and the road leading from Hartford to Boston; returned to Georgia in 1836 and became assistant engineer on the Central Road, under Mr. Randell, then Chief Engineer and afterwards President of South-Wester (Ga.) Road; his remains arrived here Saturday night, and were taken to the residence of his friend, R.R. Cuyler, Esq., whence they were conveyed to Laurel Grove Cemetery yesterday afternoon at 5 o'clock, and interred.
(Savannah Republican of Monday morning)

Aug. 15, 1855

    State of Georgia, Americus, 2d District, 10th July 1855 - a tribute of respect on life of HON. WALTER T. COLQUITT.

Aug. 22, 1855

    We regret to learn that a personal difficulty occurred at the Madison Springs on Monday night, between MR. COX of Mississippi, and WM. J. MORTON of this place, in which the latter was supposed to be fatally wounded. (Athens Watchman)

Sep. 5, 1855

    Died in Vineville, on the morning of the 2d inst., LUCIA JOHNSON, daughter of T.J. and J.E. CATER, aged 8 years 5 months.

    The HON. THOMAS METCALFE died at his home in Nicholas county on Saturday evening last, in the 76th year of his age. He had been indisposed for two or three weeks, but the immediate cause of his death is said to have been cholera. (Lou. Jour., Aug. 22)

    MR. BENJAMIN BLACKFORD died at the residence of his son, MR. WM. BLACKFORD, in this city, Monday afternoon. He was one of the few men living who enjoyed the proud recollection of having voted for "The Father of his Country" for President. (Lynchburg Virginian, Aug. 22)

Sep. 12, 1855

    Died at Macon, on Tuesday evening 4th inst., NORA, daughter of JOHN B. ROSS, ESQ., aged 7 years 6 months.

    Died at her father's residence in Hayneville, Houston county, 16th ult., MISS SUSAN E. TOOKE, daughter of JOSEPH and MARY JANE TOOKE, aged 16 years 6 months 18 days. She died with typhoid fever after 16 days illness; member of M.E. Church. (Citizen please copy)

    HON. W.B.W. DENT died at his residence in Newnan, Coweta county, on Friday last, after a protracted illness; member of last Congress from the Fourth District, and declined a nomination for re-election on account of the state of his health.

    JUDGE CRANCH died at his residence in this city on Saturday evening; one of the oldest residents of the Federal city, having removed here with his family from Massachusetts in 1796 or 1797, three or four years before the Government was transferred from Philadelphia. (National Intelligencer)

Sep. 19, 1855

    DR. CHARLES WEST, Sen. of Houston county, died on the night of 8th inst., at Saratoga, N.Y. of an affection of the heart. He was travelling at the North for the benefit of his health, with a married daughter, (MRS. POWERS, of Houston); had been a resident of McIntosh, Chatham and Houston counties; at time of his death, he was a candidate for the Senate from Houston County.

    The Florida Republican reports that HON. THOMAS DOUGLASS died at Jacksonville on Tuesday night last, at the advanced age of 65 years; at time of death, he was one of the Judges of the Supreme Court of Florida - having previously held office of Circuit Court Judge.

Oct. 3, 1855

    Died near this city on 30th ult., of Paralysis, SUSAN F., wife of WM. SHIVERS, JR., and second daughter of the late GOV. WM. RABUN, in the 57th year of her age; for last 18 years a consistent member of the M.E. Church. (Augusta papers please copy)

Oct. 3, 1855

Died in this city, on the 28th ult., MR. CALEB MALDEN, SEN., aged about 90 years, (supposed to be the oldest resident of the county).

A correspondent from Telfair county writes that on the 4th inst., JOHN QUINN, of that county, eloped with MISS MARTHA WILLCOX, daughter of WOODSON WILLCOX, of Telfair county, and carried her into Coffee county to the house of Mr. John Hill, where they were married by Abner Mobley, Justice of the Inferior Court. After they had been united, the youthful couple started for the house of the bridegroom's father, but while passing a small creek on the road, John Quinn, the bridegroom was shot in the back and instantly killed. His wife went back to the first house, which was Mr. Jonathan Ashley's, and gave the information that her husband had been killed. Suspicion rests upon the father of the young lady. (So. Enterprise)

Oct. 10, 1855

Died of Consumption, at the residence of Mr. Wm. Gray, MRS. ANN A. GRAY, wife of JOHN D. GRAY, ESQ.; for about ten years a member of the Baptist Church of this city. (with eulogy) (Christian Index and the Carolina Baptist copy)

Died in Jackson co., Fla., on the 9th of Sept., SALLIE RAINES, daughter of DAVID and SUSAN BLACKSHEAR, aged 1 year 2 months and 19 days.

Tribute of respect by Pleasant Ridge Lodge, No. 103, F.A.M. - on death of JOHN P. HUMPHREYS, aged 33, who departed this life on 12th of June, 1855, at the residence of William C. Harrison.

The Montgomery journals announce the death from Yellow Fever of NAT. HARRIS, a prominent citizen and eminent Lawyer of that city.

Oct. 17, 1855

Died in Twiggs county, on the 17th ult., MRS. MARY WARE, wife of JAMES WARE, ESQ., aged about 67 years.

Died in Vineville on the 5th inst., LAURA, eldest daughter of JOHN E. and ARABELLA JONES, aged 6 years 3 months.

Died in New York, on the 3d inst., of Billious Fever, MRS. E.B. KENNEDY, wife of MR. WM. C. KENNEDY, of this city.

Died at Jeffersonville, Twiggs county, on 27th Sept., GEORGE H. ANDERSON, son of the late THOS. W. ANDERSON.

HON. SAMUEL D. HUBBARD, formerly a member of Congress, and Post Master General under President Fillmore, died at his residence in Middletown, Connecticut, on the 8th inst.

JOHN HASKIE, an engineer on the Georgia Rail Road, was shot in Decatur, on Wed. night last, by GEO. BRICE. Haskie died of the wound the same night. (Atlanta Intelligencer, 13th inst.)

Oct. 24, 1855

Died in this city, on the 17th inst., of a disease of the lungs, DR. K.H. MANLY, of Traveller's Rest, aged about 42 years. On the 18th he was buried in Rose Hill Cemetery, by Macon Lodge, No. 5, with the usual honors of Masonry.

REV. G.H. HANCOCK died on the 16th inst. about 3 o'clock A.M. at his residence in this city, of Congestive Fever; was born in Charleston in Oct. 1818; educated at Franklin College in this State; abandoned Law in favor of Christian Ministry...(with eulogy)

Oct. 24, 1855

MORRIS ABRAHAM, indicted for the murder of RICHARD J. CHOATE, of Jones Co., was tried at the October Term of Superior Court...

Oct. 31, 1855

Died in this city, on the 11th inst., HIBERNIA R., youngest daughter of C. and ADALINE S. MULHOLLAND, in the 10th year of her age.

Died at the residence of his father, near this city, on the 11th inst., JOSEPH A., son of LEROY and M.L. NAPIER, aged 23.

Died on Saturday night, 13th inst., at Sparta, Ga., MRS. FRANCES BIRD, consort of WILLIAM BIRD, ESQ., for many years a resident of Hancock county, and a consistent member of the Roman Catholic communion.

Tribute of respect by officers and pupils of Wesleyan Female College - on death of REV. GEORGE H. HANCOCK, one of the Professors in the Institution.

WILLIAM POE, ESQ., a brother of Washington Poe, Esq., of this city, died at his residence a few miles from Montgomery, Ala., on the 20th inst., of nervous fever; was President of the Montgomery Bank.

Nov. 7, 1855

Died in Worth county, on the 25th of October, SAMUEL C. LIPPITT, ESQ., aged about 56 years; a native of Providence, R.I.; he resided for several years in Clinton, and afterwards in this city, and for last fifteen years in the place where he died.

Died in Macon, Ga., July 24, 1855, after a few hours illness, ELIZA W. COTTON, daughter of the late CHARLES COTTON, ESQ., of that place...(with long eulogy)

JAMES N. NORRELL, ESQ., Cashier of the Bank of Montgomery, and a native of Augusta, Ga., died in Montgomery, on the 1st inst., of yellow fever.

DR. J.C. HABERSHAM, SEN., expired at his residence on Liberty street, about five o'clock last evening, in the 65th year of his age...of inflammation of the lungs; born in 1790; a native of Savannah, where he had always resided, with exception of the few years spent during his collegiate course at Princeton and his medical studies at Philadelphia. (Sav. Georgian, 3rd inst.)

The Wilmington (N.C.) papers announce the death, in that city, on Tuesday last, of the HON. EDWARD B. DUDLEY. Gov. Dudley twice occupied the Executive chair of North Carolina, and was once elected to Congress.

COMMODORE JOHN D. DANELS died a few days ago in Baltimore; identified with the revolutionary struggles in Columbia, South America.

Nov. 14, 1855

Died in Perry, Ga., on the 26th, after a short illness, MR. WILLIAM C. SPEIR, in the 42d year of his age.

Died in Macon, Ga., on the 7th ult., MR. WILLIAM CRICHTON, aged 51 years; a native of Edinborough, Scotland.

Died near this city, on Sunday night, the 4th inst., MRS. HESTER THOMPSON, wife of HEZEKIAH THOMPSON; a native of Richland District, S.C., and 74 years of age; united with the Baptist Church in Carolina; leaves several children and grandchildren in different parts of the State; and a husband, who is about the same age, and with whom she walked in the pilgrimage of life for period of 51 years;

(Nov. 14, cont'd) - some eight or ten years ago Mr. and Mrs. Thompson began to experience blindness, and for some time past both have been nearly totally blind.

Departed this life, on Tuesday evening, the 6th inst., after a short though painful illness, ROBERT ATKINSON, only son of AURELIA and ALBERT G. BOSTICK, aged 21 months 6 days.

Nov. 21, 1855

The Augusta Chronicle and Sentinel of 16th inst. reports that HAMILTON RAIFORD shot and killed a man named WARD in Jefferson county on Monday last.

Dec. 5, 1855

Died in Athens, on Wednesday, Nov. 21st, COL. JOHN A. COBB, in the 73d year of his age. Was father of ES-GOV. HOWELL COBB and THOMAS R. COBB, the able Reporter of the Supreme Court.

COL. N.H. CLANTON, Senator to the Legislature from Alabama from Macon county, died in Montgomery on 27th ult., of congestive chills.

Dec. 12, 1855

Died in Lee county, on the 2d inst., MRS. SARAH A. BRYAN, wife of JOHN D. BRYAN, in the 28th year of her age, leaving a husband and three children.

Died in Hillsboro, Jasper county, on Wed. 5th Dec. 1855, CUTHBERT REESE, aged 74 years and 6 days.

Departed this life on Wednesday, 5th instant, in this city, SARAH NORMAN, in the 85th year of her age; a native of Virginia, but immigrated to Georgia more than 60 years ago, and was among the earliest settlers of Bibb county... bereaved of a husband nearly forty years ago...(with eulogy)

About 11 o'clock last night, a difficulty occurred in a house at the lower end of South Broad-street, between WILLIAM HODGES and BERNARD FLANNAGAN, which resulted in the death of the former... (Sav. Rep., 4th inst.)

Dec. 19, 1855

Died at his residence in Vineville, on Sunday evening last the 16th inst., JOHN BOWMAN, an old and respected citizen of this county, aged about 73 years.

Dec. 26, 1855

Died in Oglethorpe, on Wed. morning the 28th ultimo, after a painful illness, MRS. MARY SELINE COLZY, consort of DR. E.F. COLZY of the same place. (with short eulogy)

Died in Aberdeen, Mississippi, on the 7th inst., MRS. ELIZA CLARA CUNNINGHAM, wife of WM. R. CUNNINGHAM, of that place, and daughter of BLANTON M. HILL, of Athens, Ga.

Died at the residence of Rev. P. Ogletree in Meriwether county, on the 15th Nov. last, MRS. ELIZABETH RYHMES, widow of WILLIAM RHYMES and (sister to the HON. WM. H. CRAWFORD many years deceased) at the advanced age of 82 years; a member of the Protestant Episcopal Church.

Jan. 2, 1856

Railroad accidents. On Tuesday morning last, about 3 o'clock, the passenger train on the South-Western Railroad, while passing over an embankment of some twenty feet in height, in the Tobesaufky swamp, was thrown from the track by coming in contact with a cow. The locomotive, tender, and passenger car were precipitated down the bank - the locomotive falling on MR. H.H. COLE, the engineer, who was instantly killed. JAMES HANCOCK, the fireman, was so badly scalded, that he died a few hours afterwards.

On Saturday morning last, two passenger trains came in collision near Reynolds, by which the locomotives were considerably damaged... one of the train hands was killed, and a passenger by name of PAULK, formerly of Jones county, by lately of Alabama, in jumping out of one of the trains which was backing at the time of the collision, was injured...he died of his wounds on Sunday last.

The Columbus Times & Sentinel of 28th ult. says that JACOB MERCER, who was under sentence of death in Stewart county, for the alledged murder of GREENE B. LEE, and whose petition for pardon was recently rejected by the Legislature, committed suicide by taking laudanum furnished by his wife on the night previous to the day set apart for his execution.

Jan. 9, 1856

Died in this City, on Wed. evening last, ALEX. FEW RICHARDS, son of Judge ALEX. RICHARDS, in the 27th year of his age.

Died in this county, on the 5th inst., MR. JOHN T. PATTERSON, in the 74th year of his age - formerly a resident of Jones county, and more recently, of Monroe.

Telegraphic advices from Savannah, Georgia, announce the death, at his residence in that city, on the 1st instant, of HON. JOHN MACPHERSON BERRIEN, known to the country as President Jackson's first Attorney General, and subsequently as member of Senate of United States and of the Whig party; believed to be 75 or 76 years of age. (National Intelligencer).

The Savannah Republican also relays the obituary of HON. JOHN MACPHERSON BERRIEN. He died at 9 o'clock, Tuesday morning, January 1st, of inflammation of the kidneys; his paternal ancestors were Huguenots. Fleeing from France to Holland after the revocation of the Edict of Nantes, two brothers emigrated to this country and settled, the one of Long Island, the other in New Jersey. His paternal grandfather, JOHN BERRIEN, was one of the Judges of the Supreme Court of New Jersey. His father, MAJOR JOHN BERRIEN, came to Georgia at a very early age. Toward the close of the Rev. War he married, in Philadelphia, MARGARET MACPHERSON, the sister of JOHN MACPHERSON, (aid-de-camp of General Montgomery, who fell at Quebec,) and of GENERAL WILLIAM MACPHERSON who served in the Army until the close of the war... Nov. 1809 was elected Solicitor of Eastern District of Georgia, and following year Judge of same District; was elected four times to that office; during War of 1812 he performed a short tour of service at Darien, while the British forces were upon the Island of St. Simons; in 1822 and 1823 he represented Chatham Co. in the State Senate; Legislature of Georgia in 1824 transferred him to the Senate of the United States and he took that seat 4 March 1825; in 1829 appointed Attorney General of the U.S. in General Jackson's Cabinet; resigned his seat in May 1852 and returned to private life; his funeral was celebrated at Christ Church; his body was escorted by the Georgia Hussars, of whom he was the first commander, to Laurel Grove Cemetery.

Jan. 16, 1856

MILLER, who murdered DR. HADEL and MR. FREDERICK GRAEFF, at Cumber-

(Jan. 16, cont'd) - land, Md., a few months since was hung at that place on Friday last. He died protesting his innocence.

Jan. 23, 1856

MR. ELIJAH H. CRANE, for past thirty years a respectable Cotton merchant of Savannah, died in that city on the 15th inst.; a native of Massachusetts. For some time past he had been in retirement in consequence of bodily infirmity.

Died in this city, on the 20th inst., CADWELL W. RAINES, ESQ., aged 61 years; one of the first settlers of this county; member of Methodist Church; a Trustee of Wesleyan Female College; buried with Masonic honors by Macon Lodge, No. 5.

Died at Orange Lake, Fla., on the 12th inst., of Consumption, MR. ROBERT FREEMAN, aged 38 years; had resided for several years in vicinity of this city, and visited Florida a few weeks since for benefit of his health; his body was brought to this city and interred in Rose Hill Cemetery on Sunday last.

Died in Sandersville, on the 19th inst., DR. WM. P. HAYNES, aged over 60 years, an eminent practising physician; a Mason - had held post of Deputy Grand Master of the State of Georgia; buried with Masonic honors by Hamilton Lodge, No. 58, on the 21st inst.

Jan. 30, 1856

MR. GEORGE FRALEY, a worthy citizen of Hancock, on leaving the cars at Gordon, on Friday last, sank down and died in a few minutes.

Feb. 6, 1856

Died in this city on the night of the 4th inst., very suddenly, MR. JOHN HUNT, aged nearly 70 years.

Died in Americus on the 24th ult., after a short illness, DR. JOHN J. HAMPTON, aged 49 years 8 months; a native of Richland Dist., S.C., and previous to his removal to Americus, had resided several years in Houston, and been elected to the Legislature from that county.

Died on the 20th inst., at the residence of Garrett Smith, in Houston county, MRS. SARAH C., wife of DR. THOMAS W. BELL, and daughter of MAJ. ALEX'R SMITH, aged 19 years (eulogy)

Monroe Lodge No. 18 F. & A.M. gives tribute of respect to WILSON LARY, who departed this life at his residence near Forsyth, Monroe county, Ga., Nov. 12th, 1855, in the 47th year of his age.

HON. A.J. MILLER died at his residence in Augusta on Sabbath morning last, of pneumonia; for years he stood at the head of the Augusta Bar; member of State Senate at time of his death. (with short eulogy)

Feb. 13, 1856

Died in this city on the 9th inst., MRS. ELIZABETH J. MARTIN, widow of JOHN MARTIN.

Died at the residence of his Mother, near this City, DAVID F. RILEY, in the 21st year of his age.

Died at Dublin, Laurens county, on the 30th ult., DELAMOTTA SHEFTALL, ESQ., a member of the Bar of the Southern Circuit, in the 34th year of his age.

Died on the 29th ult., of pneumonia, at the residence of John M. Robertson, Fairfield District, S.C., in the 25th year of her age, MRS. LAURA ELLEN, wife of NATHAN C. ROBERTSON, and daughter of ISAAC WINSHIP, of Atlanta, Ga.

Feb. 13, 1856

Died in Macon Jan. 30th, of Consumption, MRS. MARY D., wife of MR. H.N. BATCHELER, aged 34 years; the daughter of REV. R.G. DENNIS; removed with her family to Milledgeville in 1851 (with eulogy)

Houston, Feb. 8, 1856 by F.A. Hill - On the night of 5th February 1856 death took my brother WM. S. HILL...had Whitman in California, and brothers James and Henry at Emory College; was born on 25 Dec. 1827 (with eulogy)

Augusta Chronicle & Sentinel - Very long obituary of HON. ANDREW J. MILLER; born and raised in Camden County, Georgia, where his worthy parents lived long, and have recently died lamented; academic education completed at West Point; his professional studies preparatory to admission to Bar were commenced in St. Mary's, and completed in this city, where in 1825, before attaining age of manhood, under special act of the Legislature, he was licensed to practise law; was twice elected President of the State Senate; as the Presbyterian Church, of which he was a member, was undergoing repairs, the use of the Baptist Church was tendered for his funeral; was interred with Masonic and Military honors.

Feb. 20, 1856

Died in Columbus, on the 12th inst., of Consumption, MRS. ANN LOUISA LEVY, wife of CHAS. P. LEVY, aged 43 years - formerly of this city.

Died in Crawford county, Ga., on Tuesday, 29th ult., MRS. CAMILLA LESUEUR, wife of DR. JOHN LESUEUR, and daughter of JOB TAYLOR, ESQ., of Monroe county, Ga.

Died in Greensboro, Ga., on the morning of the 12th inst., MRS. A.H. DUNCAN, wife of REV. J.P. DUNCAN, of the Georgia Conference.

The Savannah Republican of the 12th inst. says that MULFORD MARSH, ESQ., for some years a practicing attorney in the Eastern District, died at his residence in that city yesterday forenoon.

A Milledgeville correspondent of the Chronicle reports the demise of MR. CALDWELL, of Pike, a worthy member of the House of Representatives of Georgia Legislature, from county of Pike. He died at his residence, of pneumonia, on the 10th inst.

Feb. 27, 1856

Died in this city Sunday evening, the 17th inst., CHARLES CRAY, infant son of COL. CHAS. R. and SARAH M. ARMSTRONG - aged 2 months.

Died in Montgomery, on Thursday, the 14th instant, MR. JOHN R. JOHNSON, in the 26th year of his age; a native of Hancock county, Ga., but more recently of Coffee county, in this State, where his father resides.

The Albany Patriot announces the death of REV. JOHN W. WILSON, venerable Elder of the Baptist Church. He died near Thomasville, of Paralysis, on the 1st inst., in the 63d year of his age; for 30 years a Minister of the Gospel of Christ.

Revolting murder. A most brutal murder was committed near this city on the Houston road, on the 18th inst., upon the person of an old and trusty negro man, named SAM WEST. He was a wagoner, and on his return home, had camped for the night. He was found next day with his head split open with his own axe. The blow fell near the temple. A man by name of THOS. SORRILL has been arrested as the suspected murderer.

The Marianna Patriot (Fla.) reports death by pneumonia of MRS. CAROLINE LEE HENTZ, so well known to the reading world as one of the most popular and charming of Southern writers.

Apr. 26, 1856

COL. RICHARD MITCHELL, a meritorious and prominent citizen of
Thomas County, Ga., died recently in Tallahassee, quite suddenly.
His remains were conveyed to his residence in the above County for
interment.

Mar. 5, 1856

Died on the 15th inst., at the residence of Dr. G.W. Young, in
Glynn county, Ga., MISS SAVANNAH LAMAR, of Lincolnton, Ga.

Died in Monroe County, on the 12th inst., MR. JOB TAYLOR, aged
about 77 years; a native of North Carolina and for many years a
resident of Jones and Monroe counties (short eulogy)

The Savannah papers announce the death of HON. G.W. OWEN, formerly
a member of Congress from this State and a distinguished member
of the Bar, in his 70th year.

Serious affray at Columbus. On Sunday evening the 24th inst. in
the Oglethorpe House, at Columbus, a quarrel arose between JOHN
CHISHOLM, the young man who was recently held to bail on a charge
of purloining valuable letters from the Postoffice, and JOHN WOOD,
bookkeeper at the Hotel. Wood is said to have thrown Chisholm on
the floor, and in this posture the latter drew a pistol and shot
him through the body. Wood died on Monday night.

The Rome Courier has an account of a duel lately fought near Dallas,
Paulding county, The parties were WILEY JONES and WM. BANE, relatives. They fought with rifles and fired three times. Jones
was slightly wounded, by the first two shots, after which he rushed
upon his antagonist and tried to knock him down with his rifle.
In this he failed, however, and had his brains beaten out by Bane.
Jones died immediately and Bane escaped.

Mar. 12, 1856

Died at his residence in Fort Valley, Ga., on the morning of the
2d inst., MR. NEWTON J. ALLEN, eldest son of HUGH ALLEN, ESQ., of
Houston county; member of Methodist Church; leaves a wife and two
children.

Mar. 19, 1856

Died in Madison, on the 14th February 1856, fully prepared, in the
18th year of her age, MISS MARTHA J. REESE, only daughter of COL.
AUGUSTUS and MRS. AMARINTHA REESE, of Madison.

Died in Sumter County, on the 5th inst., of pneumonia, MR. THOS.
G. JACKSON, aged about 27 years. He was son-in-law of our worthy
friend and fellow citizen, Roland Bivins, Esq.; leaves a wife and
two children.

Tribute of respect by Wells Lodge, No. 197 (Colaparchee, Ga.,
March 8, 1856) - on death of JOHN HOWARD on 6th March.

We learn from the Key at the Gulf that the house of Col. H. Snell,
at Sara Sota, was attacked by the Indians on the 3rd instant, and
a man named OWEN CUNNINGHAM killed. Col. Snell succeeded in making
his escape, but his house was fired by the savages and burnt to
the ground.

Mar. 26, 1856

Died on 4th March, at the house of his son, Mr. B.F. Chamberlain,
near Decatur, DeKalb county, Ga., REV. REMEMBRANCE CHAMBERLAIN,
in the 67th year of his age.

Mar. 26, 1856

Died at Barnesville, on the 25th February, CHARLES G. TURNER, ESQ. aged about 46 years. He was among the early settlers of that vicinity.

The Milledgeville Union of the 18th inst. reports deaths in that city. On Saturday the 8th inst., DR. BENJ. F. CARTER, late representative from county of Murray, died at the residence of his father, COL. F. CARTER, of consumption. On Tuesday the 11th, MR. RICHARD F. BUDD, proprietor of Washington Hall in this city, died. Believe he came from Canada - was an old man. On the night of the same day, DR. HOLMES, assistant physician of the Lunatic Asylum, died of Pheumonia, at the residence of Dr. T.F. Green. Dr. Holmes we believe was originally from Floyd county, Ga. On the same day, MR. CHARLES JENKINS, an aged man, drowned in the Oconee, opposite the city. On the 15th inst., MRS. MARY M. COTTING, wife of DR. JOHN R. COTTING, formerly State Geologist, died of Pneumonia.

Apr. 2, 1856

Died in this city, on the 29th inst., MR. WM. KIBBEE, aged about 55 years. He was formerly a resident of Augusta and Griffin, and for several years, of this city. On Sunday last, he was buried with usual honors of Masonry, by Macon Lodge, No. 5.

Died in Sumter county, Ga. on 30th (20th?) March, CORINNE, only child of MR. and MRS. U.A. RANSOME.

Died on the 11th inst., suddenly, at his father's house in Chattahoochee county, MARLOR BETHUNE, eldest son of BENJAMIN T. BETHUNE, ESQ., aged 11 years.

Died near Pond Town, Sumter county, on the 8th ult., ALICE MARION, eldest daughter of MR. JOHN T. LUMPKIN, aged 16 months.

Died at Midway, at the residence of her son, COL. JOHN S. THOMAS, on Sabbath, the 23d ult., MRS. JAMES THOMAS, at the advanced age of one hundred and ten years.

Apr. 9, 1856

Died in Marion county, on the 26th ult., of Scarlet fever, JOHN H., son of MR. and MRS. ROBT. T. WILKINSON, aged 6 years.

Died on 29th March, near Lanier, Macon county, SARAH LAWTON, infant daughter of JOSIAH A. and ANNE E. FLOURNOY, aged 2 years 1 month and 18 days.

MR. T.B. CARRINGTON, editor of the El dorado Union, was shot and instantly killed in Camden, Ark., on Monday, the 17th ult., by a friend of Mr. Jones editor of the Ouachita Herald.

The Columbus Enquirer of 5th inst., announces the death of THOMAS F. WOOLDRIDGE, ESQ., which occurred near the hill at almhouse in Wynnton, Thursday evening, about 3 o'clock; was 46 or 57 years of age; had formerly represented this county in the State Legislature.

Apr. 16, 1856

Died in Milledgeville, on the 1st inst., after a brief illness, MRS. JOSEPH J., wife of MR. EDWARD J. WHITE, in the 26th year of her age; the youngest daughter of MR. JOSEPH J. and MARY COTTON.

The slave EDWARD, charged with the murder of his master, JAMES MONTGOMERY, was convicted in the Superior Court of Taylor County, last week, and condemned to be hung on 8th May next.

Apr. 16, 1856

Our readers will remember the horrible death of AMOS W. HAMMOND, JR. who was found dead on the morning of Christmas last affixed to the cow catcher of the passenger engine of the Macon & Wester Railroad.. (Atlanta Intelligencer)

JOHN W. ARGOLE, an old and greatly respected citizen of Tallahassee, died at his residence in that city, on the 30th ult.

The Penfield Crusader announces the death of REV. V.R. THORTON.

Steamboat burnt. Georgians lost! Mr. B.H. Clark, formerly of Troup county, Ga. writes us from Alexandria, La. (April 5) that a fracas occurred on board the steamboat Bellfair about three miles above the junction of the Red and Mississippi rivers...the boat took fire and was destroyed. Among the deck passengers lost - either in the flames or by drowning - the following from this State are named:
    J.B. TAYLOR, of Macon county, Ga.
    N.G. RISE, of Pike county, Ga.
    JOHN C. MATHEWS, of Randolph county, Ga.
    JOHN G. HOGE, of Upson county, Ga. and
    B.M. JOHNS, of Pike county, Ala.
    (Columbus Enquirer)

Apr. 23, 1856

Died near this city on the 19th inst., MR. LEVI CALHOUN, aged 63 years; long a resident of this county.

Died in this city on the 20th inst., at the house of Wm. Taylor, Esq., MISS SOPHRONIA E. BRANTLY, daughter of JUDGE JOHN BRANTLY, of Vineville, in the 18th year of her age (with eulogy)

Died in Appling county, MRS. J.S. FULLWOOD, formerly of this city, where she was interred on Wed. last. Almost simultaneously with her death, information was received that her sister, formerly MISS ELLEN LAMAR, had also departed this life in Texas.

Died in Atlanta, a few days since, MISS JANE IRVIN, daughter of the late GOV. IRVIN of this State.

Died in Macon co., Ga., on 10th April last, GIDEON SMITH, ESQ., aged 58 years 4 months; one of our oldest and most respected citizens; member of Primitive Baptist Church; leaves a large family.

Died, in Marion co., on 26th March, of Scarlet Fever, in the 6th year of his age, JOHN HILL, son of ROBERT and ELIZABETH WILKINSON, and on April 15th, HOMER BURTON, of same disease, aged 16 months. A few months ageo, MR. and MRS. WILKINSON lost an only daughter, by Typhoid Fever (with long eulogy)

Fatal rencontre - An unfortunate difficulty transpired on Tuesday morning last, at the carriage shop of Mrssrs. H.B. and B.R. GARDNER, in this place, between these two gentlemen and Messrs. O.J. POWELL and JOHN H. SAUNDERS, which resulted in the death of MR. B.R. GARDNER. He was shot through the heart and expired instantly. He was long a resident of this place, but removed to Milledgeville about a year ago, where his family now reside...(Sparta Georgian)

The Dalton Expositor of the 17th inst. announces that JUDGE OWEN H. KENAN, a resident of that city, died suddenly on the evening of the 16th inst. Also learn that on one of the up-trains yesterday, a gentleman by name of AUSTIN, while standing on top of one of the cars, not noticing their approach to a bridge, was precipitated from his position by a stroke on the head, which broke his neck, instantly causing death. The train following found the mangled remains of the unfortunate man.

Apr. 30, 1856

Died of Typhoid Fever, at Indianola, Texas, on 2d inst., MRS. ELLEN C., wife of DR. JOSEPH H. BALBRIDGE, in her 22d year.

Died of Consumption, at the house of her brother-in-law, Alpheus Colvard, Esq., in Appling, Columbia county, Ga., MRS. REBECCA J., wife of JOHN THOMAS FULLWOOD, ESQ., in her 23d year; was sister of MRS. ELLEN C. BALBRIDGE. (with eulogy)

Died in this city on the morning of the 21st inst. of measles and pneumonia, SELINA SHIRLEY, infant daughter of MR. WASHINGTON and MRS. SALINA POE, aged 18 months 15 days.

JOHN I. RIDGWAY died in Columbus, Ga., of Schirrus of the Stomach, after a long and painful illness, on the morning of the 24th inst., in the 46th year of his age.

The Savannah Republican reports that REV. WILLARD PRESTON, D.D., departed this life, at his residence in this city, a few minutes past 7 o'clock, Saturday evening last, of paralysis or apoplexy of the heart; born in Uxbrudge, Mass. 29 May 1785; educated at Brown University in Providence, R.I., and devoted his early manhood to profession of the law; in 1811 he abandoned the Bar, and entered the Ministry, taking charge of a church in St. Albans, Vermont; immigrated to Georgia in 1829, and resided, for short periods of time, in Powelton, Madison, and Milledgeville; in Dec. 1831 he accepted a call from the congregation of the Independent Presbyterian Church in this city...(with eulogy)

The Augusta Chronicle & Sentinel mentions the death of JUDGE O.H. KENNAN of this county upon the authority of the Expositor of last week. This is a mistake. The "Judge Kenon" reported by the Expositor as having died suddenly in this place, on the 16th inst., was JOHN KEENAN, for many years depot watchman at this place. (Dalton Times)

May 7, 1856

Died in Milledgeville on the 21st ult., MRS. MARGARET P. HAWKINS, wife of NATHAN HAWKINS, in the 40th year of her age; member of Methodist E. Church; leaves motherless children (eulogy)

HON. GEORGE M. TROUP died at his residence in Lowndes county on Saturday the 26th ult. He died of hemorrhage of the lungs, and was in the 76th year of his age...(obituary gives biographical data taken from White's Historical Collections of Georgia).

The Atlanta Intelligencer reports that REV. ALEXANDER SPEER died at LaGrange Monday the 28th ult., age 63 years; had filled office of Secretary of State in South Carolina, as well as many prominent posts in the M.E. Church; buried in Culloden.

The Constitutionalist of yesterday contains an obituary notice of MILLER ECHOLS, who died at his residence on Monday last of derangement of the liver; upwards of 84 years of age, 71 of which he has been a citizen of Georgia; survived by his wife with whom he has lived upwards of 65 years, and who was a fraction older than himself.

May 14, 1856

Died in this city, of Consumption, on the morning of the 12th inst., MR. HENRY M. WEEK, (son of the late E.B. WEEK,) aged about 24 years.

Died in this city, on Wed. evening last, MRS. ANN SAULSBURY, aged 76; a native of Maryland, but for last 24 years an esteemed resident of this city; member of the Presbyterian Church.

May 14, 1856

Died in Macon county, Ala., on the 5th inst., MRS. MARY ANN MOULTRIE, wife of BRIGGS H. MOULTRIE, formerly of this city, aged 45 years. Her remains were brought to this city and interred in Rose Hill Cemetery on the 9th inst.

Died in Clinch county, on 26th April, at 6 o'clock, P.M., at the residence of S.W. Nichols, Esq., MRS. ROXANA, wife of COL. WM. N. NICHOLS, and daughter of COL. R. and MRS. MARY C. McCOMB, of Milledgeville, in her 19th year.

Died in Columbus, on the 7th inst., at the residence of her father-in-law, MRS. ANNIE G., wife of JAMES J. SLADE, ESQ., aged 20 years 9 months; been married about one year (eulogy).

Died on the 6th inst., near Hayneville, Houston county, of Scarlet Fever and Bronchitis, ALLISON SAXON, infant son of STEPHEN and MARY C. BROWN, aged 1 year 5 months 2 days.

Charleston Courier - HON. WILLIAM CROSBY DAWSON, one of Georgia's most honored citizens, died at an early hour on Tuesday, the 6th inst., at his residence in Greensboro, Ga., of an attack of billios cholic...(Obituary gives biographical data from White's Historical Collections of Georgia).

The Baltimore Sun relates details of a duel between DR. WILKINS and J. FLANNER, a commission merchant of Wilminton, N.C., in which the Doctor was killed.

A dispatch from Chicago announces the death of JAMES G. PERCIVAL, the distinguished poet and geologist; born in Kensington, Conn., in 1795; entered Yale College at age 16, and in 1815, read as a commencement exercise his tragedy of "Zamor," which was his first attempt at poetry; in 1820 published his first volume; having received his diploma of doctor of science, he went the same year to Charleston, South Carolina, and began the practice of his profession; in 1824 was appointed assistant surgeon in the army, and Professor of Chemistry at West Point Military Academy, which position he resigned after a few months, and took a place as surgeon in recruiting service at Boston; spent two years in assisting in preparation of first quarto edition of Webster's Dictionary; then translated Malte Brun's Geography; in 1842 published an elaborate report on the Geology of Connecticut; two years later was chosen as State Geologist of Wisconsin.

May 21, 1856

Died in this city, on the 19th inst., in the 7th year of his age, ALGENON GAILLARD, son of REV. O.L. and MRS. AMANDA N. SMITH. (City papers please copy)

Died at the Madison Springs, on the 15th inst., MRS. MARTHA TYNER, wife of K. TYNER, ESQ., for many years a resident of this city; member of Presbyterian Church in Macon.

Died in Perry, Houston county, on the 17th inst., GEORGE S. RILEY, ESQ., aged about 27 years; graduated at Franklin College a few years since with the first honors of his class; member of Methodist Church; was elected Judge of Ordinary of the county at the last election; left a wife and two children; in accordance with his request, he was buried in Rose Hill Cemetery, in Macon, on the 19th inst.

The Columbus Sun, of the 13th inst., states that WILLIAM McKAY, a boy about 12 years of age, the son of MR. McKAY of Columbus, was drowned on Saturday last, through the upsetting of a skiff on the river.

May 21, 1856

We are pained to learn, says the Dahlonega Signal, of the death of DR. RICHARD BANKS, one of Hall county's most worthy and influential citizens. He died at his residence in Gainesville, on Tuesday last.

May 28, 1856

Died in this city, on the 24th inst., MARY, daughter of FREDERICK WM. and CATHARINE M. SINS, of Savannah, aged 15 months.

Died in this city, on the 17th inst., MISS EMMA IVES, aged 8 years 6 months; and on the 23d inst., her father, MR. EDWIN IVES, aged 42 years; member of the Presbyterian Church.

Died in this city, on the 20th inst., WALKER R., son of ALEX M. and MARY A. SPEER, aged 6 years 6 months.

Died, in Lee county, on the 22d inst., MR. JOHN JAMES STUBBS, formerly of Putnam county, aged about 44 years - son of FRANCIS STUBBS of Bibb county. He was an overseer on the plantation of N. Bass, Esq., and his death was caused by a wound received from a knife, by a negro, the day previous; member of Rising Star Lodge, No. 4, at Eatonton, and was interred with Masonic honors by Macon Lodge No. 5, at the family burial ground, near his father's residence, on Sunday the 25th inst.

Died in Houston county, on Wednesday night, DR. CHARLES F. PATILLO, aged 57.

Died in Houston county, on the 20th inst., after a lingering illness, HUGH LAWSON, ESQ., a highly respected and influential citizen, and Senator from that county in the last Legislature.

Died in Vineville, on the 26th inst., GEORGE W.S., infant son of MR. DANIEL and MRS. ADELIA WOODRUFF, aged 3 months and 4 days.

PETER ALEXANDER, ESQ., an old and sterling citizen of Elbert county, and father to the Senior Editor of the Savannah Republican, departed this life, after a lingering illness, at his residence near Ruckerville, Thursday the 15th inst. Was born in Culpeper county, Val, and came to Georgia when only four years old (69 years ago). His father was at Yorktown, and witnessed the surrender of Cornwallis the deceased took an active part in the war of 1812, against Great Britain.

MRS. RUSK, wife of Senator RUSK, of Texas, whose death we recorded some days ago, was a Georgian by birth, and the daughter of HON. BENJ. CLEVELAND, of Habersham county. She married Mr. Rusk in 1827, when he was a young and rising lawyer in this State, and emigrated with him to Texas in 1835.

We have a dispatch from St. Louis, dated the 16th instant, conveying the intelligence of the death on the 11th inst., of HON. JOHN G. MILLER, a Representative in Congress from the fifth district of Missouri. (Nstional Intelligencer).

Judge Crawford of the Washington District Court, has decided to hold MR. HERBERT, charged with the homicide of KEATING, for trial.

June 4, 1856

Died in this city, on Saturday morning the 31st of May, after a protracted illness of ten months, MARY ELIZABETH, second daughter of JAMES H.R. and MRS. MARY ANN WASHINGTON, aged 10 years 6 months.

Died on the 28th ult., MRS. BRANTLEY, wife of MR. JOHN W. BRANTLEY; leaves seven children, the youngest five weeks of age; body taken to Jones county for interment.

June 4, 1856

Died on the 30th ult., MARY ALICE, only child of BENJAMIN and MARY A. BURDICK, aged 16 months.

Died in Perry, Houston county, Ga., on 23d of May, of Dysentery, CHARLES ERNEST, son of NORMAN C. and LAURA J. THOMPSON, aged 22 months.

Died in this city, on the 25th of May, after a few hours illness, SUSAN MARY, only child of WM. B. and ANNA T. JOHNSON, aged 9 months 15 days.

THOMAS, son of MR. LOTT MALSBY, of this city, a lad aged about 10 years, met with a fatal accident on last Sabbath afternoon. A horse that he was riding ran away with and threw him; his foot catching in the stirrup, he was dragged nearly a quarter of a mile, and so dreadfully bruised that, without speaking, he expired on the following morning.

The Wilkes Republican of May 30 states that JESSE COHRAN, of Milledgeville, was quarrelling with his son JASPER last week, both being intoxicated, when they attacked each other with knives, and the son fell, stabbed in thirteen places, from the wounds he died the following day.

June 11, 1856

Died at Fancy Bluff, Glynn county, on 30th May, of Scarlet Fever, MARY ANN R., eldest daughter of THOMAS T. LONG, aged 9 years 9 months and 24 days (with short eulogy).

Died in Monticello, May 23d, MRS. FANNIE H. LANE, wife of MR. DAVID LANE, and daughter of the late ROBERT MITCHELL, of Hancock county; scarcely a year since she left us a joyous bride...(with short eulogy).

Died at her home in Putnam county, where she had resided nearly 50 years, on the 9th ult., MRS. SARAH HURT, widow of CHARLES S. HURT, aged not quite 70 years.

Died in Eatonton, of consumption, on 5th May, AURELIUS A. WALTON, in the 24th year of his age.

Died in Macon, Ga. June 7th, 1856, MRS. FREDONIA C. WATSON, eldest daughter of the late MAJOR JAS. P. HOLMES, of Fort Gaines, Ga; husband was invalid (with eulogy).
(City and Columbus papers please copy)

The Savannah Journal of Saturday announces the death of HON. MORDECAI SHEFTALL, SR., in the 73rd year of his age; a member of the Bar 57 years.

MRS. MARY BIBB, widow of the HON. WM. W. BIBB, the first Governor of Alabama, died at her residence in Dallas county, Ala., on the 26th ult., in the 69th year of her age; a native of Georgia; her maiden name was FREEMAN; Gov. Gilmer, in his sketch of Gov. Bibb, says: "He married Miss Mary Freeman, the only daughter of COL. HOLMAN FREEMAN, then the beauty of the Broad River.

REV. ALEXANDER McCAIN, formerly of Talladega county, Alabama, expired in the city of Augusta on Sunday night last; was founder of the Methodist Protestant Church; born in Ireland, but came to this country when little over twenty years of age; became minister of the gospel, and was probably among the very first Methodist preachers, who visited Western Georgia; he preached at what is now the city of Athens, Ga. before the town was thought of; must have been somewhere near 85 years of age; died at the home of his only daughter.

June 11, 1856

Died at Orange Lake, East Florida, on the morning of the 22d ult., MRS. MARY JANE COCHRAN, wife of COL. JOHN COCHRAN, of Eufaula, Ala., and daughter of COL. ALFRED WELLBORN, of Meriwether county, Ga; member of the Protestant Episcopal Church; leaves husband and three children, of tender ages.

June 18, 1856

Died in Vineville, on Sunday evening the 8th inst., MISS MARY GEORGIA, daughter of THOMAS A. and MARY F. BREWER, aged 28 years.

Died in Columbus, on 1st June, MR. EZEKIEL D. CLARK, aged about 25 years, formerly of Twiggs county. His death was occasioned by a shot received from another individual.

Died in this city, on the 12th inst., JAMES MARTIN, only son of HENRY E. and MARY VIRGINIA BALL, aged 2 years 1 month and 18 days. (Savannah Republican please copy)

Departed this life in the 16th year of his age, MASTER JAMES ULLA GEORGE, son of A.M. and E.A.T. GEORGE, formerly Jones, now Baker county. Died of Typhoid Fever, at the residence of his uncle, Rev. J.H. George, of Albany, with whom he was pursuing his education. (with short eulogy) (Southern Recorder will please copy)

June 25, 1856

The Tallahassee Floridian announces the premature demise, on Thursday morning last of apoplexy, of MR. J.B. BULL, one of our oldest and most esteemed citizens.

Georgian & Journal - Death of CAPT. HAMILTON GARMANY, of Ringgold; brother to Geo. W. Garmany, Esq., of this city; died in hunting accident; a native of Newberry District, S.C. - born in 1802; married MISS MARGARET McDILL in 1821, and soon after removed to Gwinnett county, where he resided more than 30 years.

July 2, 1856

Died in Marion, Twiggs county, on the 25th ult., of Typhoid Fever, DR. WM. M. MORTON, aged about 40 years; was interred in Odd Fellows burial lot in Rose Hill Cemetery, Macon, by United Brothers Lodge No. 5 on 26th ult.

Died at his residence in Marion county, on 23d of June, COL. THOMAS BIVINS, in the 58th year of his age; consistent member of M.E. Church; had represented his county in each branch of the State Legislature for several years; buried with Masonic honors on 24th. (Southern Recorder please copy)

Died in Houston county, on Thursday, 12th inst., JAMES, youngest child of JAMES and MARGARET GUERRY, in the 19th year of his age. (with short eulogy)

July 9, 1856

Died in Columbus, on Monday morning 30th of June, ANNIE GRAHAM, daughter of JAMES J. SLADE, aged 2 months and 19 days.

Died on 30th May, FREDERICK LORD - on the 3rd July, GEORGE MAYNARD, infant children of J.M. BOARDMAN.

Died in Clark county, on 5th inst., COL. JOHN MORTON.

Died in Clinton, on 3d inst., JAMES AUGUSTUS BILLINGSLEA, aged about 41 years and 9 months.

July 9, 1856

Died in Crawford county, at the residence of Ewell Webb, Esq., on 22d June 1856, MRS. AILIE L. SANDERS, wife of the late WILLIAM SANDERS of Bibb county. (Columbus papers please copy)

Died in Twiggs county, on 7th June, MR. JAMES WARE, aged 72 years 4 months. (with short eulogy)

Died in Floyd county, on the 18th ultimo, the REV. JOHN HENDRICKS, (of Baptist Church,) in the 56th year of his age.

Murder. On Monday night the 30th ult., a most diabolical murder was perpetrated on the body of WM. BAKER, a short distance below this city and near the South-Western Railroad...

HON. THOMAS H. BAYLY died on 23d ult., of consumption, at his residence in Accomac county, Va.; prominent member of democratic party; representative in Congress from Accomac district for several years.

MAJ. E.J. HARDIN, long a resident of our city, formerly Clerk of our Superior Court, died suddenly yesterday - leaves a wife and several children. (Columbus Enquirer, 3d)

July 16, 1856

Died at Minerva, Houston County, on 23d June, MRS. CORNELIA A. HAVIS, daughter of JACOB RILEY, ESQ., and wife of DR. M.W. HAVIS, aged 17 years 8 months; fifteen months since she was united in marriage (with eulogy)

Died in Cobb county, on the 29th ult., GEN. JEPTHA V. HARRIS - a distinguished attorney of the Georgia Bar.

Obituary. GEORGE S. RILEY was born in Orangeburg District, S.C. 7 March 1829 and died in Perry, Georgia, on 17 May 1856; graduated at University of Georgia with highest honors (with eulogy)

ALEX. McDOUGALD, ESQ., of this city, died suddenly on Thursday afternoon; has served with distinction in both branches of the State Legislature; leaves a widow and several children. (Columbus Enq., July 12)

Homicide in Livingston, Alabama. On 27th ult. JOHN B. McLEOD shot EDWARD S. HARRIS killing him instantly...

Tribute of respect by Twiggs Lodge, No. 164 (July 5th, 1856) - on death of DR. WM. M. MORTON.

July 23, 1856

Drowned, in Tobler's Creek, Upson county, on the 12th inst., MR. JOHN R. BROWN, an amiable young man in the bloom of life.

Died in Meriwether county, on Friday 11th inst., DR. JOHN I. BLACKBURN, in the 65th year of his age; a native of South Carolina, but at an early age removed to Jones county in this State, which he represented for several years in the Legislature; afterwards removed to Pike County, which he also served in the Legislature; from Pike he removed to Harris county, thence to Meriwether, where his ashes now slumber.

Accident on the Central Railroad. On Wed. night last, the passenger train from this place to Savannah, when a few miles below the Oconee, was precipitated from the track into a break of the embankment, which had been occasioned by a heavy rain. A young man by name of WALKER, who was acting as a fireman was killed.

July 30, 1856

Died in Rome, at the residence of her step father, MR. JOB ROGERS, on the 2d inst., MRS. FANNIE ELLER PERRY, wife of THOMAS J. PERRY, and daughter of the late GEN'L R.M. ECHOLS and MRS. MARY ROGERS.

Died on the 22d inst., of Typhoid Fever, at the house of David H. Janes, Esq., in Cuthbert, Georgia, THOMAS LAMAR, son of JAMES LAMAR, ESQ., in his 25th year.

Died in Perry, Ga., June 30th, J. WESLEY McEACHIN. He had just entered upon the arena of life...(short eulogy)
(Citizen and Telgraph please copy)

Died near this city, on the morning of the 28th inst., ELBERT CALHOUN, son of ELBERT CALHOUN, deceased, in his 17th year; attended Oglethorpe University; member of the Presbyterian Church in Milledgeville.

Aug. 6, 1856

Died in Hawkinsville, on 15th July, JAMES A. MERIWETHER, after a long and painful illness, in the 31st year of his age, leaving an affectionate wife and several small children...rests in the Village Church-yard. (with eulogy)

Died in Houston county, at the residence of her son-in-law, Mr. Samuel Kinkins, on the 30th June, MRS. MARY WILLIAMSON, widow of the late STIRLING C. WILLIAMSON, SEN., and daughter of TIMOTHY and PRISCILLA REIVES, late of Richland District, S.C.; Mrs. W. was born in that district 9 Mar. 1776, and married in 1792, emigrated with her husband to Georgia in 1836, and settled in the county in which she died; joined the M.E. Church in 1808. The venerable Dr. Lovick Pierce was the preacher in charge of the Columbia Station, S.C., and received her into the Church; was afflicted for a number of years with paralysis (with eulogy) Christian Advocate copy)

Tribute of respect by Washington Lodge No. 46, Pond Town, Ga. July 5th, 1856 - on death of COL. THOMAS BIVINS.

On Monday last, a most melancholy affair occurred in Macon County, in which MR. ANDREW SHEALY was shot, and died immediately, and a son of his dangerously wounded. They were traveling on the road in the vicinity of their residence at the time, and report says that it was done by J.C. HELVINSTON, ESQ., or his son.

Aug. 13, 1856

GEORGE TROUP HOWARD, ESQ., of Savannah, Ga., while on a visit to his relatives and friends in this city, was attacked with fever, and lingering a few days, died at the residence of his father, MAJOR JOHN H. HOWARD on Saturday night, 2d inst.

DR. THOMAS HOXEY, one of our oldest and most respected citizens, died at Montvale Springs, Tenn., on Friday 1st inst. His remains were brought to this city by his afflicted family and were interred on Tuesday morning 5th inst. (Columbus Sentinel)

MR. JOHN KYLE, of the firm Kyle, Everitt & Co., died suddenly of apoplexy on the morning of the 4th inst. (Columbus Sentinel)

EPHRAIM C. RAINEY, ESQ. died at Geneva, Ga., on the 4th inst., after a protracted illness. He was on his way to Chalybeate Springs.

Aug. 20, 1856

HENRY HOPSON LUMPKIN died at the residence of his son, JOHN T. LUMPKIN, in Sumter county, Ga., on the 7th inst., in the 67th year of his age; was brought up in Oglethorpe county, where he married at an early age his wife, who still survives him. He was one of a large family of brothers, of whom Ex-Governor Lumpkin and Judge Joseph H. Lumpkin, are most widely known; held high position in politics in Forsyth and Monroe county; in 1840 united with the Baptist Church at Forsyth; leaves wife, seven daughters and two sons.

Died on the 1st inst., of a complication of diseases, CAPT. JAMES WHATLEY, of Pike county, Ga., in the 68th year of his age; among the first settlers of the county (eulogy)

Died of Typhoid Fever, on the 13th inst., at the residence of his uncle, Maj. Daniel N. Pittman, of Atlanta, MR. REUBEN PITTMAN, of Dooly county, Ga., in the 25th year of his age.

Tribute of respect by Mount Hope Lodge, No. 9 (Hawkinsville, Ga. - August 8th, 1856) - on death of JAMES A. MERIWETHER.

Aug. 27, 1856

Died in Americus, on the 19th inst., GEORGE M. DUDLEY, JR., eldest son of COL. GEORGE M. DUDLEY, after an illness of about two weeks of typhoid fever, aged 21 years 11 months and 13 days.

Died of Congestive Chill, in Albany, Ga., on the 16th inst., ISHAM D. SLEDGE, aged about 45 years, and for past 20 years has resided in Macon; leaves wife and three children.

Died on 20th August 1856 PROFESSOR A. REINHART, of the Wesleyan Female College, Macon, Ga.; a native of Switzerland, but from his early years educated in Paris (with eulogy)

The Charleston Courier announces the death of MR. ALEX. CARROLL, assistant editor of that paper.

Sep. 3, 1856

Died in Albany on the 28th ult., JOHN W. WOLFE, ESQ., Editor of the Albany Patriot, aged about 26 years; left a wife and one child.

MRS. SUSAN A. ORR, formerly Miss McCOOL, died at her residence in this city on the morning of 31st August, about 40 years of age; had professed religion in her seventeenth year, and connected with the Macon Baptist Church for thirteen years; one year ago her husband died a violent and heart-rending death. The children are now orphans. She leaves an only sister. (short eulogy)
(Carolina Baptist please copy)

Sep. 10, 1856

Died in Upson County, August 29th, JAMES BOYT, after an illness of twelve days, aged 68 years 2 months 29 days, leaving a wife and eight children; born in Burke County in this State, near Batford's Church, and there lived until the spring of 1828, then removed to Monroe county, when quite a wilderness and settled the place on which he died; he was an affectionate husband, father, and indulgent master...rests in family burying ground in Pike County (short eulogy)

DR. RAMSEY, who was recently arrested on a charge of forging land warrants in this State, committed suicide in the jail of Sparta, Conecuh county, Ala., on the 28th ult.

Philadelphia, August 6 - The Mount Vernon Hotel at Cape May has been destroyed by fire, and PHILLIP CAIN, the lessee, and his family have perished in the flames.

Sep. 17, 1856

On 27th August, a horrible murder was committed near Preston, Webster county, Ga., by JAMES PINES, on the body of his wife, SARAH ANN PINES...(Columbus Times)

Died in this city, on the 9th inst., of Billious Cholic, MR. ALEXANDER McGREGOR, aged about 66 years. He was among the earliest settlers of this city, and erected the first framed building west of the Ocmulgee, and the first bridge over that river.

Died in Henderson, Houston county, Ga., IRENE ELIZABETH JOBSON, only child of JOSEPH S. and ELIZABETH JOBSON, aged 11 months and 18 days.

The Charleston Courier of 12th inst. reports the death of REV. J.A. SHANKLIN. He was recently Pastor of the Episcopal Church in this city, which he left on account of ill health...he was acting as senior Editor of the "Southern Episcopalian" and Rector of St. Peter's Church.

24 Sep. 1856

Died at Gainesville, Arkansas, on the 6th inst., aged 25 years 5 months, MRS. MARGARET ANN INGRAM, wife of MR. CREED A. INGRAM, formerly of Milledgeville, Ga., and daughter of N.C. BARNETT, of the latter place; member of Methodist E. Church South.
(Athens papers please copy)

The Galveston (Texas) papers announce the death there on the 2d inst., of COL. MICH'L B. MENARD. He was born in Canada and became an Indian trader - the great tribe of the Shawnees electing him as their chief, in which position he continued several years; a member of the convention which declared Texas independent of Mexico; in 1839 was member of Congress...the Lady of Col. Menard is a native of this city, formerly MISS FLUKER, and daughter of MRS. SARAH Q. FLUKER, who is still a resident. (Journal & Mess.)

$1000 reward will be given for the apprehension of ALEXANDER HUMBOLDT HELVINSTON, who committed a base murder on ANDREW SHEALY, in the county of Macon, Georgia, on the 4th August, 1856. The undersigned, his sons and sons-in-law, will pay One Thousand Dollars to any person who will arrest and deliver the assassin to the Jailor of Macon county...A.H. Helvinston is about 21 years of age, five feet ten inches high, slender figure, dark auburn hair, narrow face, high cheek bones, dark eyes, and Roman nose.
      GEO. SHEALEY
      WM. SHEALEY
      JOHN SHEALEY
      A.E. SHEALEY
      M.L. SHEALEY
      C.D. SUMMERLIN
      DAN'L KLECKLEY

Oct. 1, 1856

Died in this city, on the 25th ult., MR. JOHN A. TURPIN, aged about 20 years, (recently a resident of Americus).

To the public. The two youths, ALEXANDER H. and EUGENE HELVENSTON, charged with killing ANDREW SHEALEY, and for whom a reward of $2000 had been offered are my sons, and as the case is undergoing judicial investigation, I must beg a suspension of opinion...
 Oglethorpe, August 25th, 1856. J.C. HELVENSTON

Oct. 8, 1856

Died, in Montgomery, Ala., on the 30th ult., in the 28th year of his age, after a short illness, JOHN BOLLING HINES, for many years a citizen of this place; engaged with the Editorial department of

(Oct. 8, cont'd.) - the Montgomery "Mail" and "Advertiser" last year, and recently with a Savannah daily. He had just left the city of Charleston, and gone to Montgomery, to take charge of the "Messenger," a new paper about starting; his classmates at Oglethorpe University remember him a boy of ten, the leader of the Junior class, or friends of later years, who have seen him a boy of fifteen, at the Bar of the South-Western Circuit, living at Albany, and two years afterwards doing a lucrative practice in Macon...
(with eulogy)

Oct. 8, 1856

The CAPT. JOHN BROWN, who was reported killed in the late battle at Ossawatomie, Kansas, was the bloody scoundrel, who with a band of "whiskey drinkers," murdered five pro-slavery settlers on 24th May viz: WM. P. DOYLE, WM. DOYLE and DURY DOYLE, father and two sons, and WM. SHANNON and ALLEN WILKINSON...(New Haven Register)

Oct. 15, 1856

Died in Buena Vista, Marion county, Ga., on Sunday the 5th inst., LAURA, daughter of GEORGE W. and SARAH ANN McDUFFIE, aged 15 months and 11 days.

Died near this city, on the 8th inst., MRS. FRANCES W. KILPATRICK, aged 27 years, wife of WILLIAM G. KILPATRICK, and daughter of MRS. MARTHA D. MORRIS, of this city.

Oct. 22, 1856

The death of LORENZO B. SHEPARD, in his bath tub, should be renewed caution to abstain at night from the powerful stimulus of cold water upon an exhausted system. More than one fatal result has followed this violation of hygienic law within the circle of widely known New Yorkers. (Albany Journal)

Died in Houston county, Ga., on the 10th inst., JAMES W. WILLINGHAM, aged about 13 years.

On Saturday last, the 11th inst., says the Sumter Republican, at twenty minutes past 4 o'clock, P.M., HON. E.R. BROWN died at his residence in 46th year of his age.

COL. BENJ. S. JORDAN, an old and highly respected citizen of Baldwin county, and one of the wealthiest men in this State, died at his residence near Milledgeville, on the 11th ult.

Oct. 29, 1856

MR. GEORGE A. STEELE, one of the oldest printers in New York, died on Tuesday. He has been foreman of White & Co.'s establishment for over thirty years and connected with it, altogether, for nearly half a century.

The Newburyport Mercury announces the death of MR. HENRY BARBER, who worked in the Mercury office 65 years, and died at the age of 76. During the whole of his life Mr. Barber was never five miles distant from his home.

Nov. 5, 1856

MR. HAYS BOWDRE died yesterday, at his residence in this city, after a protracted illness of several months, in the 64th year of his age. He was a native of Columbia county, but while a youth, came to Augusta, where he has resided for near half a century.
(with eulogy) (Augusta Chronicle)

Nov. 12, 1856

J.S. GUINGNARD, ESQ., one of the oldest and most influential citizens of Columbia, died on Saturday night last, and was buried Sunday afternoon; held offices of the Clerk of the Court, Ordinary, and Register. (Columbus Times)

Nov. 19, 1856

Sumter Republican of 12th inst. contains an account of the melancholy suicide of DR. B.H. PERKINS, of Cuthbert...he was brother of Judge Perkins.

ROBERT H. DIXON died at Rockbridge, Alum Spring, Va., on the 2d inst., in the 57th year of his age; frequently represented Talbot county in the State Legislature.

Another Charleston clergyman has fallen victim to yellow fever. REV. JULIUS W. STEWART, who was Assistant Pastor of Grace (Episcopal) Church, died at Beaufort a few days ago, having gone there after contracting disease in Charleston.

Nov. 26, 1856

Died at Beallwood, near Columbus, on the 21st inst., in the 24th year of her age, MRS. CAROLINE MATILDA, wife of WM. H. GRISWOLD, ESQ., Junior Proprietor of the Columbus Enquirer, and daughter of DR. L.F.W. ANDREWS, of Macon.

JOHN THOMAS SATTERWHITE, a resident of Dawson, Terrell county, Ga., died at his residence in Randolph county, Ga., Oct. 28th, 1856, aged 21 years 6 months 21 days. (eulogy)

MAJOR JOHN H. EATON, Secretary of War under Gen. Jackson, and once Governor of Florida, died in Washington on the 17th, aged 70.

The Columbus Sun of Saturday relates the death of COL. SEYMOUR C. BONNER, which occurred sometime during Friday night, of apoplexy; in his 48th year.

VIRGIL POWERS, ESQ., has been appointed Chief Engineer of the Georgia and Florida railroad, in the place of MR. W.M. MUSSEY, deceased.

Dec. 3, 1856

Died in Wynnton, Ga., on the 25th ult., JOHN L. CHAMBERS, in the 16th year of his age - youngest son of JAMES M. and MARTHA J. CHAMBERS.

Died in this city, on 18th Nov., after a painful and lingering illness of seven months, MRS. LOUISA V. CRAWFORD, aged 45 years; leaves bereaved children.

Died at Graysville, Catoosa county, on the 28th ult., of Consumption, MISS ELIZABETH GRADY, aged about 17 years; a native of Brooklyn, N.Y. She was interred in Rose Hill Cemetery in this city, on the 30th ult.

MRS. HARRIET FRANCES CORNOCHAN departed this life at Belair, on the 18th of October last, in the 69th year of her age. (with short eulogy) (Florida Sentinel)

MRS. VALENTINE AUSTIN was killed at Memphis on the 12th by the premature discharge of a cannon while firing a salute in honor of the election of Buchanan.

Dec. 10, 1856

Died at Fort Valley, on the 30th ult., MRS. FRANCES R. JENKINS, wife of MR. ELI JENKINS, of Montezuma, aged 23 years 9 months.

Died in Webster County, of Pnewumonia, DR. E.B. SWINNEY, aged about 33 years; first Judge of Ordinary elected in that county, and Senator in the last Legislature.

Died in the same county, on the 20th ult., CLAYTON BELL, aged about 20 years - son of SAMPSON BELL, ESQ.

MRS. EXER A. MARTIN, wife of A.W. MARTIN, ESQ., was born in Baldwin County, Ga., 9 Nov. 1813 and died in Macon county, Ga. 16 Oct. 1856; member of Methodist Episcopal Church (eulogy)

The Baton Rouge (La.) Gazette of 23d announces the death of its late Editor, HON. GEO. C. McWHORTER.

Dec. 17, 1856

Died in this County, on the 10th inst., MR. WM. KILPATRICK, aged 74 years - a much respected citizen.

Dec. 24, 1856

HON. JOSEPH B. LANCASTER, a distinguished jurist and politician, died at Tampa Bay Florida on Tuesday, the 25th ult., at his residence of Pneumonia.

Died at the residence of her husband, (MAJ. JOHN MARSH,) on the morning of the 14th instant, at 6½ o'clock A.M., MRS. SARAH MARSH, in the 83rd year of her age. She emigrated with her husband to Georgia from Chatham County, N.C., many years since. (Citizen please copy)

Dec. 31, 1856

Died in Dooly County, near Drayton, on the 3d inst., after a short and painful illness, MARY FRANCES, daughter of ROBT. L. and SARAH A.F. MIMS, in the 5th year of her age. But a few days intervened between the death of Mollie and her beloved father...(with eulogy)

REV. JOSIAH EVANS, venerable minister of the Methodist Episcopal Church, formerly of Georgia, fell in the streets of Tuskegee, Ala., on the 18th, and died a few hours afterwards. His disease apoplexy.

Homicide in Laurens county. WM. E. GREEN was shot at Rozar's store, in Laurens county, on the 24th inst., by a young man about 20 years of age, by name of GEORGE SLAUGHTER, and it is said without any known cause or provocation. Slaughter fled immediately, and has not been arrested. A reward of five hundred dollars is offered for his arrest by the relatives of Green.

Jan. 7, 1857

Died in this city, on the 6th inst., very suddenly, MR. HARDY MORRIS, aged about 48 years.

DR. THEODOSIUS BARTOW, for many years a highly respected citizen and physician of Savannah, died at his residence in Floyd county, on Friday last, at an advanced age. Dr. Bartow was the father of HON. FRANCIS S. BARTOW of this city. (Savannah Republican, Dec.31st

REV. MR. STITELER, lately pastor of the First Baptist Church of this city, died at Orange Springs, Florida, Christmas day, of consumption. (Savannah Georgian and Journal)

Jan. 14, 1857

Died in Pilatka, E.F., on Monday, Dec. 22d ult., of Consumption, MR. K. McARTHY, of Macon Ga.

Died in Sumter, at the residence of his father, of Congestive Chills, MR. WM. M. BRADY, in the 28th year of his age.

Died in this city on the 11th inst., at the residence of P.E. BOWDRE, AMELIA BOWDRE, youngest daughter of JOSEPH and AMELIA McALPIN, aged 21 months.

Died, in this city, on the 7th inst., HENRY G. ROSS, ESQ., aged about 56 years. At the time of his death, it is believed that he was the oldest resident of this city, having settled at Fort Hawkins, (then the frontier of Georgia) in the year 1818. He was the Second Clerk of the Superior Court in this county after its organization, which office he held from 1827 to 1856.

Jan. 21, 1857

Died in Macon county, 24th Dec. 1856, MR. JOHN R. FELTON, age about 59 years.

Died, on the 6th inst., at his residence in Bibb county, in the 75th year of his age, EDMUND GILBERT, ESQ., after an illness of 28 hours. He visited Macon on Monday, was attacked in the evening with Pneumonia, and died on Tuesday evening between 7 and 8 o'clock; was born in Virginia, but removed to Hancock county, Ga.; from early childhood - lived several years in Jones county, then moved to Bibb; an exemplary member of Baptist Church for 25 years (with short eulogy).

MR. EBENEZAR HAYWOOD, who has been languishing since Friday last from injuries received on that day by a fall from his buggy, died at 3½ o'clock, a.m. yesterday, in the 20th year of his age; a graduate of Georgia Military Academy at Marietta. (Savannah Republican of Sat.)

Jan. 28, 1857

Died in this city, on Saturday night last, SARAH SOPHIA, only daughter of MR. CHARLES and MRS. SOPHIA F. COLLINS, aged 12 years 8 months 4 days.

Died at his residence in Houston County, on the morning of the 22d inst., of measles and diseased liver, MR. CHARLES F. CARDIN, aged 26 years; leaves wife and two orphan children. (City papers and Augusta Constitutionalist please copy)

Obituary. Died, on the morning of the 8th Jan. 1857, in the 57th year of his age, HENRY G. ROSS; native of North Carolina...among the first, if not the very first, store house of any size, that was erected in Macon, west of the Ocmulgee, was one built for Mr. Ross, in connection with his partner, Dr. Ingersold, now of Alabama; leaves widow and large family of children and relatives...

REV. CHARLES S. WALKER, of the South Carolina Conference, Spartanburg Circuit, died in Spartanburg, S.C., on Sunday last. He was a brother of R.D. WALKER, ESQ., of Savannah.

Feb. 4, 1857

Died in this city, on the 29th ult., of Consumption, MISS EMMA HOWELL, of Haddenfield, N.J., in the 24th year of her age.

Died in this city, on 9th of January, THOMAS COSPER, youngest child of THOMAS C. and MARY C. NISBET, aged 17 months. Died also, on the 24th of January, after a lingering illness, ELIZA CLAY, aged 5 years - eldest child of THOMAS C. and MARY C. NISBET.

Feb. 4, 1857

Died in Henry County, Ala., on 22d December, MITCHELL COXWELL, aged about 56 years, formerly a resident of Bibb County.

JOHN BARNEY died of pneumonia, in Washington city, on 26th ult.

HON. PRESTON S. BROOKS, of South Carolina, died suddenly at Washington on the evening of the 27th ult. His disease was an affection of the throat.

Another Revolutionary soldier gone. Died, on the 3d of January 1857, MR. WILLIAM BUTTRILL, in Butts county, Ga., at the residence of his son, MR. BRITTON BUTTRILL, at the advanced age of 93 years 10 months 13 days. Was born in Brunswick county, Va., 20 Feb. 1763; shortly after he was grown, he moved to Chatham county, N.C., where he married and remained until latter part of 1810, when he emigrated to Warren county, Ga.; about two years later, he removed to Jasper county, where he remained until 1824, then moved to Butts county, during Rev. War he entered the army as a volunteer under Gen. Green, and fought the battle at Guilford Court House, N.C.; raised a large family of children, most of whom are still living.

Tribute of respect by Mount Hope Lodge, No. 9 F.&A.M. (Hawkinsville, Jan. 24th, 1857) - on death of HENRY PHELPS.

Feb. 11, 1857

Died in Houston County, on 28th January, CAPT. L. BACON, aged nearly 81 years; a native of South Carolina, but had resided in Georgia, and at the place where he died, over twenty years (with eulogy).

Regret to announce the death of MRS. EMELINE STEPHENS, late consort of LINTON STEPHENS, ESQ., of this place; member of the Baptist Church. (Sparta Georgian, 4th inst.)

MAJ. MATTHEW ROBERTSON died at his residence in Harris County, very suddenly, about four weeks since, aged about 60 years. He was the original proprietor and publisher of this paper, then called the "Georgia Messenger"...when quite a young man, he was elected Sheriff of Jefferson County, and soon after his removal to this county (in March 1823) he was elected a Justice of the Inferior Court, and was among the first Deacons of the Presbyterian Church of this city; in 1829 he removed to Jeffersonville, Twiggs County, and some years after to Harris County. For a few years he resided in Columbus, and again returned to Harris, where he died.

The Knoxville Register of the 5th inst., says that DR. ISAAC ANDERSON, one of the "fathers" of Presbyterianism in this section of the country, and for many years President of Maryville College, died at his residence in Maryville, on Wed. 28th ult.

Melancholy occurrence. MR. JACOB BINDER, of Macon, Georgia, having become a lunatic, a friend started to bring him to our Asylum. On Wed. last, when the car stopped at Orangeburg Depot, he managed to get out, and to escape...his body was found, drowned in a mill pond. (Columbia South Carolinian)

On the 31st ult., MR. JOHN HILL, overseer on the repairs of the Rome Rail Road in Floyd county, Ga., while attempting to chastise a negro man, was struck a blow on the head by the negro with a club, from which he died the next day.

Feb. 18, 1857

Died in this city, on the 10th inst., ANNA FLYNN, aged about 6 years.

Feb. 18, 1857

Died in Americus, Ga., on the 6th inst., MR. CALEB MALDEN, a worthy citizen, aged 52 years. Obituary next week.

Died near Athens, on the 20th ult., MRS. NANCY MITCHELL, consort of the late MAJ. THOS. MITCHELL, aged 82 years.

Died on the 7th inst., in Columbus, of Phrenitis of the brain, BOBBIE, youngest son of MRS. E.B. and DR. J.L. CHENEY, aged 9 months.

Died in this city on the 8th inst., MR. FRANCIS M. WRIGHT, in his 30th year, after a brief but severe illness of cold and Pneumonia. From early boyhood he had been a resident of this city; member of Macon Guards in the Mexican War.

Died on the 7th inst., at his residence in Houston county, DR. CREED TAYLOR WOODSON, in the 56th year of his age. Born and raised in Cumberland county, Va., and read medicine in the office of the late Dr. Southall, of Jamestown. After completion of medical education in Transylvania University, in 1825, he came to this State, and located in Marion, Twiggs county. In 1829 he married the daughter of the late MAJ. PHILIP COOK, of the US Army, and in 1832 moved to West side of Ocmulgee River, in Houston county (with eulogy)

EDWARD R. ANDERSON, a most excellent citizen of Wilkes county, and for ten or twelve years past its Representative in the lower house of the State Legislature, died of cancer, at Murphreesboro, Tenn., on the 9th instant.

Feb. 25, 1857

Last week the Savannah papers announced a duel between MESSR. ELLIOT and DANIEL, of that city, in which the latter fell mortally wounded on the first fire. The Columbus Enquirer of yesterday, says a telegraphic dispatch from Savannah, announces that O.S. KIMBROUGH mortally wounded MR. J.P. HENDRICKS on the second fire, in a duel near that city, on Monday last. The parties were from Columbus.

Mar. 4, 1857

JOSEPH LUTIER, second mate of the British ship Middleton, lying at Savannah, killed GEORGE HASLIP, the cook, by beating him with his fist, on Saturday last. Lutier is now in the Chatham county jail.

Child killed. The Atlanta Rep. & Discipline says that a lad 10 or 12 years of age, named FARRALL, fell while attempting to get on the platform of one of the cars in that city, on Tuesday last, and was crushed by the wheels of the two cars passing over him.

Mar. 11, 1857

Died in New Haven, Conn., Feb. 26th, of Consumption, REBECCA H., wife of WM. T. FITCH, aged 27 years.

Died at their residence, on Monday, the 23d ult., LUCINDA, wife of PEYTON HOLT, in the 25th year of her age.

MR. DAVID HUME, a highly respectable citizen of Alexandria, was killed in the Pension Office at Washington, on the 28th ult., by COL. D.C. LEE, of that Department, and recently a member of the Washington City Council...

During the thunder storm on Friday, the 27th ult., a negro man, belonging to MR. THOMAS D. WEEMS, of Henry county, while passing from the field in which he had been plowing, with the plow chains around his neck, was struck by lightning and instantly killed. (Griffin Union)

Mar. 18, 1857

Died in Knoxville, Ga., on the 8th inst., of disease of the heart, ADELAIDE WATTS, infant child of MR. and MRS. GEO. W. NORMAN.

A fracas occurred at Dalton on the 7th inst., between JAMES TONEY and JAMES SHIELDS, in which the latter was so severely injured that he died on the following morning. The parties had been indulging in liquor.

Died, in Columbus on Saturday the 7th inst., MRS. ELIZABETH R. CROOK, in the 58th year of her age. She was the daughter of LIEUT. WM. JENKINS, of the Virginia Continental Line. Her first marriage was with MR. HARDY CRAWFORD; her second was with MR. O. CROOK, late of Harris county. She leaves three children, of whom HON. M.J. CRAWFORD is one.

JAS. A. PRICE, who murdered a man by the name of HUGHES, about two years ago, in Union District, S.C. was convicted of murder in the first degree, and sentenced for the offence last week at Union Court.

Tribute of respect by Twiggs Lodge, No. 164 - March 7th, 1857 - on death of WILLIAM C. FINCH who died on Tuesday the 17th of February in Twiggs County of Consumption.

Mar. 25, 1857

Died in Macon County, of Scarlet Fever, on the 14th inst., JOHN HILLSMAN POOL, son of JOSIAH and MARTHA POOL, in the 13th year of his age.

Died in Macon County, on the 25th February, of Dropsy of the heart, MR. WM. SIMPSON, aged about 60 years.
(Augusta Chronicle & Sentinel and Thomasville Watchman copy).

Died in Albany, on 27th February, MRS. SARAH ELIZABETH WARREN, wife of L.P.D. WARREN, ESQ., in the 22d year of her age; better known as BESSIE HINES: graduated at an early age with the first honor in the Wesleyan Female College, afterwards attending one of the best institutions in the North; united with the Presbyterian Church in Macon in 1853, but a year since transferred her membership to Presbyterian Church in Albany; leaves husband and babe (with eulogy)

REV. CALVIN COLTON, L.L.D., eminent divine, scholar and writer, died in Savannah on Friday the 13th inst.

DR. JOHN WINGFIELD expired at his residence in Madison, Morgan county on Friday evening, the 20th inst., at 11 o'clock; had lived in Madison nearly forty years. (Augusta Constitutionalist)

MR. EVERETT H. PIERCE, of Baldwin, recently died after a protracted illness.

The Woodstock Tenth Legion says: On returning home from a visit to his friends in Richmond, two weeks ago, REV. JOHN HOWARD, the esteemed Pastor of the Presbyterian Church in this place, exhibited strong symptoms of mental derangement...he committed suicide by hanging. (Virginia Herald)

Apr. 1, 1857

REV. JAMES R. McCARTER, formerly of Franklin county, in this State, died on Manitee river, Florida, on 16th of February last.

Apr. 1, 1857

REV. ELIZUR BUTLER, M.D., the missionary among the Cherokees whose imprisonment in Georgia and subsequent release after a decision in his favor by the Supreme Court of the United States, made him so well known, died of pneumonia on the 4th February last, at Van Buren, Ark., in the 62d year of his age.

Apr. 8, 1857

Tribute of respect by Mount Hope Lodge, No. 9, F.A.M. March 27th, 1857 - on death of JOHN D. GORDON.

Died in this city, on the evening of the 1st inst., W.B. WATTS, ESQ., a native of South Carolina. He removed to Macon in 1836, and has been a citizen of this place ever since. (with eulogy)

MR. SAMUEL DUFFEY, the gentleman whom we noticed last week as having the Small Pox, died on Thursday evening at about three o'clock... (Griffin Union)

Intelligence has been received at the War Department of the death on the 13th instant, at San Antonio, Texas, of EDWARD D. STOCKTON, first lieutenant in the first infantry.

MAJOR JAMES JACKSON, formerly Professor in Franklin College, died on the 26th ult., in Gainesville, Ala.

HON. SAMPSON W. HARRIS, a Representative from the State of Alabama, died yesterday morning at his late lodgings in this city, after an illness of several weeks duration; 48 years of age, of which the last ten were spent in the National Councils; the disease was laryngitis complicated with pneumonia.

Apr. 15, 1857

Died on Monday morning, the 5th inst., SALLIE LOUISE, daughter of HENRY L. and MARTHA J. JEWETT - aged one year and nine days.

MRS. JANE DAY, wife of HON. JOSEPH DAY, died in Houston County on April 7th. She was born in Richmond county, and was the daughter of NEHEMIAH and ANN DUNN; a member of the Methodist Church; lived three score years and ten.

DR. MARTIN G. SLAUGHTER died at his residence in Marietta, on Thursday night last.

COL. ROBERT McCOMBS, well known citizen of Milledgeville, died last week. He had been for some months in declining health. He was long connected with the Hotel business.

Tuscaloosa (Ala.) Monitor of April 2d reports the death of PROFESSOR TUOMEY, so widely known by his labors for the advancement of science and the promotion of educational progress in Alabama and other Southern states; his death, caused by disease of the heart, took place on Monday night last, at his residence at the State University, in which he filled the Professorship of Geology and Agricultural Chemistry.

Raleigh (N.C.) April 8 - A fire damp occurred at Governor's Creek coal mine, Chatham county, NC on Monday last. SUPERINTENDENT DUNN and four other men were instantly killed.

Apr. 22, 1857

Sav. Georgian of 5th announces the demise of COL. JAMES SULLIVAN, who suddenly breathed his last about midnight last night. He had been out yesterday as usual, and seemed well on retiring to bed. He leaves a wife and four children.

Apr. 22, 1857

Died in this city on yesterday morning, MRS. CLAUDIA A. RUSSELL, the estimable and pious wife of PROFESSOR RUSSELL of the Wesleyan Female College.

Died in Vineville on Sunday night last, MR. ELISHA C. GRISWOLD, in the 89th year of his age.

WM. M. SIMMONS, charged with the murder of JOHN CAMPBELL, in Harris county, in 1855, had his second trial last week in that county, and was acquitted.

Apr. 29, 1857

Departed this life on the evening of the 17th, in Vineville, THOMPSON CHERRY, aged 65; a native of North Carolina.

Died in Laurens county, Ga., on the 13th inst., of inflammation of the brain, JAMES DAVID, son of HON. E.J. BLACKSHEAR, aged 8 years 11 days.

Died after a short illness, on the 5th inst., at his residence in Sumter county, ELI TUCKER, aged 45 years.

Tribute of respect by Pinta Lodge, Barnesville, Ga., April 18, 1857 - on death of CHARLES JEFFRIES.

Southern Statesman (Prattville, Alabama) - Died on Tuesday evening, the 16th inst., in Prattville, MRS. MARY S. GLENN, wife of WM. GLENN. The cause of the disease of Mrs. Glenn was the intemperate use of snuff.

MAJOR SAMUEL W. FLOURNOY died at his remporary residence in Russell county, Alabama, three miles above Columbus, on the evening of the 22d instant. For several years past he has been a valetudinarian; for over twenty years he was a resident of this city, and during the larger part of that time, conducted the editorial department of the Columbus Enquirer; a native of Morgan county, Georgia, and over 50 years of age at his death. (Columbus Sun of 24th).

LIEUT. WM. GARDNER, of this city, says the Augusta Dispatch of the 22d, died very suddenly this morning of disease of the heart... about forty years of age, and a Lieutenant in the US Navy; leaves wife.

Augusta Sentinel of 23rd announces the death of GERRARD McLAUGHLIN from a violent attack of pneumonia; a native of Ireland, but had been for thirty years or more a resident of Augusta.

May 6, 1857

Died in this county, of pneumonia, on the 3d inst., MR. ROBT. S. HOLT, aged 34 years; leaves wife and three children.

Died, at his residence, in Pike county, Ga., on the 22d inst., of asthetic Pneumonia, WILLIAM WILLIAMS, son of W.F. and AGNES WILLIAMS of Pike county, Ga., being in his 31st year. (with short eulogy)

Died, in Lowndes county, on the 14th ult., MRS. HARRIET PAULETT, wife of MR. J.C. PAULETT, aged 59; for nearly 30 years a member of the Methodist Church (short eulogy)
(Southern Christian Advocate, and Athens and Madison papers please copy)

Died, near West Point, Georgia, on 13th ultimo, MRS. HESPERIA D. WHITMAN, consort of MR. J.T. WHITMAN, and eldest daughter of MR. THOS. S. and MRS. SUSAN A. REESE - aged 20 years 11 months and 27 days.

May 6, 1857

MRS. JOHN H. NEEL, of Hancock county, was accidentally burned to death on Friday 24th ult. Her clothes caught on fire while engaged in cooking, at an open fire place.

HON. EBENEZER ALEXANDER died at his residence in Knoxville, Tenn., on Wednesday last, 29th ult.; a Judge.

MR. ROBERT RAIFORD, for many years a citizen of Savannah, and well known as a Justice of the Peace, died Saturday evening from an attack of apoplexy; a native of Jefferson county (Republican).

May 13, 1857

Died in Macon County, Ga., on 30th April last, of Typhoid Pneumona, WILSON GRAHAM, son of HOSEA and ELIZABETH C. YOUNG, in the 17th year of his age. He was a dutiful son and loving brother. (Chronicle & Sentinel, of Augusta, please copy)

Died in Covington, Newton county, on the 4th inst., GEN. JOHN N. WILLIAMSON, aged about 56; extensively known to the people of Georgia, as a member of the Legislature; one of the most liberal contributors to the Masonic Female College, at Covington; funeral was attended by a large body of Masonic Brothers.

REV. J.A. COLLINS, a much esteemed divine of Baltimore, died, of pneumonia, in that city, Thursday last.

JOHN EDWARDS, of Talbot county, Ga., was shot at Talbotton on Saturday 2d inst., by young Giddings, in an affray. He died on Monday following.

May 20, 1857

Died in this city on the 16th inst., DANIEL MILFORD MEARA, son of MR. JAS. MEARA, aged about three years.

Died in this city, on the 10th inst., MISS JULIA M. HOLT, in the 16th year of her age. Also in this city on the 18th inst., of congestive fever, PEYTON C. HOLT, aged about 24 years. He was interred yesterday, and his funeral attended by the Macon Volunteers, and the members of Hook & Ladder Company No. 1, both of which he was a member. Also on the 19th inst., GRIMES T. HOLT, in the 14th year of his age - all children of PULASKI S. HOLT, ESQ.

Died near Macon, on the 6th inst., MRS. SUSAN KING, in the 73d year of her age.

Died in Hawkinsville, Ga., on Friday evening, the 8th inst., EMILY L. GRACE, a daughter of SAMUEL and NANCY M. GRACE, and wife of MATHEW GRACE, ESQ., aged 32 years 2 months and 25 days.

Died, May 17th in the 17th year of her age, ELIZABETH W., daughter of WILLIAM and ELIZA D. CLAYTON, and a member of the Sophomore Class of Wesleyan Female College. Was received into the Methodist Church about 18 months ago (with eulogy)
(Citizen and Telegraph will please copy)

Died in Savannah, on evening of 18th inst., in the 63d year of his age, MR. JOHN JONES, long resident of this city.

Died in this city on the morning of May 12th, MARTHA E.E. SANDERS, daughter of T.J. and M.A. SANDERS, aged about 16 years; attached to Methodist Church at Lebanon, Macon County, Ga. in Sept. 1856; was attacked with measles in March last...was attacked on Sabbath with Cholera Morbus and died at 3 A.M. Monday morning.

May 20, 1857

Departed this life, on Saturday, the 22d instant, at the residence of her brother, Col. Wm. L. Calhoun, in Abbeville district, MARTHA CORNELIA CALHOUN, in the 31st year of her age; communicant of Episcopal Church. (Charleston Courier)

A gentleman named SAMUEL TURNER died in Yorkville, S.C., a short time since, at the nearly centenarian age of 98 years. Two days after his death, a maiden daughter died, aged 72. (Natchez Courier)

JAMES BOATWRIGHT, ESQ., one of the patriarchal landmarks of Columbia S.C., died on Wed. last, upwards of 80 years.

Tribute of respect by Golden Fleece Lodge, No. 6 (Covington, Ga.) - on death of JOHN N. WILLIAMSON.

HON. STEPHEN ADAMS, late US Senator from Mississippi, died at his residence, near Memphis, Monday morning, at 5 o'clock.

May 17, 1857

MRS. AMANDA V. GOODE, wife of THOMAS W. GOODE, ESQ., died near Thomaston, Upson county, Ga., May 6th, 1857, aged 47 years 15 days, after a protracted and painful illness; member of Methodist Church in Thomaston. (with eulogy)

MR. J. WOOD, proprietor of the Oglethorpe House at Brunswick, was deliberately murdered by CHAS. MOORE, Marshal of that town, Saturday night last...Mr. Wood leaves a wife with several small children. (Sav. Rep., May 20)

In a difficulty between JAMES A. TATUM, Sheriff of Jefferson county, and WM. B. GODDARD, formerly of Georgia, at the residence of the former, on Saturday last, in Osawkee, Jefferson county, in this Territory, Tatum shot Goddard, the ball passing near his heart, causing his death immediately...(Leavenworth Journal) (The name of Wm. B. Goddard, is familiar to our citizens, having been born and raised in this city)

June 3, 1857

Died in East Macon, on the 28th ult., at 7 o'clock, MRS. GOVE, wife of MRS. SAMUEL F. GOVE, aged 29 years; a member of the Baptist Church of this city.

Died in Hawkinsville on Sunday the 20th ult., at 10 o'clock, A.M., after a severe illness, MRS. SUSAN A. DANIELS, wife of REV. W.B. DANIELS, in the 28th year of her age; in 1854 joined the Baptist Church of this place. (with eulogy)

Died at his residence near Notasulga, Ala., on the 17th inst., REV. C.F.R. SHEHANE, aged about 54 years.

HON. JAMES BELL, Senator from New Hampshire, died yesterday at his residence in Concord. He was the son of former eminent Senator from that State, the HON. SAMUEL BELL, who represented his State some twenty years ago. (National Intelligencer)

HON. ANDREW P. BUTLER, Senator from South Carolina, died at Edgefield on the evening of the 25th instant. (National Intelligencer)

COL. L.M.H. WASHINGTON, well known in Texas, was wounded at Castillo, and taken prisoner by the Costa Ricans, after the disgraceful retreat of Col. Titus on the 19th of February, and afterwards shot. (Houston Telegraph). The widow of Col. Washington resides we understand in this city (Austin Gazette) Col. W. moved from this city in 1836, and took an active part in the Texas Revolution; and has been ever since a citizen of Texas. He has an aged mother still living in this place. (Southern Recorder).

June 3, 1857

Tribute of respect by Mount Hope Lodge, No. 9, F.& A.M. - on death of RICHARD C. CARRUTHERS.

June 10, 1857

A telegraphic dispatch from St. Louis announces that PRATT the Mormon Elder was killed on the 14th, near Van Buren, Ark., by HECTOR MANN, whose wife Pratt had secuded. The name of the avenger is probably HECTOR H. McLEAN, whose wife Pratt ran off with from New Orleans, and who returned from California to recover his children.

Died in this city, on the 2d inst., MRS. MARGARET GROCE, wife of LEWIS J. GROCE; nearly 43 years of age; had been ill for several months; leaves husband and seven children; member of Baptist Church of this city for 22 years.

THOMAS SORRELLS, who was recently convicted in this county, of the murder of SAM WEST, a negro wagoner, and sentenced to the Penitentiary for life, managed to escape a few days since. He went to Houston county, where, with another escaped convict, by the name of JOHN HEATH, he broke into the store of MR. JOHN A. SPERRY, where they took two double-barrelled guns, and sundry other articles. They were making their way to Florida, but were overtaken and arrested by GEN. A.G. BOSTWICK, of Wilkinson county, and have been returned to their old quarters in the Penitentiary.

Company meeting of the Macon Volumteers May 26th, 1857 - to give tribute of respect on death of PRIVATE PEYTON C. HOLT.

June 17, 1857

Died at his residence in this county on the 13th inst., RANDOLPHUS M. GILBERT, aged 54 years.

Died in Monroe co., June 9th, CHARLES T. DOUGHTRY, only son of REV. T. & M.E. DOUGHTRY, age 1 year 8 months 10 days.

Died in Monroe county, on the 4th inst., SALLIE POWERS, daughter of MR. JOEL R. and MRS. N.A. SIMONTON, aged 17 months 5 days.

HON. C.B. GUYTON died at his residence in Dublin, Laurens County, on the 16th ult. Was an eminent physician, and had represented Laurens County with ability in both branches of our State Legislature; leaves a family to mourn.

GEN. ALLEN LAWHON, prominent and influential citizen of Cherokee County, died at his residence on Friday last, of cramp cholic.

The Sacramento Union relates that on the 7th instant a young man by name of CHURCH was killed by a grizzly bear in Round Valley, in Napa county. Mr. Church had been engaged in school teaching on the Mokelumne river, and was in the Valley on a visit to his relatives...

CHRISTOPHER NOBLE clung on the rear portion of a car of the Great Western Railroad last Tuesday in such a manner as to be concealed from sight, and, while the train was going at full speed, let go his hold and got off, intending to proceed to his house close by. He fell on his head...was picked up dead. (Cincinnati Gazette)

June 24, 1857

Died on the 16th inst., at his residence in Upson county, Ga., the HON. HENRY GLOVER, in the 76th year of his age.

June 24, 1857

Died near Oglethorpe on 30th May, after a long and painful illness of Pleura-Pneumonia, J.A.C. FLEMING, second son of BENJAMIN F. and FRANCIS FLEMING, age 21 years 6 months (with short eulogy).

We learn from the Sumter Republican, that on the 9th inst., the residence of MRS. McKINLEY, near Danville, Sumter county, Ga., was destroyed by fire, and horrible to relate, Mrs. McKinley and child both perished in the flames.

July 1, 1857

Died in Vineville, on Sunday morning last of Typhoid fever, MRS. BIVINS, wife of ROLIN BIVINS, ESQ., of this county; an exemplary member of the M.E. Church.

Died in Perry, Ga., June 16th, WILLIAM NEWMAN, only child of WILLIAM M. and ANN T. ELDER, aged 2 years 2 months 21 days. (Telegraph please copy)

Died in this City on 29th June of Bowel affliction, JAMES JACKSON SCARBOURGH, son of JONATHAN H. and MARY A.E. POOL, age 1 year 7 months 13 days. (Christian Index, and Chronicle & Sentinel will please copy)

HON. LANGDON CHEVES, of South Carolina, died in Columbia on Thursday last. He was born in 1776.

Tribute of respect by Twiggs Lodge, No. 164 June 20th, 1857 - on death of BENJAMIN B. SMITH who died at his residence in Twiggs county on the morning of the 15th inst., in the 67th year of his age; gave distinguished public services as Representative, Senator, and State Treasurer.

July 8, 1857

Died in Vineville on the morning of the 1st inst., THOMAS WIMBERLY, son of T.J. and A.E. CATER, aged 14 months. (with eulogy).

JIM DANIELLY was killed at Freeman & Roberts' workshop, on Tuesday. Jim was a member of the colored Brass Band of this city, and his comrades turned out and buried him handsomely with the honors of military music. There were about twenty carriages in procession, besides many colored persons on foot followed the poor fellow to the Grave! (Citizen)

July 4 - HON. WM. L. MARCY was found dead in his room at Ballstown Springs today. He appeared in his usual health in the morning.

July 15, 1857

Died in Americus on the 1st inst., OLIVIA MELINDA, only daughter of THOS. M. and MELINDA H. EDEN, aged 1 year 10 months 20 days.

Died in Crawford county, Ga., at the residence of Dr. J.C. Harvey, on the 25th June at 6 o'clock, A.M., FRANCIS E. BACON, aged 26 years, after a protracted illness of 18 days; interred with Masonic honors by Knoxville Lodge, No. 55.

HON. LANGDON CHEVES died in Columbia, South Carolina, on Tuesday night last. Born in Sept. 1776 in Abbeville district, S.C., and consequently was in the 81st year of his age. In 1811 was elected to Congress, and during his term casting vote in the negative, as Speaker of the House, on the question of rechartering the old United States Bank. Upon his return to his own State, he was elected Judge of the Court of Common Pleas, but subsequently became President of the United States Bank.

July 15, 1857

Our city was yesterday the scene of intense excitement, occasioned by a street rencontre between MESSRS. NEWMAN McBAIN and CHARLES W. HANCOCK on the one side and MESSRS. HARVEY W. and WILLIAM SHAW on the other, in which H.W. Shaw was killed...(South-Western News)

From a letter in the San Antonio Texas, dated Laredo, Texas, May 25th, we learn that "Wild Cat," the celebrated Seminole Chief, who gave the US so much trouble during the Seminole war, is dead, he with forty of his followers having fallen victim to the small pox.

July 22, 1857

COL. J.J. WORD died suddenly at Montvale Springs on the 7th inst. His health had been feeble for some time.

Tribute of respect by Mount Hope Lodge, No. 9, F.& A.M. (Hawkinsville Ga. July 10th, 1857) - on death of JOHN W. RAY.

July 29, 1857

Died on 16th May, MRS. ELIZABETH M. PITTS, daughter of O.D. TUCKER, Houston county, aged 29 years; member of the Baptist Church; leaves a husband, two children, father, sister, brother and servants to mourn. (Pulaski county, Ga. July 1857 J.R.H.)

Died in this city on the 23d inst., ANNA BEVERIGE, infant child of COL. and MRS. R.H. CLARK, aged 1 year 7 days. (with eulogy).

Died at her late residence in Bibb county, Ga., on the 19th July 1857, of Typhoid Fever, MRS. ELIZABETH THARP, in the 69th year of her age.

MARMADUKE J. SLADE died in the vicinity of Tuscaloosa, Ala., on the 16th inst. Was connected with the establishment of the "Georgia Messenger," from 1826 to 1830 - afterwards with the Press in Milledgeville. For many years, he has published the "Independent Monitor" of Tuscaloosa; a native of North Carolina.

Aug. 12, 1857

Died in this city on the 7th inst., MRS. MARY VIRGINIA BALL, wife of MR. HENRY E. BALL, aged about 24 years.

Died in Baltimore on the 3rd inst., DR. JOSEPH LOYAL COWLES, aged 23 years - son of MR. LOYAL COWLES, formerly of this City, after a lingering and painful illness of twelve months. (with short eulogy)

Died in Houston County July 20th, MRS. ANNIE ANDERSON, wife of WM. R. ANDERSON, in her 71st year. Born in Pendleton District, S.C. 14 Jan. 1787, moved to Georgia with her husband in 1816; connected with the Baptist Church in 1812; leaves husband and large family of children and grandchildren, brothers and sisters. (Southern Christian Advocate please copy)

Died at his residence in Sumter County on the 25th ult., in the 51st year of his age, REV. JOHN U. FLETCHER; preacher of the Baptist persuasion.

Died suddenly, July 30th, at the residence of Dr. James Worsham, near this city, in the 30th year of her age, MISS SARAH WORSHAM, daughter of the late DAVID G. WORSHAM, of Hopewell; member of the Presbyterian Church (with eulogy).

News of GEN. RUSK'S death by suicide comes to us by telegraph from New Orleans. A native of one of the upper Districts of South Carolina, he has for many years represented Texas in the US Senate.

Aug. 19, 1857

   Died in this city on the 7th inst., in the 24th year of her age,
   MARY VIRGINIA, wife of HENRY E. BALL, and daughter of the late
   MARK D. and NANCY M. CLARKE; member of the Baptist Church (with
   eulogy).

   The Sumter Republican of the 13th inst. says that a young man named
   THOMAS DURHAM died yesterday morning, at COL. McBAIN's Hotel, from
   the effects of Laudanum. The deceased was about 21 or 22 years
   of age.

Aug. 26, 1857

   Died near this city on the 24th inst. after a short illness, MRS.
   FRANCES M. GREER, aged about 25 years - wife of E.C. GREER, ESQ.
   and daughter of the HON. WASHINGTON POE of this city. (obituary
   in 2 Sep. 1857 issue).

   Died in Marion county on the 8th inst., MR. JOURDAN WILCHER in the
   72nd year of his age; one of the oldest and best citizens of that
   county; also one of the earliest settlers of Bibb, from which he
   removed several years since.

   DR. HENRY BRANHAM of Eatonton, Putnam county, died at the White
   Sulphur Springs, in Va., on the 14th inst., where he had gone for
   his health; an eminent physician and formerly a prominent political
   leader - and had several times occupied a seat in our Legislature.

Sep. 2, 1857

   Died in Atlanta on the 12th inst., in the 36th year of her age, of
   consumption, MRS. MARTHA E. JONES, wife of JOHN JONES and daughter
   of AUGUSTIN and SUSAN J. COOK; a member of the Baptist Church
   (with short eulogy).

Sep. 9, 1857

   Died in Americus on the evening of the 7th inst., PARTHENAI R.
   HOLT, daughter of the late DR. ABNER HOLT, aged about 10 years.

   Died in Crawford county, Georgia, at his residence after a short
   illness, JOHN STEMBRIDGE, in his 67th year; interred with Masonic
   honors by Knoxville Lodge, No. 55.

Sep. 16, 1857

   Died in this city on Friday the 11th inst., COL. I.D.N. JOHNS in
   the 31st year of his age.

   Died near Zebulon on the 7th inst., EMMA LUCINDA, infant daughter
   of DR. J.W. and LUCINDA WALKER, aged 1 year and 11 months
   (with short eulogy).

   DR. WILLIAM WINANS, venerable minister of the Gospel, died on
   Monday evening, August 31, at 4 o'clock. Born in Pennsylvania
   3 Nov. 1788; nearly half a century of his life has been devoted to
   service of Methodist Church, during 34 years of which period he
   has been a prominent actor in all its interests; in 1812 came to
   Mississippi as a Missionary. (Natchez Courier, 2d inst.)

Sep. 23, 1857

   Died in Macon on the 13th inst., JAMES S. HOLLINSHEAD, ESQ., aged
   about 50 years.

   Died in this City on the 21st inst., MRS. MARY E. JOHNS, relict of
   the late COL. I.D. JOHNS, and daughter of DR. HAMMOND of this
   city.

Sep. 23, 1857

From the Southern Christian Advocate - DR. HENRY BRANHAM, of Eatonton, Georgia, died at his summer residence, Sulphur Springs, Hall county, August 14th, 1857, in his 69th year. Before reaching his 21st year, he settled in the practice of medicine in Eatonton; for more than thirty years a member of the Methodist Church (with eulogy)

From the Southern Christian Advocate - SAMUEL BEALL, ESQ., was born near Guilford C.H., N.C., joined the M.E. Church in 1812, removed to Irwinton, Ga., in 1819, where he died, Aug. 14th, 1857, in his 75th year; a legislator in the Senate eighteen successive years; served the county as a Justice of the Superior Court upwards of 32 years, and afterwards in Office of Ordinary in his county; in 1836 enlisted with a company whose object was to protect the citizens of Southwestern Georgia against the depredations of the Indians (with eulogy).

Sep. 30, 1857

Died in this city on Sunday morning, MATTIE, daughter of DR. ROBT. and MRS. E. COLLINS, aged 2 years 8 months 9 days.

Died at his residence in Pulaski county on Tuesday the 23d inst., JOHN H. LUMPKIN, ESQ., in the 74th year of his age (with eulogy).

Montgomery Messenger of 23rd - MAJOR JOHN C. BATES died yesterday at 2 p.m. at the country residence of the late Major Cowles, four miles from this city. Born in Vermont and educated at Middleburg College, of which his father (now deceased) was the President for many years; came South about 1839, and soon took charge of the Whig paper at Wetumpka. After a year or two, he removed to Montgomery, where he married, the only daughter of the late GEN. TALIAFERRO. His connection with the Journal has been continuous for fifteen or seventeen years. We suppose his age to have been about 45. Was buried with Masonic and Military honors on Wednesday.

The numerous friends and relatives of the late DR. A.S. SPEER, of Florida, who was accidentally drowned in Lake George, a short time since, will be gratified to learn, that his body has been recovered and identified, and was buried at Bolusia, Florida, September 7th, 1857.

Oct. 7, 1857

Died at his residence in Pulaski county on Tuesday the 22d inst. JOHN L. LAMKIN, ESQ., in the 74th year of his age (with short eulogy)

Died on 3d September in Dooly county, near Drayton, JULIUS E., son of ROBT. S. and SARAH A.F. MIMS, in the 9th year of his age (with eulogy).

Oct. 14, 1857

Died at her father's residence in Floyd county, at half past two o'clock, on the morning of Monday the 5th inst., LULA REBECCA, only daughter of JOHN R. and MARY T. FREEMAN, aged 17 months 23 days.

Died at the residence of her son-in-law, at Washington, Ga., on the 2d inst., MRS. HENRIETTA ANN MANN, wife of JOHN H. MANN, ESQ., of Augusta, Ga., in the 67th year of her age; for 48 years a faithful member of the Methodist Episcopal Church, and for 30 years a teacher and superintendent in the Sabbath School.

Died in Taylor County, on 20th September, MR. DANIEL WHATLEY, aged nearly 114 years. He was probably at the time of his death, the oldest inhabitant in the State.

Oct. 14, 1857

Died at the late residence of his Grand Father, EDMUND GILBERT, ESQ., M.L. GILBERT, son of M.T. GILBERT, deceased, after a few days illness, on the 6th inst., in the 12th year of his age; leaves a mother, sister and many relatives.

The HON. WM. E. VENABLE, our lately appointed Minister to Guatemala, who died of Cholera, soon after his arrival in that country, was a native of North Carolina. For some years past, he has resided in Tennessee, where he leaves a widow and six children.

Oct. 21, 1857

J.C. CURTIS, a worthy and much respected colored man, and well known in this community, was found dead in his bed on Monday morning last. His family was absent. It is supposed he died of disease of the heart.

Oct. 28, 1857

Died in Jeffersonville on the 20th inst., of consumption, MR. F.M. FULTON, aged 27. Will be remembered as an esteemed member of the board of instruction of Wesleyan Female College last year. His remains were brought to this city and interred in Rose Hill Cemetery.

Nov. 4, 1857

Died in this city on Wed. morning ult., of Typhoid Billious Fever, A. LOUISA, second daughter of A.K. and E.W. McLAUGHLIN, aged 21 years.

Died at Fort Gaines, Ga., Sept. 30th, WILLIAM P. FORD, in the 24th year of his age; member of M.E. Church, South; suffered much and frequently from Asthma; leaves wife, mother and sister (with eulogy) (Savannah Georgian please copy)

Died at his residence in Upson county on the 8th ult., the REV. RALEIGH GREEN, aged 60. On the 29th ult., MRS. ELIZABETH GREEN, relict of the REV. RALEIGH GREEN.

Nov. 11, 1857

WILLIAM HILL, Secretary of the State of North Carolina, died on Thursday last, in the 84th year of his age. Was elected Secretary of State in 1811, and filled the office to the day of his death, a period of 46 years.

Died in East Bumbleton on the 2d inst., COL. LEWIS LEE, aged 74 years 3 months 8 days.

Died in the Georgia Lunatic Asylum on the 5th inst., JAMES DENTON, ESQ., an old and worthy citizen of East Macon, aged 45. Had been confined to the Asylum about seven months - leaves a wife and child.

MRS. ELIZABETH BOLTON DYSON, wife of THOMAS DYSON, ESQ., died in Thomasville about ten o'clock at night, on Friday the 18th Sep. 1857, aged 50 years 8 months 13 days; in early life became a member of the Baptist Church in Baldwin county, where she was born and brought up (with short eulogy).

An affray, we are told, occurred at a "Corn Shucking" last Saturday night week, at Nelson's Place, near this city, between WM. HOLT and GEORGE KNIGHT, in which the former was severly cut in several places and died yesterday morning. (Telegraph)

Nov. 18, 1857

Died in Twiggs county on the 7th inst., MRS. LUCINDA PEARCE, wife of ELIAS PEARCE, aged about 52 years - formerly the widow of COL. HENRY SOLOMON of that county.

Died in Houston county on the 9th inst., JOHN SAMUEL, son of DR. EDMUND McGEHEE, aged 14 years 11 months 21 days. His disease was Catarrh and Inflammation of the brain.

Died at his residence near Americus on the 3d inst., MR. WILLIAM BRADY, aged 69 years 10 months 20 days; member of the Baptist Church for last fifteen years.

Died in Dublin, Laurens county, on Monday the 9th inst., DR. FREDERIC CULLENS, aged 28 years 1 month 24 days.

MR. CHARLES MUNNERLYN, SR., an old and estimable citizen of Decatur county, died at his residence on the 9th inst.

MR. DUNCAN J. DAVIS, representative from Early county, died at Milledgeville Thursday morning last, of Pneumonia.

Nov. 25, 1857

On Saturday morning last, when the doors of the Baptist Church in this place were opened for public worship, HUGH KELLY was found lying in the pulpit. He had worked in the carriage shop of Gardner & Martin...(Sparta Georgian)

Died at five and a half o'clock P.M. on the 1st inst., at his residence in Sumter county, DR. ALEXANDER B. GREENE, in the 47th year of his age. His disease was dysentery of the most violent form; was son of REV. MILES GREENE; member of M.E. Church.

Died near Fort Scott, Kansas Territory, on the evening of 18 Oct., 1857, MACON CRAWFORD, youngest child of BENJAMIN and SUSAN F. BRANTLY, aged 17 months 11 days.

Died in Houston County, Ga., on the 18th inst., JACOB RILEY, SENR., in the 68th year of his age; a native of Orangeburg District, S.C., but a resident of the above county and state for nearly 22 years; for over 40 years a member of the Methodist Episcopal Church.

Tribute of respect by Young America by Young America Fire Company No. 3 Nov. 2d, 1857 - on death of JOSEPH B. CRAWFORD, who died in this city on the 31st October last, of Congestion of the Brain, in the 19th year of his age.

Dec. 2, 1857

Died in Madison, Texas on 3d November, CAPT. ROBERT S. PATTON, aged about 56 years; a native of this county and among the earliest emigrants from this section to Texas.

Died at the residence of Norman McDuffie in Pulaski county, on the 14th inst., DR. JOHN A. TUCKER, aged 22 years 6 months and 17 days. (Fed. Union please copy)

Dec. 9, 1857

Died at the Military Institute in Marietta on the 7th inst., HENRY G. LAMAR, JR., son of COL. H.G. LAMAR of this city; interred in Rose Hill Cemetery in this city.

Died in Vineville on the 2d inst., at an advanced age, MRS. CHLOE N. KELSEY, widow of the late CAPT. NOAH KELSEY, formerly of Powelton, Georgia.

Dec. 9, 1857

The Milledgeville Recorder says that a negro man named VAL BELLAMY died at the advanced age of 110 years, in the neighborhood of Island Creek, Hancock county, on the 20th ult. He was a cook for the American troops stationed at Charleston during the Rev. War.

Dec. 16, 1857

Died in Houston county on the 20th October last, DAVID HOWARD, son of JOHN A. & SUSAN HOWARD, aged about 3 years 6 months.

Dec. 23, 1857

SAMUEL WRIGHT MINOR, probably the oldest printer in Georgia, died in this city, last Thursday, after a lingering illness of three months. He was born in Queen Anne's County, Maryland in 1781, and removed to Georgia in early life. Served apprenticeship in office of William J. Bunce, of Augusta. His first adventure in business was the publication of the Athens Gazette; removed to McDonough and published the McDonough Jacksonian; then removed to Fayetteville and published Fayetteville Advertiser; was son of COL. WILLIAM MINOR, an officer of the Rev. Army. (Telegraph of 15th).

The Charleston Mercury of Thursday last reports the death of MR. JOHN MILTON CLAPP, who for nearly 20 years was associated with the editorial department of that journal. Was a native of Ohio and educated at Yale College, where he graduated 1831 with high distinction. Was appointed Principal Teacher in the Beaufort College. Removed to Charleston and became Assistant Editor of the Charleston Mercury; at one time edited the Southern Quarterly Review.

Dec. 30, 1857

Died in this city on the 22d inst. of Irresypilis, MR. JAMES V. LOYD, aged 18 years 2 months, son of MR. JAMES C. LOYD, of Crawford county. Been employed in this office about ten months as an apprentice to Printing Business (with short eulogy).

Died in this city on the 29th inst., MRS. SARAH Q. FLUKER, aged 66 years - widow of the late BALDWIN FLUKER.

Died on Thursday 17th Dec. last, in the 43d year of her age, MRS. NANCY H. TRICE, wife of JAMES TRICE, ESQ., of Upson county, Georgia, after a long and painful affliction; leaves husband and children (with eulogy).

Murder. On Christmas morning, the body of MICHAEL HICKEY was discovered on the bank of the Macon and Western Railroad, between the city and Vineville, about twenty feet below the track...was recently from Savannah, where he has a wife and two children... had worked at Findlay's foundry.

We regret to learn that an affray occurred at the Academy in Brunswick, on the occasion of a public meeting, Friday night last, which resulted in the death of MR. JACOB W. MOORE, Representative of Glynn county in the late Legislature.

Tribute of respect by Eureka Lodge, No. 95 (Starkville, Ga. Dec. 18, 1857) - on death of GEORGE A. DEAVORS.

Jan. 6, 1858

Died on 21st Dec. 1857, in Macon county, Ga., MRS. MARY ANN DAVIS, wife of ICHABOD DAVIS, in the 53d year of her age; for 29 years en exemplary member of the Baptist Church.

Jan. 6, 1858

Died in Barnesville, the 17th ult., MRS. MARTHA HIGHTOWER, daughter of the REV. JOSEPH BATTLE, and widow of DANIEL HIGHTOWER, in her 36th year (with short eulogy).

Died in this city, on Friday evening last, MRS. MARTHA L. ROSS, wife of J.B. ROSS, ESQ., and daughter of COL. W.C. REDDING of Monroe county, Ga., aged 29; a member of the Methodist Church; leaves an interesting family of children; buried in Rose Hill Cemetery.

On Thursday evening last, says the Texas State Gazette, REV. DANIEL BAKER, D.D. died at the residence of Joseph Walker, Esq.. He was in his 60th year, and had been in service of the Presbyterian Church for over a quarter of a century; President of Austin College.

The Tallahassee Floridian says: From Lieut. Shehee, of Capt. Parkhill's company, who arrived here on the last steamer from Tampa, we have the painful assurance that the lamented CAPT. PARKILL is indeed no more. He died in about ten minutes after the fatal wound was inflicted, and was buried some distance from the battle ground, in an old Indian house which was burned down over him to conceal his remains from the searching eye of the savage.

REV. GEORGE LUMPKIN, of the Baptist Church, died at his residence in Oglethorpe county, on the 14th inst., in the 70th year of his age.

We regret to notice the death of REV. R. HOOKER, formerly Pastor of the Presbyterian Church in this city; announced in the New Haven Palladium; he died in New Haven, on 19th December last, in the 49th year of his age.

We learn from the Atlanta American that young WITCHER, who killed his father last summer in that place, escaped from the jail of Atlanta a few days since, and is yet at large.

We understand that a difficulty took place at the store of N.B. ALLEN at Stevensville, Wilkinson county, in which JAS. B. BOSTWICK was shot by Mr. ALLEN, and died in a few minutes.

Jan. 13, 1858

The City Council have offered one hundred dollars reward for the detection and apprehension of the murderer of MICHAEL HICKEY.

The Philadelphia Bulletin announces the death, in Gloucester, N.J., on Saturday last, of MISS ELIZA LESLIE, a lady of well known literary celebrity. Miss Leslie was most distinguished by her works on cookery and housekeeping.

Jan. 20, 1858

Died in Oglethorpe, on the 6th inst., EDWIN ENGLISH, ESQ., an old and much esteemed citizen.

Died in Reynolds, Taylor county, ALEXANDER H.K. SWIFT, ESQ., formerly a resident of Upson and Crawford counties, aged about 59 years.

Jan. 27, 1858

Augusta Dispatch of 20th announces the death of AUGUSTIN S. WINGFIELD, ESQ., of Madison. He died yesterday morning, in that town, aged about 38 years.

Feb. 3, 1858

Died at the residence of his mother in East Macon; on the 25th ult., CRAWFORD W. BROWN, ESQ., aged 26 years; for several years past Superintendent on the Waynesboro Railroad; for months laboring under Chronic Diarrhea.

Died at Thibadeaux, La., on the 15th ult., of Consumption, MRS. MARY ANN SMITH, widow of the late GENERAL WILLIAM G. SMITH, of this city.

MR. HAMILTON CAPPS, residing some ten miles west of Americus, committed suicide on the night of the 12th ult., by hanging himself.

COL. HUGH ARCHER died at the residence of his son, in this city, on Saturday morning last, after a long illness, and was buried on Sunday following. At the time of his death, he was Collector of the Port of St. Marks, to which office he was appointed by President Pierce, in 1853; a native of South Carolina but emigrated to Florida with family many years ago; served Leon county in a legislative capacity; member of the Baptist Church (Floridian of 30th ult.)

Feb. 10, 1858

Died in Houston county, on the 3rd ult., MR. JOEL SKIPPER, an old and worthy citizen; member of the Methodist Church.

On Friday last, WILLIAM H. COATS, generally called HENRY COATS, came to his death in a singular manner...he cut a piece of beef and put it into his mouth, and finding it too tough for his teeth he attempted to swallow it, when it lodged in his throat, and literally choked him to death; formerly resided in Pike, about eight miles from this place, but had moved his family to Early county, and was here arranging matters to go there himself... (Griffin Union)

Another Revolutionary soldier gone. GIDDEON BENTLY, of Constantia, Oswego county, who died a few days since, was born in the town of Exeter, (R.I.) August 12th, 1750. Served under Col. Barton in a Rhode Island regiment one year, and as a minute-man three years. Was a volunteer in a company under Capt. Barton, who crossed over to Long Island in boats and captured a body of tories, killing 15 and taking 75 prisoners...voted at every Presidential election from Washington to Buchanan, had at time of his death 13 children; also, grandchildren and great-grandchildren numbering 225 - all of whom are now living.

Feb. 17, 1858

REV. DANIEL F. WADE, an old and worthy citizen of Houston county, recently died whilst on a visit to Alabama. ORIN D. TUCKER, ESQ., an old and much respected citizen of the same county, died at his residence on the 20th ult. Obituary next week.

The Charleston Courier of Wed. announces the death of REV. DR. SAMUEL GILMAN - at the residence of his son-in-law, Rev. C.J. Bowen, at King, Mass., yesterday.

Papers announce the death of GEORGE M. TROUP, only son of the late GOV. TROUP. He died on the first instant.

The Tallahassee Sentinel of the 9th inst. announces the death of HENRY BOND, ESQ., one of the oldest citizens of that place, and, at the time of his death, Receiver of Public Monies for the US in the Tallahassee District.

Feb. 17, 1858

The N.Y. Evening Post of the 9th announces that BEVERLY WAUGH, Senior Bishop of the Methodist Episcopal Church, died this morning, at one o'clock, at his residence in Baltimore; died of erysipelas which followed a sudden attack of apoplexy; elected to the Episcopal office in 1836; previous to that time, he was resident of New York city, and for several years had charge of the Methodist Book Concern.

$1000 reward will be paid for the apprehension and delivery to the Jailor of Lee County, Georgia of THOMAS THOMAS, under sentence of death for the murder of JOSEPH S. CROSS. The said Thomas broke Jail on the night of 7th February, 1858. He is between 21 and 22 years of age, and weight about 150 pounds, and about 5 feet six inches high, of light complexion, hazel eyes, light hair, fine white teeth, left handed ans one of his thumbs disfigured very much, occasioned by a bone-felon. (Wm. G. Cross, Adm'r)

Feb. 24, 1858

MRS. LIZZIE BIGSON, wife of MR. WILLIAM GIBSON, and daughter of MAJ. REUBEN WRIGHT, died at her father's residence, in Monroe co., Ga., 11th Jan'y 1858, aged 28 years; in 1847 joined the Baptist Church at Shiloh, Ga.; had daughter of six years and son of four. (with eulogy)

Departed this life, at Seymour's Point, East Florida, aged 24 years, HENRIETTA L., wife of REV. WILLIAM DAVIES, and eldest daughter of FRANCIS L. and MARGARET S. ROUX, of Charleston.

Died on 27th January, at his residence in Houston county, MR. ORIN D. TUCKER, in the 63d year of his age. He was born in Nash County, N.C., and came to Georgia when about 18 years old; a member of Missionary Baptist Church for eighteen to twenty years; only surviving member of his family is a widowed daughter (with eulogy) (Christian Index please copy)

MR. H.A. LIVINGSTON, Associat editor of the Newnan Blade, died at his residence in Newnan, on the 5th inst., of pulmonary consumption; in later life expressed belief in salvation by faith and grace, but in early life was a believer of the Unitarian Universalist School. (Augusta Dispatch)

Died in Columbus, Ga., on the 16th inst., MRS. ANNE L., wife of ROSWELL ELLIS, ESQ., (one of the editors of the Columbus Times and Sentinel,) and daughter of the REV. THOMAS B. SLADE of that city, aged about 23 years; had been married but a few months. (with long eulogy)

Mar. 3, 1858

Died in Jones county, on the 15th inst., MR. JOSEPH STILES, aged about 79 years, one of the earliest settlers of Jones county, and probably its oldest citizen at the time of his death.

Died in Houston County, on 22d February, of Erysipelas, MR. ABNER P. STUBBS, aged about 25 years - son of the late PETER STUBBS, of Bibb County; a member of the Baptist Church.

The funeral of the venerable JESSE ANTHONY was attended from the North Second Street Methodist Church on Thursday. The funeral sermon was preached by Rev. Mr. Washburne. At the conclusion of the discourse, an old gentleman, REV. SAMUEL HOWE, of Lansingburg, a superannuated member of the Troy conference, rose near the pulpit and proposed to say a few words in reference to the deceased ...afterwards Mr. Howe left the main room of the church, and entered the basement, where, seating himself in a rocking chair, he almost immediately expired; aged 78 years. (Troy, N.Y. Whig)

Mar. 10, 1858

Died in Vineville, near Macon, March 3rd, MRS. CAROLINE, wife of MR. PHILEMON TRACY, and daughter of the late JOHN RAWLS, aged 24 years.

COMMODORE PERRY died in New York on Thursday last.

Mar. 17, 1858

Died in this city on Sunday, the 14th March, MR. J.F. WHITFORD, aged 23 years; from Rhode Island (with short eulogy).

At a term of the Superior Court of Crawford County, held last week, JAMES REVEL was returned to the Grand Jury as guilty of the crime of Murder, for shooting W.W. HAMMACK and GEORGE ADAMS. He was tried for the murder of Hammack, and found guilty, and sentenced by Judge Lamar, to be hung on Friday the 7th May.

The venerable JOHN WARRICK, who died at Richmond on Saturday, had been printer to the Virginia Senate for the last 38 years, a member of the Masonic fraternity for 48 years, and the treasurer of a lodge for 34 years.

The Rome Courier says that on Wed. or Thursday of last week MR. JACOB SMYER, the owner of a mill some three or four miles below Coosaville, in this county, was caught in his machinery by his clothes, and drawn in between two cog-wheels, and most horribly mutilated, causing his immediate death.

Mar. 24, 1858

Died in this City, on the 20th inst., MR. JOHN T. NISBET, aged about 25 years; a member of the Presbyterian Church.

The Atlanta American of Friday announces that MRS. TURNER, wife of REV. MR. TURNER, while riding in a buggy with her husband yesterday near Palmetto, Coweta county, was killed instantly by a kick from the horse, which, taking fright, became unmanageable.

We learn from the Times & Sentinel that on Sunday night last, MR. WALKER, a respectable planter in Macon County, Ala., some seven miles west of Auburn, while reading, was shot by some person outside and instantly killed...

Mar. 31, 1858

Died in this city, on the 23d instant, of Consumption, MR. WILLIAM S. WILLIFORD, in the 37th year of his age; a native of Greenville, S.C.; at an early age settled in Savannah, and about fourteen years ago, removed to Macon; a zealous advocate of Temperance Reform and a worthy Mason; member of the Macon Volunteers; was a kind father, an affectionate brother, a dutiful son, a devoted husband.

Died in Lumpkin, on Sunday morning, the 21st inst., after a painful illness of several weeks, GEN. J.C.P. EWING, aged about 45 years.

Died in Griffin, on the 19th inst., ETTIENE SCHULER, mother of Augustus P. Barr, after a long and painful illness in the 58th year of her age; a native of St. Johns, New Brunswick; a member of the Episcopal Church.

Died in Barnesville, on the 11th inst., MRS. H.E. McCOY, wife of HENRY McCOY, ESQ., in the 28th year of her age.

Died in Atlanta, on the 18th inst., MARY WILLIAM SPENCER, only child of DR. THOMAS S. and MRS. JULIA L. POWELL, aged 4 years 6 months.

Mar. 31, 1858

Died in Laurens county, on Thursday the 18th of March, IRA STANLEY, ESQ., aged about 59.

The LaGrange Reporter announces the death of MRS. HARRALSON, widow of the late HON. H.A. HARRALSON. She died of pneumonia on the 23rd inst.

A young man by the name of THOS. M. BLACK, living in the upper part of Henry County, being out "Coon Hunting" on Tuesday night last came to his death in a very sudden and unexpected manner. It appears that the Coon was up a very large tree which had to be felled by the party in order to catch him; and when the tree fell a broken limb struck Mr. Black on the head causing instant death. He leaves a wife and two children. (Griffin Empire State)

Apr. 7, 1858

Died in Macon, Ga. on 23d inst., WILLIAM S. WILLIFORD. Born in the village of Greenville, S.C. 30 May 1821, where he resided with his parents until 1843. Then went to Savannah, Ga., and there remained about two years. Was married, and changed his residence to Macon, where he lived the last thirty years. Leaves a wife and two children, a mother and four sisters (one of whom is now a missionary in Africa); member of the Episcopal Church; Grand Scribe of the Sons of Temperance; also a Mason and an Odd Fellow; an officer in the Marine Branch Bank at Macon. (with eulogy).

S.C. DUNNING died at his residence in this city yesterday in the 79th year of his age; for many years a citizen of Savannah (News)

The demise of DR. FRANKLIN on Saturday morning last was not unexpected, though sincerely regretted by a large circle of kindred and friends.

From a letter addressed to Col. Sims, of this place, we learn that a fatal rencounter took place on Saturday, the 28th ult., in Fort Gaines, Ga., between ALEXANDER MARSHALL and WARREN SUTTON, in which the latter was killed on the spot...(Southern Georgian). Alexander Marchall was tried and acquitted.

Tribute of respect by Macon Lodge, No. 5 April 5, 1858 - on death of WILLIAM S. WILLIFORD.

Apr. 14, 1858

Died at his residence in Early county, on the 4th inst., HON. JOEL CRAWFORD. The deceased read law in the office of Hon. Nicholas Hare, in Augusta, and having taken course of law lectures in Litchfield, Connecticut, under auspices of Judge Reese, was admitted to plead and practice in the courts of Georgia, at the spring term of Wilkes Superior Court, in 1808. Commenced career at the bar in Sparta, but in 1811 removed to Milledgeville, where he resided to the close of his professional labors. In war of 1812 enlisted as a volunteer in a corps of dragoons commanded by Captain Steele, and shortly afterward was brevetted aid-de-camp to Gen. Floyd, a post which he retained to the end of the campaign. This bret gave Mr. Crawford the rank of Major and imposed on him perils in our Indian wars of that day...was elected for two terms a representative in Congress from Georgia, under the general ticket system, and declined a nomination for a third term...in 1826 commissioned by Gov. Troup to service of adjusting the boundary line between Alabama and Georgia; in 1837 was one of a board of commissioners for survey, location and construction of the Western and Atlantic Rail Road...

Died in this city on 31st March, at the residence of Mr. John L. Jones, JULIA P. YOUNG, daughter of the late GUILFORD D.YOUNG, of New York (with eulogy).

Apr. 14, 1858

Died in this city on the 7th inst., in the 29th year of her age, MRS. AMANDA M. HAFER, consort of MR. JOHN HAFER; a member of the Methodist Episcopal Church (with eulogy).

Died in this city on Easter Sunday, DERMOT ALDEN DEMPSEY, only child of THOMAS C. and MARIA L. DEMPSEY, aged 5 years 7 months 11 days.

We learn that a dreadful crime was committed on Maj. Belvin's Plantation in Houston Co., last Tuesday afternoon, upon the person of MRS. BRYANT, the young wife of Major Belvin's overseer. She had retired after dinner to take a nap, and some time thereafter the servants outside the house, hearing moans, entered her room and found her frightfully mutilated about the head and shoulders by blows from an axe...
(Telegraph of Tuesday)

DR. THOS. R. LAMAR died on yesterday morning, after a most painful and lingering illness, aged 58.

MIKE DAVIS, charged with the murder of MR. GAY, of Jasper county, has been arrested.

COL. BENTON died at his residence in Washington, at quite an advanced age; a contemporary of Clay, Webster, and Calhoun...

Apr. 21, 1858

Died, at his residence in Upson County, on the 2d inst., MR. EDMUND RAINES, aged 57 years. He had an attack of Dyspepsia in early life, together with other nervous derangements from which he never fully recovered (with eulogy).

GEORGE CRAWFORD died at his residence in Griffin, on Monday evening last, at the advanced age of 84, says the Griffin Union.

The National Intelligencer, of Monday, in noticing the death of Mr. Benton says: It is a curious and affecting circumstance that the youngest and oldest of the family should have died within a few hours of each other, under the same roof. An infant grandson of Col. Benton, the child of MR. WILLIAM CAREY JONES, died in the house of his grandfather yesterday morning.

Tribute of respect by Young Men's Christian Association, held at Macon, April 12th, 1858 - on death of JOHN T. NISBET.

Apr. 28, 1858

Departed this life at LaGrange, Ga., on the 5th instant, JAMES A. RUSSELL, ESQ., aged 34 years; born in Morgan county, Ga., the son of BURWELL and MARTHA RUSSELL; studied law (with eulogy).

W.T. INGRAM of the firm of W.O. Price & Co., committed suicide in Augusta on Sunday last, by shooting himself through the heart - cause, pecuniary embarrassments.

RADFORD CROCKETT, aged 21 (who was engaged in the coldblooded murder of SAMUEL LANDRUM, near Atlanta on the 8th inst.,) was on Saturday morning last sentenced to be hung on the 18th of June.

Tribute of respect by Traveller's Rest Lodge, No. 65 April 1, 1858 - on death of JONES M. TAYLOR. He died on the 31st March at the residence of Wm. P. Dunnwright, Dooly county, Ga. He was born 10 Oct. 1810 in Mecklenburg county, Va., and for the last five years a citizen of this neighborhood.

May 12, 1858

Died in Rutherford County, N.C., May 1st, after a short illness, EFFIE, second daughter of W.M. and MARY McAFEE, of Fort Valley, Ga., in the 16th year of her age.

Died on March 22d, 1858, BRO. ELISHA P. TURNER, aged about 60; a Mason - member of Knoxville Lodge, No. 55.

HON. JOSIAH J. EVANS, US Senator from South Carolina, died about eleven o'clock last night, at his residence on Louisiana avenue, near Four-and-half-street. (<u>Washington Star</u> of Friday afternoon)

GEN. CHARLES FENTON MERCER, a gentleman widely known throughout Virginia and the country, died at Howard, Fairfax county, Va., on Friday last, in the 80th year of his age.

CAPT. THOMAS C. EVANS of LaGrange had a stroke of Paralysis in that city, on the evening of the 4th inst., which resulted in his death before morning. Was the Ordinary of Troup County and commanded the Cadet Riflemen in the war of 1836 against the Florida Indians.

May 19, 1858

Died in this City, on the morning of the 6th inst., at the residence of her mother, (MRS. ELIZA TRAP,) MRS. LUCIA M. BROWN, wife of DR. WM. T. BROWN, of Lafayette, Ala., aged 29 years 9 months 2 days.

Died in New Orleans, on the 13th inst., of Apoplexy, MRS. CAROLINE E. SEYMOUR, consort of COL. ISAAC G. SEYMOUR, Editor of the "Commercial Bulletin," and for many years associated with the Journal & Messenger of this city.

HON. J.J. GILCHRIST, the presiding Judge of the US Court of Claims, died in Washington on Thursday, the 20th (29th?) ult., in the 49th year of his age; an eminent lawyer and formerly Chief Justice of New Hampshire.

May 26, 1858

Died near Tarversville, Twiggs County, May 5th, 1858, MR. JAMES H. FOREHAND, aged about 35 years. Also, MRS. PENELOPE ELLEN FOREHAND his wife, died May 18th, aged about 32 years; member of Methodist Church.

Died in Charleston, Mass., on the 10th inst., MR. JACOB DENSE, father of MAJ. B.F. DENSE, of this City, aged about 77 years.

Died in Milledgeville, on the 20th inst., FREDERICK H. SANFORD, ESQ., of Hancock county.

The telegraph announces the death of GEN. PERSIFER F. SMITH, who was in command of the Army of Utah.

DR. WM. BOOTH, a prominent and worthy citizen of Quincy, Fla., died on the morning of the 1st inst.

Obituary of MRS. CAROLINE E. SEYMOUR who died in New Orleans on the 13th of May, 1858. She was the wife of CO. ISAAC G. SEYMOUR of that city; became a member of Christ Church, Macon, in 1835 (with eulogy)

June 9, 1858

Died on 25th May, in Macon county, MR. JOHN C. ROGERS, aged about 70 years.

Washington, June 5 - SENATOR HENDERSON, of Texas, died yesterday.

June 16, 1858

Died in Griffin, the 10th inst., THOWNSEND S., infant son of MR. NATHAN and MRS. ELIZABETH A. WEED, aged 1 year 10 days.

St. Louis, June 7 - The details of the affray at Lawrence, Kansas, between JIM LANE and MR. JENKINS, have been received. It appears that Lane and Jenkins were living upon contested claims...Lane fired, killing Jenkins instantly.

June 23, 1858

Died in this city on June 5th, MRS. GEORGIA A. CLARKE, consort of MR. S.P. CLARKE, and daughter of the late JOHN P. and MRS. R.A. EVANS, in the 23d year of her age.

Died in Vineville, June 12th, of Brain Fever, JAMES JACKSON, son of JOHN W. and CATHARINE C. STUART, aged 3 years (with short eulogy) (Albany papers, please copy)

Died in Jones county, on 31st May, very suddenly, CAPT. ABRAM CARD, aged 82 years 10 months 4 days. Was born in Maryland, principally raised in Wake co., NC, in early life settled in Jones co., and resided there 56 years.

Died in McDonough, on the morning of the 9th inst., of billious fever, MRS. MATILDA DOYAL, wife of COL. LEONARD T. DOYAL; joined the Baptist Church at Mount Pleasant, Monroe county, on fourth Sabbath in Oct. 1837.

The Atlanta American announces that GEN. W.B. WOFFORD, late Treasurer of the State Road, died at his residence in Habersham county, on the 10th instant, of chronic diarrhea.

June 30, 1858

The Republican of Monday, comes to us in mourning on account of the death of DR. RICHARD WAYNE, Mayor of Savannah. He died at half past five Sunday morning, after one week's illness.

The Athens Banner announces that GEN. COFFEE died at his residence in Rabun county, on 30th ult., of dropsy of the chest, in the 65th year of his age; a native of South Carolina, but moved to Georgia soon after arriving at manhood, and for near thirty years represented Rabun County in the Legislature; held office of State Senator from that county at the time of his death.

July 7, 1858

Died in Forsyth, Monroe county, on the 19th inst., JOHN H. THOMAS and WILEY CURRY.

Died in Marianna, Florida, on the 16th July (NOTE: this is obviously an error on the part of the paper), of apoplexy, JOHN G. ROULHAC, ESQ., aged about 69 years; a native of Martin Co., NC, but had resided in Florida for the last fourteen years (with short eulogy).

The St. Louis Republican states that MR. STOFER, editor of the Lexington (Missouri) Expositor, was killed on board the steamer A.B. Chambers, in an affray with a gambler named CLARK...

The Columbus Enquirer of the 3rd inst. announces the death yesterday morning of COL. A.K. AYER, of this city, after a severe illness.

The Philadelphia papers announce that JUDGE ROBERT T. CONRAD, of that city, died at his residence on the 27th ult.; a prominent member of the old Whig party; was first Mayor of Philadelphia after the consolidation. The HON. JOB R. TYSON also died in Philadelphia on the same day. He was a member of Congress in 1856.

July 7, 1858

A boy fifteen years old, a son of HENRY VIELSTICH, of Savannah, Ga., was killed, by being shot with a shot gun, on the night of the 25th ult., while in a garden stealing watermelons...WM. GAIN and NICHOLAS PENNERGAST were arrested on suspicion of the shooting.

July 14, 1858

Died in Dougherty County on the 19th ult., MR. PAUL E. TARVER, son of the late GENL. HARTWELL H. TARVER of Twiggs Co., in the 35th year of his age.

Died in Oglethorpe, on the 10th inst., MISS SALLIE PAUL. Her death was occasioned by a serious burning from a fulid lamp, some four weeks since.

The Augusta Constitutionalist announces that JAMES B. LONGSTREET, ESQ., of Calhoun, Gordon county, died at his residence in that place on Tuesday evening, the 8th inst., of Pneumonia. At the time of his death, he held the office of Solicitor General of the Cherokee Circuit.

July 21, 1858

Died in Talbotton on the 14th inst., in the 24th year of her age, LUCY CARTER, wife of EWDIN W. POU.

Natchez (Miss.) July 17 - The HON. JOHN A QUITMAN died near this city this morning, from a disease contracted in Washington. Was a boarder at the National Hotel in Washington at the time of his death.

July 28, 1858

Died in Dawson, Terrell County, Ga., on the 6th inst., MRS. ANN H. LAMAR, consort of DR. JOHN Y. LAMAR, aged 24 years 4 months, leaving one child and an affectionate husband.

MR. WILLIAM T. PORTER, the accomplished editor of "Porter's Spirit of the Times," died on the 18th inst., at his residence No. 51 Bleecker Street...(New York News, 20th)

Tribute of respect by Twiggs Lodge, No. 164 F.A.M. - on death of THEOPHILUS PEARCE.

Aug. 4, 1858

The Gallatin (Tenn.) Examiner says that a child of MR. READ, in that place, died in a very few hours the past week from the effects of eating a small quantity of wild cherries.

Died in this city on the 26th ult., of Brain Fever, PARANELLA, daughter of JOHN and ELIZABETH KNIGHT, in the 11th year of her age.

Died in Irwinton, on the 25th ult., MRS. REBECCA M., wife of JUDGE A.E. COCHRANE, of Brunswick, aged 31 years.

Hamilton (Ohio) Intelligencer, 24th - MR. DANIEL ELLIOTT, who lives in Princeton, hung himself in fun in his slaughter house... (details given in the article).

Aug. 11, 1858

Died at his residence in Houston county, on the 4th inst., MR. A.S. EDGEWORTH, in the 67th year of his age. (City papers please copy)

Aug. 18, 1858

Died in the city of New York, on the 22d July, MRS. MARY J. DAY, wife of CHARLES B. DAY, and for many years a resident of the city of Macon.

Died in Philadelphia, on the 11th inst., after a brief illness, MRS. TABITHA E. MUNROE, aged about 45 years, wife of NATHAN C. MUNROE, ESQ., of this city. Her remains are expected here to-day for interment.

Died at her residence in Houston County, MRS. CAROLINE E. SUSAN HOWARD, wife of JOHN HOWARD, aged 32 years 8 months and 2 days; a member of the M.E. Church; leaves husband and five little daughters.

Died in Cuthbert, Randolph County, Ga., August 5th, 1858, MISS SALLIE C., daughter of JOHN T. and MARY A. BROWN, in her 18th year (with eulogy).

Aug. 25, 1858

Augusta Dispatch 17th - On Sunday last the Sheriff of Lincoln county called on MR. JAMES HEGGIE to assist him in arresting MR. EZEKIEL JETER, who stands charged with killing a negro. As they approached Jeter he fired at them...Mr. Heggie, having a gun in his hands, returned the fire, killing Jeter immediately.

HON. JOHN DUER, chief justice of the Superior Court of New York, died on Staten Island on the 8th inst.. Was born in 1786, and came of a well known English family. His father was COL. WM. DUER, and his mother, LADY CATHERINE, was a daughter of LORD STERLING.

Died in Lexington, Ga., on the 10th inst., GEORGE T. LANDRUM, ESQ., in the 29th year of his age. He graduated at Franklin College in 1851, and has since been engaged in the practice of Law. He was the youngest brother of REV. S. LANDRUM, of Macon, Ga., and the brother also of DR. WM. T. LANDRUM, who graduated last summer in this city.

Sep. 1, 1858

Died in Tallahassee, Florida, on the 17th ult., MR. JOHN M. GIBBS, (Printer), formerly of Georgia, aged about 50 years.

Died on the 15th ult., near Milledgeville, GEORGE R. TUCKER, son of the late HARPER TUCKER, ESQ., aged 19 years.

Died in Dooly county, on the 7th Aug., MR. JOHN Q. ADAMS, aged about 29 years. Obituary notice next week.

MRS. BURFORD, of Butts county, while passing through the streets of Jackson, on Thursday last, was thrown from a buggy, and her skull so severely fractured that she survived but a short time. She was but recently married.

MR. A. GRAVES, of the firm of Hand, Williams & Graves, Augusta, died in Madison on the 24th ult.

Sep. 8, 1858

Died in Ashley county, Arkansas, on 18th July, MR. ABNER WIMBERLY, brother of COL. JAMES WIMBERLY, of Muscogee county, and for many years a resident of Twiggs and Houston counties in this State.

Died at Gasters' Landing, Arkansas, on 10th August, MR. JOHN A. TOOKE, aged 35 years, formerly of Talbot county.

Sep. 8, 1858

Died, at his residence in Dooly county, a few minutes before 8 o'clock, on the night of 7th of August, 1858, JOHN Q. ADAMS, in the 39th year of his age. Two months and more previous to his death, his family had been sorely afflicted with fever. The life of his eldest daughter had been despaired of; his little son at the point of death when he died; his other two children only so as to be about a little; (with eulogy)

Sep. 15, 1858

Died in Dougherty county, on the 7th inst., after a few days illness, MRS. ELIZABETH RUTHERFORD, (wife of COL. SAMUEL RUTHERFORD,) in the 40th year of her age.

Sep. 22, 1858

Died in Savannah, on the 17th inst.,MRS. CATHARINE M. SIMS, wife of FREDERICK W. SIMS, one of the Editors of the Savannah Republican, and daughter of M. SULLIVAN, ESQ., of this city. Her remains were brought to this city and interred in Rose Hill Cemetery, on the 18th inst.

Died in Savannah, on the 18th inst., MRS. MARY L. PALMER, aged 25 years, wife of SAM'L B. PALMER, and daughter of F.F. LEWIS, of this city. Her remains were interred in Rose Hill Cemetery on the 19th inst.

Obituary with long eulogy on MRS. ELIZABETH RUTHERFORD (see notice in 15 Sep. 1858 issue of paper)

From Augusta Chronicle & Sentinel of 17th inst. - Details of the deaths incurred in a disastrous railroad accident on the August and Savannah Railroad. The accident occurred about ten miles this side of Millen, near Station No. 1, and was caused by a wash in the road-bed...L.M. NORTHEY, Engineer, and two firemen, PATRICK FLEURY and JAMES COGGINS, were killed, and JESSE FARRAR, machinist and workman, had his left arm broken above the elbow, and his right leg torn and bruised. L.M. Northey was a young man and has relatives near Great Falls, New Hampshire. James Coggins has relations residing in this city. Patrick Fleury, native of Ireland, and we could not hear that he had any relatives in this section. Mr. Farrar has since died.

The Lexington (Miss.) Advertiser announces the death, in Holmes county, of the REV. MR. COOPER, the original dreamer of Cooper's Well; a noted preacher and member of the Mississippi Conference.

Sep. 30, 1858

Died in this city, on the 26th inst., MR. DERMOT DEMPSEY, aged about 71 years.

Died in this city, on the 18th inst., after an illness of three weeks, MISS JULIA A. POWERS, aged 42 years (with eulogy).

Died near Hawkinsville, on the 20th inst., MRS. ELIZA ANDERSON, wife of JOHN I. ANDERSON, ESQ.; after a severe and protracted illness of twelve weeks; a member of the Baptist Church (with short eulogy).

JAMES H. MANGHAM, ESQ., Ordinary of Spalding County, died in Griffin on Friday last, and was buried on Saturday with Masonic honors.

MICHAEL N. CLARK, ESQ., an old and respected citizen of Columbus, died in that city on Friday last.

JAMES L. HATCH, ESQ., one of the Assistant Editors of the Charleston Courier, died in that city of yellow fever on Saturday last.

Sep. 30, 1858

The Charleston papers also announce the death of REV. REUBEN POST, D.D., the esteemed Pastor of the Circular Church of that city.

The Abbeville Banner records the decease of WILLIAM LOWNDES, youngest son of the late JOHN C. CALHOUN, who died on the 19th inst., on his plantation, in Abbeville District.

The venerable JAMES ADGER, a name long identified with the commerce of Charleston, died at a very advanced age recently in New York.

DRED SCOTT, the subject of the famous Dred Scott case, died at St. Louis on Friday week.

HON. ARTHUR P. BAGBY has died at Mobile. He was formerly Governor of Alabama, a Senator to the Congress of the United States from Alabama. He had been for several years in private life.

Tribute of respect by Twiggs Lodge No. 164 A.Y.M. Sept. 18th, 1858 - on death of JAMES C. HALL, who died at his residence on the 15th inst. of a long and severe attack of Typhoid Fever.

Oct. 6, 1858

MRS. F.A. GAULDING, wife of COL. A.A. GAULDING, late of the Empire State, now of the Atlanta Intelligencer, has died.

HON. S.A. WALES, distinguished citizen of Columbus, departed this life yesterday, says the Times of the 28th ult. He was born in Connecticut and moved to Georgia at an early age. Was admitted to the Bar and practiced law in Middle Georgia forty years ago. Represented Habersham county in the Georgia Legislature when a young man, and Jasper and Putnam counties in 1847. In 1855 he was Senator from Muscogee county. In 1857 was elected one of the Judges of the Inferior Court of this county - which position he held at the time of his death. Was in his 60th year.

EMERSON FOOTE, so well known in our community as the Superintendent of the Macon and Western Railroad, and for the past year of the Central Railroad, died in Savannah on Thursday night, the 30th ult., about 9 o'clock, of the yellow fever...

REV. H.M. DENISON, Rector of St. Peter's Church in this city, has fallen victim to the prevailing epidemic. Was a native of Pennsylvania, and educated at the Protestant Episcopal Seminary in Fairfax county, Va. His first official act was at Greenville, in this State, whence he removed to Brooklyn, N.Y., where he continued to serve as an assistant to Rev. Dr. J.S. Stone. He subsequently became Rector in Louisville, Kentucky, whence he removed to this city as the successor to the Rev. J.A. Shanklin, who died of yellow fever in 1856. Had been united in marriage with a daughter of the HON. JOHN TYLER (of Virginia), deceased some years since, and has a daughter residing in Brooklyn, N.Y. (Charleston News, 29th inst.)

Oct. 13, 1858

DR. CHAS. A. WARD, son-in-law of DR. BORING of this city, and formerly of Columbus, died of yellow fever, at Galveston, Texas, on the 1st inst. He was highly esteemed as a physician.

Wilkinson Superior Court convened on Tuesday last, but was on Wednesday evening adjourned. After the adjournment of the court, a serious affray occurred between JOHN E. WIGGINS and DR. JOSEPH A. GOLDEN, in which Golden was stabbed and killed immediately.

Oct. 20, 1858

Died in Northampton, Mass., on the 4th inst., while on a visit to his relatives, MR. MOSES D. BARNES, aged 42 years.

Oct. 20, 1858

Died in this place at the residence of her uncle, Dr. E.C. Williamson, MISS CARRIE CLAYTON, second daughter of MR. and MRS. P.A. CLAYTON, aged 17 years 7 months 14 days.

Homicide in Upson. A difficulty occurred at Double-Bridges on Sunday the 10th inst., between NATHANIEL DENHAM and a man named BROWN, in which the latter was shot by the former, with a rifle, and immediately expired.

The trial of JOHN COBB, JR., of Atlanta, for participating in the murder of SAMUEL LANDRUM, in April last, was concluded on Friday night last. Verdict - Guilty of Murder.

Our city was startled yesterday morning, says the Columbus Sun, of Monday, by the announcement that MR. S.D. CLARK, of the firm of Clark & Iverson, Druggists of this city, was found dead in his room this morning.

REV. DR. McGUIRE, of Fredericksburg, Va., was struck with paralysis on Thursday, and on Friday his spirit was wending its way to the invisible world.

Tribute of respect by Wornum Lodge No. 116, Clinton, Ga. Oct. 17, 1858 - on death of WM. B. GEORGE.

Oct. 27, 1858

Died in Baker county, on the 18th inst., MRS. MARY VICTORIA, wife of MR. EZEKIEL WIMBERLY, and daughter of the late ABNER HOLT, of this city.

JOHN S. WALKER, ESQ., for many years Postmaster at Madison, Georgia, of which place he was an old and highly respected citizen, died on the 14th instant.

J.T. HEADLEY, author of the "Sacred Mountains," "Napoleon and his Marshals," and other interesting works, died at Buffalo, New York on Tuesday of last week.

Nov. 3, 1858

Died at Audaston, near Sparta, at the residence of his father, Oct. 16, 1858, of consumption, THOMAS C. AUDAS, only remaining son of TUTTLE H. and HENRIETTE M. AUDAS.

The Atlanta Intelligencer of Wednesday says: We regret to learn that COL. HARRALSON, the Collector of Customs at Brownsville, Texas, died a few days ago there, of yellow fever. He was a brother of the late HON. HUGH A. HARRALSON, of Troup.

During a recounter near Ashville, N.C., on the 13th inst., COL. SAMUEL W. DAVIDSON, was killed by MR. D.N. SHOPE. His death was caused by a kick on the neck.

Nov. 10, 1858

THOMAS BALTZELL, a civil engineer, and son of JUDGE BALTZELL, of Tallahassee, Fla., was recently drowned at Appalachicola while attempting to save the life of a child which had fallen into the bay.

REV. MR. DALE, a Baptist clergyman, met with a sudden death at Sandoval, Ill., on Friday last. While resting his chest on the muzzle of a loaded gun, his foot slipped so as to cause the gun to go off, and thus almost instantly killed him.

Nov. 10, 1858

COL. KINCHEN L. HARALSON, formerly of Georgia, brother of HON. HU. A. HARALSON, died at Point Isabel, Texas, a short time since, of yellow fever. He was Collector of Customs at that port.

Nov. 17, 1858

TALBOT RALEY, ESQ., one of the Deputy Sheriffs of Bibb County, died on Saturday last. (Telegraph)

A man by the name of GREEN BROWN, was recently run over and killed, near the Plains of Dura, Sumter county. His relatives are said to reside in this vicinity.

Nov. 24, 1858

Died in Madison county, Florida, on the 23d ult., MRS. ELIZABETH RUSSELL, aged 65 years - wife of BENJAMIN RUSSELL, and formerly a resident of this city.

Died in Savannah, on the 18th inst., COL. SAM'L S. SIBLEY, after a lingering illness, aged about 50 years; was for several years Editor of the Floridian at Tallahassee, and for last ten years resided in Savannah. In that city he was for some time one of the Editors and Proprietors of the Georgian.

Died at the residence of her mother, in Bibb co-nty, on Sunday the 14th inst., MRS. HARRIET R. McLENNAN, consort of RODERICK McLENNAN, in the 28th year of her age.

Augusta Dispatch of Thursday announces the death of SAMUEL M. THOMPSON, ESQ., late news and commercial editor of the Evening Dispatch. He expired at forty minutes past three o'clock this morning, at the residence of his sister-in-law, Mrs. A.G. Willis, after a painful illness of about three weeks. Was born in Charleston, S.C. 29 Oct. 1808, and therefore 50 years and 19 days old at death.

Dec. 1, 1858

HON. T.L. HARRIS, member of Congress from the 6th district of Illinois, who has for some time been in bad health, died on the 23d ult.

On Wednesday last, the Macon Volunteers turned out to pay tribute of respect to MOSES D. BARNES, who died a short time since in Northampton, Mass., and whose remains were brought to Rose Hill Cemetery for interment.

EX-GOVERNOR WILLIAM SCHLEY died at his residence in Augusta on Nov. 20th of paralysis.

An affray occurred in Floyd, Ga., on Saturday last between S. DEAN and HOSEA HORTON, Marshal of the town, in which Dean struck Horton on the head with a hatchet, causing his death in a few minutes.

The City of Washington brings intelligence of the death of HON. B.F. BUTLER, of New York, at Paris, on the 8th instant.

Dec. 8, 1858

Died at the residence of his father, COL. R.H. LONG, on the 17th inst., of chronic bronchitis, WILLIAM H. LONG, born in Washington, Wilkes county, Ga., on 5th Dec. 1825, and was in the 33d year of his age, near its close. Removed to this county while a child, with his father at an early day of its settlement. Passed greated part of his life in the cities of Apalachicola, Savannah and Macon, where he acquired a high character as a Merchant. (Marianna, Jackson co., W. Fla., Nov. 20th)

Dec. 8, 1858

Died in Wilkinson county, on 29th Nov., MR. RICHARD HATFIELD, aged 89 years; member of the Methodist Church about 40 years.

Died in Dooly county, on 29th of Nov., of Pneumonia, JAMES S. BEAL, ESQ., aged about 43 years; a Deacon of the Baptist Church for many years; a devoted Mason; founder, and for many years, Master of Farmers Lodge, at Vienna, and at time of his death, the Master of Patrick Henry Lodge, at Drayton.

Died, at her residence in Lee county, on Saturday morning, 28th Nov., MRS. CAMILLA M. MOUGHOUN, wife of THOS. H. MOUGHOUN, in the 38th year of her age.

MR. B.T. THEUS died suddenly at his breakfast table yesterday. In earlier life resided in Charleston, where he commenced career as a practical printer; subsequently removed to Savannah and continued in same vocation, and in 1840 was foreman of this office; too enfeebled by age he resigned his post and was appointed City Sexton; subsequently filled the office of Receiver of Tax Returns (Sav. Rep.)

Suicide by a printer. MR. JAS. W. BENNETT, a printer by occupation, and for ten or twelve years past foreman of the Southern Recorder office at Milledgeville, disappeared Tuesday night last says the Savannah Republican of Monday last...late Saturday afternoon, his body was discovered in a well, in the street, nearly opposite the office. Mr. B. had been for some time, much addicted to intemperance, and it is supposed threw himslef into the well while laboring under mania from that cause. He was about 42 years of age, and left no family.

COL. WILLIAM H. HARPER, an old and valued citizen, died at the Oglethorpe House, in this city, says the Columbus Sun of the 1st inst., at 20 minutes to 6 o'clock, yesterday evening. Col. H. was one of the first settlers of the place.

A sad and fatal accident took place on one of the Freight trains on the South-Western Rail Road, just above Americus, last Friday. While the train was in motion, one of his hands, named SCARBOROUGH, in the act of stepping from one car to another, slipped and fell between them, and the wheels passed over his legs severing them both...he survived for only about an hour after the accident. (Telegraph)

The Augusta Sentinel reports that REV. JOSEPH POLHILL expired on Thursday 2d inst., at his residencd in Burke county, from a fall from the second story of his gin house four days before.

The REV. JOHN HICKLING, the oldest Methodist preacher in the world, and the last survivor of the "helpers" of John Wesley, is reported dead. Mr. Hickling was in the 71st year of his ministry, and was nearly 93 years old. He died at Audley, New Castle-upon-Tyne.

Dec. 15, 1858

Obituary notice submitted by Patrick Henry Lodge, No. 173 (Drayton, Dooly Co., Ga., Nov. 28th, 1858) - on death of member JAMES S. BEALLE.

The Right Rev. BISHOP ONDERDONK, an eminent divine of the Episcopal Church, died in Philadelphia on Monady last, of Dysentery.

MR. O.A. OWEN, a student in the Medical College of this city, we regret to learn, died of Pneumonia, on the 8th inst.

A Judge killed. JUDGE HART, city solicitor of Cincinnati, was run over on Wednesday by a railroad train at Loveland, Ohio. The accident was caused by his attempting to jump on the train while in motion.

Dec. 22, 1858

Died in Americus, on the 3d inst., MRS. MARY A. FURLOW, wife of JAMES W. FURLOW, aged about 40 years, a daughter of STEPHEN BIVINS, of Jones county.

Died in this city on the 18th instant, PULASKI S. HOLT, JR., in the 29th year of his age.

Died in Leon county, Fla., on the 10th inst., after a long and painful illness, J.P.K. SAVAGE, ESQ., a native of Augusta, Ga., aged about 29.

Regret to announce the death of COL. ALBERT PIKE, of Arkansas. He was a distinguished lawyer, poet and scholar. He commanded "C" company of Arkansas cavalry in Mexico.

From the Savannah Republican of Monday last comes a letter headed Dawson, Geo. Dec. 16th, 1858 and announcing the death of COL. JNO. A. TUCKER, (the Democratic nominee for the Judgeship of the South-Western Circuit, and also Senator to the last Legislature of Georgia, from Stewart)...the jury's verdict was that he came to his death by morphine administered by his own hands.

CAPT. JAMES N. WARD, of the 3rd Regiment of U.S. Infantry, died at St. Anthony, Minnesota, on the 16th inst. Capt. Ward was a native Georgian. He died of consumption.

Dec. 29, 1858

Died in Vineville, on the 26th inst., MRS. E.C. OUSLEY, wife of ROBT. F. OUSLEY, ESQ., aged about 33 years - and daughter of the late CHARLES Y. CALDWELL, of Meriwether county.

Charleston papers announce the death of GEN. JAMES GADSDEN, a distinguished citizen of South Carolina, but who resided many years in Florida. He had just completed three score years and ten.

Halifax, Dec. 20 - The steamship Ariel arrived here to-day short of coal, in charge of the first officer. During a gale on the 8th inst., a heavy sea struck the steamer and killed CAPT. CHARLES D. LUDLOW, and seriously injured the second officer and two seamen. Capt. Ludlow commanded the Knoxville, between this port and New York, for a number of years, and until about two years ago, when he took charge of the Ariel, a steamer belonging to the Vanderbilt line, between New York and Havre, via Southampton. (Savannah Republican)

Jan. 5, 1859

EX-CHIEF JUSTICE GEORGE EUSTIS, of the Louisiana Supreme Court, died at his residence in New Orleans, on the morning of the 22d ult., in the 63d year of his age.

The citizens of Atlanta were greatly excited on Friday and Saturday last, by the shooting of CALVIN WEBB, a baliff of that city, by W.A. CHOICE...Webb leaves a wife and children.

Died, at his residence in Fort Valley, on the 26th ult., Christmas day - MR. SAMUEL DINKINS, aged 52 years and 22 days, leaving a widow and nine children. Was born in Richland District, S.C. on 3 Dec. 1806. Married a daughter of the late STERLING WILLIAMSON, SR., and commenced the life of a planter. Removing to Georgia in 1836, he settled in the upper part of Houston county (with long eulogy) (Columbus papers please notice death)

MR. HUGH T. POWELL, a well known citizen of this place, died very suddenly on Monday morning last, from apoplexy.

Jan. 12, 1859

Died at the residence of his son in Walker Co., Texas, ELDER RICHARD PACE, near 80 years of age. Born in South Carolina, Edgefirld District, where he lived till he arrived at the age of manhood, when he moved to Lincoln county, Ga., where he married MISS AMEY BISSEY; moved to Putnam county, joined the Baptist Church and was baptized at Crooked Creek, by Rev. E. Mosely; served his country in 1812; a laborious and devoted Minister of the Gospel until he died 28 Nov. 1858; left six children - one son and five daughters, all of whom are consistent members of the Baptist Church.

The Tampa Peninsular of the 1st inst., says Mr. Kilburne, who arrived at that place the day previous, states that the celebrated Seminole Indian Chief, SAM JONES is dead, and that Tiger Tail has been appointed in his stead.

From the Columbus Times of the 3rd inst. The railroad catastrophe. Gives details of accident in which the following persons were killed:

MRS. THOMAS LEVERETTE and 3 children, Benville Parish, La.
two MISSES GUY, daughters of THOMAS GUY, Russell co., Ala.
MRS. SMITH, Texas
ALLEN E. ELY, of the firm Durie & Ely, N.Y. city (has a wife and two children)
HENRY MILLER, engineer
M. BOUCHE, fireman, Columbus, Ga.
WM. H. SNELL, train hand, Columbus, Ga.

The Augusta Constitutionalist of Friday last announces the death of DR. GEORGE M. NEWTON, M.D. He died at his residence in this city, yesterday morning, at nine o'clock, of tetanus, caused by injuries received some weeks ago, when he was thrown from his buggy. Was born in this city in 1810. After completing collegiate course at the University of Georgia, he engaged in the study of medicine; and graduating with honor at the University of Pennsylvania, he spent several years in the schools and hospitals of Paris. Soon after his return to his native city, he was elected to the chair of Physiology in the Medical College of Georgia; but was subsequently transferred to the chair of Anatomy, which he filled for about twenty years.

JUDGE GREEN B. SAMUELS, of the Court of Appeals of Virginia, died Wednesday afternoon, at the Powhattan Hotel, in Richmond, of an attack of apoplexy, with which he was stricken down the night previous.

HON. HENRY L. ELLSWORTH, of Lafayette, Ind., died in Fair-Haven, Connecticut, on Monday, the 27th inst., aged 68 years.

MR. JOHN F. McLEOD's little daughter HATTIE, was killed on the 21st ult., by the falling of a tree. She was 8 years and 9 days old. (Pulaski Times)

A few minutes before 10 o'clock Sunday night, says the Savannah Republican the REVEREND PATRICK HOOK, of St. John's (Catholic) Church, died in this city, aged 26 years. He had been educated by this diocese and had been officiating in Savannah about a year. During his visits to the sick in the late epidemic season, he contracted the fever under which he gradually sunk.

Jan. 19, 1859

Died in Macon county, East-Florida, on 24th of November last, at the residence of his uncle, BARNARD B. TYNER, (son of K. TYNER, ESQ.,) in the 28th year of his age.

Died on the 2d inst., near Hillsborough, Jasper Co., Ga., of Chronic Bronchitis, AUGUSTUS C. PHILLIPS, son of WILLIAM and SUSAN PHILLIPS, aged 25 years 9 months 15 days (with eulogy)

Jan. 26, 1859

Died in Twiggs county, on the 17th inst., MR. HENRY LAND, aged about 56 years.

Died in this city, on the 21st inst., of Conxumption, MR. PHINEAS U. BLODGETT, aged about 29 years. Was well known for four years as the Agent and Superintendent of Harnden's Express Office in this place. His father arrived here soon after his death, and conveyed his body to East Haverhill, New Hampshire, (the family residence) for interment.

Feb. 9, 1859

The following notice was communicated to the Baltimore American of Wednesday 2d instant: The death of the REV. DR. THOMAS CURTIS, on board the burning steamer North Carolina, on Saturday morning last, on her passage from here to Norfolk...he was an Englishman by birth, far advanced in life, and was for many years a leading Reporter of the debates in the English Parliament...came to this country some twenty years ago - was settled at some time at Bangor, in Maine; was subsequently, for several years, Pastor of Wentworth Street Baptist Church, in Charleston, South Carolina, and for eight or ten years past has presided over a flourishing Female Institution in the upper part of that State, in connection with one of his sons, also a Baptist minister; another son, Rev. T.F. Curtis, is a Professor in the Lewisburg University of Pennsylvania..

WILLIAM H. PRESCOTT, a famous American writer, died on the 29th ult., in Boston, in his 65th year.

Regret to announce the unexpected death of GEN. THOMAS FLOURNOY, which occurred on Saturday morning last, after a brief illness. What made the event particularly distressing was the fact that the deceased had been on Tuesday, just four days before his death, united in marriage to an amiable and accomplished lady. Gen. Flournoy was formerly Intendent of the town, and at the time of his death was commander of this brigade of Alabama Militia. His funeral was attended on Sunday evening by the "Eufaula Rifles," the Independent Order of Odd Fellows, and a large number of relatives and friends. (Eufaula Spirit, 1st inst.)

On Tuesday last, MR. JOHN RICHARDS, the "Spirit's" Governor was in health; on Tuesday morning, at 5 o'clock, he was a corpse. His death was caused by congestion of the lungs. (N.Y. Spirit of the Times)

Feb. 16, 1859

Died in Monroe county, on Monday morning, Jan. 31st, 1859, at half past 1 o'clock, MRS. AMANDA FINLISON, consort of MR. JOHN FINLISON and daughter of MR. and MRS. NOBLE, aged 20 years 7 months 10 days.

Died at Fort Valley, Georgia, Houston county, on the 7th inst., DR. HAMILTON R. PIERCE, son of REV. DR. LOVICK PIERCE, in the 32d year of his age.

Died in Crawford county, on the 4th inst., MR. ALLEN G. SIMMONS, aged about 63 years.

Died in DeSoto Parish, La., January 27th, 1859, after a painful illness, MRS. MARIA JACKSON, wife of WARREN JACKSON, late of this city, and daughter of BALDWIN DAVIS, deceased, of Monroe county, Gal. (City papers, please copy)

We regret to observe in our Milledgeville exchanges, the death of DR. C.J. PAINE, for 41 years a resident physician of that place.

Feb. 16, 1859

The Savannah Republican relays an account of the twin boys of MRS. EMILY P. LESDERNIER - a lady who gave some very effective dramatic readings at St. Andrews' Hall some weeks ago. One died in New York on 23d January. The other died the next day. Their remains were taken to Roxbury, Mass., for interment.

MR. BENJAMIN T. BRANTLEY died near Ft. Scott, Kansas Territory, on the 13th ult., aged about 22 years. Was born in Augusta 4 Dec. 1836; graduated at Mercer University in 1855, studied law, and had made his arrangements to enter upon the duties of his profession within a month from the time he was smitten down by disease. (Augusta Constitutionalist)

Tribute of respect by Masonic Lodge (not named) Feb. 5th, 1859 - on death of WM. CHAPPELL, who died on the 12th ult.

Feb. 23, 1859

Died near Dadeville, Ala., on the 8th inst., at the residence of her mother, MRS. TINSLEY, MRS. MARY M. NORMAN, aged 20 years 5 months, wife of OLIVER P. NORMAN, of Union co., Ark. Was born and raised near Forsyth, Ga., and was the youngest daughter of the late JAMES W. TINSLEY, of Monroe county.

Mar. 2, 1859

Died on the 4th ult., at the residence of Mr. A.R. Beall, Columbia co., after a protracted illness, MR. HOMER L. GARTRELL, in the 30th year of his age.

Departed this life at her residence in Lee county, Ga., on Thursday 10th instant, MRS. NANCY G. GARDNER, in the 64th year of her age.

MR. EDWARD O. SHEFFIELD, one of the oldest residents of Dooly Co., died on the 11th instant at his residence in that county. Mr. Sheffield was born 30 May 1810, being in his 49th year at the time of his death. His disease was Paralysis.

MRS. FLORIDA H. LANE, wife of REV. JAMES S. LANE, and daughter of MR. T.H. and MRS. H.W. AUDAS, of Sparta, Ga., died at the residence of her husband, near Talladega, Ala., January 28th, 1859.

Died of Croup, in Barnesville, Ga., on the 10th of February, JULIA POPE, infant of MR. C.S. and MRS. MARY E. SNEAD, aged 6 weeks.

Tribute of respect at Armory Hall, Fort Valley, Feb. 7, 1859 - on death of LIEUTENANT H.R. PIERCE, son of DR. LOVICK PIERCE.

PHILIP BARTON KEY, the U.S. Attorney for the District of Columbia, was shot and killed today in the street nearly fronting the Executive Mansion, by DANIEL SICKLES, a member of Congress from New York. The reported cause for the perpetration of this murder, is criminality between Mr. Key and Mr. Sickle's wife.

Mar. 9, 1859

MRS. LURANY CLOWER, aged 85 years 6 months 7 days, died at her residence in Clinton on the 3d inst.

JOSEPH W. THOMAS died yesterday (Sunday) about 12 o'clock. For five or six weeks he had been confined to his room with a violent attack of a disease of the stomach. (Columbus Enquirer of Monday)

Mar. 16, 1859

MR. W.B. GAMBLE, one of our oldest citizens, died very suddenly on Monday night last, from apoplexy.

Mar. 16, 1859

CAPT. JAMES DANIEL, an infulential citizen of Madison county, Ga., died of pneumonia, at the Flint House, in this city on the 5th inst.

The National Intelligencer of the 9th inst. announces the death of the HON. AARON V. BROWN, Postmaster General, who expired at his residence in this city yesterday morning about nine o'clock, in the 64th year of his age; a native of Virginia, but educated at the University of North Carolina, and then removing to Tennessee... until finally called by President Buchanan to take a place in his Cabinet as Postmaster General...

Telegraph of yesterday gives details of the violent and sudden death of COL. JOSEPH BOND. The remains of Mr. Bond were brought to this city on Sabbath last, and on Monday, interred in Rose Hill Cemetery, escorted by the Bibb Cavalry, (of which company he was a member...)

The Bainbridge (Ga.) Argus, of the 9th inst. says: The REV. THOMAS COLBERT, seriously injured by the running away of his horse, died from the effects of his injuries on Sabbath evening last, at about nine o'clock.

Mar. 23, 1859

JUDGE VESPASIAN ELLIS, late of Virginia, and for the last few years editor of the American Organ, at Washington, died in that city, of dropsy, Monday last. Judge Ellis once represented this country, in a diplomatic capacity, in South America.

The following dispatch from Hopkinsville, Ky., appears in the Nashville News: GEN. W.T. HASKELL, of Tennessee, died at the Lunatic Asylum here on Sunday the 13th.

SARAH MALLORY, a colored woman, belonging to the estate of the late Captain Gilbert, died at Norfolk on the 22d ult. She is said to have been born in 1740, and was, therefore, in the 120th year of her age. The Day Book says: Her youngest child attended her funeral as the last of the family; his back is bent, and his locks frosted o'er with the snows of eighty-seven winters. Sarah Mallory lived one hundred and eleven years a disbeliever in the teachings of scripture. At that advanced age her mind became much exercised on the subject of religion. She accordingly professed conversion and was baptised, and for the last ten years has been a firm and consistent Christian. She remembered many of the exciting scenes which were enacted during the revolution; and the surrender of Cornwallis, at Yorktown, was but as yesterday to her. At the time she was forty-one years of age, and her youngest child nine years old.

Homicide. We learn that on Saturday last, a homicide was committed at Bunkerhill, in the Eastern part of this county, on the person of a MR. MORELAND, by a man by the name of GRANTHEM. (Pulaski Times)

Tribute of respect by the Bibb Co. Cavalry March 17, 1859 - on death of COL. JOSEPH BOND.

Mar. 30, 1859

Died in Louisville, Ga., on Wednesday 23d inst., CARRIE H., daughter of COL. and MRS. A.R. WRIGHT, aged 7 months 12 days.

Died in Crawford county, on the 14th inst., ELIZABETH DENT, consort of JOHN W. DENT, in the 40th year of her age, after an illness of upwards of four weeks, of Typhoid Pneumonia; leaves a husband and six children, the youngest of whom is 14 months old.

Mar. 30, 1859

Died in Trenton, N.J., on the 19th inst., MR. WILLIAM H. BURDSALL, formerly of Macon, and for many years one of our most enterprising merchants.

MR. J.H. OLDERSHAW, of Vineville, one of our oldest citizens, and much esteemed for his piety, benevolence and uniform uprightness, died on Thursday last, from an attack of apoplexy, age 73.

The North East Reporter, published at Canton, Missouri, states that REV. JAMES SHANNON died at his residence in Canton, on the 25th ult., of asthma, aged 59 years 9 months. He was a Georgian, and at one time held a professorship in the University of Georgia, at Athens. Was a native of Ireland.

Apr. 6, 1859

Learn from our Augusta exchanges that the steamer Augusta, on its way from that city to Savannah, was burned on Friday last. MR. H.G. DAY was drowned, and two negroes burned to death...

HON. HOPKINS HOLSEY died very suddenly at his residence, in Butler, Ga., on Thursday last. In 1836, we believe, he was a Representative from this State, under the general ticket system. He was a democrat of the Jacksonian school. In 1852 he was editor of the Southern Banner, and an able leader in the Union party. His age was 61.

JAMES B. FOLEY, proprietor of the Screven House, died last evening about 8 o'clock, from injuries caused by his being thrown from his buggy while driving on the Bay. (Savannah News of Tuesday)

The Thomasville Enterprise records the death of LUCIAN H. RAINES and JOHN GROOVER, two of the oldest citizens of Thomas county.

We learn from the Batesville (Ark.) Sentinel of the 11th instant, that a young man named LESTER, from Georgia, was murdered and robbed in that place on the night of the 6th inst., by a man named CHAS. COSGROVE...

Apr. 13, 1859

Died in Griswoldville, Ga., April 4th, 1859, MRS. MARY S., consort of GEN. D.N. SMITH, and daughter of MR. SAMUEL GRISWOLD, in the 37th year of her age.

Died of Scarlet Fever, in Fort Valley, Ga., on the 11th of March, ANNA G., eldest daughter of VIRGIL and ANN E. POWERS, aged 10 years 11 months.

Died suddenly in this city, on the 9th inst., MRS. ELIZA B. SHAD, relict of MR. JOHN R. SHAD, formerly of Savannah, and daughter of MR. S. BUTTS, of South Hadley, Massachusetts.

MR. WM. G. LOCKETT died at his residence in this city on Saturday afternoon, the 9th inst., of pneumonia; leaves a wife and several children. (State Press)

Apr. 20, 1859

Died in this City, on Tuesday evening, the 12th inst., of Scarlatina, ANNIE TEFFT, daughter of COL. J.H.R. WASHINGTON and MRS. MARY ANN, his wife - aged 11 years 4 months 6 days. (City and Milledgeville papers, and Savannah Republican please copy)

DR. H.A. THORNTON, says the Columbus Enquirer, died on the night of the 14th inst., after a lingering and painful illness of two or more months. He was one of the early settlers of this place - had long been connected with the Baptist Church...

Apr. 20, 1859

The Richmond Dispatch says: His majesty, the King of Dahomey, the great negro seller of Africa, has departed this life. He was in the habit of ransacking all the neighboring African kingdoms, for the purpose of making captives, whom he sold to the slavers. At his funeral obsequies, his loving subjects manifested their sorrow by sacrificing eight hundred negroes to his memory. He is succeeded by his son, King Gezo II.

COL. WM. J. PEEPLES died at his residence in this place on the 8th inst., after an illness of eight weeks; member of the Methodist Church. Was buried at the cemetery in this place on the evening of the 9th with Masonic honors. (Laurensville News)

Tribute of respect by the Bibb County Cavalry April 11th, 1859 - on death of WM. G. LOCKETT.

Apr. 27, 1859

Died in Milledgeville, on the 18th inst., MISS SUSAN E. FORT, daughter of DR. TOMLINSON and MARGARET L. FORT, aged 23 years.

Died, at his residence, in Lee county, Ga., on the morning of the 5th inst., REV. THOMAS SPEIGHT, in the 73d year of his age. The deceased was a native of Green county, North Carolina. He emigrated to Georgia in 1836, and settled in Houston county - in 1852 he moved to Lee county; was an affectionate husband, a kind father and master. (City papers please copy)

DOLLY ANN, daughter of HENRY S. and CAROLINE WIMBERLY, died in Twiggs county, Georgia, on the evening of the 10th inst., in her 7th year, of Croup.

COL. RAGIN, an old and worthy citizen of Houston, died early on Monday morning, the 18th inst.

The Baltimore American of Saturday announces the death of REV. HENRY V.D. JOHNS, Rector of Emmanuel Protestant Episcopal Church...

HON. JAMES E. BRYCE, late Senator from Crawford county, died at his residence in that county, on Monday, the 18th inst. We hear from private information, that there has been lately an unusual amount of sickness and mortality in Crawford, principally from erysipelas. (Telegraph of Tuesday).

May 4, 1859

Died at Clinton, on the 25th ultimo, in the 43d year of her age, MRS. LUCIA JOHNSON, wife of MR. F.S. JOHNSON, and daughter of SAM'L. and LOUISA GRISWOLD; leaves husband and eight children (with eulogy) (Georgia Telegraph and Savannah Republican, please copy)

CHARLES P. WORNUM, ESQ., of this city, drowned in the Flint river, Crawford county, on the 15th inst. He was buried in Crawford county. Was 27 years old. (Columbus Times)

MR. J.W. PENN of or near Palmetto, killed MR. MELVIN JONES, son of the REV. DABNEY P. JONES, of the same place. The parties were with others out on a fishing excursion on the river, when the killing took place. Jones was struck on the head with an axe, and died soon afterwards. We understand that Penn committed the act in self-defence, and has given himself up to the proper authorities for the investigation of the case. (Newnan Banner)

The trial of ALFRED SEARS for killing MAJ. GREGG at Jacksonville, Fla., a short time since, took place on Friday last, the verdict guilty of voluntary manslaughter, and fixing the punishment at a fine of one thousand dollars and imprisonment for twelve months.

May 11. 1859

We learn from Mr. Geo. M. Aird, who arrived here yesterday from the Seminole country, that BILLY BOWLEGS died suddenly, at the home of John Jumper, on Friday, the 11th inst... (Fort Smith Times, 31st ult)

ZACHARIAH BRANTLEY, of this county, lost his life at Isabella, Ga., on Tuesday evening last, in a rencounter with JOHN GILES, JOHN HOWELL, and JAMES A. HOY...(Albany Patriot, April 21)

Died in Houston county, on the 16th ult., DR. HENRY SANDERS, aged about 56 years. Obituary notice next week.

The celebrated MATT PEEL, of the "Campbell Minstrels," died at Buffalo, a few days since.

May 18, 1859

Departed this life at Oglethorpe, on 12th instant, May 1859, DR. WILLIAM ELLIS, aged 55 years. He was born in Virginia, April 3d, 1804, and in his eighth year was brought by his parents to Georgia, who settled in Baldwin county, His father, REV. WILLIAM ELLIS, was a minister of the Baptist Church. In his youth, Dr. Ellis pursued his preparatory studies under Dr. Thomas Hamilton, then a resident of Jones county, now of Rome, and received his diploma from the Charleston Medical College. In 1830 he married VIRGINIA A. WORSHAM, daughter of ARCHER WORSHAM, and in 1835 moved from Baldwin to Talbot county, where he remained three or four years in the practice of his profession. From there he went to Auburn, Alabama, where he resided six years, and his next location was in Lumpkin, Stewart county. He continued to practice there eight years, until his removal to Oglethorpe in 1852. Having purchased a plantation in that vicinity, he employed his leisure in improving the science of agriculture...for last twenty years was a Deacon in the Baptist Church. (Editors of papers at Macon, Columbus and Milledgeville are requested to copy)

Obituary of DR. HENRY SAUNDERS. (See issue of 11 May 1859). Was born 16 Oct. 1803; for many years resided in Savannah, and was Elder in Presbyterian Church there; died 16th April in Houston county; his wife had died some years ago...(with eulogy)

MATT PEEL, the celebrated negro minstrel and performer, died at the American Hotel in this city about five o'clock this morning, of pulmonary and heart disease...his wife was with him when he died. His remains will be taken to New York for interment. (Buffalo Commerical of Wed. evening)

On yesterday afternoon, the four o'clock Passenger train from Macon ran over and killed a man named HENRY SPELLERS, near East Point. The cars passed over his head severing a portion of it from the body, which fell over the rail and remained in his hat... (National American, Atlanta)

Died in Covington, on the 9th inst., COL. ROB'T. G. USHER, of paralysis, in the 57th year of his age.

Died in Perry, on the 14th inst., MRS. CATHARINE DUNCAN, aged 65 years - widow of the late JAMES E. DUNCAN, dec'd.

Died of Serofula, on the 17th inst., JAMES EDWARD WILLIAMS, son of JAMES and CATHARINE WILLIAMS, after a protracted and painful illness of nearly ten months, aged 15 years 3 months 10 days. (City papers please copy)

Died in Milledgeville, of erysipelas, on the 11th inst., DR. TOMLINSON FORT, aged about 73 years; distinguished in his profession as a Physician, as a man of general science, and as a leading politician - also as a soldier in the Indian war of 1812 and '13.

May 25, 1859

The Mobile Mercury of the 13th inst., publishes a letter dated Greenville, Ala., May 10th, announcing the death of J.W.M. BERRIEN, ESQ., a brother of Senator Berrien, of Georgia...was a citizen of Rome, Georgia and was traveling as an agent for the house of Lockett, Belcher & Co., 26 Pearl Street, New York; leaves a wife and children.

June 1, 1859

Fatal duel. A hostile meeting took place at Bascombe race course, just below this city, yesterday, between two citizens of New Orleans, MESSRS. M.G. VICK and _____ STITH, in which Mr. Vick was killed. He was originally a resident of Vicksburg, Miss. Mr. Stith, we learn, is a native of New Orleans, and a nephew of Mayor Stith. (Mobile Tribune, 18th)

On the evening of the 13th instant, DR. S.J. SAFFOLD, for thirty-five years a successful practicioner of medicine in this place, died; is believed to be a native of Washington county, in this State, and had nearly reached his 70th year. (Madison, Georgia Visitor, 18th)

MRS. MARY TAYLOR KEY died at Baltimore on Wednesday last, at the advanced age of 75 years. This venerable lady was the widow of FRANCIS S. KEY, author of the "Star Spangled Banner," and mother of the unfortunate P. BARTON KEY, of Washington City.

June 8, 1859

MRS. EMILY FLEMING, wife of MANAGER WM. M. FLEMING, of the Savannah theatre, and an actress of some eminence in her profession, died in this city, Thursday last, after a short illness... (Savannah Republican, June 4th)

We are pained to announce the death of SETH C. STEVENS, of Baker county, which occurred in this place on Tuesday night last. He was a native of New Hampshire, but was a citizen of Georgia for the last 25 years. For fifteen years was Clerk of the Superior and Inferior Courts and of the Court of Ordinary of Baker county... was buried in this city yesterday evening by the Masonic fraternity, of which he was a member. (Albany Patriot, June 2)

June 22, 1859

It is our melancholy duty to record the death of MRS. MARY DUNLAP, wife of SAMUEL DUNLAP, ESQ., which occurred in this city at the time of the storm on Friday afternoon of last week...leaves aged parents, an affectionate husband and two small children. (Albany Patriot, June 9th)

Died at Pleasant Hill, DeSoto Parish, Lou., on the 19th inst., JOHN S. CHILDENS, ESQ., aged about 62 years; one of the earliest settlers of this county and city; was elected sheriff of city within a few years after its organization, and represented it in the State Legislature; afterwards resided in Houston several years, then removed to Louisiana. (City papers please copy)

Died in Wynton, Ga., on the 13th inst., MRS. ELVIRA FLEWELLEN, consort of the late DR. ABNER FLEWELLEN, in the 51st year of her age.

Died on 30th of May, JOHN CARLTON, son of JOHN M. and MARY F. GREER, of Oglethorpe, Ga., aged 2 years 2 months 3 days.

JOHN LAMAR, ESQ., died in Vineville on Monday night, the 20th inst., at about the age of 22 years. He was the son of JUDGE H.G. LAMAR, and a young man of high character and great promise as a member of the Bar.

June 22, 1859

    Tribute of respect by the Faculty and Pupils of the Wesleyan Female College, Macon, Ga., June 17th, 1859 - on death of MRS. MARY B. CLAYTON - who was for nearly eight years the Matron of that Institution.

June 29, 1859

    Died in Savannah, on the 28th inst., CATHARINE FAY, aged 1 year 15 days - daughter of F.W. SIMS, ESQ., one of the Editors of the Savannah Republican. She was interred in Rose Hill Cemetery on the 26th inst.

    Died in Americus, on the 17th inst., MRS. AMANDA BARLOW, wife of DR. W.W. BARLOW, aged 37 years 6 months.

    The Savannah News of Thursday last says the body of CAPT. KEEBLER, of the ill-fated steamer Jno. G. Lawton, was recovered on Monday afternoon last but a short distance from the scene of the late accident. The body was teken to Purysburg for interment.

    Tribute of respect by the Macon Bar on the 22d inst. - on death of JOHN LAMAR, ESQ., who departed this life at the residence of his father, the HON. HENRY G. LAMAR, in Vineville, near this city, at 10 o'clock yesterday evening.

July 13, 1859

    The venerable NATHANIEL RAY GREENE, son of MAJOR-GENERAL GREENE, of the Revolution, died June 11th, 1859, at his residence, Greenesdale, Rhode Island. Mr. Greene was born at the winter encampment of the American army, at Morristown, January 11th, 1780. He leaves two children, Nathaniel Greene, an eminent homeopathic physician, who lives at Newport, and George Washington Greene, formerly Professor at Brown University...

    Died in Jones County, on the 4th July, MR. GREEN G. GUNN, aged about 52 years.

    Died in Savannah, on June 28th JOHN FULTON, aged 8 years 8 months, eldest son of WM. OSCAR and MARY THERESA CHARLTON.

    JOHN COBB, JR., was hung in Atlanta, on Friday, the 8th inst. He was convicted of being engaged in the murder of MR. LANDRUM. RADFORD J. CROCKETT, another of the parties engaged in the murder, was hung some time since; and GABRIEL JONES, also implicated, has not yet had his trial.

July 20, 1859

    Died in this city on Wednesday morning, July 13th, ROBERT HARDEMAN LOGAN, youngest child of MR. and MRS. GEO. M. LOGAN, aged 1 year 10 months 13 days.

    Killed. DR. WM. G. NELSON, of Pleasant Hill, Talbot county, was shot on the 4th inst., by MR. HENRY C. WORTHEN, of Upson county. Worthen has made his escape. (Columbus Times, July 6th)

    MR. JAS. WRIGHT, an old citizen of Cincinnati, but who moved to Vancebury (Ky.) last August, on the 4th instant, died from the bite of a rattlesnake...(Cincinnati Gazette)

    Regret to announce the accidental death of MR. JOHN POLHILL, brother of our friend and townsman, B.M. POLHILL, ESQ., which occurred yesterday about eight miles from town on the survey of the Macon & Brunswick Railroad. Mr. P. was a member of the Engineering corps, and was killed by the falling of a tree which struck him on the head. He was brought to this city and died from his injuries last night at his brother's residence. (Macon State Press, 13th inst.)

July 27, 1859

Died in Perry, on the 13th inst., MR. DAVID KING, aged about 50 years.

Died in Milledgeville, on the 18th inst., (from inflammation of the bowels) COL. JOSEPH DUNCAN, aged 62 years.

The trial of CAREY W. STILES for the murder of J.W. MOORE, in Brunswick, in December last, was concluded on Wednesday last, 20th inst. The jury returned a verdict of acquittal.

DR. JAMES P. SCREVEN died at the Hot Springs, Virginia, on the 16th inst...(Savannah Republican, July 21)

HON. RUFUS CHOATE died Wednesday morning, the 13th inst., from an affection of the heart. His remains were temporarily interred at Halifax, to await the action of his friends. Was born in Essex, Essex county, Mass., October 1, 1799; entered Dartmouth College in 1815, and graduated with the highest honors in 1819; was a tutor in college one year after he graduated, when he entered the law school of Cambridge, Mass., after which he went to Washington City where he studied almost one year in the office of Wm. Wirt; closed his legal studies at Ipsqich and Salem, Mass., in the offices of Messrs. Andrews and Judge Cummins; in 1824 was admitted to the bar in the town of Danvers, and after two or three years removed to Salem; served in the Senate and House of the State Legislature, and in 1832 allowed his name to be used as a candidate for Congress; was elected, but served for single term only, and in 1834 took up residence in Boston; in 1841 was elected to the US Senate...

Aug. 3, 1859

Died in this city July 28th, HENRY FULLER, youngest son of GEORGE T. and ELIZABETH L. ROGERS, aged 8 years.

Died in Vineville, July 27th, HENRY LAMAR GILMER, aged 18 months and 19 days, son of E.H. and G.E. GILMER, of Montgomery, Ala.

Died in Oglethorpe, July 1, 1859, DR. TERRY QUINN, in the 48th year of his age. He was born in Edgefield District, SC Dec. 31, 1811. When he was quite young, his parents moved to Monroe county, Ga. About his twentieth year he engaged in Merchandise in the city of Macon, which business he pursued five years. In 1833 he married CLARINDA NOBLES, of his native District; within a year thereafter, having taken a course of Lectures, he removed to Chambers county, Ala., where he practiced medicine ten years, and came back to Georgia in 1844. He located at Evansville, Macon county, and in 1853 he removed to Dooly county. In 1854 he joined the Methodist Episcopal Church. Having purchased a farm in the vicinity of Oglethorpe, he settled there in 1858, and gave his time to agracultural pursuits. His death was occasioned by chloroform, to relieve pain caused by the extraction of a tooth...left a widow and seven children. Buried by his Masonic brothers at Travellers Rest.

A few days ago a forgery to a small amount was perpetrated on the banking house of W.H. Barksdale & Co. of this city, and three persons were suspected of participating in the crime. Among the number was FRANCIS A. MAFFIT, who is said to be a son of JOHN NEWLAND MAFFITT, the eloquent preacher, who flourished in the West some time ago...Francis A. Maffit in his cell, on Sunday night, was siqzed with an apoplectic fit and died at 9 o'clock. (St. Louis Repub.)

Aug. 10, 1859

Died at the residence of her father, on the 2d inst., in Wilkinson county, of consumption, CALISTA MATILDA, daughter of SOLOMON D. and ELIZABETH MURPHEY, aged 21 years 3 months and 4 days.

Aug. 10, 1859

THOMAS P. STUBBS, ESQ., died on the morning of the 4th inst., after
a short illness of typhoid fever. Was a native of Jones county,
Ga., and had resided in this city about thirty years - his age,
48 years 2 month. He leaves an aged mother, a widow and four
children. He was interred in Rose Hill Cemetery on the 5th inst.,
with Masonic honors, by Macon Lodge No. 5 - the Odd Fellows Lodges,
and the Macon Volunteers, of which bodies he was a member - also
by members of the Macon Bar. (with long eulogy and also tributes
of respect by the Macon Bar, Macon Lodge No. 5 F.A.M., and Franklin
Lodge I.O.O.F.)

A most terrible and disastrous accident occurred on the South
Carolina Railroad on Thursday afternoon last, between three and
four o'clock, by the explosion of the boiler of the locomotive
F.H. Elmore, instantly killing five men - all who were on the
engine. The accident occurred near the seventy-six mile post,
about fourteen miles above Branchville. The names of the killed
are THOMAS KINGDOM, the engineer, a native and resident of Charleston, leaves no family we believe; H. VONDELKIN, the conductor, a
native of Germany; A. DONEGAN, fireman, also a native of Germany;
L.M. CHITTY, freight conductor, has a family residing at or near
Graniteville, whither his remains were yesterday brought for interment; MR. MITCHELL, known as a conductor's man. The remains of
all except Chitty, were taken to Charleston, where most of them
have families. (Augusta Chronicle & Sentinel, Aug. 5)

JUDGE WILLIAM H. UNDERWOOD, while on a visit to Marietta, on yesterday, fell dead. (Atlanta American, 5th inst.)

The Washington Constitution announces the death of HON. RICHARD
RUSH at Philadelphia, on Saturday last, at an advanced age. He
was the son of BENJAMIN RUSH, one of the signers of the Declaration
of Independence. Was appointed Attorney General by President
Madison in 1814, upon the resignation of William Pinckney, of
Maryland. In 1817 was appointed Minister to England by President
Monroe, and he afterwards published a volume of his "Recollections
at the Court of St. James." In 1825 was appointed Secretary of
the Treasury, by John Quincy Adams...(Daily Sun)

Aug. 17, 1859

No Friday, the 5th inst., says the Rome Courier, HON. WM. H.
UNDERWOOD, died at Marietta; one of the earliest settlers in this
section of Georgia; was an able lawyer; his remains were brought
to Rome, and buried on the 6th inst.; was about 80 years of age;
a member of the Episcopal Church.

A notorious ruffian, known in Southwest Arkansas, as JACK CADE,
was recently killed by a woman whose husband he had shot. The
widow challenged him to fight a duel, and as the ruffian declined,
she attacked him with a revolver and lodged three balls in his
body, one of which passed through his heart.

Aug. 24, 1859

Died very suddenly, at the residence of her son, J. Thomas Slappey,
near Marshalville, Macon co., Ga., on Saturday, the 20th inst.,
MRS. ELIZABETH SLAPPEY, relict of the late JACOB SLAPPEY, in the
69th year of her age.

Died, in Monroe, Walton county, on the 14th July 1859, LEROY PATTILLO
in the 62d year of his age; a member of the Methodist E. Church
for the last 36 years of his life.

We regret to learn that the only son (and child) of COL. L.T. DOYAL
of Griffin, was shot and instantly killed by the accidental discharge of his gun, on the 15th inst. He was a young man of much
promise, and had been married but a few months.

Aug. 24, 1859

   The Memphis Appeal of the 6th, learns by passengers on the steamer
   Jennie Whipple, from Napoleon, Ark., that about twenty-five citizens
   of that place, took a river gambler, named JOHN LEWIS, from his
   room in the hotel there on the night of the 3d, killed and threw
   him in the river. He was charged with having a hand in the murder
   of DR. HARDING there a few weeks before...

Aug. 31, 1859

   Died at his family residence, in Vineville, near Macon, on the 27th
   inst., MR. BENJAMIN B. BRYAN, aged about 52 years; a native of
   Twiggs county - afterwards removed to Houston.

Sep. 7, 1859

   Died in Upson county, on the 26th August, MRS. FRANCIS, wife of
   MATTHIAS MAUK, aged 74 years 8 months 11 days.

   The Louisville Democrat says that MAJOR A.S. DONELSON died recently
   in Louisiana of erysipelas; was formerly private Secretary of
   President Jackson, and editor of the Washington Globe; in 1856 he
   was a candidate of the American party for Vice President; he removed
   from Tennessee to Louisiana a few years since.

   Oglethorpe, Sept. 5, 1859 - NAHUM H. WOOD died at the Hotel in
   this place today at 40 minutes past 1 o'clock, P.M. He resided
   in Marion county, Florida, from whence he came here on business.
   He has been Professor of Mathematics in Franklin College, Georgia.

Sep. 14, 1859

   We are grieved to learn that HON. HENRY G. LAMAR and Family have
   sustained another sore affliction in the death of ANDERSON LAMAR,
   ESQ., of Baker county, a young gentleman of worth and promise,
   whose corpse has just been brought up to Macon for interment.
   This is the fourth grown child deceased within the space of two
   years!

Sep. 28, 1859

   Died of Typhoid Fever, on the 11th inst., in the town of Isabella,
   Worth county, Ga., GAREY G. FORD, ESQ., in the 55th year of his age.

   Died of Cancer, on 22d Sept., THOMAS M. CARDIN, in his 68th year.
   He was for many years, a respected citizen of Randolph county,
   then of Baker, last of Houston.

   Died in this city, on 12th inst., MRS. MARY KIBBEE, aged 61.

   The Augusta Dispatch says that DR. WM. Q. ANDERSON, well known and
   estimable citizen of Wilkes county, died at his residence on
   Tuesday night last. At the time of his death, he was again a
   candidate for the Legislature.

   HON. ALBERT H. TRACY, an old and worthy resident of Buffalo, N.Y.,
   died in that city on the 19th instant, aged 66 years. He was a
   member of Congress from 1819 to 1825, representing the district
   comprising a large part of western N.Y. Subsequently he served
   eight years in the Senate of that State.

Oct. 5, 1859

   Died in Vineville, near this city, on the morning of the 28th inst.,
   MR. THOMAS A. NAPIER, son of SKELTON NAPIER, aged about 28 years.
   His death was occasioned by a pistol, while in his room, by himself,
   and from the attending circumstances, it would appear that it was
   from an accidental discharge of the weapon.

Oct. 5, 1859

Died in this city, on the 29th inst., MR. GEORGE GRIMES, aged 48 years.

Died in this city, on the 28th ult., COL. JOHN MITCHELL, aged about 66 years. He served in the US Army as a Lieutenant of Artillery, and resigned his commission at the close of the Creek war. He was afterwards elected Colonel of the Baldwin county Militia, which commission he held for several years. His nearest relatives, we believe, reside in Tennessee.

Died in this city, on Thursday, the 29th Sept., MAJ. H.H. BOSTICK, in the 47th year of his age, leaving a wife and children.

Died at Fort Valley, on the 23rd ult., COL. JOHN LAMAR, aged about 72 years; was among the early settlers of that vicinity.

Died in Harris county, a short time since, QM. G. FLEMING, Past Master of Rose Lodge, No. 102, and Grand Lecturer of the Second Masonic District of F.A.M. of the State of Georgia.

By intelligence from Old Point Comfort we learn that MAJOR W.W. CHAPMAN, of the US Army, and connected with the artillery stationed at Fortress Monroe, committed suicide on Tuesday last, at the fort, by cutting his throat with a razor... (Baltimore Patriot)

WM. A. GREEN, of Fulton county, was accidentally killed, on Tuesday last, by the premature discharge of his gun while on a hunting excursion in the neighborhood of his plantation.

We regret to announce the decease of the HON. A.P. POWERS, at his residence in Vineville, on Sunday morning last at 4 o'clock. His body was interred in Rose Hill Cemetery Monday morning... (Telegraph)

The editor of the Fort Smith (Arkansas) Times, learns that on Tuesday, the 13th, at Fort Belknap, MAJOR NOBLES and a man by the name of MURPHY, had some words and relative to some horses belonging to the reserve Indians, and while engaged in the dispute a man by the name of McKNETT shot Maj. Nobles in the back with a double barrel gun, killing him instantly. Major N. is extensively known as an Indian agent on the frontier of Texas.

Oct. 12, 1859

Died on the 22d of Sept., in the city of Memphis, Tenne., MRS. MARY E. HAMILTON, consort of MR. JAMES HAMILTON, formerly of Columbus, Ga.

Died in Lumpkin, Stewart co., Ga., on Sept. 2d, JULIA, only child of JESSEE B. and M.O. WRIGHT, aged 1 year 3 months 10 days.

Died in Columbus, on Wednesday, the 27th inst., MRS. ELIZABETH GAMMELL, aged 115 years.

Died near Jamestown, Chattahoochee Co., Ga., on the 25th of September, MRS. MARTHA BIBB, wife of MAJOR R.S. HARDAWAY. She was born in Elbert county, Ga.

Died in Griffin, Ga., on the 2d inst., LUCY WILHELMINA, infant daughter of MR. and MRS. ANDREW H.H. DAWSON, of Savannah.

Homicide in Thomas. Extract from a letter dated Thomasville, Oct. 6th: A serious difficulty occurred last night between MATTHEW J. ALBRITTON and a man by the name of BOWEN...in which Albritton died. He was a young lawyer of this place.

Oct. 26, 1859

Died in Jefferson county, Ga., on Sunday morning last, MRS. GERALDINE E. JOHNSON, wife of E.R. JOHNSON, ESQ., in the 27th year of her age. Mrs. J. was the daughter of the late LARKIN GRIFFIN, ESQ., of Macon, and daughter-in-law of the HON. H.V.JOHNSON. Her remains were brought to this city on Monday, and interred in Rose Hill Cemetery. Services were conducted at the Episcopal Church, by Rev. Mr. Reese.

Died in Linwood, near Columbus, on the 13th inst., DR. THOMAS W. DAWSON, son of the late HON. WILLIAM C. DAWSON.

We noticed, on Monday last, in our streets...the funeral of a negro slave called JOHN BUTLER. The hearse was preceded by a band of music - to which he belonged - playing the "Dead March" and followed by sixteen carriages and a numerous procession.

JAMES REVEL was executed at Knoxville, Crawford county, on Friday last. He was sentenced to be hung sometime since, for the murder of (by shooting) two men by the names of ADAMS and HANCOCK...

Nov. 2, 1859

Died in Jefferson county, Georgia, on the 16th inst., at the residence of the HON. H.V. JOHNSON, MRS. GERALDINE E., wife of E.R. JOHNSON, ESQ. (with very long eulogy)

Died, in Spaulding county, of inflammatory croup, on the 28th day of October last, EUGENE SKELTON, son of MR. JOHN T. and MRS. FANNY C. NAPIER, aged about 7 years 5 months. His remains were brought to this city and interred in Rose Hill Cemetery on Sunday last.

Nov. 9, 1859

MRS. WARD, wife of our old and esteemed friend, MAJ. GEO. T. WARD, of Florida, died in this city, on the 30th ult. She was the daughter of the late MAJ. BEN CHAIRS, of Florida. Her remains were taken to Florida.

HON. JAMES C. JONES, Ex-Governor of Tennessee, died at his residence near Memphis on Saturday morning.

OWEN F. SOLOMON, First Lieutenant, 4th Artillery, U.S.A., died at Fort Laramie, Nebraska Territory, on the 27th September. He was a graduate of the West Point Military Academy, in 1854, and had been in active service ever since. His parents reside in Atlanta.

JUDGE GABRIEL JONES died of the Dropsy, at his residence in this county, says the Rome Courier, on Monday night, the 31st ult. He came to this county from Columbia, some ten years since, where he held the office of Clerk of the Superior Court for twenty years.

The Fort Valley Nineteenth Century comes to us in mourning for the death of EUGENE EUGENE VASTINE RUMPH, a young man of great promise.

REV. JOHN W. MOSELY, member of the Presbytery of Cental Mississippi, shot and killed a DR. WILSON, at Sarcoxie, Mo., on the 1st instant. Dr. Wilson was an old settler of that place and had a wife and several children, one son grown and a daughter married. He had for some time been making unlawful advances to Mosley's sister, who is the mother of six children...

Nov. 16, 1859

We learn, from a gentleman just from Fort Valley, that a young man by the name of NICHOLAS TAYLOR, a son of MR. NICHOLAS TAYLOR, of Macon county, while hunting on Saturday last, was shot by the accidental discharge of his gun. He was a member of the Governor's

Nov. 16, cont'd.) - Guards at Fort Valley, and by them buried on Sunday last with Military honors.

Died in Tennessee, on the 7th inst., CAPT. SPENCER RILEY, aged about 60 years - formerly a resident, and one of the earliest settlers of Macon. He was Sheriff of Bibb county in the years 1827 and 1828. His body was brought to this city and interred in Rose Hill Cemetery, on the 9th inst.

Died at McComb's Hotel, in Milledgeville, on the 12th of Novermber. JOHN WINN, ESQ., aged about 32 years - formerly Solicitor General of the Southern Circuit.

Nov. 23, 1859

Died in this county, on the 20th inst., MR. THOMAS M. ELLIS, aged about 75 years. He was a resident of this vicinity before the organization of the county; of the Baptist denomination and one of the Deacons of that church in this city at the time of his death.

Died in Schley county, on the 16th instant, MR. BURTON A. CONGLETON, aged about 35 years. He was a member of Washington Lodge, No. 47, at Ellaville, in that county. According to his request his remains were brought to this city for interment in Rose Hill Cemetery; and on the morning of the 19th, they were deposited in their last resting place on earth, by Macon Lodge No. 5, with usual Masonic ceremonies.

Died in Savannah, on the 16th instant, MAJ. WM. P. BOWEN, a well known citizen of that place.

Died in Burke county, on the 16th instant, MR. SEABORN H. JONES, father of the HON. JOHN J. JONES.

MR. OMER RICHARDSON, young equestrian of extrordinary talent, died of consumption at Covington, Ky. on Monday, 7th inst.; leaves a widowed mother.

From Augusta Constitutionalist of Nov. 18 - HON. GEORGE R. GILMER, ex-Governor of Georgia, died at his residence in Lexington, on Wednesday morning at nine o'clock. Born in Oglethorpe County 11 April 1790 when that county was part of Wilkes County; when a lad of thirteen, he was sent to Dr. Wilson's classical school near Abbeville Court House, SC, and afterwards to the celebrated academy of Dr. Moses Waddle, at Willington, in the same State, where his education was completed; subsequently studied law in office of distinguished Judge Upson, and was admitted to the bar; obtained a commission as first Lieutenant in the US Army, and was entrusted with command of a force which was stationed in the Creek Territory, during the War of 1812, to overcome the Indians; returned to Lexington in 1818 and commenced the practice of his profession; soon afterwards was elected to State Legislature, where he served two terms, then to Congress, where he served two terms; in 1828 was elected to third term in Congress but was refused his certificate of election by Gov. Forsyth because he had failed to notify the Executive of his acceptance within the time prescribed by law; the next year he was elected Governor of the State, and after serving a term in Congress was again elected Governor in 1837...

Nov. 30, 1859

Learn from the Chattanooga Advertiser that a dispatch was received in that city stating that MAJ. E.G. EASTMAN, senior proprietor and editor of the Nashville Union & American, died of apoplexy in Nashville on Wed. last.

Died, at the residence of Jeremiah A. Tharp, in Twiggs county, on the 19th day of October 1859, J. McDUFFIE LILES, aged about 22 years; member of the Baptist Church. Tribute of respect by Twiggs Lodge, No. 164.

Dec. 7, 1859

A brief telegraphic dispatch was received on Tuesday evening announcing the death of WASHINGTON IRVING, at Irvington, on the evening of the 28th Nov...

Died in this city, on the 30th Nov., of Pneumonia, MR. ROBERT FINDLAY, aged about 52 years. A native of Scotland, emigrated to this country in early life, and resided some time in Philadelphia. Came to this city in 1836, in charge of Steam Machinery for the old Monroe Railroad, and put up and ran the first locomotive on that road to Forsyth. A short time afterwards, he put up a small shop for castings, in which he was the pioneer in this section of the state. Was Chief of the original Fire Dept. and an Alderman; active member of the Baptist Church; leaves a large family; interred in Rose Hill Cemetery on 1st inst. by a large concourse of the Masonic fraternity - also attended by the Fire Companies.

THOMAS H. TURNER died in Tuskegee, Ala., on 7th Oct., after an illness of six weeks. He was a brother of Rev. W.S. Turner, of the Georgia Conference; his eldest daughter of two years entered the heavenly city just a few days before him; leaves a bereaved companion, parents, brothers, and sister.

Died in this city, on the 6th inst., of apoplexy, MR. THOMAS H. FINT, aged about 67 years.

Died at the residence of Dr. Jameson, in this city, on Thursday morning the 1st inst., of Croup, ANNA JOSEPHINE, only daughter of JOHN T. and FANNIE C. NAPIER, aged 2 years 5 months.

Died in this city, on 27 Nov. 1859, EMMA FLORENCE WALKER, daughter of MARY ANN and ROBERT B. WALKER, aged 6 years 13 days.

Died of pneumonia, in Houston county, on the 1st instant, JAMES THARP LUNDY, son of WILLIAM and JULIA A. LUNDY, of this county, aged 4 years.

The Americus papers announce the death of DR. L.B. MERCER. He expired at his residence in Terrell county on the 27th ult.

B.H. OVERBY, ESQ., of Atlanta, died at Williamson Springs, SC a few days since, of a disease of an apoplextic nature, aged about 46 years. Mr. O. was well known to the people of Georgia. In 1855 he was the Temperance candidate for Governor. (Recorder)

The REV. DR. NEWTON, a distinguished Minister of the Presbyterian denomination, died in Jackson, Miss., on the 28th ult.

Dec. 14, 1859

Died in this city, on the 13th inst., MR. WILLIAM COWLES, aged about 24 years, son of JERRY COWLES, formerly of this city, now a resident of NY.

Died on the 9th inst., in Memphis, DR. THOMAS F. GIBBS, late of Georgia, aged 63 years.

Died at his residence near Thomaston, on the 30th ultimo, THOMAS W. GOODE, aged 57 years 19 days. The deceased was the son of JOHN and ELIZABETH GOODE, and was born in Hancock county, in the year 1802; a lawyer; member of State Legislature (with long eulogy).

Eulogy on the late B.H. OVERBY (see 7 Dec. 1859 issue).

Dec. 21, 1859

Died in Savannah, on the 14th inst., of Consumption, MR. GEO. A. BOIFEUILLET, aged about 36 years; Conductor on the Central Railroad.

Dec. 21, 1859

Died in Hamburg, Arkansas, on 16th Nov., JOHN ARMAND LEFILS, aged 3 months 14 days; and three days thereafter, CARRIE ALABAMA, aged 2 years 7 months - children of ARMAND LEFILS, formerly a much esteemed citizen of Macon (with eulogy).

Departed this life on Saturday, 10th inst., after a brief illness, MRS. LAURA M. WALKER, aged 28 years 8 months, consort of SAMUEL W. WALKER, and daughter of the late JOHN P. and MRS. R.A. EVANS (with long eulogy).

A dispatch from New York, the 9th, announces the decease of THEODORE SEDGWICK, US District Attorney, of the Southern District of NY. He was the author of "Measure of Damages," and other works of authority.

We are grieved to announce the death of DR. ROBERT E. MARTIN, of this city, says the Southern Recorder of the 14th inst. Clerk of the Supreme Court. He was found, this morning at 3 o'clock, on the pavement at the foot of a staircase, opposite the Milledgeville Hotel, with his head fractured near the top of the spinal column. The wound may have been occasioned by a fall from the steps. He was immediately taken to his residence, where he expired about 12 o'clock yesterday.

Dec. 28, 1859

The telegraph announces the death of HON. LINN BOYD, of Kentucky. He was a native of Tennessee, having been born at Nathville, Nov. 22, 1800. His first entry into public life was as a member of the Tennessee Legislature, in 1827, where he served four sessions. He entered Congress as a Rep. from Kentucky in 1835 and continued in Congress until 1855, with the exception of a single term - from 1837 to 1839. He was Speaker of the 32d and 33d Congress. In politics, he was a National Democrat.

Jan. 4, 1860

GENERAL MIRABEAU B. LAMAR died on the 19th Dec. 1859 at Richmond, Texas, of apoplexy. He was born in Warren county, Georgia about 1795, went to Alabama when a Territory, and established a newspaper in Catawba, then the capitol. Returned to Georgia, and was Secretary for Gov. Troup. Raised the "Lafayette Guards" and escorted Lafayette into Milledgeville in 1825. Was one of the earliest settlers of Columbus and established the Columbus Enquirer. Was Senator from Muscogee in 1829. Went to Texas during their revolution...afterwards elected President of the Republic of Texas. (very long obituary)

The sad news of the death of DR. WHITMILL HORNE (says the Pulaski Times) has but just reached us. Dr. Horne was born in Halifax county, N.C., but his youthful days were spent in Putnam county, Ga. For 20 years he was engaged in the duties of his profession in Arkansas and Louisiana, and returned to Georgia in 1853, in time to render important services to Savannah during the prevalence of yellow fever in that city in 1854. Dr. H. has been a resident of Macon but for two years previous to his death.

Serious railroad accident - the up freight train, on the Western & Atlantic Railroad at Vining Station, ten miles from this city, between 7 and 8 o'clock this morning. The freight engine "Oconee" exploded, instantly killing THOMAS CROFT, Conductor and JAMES RHINEHART, Woodpasser, and wounded JAMES SULLIVAN, Fireman, and WM. FLOYD, Engineer, so severely that their recovery is despaired of. (Atlanta American, 29th).

DR. THOMAS B. WINN, one of the oldest and most substantial citizens of Thomas county, died on Sunday, 18th ult.

Jan. 11, 1860

JAMES BOWEN, charged with the murder of MATHEW J. ALLBRITTON, in Thomas county, on 3rd of October last, was tried before the Superior Court of that county last week, and acquitted.

Died in this city, on the 6th instant, MR. CHARLES CAMPBELL, aged about 61 years. A native of New Jersey, and one of our most prominent business men and merchants since about 1830. At his death, he was the oldest resident merchant of our city, west of the Ocmulgee river; for many years a Deacon of the Presbyterian Church of this city.

Died in Twiggs county, on the 4th inst. - HENRY FAULK, ESQ., aged about 37 years; recently a member of the Legislature, and for several years served his county as a Justice of the Inferior Court.

Died at the residence of her father, near Mt. Zion, Hancock county, Ga., on the 28th Dec. 1859, MISS KATE BEMAN, only daughter of REV. DR. BEMAN. On the third day after the death of his sister Kate, died of the same fatal disease, (typhoid fever,) EDWARD D. BEMAN, M.D., youngest son of Rev. Dr. Beman.

Died near Monticello, Jasper county, Ga., on the evening of 24 Dec. 1859, aged 35 years, MRS. ANNA S. GLOVER, wife of HENRY S. GLOVER and daughter of HON. DAVID A. REESE.

JUDGE ISAAC RAMSEY, of Columbia county, died at his residence on Wed. morning, the 4th instant. (Chronicle & Sentinel).

DR. W.R. PALMER, whose name was mixed up with the Harper's Ferry forray, and whose arrest at Memphis, in November last, caused no little talk and excitement at the time, died in that city on Saturday last, 31st of Dec., of Consumption.

COL. R.W. ALSTON died at his residence, near Thomasville, on the 24th ult. He was an aged planter, and died very suddenly, without disease.

MRS. A.A. GAMBRILL, second daughter of DR. LOVICK PIERCE, died after a long and suffering sickness, in Columbus, Georgia, Dec. 1st, 1859.

ELDRIDGE F. PAIGE, well known as "Dow, Jr." the author of the famous "Patent Sermons," was found dead in a house of prostitution in San Francisco on the 4th ult. He was a native of Litchfield, Conn. Ten years ago he was editor and proprietor of the New York Mercury, but meeting with reverses he went to Calif., where he became addicted to liquor, and died in the most utter degredation and misery.

ROBERT BAXTER who was charged with killing a man by the name of DUNBAR, in Warren county, Miss. during last winter, was hung at Vicksburg on Friday, Dec. 30th.

MR. ISAAC HURST, of Sandersville, Ga. was stabbed in the heart and instantly killed on Monday last, while endeavoring to prevent two men from fighting, as we learn from the Sandersville Georgian.

BURRELL K. HARRISON, ESQ., of Stewart county, says the Columbus Times, died at Lumpkin Wed. night, January 4th. He was a lawyer of prominence in this section of the State. Held the position of Clerk of the House of Representatives of Georgia in 1849, and was the candidate of the Southern Rights Party for the Senate in 1851, for the counties of Muscogee and Stewart.

Jan. 18, 1860

The venerable WILLIAM ARNOLD, a well-known and much esteemed minister of the Methodist church, died at his residence on Thursday last.

Jan. 18, 1860

COL. ROBERT W. ALSTON was born in Halifax county, N.C. 2 March 1781, and was among the first students of Chapel Hill College, in that State, where he was educated. He married, at age 19, and removed to Georgia, Hancock county, where he resided until 1834, when he emigrated to Florida. In 1855 he moved back to Georgia, Thomas county, where he died, at his residence, near Thomasville, on the 24th Dec. 1859 in the 79th year of his age (with eulogy).

Died, on the 13th inst., at the residence of Capt. E. Wimberly, Baker county, REBECCA, only child of WM. F. and HELEN PLAUE, aged 18 months.

Jan. 25, 1860

Homicide. MR. SIMEON HARRISON, living near Hayneville, Houston county, was killed by a man by the name of BRASWELL. The killing occurred at the plantation of Jeremiah Bunn, for whom Braswell was overseeing. (Hawkinsville Times).

JAMES W. JONES, ESQ., the veteran editor of the Augusta Chronicle and Sentinel, died about one o'clock yesterday morning, in the 52d year of his age, after six days' illness, of Pneumonia. Was a native of Oglethorpe county, Ga. Funeral service was performed at St. John's Methodist church, by the Rev. Mr. Graham (with long eulogy). (Constitutionalist of Sunday)

JAMES B. AYRES died on the 18th inst., aged about 50 years. He was a native of Woodbridge, New Jersey, and had resided here since 1835. He was an accomplished architect and builder, and erected many of the best edifices of our city. He was interred in Rose Hill Cemetery on the 20th inst. by the Firemen, Odd Fellows and Floyd Rifles, of which bodies he was a member (with a tribute of respect by Franklin Lodge, No. 2, I.O.O.F.).

MR. BENJ. LEVY, one of the pioneers of journalism in New Orleans, and by whom the New Orleans Prices Current was established in 1818, died in that city on the 10th inst.

Tribute of respect on death of HENRY FAULK. Given by Twiggs Lodge, No. 164, Jan. 7, 1860.

Died on the 18th of the present month, MR. JOHN CASTTIN, in the 73d year of his age (with eulogy). (City papers please copy).

Died at Fort Gaines, on the 15th inst., GEO. B. WARDLAW, ESQ., aged about 62 years. He was a native of South Carolina, and a resident of Fort Hawkins, (now known as East Macon,) when our city was located.

Died in this city, on Sunday morning last, of consumption, MRS. SARAH LOCKETT, wife of MR. BENJ. G. LOCKETT; leaves a husband and 3 children.

Feb. 1, 1860

Died at his residence in Tallokas, Brooks county, Ga., on the 13th inst., DR. WILLIAM R. COLEMAN, in the 34th year of his age. Born near Macon, Ga. and unfortunately deprived of parental protection at quite an early age; graduate of New York Medical College. He had been engaged in the practice of his profession some four years when he came to this place some ten years since. Was married to MISS LAURANAH EDMONDSON in March 1851 (with eulogy).

Feb. 15, 1860

Died on the 8th inst., after an illness of three months, MARY, only daughter of REV. H.B. TREADWELL, aged about 9 years.

Feb. 15, 1860

Died in Knoxville, Tenn., MR. NATHANIEL BARKER, aged 58 years. He was a native of Mass., and resided in this city almost from its earliest settlement, until within a few years past, when he removed to Montgomery, Ala. Recently he removed to Knoxville, Tenn., where he died on the 22d ult.

Died in the vicinity of Oglethorpe, of consumption, on 11th inst., MRS. SARAH G. COOK, wife of PHILIP COOK, ESQ., and second daughter of HENRY H. and LUCY LUMPKIN...her mother and oldest and youngest sisters were present to soothe her last moments; was an amiable wife and fond mother.

Died in this city on the 11th inst., of congestion of the brain, CHARLES VAUGHAN WAGNON, aged 5 years 4 days, son of W.W. and MARY V. WAGNON.

Died in this city, on the night of the 10th inst., of Pneumonia, JOHN W. LUNDY, after an illness of two weeks, aged 22 years. The deceased was a native of Newnan, Coweta county, in this State, whither his remains were carried, on Saturday morning, accompanied by his afflicted mother and sister.

From the Waynesboro News, Feb. 8 - On last Monday afternoon a most lamentable tragedy was enacted in and near our town. MR. JOHN B. OWEN, a respected citizen, was shot dead in front of his store by a MR. JOHN WALKER, a South Carolinian, who has resided for the past year in our county...(long story giving details).

Homicide in Warren County. The Constitutionalist learns from a gentleman in Warren county, that MR. AUGUSTUS BRINKLEY, the former Sheriff killed his stepfather, EDWARD BAKER, at his residence near by, or at Double Wells, on Thursday last.

HON. CHARLES J. INGERSOLL, one of the Judges of the United States district Court died at New Haven on Wed. last.

Feb. 22, 1860

Died in Upson county, on Sunday, the 12th inst., MISS LOUISA F. SHARPMAN, daughter of THOMAS S. SHARMAN, ESQ., aged about 18 years.

Died in Bienville Parish, La., on the 21st of January, MR. WM. WIMBERLY, brother of Col. James Wimberly, of Muscogee county, Ga., and Lewis Wimberly, Esq., of Talbot county.

HON. OWEN H. KENAN died at his residence in Whitfield county on the 27th of January last, in the 75th year of his age. He had filled the office of Judge first in Ocmulgee, and then in the Cherokee Circuit.

Our city says the Sumter News was shocked last Friday evening by the announcement of the death of MISS MEDORA NUNN, eldest daughter of HAWKINS H. NUNN, ESQ., R.R. Agent at this place. Miss Nunn, was on a visit to Cuthbert. In an afternoon's ride with some friends she was thrown from her horse, and so injured that she expired within 24 hours.

We are pained to learn this morning, by a letter from Mr. J.D. Strother, that our old and valued friend, GEN. THOS. S. WOODWARD, died, after a long and painful illness, in Winn Parish, Louisiana, at five o'clock on the morning of the 4th inst. He was born in Elbert county, Georgia, about the year 1796, but the greater part of his life was spent in Alabama. His only surviving child is Col. Thos. Woodward, of Louisiana. (Montgomery Mail)

Feb. 29, 1860

From Nashville Union and American of Feb. 22d - BISHOP MILES, of

(Feb. 29, cont'd) - the Catholic Church, died at his residence in this city yesterday afternoon, of hemorrhage of the lungs; was upwards of 70 years of age.

On Saturday afternoon, JAMES SMITH, a lad employed in this office and about 15 years old, went out shooting, in company with two others, in the woods below the Central R. Road track, known as the Reserve...died in gun accident (details given in story).

A telegraphic dispatch to Washington announces the murder of DR. W.J. KEITT, of Florida, by his negress. The Ocala (Fla) Companion of the 21st gives details...Dr. Keitt had been living by himself on his plantation about three miles from Ocala; was a native of South Carolina, and a brother of HON. L.M. KEITT, the brilliant Senator (Rep) of that State; had moved to this State about six years ago.

A little girl aged about two years, the daughter of OWEN REICH, of Easton, Pa., died the other day from having eaten the tops of two or three matches (Harrisburg Union).

Mar. 7, 1860

Died in Covington on the 16th ultimo, MRS. SALLIE ZACHRY, consort of LEWIS ZACHARY, ESQ., in the 65th year of her age. She was an affectionate wife, devoted mother, and kind neighbor.

Died at her residence near Linden, Ala., on the 25th ult., suddenly, MARY E., wife of ADLAIS O. HOUSTON, and second daughter of DR. THOMAS F. and MRS. A.E.A. GREEN, of Midway, Ga.

A bloody affray occurred in Franklin county, Va., on Saturday last, the 25th ult., in which three brothers, MESSRS, JAMES, WILLIAM, and RALPH CLEMENTS, were killed by VINCENT WITCHER, former President of the Richmond and Danville Railroad, and his grandson, MR. JOHN A. SMITH...(Richmond Dispatch)

MRS. MILLEGE, relict of the late GOV. MILLEGE of Georgia, died the morning of the 23d at her residence near Augusta.

Mar. 14, 1860

Died in this city on the 6th inst., of Scarlet Fever, TALLULAH F., infant daughter of JOHN H. and FLORENCE ENGLISH, aged 1 year 7 months 6 days. (Columbus Times please copy).

MISS CATHERINE McDONALD departed this life in Scottsboro, on the 8th inst., after a protracted illness.

Died, at her residence in Pulaski county, on the morning of the 26th ult., MRS. MARY ANN PHILIPS, wife of JAMES PHILIPS, SEN., in the 73d year of her age.

The Dallas (Tex) Herald of the 22d ult. relates that MRS. ELIZABETH CROCKETT, widow of DAVY CROCKETT, ex-member of Congress from Tennessee and the hero of the Alamo, died on the 2d inst., of apoplexy, in the 74th year of her age. Mrs. Crockett had lived for several years in Johnson county.

The Madison (Fla) Messenger gives an account of a most brutal murder committed in that county, by negroes, on the 3d instant. MR. MATTHEW D. GRIFFIN, overseer of Maj. Watts, at his plantation nine miles from Madison C.H., was set upon by a number of negroes as they were returning from work, and shockingly mutilated with axes. The body of the murdered man was then taken to a neighboring lake and there sunk in the center of it, with an anvil attached to weight it down.

REV. THOMAS W. COOPER, of the Methodist Church, died at his residence in Micanopy, East Florida, on Friday evening, Feb. 24th, of

(Mar. 14, cont'd) - disease of the throat. At the time of his death, he was Presiding Elder of the St. John's District.

Mar. 24, 1860

JAMES AIKEN, found guilty of the murder of MIKE HIBBETTS, was hanged at Kingston, Alabama on Friday last...

MISS TENNESSEE GIBSON, a beautiful young lady, died from the effects of snuff dipping, in Arkansas...

The boiler of the Steamer S.M. Manning of Hawkinsville, exploded on the Altamaha River, not far from Jacksonville, Telfair Co., on the 12th inst. Nearly all the persons on board were killed... CAPT. TAYLOR's son JEFFERSON, and JOSEPH B. WILLIAMS, JACOB PARKER and JOHN HARRELL, three last citizens of Telfair county, are killed. Among the negroes killed are two belonging to James Y. Wilcox, tow belonging to Wm. Wilcox, and one to John F. McRae. (two separate articles)

A little son of MR. L. KENDRICK, about 8 or 10 years of age, was run over by one of the trains on the State Road on Wed. night last, at "Big Shanty," in Cobb county. He was instantly killed... (Atlanta Intelligencer)

Mar. 28, 1860

Died on the 15th Feb., at the residence of her father, WM. A. CARR, ESQ., near Lake Jackson, Leon county, Fla., MRS. SUSAN A. THOMAS, consort of MR. JOHN G. THOMAS. The deceased was in her 24th year, and had passed most of her life in Athens, Ga. (with short eulogy)

Died in Oglethorpe, Ga., on the 17th inst., MR. JOHN W. WILSON, in the 29th year of his age, of consumption; at time of his death was Judge of Ordinary of the county (with short eulogy).

JOHN PASS, aged about 40 years, and a printer by trade, was found dead in bed at 2 o'clock yesterday morning, at the residence of his sister's husband, Mr. Shira Cunningham, in the Warrior District, twelve miles from Macon. The night before he was under influence of liquor and his sudden death is attributed to that cause.

A man was killed on the South Western Railroad on Monday, the 19th inst., a short distance below "Anderson Station" in Sumter county. It would appear that he was sitting on the track intoxicated, and asleep...the only evidence of his identity were two letters found in his hat, addressed to HENRY TURNER, at Richland, Stewart county, apparently from his sons - and mailed at Eatonton, the other at Milledgeville.

BROTHER JAMES G. WHATLEY, of Pinter Lodge, No. 88, departed this life on the 7th of March 1860. Tribute of respect by that lodge, Barnesville, March 1860.

Apr. 4, 1860

The Raleigh (NC) Press of the 22d learns that a fight occurred at Chapel Hill last Sat. evening between a young man named FORD of that State, and a young man named WATSON of Chapel Hill, son of JONES WATSON, both students, which terminated in the death of Watson. It is said that Ford struck Watson with a loaded whip and then stabbed him; from which wounds he died Tuesday evening last. Ford has made his escape.

Died in this city, on the 31st ult., of constipation of the bowels, MR. BENJAMIN T. SMITH, of Twiggs county, aged 36 years.

Died on Sunday afternoon, of consumption, C.P. BRICKHOUSE, of Norfolk Va., whither his remains were carried on Sunday night. He was probably 30 years old.

Apr. 4, 1860

We regret to learn of the death of DR. JAMES TINSLEY, of Line Creek, which occurred Sat. last. Dr. T. was an intelligent planter of this county, and, we belive, was formerly editor of a newspaper in Georgia. (Montgomery Mail). Resided for many years in Athens, where he at one time edited the Southern Whig; was about 65 years old.

Apr. 11, 1860

Homicide in Lumpkin. Columbus Enquirer reports that on Sunday last, the first day of April, a difficulty occurred between two young men in Lumpkin, named GAULDING and ALDAY, the former charging the latter with sending him an "April fool" letter just received; and the sad termination of the affair was that Gaulding stabbed Alday with a pocket-knife, the wound proving fatal in a short time. We learn that the parties were relatives.

JAMES KIRKE PAULDING died on the 4th instant, at Tarrytown, NY, in the 81st year of his age.

The Southern Recorder announces the death of MRS. LOUISE EUGENIA CUTHBERT, wife of HON. JOHN A. CUTHBERT, formerly of Georgia, and for many years a highly respectable citizen of Mobile.

Apr. 18, 1860

Died in Tallahassee, Fla., on the 7th inst., MR. E.J. STOW, aged 36 years - formerly a resident of this city.

Died in this city on the 15th inst., of pneumonia, WILLIAM E. O'CONNER, in the 22d year of his age (with short eulogy).

From the Southern Christian Advocate - CHARLES, a servant of ISAAC WINSHIP, of Atlanta, Georgia, died on the 10th of March, at the advanced age of 106 years. Was taken prisoner by the British and Tories in SC. Later was exchanged in an even swap for a white Tory. He was for many years in the Hampton and Cook families; but for 25 years past has been in the family of brother Winship; was preacher among the colored people of M.E. Church (with long eulogy).

MR. BENJAMIN CARR, for the last 20 years a citizen of Covington, died at the residence of John P. Carr, in this city, on the night of the 7th inst., in the 93d year of his age; leaves a wife who is 100 years of age. (Covington Times).

Apr. 25, 1860

Died in this city, on the 21st inst., MRS. ANTOINETTE VIRGINIA WOOD, wife of GRANVILLE WOOD, aged about 36 years. Also on the 18th, their child, ROSA IRENA, aged 2 years 4 months.

The trial of JACKSON ROBERTS, for the killing of his brother AUGUSTUS ROBERTS, came off in Clinton last week...

May 2, 1860

Died near Butler, Taylor county, on the 21st ult., WM. W. CORBITT, ESQ. He was a native of Virginia, and had resided for many years in Macon and Taylor counties. For some years he was Deputy Grand Master of the first District F.A. Masons of Georgia.

Died in Marietta, on the 19th ult., MRS. ELIZA McDONALD, wife of the HON. CHAS. J. McDONALD, aged 58 years. She was the daughter of JUDGE ROANE of Virginia, and sister to the HON. WM. H. ROANE, late Senator from that State.

May 2, 1860

Columbus, April 30 - The Steamer J.C. Calhoun exploded yesterday, at Ridleyville, mortally injuring CRAWFORD, the acting Captain, and dangerously wounding HUGH ATKINS, the second Engineer, and two passengers. Six negro deck hands were killed.

MRS. LUCY CLARK, probably the oldest lady in this county, died at the residence of her son, DR. E.E. JONES, on the evening of the 22d inst. She removed from Virginia to this county many years ago, and was, at the time of her death, in her 93rd year. (Madison Visitor)

We learn from the Southern Home Journal, that a man by the name of STOKES, living in the lower edge of Pike county, on Three Notch road, hung himself last Friday. His wife threatened to leave him, and he concluded to go first. This is supposed to be the only cause of the rash act.

W. COST JOHNTON recently died in Washington, in the 54th year of his age. He was a man of commanding talents, and for many years past, a leader of the Clay school, in the Congress of the U.S.

May 9, 1860

Died in Macon county, Ala., on the 17th ult., of apoplexy, MRS. M.R. ADAMS, wife of REV. ROBERT ADAMS, in the 68th year of her age. The deceased was, before her marriage with Mr. Adams, the widow of CHARLES ABERCROMBIE, formerly of Russell county, Ala., from which county she removed to Macon about 12 years ago.

Philadelphia papers of the 27th ult. report the death, on the previous day, of LAWRENCE JOHNSON, the well-known type-founder of that city. He was about 60 years of age, and an Englishman by birth.

We are truly sorry to announce the death of JOHN B. REID, ESQ., of this place, says the Griffin Democrat; one of the first settlers of this part of the country; member of Presbyterian Church; leaves a widow and two children.

We learn that a MR. BLAKEY was drowned in Cubahatchee creek, in this county, on last Sat., in attempting to save his nephew, a son of DR. BLAKEY. The corpses were found clinging to each other. (Tuskegee, Ala. Rep. 3d)

May 16, 1860

We learn from the Forsyth Journal, that MR. PETER A. CURRY died in that place on the 6th inst.

May 23, 1860

Died in Americus, Ga., at the residence of her father, DR. WM. N.L. CROCKER, on the 10th day of May inst., after a long and protracted illness, MRS. VICTORIA E. TOMLINSON, consort of MR. J.J. TOMLINSON, in the 23d year of her age, leaving a husband, a little daughter aged 5 months, a father, mother, two sisters, three brother; in Oct. 1858 was married to her bereaved husband; member of Methodist Episcopal Church.

May 30, 1860

Died in this city, on Friday last, ELLIOTT CHASE, infant son of REV. J.W. and MRS. C.A. BURKE, of this city, aged 3 months 27 days.

From the last Louisville Journal - MR. JOSEPH BERND, the local editor of the Louisville Journal and the sole editor of the Louisville Bulletin, died at the Louisville Hotel on Sat. morning of pneumonia after an illness of five days.

May 30, 1860

(Columbian of the 23d) - HON. WILLIAM CAMPBELL PRESTON, on the 22d inst., died in Columbia, S.C. at the residence of his brother, John S. Preston, Esq., in his 67th year. He was the eldest son of GENERAL FRANCIS PRESTON, of Virginia, and was born in Philadelphia on 27 Dec. 1794 - his father being a member of Congress of the US, then sitting in that city. His mother was the only child of GENERAL WILLIAM CAMPBELL, who commanded the American forces at the battle of King's Mountain. Her mother was a sister of PATRICK HENRY. In 1809 Mr. Preston entered as a student in the South Carolina College, where he graduated with distinciton in 1812; then became student of the eminent William Wirt, at Richmond, and left his office for an extended tour of Europe. Returning in 1819, he soon married MISS COALTER, daughter of DAVID COALTER, ESQ., formerly of Columbia, In 1820 he was admitted to the Bar, and in 1822 adopted Columbia as his home. His wife died in 1825, and in 1830 he married MISS DAVIS, daughter of DR. JAMES DAVIS of Columbia. S-e died about five years since, and he leaves neither wife nor children. He served our city as Mayor, and the State in the Legislature, re-elected for several terms, then served in the US Senate; after retirement from that office, he became President of the South Carolina College...

June 13, 1860

COLONEL COLIN C. CAMPBELL, one of the editors and proprietors of the Memphis Avalanche, died at his residence, near Columbia, Tenn., on the 31st ult.

On the 1st Friday of this month ELLEY H. GORDON was executed at Abbyville, Wilcox county, in this State, for the murder of ABRAHAM PYTAS, in December last...

The Milledgeville papers announce the death of MRS. E.A.E. GREEN, the pious and esteemed wife of DR. THOS. F. GREEN, after years of patient suffering.

A murder was committed in Upson county, on Friday of last week, by a DR. CHATHAM, upon H.C. HOWELL. It appears that Chatham rode up to a field where Howell was at work, and calling him aside, after some words, shot him through the heart with a pistol.

We learn from the Savannah Republican that DR. CHAS. W. WEST, of that city, was thrown from his buggy, at Newton, Baker county, a few days since and fatally injured. After lingering for some time, he died on Tuesday, and his remains were brought to Savannah for interment.

June 20, 1860

Died in this city, on the 15th inst., JOHN M., infant son of M. and JOSEPHINE McCARDLE, aged 13 months 25 days. (Telegraph and Citizen please copy)

PETER S. HUMPHRIES, ESQ., a well known lawyer of Perry, Ga. died at the Indian Springs on the 13th inst.

The Dahlonega Signal announces that their townsman MAJ. M.J. WALKER died on Sunday evening the 3d inst., at about 8 o'clock, of disease of the heart. He had been a resident of Dahlonega for many years; an attorney at the bar; member of the Methodist Church.

Notice of death of MAJ. DOZIER THORNTON, for many years a resident of Columbus, but more recently of Coosa county, Ala. He died at his residence in that county on Sunday night, 10th inst., of apoplexy He was about 60 years of age. His remains were brought to this city and deposited in the family burying ground yesterday afternoon. (Sun)

June 20, 1860

GEN. THOMAS S. JESSUP, Quarter Master General of the US Army, died in Washington of paralysis on the 10th inst. Known as an active and efficient officer - particularly in the "Black Hawk" and other Indian wars.

June 27, 1860

Died in this city, on the 11th inst., MRS. M.E. MALSBY, aged 87 years - wife of MR. LOTT MALSBY.

Died in Columbus, on the 12th inst., MR. T.S. KILPATRICK, aged about 45 years - formerly of this city.

Died in this city, on the 19th instant, ALICE, only daughter of JOHN A. and MRS. T.A.E. McMANUS, in the 4th year of her age.

WADE H. LESTER, ESQ., for a few months a resident of this city, says the Atlanta American, and engaged in business here, died a few days since at the Georgia Lunatic Asylum, whither he had been taken in consequence of a very sudden bereavement of reason, caused by unusual exposure to the intense heat of the sun while seining. The corpse passed through the city on yesterday, in charge of his brother, REV. R.B. LESTER, on the way to Marietta, for interment. Leaves an interesting family to mourn his loss.

July 4, 1860

DR. PHILIP A. BRANHAM died at the residence of his father, DR. JOEL BRANHAM, on Monday night. He had but recently become a resident of our city. His age was about 23 years.

Columbus papers record the death of MRS. SARAH ANN RAGLAND, the estimable wife of THOMAS RAGLAND, ESQ., of the Enquirer, of that city. She died of consumption, at Wynnton, Wed. last.

Tribute of respect by Twiggs Lodge, No. 164 June 24th, 1860 - on death of MOSES HARRELL who died on Sunday the 10th inst., of congestive fever; leaves an aged mother, a widow and 3 small children.

July 11, 1860

MAJ. E.R. YOUNG, a beloved and valued citizen of Thomas county, Ga., died on Friday, 29th ult., aged 62 years. He had accumulated a large fortune, and had set apart in his will $30,000 for the erection of a Female College in Thomasville - also a donation of $2500 to the St. Thomas Lodge of Free Masons.

Macon, Ga. July 4th, 1860 - tribute of respect by the physicians of Macon on the death of DR. PHILIP A. BRANHAM. Signed by Drs. J. Dickson Smith, R.H. Nisbet, W.S. Lightfoot, G. Harrison, A. Pye.

July 18, 1860

MAJ. E. BROUGHTON, Assistant Engineer of the South Western Railroad, died in Eufaula, Ala., on Sat. night last, from the effects of a sun stroke.

HON. JNO. H. LUMPKIN died at the Choice House in this city, on Tuesday morning last, at 6 o'clock; a Judge of Superior Court; Rep. in Congress. (Rome Southerner, 12th)

July 25, 1860

Long obituary of PETER S. HUMPHRIES who died at the Indian Springs, June 13th, 1860, in the 34th year of his life. - Perry Ga., July 19th, 1860, (ED. NOTE: See 4 July 1860 issue)

July 25, 1860

REV. A.J. ORR departed this life at his residence in Thomasville, on Friday, the 13th inst., after a severe illness of two months; aged about 43.

JOSEPH GALES, Senior Editor of the National Intelligencer, has died. Was born at Eckington, near Sheffield, England, April 10, 1786. Came to America at age 7, with his father, who had published the Register at Sheffield, until his sympathies with the French Revolution drove him from England. Was educated at the University of North Caroiilina, and in 1807 went to Washington as assistant and finally partner in the National Intelligencer. In 1812 he took into partnership his brother-in-law W.W. Seaton...(Augusta Chronicle & Sentinel)

Aug. 1, 1860

Died in Twiggs county, on the 27th ult., after a short illness, HARDY DURHAM, ESQ., aged 76 years. He was among the oldest residents of the county.

MRS. SUSAN DECATUR, widow of COMMODORE STEPHEN DECATUR, died at Washington City, on the 12th inst., aged 84 years.

MR. JAMES STUBBS, a citizen of this county, was drowned in Echeconnee Creek, about nine miles from this city on Wed. evening last, while bathing. Mr. Stubbs has for a long time been subject to paralytic strokes and it is supposed that he was attacked with this disorder while in the water, and drowned. (Telegraph)

Aug. 8, 1860

Died in Upson county, a few days since, DR. DAVID KENDALL. Also, SAM'L GRANDLAND, ESQ., - both old residents and highly respected citizens of that county. Also, DR. JAMES ANDERSON, of that county, died at his plantation in Louisiana, and was brought here for interment.

South Carolina papers report the death on the 24th ult., at Orangeburg in that State, of REV. REDDICK PIERCE, an elder brother of DR. L. PIERCE of this city. He entered the South Carolina Conference in 1805, and was its oldest member at the time of his death; his age was 78. (Columbus Enquirer)

Aug. 15, 1860

Died in this city, on the 14th inst., DR. ANDREW PYE, in the 49th year of his age, after a short illness of a congestive nature. He was a native of Oglethorpe county, and had resided in this city several years.

Died at the Indian Springs, on the morning of the 8th inst. JAMES DEAN, JR., only son of JAMES DEAN, ESQ., of this city. His remains were brought home, and interred in the family lot, in Rose Hill Cemetery, and the last sad rites of respect paid by the Floyd Rifles.

Died at Chatham, Four Corners, NY on Tuesday August 7th, after a short illness, JOHN B. STWO, formerly a resident of this city, in the 42d year of his age.

JAMES S. SLAUGHTER committed suicide on yesterday by taking laudanum. Was a young man of genius, and was connected in 1856 with the Alabama Press, and in 1858 and 1859 with the National American of this city. Leaves a wife and an infant child. (Atlanta Confederacy, 9th).

Tribute of respect by Supreme Court of Georgia in chambers at Macon, July 21, 1860 - on death of JUDGE ABNER P. POWERS.

Aug. 22, 1860

Died in Griffin, Aug. 9, 1860, MRS. ELIZABETH SIMMONS, wife of REV. JOHN SIMMONS, in her 74th year; member of M.E. Church for 49 years.

Died in Oglethorpe, Ga., Aug. 13th, 1860, little FANNIE GREER, infant dau. of JOHN M. and MARY F. GREER, aged 10 months 9 days.

WM. M. MILLER, ESQ., Clerk of the Superior Court of Houston County, died in Perry on the 15th inst.

Aug. 29, 1860

Died near Fort Valley, Houston county, on the 27th instant, MAJ. JAMES H. HARDAWAY, aged about 75 years. He was a native of Virginia, and one of the earliest settlers of this city; member of Presbyterian Church; was brought to this city and interred yesterday at 4 o'clock by the brethren of Macon Lodge, No. 5.

Tribute of respect by Houston Lodge, No. 35 F.A.M., Perry, Ga. Aug. 27th, 1860 - on death of WM. H. MILLER.

Sep. 5, 1860

Died in this city, on the 2d inst., MR. JAMES RICHARDSON - an old and much respected citizen.

Died in Savannah, on the 1st instant, while on his way home from a Northern tour, WM. H. MORELAND, ESQ., a well known citizen of Jones county.

Died in Dooly county, on the 22d July, JOHN A. REDDING, aged 25 years - son of ROLAND REDDING, of Monroe county.

Died at Morristown, N.J. on the 26th ult., MR. EDWIN GRAVES, well known here for many years, as one of our active citizens.

Died in the vicinity of Oglethorpe, on 2d inst., after a long and painful illness, HARRIET THOMAS, wife of MAJOR STEPHEN F. MILLER.

Died near this city, on the 2d inst., MRS. ELIZABETH BURGE, wife of J.L. BURGE, aged 54 years.

Regret to announce the death of MAJ. W. LETCHER MITCHELL, one of our old and highly respectable citizens. He died at the Franklin House in this place on Sunday night, the 26th inst.
(Athens Banner, 29th).

The Memphis Appeal learns that on Thursday, 23d, a duel was fought in the Indian Nation between DR. MITCHELL and MR. GANTT, opposing candidates for Congress in the last election in Kansas, in which Mr. Gantt, the successful aspirant was killed. The deceased was brother to Geo. Gantt, Esq., well known lawyer, and policitician of Columbia, Tenn.

Sep. 12, 1860

Died at Geneva, Talbot county, Ga., 12th of July, aged 17 years 2 months - MISS MARY J. McCRARY, eldest daughter of MR. J.B. McCRARY had just returned home from Wesleyan Female College, where she was a pupil; (with eulogy)

Died in Polk county, Texas, on the 4th instant, MRS. VIRGINIA HUBERT, consort of ROBERT HUBERT, and daughter of REV. J.P. DUNCAN, of Americus.

Sep. 12, 1860

Died in this town, at the residence of his son-in-law, W.W. Hartsfield, Esq., after a lingering illness, EDWARD TRAYLER, on Tuesday morning, Sept. 4th, aged 77 years 1 month 14 days. He was born in Virginia - settled in Green county - moved to Putnam, and in 1827 to Upson; was married over 40 years and a widower ten; he tented over 20 consecutive years in the same tent at Upson Camp Ground. (Upson Pilot)

COMMODORE JAMES M. McINTOSH, of the US Navy, died at Pensacola at 35 minutes past six o'clock of Sunday morning, the 2d inst., age about 65 years; native of Liberty county, Ga. and had been in the naval service for more than a half century.

Letter from Dawson announces the death of MATHEW E. WILLIAMS, ESQ., of Terrell county. He died on Tuesday last, after an illness of 36 hours. Was Senator from Terrell county in 1857 and 1858 (Sumter Republican).

The Nashville Gazette announces the death of fellow-citizen A.A. STITT, ESQ. He died in Philadelphia yesterday morning, after a lingering disease. For several years past, Mr. Stitt has been acting as Superindendent of the Southern Methodist Publishing House.

Sep. 19, 1860

GEORGE ECKLEY. An old and faithful servant of Mr. Damour, of this city, died last week, and was followed to the grave by a very large procession of colored friends and several of our citizens. He was a leading and cinsistent member of the Methodist Church - usually "raised the tunes," and was much esteemed by white and black.

The REV. ABEL McEWEN, D.D., died at his residence in New London, Conn., on Friday morning last, at the advanced age of 80 years. He had been the pastor of the First Congregational Church of that city for more than half a century, but during the last few years had been assisted by a colleague. The New London Star says that he was a classmate at Yale College of John C. Calhoun, and his successful competitor for the Valedictory.

Died at the residence of Mr. Story, in Twiggs county, on the 8th inst., DR. ANDERSON KING, son of WESLEY KING, age about 22 years.

Sep. 26, 1860

Death of L.C. SIMPSON, ESQ. Died at his residence in this city, says the Atlanta American, at about half past 9 occlock last night. His funeral will take place this afternoon at 4 o'clock. Mr. Simpson was one of our oldest citizens, and was honored by his fellow citizens with various public offices. He leaves a widow and five children.

Oct. 17, 1860

The body of the HON. I.T. IRVIN has been buried, for the present, in Texas, near the scene of the disaster, by which he lost his life.

The sad intelligence which we received last Saturday of the death of HON. I.T. IRVIN, Speaker of the Georgia House of Representatives, is confirmed. Away from home and family and friends, he has met a cruel death by drowning, having jumped overboard of the boat whose boilers had exploded. Was a planter, about forty years of age...last November was speaker of the House of Representatives. (Chronicle and Sentinel).

Oct. 17, 1860

Homicide. On Tuesday evening the 9th inst., says the Americus Georgian, a couple of pistol shots each were exchanged between MAJ. WILLIAM BLACK, of Ellaville, and JAMES HUMPHIRES, formerly a resident, we believe, in the same community. Humphries had for some time been threatening the life of Black, and a peace warrant was at the time in the hands of the Sheriff for his arrest. There is a difference of opinion as to which fired the first shot. Humphries received a shot in the lower part of the abdomen, of which he died in about 24 hours. The whole current of public sentiment justifies the killing as clearly in self defense.

Died in this city, on Sunday morning, the 7th inst., MRS. MARIAH MALSBY, widow of JOHN MALSBY, in the 63d year of her age. She was one of the oldest citizens of the place, having lived here 33 years. Leaves a large family and numerous friends to mourn her loss.

Oct. 24, 1860

An old citizen gone! We are pained to announce the decease of so excellent a man as JONATHAN WHITESIDE, ESQ. who died on Lookout Mountain, at the residence of his son, W.B. Whiteside, on Sunday last. He was about ninety years of age. He was afflicted with a cancer on his throat which was the immediate cause of his death. He was the father of Col. A. Jas. and Dr. W.B. Whiteside. (Chattanooga Gazette).

MR. JOHN SMITH, one of our oldest and best citizens, died at his residence in this city on Saturday morning the 6th inst. Mr. Smith was a native of Conn., came to Georgia when but 19 years old, and for a long time lived in Green county. He was 75 years old, and came down to the grave like " a shock of corn fully ripe for the harvest." (Rome Courier).

Oct. 31, 1860

JOHN J. MADDOX, convicted last week in the Superior Court of Jones County for the murder of LEVI A. LLOYD, was yesterday brought to Macon by Sheriff Balkcom of Jones County and committed to Bibb county jail to await his execution on the 7th of Dec. next, the Jones county jail being considered insecure. (Macon Telegraph).

The Sumter Republican of Friday last announces the decease of HON. HUGH M.D. KING. His disease was dropsy of the chest. He was aged 53.

Nov. 7, 1860

Fatal railroad accident. A collision occurred near No. 9, on the Savannah, Albany & Gulf Railroad on Wed. morning last, says the Savannah News, by which we regret to learn that MR. WM. GODFREY, a worthy young man of that city and engineer of the down passenger train, lost his life.

Death of JAMES SHERIDAN KNOWLES. This eminent dramatic author died lately, while on a voyage from England to Russia. He was a native of Cork, where he was born in 1784. "The Wife, a tale of Mantua," "Virginius," "The Hunchback," "The Love Chase," "William Tell," the opera of "The Beggar of Bethnal Green," were from his pen.

Nov. 14, 1860

Died in this city, on the 9th inst., MRS. MARY L. CRAY, in the 73d year of her age - widow of the late SCOTT CRAY, ESQ.

Nov. 21, 1860

Died on the 10th inst., in this city, MRS. ELIZABETH L. DURRETT, wife of DAVID M. DURRETT, in the 26th year of her age.

Nov. 28, 1860

REV. J.E. DAWSON. The funeral obsequies over the remains of this able and distinguished Baptist Minister were performed in this city on Tuesday says the Columbus Enquirer, of Wed. last. Mr. Dawson died at Tuskegee, Ala., of consumption, after a lingering decline, and his remains were brought here for interment. He was lately one of the editors of the South-Western Baptist, from which station he had to retire on account of his declining health.

Death of JUDGE HILL. In the LaGrange Reporter of the 23d inst., we find the melancholy intelligence of his sudden death...while making a speech Sat. last, he was stricken with paralysis...was removed to the residence of Mayor Bacon, where he lingered until half past 9 o'clock, on Tuesday night.

Died, in Clinton, on the 18th inst., DR. HORATIO BOWEN, aged about 68 years. He was, at the time of his death, one of the oldest residents of Jones county, having settled there soon after the war of 1812. He was a surgeon in that war, in the army of Gen. Floyd.

Died on the 26th inst., in this city, ALEXANDER HOLZENDORF, son of U. and E.T. VAN GIESEN, aged 13 months and 26 days.

Dec. 5, 1860

Died in this city, on Wed. morning last, after a painful and protracted illness, of years, MR. EDWARD CURD, in the 34th year of his age.

Tribute of respect by Pleasant Ridge Lodge, No. 103 - on death of JAMES DUNCAN.

Dec. 19, 1860

A sad accident. On Wed. evening last, MISS MARTHA BIVINS, daughter of ROLAND BIVINS, ESQ., of this county, was accidentally shot by a pistol in the hands of a lady of the family. The pistol had been used in practicing, and while she was handling it, it exploded. The wound was not, at first, considered dangerous, but terminated fatally on the third day afterwards.

Died in this city, on the 12th instant, MRS. ELEANOR BLAKE, in the 74th year of her age.

Dec. 26, 1860

A despatch from Columbus, Dec. 19 says: B.Y. MARTIN, ESQ., long the efficient Reporter of the Supreme Court of Georgia, and elector for the Second District on the Douglas and Johnson ticket in the late Presidential canvass, and an able lawyer and highly esteemed gentleman, died in this city, at 2 o'clock in the morning.

The following is a list of revolutionary soldiers on the rolls of the State of Georgia and Alabama, who are regularly receiving their pensions, and their ages in 1859:

MICAJAH BROOKS, Polk county, Ga., 98 years of age

WM. COGGIN, Gordon county, Ga., 104 years of age

JOHN HAMES, SR., Murray county, Ga., 107 years of age

JOHN McMILLEN, Habersham county, Ga., 99 years of age

JOHN NICHOLSON, Union county, Ga., 96 years of age

REUBEN STEVENS, Chambers county, Ala., 97 years of age

Jan. 2, 1861

Departed this life in Macon county, Nov. 30th, 1860. E. PLURIBUS UNUM, youngest son of JOHN T. and CATHARINE OLIVER, aged 1 year 10 months 9 days.

Died on the 26th inst., in the city of Oglethorpe, WM. DRAYTON, youngest son of WM. B. and ELLEN JONES, aged two years, two months and 23 days - after an illness of two days of congestive chill.

Died in Baldwin county, on the evening of the 20th ult., after a long and protracted illness, ELIZABETH, wife of WILLIAM SANFORD, in the 77th year of her age; an exemplary member of the Methodist E. Church.

Died in Milledgeville, on Thursday morning, 19th ult., aged 33 years, MRS. MARY A. SNEAD, wife of JOHN W.W. SNEAD.

Died in St. Louis, Mo., on the 15th inst., of Consumption, JOSIAH H. OBEAR, aged 43 years, a native of Salem, Mass., and at one time a resident of this city (long notice copied from the St. Louis Republican of 16th ult).

Jan. 9, 1861

RALPH FARNHAM, the last survivor of the battle of Bunker Hill, died while on a visit at Great Falls, New Hampshire, on the 26th ult., aged 104 years 5 months and 19 days...

Died in Sumter county, on the 1st instant, of Pneumonia, MRS. MARY H. KITCHENS, aged 48 years 2 months - wife of BOAZ KITCHENS, late of Jones county.

Jan. 16, 1861

Long obituary notice on HON. CHARLES J. McDONALD, Ex-Governor of Georiga (not copied - in standard biographical sources).

We regret to learn says the Telegraph that the HON. JOHN T. DUNCAN, late Senator from Chattahoochee, died last week at his residence after a very short illness.

Died January 1, at half-past 7PM, MRS. MARY HOLT, wife of MR. ASA HOLT, of Macon, Ga. She was in her 68th year, and the 44th year of her married life (with long eulogy).

Jan. 23, 1861

HON. CHAS. MURPHY died at his residence in DeKalb county, on Tuesday 15th inst., a most worthy citizen; for number of years was a member of the Georgia Legislature; also for two years a member of Congress from the 4th District; at time of death was an elected member of the Georgia Convention (Atlanta Intelligencer).

Jan. 30, 1861

Fatal affray. We copy from the Daily Telegraph of the 28th inst... There has been some difficulty existing between the parties for some time, and accidentally meeting at Byington's Hotel, MR. JOHNSON accosted CAPT. WIMBERLY in an insulting manner, whereupon the latter unarmed, the affair was adjusted, apparently to the satisfaction of the parties concerned. Afterwards meeting at the bar-room of King & Walker, Johnson drew a Derringer pistol and snapped it twice, the third time it fired...Mr. Johnson died about ten minutes after being shot.

The Sumter Republican relates the death of GRIFFIN SMITH, ESQ., formerly of Starkville, but late a resident of Smithville. He died suddenly in his chair, at the Hotel at Milledgeville, on the 23rd instant, and his remains have been accompanied to this city, by his son-in-law, the HON. W.A. HAWKINS, for interment.

Feb. 6, 1861

JOSEPH FELT, an old and respected citizen of Savannah, says the Republican of Friday, and well-known as a Justice of the Peace, died yesterday morning. He was a native of Wrentham, Massachusetts, and had resided in this city for 46 years.

Died in this city, on Monday last, after a brief illness, MISS KITTY TOOKE, daughter of MR. JOSEPH TOOKE, of Houston County.

Feb. 13, 1861

Died at the residence of Rev. Jno. W. Burke, in this city, on Monday the 4th inst., at 8AM, MISS KITTIE TOOKE, the daughter of JOSEPH TOOKE, ESQ., of Hayneville, Houston county, Ga. At the time of her death was a member of the Senior Class of Wesleyan Female College (with eulogy).

Feb. 20, 1861

MR. WILLIAM DANIEL of Jones county died very suddenly on Thursday last, at the residence of his mother, MRS. SINGLETON, some eight miles from Clinton. He was in bad health and said he would go out to the family buring ground and select a spot for his grave. He had scarcely left the ground he had marked out for that purpose before he fell and expired.

REV. WHITMAN C. HILL, a venerable member of the Georgia Methodist Conference, died near Fort Valley, on the 9th instant, of dropsy of the heart.

REV. NOBLE DeVOTIE, of this city, was drowned at Fort Morgan on the evening of the 12th inst. He was Pastor of the Selma Company stationed at that point. (Times).

Died suddenly near Villula, Russell county, Ala., on the night of the 7th inst., THACKER ADOLPHUS, an interesting and promising child, aged about 8 years, eldest son of JOHN and JULIA D. THWEATT.

Feb. 27, 1861

Died at his residence in Monroe county, on the 13th inst. COL. OWEN J. WILLIS, in the 54th year of his age.

Mar. 6, 1861

MRS. BURCH died recently in the town of Junius, New York, aged 112 years. She was married 90 years.

One of the oldest and most respectable citizens of Thomas County, THOMAS G. MITCHELL, says the Enterprise, died on the 22d inst., at the age of 67 years. He had been an invalid for several years, and only recently returned from Tennessee, where he had been in hope of improving his health. Mr. Mitchell lived a Universalist to within a few days of his death when he was comverted to the orthodox faith, and to the great joy of his family renounced Universalism and embraced true Christianity. A few hours after his death he was followed to the grave by an elder sister, MRS. ANN BLACKSHEAR.

COL. WILLIAM H. REYNOLDS, another of our most valuable citizens, died on Monday morning, the 25th inst., at his residence near Duncanville; formerly resided in this city.

Tribute of respect headed Christ Church, Macon, Ga. and dated January 25, 1861 - on death of REV. SENECA G. BRAGG, who died at Kingston, New York on Monday the 21st inst., in his 68th year; was the first pastor of Christ Church in Macon, Georgia (with long eulogy).

Mar. 27, 1861

Died in Charleston on Tuesday the 5th of March 1861, ADIE E., wife of JAMES A. HALL, and daughter of DR. THOS. F. GREEN, of Milledgeville, aged 29 years (with short eulogy).

Apr. 3, 1861

Died in this city on the 25th inst., DR. DAVID JAMISON, aged 70 years. Was born in Greene county, and served in the War of 1812, as a soldier and Assistant Surgeon. Commenced practice and resided many years in Twiggs and Houston counties before his removal to this city.

Apr. 10, 1861

COMMODORE ROBERT B. CUNNINGHAM, of the U.S. Navy, died at San Francisco on the 13th ult. Was a native of Virginia and had an extensive family connection in the vicinity of Petersburg.

LEMUEL SHAW, late Chief Justice of Massachusetts, died at his residence in Boston on Saturday. He fell dead while conversing, being in the act of dressing himself in his room.

On Thursday last, after a protracted and painful illness, DR. COLLINS died at his residence in this city. He was a native of North Carolina, and came to this State in his early years. He resided first in Washington county, studied the medical profession in Philadelphia, commenced practice in Twiggs, and removed to this city soon after its organization.

We regret to observe, by the Madison Visitor that REV. M.H. HEBBARD, of the Georgia Conference, and well known to many of our citizens, died in Morgan county, on the 13th ult.

The telegraph announces the death of Associate Justice McLEAN, of the U.S. Supreme Court, which occurred at Cincinnati, Thursday morning last. Was appointed to the Supreme Bench by General Jackson in March 1829. (Sav. Republican).

MR. SCOTT, overseer of G.A. Croom, Esq., on Lake Jackson, Fla., was shot dead by a runaway negro belonging to Mr. C., on Sunday last, says the Floridian of Saturday; while in the effort by Mr. S. to capture him.

Obituary. MRS. MARY A. DUPONT, daughter of the late COL. R.A.L. and MRS. E.A. ATKINSON, of Macon, Ga., was born in Louisville, Ga., April 30th, 1836. She was united in marriage to her now disconsolate husband, JOSEPH H. DUPONT, ESQ., March 16th, 1858, and died near Quincy, Fla, March 24th, 1861, after an illness of four years (with eulogy). (headed Quincy, Fla. March 28th, 1861).

Died in Milledgeville, the 28th ult., CAPT. ANTHONY NEWSOM, about 85 years of age. He was perhaps the oldest citizen of the city.

Apr. 17, 1861

Detailed obituary of the distingushed Statesman and Jurist JOHN McLEAN as taken from the Cincinnati (not copied - in standard biographical sources).

Apr. 24, 1861

We are sincerely grieved to record the death, on Monday night last, of MRS. CHURCH, the wife of REV. DR. CHURCH, Ex-President of Franklin College. (Athens Banner).

May 1, 1861

Death of CAPT. McCONNELL. The Mobile Register of Sunday chronicles the death of this officer, which occurred at the residence of Major Hessee yesterday. The deceased was an accomplished officer and gentleman. He was formerly of the US Army, and resigned and became the Commandant of the Georgia Military Institute. At the time of his death he was a Quartermaster in the Confederate service. His funeral takes place at ten o'clock this morning, from the residence of Major Hessee. The Mobile Cadets will form a military escort.

Died suddenly on the morning of April 12th, 1861, in Talladega, Ala., MRS. MARY ANN HARRIS, wife of DR. JOHN L. HARRIS, and daughter of G.A. and HARRIET PEASE.

Died in this city, 24th ult., MRS. JULIA ANN, wife of MR. J. JOSEPH HODGES, aged 44 years. Her remains were taken to Savannah for interment.

Died at his residence near Montpelier, on 18th of April, DR. E.H. JACKSON, with Gastro-Enterritis. Was 39 years old and leaves a wife and four children.

May 8, 1861

Died April 10th, in Meriwether county, at the residence of her father, JORDAN REES, ESQ., MRS. ELIZA J. MARTIN, wife of the REV. C.P.B. MARTIN, of Montpelier. (A more extended notice will be given.)

Died at her residence in Jackson Parish, La., MRS. MARTHA HARGROVE, consort of A.H.L. HARGROVE, and daughter of MR. ELIJAH BUTTS, of Dooly county, Ga.

May 15, 1861

HON. CHARLES H. POND, late Lieut.-Governor, and part of his official term, Governor of this State, died at his residence in Milford, on Monday the 28th inst. His age was about 80. He was the son of CAPT. CHARLES POND, an intrepid and patriotic veteran of the war that "tried men's souls." Was educated at Yale College and graduated in the class of 1802. (New Haven Register).

REV. THOMAS DOUGHERTY died in Memphis on Friday last. His remains reached this city on Sunday evening, and were met at the depot and taken in charge by the Masonic fraternity, and buried in Rose Hill Cemetery. At the time of his death he held a responsible position on one of the Memphis railroads.

Died in Houston co., Ga., May 6th, 1861, MRS. CATHERINE H. BRYAN, relict of the late JAMES A. BRYAN, in the 58th year of her age.

Died on the 3d inst., at his plantation near Montezuma, Macon co., MR. REUBEN WRIGHT, a well known citizen of Monroe. He died very suddenly of Paralysis.

Died in Laurensville, on the 3d inst., GEN. L.A. JERNIGAN, an old and much respected citizen, and for 28 years Clerk of the Superior Court of Washington County.

Died at Drayton, Dooly county, on the 10th inst., DR. ANDREW W. DENNY, aged about 30 years. His remains were brought to this city and interred in Rose Hill Cemetery, by Macon Lodge No. 5, with the usual Masonic ceremonies.

Died in this city, May 13th, NINA CLOPTON, youngest daughter of MR. and MRS. J.L. SAULSBURY, aged 14 months.

May 15, 1861

Died in New Orleans, May 9th, MRS. FANNY M. BOZEMAN, wife of DR. NATHAN BOZEMAN, and daughter of MRS. B.B. LAMAR, of Vineville.

Died on the morning of the 5th of May, 1861, MR. ANDERSON G. KILLINGSWORTH, aged 50 years. He was long a citizen of Macon, and well known as an honest man a devoted and consistant Christian.

May 22, 1861

A correspondent of the Richmond Dispatch, under date of Portsmouth, Va., 14th inst., says: Another sad accident, resulting in the death of an estimable officer occurred on Sunday night, near norfolk. LIEUT. RICHARD HENRY STORRS, of the Third Alabama Regiment, was returning to camp from the city about 9 PM. He was hailed by the sentinel, whose gun was accidentally discharged, and in an hour or so the victim was a corpse. He was from Wetumka, Alabama.

The same letter has the following: HENRY C. SMITH, of the Macon County Volunteers (Ga.) died at the Ocean House, and was buried on Sunday morning. Our Home Guards and a large number of citizens attended the remains to their last resting place.

On Tuesday morning last, says the Educational Journal, DR. J.M. PARSONS, for a number of years a resident of this county, died of paralysis. He leaves a wife and several children.

Also, a few days ago, FATHER CHIPMAN, an aged and estimable man, a useful Minister of the Gospel, was taken from us by the same disease. He was about 90 years old, and has been preaching more than forty years. MRS. JUDGE CABANISS has lost one of the best of fathers.

We publish today, says the Corner Stone, an account of an accident resulting in the death of LIEUT. NELSON, and the serious if not fatal injury of COL. MILLER GRIEVE, of Milledgeville, by the firing of a salute on passing Fort Pulaski.

Died in Twiggs county, on the 20th April, CELINA RICE, wife of DR. U.A. RICE, aged 29 years and 4 months; worthy member of the Baptist Church for several years.

Died in this city on the 17th inst., MR. JAMES C. EDWARDS, aged about 60 years. His death was occasioned by a carbuncle on the spine, which terminated fatally in a few days.

Died in this city on the 17th inst., MR. JAMES W. GRIFFIN (of the firm of Hardeman & Griffin) of a pulmonary complaint, aged about 31 years.

Tribute of respect headed Camp Macon County Volunteers, 4th Regiment Geo. Volunteers, Portsmouth, Va. May 61 - on death of YOUNG H.C. SMITH.

May 29, 1861

The New York Tribune says that COL. ELLSWORTH was shot as he was descending the stairs with the secession flag by MR. JACKSON, keeper of the Marshall House, and died almost instantly, dyeing the flag with his blood. Mr. Jackson was killed by FRANCIS B. BROMWELL.

Died in this city, on Saturday 25th inst., MISS EUGENIA A. NISBET, daughter of HON. E.A. NISBET, aged 16 years 7 months and 24 days.

Died at the residence of her son, Mr. Mark A. George, Chattahoochee county, MRS. MARY GEORGE, aged 85 years. Born in Rockingham county, N.C., and was the sister of that noble band of brothers, "the Hardens" whose prosperity is now numerous and occupying worthy and distinguished positions in society; for many years a consistent member of the Methodist church.

May 29, 1861

   Died in Macon county on the 28th inst., after a short illness,
   SLAUGHTER HILL, ESQ., aged 59 years.

June 5, 1861

   It is with regret that we record the death of H.H. PARKYN, ESQ.,
   a member of the Clinch Rifles of this city, says the Augusta
   Constitutionalist. His death was caused by the bite of an adder,
   and the sad event took place on Friday last, near Pensacola, where
   his company is now stationed.

   Montgomery, June 2 - MARK BRANTLY, a member of the Quitman Guards,
   of Forsyth, Georgia, was killed last night on the Pensacola Railroad. It is supposed that he fell from the top of the cars and
   was crushed. His body is here and will be sent home for interment.

   Died in Portsmouth, Va. on Sunday the 26th ult., WILLIAM LeCONTE,
   son of CLIFFORD and ANNA L.C. ANDERSON, of Macon, Georgia, aged
   10 months 20 days.

   Tribute of respect by Patrick Henry Lodge No. 173 Free and Accepted
   Masons, Drayton, Dooly county, Ga., May 17th, 1861 - on death of
   A.W. DENNY.

June 12, 1861

   Papers announce the death of HON. STEPHEN A. DOUGLAS.

   Private L.H. BALDWIN of the Southern Rights Guards, 4th Regiment,
   Georgia Volunteers, died at Kingsville last Saturday.

   CHARLES MALLRY, a member of the "Stephens Light Guards," from
   Greene county, Ga., died at the Augusta Hotel at half-past 6 o'clock
   yesterday morning, says the Sentinel of Thursday, from injuries
   received on the South Carolina Railroad on Monday night last...
   was a single man, and previous to his enlistment, resided near
   Union Point. He was about 24 years of age. His funeral was attended yesterday by the Clinch Rifles and a numerous delagation from
   the Augusta Fire Department. He was buried in the city cemetery.

   The Richmond Enquirer of June 3rd details fight at Fairfax Court
   House in which CAPT. JOHN Q. MARR of the Warrenton Rifles, was
   killed. Was a member of the Virginia Convention.

June 19, 1861

   The Memphis papers announce the death of MRS. OTEY, the wife of
   BISHOP OTEY, of Tennessee.

   Died in this city on the 7th inst., WALTER, infant son of MR.
   JOHN B. and MRS. JOSEPHINE LIGHTFOOT, aged 5 months 8 days.

June 26, 1861

   JAMES CAMPBELL, who was on the floating battery at Charleston
   during the bombardment of Fort Sumter, and who did effective
   service at that time, was accidentally drowned at Norfolk on the
   11th instant.

   Melancholy occurrence. On the night of the 16th inst., private
   B.H. MEYER, of the Newnan Guards, was shot by private STOKES, of
   the Quitman Guards, of Monroe, at Shaw's Pass in Virginia. Meyer
   was on guard and refused to let Stokes pass without "the word."
   Stokes loaded the gun and shot him. It is understood that he
   was tried and shot the next day.

June 26, 1861

HON. LOTT WARREN died in Albany on the 17th inst. He was in the court-house delivering a speech in a criminal case for commitment, when he was suddenly stricken and fell lifeless to the floor... was once Judge of the Superior Court and a member of Congress; a prominent and active member of the Baptist Church, of which he was a minister.

Died in this city on Wednesday morning the 19th inst., of typhoid fever, MISS MARION PRESTON ROSE, daughter of MR. SIMRI ROSE, aged 20 years 9 months. In 1859 she graduated at the Wesleyan Female College with the first honor; a member of the Baptist Church; and a most useful and effective teacher in the Sabbath School (with eulogy).

Died in this city on the 22d instant, DR. JOHN B. WILEY, in the 58th year of his age. A native of Hancock county, Ga. In early manhood he removed to Macon and commenced the practice of medicine (with short eulogy).

Died in Perry, Houston county, on the 17th inst., at the residence of Dr. Cullur, her son-in-law, MRS. REBECCA COBB, wife of the HON. HOWELL COBB, of that county.

July 3, 1861

Died after a protracted illness, at Scottsboro, near Milledgeville, on the 18th ult., in the 81st year of his age, COL. FARISH CARTER, one of our oldest citizens. Was, we believe, a native of South Carolina, but had been for the last fifty years a resident of Baldwin county, Ga.

Died in this city on the 26th ult., CLIFFORD WILLIS, only child of NATHAN M. and CATHERINE E. BRAY, of Eufaula, Ala.

July 10, 1861

A telegraphic dispatch to the Richmond Dispatch, dated Raleigh, July 8, announces the death of JOHN W. ELLIS, Governor of North Carolina, at Red Sulphur Springs, Virginia, on Sunday, 7th inst.

Died at the Indian Springs on the 5th inst., MR. JAMES WAKEMAN, aged 57 years; for many years a resident of this city; member of the Presbyterian Church.

Died in Macon county, Ga. on 18th of June, 1861, SARAH AMME, infant daughter of THOMAS W. and C. AMANDA SUTTON, aged 1 year 7 months 9 days. Also, near the same place, only a few days after, on the 23rd, MARY FRANCIS, daughter of S.L. and P.M. TURNER, aged 7 years 9 months. (their Grand Pa)

We regret to learn by telegraph of the death yesterday morning, near Pensacola, of HON. JAMES ABERCROMBIE. A native of Hancock county, Ga., and was at the time of his death 60 years of age. He resided in Russell county, Ala. for many years, and twice represented his District in the US Congress. For the last two years he has resided near Pensacola. We learn that his remains will be received in this city for interment today. (Col. Times, 3d inst.)

Tribute of respect by the Macon Baptist Sunday School - on the death of MISS MARION P. ROSE.

July 17, 1861

Death of COLONEL CHARLES D. DREUX, of the Louisiana Cadets, in an encounter with a body of Federalists near Newport News...a member of one of the oldest Creole families in New Orleans; as a lawyer he had acquired a distinguished position at the New Orleans bar; was one of the finest popular orators of the famous French school

(July 17, cont'd.) - of Louisiana; a graduate of Georgetown College, and had been a prominent member of the Louisiana Legislature; had not yet reached his thirtieth birthday; leaves a wife and one child. (Richmond Whig).

MR. HOLLAND, of Chattooga county, was brutally murdered a few evenings since by her negro woman and thrown in the well. The negro has confessed the crime, and is now in the Summerville jail. Mrs. H. was about 70 years of age. Her friends arrived here on Saturday with her remains, on their way to some point down the country. (Rome Courier, 8th)

WILLIAM A. ROSS died at Baily's Springs, Ala., whither he had gone for his health. His remains reached this city on last Wednesday evening, and were deposited in Rose Hill Cemetery on Thursday morning; an active and useful member of the Methodist Church. (with eulogy).

The Athens Banner, of Wednesday last, reports the unexpected death of MRS. P.H. MELL, on Saturday.

Unfortunate rencountre. The Macon Telegraph of the 13th inst. reports a difference arose between THEODORICK L. MONTFORT, ESQ., and DR. J.E. BARTLETT, of Oglethorpe...a recontre took place in which Bartlett was supposed to be mortally, and Montfort severely wounded.

Charleston, July 14 - Ex-GOVERNOR ADAMS, of this State, died at his residence near Columbia, last night.

The Jacksonville (Ala) Republican of the 4th, learns that on Thursday previous, an affray occurred near the steam sawmill in that county, between four persons named STEADMAN, father and three sons on one side, and GREEN SKELTON, baliff, Mayfield, and one or two others, whom he had summoned to his aid in arresting the Steadmans, in which JOHN STEADMAN was shot dead, one of his brothers mortally wounded, and Skelton shot in the knee and arm. There had been some fighting between the Steadmans and a Mr. White, and the affray occurred in resisting the arrest of the Steadmans.

Died in Savannah on the 12th inst., MR. FRANCIS H. WELMAN, aged about 80 years. A native of Bermuda, had resided in Savannah for 63 years, and been one of its most prominent business men. In early life he was a Midshipman in the English navy - a member of the Chatham Artillery forty-nine years, and for many years the Swedish and Norwegian Consul, and also held the agency of "Lloyds," London.

Died at Meridian Depot, on the Mobile and Mississippi Railroad, COL. SHADRACH SLAUGHTER, formerly of Clinton, Ga., and for many years a resident of New Orleans.

Died in this city, of apoplexy, on the 11th inst., DR. JOHN H. ELLIS, a native of New Jersey, and well known in this city as a Druggist, for about thirty years.

Died at the Indian Springs on the 10th inst., MR. JONATHAN PARISH, of Clinton, Jones county. He died very suddenly, apparently from the infirmities and debilites of age. He was probably the oldest resident of Jones county, and about 80 years of age.

July 24, 1861

Tribute of respect headed Camp Gwynn, Headquarters, 3d Regiment Georgia Volunteers, Portsmouth, Va., July 17th, 1861 - on the death of Private WILEY D. CLARK who died this evening at 4 o'clock.

July 31, 1861

Killed and wounded of the 7th Georgia Regiment. Members of Coweta and District Guards killed: C.N. BROWN, MARCUS A. NORTH, GEO. B. CARMICHAEL. Atlanta Confederate Volunteers killed: WM. M. BALLARD, WM. E. SIMPSON, JOHN E. WOODRUFF, JOHN F. WHITE, WM. TODD, WM. H. WHITAKER. Members of Heard Volunteers killed: LIEUT. E.F. GLOVER, A.J. MILIRONS. Members of Roswell Guards killed: THOMAS KIRK, JAMES PADDOCK, B.F. SMITH. Members of Davis Infantry killed: JOHN A. PUCKETT, WM. A. BAGWELL.

Obituary of GEN. BARNARD E. BEE as taken from the Charleston Mercury. Was about 35 years of age; leaves a widow and infant son; entered West Point a cadet in 1841; was made Brevet Second Lieutenant, 3d Infantry, in 1845; during the Mexican War served with marked distinction, winning two brevets before the close of the war - that of First Lieut., "for gallant and meritorious conduct in the battle of Cerro Gordo, on the 18th April, 1847," in which he was wounded; that of Captain, in the storming of Chepultepec, on the 13th of September, 1847; since 1848 he has served as Adjutant, and rose to a full First Lieutenancy March 1851...President Davis appointed him Brigadier General in the Provisional Army.

Death of LIEUT. COL. BENJAMIN J. JOHNSON, the second in command of the Hampton Legion. A native of Beaufort, S.C. and about 45 years of age at his death. His brothers reside in this State - two of whom are clergymen of the Episcopal church - one, the Rev. Rich'd Johnson, being the Chaplain of Hampton's Legion. Col. Johnson was educated at Williamsburgh, Virginia, and commenced life as a planter; but afterwards studied law with Col. DeTreviole, and came to the bar of Beaufort, where he practiced a few years. During his residence in Beaufort he commanded the 12th Regiment of Indantry. In 1837 was elected a member of the House of Representatives from St. Helena Parish, where he served many years, until he was transferred to the Senate by the same constituency. Served in the Senate for two terms, and until his removal to Christ Church Parish, about three years ago. Here was elected a member of the House of Representatives and continued a member to his death.

Death of GEN. ROBERT SELDEN GARNETT. Entered West Point Academy as a Cedet from Virginia in September 1836. Graduated in 1841 and received appointment of Brevet 2d Lieutenant, 4th Artillery. In July 1843 was detailed as instructor of infantry tactics at West Point, and continued there until October 1844, when he was attached to Gen. Wool's staff in capacity of Aid-de-camp. Distinguished himself in the Mexican War at the battles of Palo Alto and Resaca de la Palma. In August 1846 was made 1st Lieutenant, and called by General Taylor to his personal staff, on which he served until January 1849. For service at Monterey, Mexico, he was breveted Captain; and for service at Buena Vista was breveted Major. Since the close of the Mexican War, he has been attached to the 7th Infantry US Army. Upon the dissolution of the Union he resigned his commission and joined his fortunes with those of his native States. Was appointed Brigadier General by President Davis and placed in command of one of the corps d'armees sent to crush the Abolition traitors of the Panhandle. He died in the performance of his duty, the first general officer to fall in the cause of southern Independence.

Death of THOS. FRANCIS MEAGHER. The Richmond Dispatch says this notorious individual was killed at Manassas on the 21st inst.

Loss of the Macon Guards. Killed: LEONIDAS LAMAR, son of JUDGE H.G. LAMAR, of this city; WALTER C. ALLEN, of Houston; and WM. W. JONES. We learne that the remains of Leonidas Lamar will be interred in Richmond, where they will remain until next winter, before they are brought to this city.

Aug. 7, 1861

L.W.S. of the Mercury says that SENATOR FOSTER of Connecticut was one of the killed at Manassas. He had come over to see the fight and celebrate a victory, but in the precipitation of the flight his carriage was broken to pieces, himself shot, and Ely, his companion, taken prisoner.

WM. GAREY, of the Macon Guards was severely wounded in the head and taken prisoner - afterwards fell in the hands of the Confederates and has since died of the wound. A letter from Mr. Manard, of that company, has just been received, stating the facts, accompanied with his watch, which was sent to his brother, F.P. Garey.

Savannah Republican of the 29th reports obsequies of GENERAL BARTOW. Was buried by the side of his father. Burial service was read by Bishop Elliott, the military firing three vollies in honor of their departed friend and fellow-soldier.

Casualties in the Eighth Georgia Regiment. Killed: COL. F.S. BARTOW, Adjutant JOHN L. BRANCH. Members of Rome Light Guards killed: J.B. CLARK, J.T. DUNCAN, D.C. HARGROVE, C.B. NORTON, G.T. STOVALL. Members of the Oglethorpe Light Infantry killed: W.H. CRANE, G.M. BUTLER, J.A. FERRELL, B. MOREL, THOS. PURSE, JR. Members of the Macon Guards killed: W. ALLEN, LEONIDAS LAMAR, WM. M. JONES. Members of Echols Guards (from Meriwether) killed: CAPTAIN C.W. HOWARD, W.H.C. GADBY. Members of the Miller Rifles (from Floyd) killed: FRANK LATHROP, (Color Guard,) T.S. MOBLEY, L. YARBOROUGH. Members of the Atlanta Grays killed: SERGEANT J.S. GEORGE, A.M. ORR, R.B. HAMILTON. Members of the Pulaski Volunteers killed: J.W. CARUTHERS, A. GOODSON, JOHN LOWRY, J.A. SCARBOROUGH. Members of the Floyd Infantry killed: F. MADREY, WM. CHASTAIN, A HARSHAW, A. WARNOCK, SERGEANT G.G. MARTIN. Members of the Stephens Light Guards killed (from Greene): AUG. DANIEL, JAS. PALMORE, T.S. HOWELL, JAS. HARPER, GEO. HEAD.

A son of COLONEL GARTRELL, of one of the Georgia Regiments, who was severely wounded in the late battle, died at the residence of Rice W. Payne, Esq., in Warrenton, Va., on Sunday last, and was buried with military honors. He was but 17 years of age.

Louisville, Aug. 3 - GENERAL FLOURNOY, of Arkansas, a Confederate officer, died in this city today.

Died in Milledgeville on the Morning of the 22d inst., after a short but distressing sickness, WM. P. BOUGHTON, only child of S.N. BOUGHTON, of the Federal Union, in the 19th year of his age.

Died at the Indian Springs on the 25th ult., MRS. NANCY PARRISH, relict of CAPT. PARRISH, recently deceased. Her remains were brought to Clinton and deposited by the side of her husband. These old people left no children.

Died in Jones county on the 30th ult., WILLIAM REYNOLDS, aged over 70 years.

Died in Yorktown, Va., on the morning of the 19th ult., MR. WM. HAMPTON, son of JACOB HAMPTON, of Houston county, Ga., and a member of the Beauregard Volunteers, 6th Ga. Regiment. Leaves bereaved parents.

Aug. 14, 1861

WILLIAM NEAL, of Worth, while in conversation with some friends at McLellan's Mills, on Sunday morning last, fell suddenly dead. He is probably a native of Washington City as he has relatives there. He served in the Florida War, and was a Lieutenant in the Mexican war. He was about 60 years of age.

Aug. 14, 1861

MR. THOMAS HARDEMAN, SEN., an old and highly esteemed citizen, died at his residence in Vineville, on Sunday morning last. Had suffered severly from rheumatism for several years...funeral took place at the Methodist Church on Monday morning. Mr. H. was in the 65th year of his age.

On Saturday last two persons were killed on our Railroads in this city, at nearly the same moment. One of them was a young man from the upper part of Twiggs county, named ROWELL BATES...the other one killed was a lad, about 12 years, named WM. FERRELL...(story gives details of the accident).

LIEUT. JOHN R. FELDER, of the Southern Rights Guards, Houston county, died of Typhoid fever, in camp at Monterey. His remains passed through this city on Friday last, accompanied by the sorrowing father of the deceased.

Died in Albany on the 10th inst., MRS. AMANDA HOBBS, wife of RICHARD HOBBS, ESQ. and daughter of the late R.K. HINES, ESQ. She was brought to this city and interred in Rose Hill Cemetery on the 12th inst.

Departed this life on the first day of July last, JOSEPH KEY, at his residence in Butts county, in the 72d year of his age.

Aug. 21, 1861

A.J. BOGGESS, Surveyor General of the State, died in Richmond on the 15th, of the Typhoid Fever. He was a citizen of Carroll county.

COL. ROLAND BIVINS died at his residence in this county on Saturday last, of bilious colic, after a few days illness. His age was 60 years.

Railroad accident. On Thursday last, the train which left Columbus for this city was thrown from the track some sixteen miles from the former place, near Odom's...MR. MOORE, of the Columbus Volunteers was killed...

Tribute of respect headed Sixth Regiment Georgia Volunteers, Yorktown, Va., Aug. 9th, 1861 - the Twiggs Guards give a memorial to SERGEANT J.H. BUSH. He leaves a bereaved mother and sisters.

Aug. 28, 1861

AHAZ J. BOGGESS, ESQ., Surveyor General of Georgia, died at Richmond, Virginia, on 15th inst., of Typhoid Fever. Was a native of Tennessee, but removed early in life to Carroll county, Georgia, from whence he volunteered in the Florida War of 1836, and served in the Commissary Department under the late General Nelson. He represented Carroll in both branches of the Legislature. Was elected Surveyor General in 1859. When the present war began, he joined the "Iverson Invincibles", Capt. Burke, and took part in the battle of Manassas, where his face was grazed by a cannon ball, which knocked him down. Fever ensued which terminated fatally, in the 45th year of his age. A wife and six children survive. (So. Rec)

Sep. 4, 1861

Death of GEORGE T. STOVALL at the battle of Manassas; member of the Methodist Church; a private in the Rome Light Guards; Superintendent of the Sabbath School (with long eulogy).

GENERAL LYON, recently killed in Missouri, was born at Ashford, Connecticut. Was graduated at West Point Academy in 1841. Served in all the United States wars afterwards, and was breveted for gallant service in the battle of Mexico.

Sep. 4, 1861

HON. H.G. LAMAR died on Friday evening at his residence in Vineville; member of the Methodist Church (with eulogy).

Early on Saturday morning, MR. JAMES REA, perhaps the very oldest citizen of Macon, died at his room in the Lanier House. He died in the 83d year of his age, of general debility.

OSWELL B. EVE, who died on the 21st ult. in Virginia, near Manassas, says the Louisville Gazette, formerly lived in this county. His father owned at one time the mill now known as Clarke's Mill. Was a member of the Miller Rifles, of Rome Ga.; leaves a wife and several children.

CAPT. W.C. CLEVELAND, JR., of the Crawford Grays, son of an old and venerable friend, REV. W.C. CLEVELAND, recently died at Yorktown, Va.

Died at his father's residence near Jeffersonville, Twiggs county, Ga., on the 21st ult., JOSEPH J. SANDIFORD, aged 19 years 3 months 12 days. Was a volunteer of the Twiggs Guards, under Capt. Barclay of the 6th Georgia Regiment in Virginia.

Sep. 11, 1861

SERGEANT THOMAS M. NEWTON, of the "Sparks Guards," was buried on yesterday in Rose Hill Cemetery. Detachments of the Jackson Artillery Reserve, Macon Volunteers, and Fire Company No. 3, participated in the military honors of the occasion. Funeral service was preached by Rev. Dr. Mann. (Telegraph of 5th inst.).

MR. JOHN SCOTT, a member of the Bibb Greys, died at Camp Stephens, near Griffin, on Sunday last. His remains reached this city and were interred on Monday.

Grieved to learn of the death of HON. HENRY C. LAMAR, Judge of the Macon Circuit. Died at Macon on the 30th ult., aged about 65. Two sons survive. Was aid to Gov. Troup in 1825 when Gen. Lafayette visited Georgia. In 1829 he was elected a Representative in Congress to fill a vacancy declared by Gov. Forsyth, in the case of Mr. Gilmer, and was subsequently reelected.

A little son of MR. JOHN DONOHOE of this city was so seriously injured by the falling of a plank upon him on Sunday last, that he survived but a few hours. His age was about five years.

Tribute of respect by Millwood Lodge, No. 198, F.A.M. on the death of MARTIN KENDRICK who died near Staunton, Va. Aug. 6, 1861, aged 39 years 9 months; was made a member of this lodge Nov. 27, 1858.

Sep. 18, 1861

Two more of the Jefferson Guards have been consigned to their last earthly resting place, says the Louisville Gazette, viz. MR. _____ SIMMONS and MR. R. TARVER.

Died in Marion, Twiggs county, on the evening of the 18th inst., of Pulmonary Consumption, MR. JAMES LOYLESS EVANS, age 22 years 9 months 18 days; was the only son of a widowed mother (with eulogy).

Within the past week we have received the sad tidings of the death of JOHN LAIDLER, MOSES DANIEL, W.N. BOWEN, and ISAAC RAINS, members of the Pulaski Volunteers. Messrs. Laidler and Daniel were formerly residents of our immediate community...all of the deceased were engaged in the battle of Manassas. The remains of Mr. Laidler arrived here on Sunday last, and on Monday were conveyed to Houston county for interment. The others repose in the soil of Virginia. (Hawkinsville Times)

Sep. 18, 1861

Died in this city on Friday last, at two o'clock PM, ROBERT N. BAILEY, about 26 years old, son of the late JOHN BAILEY of this county.

Died at her residence in Houston county, on Tuesday the 10th inst., of Pulmonary Consumption, MRS. NANCY BRYAN, widow of the late BENJ. BRYAN, late of Vineville, in the 47th year of her age.

Died at the camp of the 18th Georgia Regiment, Richmond, Virginia, of congestion of the brain, on the 29th of August, MR. JOHN H. PEACOCK, of the Dooly Light Infantry, aged 20 years 25 days.

SERGEANT T.B. ELLIS of the Crawford Greys, 6th Georgia Regiment, died at the residence of his father-in-law, near Knoxville, Crawford county, on the morning of the 28th August, in the 21st year of his age.

Died at Green Brier River, in the state of Va., on the 28th day of August, MR. A.J. BUTLER, of Dooly county, in the 22d year of his age, a volunteer in the Davis Guards, 12th Georgia Regiment. His disease was the measles; leaves a mother and several brothers and sisters.

Died in this city at the residence of his father, on the morning of the 14th inst., LEROY HOLT, aged 23 years 28 days.

Sep. 25, 1861

COL. JOHN A. WASHINGTON. News from General Lee's camps, says the Richmond Dispatch, confirm the Federal report of the death of this officer, who was an aid to Gen. L. He was shot near the Fort of Cheat Mountain. Col. W. was the owner of Mount Vernon prior to the sale to the M.V. Association.

COL. OWEN CLINTON POPE, an old and much respected citizen of this county, says the Sandersville Georgian, died of paralysis at his residence near Sandersville, on Tuesday the 10th inst. He was born in Roberson County, North Carolina, and served his time of seven years at the printing business in Fayetteville. He removed to this county in 1831. For more than thirty years has been connected with the Southern Recorder in various capacities. Leaves a large family.

Augusta Sentinel of Thursday announces the death of WM. D'ANTIGNAC, at Bailey's Springs, Ala. At time of his death he was President of the Insurance & Banking Company.

Camp Bartow, Quarters of the Jones Volunteers, Sep. 8th, 1861 - announces the deaths of JAMES SEABORN, FRANKOIN WELLS, WILLIAM T. SMITH and WILLIAM G. GIBSON.

JAMES HAMILTON, ESQ., formerly of this city, says the Columbus Enquirer, but for two or three years past a citizen of Memphis, Tenn., was killed in the late Federal attack upon Columbus, Ky.; was a lawyer of ability and promise.

Camp at Edray, Virginia, 14th Regt. Ga. Volunteers, Sep. 8th, 1861 - announce death of LIEUT. ROBERT I. WEEKS.

Died on Sunday the 1st inst., HENRY CLAY SHROPSHIRE, of typhoid diarrhea, aged about 30 years. Mr. S. was a member of Capt. Wallace Jordan's company from Jasper county, Georgia.
(Lynchburg Virginian)

Oct. 2, 1861

Another military train thrown through a bridge - Cincinnati, Sept. 18. Last night a train containing a portion of Colonel Torchen's Nineteenth Illinois Regiment, while passing the bridge near Huron,

(Oct. 2, cont'd) - Indiana, fell through into the river...CAPTAIN HOWARD, of Company I, was killed...

EDWARD F. CAMPBELL, an old and highly esteemed citizen of Augusta, died at the Georgia Railroad Bank Friday morning, in a fit of apoplexy.

Died near Cheat Mountain, Virginia, MR. WM. JOHNSON, a member of the Quitman Guards, of Monroe County.

Died at Albany on the 12th inst., of congestive fever, MR. ROBERT LUNDY, aged 63 years.

Died in this city on the 27th September, MRS. MARY SEYMOUR, aged 66 years.

Oct. 9, 1861

LIEUT. J.M. STUBBS bravely fell at his post at the battle of Green Briar River, Virginia on the 3d inst...one of our estimable young men; had but recently entered upon the legal profession; but a few months ago married the daughter of DR. N. TUCKER of Laurens.

CAPT. ISAAC S. VINCENT, of the Clark County Rifles, died suddenly in Portsmouth, Virginia, on the 27th ult. of apoplexy.

Richmond, Va., 5th...B.B. Lewis: COL. MATT WARD, of Texas, died this morning at Yarborough's Hotel, Raleigh, N.C.

Staunton, Va., via Richmond, 7th...Georgians killed: DAVID BROWN, Gate City Guards; RICHARD COLEMAN, of the Marion Guards.

LAURA JANE, only child of B.C. ALFRIEND of White Plains, Ga., was born 31st Aug. 1838 and died Sept. 26th, 1861. She and other young ladies of the village were giving a concert and during the entertainment her dress came into contact with a candle...she lived only five days...was converted at Liberty Camp Ground of Greene county, some 12 or 13 years ago, very soon became a member of the M.E. Church.

Oct. 16, 1861

We are gratified to learn that LIEUT. STUBBS, whose death was announced last week, is alive, and at last accounts, was well.

LIEUT. L.A. NELMS - the fall of this gallant young Georgian, says the Savannah Republican, in the battle of Santa Rosa Island - a native of Elbert county, but after admission to the Bar, settled in Warrenton; was a delegate to the Charleston Democratic Convention...

Died in Macon county, Sept. 26th, 1861, MR. JAMES DRAWHORN, son of THOMAS DRAWHORN, aged 26 years 8 months 4 days. Enlisted in the Southern Confederacy under Capt. Griffin of the Butler Van Guards, and was stationed at Yorktown...he was attacked with measles first, and then came fever, which resulted in his death; he lay sick in Yorktown nine weeks after which time he came helpless as an infant, and told his parents he had come home to die...

Oct. 23, 1861

Among the slain at Pensacola appears the name of MR. J.E. HOLMES, a printer and member of Atlanta Typographical Union... (Atlanta Confederacy)

A father in Israel has fallen. The Columbus Corner Stone says: JOHN BETHUNE, the father of the Editor of this paper, died on Friday last, in the 92d year of his age...native of Scotland, but was brought to this country when quite an infant, residing first in North Carolina, and afterwards for many years in Georgia.

Oct. 23, 1861

Died in Baker county on the 8th inst., at the residence of her son, REUBEN S. WILLIAMS, (very suddenly) MRS. ANN R. WILLIAMS, aged 84 years - widow of the late JOHN WILLIAMS, formerly a resident of Milledgeville. She was brought to this city and interred in Rose Hill Cemetery on the 10th inst.

Died at Yorktown, Va., October 13th, 1861, ANSON McCOLLUM SPERRY, of the Beauregard Volunteers, 6th Georgia Regiment, in the 19th year of his age, and son of JNO. A. and MARY B. SPERRY, of Marshallville, Ga.

Oct. 30, 1861

MEADE LeSEUR, SEN., died at his residence in Colaparchee, Monroe county, Ga., 45 minutes after 5 o'clock, on the evening of the 12th inst., in the 68th year of his age. (Educational Journal)

Died in this city on the 23d inst. of consumption, DR. ALFRED PIERCE, aged about 38 years - a native of Winchester, N.H., but for several years a resident of this city. He was buried on the 24th inst. in the Masonic burial lot in Rose Hill Cemetery by Macon Lodge No. 5, of which he was a worthy member.

Nov. 6, 1861

HON. W.A. LAKE, lately killed in a duel in Arkansas, had for more than twenty-five years been a member of Christ Church, Episcopalian, in Vicksburg...

Died in our city this morning of fever, MRS. JANE LEWIS, companion of MR. CURTIS LEWIS. (Griffin paper)

Melancholy accident. We learn from Cumberland Gap, that N.P. JACKSON, son of Quartermaster GENERAL A.E. JACKSON, accidentally shot himself through the heart a few nights since. Mr. Jackson, who was acting as Assistant Quartermaster at Comberland Ford, had gone to bed with a pistol upon his person, which by some unexplained accident, during the night, became discharged, the ball piercing his heart and producing instant death. The deceased was a lawyer by profession, and resided at Jonesboro, Washington county; leaves a wife and several children. (Knoxville Register, 26th)

Nov. 13, 1861

We regret to announce the death of MRS. IVERSON, wife of HON. ALFRED IVERSO_, which occurred in this city says the Columbus Sun, on Saturday last. Her remains were conveyed to their last resting place Sunday.

Died in Dooly county on the 10th inst., WM. F. BEALLE, aged about 85 years.

Nov. 20, 1861

Fatal accident in Kentucky. A dispatch was received yesterday at the War Department, says the Richmond Dispatch of Friday, giving an account of a fatal accident from the busting of a Dahlgren gun at Columbus, Kentucky, by which two officers and seven privates were killed on the spot. The names of the officers who were victims of the sad casualty are: LIEUT. SNOWDEN, of the Confederate States Infantry, and CAPT. KEITER, of the Artillery.

Tribute of respect by Wells' Lodge No. 187, Monroe County, Oct. 26, 1861 - on the death of ENNELS McPHERSON. Leaves a widow and orphans.

Nov. 26, 1861

MR. EDWARD WARE died at his residence, says the Rome Courier of the 21st - died yesterday at his residence eight miles from this place, at a very advanced age. He had been in very bad health for several months. He was a member of the Georgia Convention in 1850, from this county.

A dispatch was received in this city yesterday, from Warrenton, Va., conveying the sad intelligence of the death of CAPT. LAFAYETTE LAMAR. Was in command of the "Lamar Confederates" attached to Col. Thomas' Regiment (15th Georgia). He was from Lincoln county, Georgia, and in the 37th year of his age. His remains are expected to pass through Augusta on Thursday next. We regret to see the above announcement in the Augusta Sentinel of the 19th inst.

Died in Clinton on the 10th inst. of Paralysis, CHAS. MACARTHY, aged 63 years and 10 months. For the past forty years he has held the offices of Clerk of the Superior and Inferior Courts and Judge of the Court of Ordinary.

Died in Montgomery, Ala. on the 18th inst., MR. E.C. ROLAND, a native of this city, and recently the editor of the "State Press." His remains were brought to this city and interred on the 20th inst.

Died on the 20th ult., at Rock Bridge, Allum Springs, Va., of Typhoid fever in the 21st year of his age, CALEB W. KEY, of the Jasper Infantry - Company C, 14th Regiment Geo. Vols., and 5th son of B.P. and TEMPERANCE KEY, of Jasper county.

Also on the 18th ult. at Warm Springs, Va., of Typhoid fever, in the 20th year of his age, PRIVATE GEORGE W. PRICE, of the Jasper Infantry - Company C, 14th Reg't Geo. Vols., son of L.M. and A.W. PRICE of Jasper county, and grandson of B.P. and TEMPERANCE KEY.

Died in the 3d Ga. Hospital, Richmond, Va. on the 15th inst., JOSEPH Y. HALL, of Meriwether co., Ga., and a member of the Jackson Blues - aged 19 years. A widowed mother, brothers, sisters and numerous friends mourn his loss.

Died on pneumonia at his residence in Americus on the 22d inst., DR. JOSEPH McDONALD, formerly of Kentucky.

Dec. 4, 1861

Tribute of respect on the death of THOMAS J. HATHORN, a Mason.

Tribute of respect headed Pleasant Ridge Lodge (Macon County, Ga.), No. 108, F.A.M. - on the death of BENJAMIN D. CHILDS. Was a Sergeant and died in the Confederate service at White Sulphur Springs, Va., Oct. 22nd, 1861 - aged 27 years 8 months 5 days.

Tribute of respect headed Pleasant Ridge Lodge No. 108 F.A.M. (Macon County, Georgia) - on the death of GEORGE M. GAINES who died in the Confederate service at White Sulphur Springs, Va. on Nov. 8th, 1861 - aged 28 years 5 months 27 days.

Died in Forsyth on the 22d inst., MR. DULANE F. PONDER, in the 44th year of his age, after a short illness of typhoid pneumonia; a Mason.

Dec. 11, 1861

WM. C. DUNSON, ESQ., late our fellow citizen, recently died of the typhoid fever in Virginia. He was a member of the Macon Guards, and wounded in the battle of Manassas. His remains were sent to La Grange for interment.

Dec. 11, 1861

DR. VAN WICKE, Surgeon to Col. Forrest's Kentucky Regiment, was killed by a Lincolnite, named Best, near Madison, Kentucky a few days since. Dr. Van W. was formerly of citizen of Huntsville, Ala.

Tribute of respect by Hunter Lodge No. 134, Marshallville, Ga. Dec. 6, 1861 - on the death of JOHN W. SHORT. He was a member of the Davis Rifles attached to the 12th Regiment Georgia Volunteers in western Virginia.

Camp Bartow, Green Brier, Va., Nov. 15, 1861 - a resolution by the Blues on the deaths of privates W. HENDERSON and H.S. BRADDY, who died at Camp Bartow of pneumonia on the 2d of November.

Died in Thomaston, Ga. on the 4th inst., MISS CORNELIA PARANELLA CUNNINGHAM, daughter of W.W. and A.S. CUNNINGHAM, aged 4 years 11 months 14 days.

Died in Macon Nov. 30th, 1861, MISS ISABELLA S. BLACKSHEAR, daughter of MRS. C.L. and the late MAJOR JAS. HAMILTON BLACKSHEAR, of Laurens county.

Dec. 18, 1861

Departed this life on the 27th of November at the residence of her mother, MRS. CAROLINA DAY - in Upson county - MISS CHARLOTTE M. DAY. She embraced religion at an early age and united herself with the Baptist Church in Milledgeville, whilst under the charge of Rev. Adiel Sherwood. (Southern Recorder and Columbus Enquirer please copy).

Died suddenly at his residence in Macon county on the 12th inst., EZEKIEL H. ADAMS, ESQ., in the 55th year of his age.

Died in Newardk, N.J. on the 22d of November, after a protracted illness, MRS. EMMALINE H., wife of J.C. THORNTON, of Macon, Ga.

Dec. 25, 1861

In the battle at Valley Mountain, of the O-tnam Infantry, CAPT. DAVIS, W. DAVIS was killed...

Death of MAJ. FRANKLIN S. BLOOM on the night of the 19th inst. He was buried in Rose Hill Cemetery on the 21st inst., with military honors by a battalion of the Macon Volunteers and Floyd Rifles.

Fight at Dranesville...Killed of Capt. Cutts' Artillery are: J.L. GARRETT, B.F. WILLIAMS, W.P. LANEY, J.A. CAPHS.

Died on the 22d inst. after an illness of three months, ERASMUS DARWIN WILLIAMS, in his 50th year, a native of Northampton, Mass., but a resident of this city for the last thirty years.

Died at Camp Thomson, near Brunswick, Ga., R.W. WHITAKER, a member of the Thomason Guards, on the 10th inst., in the 22d year of his age.

Died in Lee County, Ga. on the 10th inst., MRS. ADA V., daughter of DR. R.C. BLACK, and wife of JOHN TOMLINSON.

Jan. 22, 1862

AMOS BENTON, ESQ., died in Savannah, on the 19th inst. after a short illness. He was in the Confederate service, as a member and Quartermaster of the Bibb Cavalry, and among the oldest members of that corps. He also served in it in the Creek war of 1836... was fulfilling the duties of a Magistrate of this city, which he held many years. Was yesterday interred in Rose Hill Cemetery with Masonic honors by Macon Lodge No. 5, of which he was for several years the W. Master. Also the presiding officer of the other Masonic Bodies of the city, and a Deputy Grand Master of the Grand Lodge of Georgia. His funeral was also attended by the Macon Volunteers.

DR. HENRY LOCKHART, an old and much respected citizen, died at his residence in Beallwood near this city, on Wednesday night. He was formerly of Warren county, Ga., more recently was engaged in business at Apalachicola, and for the last fifteen or twenty years he resided in this city. (Columbus Enquirer)

Tribute of Respect by Macon Lodge No. 5 on the death of JOEL G. STUBBS, who departed this life in Richmond, Va., of pneumonia, in the 34th year of his age, on the first day of January while serving his country in the Bibb Greys, commanded by Capt. J.W. Stubbs of the 31st Ga. Regt.

PRIVATE L.M. FRENCH, of the Jackson Artillery, died at the Hospital on the 12th inst., of dyptheria, after an illness of 18 hours, aged 39 years.

Died in Montezuma, Ga. on the 6th inst., from an attack of Paralysis, MORTON N. BURCH, ESQ., in the 67th year of his age. A native of Hancock county, and for a number of years a resident of this city, where he was well and favorably known.

Died at Bowling Green, Ky. on the 25th of Dec. 1861, of typhoid fever, A.C. CALLAWAY, in the 24th year of his age.

Jan. 29, 1862

Death notice of EX-PRESIDENT JOHN TYLER.

MR. MARCUS A. WINGFIELD died suddenly on the 25th inst., near Norfolk, in the camp of the Floyd Rifles, of which company he was a member. He was aged about 35, and for several years a resident of this city. His remains are sent to Madison (his native place) for interment.

WALTER SCOTT HARDEN, son of A.T. HARDEN, our Postmaster, died of Camp Fever, at Richmond on Monday, the 13th inst...a lovely youth of some 18 years. (Rome Courier)

Tribute headed Camp Whittle, Headquarters Jackson Artillery, St. Simons Island, Jan. 18, 1862 - on death of L.M. FRENCH.

Died in this city on the 6th inst., MR. CHARLES G. BEAVERS, aged 32 years 11 months 24 days. The painful circumstances attending the death of Mr. Beavers having already been published in the city papers, we deem it unnecessary to recite them in this connection... born near Chattanooga 29 Jan. 1829, and was a son of MR. RICHARD M. and MRS. MARY BEAVERS. His father and sister (Mrs. Majors) now reside near Knoxville, Tenn., and he has a brother (Spencer M. Beavers) in the Confederate Service, at Valley Mountain, Va. (with long eulogy)

Died on the morning of the 18th inst. at his residence near Athens, DR. HUGH NEISLER, in the 90th year of his age...one of the early settlers of Athens...his father was an elder in the Presbyterian Church in North Carolina.

Feb. 5, 1862

Warning to snuff dippers. MISS GIBSON, a beautiful young lady, died from the effects of snuff dipping, in Arkansas...

Died at Camp Alleghany, Va. on the 15th January, MR. WM. H.H. SUMMERFORD, of Dooly county, aged 18 years.

Tribute of Respect headed Georgia Barracks, near Norfolk, Va. Jan. 28th, 1862 - on the death of MARK A. WINGFIELD.

Feb. 19, 1862

COL. WILLIAMS died on Monday 3rd inst. of consumption...a member of the Methodist Church (Corner Stone)

Mar. 19, 1862

REV. JAMES H. REESE of the Georgia Conference departed this life at the residence of James Coachman, Decatur co., Ga. (taken from the Southern Christian Advocate of Thursday last).

A member of the Southern Rights Guards named SPEER, from Houston county, died at the Globe Hotel in this city last night. He had just been mustered out of service with his regiment (First Georgia) and was on his way home when taken sick... (Augusta Sentinel of Thursday)

Died on the 18th inst. of inflammation of the bowels, in Augusta, Ga., PRIVATE JOHN R. SPEIR, of the Southern Rights Guard, Company C, 1st Georgia Regiment, aged 26 years 1 month 14 days.

Died in Oglethorpe county on the 4th inst. after a brief illness, RICHARD E. BURKE, aged 77 years.

Apr. 16, 1862

The Augusta Constitutionalist of yesterday says: A private despatch from Corinth, to his friends in this city, brings us the painful intelligence that LIEUT. J.J. JACOBUS, of the Washington Artillery, was killed in the battle of Shiloh.

COL. DAVID C. CAMPBELL, one of our most prominent and influential citizens, died suddenly from disease of the heart on Friday evening last at his residence in this vicinity, in the 62d year of his age. Was a native of New Jersey and a graduate of Hamilton College, New York. Soon after completing his education, he removed to South Carolina, and for several years practiced law in partnership with the HON. C.G. MEMMINGER, the present distinguished Secretary of the Treasury of the Confederate States. About 1835 he changed his residence to Macon, Georgia, and soon afterwards represented the county of Bibb in the Legislature. In 1845 he became proprietor and editor of the Federal Union...a trustee and member of the Executive Committee of Oglethorpe University...appointed by the late State Convention as Commissioner to Delaware...member of Presbyterian Church...two of his sons are in the army - one, Capt. Charles Campbell near Manassas, and the other, Memminger Campbell, a member of the "Baldwin Blues" of the Fourth Ga. Regt., near Norfolk, Va.; another son was J.B. Campbell; funeral discourse was preached at the Presbyterian Church by Rev. Dr. Talmage, who was aided in the services by Rev. Dr. Beman, former President of Oglethorpe University. (Southern Recorder).

Died near this city on the 12th inst. after an illness of fourteen days, of Pneumonia, ASA E. EARNEST, ESQ., in the 75th year of his age. Was distinguished for his agricultural knowledge and successful experiments in that line.

Apr. 23, 1862

Details of skirmish at Whitmarsh Island. Killed were TOLCOT B. ANDREWS, Co. G, shot through the head; THOMAS ALLEN, G, shot through the thigh; MATHEW McCORMACK, G, shot through the bowels; JAMES PILKENTON, A, shot through the thigh.

JUDGE JOB JOHNSON, Associate Justice of the Court of Appeals, died at his residence in Newberry recently, after a protracted and painful illness, at the advanced age of 68 years.

COL. E.R. GOULDING, commander of the Ninth Georgia Volunteers, died suddenly of apoplexy, at Orange Court House, Virginia, on Thursday, the 3d April instant.

Tribute or Respect by Ross Volunteers at Camp Lee on 13th April - on the death of PRIVATE ROBERT C. OUSLEY.

Apr. 30, 1862

HON. GEORGE W. JOHNSON, Provisional Governor of Kentucky, died at General Buell's headquarters on the 9th inst. He was severely wounded in the fight on Monday. He died in two days after of his wounds. (Atlanta Confederacy)

Died in Savannah on the 19th inst., JOHN W. KELLY, aged 42 years.

May 14, 1862

Died in this city on the 12th inst., MR. JOHN H. DAMOUR, aged about 52 years. Was a native of Beauvoir in France, and emigrated to this country in early manhood. He located in this city in 1833.

June 4, 1862

Poem to the memory of A.E. SHERWOOD, who fell at the Battle of McDowell, Va., May 8, 1862.

BRITTON S. WARE, of Twiggs County, who was confined in our jail for several weeks past, on the charge of killing WM. S. LINGO (also of Twiggs) was admitted to Bail on the 29th ult., by Judge Lochrane, on a bond of $20,000.

HON. CHARLES J. INGERSOLL died in Philadelphia on the 14th inst. in the 80th year of his age. He had occupied many important political positions in the country.

Tribute of Respect by Hunter's Lodge No. 134 F.A.M., Marshallville, Ga., May 23, 1862 - on the death of JOHN McMILLAN...fell pierced by a ball in the left breast, whilst gallantly leading the left wing of the 12th Ga. Regt. in the bloody conflict at McDowell. He was born in Chesterfield District, South Carolina 4 Jan. 1832, and was in his 30th year. He was the only child of an aged and very pious mother...graduated with honor at Franklin College, Athens, Georgia in 1852...educated with a view to the medical profession, but turned his attention to teaching; was Principal of school at Marshallville; entered war and tendered services of his company, the Davis Rifles, and was attached to the 12th Ga. Regt...(with long eulogy)

June 11, 1862

The Forsyth Educational Journal of June 6th relates the death of DR. J.H. ETHRIDGE, who fell on the battlefield near Richmond, Va.

Died in this city on the 8th inst., HENRY A., son of DR. M.S. THOMPSON, aged 5 years 5 months.

July 2, 1862

Among the killed on the Yankee side in the battle of the Chickahominy is the name of THOMAS FRANCIS MONGHER (?), the "much lauded and highly applauded" Irish patriot. He had led the 69th Erin regiment into the fight at Manassas. (Richmond Enquirer)

COL. ROBERT A. SMITH died at Richmond, Va. on the 29th...He had fully proved himself as a good officer in commanding the Macon Volunteers from the commencement of the war, until he was promoted to the command of the 44th regiment; was a member of the Methodist Church of this city. His body was expected here last night, and to be buried today. (A separate article details the funeral procession).

Died in Perry, Ga. on Friday evening, 20th June, MRS. JEANNETTE DUMAS, wife of J.J. DUMAS, ESQ., and daughter of the late JAMES POPE, ESQ., of Houston. Less than a twelve month before her decease, the subject of this notice was happily united in marriage. (with long eulogy).

July 16, 1862

Tribute of Respect by Worth Lodge No. 194 F.A.M. - on the death of WARREN DYKES, who died at his residence in Worth county, Ga. on the 20th of May - aged about 70 years; was a subscriber on the petition for the charter of this Lodge, and acted in several offices; for long time was a Minister of the Gospel of the Primitive faith.

Died in Hawkinsville on the 1st of June last, MRS. MARY M. ROSS, aged 25 years, after a painful and protracted sickness of three weeks; a member of the Baptist Church.

Died in Savannah on the 12th inst. of the typhoid fever, SERGEANT GEORGE E. RICKS, of this city, aged about 22 years. Was a member of the Lamar Infantry, and was brought to this city and interred in Rose Hill Cemetery on Sunday by the Floyd Rifles and Young America Fire Company.

Died at her residence in Macon county on the 25th of June, MRS. NAOMI WATTS, aged 26 years (short eulogy).

July 23, 1862

Tribute of Respect headed Camp Oglethorpe, Macon, Ga. July 15, 1862 - on the death of E. PLEURIBUS PARTRIDGE, who died at home on furlough on the 13th of this instant. Was a member of the Macon County Guards, Mess No. 7.

Died in Houston county on the 14th inst., MRS. ELIZABETH BRYAN, wife of JNO. BRYAN, ESQ., in the 53d year of her age; for over thirty years a member of the Methodist Church.

Died at Mr. Firman Chaires' plantation in Leon county, Fla. on Tuesday the 24th June, WILLIAM CANNON, a native of Oxford, Ga., aged 52 years.

Aug. 6, 1862

Tribute of Respect by Franklin Lodge No. 2 I.O.O.F., Macon, Ga. dated July 18th, 1862 - on the death of ROBERT A. SMITH.

Tribute by the Macon Volunteers, 2d Georgia Battation, held July 21st at Camp Lee, near Petersburg, Va. - on the death of PRIVATE J.W. HOGG, who died of fever at the Ladies' Hospital, Petersburg, Va., July 14, 1862.

Aug. 6, 1862

Tribute headed Camp Oglethorpe, July 25, 1862 by the Macon County Guards - on the deaths of WILLIAM CARNALD, BURWEL McCOY, TARPLEY HAMBRICK, E.P.W. PARTRIDGE, JAS. LEGGITT, and JOHN H. McBRIDE.

Died near Richmond, Va. July 26, 1862, at Wright's Brigade Hospital, of typhoid fever, SERGT. JAMES C. YARBROUGH, of the Macon County Volunteers, 4th Ga. Regt., aged about 22 years.

Aug. 13, 1862

Died in Thomaston, Upson county, on the 3rd inst., WM. LOWE, ESQ., aged about 60 years. Was among the oldest settlers of that county. He died quite suddenly, of an affection of the heart.

Aug. 27, 1862

LIEUT. C.S. WEBSTER, U.S.A., a grandson of the great lexicographer, Noah Webster, and great grandson of Martha Washington, died at New Haven, Conn. on the 10th inst.

Died at the 15th Georgia Hospital, Richmond, Va., on the 11th inst. of typhoid fever, in the 23d year of his age, JAMES K. PARKS, of Macon county, Ga.

Sep. 3, 1862

At a hospital in Lynchburg, Va. on Monday, C. McDANIEL, of the 14th Tenn., was killed in an affray with J. HOLMES, of the 13th Ga., who stabbed him in the heart. JAMES READ was accidentally killed on the same day. (Raleigh Register).

PHILIP T. SCHLEY, EDQ., died in Savannah on the 31st ult., aged 64 years. Was distinguished as an Attorney, and prominent member of the Masonic Fraternity. Was Grand Master of the Grand Lodge of Georgia seven years and the presiding officer of the Grand Council and Grand High Priest of the Grand Chapter of the state at the time of his death.

Tribute headed Bivouc near the Rapidan Aug. 18, 1862 by the commissioned officers of the 49th Regt. Ga. Vols. - on the death of LIEUT. E.A. SMITH, of Co. K, which took place in Richmond on Friday the 15th inst.

Tribute of Respect headed Traveler's Rest Lodge No. 65 F.A.M., Montezuma, Aug. 1862 - on the death of DANIEL S. HARRISON - who departed life on Thursday the 14th inst.

Tribute of Respect by Millwood Lodge No. 198 F.A.M., Dooly County, Ga., - on the death of BRIGHT B. HERRING, who ided of typhoid fever at the hospital, Atlanta, on 17 Aug. 1862.

Died in Houston county on the 8th inst., after a few hours illness, COL. LEWIS RUMPH, aged 70 years formerly of Marlborough District, South Carolina.

Died at Traveler's Rest, Dooly county, on the 18th inst., of camp fever taken while on a visit to his son in the army near Richmond, DANIEL SHINE HARRISON, ESQ., aged 55 years, a native of Jones county, North Carolina.

Oct. 8, 1862

COL. LEVI B. SMITH was killed in the recent bloody conflict in Maryland. Was the late Senator from Talbot county, and occupied a distinguished rank at the Bar. At one time he was the partner of the late Gov. Towns in the practice of law.

Oct. 8, 1862

Death of MAJOR SPAULDING McINTOSH in battle near Shepherdstown, Maryland, Sept. 17, 1862. Was shot through the heart with a musket ball. His remains will be carefully cared for - if possible be placed in the vault of Mr. Rutherford, Charlestown, Va. along with those of COL. JNO. B. LAMAR, Macon, Ga.

MAJ. JOHN D. WALKER, who was severely wounded during the recent battles in Virginia, has died of his wounds. He was a brother of the gallant Gen. W.H.T. Walker, of this city. (Augusta Chron. & Sent.)

Oct. 15, 1862

GEO. A. WINN, of Monroe county, died of typhoid fever on the 7th inst. Was among the oldest residents of that county and was State Senator at the time of his death representing the counties of Monroe, Bibb, and Pike.

Died in this city on the 12th inst., MRS. MARY L. FRANKLIN, widow of the late DR. M.A. FRANKLIN.

Tribute of Respect by Houston Lodge No. 35 Oct. 3d, 1862 - on the death of JAS. A. ROQUEMORE.

Dec. 10, 1862

THOMAS L. ROSS, ESQ., Confederate Marshal of this city, was most wantonly murdered at Marietta, on Saturday last...

Died in Hamilton, Ga. on the 28th inst., of paralysis, MR. JOHN MURPHY, aged about 65 years. Was a native of Jefferson county, and was among the very first settlers of this city, where he resided and carried on a mercantile business for several years - then returned to Jefferson, and a few years afterwards removed to Hamilton.

Feb. 11, 1863

On yesterday an unfortunate recontre took place in this city between CAPT. G.W. ANDERSON of the first Georgia Regulars - who from a wound received in one of the battles before Richmond has been absent from his Regiment - and one of the Marshals of this city, MR. THOMAS SHIVERS, in which encounter, several pistol shots were fired by both, from one of which the latter was killed...(Atlanta Intel., Feb. 3d)

Died at the residence of John M. Blakey, Esq., of Richmond, Va., on the morning of the 22d December 1862, CAPT. H.J. MENARD, Co. C (Macon Guards) Eighth Georgia Regiment (with eulogy).

Feb. 18, 1863

Died at Forsyth on the 16th inst., ZACHARIAH E. HARMAN, ESQ., an able practicing Attorney; a sufferer from paralysis for several years.

Feb. 25, 1863

Died Feb. 14th, 1863 at her father's residence, Columbus, Ga., MISS MARY L. SLADE, aged 36 years, daughter of the REV. THOS. B. SLADE (with eulogy).

Died in this city on the 20th inst. JOSEPH E. BROWN - aged about 19 years - son of E.E. BROWN, ESQ., of disease contracted in the army in which he had served as a member of the Jackson Artillery since the commencement of the war.

Feb. 25, 1863

COL. WM. CUMMING departed this life at his house in this city about two o'clock in the morning. For the last four years he has been an invalid and for several years previous, was in comparative retirement. (Augusta Chronicle & Sen., Feb. 18th).

Mar. 4, 1863

A.G. WARE, whose name is well known as being for many years connected with the press, and for some time past the Agent of the Macon and Western Railroad at Atlanta, died in that city of a carbuncle, on the 27th inst.

Died in this city on the 1st inst., MR. JOHN MASSETT (?) - aged about 50 years.

Mar. 18, 1863

The Charleston papers announce the death of HON. JAMES L. PETTIGRU. He died on Monday afternoon last, in the 74th year of his age. Was born in Abbeville District, South Carolina in 1789; was a pupil of the celebrated Dr. Moses Waddell, of the Wilmington Academy; graduated at Columbia in 1809; was admitted to the Charleston Bar in 1812, with the celebrated Robert Y. Hayne.

Tribute of Respect by the Physicians of Macon - on the death of DR. ROBERT C. HARDIE.

Died in this city on the 6th inst., COL. E.D. HUGUENIN, a much esteemed citizen.

Died in Americus on the 3d inst., DR. THOMAS C. LAMAR, aged 44 years.

Died in Monroe county on the 17th inst., of Pneumonia, MR. GEO. W. TAYLOR, aged 35 years.

Died in the Georgia Hospital at Richmond, of Pneumonia, HENRY CLAY GREEN, aged 19 years - son of Burwell Green, Esq., of Macon county.

Mar. 25, 1863

W.S. Granville, late Clerk of the Supreme Court of Missouri, in a letter to the Southern Crisis, gives account of the murder of JOSHUA CHILTON, State Senator from Shannon county, Missouri...

Tribute of Respect by Millwood Lodge No. 128 F.A.M. March 14, 1863- on the death of JESSE W. CONE, who died of Typhoid Pneumonia in the hospital at Cumberland Gap, Tennessee, on the 18th February last. Was born in Houston county, Geo. on the 11th June 1835, and was a resident of Dooly county, Geo. at the time of his death (with eulogy).

Died of Pneumonia in the first Georgia Hospital, Richmond, Va., on the 23d day of January, 1863, HENRY CLAY GREENE, in the 19th year of his age; son of BURWELL GREENE, ESQ., of Macon County, Geo. (with eulogy).

Died in Itawamba county, Miss. on the 7th February, JOHN C. HELVINSTON, ESQ., aged about 73 (78?) years. He was for many years a resident of this city, and afterwards of Macon county, Ga.

Died in Macon county on the 14th inst., of Pneumonia, MASTER JAMES POPE, aged about 13 years - son of the late GIDEON POPE.

Apr. 1, 1863

ELAM ALEXANDER died in this city on the 29th inst. after a brief illness, of inflammation of the bowels - aged about 68 years. Was one of the earliest residents of this city...well known as an extensive railroad contractor - was for several years President of the Washington and New Orleans Telegraphic Company, and at the time of his death, President of the Empire State Iron and Coal Mining Company.

Apr. 15, 1863

Died in Americus on the 4th inst. from the effects of a fall, MR. ISAAC C. WEST, in the 56th year of his age.

Apr. 22, 1863

Died in this city on the 14th inst., MRS. DELIE MAUSSENET, aged 38 years.

Apr. 29, 1863

ROBERT EMMETT DIXON, Clark of the House of Representatives, was killed in Richmond by R.E. FORDE of Kentucky, the 24th inst. Dixon was a native of Talbot county in this state, and a resident of Columbus. (long story gives details).

May 6, 1863

GEN. TRACY was killed at Port Gibson, Miss. on the 1st inst. The particulars have not been received. Was a native of Macon and brother of the gallant Major Phil Tracy; was aged about 28 (from Daily Telegraph of 2d inst.).

May 13, 1863

STONEWALL JACKSON expired at Guiney's Station, at a quarter past three o'clock on the 10th inst., from the combined effects of his wounds and an attack of pneumonia...

BRIG. GEN. FRANK PAXTON who was killed at Chancellorsville was a citizen of Lexington, Va., and was well known as the President of the Bank of Rockbridge. He commanded the Stonewall Brigade when killed.

May 27, 1863

Detailed obituary of THOMAS J. JACKSON (Stonewall Jackson).

Details of the killing of GEN. VAN DORN (Cor. Rich. Enq.).

June 10, 1863

DR. GABRIEL HARRISON died on the morning of the 3d inst. from an attack of congestive chills and pneumonia. Was interred with Masonic honors by Macon Lodge No. 5 (of which he had been presiding officer) on the 4th inst.

June 24, 1863

Honicide in Worth county. GEORGE & JOHN DERCE the victims - George Kerce was an old man of sixty years or more, and John, his son, from thirteen to fourteen years of age (details in article).

CHARLES A. BYINGTON, son of CAPT. A.F. BYINGTON, was born in Hancock county, Ga. 29 Oct. 1835, and joined the Baldwin Blues as a recruit in August 1861, and was killed in the battle of Chancellorsville, Va. 2d May 1863. Has left a widow and four small children (the eldest 6 years) and an aged father and seven brothers and sisters to deplore his untimely death. (with eulogy).

July 1, 1863

    Tribute of Respect by Millwood Lodge No. 198 F.A.M. - on the death of ORDERLY JOHN ROBERTS of Co. C, 55th Regt. Ga. Vols., who died of Typhoid Pneumonia, at Cumberland Gap, Tenn., aged 24.

July 8, 1863

    Departed this life on 25th June, MRS. ELIZABETH REDDING, wife of COL. A.W. REDDING, of Jamestown, Chattahoochee county, Ga.

July 22, 1863

    THOMAS J. DYSON, ESQ., adjutant of the 57th Georgia Regt., and a prominent young lawyer of Thomasville, was mortally wounded in the bloody battle at Champion's Hill, about 35 miles (from) Vicksburg on Saturday the 16th ult. (Sav. Republican).

    Died at Farmville, Va. on the 18th June of chronic diarrhea, SERGT. V.A. HARVARD, aged 21 years - a member of Capt. Armstrong's company, of Dooly county. He was wounded in the second battle of Manassas, from which he recovered, and re-joined his command to fall the victim of disease.

    Tribute of Respect by Wells Lodge No. 198 F.A.M., Monroe Co., Ga. May 23rd - on the death of GEORGE W. TAYLOR, who died at his residence in Monroe County on 8th March, 1863.

    Tribute of Respect by Millwood Lodge No. 198 F.A.M. dated June 8, 1862 - on the death of W.G. CONE - was born in Houston county, Ga. 21 Dec. 1840, and died in the Hospital at Staunton, Va. 14 Jan. 1863. He left his home 24 Aug. 1862 to join the 13th Georgia regiment, but was overtaken by sickness, which proved to be fatal.

Aug. 5, 1863

    COL. WM. T. HARRIS fell in the battle of Gettysvurg on the 2d inst. - was shot through the heart...

    HON. WM. L. YANCEY died at Montgomery, Ala. on the 28th ult. after a sickness of four weeks of a kidney disease. He was about 49 years of age.

    Obituary of JOHN W. PARKS. Was shot by the enemy's pickets at Gettysburg while attempting to remove a wounded man from the field on the morning of 3d July. He was in his 32d (?) year, was native of Wilkinson county, but removed to Macon county in 1859, where he married the following year (with eulogy).

Aug. 19, 1863

    Died on Monday the 10th inst. of Diphtheria, MARGARET BELL, daughter of THEODORE and VIRGINIA PARKER, aged 6 years 10 months.

    Tribute of Respect by Millwood Lodge No. 198 F.A.M. - on the death of J.D. GORDON of Co. G, 8th Geo. Vols. - who fell at Gettysburg.

    Yankee outrage at the grave. The body of CAPTAIN W.D. BROWN of the Chesapeake Artillery, who was mortally wounded at Gettysburg, and who died subsequently in Baltimore, was delivered to his family. While the last solemn services were being conducted around the grave, a squad of Yankee soldiers appeared and arrested all present, and confined them in the Gillmer House until the next day, when they were paroled. (Richm'd Enquirer).

Aug. 26, 1863

    Died in East Macon on the 19th inst., MR. THOMAS WOOLFOLK, aged 87 years 6 months - a long resident and well known citizen of this vicinity. Was born in Wilkes county, North Carolina, and removed

(Aug. 26, cont'd) - to Jones county, Ga. in 1800, and to Bibb in 1819, where he has since resided.

Sep. 2, 1863

EX-GOV. FLOYD, of Virginia, died at Arlington, Va. on the 26th ult.

Death notice of REV. GEO. W. MOORE, a venerable and beloved Charlestonian, who for 43 years has labored among the people in winning straying souls. Died Sunday afternoon while attending a Camp Meeting near Anderson Court House. (Chas. Courier).

Died near Oglethorpe, Macon county, Ga., on the 25th August, of intermittent fever, ELIZZIE ELLEN, daughter of J.R. and S.V. HOLSONBAKE, aged 2 years 7 months.

Sep. 16, 1863

Died in Tallahassee on the 31st August of a congestive chill, MR. JOHN S. (?) HARRIS, of this city, aged about 57 years.

Sep. 30, 1863

The body of MAJ. GEO. W. ROSS, who died of wounds received in the battle of Gettysburg, was received here, and interred on Monday afternoon in Rose Hill Cemetery.

Oct. 7, 1863

MAJ. JOHN S. ROWLAND, the Superintendent of the Western & Atlantic Railroad, died at his residence in Bartow county, on the 18th ult. after a short illness.

A fatal recontre took place on the train which left Augusta on Friday evening on the Augusta and Savannah railroad. An altercation took place between conductor Adams and a passenger by the name of JAMES CURREN, who refused to pay his fare. Curren violently assaulted the conductor...when Mr. Adams recovered himself, he drew a knife and inflicted a wound upon Curren in the stomach, from which he soon after died. Mr. Adams immediately returned the train to Augusta and gave himself up to the authorities. (Charleston Courier).

Died at his residence near Fort Valley, Ga., MR. WILLIAMSON MIMMS, at the advanced age of 80 years; an exemplary and pious member of the M.E. Church.

Oct. 28, 1863

Tribute of Respect by Southwestern Lodge No. 143 - on the death of WILLIAM J. TAYLOR.

Nov. 4, 1863

The Augusta Chronicle & Sentinel of the 29th says: We learn that a hostile meeting took place Wednesday afternoon at the Sand Bar Ferry, on Carolina Shore, between MR. C.A. RED of this city, and MR. RICHARD COPELAND, of Maryland - resulting in the death of the latter...

Nov. 18, 1863

Died in Monroe county on the 13th inst. after a very short illness, MRS. _____ PINCKARD, wife of COL. J.S. PINCKARD.

Died in Schley county on the 10th inst. of a congestive chill, HENRY D. HOLT, ESQ., an old and highly respected citizen, and a true brother of the Masonic Fraternity in heart and action.

Nov. 25, 1863

JAMES B. CARLISLE, junior Editor of the Floridian, died at Tallahassee on the 8th inst. Several years since we knew him as the Editor of the "Wakulla Times," at Newport, and since in connection with the Floridian.

GRIG. GEN. POSEY, commander of Posey's Brigade, attached to General Lee's Army, died on Sunday last, at Charlottesville, Va., of a wound received at Gettysburg. The remains were interred at Charlottesville on Sunday with military honor.

JUDGE JOHN C. NICHOLL died at his residence in this city on Monday evening about six o'clock. Was a native of this city and in the 69th year of his age. For upwards of twenty years was Judge of the United States District Court, and for sometime past had been the Confederate States District Attorney. (Savannah News).

Dec. 2, 1863

Horrible murder. MR. IRWIN, an old and highly respectable citizen, was assassinated by one of his servants on last Friday in Carroll county...(Atlanta Confed.).

Died in this city on the 30th ult., MRS. MARTHA HUGUENIN, wife of the late COL. E.D. HUGUENIN and daughter of the late DR. TOMLINSON FORT, of Milledgeville. Her death was caused from injuries received in jumping from a carriage, a few weeks since.

Died on the 29th ult. of typhoid fever, MRS. PAMELA DeGRAFFENRIED, wife of LIEUT. MARSHALL DeGRAFFENRIED, aged about 20 years, and daughter of CAPT. B.F. ROSS, of this city.

Dec. 9, 1863

PLEASANT STOVALL, ESQ., of Augusta, but who has resided in this place for many years past, died at his residence in this town on Sunday the 29th Nov. (Athens Watchman).

Obituary notice of MRS. JULIA E. HUGUENIN, wife of the late COL. E.D. HUGUENIN.

Died at his residence in Houston county, of typhoid fever, on the 3d day of November 1863, MR. WILLIAM BURNAM, aged 50 years. (with eulogy).

Dec. 30, 1863

The Petersburg (Va.) Intelligencer says that any remittance in aid of the family of DR. DAVID L. WRIGHT, who died the death of a martyr at Norfolk, may be mailed to that office...

Jan. 6, 1864

Died in this city on the 30th ult. of pneumonia, COL. GEORGE R. HUNTER, aged about 55 years - for many years a resident of Knoxville, Crawford co., and well known as one of the leading members of the Bar.

Jan. 20, 1864

A shocking affair occurred in this city on Third street, about six o'clock on Friday evening last, between ROBERT MARTIN, of this city, and JAMES BURNS of Twiggs county, in which Martin was killed...

Jan. 27, 1864

LIEUT. COLONEL EDWIN W. BUKER, of the First Regt. Georgia Militia, died in this city on Saturday afternoon last, in the 46th year of his age. The deceased was a native of Maine, but has resided in

(Jan. 27, cont'd) - in this city from his early youth to the period of his death. For a number of years past he has served as a Master of the Masonic Lodge in this city, and his funeral yesterday afternoon was attended by a large number of the fraternity. (Sav. News).

Died in this city on Sunday morning the 9th inst., MR. JOHN P. HARVEY, aged about 50 years, leaving a large family and a numerous circle of friends to mourn their loss.

Tribute of Respect by Wells Lodge No. 197, Monroe Co., dated Dec. 26th, 1863 - on the death of ARCHIBALD H. ERWIN, LIEUT. commanding Co. K, 59th Ga. Regt. in the battle at Funkstown, Pa., July 10, 1863, where he fell mortally wounded and died on the battlefield.

COL. R.S. CLUKE, acting Brigadier General in Gen. Morgan's command, died in the Ohio Penintentiary, in a dungeon, in close confinement... (Atlanta Intel. 22d).

Feb. 3, 1864

Died in Upson county, Ga. Jan. 18th, 1864, MARY D. MATTHEWS, youngest daughter of FRANCIS S. and ELIZABETH MATTHEWS, aged 11 years 11 months 27 days (with long eulogy).

Feb. 10, 1864

Died near Hudson, Pike county, Alabama, on the morning of the 21st January 1864, MISS MARGARET E. LAW, youngest daughter of JOHN A. and SARAH LAW, in the 19th year of her age (formerly of Macon co., Ga.).

Feb. 17, 1864

COL. JOHN BOSTON, an esteemed citizen and Collector of the port of Savannah, died this forenoon at his residence in this city, after an illness of some 12 days (Sav. Rep. 12).

Feb. 24, 1864

Died on the 8th inst. at the residence of his mother in this place, PETER J. WILLIAMS, in the 29th year of his age. (with short eulogy) (Milledgeville Union).

Mar. 9, 1864

Died in Macon on the 8th inst., MINNIE E. FORRESTER, eldest daughter of CHAS. A. and SARAH C. FORRESTER, aged 5 (?) years 7 months 3 days.

Apr. 13, 1864

Tribute of Respect by Hunter Lodge No. 134 F.A.M. - on the death of WM. FELTON - was a native of Gates co., North Carolina, but for 45 years a resident of this county; attached himself to our Order in 1847.

May 4, 1864

JUDGE THOMAS W. THOMAS, of Elbert county, died at his residence in Elberton on Sunday night last. (Augusta Chron. & Sent.).

May 18, 1864

Death notice of THOMAS BUTLER KING. The remains of Dr. King will arrive here today by the Gulf train, and the funeral services will take place at Christ Church at 5 p.m. (Sav. Rep.).

June 1, 1864

Died in this city on the 23d ult. after a painful illness of five months, in the 59th year of her age, MRS. EMILY BRANHAM, wife of DR. JOEL BRANHAM.

Killed on the battle field near Spotsylvania C.H., Va., on Friday, 6th ult., SENECA BRAGG BULKEY, son of EDWARD C. and ANNA BULKEY, of this city, in the 19th year of his age.

Died in Eatonton on the 21st ult., JEFFERSON ADAMS, ESQ., a much esteemed citizen and a Senator in the present Legislature.

June 8, 1864

GEN. GEORGE P. DOLES was among the killed in recent battles in Virginia. He was a native of Milledgeville, and early entered the service as Captain of the Baldwin Blues, and soon distinguished himself by his conspicuous gallantry, which was appreciated by his being elected Colonel of the 4th Ga. Regt. After the battle of Sharpsburg, he was immediately promoted to the rank of Brigadier General.

Killed at the same time with Gen. Doles was MAJOR J.E. RYLANDER, a native of this city.

CAPT. EUGENE A. HAWKINS, also a native of Milledgeville, was killed a few days previous, at the battle of the Wilderness.

Died at his residence near Hawkinsville on the 22d inst., JOHN I. ANDERSON, ESQ., in the 59th year of his age. In 1862 he became a member of the Baptist church (with eulogy).

June 29, 1864

COL. C.H. WALKER, of Giles county, Tenn., commanding the 3d Tennessee Regt., was killed last evening at the front. Was a graduate of West Point.

Died in Twiggs county on the 26th inst., MR. JOHN DAVIS - aged about 58 (?) years.

July 20, 1864

Among the casualties of the late battle on John's Island, noticed in the Charleston papers, is that of CORPORAL J.P. DENNIS, of Co. C, Baraud's Artillery Battalion (with short eulogy).

Explosion of a locomotive. The new locomotive "Sunshine," recently completed in this city, and has been on the track but a few days, exploded on Monday, while bringing down a freight train, a few miles below Jonesboro. The engineer, JOE HUSKQITH, DR. DENNIS, DR. HARRIS, and a negro wood passer killed.

July 27, 1864

LIEUT. COL. JOHN M. BROWN, brother of Gov. Brown, was severely wounded near Atlanta on Friday last and was carried to Milledgville. He died on Monday.

Death notice of CAPTAIN JOHN C. MITCHELL, the commander of Fort Sumter. The remains were brought to this city last evening. His funeral will take place at St. Paul's Church at 5 o'clock this afternoon. In accordance with his last wishes, he will be buried in Magnolia Cemetery. (Charleston Mercury).

Fell on the battle-field at James' Island July 9th, OWEN J. WILLIS, JOHN S. HARPER, and DOUGLAS P. WATSON, of the 32d Ga. Regt., Co H (?) (with short eulogy).

July 27, 1864

   Departed this life in Waynesville, Wayne county, Ga., on the 15th of July, 1864 JOHN _____ FORD MABRY, aged about 18 years, son of _____ FORD and LAURA MABRY. He was at East Point, Ga. to protect the bridge, and was taken sick and remained in the hospital two weeks...

Nov. 16, 1864

   Article about the siege of Charleston... A man and wife named JOHN and MARY MULLANY were killed about half past eleven o'clock Sunday night, by a fragment of a shell which entered the room where they were sleeping...

   Died at his residence in Dahlonega, Ga. on the 17th Oct. 1864, COL. WILLIAM MARTIN, of the First Ga. Regt. of Regulars. Col. M. was in the 53d year of his age.

Jan. 4, 1865

   Accident on the Brunswick Railroad. On Thursday last, while the passenger train coming to this city, with the locomotive pushing a wood car before it, in passing over the bridge and trestle work at Flat Creek, the wood car ran off the track, falling into the creek and carrying with it the locomotive and tender...MR. E.P. COLLINGS, the engineer, and B.B. CARTER, the fireman, were both thrown into the mass of rubbish and instantly killed.

   Died in Monticello, Jasper county, on the 8th December, GEN. JOHN W. BURNET, aged about 68 years. He has been well known to the people of Georgia in public life, and was a most esteemed and worthy citizen.

Jan. 18, 1865

   Died in this city on the 26th ult. very suddenly, MR. CHARLES COLLINS, aged about 65 years. While in apparent good health, he was, as is supposed, attacked with a fit of apoplexy, of which he soon expired.

   Died on the 25th inst. MR. JAMES H. GILLIN, probably about 40 years of age. He has long been known as an engineer on railroads, and was at this time employed on the Macon and Brunswick road. The cause of his death is somewhat a mystery, but it is supposed to be from inhaling coal gas. He was employed in lighting the furnace in the basement of the Baptist church, on Saturday night where he laid down. A lad a nephew of his who was with him was much overcome by its effects and barely escaped with his life...he was buried on Monday in the Rose Hill Cemetery by Franklin Lodge Odd Fellows.

   Died in this city on the 31st ult., MR. FRANCIS H. MURDOCK, aged about 50 years.

Apr. 5, 1865

   Tribute of Respect by Jeffersonville Lodge, U.D. 5865 - dated March 22d, 1865 - on the death of JOHN GLOVER.

Apr. 12, 1865

   LIEUT. E.P. HOLSTEAD, of the Bartow Artillery, was killed in one of the recent battles in North Carolina...

June 14, 1865

   The first man killed in this war was DANIEL HOWE, of New York, at Fort Sumter in 1861, by the premature discharge of a gun.

June 30, 1865 (daily)

Died at the residence of D.W.L. Peacock, Esq., in this city, on the 27th inst., JOHN LATIMER, only son of DR. WM. H. and MRS. REBECCA A. FELTON, aged about eleven years.

July 12, 1865

The Columbus Enquirer announces the death of JUDGE GRIGSBY E. THOMAS. Died at his residence on the night of the 4th inst. Was in his 70th year and was a consistent member of the Presbyterian church.

July 19, 1865

MR. HENRY AMOS, of Hancock county, was shot dead in his bed on Tuesday night July 4. No clue has yet been obtained of the murder.

The death is announced of STEPHEN ALLEN BENSON, for eight years President of Liberia, who died on the 24th of January last.

July 22, 1865 (daily)

Friday afternoon, the 7th, a Government employee named JOHN ARRISON was shot and instantly killed at Nashville by one of the guards belonging to the 48th Wisconsin infantry...(Constitutionalist)

Sep. 13, 1865

MAJOR JOHN P. HEISS, a native of Kentucky, for many years the conductor of a newspaper in Washington, D.C., first as an associate of Mr. Ritchie, in the editorial conduct of the Washington Union, died recently in New York City. Subsequently to Mr. Polk's Administration, he had charge of the Washington States.

A horrible tragedy occurred in South Dedham, Mass. on Thursday night, the 31st ultimo. A MRS. CARLOS MARSTON, the wife of a homeopathic physician in that place, shooting her husband and a beautiful and interesting daughter ten years of age, and ending her tragic performance by shooting herself. She is supposed to have been insane.

Desperate fight in Pickens County in which BEN SMITH and BELL COLLINS were killed (details in article).

GEN. JOSEPH G. SWIFT, the first cadet appointed to the Military Academy at West Point, died lately in New York, at the age of 85 years - and 63 years after he entered West Point, which was in 1802.

MR. BROAD, of Boston, one of the principal submarine divers employed by the Philadelphia, Wilmington and Baltimore Railroad Company, in constructing a bridge was smothered to death in his diving dress on Friday afternoon, owing to a defect in the air pumps.

The Atlanta Intelligencer reports the death of JAMES M. JONES which took place at his residence in this city on Sunday last. The deceased was in the 69th year of his age, was a native of Delaware, but had been a resident of Savannah upwards of thirty years, during which time he filled the position of Secretary of various Masonic bodies.

Sep. 20, 1865

Tribute of Respect by Monroe Lodge No. 18 F.A.M., Forsyth, Ga. Sep. 8th, 1865 - on the death of WM. J. THOMAS.

A coroner's inquest was held on the 8th inst., in New York, over the remains of a woman named MARGARET BETTS and her infant daughter, whose dead bodies were found lying in a room occupied by them at 335 East Eighth Street. The jury returned a verdict that the mother's death was caused by intemperance and the child's by starvation.

Sep. 27, 1865

A horrid and brutal murder was committed in Williamson county, Tenn. on Saturday last by a man named JOHN SCALES, the victim being MR. ALFRED OGILVIE. The ruffian shot him while riding in his carriage by the side of his daughter, without the slightest provocation.

Oct. 4, 1865

MR. GEORGE WALKER died of Bilious Fever at his residence in Longstreet, Pulaski county, on the 30th ult., in the 73d year of his age. Was born in Burke county, Ga. 13 Aug. 1793, and about 1808 moved with his parents to Pulaski county, where he ever after lived. (with long eulogy).

Philadelphia, Sep. 27 - The morning papers announce the death of HON. WILLIAM DUANE, aged 85. He was Secretary of the Treasury under Jackson, and resigned his office rather than consent to the removal of deposits from the United States Bank.

Oct. 18, 1865

A young man named WILLIAM BLOOMFIELD, near Akron, Ohio, had some difficulty with his sweat-heart, Miss Alice Mann. He took her out riding in a buggy, drew a pistol, and shooting himself through the head, fell a corpse across her lap.

Oct. 25, 1865

Story about the death of JAMES NISBET, of the San Francisco Bulletin. He was lost on the steamship Brother Jonathan, and his body was found floating in the ocean seven miles from land...

Nov. 1, 1865

HENRY C. MAGRUDER, a Confederate guerilla in Kentucky, was hung by order of a Military Court in Louisville on the 20th. He was charged with having committed murders and a rape, while he was a guerilla. Magruder was only 22 years of age. Some weeks previous to the execution he professed the Catholic religion. When seventeen years of age, he joined Gen. Buckner's command, escaped from Donelson, afterwards was a member of the body guard of Gen. Sidney Johnston; after his death joined Morgan's command, escaped capture in Ohio, and since then has been a guerilla in Kentucky.

Announce the death of MR. A.P. BURR, who has for several months past been as associate Editor of this paper, and its principal writer. His death has been very sudden and unexpected. His age was about 48 years, having been born July 29th, 1817...was an apprentice in this office in the years 1835, '36 and '37, during which time he served a tour in the Seminole war, under our former associate, Col. I.G. Seymour. He was, after being Editor and proprietor of one or two papers, foreman of this office for some time. Then Editor in Griffin, Atlanta, Marietta and Albany. Then served in the present war until severely wounded, and compelled to retire to a rural life as a quiet farmer in the vicinity of Griffin.

On Thursday last Officer Eagan arrested a young man named CHARLES TUCKER alias J.B. WALSTON, on suspicion of having murdered CHAUNCEY P. EARL, a sutter at Duvall's Bluff on the 11th of September last... (St. Louis Democrat, 26th)

WILLIAM F. LYNCH, formerly a Captain in the US Navy, and latterly holding the position of Flag Officer or Commodore in the rebel navy, died at Baltimore, Maryland, on the 17th inst.

A Boston dispatch of the 24th says that Commodore JOHN S. MISSROON, US Navy Ordnance Officer at the Charleston Navy Yard, died yesterday. He was a native of South Carolina, and entered the service in 1824.

Nov. 1, 1865

The funeral services over the remains of the late JOHN DOWNS, U.S. Navy, who died at New Orleans Sep. 21, took place today at the residence of his brother-in-law, in this city. (Boston dispatch of 24th).

The Times-Washington Special states that the murder of HARRIET WELLS by her paramour, LEVI FAREWELL, which occurred yesterday morning on Thirteenth Street, proves to have been a more diabolical scene than was at first supposed. The evidence before the Coroner's Jury today shows that the murderer deliberately administered chloroform to his victim, while she was asleep, then strangled her to death and put her body in a closet, robbed her of her watches, jewelry, etc. and then fled. He has not been arrested. The cause of the murder is said to have been the refusal of her to marry. Although the keeper of a house of prostitution here, she is said to be respectable connected, and has a son at school, at New Brunswick, N.J., for which place she intended to start this evening. She came to this city from Albany, New York. Farewell was originally from Massachusetts.

Tribute of Respect by Pinta Lodge No. 88, Barnesville, Oct. 21 - on the death of JOHN E. SMITH.

Nov. 8, 1865

The New Orleans Times relates details of the death of DR. J.L. RIDDELL. Was one of the best botanists and chemists of Louisisna, or of the South, and very widely known. Was Postmaster at New Orleans under Mr. Buchanan, and also under the Confederacy, though he was always a Union man. His death was singular.

A special dispatch to the Mobile Tribune announces: Columbus, Miss., Nov. 1 - JUDGE A.B. MEEK died this morning about two o'clock, of an affection of the heart.

Died in Richmond, Kentucky on the 18th of October, MRS. MARTHA R. BRECK, wife of REV. ROBERT L. BRECK. Was the wife of the former pastor of the First Presbyterian Church of Macon, Ga. (eulogy)

Coroner Coleman was notified last last evening of the fact that a man named MARTIN GLESE had been found dead in his store on Broad street, a short distance this side of the Chattanooga railroad... (Nashville Gazette, 29th)

DR. OCTAVUS W. TREZEVANT, a native of Charleston, S.C., was killed by a negro soldier in Carrollton, Ga., on Thursday the 26th ult. The True Delta says the deed was committed without provocation.

About 9½ o'clock Thursday night a policeman discovered a man lying on the pavement on Elm street, opposite the Southern Hotel, in an insensible and dying condition...from papers on his person it was discovered that his name was C.P. CHANDLER, formerly a major in the Confederate service, belonging to the 15th Arkansas, and that he was paroled in May last, by Major General Wilson, and furnished transportation to Louisville via Richmond. From a photograph of himself taken in full uniform, it appears from his left eye being bandaged that he had probably lost an eye by a wound in battle... (St. Louis Republican)

Nov. 15, 1865

JOSEPH WORCESTER, distinguished scholar and eminent lexicographer, died on the 28th of October at his residence in Cambridge, Mass. Was born in 1784, and consequently 81 at his death. In 1830 he published the "Comprehensive Pronouncing and Explanatory Dictionary".

Nov. 15, 1865

Died on the 10th instant, MARGARET E. CARTER, in the 17th year of her age. Attached to the M. Church about six years ago at Vineville, Ga. (with short eulogy).

Obituary of THOMAS ALSTON HARRIS. Was born in Edgefield District, South Carolina in 1814. At age 15 he removed to Georgia, making the city of Macon his home. In 1842 he married a daughter of GEORGE HINES...member of the Methodist Episcopal Church for many years; for 25 years an active Mason (wulogy).

Nov. 29, 1865

NELSON H. MAY and CHARLES HOPPER, captain and mate of the schooner A. Richards, of Boston, were killed by the ecplosion of a torpedo, near Jacksonville, Fla.

CAPT. JAMES R. HANHAM, aged 94 years, and the oldest resident of St. Augustine, Fla., died in that place on the 2d inst.

Dec. 13, 1865

The Columbus Enquirer says: On Sunday evening, Dec. 3d, COL. JOHN G. WINTER, long a resident of this city, died in New York, in the 67th year of his age.

A remarkable case of dropsy. Died on the 24th of November last, at the residence of Mrs. Eubanks in Crawford county, MRS. LUCRETIA EMLINGER, aged 49 years 8 months. For ten years she labored under dropsy of the abdomen, and was during that time, tapped 104 times, and the enormous amount of 862 gallons of water drawn off.

Dec. 20, 1865

A man named JOHN CULLIN was found dead near Nashville a few days ago.

Jan. 3, 1866

JAMES R. BARTREE, formerly of Columbus, Mississippi, was killed a few days since at Palo Alto by the accidental explosion of a gun which he held in his hand.

Baltimore, Dec. 30 - H. WINTER DAVIS died today of pneumonia.

COLONEL WM. A. BARSTOW, formerly Governor of Wisconsin, died a few days since at Leavenworth, Kansas.

The St. Louis papers announce the death, in that city, of MRS. ELIZABETH ORTES, at the advanced age of 106 years.

Jan. 10, 1866

Died on the 5th (?) inst. in Pulaski county, MAJOR HENRY WOOD, aged about 57 (?) years. Was a native of Pennsylvania, but a resident of Georgia for over forty years. He resided many years in Clinton then in this city, where he was a Magistrate and held several other offices. For the last three or four years he resided in the vicinity of Hawkinsville. His body was brought to this city and interred by Masonic Lodge No. 5 on the 7th inst.

On Sunday night last an old citizen of Doctortown, HENRY GRANTHAM, was fatally shot by one of Co. K, 103d U.S.C.T., stationed at Doctortown...Grantham and his family were much respected in Wayne county...Mr. Grantham's residence is about three miles below Doctortown, on the river. (Sav. Herald).

Jan. 17, 1866

GENERAL W. HACKEY, Chief Clerk of the US Senate, died this morning, aged 70 years. He has been in the employment of that body 42 years.

Tribute of Respect by Cool Spring Lodge No. 185 F.A.M., Cool Spring, Jan. 5th, 1866 - on the death of BAILY ABNEY who died on the 24th ult.

The Savannah Herald of the 8th inst. announces the death of old PETER CONE. His death occurred at his residence in Bulloch county on Saturday morning last. The deceased was over 70 years of age. For 42 years, or 21 terms, he served Bulloch county with ability in the State Senate, in which body he was known as the senior member. For many years was Major General of the First Division Georgia Militia, to which position he was elected by the Legislature over his competitor, Gen. Charles Floyd. In the last war he served under Gen. Andrew Jackson as captain, and was in command of his company at the taking of Tallahassee by the Indians. General Cone was born in Bulloch county. His funeral will take place today, and his remains will be deposited in the family vault in that county.

Jan. 31, 1866

Death notice of HENRY BURGEVINE, the "Hero of China." How a North Carolina boy became a Mandarin of the Red Button. Was born in Newbern, North Carolina in 1836. His father was a Frenchman - an officer in the Grand Army of Napoleon. Subsequently he was in the service of Spain, and came to America in the capacity of Surveyor General of Florida, married an American lady, and died in 1843, leaving a family consisting of his widow, two sons and a daughter... HENRY BURGEVINE, the youngest of the family, came to Washington City with his mother and sister in 1846...(very lengthy).

Feb. 7, 1866

Died in the city of New Orleans on the night of the 23d January, COL. WILLIAM H. HOBSON, of Nashville, Tenn.

A man named MOORE lately died near Indianapolis, Indiana, from nervous exhaustion caused by fear of hydrophobia.

Memphis, Jan. 30 - The steamer Miami, hence for Little Rock, on Saturday night, when six miles up the Arkansas river, exploded her boiler, tearing away her forward deck, when she took fire and burned to the water's edge and sank. She had on board fifty passengers (cabin passengers), one hundred of Company B, US Cavalry, and 150 persons on deck, including the crew. LUSK and JOHNSON, Clerks were lost; also the wife and child of the former...

Feb. 14, 1866

ELIPHALET MOTT, D.D., President of the Union College, at Albany, New York, died Monday morning in the 93d year of his age. He had been for 62 years President of the Union College.

Feb. 21, 1866

BEATIE NABERS, actress, died not long since in Memphis, at the advanced age of 112 years.

The supposed oldest man in the United States, JOSEPH CRELE, died on the 27th ult. at Fortage, Wisconsin, at the ripe old age of 141 years.

Mar. 7, 1866

Died near Montezuma, Macon county, Ga., on the 24th of January, 1866, MRS. FARMILLA M. TURNER, thirty years of age, wife of CAPT. SAMUEL L. TURNER; member of the Baptist church.

Mar. 21, 1866

The death of the able historian, JARED SPARKS, President of Harvard, is announced.

Apr. 4, 1866

Paris, Ky. True Kentuckian, March 29 - On last Monday a fearful tragedy was enacted in Millersburg...the first shot killing F.F. WATERS, the son of H.H. WATERS, of Columbus, Ga., and formerly Auditor of that State. Waters was about 21 years of age, and had lost a leg before Atlanta, during the war, having been a Major in the 4th Georgia regiment. He was a student in the college at Millersburg...

Apr. 11, 1866

Died in Bibb county on the 25th ult., SARAH ELIZABETH, eldest daughter of D.R. and MARY J. McARTHUR, in the 17th year of her age; died of pneumonia (with eulogy).

Apr. 18, 1866

Terrible murder in Philadelphia. A terrible massacre occurred in Philadelphia, in the lower section of the city on Friday before last, of a family of seven members - CHRISTOPHER DEERING, his wife, niece and four children, on Mr. Deering's farm, at Point House and one JAMES LANE...

May 9, 1866

Obituary and tribute of respect by Burn's Lodge No. 56 F.A.M., Oak Grove, Macon Co., May 1st, 1866 - on the death of DAVID WORSHAM.

June 13, 1866

Horrible murder and robbery. On Sabbath morning last a fisherman on his way to his basket discovered the body of MASTER RILEY MARTIN, near the cemetery of this city...member of the Baptist Church; his parents reside near Cuthbert, Ga. (Bainbridge Chart and Compass,2d)

Disaster at Bamburg, S.C. by the storm on Tuesday afternoon... killed are: CARRY SIMMONS, AGNES BRABHAM, HATTIE BRABHAM, ELMORE SINBRIS, CHARLES STEWART, ERBANNA RENTS and BALOFFE HUFFMAN.

June 20, 1866

Titusville, Pa., June 10 - About 12 o'clock this morning a young man named JOHN DALE left here in a wagon, to be married to MISS HATTIE MATHISON, living about six miles north of here. When about two miles on the road, he received a rifle ball through his body... the rifle was found near where he was shot, evidently showing that the murderer had been within twenty feet of his victim. A rival for the hand of the young lady had threatened to shoot him, and he is supposed to be the guilty party.

July 25, 1866

On last Saturday night, BUD HAMMOND, of Atlanta, about 18 years of age, was killed by a negro boy. The mother of the negro held young Hammond while her son inflicted a terrible wound near his neck with a long knife. Young Hammond died instantly.

A young, educated and attractive woman named MAGDALENA KABLE, formerly from New Hampshire, committed suicide recently in Chattanooga - Cause, desertion by her husband, and then by a Dr. O.L. Gilman, under whose protection she had been after her husband left her.

July 25, 1866

Thirty years ago a widow named PATTY POLK was murdered in Cecil County, Maryland. The perpetrator was first discovered last week, by his own confession on a sick bed.

A tallahassee paper states that William, who murdered MRS. ROLLINS, in Wilkinson county, has been arrested near that city, and confined in jail. Mr. Rollins has been telegraphed to come and identify him.

Aug. 1, 1866

A private letter gives some details of the case of child-murder in Medina, New York, (already reported), in which a clergyman named JOEL LINDSLEY whipped his little boy to death because he would not say his prayers...(N.Y. Evening Post).

COL. HENRY LONG, formerly Mayor of LaGrange, and one of the best citizens of that county, died on Wednesday morning last, at the age of 69 years.

Aug. 15, 1866

A correspondent at West Point (Georgia) writes that on Saturday evening, a man by the name of CARRINGTON was shot down by one HARMAN BLACKBURN...(Atlanta Intelligencer).

An inquest was held in London, on the 10th ultimo, upon the body of MR. JOSEPH TONYBEE, physician of Saville Row, Burlington Gardens, whose death was caused by medical experiments...

Aug. 22, 1866

On Monday morning last, our vigilant and effecient chief of police, arrested a freedman named LUM JONES, formerly of Newberry, on suspicion that he was of the gang who murdered MR. LANE, of that District. Since then however, Mr. Green has found on the negro a watch that was taken from MR. WALKER, recently murdered near Chester, C.H., and it is presumed that the prisoner was involved in both murders. (Columbia Phoenix, 15th).

Sep. 19, 1866

DISHROON, who killed his brother-in-law two months ago near Danville, Va., has been found guilty of manslaughter, and sentenced to the penintentiary for five years.

A terrible boiler explosion took place near Newbern, North Carolina, on Friday last, at the steam saw mill of Jones & Whitcomb, by which MR. C.H. ALEXANDER was instantly killed, and five others were wounded. Loss, $20,000.

Sep. 26, 1866

A destructive tornado occurred at Mount Holly on Friday evening last. The Mirror says, it commenced about a mile and a half from Buddtown, uprooting trees, prostrating corn and fences. A mile and a half from Pemberton, the house of the MISSES ALCOTT was torn in pieces and one of the sisters fatally injured.

Terrible tragedy in Virginia. A correspondent of the Richmond Dispatch, writing from Buckingham Court House, Va., September 6, gives the following particulars of the terrible tragedy which recently occurred there: About three weeks ago or more, MR. ANTHONY WALTON, a wealthy mill-owner of this town, arose early in the morning with the alledged intention of visiting his mill and plantation, but suddenly changing his route, returned to the house. There he found MR. JAMES LEACH (a young lawyer who makes Mr. Walton's house his home during the sessions of court) in the room with his wife. Their positions relative to each other were such as to excite

Sep. 26, cont'd) - suspicion on the part of the husband, who at once ordered Mr. Leach out of the house, and forced the execution of his mandate at the point of a revolver; after which, he called for the carriage, and putting madam in, sent her to her mother. Nothing farther of interest transpired in the case, except that a bill of divorce was filed by Mr. Walton, until last Saturday, when Leach again rode into town. After strolling about the village for some time, he met ANDERSON WALTON, a son of Anthony by a first wife. Anderson reproach-d Leach at once with the scandal...and drawing his six-shooter, Leach fired, and young Walton fell pierced through the lungs...Just then Mr. Walton the elder rushed up and fired three shots from his pistol directly at Leach, but missing him entirely, slightly wounding Captain A.T. Moseley and a negro. Once more Leach fired, and the elder Walton lay a corpse...Anderson lingered until Monday evening about 2 o'clock, when as they were closing the grave over all that was mortal of his father, his soul joined him in the spirit world. But the tale of death does not end here. The REV. JAMES H.C. LEACH, D.D., a highly respected Presbyterian minister, died soon after hearing of the bloody drama in which his son had acted so prominent a part...Leach has been justified on the plea of self-defense.

Nov. 7, 1866

A correspondent at Edgefield Courthouse relates a curious incident which occurred last week, during the trial of R.J. BUTLER, for killing COL. TWIGGS...

Nov. 21, 1866

Information wanted. BENJAMIN SMITH, Company H, 40th Regt. N.C.T., has not been heard from since the fall of Fort Fisher. His father, H.H. SMITH, of Rockingham, Richmond county, N.C., would feel consoled to learn with certainty the fate of his son.

MARY KNIGHT 18 years old, died recently in Topham, Mo., of a peculiar disease. Her blood changed to sugar, and during her illness, which lasted six months, she would drink as much as a pail of water nightly.

By the recent death of COLONEL SAMUEL SWETT, Mr. Isaac Lincoln is left the sole survivor of the Harvard class of 1800.

Nov. 28, 1866

DR. GEORGE FRIES, a well known citizen of Cincinnati, died in that city on the 14th inst.

Dec. 19, 1866

Horrible murder and robbery at Palatka. MR. WILLIAM B. STEVENS, Sheriff of Putnam County, and exOfficio Tax Assessor and Collector, attended an appointment on Thursday, the 29th ult., at John Register's for the purpose of receiving the State and County tax from the citizens of that precinct. About 4 p.m. he left for Palatka on horseback, taking with him what money he had collected, supposed to be between two and three hundred dollars. On the Monday following his body was found about two miles from Register's, pierced in the breast by a rifle or pistol ball...(Jacksonville Union, Dec. 8).

Dec. 26, 1866

RT. REV. BISHOP STEPHEN ELLIOTT, of the Protestant Episcopal Church of this State, died suddenly in Savannah on Friday evening, the 21st inst...supposed from disease of the heart.

LYON J. LEVY, at one time the most prominent merchant of Philadelphia, died on Friday. He occupied at one time the site now occupied by the postoffice, on Chestnut street, from which he removed to the building now occupied by the National Bank of the Republic, which he erected at a cost of more than $100,000.

Jan. 9, 1867

Cincinnati, Jan. 7 - The train on the Dayton & Lake Erie R.R. was thrown from the track today, by a broken rail, near Green Springs, and several persons killed and many injured. The killed were MRS. JAS. EDMONSON, MRS. DENNIS, of York, Ohio, HENRY STARR, of Dayton, and a boy named PHILLIPS. Among the Injured were Miss Hughes, of Tiffin, Ohio, collar bone broken, and J. Palucie, road master, badly hurt.

Supposed murder. On the 22d of December last, an old lady named MARY STEVENS, disappeared from her home, on the Louisville road, about ten miles from the city, and since has not been heard of... it was found that the last seen of Mrs. Stevens she was in company with a man named Nathan Cohen, who, it appears, used to butcher for her occasionally...(Savannah Herald).

MAJOR JEROME WILSON, formerly adjutant on General Hood's staff, died of cholera on Wednesday, at Memphis, Tenn.

FRANKLIN W. ABBOTT died at Tyngsboro, Miss., on Wednesday, of lockjaw. He had served in the army during the rebellion, losing part of the finger of his left hand. Sometime since he removed to Tyngsboro, he having purchased a small farm, which he was cultivating. While at work in a saw mill on Thanksgiving Day, he caught his left hand in a saw and cut off the balance of the fingers, which resulted fatally, as stated. The deceased leaves a widow and two children.

Jan. 16, 1867

G.A. and D. PEAK, from Georgia, were crushed to death by a fall of rock in a coal bank, near Wheeling, on Monday week.

JOHN A. DARGAN, a poet of exceeding great promise, died in Philadelphia on Tuesday, at the early age of 31 years.

Jan. 23, 1867

A shocking affair. Details of the killing of "MAGE" HENDERSON, a son of JUDGE H.L. HENDERSON, by SAMUEL HARDAWAY, in Wakulla county, on last Sunday afternoon...(Tallahassee Sentinel).

WILLIAM S. HAMMIL, ESQ., died at his residence in Montequma, Macon county, Georgia, on the 3d day of January, 1867, aged 69 (?) years and 5 months...his remains repose near the sequestered shades of Traveller's Rest. (with short eulogy).

Tribute of Respect by Eureka Lodge No. 55 F.A.M. dated January 18th, 1867 - on the death of WILLIAM GREGG MEALD. He died of dropsy on the morning of the 15th instant, in the 52d year of his age.

New York, Jan. 21 - N. PARKER WILLIS, the poet, is dead. He was aged 60 years.

Feb. 20, 1867

MOLLIE TRUSSELL, who killed her paramour in Chicago a short time since and was sent to the penintentiary, has been pardoned.

Tragedy in Savannah. One man murders another and then commits suicide. The melancholy affair took place in the kitchen attached to the "Our House" dining saloon, and the principal actor was a Frenchman named ALFRED MEUILLOT, who was the chief cook in that establishment. His victim was a young man named PHILIP JUDGE, about twenty years of age, who, up to within a short time since, has been employed there as waiter...(from the Savannah News, of Monday).

Feb. 20, 1867

Distressing accident. We regret to learn that a daughter of MAJ. WEST, of the firm of West & Guthrie, of this city, was burned to death on Monday afternoon. It appears that she was alone in a room, and her clothing taking fire in a way unknown, she was dreadfully burned before assistance reached her. Her two sisters were burned in attempting to relive her. She was aged 27 years. (Atlanta Intelligencer, 12th).

Terrible marine disaster. Burning of the steamship City of Bath at sea. Only four lives saved. Twenty-two lives lost! Details from the Charleston Courier of the 15th...amongst those supposed to be lost are the three passengers, CAPTAIN CONY, MR. MEAD, FIRST MATE, MR. BACON, SECOND MATE, The Savannah Pilot (name unknown), A. CALDEN, CHIEF ENGINEER, JOHN WIGGIN, FIRST ASSISTANT ENGINEER, CHAS. A. CLARK, SECOND ASSISTANT ENGINEER, TALBERT, FIRST STEWARD, MOSES TAYLOR, SECOND STEWARD, MR. BANKS, QUARTERMASTER, JOHN RYAN, FIREMAN CHARLES POTTER, COOK, SECOND COOK, (name unknown), and three coal passers, JOHN HAMILTON, WM. FLINN, and one whose name is unknown...CAPTAIN JOSEPH S. CONY was a native of Maine and a relative of ex-Governor Cony, and during the war distinguished himself in several naval engagements as commander of one of the US gunboats, participating in the Fort Fisher attack with great gallantry. Capt. Cony commanded the steamship Wm. Tibbets, consort of the "City of Bath" until within the last two months, when he assumed command of the latter vessel. (Another account quoted in the same issue states that Albert A. Calden, John L. Wiggin, and Mead were rescued).

REV. DR. NATHAN HEWITT, so well known as one of the ablest temperance advocates thirty or forty years ago, died on Sunday, Feb. 3, at his residence in Bridgeport, Conn., in his 80th year.

Mar. 6, 1867

A well authenticated case of spontaneous combustion occurred at Columbus, Ia., Friday morning. ANDREW NOITE, a German, very intemperate in his habits, was found dead in his shop, his lips entirely burned away, leaving a ghastly hole; his tongue charred to a crisp. His nose was also burned, as if by fire coming out of his nostrils, and his clothes were still burning when found. No other part of the body save the air passages were burned. Physicians who examined the body pronounce it a clear case of spontaneous combustion. It is supposed that the fire was communated by attempting to light a cigar.

MR. ROBERT M. WELLS, aged about 22 years, a resident of Petersburg, and a printer by trade, was accidentally killed while out hunting in Chesterfield county Friday afternoon.

Mar. 20, 1867

Died near Perry, March 9th, 1867, MRS. LAURA J. BASKIN, wife of ALONZO P. BASKIN, and daughter of MR. JOHN G. WHITE, aged 19 years and 16 days; member of the Methodist Episcopal Church. (with eulogy)

Mar. 27, 1867

A negro named ADAM PAGE died in King George county, Virginia, on the 4th inst., in the one hundred and twenty-second year of his age.

Apr. 3, 1867

COLONEL LEVI C. TURNER, Judge Advocate of the War Department, died at his residence, in this city, on Thursday evening, in the 61st year of his age. A considerable portion of his time was spent in the profession of journalism. Over twenty years ago he was past proprietor and editor of the Cincinnati Gazette, and subsequently was an editorial writer on the New York Tribune. (Washington Intelligencer).

Apr. 3, 1867

An unfortunate affair transpired in Chattanooga county, in the neighborhood of Melville, on Monday, the 25th inst. It had been reported that a white man, supposed to be a horse thief, or some outlaw, was stopping at some negro cabins, in a very out of the way place. Several of the neighbors - Messrs. Allison, Cook, Fry, R.S. Foster, and two of his sons, Kinchen and Mose, all went together to the vicinity for the purpose of arresting the supposed refugee from justice. They surrounded the house, and Mr. R.S. Foster went to the door and ordered the man, whose name has since been ascertained to be STAFF, to surrender and he should not be hurt. Staff started towards the back door as if to make his escape. Mr. Moses Foster met him there, and again ordered him to surrender, but Staff started back towards a window, over which two guns were suspended. Mr. Moses Foster, supposing that he intended to take one of the guns to use against him, shot him with a pistol, producing instant death. Mr. Foster immediately gave himself up to the civil authorities, but as it was actuated by good intentions, he was discharged. (Rome Courier).

Terrific explosion on the Baltimore and Ohio Railroad. A terrible locomotive explosion occurred near Littleton, on the Baltimore and Ohio railroad, about 35 miles from Wheeling, on Thursday afternoon, by which three men, OTTO BURRELL, GEORGE ARTIS and R. JOHNSON were almost instantly killed...(Wheeling Register).

Apr. 5, 1867

R.G. PORTER, Mayor of Apalachicola, and an old and esteemed merchant, died at that place last Saturday afternoon.

It is stated that six cases of trichina spiralis have occurred in Springfield, Mass. - all in the family of RANSLEY HALL - from the eating of ham, and a daughter of Mr. Hall died on Monday from that terrible disease...

On Saturday evening about 3 o'clock, a mulatto prostitute named ANNA GARDNER, was shot and almost instantly killed...the deceased had been but a few months in the city, having come from Augusta, where she left a husband. The body was sent to Augusta by yesterday morning's train. (Savannah News).

Apr. 17, 1867

Died in Houston county on the 11th instant, JOHN P., infant son of F.P. and FANNY C. GAREY, aged 8 months 13 days.

Apr. 24, 1867

Fulton Superior Court - JOHN JOHNSON, a colored man, implicated in the BRIDWEL murder, was arraigned, and plead guilty of voluntary manslaughter. He was sentenced to the penintentiary for a period of nineteen years. ___ CARTER HEARD (a person of color) was found guilty of the murder of BUD HAMMOND (white) at the April term of the court 1866, and sentenced to be hung. The case was carried up to the Supreme Court by the prisoner's counsel, asking for a new trial. That tribunal having refused to grant a new trial, the prisoner was today 43-sentenced to death - the sentence to be executed on the 7th of June proximo, between the hours of 10 AM and 2 PM.

THEOPHILUS CISNEY died in Hill Valley, Huntingdon county, Pa., on the 20th ult., at the age of 104. He was in sufficiently good health to manage his farm until the age of 94.

The death is announced of the REV. DR. JOHN CAMPBELL, a well-known minister of the English Congregationalists. The deceased was born in 1795 in Scotland, and received his education at the universities of St. Andrews and Glasgow.

Apr. 24, 1867

Details of the murder of a man named PARRISH by Brownlow's militia in DeKalb county. (Nashville Banner).

May 8, 1867

Information wanted. Of R.N. BRADEN, WILLIAM C. KERCE, and JAMES H. KERCE. These young men were enlisted in Co. C, 40th Regt. Ga. Vols. by Capt. Hargrove, at Rome, Ga., on the 4th of March, 1862. After the fall of Vicksburg, they left with other paroled soldiers for their homes, in Georgia, and have not been heard from since by their relatives and friends. Any information in reference to said parties will be thankfully received by R.M. BRADEN, Rome, Ga.

RANDALL FULWOOD, a colored boy about eight years of age, was drowned while bathing in a round hole in Hoges' brick-yard on the morning of the 5th instant...

May 15, 1867

CAPT. F.C. CLEWALL, an ex-Confederate Officer, swallowed prussic acid in a St. Louis hotel on Friday, and died. He belonged to Mississippi, and is said to have left that State in consequence of a difficulty with a negro whom he killed. He was arrested and tried by the civil authorities, and was discharged; but fearing further prosecution by military authorities, he left the State.

The Dawson Journal states that MR. JOHN WISEMAN accidentally inflicted upon himslef a gunshot wound, which, it is feared, will result in his death. He was alive on Friday, but with little hope of recovery.

May 22, 1867

On Monday afternoon, at 126 Mott street, MICHAEL FARRELL, a tailor, was murdered in his room by another tailor named EUGENE SULLIVAN, living at 25 Pell street. The instrument used was a large-sized knife. Sullivan's wife had deserted him and cohabited with Farrell. The murderer surrendered himself. The case is in the hands of the coroner. Full particulars in our next.

Murder in a ball-room. On the night of Easter Monday, one of the civic societies of this city held a ball at the house of Mrs. Helather, No. 434 Second avenue...soon after midnight four men forced their way into the ball-room despite the efforts of the door-keeper. The President of the Society, MR. CHARLES ANERCHACIM, was called...one of the men by name of HORTON struck the President, and was incontinently kicked down stairs, followed by the rest of the gang. Horton turned and fired a pistol up the stairs, when Mr. Anerchacim ran down to stop him, and in doing so received another bullet in his side. Horton also fired three more shots, one of which struck Mr. Charles Kirchoff, when he ran off, and he was subsequently arrested. Dr. Simon, of East 6th Street, was called and found that the wound was of such a character that death might occur at any moment...on Monday afternoon the infured man died at his residence, 612 East 12th street. Coroner Schirmer will hold an inquest.

Horrible murder committed in the western part of this county, in what is familiarly known as the "Warrior District." MR. ISAAC HEARD, the man murdered, had missed some of his hogs, and an intimation had been given him by some parties, that he could find the thief...Mr. Heard was a man about 28 years of age, with a small family.

The sad intelligence of the death of our friend and former active citizen, MR. IRA H. TAYLOR, reached us on Monday. Was a native of New York State. He removed to Macon when about 20 years of age, and was employed as chief accountant in several of our most flourishing institutions, until in 1859 he was made Secretary and Treasurer of the Macon and Western Railroad Company, which office he held twelve

(May 22, cont'd) - years. He then removed to his plantation in Jefferson county at No. 10 on the Central Rail Road...on last Sunday morning, after penning a few lines to his family, in a state of partial mental derangement, at twelve o'clock he terminated his earthly existence by shooting himself through the head...his age was about 48 years; leaves a wife and two lovely daughters. His family passed through Macon yesterday to the place of his remains.

Death of BISHOP LAVIALLE, pious prelate of the Roman Catholic Church. He died at half past nine o'clock on the evening of Saturday last, May 11th, at the residence of the Ecclesiastical Superior of the Nazareth community of Sisters of Charity, near Bardtown, Kentucky. (Louisville Courier).

General Stonewall Jackson's colored nurse died in Jackson, Madison county, Tennessee, on the 30th of April, 1867, at the advanced age of 113 years 9 months 12 days. She was a slave in the Jackson family from early life until about 25 years ago, when the General set her free. Shortly after being liberated, she moved to Madison county, Tennessee, to live with some relatives, and remained there until the time of her death.

REV. G.G. NORMAN, of Wilkes county, died on the 9th. The Gazette says that he was Ordinary of that county from the creation of the office till his death.

June 5, 1867

Bibb Superior Court. The case of ISAAC HARRIS, charged with the murder is ISAAC WINGFIELD (colored) was tried on yesterday...

Details of shooting accident in Crawford county, Ga., near Hopewell - in which young MORDAUNT SHARP was killed and his brother Peyton Sharp slightly wounded. (Letter to the paper from the boys' father, JOHN M. SHARP).

PROF. JAMES P. WADDELL died at his residence this morning at four o'clock, of paralysis. The deceased was a son of MOSES WADDELL, one of the early Presidents of Franklin College, and was himself a member of the Faculty for many years.

Information wanted. Any person knowing the whereabouts of A.M. COOK, native of Watauga county, Ala., will confer a favor upon his distressed mother by addressing MRS. EMILY J. COOK, Montgomery, Ala. He was a member of the 59th Alabama Regt., Col. Hall; was captured, and has not been heard from since the close of the war.

July 17, 1867

CAROLINE BREMER, an inmate of the Portland (Me) almshouse for thirty years, died there on the 38th ult. In all that time she had never spoken a word.

ROBERT STRATTON, a well known miller, near Gainesville, Ala., was murdered on the 6th while sleeping in his bed. The weapon with which he was shot was held so near his body as to burn the flesh.

MR. THOMAS MILLS, well known in Montgomery, was murdered in Greenville, Ala., on Tuesday. No particulars, as yet, have been made public.

SILAS BRAGG, believed to be one of a gang of outlaws in Baldwin county, Ala., murdered on the 3d instant, a citizen of that county named BRUTON. On the 6th he was found dead in the woods.

DINAH, an ex-slave of DR. GODWIN, of Autauga county, Ala., died on Tuesday in that county, aged 110 years.

We are pained to learn, from the Intelligencer, that ALBON CHASE, one of the best citizens of Athens, died in that place on the 10th inst.

July 17, 1867

LOTTIE SHERWOOD, a "pretty waiter girl," shot and killed WAREN PETTIT, her lover, and who was employed in the same saloon, in Memphis, on Monday night.

DR. ROBERT J. BRECKENRIDGE, well known in medical circles in the Confederate States army, and at one time acting Cheif Medical Director of the Army of Northern Virginia, died a few days since in Houston, Texas.

MRS. RUTH, a daughter of the late GEN. QUITMAN, of Mississippi, died on the 10th in Louisville.

EX-GOV. JOHN A. KING, of New York, died on Long Island, on Sunday. He was the first Governor elected by the Republican party after its formation in 1854, in that State.

July 24, 1867

The relatives of MR. CLARENCE H. SELLECK, who have been in suspense as to his fate since his disappearance over four years ago, have received intelligence of him in Savannah, Ga., from a lady in Tennessee. He was killed in a skirmish near Fairfield, Bedford county, Tennessee, while General Bragg was in command of the Western Army. A lady, who lives in sight of the ground where the engagement took place, took care of his body and had it buried, but the officer in charge of the Federals refused to give her his papers and letters. Mr. Selleck was well known in this place, and also in Due West, where he was a student at Erskine College...The Savannah Oglethorpe Light Infantry, the original company of the lamented F.S. Bartow, were his first comrades in the war, and he will be remembered by the survivors of Kershaw's brigade, with which he served in Virginia from the spring of 1861 until the summer of 1862. When killed, he was a member of a Confederate cavalry regiment, the 2d, attached to General Wharton's division. (Abbeville, S.C. Banner).

CAPTAIN BRIDGEWATER, a notorious desperado, was shot and killed at Stanford, Ky., on the 19th instant. Sixteen balls were lodged in his body.

RICE PUCKETT killed DR. WITT, a dentist, at Gaylesville, Ala., on the 16th, for seducing his sister.

BISHOP SCOTT, of California, died in New York on the 14th instant. He was formerly a Presbyterian minister.

A railroad employee named BROWN stabbed and killed a man named BERAGLIE, proprietor of a restaurant in Columbia, S.C. on Wed.

A German butcher named OFF was murdered Sunday night, in Louisville, by some of his fellow Teutons. Beer and ten pins inciting thereto.

JOHN ROBINSON, of Blount county, Illinois, died lately aged 110 years. He was born in Scotland, and married first at 51.

MR. WILLIAM N. WHITE, editor of the Southern Cultivator, died at Athens on Sunday last; a Northern man by birth...

Aug. 14, 1867

The Sumter Republican of the 13th says that JUDGE J.C. HORNE of that county was shot by two negroes, and so seriously wounded that he was not expected to recover.

Sep. 11, 1867

On Thursday last JACOB RENNER stabbed and killed HENRY SCHWARTZ, in Columbus, Ohio. Benner was 15, and the murdered boy, 12 years of age.

Sep. 11, 1867

FRED KOELER, a German, committed suicide Thursday night, in Cincinnati, by swallowing a dose of arsenic. The next morning, PETER BAXTER, a Dane, hung himself.

Sep. 18, 1867

CHARLES T. WHEELER plunged into the water of St. Clair, Mich. and saved a young girl from drowning only to meet his own death, being struck by a propeller, and to lose the enjoyment of $22,000 which he had gained a few days before.

On Wednesday last at Jackson, Tennessee, one of Brownlow's militia, without the slightest provocation, deliberately shot down in the street MAJOR HARTMUS, formerly of Gen. Bate's Staff, one of the worthiest citizens of that place.

Two suicides in New York City on the 13th by shooting - WM. PULLMAN, shopkeeper under St. Nicholas Hotel, and HERMAN MELVILLE.

Sep. 25, 1867

WILLIAM BROBERG, of Montgomery, Ala., shot himself through the heart, on Friday last, in that city.

A man named PRITCHARD, lying asleep on the track of the Alabama & Florida Railroad, on Friday night, was run over and instantly killed.

Oct. 2, 1867

SAMUEL GRISWOLD. We inadvertantly omitted to notice the death of this well-known gentleman, who died at his residence in Griswoldville, in Jones county, on the 14th inst. aged about 77 years. He was probably better known to planters than any other men in all the cotton States for his "cotton gins," having first perfected his machinery for their manufacture under skillful mechanics (one of which was A.D. Brown of Columbus)...

COL. E.E. CROCKER died at his residence in Marion, Twiggs county, on the 24th inst. His age was about 64 years. He has long been known as a practicing attorney in several counties.

An ex-Confederate soldier named MAGRATH was shot and killed by a negro, near Pocataligo, SC, on Friday last.

A daughter of the REV. JOSEPH CROSS, a minister well known in this section, died recently in Houston, Texas, of yellow fever.

Oct. 9, 1867

Our community was shocked to learn of the death of MR. L.S. BENNETT, who has been for some fifteen or twenty years a resident of this city. We learn that he had been feeling unwell for two or three days, and on Sunday morning took a cold bath. Within five minutes after leaving the bath, he was in a state of congestion, and died yesterday morning at 8 o'clock. (Sav. Adv. 1st).

COL. STROTHER JONES HAWKINS died recently at his residence, near Henderson, Kentucky, aged 77 years. He was born in 1790, in Fayette county, in the District of Kentucky. He served in the war of 1812, was at the battle of the Thames.

WILLIAM H. HESS, living twelve miles from Pittsburgh, was gored to death by a bull on Saturday. Mr. Hess was about 60 years of age.

LIEUT. OWEN THOMAS THWEATT, for a long time the faithful courier of General Benning, died in Columbus on Thursday night.

Nov. 1, 1867

JAS. S. EVERITT, a worthy citizen of Thomas county, died in that county on Thursday.

COL. DANIEL WARD, a "fine old" Virginia gentleman, died in Culpepper county, in that State, last week, aged 82 years.

DR. ROBERT J. WARE, a native of Georgia, but for forty years a wealthy and prominent citizen of Alabama, died in New York city on Saturday.

JOHN NANCE, who murdered WM. McBEE near Strawberry Plains in 1865, has been refused a new trial by the Supreme Court of that State.

The Loyal Leaguers who killed YOUNG HUNNICUTT in Pickens District, South Carolina on the 12th of October have had sharp justice meted out to them. Six negroes will be hung on the 6th of December, and eighteen others sent to the penitentiary.

Nov. 20, 1867

A man named SHEPHERD shot and killed his wife near Worcester, Massachusetts on the 15th inst.

HENRY G. DEAN, well known in Atlanta, died of yellow fever recently in Texas.

ROBERT H. POMEROY, cashier of the Mohawk Valley National Bank, committed suicide at Uitca, New York on the 16th inst.

MR. SAMUEL SPELSSEGER, a resident of Savannah for more than half a century, died in that city on Saturday.

MRS. MARY CANNON has recovered $5000 damages in Fulton Superior Court, from the State Road, for the killing of her husband, an employee of that road, in 1862.

EMERSON, who was killed at Albany by BETTS a short time since, was formerly a citizen of Anderson, South Carolina, and during the recent civil war, a brave soldier of the Palmetto Riflemen.

Died in Houston county on the morning of Thursday the 13th inst., after a protracted illness of Typhoid fever, MR. FREDERICK WARREN, aged about 68 years. Was born in East Hartford, Conn. 14 Dec. 1799, but on attaining his majority came to North Carolina, where he married and lived until 1830, when, with his young family he moved to this State and settled in the upper part of Houston; continued to reside in the same neighborhood for 37 years (with long eulogy).

A man named McCLELLAN was drowned in an oil tank at Spring Creek, Tennessee last week.

MAJOR JOSEPH WORK, an old and worthy resident of Nashville in happier days, but his throat in that city on Tuesday. He was over sixty years of age.

A man named GEORGE CLOUD, while working on a railroad bridge at Bridgeport, Ala., on Tuesday, was knocked off by the passage of a hand-car, and falling sixty feet was so shockingly mangled as to died in one hour and a half after his fall.

A horrid murder was committed in Baldwin county, on the plantation of Mr. Benjamin Myrick, on the 7th inst., by JACKSON THOMAS, a negro. He cut his victim (another negro) to pieces, then buried him.

The Southern Recorder learns the death, at Nava-Sotia, Texas, recently, of GENERAL THOS. BLACKSHEAR, formerly a resident of Thomas county, and at one time, a Senator from that county. He was about 58 years of age.

Nov. 27, 1867

The REV. THOS. WOLSTEN HOLM, a Presbyterian minister, and the oldest Odd Fellow in the United States, died in Columbus, Mississippi, last week. He had belonged to the Order fifty years.

JIM HARRISON, "manhood," made a "cold corpse" of HENDERSON SMITH, on Tuesday last in Memphis, by shooting him through the head.

JOE WARFIELD, a negro who murdered MR. WM. LANG, Cashier of the First National Bank of Zenia, Ohio, in April 1866, was arrested on Sunday on board a steamboat at Memphis.

WILEY W. BARNUM was shot and killed in Marietta, on Monday last, by THOMAS J. AINSLEY.

MR. N. ARNOLD was shot and killed by JOHN WILLIAMS, in Morgan, Calhoun county, on Monday last.

EDWARD F. KINCHLEY, a prominent and respected citizen of Augusta, died in that city on Monday night.

MR. WILLIAM CARR, aged 92 years and for 34 years a resident of Floyd county, died last week at his residence in that county.

COL. ALFRED HILL, one of the editors of the Chicago Tribune, died in that city on the 17th inst. He was a member of the Louisiana Constitutional (?) Convention of 1864, and an officer on Banks' staff at the same time.

Dec. 18, 1867

SILAS BRONSON died in New York a short time since. He left $15,000 a piece to about twenty-five nieces and nephews scattered all over the country. Hurry up, all you Bronsons.

MRS. BARCLAY, born in February 1765 and since 1816 a resident of Bullitt county, Kentucky, died in that county last week. She once dined with Gen. Washington, and often referred to this fact with pride.

ZEB WESTWOOD, of Cincinnati, while engaged in stealing a corpse from a cemetery in that city on Wednesday night last, was shot and killed by the watchman of the grounds.

MRS. MARGARET A. JOHNSON died in St. Louis on Monday, a few hours after the demise of her husband, EDWARD WILLIAM JOHNSON, a brother of General Joseph E. Johnson.

The Athens Banner learns that a serious collision occurred at Elberton a few days ago between a party of negroes and the civil authorities...the SHERIFF, MR. GEORGE ALLEN, was killed.

Death of the REV. RICHARD T. MARKS. We find in the Sumter Republican of the 10th inst. a notice of the death of this most esteemed and well known gentleman. This sad event occurred at the residence of his son-in-law, Dr. A.D. Bruce, in this place on Friday the 6th inst. The deceased was born in Louisville, Ga. 24 Sep. 1809; joined the Presbyterian church at Augusta, Ga. in 1826; was married in 1827; licensed to preach the Gospel by the Flint River Presbytery at Columbus in 1837, and ordained by the same Presbytery in Oct. 1839...

Jan. 1, 1868

A shocking occurrence at Whitesville, Harris County. (Taken from the Columbus Enquirer) - Details of the killing of FRANK DAVENPORT.

Jan. 1, 1868

The ring marked "C.L.," found on a charred body, one of the victims of the Angola disaster, is supposed to belong to CHARLES LOBDELL, the assistant editor of the LaCrosse (Wis.) Democrat, who it is thought, was on the train.

We regret to learn that an unfortunate difficulty occurred at Lowndesboro on Monday last, between MR. JAMES D. McCALL and MR. SAURIN, which resulted in the death of the former... (Montgomery Mail, 26th).

Jan. 8, 1868

MRS. NANCY CARTER, aged 115 years, died at Alexandria, Va., on Thursday last.

While the last down West Point freight train was at LaGrange last Thursday, a lad about 16 years of age, HARRISON SLOPER, stepped upon the engine to sell apples; as the train started he endeavored to step off, but fell between the engine and tender, the wheels of the latter passing over and dreadfully mangled his body. He lived in great agony until about five o'clock the next morning, when he expired. We understand his family was on the eve of moving to Atlanta. (Atlanta Era, 5th).

Death of the oldest Free Mason. The funeral of JOSHUA R. JEWETT, ESQ., of Granby, took place last Saturday. He had attained the ripe age of 96 years, and had begun the 73d year of his Masonic life, having been made a Mason in St. Mark's Lodge in 1795. He was a "bright" Mason to the end of his life and filled with the highest acceptance, at the age of 90 years, the position of Principal Sojourner of Lafayette Chapter. He leaves several children who have passed middle age, though scattered widely in the States, still have had a care for his comfort, and among them the wife of Paran Stevens, the prince of hotel-kiipers in this country. (Hartford Times).

JOHN CALLAHAN, an undertaker in Montgomery, died on Friday afternoon of a fit of apoplexy. He was struck down while preparing a Federal Lieutenant for the grave.

Suicide in Montgomery. A very respectable man, GEORGE HARDT, shot himself with a pistol in Montgomery, a day of two since. He was induced to commit this act by the riotous demonstrations of Swayne's nigger pets who he feared were going to kill him in order to plunder his premises.

Even while we penned the lines upon the "oldest man in town" which appeared in our last issue, old MOSES DAVIS, the subject of our sketch, was breathing his last. After a short illness, with which old age feebly wrestled, Moses closed his eyes upon the world he has known for 96 years, and on Sunday last his body was consigned to the grave. (Wilmington Star, 31st ult.).

Died in this city, at his residence, on Friday evening Dec. 27, 1867, GEN. WILLIAM BAILEY, in the 78th year of his age. Born in Camden County, Georgia, on the 4th of April 1790, and emigrating to Florida when it was comparatively a wilderness, for quite half a century was he a resident of the State. (Tallahassee Floridian, Dec. 30th).

Feb. 5, 1868

A MR. STROBEL, a resident of Blackville, South Carolina, was found on the roadside near that place on Friday last, supposed to have been killed by a fall from a horse.

Mar. 11, 1868

    We are reliably informed that a difficulty took place at Sikes' Store, Decatur county, on last Saturday, between Wash Owens and COOTE MILLER, in which the latter received some eight or ten very severe cuts with a large pocket-knife, from the effects of which he died almost instantly...(Early County News).

Mar. 25, 1868

    MR. GEO. CHARES, a well known citizen of Chattanooga, was drowned on Sunday last, in Lookout creek while attempting to swim his horse across.

    MR. REUBEN TOMLINSON, of Monroe county, was killed last week by being thrown from his buggy, and dragged some distance through the woods.

    Funeral notice. The friends and acquaintances of MRS. CHARLOTTE J. McDONALD and Mr. and Mrs. F.H. Alley, are respectfully invited to attend the funeral of the former, from the Mulberry Street Methodist Episcopal Church, this Wednesday afternoon at four o'clock.

Mar. 26, 1868 (daily)

    PHILIP LEFTAN stabbed and killed CHARLES BOUDEL, and seriously wounded John Andrews, at a saloon, in Louisville, on Monday night.

    Died in the city of Macon, of hemorrhage of the stomach, on the 6th day of February last, MRS. PHEBE GRIER, wife of MR. JAMES V. GRIER, in the 57th year of her age. The deceased was born in Washington county, Ga. on the 25th of May 1811, and in childhood, with her parents, removed to Macon, where she lived until the day of her death. In 1830 she married MR. WM. HIGHTOWER, by whom she had six children, two only of whom lived to years of maturity. One of these (an only son) died in the prison camp at Point Lookout.. In 1848 Phebe Hightower married Mr. Grier, and in the same year, while on a visit to Lee county, she professed religion, was baptised, and became a member of the Baptist Church...(with eulogy).

    Died at the residence of her uncle, D.W. Visscher, near this place, on the 14th March 1868, MISS KATE EASTON VISSCHER, eldest daughter of FREDERICK and BETTY VISSCHER, of Owingsville, Kentucky. (with long eulogy).

Apr. 14, 1868

    We are truly sorry to learn that JUDGE WILLIAM E. GRIFFIN, of Morgan, Calhoun county, while out hunting one morning last week, on Chickasawhatchie creek, was shot by a freedman, who mistook him, as he said, for a bear. The negro carried him home, and in a few hours he breathed his last.

    Shocking accident. Yesterday evening, while MR. B.G. TILDEN and Mr. Geo. Gray were riding in a buggy on the road near Thunderbolt, the horse took fright, and running away threw Mr. Tilden and Mr. Gray out of the buggy. The latter escaped with a few bruises, but the head and shoulders of the former were caught between the spokes of the wheel...at last accounts, Mr. T. was in a hopeless condition. (Sav. News, 9th).

    The Augusta down train was the scene of a melancholy incident on Wednesday. One of its passengers, COMMODORE GEORGE A. PRENTISS, of the U.S. Navy, without exhibiting any signs of indisposition, suddenly fell dead...(Charleston Courier, 11th).

May 19, 1868

    We regret to learn from the Tallahassee Floridian the death of MRS. ___?___ ILOCLEN ALSTON, wife of his Excellency, GOV. WALKER, of that state, in Tallahassee, on the 7th inst.

May 26, 1868

DR. BELFIELD NEWSOME shot in a Railroad car. Litigation about Confederate money alleged to have been the cause. One of the most cold-blooded murders which has happened for some time in this part of that state, occurred last yesterday afternoon, about three miles from town, on the Nashville and Northwestern Railroad... (Nashville Banner, 17th).

We learn that MR. MAGOR SMITH, of Griffin, formerly of the firm of Flemiston & Smith, of that place, committed suicide yesterday morning about daylight, by cutting his throat with a razor; leaves a wife and several children.

The death of HON. JOHN A. GILMER is announced in the Greensboro (N.C.) Patriot, of the 15th instant...death occurred about ten o'clock on Thursday morning, at his residence in this place.

From a Richmond paper we learn that the grave of MAJOR J.R. STURGESS, of the 3d Georgia regiment, who was killed in the battle of Seven Pines, was found in a cornfield which was being ploughed. The body was taken up and reburied at the junction of the Charles City and Williamsburg roads, about two and a half miles from Richmond, Va. (Savannah News & Herald, 19th).

We regret to learn that COL. FRANK LITTLE died at the residence of his father, in Walker county, on Sunday the 17th inst. His disease was consumption. For a considerable time before the close of the war, Col. Little was in command of the 11th Georgia regiment.

We learn from the Athens Watchman, of the 20th, the death of COL. ROBERT McMILLAN, a prominent citizen of North Eastern Georgia, which occurred at his home in Clarksville, Habersham county, on the 6th inst. During the late civil war, he was Colonel of the 24th Georgia regiment.

Details of horrid affray in Greenville, Miss. of Wednesday afternoon in which COL. POWELL HINDS was killed.

The funeral services of MRS. W.B. BULLOCK were conducted at Christ Church yesterday afternoon. Mrs. Bullock, at her death, was 76 years of age. (Savannah News, 21st).

June 2, 1868

Terrible tragedy at Marshallville - Headed Marshallville, May 28 - tragedy occurred yesterday morning about 8 o'clock. MR. W.C. STANLEY shot a freedman by the name of HENRY WHEELER...he died last night about half past nine o'clock.

Suicide. The body of MR. EDW. CROCKER, a young man well known in this city, was found near the farm of the late Chas. Carter, Esq. The verdict of the Coroner's Inquest was that his death was caused by laudanum administered by his own hands. (Chron. & Sent.)

Vienna, Ga., May 27th - A very painful accident happened on the night of Sunday the 23d ult., in the burning of a negro cabin, the property of JACK BALLARD, a freedman, living in the vicinity of our town, which destroyed two of his children who were sleeping till the flames had enveloped the building and prevented their escape from this most horrid fate...

On last Saturday the eldest son of ED. BUSTAIN, ESQ., of Fayette county, was thrown from a skittish young mule against a tree, and instantly killed. We deeply sympathize with his afflicted parents. (Griffin Star, 29th).

Death of EX-PRESIDENT BUCHANAN.

June 2, 1868

Died in San Luis Potosi, on the 6th of January last, after a protracted illness of consumption, CAPTAIN WILLIAM MITCHELL, a native of Georgia. Capt. "Snap" Mitchell was an ex-Confederate soldier.

CAPT. HENRY C. BRANDT, well known as Freedmen's Bureau Agent for St. Peter's parish, South Carolina, but who has generally kept his headquarters in Savannah, was found dead in his bed yesterday morning, at his room, No. 16, City Hotel Building. His disease was congestion of the lungs. Deceased was a Prussian by birth, came to this country and served in the Federal army with distinction, was wounded, and received the Appointment of Captain in the Veteran Reserve Corps. (Savannah News & Herald, 27th).

June 9, 1868

JOHN S. ASHE. On Saturday evening last, with the setting of the sun, passed to eternal repose all that was mortal of this chivalric Carolina gentleman. Colonel Ashe was born in 1796, of wealthy parentage whose ancestry could be traced far beyong the first settlement of this State. For many years he occupied a seat in the Senate of this State and was a welcome compeer in the councils and domestic associations of the Hamptons, Haynes, Prestons, and other honored sons of Carolina (Charleston Courier, 1st inst.).

COL. W.L. WYNN, formerly a well known citizen of Columbus, for many years a member of the Legislature from Muscogee county, and after whom was named the beautiful suburban village of Wynnton, near that city, died in New Orleans on the 28th of May, aged 69 years.

A negro man, named JOHN WARDLAW, was killed yesterday, in the Glade road, opposite Woolfolk's bend. He had stolen a mule from Mr. Jas. Braley, of Harris county...(Col. Enquirer, 5th).

On Sunday evening last, May 30th, CAPT. JEWETT McGINNIS was killed by WALTER CHEEK, in Jasper county, near the line of Newton. Capt. McGinnis was living on a plantation adjoining the land owned by Cheek, and occupied by Mr. J.C. Bennett. Some difficulty had arisen between the parties resulting in mutual threats. Meeting at the time mentioned, Cheek being armed with a double-barreled gun, after some angry words, discharged both barrels at McGinnis, forty-nye buck shot taking effect in his breast. Cheek then left, and has not, as yet, been arrested. (Covington Enterprise, 5th).

June 23, 1868

JOHN P. EVE, one of the oldest and best citizens of this county, died at his residence near Eve's Station, on Friday, the 12th inst. We suppose his age to be not far from 70 years. (Rome Courier, 16th)

Death of COL. E.P. WATKINS. We are pained to announce the death of this gentleman in Coweta county on Saturday last, of a pulmonary disease that long preyed upon his constitution. (Constitution, 16th)

JAMES CURENTON, of Girard, Alabama, was stabbed and killed by PETER BIEHLER, of Columbus, in a bar-room in the latter place, on Saturday night; and a young man named Brock was stabbed and dangerously wounded on the same night, by a man named Pressly, at Wommockville, near Columbus - both of which facts are reported by the Enquirer of yesterday.

Sad casualty. MR. JACKSON PHIPPS, who resides about twelve miles north of the city, was thrown from a colt he was breaking, on Monday afternoon, and almost instantly killed. He was an estimable young man and leaves a large circle of friends to mourn his untimely end. (Cuthbert Appeal, 19th).

June 23, 1868

Shocking casualty. Three persons drowned. Suspicion of foul play. On Wednesday evening last, MR. B. ROSSIN, who conducted a plantation on Wardo river, about seven miles from this city, left here for the purpose of visiting his place, in company with an Irish laborer named Frank, and three negro men and one negro woman, in a small boat. Since then the melancholy intelligence of the drowning of Mr. Roddin, the man Frank and the woman, has reached us under circumstances which induce us to believe that foul play has been practiced...(Chas. Courier, 19th).

July 14, 1868

MAJOR LAWRENCE VAN BUREN, brother of President Van Buren, and for many years postmaster at Kinderhook, died suddenly on the evening of the 2d instant, at his residence in that village, in the 85th year of his age.

July 21, 1868

WILLIAMS, the negro murderer of the brothers LUKE, in Irwin county, was burned to death in the jail of that county last week. The building was entirely destroyed.

COL. YELVERTON P. KING, of Greensboro, died on the 5th inst. He probably was the oldest member of the Bar in Georgia. Was Solicitor General of the Ocmulgee Circuit in 1823, Minister to Bogota during Mr. Filmore's administration. (Milledgeville Recorder).

Aug. 11, 1868

CAPTAIN SAMUEL BARR, indicted as accessory to the murder of HENRY ANDERSON on the steamer Great Republic, was admitted to bail yesterday in the sum of $20,000. Captain Dan Able and W.H. Thorwegan are his sureties.

Sep. 1, 1868

Died at Magnolia Hill, Johnson County, on Sunday, August 30th, 1868, NORA COHEN, youngest child of JAMES R. and NORA C. SNEED, aged 19 months and 24 days.

Died in Griffin, Georgia on Sunday afternoon, August 30th, at five o'clock, EMORY, aged 14 months, infant son of MR. and MRS. EMORY WINSHIP.

Died in this city on the 28th Aug., ROBERT BIRDSONG, ESQ., aged about 71 years. He was one of our older residents, having settled here in 1824, as one of the firm of Gillespie & Birdsong; for many years a member of the Inferior Court, and one of the City Council. On the formation of the Macon Volunteers, he was elected First Lieutenant, and was the third member initiated into Macon Lodge, in which he held office for several years. On Sunday his remains were consigned to their resting place in Rose Hill Cemetery, by Macon Lodge No. 5, by the largest assemblage of the Order ever congregated on a similar occasion.

Departed this life on the morning of the 26th August, at his residence in Twiggs county, Georgia, DANIEL O'DANIEL, aged about 62 years; leaves a son, wife and grandchildren. (with short eulogy).

The riot in Twiggs County - On last Monday week two negroes, by the names of NELSON and CAROLINUS, engaged pulling fodder on the plantation of A.F. Beckome, got into a fight, in which Nelson killed Carolinus...

Sep. 8, 1868

From the Fort Gaines Mirror, Sept. 5th - This morning about 8 o'clock, the new bridge being built across the Chattahoochee river, in consequence of the rising waters, which drifted rafts of timbers against the temporary structures, washed them away, and the whole came down with a tremendous crash and fatal results...Among the killed and wounded we could only learn the names of the following: Killed, JOHN C. HILL, SHERIFF of Clay, HOOKER STEVEN, missing and supposed to be killed, JAMES MIDDLETON, COL. and JERRY SUTTON. Wounded mortally: WM. A. JACKSON, R.L. PETERS and ROBERT BROWN. Wounded slightly: Wm. Walden, W.H. Jernigan, W.G. Jernigan, Wm. Mount and ANDREW NEWSON, COL., mortally.

Our circus going citizens remember HERR LENGEL, the lion tamer, who has been here with Ames' show. He was bitten through the leg a few days ago by the lioness, at Madison, Indiana, and afterwards died from the loss of blood...

An eagle killed a child. A Tippah county (Miss.) school-teacher writes details to the Winona Democrat: A sad casualty occurred at my school a few days ago. The eagles have been very troublesome in the neighborhood for some time past, carrying off pigs, lambs, etc. No one thought that they would attempt to prey upon children; but on Thursday, at recess, the little boys were out some distance from the house, playing marbles, when their sport was disturbed by a large eagle sweeping down and picking up little JEMMIN KENNY, a boy of eight years, and flying away with him. The children cried out; and when I got out at the house the eagle was so high that I could just hear the child screaming. The alarm was given, and from screaming and shooting in the air, etc., the eagle was induced to drop his victim; but his talons had been buried in him so deeply, and the fall was so great that he was killed; or either would have been fatal.

Sep. 15, 1868 (? - date illegible)

Died at Enterprise, Miss. on the evening of the 22d August, MRS. E.E. SMITH, wife of COL. H.S. SMITH, of Mobile, Ala.

Died in Baker County on the 2d inst. at his residence, HENRY J. SLAPPEY, at the age of 41. When quite a young man, Mr. Slappey removed from Twiggs to Baker County, and engaged at once in the business of agriculture; was a Methodist. (with long eulogy).

Little "Johnnie," son of MRS. S.A. DRAPER, aged six years, died on the 25th day of August, 1868. (with eulogy).

REUBEN SIKES, a butcher of Bennington, Vt., during a fit of delirium tremens a few days since, chopped of the hands and feet of his little three year old son with a meat ax, and would have gone further had not the screams of the child attracted the neighbors.

Supposed murder. Early Monday morning CHARLEY WILSON, about fifteen years of age and son of the late EDWARD G. WILSON, started out hunting with FRANK GUE, a son of Alderman P.L. Gue, and hunted along the White Bluff road. About 12 o'clock Frank headed back, stating that as he had come out without permission, he wanted to get back before his father came home to dinner. Charles said he would not go back then but would sit down and rest awile, and this was the last that Frank saw of him...as Charlie had a fine gun and wore a good suit of clothes, it is supposed that his two companions murdered him in order to get possession of those articles. (Savannah News & Herald, 2d).

Oct. 6, 1868

A large audience assembled at the Catholic Church yesterday morning to pay a last tribute to the earthly remains of HENRY HORNE. A solemn funeral dirge was sung by Mrs. Blackshear, Misses Connor,

(Oct. 6, cont'd) - Mr. Maas, and others in the choir, and an appropriate service read by the Priest; was interred in Rose Hill Cemetery.

Oct. 13, 1868

Double murder in New Kent. The murderers and incendiaries arrested and in jail. In Tuesday's Dispatch appeared the record of the most startling and cold-blooded tragedy that has ever been entered upon the criminal calendar of Virginia. The paragraphs referred to contained an account of the inhuman murder of MRS. JULIA STEWART, of New Kent county, the burning of the dwelling-house over the head of the corpse, and the killing of JOHN BAKER, a half-breed Indian in the employ of the unfortunate woman...(Rich. Dispatch, 2d).

Death on the gallows. Execution of AMOS GORMAN, LEVI JENKINS and ROBT. WHITUS for the murder of JONATHAN SHEFFIELD -- was murdered on the night of the 25th of last August. Was the proprietor of a small grocery and provision store near Vineville, a few steps beyond the city limits.

Obituary notice of MRS. NANCY FAULK, relict of MARK FAULK, which occurred at the residence of her son, in Twi-gs county, September 21st ult., in the 66th year of her age. (with a very long eulogy).

Oct. 27, 1868

MR. WM. BEADLEN died in Coweta county on the 6th inst. He was born July 13th, 1773.

Paragraph on burial of GEN. COBB at Athens. Funeral service and honors.

MRS. BATHSHEBA F., consort of RICHMOND RALEIGH, died in Macon, Ga., October 10th, 1868, in her 42d year. She embraced religion in 1850 (?) and joined the M.E. Church, South, at Fort Valley, Ga. (with short eulogy).

JOHN WATKINS PATE, son of DR. R.H. and MRS. E.V. PATE, was born on the 3d of August 1863 (?) and died of brain fever on the 28th of September, 1868. He was the first born of his parents. Central Georgian please copy. (short eulogy).

Dec. 1, 1868

MRS. BEACHNIAN, wife of a Federal soldier stationed at Columbia, died on Saturday, from the effects of wounds received the previous Thursday, at the hands of a sweet tempered "colored" lady.

DR. JOHN MAYO, one of the old time "Virginia gentlemen," died in Richmond on Sunday. He wore a cocked hat to the day of his death.

MR. PARIS J. TILLINGHAST died at his residence beyond Wynnton, Monday night, in his 89th year. He was originally from Providence, Rhode Island. For many years he was one of the most prosperous merchants in Fayetteville, North Carolina. He came to Columbus in 1838, and since has resided in or near the city. For ten or twelve years he had charge of one of the leading houses in our city, but being unsuccessful in cotton speculations, he retired from business, and since has been living a very quiet existence. A year or two ago his wife, at the advanced age of 93, breathed her last. (Columbus Sun, 25th).

Richmond, Nov. 28 - DR. ARTHUR E. PETTICOLAS, Superintendent of the Lunatic Asylum at Williamsburg, committed suicide there this morning by leaping from a window of the Asylum, dashing his brains out on the bricks below. The deceased was a distinguished physician, and was former Professor of the Medical College here. His mind has been unsettled for some time past.

Dec. 1, 1868

Died in Twiggs county, October 13th, 1868, DANIEL W. SHINE, ESQ., aged 82 years. He was born July 30, 1786, in Jones county, North Carolina, and immigrated to Georgia in the year 1810, settling in Pulaski county, then on the Indian frontier. In the war of 1812-14 he held the commission of Lieutenant in the command of the late Gen. David Blackshear, as may be seen by the published muster roll. His father, JOHN SHINE, was a soldier of the Revolution, whose services in the battle near Camden, South Carolina, in 1786, are referred to in White's "Historical Collections of Georgia." At the close of the war in 1815, D.W. Shine opened a store in Twiggs county, and for ten or fifteen years pursued the trade of a merchant, in which he was eminently successful. Retiring from business more than thirty years ago, he devoted himself to his large planting interests, and to the education and settlement of his children. For several years he was a Representative in the Legislature. About his fifteenth year he connected himself with the Baptist Church and continued faithful to the last. In February 1861 he was smitten with total blindness.

Dec. 8, 1868

The dead POLLARD. Radical reflections on the late editor of Southern Opinion. (From the Cincinnati Commercial 25th). The death of H. RIVES POLLARD by violence was only a question of time. He was morally certain to come across a man who would respond to his virulence by shooting him. Pollard was a social porcupine not to be approached without danger of a wound from his poisonous quills...

Another Tennessee horror. Butchery of an entire family near the Kentucky border. Capture of the murderer with the blood stains still upon him. A little over a week ago a frightful tragedy was enacted in Fentress county, Tennessee, near the Kentucky line. There lived in that section a family composed of an old lady, some eighty years of age, and her three grandchildren - one a young lady, another a boy of twelve, and the third a small girl. In the neighborhood was a man named LOGSDON, ill-favored of face, and of little character, who in some way became cognizant of the fact that the old lady had in her possession a considerable amount of money, the back pay of her dead son, who had been a soldier, and he resolved to secure it at all hazards. Proceeding one night to the house she occupied, Logsdon, with knife and revolver, murdered the grandmother and granddaughter, and left the boy for dead also...
(Louisville Courier-Journal, 30th ult.)

Washington County mourns the loss of one of her best citizens, MR. DAVID E. CUMMING, who died on the 24th inst.

Death of a distinguished native Georgian. The Memphis papers announce the death in that city, on the 26th ult., of JUDGE WM. L. HARRIS, a native of this State, but long a resident of the State of Mississippi. Judge Harris was one of the ablest, purest and most influential men in the State of his adoption. He served with great distinction upon the Circuit and Supreme Benches of Mississippi. He shunned politics and refused a seat on the Supreme bench of the United States to link his own fortunes and destinies with those of the South; was in the 61st year of his age. (Columbus Sun, 2d) If we are not mistaken, Judge Harris was a son of the late Gen. Jeptha Harris, of Athens, and was probably a native of Elbert County, removing, however, to Mississippi from Athens.

A strange story. A maniac named JACQUES CONSTADT died in New Orleans on Tuesday, the 24th instant. The Picayune gives his history as follows...

A.M. MATTHEWS, an employee of the Muscogee railroad, was fatally crushed between two cars on Thursday.

Dec. 8, 1868

Tribute of Respect by Austin Lodge No. 247, Smithville, Ga., Nov. 28, 1868 - on the death of FRANCIS H. CHEVES, who departed this life on Nov. 15, 1868.

Tribute of Respect by Houston Lodge No. 35 F.A.M., Perry, Ga., Nov. 16, 1868 - on the death of JOHN G. MOORE, who departed this life September 21st, 1868, aged 23 years and 1 day.

MARY ANNIE BRASSEY, the only child of MRS. PETRONIA WALKER, fell asleep in Jesus December 3d, 1868, aged three years nine months four days. (with short eulogy).

Dec. 15, 1868

MR. WILLIAM BIRD, the oldest (illegible) of Hancock county, died in that county on the 28th ult.

Horrible outrages by the radical militia of Arkansas. The following dispatch from Little Rock appeared in the Memphis Avalanche of the 9th. The scene of the outrages was Louisburg, Conway county. On the night of the 3d, a disguised party went to the house of ALVIN and WASH LEWIS, colored, living near that town with two white prostitutes who had been repeatedly ordered to leave the country on account of bad character. The party broke into the home, killed Wash and run Alvin off. Saturday, Captain Matthews' company of colored militia went to the neighborhood. Meeting JOE JACKSON and ROBERT PERRY on a cotton wagon, they immediately arrested them. Four negroes took Perry into his care, stood him against a tree and shot his ear off. He then broke from them and escaped. They then shot Jackson mortally, and left him. He was found, and told who did it before expiring. They then went to the home of THOMAS HOOPER, aged 60, took him off and shot him down the road, afterward saying he tried to escape...

Melancholy suicide. MR. THOS. J. PRICE, SR., a very aged man, committed suicide in this city on Friday night last by taking poison. He was well known here as Assistant Bridge-keeper under Mr. Robert Cunningham. He had been laboring under a fit of insanity for several days previous to his committing this rash and fatal act. Mr. Price was a native of South Carolina, and lived in Columbia, S.C. for many years, where we knew him in better days.

Fatal rencounter. MR. FLOYD SAWYER was killed on Saturday morning last, in Houston county, by a man named ETHERIDGE, one of his tenants. Sawyer was attempting to cross the fence around Etheridge's house, for the supposed purpose of attacking him, when the latter fired, and Sawyer fell mortally wounded.

Died in Smithville, Lee county, Ga., November 12th, 1868, THOMAS M. SKINNER, infant son of DR. T.T. and MRS. MATTIE SKINNER, aged 5 months 18 days. (with eulogy).

Another victim of negro malice. FREDERICK BRICKMAN, who was wounded in the abdomen and groin, in the attack upon the special police force on Thunderbolt road last Saturday night by an organized gang of negro murderers, died from the effects of his wounds yesterday. Mr. Brickman resided upon the same place as the late Mr. Broadbacker, and assisted in cultivating the extensive vegetable gardens of the latter. He was a native of Germany, was upwards of forty years of age, and leaves a wife and family. His funeral will take place at three o'clock this afternoon. (Savannah News, 9th)

Dec. 22, 1868

A few days since a son of DR. H.W. HILL, of Rowan county, N.C., and about 17 years, charged a musket for the purpose of firing at a flock of wild geese, but having unfortunately overcharged the piece, the concussion produced by the discharge was so great as to discharge

(Dec. 22, cont'd) - the barrel of the gun from the stock, which, striking the young man upon the forehead, inflicted a mortal wound. Two of the wild geese were also killed by the shot.

Foul play. Body of a dead man found near the city. On Sunday morning, while some little boys were skating on Proctor's creek, to and a half miles beyond the Rolling Mill, on the Mason and Turner's Ferry road, they discovered under the ice the body of a dead man... An investigation of the mystery at once was had, when the body was recognized by several neighborhood acquaintances as that of MR. HIRAM PROVINCE...(Atlanta Constitution, 14th)

Shocking accident. JOHN BRITT came to his death on Saturday night under the most horrible circumstances, having been literally roasted alive. He was a workman at J.V. Rice & Co.'s iron foundry, where he has been employed seven or eight years...(Wilmington, Del. Commercial)

On the 10th of November, died, in Valparaiso, MRS. DAVIDSON, one of the sufferers by the terrible earthquake of the 13th of August. She was a widow and was living at Arica with her son when this catastrophe occurred...

MR. WILLIAM BURGAY, who killed MR. MORTIMER MINCHEW, in a rencontre in the Rutland District of this county on Friday the 11th inst. - an account of which we published at the time - came to this city on Friday last, and voluntarily surrendered himself to the custody of Sheriff Martin, and was admitted to bail.

Died at his residence in Twiggs county, Ga., on the 18th of December, JAMES G. WALL, in the 72d year of his age. This venerable man was prostrated by successive carbuncles through a period of several weeks; member of the Methodist Church. (with short eulogy).

It was rumored on our streets yesterday, that DR. WM. WEST, in an altercation with DR. GEORGE PATTERSON, of Edgefield District, S.C., lost his life. The particulars of the difficulty arising between these gentlemen have not come to our knowledge, and we refrain from speculation in the matter. Dr. West was in this city only a few days since - Friday last - on the night of which he is reported to have been killed. He leaves a family of ten children, who have within the last six weeks been called upon to mourn the decease of a loved mother. The widowed mother of Dr. West, MRS. STARR, known in connection with the Globe Hotel of this city, and the Trout House of Atlanta...(Augusta Republican, 16th).

Dec. 29, 1868

Death of GEN. J.W. ARMSTRONG, who died at his residence in Bartow county on the 21st inst. His remains are expected to arrive here this morning, and his funeral will take place from the Presbyterian Church at 3 o'clock in the afternoon.

Hanging of the Seymour Express robbers. A New Albany dispatch to the Chicago Tribune, dated December 12th, gives some additional particulars of the hanging of the Reno brothers (FRANK RENO and SIMEON RENO) and CHARLES ANDERSON at that place on the 12th inst. by a Vigilance Committee from Seymour, Indiana...

Two difficulties in Stewart County - Both on the same day. On the 16th instant CAPT. J.C. BYRD had a misunderstanding with MESSRS. JOHN and WILLIAM BEALL, about some settlement of rent, which resulted in the killing of Captain Byrd by the Bealls...On the same day a difficulty between DANIEL HORTON and J.N. ARNOLD and a son of Mr. Arnold occurred, in which the latter was shot and so seriously wounded that he has since died. This difficulty, like the one between Byrd and the Bealls, grew out of a settlement of business, and at Mr. Horton's house. (Columbus Enquirer, 23d)

Dec. 29, 1868

More outrages in Arkansas. Memphis, December 19 - The Avalanche's Little Rock special tonight says, reliable information states that on the morning of the 16th, four companies of militia, commanded by Colonels Gray and Williams, from Roane and Matthews counties, the latter colored, entered Louisburg, shooting in every direction, marched to the store of Bream & Casey and set it on fire...during the fire MR. CASEY was shot down and his body thrown into the flames after rifling his pockets...

We learn that a fatal rencounter took place on Saturday evening last between MR. JAS. NEWNAM and JAS. HARTLEY in which the latter lost his life at the hands of the former...

Tribute or Respect by Reynolds Lodge No. 255 - on the death of JOHN W. JAMES - died at his residence in Taylor County on the 7th of November, 1868, in the 45th year of his age.

Augusta, December 26 - GABRIEL MARTIN and two maiden sisters, residing in Columbia County, were murdered and robbed on Thursday night, and their house set afire and bodies consumed. Suspicion is said to rest on negroes who reside in the neighborhood.

Apr. 20, 1869

Terrible tragedy near St. Paul, Minnesota. Chicago, April 9 - A special from St. Paul to the Times, gives the full particulars of the murder of his wife and four children by JOHN B. GRAY, at Oakdale Township, Washington county, Minnesota, on the 7th inst. The murderer is a farmer, and was laboring under temporary insanity at the time he committed the deed. Gray is a man about 40 years of age, a native of Harrisburg, Pennsylvania. His wife, ALICE, formerly MISS FARLEY, was 38 years of age. They were married at Hasting eleven years ago. The children were two boys an two girls, as follows: MARGARET, aged nearly 10; JAMES B., aged 8; DAVID, aged 5; and NELLIE JANE, aged 3...

Terrible tragedy at Courtland. A conductor shot dead by a hotel keeper. From the Huntsville Democrat, 8th - One of the saddest tragedies we have ever had to record, was enacted at the little town of Courtland on the M. & C.R.R. on yesterday morning...the body of THOS. J. OATES...was killed by a man named PARSHALL, who keeps the railroad eating house at Courtland. The difficulty originated about the payment of a board bill of a brakesman on the road, who had left the employ of the road, and gone o-f in debt to Parshall. It is said that Parshall claimed that Conductor Oates was responsible for the payment of the board bill, which Oates would not admit, and from this sprung the quarrel...

GEN. JOHN SCHNIERIE, of Charleston, for many years Mayor of that city, and member of the Legislature, died there Wednesday.

Regret to announce the deaths of GEORGE H. TRAYLOR and JOHN T. BOYKIN - the former of whom died at his home on Friday last of dropsy; the latter on Tuesday following, stricken down by paralysis while going over his farm, and found dead where he fell. (LaGrange Reporter, 16th).

By letter we learn of the death of a most estimable lady in Athens - MISS SUSAN CRAWFORD. She was a daughter of one of the great men of this country, HON. WILLIAM H. CRAWFORD. (Atlanta Intelligencer, 17th)

Homicide in Houston County. A correspondent writing under date of the 12th instant, from Henderson, Houston county, gives us the particulars of a homicide there on Friday night, the 9th instant. The parties were RUFUS SHANNON and WILLIAM THOMPSON, both negroes. Shannon was beating his wife, who is a sister of Thompson's, and the latter very naturally remonstrated whereupon Shannon struck him with a board on the head, from the effects of which he died the next night. The murderer made his escape.

Apr. 20, 1869

On yesterday evening at about six o'clock, MR. WILLIAM SHACKLEFORD, of this city, fell into the Savannah river and was drowned... (Chronicle & Sentinel, 18th)

Supposed murder of DR. BENJAMIN AYER in Jefferson county. Was a native of Maine, between 65 and 70 years of age. He emigrated to Georgia and settled in Louisville when quite young, where he followed the practice of medicine with considerable success. Some time prior to the war, he moved into Emanuel county...whether he had committed suicide of fell by the hand of an assassin is yet unknown. (Savannah Advertiser, 18th).

Augusta, April 19 - The Chronicle & Sentinel contains the particulars of the murder of BENJAMIN AYER, Republican member of the Legislature, killed near Louisville, which states that Ayer was murdered and robbed by a negro named WILSON...

Tribute of Respect by Jeffersonville Lodge No. 349 F.A.M., Jeffersonville, Ga., April 10, 1869 - on the death of DR. IRA E. DUPREE.

Apr. 27, 1869

Death of LUKE P. HAMES at the hands of MR. AP. SMITH. We understand that Hames was at his mother-in-law's, Mrs. McLeod, last night about 10 o'clock very much intoxicated; Mr. Smith, a neighbor, being on a visit at the house the same time...(Americus Republican, 21st).

Murder in Brooks County. A correspondent of the Savannah Morning News writing from Quitman April 20 says: On last Sabbath a little boy, aged about 10 years and son of MR. ALEXANDER HUMPHREYS of this county, went fishing with a negro boy about 15 years of age. During the day the negro killed the white boy and ran off. He was apprehended and confessed the deed.

Acquitted - A.W. JACKSON, tried before Washington county Superior Court, April 15-17, for the murder of WILLIAM A. TAYLOR, on the 30th of August, 1868, was acquitted, as we learn from the Central Georgian - the jury returning a verdict of "not guilty" Sunday morning.

MR. ARCHIBALD BRUCE, SR., aged 90 years, died in the valley on the 20th inst. Mr. Bruce, says the Talbotton Gazette, was for many years a ruling elder in the Presbyterian Church.

MRS. POTTER, aged about 70 years, widow of WASHINGTON POTTER, late of Calhoun county, committed suicide on the 13th inst., at the house of her son-in-law, MR. THOMAS WILKERSON...(Dawson Journal, 22d).

Starved to death. The lifeless body of a negro man, named ALFRED WILLIAMS, was found yesterday in a house in Cooleyville, beyond the brickyard...His wife had left him because he would not help support their children. He had been on the chain gang for stealing meat from Major R.J. Moses, and having served his time, was discharged last Thursday. (Columbus Sun, 21st).

More details on the murder of DR. BENJAMIN AYER. (See previous issue).

Tribute of Respect by Macon Lodge No. 5 F.A.M., Macon, Ga., April 19th, 1869 - on death of SIMRI ROSE.

Death of COL. R.T. PRIDE. He died of pneumonia early yesterday morning, his health having been feeble for several years past. He served most gallantly in the late sectional war, entering the service as Captain in the 31st Georgia regiment, and at its close being Lieutenant-Colonel of the regiment. Was wounded five times in service...leaves a widow but we believe no children. (Columbus Enquirer, 20th).

Apr. 27, 1869

Terrible railroad accident. New York, April 23 - A horrible accident is reported on the Long Island Railroad...Among the passengers killed are WM. PUSHMAN, President of the Atlantic Bank, Brooklyn, and P. STRAUNTON, a railroad contractor.

COL. SUMNER J. SMITH died at his residence in Banks county last Saturday. He had been in bad health for some time. He served in the Georgia Legislature about the year 1859, from Towns county.

We are pained to announce the death of MR. EZEKIEL M. PARK, son of DR. COLUMBUS M. PARK, who died of meningitis in our city on Tuesday morning last.

COL. THACKER HOWARD, one of our oldest and most esteemed citizens, died at his residence near this city yesterday morning. He had been in bad health for some time and was over 70 years of age. He was a brother of Major John H. Howard, deceased, and leaves behind a widow and several children. (Columbus Sun, 25th).

Philadelphia, April 20 - Mathematician MITCHELL, aged 76, died of debility at Vassar College today.

June 15, 1869

Horrible murder by negroes. The New Orleans Picayune says that a most horrible outrage was perpetrated on Saturday last, near Natchez, Miss. A young planter named MARR, son of R.H. MARR, a prominent lawyer of New Orleans, was waylaid and murdered on his plantation by negroes. When found he had been dead probably two hours, and 132 buckshot were discovered in his body. He had gone out, it is said, for the purpose of arresting a negro, and was waylaid and murdered by a gang.

Death of MR. PETER RANDALL occurred here yesterday morning after an illness of about ten days. Mr. Randall was nearly or quite 80 years of age.

Also regret to announce the death of MR. AQUILA CHENEY, one of the oldest citizens of this county, which occu-red on the 1st instant. He was 84 years old, and had been a resident of Monroe for fifty years.

We regret to learn from the Milledgeville papers of Tuesday that MRS. FANNIE HUNTER, wife of COLONEL R.L. HUNTER, formerly Secretary of the Executive Department, and daughter of the HON. IVERSON L. HARRIS, died in that city on Wednesday night the 2d inst.

MR. WM. KNOX, one of the oldest and most popular citizens of Montgomery, Ala., is dead.

About two weeks since a MR. STRICKLAND, recently from Grantville, Ga., married a lady near Tallahassee, or Cowles' Station, on the Montgomery and West Point Railroad. Returning to Grantville on his bridal tour, he met a man between whom and himself an old feud existed. An altercation ensued in which Strickland was killed. The widowed bride, with the corpse, came to Cowles' Station on Monday evening's train. (Montgomery Advertiser, 9th).

Homicide in Meriwether County. A friend informs us that a difficulty occurred near Lutherville, in the upper part of Meriwether county, on Saturday last between a MR. STRICKLAND, from Alabama, and MR. GEO. TEAGLE, in which Strickland was shot through the body and died, and Teagle was shot twice through the arm and once in the body. (LaGrange Reporter, 11th).

June 15, 1869

One man killed and two wounded in Hancock County. We learn from the Hancock paper that, on last Saturday night, MR. JOHN TAYLOR, Superintendent of the Montour Factory, was shot and killed by a young man named JAMES OXFORD, in the adjoining village of Montour... (Chronicle & Sentinel, 13th).

From the Memphis Appeal, June 9 - We learned last night by a special telegram from a correspondent at Jackson, Mississippi, the particulars of a horrible tragedy enacted in the city yesterday by COLONEL E.M. YERGER...the victim was COLONEL J.G. CRANE, of the U.S. Army, Chief of Subsistence for the Department of Mississippi, and lately the Acting Mayor of Jackson...

MISS LIZZIE MASON, whose mother lives at or near Wetumpka, committed suicide at the residence of Colonel Butts, in this county on Friday morning last, by taking strychnine. Some eighteen months since her father died, leaving her mother with several young and almost helpless children...(Talladega Mountain Home).

MRS. KOLB, who recently died in Madison, Morgan county, left an estate valued at near $100,000, almost all of which if bequeathed to the Ordinary of the county in trust, for the purpose of educating the poor children (orphan) of the county.

Full particulars of the killing of COL. FLOURNOY. From the Chronicle & Sentinel, of Saturday...

Staunton, Va., June 14 - JESSE EDWARDS, a negro who raped and afterwards murdered MISS SUSAN PYLE, a respectable young lady, was taken from jail today and hanged.

Died at the residence of Mr. Thomas T. Lytle, in Macon county, Ga., on the 5th of June, MRS. MARTHA SHEALY, aged 24. She attached herself to the Baptist Church at Traveler's Rest in 1863 (?)... (with eulogy).

Untimely death of little boy JOHN H.J. HOOK, who died on the night of the 2d of March, 1869, with laryngitis, aged 2 years 5 months. (short eulogy).

July 6, 1869

Another murder. This morning about two o'clock, the quiet of the city was disturbed by the firing of six pistol shots, in rapid succession, in the eastern portion of Atlanta. Our vigilant police repaired promptly to the spot, and ascertained that a murder had been committed by a negro named SAM JOHNSIN, upon the body of MR. R. FOX. The deceased has a large number of relatives if DeKalb, Gwinnett and Fulton counties...(Atlanta Constitution, 28th).

CAPTAIN L.B. DUCK, one of our busine-s men of long standing, died after a very brief illness on Sunday afternoon. The attack was probably an apoplectic one. Captain Duck was about 43 or 45 years of age, and has long been engaged in business in Columbus. (Columbus Enquirer, 29th).

From the Valdosta Times - Died at his residence in Clinch county, Ga., on the 8th of April last, SAMUEL REGISTER, aged 83 years and 9 months. He had seven sons and seven daughters - 112 grandchildren - and 155 great-grandchildren.

Fatal affray in Scriven. Occurred near Mobley's Pond on the night of the 21st inst. Resulted in the death of a negro named GEO. WASHINGTON...(Waynesboro Sentinel, 30th).

July 27, 1869

Reprieved. HENRIETTA GREER, the negress under sentence of death for the murder of MISS NANCY WRIGHT, and held for execution today, has been reprieved by Governor Bullock until the 20th of August.

JAMES R. BUTTS, one of Macon's oldest, most prominent and best known citizens, died at 5 o'clock yesterday evening, after a short illness. For more than thirty years he was identified with the commerce and businces enterprise of Macon. He may be said to be one of those who founded her prosperity, and from the time that he started the line of cotton boats to the day of his death, he was actively interested in her growth and success. In latter years he was chiefly engaged in the land agency business, and in that connection prepared and published the best map of Georgia which is now extant...One by one the familiar faces are disappearing from amongst us. It is but a few days since we chronicled the death of GEO. T. ROGERS...the funeral will take place from the Baptist Church this evening at 4 o'clock.

MR. M.T. HARRIS, of this county, died suddenly at Tazewell, in Marion County, last Friday. His remains were buried on Sunday near his residence, about eight miles east of Talbotton.

An election row in Barnwell. Two men killed. Another man fatally shot. Four men stabbed. (From the Augusta Constitutionalist of Friday) - The bloody row occurred at the election precinct of Sleepy Hollow, Barnwell county, S.C., on Thursday...killed: JOHN H. HOLLAND, JOHN S. GREEN, SR., and A.P. WOODWARD.

Alexandria, Va., July 22 - COMMODORE S.S. LEE, brother of General R.E. Lee, died at his home in Stafford county today.

Memphis, July 24 - WADE BOLTON, who was shot some days since by DR. DICKENS, is dead. He bequeathed $100,000 to charitable purposes, including $10,000 to Stonewall Jackson's widow, and fifty acres of land to each of Jackson's former slaves.

Oct. 5, 1869

ARCHIBALD W. OXENDINE, one of "Marion's Men" during the Revolution, and for forty years of his life a Baptist preacher, died recently in Missouri, at the age of 110.

Unparalleled outrage. MR. FERGUSON, of Jefferson county, while lying sick upon his bed, was so severly beaten on Saturday night that it is feared he will not recover. The negroes who inflicted this severe punishment are marked, and many of them can and will be identified. His wife and daughter made their escape to the woods, where they remained till daybreak.

The homicide at Coley's Station. Details relative to the killing of MR. W.F. MASON...

Information was received in New York on the 30th of September of the death at Chicago on the 29th of ex-Postmaster ISAAC N. FOWLER. His remains are on the way to New York for interment.

Arrest of a murderer. Officers Ferrill and Plunkett night before last arrested a noted scoundrel by the name of ROBERT NAPPER, who had recently murdered another negro by the name of JUDGE FREEMAN, an overseer on the plantation of T.J. Williams, Esq., in Jones county...

The Augusta papers announce the death of WM. H. CRANE, SR., an old merchant and esteemed citizen, who died suddenly Wednesday of paralysis.

The Covington Enterprise announces the death of MR. RICHARD BRYNE on the night of the 28th of September, a well known citizen of Covington, aged about 70 years.

Oct. 5, 1869

    MR. JAMES WOODRUFF, of Newton county, killed himself Saturday week by the accidental discharge of a Colt's repeater...

    The Athens Banner reports that a few evenings since, MRS. MARION JOHNSON, of Hart county, in attempting to fill a lighted lamp, ignited the kerosene causing an explosion which burned her so seriously that she died in a few hours. The house took fire also but was extinguished by a little son of deceased, a lad of age ten.

    Tribute of Respect by M.S.L., Thomaston, Ga., Sept. 17, 1869 - on the death of GEORGE E.F. BIRDSONG, who died August 18th, 1869.

SEE INTRODUCTION
THESE ARE ADDITIONS

Jan. 30, 1867

    Died in this city Dec. 17, after a few days of severe illness, MAJOR A.G. NEGEL, in the 80th year of his age. Was a native of Anhalt, Germany, and came to this country in early life. Sor some years he resided in Savannah and was the last surviving member of the old Savannah Guards of 1812. He was a faithful Master Mason (with eulogy).

June 12, 1867

    Death of Chief Justice JOSEPH HENRY LUMPKIN, which occurred at his residence in Athens on the morning of the 4th instant. Was born on 23 Dec. 1799, and thus in the 67th year of his age; came to the Bar in 1820; was an elder in the Presbyterian Church (long eulogy).

    Fatal accident. A fatal accident occurred at the saw mill of Loomis & Bennett on Sarurday. While some logs were being hurled up the inclined plane, the belt which works that part of the machinery broke. A man named TIDWELL, from the southern part of Georgia, who was an employee in the mill, attempted to check the descent of the truck by applying the brakes, but was unable to do so, and while so occupied, the impetus of the truck caused the drum, upon which the rope attached to the truck was wound, to revolve with such rapidity that it flew into pieces, one of which struck Mr. Tidwell on the head, breaking his scull and causing death in a few hours. (Chattanooga Union, 4th).

June 26, 1867

    Death of JOHN L. WOODWARD. Died a few days since at the Indian Springs, his present place of residence. He had for many years been a well known and prominent citizen of Monroe and Crawford counties, and one among their earliest settlers, and a patron of this journal nearly forty years.

    Died in this city of paralysis on the 20th instant, MR. JOHN M. ELLIS, age 28 years 6 months 22 days.

July 3, 1867

    SAMUEL B. WIGGINS died in St. Louis recently from a cancer in his nose, caused by pressure of his spectacles.

July 3, 1867

WM. KING and ABRAHAM OWENS, ex-captain and ex-private in Kentucky regiments in the Federal service during the war, were hung on Friday the 28th at Franklin, Ky. for the murder of HARVEY KING.

Portsmouth, July 1 - REAR-ADMIRAL GEORGE F. PEARSON died - aged 68 years.

The "Intelligencer" of Friday reports JOSEPH O. KELLEY, of Newton county, as committing suicide by shooting himself through the head with a rifle.

ROBERT McKNIGHT, father of "ASA HARTZ," died recently. He learned the "art preservative" in 1788, and set type nearly 78 years.

CAESAR ROUNTREE, f.m.e., aged 13 years, made a dead tree of another boy of the same name, in Lowndes county, on the 20th inst., with a knife.

ABRAM SPANN, a colored delegate to the Radical Convention to be held on 4th July at Atlanta, shot and killed HENRY CLEMENTS, another colored man in Louisville, Jefferson county, on the 25th - says a letter to the Augusta Chronicle & Sentinel.

July 10, 1867

A negro man 112 years of age died on the 1st inst. at Shelbyville, Ky.

COL. GEO. A. SMITH. The remains of this gallant soldier reached here on yesterday. Was a native of our city. When the war commenced, he raised a company in this county - the Brown infantry - and was ordered to Pensacola...was buried in Rose Hill Cemetery.

REV. JOEL HAWES, D.D., for nearly fifty years pastor of the First Congregational Church in Hartford, Conn., died in Gilead, of congestion of the lungs...was in his 78th year, being 77 years old in December last.

GEO. W. CUYLER, for many years Cashier of the Central Railroad Bank at Savannah, died on the 12th of June in Munich, Bavaria.

The Valdostian Times of the 3d says that NAT ASHLEY, of Coffee county, was shot and killed at Jacksonville, Telfair county, on Monday, by WASH WELLS, of Telfair.

FREDERICK THOMPSON, captain of a negro volunteer company in Montgomery, Ala., was drowned in the Alabama river, at that city, on Sunday.

PAUL TAYLOR, a one-armed negro recently convicted of murder in Montgomery, will be hung on the 27th inst.

July 31, 1867

MAJOR EDWARD W. WRIGHT died at Camden, Arkansas on the 30th of June, aged probably about 67 years. He was a native of Maryland, and settled in this city about 1824, and was engaged in mercantile business with John S. Childers, and between them they built the old "Washington Hall" block (with other buildings) which still retains its name (although it has once arisen from the ashes). On the organization of the Macon Volunteers on 23d April 1825, he was selected as its commander. Was early associated with the Macon Lodge as an active member, and superintended the construction of its first Hall. In 1826 he married ELIZABETH MORGAN, of this county, who survived but two or three years, leaving one son. Maj. Wright, a few years after the death of his first wife, married the daughter of HENRY CROWELL, of Crawford county, and removed to Camden, Arkansas, where he has since resided; member of Presbyterian Church.

July 31, 1867

GEN. L.L. GRIFFIN died at Aberdeen, Mississippi on the 9th inst., aged about 75 years. He was projector of the present "Macon & Western Railroad."

A man named ROCKWELL, hailing from Memphis, fell from the third story of a building in St. Louis last week, and was instantly killed.

A negro man named CORA RICE made cold pudding of himself on last Saturday at Memphis, by taking a large vial of laudanum.

Two men named BRIDGEFORD and NICHOLS shot each other at Frankfort, Ky. on Friday with the following results - Nichols dead, and Bridgport mortally wounded. (Ed. note: Name was listed by two different spellings).

PAUL TAYLOR, the one armed negro who was to have been hung on Friday last at Montgomery, Ala., has been respited till the 23d of August.

A farmer named GOWAN and his wife, at Weathersfield, Vt., were murdered on the 23d by a Frenchman. He knocked them down and beat their brains out with an axe.

RICHARD G. WALKER, a native of this State, but long resident in Montgomery, Ala., died in that city on Thursday of a congestive chill.

WILLIAM BLACKWELL, aged 17, was drowned while bathing in the Chattahoochee river at Columbus on Thursday afternoon - the second case at that place within four weeks.

A wretch named HUNTER killed his mother at Cincinnati on the 25th because she begged him to go home from a drinking saloon.

A man named NORMAN shot and killed a companion named BAMFORD the same day in the same city. They both belonged to Newcomb's Minstrels.

L.D. TYSON, the "swell" tailor at Louisville, shot himself on Saturday and died almost instantly. "Young Louisville" mourns, as he was the neatest hand on tight pantaloons in the city.

Aug. 28, 1867

JAMES CUTTING, inventor of the ambrotype process for taking pictures, died last week in the Insane Asylum at Worcester, Mass. He went crazy experimenting with an aquarium.

MRS. AMAR (?), a lady of Charleston, died very suddenly on Sunday morning of apoplexy, in St. Patrick's Church as she was attending early mass.

A young man named WORTHEN, a resident of Wilkes county, was recently killed by the accidental discharge of his gun while he was out hunting.

Two men named GRAHAM and HUGHES shot and stabbed each other on the 19th at Lebanon, Ky. Cause of the quarrel - the price of a glass of whiskey!

JANE WILLIAMS cut the throat of her sister-in-law, at Gibson township, Indiana, on the 22d inst., almost severing the head from the body.

GEORGE EBERLEIN, an old citizen of Moblie, shot himself Friday night and died almost instantly. In the great explosion shortly after the surrender, he lost all his property, and was permanently crippled.

MR. B.J. QUINN, a citizen of Wilkes county, temporarily residing in New York City, died in that county on the 12th, very suddenly.

Aug. 28, 1867

CAPT. J.B. HARRISON, one of the oldest citizens of Dallas county, Ala., was murdered and robbed on Saturday, a few miles from Selma.

PAUL TAYLOR, a one armed negro, was hung in Montgomery, Ala. on Friday last, for the murder of a white peddler.

COLONEL W.H. FOWLER, Clerk of the Alabama House of Representatives at its last session, was killed in Jefferson, Texas recently by a U.S. Internal Revenue Collector.

MRS. ANNIE A. HUNTER, wife of COMMODORE THOS. T. HUNTER, late of the Confederate States Navy, died very suddenly on the 20th inst. near Washington, Wilkes county.

MRS. BREWSTER, an aged lady residing in Newton county, was found dead in her house one day last week. It is believed she was murdered.

MRS. DR. CARTER, of Mobile, lost her life Friday night at the hands of her own son. She thought there were burglars in the house and going to her son's room to arouse him, he, mistaking her for the burglars, drew a pistol from under his pillow, and shot her dead.

Oct. 30, 1867

One bright afternoon in the winter of 1863, I was wandering through Greenwood Cemetery, and suddenly came upon an humble grave, in a small three cornered lot, quite unadorned, and only marked by a plain white stone, bearing this simple inscription:
    MRS. ELIZA GILBERT
    Died February 17, 1861. Age 42.
It was the grave of LOLA MONTEZ. I could hardly realize that after such a free, wild swing at life, from continent to continent, she had been limited to such a narrow domain...

A young man named WHEAT committed suicide on Saturday near Atlanta by taking strychnine.

A chicken thief named DICK EDWARDS was shot and mortally wounded Thursday night, in Savannah, by MR. JOHN COOPER.

CAPTAIN JOSEPH ALPHOUSE, of Charleston, dropped dead in a street of that city on Wednesday.

MRS. FANNY HAYMAN, a native of this place, but lately residing in New Orleans, died in that city on Tuesday of yellow fever.

Another horrible tragedy in Brooklyn, New York on Monday. THOMAS MULLAN cut his wife's throat and then his own. They both died within an hour.

A school boy named FERGUSON, while running in front of a swing in Louisville on Friday, was struck by the feet of a boy who was swinging, and had his eye put out and his skull fractured. He died almost instantly.

LIEUT. MYERS, who served in the Second South Carolina Infantry, Confederate States Army, in the late war for Independence, and a resident of Columbia, died in Houston, Texas recently of yellow fever.

J.T. STEVENS, of Boston, in the employ of the Congressional Commission engaged at Boston, in recording perjuries by Yankee soldiers who have been in Confederate prisons, committed suicide in that city on the 22d. He heard so many lies told that it disgusted him with life and his fellow men.

Oct. 30, 1867

Correspondence of the Springfield Republican. - Full particulars of the Hoosick Tunnel disaster. North Adams, October 20 - Details of the disaster in which are listed the following victims: PATRICK CONNOLLY, who leaves a wife and six children, JAMES BENNETT, JAMES FITZGERALD, brother of the foreman, THOMAS MULCARE, JOHN HARKNESS, THOMAS and PATRICK COLLINS, brothers, MICHAEL WHALEN, JAS. CARVENOUGH, who leaves a wife and two children, JOHN CURRAN, THOMAS COOK, who leaves a wife and two children, JAMES McCORMICK, and JOSEPH MESSIER, a Frenchman.

MR. JOEL KELSEY, one of the oldest citizens of Atlanta, died in Jefferson, Texas on Tuesday, aged 74 years.

CAPT. W.W. AUSTIN, of the steamer Metcalf, died in Savannah on Wednesday of congestive chill.

A MR. THOMPSON, of Savannah, died on board the steamship Montgomery, on her passage from New York to Savannah, a few days ago.

MR. WILLIAM RAY, one of the oldest citizens of Baldwin county, died in that county on the 11th instant, aged 87.

JOHN WOOD, quartermaster of the Washington Artillery battalion during the late civil war, died in that city on Sunday, of yellow fever.

Nov. 13, 1867

An English physician, formerly of St. Louis, Missouri, murdered in Minnesota. A curious chain of circumstantial evidence. The St. Paul Press of October 22nd contains an account of the exhumation of the remains of DR. HARCOURT, who was interred there in August 1865, and the bringing to light of circumstantial evidence very strongly reflecting upon GEORGE L. VAN SOLEN as the murderer...

DAVID L. ROATH, Clerk of the Court and Ordinary of Richmond county, died in Augusta on Tuesday.

WM. CARY JONES, son-in-law of the late Thos. H. Benton, and a prominent lawyer of San Francisco, died in that city on the 5th inst.

ADOLF DEUTCH, a German, was found dead in the road near Chattanooga on Wednesday, with his head horribly mutilated. He was murdered by a negro.

JUDGE JOHN S. BRIEN, a native of Virginia, but for more than fifty years a resident of Tennessee, and one of her foremost lawyers, died in Nashville on Wednesday.

On Thursday night in Savannah the HON. POMPEY SMASH, a delegate to Pope's odoriferous Convention, was found dead in his bed. He was from the "rural districts," and blew out the gas instead of turning it off.

SAMUEL WHARTON, one of the prominent merchants of Louisville, died in that city on Saturday.

JAS. DUFFEY and one HOOBERRY, citizens of Rutherford, Tennessee, are now lying mortally wounded, as the result of a "little unpleasantness" last week.

CAPTAIN MARTIN, who killed WESTMORELAND at Brunswick last summer, has been liberated from Chatham county jail, on $20,000 bail.

Dec. 11, 1867

MR. WILLIAM SCHLEY, of Augusta, died at sea a few days ago, while returning home from a Northern tour.

Dec. 11, 1867

   Our Frankfort dispatches bring us the intelligence of the death of
   ROBERT ATTCHERSON ALEXANDER of Woodford county. He was a native of
   Woodford but inherited estates in Great Britain, from which he
   received a very larg annual income, and from the circumstances he
   was sometimes spoken of as "Lord Alexander."...(Louisville Courier,
   Dec. 2).

Dec. 25, 1867

   CAPT. MOBLEY, a member of Crisp's theatrical corps, and son-in-law
   of Mr. Crisp, died in Atlanta on Saturday.

   CAPT. MITCHELL G. HESTER, formerly of Augusta, died of consumption
   in Louisville, Ky. on Thursday last.

   WILLIAM CAMP, son of G.H. CAMP, of Green county, was drowned in the
   Oconne river on Sunday last.

   BARTON PRINGLE, Pope's Registrar for the 22d Senatorial District,
   made a "cold corpus" of himself on Thursday last by taking strychnine.

   JAMES L. PRICE, ESQ., a prominent citizen of Perry county, Ala.,
   formerly President of the Selma and Meridian R.R., died last Friday
   at his residence near Uniontown.

   Died near Butler, in Taylor county, DANIEL W. MILLER, ESQ., on the
   7th inst., aged 55 years; a practicing attorney.

   R.B. LYLES killed his father-in-law, a man named DEAN, in Laurens
   District, S.C. last week.

Jan. 22, 1868

   Homicide. MR. J.W. HALL, long a citizen of this county, but who
   some time ago removed to Mississippi, returned here on a visit to
   his friends and relatives about two weeks since. Before he left
   for our sister State, he had two or three difficulties with a man
   of the name of DANIEL McLEOD, a planter in the same neighborhood
   in which Hall formerly lived...when McLeod killed him. The affair
   occurred in the vicinity of Fort Browder. (Eufaula News, 17th).

   A fatal occurrence. On Sunday evening last, at the room of Mr.
   Wm. Dougherty, Esq., an unfortunate affair, resulting in the death
   of T.W. DAVIS, startled our quiet town...(Tuskegee News).

Feb. 19, 1868

   Death of Conductor VERDERY. We regret to announce that the injuries
   received by MR. JOHN P. VERDERY three weeks since terminated fatally
   yesterday morning. After the amputation of his feet he seemed for
   a time to be getting along favorably, but subsequently the wounds
   sloughed, and gangrene and mortification set in. On Sunday night
   he was seized with lockjaw, and gradually sank till received by
   death about 4 o'clock yesterday morning. (Sav. Adv., 16th).

   Philadelphia, Feb. 16 - WILLIAM M. SWAIN, the founder of the Public
   Ledger newspaper, died today, aged 59.

   MRS. MARY H. BIRDSONG was born 2 Nov. 1807 and died 16 Jan. 1868
   in Macon, Georgia. Her death was sudden, though not unexpected.
   On the 15th of November last, she had a violent and sudden attack
   of disease, which was variously supposed to be paralysis, congestion,
   or apoplexy...(with long eulogy).

Feb. 19, 1868

Died at Marion, Ga. on the 25th of January last, of puerperal peritonitis, MRS. GERALDINE BECKOM, wife of W.H. BECKCOM, in the 25th year of her age; leaves a husband and four children (with eulogy).

San Francisco, Feb. 17 - A boat capsized in Osaka river, drowning ADMIRAL BELL, of the United States Navy, LIEUT. REID, and ten seaman.

Feb. 26, 1868

Homicide. About 5 o'clock on Wednesday afternoon two negro boys, about 15 years of age, while engaged in a game of marbles on the corner of West Broad and South Broad streets, got into an altercation and after some rough words both drew their pistols. One of them named ISAAC MORRELL fired first, the ball taking effect in the neck of PRINCE JOHNSON, his opponent, inflicing only a flesh wound. Prince then fired and shot Isaac through the stomach...he died about 6 o'clock in the morning. (Sav. Advertiser, 21st).

The HON. JOSEPH R. INGERSOLL, formerly a member of Congress and U.S. Minister to England during Mr. Fillmore's administration, died in Philadelphia on Thursday, in the 82d year of his age. He was a brother of the Hon. Charles Jared Ingersoll, also formerly a member of Congress.

JUDGE O.A. BULL departed this life in this city on Wednesday morning last, the 19th inst. (LaGrange Republican).

The Savannah News & Herald learns that the REV. MR. JACKSON, a Methodist minister living near Quincy, Florida, while jumping aboard the train as it was leaving Baldwin for Lake City, on last Tuesday, fell under the wheels and was so badly crushed as to leave little hope of his recovery.

A correspondent of the Savannah Advertiser, writing from Bainbridge on the 18th inst., says that morning a DR. PARSONS, who keeps a drug store in that place, deliberately put his neck on the track as the cars were leaving town, and had his head severed from his body. He was originally from Eufaula, and leaves a wife and several children.

Mar. 4, 1868

Yesterday morning about 5 o'clock the body of policeman JOHN CURTIS was found lying in Congress street lane, near Habersham street. Mr. C. got off duty at 12 o'clock, and left the barracks for home apparently in perfect health. His body was taken to the barracks, where a post mortem examination was held and it was found that he came to his death from disease of the heart. Mr. Curtis was about 42 years of age, a native of county Wexford, Ireland, but a resident of this city since the year 1852. He leaves a wife and family. (Sav. Advertiser, 29th instant).

The death of SIDNEY McWHORTER, ESQ. occurred yesterday morning at his residence in this city. (Chron. & Sen., 29th).

Apr. 1, 1868

Died in Twiggs county, Ga. 25 Feb. 1868, MRS. MARY JONES, wife of MAJOR JOHN JONES, daughter of S.W. and M.L. WATTS of LaGrange, Ga., in the 24th year of her age; a member of the Methodist Church. (with long eulogy)

Apr. 7, 1868

From the Columbus Enquirer of April 1st - Our citizens were greatly startled on Monday night and yesterday morning by the news that GEO. W. ASHBURN had been killed in the house in which he was living, in the upper part of Oglethorpe street, by a body of men in disguise;

(Apr. 7, cont'd) - the deceased was a formenter of discord and a man of strife. He was obnoxious to the white people of the city, not merely on account of his disorganizing political course, which had been greatly instrumental in creating and keeping alive bad feeling between the races, but because of his social habits...

CHARLES L. STEWART, of White Plains, New York, dropped dead in the street one day last week. He leaves a young wife and a million of dollars.

Apr. 21, 1868

We regret to learn the death, on Thursday last, at his plantation in Barbour county, Alabama, of MR. LEROY M. WILEY. Mr. W. had long held a prominent position in commercial circles in Charleston and New York, and was well and favorable known to the business community of this and other Southern States.

We learn that a serious difficulty occurred in Pickens county, Ga., on the 9th inst., in which MR. RILEY CORBIN was killed by WILLIAM MARTIN...(Marietta Journal, 17th).

Wilmington, April 17 - During the storm yesterday at Lawrenceburg, Richmond county, the REV. JOHN B. McKINNON and L. McLAUREN were struck by lightning and instantly killed.

Apr. 28, 1868

Strange case with a fatal ending. The Jackson, Michigan correspondent of the Detroit Tribune relates the details of a case of insanity, followed by death, of a man named MR. ELBERT WILBUR...

Homicide and fatal accident. Falling of a floor. At 5 o'clock yesterday afternoon one of the most horrible accidents ever recorded in the annals of this city occurred...death of MR. H.A. TROUTMAN of the firm of Farrar & Troutman, hardware merchants, Third street...

Richmond, April 26 - Telgrams from Charlottesville announce the death yesterday of WM. C. RIVES, former U.S. Minister to France and Senator from Virginia. Aged 75 years.

The mortal remains of GEN. JOHN H. MORGAN were interred in their final resting place at Lexington, Ky. on the 17th inst.

May 5, 1868

Baltimore, May 1 - JOHN BROOKS, a famous snake fancier, was bitten today by a pet rattlesnake, and died in fifteen minutes.

Detailed obituary of HON. WM. C. RIVES, of Virginia. Was born in Nelson county, Virginia 14 May 1793. Was educated at the colleges of Sidney and Hampden and William and Mary. After leaving college, he studied law under the direction of Thos. Jefferson. In 1814-15, he was in the militia forces which were called out for the defence of Virginia. He was a member of the Convention which met at Staunton in 1816 to revise the Constitution of Virginia. From 1817-1819 he served in the Legislature as a member from Nelson county. In 1822 was elected from the county of Albemarle. Was elected a Representative in Congress in 1823, and successively re-elected in 1825 and 1827. When General Jackson became President in 1829, he appointed Mr. Rives Minister to France...

May 12, 1868

COL. JOHN G. COLTART, of Huntsville, died in the L-natic Asylum at Tuscaloosa on the 16th ult., where he had been taken a few weeks previous at his own request. He was Colonel of the 7th and 50th Alabama Regiments during the late war, and distinguished himself in several battles, especially that of Bentonville, in which he commanded a division.

June 16, 1868

DR. JOSEPH A. MURRELL, formerly a citizen of Covington, died in Minden, La. on the 7th inst. He had many relatives and friends in this State.

It is our melancholy duty to record the death of MR. THEODORE BLOIS, which took place at his residence in this city last evening after a lingering illness. The deceased was a native of Savannah. Early in life he engaged in commercial pursuits, some twenty years ago became connected with the press of the city. In 1858 he became part owner in this paper, then the Morning News, of which he was the Business Manager till near the close of the war, in which, notwithstanding his feeble health, he served as a Confederate volunteer in the field; he died of pulmonary disease. (Savannah News & Herald, 11th).

CAPT. W.S. HARDIN, the oldest resident of LaGrange, died in that place on Wednesday last. He had been living there since 1827.

MR. NATHAN LIPSCOMBE, of Troup county, was poisoned one day last week by chewing what he supposed was angelica root. He died in half an hour.

A most horrid butchery. A sleeping man sought in his bed and his head nearly severed from his shoulders with an axe. Details of the death of CAPTAIN MATT. DWYER, who resided near Raleight...Capt. Dwyer served in the war as a Captain in the Fifteenth Tennessee (Confederate) Regiment.

DAVID BRYANT, freedman, living on the plantation of Mr. McGough, in this county, was murdered last Thursday evening just before dark, while sitting in his cabin. An inquest was held, and the jury returned a verdict that said Bryant was killed by another freedman named WILLIAM LUCAS. Lucas' wife had deserted him, and at the time of the murder, was living with Bryant in the relation of husband and wife. (Monroe Advertiser, 2d inst.).

June 30, 1868

DR. CHARLES F. THORNTON, a grandson of General Harrison, ex-President, committed suicide at Clevels, a few miles from Cincinnati, today by cutting his throat and stabbing himself in the heart with a penknife. Thronton made the attempt to take his life some weeks ago, but was prevented by his friends.

Murder in Irwin County. Two young men murdered by a negro! Escape of the murderer! On Saturday night last a dreadful tragedy occurred in Irwin county, about five miles from Bowen's station, by which a family lost two sons by the murderous hand of a negro. The names of the young men were WILLIAM and DANIEL LUKE, sons of MR. JAMES LUKE. The name of the murderer is JOSHUA WILLIAMS...the young men were from 18-20 years of age. (Savannah Republican, 25th).

From the St. Charles (Winona county, Minn.) Herald - A man buried alive forty feet deep in a well. A sad and fatal accident occurred on Saturday last, May 30, at the residence of James Bennett, in the town of Quincy, about seven miles from this village, by which O.L. BRYANT lost his life...The deceased was a widower, aged about 32 years. He had no children, but was living with his aged mother, who kept house for him. For two years past he has been Superintendent of the Union Sabbath school in the vicinity in which he lived.

Aug. 4, 1868

New York, Aug. 3 - CHAS. G. HALPINE, alias MILES O'RILEY, editor of the Citizen and State Register, of this city, died this morning from an overdose of chloroform taken to relieve neuralgia.

Sep. 15, 1868

There resides in Henry county, near the Spalding line, a remarkable old lady named ELIZABETH STILWELL. She was born in Mecklenburg co., N.C. on 3d of November 1773, and is therefore in her 95th year.. (Griffin Star, 5th).

Oct. 20, 1868

Funeral obsequies of the HON. HOWELL COBB in Athens...

MRS. CAROLINE WATERMAN, wife of JOSEPH WATERMAN, and daughter of THOMAS and ANN MORRIS, was born in Jones County, Georgia, 6 Aug. 1826 and died in Talbotton, Georgia 12 Oct. 1868. Nearly two years ago she had an attack of apoplexy, from which she never entirely recovered; was attacked suddenly on the morning of her death with the same disease, and died about one o'clock.

Departed this life at Knoxville, Tenn., on the evening of the 8th of September 1868, after a short illness, GEORGE W. TOWNS, youngest son of MRS. MARY W. and the late EX-GOVERNOR TOWNS, of Georgia, in the 18th year of his age...(long eulogy).

Died on the 4th of September 1868 at the residence of Mr. and Mrs. William Methvin, Twiggs County, their little daughter, EMILY MINNIE, aged 5 years 1 month. (with eulogy).

Died in Twiggs County on the 13th of October, MR. DANIEL W. SHINE, aged 82 years. (Ed. Note: See 1 Dec. 1868 issue for extensive obituary).

Died in Perry, Ga. on Tuesday evening, 15th September 1868, JOSEPH HIGGINS, infant son of FRANCIS A. and FIDELIA JOBSON, aged 1 year 3 months 6 days.

Nov. 3, 1868

Died near Knoxville, Georgia, October 7th, 1868, MRS. ERNANA M. HORTMAN, in her 24th year. (with long eulogy).

Died in Quitman county on the 7th inst., MRS. MARY A. OLIVER, relict of JAMES M. OLIVER, ESQ., in her 43d year; member of the Methodist Church.

Died in Houston County on Tuesday evening, October 13th, after a short illness, EDDIE McGEHEE, son of MR. G.B. and MRS. L.F. PLANT, aged 2 years 7 months.

Nov. 10, 1868

Yesterday morning about ten o'clock policeman SAMUEL BRYSON, who was wounded in the riot at the Court-house on Tuesday, drew his last breath...(Sav. News, Nov. 5th).

From the Lynchburg Virginian. The death of MRS. BASIL WILLIAMSON is announced in the Charlestown, Jefferson county, papers. She died in Tyler county at the advanced age of 89 years; was one of the first settlers of Harper's Ferry, after the death of her great uncle, Robert Harper, the earliest proprietor, who purchased the land from Lord Fairfax, the Baron Cameron...

MR. WM. L. BRUNSON, of Sumter, South Carolina, who died last Thursday, bequeathed to his old and faithful servant Washington, who, with his family had never left him, forty acres of land, a mule, a wagon, a cow and calf, a fine stock of hogs and one-half the crop grown upon the farm the present year.

Fell asleep in Jesus, October 2d, after a severe illness of a few weeks, MISS JULIA E. ARTOPE; member of the Episcopal Church (with long eulogy).

Nov. 10, 1868

Died in Albany on the 27th ult., of a congestive chill, MRS. CAROLINE
A. SMITH, wife of the HON. WM. E. SMITH, and daughter of REUBEN
WILLIAMS, ESQ., of Dougherty county; was a student in our Female
College. (with short eulogy).

Nov. 17, 1868

Tribute of Respect by former members of the 45th Georgia Regiment
convened at Gentlemen's Parlour, Lanier House, Macon, Ga., Nov. 12th,
1868 - on the death of CAPT. JOHN T. BROWN.

We sincerely regret to hear of the death of the REV. JEREMIAH F.
O'NEAL, JR., Roman Catholic priest, late of this city, which occurred
on last Friday at St. Agnes Hospital, on the York road, near the
city of Baltimore. Father O'Neal was a nephew of the venerable
Father of the same name so well known and so highly respected by
all denominations in Georgia and South Carolina. He was about 42
years of age, and was born, we think, in Ireland, but his parents
came to this country and settled in Taliaferro county when he was
very young, and his widowed mother now resides in that county.
Father O'Neal has been in bad health for some years, and had been
travelling North for its benefit.

Jan. 5, 1869

MR. GEORGE P. WAGNON, once an old resident of Macon, but lately
of Alabama, was found dead in his bed at the Isaacs House yesterday
morning. The deceased had been suffering from the insidious inroads
of that fell destroyer, consumption, and this, no doubt, was the
cause of his death. He was a resident of our city probably as far
back as 1836, and well known as an active man on our streets as
a cotton buyer, and in other business egagements. He was several
times a member of the City Council. After leaving this city some
twelve or fifteen years since, he resided at West Point, and afterwards in Russell county, Ala., near Columbus, where he lost his
home by fire, with all its contents.

Horrible crime in Columbia County. Under this head the Chronicle
& Sentinel, of Sunday, notices the murder and arson case...On Christmas night a house situated five miles from Appling Court House,
the county seat of Columbia county, and occupied by MR. GABRIEL
MARTIN and his two sisters was burned to the ground and its three
occupants consumed in the flames...

MRS. W.H.T. WALKER, widow of the late MAJOR GENERAL WALKER, C.S.A.,
who was killed in 1864 near Atlanta, died of heart disease in Albany,
New York on Monday.

DR. JOSEPH D. BROOKS, of Pleasant Hill, Georgia, died on the morning
of the 20th ult. His disease was affection of the heart. He was
a member of the Georgia Masonic Mutual Life Insurance Company, so
that his heirs will receive a handsome sum from this Company.

MR. A.W. WHEAT, a prominent citizen of Campbell county, died last
week of apoplexy.

DR. N.N. SMITH, for thirty-one years a prominent physician of
LaGrange, died there last week.

Richmond, Dec. 30 - MOSELY CLARK, born in 1747, died yesterday,
aged 121 years. He was a wagon driver in the Revolutionary war.

Wilmington, Del., January 2 - MARTIN W. BATES is dead.

New York, Jan. 4 - By a premature explosion at the wreck of the
steamer Scotland, off Sandy Hook, CAPT. WM. L. CHURCHILL, late of
the navy, and three others were blown to atoms, and several others
injured.

Jan. 12, 1869

MRS. ELLEN BARFIELD, wife of B.F. BARFIELD, proprietor of the Bainbridge Georgian, died last Saturday.

Death of GEO. L. BARRY. Highly esteemed by the Masonic Fraternity, as Deputy Grand Master, and Grand Lecturer for some years past of the Grand Lodge of Georgia. A Tribute of Respect by Osgood A. Barry dated January 6th, 1869, at Cuthbert, Ga.

New York, January 5 - MR. EASTON, a prominent cotton merchant, is dead - aged 65 years.

Washington, Jan. 5 - COMMODORE WILLIAM D. SLATER is dead. He was 75 years of age.

Alexandria, Jan. 8 - HON. JOHN M. BOTTS died at his home, in Culpepper county, this morning at one o'clock. His funeral will take place in Richmond on Sunday.

Richmond, Jan. 8 - COLONEL THOMAS N. BURWELL, a captain in the war of 1812, died today, aged 81 years.

New Orleans, Jan. 7 - F.P. PIERPONT, formerly Adjutant General, West Virginia, died here this morning of consumption.

New Orleans, Jan. 8 - GENERAL ROUSSEAU died very calmly last night at eleven o'clock. He had been ill with inflammation of the bowels.

Died in Geneva, Talbot county, Ga., WILLIAM BURT TOOKE, son of REV. J.J. TOOKE, aged 16 years 10 months. He professed religion four months ago, and lived a consistent member of the Methodist Episcopal Church, South, until he died.

A few days ago a man in Platte county, Missouri, named WILLIAM MARSHAL, murdered in cold blood his own mother and brother, in order to get possession of property of which they were possessed, and which would revert to him on their death. A reward of $3000, of which the guilty wretch himself cunningly offered $1000, put detectives to work, who traced the deed to him, and a few days ago he was arrested and lodged in jail.

Jan. 19, 1868

Monroe County Item. From the Forsyth Advertiser of yesterday. MR. ZACHARIAH CHAMBLESS, aged 96 years, is the oldest inhabitant of this county. He lives on Deer Creek, about seven miles east of Forsyth, where he settled about fifty years ago, when this thrifty and populous section was covered with the primitive forest, and the wild deer and Indian roamed free over their own native hills.

DR. C.T. CUSHMAN, who accidentally shot himself on Saturday afternoon, died Sunday morning about nine o'clock at his residence, upper part of Randolph street. (Columbus Sun, 12th).

What forty acres of land did for a man. WALTER L. NEWBURY, of Chicago, died on board the Persia last month while on his way to join his family in Paris. He went to Chicago in 1833, purchased at an early day, among other property, forty acres of land, on either side of North Wells street, and persistently retained possession of it to the time of his death. This property cost him $1100 and is worth $3,500,000. And this is only a part of his vast estate. He was formerly a resident of Oneida county, and was a poor boy when he went to Chicago. (N.Y. Express).

The murderer of CHAS. M. RODGERS, in New York, has surrendered himself.

Jan. 19, 1869

Unoffending citizens murdered in cold blood near Madison, Arkansas. (From the Memphis Avalanche of the 8th) - Clayton's loyal bloodhounds are still murdering, plundering and outraging the unfortunate people of Arkansas. Only a day or two since they fell upon a most peaceable and unoffending citizen by the name of DILLARD, as he was returning from his place of business, and for attempting to escape, murdered him in cold blood. Yesterday a MR. JOHN ORGAN was shot dead at Fifteen Mile Bayou, near Madison, where they have eight or nine hundred head of horses and other property, stolen from citizens of the surrounding country...

For two days rumors have been floating around that the real murderers of G.W. FEAGAN, killed by an assassin near Silver Run, Ala. on Tuesday evening, October 27th last, had been discovered...

New Orleans, Jan. 15 - BREVET MAJOR R.M. MARSTON, first Infantry, one of the victims of the Glide disaster, died last evening and was buried today. He had been temporarily assigned to staff duty, and was ordered by Gen. Rousseau to make some investigations in western Louisiana.

Jan. 26, 1869

The friends and acquaintances of Dr. George N. Holmes and family, and of his sister-in-law, MRS. PHETIS A. PHILLIPS, are respectfully invited to attend the funeral of the latter, from the residence of the former, on Third street, this afternoon at 2 o'clock.

Funeral of the murdered victims of Marion to take place in Memphis today. We learn that the bodies of the three citizens murdered by the Arkansas militia at Frenchman's Bayou a few days ago arrived in this city last night, at midnight, and their funerals will take place today - probably from the Cumberland Presbyterian Church. The body of MR. McALISTER will be regularly buried; the others - MESSRS. LEWIS and HARNEY - will be deposited, for the present, in the vault at Elmwood. (Avalanche, 24th).

COL. JOHN PINCKARD, the oldest citizen of Forsyth, died there Friday last.

Feb. 2, 1869

Four negroes and a white man, charged with the crime of stealing the body of a COL. WILLIAMS from a tomb about four miles from Kinston, N.C. were taken from the jail at that place last week and hung.

Augusta, Jan. 27 - EX-GOVERNOR PICKENS, formerly Minister to St. Petersburg, died at his residence in Edgefield, S.C. on Monday last.

Washington, Jan. 28 - The Catholic priest O'CALLAHAN, killed at Periere, was a member of the Georgetown College Faculty.

Wilmington, Del., Jan. 31 - CHAS. J. DUPONT is dead.

Feb. 9, 1869

We see that MISS AUGUSTA ST. CLAIR, who will be recollected as proposing to lecture here sometime last year, on "woman," died at Salt Lake, Utah, on the 27th of January.

Departed this life on the 5th of January, at his residence in Houston county, ISAAC HOLMES, in the 65th year of his age. Was born in North Carolina. His father, soon after the birth of his son, moved to Jefferson county, of this State, where he soon died, leaving young Isaac penniless orphan, at the early age of six years, with no counselor except a widowed mother. His mother having contracted a second marriage, the family removed and settled in Houston county...(short eulogy).

Feb. 9, 1869

Tribute of Respect by Fort Valley Lodge No. 110, Fort Valley, Ga., January 27th, 1869 - on the death of JAMES L. BYINGTON, who died on the morning of the 23d instant.

From the Memphis Avalanche, 30th ult. Arkansas. The militia take a cripple from his sick bed, and murder him in the woods. One of the most heinous atrocities yet committed by the Arkansas militia, occurred last Monday in Mississippi county. It was nothing less than the cold-blodded murder of MR. ALEXANDER BAUGH...Mr. Baugh lived on Carson's Lake, ten miles from Osceloa...

Feb. 16, 1869

Horrible results of religious insanity. St. Louis, Feb. 6th - A man named HOEFER, living in the outskirts of Hannibal, Missouri murdered his daughter, ten years old, yesterday...he replied that Christ died, that Christ was killed, and it was no worse for his child to died than Christ; that he offered her as a sacrifice to Christ.

The death of four members of a family named WILBRECHT, in Oneida county, New York from trichinasis was recently noticed...

New York, Feb. 9 - JAMES T. BRADY died today of apoplexy, aged 54 years. All the Courts adjourned, as a token of respect to his memory.

Richmond, Feb. 10 - REV. HENRY A. WISE, JR., died today.

New Orleans, Feb. 12 - A dispatch from Jefferson, Texas reports the burning of the steamboat Mittie Stephens, in Caddo Lake, Red River last night at midnight. Sixty-three lives were lost; among them were W.A. BROADWELL, T.L. LYON and his son FRANK, of New Orleans.

Philadelphia, Feb. 14 - JAMES DOYLE, a well known lawyer, was found in the streets this morning badly wounded. He has since died. No arrests.

Feb. 23, 1869

We regret to announce the death of JUDGE ALEXANDER B. CLITHERALL, which occurred at his residence, near this city, yesterday. Had been in very feeble health for many years, from dropsy; had been a member of both branches of the State Legislature; was for a number of years Clerk of the House of Representatives; was born in North Carolina, and was at the time of his death 45 or 50 years of age; had lived in Montgomery for the last nine years, previous to which he lived in the Western part of the State; leaves a wife and children to mourn. (Montgomery Mail, 18th).

MISS AGNES BATES, long and favorable known as one of the first teachers in the South, died recently in Charleston, S.C., where with her sisters she had been teaching several years.

Richmond, Feb. 16 - The Grand Jury today indicted JAMES GRANT for the murder of RIVES POLLARD. The trial to commence Monday next.

Baltimore, Feb. 20 - CHAS. A. GAMBALL, an extensive manufacturer, is dead, aged 64.

Dispatches published in the Chicago Times, of the 11th, give particulars of the assassination of MR. O'CONNELL, at Jacksonville, Illinois...

Shortly after five o'clock on yesterday afternoon this community was startled by the announcement that MR. D.G. OLCOTT, of the well-known firm of Cooper, Olcott & Co., had committed suicide by placing a pistol in his mouth, pulling the trigger and sending the charge

Feb. 23, cont'd.) - crashing through his brain, producing instant death... (Savannah Republican, 18th).

Mar. 2, 1869

The news yesterday morning that COL. W.M. SMITH, of this city, had died the evening before in New York was received with the profoundest feeling by the entire community; had been a resident of this city from fifteen to twenty years. (Times and Messenger, Selma).

THOMAS JONES, SR., died at his residence near Thomasville, at 6 o'clock this morning, aged 67 years. (Thomasville Enterprise, 24th).

HENRY A. SWIFT, EX-GOVERNOR of Minnesota, died at St. Paul, the capital of that State, on Friday last.

Louisville, Feb. 26 - THOMAS E. WILSON, senior partner of the firm of Wilson, Isler & Co., druggists, committed suicide today. Aged 61 years.

Mar. 9, 1869

MR. HENRY E. LUCAS, JR., one of the most esteemed and successful citizens of St. Thomas parish, near Charleston, accidentally shot and killed himself with a pistol on Monday last.

Detroit, Michigan, Mar. 5 - BISHOP LEFEVRE is dead, aged 60. He was ordained a Bishop in 1841.

Mar. 23, 1869

MR. JAMES H. GOUGH, of Jasper county, Mississippi, was instantly killed a few days ago by the explosion of a mill stone. He was feeding the hopper when the stone burst into numberless pieces, one fragment striking him on the forehead and producing instantaneous death.

Letter from Jeffersonville, Twiggs county, relates news of the death of DR. IRA E. DUPREE. He died of dropsy on the night of the 17th, after suffering for near six months. Was in the 69th year of his age. (a long eulogy is given in a separate notice in same paper).

Washington, Mar. 22 - T.B. LAWRENCE, the former husband of SALLIE WARD, of Louisville, is dead.

Apr. 13, 1869

The friends of MR. HENRY SINGLETON will regret to learn of his death, which occurred at his residence in this county on the 2d instant. Mr. Singleton was one of the oldest citizens of Monroe. (Monroe Advertiser, 6th).

The Savannah News reports the killing of MR. WILLIAM LIBBY, at Valdosta on Friday night...

SIMRI ROSE died at his residence in Macon, of pneumonia, on Sunday morning. Was in his 70th year; had been Secretary of Macon Lodge for about thirty years, and Grand Secretary of the Grand Lodge for the past 24 years; has been connected with the Journal & Messenger for 46 years, up to the time of our sale to J.W. Burke & Co... (two more columns give various obits as appeared in the Telegraph, the Middle Georgian, the Atlanta Intelligencer, the Monroe Advertiser, the Americus Republican of the 7th, the Eufaula News of the 6th, and the Rome Courier of the 8th).

On Saturday evening last about 8½ or 9 o'clock, CHARLES MATHIS, a lad about 15 or 16 years old, but quite small for his age, had a difficulty with a negro woman named SUSANNAH DUMAS...she was cut in the left breast and died in about half an hour after being cut. (Southern Recorder, 6th).

Apr. 13, 1869

MRS. MARTHA CALHOUN BURT, of Abbeville, C.H., South Carolina, died there on the 27th ult. She was the wife of GENERAL ARMISTEAD BURT, ex M.C. of that State, a very prominent lawyer and politician, and a niece of the great Calhoun.

Tribute of Respect by the Macon Typographical Union No. 81, held on the 7th inst. - on the death of SIMRI ROSE.

The LaGrange Reporter announces the death of MAJOR MIDDLETON THORNTON, who died at his residence in Campbellton, Ga. on the 3d inst., aged 69 years 4 months 8 days - having been born Nov. 25th, 1799. Was the oldest citizen of Campbellton; a Mason and member of the Baptist Church.

MR. WILLIAM P. HUNTER breathed his last at half past three o'clock yesterday afternoon. Was about 70 years of age; for many years was Chasier of the Marine Bank; member of Chirst Church, having for many years been a member of the Vestry of that church; his funeral will be preached at Christ Church at four o'clock this afternoon. (Savannah Morning News, 12th inst.)
  Mr. Hunter resided in Macon many years ago, and removed from this place to Savannah. He was one of the first wardens of Christ Church, Macon, and was elected warden in 1833, which position he held until the 20th of June, 1834, when he resigned, preparatory to removing to Savannah.

SABIN SHERWOOD, of Dover, N.H., and lately of Henderson, Ky., was killed recently by being run over by a passenger train on the Kentucky Central Railroad, at Lair's station...

GEORGE F. NESBIT, a well known New York printer and stationer, died in that city on the 7th inst., aged 61.

Tennessee papers announce the death of W.G. SWAN, who figured prominently some years since in Tennessee politics. He was a member of the Confederate Congress.

Philadelphia, April 8 - TWITCHELL, convicted of the murder of his wife's mother, and whose execution was to take place today, was found dead in his bed this morning. It is supposed that friends who visited him yesterday left poison.

Apr. 20, 1869

Justice P.M. Russell, Sr. held an inquest yesterday, in view of the body of GEORGE W. STROBHART. The jury found that the deceased came to his death by a gunshot wound, inflicted in the left side of the abdomen by JOHN CHAPLIN, of which wound, he died, in the county of Chatham, in the 12th of April, 1869. It appeared from testimony that the deceased lived at a place on Daufauskie island, in South Carolina, called No. 6, owned by Mr. John Stoddard...
(Savannah Republican, 14th).

We are pained to chronicle the death of MRS. MITCHELL, wife of COL. DANIEL R. MITCHELL, of this city, who died very suddenly on Friday night last. Mrs. Mitchell was one of the oldest citizens of Rome, her husband moving to this place about the year 1834. She was about 70 years old. (Rome Commercial, 15th).

May 4, 1869

Another kerosene accident. We learn that the colored man named ADAM DOOLIE, residing in Mill street, who was dreadfully burned on Sunday night last by the explosion of a kerosene lamp, is dead. (Savannah Republican, 29th).

We regret to learn of the death, at Atlanta, of MAJOR J.R. BARRICK, editor of the Constitution of that city. He was a Kentuckian by birth.

May 4, 1869

Chicago, April 28 - A horrible death from hydrophobia occurred here today. The victim was a young man, twenty five years old, named WM. GOODWILLIE, foreman in a box manufactory on North Pier...

Fatally burned. MRS. BLAKE, residing on Mill street, has been subject to epileptic fits, in a mild form, for some time, and her husband kept a colored servant woman to attend her. Yesterday morning the servant made up a fire in the back yard to heat water for washing purposes. She then went ot pump for a bucket of water, and when she returned she found Mrs. Blake lying in the fire in an insensible condition...(Savannah Republican, 30th).

Departed this life near Knoxville, Crawford county, Ga., on the 19th of April 1869, at 11½ o'clock P.M., MRS. KIZZIAH LOWE, wife of JACOB LOWE, in the 61st year of her age; became a member of the Missionary Baptist Church about 29 years ago. (with long eulogy).

May 11, 1869

Washington, May 4 - JOSEPH HELMES, a colored member of the State Constitutional Convention, was killed at Charlotte Court House yesterday. A personal difficulty occurred between him and John Marshall, son of Judge Marshall, of whose family Helmes was formerly body servant.

Died at his residence in Savannah, Ga., on Sunday, April 11, 1869, WILLIAM P. HUNTER, aged 70 years. (short eulogy).

May 18, 1869

Assassination in Terrell county - the murderer not yet arrested. Dawson, May 12th, 1869 - Our community was shocked last evening by learning that one of our most useful and respected citizens, CAPT. RICHARD H. FLETCHER, had been waylaid and shot and instantly killed. It is supposed that the demon-incarnate who committed this deed is one JOHN LEE, a young mane aged about 20 years, and who moved with his mother (a widow) from near Marianna, Fla., to this county during the last winter...

COL. EDWARD CONNOR died on Monday morning, the 10th of May 1869, at Fayetteville, Ga. He had been a citizen of Fayetteville for more than twenty years. He was a sound lawyer and an excellent Judge of the Court of Ordinary, which office he held at the time of his death. (Atlanta Intelligencer, 13th).

Yesterday afternoon about six o'clock CAPT. GEO. A. BICKFORD, of the ship Ellen Southard, was drowned...was 46 years of age and a native of Richmond, Maine. His wife was on his vessel, a short distance from the scene of the accident, but fortunately did not behold it.

On yesterday morning it was rumored on the streets that JOSEPH ADKINS, a notorious scalaway and Senator in the Georgia Legislature from the Warren District, had been killed on the previous day in Columbia county. By the mail of yesterday evening letters were received in this city from that county giving the particulars of the tragedy...

Shortly after 12 o'clock last Friday, a tragedy was enacted in the streets of Jackson, Tennessee, which resulted in the death of a young man named JOHN HODGES, better known as one of General Forrest's orderlies during the war, and who went by the sobriquet "happy Jack."

MRS. ELIZABETH WINN, residing near Barnett, in Warren county, who celebrated her 96th birthday on the 5th instant, is in possession of her faculties of sight, hearing and action, almost unimpaired... (Constitutionalist).

May 18, 1869

On Thursday last MRS. WEBB, widow of JOHN WEBB, deceased, was found dead in her house. (Greensboro Herald, 13th).

A minister probably murdered. We learn from the Eufaula News of Thursday that the horse, buggy and some of the clothing of the REV. MR. McKEE, a travelling Presbyterian Minister, were found last Monday at Joiner's bridge, on Pea river. Mr. McKee himself could not be found...

The jury in the case of JESSE WATKINS, negro, charged with the murder of CHARLES WILSON, a white youth, about 25 (?) years of age, in August 1868, near Savannah, on Wednesday last found a verdict of guilty. They were out only about twenty minutes.

We regret to chronicle the sudden demise of DR. F. FICKLIN, an old and highly esteemed citizen of this place, who expired about one o'clock on Friday morning. He was at church the night previous, and seemed to be as well as usual. (Washington Gazette, 15th).

The grand jury of Jefferson county found a true bill for the murder on Tuesday last against WILSON FLOURNOY, a freedman, for the killing of DR. AYER, Radical member of the Legislature from that county... (Chronicle and Sentinel, 16th).

On the morning of Wednesday last, the 12th instant, REV. LEVI STANSELL, an esteemed minister of the Methodist Church, died at his residence near Oxford, Ga., aged about 76 years; was one of the oldest citizens of Newton county. (Covington Enterprise, 15th).

Atlanta, May 15 - CAPTAIN E. McBAROM TIMONY, late of the U.S. Army, who last fall at the American Hotel in this city shot and killed, in self-defence, RICHARDSON, a member of the Georgia Constitutional Convention, was today found not guilty of the charge of murder, and released from custody.

Died in Crawford County on the 10th instant, REV. WASHINGTON C. CLEVELAND, in the 66th year of his age; was born in Jasper county, Ga., 20 May 1803; joined the Baptist Church in Jasper county (Falling Creek Church) and was baptised by James Henderson in 1828; was licensed to preach at Mount Carmel Church, Crawford county, on 19th May 1838; was ordained January 13 (?), 1840 by Revs. Bryant Bateman, Allen Cleveland, John Barker, and James Mathews; when the division took place in the Baptist church, he adhered to the Primitive wing; was married thrice - first, to MRS. EDNA McCLENDON; secondly, to MRS. NANCY MATTHEWS; third, to MRS. AMANDA BAILEY who survives him. Three daughters and two sone - the fruits of the first marriage still survive him; the second marriage bore no fruits; two children, a son and a daughter, of his last marriage also survive him. (with long eulogy).

June 8, 1869

Misstrial. We learn that the jury at Dawson Court, on Friday last made a misstrial in the case of the State vs. LEE, charged with the murder of CAPT. FLETCHER. (Albany News, 1st).

We learn that a negro named WARREN HAYS was killed last week near Lexington, while resisting an arrest by the civil authorities... (Athens Watchman, 2d).

A negro man named ALFRED PICKETT was shot and killed by a white man named JOHN MORAND at the bridge, near this city, on Saturday... (Americus Courier, 1st).

June 8, 1869

A terrible tragedy was enacted in Dawson County on Saturday the 22d...JACK and WILLIAM THOMPSON were twin brothers, and lived together. The former had a family, and was an intemperate fellow. The other was single, and was a sober, industrious man and a good citizen. On the day above named, Jack wanted his garden hoe and was informed that one of the negroes had carried it to the field. He immediately took down his double-barreled shot-gun, and swearing he would kill the negro, mounted his mule and started to the field to carry out his threat. His brother, William, knowing what kind of man he was, endeavored to get to the negro first; but he was outstripped by Jack, who got there and fired at the negro before William came up; but failed to hit him. Seeing his brother advancing, Jack asked if he took the negro's part. Before time was given for a reply, he fired the other barrel of his gun killing William instantly. Leaving his dead brother's body on the field, Jack went home and told his wife what he had done, and asked for some of his best clothes. Taking his clothes, gun, repeater, and a jug of whiskey, he left and had not been heard from up to the date of our letter. William Thompson's remains were buried last Monday with Masonic honors. (Atlanta Era, 1st).

The State vs. NEWTON AWTREY. This case took two days in the Superior Court last week. HIRAM PROVINCE, then a citizen of this county, was missing the 26th of November last. The 16th of December he was found in Proctor's creek, fastened under a log ten to fourteen feet long, and ten to twelve inches thick...the jury returned a verdict of "Not Guilty" (Atlanta Constitutionalist, 31st).

DR. JAMES MOULTRIE, grandson of GENERAL MOULTRIE of revolutionary fame, died in Charleston on Saturday, May 29, aged 77 years. He was a very eminent physician, and for thirty-three years Professor of Physiology in the Charleston Medical College.

Portland, Me., June 2 - LAWYER BARER's wife was fatally shot today by a milliner. Cause - jealousy.

New Orleans, June 4 - A sub-marine diver named ROBERT SPENCER was drowned in the Southwest Pass today, while wrecking the steamship Pantheon. The face-glass on his armor broke, and he became fouled among the timbers, and it was impossible to haul him up. A man named W.E. Buck descended twenty-five feet under water, without armor, and recovered the body.

MRS. MATILDA ELIZABETH FUTCH, consort of JOHN A. FUTCH, and daughter of HOPE H. and MARTHA A. COLSON, was born in Charlton county, Georgia, February 16th, 1845, and died at the residence of her father, in Bradford county, Florida, April 11, 1869, aged 24 years 1 month 24 days; member of the Methodist Church. (with eulogy - signed C.F.H. and dated Levyville, Fla. Apr. 18).

It now becomes our painful duty to record the death of DR. JOHN W. QUINCY, who died of pneumonia, after a short and painful illness, at his residence in Levy county, Florida, March 25, 1869, aged 40 years 1 month 24 days. He was born in Cambridge, England on the 31st of January 1829, and emigrated to this country in the twenty-second year of his age, and shortly after his arrival here, commenced the study of medicine, in which profession he graduated in South Carolina Medical College; united with the Methodist Church at Levyville about two years ago; leaves a wife and two children - a little boy and girl. (long eulogy).

MRS. JANE McNAB, wife of JOHN McNAB, ESQ., died at their residence in Eufaula, Ala. on the morning of the 2d of May, in her 48th year; was born on the beautiful and romantic island of Islay, near the northwest coast of Scotland. Her parents, while she was yet a child, removed to North Carolina, where she lived until after her marriage. In 1835 she came with her husband to Alabama. Eufaula was then a mere frontier settlement, whose possession was still

(June 8, cont'd) - disputed by the Indians; member of the Baptist Church. (long eulogy).

June 22, 1869

On Wednesday evening the 9th instant, MR. JOHN W. HUTCHINSON, an old and highly esteemed citizen, died very suddenly of dropsy of the heart. (Brunswick Appeal, 14th).

Bibb Superior Court - Wed. The case of the State vs. HENRIETTA GREER, col'd, charged with the murder of NANCY WRIGHT, a white girl, in March last, was taken up...

Another homicide in Meriwether. We regret to hear of another killing scrape a few days since near Rocky Mount. MR. WM. BRITTON shot and instantly killed one of his neighbors named LAPSEY... (Griffin Star, 18th).

We were informed yesterday of the death of MRS. NANCY STROUD, of Lee county, Ala., who was born Feb. 10, 1785. She died on May 13, 1869, aged 84 years 2 months 3 days. She married sixty-six years ago, in her eighteenth year, to the husband who survives her. Her husband, JAMES STROUD, was born May 18, 1779. He is now in his 90th year, lives in Lee county...of the Primitive Baptist faith. (Columbus Sun, 20th).

Knocked into eternity. In a prize fight at Cayugh, New York last Saturday, one of the contestants, named McGUIRE, was killed in the ninth round by his adversary, a man named DONNELLY, who escaped to Canada.

Suicide. We learn that a most shocking suicide occurred at Bonesville, in Columbia county, yesterday morning. It appears that a gentleman by the name of WALKER had a little quarrel with his wife at breakfast time on yesterday, during which the husband got up and left the house, saying to his wife that he would go down to the mill and remain until she recovered her temper. He walked down to the mill, which was but a short distance off, but had not been there long when one of his children came running from the house and told him that her mother had killed herself. Returning to his home, Mr. Walker found his wife lying on the floor in a pool of blood, dead. She had cut her throat from ear to ear with a razor. (Chronicle and Sentinel, 17th).

Editors: Chronicle & Sentinel - ADKIN B. LEWIS, a good and useful citizen, residing about seven miles from this place, was murdered in his field about 8 o'clock A.M. today. The murderer is a negro named "Ben" about 40 years old - a round, plump fellow, weighing about 150 pounds...a little son of Mr. Lewis, about ten years old, was present at the killing. (signed from Waynesboro, Ga. June 16, 1869).

A horrible accident occurred about six o'clock yesterday evening, at the machine shop of the Albany and Gulf road, in this city, by which MR. THOMAS GAERON, a young man 18 years of age, and by trade a painter, was most horribly and perhaps fatally injured. It seems that Mr. Gaeron was endeavoring to adjust a belt on the main shaft running from the machine shop to the paint shop, when by some means he slipped, and was caught by the belt and whirled around with great violence, making, it was thought, a hundred or more revolutions before the machinery was stopped...(Sav. Advertiser, 20th).

Trouble in Sparta. One man killed, another mortally wounded. Details of the killing of WASHINGTON PIERSON and the wounding of a negro named MARSHALL. Washington Pierson was a notorious scoundrel and desperado, who has for some time past been known as the ringleader in nearly act of rascality committed in Hancock county... (Chronicle and Sentinel, 19th).

June 22, 1869

Death in a railroad car. The Gulf Railroad train that arrived here on Saturday morning brought the body of a man who had died in a car a short time before reaching Savannah...Deceased was a MR. MILLEN, a citizen of Valdosta. Had been for some time a sufferer from dropsy of the heart, and latterly confined to his bed. Had started on Friday evening, in company with his wife, for his former home in Connecticut...upon arriving at Savannah, the body was taken in charge of by Messrs. Ferguson & Dixon, who had it interred temporarily in Laurel Grove Cemetery. (Savannah News, 21st).

June 29, 1869

Attempted buring of a dwelling. Five persons burnt - one fatally. About two o'clock yesterday morning, MRS. E.E. CALDER, residing with her father, MR. E.C. PRINCE, at No. 1 Ann, near Elizabeth street, was aroused by a light in her chamber, in which she, with her two children, one an infant four months old, slept. She immediately jumped up and discovered that the bed was on fire, burning from the bottom. She gave the alarm and her father and brother, MR. J.E. PRINCE, came to her assistance. They rescued the children from the flames...Mrs. Calder, her brother and father were burnt about the hands and arms while rescuing the children, both of whom were severely burnt. One of them, EDWIN CHARLES, about three years of age, lingered in excruciating agony until seven o'clock yesterday afternoon, when death put an end to his sufferings. At a late hour last night no hopes of the recovery of the babe were entertained. (Savannah News, 22d).

Death of MAJOR PHILLIP C. PENDLETON. In our issue of Friday last we noticed the fact that Major P.C. Pendleton, editor of the Valdosta Times, had sustained severe injuries by being thrown from his buggy, while riding in the vicinity of his home...we are pained to learn that Major Pendleton died on Saturday last, having remained unconscious from the time he received the injury to the hour of his death. (Savannah News, 24th).

We learned late yesterday that a dispatch had been received during the morning announcing the death of MR. WILLIE CARTER, son of DR. ROBERT CARTER, of this city. He died during the night of yellow fever at Key West, Fla. We suppose his age to be 17 or 18 years. (Columbus Sun, 24th).

The Wilkes County murderers. From the Washington Gazette we learn that a special session of the Superior Court was called in Wilkes county on Monday last for the trial of ROBERT ARNOLD and LUKE ARNOLD, colored, under the charge of murdering MR. THOMAS THAXTON in March last...(Chronicle & Sentinel, 26th).

"In Memoriam" notice by Houston Lodge No. 35 F.A.M. - on the death of JOHN L. BIRCH, Past Master of this Lodge, who died suddenly at his residence in Perry, Georgia, January 11, 1869, aged 40 years 3 months 9 days.

Sudden death. Between six and seven o'clock on Wednesday evening, MATTHEW HENRY was found wandering about the streets by Police Officer Thomas Maguire. He imagined that he was in the city of New York, and the officer perceiving that he was insane and totally incapable of taking care of himself, arrested him and lodged him in the Police Barracks. He was apparently a healthy, strong man, who was laboring under the influence of delirium tremens. He was put to bed, and at eleven o'clock found to be in a dying condition, and expired at about half past eleven o'clock p.m. A letter of introduction to Messrs Meinhard & Bro. was found on his person, from which it appeared that his name was Matthew Henry, and that he was a "boot and shoe packer," who had been sent from the city of New York, by Mr. Meinhard of that city, to his brother in Savannah... (Savannah Republican, 25th).

June 29, 1869

Death of an old citizen of Oglethorpe. A correspondent writes us as follows from Lexington, June 25th, 2 P.M. _____ DANIEL DUPREE JOHNSON, ESQ., the foreman of the last Grand Jury in this county, and a highly respected citizen, died this forenoon very suddenly while engaged in his business. Mr. J. was a member of the Secession Convention, and held a high place in the Baptist Church. (Chronicle & Sentinel, 26th).

July 13, 1869

A sad and sudden death. On last Sunday night, the REV. JOHN LONG, of Thomasville, North Carolina, a Methodist divine of 25 years' faithful service in the pulpit, began preaching to a large congregation in Wesley Chapel - the church of the Rev. Mr. Kimball... had an apoplectic stroke from which he never recovered. He died Monday morning about 5 o'clock. Was 58 years old; was buried this morning with Masonic honors. (Atlanta Constitution, 6th).

We learn that a horrid murder was committed at the residence of Mr. Hampton Penny, who lives near Judge J.W. Thomas, in the lower part of this county, last Sunday evening. DAVID PARTIN, a young man, killed STILES MONTGOMERY, a grandson of Bartly Montgomery, who was a sober, industrious young man, about 19 or 20 years old. He was stabbed three times. The origin of the difficulty is said to have been about some woman. Partin made his escape. (Rome Courier, 6th).

REV. T.W. DORMAN, member of the Mobile Conference, M.E. Church, South, died at his residence in Mobile on the night of the 3d inst., as we learn from the Moblie Register.

MR. JACOB CRANE, a prominent New York merchant, died on the 6th inst.

We learn from the Wilmington Journal that a young lad, named LEONIDAS BEATTIE LAMB, aged 13 years and 9 months, a son of G.W. LAMB, ESQ., was struck by lightning and instantly killed, while hunting on the beach at Myrtle Grove Sound, Saturday afternoon last.

Acquitted. HILLORY B. HUMPHRIES, who was tried last week in Thomas Superior Court, for the killing of GABRIEL WILSON, Sheriff of this county, was found not guilty by the jury, after an absence from the court of about fifteen minutes.

From Coweta County and the Newnan Herald of the 3d - MR. FRED GERRALD, a young man about 20 years old, killed HENRY DAVIS, colored.

Bangor, Me., Tuesday, July 6 - MISS NORA GILES, daughter of REV. HENRY GILES, the well known lecturer and essayist, a beautiful and highly educated young lady, was drowned at Bucksport on Saturday, by the upsetting of a boat in which she was sailing, in company with her sister, another young lady, and a gentleman. Her body had not been recovered at last accounts.

The Talbotton Gazette of the 8th announces the death in that place, on the 2d instant, of MR. T.H. PERSONS, at the age of 68 years.

The Americus Republican of Thursday chronicles the sudden death, on the 6th instant, of CAPTAIN JOHN M. SHIVER, a talented citizen of that place. Was a member of the Sumter Light Guards during the Civil War; a Mason; was elected Assistant Foreman of Fire Company No. 1.

Died on the 18th ultimo at the residence of Mr. A.H. Moore of Twiggs county, Ga., of Typhoid Dysentery, in the 25th year of her age, MISS MARY S.W., youngest daughter of the late WILLIAM KILLPATRICK, of Jefferson county, and his relict - now MRS. S.A.E. STEVENS. Mollie was born in Jefferson county on the 2d day of March, 1844; member of M.E. Church; her step-father settled in this

(July 13, cont'd) - county in 1859; the deceased was on a visit at her sister's, Mrs. Burkett, when she died. (long eulogy).

Tribute of Respect by Patrick Henry Lodge No. 173 F.A.M., Drayton, Ga., July 3, 1869 - on the death of WILLIAM J. BASON.

July 20, 1869

A young man named JOSEPH WARNER, living in Charleston, West Virginia, died on Thursday under curious circumstances. He professed to have the power of charming snakes. Last Thursday, having captured a rattlesnake, he was giving some friends an exhibition of this power.. the snake bit his tongue, and he died in about an hour afterwards.

MR. MOSES E. McWHORTER died at his residence in Athens on Sunday night, after an illness of several days.

MR. JOHN SAMUEL PEAKE, one of the oldest adopted citizens of South Carolina, died at his residence in Summerville on Monday last, in the 83d year of his age.

We sincerely regret to learn the death of REV. R.K. PORTER at Atlanta on the 15th inst. Was pastor of the Central Presbyterian Church in that city; was born at Cedar Springs, S.C., January 1, 1827, graduated at the University of South Carolina, and immediately entered the ministry after he left the University.

Death of "old aunt JENNY LAMAR" is announced in the Milledgeville papers. Jenny was the slave of Col. Jack Lamar, father of our lamented fellow-citizen, Col. John B. Lamar, and of Mrs. Howell Cobb.

CAPTAIN HAYNES, the notorious Arkansas militiaman, was killed by CLARENCE COLLIER at Marion, Arkansas, on the 15th inst.

HON. JAMES SHANNON, of Kentucky, for thirty-five years previous to 1860 a member of the Democratic State Central Committee, died in Frankfort on Friday last, aged 80 years. He was the intimate friend of Amos Kendall, and afterwards of Governor Powell.

CAPTAIN MATTHEW MERCER, a section-master on the Virginia and Tennessee Railroad, near Mount Airy, Virginia, was shot and mortally wounded about sunset Thesday evening by a party of negroes...

MR. J.W. WELDON, an old citizen, died very suddenly at his residence in this city last night about 8 o'clock, with congestion of the brain.

Aug. 3, 1869

A correspondent of the New York Herald, writing from Santiago de Cuba on the 8th instant announces the death on the 6th of GEN. STEADMAN, U.S. Consul at that port. The General only arrived on the 29th ult., and was soon after attacked by yellow fever...

Details of the killing of MR. THOS. EDWARDS by a MR. COLUMBUS REESE in Crawfordsville on Saturday. (Augusta Constitutionalist).

A correspondent informs us that a lad named JAMES LAWSON was bitten by a rattlesnake on the 14th inst., on the plantation of W.S. Bush, near Ellisville, Florida, and died in twelve hours after he received the bite.

A.H. LEE,"the man who drew the Crosby Opera Houe," died suddenly last week while pleasuring in Cincinnati.

MR. WILHEMUS BOGGART died in New Orleans, 27th July, at the advanced age of 78.

Aug. 3, 1869

Tribute of Respect by Lumber City Lodge, Lumber City, Ga., July 17, 1869 - on the death of ALEXANDER POWELL, who departed life at his residence in Telfair county, Ga. 1 July 1869, aged 62 years 4 months; member of the M.E. Church.

Buffalo, July 27 - EDWARD HALPIN, an elderly man, fell into Niagara Falls, a distance of 180 feet. He was instantly killed.

Aug. 10, 1869

MISS SUSAN CAROLINE GODSEY, the sleeping wonder, died at her mother's home, some eight miles from Hickman, Kentucky, on Wednesday the 14th instant. The history of Miss Godsey is well known to the public, a statement of her wonderful condition having been published extensively by the press of the United States. At the time of her death, Miss Godsey was about 26 years of age, and had been asleep about fourteen years...

HENRIETTA NICHOLS, the oldest colored woman in Maryland, died last week, aged 110 years.

MANSON JOLLY, a bold and daring Confederate soldier, was drowned on the 8th July, near his home in Texas, so says the Anderson, S.C. Intelligencer.

Augusta, Aug. 5 - A report comes from Edgefield, S.C. that CHAS. and J.D. CRESSWELL, who left this city yesterday, were shot this morning near Edgefield, the former being killed instantly, and the latter seriously, if not mortally, wounded. The affair is entirely of a private nature - alleged to have grown out of family troubles. Aug. 6 - GEORGE B. and JAMES ADDISON have surrendered themselves to the authorities for the shooting of Chas. and J.D. Cresswell. Chas Cresswell, charged with criminal intercourse with a sister of Addison's, is dangerourly, but mortally wounded.

Aug. 17, 1869

Tragedy in Boston. The wife of a prominent physician shot dead in her parlor in presence of her family. From the Boston Journal, July 4 - Details of the shooting of MRS. ALVAH H. HOBBS.

HENRY DICKINSON committed suicide in West Springfield, Ohio last Tuesday week, by pounding his head with a mallet.

A man and wife named CONYNGHAM, living near Floyd, Iowa, were instantly killed by lightning while in bed asleep. Their bodies were perfectly black from the effects of the stroke. The man's mother was rendered insane by the same shock.

MR. CHARLES C. LITTLE, the founder and senior partner of the firm of Little, Brown & Co., of Boston, died recently at his house in Cambridge. Was born at Kennebunk, Me. on 25 July 1779, and was consequently a few days over 70 at the time of his death.

Aug. 24, 1869

MR. CHRISTIAN ARANT, an old and respected citizen of Orangeburg district, S.C., was thrown from his buggy last week, and was so seriously hurt that he died from the injuries.

MR. JAMES C. DOBBIN, a particularly promising young lawyer of North Carolina, a son of the Secretary of War under Pierce's administration, was killed on Friday last by falling from a window in the third story of his residence in Fayetteville.

MRS. GIFFORD, living in Marion county, Iowa, died from the effects of fright at the eclipse.

Aug. 24, 1869

CHARLES WHITE, the lion tamer, travelling with Thayer's menagerie, was eaten by the lions, in a small town in Michigan.

E.O. HAILE, extensively known as a humorous contributor to the press under the name of "A. HEAD," died at Austin, Texas on the 15th inst.

Aug. 31, 1869

MR. HENRY K. WALKER, of the house of L.J. Guilmartin & Co., Savannah, died at the Sandersville Hotel on Wednesday last.

REV. BERRY PEELER, of Hancock, and one of the oldest ministers of the Washington Baptist Association, died a few days since.

MR. THOMAS NIX, for more than 35 years a citizen of Columbus, died at Whistler, near Mobile, Ala., on the 17th instant.

EDWARD HOWLAND, son of the well known ship owner of New Bedford, Mass., committed suicide at Lake Lahoe, Cal. on Monday last, by blowing out his brains.

The quiet village of Monroe was startled on Sunday night of last week by the announcement that a young lady - MISS MARY CUNNINGHAM - daughter of MRS. CUNNINGHAM of that place - had committed suicide by poisoning herself with strychine... (Athens Watchman).

MR. JAMES M. DURYEA, of Charleston, S.C., was instantly killed Thursday morning by the discharge of a pistol which he was examining, preparatory to cleaning.

JOHNNY PENDERGRAST, the minstrel, chose his coffin in jest from a wharehouse in Pittsburgh the other day, and in twenty-four hours he occupied it.

MAJOR WILLIS H. CLAIBORNE, only son of COL. J.F.H. CLAIBORNE, died on the 13th inst., near Natchez, aged 34 years, and in conformity with his last request, was buried in his Confederate uniform.

The Nashville Banner reports that W. BRITT, I. BRITT and W. ANDREWS were killed, and T.L. Taylor, Bug Steward, Bell Andrews and James Henry badly wounded, at Wilderville, West Tennessee, a few days ago during a drunken quarrel.

A man named SHY was found dead, with a bullet-hole through his head, in Sumner county, Tennessee a few days since. This is the same man that was tried for killing negroes some time since, and was not convicted.

Sep. 7, 1869

We learn by telegraph that GENERAL JOHN A. RAWLINS, U.S. Secretary of War, died yesterday afternoon at Washington City. Hemorrhage of the lungs was the immediate cause of death.

Sep. 14, 1869

The telegraph announces the death, September 8, of WILLIAM PITT FESSENDEN, one of the U.S. Senators from Maine...

OVIDE GREGORY, member of the Alabama Legislature from Mobile county, died in Mobile on the 1st instant. The Montgomery Mail says Ovide was one of the most respectable members of the House, though he was a negro.

From the Nashville Banner of the 11th - The HON. JOHN BELL, Tennessee statesman, died at two o'clock yesterday morning at Cumberland Iron Works after a long illness...

Oct. 12, 1869

COL. MALCOLM D. JONES, one of the most promising and enterprising citizens of Burke county, died at his residence near Bark camp in that county on Friday last...(Chronicle and Sentinel, Oct. 7).

Oct. 19, 1869

Notice of the death of EX-PRESIDENT FRANKLIN PIERCE.

DR. THOMAS ANDERSON, once a leading physician and influential citizen of Vicksburg, died recently at Memphis, aged 80 years.

We are pained to chronicle the death of MR. WM. HENRY HUGHES, son of HAYDEN HUGHES, and a brother of Col. Daniel G. Hughes, of Twiggs county. Mr. Hughes died of a congestive chill in Athens, Ga. on Friday last. His remains were brought to Macon Saturday evening by Mr. Nathan Monroe Solomon, one of his classmates in the University of Georgia, and were taken by private conveyance yesterday to the residence of his father, in Twiggs county, for interment.

On Monday last MR. THOMAS H. FIELD, a retired merchant and a resident of New Rochelle, was killed instantly by a trap-gun he had set up to keep trespassers from entering his property and robbing his grapery...

COL. JAMES F. COOPER, formerly Superintendent of the U.S. Mint at Dahlonega, and of the W. & A.R.R., died in Atlanta on Wednesday, aged 55 years.

MR. JOHN SUTTON died at his residence in Macon County, Georgia, September 29th, 1869, aged about 68 years.

From Macon Daily Telegraph of 4 March 1866

Confederate Dead at Elmyra:

    Through the kindness of a young lady a "Southern sympathizer," residing in Albany, New York, I have procured a "Death Roster" kept by a Surgeon of the hospital at Elmyra prison. I send it to you, editors of a Southern paper, with a request that it be published throughout the South, for the benefit of those bereaved families who have an interest in "the missing" of the battle-field. Hoping that this list of buried braves may not blight too suddenly the lingering hopes of many fond mothers and wives, who seek comfort in the thought - "he is not lost, he will be found" and that it may comfort those who entertain no hope, by revealing to them the spot where their treasures are sleeping.

NORTH CAROLINA

1st Regt., Co E - A.C. GESNER; Co F - J.A. BRISTON; Co I - A.H.
        ROLLIN, J.D. WITHERS; Co K - J. WATSON; Co E - R. FAUCETT
3rd Regt., Co E - ELIJAH E. SHELFER; Co F - GEORGE L. POWELL
5th Regt., Co E - N.M. CLOUD; Co H - MADISON MINER
7th Regt., Co D - JOHN MEREDITH
8th Regt., Co E - T. MORRIS
10th Regt., Co F - K. JORDAN, MATHIAS CRAWFORD; Co K - G.A. HOBBS
12th Regt., Co C - OCTAVUS SATTLINGS
13th Regt., Co D - DAVID ORWOOD
18th Regt., Co A - GILBERT WILLIAMS; Co B - J.A. HAGLER; Co D -
        W.O. ANDREWS; Co E - NATHAN LEWIS; Co F - N. BROWN
20th Regt., Co G - CALVEN CHURCH
21st Regt. Co K - P. ROND
22d Regt., Co I - GEO. W. TYSON
24th Regt., Co B - MARTIN HUMPHRIES
28th Regt., Co B - JONATHAN BAILEY; Co G - WM. J. WART
30th Regt., Co A - J.R. REYNOLDS; Co H - H.T. CAMPBELL
31st Regt., Co B - WM. R. DIGGS; Co H - JOEL WALKER
32d Regt., Co B - JOHN LAWER; Co D - JAS. PILAN; Co H - J.N. COGGIN
33d Regt., Co E - THOMAS BANCHUM
36th Regt., Co E - T. FAIRCLOTH; Co F - W.T. CUTCHIN; Co G - ED
        HARRIS, WM. MERITS; Co B - J. STEWART; Co C - DUNCAN PERCELL
37th Regt., Co A - WM. ROYAL
40th Regt., Co K - EPHRAM EVERS, ALFRED FELTON
42d Regt., Co C - FRANKLIN CAUBLE
43d Regt., Co B - T.M. MAMS; Co F - H.H. LELIS
45th Regt., Co A - N. GIPSON; Co H - J.B. HOLMAN
51st Regt., Co H - WM. J. PENNY; Co G - WARD RENEN; Co K - C. VANN
53d Regt., Co F - B.A. RAY
56th Regt., Co F - JOHN M. LINDSAY, C.J. PAYNE

VIRGINIA

2d Regt., Co G - F. MOWRY
3d Regt., Co G - WM. H. DOWDY
4th Regt., Co G - WALKER WILLIAMSON
11th Regt., Co C - ISAAC A. MILLEN

(Confederate dead of Virginia, cont'd)
14th Regt., Co I - MATTHEW HELMS
22d Regt., Co D - MATTHEW REESE
26th Regt., Co C - GEORGE GOODE, J. CARDWELL; Co D - J.S. CHEWING;
    Co F - ALLEN MEADOWS; Co G - WM. U. WYATT, J.H. MARSHAL:
    Co H - F. CLEGG
40th Regt., Co F - JOHN O. BLACKWELL; Co H - O.A. SMITH
42d Regt., Co E - J.E. NEIGHBORS; Co B - JERRY UNDERWOOD
48th Regt., Co C - M.V. DARNEL; Co I - J.H. FLEENIN
50th Regt., Co B - WM. HALL; Co E - AARON CYPHERS; Co F - JOHN
    KNOYLE; Co I - J.L. BREDING, J.O. SMITH, R. TUGET, C. KING
52d Regt., Co I - T.R. LEIGHTNER
59th Regt., Co A - Corporal WILLIAM HIGGS

GEORGIA

4th Regt., Co D - HORACE WHITTON
7th Regt., Co D - JOHN WALKER, DANIEL E. DOUGLAST
21st Regt., Co J - LEIN SAPP
27th Regt., Co K - THOMAS HARDY
31st Regt., Co G - WM. L. SHIP
35th Regt., Co I - JOHN RUTHERFORD
44th Regt., Co D - WILLIAM ALL, WILLIAM B. STEWART
53d Regt., Co E - JAMES A. STEPHENS
Co-b's Legion, Co C - J.M. ANDERSON; Co E - NOAH ROYNE, J.L. MADRAY

SOUTH CAROLINA

1st Regt., Co L - FREDERICK WIECKING
4th Regt., Co A - W.R. SELLERS; Co C - P.A. COLLINS
11th Regt., Co J - JOHN B. BAILY
14th Regt., Co F - R.P. CARTER
15th Regt., Co B - JOHN GROSS
17th Regt., Co I - J.L. HOWARD, ALLEN J. ROBERTSON
7th Regt., Co G - WM. J. COOPER
21st Regt., Co F - G.W. BRANCY, M. BIRD; Co I - E. STEPHENS
22d Regt., Co C - M.A. WOOD
25th Regt., Co G - H.L. BAILY; Co I - S.B. HODGE; Co K - W.H. OWENS

ALABAMA

1st Regt., Co A - C.F. HIGDON, DAVID M. TURNER, NOAH DUNCAN,
    Corporal L.D. WARKER, JAMES HARRISON, J.A. PRESBY, JOHN
    EDWARDS, J.W. STENSON; Co E - HIRAM KING
1st Artillery - DAVID BENNEYFIELD, R.J. LANE, J.D. SWAIN, J. SMITH
3d Regt., Co K - J.D. BURDSHAW
5th Regt., Co I - J.B. SOMERS
12th Regt., Co H - J. McMEIN
21st Regt., Co A - WM. M. CRON, WM. T. CALDWELL
59th Regt., Co B - H.A. JOHNSON
61st Regt., Co C - JAMES CULLAN; Co E - W.A. GRIFFITH

(Confederate dead, cont'd)

LOUISIANA

2d Regt., Co F - SAMUEL SMITH
4th Regt., Co A - JAMES E. POWELL
10th Regt., Co K - EMILIE RUBLEAN
15th Regt., Co F - F.W. LEAVENS

FLORIDA

1st Regt., Co A - JOEL BROWN
2d Regt., Co I - W.T. McNEER
5th Regt., Co F - JAMES R. TERREL; Co E - F.M. KAMEN; Co K - J. CARTER

TENNESSEE

1st Regt., Co B - WM. J. TROXELL
31st Regt., Cavalry, Co C - J.M. JEFFRIES
63d Regt., Co K - JOEL COOK

ARKANSAS

3d Regt., Co G - J.H. THOMAS, H.W. WALKER

HOOD's BATTALION

Co B - THOMAS W. KITCHEN
Co B - JOSIAH SUDKINS

From Macon Daily Telegraph of 26 April 1866

Confederate Dead Buried in Rose Hill Cemetery (Macon, Ga.)

L.O. Tait, co I, 8th Confederate Regiment, died,_____
J.W. Swiney, _____, _____, died Dec. 13th '63
Capt. Erasmus Collum, co F, 8th Tenn. (killed near Griffin) Nov.16,64
W.H. Bird, co A, 32d Miss, Dec. 7th '63
J.F. McGraw, co D, 9th Ga., Dec. 11th '63
Thos. Copeland, Co A, 1st Ga., Dec 6th '63
J.H. Yates, _____, _____, '63
Willie C. Ross, from Rome, May 21st '63
Robt M. Bee, co B, 1st Ga., '63
M.F. Downs, co H, 50th Ala., Dec 14th '63
W.B. Humbers, co G, Ala., Dec 16th '63
M. Kaugh, co B, 2d Tenn., Dec 28th '63
Thos Alderman, 29th Ga., Dec 30th '63
Thos Ohara, co A, 12th Ga., Dec 28th '63
C.H. Stewart, 1st Fla, Jan 4th '64
Jas F. Hewston, Newnan's Tenn. Battery, '64
Jas Smith, co C, 3d Tenn., Jan 15th, '64
J.W. Shaw, 1st Ga., Jan 15th '64
S. Daniels, co K, 51st Ga., Jan 31st '64
Jas Raley, co G, Finley's Battalion, '64
Jas A. Hobbs, co D, 66th Ga., Feb 3d '64
J.G. Hammonds, _____, _____, Feb 8th '64
S. Miles, co A, 10th S.C., '64
G.W. Deerson, co F, 7th Fla., March 25th '64
W.H. Ross, 4th Ky, March 27th '63
Capt. J.D. Agilvy, co K, 4th Ala., _____
J.M. Davie, co D, 29th Ga., _____
Wm. Vickory, co K, 50th Ga., _____
W. Lester, from Camp Cooper, Macon, Ga., April 19th '64
E.A. Davis, co H, 45th Tenn., May 4th '64
Allen Raines, co E & F, 28th Ala., May 15th '64
J.W. Rodgers, co K, 25th Ga., '64

(Confederate dead buried in Rose Hill, cont'd)
Jno McDoe, co A, 38th Tenn., age 10 years, '64
Solomon Sagers, co K, 63d Ga., May 22d '64
Benj Cadish, co A. 37th Ala., May 31st '64
J. Radiford, co D. 17th Ala., May 24th '64
F. Reedy, co D, 63d Ala., '64
Geo Rentz, co F, 47th Ga., May 24th '64
J.H. Groover, co F, 29th Ga., May 24th '64
J. Lovett, co I, 10th S.C., May 25th '64
N.A. Lawson, co I, 52d Ga., May 26th '64
J.W. Bell, co B, 8th Confed. Cav., '64
A.L.K, '64
P.E. Banks, co C, 5th Ga., June 22d '64
Jas Smith, co H, 40th Ala., June 21st '64
J.J. Sanders, co A, 40th Ga., June 20th '64
E.J. Bardwell, co K, 35th Miss., 19th '64
A.L. Johnson, co E, 31st Miss., '64
John Riley, co B, 33d Ala., June 8th '64
A.J. Pearson, co G, 15th S.C., June 16th '64
A.G. Smith, Perrin's Miss Cav., June 16th '64
Jas Andrews, 38th Ala., June 16th '64
R. Woodford, 57th Ala., June 16th '64
M. Motby, 58th Ala., June 14th '64
G.J. Morris, 11th Tenn., June 15th '64
Name unknown, died on train coming from Columbus to Macon
M.M. Carter, 56th Ga., June 10th '64
Benj. Lewis, 57th Ala., June 10 '64
R.F. Yarborough, 17th Ala., June 6th '64
J.W. Sullivan, 17th Ala., June 6, '64
Wm. Wray, 49th Ga., June 6, '64
M.V. Nichols, 1st Tenn. Cav., June '64
T.J. Roberts, 39th Miss., June 5, '64
J.M. Hill, 63d Ga., June 5, '64
H.C. Kyle, 51st Tenn., June 1, '64
Rufus Dean, 24th Texas, June '64
Joshua Harrald, Cobb's Reserves, May 30, '64
A.M. Brewton, 23d Ala., May 29, '64
J.A. Black, 17th Ala., May 29, '64
W.T. Belcher, 30th Ga., May 29, '64
J.W. Elliott, 54th Ga., May 28, '64
Corp. W.G. Smith, 24th S.C., May 28, '64
J. Batchelor, 63d Ga., May 27, '64
D.J. Hanney, 3d Miss., June 23, '64
J.Q. Thomas, co D, 18th Ala., June 24, '64
J.A. Weaver, co D, 34th Ga., June 26, '64
W. Crenshaw, co D, 36th Miss., June 27, '64
Henry Davis, co B, 29th N.C., June 27, '64
B. McPeek, co D, 54th Va., June 28, '64
J. Roberts, co F, 20th Miss., June 29, '64
W.T. Bailey, co A, 30th Ala., July 1, '64
J.P. Hunter, co K, 18th Ala., July 1, '64
G.J. Brantley, co H, 63d Ga., July 1, '64
C.A. Breland, co C, 49th Ala., July 1, '64
Robt. Lewis, co C, 5th Ga., July 2, '64
W. Thomas, co I, 8th Tenn., July 4, '64
W.L. Shaver, co A, 58th N.C., July 6, '64
W.W. Lowell, co D, 46th Miss., July 8, '64
J.T. Phipps, co I, 35th Miss., July 9, '64
J. Martin, co G, 49th Ala., July 10, '64
J.R. Rustin, co D, 5th Ga. Cav., July 10, '64
D.B. Reed, co E, 4th Tenn., July 11, '64
J. Powell, co E, 42 Ala., July 12, '64
B.L. Pollard, co C, 28th Tenn., July 11, '64
T. Anderson, co C, 45th Ala., July 12, '64
Jno. Asken, 5th Ga. Res., July 12, '64
C.A. Friday, 24th Ala. Bat., July 13, '64
M. Collier, co C, 34th Ala., July 14, '64
T.A. Motes, co C, 40th Ala., July 15, '64
J.B. Wheeler, co K, 12th Tenn., July 24, '64
W.C. Rouse, co K, 7th Fla., July 23, '64

(Confederate dead buried in Rose Hill, cont'd)
D.W. McIlheny, Ward's Art'y, July 22, '64
M.J. Grimes, co E, 46th Miss., July 22, '64
M.V. Boydston, co F, 15th Miss., July 22, '64
B.J. Bush, co I, 2d Tenn., July 22, '64
J. Battle, co A, 12th Ala Bat., July 23, '64
C.C. Clay, co C, 37th Miss., July 21, '64
D. Lester, co K, 29th Ala., July 22, '64
J.K.P. Smallwood, co I, 1st GM, Sept. 10, '64
R.H. Morgan, co G, 15th Miss., Sept. 8, '64
Wm. Stevens, Co H, 2d Ark., Sept. 8, '64
J.F. Vickers, co K, Ga. S L, Sept. 9, '64
Allen Daughtry, co D, 6th Ga., Sep. 9, '64
R. Jacobs, co A, 9th Ga., Sep. 10, '64
A. McCorkle, co C, 15th Texas, Sep. 12, '64
M. Harrall, co G, 29th Ga., Sept. 11, '64
Wm. G. Albright, co E, 22d Ala., Sept. 12, '64
Jno Comas, co I, 8th G M, Sept. 12, '64
R.H. Edwards, co I, 41st Ga., Sept. 11, '64
H.A. Phillips, co D, 16th La., Sept. 12, '64
Henry Crosby, co I, 12th Ga., Sept. 12, '64
Amos Rollins, Ethridge, N.C. Art'l., July 21, '64
A.J. Teague, co A, 2d Ala., July 21, '64
G.T. Crone, co A, 9th Tenn., July 21, '64
E.S. Walson, co G, 15th Miss., July 20, '64
R. Jones, co K, 30th N.C., July 18, '64
W.J. Gordon, co F, 46th Ala., July 18, '64
E.A. Hill, co D, 49th Ga., July 18, '64
Jos. Watson, co H, 63d Ga., July 17, '64
J.B. Hooper, co K, 42d Tenn., July 16, '64
J.M. Beach, co D, 8th Tenn., July 16, '64
T.A. Hogan, co B, 41st Ga., Sep. 6, '64
W.M. Murray, co E, 54th Va., July 15, '64
A.L. Smith, July '64
Sgt. R. Braden, co K, 9th Tenn., July 25, '64
F.J. Polk, co E, 56th Ga., July 25, '64
Joaish Crawly, co G, 6th Miss., July 25, '64
Col. Jas. Barr, 10th Miss., July 25, '64
Newton L. Moore, co A, 15th Miss., July 26, '64
J. Bellow, Miller's regt., July 26, '64
J. Anderson, co K, 7th Fla., July 29, '64
J.A. Maden, co A, 21st Tenn., July 29, '64
H.W. Magee, co K, 39th Miss., July 29, '64
Wm. Cox, co A, 7th Ala., July 29, '64
Samuel Hall, Musician, 19th La., July 29, '64
H. Patton, 54th Ga., July 29, '64
V.D. Spyker, Winchester, July 28, '64
B.A. Kelly, co E, 55th Ala., July 28, '64
C. Cowart, co E, 54th Ga., July 29, '64
J.F. Gray, co F, 42d Tenn., July 28, '64
J.M. Barrentine, co C, 4th Ark., July 28, '64
S. Horton, co B, 2d Ala., July 28, '64
F.M. Lynchburger, co H, 1st Ga., July 28, '64
R.L. Davis, co B, 1st Ark., July 28, '64
W.B. Jones, co E, 3d Ga. Cav., July 28, '64
J.T. Miles, co A, 25th Ala., July 28, '64
W. Martin, co C, 10th Confed. Cav., July 29, '64
T.J. Richards, co D, 26th Ala., July 30, '64
J.A. Straton, co K, 26th Ala., July 30, '64
W.J. Vaughan, Ga. Mil., July 30, '64
C. Waters, co B, 1st Ga. S.L., July 30, '64
Corp. J. Bunyards, co D, 6th Miss., July 30, '64
Barnabas Taylor, co A, 22d Ala., Aug. 1st, '64
Moses Whitton, co D, 42d Ala., July 31, '64
Sergt. Maj. J.M. Bennett, 54th Ga., Aug. 2, '64
Sergt. T. Obarr, co F, 31st Ala., July 30, '64
M. King, co F, 54th Ala., July 31, '64
J.A. Messer, co A, 37th Ala., July 30, '64
R.P. Smith, 18 years old, July 28, '64
J. Johnson, co C, 29th Ala., Aug. 9, '64

(Confederate dead buried in Rose Hill, cont'd)
B. Upchurch, co E, 17th Ala., Aug. 9, '64
M.G. Arrington, co B, 66th Ga., Aug. 9, '64
R. Comfort, co E, 15th Miss., Aug. 8, '64
J.A. Harris, co C, 14th Texas, Aug. 8, '64
T. Carrell, co I, 29th Ala., Aug. 7, '64
G.P. Ragan, Gate's Ala. Batt., Aug. 7, '64
W.H. Hammond, Rowan's Bat., Aug. 7, '64
R. Richbourg, co E, 19th S.C., Aug. 7, '64
Wm. Anderson, co A, 12th Miss., Aug. 7, '64
S.R. Neal, Phelin's Miss. Batt., Aug. 7, '64
J. Tidwell, co H, 45th Ala., Aug. 8, '64
Jas. Cooper, co A, Ga. Mil., Aug. 7, '64
J.F. Gardner, co A, Stiggs Battery, Aug. 7, '64
J. Stanton, co B, 3d Ala. Cav., Aug. 8, '64
Jno. Burton, co D, 1st Ga. Res., Aug. 4, '64
A. Morgan, co G, 66th Ga., Aug. 5, '64
J.G. Benton, co E, 50th Tenn., Aug. 5, '64
D. Smith, Aug. 5, '64
J. Pilojean, co F, 30th La., Aug. 4, '64
A. Tonton, co A, 2d Ga. S L, Aug. 4, '64
R. Coode, co F, 42d Tenn., Aug. 4, '64
W.T. Jones, co D, 25th Ala., Aug. 3, '64
Wm. R. Mabrey, co K, 4th Ga. Mil., Aug. 4, '64
L.F. Young, co I, 39th N.C., Aug. 3, '64
J.E. Gibbers, co C, 4th Miss., Aug. 2, '64
W.H. Hammond, co A, 1st Ga. Ba'n. Mil., Aug. 2, '64
J.T. Barbee, co K, 57th Ga., Aug., 2, '64
J.A. Crawford, co G, 29th Ga., July 31, '64
W.J. Johnson, co C, 66th Ga., Aug. 1st, '64
Thos. Wolfe, co K, 5th Ga. Reserves, Aug. 1st, '64
A. Robertson, co H, 12th Miss. Cav'y, Aug. 1st, '64
W.W. Mills, co I, 29th Ala., Aug. 1st, '64
J.W. Wilkinson, co A, 4th Ky., Aug. 9th, '64
A.A. Binwiddie, Ensign 5th Tenn., Aug. 8th, '64
Capt. W.G. Reynolds, co A, 29th Miss., Aug. 3d, '64
J. Ramey, co H, 56th Ala., Aug. 8th, '64
J. Russell, co C, 3d Miss., Aug. 8th, '64
L. Blackman, co B, 17th Ala., Aug. 10th, '64
T.L. Davis, Torren't Battery, Aug. 10th, '64
A.J. Council, co E, 10th S.C., Aug. 10th, '64
G.W. Bryan, co H, 23d Ala., Aug. 10th, '64
T.A. Bagley, co E, 63d Ga., Aug. 10th, '64
Lt. L.C. Isey, Cooper Battery, Aug. 11th, '64
Corp'l J. Maxwell, co A, 6th Texas, Aug. 10, '64
Thos. J. Chambers, _____, Aug. 11, '64
D. Cardry, co H, 1st Ga., Aug. 12, '64
L. Anderson, co B, 18th Ala., Aug. 12, '64
O.W. McGee, co E, 22d Miss., Aug. 13, '64
Jas. B. Varnado, co B, 22d Miss., Aug. 12, '64
C. Adams, co E, 63d Ga., Aug. 12, '64
U.R. Teagle, co A, 9th Miss., Aug. 13, '64
J. Pettigrew, co K, 30th Miss., Aug. 14, '64
F. Luts, Jeffrey's Battery, Aug. 18, '64
Jno. Phillips, co H, 63d Va., Aug. '64
M. King, co C, 1st Fla., Aug. 13, '64
J.C. Hancock, co I, 5th Ga. Mil., Aug. 13, '64
J.O. Bailey, co B, 42d Ala., Aug. 15, '64
W.M. Jordan, co A, 41st Tenn., Aug. 18, '64
J.C. Barclay, co K, 10th Miss., Aug. 17, '64
G. Lovell, co C, 33d Miss., Aug. 17, '64
A.J. Thompson, co K, 1st Ala., Aug. 17, '64
J.F. Scorggins, co K, 3d Miss., Aug. 17, '64
John Hart, co A, 57th Ga., Aug. 17, '64
J.D. Weed, co I, 3d N.C., Aug. 17, '64
L. Bailey, co K, 57th Ala., Aug. 27, '64
C.C. Ward, co K, 14th Miss., Aug. 27, '64
E.C. Johnson, _____, Aug. 27, '64
L. Griffith, co C, 12th G M, Aug. 27, '64
T.V. Belwe, Ensign 31st Miss., Aug. 25, '64

(Confederate dead buried in Rose Hill, cont'd)
A. Ledbetter, co F, 29th N.C., Aug. 24, '64
S.E. Robins, co B, 17th Ala., Aug. 25, '64
W.F. Cochrane, co A, Miller's Cav., Aug. 24, '64
B.P. Evans, co D, Miller's Cav., Aug. 24, '64
M.B. Garrett, co G, 27th Ala., Aug. 22, '64
A.P. Holston, co G, 3d and 5th Mos., Aug. 22, '64
F.W. Otto, co E, 9th Miss., Aug. 22, '64
W.H. Woodford, co B, 33d Ala., Aug. 22, '64
Jas. Winslett, co A, 30th Ala., Aug. 21st, '64
Jno. Nelson, co A, 25th Ala., Aug. 21, '64
R. Hester, co K, 10th S.C., Aug. 21, '64
David Golhard, co C, 50th Tenn., Aug. 21, '64
Josiah Payne, co B, 34th Miss., Aug. 21, '64
J.T. Scott, co B, 4th Tenn., Aug. 19, '64
J. Nothcut, co C, 1st Ala., Aug. 20, '64
N. McIlhane, co I, 29th Ala., Aug. 19, '64
Sgt. R.J. McKnight, co C, 55th Tenn., Aug. 19, '64
J.P. Knowles, co B, Bellamy's Bat'y, Aug. 19, '64
P. Gilmore, co F, 2d Ala., Aug. 19, '64
D. Faulinberry, Aug. 19, '64
W.H. Graham, co K, 8th Miss., Aug. 19, '64
J.W. Vickery, co I, 20th Tenn., Aug. 19, '64
Lt. J.B. Marshall, co A, 42d Ala., Aug. 18, '64
F. Nutt, co G, 5th G Res., Aug. 18, '64
J.R. Wilkinson, co A, 40th Ala., Aug. 18, '64
J.E. Scott, co B, 3d Miss., Aug. '64
L. Shaham, co B, 1st Confed., Aug. 28, '64
Wm. Isler, co H, 10th G M, Aug. 29, '64
P.P. Womack, co F, 2d Miss., Aug. 30, '64
Judson Jones, co C, 34th Ark., Aug. 30, '64
J.E. McAbee, co C, 39th Ga., Aug. 30, '64
S. Long, co C, 54th Va., Aug. 31, '64
W.T. Fisher, co F, 42d Ala., Sept. 1, '64
A.H. Alveston, co F, 3d G M, Aug. 31, '64
L. Freedon, co A, Perrin's Miss. Cav., Sept. 1, '64
M.J. Hudson, co D, 46th Ga., Sept. 2, '64
J. McCoy, co C, 54th Ga., Sept. 1, '64
J. Abernatha, co A, 54th Ala., Sept. '64
J.T. Crittenden, co E, 56th Ala. Cav., Sept. 2, '64
S.M. Vancleave, co D, 46th Tenn., Sep. 5,'64
J.R. Johnson, co D, 34th Ala., Sept. 4, '64
Lt. W.H. Simmons, co E, 30th Miss., Sep. 3, '64
W. Rogers, co I, 43d Ga., Sept. 4, '64
A.B. Whittlesey, co G, 1st Mo., Sep. 4, '64
S.J. Anderson, co D, 56th Ga., Sep. 4, '64
J.F. Smith, co C, 17th Ala., Sep. 4, 1864
S.W. Adams, co B, 3d Miss., Sep. 4, 1864
A. Vignes, Cooper's Bat'y, Sep. 5, '64
W.A. Taylor, co E, 1st Ark., Sep. 5, '64
J.W. Shackleford, co B, 46th Ala., Sep. 4, '64
I.B. Hawkins, co F, 12th Miss. Cav., Sep. 6, '64
N. Simmons, co B, 2d Ga. Batt., Sep. 5, '64
Jas. Ryals, co K, 1st Fla., Sep. 6, '64
W.H. Holland, co I, 32d Tenn., Sep. 6, '64
Sgt. A.L. Thomas, co E, 50th Ala., Sep. 6, '64
B. Hampton, co K, 1st Ga. Cav., Sep. 5, '64
Sgt. C. McGuire, co B, 4th La., Sep. 5, '64
Jno. Corley, co K, 50th Tenn., Sep. 5, '64
Jno. House, co I, 2d Ark., Sept. 5, '64
L.H. Johnson, co B, 22d Miss., Oct. 13, '64
R.D. Cade, co I, 35th Miss., Nov. 2, '64
Patrick L. Henry, Com. Dept., Oct. 15, '64
J.S. Cunningham, co H, 45th Ga., Sept. 10, '64
J.B. McCain, co I, 30th Ala., Sept. 10, '64
J.S. Hall, co A, 28th Ala., Sept. 10, '64
R.F. McMillan, co K, 10th Ga., Sept. 10, '64
Wm. Henderson, co K, 1st Ga. Mil., Sept. 16, '64
W. Carpenter, co E, 2d Ala., Sept. 18, '64
G.T. Dempsey, co F, 30th Tenn., Sept. 9, '64

(Confederate dead buried in Rose Hill, cont'd)
J.P. Davis, co D, 57th Ga., Sept. 9, '64
H.W. Johnson, co A, 4th La., Sept. '64
E. Graham, co H, 34th Ga., Sept. 9, '64
A.N. Wise, co D, 6th and 7th Ark., Sept. 5, '64
Jno Bryant, co A, Perrin's Miss. Cav., Sept. 8, '64
Sgt. F.T. Green, co A, 15th Ala., Sept. 8, '64
Z. Rogers, co B, 46th Miss., Sept. 8, '64
H.C. Gayne, co F, 16th Tenn., Sept. 7, '64
G. Wellington, co F, 2d and 3d Mo., Sept. 8, '64
G. Herring, co F, 2d Ga., Sept. 9, '64
J.M. Johnson, co B, 44th Miss., Sept. 7, '64
W. Johnson, Sept. 7, '64
Jno P. Brooks, co E, 29th Tenn., Sept. 7, '64
Sgt. O.H. Bushing, co E, 33d Ala., Sep. 6, '64
W.C. Hailes, co H, 36th Miss., Sept. 5, '64
Robt. H. Harris, co H, 25th Ga., Sept. 5, '64
B. Owens, co G, 7th G M, Sept. 7, '64

From Macon Daily Telegraph of 26 April 1866

Confederate Dead Buried in Old City Cemetery in Macon, Georgia

W. Byres, co D, 9th Ark., Sept. 22, '64
J.L. Gibbs, co I, 32d Tenn., Sept. 24, '64
Sergt. T.L. Littlejohn, co F, 13th Tenn., Sept. 23d, '64
Louis Corturiet, co B, 6th & 15th Tex., Sept. 22, '64
Sergt. Horrel, Bellamy Battery, Sept. 22, '64
J.E. Bowen, co E, 1st Ga. S L, Sept. 29, '64
Lieut. G.P. Green, Pruden's Battery, Sept. 29, '64
J.J. Reynolds, co I, 24th Ala., Sept. 29, '64
S.M. Pendly, co B, 1st Confederate, Sept. 27, '64
J.B. Blakely, co H, 5th Va., Sept. 28, '64
P.A. Avant, co E, 29th Miss., Sept. 27, '64
Wm. Roy, co K, 53d Ala., Sept. 27, '64
James Morris, co B, 34th Ala., Sept. 27, '64
Ed. J. Watley, co K, 20th Ala., Sept. 26, '64
I.E. Cooper, co I, 19th Tenn., Sept. 27, '64
W.J. Robinson, co K, 40th Miss., Sept. 26, '64
Sergt. A.H. Furgerson, co B, 55th Ala., Sept. 26, '64
D. Saunders, 5th Ga. Res., Sept. 21, '64
D.M. Habfield, 3d Reg. Eng. Corps, Sept. 25, '64
Jackson Kelley, co B, 2d Ga., Sept. 25, '64
R.H. Andrews, co G, 3d Ga., Sept. 26, '64
John Wilson, 12th Miss Cav., Sept. 25, '64
Wm. Fiddy, co H, 16th S.C., Sep. 26, '64
Maj. Smith, 39th Ala., (died at Barnesville), Sept. 23, '64
T.C. Heidelberg, co H, 27th Miss., Sept. 24, '64
Wm. H. Scott, co E, 50th Ala., Sept. 23, '64
Lieut. A. McGrath, co A, 154th Tenn., Sept. 23, '64
J.B. Stroman, co I, 11th Ga. Mil., Sept. 22, '64
J.H. Smith, co E, 6th Ga., Sept. 24, '64
E. Dooly, co E, 3d Miss., Sept. 21, '64
W.J. Bayliss, co H, 17th Ala., Sept. 21, '64
L.F. Newton, co E, 6th Texas, Sept. 21, '64
L. James, co A, 5th Ga. Res., Sept. 21, '64
W.H. Gideon, co G, 35th Miss., Sept. 22, '64
Wm. F. Harniss, co B, 55th Tenn., Sept. 20, '64
A.H. McBee, co G, 10th Ga. Mil., Sept. 21, '64
W.J. Andres, co D, 3d & 5th Miss., Sept. 20, '64
J.M. Harris, co B, 63d Ga., Sept. 20, '64
J.A. Jackson, co C, 39th Ga., Sept. 20, '64
Wm. Lusk, co B, 27th Tenn., Sept. 20, '64
M.B. Wilbon, Conscript., Sept. 20, '64
C.P. Alverson, co F, 4th La., Sept. 20, '64
J.M. Spinks, 5th Ga. Res., Sept. 20, '64
J.A. Kilpatrick, co H, 2d Ark., Sept. 18, '64
Joe Ball, co E, 24th Ala., Sept. 18, '64

(Confederate dead buried in Old City Cemetery, cont'd)
M. Young, co C, 11th Ga. Mil., Sept. 18, '64
James L. Gregory, co K, 2d Ga. Mil., Sept. 19, '64
Sergt. Miller A. Young, co B, 1st Miss. Cav., Sept. 18, '64
Jas. P. Carson, co I, 3d Miss., Sept. 18, '64
David W. Tanner, co F, 34th Ga., Sept. 18, '64
Robert Willson, Rees' Battery, Sept. 19, '64
M. Short, co K, 30th Ala., Sept. 19, '64
Sergt. Wm. Anglin, co C, 58th N.C., Sept. 18, '64
Holliday Harrell, co E, 8th Ga., Sept. 17, '64
R.R. Radway, co K, 28th Ala., Sept. 17, '64
W.O. Edwards, co I, 28th Ala., Sept. 17, '64
R. Harralson, 7th Ga. Mil., Sept. 17, '64
John J. Johnson, co E, 10th Ga. Mil., Sept. 16, '64
Peter A. Domingues, co H, 19th La., Sept. 17, '64
D. Jirogg, co I, 54th Va., Sept. 17, '64
Joseph Goodwin, co B, 34th Ala., Sept. 17, '64
Thos. Simmons, co E, 15th Texas, Sept. 17, '64
Wm. P. Cheek, co K, 52d Ga., Sept. 17, '64
W.A. Hays, co F, 1st & 3d Mt. Cav., Sept. 16, '64
J.J. Webb, co E, 24th Texas, Sept. 15, '64
A.D. Partin, co H, 36th Miss., Sept. 15, '64
A. Bright, co F, 58th N.C., Sept. 16, '64
Henry R. Tucker, co E, 5th Ky., Sept. 16, '64
J.T. Isom, co G, 41st Miss., Sept. 15, '64
M. Bronly, co H, 4th Ga., Sept. 15, '64
Jacob W. Hutchinson, co K, 12th Tenn., Sept. 16, '64
H.J. Simmons, co H, 18th Ala., Sept. 15, '64
Robt. A. Witherall, co G, 31st Miss., Sept. 15, '64
H.J. Butler, co A, 29th Miss., Sept. 14, '64
Victor Ryan, co A, 3d Miss., Sept. 14, '64
Martin Cooper, co B, 12th Ga. Mil., Sept. 14, '64
Wm. Honnell, co D, 24th Miss., Sept. 14, '61
Wm. Adams, co E, 11th Ga., Sept. 14, '64
J.F. Culpepper, co D, 11th Ga., Sept. 14, '64
Calvin Land, _____, Sept. 13, '64
G.A. Wilson, co D, 5th Miss., Sept. 13, '64
J.A. Robertson, co B, 2d Miss., Sept. 12, '64
R.C. Graves, co E, 37th Ga., Sept. 13, '64
James Powell, co G, 57th Ala., Sept. 12, '64
W. Lahay, co H, 15th & 37th Tenn., Sept. 12, '64
M. Hartfield, Stanford's Battery, Sept. 12, '64
Lieut. W. Johnson, co ___, 11th Ga. Mil., Sept. 12, '64
David Hudson, co D, 12th Ga. Mil., Sept. 12, '64
James D. Baxter, co I, 4th Fla., Sept. 13, '64
Jabez Robertson, Perry's Fla. Batt., Sept. 13, '64
O.F. Meekin, co B, 24th S.C., Sept. 13, '64
Lt. J.S. Wilson, co H, 24th Miss., Sept. 12, '64
W.E. Camp, co F, 29th Ala., Oct. 10, '64
A.J. Still, co K, 9th Texas, Oct. 11, '64
J.J. Crosby, co A, 6th Fla., Oct. 11, '64
John Watts, co B, 3d Tenn., Sept. 23, '64
John F. Vick, co C, 3d Ala. Cav., Jan. 16, '65
W.F. Mitchel, co H, 4th G M, Jan. 11, '65
R.A. Gibbs, co G, 7th Ga., Dec. 26, '64
J.J. Robinson, co I, 15th Ark., Oct. 29, '64
J.L. Dickey, co D, 15th Texas, Oct. 27, '64
J.T. McGrady, co E, 5th Ga. Res., Oct. 28, '64
Wm. Sexton, Garrison Guards, Oct. 29, '64
G.W. Street, co C, 66th Ga., Oct. 27, '64
Henry Arnold, co I, 5th Ga. Res., Oct. 27, '64
A.J. Campbell, co C, 3d Tenn., Oct. 27, '64
J.C. Huckaby, co H, 54th Ga., Oct. 27, '64
Amos Jones, co F, 18th Ala., Oct. 25, '64
S. Galager, co B, 5th Confed., Oct. 25, '64
J.B. Craig, co E, 15th Texas, Oct. 24, '64
J. Johnson, co F, 1st Ark., Oct. 25, '64
S. Odum, co G, 14th Tenn., Oct. 24, '64
Ed. Frank, Hoskin's Battery, Oct. 25, '63
David Tumblin, co G, 19th Ala., Oct. 23, '64

(Confederate dead buried in Old City Cemetery, cont'd)
Moore, Lee, co F, 7th G M, Oct. 24, '64
J.M. Hardage, co I, 2d Ga. S T, Oct. 22, '64
J.J. Armstrong, Garrison Guards, Oct. 23, '64
John Manning, co I, 7th Fla., Oct. 1, '64
G.M. Mathews, co A, 33d Tenn., Oct. 1, '64
Thos. Bechus, co G, 16th Tenn., Oct. 2, '64
Henry Walls, co A, 25th Ga., Oct. 1, '64
N. Brown, co G, 16th Tenn., Oct. 2, '64
Alfred Seal, co A, 58th N.C., Oct. 2, '64
Philip B. Snead, co H, 19th Ala., Oct. 2, '64
Joseph J. Seward, co H, 4th Ga. Cav., Oct. 2, '64
J.L. Thompson, co K, 2d Ga., S L, Oct. 4, '64
Capt. G.W. Stockburg, co B, 39th Ga., Oct. 2, '64
Thos. Winslett, co A, 36th Ala., Oct. 2, '64
Jackson S. King, co D, 12th Tenn., Oct. 3, '64
J.S. Saunders, co I, 3d Miss., Oct. 2, '64
Lt. Wm. J. Barefield, co D, 17th Texas, Oct. 3, '64
Arnold Norwell, co E, 57th Ala., Oct. 3, '64
Sol. R. Taylor, co A, 38th Ala., Oct. 3, '64
J.N. Ammond, co B, 6th & 7th Tenn., Oct. 3, '64
John C. Craig, co E, 44th Miss., Oct. 3, '64
Andrew Smith, Darden's Battery, Oct. 3, '64
Nathan Angel, co G, 9th Ky., Oct. 4, '64
R.A. Clinton, co G, Garrison Guards, Oct. 3, '64
James Gray, Baxter's Bat'y., Oct. 5, '64
D.C. Dubbs, co B, 20th Miss., Oct. 5, '64
Lt. Jno. D. Cooper, co G, 7th Miss., Oct. 4, '64
Jas. A. Willshiese, co C, 10th Texas, Oct. 5, '64
Lewis Roberts, Miller's Regiment
Jno. D. Mock, co A, 7th Miss., Sept. 29, '64
Wm. E. Slack, Conscript, Sept. 29, '64
Gibhard Gunby, co I, 1st Ga., Sept. 30, '64
Thos. A. Austin, co D, 55th Ala., Sept. 29, '64
D.J. Hancock, co E, 54th Ga., Oct. 1, '64
W.D. Nelson, co D, 3d Miss., Oct. 1, '64
W.R. Corn, co C, 2d Tenn., Dec. 3, '64
M. Russell, co H, 22d Ala., Feb. 2, '65
James Welch, co I, 24th S.C., Feb. 2, '65
Sgt. W.J. Martin, co C, 1st La., March 1, '65
Joel Eaton, co D, 10th Tenn., March 17, '65
Silas P. Smith, co G, 59th Ga., March 18, '65
T.M. Chandler, co I, 34th Ala., March 18, '65
Wm. Hays, co H, 29th Ala., March 25, '65
Jno. Flamugan, co K, 6th La., Apr. 9, '65
Patrick Barnes, co A, 4th Tenn., Apr. 15, '65
Chas. Fogarty, 4th Tenn., April 21, '65
J.T. Ellis, co F, 11th Tenn., April 21, '65
Henry Jones, co G, 5th Ga. Res., Feb. 5, '65
E. Thomas, co G, 37th Ga., Feb. 2, '65
Pat Donald, co I, 6th Texas, Feb. 2, '65
W. England, co K, 25th Tenn., Feb. 2, '65
J.H. Morris, co H, 43d Ga., Feb. 20, '65
Jno. Benson, co I, 2d Ala., April 8, '65
Wm. J. Briant, 5th Ga. Cav., Jan. 16, '65
Jos. K. Morgan, co D, 37th Tenn., Oct. 4, '64
A.D. Hubbard, Gibosn Mo. Bat'y., Oct. 4, '64
Lt. E. McClure, co I, 1st Ark., Oct. 5, '64
H.E.T. Dominy, co B, 4th Ga. Cav., Oct. 4, '64
A.S. Jared, co K, 28th Tenn., Oct. 6, '64
Wm. Brown, co K, 59th Ga., Oct. 8, '64
S. Hammonre, co H, 20th Ala., Oct. 7, '64
W.W. McMill, co E, 37th Miss., Oct. 7, '64
S.H. Thompson, co D, 54th Ga., Oct. 8, '64
J.L. Goodman, co E, 46th Ga., Oct. 8, '64
J.W. Duke, co I, 39th Ga., Oct. 18, '64
J.C. Smith, co H, 5th Ga. Cav., Oct. 18, '64
Jno. Harris, co F, 56th Ga., Oct. 17, '64
J.J. Massey, co H, 54th Ga., Oct. 17, '64
H. Floyd, co K, 11th Tenn., Oct. 17, '64

(Confederate dead buried in Old City Cemetery, cont'd)
W.M. Ellison, Baxter Batt'y, Oct. 16, '64
J.M. Coffee, co F, 50th Ala., Oct. 15, '64
Jno Smith, co G, 33d Ala., Oct. 17, '64
B.F. Betlay, co C, 3d Miss. Batt., Oct. 17, '64
J.A. Reaves, co G, 20th Miss., Oct. 14, '64
D.F. Dalton, co H, 9th Miss., Oct. 15, '64
R.J. McGinnis, co E, 34th Ga., Oct. 15, '64
J.W. Hudgins, co H, 34th Miss., Oct. 14, '64
S.M. Jones, co I, 24th Miss., Oct. 13, '64
J.J. McCraney, co G, 29th Ga., Oct. 18, '64
W. Welch Braxton, Bat'y, Oct. 12, '64
E. Kerr, co F, 12th G M, Sept. 11, '64
T.J. Abernathy, co A, 46th Ala., Oct. 12, '64
S. Weston, co A, 35th Miss., Oct. 13, '64
W.M. Driscoll, Macon Arsenal, Oct. 13, '64
J.H. Harris, co B, 66th Ga., Oct. 9, '64
G.W. Simmons, co F, 32d Tenn., Dec. 20, '64
R.M. Wade, co E, 1st Ga. R-s., Oct. 17, '64
A.L. Payn, co A, 2d Ga. S L, Oct. 16, '64
Jas. A. Brandon, co G, 4th Tenn. Cav., Oct. 14, '64
P.H. Carter, co F, 12th G M, Oct. 14, '64
W.R. Ryalds, co C, 7th Ga., Oct. 16, '64
Thomas Barnes, co H, 5th Ga. Res., Nov. 4, '64
Wm. Sexton, co C, 8th Miss., Nov. 5, '64
Wm. Burgamy, co K, 5th Ga. Res., Nov. 4, '64
Henry C. Smell, co B, 8th Ga. Batt., Nov. 3, '64
Chas. H. Taylor, Richard's Bat., Nov. 3, '64
Henry M. Carthy, co B, 6th Miss., Nov. 2, '64
Thomas Owen, co I, 10th Miss., Nov. 2, '64
Wm. Grimesly, co I, 5th Ga. Res., Nov. 2, '64
Lott Bradshaw, co E, 6th Ky., Oct. 31, '64
John Hewell, co I, 5th Ga. Res., Oct. 30, '64
Samuel C. Patton, co C, 13 Ga., Dec. 14, '64
Jas. S. Stewart, co C, 21st La., Dec. 11, '64
J.M. Allen, co C, 5th Ga. Res., Dec. 10, '64
R. Benjamin, Conscript, Dec. 6, '64
F.W. Garner, co I, 5th Ga. Res., Dec. 7, '64
John W. Jones, co H, 1st & 4th Mo., Dec. 5, '64
James R. Marks, co I, 5th Ga. Mil., Dec. 6, '64
Wm. Sanford, co G, 5th Ga. Res., Dec. 5, '64
Wm. Spradly, co I, 3d Ga. Mil., Dec. 3d, '64
E. Lublin, co C, Augusta Batt., Dec. 1, '64
Albert Domony, co K, 5th Ga. Res., Dec. 2, '64
A.J. Emerson, co K, 37th Ga., Dec. 1, '64
James Barber, ____, ____, Oct. 22d, '64
John Chaffin, co F, 28th Tenn., Oct. 21st, '64
Armand Dillery, Washington Artil'y, Oct. 22d, '64
James Hendricks, co E, 58th N.C., Oct. 22d, '64
John Connor, co B, 4th Ga. Res., Oct. 22d, '64
Marion Brazil, Oct. 19th, '64
Lewis Cornan, co A, 30th Ga., Oct. 19th, '64
J.W. Thompson, co K, 6th Ga. Res., Dec. 1, '64
W.C. Carswell, co A, 5th Ga. Mil., Nov. 24, '64
Steward Cash, co H, 30th Ga. Batt., Nov. 25, '65
James Grace, co G, 5th Ga. Res., Nov. 23, '64
Bascom Shelton, co I, 5th Ga., Nov. 22, '64
S.T. Roberts, co A, 4th Bat. Tenn. Cav., Nov. 20, '64
J.B. Hollingsworth, co B, Con. Res., Nov. 9, '64
J.A. Cooper, co D, 31st Miss., Nov. 13, '64
G.J. Graycore, co A, 53d Ala., Nov. 11, '64
J.S.W. Scarborough, co A, 5th Ga. Res., Nov. 11, '64
James J. Bathrop, co F, 7th Tenn., Nov. 10, '64
W.A. Weatherspoon, co A, 44th Miss., Nov. 9, '64
Joshua Grant, co C, 60th N.C., Nov. 9, '64
M. Murphy, Garrison Guards, Dec. 6, '64
Lt. Dan McCarthy, co D, 4th La., Nov. 5, '64

From Georgia Weekly Telegraph of 7 May, 1866

List of Confederate Dead Buried in the Cemeteries at Macon, Ga.

We have been furnished by the ladies with the following additional names of Confederate soldiers who died in the city of Maocn, or were buried there during the war. It is gathered from identified graves, and the books of the hospitals and undertakers.

1862

Hugh Middleton, co C, 27th Regiment, April 23
Corpl. Griffit, ___ Ala., April 23
Capt. Spencer, co C, Coffee Rangers, 50th Ga., April 30
Jno B. Evans, co H, 50th Ga., April 30
L.N. Harrell, Decatur if, 50th Ga., April 30
Alfred Smith, co H, 50th Ga., May 1
Geo. H. Fereter, 50th Ga. regt., May 5
W.Y. Holly, co C, 10th Ga. Batt., May 14
O. Walden, 50th Ga. regt., May 14
Isham Walker, 50th Ga. regt., May 28
Robt. Lovett, co K, 50th Ga. regt., May 29
Homer Yerby, co B, 10th Batt., June 6
Richard Thomas, co B, 50th Ga., June 7
John Fulwood, 50th Ga., April 24
A.C. Fulbright, Stiles' Batt., April 24
Wm. Carter, Wright's Legion, April 24
Thos. Mullins, co K, 4th La. Batt., June 13
Jo-n Handcock, Macon Lt. Art., June 25
Lieut. Ellison, June 30
P.W.S. Maskill, co C, 31st Ala., July 8
Henry Moore, Conscript, Brown's Reg., July 14
W.Y. Carter, co B, Conscript, Brown's reg., July 14
Jno. Neeves, Cobb's Plant Guards, July 22
J.P. Brantly, Sr., July 22
J.B. Murray, co B, 10th Ga. Batt., Sept. 15
English Long, co B, 10th Ga. Batt., Sept. 15
Wm. J. Byrd, co C, 59th regt., Sept. 15
Geo. McDonald, co H, 59th Ga. Vol., Oct. 24
H.L. Alexander, co E, 10th Ga. Batt., Oct. 28
Thos. Cunningham, co D, 10th Ga. Batt., Nov. 2
A.H. Calts, 9th Tenn., Nov. 11
John A. Pate, co B, 10th Ga. Batt., Nov. 13
Josiah S. Taylor, co A, 10th Ga. Batt., Nov. 15
P.R. Sarell, co C, 10th Ga. Batt., Nov. 19
O.F. Dumas, co K, 9th regt., Nov. 27
___ Whatley, co A, 10th Ga. Batt., Nov. 27
Jno. H. Summerford, co D, 10th Ga. Batt., Nov. 27
H. Strange, co H, 10th Ga. Batt., Dec. 2
H.W. Taylor, co H, 10th Ga. Batt., Dec. 10
E.J. Rape, co C, 10th Ga. Batt., Dec. 11
Alex McAlpir, co E, 10th Ga. Batt., Dec. 12
Henry Yertz, co B, 10th Ga. Batt., Dec. 18
E.R. Taylor, co B, 10th Ga. Batt., Dec. 20

1863

Jos Conn, co B, Camp Inst, Jan. 22
K.D. Watson, co D, 10th Ga. Batt., Jan 24
John Grey, February 20
Wm. Corland, co B, 25th Ga. Vol., Feb. 23
R.B. Stevens, co F, 29th regt., Feb. 29
Michael Conroy, co B, Phoenix Rifles, March 20
Jas. L. Bryant, Camp Inst., March 26
R.M. Bell, co B, 1st Ga. Regs., April 8
W.W. Darnell, May 24
J.C. Rodgers, co K, 47th Ga. Reg'l., June 5
J.J. Ramey, Aug. 22

(Confederate dead buried in Cemeteries at Macon, Ga., cont'd)
1863

F. Colquitt, Aug. 24
T.C. Jones, co G, 63d Ga., Aug. 10
J.J. Barney, Aug. 22
Pri Babb, Sept. 12
J. Walch, co K, 1st Ga. Regulars, Sept. 19
E.S. Beall, co M, 1st Ga. Regular, Sept. 26
J.F. Shadd, co D, 4th Fla., Oct. 1
John Langston, Oct. 5
John Hollomon, co E, Findlay's Batt., Nov. 23
Wm. Julort, co A, Provost Batt., Dec. 8
F.M. Wall, co E, 47th Ga. Vol., Dec. 8
J. Henderson, 37th Ala., Dec. 11
D. Fears, co E, 35th Ga. Vol., Dec. 11
Capt. M.T. Donn, 50th Ala., Vol., Dec. 13
D.B. Davis, co G, 13th Ga., Dec. 18
G.B. Roul, co H, 37th Ga., Dec. 28

1864

C.A. Stewart, Jan. 4
G.W. Horton, Conscript, January 11
John Crump, co C, Provost Batt., Feb. 26
G.W. Dickerson, co F, 7th Fla., Feb. 23
C. Butts, Ga. State Line, May 4
Joseph Fullinder, co A, 55th Ga., May 12
B. Ledlow, May 13
Charles Gilliam, 28th Ala., May 15
W.J. Reagan, Floyd's Company, May 18
J.W. McDonald, 1st Ga. Reg'l., May 21
L. Lingers, co K, 63d Ga., May 23
J. Caracter, co L, 46th Ga., May 23
Henry Gilbert, co K, 63d Ga., May 28
V. Carlisle, co A, 37th Ala., May 30
J.F. McCarey, co B, 20th Ala., May 31
B.F. Collin, co H, 6th Ga., June 3
W.E. Davis, Rowan's Batt., Ga. Mil., June 3
James W. Strippling, Massenburg's Batt., June 10
Sergt. E.E. Brown, co D, 30th Ga., June 10
A.C. Whitman, co H, 46th Ga., June 11
J.C. Wallen, co B, 29th Ga. Batt., June 11
Sergt. A.J. Gonnell, co C, 16th SC, June 11
Rob Glen, co C, 5th Regt. Res., June 11
Daniel P. Darden, co L, 29th Tenn., June 17
D.P. Hanly, co D, 17th Ala., June 23
J.S. Roy, co B, 36th Ga., June 23
L.B. Price, co E, 57th Ala., June 28
V.H.W. Kerler, co L, 54th Ga., June 28
Benj. McPhures, co D, 54th Va., June 28
Allen Kendrick, co C, 5th Ga. Res., June 28
Lt. C.C. Smith, co H, 9th Miss., July 1
Charles Moon, co F, 5th Ga., July 7
Nathan Renno, Ward's Batt. Ala. Vol., July 9
James Shelly, co K, 1st Con. Cav., July 9
N.M. Thompson, co D, 66th Ga., July 9
Thos. Henderson, co C, 35th Ala. regiment, July 12
Lt. G. Hardwick, co B, 2d Ga. Batt. Cav., July 13
J.C. Poplean, Beckham's Art., July 13
T.A. Webb, co G, 46th Ga., July 13
Wm. Carr, Balentine's Miss. regiment, July 15
Thos. Murphy, co D, 5th Ga. July 15
W.W. Buchanon, co G, 4th Ga., July 15
J.J. Terry, co A, 20th Ala., July 18
E. Attany, co B, 14th Texas, July 18
J. Merritt, co K, 5th Ga., July 18
P.H. Edwards, co B, 2d Ky. Cav., July 21
Wm. Auldy, co K, 46th Miss., July 21
Capt. H. Parks, 66th Ga., died on cars, July 21
Andrew Leml, co D, 31st Ark. Vol., July 21

(Confederate dead buried in Cemeteries at Macon, Ga., cont'd)
1864
David Tate, co A, Camp Instruction, July 22
A.J. Smith, co B, 3d Miss., July 24
Newton Laurimore, co A, 15th Miss., July 25
J.A. Nobles, co D, 5th Ga., July 25
James Vaden, co A, 31st Tenn., July 26
T. Cashon, 1st Ark. Rangers, July 27
John J. Cole, co H, 5th Ga., July 27
Jno. Meeks, 9th Ky., July 28
T.P. Wedgeworth, co G, 37th Miss., July 29
G.W. Cash, co K, 12th Ga. Vol., July 30
T.J. Richardson, co D, 26th Ala., July 30
H.M. Nareri, co A, 41st Miss., July 31
John Roberson, co F, 1st Con., July 31
G.P. Webb, co C, 20th Ala., July 31
B. Taylor, co D, So. Car. reg't., Aug. 1
Wm. J. Johnson, co C, 66th Ga., Aug. 1
James Wilson, co K, 5th Ga., St. Line, Aug. 1
W.D. Robinson, co C, 12th Miss., Aug. 1
W.P. Myers, co B, 46th Ga., Aug. 1
Henry Patton, co G, 54th Ga., Aug. 1
Jas. P. Barber, co K, 57th Ga., Aug. 2
J.E. Gilbert, co C, 41st Miss., Aug. 2
John Howard, co E, 29th Ala., Aug. 2
Sergt. W.H. Burk, co B, 4th Tenn., Aug. 3
Stafford, co F, 2d Ark., Aug. 3
Jas. J. Tucker, co E, 4th Ark., Aug. 3
Sergt. A.A. Childress, co C, 19th La. Vol., Aug. 3
A. Lawton, co A, 2d Ga. St. Line, Aug. 3
Oliver Hicks, co C, 5th Ga. Res., Aug. 5
J.M. Wilkerson, co A, 4th Ky, Aug. 5
C. Burrell, co E, 3d Miss., Aug. 9
G.W. Bryant, co H, 28th Ala., Aug. 10
John M. Sneer, co A, 6th Texas, Aug. 10
L.C. Newman, co I, 22d Ala., Aug. 10
T.J. Chambers, co P, Miss. Cav., Aug. 10
J.M. Tullis, co K, 33d Ala., Aug. 10
J. Gross, co B, 63d Ga., Aug. 11
Maj. A. Stewart, Aug. 11
J. Thornton, co G, 45th Miss., Aug. 11
M.L. Muce, co F, 15th Miss., Aug. 11
Jarrett J. Jones, co K, 3d Ga. Mil., Aug. 12
Jas. M. Corbill, co G, 4th La. Reg., Aug. 12
W.B. Taylor, co A, 9th Miss., Aug. 13
Henry Tangle, co H, 2d NC, Aug. 14
J.J. Reussam, co K, 6th Miss., Aug. 14
Wm. H. Pate, co D, 36th Miss., Aug. 14
J.A. Hollingsworth, co D, 6th Miss., Aug. 14
M.A. Nixon, co E, 63d Ga., Aug. 14
W.D. Hadley, co C, 10th Texas, Aug. 14
R.M. Bailey, co E, 31st Miss., Aug. 14
Jesse M. Thompson, co A, 50th Ala., Aug. 14
J.P. Stalworth, co F, 23d Ala., Aug. 14
James Blith, co K, 12th Miss., Aug. 14
W. Turnhill, co E, 43d Ga., Aug. 16
H. Johnson, Ga. Mil., Aug. 16
A.W. Lee, co E, 25th La., Aug. 16
T. Cockerell, co D, 46th Miss., Aug. 16
J. Shirley, co R, 40th Ala., Aug. 17
J.M. Slator, co C, 3d Miss., Aug. 17
M.A. Gardner, co A, 46th Ala., Aug. 17
T.M. Guarded, co F, 4th La. Reg., Aug. 17
W.A. Graham, co R, 8th Miss., Aug. 17th
G.B. Gressom, co H, 2d Miss. Cav., Aug. 17
W.J. Stoney, co C, 26th Ala., Aug. 17
W. Dabbs, co F, 33d Miss., Aug. 17
Lt. J.W. Murphy, co H, 37th Ala., Aug. 17
J. McKnight, co C, 55th Tenn., Aug. 17
D. Talkinberry, co A, 17th Ala., Aug. 17

(Confederate dead buried in Cemeteries at Macon, Ga., cont'd)
1864

John M. Bell, co B, 2d Ark., Aug. 20
J.W. Grimes, co C, 49th Tenn., Aug. 20
W. Cotton, co A, 4th Ala. Cav., Aug. 20
Robt. Martin, co A, 1st Confed. Ga., Aug. 20
James Collier, co F, 5th Ky., Aug. 20
S.B. Shedamn, co F, 38th Tenn., Aug. 20
Sergt. R.M. Patterson, co H, 46th Tenn., Aug. 20
W.B. Garnett, co G, 12th Ala., Aug. 21
T. Halpin, co F, 17th Ala., Aug. 21
J.T. Nichols, co H, 29th Ala., Aug. 21
Capt. A.J. Brock, co E, 34th Ga., Aug. 22
D. Lucas, co H, 1st Confed. Ga., Aug. 22
Lt. E.D. Vance, co B, 4th Ala. Reg., Aug. 23
T.T. Lawyer, co H, 1st Ga. Mil., Aug. 23
J. Robison, co K, 4th La. Reg., Aug. 23
Daniel Hartley, co C, 44th Miss., Aug. 23
Sergt. Jessie M. Walch, co F, 39th Miss., Aug. 24
James Spear, co G, 2d Ga., Aug. 24
Jas. M. Herrington, State Troops, Aug. 24
J.M. Tilter, co K, 1st Ga. Mil., Aug. 25
Sidney R. Cox, co D, 10th Texas, Aug. 25
Ralf Narvis, co L, 34th Tenn., Aug. 25
S.F. Kerr, co H, 25th Ark., Aug. 27
S.B. Harroll, co F, 1st Ala., Aug. 27
Benj. Bird, co G, 59th Ala., Aug. 27
E.K. Suttlemore, co A, 9th Miss., Aug. 29
W.T. Barron, co G, 46th Miss., Aug. 29
J.H. Wright, co L, 1st Ala., Aug. 29
W.L. Smith, co K, 8th Ark., Aug. 29
W.J. Tuller, co H, 1st Tenn., Aug. 29
John E. Jeffers, co F, 36th Ga., Aug. 29
L.G. Mitchell, co G, 10th Texas, Aug. 29
Lt. A.L. Reed, Pioneer's Corps, Aug. 29
W.B. McInvals, Havy's B'y., Aug. 19
J.B. Chancy, co I, 1st Ala., Aug. 31
L.T. Pendin, co A, Perrin's Miss. Cav., Aug. 31
W.J. Motherhead, co F, 16th Ala., Sept. 1
W.B. Smith, co C, 14th Miss., Sept. 4
James Bales, co E, 3d Ga. Mil., Sept. 5
T.A. Bryan, co B, 21st Ga. Sept. 5
P.E. Simmons, co I, 20th Miss., Sept. 6
Benj. F. Underwood, co E, 19th Ala., Sept. 6
Sergt. G. Harris, co I, 2d Ga. S L, Sept. 7
Aaron H. Hollingsworth, co K, 10th Texas, Aug. 7
H. Hammonds, co F, 45 Ala., Sept. 7
David Long, co B, 4th Ga. Mil., Sept. 8
J.R. Burdell, co K, 46th Ga. Vol., Sept. 8
James Byers, Sumer's By., Sept. 8
J.H. Thomas, co I, 3d Miss., Sept. 8
S'gt. M.A. McCauly, co K, 84th Miss., Sept. 9
Isaac Harden, co D, 2d Ga., Sept. 9
T.L. Staunton, co F, 1st Miss., Sept. 11
J.T. King, co C, 40th Ala., Sept. 11
J.L. Crump, co H, 2d Ga., Sept. 11
B. Bell, co B, 4th Tenn., Sept. 12
J. Stewart, co C, 37th Ga., Sept. 12
J. Joiner, co F, 8th Ga. Mil., Sept. 12
M. Cartfield, Stanford's B'y., Sept. 12
G.A. Wilson, co D, 5th Miss., Sept. 13
W. Adams, co E, 11th Ga., Sept. 13
J.P. Nalar, co C, 13th Ark., Sept. 14
J.W. Bowles, co D, 1st Tenn., Sept. 14
Lt. Nolins, Sept. 15
J.H. Mercer, co K, 46th Ga., Sept. 15
J.H. Gunly, co C, 12th Ga. Mil., Sept. 15
Jas. L. Gegon, co K, 2d Ga. Mil., Sept. 17
J.J. Kilpatrick, co H, 2d Ark., Sept. 17
P.A. Syker, co E, 11th Ga., Sept. 17

(Confederate dead buried in Cemeteries at Macon, Ga., cont'd)
1864
J.H. Conley, co D, 2d Ark., Sept. 19
W.J. Lark, co A, 28th Ga., Sept. 20
D. Landers, co I, 5th Ga. Res., Sept. 21
L. Courtney, co B, 6th Texas, Sept. 22
Capt. Thos. Northcut, Sept. 22
H.H. Scott, co C, 25th Tenn., Sept. 24
Author D. Larmer, co D, 4th La., Sept. 24
J.C. Hillsborough, 27th Miss., Sept. 24
W. Owins, Sanford's B'y., Sept. 24
J.A. Motherhead, co I, 45th Ala., Sept. 24
D.H. Halfield (or Hollifield), co E, Regt. English Corps, Sept. 26
W.S. Fumnier, co L, 1st Tenn., Sept. 26
S.M. Pardly, co B, 1st Cav., Sept. 26
J.W. Turner, co G, 5th Ga., Sept. 26
W.H. Hayden, co G, 5th Ky., Sept. 26
J.D. Mock, co A, 1st Regt. Vol., Sept. 26
Sergt. Geo. Setler, co G, 50th Tenn., Sept. 26
W.H. Daniels, co A, 55th Tenn., Sept. 29
J. Brown, co A, 9th Miss., Oct. 1
P. Frances, co H, 18th La., Oct. 1
G.F. Gibson, co D, 6th Ky., Oct. 1
T.C. White, co F, 22d Ala., Oct. 2
J.R. Morgan, co D, 37th Tenn., Oct. 2
Willshire, co C, 10th Texas, Oct. 5
R.H. Vinson, co H, 31st Ala., Oct. 10
G. Frazier, co F, 4th La., Oct. 10
M. Reese, co D, 9th Ky., Oct. 10
B.T. Comico, Selden's Bat'y., Oct. 10
Thos. Nesbet, Austin's La. Bat'y., Oct. 10
W.T. Cluar, co A, 33d Tenn., Oct. 12
W. Wallace, co D, 14th Texas, Oct. 12
W.F.B. Francher, co D, 41st Miss., Oct. 12
B. Tenell, co K. 10th Miss., Oct. 14
Wm. Beckley, co F, 5th Ga., Oct. 14
John Smith, co G. 33d Ala., Oct. 15
Serg't. H.W. Parish, co E, 16th La., Oct. 15
S.M. Green, co A, 58th NC., Oct. 15
T.A. Blatchford, co D, 29th Ala., Oct. 15
J. Golden, co C, 15th Tenn., Oct. 18
J. Lamemi, co H, 1st Con., Oct. 19
R. Leslie, co G, 1st La., Oct. 19
T.W. Brock, co K, 31st Ark., Oct. 19
S. Gallagher, co B, 5th Con., Oct. 19
W. Wyley, co G, 5th La., Oct. 26
W. Duncan, co K, 16th SC, Oct. 26
T.W. Florence, co C, 2d Ga., Oct. 27
J.T. Belany, co D, 9th Miss., Oct. 29
W.J. Armstrong, co F, 29th Ala., Oct. 31
T.C. Discol, co B, 31st Tenn., Oct. 31
J. Ammons, co H, 29th Ala., Oct. 31
J.J. Cooper, co G, 9th Ark., Oct. 31
C.T. Cox, co D, 29th Miss., Oct. 31
R.D. Cade, co I, 31st Miss., Oct. 31
J. Barnes, co H, 5th Ga. Res., Nov. 5
P. Ward, co G, 2d Miss., Nov. 5
J.L. Johnson, co K, 19th Ala., Nov. 7
J.H. Coleman, co H, 2d Ga., Nov. 7
T. McCarroll, co F, 13th Ark., Nov. 7
J.J. Dudley, co C, 31st Miss., Nov. 7
E.C. Dickly, co A, 5th Ga. Res., Nov. 10
J.W. Fleming, co K, 49th Ga., Nov. 10
L.L. Most, co B, 33d Ala., Nov. 17
Lt. Thomas, Gen. Smith's escort, Nov. 17
W.C. Carnell, co H, 9th Ga., Nov. 23
Wm. Rathmore, co C, 9th Ga., Nov. 23
L.T. Lewis, co A, 2d Ga. St. Line, Nov. 23
Thos. Lanier, co C, 10th Ga. Mil., Nov. 23
Lieut. McNair, Nov. 25

(Confederate dead buried in Cemeteries at Macon, Ga., cont'd)
1864

A. McCloud, Nov. 25
M.C. Carry, co K, 12th Ga. Mil., Nov. 25
M.C. McNear, co C, 3d Miss., Nov. 25
J.B. Lyles, co F, 9th Ga., Nov. 25
Renry Smith, co C, 9th Ga., Nov. 25
H.N. Vinsin, co G, 9th Ga., Nov. 25
A. Lanery, co C, 5th Ga., Nov. 25
David Richardson, co D, 23d Ga., Nov. 25
Dilbert Dunning, co K. 5th Ga. Res., Dec. 2
Capt. J.H. Wood, co L, 27th Miss., Dec. 2
R.B. McElroy, Pioneer, Dec. 2
A. Simmons, co D, 9th Ga. Mil., Dec. 2
_____ Carey, co K, 8th Ga. Mil., Dec. 2
E. Dowling, Augusta Battery, Dec. 2
V.J. McDuffie, co L, 7th Ga. Mil., Dec. 2
Wm. Hawkins, co H, 5th Ga. Mil., Dec. 4
W. Sawyer, co A, 5th Ga. Mil., Dec. 4
Wm. E. Fields, co G, 5th Ga. Mil., Dec. 4
Lt. Col. Frank George, 6th Ga. Res., Dec. 4
D.S. McNair, Waddell's Batt'y., Dec. 4
M.K. Wilcox, co C, 7th Ga., Dec. 4
D. Ruff, co H, Ga. Mil., Dec. 14
D.H. McCloud, co G, Ga. Mil., Dec. 14
Capt. M. Gray, Dec. 14
W.J. Boal, co H, 9th Ga. Mil., Dec. 14
D.C. Jones, co L, 5th Ga. Mil., Dec. 15
W.Y. Graves, co D, 1st Ga. regt., Dec. 15
H. Sherman, co C, 5th Ga. Res., Dec. 15
M. McIntosh, co C, 12th Ga. Mil., Dec. 15
R.F. Drawhan, co H, 5th Ga. Res., Dec. 23
C.F. White, co A, 8th Ga. Mil., Nov. 23
C.C. Yarbrough, co B, 10th La. Mil., Dec. 23
J.L. Fluman, co C, Athens, Dec. 23
W.J. Lenore, co F, 1st Confed., Dec. 23
C.A. Tupper, Pioneer Corps, Dec. 26
J.A. Powell, co L, 7th Ga. Mil., Dec. 26

1865

Lieut. J.L. Dyer, co E, 1st Ga. Cav., Jan 4
J.F. Vicks, co C, 3d Ala., Jan 9
W.F. Mitchell, 4th Ga. Mil., Jan. 9
L.O. Tate, co J, 8th Confed. Cav., Jan 18
T. Rich, co H, 12th Ga. Mil., Jan. 24
E. Thomas, co G, 37th Ga., Feb. 2
D. Thompson, co E, 57th Ga., Feb. 3
H. Jones, co G, 5th Ga., Feb. 3
P. Donold, co I, 6th Texas, Feb. 8
M. Ryar, discharged soldier, Feb. 14
A.S. Dowling, co K, 8th Ga. Cav., Feb. 14
W.J. Bryant, 4 Ga. Cav., Feb. 28
J. Welch, co I, 24th SC, Feb. 28
W.J. Martin, co C, 1st La. Art., Feb. 28
T.A. Peirson (Conscript), Feb. 28
J. Eaton, co D, 10th Tenn., March 16
T.M. Chandler, co I, 24th Ala., March 16
W. Hayes, co H, 29th Ala., March 25
S.R. Smith, co G, 59th Ga., March 25
S.H. Edwards, co C, 14th Ala., April 3d
John Finigan, co K, 6 La., April 3
John Benson, co I, 2d Ala., April 3

From the Macon Daily Telegraph (Macon, Georgia)
of May 8, 1866

Confederate Dead at Cuthbert, Georgia:

B.A. Graham, 1st Lieutenant, co B, 47th Ga. Infantry
Vincent Wilson
J.P. Edwards, 4th G.M.
L.V. Smith, co ___, 3d Engineers
M.W. Cochran, co I, 20th Mississippi
T.O. Turner, co F, 7th Florida
Geo. P. Crenshaw, Cheatham's Escort
James G. Brooks, co A, 47th Ga.
W.R. Coleman, co ___, 2d G.M.
L.C. Jennings, co ___, 2d Ga. Reserves
W.J. Andrews, co G, 50th Tennessee
G.W. Jenkins, co A, 65th Ga.
A.G. Morris, co H, 15th Tenn.
Abraham Gurganus, co A, 12th Tenn.
James Barrier, co H, 8th North Carolina
Hardy J. Bullion, co F, 1st Arkansas
W.H. Allen, co D, 45th Tenn.
A.J. Moss
Y.B. Childers, co C, 1st Alabama
Robert Paul, co G, 48th Georgia

From the Macon Daily Telegraph 20 May, 1866

Georgians buried at Charlottesville, Virginia. List sent
by Mr. J.W. Schofield, a resident of this city, but who is
now a student at the University of Virginia.

Anderson, Sergt. J.L., co B, 21st, April 19, 1862
Alderman, Daniel, co C, 26th, June 11, 1863
Allen, D., 61st, June 25, 1862
Allem, H.D., co A, 24th, Nov. 10, 1862
Abernathey, J.J., co H, 38th, Nov. 12, 1862
Adams, N.A.G., co E, 61st, Dec. 29, 1862
Abbott, J.A., co I, 31st, Jan. 3, 1863
Anderson, Corpl. W.T., co C, Cuft's Art'y., Dec. 10, 1863
Anderson, J.M., co D, 59th, May 3, 1864
Argo, A.J., co O, Phillips' Legion, Oct. 27, 1864
Baggett, H.H., Confed. Guards, 7th Ga., Aug. 3, '61
Bryant, J.R., co K, 9th, Sept. 11, 1861
Braxton, W.J., co D, 9th, Oct. 26, 1861
Bookout, T.J., co D, 7th, Nov. 17, 1861
Bivins, W.R., co B, 17th, Nov. 17, 1861
Burns, J.W., co K, 1st, Jan. 6, 1862
Bently, H.L., co H, 27th, March 13, 1862
Bagley, J.M., co K, 27th, Apr. 27, 1862
Banks, G.H., co I, 21st, Apr. 27, 1862
Beckum, G.W., co H, 21st regt., May 11, 1862
Bridges, W.H., co K, 21st regt., May 30, 1862
Brown, John, co D, 21st regt., June 13, 1862
Bridges, J., co B, 61st regt., June 29, 1862
Benard, John J., co E, 7th, July 1, 1862
Boum, B., co A, 31st regt., July 4, 1864
Bennett, R., co N, 38th regt., July 6, 1864
Brown, J.A., co I, 26th regt., July 8, 1862
Barns, Sergt. Jas. H., co ___, 18th regt., July 15, '62
Brown, J.Y., co I, 24th regt., Nov. 22, 1862
Brook, J.D., co C, 9th regt., Dec. 27, 1862
Brown, M.V., Phillips' Legion, Jan. 7, 1862
Baker, W.M., co A, 38th regt., Feb. 14, 1863
Bannkston, A.J., co A, 44th regt., Feb. 20, 1863
Brown, C., co E, 49th regt., May 29, 1863
Baggs, W.A., co E, 20th Cav., June 28, 1863

(Georgians buried at Charlottesville, Va., cont'd)
Brown, A.J., co D, Phillips' Legion, July 3, 1863
Crosby, Lt. W., co E, 17th regt., Nov. 21, 1862
Copeland, T., co ___, 17th regt., Apr. 13, 1862
Crymes, T.T., co K, 17th regt., Apr. 18, 1862
Cleveland, W., co C, 11th regt., May 13, 1862
Conner, T.B., co E, 61st regt., June 24, 1862
Connor, F., co F, 31st regt., April 26, 1862
Collier, J. co K, 38th regt., April 29, '62
Cadwell, A.T., co F, 31st regt., July 4, '62
Carroll, Turner, co E, 31st regt., July 8, '62
Cross, W., co f, 61st regt., July 8, '62
Clark, W.F., co ___, 61st regt., July 18, '62
Cassels, R.K., co D, 35th regt., Aug. 28, '62
Curry, B.M., co F, 7th regt., Nov. 11, '62
Cothran, H.T., co B, 52d regt., Nov. 15, '62
Comer, W.W., co F, 61st regt., Dec. 16, '62
Crisson, E.A., co I, 48th regt., Jan. 12, 1863
Clemens, U.J., co D, 16th regt., March 16, '63
Conner, J.C., co K, 61st regt., Dec. 12, '63
Cobb, A., co I, 59th regt., April 27, 1864
Clarke, J.G., Corp., co I, 61st regt., May 21, '64
Cutts, H.H., co H, 13th regt., Aug. 10, '64
Chaffin, G.W., co F, 4th regt., Jan. 27, 1865
Dun, J.H., co H, 8th regt., Jan. 24, 1861
Daniel, J.N., co I, 7th regt., Jan. 28, '61
Daniel, W.R., co I, 7th regt., Aug. 16, '61
Duke, T.F., Sergt., co E, 7th regt., Aug. 9, '61
Daniel, Moses, co D, 8th regt., Aug. 31, '61
Duggon, R., co A, 21st regt., April 27, 1862
Denson, E.Y., co E, 27th regt., May 6, '62
Duggon, J.A., co C, 7th regt., J-ne 22, '62
Daily, John, co ___, 26th regt., June 29, '62
D___, John A., co ___, 38th regt., July 1, '62
Doest, Newton, co I, 61st, July 9, '62
Dean, J.C.H., co ___, 26th regt., July 15, '62
Dailey, S.R., Sergt., co C, 35th regt., Aug. 24, '62
Davenport, W.A., co D, 2nd regt., Nov. 16, '62
Denby, E., co B, 10th regt., March 1, 1863
Erwin, E.T., co D, 7th regt., Aug. 6, 1861
Edwards, J.C., co D, 8th regt., July 4, 1862
Ester, J.T., co D, 38th regt., July 6, '62
Eaton, S.F., co B, 21st, July 15, '62
Eslinger, J., co G, 11th regt., Nov. 17, '62
Ernis, G.M., co A, Phillips' Legion, Feb. 25, '63
Elliot, G.I., Sergt., co G, 19th regt., April 7, '63
Funderbank, J.F., co E, 8th regt., April 28, 1861
Fowler, G.C., co D, 28th regt., April 18, '62
Fowler, J.J., co B, 28th regt., May 1, '62
Flourney, W.H., co A, 27th regt., May 16, 1862
Flemming, D.F., co F, 38th regt., Aug. 26, 1862
Freeman, G.H., co G, 16th regt., Nov. 14, 1862
Frazier, R.B., co I, 59th regt., April 25, 1864
Griffin, W., co F, 9th regt., Jan. 27th, 1862
Gatewood, P., Sergt., co G, 21st regt., June 4, 1862
Gregory, Eph., co C, 38th regt., Aug. 5, 1862
Gay, M., co F, 61st regt., Dec. 11, 1863
Hagans, J.T., co A, 7th regt., Aug. 30, 1861
Holt, J.G., co A, 28th regt., April 8, 1862
Herndon, G., co K, 21st regt., April 24, 1862
Huckaby, W.J., co H, 8th regt., April 30, 1862
Hardeman, J.J., co A, 31st regt., July 6, 1862
Hambrick, Jas., co I, 61st regt., July 9, 1862
Harris, G.W., co C, 18th regt., July 15, 1862
Hambrick, J.E., co D, 38th regt., Nov. 11, 1862
Hall, J.G., co G, 59th regt., Nov. 26, 1862
Hysmith, S., co C, 26th regt., April 3, 1863
Aubert, M.D., co B, 48th regt., Dec. 5, 1863
Johnson, J., co H, 28th regt., Jan. 8, 1862
Jones, J.A. Corporal, co E, 28th regt., April 16, 1862

(Georgians buried at Charlottesville, Va., cont'd)
Johnson, H.M., co C, 26th regt., June 19, 1862
Jones, Paul, co F, 31st regt., June 20, 1862
Jones, J.B., co F, 61st regt., July 17, 1862
Jones, Jno. H., co A, 59th regt., March 21, 1863
Jackson, R.W., co I, 44th regt., Dec. 12, 1863
Kimbrough, C.M., co I, 45th regt., May 16, 1864
Kerlen, W.J., co I, 13th regt., Oct. 2, 1864
Lawrence, R., co B, 28th regt., Dec. 30, 1861
Lindsay, G.B., Sergt., co A, 11th regt., April 28, 1862
Laggett, Jordan, co D, 26th regt., June 27, 1862
Lister, J., co P, 31st regt., June 29, 1862
Lewis, Joseph, co B, 51st regt., Nov. 30, 1862
Lindsey, Moses, co F, 61st regt., Feb. 17, 1863
Lancaster, H.H., co G, 8th regt., March 9, 1863
Lynn, Phillips' Legion, co B, Aug. 24, 1863
Lang, W., co H, 61st regt., May 15, 1864
Lindley, J.T., co C, 49th regt., May 24, 1864
Lugg, Arnon, co F, 26th regt., May 28, 1864
McSwayne, Dav., co G, 7th regt., Aug. 1, 1861
Mullins, Thos., co I, 7th regt., Aug. 2, 1862
Megarity, L.W., co I, 7th regt., Aug. 9, 1861
Mason, D.H., co G, 8th regt., Aug. 23, 1861
McDaniel, Jas., co G, 8th regt., Sept. 16, 1861
McWilliams, S.G.I., co C, 23rd regt., June 18, 1862
Mozeley, W.D., 15th regt., June 16, 1862
Mack, J.M., Lieut., co B, 21st regt., June 21, 1862
Ninor, Riley, co D, 61st regt., July 4, 1862
McRae, T.W., co F, 61st regt., July 9, 1862
Moore, P.E., co E, 61st regt., July 12, 1862
Minshew, J., co A, 26th regt., Sept. 5, 1862
Medlin, T.W., co F, 19th regt., Oct. 4, 1862
McAlhannon, co I, 2d regt., Nov. 29, 1862
McBee, Lieut., co B, 21st regt., Jan. 21, 1863
McGintry, R.C., co C, 59th regt., July 22, 1863
Mays, G.W., co D, 46th regt., May 15, 1864
Morris, W., co B, 16th regt., May 16, 1864
McDonald, J.T., co B, 11th regt., May 22, 1864
Moore, H.C., co A, 26th regt., May 23, 1864
Mathews, A.J., co K, 45th regt., Aug. 6, 1864
Mash, J.T., co E, 7th regt., May 7, 1862
Nesmith, C.M., co C, 61st regt., June 23, 1862
Nolan, T., co F, Phillips' Legion, Nov. 15, 1862
Norris, Thomas, co B, 48th regt., Dec. 1st, 1864
Newnan, E.L., co D, Cobb's Legion, July 31, 1864
Night, J.D., 44th regt., co I, Oct. 27, 1864
Olden, W., co K, 61st regt., July 8, 1862
Osteen, W.D., co E, 26th regt., July 8, 1862
Owen, W.J., co I, 21st regt., July 23, 1862
Oliver, W., co E, 12th regt., Nov. 23, 1862
Pry, Hugh, co I, 17th regt., May 6, 1862
Porter, Dr. A., co F, 21st regt., June 10, 1862
Pulline, Jas., co H, 38th regt., June 30, 1862
Pye, Freeman, Sergt., co F, 61st regt., July 6, 1862
Phillips, J.T., co D, 2d regt., Nov. 10, 1862
Pitts, J.W., Corporal, co F, 19th regt., Dec. 17, 1862
Pennington, L.J., co K, 31st regt., Aug. 10, 1862
Rosser, F.A., co B, 9th regt., Sept. 29, 1861
Roberts, R., co B, 27th regt., April 11, 1862
Robind, W.M., co D, 2d regt., May 7, 1862
Reeves, N., co H, 8th regt., May 6, 1862
Roland, Jas., co D, 26th regt., June 22d, 1862
River, G.W., co R, 39th regt., Aug. 1, 1862
Rawls, J., co K, 44th regt., Oct. 12, 1862
Reeves, W.L., co C, 10th regt., Nov. 20, '62
Russell, J.F., co D, Phillips' Legion, Jan. 25, '63
Rolind, W., co F, 31st regt., Oct. 20, '63
Rich, J.T., co A, 59th regt., May 1, '64
Redding, J.M., co D, 45th regt., May 16, '64
Simpson, Edward, Ass't Surg., 15th regt., Oct. 23, '61

(Georgians buried at Charlottesville, Va., cont'd)
Simpson, J.W., co B, 27th regt., Nov. 28, '61
Sayers, W.P., co G, 8th regt., April 21, '62
Skipper, Eli, co L, 21st regt., May 1, '62
Stricklin, S., co I, 26th regt., June 16, '62
Strickler, W., co F, 61st regt., July 9, '62
Seigler, L.M., co G, 45th regt., Aug. 17, '62
Shepherd, W.R., co E, 45th regt., Aug. 20, '62
Senter, J.R., co D, 45th regt., Aug. 24, '62
Sawyer, G.B., co C, 51st regt., Sept. 5, '62
Solomon, H.L., Lieut., co G, 48th regt., Oct. 16, '62
Simpson, Aiden, co A, 48th regt., Nov. 14, '62
Saunders, R., co M, Phillips' Legion, Nov. 26, '62
Sapp, Riley, co I, 26th regt., Dec. 7, '62
Simmonds, W., Corpl., co C, 45th regt., Feb.16, '63
Sturat, W.W., co D, 45th regt., Dec. 19, '63
Sullivan, W.J., co B, 45th regt., May 15, '64
Spradley, L.J., co B, 45th regt., May 15, '64
Stovall, J.B., Sergt., co F, 15th regt., May 28, '64
Simms, L., co E, 20th Cav. regt., July 20, '64
Shores, J.W., co B, 31st regt., Nov. 24, '64
Thompson, R.L., co E, 19th regt., Nov. 5, '61
Thompkins, W.P., co B, 28th regt., May 6, '62
Toole, Jas. A., co G, 13th regt., July 2, '62
Thackson, J.M., co A, 38th regt., July 28, '62
Thompson, J.E., co G, 19th regt., Sept. 16, '62
Turner, E.J., co G, 24th regt., Nov. 17, '62
Turner, J.B., co G, 24th regt., Nov. 20, '62
Thrift, J., co B, 50th regt., Nov. 20, '62
Thornton, T.T., co E, 31st regt., Sept. 29, '64
Vaughn, W.W., co A, 31st regt., June 14, '62
Vincent, M., co A, 19th regt., March 29, '63
Ware, J.B., co B, 7th regt., Sept. 11, '61
Wilkerson, R.B., co G, 20th regt., May 5, '62
Whiddon, Edwd, co I, 38th regt., June 18, '62
Whitehead, Jas. A., co C, 24th regt., Jan. 14, '63
Whitehead, W.L., co C, 44th regt., Dec. 11, '62
Warren, M.D.L., co G, 13th regt., April 1, '63
Webb, T.M., co D, 11th regt., April 28, '64
Wynn, J.H., co K, 35th regt., May 11, '64
Walker, J.A., co K, 45th regt., May 26, '64
Wallace, F.B., co I, 9th regt., Nov. 29, '64
Yates, J.D., co A, 27th regt., April 29, '62
Young, G.L., co E, 26th regt., July 19, '62
Young, Thomas, co F, 49th regt., Dec. 7, '63

From the Macon Daily Telegraph of 31 May 1866

The Louisville Courier, of the 22d inst. contains a list of the Confederate dead buried in Cave Hill Cemetery, near that city.

We publish herewith, the names of the Georgians and Floridians which appear in the list.

1862

Nov. 9   Thos. Jackson, F, 6th Georgia
Nov. 14 J.A. Black, Forsyth co, Florida
Dec. 7   F. Backly, _____, Georgia
Dec. 10 Wm. Kendrick, _____, Georgia
Dec. 13 R.T. Pullion, G., 4th Georgia
Dec. 17 J.T. Atkinson, _____, Florida
March 15 Lt. Alec Moss, _____, Georgia

1863

Dec. 15 F.C. Gidding, K, 29th Ga.
Feb. 23 Wm. Hastings, 3d Fla.

(From the Louisville Courier, of the 22d, Georgians & Floridians)

1864

July 23	Geo. Turner, H., 63d Georgia
June 23	John H. Odom, F., 4th Georgia
June 1	Wm. McCantery, H., 14th Georgia
March 31	R. O'Neal, C, 9th Georgia
March 26	A. Everett, A., 51st Georgia
Feb. 19	T.F. Todd, H., 16th Georgia
Feb. 7	A.P. Dunn, C., 59th Georgia
Jan. 20	John Lindsay, G., 18th Georgia
Jan. 14	G.H. Veale, B., 8th Georgia
Jan. 12	William H. Wilburn, K, 16th Ga.
Jan. 11	H.J. Parish, C, 47th Georgia
Jan. 3	J.W. Powel, C., 16th Georgia
Aug. 1	Geo. W. Mooney, 13th Ga. Cav.
Aug. 2	Lewis Potts, C, 61st Georgia
Oct. 1	Elizabeth Tennans, Calhoun, Ga.
Nov. 13	C.L. Ayers, 1st Ga. State troops
Jan. 28	James D. Lenar, B., 36th Georgia
Jan. 30	Reuben Garden, C., 25th Georgia
Jan. 10	James Johnson, A, 1st Georgia
Jan. 9	Wright Pesmeter, H., 22nd Ga.

From the Macon Daily Telegraph of 31 May 1866

Confederate Dead at Danville, Ky.

In the Danville Advocate we find the following list of Confederates who were buried in the cemetery at that place, between Sept. 28th and Nov. 30th, 1862:

W.S. Paten, B., 24th Georgia
Geo. Thompson, H., 42d Georgia
F.I.C. Flitz, Maison Battery, Florida
M. Compton, B, Smith's Legion, Georgia
C.W.M. Grow, B., 56th Georgia
Warner Jackson, K., 54th Georgia
Thos. Hormon, F., 42d Georgia
L.M. Hicks, Smith's Legion, Georgia
Jas. Mitchell, B., 19th Georgia
W.M. Packer, Gibbon's Battery, Florida
J.B. Hindman, I., 42d Georgia
Andrew I. Beggs, C., 3d Florida
Joseph Wray, C., Smith's Legion, Georgia
Wm. Dunn, G., 10th Florida
Thomas Mormon, F., 41st Georgia

From Macon Daily Telegraph 4 August 1866

Names of those who are buried at the Confederate Grave Yord near Milner, Pike County, Georgia

Capt. D.B. Lattimore, co G, 54th Miss.
Capt. C.C. Wood, co B, 4th Tenn. cavalry
Lt. J.E. Harril, co A, 6th Texas
Lt. W. Fulghum, co F, 3d Ga.
Dr. J.W. Morrison, Lt. co B, 6th Ark.
Lt. F. McCulloch, co A, 154th Tenn.
Lt. G.G. Ussery, co D, 24th Miss.
Lt. W.H.H. Barker, co D, 15th Texas
Lt. J.M. Fulghum, co G, 9th Miss.
Lt. D.S. Coleman, co D, 33d Miss.
Sergt. Maj. J.R. Delf, 66th Ga.
Sergt. D. Johnson, co C, 10th SC
Sergt. J.H. Ramsey, co H, 5th Tenn.
Sergt. R.S. West, co F, 16th Tenn.
Sergt. T.F. Smith, co F, 4th Fla.
Sergt. M.P. Berry, co A, 55th Tenn.
Sergt. S.C. Hester, co K, 18th Ala.
Corporal M. McAdee, co H, 46th Tenn.
Corporal J.H. Duke, co D, 27th Miss.

PRIVATES

J.R. Skinner, 35th Miss.
J.J. Johns, co F, 4th Fla.
P.P. Seaton, co B, 28th Miss
W.M. Wright, co K, 12th Tenn.
E. McClure, co A, 1st Ala.
W.H. Richards, co A, 154th Tenn.
G.E. Williams, co B, 30th Tenn.
John See, co C, 10th Texas
James Guthrie, co H, 19th La.
W.H. Vanmeter, co H, 6th Ky.
A. Appling, co F, 57th Ala.
G.W. Mills, Sheldon's Battery
A. Cobb, co I, 3d Florida
E. Grigsby, co K, 10th Texas
J.S. Williams, co K, 24th SC
F.G. Manse, co C, 11th Texas
J.C. Parmalee, co K, 57th Ga.
D. Montgomery, co H, 11th Tenn.
R.C. Patton, co C, 10th Texas
D.L. Wade, Stanford's Battery
W.O. Ward, co K, 32d Texas
J. Vanderskee, co B, 51st Ala. Cav.
H.C. Hawkins, co B, 11th Tenn.
A.H. Duncan, co B, 29th Ala.
G.W. Burton, co K, 9th Ark.
F.W. Oppelt, co A, 35th Miss
N.F. Cavr, co G, 17th Ga.
B.R. Benson, co B, 25th Ala.
J.D. Bryant, co B, 46th Ga.
J.A. George, co K, 17th Ala.
T.J. Withers, co K, 17th Ala.
G.M. Tucker, co A, 25th Ala.
W. Thomas, co F, 1st G M
W.D. Nimo, co D, 12th Tenn.
W.C. Aycock, co A, 20th Tenn.

W. Jolly, co G, 20th Ala.
J.P. Hall, co H, 1st G M
W.W. Weed, co E, 53d Ala. Cav.
B.F. Rountree, co B, 55th Ala.
T.M. Hoy, co H, 27th Miss.
E. Freeman, co D, 24th SC
H.B. Hammond, co G, 15th Texas
A.J. Chandler, co D, 40th Ga.
M. Hawkins, co H, 50th Ala.
J. Shaw, co E, 29th Ala.
T. Nichols, co K, 10th Texas
E.M. Harris, co E, 1st Ga. Batt
J.A.A.S. Carden, co E, 30th Ala
A. Rosenthum, co B, 54th Ala.
G.W. Waters, co B, 9th Tenn.
A. Troy, co B, 4th Ala.

From the Macon Daily Telegraph 8 August 1866

List of Confederate Dead on the Battlefield of Resaca, Ga.

GEORGIA

H.G. Collins, co A, 4th Ga. Bat.
One unknown, 8th Ga. Bat.
Wm. A. Ch____ing, co G, 19th Ga. Reg.
J. Hix, co E, 34th Ga. reg.
Capt. Morgan, 36th Ga. reg.
Rufus Bray, 40th Ga. Reg.
_____ Steadman, 40th Ga. reg.
_____ Estis, 40th Ga. reg.
B.B. Ayres, 42d Ga. reg.
J.B., 42d Ga. reg.
J. Jones, 42d Ga. reg.
A.C. Haines, 43d Ga. reg.
J.D. Youngblood, 43d Ga. reg.
J.H. Martin, 43d Ga. reg.
J. Mathews, co B, 47th Ga. reg.
J. Williamson, co I, 52d Ga. reg.
Arnold Gates, 52d Ga. reg.
One unknown, 56th Ga. reg.

ALABAMA

Col. F.R. Beck, Alabama
J.R. Morvan, 16th Ala. reg.
W.T. Smith, 18th Ala. reg.
G.H. Henderson, 18th Ala. reg.
R.D. Harp, 18th Ala. reg.
R.D. Harp, co F, 19th Ala. reg.
Wm. M. Palmer, co C, 31st Ala. reg.
D.F. Stolter, 2nd Lt., co C, 32d Ala. reg.
S. Lone, co H, 32d Ala. reg.
J. Dixon, co F, 32d Ala. reg.
W.P.H. Gordon, 2d Lt., co B, 36th Ala. reg.
John Shelton, co B, 36th Ala. reg.
M. Shelterfield, 36th Ala. reg.
James M. Elliot, co D, 41st Ala. reg.
D.G. Barneard, co B, 42d Ala. reg.
David Parkman (or Bookman), co D, 54th Ala. reg.
S.A. Butterworth, co H, 58th Ala. reg.
J.W. Williams, co H, 63d Ala. reg.
D____bery, co F, ____Ala. reg.

SUPPOSED TO BE ALABAMIANS

Corp. R.E. Mayfield, co G, 4th reg.
T M, and J F M

MISSISSIPPI

A.J. Jaquors, 4th Miss. reg.
Lt. L.M. Clark, co G, 8th Miss. reg.
Lt. Watts, 10th Miss. reg.
J.L Williams, co E, 10th Miss reg.
_____ Reed, 10th Miss. reg.
John Andrews, co B, 14th Miss. reg.
Jake Branan, co D, 14th Miss. reg.
Wm. S. Parkham, 15th Miss reg.
Lt. J.S. Reed, 24th Miss reg.
H.L. Mayoe, 29th Miss. reg.
J.J. Russel, 30th Miss reg.
W.J. Keenim, co H, 35th Miss reg.
W.W. McGill, co B, 37th Miss reg.

Mississippi cont'd

R. Baynes, co B, 37th Miss reg.
Isaac Land, co B, 37th Miss. reg.
Serg't S.G. Gilmore, 39th Miss. reg.
Two unknown

TENNESSEE

John McAfee, co F, 1st Reg't
Lt. Dunham, 3rd Reg't
W.J. Jackson, 3rd Reg't Cav.
J. Gambele, 3rd Reg't
J. Cambell, 3rd Reg't
Capt. D.O. Puryear, 8th Reg't.
Capt. John S. Brown, co F, 8th Regt
Lt. D.E. Tally, 8th Regt
Lt. J.O. Call, 8th Regt
John Ingles, co D, 8th Regt
Jacob Lipshut, co G, 8th Regt
J.W. Ruthers, co C, 8th Regt
W.D. Bryant, co G, 9th Regt Cav.
O.D.T. Roberts, co E, 9th Regt Cav.
A. Theston, co E, 15th (or 18th) Regt
T.S. Mordy, 19th Regt
J.H. Savage, 10th Regt.
J.S. Parmento, 27th Regt
J.M. Smith, 27th Regt
T. Jourdon, co D, 29th Regt
S____, 32d Regt.
J.H. Wardy, 32d Regt.
G. Sackton, co G, 32d Regt
Lt. R.H. Calhoun, co F, 33d Regt
J.R.P. Benton, co D, 41st Regt.
N.B. Brown, 47th Regt, Vaughn's Brig.
Amos Nation, 154th Regt
Thomas McHenry, Forest's Cav., died of disease in 1863

KENTUCKY

____ Howard
1st Lieutenant, unknown

LOUISIANA

Corp S.T. Russell, 5th co, Washington Art'y, N O
J.H. Simmons, Steven's Batt'y, N O
J. Daugherty, co A, 4th La. Batt'y.

FLORIDA

Sergt. Wm. Wright, co G, 3d regt.

TEXAS

Wm. Boyd, co A, 18th regt.

STATE UNKNOWN

B. Parker, CSA
F. D____
Alfred Grangir
Bethune
W. Graham

In addition to the above 175 unmarked graves have been discovered.

From the Georgia Journal and Messenger (Macon, Ga.)
of April 17, 1867

List of Georgians Buried in the Cemetery at Spotsylvania
Court House up to the 20th of March 1867

W.I. Fitzgerald, co H, 46th Ga.
J.C. Upshaw, co B, 13th Ga.
J.M. Mercer, bo C, 45th Ga.
G.M. Bandy, co D, 60th Ga.
Lieut. L.H. Page, co H, 31st Ga.
H.P. Baskin, co A, 4th Ga.
H.N. Battle, co I, 13th Ga.
J.W. Bedingfill, co H, 14th Ga.
J.P.A., co G, 38th Ga., killed May 10th
Lieut. Col. S.W. Jones, 13th Ga.
T.J. Warren, co H, 14th Ga.
L.L. Smith, co G, 13th Ga.
H.B. Light, co E, 14th Ga.
J.W. Williams, co C, 4th Ga.
W.W. Loper, co E, 26th Ga.
James H. Giddens, co E, 26th Ga.
Lieut. H.M. Broadwell, co A, 26th Ga.
J.W. Jones
J.R. Hooks, co I, 3d Ga.
J.S. Lewis, co D, 7th Ga.
Capt. H.B. Stanley, co G, 49th Ga.
J.S. Parker, co A, 4th Ga.
E. Meeks, co G, 38th Ga.
J.D. Herring, co D, 26th Ga.
Sergt. J.S. Smith, co B, 49th Ga.
C.W. Grines, co G, 12th Ga.
Robt. L. Dishman, co A, 15th Ga.
J.C. Booker, co A, 11th Ga.
Sergt. T.M. Huington, co E, 59th Ga.
W. Dukes, co H, 59th Ga.
B.L. Johnson, co H, 59th Ga.
D.M. Blue, co G, 8th Ga.
Sergt. J.P. Russel, co I, 20th Ga.
W.S. Johnson, co G, 59th Ga.
W.T. Smith, co H, 59th Ga.
C.T. Mason, co G, 10th Ga.
O.P. Scott, co R, 9th Ga.
Wm. Register, co H, 14th Ga.
M.C. Anthony, co C, 59th Ga.
A.J. Amerson, co C, 59th Ga.
W.M. Williams, co R, 26th Ga.
Lieut. J.A. Patterson, 13th Ga.
W.A.S. Davis, co C, 4th Ga.
T.D. Anderson, co C, 26th Ga.
J. Dampler, 56th Ga.
A.M. Roberds, co F, 61st Ga.
Sergt. E.W. Wincey, co C, 61st Ga.
S.T. Farmer, 38th Ga.
Sergt. J.T. Calley, co B, 13th Ga.
C.H. Billette, co I, 31st Ga.
R.C. Fair, co H, 13th Ga.
J.L. Ogletree, 13th Ga.
Corp. D.N. McLane, co I, 26th Ga.
James White, co E, 26th Ga.
J. Shaw, co A, 44th Ga.
Sergt. R. Vickery, co C, 26th Ga.
Corp. W.C. Driver, co A, 15th Ga.
L.B. Pulliam, co D, 15th Ga.
Sergt. C.G. Wright, co B, 60th Ga.
A.H. Cloud, co I, 4th Ga.
Capt. R.A. Holt, co K, 14th Ga.
J.M. Garrett, co D, 35th Ga.
D. Wood, co D, 10th Ga.

(Georgia Journal & Messenger, con't)
G.R. Bailey, co C, 22d Ga.
J. Wallor, co D, 10th Ga.
D.H. Linch, co B, 3d Ga.
J.A. Aldred, 22d Ga.
G.M.H.F., co D, 15th Ga.
Sergt. J.W. McHugh, co F, 24th Ga.
H. Mars, co A, 22d Ga.
Cook, 3d Bat. S S, Ga.
M.N. Wall, co E, 3d Ga.
J.Y. Dennis, co K, 44th Ga.
A.J. King, co E, 26th Ga.
Sergt. James Blackwell, co D, 60th Ga.
J.W. Cremer, co F, 12th Ga.
Wm. Potts, 61st Ga.
J.M. Hall, co H, 16th Ga.
Lieut. D.L. Gray, co K, 61st Ga.
J.A. Dozier, co F, 12th Ga.
Lieut. H.A. Maddux, co C, 60th Ga.
E. Dobarty, co K, 12th Ga.
A.F. Clark, co D, 20th Ga.
A.J. Hammock, co D, 4th Ga.
Jason Rijell, co A, Ga.
A.L. Rijell, co A, Ga.
J.N. Mauldin, co B, 12th Ga.
Rev. Robt. A. Ellis, co C, 60th Ga.
Lieut. Col. C.W. McArthur, 61st Ga.
Sergt. S. Tallings, co A, 4th Ga.
Ricks, co C, 35th Ga.
Lieut. J.T. Cally, 12th Ga.
J.P.M., co A, 18th Ga.
W.B. Kimbro, co B, 3d Ga.
Lieut. G.A. Worsham, co F, 17th Ga.
B.F. Mills, co B, 59th Ga.
J.R., 44th Ga.
J.P. McNeely, co C, 20th Ga.

From the Georgia Journal and Messenger of 11 May 1869

Confederate Dead at Thomaston, Georgia

Mr. Editor: As the names of the Confederate soldiers who died in hospital and were buried here have never sppeared in print, I send you a list of this late day for publication. The names of a few having not been ascertained.

Respectfully,
E.A. Flewellen
Thomaston, Upson County, Ga.
May 3

B.F. Johnson, Company B, 1st Mississippi Regiment
R.J. White, Company G, 20th Mississippi Regiment
J.M. Carter, Company B, 35th Mississippi Regiment
J.W. Brady, Company I, 20th Mississippi Regiment
W. Shepard, Company G, 46th Mississippi Regiment
J.C. Sprawls, Company B, 15th Mississippi Regiment
A. Baker, Company G, 1st Mississippi Regiment
E.M. Wright, Company E, 44th Mississippi Regiment
Abel Warr, Company D, 3d Mississippi Regiment
S.T. Brown, Company H, 9th Mississippi Regiment
J.R. Ford, Company E, 15th Mississippi Regiment
E.J. Dunham, Company H, 23d Mississippi Regiment
S.J. Chambers, Company ___, 4th Mississippi Regiment
W.A. Hartsfield, Company F, 3d Mississippi Regiment
J.B.L. Dear, Company A, 6th Mississippi Regiment
Samuel Brown, Company C, 1st Mississippi Sharpshooters
W.H. Harrison, Company B, 4th Mississippi Regiment
Elrich Henderson, Company B, 4th Mississippi Regiment
J.W. Clopton, Company C, 1st Mississippi Regiment

(Confederate Dead at Thomaston, cont'd)
W.A. Corley, Company B, Perrin's Regiment
W.T. Blair, Company B, Perrin's Regiment
R.L. Loyd, Company A, Perrin's Regiment
James Quigly, Company F, 5th Confederate
W.L. Rumley, Company G, 5th Tennessee Regiment
J.H. Shoemaker, Company C, 29th Tennessee Regiment
W.H. Michael, Company F, 29th Tennessee Regiment
Wm. Rowan (?), Company C, 50th Tennessee Regiment
J.A. Jones, Yates' Battery
J.T. Ussery, Yates' Battery
A.G. Marble, Swett's Battery
W.A. Smith, Company E, 60th North Carolina Regiment
L.D. Dunlap, Company E, 19th South Carolina Regiment
J.T. Gentry, Company D, 19th Arkansas Regiment
S.A. Wells, Captain 15th Arkansas Regiment
W.H. Delahaunty, Company G, 1st Arkansas Regiment
Wm. Henley, Company B, 18th Alabama Regiment
O.R. Ingram, Company A, 20th Alabama Regiment
L.A. Roustan, Company E, 4th Louisiana Regiment
H.F. Wagoner, Company ___, 5th Georgia Regiment
W.A. Gillespie, Company C, 59th Georgia Regiment
A.B. Bryan, Company A, 57th Georgia Regiment
James Raley, Company A, 54th Georgia Regiment
H. Roston, Company H, 40th Georgia Regiment
J.B. Mulkey, Company F, 8th Georgia Regiment
C.C. Raley, Company A, Georgia Battalion of Sharpshooters
____ Drinkard
J.H.K.
Four unknown

MARRIAGES
FROM THE
MACON MESSENGER

MARRIAGES
From the Georgia Messenger
Macon, Georgia

Apr. 28, 1823

Married in this town on the 27th inst. by John W. Beard, Esq. MR. MOSES PETTIS to MISS LUCINDA LAWSON, both of this county.

Aug. 18, 1823

Married in Fort Hawkins, on the 13th inst. by the Rev. Mr. Tharp, MR. ENOCH T. BOWERS, merchant, to MISS TABITHA GUYTON.

Sep. 22, 1823

Married in this place, on the 17th inst. by Mr. Robertson, Esq., MR. GEORGE JEWETT, Merchant, late of Granby, Conn. to MISS ELIZA GUYTON, of Dublin, Geo.

Jan. 7, 1824

Married on 30th inst., MR. HANNON B. POUND of Putnam Co. to MISS MILLY GAY of Jones Co.

Mar. 17, 1824

Married in this county by E. McCall, Esq. MR. ARTHUR McFERSON of Jones Co. to MISS MARGARET MOODY.

Apr. 28, 1824

Married in this place on the 22nd inst. by F.H. Godfrey, Esq., DR. THOMPSON BIRD to MISS LUCINDA HARRIS.

July 21, 1824

Married on the 8th inst. by the Rev. Thomas Darley, MAJ. PHILIP T. SCHLEY of Sandersville to MISS FRANCES V.L. BROOKING of Hancock County.

Aug. 4, 1824

Married in this county, wodow ELIZABETH BAGBY, aged 40, to MASTER JAMES THOMPSON, aged 19.

Married on the 28th ult. by the Rev. V.A. Tharp in Twiggs Co., CAPT. WILLIAM SIMMONS of Monroe Co. to MRS. BETHIA HATCHER.

Married in Crawford Co., on the 22 ult. by P. Calhoun, Esq., MR. _____ ETHERIDGE of Wilkinson County, to MISS ELIZABETH G. HENDRICK.

Sep. 1, 1824

Married in this county on the 29th Aug. by Edmund C. Beard, Esq. CAPT. CHARLES INGRAM, to MISS SARAH ANN CAROLINE ISLER.

Sep. 22, 1824

Married in this county on the 16th inst. by his Honor Judge Shorter, MR. GEORGE B. WARDLAW to MISS MARINA ROSS.

Jan. 19, 1825

Married on the 6th inst. MR. JAMES HOLDERNESS, of Pike County, to MISS ELIZABETH BRYAN, of Twiggs County.

Feb. 9, 1825

Married in this town, on the 3d inst. by E. Keeney, Esq. MR.
ALEXANDER D. BROWN to MISS EMILY CRAWFORD.

Mar. 2, 1825

Married in this county on the 23d ult. by E. McCall, Esq., MR.
WILLIAM CARR, to MISS VIRGINIA HAWKINS, daughter of the late Col.
Benjamin Hawkins.

Married on the 17th ult. by James Flewellen, Esq. ROBERT PATTON,
SEN. to MRS. MARTHA ROSS.

Married in Milledgeville, on the 21st ult. RICHARD M. ORME, ESQ.
one of the Editors of the Southern Recorder, to MISS JUNE M. PAYNE.

Nov. 30, 1825

Married in Crawford county on the 6th inst. by B.F. Lane, Esq.
MR. WILLIS HARE, to MISS MARY McGEE.

Married in Twiggs county, on the 24th inst. by the Rev. John Ross,
GEORGE GRANBERRY, ESQ. merchant, to MISS SARAH S. HILL.

Feb. 1, 1826

Married on Thursday the 19th ult. at Marion, MR. ROBERT BEAL, of
Eatonton, to MISS ELIZABETH GRIFFIN of the former place.

Married in Perry county, Alabama, on the 5th inst. by the reverend
Mr. Hilhouse, MR. MIRABEAU B. LAMAR of Milledgeville, Ga. to MISS
TABITHA B. JOURDAN, late of Georgia. (Cahawba Press).

Feb. 22, 1826

Married in this county, on the 15th inst. by the Hon. Charles J.
McDonald, MR. JOHN W. ROBARTS, Merchant of this place to MISS PERMELIA
S. BOOTH, daughter of Col. David S. Booth.

May 24, 1826

Married in Telfair county, on the 11th instant CAPT. DAVID FLANDERS,
of this place, to MISS MARTHA J. MITCHELL.

Married on the 16th inst. by the Rev. Mr. Ogletree, MR. WILLIAM
STALLINGS, to MISS SHADY ANN WRIGHT, daughter of Mr. William D.
Wright, all of Monroe county.

Married in Milledgeville, on the 9th inst. DR. WM. B. BALL to
MISS MARY M. HINES - and on the 10th inst. MR. ROBERT B. CLAYTON,
to MISS MARY B. ROSSETER.

May 31, 1826

Married on Thursday evening last at the upper cakery MR. THOMAS
HAMILL, Rockmason, a native of the Emerald Isle, to MISS BERSHEBA
CARSON; late house-keeper to Esq. Belknap, all of this vicinity.

July 5, 1826

Married in this place, on Wednesday last by the Rev. Mr. Jones,
MR. SUMNER STONE to MISS ELIZABETH WICK.

Married in Clinton, on the 29th ult. WILEY WILLIAMS, ESQ. attorney
at Law to MISS _____ FLETCHER, both of that place.

Married in Jones county, a few days ago, HOPKINS HOLSEY, ESQ. of
Hancock county to MISS ELIZABETH MITCHELL, daughter of James Mitchell
Esq.

July 18, 1826

    Married in this county, on the 6th inst. by the Rev. J. Neel, MR. JOHN BAKER, to MISS CHARLOTTE SNELGROVE.

Aug. 15, 1826

    Married in Jones county, on the 10th inst. by the Rev. Mr. Calloway, MR. MARMADUKE J. SLADE, junior editor of the Messenger, to MISS ANN G., daughter of THOMAS BLUNT, ESQ.

Aug. 22, 1826

    Married at Taliahassee, ACHILLE MURAT, ESQ. of Florida, formerly of Italy, oldest son of his late Majesty, King Joachim, of Naples, to MRS. CATHERINE DANGERFIELD GRAY, of Taliahassee, formerly of Fredericksburt, (Va.) and daughter of Major Byrd C. Willis.

Sep. 12, 1826

    Married in New-Haven, Conn. on the 20th ult. by the Rev. Dr. Taylor, MR. LEWIS FITCH, merchant of this town, to MISS GRACE L. HILL, of that city.

Oct. 3, 1826

    Married in this County, on the 24th ult. by Daniel Matheson, Esq. MR. FREDERICK FOY, to MISS CHARLOTTE WHITE.

Oct. 10, 1826

    Married in this County, on the 4th inst. by Z. Holloman, Esq. MR. JOSEPH SHAW, of this town, to MISS LUCY A.M. ROGERS.

Oct. 17, 1826

    Married on the 15th instant by M. Robertson, Esq. COL. PHILO P. ATWELL, to MI_S SARAH DEES, both of this town.

Oct. 24, 1826

    Married in this town, on Tuesday last, by the Rev. Joseph C. Stiles, ROBERT BIRDSONG, ESQ. to MISS MARY H. STOVALL.

Nov. 7, 1826

    Married in this county on Thursday evening last, by the Rev. Mr. Stiles, MORTIMER R. WALLIS, ESQ. of this place, to MISS SARAH ANN NORMAN.

    Married in this town, on the same evening, by M. Robertson, Esq. MR. JEREMIAH SMITH, to MISS MILLEY BAILEY.

Nov. 28, 1826

    Married in this county on Thursday evening last, by H. Carr Esq. MR. JOHN M. POWLEDGE, to MISS FRANCES FOY.

Dec. 5, 1826

    Married in Augusta, on the 22d ult. by the Rev. Hugh Smith, MR. JOHN T. LAMAR, of this place, to MISS LOUISA VIRGINIA, daughter of DR. THOMAS I. WRAY, of Augusta.

Dec. 19, 1826

    Married in this county on Tuesday evening last, by the Rev. Lot Jones, MAJOR EDWARD W. WRIGHT, of this town to MISS ELIZABETH MORGAN.

Dec. 26, 1826

Married on the 21st inst. in Monroe county, MR. FRANCIS NUNN to MISS CLEMENTINA GAULDING.

Married on the 24th, in Monroe county, DAVID TARASH, ESQ. to MISS MATILDA PRATT.

Married in Monroe county, MR. WM. SHIPIRINE to MISS ELIZABETH LAWSON.

Married in Monroe county, MR. JOSEPH HORTON to MISS HANNAH ASHLEY.

Married ----- MR. JAMES OGLETREE of Monroe county, to MISS EMILY SANDERS, of Houston county.

Jan. 2, 1827

Married in this town on the 28th ult. by the Rev. Mr. Gardner, MR. FRANCIS H. HICKIMBURG to MRS. MARY ANN KIMBLE.

Jan. 23, 1827

Married at Waynesborough on the 17th inst. MAJOR A. MANDAL, Attorney at law of this place, to MISS MARY E. PORTRESS, daughter of Major Portress of Laurens county.

Feb. 20, 1827

Married in this town, on Tuesday last, by the Rev. Mr. Darley, MR. CHARLES COTTON, to MISS ELIZABETH W. BULLOCK.

Mar. 13, 1827

Married in this county, on the 6th inst. by the Rev. Mr. Buchanan, MR. WM. SHEPHERD NORMAN, to MISS MARTHA ADELINE WATTS.

Mar. 20, 1827

Married on the 12th inst. at Mount Pleasant, Monroe county, by A. Ginn, Esq. CAPT. LEWIS ATKISON to MISS ROLTHA HILLIARD.

Married in Upson county, on Thursday the 8th inst. by James R. Harwell, Esq. MR. SAMUEL GRESHAM to MISS MARTHA, daughter of ABNER McCOY, ESQ. all of Upson county.

Apr. 3, 1827

Married on the 1st inst. at Laurel Hills, Laurens county, by Rossel Kellam, Esq. DR. NATHAN TUCKER, formerly of this place (Macon), to MISS ELIZA MADDOX, daughter of CAPTAIN LEWIS MADDOX.

May 1, 1827

Married on the 26th inst. by James Pierson, Esq. MR. JAMES SMITH aged 75 years, to MISS MARY JANE JESSOP, aged 17.

Married also on the same day, by Wm. Melton, Esq. MR. JEREMIAH JOHNSON to MRS. LUCRETIA SMITH - all of Twiggs county.

May 8, 1827

Married in this place on Tuesday evening last, by the Rev. Mr. Darley, MR. CHARLES S. LEWIS, to MISS MAHALA WHITE.

Married in Clinton, on Sunday the 6th inst. by Solomon Hoge, Esq. LIEUT. ISAAC T. WHEATON to MISS MARTHA ROBINSON, all of Clinton.

May 15, 1827

    Married in this place, on Monday evening the 7th inst. by the Rev. Mr. Buchanan, MR. THOMAS M. ELLIS, to MRS. CATHARINE WILSON.

    Married in Twiggs county, on the 29th ult. by Henry Bunn, Esq. COL. MICHAEL WATSON, of Houston county, to MISS MARY WIMBERLY, daughter of James B. Wimberly, Esq.

    Married on the 1st inst. by Henry Buen, Esq. MR. HUGH LAWSON, of Houston co. to MISS SARAH BRYAN, daughter of MAJOR JAMES C. BRYAN.

June 12, 1827

    Married in this county, on Tuesday evening last, by T. Bird, Esq. MR. CHARLES CRAWFORD, to MISS LOUISA BORIN.

July 3, 1827

    Married in Macon, on the 24th ult. by Thos. G. Bates, Esq. ARCHIBALD C. M'INTYRE, ESQ. to MISS MARGARET BOSEMAN.

    Married in this county, on the 25th inst. by Judge McDonald, WM. J. HEAD of Monroe county, to MISS LUCY L. LUNDY, daughter of THOS. LUNDY, ESQ.

    Married in this county on the 1st inst. ELEAZER McCALL, ESQ. to MISS _____ PATTON, daughter of the late MAJOR JAMES H. PATTON.

July 17, 1827

    Married in Macon on the 12th inst. by Judge McDonald, MR. ALBERTO FIELDING WALLIS, to MISS ANN MOORE.

Sep. 4, 1827

    Married in the vicinity of Pittsburg, Jones county, on the 30th ult. MR. ISAAC PITTS to MISS DRUSILLA PITTS all of said county.

Sep. 18, 1827

    Married on the 9th inst. by T. Holt, Esq. MR. NATHAN PARISH to MISS JANE BAZEMORE, all of this county.

    Married in Jones county, a few days ago, MR. DANIEL PRATT to MRS. ESTHER TICKNER.

Oct. 9, 1827

    Married at the Falls of Chatahoochy, on Thursday 4th October, by Luther Blake, Esq. MR. ZACHARIAH DUELL, to MISS NANCY DAY, all citizens of the Vilage at the Falls.

Oct. 16, 1827

    Married in this place, on Tuesady evening last, by the Rev. Mr. Stratton, ROBERT COLEMAN, ESQ. to MISS MARY B. TAYLOR, both of Macon.

    Married in this county, on the 4th instant, by John J. Harper, Esq. MR. AMBROSE EDWARDS, of Monroe county, to MISS EMELINE J. GAULDING, of Bibb county.

Nov. 27, 1827

    Married in Monroe county, a few days ago, MR. ABNER F. GIBSON, of Clinton, to MISS CAROLINE POPE.

Dec. 4, 1827

    Married in Twiggs county, on Tuesday evening last, by Geo. W. Welch, Esq. HENRY C. ABERNATHY, ESQ. of Macon, to MISS MARY A.K. GUERRY, of the former place.

Dec. 25, 1827

    Married in this place, on Thursday evening last, by the Rev. Mr. Darley, MR. LEMUEL NEWCOMB, merchant, to MISS MARTHA SNOW, both of Macon.

Jan. 28, 1828

    Married in this place, on Thursday evening last, by the Rev. Thomas Darley, CAPT. WM. J. DANELLY, to MISS ANN ELIZA SLADE, formerly of Warrenton, N.C.

Feb. 4, 1828

    Married in Milledgeville, on Wednesday last, by the Rev. Mr. Stiles, CAPT. CHARLES BULLOCK of Macon, to MRS. ELIZA A. GRANTLAND, of that place.

    Married in this county, by the Rev. Mr. Gardner, on Tuesday last, MR. GIDEON POWLEDGE to MISS SUSAN GODFREY.

    Married in Upson county, on the 29th of Jan. MR. ROBERT PARHAM, to MISS SARAH, daughter of ROBERT COLLIER, ESQ.

    Married in Twiggs county, a few days since, MR. WM. M. TARVER, to MISS JOANNA SLAPPEY.

Feb. 11, 1828

    Married in this place, on Thursday evening last, by the Rev. J.C. Stiles, MR. ISAAC B. ROWLAND, to MISS FRANCES A.M. CAMPBELL.

Apr. 14, 1828

    Married on the 1st of April, on the banks of the Chattahoochee river, in the county of Muscogee, by Edwin E. Bissell, Esq. MR. ROBERT B. SIMMS to MISS MARCELLA RANSOM, both of Montgomery county, Alabama.

    Married at Columbus, on the 19th of March, by Edwin E. Bissell, Esq. MR. STODDARD RUSSELL to MISS CLARISSA SWIFT, both of that place.

    Married on the 20th ult. by Edwin E. Bissell, Esq. MR. JOSEPH C. DANFORTH to MISS MILDRED PONDER, both of Columbus.

Apr. 28, 1828

    Married in Twiggs county, on Sunday night 15th inst. JAMES PARK ESQ. formerly of North Carolina, to MISS MARTHA WODDARD, both of said county.

    Married about the same time, in Wilkinson county, MR. JAMES HATFIELD, to MISS ELVIRA VINSON, both of the same county.

May 5, 1828

    Married in this place, on Thursday evening last, by the Rev. Mr. Hardy, MR. ISAAC WINSHIP to MISS MARTHA A.P. COOK, daughter of MAJ. PHILIP COOK.

May 24, 1828

    Married on the 8th inst. COL. E.B.W. SPIVEY to MISS SARAH GEORGIANNA, daughter of THOMAS McCALL, ESQ. of Laurens county.

May 24, 1828

    Married at Morristown, N.J. on the 30th ult. MR. JOSEPH BLACKLEY, of Cincinnati, Ohio, to MISS MARY C. TUTTLE, of the former place, (late of Macon).

June 14, 1828

    Married on the 29th ult. at Byron, Baker county, ISAAC WELCH, ESQ. of Monroe county to MISS E.W., eldest daughter of MAJ. THOMAS PORTER, formerly of Lawrensville, Lawrence county, S.C.

    Married in Monticello, on the 11th inst. by the Rev. Dr. Brown, MR. BAILEY GODDARD, of this town to MISS CATHARINE USHER.

Aug. 9, 1828

    Married on Sunday evening last, by E.E. Bissell, Esq. COL. PHILIP H. ALSTON to MRS. SARAH D. PARKS, all of Muscogee.

Aug. 23, 1828

    Married in Macon, at the residence of Henry G. Lamar, on Thursday evening last, by the Rev. Mr. Hodges, MR. JEFFERSON J. LAMAR, of Putnam county to MISS REBECCA LAMAR, of this place.

Sep. 27, 1828

    Married in this county, on Tuesday evening last, by the Rev. Mr. Gardner, MR. JOHN CORBETT, of this town, to MISS MARY H. WATTS.

    Married in this town, on Thursday evening, by the Rev. Mr. Patterson, DR. THOMAS R. LAMAR, to MRS. NANCY J. FULLWOOD.

Oct. 4, 1828

    Married in this county, on Tuesday evening last, by the Rev. Mr. Gardner, MR. ANGUS GILLIS, of this town, to MISS MARGARET ALSTON.

Oct. 11, 1828

    Married in Monroe county, on the 11th Sept. last, by James A. Henry Esq. MR. WM. _____ SLATTER (?) of Crawford county, to MISS LUCINDA MILLS, of Monroe county.

Oct. 18, 1828

    Married in Clinton, on Wednesday the 15th inst., by the Rev. Mr. Gardner, MR. SIMRI ROSE, one of the Editors of this paper, to MISS LAVINIA E.H. BLOUNT.

    Married in Houston county, on the 2d inst. MAJOR ROBERT A. BEALL, of Marion to MISS CAROLINE SMITH, daughter of the late RICHARD SMITH, ESQ.

    Married in Milledgeville, on the 2d inst. REV. CHARLES HARDY to MISS EMILY REYNOLDS.

Oct. 25, 1828

    Married in Milledgeville, on Thursday evening the 16th inst. MR. PHILIP AUGUSTUS CLAYTON, to MISS ELIZABETH WILLIAMSON, both of that place.

    Married recently, in Milford, at the residence of Lowther Layton, the REV. MR. SMITH to the REV. MISS ELOIS M. MILLER. This is an extrodinary circumstance, two preachers married together, and not Quakers either, but Methodists.

Nov. 15, 1828

    Married in Milledgeville on Friday evening the 7th inst. by the Rev. Thomas Goulding, DR. BENJAMIN F. OWENS, to MRS. ALMIRA HARGRAVE.

Nov. 29, 1828

    Married in this town, on Tuesday evening the 25th inst. by the Rev. Mr. Hodges, EDWARD D. TRACY, ESQ. to MISS SUSAN CAMPBELL.

    Married on the 23d inst. MR. JOHN B. LUMPKIN, to MISS MARY GRIMES (?), both of Crawford County.

Dec. 13, 1828

    Married at Powelton, on the 4th inst. THOMAS F. GREEN, ESQ. of Milledgeville, to MISS ADELINE A.E. CROWDER, of the former place.

Dec. 20, 1828

    Married on Tuesday Dec. 2d at St. Michaels Church, Trenton, N.J. by the Rev. W.L. Johnson, ISAAC G. SEYMOUR, ESQ. of Macon, Geo. to MISS EULALIA daughter of the late REV. HENRY WHITLOCK, of New-Haven, Conn.

Dec. 27, 1828

    Married in Marion, on Thursday the 18th inst. GEN. THADDEUS G. HOLT, to MISS NANCY FLEMING.

Jan. 17, 1829

    Married in Twiggs county, on Thursday last, by the Rev. C.A. Tharp, THOMAS G. BATES, ESQ. of this place, to MISS MARY SOUTHALL.

    Married in Greensborough, on the 18th ult. MR. WILLIS ALSTON, of Sparta, to MISS ELIZABETH SARAH, daughter of the REV'D JOHN HOWARD of the former.

    Married in Columbia county, by the Rev. Mr. Talmage, on the 1st January, WILLIAM H. TORRANCE, of Milledgeville, Counselor at Law, to MISS JANE M. daughter of PETER CRAWFORD ESQ.

Jan. 31, 1829

    Married on the 8th instant, in Milledgeville, by the Rev. Lovick Pierce, MR. JERRY COWLES of Eatonton, to MISS SARAH C. WILLIAMS, of the former place.

Feb. 21, 1829

    Married in Columbus on Thursday the 12th inst. by the Rev. Mr. Hollenbek, MR. RICHARD T. MARKS, to MISS JACINTHA E. DAWSON.

    Married in Clinton, on Thursday evening the 12th inst. COL. FRANCIS A.D. WEAVER, of Greensborough to MISS CAROLINE COOK, of the former place.

Feb. 28, 1829

    Married in Jones county, on the 23d inst. by the Rev. Thomas Gardner, of Macon MR. ARCHIBALD P. BENTON, of Clinton, to MISS MARTHA F.W. BREEDLOVE, of Jones.

    Married in the Court-House in Thomaston, in the office of the Clerk of the Court of Ordinary, on the 24th inst. (before a large assemblage of members of the bar, and other respectable citizens) by Wm. P. Yonge, Esq. MR. JAMES SMITH to JANE LUNDY, after a courtship of the most intimate kind for eight years. Their attendants were the Sheriff, his Deputy and Bailiffs.

Mar. 7, 1829

   Married in Twiggs county on the 9th Feb. by the Hon. T.G. Holt,
____ Boynton of the House of Boynton & Brown to MISS RUBY BRYAN
daughter of BENJAMIN BRYAN, ESQ.

Apr. 25, 1829

   Married in this town on the 22d inst. by the Rev. Mr. Gardner,
MR. MATTHEW E. RYLANDER, to MISS ANN GAMBLE.

   Married on Thursday 2d instant, by the Rev. Mr. Hand, MR. ASA B.
COOK, of Jones county, to MISS ELIZABETH W. IVEY, daughter of
ROBERT IVEY of Baldwin.

   Married in Sparta, at the residence of Captain Duke Hamilton, on
the 13th inst. by the Rev. Mr. Darley, JOHN BONNER, ESQ. to MISS
FRANCIS M. REEVES, all of Hancock County.

   Married in Monroe County on Tuesday the 14th instant at the house
of Mr. Enos Young, by R.L. Barnes, Esq. MR. COOPER JONES to MISS
MARIA D. TARVER of Hancock County.

May 2, 1829

   Married in Macon on Wednesday the 29th inst. by the Rev. Thos.
Gardner, COL. SAMUEL T. BAILEY of Columbus, to MISS MARTHA D.
STRONG, daughter of the HON. C.B. STRONG.

May 9, 1829

   Married in Jones county, on the 3d inst. by the Rev. Joshua S.
Callaway, THOMAS BLUNT, ESQ. to MISS MARY RICKETTS.

May 23, 1829

   Married on the 7th inst. by the Rev. Joshua Key, MR. PHILIP ROBINSON,
to MISS ELIZABETH EMANUEL, all of Burke county.

June 13, 1829

   Married in Augusta on the 4th instant, by the Rev'd Hugh Smith,
CAPT. GERALD M'LAUGHLIN, merchant, to MISS LAURA CAMILLA, daughter
of DOCT. T.I. WRAY, all of that city.

   Married on the same evening by the Rev. Mr. Tallmage, MR. BENJAMIN
BARTON merchant, to MISS MARY SIMS, daughter of BENJAMIN SIMS, ESQ.

   Married on the 27th ult. by the Rev. Mr. Converse: the HON.
GEORGE M'DUFFIE to MISS MARY REBECCA SINGLETON, daughter of RICHARD
SINGLETON, ESQ. of Sumpter District, S.C.

June 27, 1829

   Married on Tuesday evening by the Rev. Mr. Neufville, DR. AMBROSE
BABER, of Virginia and at present a resident of Macon, Ga. to MISS
MARY E. SWEET, daughter of the late GEO. C. SWEET, ESQ. of this
city. (Sav. Georgian).

July 18, 1829

   Married in Twiggs County on the 12th(?) inst. by James M. Granberry,
MR. ELIJAH ANDERSON to MRS. ELIZABETH POWEL both of Twiggs County.

Aug. 15, 1829

   Married near Brunswick (New-Jersey) on the 28th July, by the Rev.
Mr. Romain, MR. JOSIAH FREEMAN, merchant of Macon, to MRS. ANN H.
WILLIAMSON, daughter of MR. ENOS AYRES.

Aug. 29, 1829

    Married in Newton county, on the 23d inst. COL. MATTHEW PHILLIPS, of Monticello, to MISS _____ BACON.

Sep. 19, 1829

    Married on the 7th inst. by the Rev. James C. Patterson, MR. EZEKIEL SMITH to MISS JANE WARDLAW, both of this place.

Sep. 26, 1829

    Married in this county, on the 24th inst. by the Rev. Mr. Patterson, MR. WM. E. BOREN to MISS MARIA DANELLY.

Dec. 26, 1829

    Married in this place, on Thursday evening last, by the Rev. Mr. Patterson, WASHINGTON POE, ESQ. to MISS SALINA S. NORMAN.

    Married in Clinton, on the 22d inst. by the Rev. Dr. Pierce, MR. JOSIAH BEALL to MISS MARTHA COOK.

Jan. 30, 1830

    Married in Jones county, on Thursday evening last, by the Rev. Gideon Mason, MR. HENRY KELLY to MISS MARY ANN JENKINS.

    Married in Jasper County on the 20th ult. by the Rev. James Hunter, MR. ALFRED A. COMER of Jones County to MISS MARY R. RIVERS, daughter of THOMAS RIVERS, ESQ.

Feb. 13, 1830

    Married in Upson county, by Wm. P. Yonge, Esq. DR. JAMES W. STINSON, of Thomaston, to MISS _____ JACKSON.

Feb. 20, 1830

    Married in Twiggs County, on the 11 inst. by James Solomon, Esq. MR. LAWRENCE JOINER to MISS MARY GLOVER.

    Married by Joel Denton Esq. MR. WILLIAM PAUL of Jones county to MISS MARY WARE, daughter of JAMES WARE, ESQ.

    MAJOR WILLIAM CASWELL married to MISS _____ GILBERT.

Mar. 20, 1830

    Married in this place, on Thursday evening last, by the Rev. Mr. Patterson, MR. CHARLES PECK to MISS JANE ELLIS.

    Married on Wednesday morning, the 3d inst. by the Rev. Dr. Pierce, MR. HARPER TUCKER, to MISS MARY BIVINS, all of Baldwin county.

Mar. 27, 1830

    Married in Houston county, on Thursday evening, the 13th inst. by John Chain Esq. DOCT. EDWARD T. McGEHEE of Perry, to MISS CLARA A. daughter of MR. JOHN J. OWENS of that county.

Apr. 10, 1830

    Married on Thursday evening last, MR. BRYAN F. LANE, of Macon, to MISS CAROLINE T. DICKSON, of Crawford County.

May 8, 1830

    Married in Monroe county, on the 4th inst. by C. Bayne Esq. CHRISTOPHER PARKER to MISS SARAH STROUD.

June 5, 1830

Married in this place, on Thursday evening last, by the Rev. Mr. Patterson, CAPT. ROBERT S. PATTON, to MISS REBECCA PACE.

Married in Clinton, on Thursday evening, the 27th ult. by the Rev. Daniel Duffie, DR. JOHN TURNER, of Monroe county, to MISS ELIZA L. IVERSON, of Clinton.

June 12, 1830

Married in Thomaston, on the 29th ult. by James McBryde, Esq. MR. JAMES BOWDRE, to MISS PEGGY BEALL, in presence of a large collection of the most interesting inhabitants of this place.

June 19, 1830

Married in this county, on Sunday evening last, by Charles Ingram, Esq. MR. ALFRED BRADY to MISS SUSAN JOHNSON.

July 24, 1830

Married in Forsyth on the 14th instant, by the Rev. J. Patterson, BUTLER KING to LOUISA M. second daughter of WILLIAM F. JACKSON.

July 31, 1830

Married in Thomaston, Upson co. on Tuesday the 20th inst. by Green Ferguson, Esq. DANIEL WALKER, to MRS. MARIAH MILLING.

Married in Laurens county on the 21st inst. by the Rev. D. Buchanan, JOHN G. COATS, ESQ. formerly of this place, to MISS CELIA THOMAS daughter of JOHN THOMAS ESQ. of Laurens.

Aug. 7, 1830

Married in Talbotton on Sunday the 25th inst. by Rev. Mr. Manly, MR. JAMES BLANTON to MISS CYNTHIA CUNNINGHAM.

Aug. 14, 1830

Married on 20th ult. MIDDLETON, Connecticut MR. JOHN LEWIS JONES, merchant of Macon, Geo. to MISS JULIA PARKMAN, of Berlin, Con.

Sep. 4, 1830

Married in Houston county, on Wednesday the 25th inst. by John Chain Esq. JOHN H. McCARTER, to MISS CLARA JANE, daughter of CAPT. GEORGE TERVIN, all of said county.

Oct. 23, 1830

Married in Augusta, on the 12th inst. by the Rev.'d Mr. Bass, CAPT. ROBERT W. McKEEN, to MISS MARY DANFORTH, all of this city.

Oct. 30, 1830

Married in Houston county, on Thursday evening, by John Chain, Esq. MR. ABRAHAM C. BYRD to MISS ELIZABETH REID, all of said county.

Nov. 13, 1830

Married in this county, on the 3d instant, by Mr. Elbert Calhoun, MR. EDWARD FOLDS to MISS LUCRETIA HOLMES.

Nov. 20, 1830

Married on Thursday evening last, the 9th instant by John T.B. Turner, Esq. MR. THOMAS MAFFORD(?) to MISS FRANCES E.A. WYNN, both of Monroe county.

Nov. 27, 1830

    Married in Twiggs county, on Wednesday evening last, MR. AUGUSTUS HOWARD of Houston, to MISS MARTHA WIMBERLY, daughter of GENERAL E. WIMBERLY.

Dec. 13, 1830

    Married on the 16th inst. by the Rev'd I. Few, MR. G. CHAMPLIN, to MISS MARY ANN B. ELLIS, all of this place.

Jan. 8, 1831

    Married on Tuesday the 28th ult. by the Rev. Hugh Smith, MR. ALEXANDER R. McLAUGHLIN, Merchant of Macon, to MISS ELIZABETH W. BUGG of this place.

    Married in Montgomery, (Ala.) on Thursday evening 16th ult. by the Hon. N.E. Benson, MR. GEORGE WHITMAN, Merchant of that place to MISS HARRIET P. BRAME, recently of Macon.

Mar. 19, 1831

    Married in Monroe county, on the 10th inst. by the Rev. Thos. Battle, MR. BERNIER PYE, to MISS CUZZIAH ROBINSON.

Apr. 30, 1831

    Married in this county, on the 13th(?) instant, JOHN BUTTRILL, ESQ. of Zebulon, to MISS _____ ALSTON, daughter of COL. JAMES ALSTON.

    Married near Augusta, on the 7th last ALFRED IVERSON, ESQ. of Columbus, to MISS JULIA FRANCES, daughter of the HON. JOHN FORSYTH.

    Married in Talbot county, on the 21st inst. by Thomas Howard, Esq. MR. WM. SEARS, to MRS. MARTHA LOCKHART.

June 4, 1831

    Married in Thomaston, on the 26th ult. by A. Brown, Esq. MR. W. DOLES, aged 70 years to MRS. _____ BUTLER, aged 65. From the infirmities of old age, the bridg-groom was under the necessity of being held on his feet by his attendants, during the ceremony. (NOTE: The notice contains a description of the ceremony).
-- P.S. - May 30 - The Bride ran away last night, taking from her husband all his Cash and Notes; and has shaved the latter at 33 1/3 per cent.

June 11, 1831

    Married on Thursday Evening last, by the Rev. Mr. Pope, MR. JAMES A. HALL, to MISS ELIZABETH, eldest daughter of ELIJAH COTTON, ESQ. all of this county.

    Married on the 1st inst. in Edgefield District, S.C. by the Rev. C.D. Mallary, the REV. IVERSON L. BROOKS, of Jasper county, Ga. to MRS. SARAH JANE MYERS, of the former place.

    Married in this county on Thursday 2d inst. by the Rev. Mr. Campbell, MR. THOMAS M. ELLIS, to MISS ELIZA CUNNINGHAM, daughter of ROBERT CUNNINGHAM, ESQ. both of Jones county.

June 18, 1831

    Married in this county on Thursday Evening last, by the Rev. Mr. Pope, MR. WILLIAM L. SOUTHALL, to MISS MARIA BAILY, all of Bibb.

June 25, 1831

   Married in Clinton, on Thursday evening last, MR. GILES B. TAYLOR,
   ESQ. of Perry, Houston county, to MISS ANN HARVEY, daughter of
   JOHN HARVEY.

July 2, 1831

   Married on Tuesday evening the 28th inst. by John Chain, Esq. MR.
   VINCENT A. WITHERSBY, to MISS MARGARET BARR(?), all of the county
   of Houston.

July 9, 1831

   Married in Monroe county, on Thursday evening the 30th ult. MR.
   SAMUEL T. BEECHER to MISS LAURA P. BROWN, daughter of DOCTOR GEORGE
   A. BROWN.

July 16, 1831

   Married on the 30th June, by John Gardner, Esq. MR. BENJAMIN GIBSON,
   of Upson county, to MISS JULIA ANN FREENY, of Pike county.

July 23, 1831

   Married on Tuesday evening last by the Rev. Benj. Pope, DR. MYRON
   BARTLETT, Editor of the Macon Telegraph, to MISS TABITHA NAPIER,
   daughter of ISAAC HARVEY, ESQ. of this town.

July 30, 1831

   Married in this place, on the 28th ult. by H.B. Hill, Esq. MR. WM.
   MOBLEY, to MISS LEVINIA CLARK.

   Married in Twiggs county, on the 14th inst. by Wm. H. Perkins,
   Esq. MR. ISAAC ANDREWS, (son of ROBINE ANDREWS, ESQ.) to MISS
   _____ JONES.

Aug. 6, 1831

   Married at Washington City, on the 13th ult. MR. PHILIP HENRY
   ECHOLS, of Monticello, Ga. to MISS MARGARET L.M. BERRIEN, daughter
   of the HON. JOHN M. BERRIEN of Georgia.

Aug. 27, 1831

   Married on the evening of the 25th by the Rev. Mr. Pope, MR. JORDAN
   T. COUNCTZ, formerly of Tennessee, to MISS SOPHIA, daughter of
   JAMES S. FRIERSON, ESQ. of this place.

Sep. 3, 1831

   Married in Jones county, on Sunday evening last, by Thomas Humphries,
   Esq. MR. SAMUEL W. COURSON to MISS ELIZA TOWNSEND, all of Jones
   county.

   Married in Columbus, on Monday evening 15th ult. by the Rev. Jesse
   Boring, MR. JONATHAN A. HUDSON, to MISS MARTHA ELIZABETH ABERCROMBIE,
   of Hancock county.

Sep. 10, 1831

   Married in Darien, on the 23d ult. by the Rev. Mr. Pratt, ANSON
   KIMBERLY, ESQ. to MRS. SARAH ANN STREET, both of Darien.

Oct. 1, 1831

   Married in Twiggs county on Thursday the 15th inst. by Edward B.
   Young, Esq. MR. TOMLINSON FORT to MRS. MARY E. BELCHER, all of
   said county.

Oct. 22, 1831

Married on the 12th inst. by the Rev'd. Mr. Patterson, DR. GEORGE A. BROWN, of Monroe county, to MRS ELIZA ALLEN, of Milledgeville.

Oct. 29, 1831

Married in Augusta, on the 23d inst. by the Rev. Jas. O. Andrew, HENRY B. HILL, ESQ. of this place, to MRS. ANN P. WALSH, widow of the late DR. WALSH, of Columbia, S.C.

Nov. 5, 1831

Married in Monroe county, on the 13th October, by the Rev. Mr. Pope of Macon, AMASA R. MOORE, ESQ. to MISS ELIZABETH L. GREER, daughter of DR. THOMAS GREER, deceased, of Green county.

Nov. 19, 1831

Married in Hawkinsville, Pulaski county, on Sunday morning the 6th inst. by John Bozeman, Esq. DR. ISAAC D. NEWTON, to MRS. LOUISIANA B. LLOYD, daughter of JOHN McCOLL, ESQ. all of that place.

Nov. 26, 1831

Married on the 20th inst. by the Rev. Mr. Pope, MR. JAMES WILLIAMS to MISS CATHARINE ARNETT, all of this place.

Dec. 3, 1831

Married in this county, on the 20th inst. by the Rev. Wm. Henderson, MR. JAMES JONES, of Talbotton, to MISS THIRZA-ANN FITZPATRICK.

Dec. 24, 1831

Married on Thursday night last, by the Rev. Mr. Holt, MR. GEORGE DOUGLASS, to MISS MARY ANN CURBOW.

Jan. 7, 1832

Married on Thursday evening the 5th inst. at the house of Dr. James Thweatt of Monroe county, by the Rev. Charles Williamson, MR. J.P. SMITH to MISS ELIZA ROWENNA BENNING all of this town.

Jan. 28, 1832

Married in Baldwin county on Tuesday evening the 24th inst. by the Rev. Mr. Holt, of this place, MR. JOHN HAYS, to MISS SARAH ANN WILEY, all of that county.

Feb. 4, 1832

Married on Thursday evening the 2d inst. by the Rev. John Howard, MR. BENJAMIN R. WARNER, to MISS MARY CAPERS, daughter of the REV. G. CAPERS, all of this place.

Married on Wednesday Evening the 25th inst. at Cullodenville, Monroe county, by the Rev. Charles Hardy, MR. EARLY CLEVELAND, of said county to MISS LUCY B. daughter of NAHUM WILDER, of Princeton, Massachusetts.

Mar. 3, 1832

Married on Thursday Evening 16th ult. by Wm. H. Calhoun, Esq. MR. JOHN PITTMAN, to MISS NANCY JAMES, all of this county.

Married on Thursday Evening, 1st of March, by W.H. Calhoun, Esq. MR. ALLEN JAMES, to MISS RACHEL BURNETT, all of this county.

Mar. 3, 1832

Married in Thomaston, on the 21st ult. MR. WILLIAMSON FREEMAN, of Talbotton, to MISS DRUSILLA BOWDRE, of the former place.

Mar. 24, 1832

Married in Jasper county, on the 14th inst. MR. THOMAS M. TURNER, of Monroe county, to MISS CAROLINE VIRGINIA RIVERS, of Jasper county.

Apr. 7, 1832

Married in Houston county on Sunday evening the 25th inst. by John Chain, Esq. JAMES DEAN, ESQ. to MISS OBEDEANCE H. LOW, all of said county.

Married in Darien on the 25th ultimo, by B.B. Stubbs, Esq. MICHAEL J. KENAN, ESQ. of Baldwin county, to MISS CATHARINE A. SPALDING of McIntosh county.

Apr. 14, 1832

Married on Sunday evening last, by the Rev. B. Pope, MR. JOHN H. SIMS, to MISS ELIZA SMITH, both of Macon.

Married on Monday evening, by the Rev. E. Holt, MR. FREDERICK F. LEWIS, to MISS JULIA ANN THOMAS, all of this place.

Married in Hillsboro, Jasper Co. on the 4th inst. by the Rev. Thomas Mabery, MR. JOHN G. MORRIS to MISS LUCINDA B. BELL.

Apr. 21, 1832

Married in Jones county, on the 10th inst. by B. Paterson, Esq. MR. ROBERT M. JACKSON, to MISS ELIZABETH P. daughter of KINCHEN P. THWEATT.

Married in Twiggs county, on Thursday Evening, 19th inst. by the Rev. Charles Hardy, MR. ARCHIBALD M. CAMPBELL, of Macon, to MISS MARY W. WILLIS, of the former place.

May 5, 1832

Married in Crawford county, on Wednesday evening last, by the Rev. E. Holt, MAJOR EDWARD W. WRIGHT, of this place, to MISS MARTHA W. CROWELL, daughter of HENRY CROWELL, ESQ. of the former place.

May 19, 1832

Married at the residence of Geo. W. Welch, Esq. in Twiggs county on the 10th inst. DR. JOSHUA R. WIMBERLY to MISS CAROLINE STARR.

Married on Thursday evening 3d inst. WILLIS S. BREAZEAL, ESQ. of Upson county, to MISS HARRIET E. JONES, daughter of COL. JONES of Burke county.

June 14, 1832

Married in Warrenton on the 11th inst. by the Rev. Joseph L. Moultrie, MR. EDWARD B. YOUNG of Marion, to MISS ANN F. BEALL, of the former place.

July 5, 1832

Married in Bibb County, on Thursday evening the 28th June by the Rev. Thomas Battle, MR. ROBT. CAMPBELL REDDING, of Monroe County, to MISS PARASADE H. WATTS, of the former county.

July 12, 1832

Married on Thursday 5th inst. in Laurens County, by the Rev. B.B. Buchanan, MAJ. GEORGE GRANBURY of Harris County, to MISS MARY G. FULSOM of the former place.

Aug. 2, 1832

Married at Clinton, Jones county, on the 18th instant, MR. GEORGE W. DILLINGHAM to LUCY ELIZABETH TICKNER, daughter of the late DR. ORRAY TICKNER of Jones county.

Married in Columbus on Wednesday evening the 25th inst. by the Rev. I.A. Few, GEN. JAMES N. BETHUNE, to MISS FRANCES GUNBY, of Columbia county.

Aug. 9, 1832

Married in Jasper county, on the 31st ult. by the Rev. Charles Hardy, DR. ABNER F. HOLT, of Bibb county, to MISS ELIZA ADDISON, of Jasper county.

Aug. 23, 1832

Married on the evening of the 16th instant, at Milford, Jefferson County, by the Rev. C. Harrison DR. JAMES R. SMITH of Louisville, to MISS SUSAN, only daughter of DR. JNO. J. JENKINS.

Sep. 6, 1832

Married in this county, by James Thompson, Esq. on the 1st instant, MR. EDWARD C. BUCKLEY to MISS HARRIET J. HILL - daughter of HENRY B. HILL, ESQ.

Sep. 13, 1832

Married at Wm. Hodges's Esq. in Bibb county on Sunday morning the 9th inst. MR. GUY E. FOOTE, to MISS AMELIA E. FULLER, both of Perry.

Married in this vicinity, on Thursday last, by the Rev. John Howard, MR. GEORGE W. MALLORY, to MISS EMILY P. BOREN.

Sep. 20, 1832

Married on Thursday evening, 12th inst., by the Rev. Isaac Smith, DR. GEORGE G. SMITH to MISS SUSAN HOWARD, daughter of the Rev. John Howard - all of Macon.

Sep. 27, 1832

Married on the 22d inst. by the Reverend Mr. Pope, MR. ALFRED M. HOBBY to MRS ANN ELIZA DANELLY, both of this place.

Married by Ephraim Kendrick Esq. on the 18th inst. ELIJAH S. OWENS ESQ. to MISS REBECCA T.E. SAUNDERS, all of the county of Houston.

Oct. 11, 1832

Married in this place, on the 4th inst. by the Rev. Mr. Pope, MR. FREDERICK SIMS, of Crawford County, to MRS. SUSAN WELLS.

Nov. 8, 1832

Married in Talbot County, on the 1st inst. by William Barron, Esq. WILLIAM R. DAVIS of Upson County, to MISS SARAH STALLINGS daughter of JAMES STALLINGS, ESQ.

Nov. 22, 1832

Married in Winchester, Connecticut, on the 24th ult. JOHN RUTHERFORD, JR., ESQ. of Macon Geo. to MISS CAROLINE HURLBUT, daughter of LEMUEL HURLBUT, ESQ.

Dec. 6, 1832

Married on Thursday evening the 15th ult. by B.P. Stubbs, Esq., MR. ZADOCK J. DANIEL of Macon, to MISS NANCY ANN WEST, of Baldwin County.

Jan. 3, 1833

Married on Thursday evening 20th inst. by the Rev. Thomas Samford, REV. THOMAS HUMPHRIES CAPERS to MISS JANE ANN, daughter of the late DOCTOR JAMES HAMILTON of Elbert.

Jan. 24, 1833

Married in Henry County, on Thursday evening the 10th inst. by Benjamin Cagle, Esq. MR. JOSHUA SHUPTRINE of Pike County, to MISS SARAH M. STEAGALL of the former place.

Married in this county, on the 17th inst. by Jehu Campbell, Esq. MR. JAMES CLACK to MISS NARCISSA BRITTINHAM.

Feb. 7, 1833

Married on the evening of the 30th of January, by the Rev. Charles Hardy, MR. SAMUEL W. HARRIS, of Harris County, to MISS ANN, the daughter of MR. ROBERT JACKSON, of Upson County.

Married on the evening of the 28th of January, by the Rev. Mr. Rayford, MR. NICHOLAS W. PERSONS, of Lagrange, Troup County, to MISS ELIZA, daughter of MR. THOMAS STANFORD, of Cullodensville, Monroe County.

Feb. 28, 1833

Married in Scottsborough, on Thursday evening the 21st instant, by the Rev. Mr. Lowrey, CAPT. LEWIS J. GROCE, merchant of East Macon, to MISS MARGARET GILBERT, of Scottsborough.

Mar. 7, 1833

Married on the 21st ult. by the Rev. William Mosely, DR. J.H. STARR, of Pleasant Grove, Henry County, to HARRIET J. eldest daughter of SAMUEL JOHNSON, ESQ. all of the above place.

Married on the 6th inst. at the Montpelier Springs, Monroe county, by the Rev. E. Holt, SAMUEL W. JACKSON, ESQ. of Augusta, to MISS CAROLINE AMERICA, daughter of the REV. CHARLES WILLIAMSON.

Apr. 4, 1833

Married in this city, on Thursday evening last, by Rev. Mr. Holt, MR. THOMAS WOOD to MISS MATILDA E. GRAVES, formerly of Sunderland, Mass.

Apr. 11, 1833

Married in Twiggs County, on Thursday evening, the 4th inst. by James N. Granberry, Esq. MR. ALEXANDER BELLAMY, of Brownsville, Monroe County, to MISS LODOISKI P. HARDIN, daughter of MAJ. JOHN HARDIN, of Twiggs County.

Apr. 18, 1833

    Married in this place on Wednesday evening last, by the Rev. Mr. Mitchell, MR. WILLIAM ROUNTREE of Augusta, to MRS. ELIZA A.M. ROBINSON of this city.

Apr. 25, 1833

    Married in Houston County, on the 28th March, by the Rev. Wm. Mizell, MR. L.D. McMILLAN, of Marion County, to MISS MARY P. daughter of MAJ. JOHN YOUNG, of Houston.

May 9, 1833

    Married in Clinton on the 1st instant, by the Rev. Miles Green, JOHN LAMGDON LEWIS, ESQ. to MISS MARTHA C. SMITH.

May 23, 1833

    Married in Monroe County, on Thursday last, the REV. ISAIAH LANGLEY to MISS CAROLINE, daughter of EDWARD CALLOWAY.

    Married in this city, on Wednesday night, by the Rev. Mr. Holt, MR. CHARLES DAY to MISS MARY CROCKER.

June 13, 1833

    Married in Monroe county, on Thursday evening last, by the Rev. Mr. Howard, MR. A.W. MARTIN of this city, to MISS EXER ANN SMITH, of the former place.

July 18, 1833

    Married in Savannah, on Wednesday evening the 10th instant, by the Rev. Mr. Preston, the HONORABLE JOHN MACPHERSON BERRIEN to ELIZA CECIL, oldest daughter of COL. JAMES HUNTER - all of that city.

Aug. 22, 1833

    Married near Milledgeville, on the 20th inst. by the Rev. Dr. Brown, MILLER BRIEVE, ESQ. Editor of the Southern Recorder, to MISS SARAH C. GRANTLAND, daughter of the late FLEMING GRANTLAND.

Sep. 19, 1833

    Married in this city on Tuesday evening, the 10th inst. by the Rev. Mr. Mitchell, MR. THOMAS S. HUNT, to MISS ANN ELIZA FRIERSON, both of this city.

Oct. 3, 1833

    Married on Monday evening 23d September, by the Rev. Dr. Spring, MR. THOMAS TAYLOR, of Macon, Geo. to MISS MARY H. daughter of MR. STEPHEN HOLT, of N. York.

Oct. 17, 1833

    Married in this county on the 10th inst. by William F. Clark, Esq. MR. WILLIAM B. JOHNSTON to MISS CAROLINE BAILEY.

    Married in Upson county, on the 9th inst., by William Robertson, Esq. MR. ABSALOM C. CLEVELAND of Crawford county, to MISS LUCINDA D. HARP of Upson.

Oct. 24, 1833

    Married on Thursday evening 17th inst. by the Rev. Mr. Mitchell, MR. JOHN HOLMES to MISS CAROLINE L. BIVINS.

Nov. 21, 1833

Married on Sunday evening the 17th inst. by Henry B. Hill, Esq. MR. GARLAND HIGHTOWER, to MISS MARTHA CUMBY, all of this county.

Dec. 12, 1833

Married in Upson County, on the 8th inst. by the Rev. Henry Hooten, at the residence of Ichabod Davis, Esq. MR. JAMES B. HOOTEN, of Talbot County, to MRS. CLARISSA L. GLINN, of Twiggs.

Dec. 19, 1833

Married on the 12th inst. by the Rev. Wm. C. Parker, MR. FREDERIC B. McNEAL, of Mobile, to MISS HENRIETTA J. POPE, of this county.

Jan. 30, 1834

Married on Thursday, the 23d inst. by the Rev. William Mizell, MR. ELDRIDGE S. RUTH to MISS MALINDA SMITH, all of Houston County.

Married in Twiggs County, on the 16th inst. by the Rev. James Lowery, MR. FREDERICK D. WIMBERLY, of Houston County, to MISS HARRIET M. daughter of HENRY BUNN ESQ. of Twiggs County.

Married on the 22d inst. by Josiah Daniel, Esq. DR. HENRY S. WIMBERLY, of Houston County, to MISS CAROLINE C. daughter of HARDY DURHAM, of Twiggs County.

Feb. 27, 1834

Married in Bibb County, on the 20th inst. MR. WILLIS H. HUGHES to MISS FRANCES M. BAGBY.

Mar. 6, 1834

Married in East Macon, on Thursday evening, the 20th ult. by the Rev. Mr. Holt, MR. DAVID J. DAVIS to MISS MARY ANN HOGE, all of East Macon.

Apr. 10, 1834

Married on Thursday morning the 3d instant, by Alexander H. Dougherty, Esqr. MR. DAVID SPENCER, merchant, to MISS JANE LEMON, both of Butts, Ga.

May 22, 1834

Married on Thursday evening last, in Bibb county, MR. JOHN BENNETT ROSE of this city, to MISS ANN LANE, daughter of MAJOR TARPLEY HOLT.

Married in Nansemond county, Va. on the 1st instant, MR. ZEPHANIAH T. CONNER, of this city to MISS LOUISA ANN GODWIN.

June 5, 1834

Married in Warrenton, on the 28th ult. by the Rev. P.N. Maddux, MR. WM. H. YOUNG, of Marion, to MISS ELLEN A. BEALL, of the former place.

Married in this place, by the Rev. Mr. Few, COL. THO. N. BEALL, of Forsyth, to MISS ANTOINETTE C. SCOTT.

June 19, 1834

Married by the Rev. E. Holt, on Thursday evening last, in Clinton, MR. JAMES JOHNSON, to MISS ANN HARRIS, both of that place.

July 3, 1834

    Married in Bibb county, on the 26th ult. MR. ZACH LAMAR, to MISS MARTHA A. RICE.

July 31, 1834

    Married in Macon on the 27th inst. MR. GEORGE W. _____ to MISS PIETY PRICHARD, both of this city.

Aug. 7, 1834

    Married in Twiggs co. on the evening of the 31st July, by the Rev. A.T. Holmes, MR. AMARIAH DANIEL, to MISS ELIZABETH CAROLINE PIERSON, daughter of MAJOR JAMES PIERSON.

Aug. 21, 1834

    Married on Monday evening last, by the Rev. Mr. Sinclair, COL. A.C. COLDWELL, formerly of Augusta, now of Macon to MISS MARY PAYNE, only daughter of MR. PAYNE of this city.

    Married in Twiggs county, on the 5th inst. by the Rev. Mr. Tharp, MR. ISAAC NORRIS of Bibb county, to MISS RUTHY M. ANDREWS daughter of ROBBINS ANDREWS ESQ. of the former county.

Aug. 28, 1834

    Married on the 21st August, by Matthew G. Jordan, Esq. MR. SAMUEL G. TINSLEY, formerly of Macon, to MISS PENELOPE LANE, of Monroe county.

Sep. 18, 1834

    Married in this county, on Sunday evening, September 14th, by the Rev. A.T. Holmes, MR. ROBT. P. ROBINSON, to MISS MARY ANN MORGAN, daughter of LUKE J. MORGAN, ESQ.

    Married in this city, on Tuesday morning, the 16th inst., by the Rev. Mr. Bragg, MR. WM. G. BROWN to MISS FRANCES JEANETT JONES.

Oct. 9, 1834

    Married on Thursday evening the 25th ult., by Wm. F. Clack, Esq. MR. WILLIAM HARRINGTON to MISS ELIZA JOHNSTON

    Married on Thursday evening the 2d instant, by the Hon. C.B. Strong, MR. JOSEPH J. HOLLEMAN to MISS MARTHA JOHNSTON. The ladies are twin sisters and daughters of WM. JOHNSON ESQ. of this county.

Oct. 16, 1834

    Married on the evening of the 9th inst. by the Rev. Mr. A.T. Holmes, MR. SAMUEL F. DICKINSON to MISS SUSAN W. COOKE, daughter of MR. COOKE, all of this city.

    Married in this city on the 12th inst. by the Rev. J.D. Mann, MR. ALBERT G. TUCKER of Fort-Gains (Georgia) to MISS REBECCA WYCHE of the former place.

Nov. 27, 1834

    Married on the evening of the 20th inst., by the Rev. Mr. Bragg, in Clinton, MR. F.S. JOHNSON, of this place, to MISS LUCIA, daughter of MR. SAMUEL GRISWOLD, of the former place.

    Married in Twiggs county, on Thursday evening 20th inst. by the Rev. C.A. Tharp, MR. ELISHA DAVIS, of Bibb county, to MISS MAZY G., only daughter of JOHN PARKER, of the former county.

Nov. 27, 1834

Married on Thursday evening last 20th instant, at the house of Col. Farish Carter, in Baldwin county, by the Rev. Mr. Sherwood, DR. MARCUS AURELIUS FRANKLIN, of this city, to MISS MARY LOUISA BOND, of Baldwin county.

Dec. 4, 1834

Married on Tuesday morning the 18th inst. by Judge Beall, MR. MIDAS L. GRAYBILL, of this city, to MISS MARY BAILEY, of Thomaston, Upson county.

Dec. 11, 1834

Married in Pike county, on Sunday the 7th inst. by the Rev. John Milner MR. JOHN NEAL, to MISS MARY JANE CAMPBELL, daughter of JAMES A. CAMPBELL.

Dec. 18, 1834

Married on Thursday evening, by the Rev. Mr. Bragg, MR. A.C. PARMELEE to MISS CATHARINE McCALLUM, of this city.

Jan. 15, 1835

Married in Upson county, on the 8th inst., at the house of Ichabod Davis, Esq., by the Rev. Henry Hooten MR. WILLIAM W. BATTLE to MISS PARSILLA C. WESTBROOK - all of said county.

Jan. 22, 1835

Married on the 13th inst. by the Rev. Mr. Everitt, MR. DANIEL SANFORD to MISS JULIA ANN, daughter of GEN. ELIAS BEALL, all of Forsyth, Monroe county.

Mar. 12, 1835

Married on Tuesday the 24th ult. in Athens, MR. JAMES D. FRIERSON, of Macon, to MISS MARGARET R.H. BOSTWICK of the former place.

Mar. 26, 1835

Married in Jones county, on the 23d inst. by C.A. Higgins, Esq. MR. JAMES DOYLE, to MISS MARY BROWN, both of Baldwin county.

Apr. 2, 1835

Married in this City, on the 1st inst. by the Rev. Adam Holmes, MR. THOMAS B. WARD, to MRS. JANE M. ROGERS, all of this city.

Apr. 9, 1835

Married in Talbot county, on Tuesday night, the 24th ult. by the Rev. Mr. Groves, MR. HARRISON M. OSGOOD, of Talbotton, to MISS SUSAN LEONARD.

May 14, 1835

Married in Monroe County, on the 26th ult. MR. GEORGE A. BROWN, of Milledgeville, to MRS. MATILDA ALISON, of the former place.

May 21, 1835

Married by the Rev. James E. Evans, the REV. RICHARD DOZIER, of Harris county, to MRS. LUCY CLEMENTS, of Monroe county.

June 4, 1835

Married in Twiggs county, on Thursday evening the 28th ult., by the Rev. John Hughs, MR. ETHELDRED GRIFFIN, to MRS. MALINDA CHILDERS.

June 11, 1835

    Married in Monroe county on the 28th ult., by the Rev. Thomas Battle, MR. JOSEPH GAINER, of this city, to MISS CINDERILLA, daughter of ARTHUR REDDING, ESQ. of that county.

    Married on Tuesday evening the 25th ult., by the Rev. Samuel Anthony, MR. JAMES N. OWENS, of Perry, to MISS LOUISA, daughter of ROBT. SANDERS, ESQ. of Houston County.

    Married in Columbus, on the 20th of May, by the Rev. Mr. Sanford, JAMES RANDAL JONES, to MISS ANN C. BOYKIN, daughter of JAMES BOYKIN.

July 2, 1835

    Married on the evening of the 25th inst. in Milledgeville by the Rev. Mr. Sinvlair, COL. N.B. WILLIAMS, of Macon, to MISS FRANCES L. ROBB, of the former place.

July 16, 1835

    Married in Greensboro, Georgia, on Thursday evening, 2d inst. by the Rev. Mr. Chappel, MR. WILLIAM M. MARTIN, of Augusta, to MISS JULIA E. NICHOLSON, of the former place.

July 23, 1835

    Married on the 19th inst., in Bibb county, by the Rev. Mr. Neal, MR. CAMPBELL RAYNFROUGH, of Crawford, to MRS. ELIZABETH VICTORY.

July 30, 1835

    Married in this place on the 15th inst. by the Rev. Mr. Bragg, DR. RICHARD McGOLDRICK, to MISS MARTHA L. MUNSON.

Aug. 6, 1835

    Married on 29th July, at Mount Vintage, Edgefield dist. S.C. by the Rev. Senaca G. Bragg, pastor of Christ Church Macon, Ga., MR. OSSIAN GREGORY of Macon, to MISS ANNA E., daughter of COL. CHRISTIAN BREITHAUPT.

Aug. 13, 1835

    Married in Scott County, on the 8th inst. by the Rev. Mr. _____, MR. THOS. W. SCOTT, a white man, to MISS ADELINE J. JOHNSON, a mulatto girl, and reputed, or acknowledged, daughter of the HONORABLE RICHARD M. JOHNSON, one of the Representatives of the State of Kentucky to the Congress of the United States.

    Married on Tuesday evening, 4th last, by the Rev. Mr. Ford, EDWARD D. TRACY, ESQ. to MISS REBECCA CAROLINE CAMPBELL, both of Macon.

Sep. 17, 1835

    Married in Forsyth on the 10th inst. MR. WILLIAM S. WILSON of Danville, Va. to MISS MARION M. LUMPKIN, daughter of H.H. Lumpkin, Esq.

Oct. 1, 1835

    Married on Monday evening last, at the residence of Wm. M. Morton, Esq. in this place, by the Rev. A. Church, MR. THEODERIC L. SMITH, of Macon, to MISS FRANCES A. BROADNAX, of Athens.

Oct. 8, 1835

    Married on the 13th of Sept. by the Rev. Z.H. Gordin, MR. WILLIAMSON WORTHY, to MRS. MARY PACE.

Oct. 8, 1835

   Married on the 20th of Sept. by the Rev. Z.H. Gordin, CAPT. SAMUEL
   WILSON, to MISS ELIZABETH HARP, daughter of DICKSON HARP, ESQ.

   Married on the first of Oct. by Philip Cunningham, Esq. MR. JOHN
   W. ROBERTSON, to MISS SUSAN BRIDGES, all of Upson county.

Oct. 29, 1835

   Married in this county on Thursday evening last by the Rev. Mr.
   Christian, MR. WILLIAM FOWLER of DeKalb, to MISS MARTHA WINBUSH.

   Married in this county on Friday evening 23 inst. by John Smith,
   MR. ABSALOM JAMES, to MISS CAROLINE YOUNGBLOOD of Twiggs county.

Nov. 5, 1835

   Married on Thursday evening, 29th ult., by Judge Collines, MR.
   NATHANIEL F. WALKER, to MISS SUSAN PALMER, all of Upson county.

   Married in Hanover, Va. at the residence of Mr. Wm. Pollard, on
   Tuesday the 21st inst. the HON. SEATON GRANTLAND, member of Congress
   from Georgia, to MISS CATHARINE M. DABNEY, daughter of the late
   CAPTAIN GEORGE DABNEY, of Hanover.

Nov. 22, 1835

   Married at the Baptist church, in this city, on Sunday morning
   last, by the Rev. Mr. Holmes, MR. SAMUEL S. VIRGIN, formerly of
   Concord, N.H. to MISS SARAH ANN, daughter of the REV. JOHN ELLIS,
   of Stamford, Conn.

Dec. 3, 1835

   Married on the 22d ult., in Twiggs county by the Rev. Mr. Mellson,
   the REV. JAMES R. LOWERY of Bibb county to MRS. BARBARA FRANK BROWN.

Dec. 10, 1835

   Married in this city, on Sunday evening the 6th inst., by the Rev.
   John W. Tally, MR. JOHN S. TRAVIS of Fayette county, to MISS ELDECIA
   PARKER, daughter of WM. C. PARKER, ESQ.

Dec. 17, 1835

   Married in Forsyth, Monroe county, on Tuesday the 8th inst. by the
   Rev. Jacob King, WILLIAM L. GWYN to MISS AMANDA F. eldest daughter
   of STEPHEN JONES, of S. Carolina.

   Married in Monticello on the 15th inst. MR. U.I. WRIGHT of this
   city to MISS MARY, daughter of JEREMIAH PIERSON.

Dec. 31, 1835

   Married in Putnam County, on the 23d inst., by the Rev. C.W. Key,
   MR. JOHN W. HAMPTON, to MISS MARY ANN LINCH.

Jan. 28, 1836

   Married in Macon on 21st (?) inst. by R.B. Washington, MR. PETER
   J. CARNES, to MISS EMILY S. CAMPBELL.

   Married in Macon on the 24th inst. by the Rev. John Howard, MR.
   THOMAS J. NEWTON, to MISS SARAH ANN RICHARDS, both of this city.

Feb. 25, 1836

   Married in Vineville, on the 18th inst. by the Rev. Mr. Sinclair,
   DR. J.B. WILEY, to MISS ANN G. CLOPTON.

Mar. 3, 1836

    Married in Fayetteville on the 22 ult. by the Rev. J.D. Mann, DR. J.I. EARLY to MISS ELIZABETH GARRISON.

Apr. 14, 1836

    Married in this city, on Tuesday evening, in the Baptist church, by the Rev. Mr. Holmes, MR. ROBERT KELTON to MRS. LUCINDA BIRD.

    Married on the 30th of March, by the Rev. Thomas Shelman, MR. WM. K. JOHNSTON, of Irwinton, Alabama, to MISS MORGIANAH NICHOLS, of Jefferson County, Georgia.

Apr. 21, 1836

    Married on Thursday evening, the 14th instant, by the Rev. W.H. Moseley, DR. THOMAS R. LAMAR, of Macon, (Georgia,) to MISS ELIZA W.W. LAMAR, daughter of JAMES LAMAR, ESQ. of Bibb County.

June 16, 1836

    Married in Crawford county, on Thursday the 9th inst. by R.B. Washington, Esq., JAMES MONROE ELLIS of this city, to MISS MARY F. WATSON, of the former county.

June 23, 1836

    Married on the 22d inst. by R.B. Washington Esq. MR. DANIEL F. CLARK, to MISS ELIZA CLARK, formerly of Augusta.

July 14, 1836

    Married in this County, on the 7th instant, by H.B. Hill, Esq. MR. LEIGHTON SOWELL, to MISS LUCY ANN HUGHES, all of this County.

Sep. 1, 1836

    Married in Perry, on the 18th inst. by the Rev. Noah Laney, MR. JOHN M. CHASTAIN to MISS SOPHIA, only daughter of the late COL. LITTLETON SPIVEY.

Sep. 8, 1836

    Married in this county on the 1st inst. by the Rev. Mr. Dunwoody, MR. WM. H. ELLISON, to MISS ANNA S. JOHNSON.

    Married in Monroe county on the 4th inst. by the Rev. Mr. Taylor, MR. WINFREY SHOCKLEY, to MISS ADELINE WILLIAMS.

Nov. 17, 1836

    Married in Savannah on the 8th inst. the REV. JOHN W. TALLY, to MISS ROSETTA B. RALSTON.

Dec. 1, 1836

    Married on Thursday, the 24th inst. in Columbia county, by the Rev. J.W. Reid, JOHN LAMAR ESQ. of this city, to MISS MARY LOUISA HILL.

Dec. 15, 1836

    Married on Thursday the 8th inst. by the Rev. S.G. Bragg, MR. THOMAS HARROLD to MISS MARY ANN BULLOCK, both of this city.

Dec. 29, 1836

    Married in Forsyth on the 21st inst. by Judge A.M.D. King, MR. ARCHIBALD NALL to MISS CORDELIA S. daughter of NICHOLAS WAGNER ESQ.

Jan. 12, 1837

Married in this City on the 10th inst., by the Rev. Adam T. Holmes, MR. ISAAC HOLMES of Columbus, to MISS LOUISA J. MOTT, of this city.

Jan. 19, 1837

Married in Bibb county, at the residence of Mr. Absalom Jordan, on the 10th ult. by the Hon. John Baily, MR. BARWELL PARKER to MISS NANCY JORDAN.

Jan. 26, 1837

Married in this City on the 24th inst. by the Rev. Mr. Holmes, MR. TREAT HINE of Milford, Conn. to MISS CHARLOTT SETTLES of Richmond, Va.

Married in Jones county, at the house of Joshua Harris, on Sunday the 22d inst. by the Hon. Jehu Campbell, MR. ELBERT MILLER of Stewart county to MRS. HARRIET S. HAMILTON, formerly of Macon.

Feb. 16, 1837

Married in Upson county on Tuesday night the 7th inst. by Edward Steward Esq. MR. McDANIEL SCOTT to MISS MARY HEATH all of this county.

Feb. 23, 1837

Married last evening, 22d February, by the Rev. Adam T. Holmes, CORNELIUS R. HANLEITER to MISS MARY ANN FORD, of New Haven (Conn.).

Mar. 2, 1837

Married in this city on the 23d inst. by the Rev. S.G. Bragg, MR. ALEXANDER H. FOSTER, to MISS ANN DUETT, both of this city.

Married in this County, on the 26th, by Henry B. Hill Esq. MR. JOHN C. SHEFFIELD to MISS NANCY WINSLOW.

Mar. 9, 1837

Married in this city on the 24th inst. by the Rev. A.T. Holmes, MR. J.M. FELD, to MISS MARTHA ANN JUSTISS, both of this city.

Mar. 30, 1837

Married in Jones county on Thursday the 23d inst. by the Hon. Jehu Campbell, MR. JAMES DENTON of this City, to MISS EMILY J. PHILIPS, daughter of MR. DAWSON PHILIPS of Jones County.

Married in Jones County on Sunday the 26th inst. by John R. Moore Esq. MR. JOHN W. POWERS of Hawkinsville, to MISS ELIZA ANN WADSWORTH of Jones County.

Married in this city, on Thursday evening last, by the Rev. Mr. Sinclair, MR. JOHN H. LUMPKIN, of Milledgeville, to MISS ANN JAMESON, daughter of DR. D. JAMESON of this city.

Apr. 13, 1837

Married in this City on the 12th inst., by the Rev. Mr. Holmes, MR. WILLIS T. SAGE, to MISS MARY GILMER, all of this city.

Apr. 27, 1837

Married in Upson county on Tuesday the 11th inst. MR. EDWARD S. MEADOWS of Eatonton, to MISS MARY ANN eldest daughter of MR. BENJAMIN WALKER of the former place.

May 4, 1837

Married in this City on the 1st inst. by the Rev. S.G. Bragg, MA. JOHN C.F. CLARK, to MISS ADELINE STEVENS, both of this City.

Married on the 25th inst. by the Rev. F.D. Lowry, MR. T. LEGRAND GUERRY, to MISS MARTHA HARRISON, all of Twiggs county.

May 11, 1837

Married in this city, on the 9th inst. by the Rev. Dr. Pierce, MR. CHARLES L. BASS of Columbus, to MISS REBECCA M. FLUKER.

May 25, 1837

Married on Tuesday evening, the 16th inst. by the Rev. Jordan Baker, MR. H. ROWE, of Fair Haven, Conn. to MISS MARGARET JANE MOORE, daughter of DR. THOS. MOORE of Dublin, Laurens county, Ga.

June 1, 1837

Married in Clinton on Thursday evening the 11th ult. by the Rev. Elijah Sinclair, MR. WILLIAM LOWTHER to MISS ELIZABETH S. GIBSON, all of Clinton.

June 8, 1837

Married in Milledgeville on the 4th inst. by the Rev. John W. Baker, MAJOR WILLIAM S. ROCKWELL, Editor of the Georgia Journal, to MISS REBECCA S. DAVIES.

July 20, 1837

Married in Vineville, this morning, by the Rev. S.L. Stevens, MR. GEO. P. COOPER to MRS. ELLEN C. WILSON.

Aug. 3, 1837

Married in this city on the 27th of July, by the Rev. A.T. Holmes, MR. E.D. WILLIAMS, to MISS ELIZA MOULTON.

Aug. 10, 1837

Married in this city on the 9th inst. by Judge Frederick Sims, MR. THOMAS H. BLOUNT, to MISS SARAH R. CLARKE.

Aug. 17, 1837

Married in Monroe County on the 10th inst. MR. STEPHEN LESUEUR to LUCY K. daughter of LARKIN WILSON of said county.

Aug. 24, 1837

Married in this county on the 17th inst. by P.B. McCready, Esq. MR. JAMES POWELL to MISS LUCINDA JACKSON.

Married in McDonough, at the residence of H. Varner Esq. on the 10th inst. by the Rev. Wm. A. Callaway, DR. ASA V. MANN, to MISS MARY ELLSWORTH, late of East Windsor, Connecticut.

Aug. 31, 1837

Married in Butts county on the 16th inst. by the Rev. J.Carter, DR. SNODDY of Jackson, to MISS MARY daughter of the late MR. ALLEN M'CLENDON of said county.

Sep. 7, 1837

Married on Tuesday the 5th inst. by the Rev. Mr. Cassels, MR. JOEL T. CHERRY, to MISS SUSAN McCALLUM, both of this city.

Sep. 7, 1837

   The marriage contract between MR. HARMAN DAVIS, of Wilkinson County, and MISS ELIZABETH McGRAW, of Bibb county, was solemnized by Absolam B. McGuire, Esq. on the 3d inst.

Sep. 28, 1837

   Married on the 26th inst. by the Rev. Mr. Bragg, HR. JOHN A. SPERRY, formerly of Waterbury, Conn. to MISS MARY McCALLUM, of this city.

Oct. 5, 1837

   Married in Monroe county on the 24th ult. by John Wooten, Esq. MR. L.W. HUNT, to MISS NANCY V. WARD.

   Married in Macon, on Thursday night 28th ult. by Wm. Cumming, Esq. MR. JAMES WILLBANK, formerly of Philadelphia, to MISS FRANCIS ARNOLD, of this place.

   Married in Monroe county on the 17 August, by S.H. Neal Esq. MR. BENJAMIN BRANTLY of Jones county, to MRS. SARAH SHOCKLY.

Oct. 12, 1837

   Married on Thursday the 21st ult. by the Rev. Mr. Hill, MR. JETHRO WILLIAMS to MISS SARAH McCALLUM both of Monroe county.

Oct. 19, 1837

   Married in Savannah, on the 5th inst., by the Rev. Stephen A. Mealy, EDWARD J. PURSE, of this city, to MISS ANN MARGARET ANDERSON, of Savannah.

Nov. 23, 1837

   Married on the 9th inst. by the Rev'd Mr. Anthony, MR. HENRY A. HARMAN to MISS AMANDA daughter of TURNER HUNT ESQ. all of Monroe County.

   Married at the residence of Williamston Archer, on Sunday the 12th inst. by Justice M. Buckner, GILES DRIVER ESQ. to MISS AMANDA E. SIMPSON (formerly of Powelton, Ga.) all of Marion county.

Dec. 7, 1837

   Married on Monday the 4th inst. at the residence of Col. S.T. Bailey, at Vineville Bibb county by the Rev. S.G. Bragg, MR. MILTON S. BAKER, to MISS CORNELIA B. YATES, Teacher of the Female Seminary at Forsyth Monroe county.

   Married on Wednesday the 6th inst. by the same, MR. EDWIN FORT of Talbotton, to MRS. MARY B. MUNSON, of Vineville.

Dec. 14, 1837

   Married in Troup County on Thursday the 3d ult. by the Rev. Mr. Harrison, MR. JOHN S. HOLMES of Barnesville Pike county, to MISS MATILDA daughter of JOHN HARDIN ESQ. of Troup Co.

Jan. 4, 1838

   Married in Houston County, on the 22d ult. by the Rev. Mr. Jenkins, the REV. ADAM T. HOLMES, of this city, to MRS. REBECCA G. NELSON.

   Married in this city, on the 3d inst. in the Episcopal church, by the Rev. Mr. Bragg, B. FRANKLIN SMITH of Charleston, to MISS SARAH L. daughter of the late COL. BREITHAUPT of S.C.

Jan. 4, 1838

    Married in St. Phillips church Charleston, MR. ALLEN P. OWEN of Upson county, Ga. to MISS EMELINE L. MATTHEWS.

Feb. 1, 1838

    Married on the 24th inst. by the Rev. Charles Harrison in Troup county, MR. WM. E. BOREN of Macon, to MISS MARIA A. DICKS.

Feb. 8, 1838

    Married on the 30th Jan. by the Rev. James Perryman, MR. WM. P. WOOD of Talbot Co., to MISS FRANCES E. GIBSON of Harris Co.

    Married at the house of Edward Latimer, in Randolph Co. Ala. on the 25th ult. by Jas. W. Furlow Esq., MR. ANDERSON J. LATIMER of Hancock Co. Ga., to MISS ELIZABETH A.T. WATTS of the former place.

Feb. 15, 1838

    Married on the 8th inst., by the Rev. J. Moultrie, MR. WM. JOHNSON, of Jones county, to MISS LOUISA, daughter of DAVID HOWARD, of Monroe county.

    Married in Twiggs county on the 13th inst. by the Rev. S.J. Cassels, COL. WM. W. WIGGINS, to MISS MARY ANN, daughter of COL. HENRY SOLOMON.

Mar. 8, 1838

    Married in Twiggs county, by the Rev. Mr. Cassells, on the 6th inst., MR. JAMES LAND, of this city, to MISS LUCRETIA FAULK.

    Married in Milledgeville on the 15th ult., WILKINS HUNT ESQ., of this city, to MISS JULIA ANN ROOT.

    Married in Randolph county, Ala. on the 22d inst. by the Rev. T.P.C. Shellman, MR. WILLIAM BARTON of Lafayette Ala. to MISS LURENA HATHOM. At the same time and place, MR. EDWARD McCOY of Lafayette Ala. to MISS LUCINDA HATHOM, both daughters of JAMES HATHOM of the former place.

Mar. 22, 1838

    Married in Vineville on Wednesday morning the 14th inst. by the Rev. S.G. Bragg, MR. THOMAS W. GATLIN, of Thomas county, to MISS MARTHA W. GATLIN, of the former place.

    Married in Christ Church, on the 20th inst., by the Rev. Mr. Bragg, MR. JOHN M. BURDINE of Athens, Ga., to MISS MARY ANN JONES, of this city.

Mar. 29, 1838

    Married in Eatonton, on the 15th inst. by the Rev. Mr. Green, COL. CHAS. J. MALONE, of Washington county, to MISS JANE A., daughter of the HON. IRBY HUDSON.

    Married in this county, on the 22d inst. by Jacob Johnson Esq., MR. D.B. HOGE to MISS ELENOR A., daughter of THOMAS HOWARD, all of Bibb county.

    Married in this City, on the 23d inst., in Christ Church, by the Rev. S.G. Bragg, MR. S.W. BENNETT, to MRS. MARTHA G. NEWCOMB.

Apr. 26, 1838

    Married on Thursday evening last, in Culloden, by the Rev. John J. Groves, MR. JAMES ALSTON of Monroe county, to MISS JANE NORWOOD.

May 10, 1838

   Married in Macon, on Sunday morning, the 6th inst. by the Rev.
   W.D. Matthews, MR. DUKE W. BRASWELL to MRS. CAROLINE S. BEALL,
   all of Macon.

May 24, 1838

   Married in Pulaski county, on the evening of the 21st inst. by
   Matthew Hodges, Esq., MR. ALEXANDER B. DUNEAN (?), of Albany,
   to MISS ELIZABETH ANN TAYLOR, of the former county.

   Married in Albany, on Thursday evening the 10th inst. by the Rev.
   Joshua Mercer, MR. NELSON TIFT, to MISS ANN MARIA MERCER, all of
   Albany.

   Married on Thursday the 17th inst. at the house of N.W. Collier,
   by the Rev. Jonathan Davis, H.B. GUNISON, to MISS SUSAN MALLARY,
   all of Albany.

May 31, 1838

   Married on the 29th inst. by the Rev. S.G. Bragg, MR. JOHN G.
   CREAGH, to MISS LUCRETIA PRATT, all of this City.

June 7, 1838

   Married on the 3d inst. by the Rev. Mr. Bragg, MR. WM. H. WALKER,
   of Forsyth, Ga. to MISS MARY A. SMITH, of this City.

   Married on the 31st ult. in this county, by the Rev. Mr. Anthony,
   MR. THOMAS NORRIS, of South Carolina, to MISS FRANCES E.A. MYRICK.

June 14, 1838

   Married in this city, on the 10th inst. by the Rev. Mr. Bragg,
   MR. WILLIAM A. GREEN, to MISS MARIAH L. JACOBS.

   Married by the Rev. Smith, on Monday last, the 4th inst. at the
   residence of Mr. Wiley Pope, in Oglethorpe county, MR. CHARLES R.
   GIBBS, of this City, to MISS MARTHA H. POPE.

June 21, 1838

   Married in Houston County on the 14th inst. by the Rev. Mr. Wade,
   MR. GEO. A. ROGERS of this city to MRS. MARY ANN WANNAMAKER, of
   Macon County, Ga.

June 28, 1838

   Married in Randolph county, (Ala.) on the 14th inst. by Jas. W.
   Furlow, Esq. MR. THOMAS K. SMITH, of Lafayette, to MISS ELIZA E.,
   daughter of HUGH HATHOM, ESQ. of Randolph.

July 12, 1838

   Married in Milledgeville on the 3d inst. by the Rev. Mr. Sinclair,
   JOHN T. LAMAR, ESQ., of this City, to MISS URIAH T. KENAN, of the
   former place.

   Married in Franklin Village, Upson County, on the 4th inst. by
   P. Cunningham Esq., MR. PHILIPS PIKE, to MISS HARRIET STORY, both
   of this County.

July 26, 1838

   Married on the 11th instant, at Christ Church, by the Rev. Seneca
   G. Bragg, MR. JACOB SHOTWELL, to MISS SATAH L. NEWHALL, daughter
   of ISAAC NEWHALL, ESQ. both of this city.

Aug. 2, 1838

Married on the evening of the 26th ult., by the Rev. Elijah Sinclair, MR. VIRGIL P. DUPONT of Florida, to MISS EMILY WHITLY, of Jones county.

Aug. 23, 1838

Married in McDonough, on the 9th inst., by the Rev. C.W. Key, MR. ANTHONY STOW, to MISS ADELINE, daughter of MAJ. T.W. KEY, of the former place.

Married on the 15th inst., by the Rev. Mr. Brown, MR. JESSE J. KENNEDY, to MISS CAROLINE S.M. STUBBS, all of this county.

Aug. 30, 1838

Married on the 21st inst. in Marion county, by the Rev. Dr. Powers, MR. DANIEL HIGHTOWER, to MISS MARTHA JANE, daughter of the REV. JOS. J. BATTLE.

Sep. 6, 1838

Married in this city on the 2d inst., by the Rev. E. Sinclair, the REV. C.W. KEY, of Milledgeville, to MISS ELIZABETH, daughter of COL. JAMES WIMBERLY, of this city.

Sep. 13, 1838

Married in McDonough, on the evening of the 2d inst. by the Rev. Mr. Callaway, MR. WM. WARREN, to MISS LYDIA STRICKLAND.

Married in McDonough, on the evening of the 11th Sept. by the Rev. Mr. Manson, MR. JOHN STILWELL to MISS ANN NOTTALL of McDonough.

Married in Henry county, on the evening of the 4th Sept. by the Hon. Chas. L. Holmes, MR. MENON N. TURNER, to MISS HAMILL - all of Henry county.

Sep. 20, 1838

Married in this county, on Tuesday evening, the 18th inst. by the Rev. E. Sinclair, MR. WILLIAM W. TRIPPE, of Culloden, to MISS ANN ELIZA BIVINS, daughter of ROLLEN BIVINS, of this county.

Oct. 4, 1838

Married on the 2d inst. by the Rev. Samuel J. Cassels, MR. JOHN P. LORD, to MISS MARY ANN FLANDERS, both of East Macon.

Oct. 18, 1838

Married in Guilford Conn. on the 3d inst. by the Rev. Mr. Darkin, MR. EDMUND RUSSELL, of this city, to MISS ELIZA A. KIMBERLY, of the former place.

Married in Butts County, on the 11th ult., by the Rev. Mr. Ogletree, THOMAS J. McMULLEN, of Spring Place, to MISS MARY ANN D., daughter of JOSEPH P. KEY ESQ., of the former place.

Married in Milledgeville, Ga. on the 3d inst. by the Rev. Mr. Brantly, of Charleston, S.C. JOSEPH W. WILSON, of Montgomery Ala. to MISS AMANDA LAWRENCE, youngest daughter of GEORGE R. CLAYTON, ESQ.

Married in Jackson, on the 4th inst. by Calvin Goins Esq. MR. PALMER A. HIGGINS, to MISS JANE HEADSPETH.

Oct. 25, 1838

Married on the 17th inst. by the Rev. E. Sinclair, MR. DAVID REID, to MRS. ELVIRA P. ARMS, both of this City.

Oct. 25, 1838

   Married in Houston county, by Wm. L. Hunt, Esq. MR. GEO. W. VINSON to MISS MARY, daughter of the REV. BRYAN BATEMAN.

   Married on Thursday, the 18th inst. MR. WM. A. ROSS, of this city, to MISS MARY ANN, daughter of COL. WM. C. REDDING, of Monroe county.

Nov. 1, 1838

   Married in this city, on Sunday last in the Presbyterian Church, by the Rev. S.J. Cassels, MR. WLAM ALEXANDER, to MRS. ANN G. STONE, of Savannah.

Nov. 22, 1838

   Married in Houston county, on the 15th inst., by the Rev. Mr. Speight, COL. EDMUND BLAKE, of this city, to MRS. ELEANOR HARRIS, of Houston.

Nov. 29, 1838

   Married on the 22d Nov. by the Rev. Chas. A. Brown, MR. JOHN W. JOHNSTON to MISS SUSAN A.M. SANDERS, all of Talbot County, Georgia.

Dec. 6, 1838

   Married on the 20th ult. in Randolph county, Ala. by James W. Furlow Esq. MR. THOMAS C. PINCKARD of Heard county, Geo. to MISS FRANCES ELIZA ROBINSON of Ala.

Dec. 27, 1838

   Married in Upson county on Thursday the 20th inst. by Thos. Beall Esq. MR. JOHN TRAYLOR to MISS LUCINTHA JANE READING daughter of the REV. ARTHUR READING, of Monroe county.

   Married on Thursday evening the 6th inst. by the Rev. Mr. Kickenson, MR. A.D. STEEL of Talbot County to MISS ADELINE, daughter of ALEX PERKINS ESQ. of Monroe county.

   Married in this city on the evening of the 24th inst. by the Rev. S.G. Bragg MR. COLLIN MULHOLLAND, to MISS ADELINE S. HUNT.

Jan. 3, 1839

   Married on Tuesday evening the 1st by the Rev. Dr. Andrews MR. ROBERT PHILIP, of Augusta, to MISS ISABELLA M. CURBOW of this place.

   Married in this city on the evening of the 30th inst. by C.A. Higgins Esq. MR. HENRY CLARKE, to MISS MARY RILEY, daughter of WM. RILEY ESQ. all of this County.

Jan. 17, 1839

   Married in this City on the 15th inst. by the Rev. Mr. Baker of Milledgeville, the REV. SAMUEL J. CASSELS, Pastor of the Presbyterian Church in this City, to MRS. SARAH ANN WALLIS.

Jan. 24, 1839

   Married in Monroe county on Thursday the 17th inst., by the Rev. Mr. Slaughter, MR. R.Y. OUSLEY of Culloden, to MISS ELIZABETH CALDWELL.

   Married on the 15th instant, by the Rev. S.G. Bragg, S.M. STONE, ESQ., to MISS MARY ELLA NIXON.

Jan. 24, 1839

    Married at the same time by the Rev. E. Sinclair, MR. MURDOCK McKASKILL, of South Carolina, to MISS ELIZA ANN NIXON - daughters of COL. WM. NIXON of Vineville

Feb. 7, 1839

    Married in Twiggs county, on the 24th Jan. by the Rev. C.A. Tharp, THOMAS LOWE, ESQ. of Jones county, to MISS ELLEN THARP, daughter of WM. A. THARP.

Feb. 28, 1839

    Married in Crawford county on the 19th inst. by the Rev. John P. Dickerson, MR. SOLOMON L. POPE, of Haynesville, Ala. to MISS JOANNA E. TROUTMAN.

    Married on the 13th inst. by the Rev. C.W. Key, MR. ROBERT H. RAINES, of Twiggs county, Ga. to MISS MARTHA F., daughter of COL. MICHAEL WATSON, of Edgefield District, South Carolina.

Mar. 28, 1839

    Married in Forsyth on Sunday evening the 24th inst. by D. Sanford Esq. MR. ALEXANDER BELLAMY to MISS LOUISA M. HILL.

Apr. 11, 1839

    Married at Culloden on Wednesday evening the 3d inst., by the Rev. Mr. Slaughter, DOCT. JOHN C. DRAKE of Nashville, N.C. to MISS MARY ANN FLEWELLEN of the former place.

Apr. 18, 1839

    Married in Twiggs county on the 11th inst. by the Rev. C. Thrap, MR. GEO. Y. LOWE of Macon county, to MISS LUCINDA THARP, daughter of JEREMIAH THARP, ESQ. of Twiggs county.

    Married on Wednesday evening the 10th inst. by the Rev. Mr. Smith, MR. R.H. HARDAWAY of this city, to MISS ELIZABETH, daughter of NATHANIEL MITCHELL, ESQ. of Thomas county.

May 2, 1839

    Married in this City on Sunday morning, the 28th inst. by the Rev. S.G. Cassels, MR. GEORGE W. JONES, to MISS MALVINA HOLLINGSWORTH, all of this City.

    Married in Upson county on Thursday the 25th inst. by the Rev. Obediah Gibson, MR. THOMAS T. WYCHE of this City, to MISS ADELINE W. daughter of MR. THOMAS B. GREEN.

    Married in Campbell county on the 25th inst. by the Rev. Joseph Moultrie, MR. JOSEPH GAINER of this City, to MISS MARGARET BEALL.

    Married in Monroe county on the 21st inst. by the Rev. W. Perryman, MR. THOS. W. CARROLL of Monroe county to MRS. FRANCES CAMPBELL of Talbot.

May 9, 1839

    Married on Sunday evening the 5th inst. by the Rev. S.J. Cassels, MR. DANIEL T. REA of this city, to MISS LOUISA G. CRAIG of Columbia, South Carolina.

    Married in Sumter county on the 18th April, at the residence of Col. Richard Picett, MR. SEABORN A. SMITH, of Cuthbert, to MISS NANCY REYNOLDS, daughter of LARKIN REYNOLDS of Stewart County.

May 23, 1839

   Married in Houston county on the 9th of April, by the Rev. James
   Hudson, GEO. R. CLAYTON, of Milledgeville, to MISS HARRIET A.R.,
   daughter of STERLING C. WILLIAMSON, formerly of South Carolina.

   Married on the 16th inst., near this city, by the Rev. E. Sinclair,
   MR. GEORGE W. BIVINS, to MISS ELIZABETH S., daughter of COL. ELBERT
   CALHOUN - all of this county.

   Married in Monroe county on the 14th inst. by the Rev. N.G. Slaughter,
   MR. WILEY FERRELL (?), of Crawford county, to MISS SUSANNAH, daughter
   of WARREN BARROW.

June 13, 1839

   Married at Culloden, on the 11th inst. by the Rev. Mr. Slaughter,
   MR. JOHN T. BROWN, to MISS MARY ANN OUSLEY.

June 27, 1839

   Married in Talbot county, on Tuesday evening last, by the Rev. B.
   Searcy, MR. M.E. RYLANDER, of this city, to MISS SARAH C. BROWN.

July 11, 1839

   Married in this place, on the 4th inst. by J.R. Perry Esqr. MR.
   WM. SAUNDERS, to MISS ALAH LUCAS.

Aug. 1, 1839

   Married on the 25th inst. by C.A. Higgins Esq. MR. THEODORE HARBRUM,
   to MISS MARTHA TERRY.

   Married in Thomaston on Wednesday evening, the 27th inst. by the
   Rev. N.G. Slaughter, MR. JAS. F. WHITE of that place to MISS LOUISA
   A. DRAKE, of Nashville, N.C.

Aug. 8, 1839

   Married on the 25th ult. by Charles Powell Esq. MR. JOSEPH E.
   KNOWLES to MISS MARY ANN daughter of THOS. SWEARENGEN ESQ. all of
   Dooly County.

   Married in Macon County on the 25th ult. by Robert Grier Esq. MR.
   ABEL HOLTON of Bristol to MISS RACHEL JANE daughter of WILLIAM
   RUSHIN ESQ.

Aug. 15, 1839

   Married in this county on the 8th inst. by Jehu Campbell, Esq. MR.
   SOLOMON R. JOHNSON, to MISS VASHTI JOHNSTON, daughter of the late
   WM. JOHNSTON, all of this county.

   Married in Vineville, on Tuesday the 8th inst. at 7 o'clock A.M.
   by the Rev. J.H. Campbell, COL. JOHN L. HODGES of Twiggs county,
   to MISS MARY B. HAMILTON daughter of MAJ. WM. HAMILTON.

   Married in Monroe county, on the 8th inst., by the Rev. M. Dickerson,
   MR. JOHN R. CANDLER, to MISS MARY A. MILLER, all of Monroe.

Aug. 22, 1839

   Married in this city on the 20th inst. by the Rev. Elijah Sinclair,
   MR. LARKIN GRIFFIN, to MISS ELIZABETH ROSSETER - all of this city.

Aug. 29, 1839

   Married in this City, on Tuesday evening, the 27th inst. by Jehu
   Campbell, Esq. MR. GEORGE J. LUNSFORD, (printer) to MISS MARIA
   MATTHEWS, all of this City.

Sep. 12, 1839

Married on the 4th inst. by the Rev. S.G. Bragg, DANIEL GRIFFIN, ESQ. Chief Engineer of the Monroe Rail Road, to MISS NARCISSA POWERS, daughter of JOHN POWERS ESQ. of Monroe county.

Sep. 19, 1839

Married on the 18th inst. at the Episcopal Church, by the Rev. S.G. Bragg, AUGUSTUS P. BURR, to MISS CATHARINE BEASLEY.

Sep. 26, 1839

Married on Wednesday 18th inst., by the Rev. John Milner, MR. JONATHAN J. MILNER to MISS SARAH M.D. SHIVERS, all of Pike county.

Married on the 19th inst. by the Rev. John Milner, MR. ISAAC P. ESKEW to MISS MIREUM M. MILNER, all of Pike Co.

(LEGAL NOTICE: WHEREAS, by and in virtue of a marriage settlement made, concluded, and agreed upon between the late JOHN MONTFORD, of Wilkes county in the State of Georgia, and SUSANNAH STONE, daughter of the late THOMAS STONE of Glynn county and the State aforesaid, bearing date the 26th February, A.D., 1796, a certain Negro Woman named Harriet, and her issue which now consists of a negro man named Titus, a boy named Will, a boy named Toney, a woman named Diannah and her two children, and a young woman named Caroline, now in the possession of the said SUSANNAH, of Crawford county in the State aforesaid, widow of the late LEMUEL TRANUM, formerly widow of the said JOHN MONTFORD...

Oct. 3, 1839

Married in Upson County on the 26th inst. by Thomas Beall Esq. MR. SIMEON BROOKS of Monroe County to MISS LOUISA C. BUTTS daughter of CAPT. HENRY BUTTS.

Married on Thursday the 26th September by Rev. George F. Pierce, MR. I.E. FORT to MISS LAURA P.M. WIMBERLY, all of this city.

Oct. 17, 1839

Married on Wednesday evening the 2d inst. in Houston County by the Rev. Jehu Humphries JOHN MASON GILES ESQ. of Lanier to MISS HARRIET NEWELL daughter of the REV. SAMUEL JENKINS.

Oct. 24, 1839

Married in Thomaston on the 17th inst., by Thomas Beall Esq. MR. JAMES ANDREWS, to MISS ACHSAH (?) M. HOLLOWAY, daughter of CAPT. EDWARD HOLLOWAY, all of Upson county.

Oct. 31, 1839

Married in Crawford Co., on the 23 inst. by the Rev. S.W. Durham, H.W. BRONSON of Macon, to MISS MARIA A. DuBOSE of the former place.

Married on Wednesday the 2d inst., in New York, by the Rev. Dr. McCauley, COL. JOHN D. WATKINS of Elbert Co. Ga. to MISS ELLEN AUGUSTA HUNT, of that city.

Married on Wednesday the 9th inst. by the Rev. Dr. McCauley, MR. JAMES C. EDWARDS of this city, to MISS ELIZABETH G. HUNT, of New York.

Married in Crawford Co. on the 24th inst., by the Rev. Mr. Dickinson, DR. WM. A. MATTHEWS of Monroe Co. to MISS MARY ANN, daughter of JAMES A. MILLER of the former place.

Oct. 31, 1839

    Married by the Rev. Dr. Empire, on the 12th inst. at the house of Dr. John Brockenborough, of Richmond Va. CHAS. J. McDONALD, ESQ. of this city, to MRS. ELIZA RUFFIN, youngest daughter of the late JUDGE SPENCER ROANE.

Nov. 7, 1839

    Married on the 31st October, by the Rev. W.H. Ellison, MR. DUKE HAMILTON HAYES of Thomas county, to MISS SARAH ANN MUNSON of Vineville.

    Married in Forsyth on Thursday evening the 31st Oct., by the Rev. John Winn, ROBERT L. RODDEY M.D., to MISS ANN E.C. DUNN.

    Married on Sunday evening the 3d inst., by the Rev. Mr. Dickinson, MR. TIMOTHY M. FURLOW to MISS MARGARET ELLA, second daughter of MAJOR TARPLY HOLT, all of Bibb county.

    Married near Clinton, on the evening of the 30th ult. by the Rev. S.J. Cassels, JOHN J. GRESHAM, ESQ. of Macon, to MISS CATHARINE B. daughter of DR. A.H. FLEWELLEN, of Jones county.

    Married in Monroe county, on the 31st ult., by Daniel Sanford Esq. MR. ALBERT E. SINCLAIR, to MISS ELIZABETH E. OWEN.

    Married in this county on the 3d inst., by the Rev. G.F. Pierce, MR. CLABERN WALL, of North Carolina, to MISS AMERICA GROCE, of this county.

Nov. 14, 1839

    Married on the 12th inst., by the Rev. S.J. Cassels, MR. THOMAS K. MILLS, to MISS ELEANOR WOODWORTH, both of this place.

    Married on Sunday evening, 3d Nov. in Louisville, by the Rev. Joseph Polhill, HENRY P. WATKINS to FRANCES ADELINE youngest Daughter of ARTHUR SIKES ESQ., all of Louisville.

Nov. 21, 1839

    Married in this City, on the evening of the 19th inst., by the Rev. Mr. Bragg, MR. MARTIN L. HARDIN, to MISS SARAH E. MACON.

Nov. 28, 1839

    Married in this city, on the 21st inst. by the Rev. George F. Pierce, MR. JOSEPH A. WHITE, to MISS MARTHA A. BALDWIN.

    Married in this city, on the 24th inst. by the Rev. Mr. Ellison, MR. GEORGE JEWETT, to MISS EUNICE FREEMAN.

    Married at Midway, near Milledgeville, Baldwin county, on Tuesday evening, the 19th inst., by the Rev. S.K. Talmage, MR. JOSEPH WOODS, of Hamburg, S.C., to MISS ELLEN HAMMOND, of the former place.

Dec. 5, 1839

    Married in this City, on Sunday morning the 1st inst., at the Episcopal Church, by the Rev. S.G. Bragg, MR. ELIHU PRICE, to MISS JULIA FORD, of New Haven Connecticut.

    Married in Talbot county on the 24th November, by the Rev. Jas. R. Thomas, MR. THOS. B. TOOKE, to MISS ELLEN E. WILLIAMS.

    Married in Clinton, on Sunday evening, 1st inst., by Major John R. Moore, MR. JOSEPH CHILES, to MISS SARAH A. GRIEVE, both of that place.

Dec. 5, 1839

    Married in Thomaston, on Thursday evening the 28th ult., by the Rev. O.C. Gibson, MR. GEORGE L.F. BIRDSONG, to MISS SUSAN F., daughter of the REV. THOS. THWEATT, all of that place.

Dec. 12, 1839

    Married at the residence of Mrs. Pope, near Forsyth, on the 5th inst. by Daniel Sanford, COL. JOSEPH M. EVANS, of Madison, to MRS. SUSAN A. LOCKETT, of Monroe county.

Dec. 19, 1839

    Married on Sunday the 15th inst. in the Presbyterian Church in this city, by the Rev. S.J. Cassels, MR. SETH HART, of Avon, Conn., to MISS MATILDA J. MILLS, daughter of the late COL. TIMOTHY MILLS of New York.

    Married in Florence on Sunday evening the 8th inst., by the Rev. Thomas Gardner, MR. HARMON H. BARROW, (late one of the Editors of the Georgia Mirror,) to MISS MARY ANN ELIZABETH, youngest daughter of WM. STAFFORD ESQ. all of this place.

Dec. 26, 1839

    Married on the 17th inst. by the Rev. S.G. Bragg, of this city, MAJOR ROBERT O. USHER to MISS FRANCES A. COLBERT, both of Covington, Newton Co. Ga.

    Married on the 19th inst. by the Rev. Mr. Bragg, MR. E.D. WILLIAMS, to MISS EMILY MENARD, all of this city.

    Married at Oak Grove, Jones county, on the 24th inst. COL. URIAH J. BULLOCK, of this city, to MRS. SARAH S. COX, of the former place.

Jan. 2, 1840

    Married at the residence of Mr. James R. Daniel by the Rev. Mr. Mooney, MR. JOHN C. DANIEL to MISS REBECCA A. GIBSON of Sumter county.

    Married in East Macon on the 27th ult. by James Denton Esq. MR. RICHARD J.H. PORTER, to MISS FRANCES AMANDA ROGERS.

Jan. 16, 1840

    Married in this City on the 25th Dec. by the Rev. S.J. Cassels, MR. GEORGE KING of Florida, to MISS FANNY R. GRAVES of this City.

    Married in this City, on Tuesday evening the 14th inst. by the Rev. Geo. F. Pierce, MR. B.F. ROSS, to MISS MARTHA J. CHILDERS - all of this city.

Jan. 23, 1840

    Married on Thursday evening last, by the Rev. Mr. Ellison, MR. H.P. REDDING, to MRS. PRISCILLA A. HAWFIELD, of Vineville.

Feb. 6, 1840

    Married in this city on the 4th inst., by the Rev. Samuel J. Cassels, MR. ALEXANDER SCOTT, of Brunswick, Ga., to MISS MARGARET WILLIAMS, of this city.

Feb. 20, 1840

    Married on Tuesday evening, the 11th inst. by the Rev. A.T. Holmes, DR. MILES K. HARMAN, of Dooly county, to MISS LAVINIA A. HOLLINSHED, of Macon county.

Mar. 5, 1840

Married in this county, on the 26th ult., by the Rev. Jonathan Neel, MR. ZACHARIAH SNEED, of Crawford county, to MISS A.G. GILBERT, daughter of EDMOND GILBERT ESQ.

Married on Sunday the 1st inst. in this city, by the Rev. S.G. Bragg, MR. TERENCE CODY of Forsyth, to MISS ANN TOBIN of this city.

Married in this City, on the 3d inst. by E.E. Brown Esq. MR. GEORGE W. CRAFT, to MISS SARAH BEARD, all of this County.

Mar. 12, 1840

Married in this city, on Thursday evening last, by the Rev. Sam'l J. Cassels, DR. G. McDONALD, of this city, to MISS HARRIET A. NORTH, of Hartford, Conn.

Married in Wetumpka, (Ala.) on Tuesday evening the 18th February, by the Rev. Mr. Holman, MAJ. F. HAYES, to MRS. MARTHA STONE, both of that city.

Apr. 2, 1840

Married March 26th, in Twiggs county, Ga. by Thos. Glover Esq., DR. A.T. CALHOUN, to MISS LAVINIA C. PERRY.

Apr. 9, 1840

Married in this City, on Thursday evening the 2d inst. by the Rev. Mr. Bragg, MR. GEO. D. COMBS, to MISS EVELINA BULLOCK, all of this city.

Married in this City on Tuesday morning the 7th inst., by Robert B. Washington, Esq. MR. THADEUS W. BRANTLEY, of Jones county, to MISS ANN E. HALL, of this city.

Apr. 16, 1840

Married in this county on Thursday evening, the 9th inst. by the Rev. Wm. H. Ellison, MR. A.F. SHERWOOD, of this city, to MISS MARTHA EARNEST.

Apr. 23, 1840

Married on Tuesday the 21st inst., by the Rev. S.G. Bragg, MR. JAMES J. FLANDERS, of this city, to MISS MARY B. HARRISON, of Jones county, Ga.

May 14, 1840

Married in Websterville, on Sunday evening, the 10th inst. MR. ISAAC S. MERRIAM to MISS JOSEPHINE BEARD, both of Bibb county.

May 28, 1840

Married in Twiggs county on Sunday morning, 17th inst. by Thomas Glover, Esq. TILLMAN R. DENSON, ESQ. to MISS TEMPERANCE, the fourth and last daughter of the late THOMAS ARRINGTON ESQ.

July 2, 1840

Married in East Hampton Mass. June 17, by the Rev. Mr. Bement, MR. S.F. WILLIAMS, of Springfield, (Cabotville) to MISS MARY FEDELIS, youngest daughter of E.B. BLOOD ESQ. of East Hampton.

July 16, 1840

Married near this City, on the 13th instant, by the Rev. Mr. Cassels, MR. ALEXANDER MELROSE, to MISS CHRISTIANA McLEOD.

July 23, 1840

    Married on the 21st inst. by the Rev. Mr. Bragg, MR. DAVID B. HAMILTON, to MISS THEODOSIA MUNSON, both of Vineville, Bibb county.

    Married on Thursday evening last, by the Rev. Mr. Cassels, FRANCIS R. SHACKELFORD ESQ. of Darien to MISS ELIZA M. BLOOM of this city.

Aug. 20, 1840

    Married in Monroe county, on the 16th of July, by the Rev. Levi Parks of Ala., MR. GEORGE W. COOK to MISS LETTY JONES, all of Monroe.

    Married in Zebulon, Pike county, on the 23d of July, by Isaac C. Parks, Esq. of Monroe, MR. JOHN W. EMPINGER, of the latter place, to MISS AMANDA B. WAGNER, of the former place.

    Married in this city, on Sunday the 2d inst., by the Rev. Mr. Cassels, at the Presbyterian Church, MR. LUCAS McCALL, to MISS MARTHA PATTON.

Sep. 17, 1840

    Married in Monroe County on Tuesday evening the 1st inst. by the Rev. Wyatt R. Singleton, MR. WM. HENRY SHARP of Forsyth to MISS ELIZABETH J. second daughter of MR. ALEXANDER PICKENS, all of Monroe County.

Sep. 24, 1840

    Married on Tuesday evening the 8th inst. by the Rev. Spencer Mattison, MR. BRADFORD T. CHAPMAN of Warrenton, to MISS ELIZABETH A. daughter of AMBROSE CHAPMAN, ESQ. of this city.

    Married on the 15th inst. by the Rev. Wm. Hunter, MR. A.J. PSALTER of Coose county, Ala. to MISS AMANDA J. daughter of J.B. WHATLEY ESQ. of Chambers county Ala.

Oct. 1, 1840

    Married on Tuesday evening, the 22d ultimo, by the Rev. G.W. Persons, A.M. SPEER, ESQ. to MISS MARY ANN daughter of REV. THOMAS BATTLE - all of Culloden.

Oct. 8, 1840

    Married in this city, on the 3d July, by the Rev. Philo Brownson, MR. HENRY PIKE to MRS. ANN BRADLY.

Oct. 15, 1840

    Married in Harris county, on the 22d September, MR. JOS. C. SALE, of Forsyth, Monroe county, Geo. to MISS SAMANTHA N. second daughter of GEORGE OSBORN.

    Married in Perry, Houston county, on Wednesday, the 30th Sept. by the Rev. Wm. H. Ellison of Macon DR. P.B.D.H. CULLER, recently of Orangeburg District, S.C. to MISS MARY S. only daughter of COL. HOWELL COBB, of Perry.

    Married in this city, on the 12th inst., by James Denton, Esq., JEHU CAMPBELL, ESQ., to MISS ELIZA M. RUTLAND.

Oct. 22, 1840

    Married on Tuesday the 13th inst., by the Rev. Mr. Holmes, MR. WILLIAM W. CHAPMAN, of this city, to MISS CAROLINE M., daughter of MR. JAMES D. LESTER, of Cullodens, Monroe county.

Oct. 22, 1840

   Married in Monroe county, on the 15th inst., by the Rev. Mr. Bragg, MR. GEORGE W. PRICE, of this city, to MISS CAROLINE W. KELSEY, of the former place.

Nov. 5, 1840

   Married on the 27th inst. by Judge J.G. Jordan, at his residence, DR. J.M. PARSONS to MISS LEONORA C. daughter of CAPT. L.B. LUCAS, all of Monroe county.

   Married on the 22d ult. by the Rev. Mr. Stell, DR. A. MEADORS to MISS SARAH E. BRAGG, all of Fayetteville, Fayette county, Ga.

   Married in Edgefield District, S.C., MR. JOHN J. WIMBERLY of Houston, Ga., to MISS ELLEN WATSON, of S.C.

Nov. 12, 1840

   Married in this city, on the 29th ult. by the Rev. James Graham, MR. WILLIAM C. KENNEDY, to MISS ELLEN B. GALLAGHER, both of this city.

   Married in Vineville, on the evening of the 10th inst. at the house of Hardy Solomon, Esq. by the Rev. C.A. Tharp, MR. ROBERT FULTON, to MISS LOUISA MELTON, all of said county.

Nov. 26, 1840

   Married on the 10th inst. by the Rev. George Granberry, MR. JOHN H. RUTHERFORD of Houston county, to MISS MINERVA D., eldest daughter of the late HARDY CRAWFORD, of Harris county.

Dec. 31, 1840

   Married in East Macon, on the 15th inst. by Rev. Dr. Curtis, MR. HENRY L. COOK to MISS S.G. DURRETT, both of East Macon.

   Married in Talbot County, on the 24th inst. by the Rev. H. Powell, MR. WADE H. FULLER, of Bibb county, to MISS MARTHA E., youngest daughter of SAMUEL FULLER.

Jan. 7, 1841

   Married in Baldwin county, on the evening of the 24th November, by Judge Goddard, MR. RICHARD BLOW, of Jones county, to MISS MARTHA H. HARRIS, of Baldwin.

Jan. 14, 1841

   Married, Dec. 3d 1840, in Twiggs Co. Ga. by Elder A.T. Holmes, ELDER C.D. MALLORY, to MRS. MARY T. WELCH.

   Married in Monroe county, on the 24th of December, by the Rev. Gabriel Christian, MR. HENRY P. CHRISTIAN to MISS SUSAN K. daughter of MR. THOMAS HATHORN.

Jan. 21, 1841

   Married on the 14th instant, by the Rev. George F. Pierce, MR. DAVID S. GRIMES, to MISS MARY S., daughter of HENRY G. ROSS, ESQ. all of this City.

Feb. 4, 1841

   Married on Thursday evening last, by John Bailey Esq., MR. ISAAC J. NEWBERRY to MISS AMARETTA S. Daughter of IRWIN BULLOCK, all of Bibb county.

Feb. 4, 1841

> Married on Tuesday evening the 19th inst., by Edmond Chambless Esq. COL. MORDICAI S. BENTON to MISS MARY ANN HOWARD, daughter of JOHN HOWARD ESQ. all of Monroe county.
>
> Married on Thursday 28th January, by C.A. Higgins Esq. MR. GOTTLEB ZIMMERMAN, to MISS WINNEFORD HAMILTON MONUK, also MR. JOHN DIEDRICK to MISS SUSAN ADELINE MONUK, all of this City.

Feb. 18, 1841

> Married near Warrenton, on the 4th inst. by the Rev. Mr. Maddox, MR. MILLER W. McCRAW, of Monroe county, to (MRS.)? CYNTHIA FLEMING, of Warren county, Ga.

Mar. 4, 1841

> Married in this city, on the 1st instant, by the Rev. Geo. F. Pierce, CAPTAIN ABSALOM D. POWELL, to MISS CATHERINE LIDDEN - all of this city.

Mar. 11, 1841

> Married in Monroe county, on the 2d inst., by the Rev. Geo. F. Pierce, MR. HENRY L. JEWETT of this City to MISS MARTHA HOWARD.

Mar. 25, 1841

> Married in Monroe county, on the 16th inst. by the Rev. Osborn Rogers, MR. STEPHEN D. CHAPMAN, of this city, to MISS CAROLINE E. JACKSON, of Monroe county.

Apr. 15, 1841

> Married in Thomaston, on the 25th of March, by the Rev'd Samuel Harwell, DR. WILLIAM E. ALLEN, to MISS ANTOINETTE E., daughter of GEN. THOMAS BEALL.
>
> Married by the Rev. N.G. Slaughter, on the evening of the 11th inst., AMOS W. HAMMOND of Culloden, Geo. to MRS. MARY ANN SHELBY of this city.

May 20, 1841

> Married in Culloden on the 12th inst. by the Rev. James Davis, THOS. G. RANDLE, ESQ. of Meriwether county, to MISS MARY A., daughter of OBADIAH GIBSON, ESQ. late deceased of Monroe county.
>
> Married on Wednesday the 5th inst. by the Rev. O.C. Gibson, MR. FRIAR MATHEWS, of Fayette county, to MISS IRRENA WILLS, of Upson county.
>
> Married on Thursday the 6th inst. by the Rev. O.C. Gibson, MR. JOHN A. SMITH to MISS MARY N., daughter of JOHN GARDNER, ESQ. of Upson county.

June 24, 1841

> Married in Monroe county on Tuesday evening the 8th inst. by the Rev. Mr. Carter, MR. WILLIAM W. TAYLOR, to MISS MARY ANN, daughter of THOMAS L. POPE ESQ. - all of Monroe county.

July 15, 1841

> Married on Wednesday the 12th July by the Rev. George F. Pierce, MR. JOHN B. STOW ESQ. of Charleston S.C., to MISS CATHARINE M. SIMS, daughter of F. SIMS ESQ. of this city.

July 15, 1841

    Married in Scottsboro, on Wednesday morning, the 7th inst. by the Rev. Mr. Hillyer MR. JAMES R. BUTTS, of this city, to MISS LOUISA M. POLHILL, daughter of the late HON. JOHN G. POLHILL.

Aug. 12, 1841

    Married in this city, in the Episcopal Church, on Tuesday morning last, by the Rev. Mr. Bragg, DR. HENRY K. GREEN to MISS THEODOSIA PARKER.

Aug. 26, 1841

    Married on Tuesday evening the 27th ult. at the residence of Maj. Brown, near Columbia, (Tenn.) by the Rev. Mr. Sherman, MR. J.L. DeLAUNEY, of Stewart county, Ga. to MISS SARAH C. NAPIER, daughter of MR. THOS. T. NAPIER of this city.

    Married on the 18th ult. by the Rev. A.H. Mitchell, THOMAS C. HOWARD, ESQ. of Covington, to MISS MARIANNA, eldest daughter of DR. E. HALL, of Crawford county.

Sep. 2, 1841

    Married in Montgomery, Ala. on the 24th ult. by the Rev. H.W. Hilliard, MR. HENRY C. FREEMAN of this city, to MISS ANN R. SCHEONMAKER, of the former place.

    Married at the residence of Wm. F. Clark, Esq. in Bibb county, on the 26th ult. by Judge Bailey, MR. CHARLES G. DOUGLASS of Monroe county, to ELIZA B. HOGAN, of Bibb county.

Sep. 9, 1841

    Married on Tuesday evening, the 7th inst. by Jesse L. Owen Esq. MR. RICHARDSON SANDERSON, to MISS EMILY DERACKIN, all of this city.

Sep. 23, 1841

    Married on Tuesday, the 14th inst. by Samuel H. Harris, Esq. MR. JOHN COLBY, of Irwinton, Ala. to MISS CHARLOTTE ANDREWS, of Crawford county, Ga.

Sep. 30, 1841

    Married in Macon county on the 23d inst. by Judge Penleton, WM. SHEELT to MISS ELIZABETH A. HIGGINS.

    Married in this city on Wednesday evening the 23d inst. by the Rev. Mr. Mann, MR. WILLIAM D. RAINEY to MISS REBECCA A.S. WYCHE - all of this city.

Oct. 14, 1841

    Married in Hartford, Conn. on the 29th Sept. by the Rev. Mr. Sprague, MR. JAMES H. BISHOP, of this City, to MISS LAURA A. LOWRY, of Hartford.

Oct. 28, 1841

    Married on the 21st inst., by the Rev. James Lunsford, MOSES H. BALDWIN ESQ. late of this City, to MISS ELIZABETH MILLER, of Randolph county.

Nov. 25, 1841

    Married in this city, on the 18th inst. by the Rev. Mr. Mann, MR. JAMES A. KNIGHT, to MISS DORCAS WILLIAMS, all of this city.

Dec. 2, 1841

    Married at Culloden, Monroe county, on the 16th Nov. by the Rev. Mr. Perryman, MR. HENRY S. COTTON, to MISS EMELINE C., daughter of JAMES BIVINS, ESQ. all of said county.

    Married in Savannah, on the 23d inst. P.C. PENDLETON ESQ. editor of the Magnolia, to MISS CATHERINE M., daughter of CAPT. F.E. TEBEAU.

Jan. 13, 1842

    Married near this city, on the 10th inst. the HON. WALTER T. COLQUITT, of Columbus, to MISS HARRIET M. ROSS, daughter of LUKE ROSS, ESQ.

    Married in Monroe County, on the 6th inst. by the Rev. Mr. Chipman, MR. GEORGE EDWARDS, to MISS ELIZA L. McMULLEN, all of said county.

Jan. 27, 1842

    Married in Macon county, on the 20th inst. by the Rev. Gray Cummings, DR. JOHN J. MILLER, to MISS ETHALINA U. BROWN, daughter of ROBERT BROWN, ESQ.

Feb. 3, 1842

    Married in Crawford County on the 24th January, by the Rev. Mr. Ansley, MR. CHAS. J. REYNOLDS of Marion, Twiggs county, to MISS MARTHA E. JORDAN, daughter of WM. W. JORDAN ESQ.

    Married in Crawford on the 16th ult., by the Rev. A.W. Hammock, MR. W. HAMMOCK, to MISS GEORGIA ANN JOLLY.

Mar. 3, 1842

    Married on the 1st inst. in this City, by S.G. Bragg, MR. BERTRAND TISSEREAU, to MISS MARTHA McNEAL.

    Married at Windsor Hill, near this City, on the 13th ult., by the Rev. S.G. Bragg, MR. JOHN F. McLEOD, to MISS HARRIET J. SMITH.

Mar. 10, 1842

    Married in Scottsboro, on Tuesday evening the 22d ult. by the Rev. Alfred T. Mann, WILLIAM T.W. NAPIER, ESQ. of Milledgeville, to MISS JULIA E., daughter of MR. JOEL T. TUCKER, of the former place.

Mar. 17, 1842

    Married on Sunday evening, the 13th inst. by the Rev. S.G. Bragg, MR. WILLIAM B. FERRILL, to MISS ANN ROBINSON, both of this city.

    Married on Tuesday evening last, by the Rev. Geo. F. Pierce, COL. R.H. WARD, of Putnam county, to MISS MARTHA SARAH HOLT, of this county.

Mar. 24, 1842

    Married in Charleston, on the 17th inst. by the Right Rev'd Dr. Gadsden, MR. GEO. W. STOW, of Columbus, Ga. to MISS SUSAN A., daughter of BENJ. FAIRCHILD, ESQ. of Stratford, Conn.

Apr. 7, 1842

    Married in Augusta, on the 31st ult. by Rev. Alonzo Church, J.B. JONES, ESQ. to MISS SARAH A. LEWIS, both of Burke county.

Apr. 21, 1842

   Married in New York, on the 26th ult., by the Rev. M.P. Parks, Chaplain U.S. Military Academy, and Bishop elect of Alabama, CAPT. ROBERT ANDERSON, U.S. Army, to ELIZA BAYARD, daughter of GEN. CLINCH, of Camden county, Ga.

   Married on the 14th inst. by the Rev. S.G. Bragg, MR. JOSEPH C. HUNT, to MISS ADELAID JULIA BOUYER, both of this city.

   Married in Athens, on the 7th inst. by the Rev. Dr. Hoyt, MR. G.W. HOLLAND, to MISS SARAH, daughter of J. NEWTON, all of that place.

   Married in East Macon, on the 19th inst. by the Rev. Geo. F. Pierce, MR. ISAAC H. MORELAND, of Jones county, to MISS MARY J. DICKSON, of this city.

May 5, 1842

   Married in this City, on Tuesday evening the 3d inst. by the Rev. Seneca G. Bragg, Esq. SAMUEL R. BLAKE, ESQ., to MISS MARY ADALINE BEAL. At the same time, COL. ABNER P. POWERS, to MISS FRANCES BEAL.

May 12, 1842

   Married on Wednesday evening the 4th inst. by the Rev. Mr. Ellison, MR. ALEXANDER J. RAYMUR to MISS MARTHA S., daughter of WM. G. MACON, ESQ. of this city.

May 19, 1842

   Married in this city on the 10th inst. by C.A. Higgins, Esq. MR. JOHN CONNER, of Conn. to MISS REBECCA ANN KIMBRO of Ala.

May 26, 1842

   Married in this city on the 24th inst. by James Denton Esq. MR. JOSEPH H. MOUNT, of Washington City, D.C. to MISS ELIZA A.E. BARNARD, of this city.

   Married in Wadesborough, N.C. WM. H. SCOTT ESQ. of this city to MISS MARTHA A.E. SINCLAIR, of Savannah.

June 16, 1842

   Married in this city on the 2d inst. by the Rev. S.G. Bragg, MR. EDMUND RICHARDSON, formerly of Berlin, (Conn.) to MISS ELIZA JANE BRADLEY, of New Haven, (Conn.).

June 30, 1842

   Married on the 23d inst. by Wm. Halstead, Esq. MONROE BAISMORE, ESQ. to MISS ANN VAUGHN, both of Houston Co.

July 14, 1842

   Married in this city on the 12th inst. by the Rev. George F. Pierce, MR. K.J.T. LITTLE, of Griffin, to MISS LUCINDA FLINT, of this city.

   Married on the 28th ultimo, by the Rev. C.A. Brown, DR. H.P. SMEAD, of Talbotton, to MISS PRISCILLA HURT, daughter of COL. BENJAMIN HURT, of Alabama.

Aug. 11, 1842

   Married in Forsyth on the 28th July, by the Rev. Mr. Cook, MR. ALLEN L. LUCE, of Macon, Ga. to MISS S.A. BRENT, daughter of WM. L. BRENT, Washington City.

Aug. 25, 1842

Married in Forsyth on the 15th inst. by the Rev. W.H. Ellison, PHILIP COOK, ESQ. to MISS SARAH G. LUMPKIN.

Married in Jones county, on the 16th inst. MR. WM. W. JOHNSON of Jasper, to MISS AMRTHA S. MORELAND.

Sep. 1, 1842

Married in Monroe county on the 16th inst. by the Rev. James Carter, COL. WILLIAM LONG, of LaGrange, to MISS SARAH M. TAYLOR, daughter of JOB TAYLOR, of Monroe county.

Sep. 15, 1842

Married on the 18th ult. by the Rev. Davis Lowry, DR. ABRAM GARNER, to MISS JANET, daughter of the late MARK FAULK, ESQ. all of Twiggs county.

Oct. 6, 1842

Married in East Macon, on Tuesday evening last, by the Rev. Geo. F. Pierce, MR. GRANVILLE WOOD, to MISS ANTOINETTE V. EANES.

Married in this city, on the 2d inst., at the house of Mr. A.R. Freeman, by the Rev. Wm. H. Ellison, MR. WOODFORD MABERY, to MISS LAURA M. WING, both of Darien.

Oct. 20, 1842

Married in Jones county, on the 4th inst. by the Rev. Mr. Ingles, MR. CHARLES S. THOMAS, of this city, to MISS MARTHA ANN ROBERTS, of the former place.

Married in Jones county, on Tuesday evening the 11th inst. by John Walker, Esq. MR. CHARLES PAUL to MISS LUCY ANN STEPHENS.

Married in this county on Tuesday evening the 11th inst. by the Rev. Sam'l Burnett, MR. SAMUEL McARTHUR to MISS MATILDA NEAL, daughter of the Rev. Jonathan Neal.

Married in Jones county, on the 16th inst. by the Rev. Mr. Bragg, MR. JAMES BAILEY, of this city, to MISS AMANDA STILES, daughter of JOSEPH STILES of said county.

Nov. 10, 1842

Married in Milledgeville, on the 1st inst. by the Rev. S.T. Hillyer, MR. JOHN JACKSON, of Albany, Baker county, to MISS ADELAIDE E. STOVALL, daughter of JOSEPH STOVALL, ESQ. of the former city.

Nov. 17, 1842

Married at Brooklyn, L.I. Oct. 26th, by the Rev. Mr. Farley, MR. CHARLES A. STRONG, of New York, to MISS FRANCES ANNA, daughter of JOSEPH L. LORD, ESQ.

Married in this City on the 15th inst. by the Rev. S.G. Bragg, MR. ROBERT NISBET of Jefferson county, to MISS MARIAN S. ABBOTT, of this City.

Married near this city, on the 15th inst. by Rev. Jesse H. Campbell, MR. CHARLES HUTCHINS of Jones county, to MISS ELIZA SMITHWICK.

Nov. 24, 1842

Married in Twiggs county on the 18th inst. by the Rev. F.D. Lowry, JOSEPH J. BOYNTON, of Lumpkin, to MISS PENELOPE, daughter of BENJAMIN BRYAN.

Dec. 1, 1842

    Married in Vineville, on the 24th ult. by the Rev. Geo. F. Pierce, MR. RICHARD A. BENSON to MISS CATHERINE E. BREWER, eldest daughter of THOMAS A. BREWER.

    Married on the 12th inst. by C.A. Higgins Esq. MR. Z.B. WADE to MISS FRANCES P.A. SACRAE, both of this City.

Dec. 8, 1842

    Married in Twiggs county on the 1st inst. by Rev. Jesse Campbell, MR. MARCUS H. BUNN to MISS CATHERINE CARDEN.

    Married on the 29th Nov. by Rev. Kader Parker, MR. SAMUEL S. POWELL to MISS RACHEL ELIZABETH, daughter of CAPT. JOHN FRENCH, all of Marion county.

Dec. 29, 1842

    Married on Tuesday, the 27th inst., by Rev. S.G. Bragg, MR. JACOB LUDWIG to MISS PHILIPINA KUH, all of this city.

    Married on Tuesday the 27th inst. by Rev. S.G. Bragg, MR. JOHN S. HOGE to MISS ADELINE L. FRIERSON, all of this city.

Jan. 5, 1843

    Married on Thursday morning the 22d ult. in this city by the Rev. Wm. H. Ellison, MR. THOMAS J. CATER to MISS AMELIA ELIZABETH WIMBERLY.

    Married in this city, on the 4th inst. MR. NEWEL BIRD, to MRS. JANE KIMBRO.

    Married at the residence of Mr. James T. White, on the 21st ult., by the Rev. C. Trussell, MR. TURNER SMITH to MISS E.A. ODOM, all of this county.

Jan. 19, 1843

    Married at the residence of Mrs. Mary Cotten in Monroe county, Jan. 16th, by the Rev. J.R. Kendrick, MR. JOHN J.B. HOXEY of Columbus to MISS CAROLINE E. COTTEN of Monroe.

Feb. 16, 1843

    Married in Houston county, on Thursday the 2d inst. by Rev. James Hudson, CUSTIS B. NOTTINGHAM, M.D. (late of Virginia) to REBECCA FRANCES, youngest daughter of HEZEKIAH THOMSON, ESQ.

    Married on the 21st January, by the Rev. B.M. Sanders, MR. B.F. THARP, of Twiggs county, to MISS MARTHA A. JACKSON, of Greene.

Feb. 23, 1843

    Married on Wednesday evening, the 15th inst. by the Rev. W.W. Roberson, MR. GEO. SANDERS, of Crawford county, to MISS CATHARINE M. STUBBS, of Bibb.

    Married on Tuesday evening the 14th inst. by the Rev. Mr. Arnold, MR. FRANKLIN S. JENKINS, of Eatonton, Putnam county, to MISS MARTHA A. JACKSON, of Hillsboro, Jasper county.

Apr. 13, 1843

    Married in Clinton, on Sunday evening last by the Rev. J.H. Campbell, MR. WILLIAM S. STARKS, of Alabama, to MRS. MARY T. SPINKS, of Clinton.

Apr. 13, 1843

Married on the 11th inst., in Macon county, MR. SHADRACK R. FELTON, to MISS LAVINIA, daughter of MAJOR JOHN YOUNG.

Apr. 20, 1843

Married in this county, on the 11th inst. by the Rev. Jonathan Neel, MR. JAMES M. DAVIS of Twiggs county, to MISS OBEDIENCE A. THARP, of Bibb.

Married in Thomaston, on the 13th inst. by Thomas Beall, Esq. WILLIAM H. STERLING, of Troup county, to MISS MARY A.M., daughter of COL. E.W. WOMBLE, of the former place.

Married in this County on Wednesday 12th inst. by the Rev. Mr. Anthony, A.C. MOREHOUSE, ESQ. of Syracuse, N.Y., to MISS REBECCA MORGAN, of Macon.

May 4, 1843

Married in Bibb county on the 30th April, by the Rev. F. Miller, MR. JAS. LAWRENCE KING, of Charleston, (S.C.) to MISS SARAH ANN, eldest daughter of PETER STUBBS, of this county.

Married on Tuesday evening, the 2d inst. by the Rev. Mr. Kendrick, MR. ISHAM D. SLEDGE, to MISS MARIA A. HEATH, daughter of P. HEATH, ESQ., all of this city.

May 11, 1843

Married on Tuesday evening the 9th inst. by the Rev. Mr. Murphy, MR. JACKSON BARNES to MISS MARY DEGNAN all of this city.

June 8, 1843

Married in Athens, on the 25th ult. by the Rev. Mr. Hoyt, D.D. JOHN J. GRESHAM, ESQ. Mayor of this city, to MISS MARY E., daughter of THOS. W. BAXTER, ESQ.

June 15, 1843

Married on Thursday evening the ____ inst. by the Rev. Mr. Anthony, MR. E.R. PEASE, of Henry county, to MISS MARTHA E. CURD, of this city.

July 13, 1843

Married in this city on Thursday evening last, by the Rev'd J.R. Kendrick, MR. JOHN S. INGRAHAM to MISS ELEANOR FLEMING, all of this city.

Married on 11th inst. by Rev. S.G. Bragg, MR. JOHN T. HARBAUM to MISS GERTRUDE FLEISCHMANN, both of this city.

Married in Houston county, on the 6th inst. by Mitchell Brown, Esq. MR. MARTIN KENDRICK to MSS ELIZA A. BROWN - all of Houston county.

Aug. 17, 1843

Married on the 10th inst. by the Rev. Mr. Anthony, MR. THOMAS RICHARDS to MISS CAROLINE A. BARR, all of this city.

Married in Vineville, on the 10th inst. by the Rev. J.C. Postell, SAMUEL P. JONES, of Houston county, to MISS ELIZABETH C. NIXON, daughter of the late COL. WM. NIXON, of the former place.

Aug. 24, 1843

   Married at the residence of Mrs. Sarah Cabaniss, in Jones Co. on
   the 17th instant, by James Gray, Esq. MR. ROBERT O. MORELAND, to
   MISS SARAH H., daughter of the late HARRISON CABANISS, deceased -
   all of said county.

   Married by the Rev. Isaiah Langley, D. PORTER EVERETT of Houston
   county, to MISS HENRIETTA A. CALLAWAY, daughter of EDWARD CALLAWAY,
   of Monroe.

Sep. 28, 1843

   Married on the 19th inst. at the house of Mrs. Nancy J. Jordan, in
   Crawford county, by the Rev. Lemuel G.R. Wiggins, MR. WILLIAM T.
   SHIRLEY to MISS ANN T. JORDAN, daughter of MRS. NANCY J. JORDAN.

Oct. 5, 1843

   Married in Vineville, on the 38th ult. (Was 28th intended?) by the
   Rev. J.R. Kendrick, GEN. ELIAS BEALL to MRS. ANN G. SANDERS.

   Married on Tuesday the 3d insts. by the Rev. S.G. Bragg, MR. JOHN
   HOLLINGSWORTH, JR. to MISS MILDRED H. JOHNSON, of the county of
   Bibb.

   Married in Russell county, Ala. on the 28th ult. by the Rev. R.T.
   Marks, JAMES V. JONES, ESQ. of Buke county (Was Burke intended?)
   to MISS ELIZABETH, youngest daughter of the late JOEL HURT, ESQ.

Oct. 19, 1843

   Married in Monroe county on the 11th inst. by the Rev. C.F. Sturgis,
   REV. JAMES R. KENDRICK of this City, to MISS ARABELLA M. RANDLE.
   Also, by the same, at the same time, MR. JUDSON A. KENDRICK of
   Houston county, to MISS ELIZA ANN RANDLE.

Oct. 26, 1843

   Married at Bellgrade, Pittsylvania County, Va. on the 10th inst. by
   the Rev. Samuel J.P. Anderson, MR. HENRY H. LUMPKIN, JUNR. of
   Forsyth Ga. to MISS ISABELLA G. daughter of COL. NATHANIEL WILSON
   of the former place.

   Married in Warrenton on the 18th inst., by the Rev. A.J. (Teel?),
   MR. CYRUS K. WENTWORTH of Milledgeville, to MISS JANE I. MATHER,
   of Manchester, Conn.

Nov. 2, 1843

   Married on the 17th ult. in the city of New York, in St. Peter's
   Church, by the Rev. Hugh Smith, D.D. MAJOR WASHINGTON SEWELL, U.S.
   Army, to SUSAN AMELIA, youngest daughter of the late JOHN M.B.____
   ESQ. formerly of Duchess county.

Nov. 9, 1843

   Married near Waynesville, Wayne county, on ____ ult. by the Rev.
   Mr. McIntosh, I.C. PLANT, of this city, to MISS ELIZABETH M.,
   daughter of ____ HURST ESQ.

Nov. 16, 1843

   Married in Savannah, on the 6th inst. by the Rev. Mr. P____, MR.
   JOHN W. BABCOCK, of this city, to MISS MARGARET A. HOOKER, of
   Savannah.

Dec. 7, 1843

   Married in Monroe county, on Thursday, the 30th ult., by the Rev.
   J.R. Kendrick, MR. JOEL R. SIMONTON, of Bibb, to MISS N.A. COTTER,
   of Monroe county.

Dec. 14, 1843

   Married in Crawford county, on the 7th inst. by the Rev. Enos Young,
   MR. LUCIUS G. EVANS, of Macon county, to MISS SUSAN C. EVANS, of
   Crawford county.

Dec. 21, 1843

   Married in this city on the evening of the 16th inst. by Eliphalet
   E. Brown, Esq. MR. ROGER McCALL to MRS CYNTHIA Y. ROCKWELL, all
   of this city.

   Married in Forsyth, Monroe county, on the 12th inst. by the Rev.
   Dr. Purefoy, MR. WM. R. BERNER to MISS JULIA A. COOK.

   Married in this city on Tuesday evening, 19th last, by the Rev. Wm.
   H. Ellison, MR. BRITAIN F. ROGERS to MISS SARAH JAMESON, daughter
   of DR. DAVID JAMESON.

Dec. 28, 1843

   Married in Talbot county, on the 14th inst. by the Rev. Mr.
   Montgomery, MR. ANDREW J. ORR, of this city, to MISS SUSAN A. McCOOK.

Jan. 11, 1844

   Married on the 4th ult. by the Rev. S.G. Bragg, of the city of
   Macon, ELIJAH P. ALLEN, ESQ. of Fayette county, to MRS. SARAH E.
   MEADOWS, of Walton county, Ga.

Jan. 25, 1844

   Married in this City on the 18th inst. by James M. _____ Esq.
   JOHN F. HEATH, to MRS. MARY M. _____ (illegible - paper torn).
   Married in Houston county, on the 17th inst. by the Rev. Dr. Moore,
   COL. JOHN R. STAPLES, of Macon _____ to MISS CAROLINE EMMA, daughter
   of the REV. _____ C. POSTELL.

   Married in Monroe county on the 23d inst. by the Rev. William
   Hardy, MR. JAMES TURRENTINE of _____ ton county, to MISS ELIZABETH A.
   daughter of _____ ROWLAND REDDING. (illegible - paper torn).

   Married in Monroe county, on the 9th inst. by the Rev. Mr. Barron,
   MR. JOHN W. BURTON of this county ot MISS CAROLINE G. MORAN.

Feb. 1, 1844

   Married on the 25th ult. by the Rev. J.H. Campbell, MR. ELISHA
   GRISWOLD, of Clinton, to MISS ELIZABETH HARDEMAN, daughter of
   THOS. HARDEMAN, of this city.

   Married on the 11th ult. in Cullodensville, by the Rev. T.F.
   Montgomery, JAMES W. CASTENS, of Talbotton, to MISS ANN V., daughter
   of MR. JAMES OLIVER, of the former place.

   Married on the 18th ult. at 9 o'clock A.M. in Talbotton, by the Rev.
   T.F. Montgomery, A.C. VAN EPPS, ESQ. of Eufala, Ala. to MISS
   CAROLINE, daughter of GEN. N. HOWARD, of the former place.

   Married on the 10th ult. at St. Louis, Missouri, by the Rev. _____
   Bullard, AUGUSTUS PEABODY, to MISS M.T.C. ECKLEY, eldest daughter
   of LEVI ECKLEY, formerly of Macon.

Feb. 15, 1844

   Married on the 1st inst. by Esq. Burdon, MR. J.J. JORDAN to MISS ELIZABETH SUMERS, daughter of NICOLES SUMERS, all of Jones county. Married on the 16th Jan. by Esquire Burdon, MR. JOSEPH STILES to MISS MARTHA ANN STRIPLING, all of Jones county.

Mar. 14, 1844

   Married on the 14th of February last, by the Rev. T.F. Montgomery, MR. JAMES SHERIDAN to MISS CATHERINE FORBES, all of Talbotton, Geo.

   Married on the 5th inst., by the Rev. T.F. Montgomery, MR. ALEXANDER F. OWEN to MISS SARAH A., youngest daughter of ROBERT GAMBLE, SR. all of Talbot county.

   Married on the 10th inst., by the Rev. T.F. Montgomery, MR. JOHN M. BRUCE, of Meriwether co., to MRS. MARTHA BUCHANAN, of Talbot county.

Apr. 4, 1844

   Married on the 21st ult. by the Rev. S.G. Bragg, MR. JAMES M. JANERETT, of Charleston, S.C. to MISS C. DALTON BIRD, of this city.

Apr. 11, 1844

   Married in this City on the 8th (?) inst. by the Rev. Mr. Payne, MR. GEO. R. FRAZER of Augusta, Ga., to MISS MALVINA C. JACKSON, of the same place.

Apr. 25, 1844

   Married on Thursday evening the 18th inst. by the Rev. Wm. H. Ellison, MR. ZACHARIAH O. WHITEHEAD, to MISS CASSANDRA M., daughter of MR. THOMAS H. FLINT, all of this city.

May 9, 1844

   Married on the 24th April, by Rev'd David Roberts, MR. SHADRACH WARE (WARD?), to MRS. CLARISSA W. GLENN, daughter of D.W. SHINE, ESQ. all of Twiggs county.

July 18, 1844

   Married in St. Marys Ga. on the 10th inst. by the Rev. Mr. Baird, MR. MILES G. STEPHENS of this place to MISS LATITIA S. ALDRICH daughter of DR. W. ALDRICH.

Aug. 15, 1844

   Married on Wednesday morning, the 7th inst. by Rev. S.G. Bragg, MR. GEORGE PAYNE, to MISS EMILY H. SIMS, daughter of FREDERICK SIMS, ESQ. all of this city.

   Married on the evening of the 7th inst. by Rev. John Hendricks, COL. JEREMIAH LEAK, of Marietta, (Geo.) to MISS MARY T. SWIFT, of Morgan county.

Aug. 22, 1844

   Married in Greenville, Meriwether county, on the 13th inst. MARCUS A. JOHNSON ESQ. (Editor of the American Democrat, of this city), to MISS JUVENIA ROSE, daughter of DAVID C. ROSE, ESQ.

Aug. 29, 1844

   Married on the 20th ult. by the Rev. C.F. Sturgis, MR. BENJ. F. TAYLOR to MISS MARY F. DURHAM, all of Monroe.

Sep. 26, 1844

Married in New York, on Thursday the 12th inst. by the Rev. Dr. McCawley, MR. WARREN FREEMAN, of this city, to MISS JULIET ANN MAIRS, of New York.

Oct. 17, 1844

Married in Guilford, Conn. on the 22nd Sept. by the Rev. Mr. Bennett, MR. GEO. I. SHEPARD of this City, to MISS SUSANNAH LOPER, of that place.

Oct. 31, 1844

Married in Macon county, Georgia on the 24th instant, by the Rev. Jas. C. Postell, MR. M.M. WINDSOR of Montgomery, Ala., to MISS EVELINE L., daughter of JOHN C. RODGERS, ESQ. of the former place.

Nov. 14, 1844

Married in this City on the 7th inst., at the house of Elam Alexander Esq., by the Rev. J.R. Kendrick, MR. NATHANIEL R. MITCHELL, of Thomas county, to MRS. LUCY HILLS, of this place.

Nov. 21, 1844

Married in Sumter county, Ga. on the 31st ult. by Logan Douglas, MR. A.A. WILLETT to MISS ELIZABETH R.A. WHITE, daughter of PETER WHITE, ESQ. all of Sumter county.

Married by the Rev. James B. Payne, on Sunday evening the 19th inst. at Haynesville, Houston county Ga. MR. BRYANT BALTON to MISS ELIZABETH ANN PATTILLO, daughter of DR. CHARLES F. PATTILLO, all of Houston county.

Nov. 28, 1844

Married on Tuesday morning the 19th inst. in Lanier, Ga. at the residence of Judge H.J. Neeley, by the Rev. W.D. Bussey, MR. GILBERT C. CARMICHAEL, of that place, to MISS MARY E. KEY, of the city of Macon.

Married in Jones county, on the 17th inst. by the Rev. David Kelly, MR. SAMUEL F. GOVE of Macon, to MISS SARAH L. LESTER, of the former place.

Dec. 5, 1844

Married on Sunday evening the 24th inst. by the Rev. Mr. Coffee, MR. WM. BRANSBY of Savannah, to MISS JOANA TOBIN, of this city.

Married on Friday evening last, at the Post Office, in Americus Sumter county, by Judge Lewis Bruner, MR. JOHN W. SMITH to MISS CATHARINE BROWN, all of Pulaski county.

Married in Baldwin county, on Tuesday evening, the 26th ult. by the Rev. Samuel Anthony, MR. ANDERSON J. HOLLINGSHEAD, of Macon county, to MISS SARAH C. MURPH, of the former place.

Dec. 12, 1844

Married on Tuesday evening the 26th inst. at the residence of Benjamin S. Tarver, Esq. in Tallapoosa county, (Ala.) by the Rev. McCarty Oliver, ELEY W. TODD to ALLEVIA ANN ELIZABETH, daughter of BENJ. S. TARVER.

Married in Savannah, on the 3d inst. by the Rev. N. Aldrich, WILLIAM S. WILLIFORD, ESQ. of Macon, to MISS SARAH A.F., eldest daughter of JOSEPH FELT, ESQ. of Savannah.

Dec. 12, 1844

    Married in Talbotton, on the 24th ult. by the Rev. C.W. Key, BARNARD HILL, ESQ. to MISS MARY C. BURCH.

Dec. 19, 1844

    Married on Tuesday evening the 10th inst. by the Rev. Mr. Kendrick, MR. A.G. KILLINGSWORTH to MISS ELIZABETH McNELL, all of this City.

    Married on the evening of the 11th inst. by the Rev. S. Anthony, MR. JOSEPH R. BANKS to MISS MARY PRICHARD of Forsyth, and both of Monroe county, Ga.

Jan. 2, 1845

    Married in this city on the 17th Dec., by the Rev. W.H. Ellison, MR. WM. S. HOLT to MISS HENRIETTA J., daughter of MR. JAMES DEAN - all of this city.

Jan. 16, 1845

    Married in Madison county on the evening of the 7th inst., by the Rev. B. (?) M. Smith, MR. EDWARD STUBBS of Bibb county, to MISS MARY B. BRONSON, of Houston.

    Married near Athens, on the morning of the 1st inst., by the Rev. Dr. Hoyt, DANIEL W. MILLER, ESQ. of Lanier, Macon county, to MISS SUSAN H., daughter of DR. HUGH NEISBER(?).

    Married in Dooly county on Sabbath evening, Dec. 20th (?), by Charles F. Pattillo, Esq. MR. OLIVER P. SWEARINGEN to MRS. NANCY COLLIER.

    Married in Mayesville, on Thursday evening, 2d Jan., by Charles F. Pattillo, Esq. MR. HENRY B. HUGHES to MISS SARAH E. CHILDERS.

Jan. 23, 1845

    Married in Culloden, Monroe county, (Ga.) on the 16th inst. by the Rev. A. Spear, MR. GEORGE CLARK, merchant of this city, to MISS SARAH E., daughter of JOHN CASTLEN, ESQ. of the former place.

Jan. 30, 1845

    Married in Monroe county on the 21st inst., by the Rev. N. Ously, MR. SAMUEL CALDWELL to MISS SUSAN LESUEUR.

    Married in this city, on the 26th inst., by the Rev. J.R. Kendrick, MR. HARTWELL P. SMITH, of Jones county, to ELIZABETH COLLINS, of this place.

    Married on the 26th inst. by the Rev. Mr. Young, MR. ISAAC H. ROYAL, to MISS NANCY, daughter of DAVID O. SMITH, ESQ., of Houston county.

Feb. 6, 1845

    Married in Monroe county, on the 23d inst. by the Rev. Mr. Cooper, MR. CALVIN W. BATTLE to MISS HARRIET G. REDDING.

    Married in Savannah, on the 23d ult., by Rev. Mr. Wyatt, GARDNER L. LILLIBRIDGE, ESQ., Editor of the Savannan(?) Daily Sun, to MRS. ADELINE CLARK, of New York.

    Married in Monroe county on the 30th ult. THOMAS COLLINS, ESQ. of this city, to MISS ARABELLA MACARTHY, daughter of ROGER MACARTHY, ESQ.

Feb. 20, 1845

Married in this city on the 15th(?) inst. by the Rev. J.R. Kendrick, DR. WILLIAM A. JARRATT, of Milledgeville, to MISS ELIZA M. MARTIN, of this place.

Married in Houston county on the 12th inst. by the Rev. John Humphries, COL. HUGH FARRIER, of Pike county, Ala. to MISS OLIVIA R., daughter of MR. DANIEL FREDRICK.

Feb. 27, 1845

Married in this city on the 25th inst. by the Rev. J.R. Kendrick, MR. ANDREW T. ANDERSON, of this place, to MRS. LORETTA JANE PARMALEE, of New York City.

Mar. 6, 1845

Married in Houston county, on the 4th inst. by the Rev. J.R. Kendrick MR. JOHN T. LAMAR, of Macon, to MISS MARTHA ELIZABETH, daughter of GEN. B.H. RUTHERFORD.

Mar. 13, 1845

Married in this city on the 5th (?) inst. by the Rev. Mr. Bragg, MR. JAMES A. RALSTON, to MISS A____ LAMAR, daughter of COL. H.G. LAMAR.

Married in Bibb county on the 3d inst. by the Rev. Mr. Ellison, MR. JOHN B. ROSS, of this city, to MISS MARTHA L. REDDING, daughter of W.C. REDDING, of Monroe county.

Apr. 3, 1845

Married on Thursday night last, by the Rev. Mr. Mallory, WILLIAM LUNDY, to MISS JULIA A.D. THARP. daughter of the late WM. A. THARP, of Twiggs county.

Apr. 10, 1845

Married on the 2d inst. at Dahlonega, Lumpkin county, MR. MONTGOMERY P. WINGFIELD, of this city, to MISS MARY E., daughter of DR. JOSEPH J. SINGLETON, of the former place.

Married in this city, on the 8th inst., by David Reid, Esq., MR. ALEXANDER ANNESLY to MISS MAHALA JONES, both of this city.

Apr. 17, 1845

Married in Monroe county on Tuesday evening last, by the Rev. Wm. Hardy, MR. THOMAS D. OUSLEY, ESQ. of this city, to MISS MARTHA C. BAILEY.

May 1, 1845

Married in the city of New York on the 31st March by Rev. Samuel B. Burchard, THOMAS MANSON to MISS ELIZA, youngest daughter of the late ABRAHAM JAQUES, ESQ., all of that city.

May 8, 1845

Married on Wednesday morning the 30th ult. by the Rev. Mr. Ellison, MR. BENJAMIN CHAIRES of Florida, to MISS GODFREY VIRGINIA GODFREY, of this county.

May 22, 1845

Married on the 14th inst. by the Rev. Mr. Bragg, MR. E.L. SHELTON to MISS MALINDA S. CUMMINS, all of this city.

May 29, 1845

Married on Thursday, May 15th in the city of New York by the Rev. Chas. H. Williamson, MR. RICHARD W. HURLBUT to MISS AURELIA M. HARRISON, daughter of the late GEORGE A. HARRISON.

June 5, 1845

Married on the 30th ult. by the Rev. S.G. Bragg, MR. FRANCIS J. OGDEN, to MISS ANNA F.K., daughter of HARVEY SHOTWELL, ESQ., all of this city.

Married in this city on the 3d inst., by the Rev. S.G. Bragg, FERDINAND HORNE, ESQ. to MISS SARAH HICKS, all of this city.

June 19, 1845

Married in Forsyth on Wednesday morning by the Rev. J.D. Stephens of Macon, THOMAS B. GORDON, ESQ. to MISS FRANCES M. GREER.

Married in Hopewell, Crawford county, (Geo.) on Tuesday evening, the 9th inst. by the Rev. J.M. Wood, DR. DUDLEY S. JONES, of Knoxville, to MISS MARY JANE, daughter of JAMES C. PEMBERTON, ESQ. of Hopewell.

July 3, 1845

Married on Tuesday, the 1st inst., by J.B. Artope, Esq., MR. JOHN K. HARMAN to MISS ELIZABETH W., daughter of PLEASANT HEATH, ESQ. - all of this place.

July 10, 1845

Married on Thursday the 3d inst. by the Rev. Mr. Castellow, MR. ABNER P. STUBBS to MISS MARTHA ANN, daughter of STEPHEN WOODARD, ESQ. - all of this county.

July 17, 1845

Married by the Rev. Wm. H. Ellison, on the morning of the 5th instant MR. ROBERT FREEMAN of Jones county to MISS HARRIETTE A., daughter of WILLIAM SCOTT, of Vineville.

July 24, 1845

Married in this place on Thursday evening the 10th instant by the Rev. Mr. Anthony, MR. H.P. WESTCOTT to MISS ANN GORDON, all of Macon.

Sep. 4, 1845

Married in Marshallville, Houston county, on the 28th July, by the Rev. Mr. Postell, MR. THOMAS A. HARRIS to MISS MARTHA HINES, all of this city.

Married on the 26th July by the Rev. A. Ogletree, MR. M.J. McMULLAN of this city, to MISS MARY A. STUART, of Marion county.

Sep. 18, 1845

Married in Vineville on the evening of the 10th inst. by the Rev. Joshua Knowles, the HON. R.B. HOUGHTON, of Gadsden county (Fla.) to MISS SARAH TAYLOR, second daughter of the HON. CHRISTOPHER B. STRONG.

Sep. 25, 1845

Married on the 11th inst. by the Rev. Enos Young, JESSE I. SWANNER, of Macon county, (Geo.) formerly of Martin county, (N.C.) to MISS MARY HAUGHABOON, of Crawford county (Geo.).

Oct. 16, 1845

    Married at Greensboro on the 1st inst. by the Rev. Frances Bowden(?) MR. ALFRED WINGFIELD, of this place, to MISS FRANCES M., daughter of JOHN CUNNINGHAM, ESQ. of the former place. (Madison Miscellany)

Oct. 23, 1845

    Married in East Macon, by the Rev. Mr. Anthony, on Sunday last, MR. A.C. PARMELEE to MISS HESTER C. FICKLING.

Nov. 6, 1845

    Married on the 16th ult. by the Rev. W.W. Hardy, MR. J.V. DAVIS, of Putnam county, to MISS MARY WALKER, daughter of D.F. WALKER, of Monroe county, Geo.

Dec. 25, 1845

    Married on the 11th inst. near Montpelier, Monroe county, by George Brown, Esq. COL. JOHN C. BRADLEY to MISS JANE, daughter of the late FELIX HUCKABY, ESQ. all of Monroe county.

    Married in Knoxville, Crawford county, on the evening of the 16th inst. by the Rev. Mr. Perryman, COL. JOHN L. WOODWARD to MRS. ADELINE AMOS, all of said county.

Jan. 1, 1846

    Married in Harris county, on the evening of the 16th inst. by the Rev. T. Goulding ____ DOCTOR ____ BRUCE, to MISS CORNELIA MARKS, daughter of REV. R.T. MARKS.

    Married near Macon, on the 2d ult. by the Rev. Mr. S. Anthony, MR. WM. A. CHERRY, of Macon, to MISS MARTHA E. WILDER.

    Married in Crawford county, on the morning of the 14th inst. by the Rev. W.W. Robinson, ____ JOHN R. JORDIN, to MISS JOANNA S. ANDREWS, all of said county.

Jan. 22, 1846

    Married in Albany, Ga. on the 15th inst. by James A. Newman, Esq. MR. HEZEKIAH A. NASH to MISS CATHERINE G. BASSETT.

Jan. 29, 1846

    Married in this city, on Tuesday Evening last, by the Rev. S.G. Bragg, HARVEY W. SHAW, late of Orleans Co. N.Y. to MISS AUGUSTA M. CUMMING.

    Married on the 22d inst. by the Rev. Mr. Ousley, DAVID SMITH, ESQ., of Fayetteville, N.C. to MISS REBECCA T. FULLER, of this county.

Feb. 5, 1846

    Married in this city, on the 31st of January, by the Rev. J.R. Kendrick, MR. TIMOTHY GOODYEAR, to MRS. ELIZABETH WILLINGHAM.

Feb. 12, 1846

    Married on the 3d inst., by Luke J. Nowell, Esq. JACKSON CHAMBLESS, to MISS MARY TAPLY, all of this county.

Feb. 26, 1846

    Married on Wednesday evening, the 18th inst. by the Rev'd A.T. Holmes, MR. EBENEZER ROBINSON, of Hawkinsville, to MISS MARIA E. HATHAWAY, of Perry.

Mar. 5, 1846

    Married in this city on the 1st inst. by the Rev. J.R. Kendrick, MR. EMANUEL ISAACS to MISS HELEN J. BEASLEY, all of this city.

    Married in the Presbyterian Church, on Thursday evening, 26th ult., by Rev. Mr. Hooker, MR. CLARK S. PUTNAM to MISS FRANCES A. WARNER - all of this city.

    Married on the 26th ult., at Warrenton, Ga. by the Rev. P.N. Maddox, MR. JOHN C. MATHER, of this city, to MISS ELIZABETH C. HUBBARD, of Bergen, N.J.

Apr. 2, 1846

    Married in East Macon, on the 25th ult. by the Rev. Mr. Ellison, MR. M.J. LOPER, of Houston county, to MISS ELIZABETH C. BUTLER, daughter of CHAMPION BUTLER, ESQ. of this city.

Apr. 16, 1846

    Married in Monroe county, on the 31st ult. by the Rev. John S. Wilson, DR. ALEXANDER JACKSON, of Decatur, to MISS LOUISA A.T. MANN, daughter of COL. STEPHEN A. MANN of Monroe.

    Married in this city on Wednesday evening the 8th inst. by the 8th inst. by the Rev. S.G. Bragg, GREEN J. BLAKE, to MISS ELIZA MORRELL, all of this city.

    Married in Monroe county, on Sunday evening, the 12th inst. by the Rev. N. Ousley, ROBERT NELSON, ESQ. of Montgomery, Ala. to MISS MARTHA G., daughter of CHAS. Y. CALDWELL, ESQ. of Monroe county.

Apr. 30, 1846

    Married in this vicinity, on the 16th inst., by the Rev. Mr. Ellison, MR. WM. S. ELLIS, of this city, to MISS MARTHA J. GRAY, daughter of MR. WM. GRAY.

May 7, 1846

    Married at the residence of Col. R.V. Hardeman in Jones county, on the evening of the 29th April, by the Rev. J.R. Campbell, DR. ASBURY KINGMAN, of Clinton, to MISS ELIZABETH, daughter of JEREMIAH CLARK, ESQ. of Savannah.

May 14, 1846

    Married in this city on Tuesday evening the 5th inst. by the Rev. Mr. Bragg, DR. JAMES M. GREEN, to MISS SARAH VIRGINIA PRINCE, eldest daughter of the late OLIVER H. PRINCE.

May 28, 1846

    Married near Forsyth, on the 13th inst. by the Rev. J.R. Kendrick, MR. J. EGBERT THOMPSON to MISS MARY ANGELINA RANDLE, daughter of PETER RANDLE, ESQ.

    Married in Forsyth, on the 20th inst. by the Rev. J.R. Kendrick, NICHOLAS W. BATTLE, ESQ. to MISS MARY CABANISS, daughter of E.G. CABANISS, ESQ.

June 4, 1846

    Married at St. Marks, Fla., on the evening of the 21st inst. by the Rev. Wm. P. Buell, MR. WM. R. PETTES, to MISS HELEN H. DANELLY.

June 4, 1846

    Married in Meriwether County, on Wednesday evening the 27th inst. by the Hon. Hiram Warner, Judge Supreme Court, COL. SEYMOUR R. BONNER of the Warm Springs, to MISS MARY LOUISA, third daughter of STERLING EDWARDS, ESQ., all of Meriwether County.

June 11, 1846

    Married in this city, on the 6th inst., by the Rev. Wm. H. Ellison, MR. JAMES D. CARHART to MISS SARAH A. CURD.

July 9, 1846

    Married at Haynesville, Houston county, on the 27th inst. by the Rev. A.T. Holmes, H.H. TUCKER, ESQ. of Forsyth, to MISS MARY E., daughter of DR. CHARLES WEST, of Houston county.

    Married in Campbell county, on the 25th June, JOHN A. NELSON, of this city, to MISS SARAH N. HOGAN, daughter of COL. WM. HOGAN, of Campbell county.

    Married on Thursday evening, the 2d inst. by the Rev. Thos. G. Wood, MR. THOMAS JEFFERSON STEWART to MISS MARTHA J., daughter of the late BENJAMIN FINNEY, all of Jones county, Ga.

July 16, 1846

    Married near Montpelier on the 9th inst. by the Rev. Mr. Nowell, MR. JOHN McCALLUM to MISS SARAH ANN, eldest daughter of JOHN HART, ESQ., all of Monroe Co.

    Married in Houston county, by the Hon. N. Ousley, MR. HARDY B. BRYAN, of Macon county, to MISS SARAH E. ROUNDTREE, of Houston county.

July 23, 1846

    Married in Hayneville, Houston Co., on the 30th June, by Rev. N. Ousley, ISAAC H. MORELAND of East-Macon, to MARY JANE TOOKE, of the above named village.

July 30, 1846

    Married on Sunday morning, the 19th inst. by the Hon. D.W. Miller, MR. THOMAS RAGLAND to MISS ANNA E.W., daughter of SAM'L F. JONES, all of Lanier.

    Married on the evening of the 21st inst., at the residence of Dr. J. Beall of Harris county, by the Rev. J.W. Attiway, of Talbotton, MR. J.B. FOSTER, of Waverly Hall, to MISS J.V. SANDERS, of Macon, Ga.

Aug. 13, 1846

    Married in Crawford county on the evening of the 4th inst. by the Rev. W.W. Robinson, WILLIAM H. BROOKS, ESQ. to MRS (MISS?) MARTHA T. _____.

    Married in New Haven, Ct., on the ___ ult. by Rev. Dr. ___, the REV. RICHARD HOOKER, of this city, to AURELIA, daughter of JAMES DWIGHT (?), ESQ., of the former place.

    Married on the 6th inst. near Travellers Rest by the Rev. Benjamin Webb, MR. JAMES BUSEY, of South Carolina, to MISS ELIZABETH WILLIAMS of the former place.

Aug. 20, 1846

    Married on the 11th inst. by the Rev. B.F. Wade, COL. WILLIAM J. PATTERSON of Americus, to MISS ANNA MARRIA EDGWORTH, of Houston County Georgia. (The Southern Recorder, Georgia Journal, Camden Journal, and S.C. Temperance Advocate will please copy).

Sep. 10, 1846

    Married in this city on Tuesday evening the 8th inst. by the Rev. Mr. Kirby, MR. J.O. HODGES to MISS ELENORA H. WATTS, daughter of WM. B. WATTS, ESQ. all of this city.

Oct. 15, 1846

    Married in this city, on Sunday last by the Rev. Mr. Crumly, MR. AINSLEY H. WYCHE, to MISS HARRIET SULLIVAN.

    Married on Monday the 14th September, at the residence of James D. Gilmer, in Bossier Parish, Louisiana, by J.C.G. Key Esq. ANDREW LANSON ESQ. of Minden, Claiborn Parish, to MRS. MARY E.W. SHOTWELL, of Nacogdoches County Texas.

Oct. 22, 1846

    Married in Houston county, by the Rev. Edw'd T. McGehee MR. JAMES A. STUBBS to MISS MARY JULIA RENTZ.

Oct. 29, 1846

    Married in Culloden on the 27th by the Rev. M. Speer, MR. A.W. CHAPMAN to MISS SARAH W. LOCKET.

Dec. 3, 1846

    Married in this city, on Wednesday evening the 25th ult. by the Rev. Mr. Hooker, ME. ALLEN FLEMING to MISS ELIZABETH C. MARTIN, all of this city.

Dec. 10, 1846

    Married in this city, on the 8th inst. by the Rev. J.R. Kendrick, MR. M.R. ROGERS to miss M.E. LEDDEN, all of this city.

    Married on Tuesday the 1st inst. by William Bateman, Esq. DR. JOHN W. WALKER to MISS LUCINDA C. CUPEPPER, all of Houston county.

    Married on the 26th ult., by the Rev. W.H. Hebbard, ELIAS MIMS ESQ. to MISS GEORGIA A.R. RICE, all of Houston county.

Dec. 17, 1846

    Married on the 9th inst. by the Rev. J.R. Kendrick, MR. ROBERT L. MIMS, of Houston county, to MISS S.A.F. GILBERT, of Bibb county.

Dec. 24, 1846

    Married in this city by the Rev. S.G. Bragg, MR. HENRY DANIELS, to MISS JOSEPHINE TISSEREAU.

Dec. 31, 1846

    Married on the 22d inst. by the Rev. Mr. Hooker, ELIJAH A. BRADLEY, to MISS CATHARINE H. CUUTER, ALL OF THIS CITY.

    NOTE: Dec. 10, 1846 - Bride's name was probably intended to be CULPEPPER but the newspaper printed it minus the "L" Dec. 31, 1846 - Bride's name probably intended to be CUTTER (an early family of Macon) but newspaper spelled it CUUTER.

Jan. 14, 1847

    Married in Lumpkin, Stewart co. on the 31st Dec. by the Rev. Jos. T. Talley, MR. JNO. B. KENDRICK, of Stewart co., to MISS SARAH M. PATTON, of Macon.

Jan. 21, 1847

Married in Dooly county on Sunday morning the 17th inst. by Norrel R. Trulock, Esq., DR. H.C.M. RAIFORD, of Travellers Rest, to MISS AMELIA, daughter of the REV. BENJAMIN WEBB, of the former place.

Feb. 25, 1847

Married in Monroe co. on the 23d inst. by the Rev. Mr. Dickinson, COL. ABRAM W. COGART, of Harrodsburg, Ky, to MISS JULIA A.E. CALDWELL, daughter of C.Y. CALDWELL, ESQ., of Monroe county.

Mar. 11, 1847

Married on the 4th inst. by the Rev. Mr. Ousley, MR. W.T. HOLLINGS-WORTH, of this city, to MISS ANN M. JOHNSTON, of this county.

Married in this county on the evening of the 2d inst. by the Rev. W.J. Stephens, THOMAS R. GATES, ESQ. to MISS PATIENCE Z., eldest daughter of WM. H. and CAROLINE A. LOWE.

Mar. 25, 1847

Married at Fort Valley, Houston county, on the 10th inst. by the Rev. D. Kelsey, MR. WM. J. ANDERSON to MISS REBECCA C. HOLLINSHEAD.

Married in Atlanta on the 14th inst. by Rev. J.S. Wilson, WILLIAM H. ROYAL, Senior Editor of the Atlanta Enterprise, to MISS SARAH FOX.

Married at the Oregon House in this city on the 23d inst., MR. JOHN S. INGRAHAM to MISS ELIZA ANN JARVIS.

Married in Upson county on Thursday evening 18th instant by the Rev. William Crawford, MR. JAMES M. BARRON to MRS. LOUISA C. BROOKS.

Apr. 15, 1847

Married on the 8th April in this city by the Rev. W.H. Crumley, ALPHEUS C. COLVARD, ESQ., of Appling, Columbia Co., Ga., to MISS ANN LAMAR, of this place.

Married on the 4th inst. by A.J. Williams, Esq., MR. HENRY F. BURKE to MISS MARY A.E. DOZIER - all of Sumter county.

May 19, 1847

Married on Thursday evening the 6th inst. by the Rev. W.H. Ellison, MR. H.M. LINDSAY to MISS MARY A. FLINT, all of this city.

Married in this city on Thursday evening May 13th by the Rev. Mr. Hooker, MR. D. CHESTER RUSSELL, formerly of Connecticut, to MISS ELODIA B., daughter of BENJAMIN TRAPP, ESQ., of this city.

May 26, 1847

Married on the 20th inst. near Travellers Rest, Dooly county, MR. FELIX JOHNSTON, of Twiggs, to MISS SUSAN JONES, daughter of ELIAH JONES

Married in Dooly county on the 20th inst. by Wm. S. Hammil, Esq., MR. MORGAN W. DAVIS, of Macon county, to MISS MARY FRANCES TURNER, of the former place.

Married in this city on the 8th inst. by the Rev. Mr. Crumley, WILLIAM S. WALLACE, of Charleston, S.C., to MISS MARTHA ANN GAMBLE, eldest daughter of WILLIAM B. GAMBLE, of this city.

June 16, 1847

　　Married in this city on the 9th inst. by the Rev. Wm. M. Crumley, WILLIS S. BREAZEAL, ESQ., of Burke county, to MISS MATILDA J. MOORE.

June 23, 1847

　　Married in Monroe county on Thursday morning the 31st by Martin Ansley, M.G., COL. EWELL WEBB, of Crawford county, to MISS GABRILLA E.A., daughter of WM. SAUNDERS, ESQ.

July 7, 1847

　　Married in Muscogee county on Sunday the 27th ult. by Rev. C.C. Willis, GEN. ELIAS BEALL, of Macon, Geo., to MRS. ELIZABETH PRUETT, of the former place.

July 14, 1847

　　Married on the 30th June by the Rev. Dr. Talmage, MR. WM. W. CARTER, of Greenville, Ga., to MISS ANN K. WARTHEN, of Midway, Baldwin Co., Ga.

　　Married on the 1st instant by the Rev. S.W. Durham, MR. WM. W. RHODES to MISS CAROLINE G., daughter of RICHARD HALL - all of Talbot county.

July 21, 1847

　　Married by the Rev. Mr. Boring of Eatonton, DR. WADE C. COX, of Americus, to MISS MARTHA A. PEARSON, of Putnam county.

July 28, 1847

　　Married at the residence of Major John Howard, near Columbus, on Tuesday evening the 13th by the Rev. Dr. Pierce, MAJOR CHARLES J. WILLIAMS to MISS MARY A. HOWARD.

　　Married in Oxford, Georgia on Thursday evening 15th inst. by the Rev. Dr. A. Means, L.Q.C. LAMAR, ESQ. to MISS VIRGINIA L. LONGSTREET, daughter of A.B. LONGSTREET, L.L.D.

　　Married in Twiggs county on the evening of the 22d instant by the Rev. Jesse H. Campbell, MR. WILLIAM FAULK to MISS VIRGINIA A. SOLOMON, daughter of the late COL. HENRY SOLOMON.

Aug. 4, 1847

　　Married in Crawford county, near Knoxville, at the residence of Mr. S.S. Wright on Sunday morning 1st inst., by the Rev. Marlin Ansley, JUDGE L.F. HICKS to MISS MARY ANN WRIGHT, all of Crawford.

Aug. 11, 1847

　　Married in Macon county on the evening of the 29th ult. by William J. Tillman, Esq., MR. MILTON S. McKENZIE, of Travellers Rest, to MISS AMERICA ANN DAVIS, daughter of ICHABOD DAVIS, of the former place.

Oct. 20, 1847

　　Married on the 5th inst. by the Rev. R.M. Hooker, MR. SAMPSON MASSEY LANIER, of this city, to MISS GEORGIA A. VIGAL, of East Macon. (Greensboro, N.C. papers please copy)

Nov. 3, 1847

　　Married in this city on Tuesday the 26th of October, by the Rev. Mr. Williams, MR. D.R. RODGERS to MISS CATHERINE E. SEYMOUR, all of this city.

Nov. 17, 1847

    Married in Madison on the 2d instant by the Rev. Mr. Herberk, COL. SAMUEL R. BLAKE, of Macon, to MRS. FRANCES P. WYATT, of Madison.

    Married in Mount Zion on the 2d instant by the Rev. Mr. Bowman, MR. J.R. BRANHAM, of Eatonton, to MISS JULIA MARIA, daughter of the HON. ALFRED IVERSON, of Columbus.

Nov. 24, 1847

    Married on the evening of the 16th inst., in Houston county, by the Rev. F.W. Baggerly, MR. JOHN H. RUTHERFORD to MISS S.M. ANDERSON.

Dec. 22, 1847

    Married on the evening of the 9th instant by the Rev. Dolphin Davis, MR. HENRY W. SMITH to MISS ISABELLA E., daughter of CALVIN MURCHISON, ESQ., all of Crawford county.

    Married on the evening of the 14th November by the Rev. Mr. Campbell, MR. HENRY E. WIMBERLY, of Twiggs county, to MISS ELIZABETH WALKER, daughter of MR. GEORGE WALKER, of Pulaski.

Dec. 29, 1847

    Married in Twiggs county on the 21st inst. by the Rev. C.A. Tharp, MR. WILLIAM FINCH to MRS. LOUISA FULTON. On the same evening DR. WILLIAM T. ZACHARY to MISS MARTHA FINCH.

    Married on the 22d inst. by the Rev. Mr. Ellison, MR. JOSEPH McALPIN, of Upson, to MISS AMELIA M.G., daughter of P.E. BOWDRE, of this city.

Jan. 5, 1848

    Married in Maocn county on 9th November last, MR. ISAAC WEBB to MISS MARY BROOKS.

    Married at the Episcopal Church in this City on Sunday the 2d inst. by the Rev. Joseph A. Shanklin, JACOB A. BURBANK, A.B., of Houston Co. (formerly of Wayne Co., N.Y.) to MISS MARGRETTE VIRGINIA MITCHELL of Macon.

Jan. 19, 1848

    Married in Pike county on Thursday evening, the 23d December last, by the Rev. Mr. Stamper, COL. DANIEL HOWARD, of Griffin, to MISS MARTHA, daughter of JOHN GREEN, ESQ.

    Married on the 16th instant by the Rev. F.W. Baggerly, REV. DANIEL KELSEY, of the Georgia Conference, to MRS. E.A. CHAINE, of Perry.

Jan. 26, 1848

    Married in Macon county on Tuesday the 18th inst. by the Rev. F.D. Wade, MR. GEORGE WALKER, of Houston county, to MISS FRANCES FREDERICK.

    Married on the 19th inst. by the Rev. W.R. Singleton, of Marion county, MR. A. CONGLETON, of Sumter county, to MISS ELIZA H. FOSTER, daughter of MR. ARTHUR FOSTER, of Bibb county.

Feb. 9, 1848

    Married on the 2d inst. by the Rev. John M. Fields, DOCTR. B.F. BONNER to MISS CAROLINE NEWSOM, all of Bibb county.

    Married in Muscogee county on the 2d inst. by the Rev. R. Dozier, MR. O.V. BROWN, of Jones county, to MRS. MARTHA W. KINBROUGH.

Feb. 9, 1848

Married in Culloden on the morning of the 3d inst. by the Rev. Richard Holmes, DR. ROBERT J. FLEWELLEN to MISS CARRIE BIVINS.

Feb. 16, 1848

Married on Thursday evening the 3d inst. by the Rev. Mr. Winn, JOHN H. POWERS, ESQ. to MISS CLIFFORD STILES, daughter of DR. CHARLES WEST, of Houston county.

Mar. 1, 1848

Married in Auburn (Ala). on the 23d ult. by the Rev. Mark Westmoreland, MR. JOHN W.W. DRAKE to MISS VOLICIA V.A. MITCHELL, both of the former place.

Married in Eatonton on the morning of the 23d inst. by the Rev. Mr. Key, THOMAS HARDEMAN, JR., ESQ. to MISS SARAH F. POOL, both of St. Marks, Florida.

Mar. 22, 1848

Married on the evening of the 15th inst. at the residence of Mrs. Fluker in this city, by the Rev. Mr. Shanklin, EDWARD J. JOHNSTON, ESQ. to MISS FLORA A. CAMPBELL.

Married in this Ctiy on the 2d of March by the Rev. Walter Branham, MR. HILLIARD J. CHERRY to MISS W. WRIGHT, all of this city.

Mar. 29, 1848

Married in Vineville on the 18th inst. by the Rev. W.B. Branham, MR. JAMES H. GILLINS to MISS MARTHA ELIZABETH HOBBS.

Married on the 21st inst. by the Rev. John W. Turner, CULLEN H. COTTLE, of Sumter county, to MARTHA, daughter of WRIGHT SHERRARD, ESQ. of Talbot county.

Apr. 19, 1848

Married on the 30th ult. at Mr. Charles Walker's in Pulaski county, by the Hon. James J. Scarborough, DR. W.N.L. CROCKER, of Macon county, to MRS. LOUISA G. WRIGHT.

Married on Thursday evening the 2d ult. by the Rev. Wyatt R. Singleton, LEONIDAS A. GAAR to MISS MARTHA TOMPKINS, all of Marion county.

May 3, 1848

Married in this city on Tuesday evening the 25th April by the Rev. Mr. Hooker, JOHN G. WOODSON, ESQ., of Russell County, Alabama, to MISS CAROLINE E. HOGE, of this city.

May 10, 1848

Married on the 5th ult. at the Florida Line by the Rev. J. Smith, MR. ANDERSON GRAHAM to MISS PERTHENA MORGAN, all of Lowndes county, Ga.

Married in Jefferson county on Tuesday evening 2d instant by the Rev. Mr. Stapleton, CAPT. D.M. CAUSEY, of Knoxville, Ga., to MISS NANCY J., daughter of JOS. OLIPHANT, ESQ.

May 24, 1848

Married in Lee county on the evening of the 11th inst. by the Rev. Ansley Philips, A.B. DUNCAN, ESQ. to MISS ELLEN A. BRYAN.

May 31, 1848

    Married at Fort Gaines, Early County, on the 16th inst. by the Rev. Mr. Turner, JNO. F. TROUTMAN, ESQ. to MISS VICTORIA J., daughter of MAJOR JAMES P. HOLMES.

June 7, 1848

    Married in Christ Church on Wednesday 24th ult. by the Rev. Mr. Shanklin, JAMES T. WELSMAN, of Charleston, S.C., to CAROLINE, daughter of LEROY NAPIER, ESQ., of this city.

    Married in this city on the morning of the 6th inst. by the Rev. Joseph Stiles, EDWIN B. WEED, ESQ. to MRS. SARAH A. LeCONTE.

June 14, 1848

    Married in Watkinsville on the 30th ult. by Rev. J.N. Glenn, MR. JOHN CALVIN JOHNSON, ESQ. to MRS. MATILDA HARDEN, all of that place.

June 21, 1848

    Married in this city on Thursday evening 15th inst. by Judge Samuel B. Hunter, MR. SETH CASON of Crawford county to MRS. SUSAN CALHOUN.

July 5, 1848

    Married in this city on the 28th inst. by the Rev. Mr. Pierce, MR. WM. H. BRAY to MISS SARAH SIMS.

    Married on the 28th ult. by the Rev. A.T. Holmes, COL. GEORGE F. COOPER to MISS LENORA DUNCAN, both of Perry, Houston county.

    Married in Culloden on the 29th ult. by the Rev. Richard Holmes, MR. J.C. MATHER to MRS. EMELINE C. COTTEN, both of Culloden.

    Married at New Port, Florida on the 22d ult. by the Rev. Joshua Phelps, MR. GEORGE S. KING to MISS MARY ANN CROOM.

July 19, 1848

    Married on Sunday morning 9th inst., in Twiggs county, by the Rev. Jesse H. Campbell, MR. ELIAS PEARCE to MRS. LUCINDA SOLOMON.

    Married on the 16th by the Rev. Wm. H. Ellison, D.D., MR. JAMES G. RODGERS of this city to MISS LUCRETIA A., eldest daughter of JOSEPH WILLET, ESQ., of Bibb County.

July 26, 1848

    Married at Clinton, Jones county, on the 18th instant by the Rev. W.R. Branham, REUBEN C. SHORTER, ESQ., of Montgomery, Ala., to MISS CAROLINE BILLINGSLEA.

    Married in Knoxville, Crawford county, Ga. on the 23d inst. by Wm. H. Brooks, Esq., MR. WM. J. CAUSEY to MISS SARAH E. WRIGHT, second daughter of the late JAMES H. WRIGHT, deceased.

Aug. 2, 1848

    Married on the 19th ult. by the Rev. Mr. Baggerly, DR. J.(?) R. COOK to MISS LAVINIA A. HARMON, both of Macon county.

Aug. 16, 1848

    Married on the 3d instant by the Rev. Dr. McGehee, JOHN C. ASHBURN, ESQ. to MISS MARTHA F. EDWARDS, daughter of REV. JOSEPH EDWARDS, of Houston county. (Savannah Republican please copy).

Aug. 16, 1848

   Married on the 10th inst. by Dr. W.S. Lightfoot, MR. SANFORD F.
   MAYNARD to MISS GILLA ELIZABETH, eldest daughter of JOSEPH MESSER,
   ESQ., all of Jones county, Geo.

Oct. 11, 1848

   Married near Travellers Rest on Sunday morning the 24th inst. by
   N.R. Trulock, Esq., MR. ELI C. THOMSON to MRS. MARY A.F. POWELL,
   all of Dooly county.

Nov. 1, 1848

   Married on the 22d ult. at the residence of Seaborn McMichael by
   the Rev. Dr. Dozier, MR. WILLIAM B. STEVENS to MISS SARAH M.
   McMICHAEL, all of Marion county.

Nov. 8, 1848

   Married on the 7th inst. in Pulaski county by the Rev. David Smith,
   MR. JAS. R. COOMBS of Laurens county to MISS SARAH E. BOOTHE,
   eldest daughter of THEOPHILUS D. BOOTHE of the former place.

Nov. 15, 1848

   Married on the evening of the 8th inst. by the Rev. W.H. Ellison,
   MR. JOHN E. JONES to MISS ARABELLA O., second daughter of MR.
   JAMES DEAN, all of this city.

Nov. 29, 1848

   Married on the 21st November by the Right Rev. Bishop Elliott,
   DANIEL GRIFFIN, ESQ., of Columbus, Georgia, and MISS MARY ELIZABETH,
   daughter of JOHN POWERS, ESQ., of Monroe county.

Dec. 6, 1848

   Married on the 28th inst. in Hawkinsville by Judge J.G. Polhill,
   MAJ. HENRY WOOD, of Macon, to MRS. CASANDER POLLOCK, of the former
   place.

   Married on the 23d November by Dr. W.S. Lightfoot (J.I.C.), MR.
   ABRAHAM JOHNSON to MRS. SARAH G. EATON, all of Jones county.

Dec. 20, 1848

   Married on Tuesday morning of the 5th inst. by the Rev. Jas. R.
   McCarter, JOHN R. WORRELL, ESQ. to MISS SARAH A. SELLECK, all of
   Americus, Sumter county.

Dec. 27, 1848

   Married on the morning of the 21st inst. by the Rev. S.G. Bragg,
   MR. JACOB V. RUMPH, of Houston county, Ga., to MISS MARY CHURCH,
   of Bethlehem, Connecticut.

   Married on Thursday evening the 21st inst. by the Rev. Richard A.
   Cain, DR. HENRY A. SCOTT to MISS ELIZABETH M. RENBERT, all of
   Bibb county.

Jan. 10, 1849

   Married on the morning of 25th December last, in this city, by the
   Rev. Wm. M. Crumly, MR. JAMES A. KNIGHT to MISS MARY E. RICHARDS,
   both of this city.

Jan. 24, 1849

Married on the 18th inst. by the Rev. James Williamson, ROBERT W. RADFORD, of Twiggs county, to MISS ELIZA E. COLEY, daughter of JOHN A.D. COLEY, ESQ. of Pulaski county.

Married in Thomas county on the 14th inst. by Isaac G. Jourdan, Esq. MR. WILLIAM J. HEARD to MISS MARGARET E. MITCHELL, daughter of THOMAS G. and ELIZABETH MITCHELL.

Married in Putnam county on the 11th instant by William Davies, Esq., MR. JAMES YANCEY to MISS LOUISA LEE - all of Putnam county, Ga.

Feb. 21, 1849

Married on the 14th instant by the Rev. Mr. Fuller, AMOS LASSETER, ESQ., of Twiggs county, to MISS ELIZABETH R. HARMON, of Monroe county, Ga.

Married in this place on Wednesday evening the 14th inst. by the Rev. Washington Baird, COL. JOHN T. SMITH, Secretary Executive Department, to MISS LAURA VIRGINIA RALSTON, of Macon.

Feb. 28, 1849

Married in this city on Thursday morning the 22d inst. by Rev. Wm. H. Ellison, MR. THOS. D. EASON, of Charleston, S.C., to MISS WILHELMINA L., youngest daughter of STERLING LANIER, ESQ. of Macon.

Married at Hawkinsville, Ga. on the 15th instant by his Hon. Thomas G. Polhill, JAMES L. MIMS, of Augusta, Ga. to MRS. AMANDA M. COOPER, of the former place.

Mar. 7, 1849

Married on the 28th ult. at the house of Dr. A.V. Mann in Forsyth, Ga., by Rev. S.G. Bragg, Prof. I.N. LOOMIS, late of Franklin College (Tenn.) to MISS SUSAN E., daughter of SAMUEL M. HAYDEN, of Essex, Conn.

Mar. 21, 1849

Married in this city on the 15th inst. by the Rev. Mr. Hooker, MR. MOSES D. BARNES to MISS REBECCA JUSTISS, all of this place.

Apr. 18, 1849

Married by the Rev. John Fullwood at the residence of U.W. Wise, Esq. in Fort Valley, on Tuesday March 27, A.B. HAWKES, M.D., of Houston county, Ga., to MISS MARY T. WALLACE, late of Cadiz, Ohio.

Married by the Rev. Dow Perry on the 22d of March, COL. WILLIAM J. HENRY to MISS N. AMELIA DENSON, all of Macon county, Ala.

May 9, 1849

Married on the 19th April by the Rev. Jno. E. Dawson, DR. G.D. ROYSTON of Oak Lawn, Baker county, Ga., to MISS MILDRED ANN, daughter of NOLAND LEWIS, ESQ. of Russel County, Ala.

Married in Crawford county on the 20th ult., MR. WM. E. HAMMACK to MARTHA MOORE.

May 16, 1849

Married in Travellers Rest on the 6th inst. by the Rev. Mr. Peurifoy, MR. WILLIAM S. TRULUCK to MISS CHRISTIANA BENDER.

May 23, 1849

    Married in this city on the morning of the 16th inst. by Rev.
    William H. Ellison, ERASTUS KIRTLAND, ESQ. to MISS ELIZA SIMS.

May 30, 1849

    Married in Jefferson county on the 24th inst. by the Rev. Wm. H.
    Ellison, IRA H. TAYLOR, of this city, to MISS MARY S. CONNALLY,
    daughter of PATRICK B. CONNALLY, ESQ.

    Married in Macon county on the 22d inst. by D.H. Brown, Esq., MR.
    STEPHEN E. RIGGINS, of Sumter county, to MISS CLARISA AMANDA,
    daughter of ICHABOD DAVIS, ESQ.

    Married in Monroe county on Sunday morning last by Rev. J.P. Duncan,
    JAMES W. GAULDING (Editor of the Bee) to MISS LUCINDA J., daughter
    of THOMAS F. MALONE, of Russell county, Ala.

    Married in Laurens county on Wednesday the 16th instant by the Rev.
    Dr. Smith of Sandersville, COL. THOMAS C. HOWARD, of Crawford county,
    to MISS ELIZABETH KELLUM.

June 20, 1849

    Married in Marion county on the 14th inst. by the Rev. D.N. Burkhalt-
    er, MR. WILLIAM J. REESE, of Thomaston, to MISS MARY BROWN, daughter
    of COL. WM. M. BROWN.

    Married in Randolph county on the 12th inst. by the Rev. J.H.
    Wilkins, MR. JOHN A. McGREGOR to MISS MARGARET J. JOHNSTON, daughter
    of JAMES JOHNSTON.

June 27, 1849

    Married in this city on Thursday morning 14th inst. by the Rev.
    Walter Branham, MRS. AGNES ISABELLA SIMONTON, of Abbeville District,
    S.C., to E. CLIFTON BLAKE, ESQ., of this city.

    Married in Houston county on the 17th inst. by the Rev. J.C.
    Postell, MR. F.L. NIXON to MISS S.E. RICE, daughter of COLO RICE,
    formerly of Barnwell district, S.C.

July 4, 1849

    Married on the 8th ult. by the Rev. John Wright, R. MANNING
    LEVERETT, ESQ. to MISS CYNTHIA LANIER, daughter of MRS. MARY LANIER,
    all of Meriwether county.

    Married in East Macon on Thursday evening 28th ult. by the Rev.
    P.A. Strobel, MR. HENRY WILKES, of Twiggs county, to MISS SRAAH
    ANN HOLLAND, of East Macon.

    Married in Lee county on the 24th ult., MR. WILLIAM WATERER to
    MISS THERESA THOMAS.

July 18, 1849

    Married at the residence of and by Judge Davis of Macon county, on
    the 10th instant, MR. HUGH LAWSON, of Houston, to MRS. MARY WORTHY.

    Married in Vineville on Sunday the 15th inst, by the Rev. Walter
    R. Branham, the REV. WILLIAM M. CRUMLEY, pastor of the Vineville
    Church, to MISS JULIA ANNE, eldest daughter of MR. JACOB J. CHOAT,
    of Vineville.

Aug. 1, 1849

    Married on the 17th inst. at her residence in New Georgia, near
    Wetumpka, Ala. by the Rev. J.D. Williams, JAMES HOLMES, ESQ., of
    Talbot Co., Ga. to MRS. J.C. GAITHER.

Aug. 15, 1849

Married by D.H. Brown, Esq. on the 9th instant, MR. JAMES P. WEST to MISS SARAH JANE SCRUTCHEN, daughter of JOSIAH SCRUTCHEN, all of Sumter county.

Aug. 22, 1849

Married on Sunday morning the 12th instant by Robert Mays, Judge Inferior Court, MR. WILLIAM GRESHAM, of Monroe county, to MISS SARAH ANN, daughter of DAVID ELDER, of Butts county.

Married on the same day by the same, JAMES M. CLOWER, of Monroe county, to MISS OLIVE J., daughter of WILLIAM A. McCUNE, of Butts county.

Married in Houston county on the 12th inst. by the Rev. J.C. Postell, MR. JACOB HILEY to MISS DORA A. MOORE.

Oct. 3, 1849

Married in Madison on the 20th ultimo by the Rev. Chas. M. Irwin, CHARLES E. NISBET, ESQ., of Lagrange, to MISS VIRGINIA E. JONES, of the former place.

Oct. 10, 1849

Married in Crawford county at Mrs. Cleveland's on Thursday the 27th ultimo, by the Rev. Washington C. Cleveland, MR. ROMULUS W. MATTHEWS to MISS LOUISA F. REEVES, both of Crawford county, Ga.

Oct. 17, 1849

Married in this city on the 10th inst. by the Rev. Dr. Ellison, GEORGE S. OBEAR to MISS HARRIET E. GRAY, daughter of WILLIAM GRAY - all of this city.

Married on the 2d instant by Hon. Joseph Day, J.I.C., DR. WM. N. STEWART, of Marion, Twiggs county (formerly of Jones county) to MISS CAMILLA S., daughter of MR. JOHN E. LESTER, of Jones county.

Oct. 24, 1849

Married on the 16th instant by the Rev. James Thomas, ROBERT B. LESTER, ESQ., of the city of Macon, to MISS MARY AUGUSTA, daughter of BARNARD HILL, ESQ. of Talbotton, Ga.

Oct. 31, 1849

Married on Sunday morning the 14th inst. at the house of Wm. Tinsley, by the Rev. Elijah Northcut, MR. PHILIP P. CLAYTON to MISS JANE E. TINSLEY, both of Cobb county.

Married in Pulaski county by John Lee, Esq., SIMEON A. ROLAND to MISS AMANDA A. ROZIER.

Nov. 7, 1849

Married in Bulloch county on Sunday morning the 28th ult., by the Rev. Wm. McQueen, COL. WM. M. BROWN, United States Marshal for the District of Georgia, to MRS. ANN E. RAWLS, of Bulloch county.

Nov. 14, 1849

Married on the 30th ultimo by the Hon. John J. Floyd, DR. JOSEPH H. MURRELL, of Covington, to MISS MARY ANN NEAL, daughter of JOHN NEAL, of Zebulon.

Married on Sunday morning the 5th inst. by Robt. Mays, J.I.C,, MR. ROBT. B. HANSFORD, of Monroe county, to MISS ELIZABETH A., daughter of WILLIAM A. McCUNE, ESQ., of Butts county.

Nov. 21, 1849

Married on the evening of the 14th inst., JAMES F. WINTER, of Columbus, to MISS C. VICTORIA, daughter of MAJOR A. COMER, of Vineville.

Married in Pike county at the house of John B. Reed on the 14th instant by the Rev. O.C. Gibson, RUFUS W. McCUNE, ESQ., of Jackson, to MISS MARY S. ALEXANDER, of Lowndes county, Ala.

Married in Cass county on the 1st inst. by the Rev. Thos. Knowles, MR. JOHN R. FREEMAN, of Jones county, to MISS MARY TROUPIANA HAMILTON, daughter of DR. THOMAS HAMILTON.

Nov. 28, 1849

Married in Vineville on the 22d inst. by the Rev. W.H. Ellison, MR. A.C. SPAIN, of Sumter District, S.C., to MISS SARAH JANE, daughter of THOMAS HARDEMAN, ESQ. of this city.

Married in Twiggs county on the 22d inst. by Rev. C.A. Tharp, REV. JESSE STALLINGS, of Sumter county, to MRS. MARY HODGES.

Dec. 12, 1849

Married on the 2d inst. by the Rev. J.A. Shanklin, MR. W.S. WILLIFORD to MRS. CAROLINE E. HOLMES - all of this city.

Married in Twiggs county on the 6th inst. by Thos. Glover, J.I.C., MR. JOHN A. CLEMENTS to MISS JULIA ASBELL, daughter of the late ELISHA ASBELL.

Dec. 19, 1849

Married in this city on the 13th inst. by the Rev. Walter H. Branham, MR. W.W. WAGNON to MISS MARY VIRGINIA CRAWFORD, all of this city.

Married in Monroe county on the 4th inst. by the Rev. J.P. Duncan, MR. W.B. MERRITT to MISS MARY JANE BOZEMAN.

Married in Laurens county on the 6th inst. by the Hon. E.J. Blackshear, MR. W.G. WRIGHT to MISS REBECCA MOWMAN, all of Laurens county.

Married in this city by the Rev. Prof. Myers, MR. GEORGE WOOD to MISS RACHAEL ANN, daughter of MR. JOHN B. NORRALL, all of this city.

Dec. 26, 1849

Married on the 19th inst. MR. JOHN EZELL to MISS EMILY, daughter of EVAN POWELL, ESQ., all of Jasper county.

Jan. 2, 1850

Married in Twiggs county on the 18th inst. by Rev. David Roberts, MR. JESSE COOPER, of Houston county, to MISS LOUISA H. BROWN, of the former place, daughter of HARDY BROWN, deceased.

Married in Houston county on the 21st inst. by the Rev. James Murray, FREDERICK WEST, of Dooly county, to MISS MARY JANE ALLEN, daughter of THOMAS ALLEN, ESQ., formerly of Burke county.

Married on the 27th ult. in Jones county by the Rev. Dr. Ellison, HENRY P. ADAMS, ESQ., formerly of R.I., now of Eufaula, Ala., to MISS ELIZABETH SEABROOK, daughter of the late SMILIE SEABROOK, ESQ.

Married in Bibb county on Tuesday evening 25th Dec. 1849 by Keelin Cook, J.I.C., MR. SAMUEL D. FULLER to MISS SARAH JANE BOWMAN - all of said county.

Jan. 9, 1850

Married by the Rev. Dr. Ellison on the evening of the 1st inst., MILES L. GREEN, ESQ., of Houston county, to MISS ANN E. PERSONS, daughter of REV. GEORGE W. PERSONS, of Crawford county.

Jan. 16, 1850

Married in this city on the 8th inst. by the Rev. Sylvanus Landrum, MR. JOHN E. POUND to MISS THURSA L. FLEMING.

Jan. 23, 1850

Married at the residence of J.B. Rowland, Esq., Montgomery, Ala., on the 11th inst. by Rev. Mr. Morrison, COL. M.B. MENARD, of Galveston, Texas, to REBECCA MARY, eldest daughter of MRS. SARAH FLUKER, of this city.

Jan. 30, 1850

Married on the 22d instant by the Rev. D.F. Wade, MR. WILLIAM H. FELTON to MISS MARY V., daughter of DR. WILLIAM N.L. CROCKER - all of Macon county.

Feb. 6, 1850

Married on the 3d inst. by the Rev. Richard A. Cain, MR. JOHN SCOTT to MRS. J.G. REMBERT, all of this county.

Feb. 13, 1850

Married on the 30th ult. by the Rev. Thomas Speight, MR. MEREDITH TAYLOR to MISS NANCY KING, all of Houston county.

Feb. 27, 1850

Married on the 21st inst. by the Rev. W.R. Branham, MR. JOHN T. PRICE to MISS SARAH P. FLANDERS, all of East Macon.

Mar. 6, 1850

Married on the 21st of December last by the Rev. J. Danforth, HAYDEN HUGHES to MISS CAROLINE M. WILLIS - all of Twiggs county.

Married in Bryan county on the 28th ult. by Rev. J.S. Law, MR. E.F.T. ROWLAND, of Savannah, to MISS MARY WINN, daughter of DOCT. RAYMOND HARRIS, of the former place.

Mar. 20, 1850

Married on the 6th inst. in Atlanta by the Rev. William G. Parks, MR. J.G.W. MILLS, of Marietta, to MISS SARAH E. PAYNE, daughter of EDWIN PAYNE, ESQ., of Atlanta.

Mar. 27, 1850

Married on Tuesday evening the 19th by Willis Allen, J.P., at Cool Spring, the REV. DAVID SMITH to MISS LIDA PEARCE, both of the same place.

Married on the 20th inst. by Eli Sears, Esq., MR. LEVI GALIMORE, of Twiggs county, to MISS ELIZABETH McNAIR, daughter of WM. McNAIR, of the county of Wilkinson.

Apr. 10, 1850

Married on Tuesday evening 2d inst. by Rev. D.F. Wade, COL. NATHAN M. MASSEY, of Dooly county, to MISS CELIA, daughter of E.H. ADAMS, ESQ., of the county of Macon.

Apr. 24, 1850

    Married on the 16th inst. in Vineville by the Rev. N. Ousley, DOCTR. STEPHEN H. CONGER to MISS JANE AMELIA SEABURY, both of Bloomfield, New Jersey.

May 1, 1850

    Married in this city on the 24th inst. by the Rev. R. Hooker, COL. C.H. DOUGLASS of Summerville, Tennessee, to MISS ELIZA B., daughter of the late DR. R.H. RANDOLPH.

    Married at Longstreet, Pulaski county, on the 17th ult. by the Rev. A. Wright, MR. JOHN W. CROCKER to MISS T.S.T. JAMIESON.

May 8, 1850

    Married in Forsyth on the 2d inst. by the Rev. Mr. Overby, CINCINNATUS PEEPLES, ESQ., of Athens, to MISS ELIZA J., daughter of E.G. CABANISS, ESQ.

    Married on the 2d instant by the Rev. Sylvanis Landrum, COL. WILLIAM F. WILBURN of Penfield to MISS FRANCES I. WILLETT, of East Macon.

    Married at Newport on the 22d instant by the Rev. William Neil, MR. DANIEL LADD and MISS ELIZABETH A. OVERSTREET, all of Newport.

May 15, 1850

    Married on the morning of the 9th inst. by the Rev. Mr. Dickison, MR. D.W. SIMMONS, of Hickory Grove, to MISS EUGENIA A. RAINES, of Talbotton, Ga.

    Married in Gadsden county, Fla. on Wednesday evening 20th of April, by Rev. W. McElroy, DOCTOR J.W. BISHOP to MISS JULIA ANN, daughter of DAVID MILLS, ESQ.

    Married in Columbus on the 8th inst. by the Rev. Wm. M. Crumley, COL. HENRY J. LAMAR, of Macon, to MISS VALERIA B., eldest daughter of WILEY E. JONES, ESQ., of that city.

May 22, 1850

    Married in Vineville by the Rev. Wm. H. Ellison on the 20th inst., GEORGE M. LOGAN, ESQ. to MISS PAULINE HARDEMAN.

May 29, 1850

    Married in Dooly county on the 21st inst. by the Rev. J.T. Smith, THOMAS A. SWEARINGEN, ESQ. to MISS FRANCIS JANE FUDGE, both of the former county.

June 12, 1850

    Married on Monday morning 10th instant by the Rev. Mr. Branham, MR. E.S. ROGERS to MISS CATHARINE McGREAL - both of this city.

    Married by the Rev. G.W. Persons on Tuesday morning, 28th of May, MR. AUGUSTUS A. PERSONS, of Culloden, to MISS MARY B. QUIGLEY, of Houston county.

July 3, 1850

    Married on the 25th ult. by the Rev. J.P. Duncan, MR. JOSEPH R. BANKS, of Pike county, Ga., to MISS AMANDA M. DAVIS, daughter of ARCHIBALD DAVIS, ESQ., of Monroe county, Ga.

    Married on the 25th ultimo by D.H. Brown, Esq., DR. ENOS SCARBOROUGH and MISS MARY ANN, oldest daughter of ROBERT PRYOR, deceased, all of Sumter county.

July 31, 1850

    Married near Fort Valley on Sunday morning the 21st July, by the Rev. Mr. Murray, MR. J.B. WRIGHT, P.M. of Daviston, Talbot county, to MISS EVALINA HAMILTON, of Houston county.

Aug. 7, 1850

    Married in Talbot county on the 31st ult. by the Rev. Thomas B. Slade, MR. JOSEPH B. ROULHAC, of Marianna, Florida, to MISS MARTHA HINES DIXON, daughter of ROBERT DIXON, ESQ.

Aug. 14, 1850

    Married in this county on the 29th ult. by the Rev. N. Ousley, REV. THOMAS DOUGHERTY to MISS MARY REDDING.

Sep. 18, 1850

    Married in Macon county on the 5th inst. by the Rev. E.T. McGhee, MR. JAMES A. SPIVEY to MISS GEORGIANA V. HAUGABROOK.

    Married at the residence of Mrs. Key on Thursday evening the 12th instant, by the Rev. John K. Morse, MR. BENJAMIN FORT to MISS ELIZA VIRGINIA KEY - all of Vienna, Dooly county, Georgia.

Oct. 23, 1850

    Married on the 10th inst. by the Rev. J.C. Postell, MR. WARREN W. DAVIS to MISS ANN ELIZABETH, eldest daughter of J.J. HAUGABROOK, deceased - all of Macon county, Georgia.

Oct. 30, 1850

    Married on the 19th instant by the Rev. Wm. L. Tucker, ISAAC B. HUFF, ESQ., of Warrenton, to MISS ICY A. TURNER, of Burke county, Georgia.

    Married on the 24th Oct. by Robert Mays, J.I.C., SHEPPARD A. STONE, of Florida, to MISS JULIA A. RODGERS, of Monroe county.

Nov. 13, 1850

    Married in Talbotton on the 7th instant by the Rev. John P. Dickinson, MR. JOSEPH T. SHELTON, of Talbot, to MISS SALLIE JACKSON, daughter of JOHN JACKSON, of Jasper county.

    Married on the 31st of October in Tallahassee, by the Rev. F.H. Rutledge, D.D., THOMAS P. DENHAM, to VIRGINIA L., third daughter of THOMAS BROWN, Governor of Florida.

Nov. 22, 1850

    Married on the evening of the 6th instant by the Rev. Wm. Caldwell, ANDREW J. COALSON, ESQ., of Pulaski county, to MISS SARAH H. PATTILLO of Hayneville.

Dec. 4, 1850

    Married on the 4th inst. by the Rev. L.W. Bassett, MR. HENRY H. GLOVER to MISS LOUISA C. ELLIS - all of Houston county, Ga.

    Married in this city on the 28th ult. by the Rev. R. Hooker, MR. T.R. BLOOM to MISS ANNA E. FLUKER.

    Married in Pulaski county, Ga. on the evening of the 12th inst., by Rev. J.E. Sharpe, MR. J.A. McGRIFF to MISS A.M. DYKES - both of Pulaski county.

Dec. 4, 1850

    Married in East Macon on the 26th Nov. by the Rev. S. Landrum, MR. NATHANIEL COATES and MISS SUSAN V. ADAMS.

Dec. 11, 1850

    Married in Monroe county on Wednesday morning 4th instant by the Rev. Davis Smith, MR. WILLIAM CLEVELAND, of Crawfo-d county, to MISS SUSAN HOLLIS, of Monroe county, Ga.

Dec. 18, 1850

    Married on the 8th inst. by Ichabod Davis, J.I.C., MR. JAMES S. COLWELL to MRS. HARRIET HAUGABROOK, all of Macon county, Ga.

    Married in Crawford county on the 6th inst., by Samuel E. Crute, Esq., MR. CURTISS W. IVEY to MISS JENCEY ELLEN RAY, of Crawford.

    Married on the morning of the 10th of Dec. 1850 by the Rev. John M. Marshall, MR. GEORGE S. RILEY, of Houston county, to MISS CAROLINE C., eldest daughter of the REV. DANIEL F. WADE, of Macon county, Ga.

    Married in this city on the 17th inst. by E.C. Granniss, Esq., MR. D. SHERMON, formerly of Connecticut, to MISS HENRIETTA NORRELL, youngest daughter of JOHN B. NORRELL of this city.

Dec. 25, 1850

    Married in Forsyth, Monroe county, on the 10th inst. by the Rev. A. Ogletree, MR. THOMAS S. HAMMOND to MISS ELIZA ANN MERITT, all of Monroe county.

Jan. 1, 1851

    Married on the 25th inst. at the house of J.D. Wilkes, by the Rev. James Pearson, MR. JAMES W. ANDREWS, of Twiggs county, to MISS WINFORD A.M. JOINER, of Sumter county.

    Married in Culloden on Wednesday the 18th inst. by the Rev. Wesley F. Smith, WILKINS W. JACKSON to MRS. VIRGINIA C. BARRON, both of Monroe county, Ga.

    Married in Twiggs county on the evening of the 24th ult. by D.H. Coombs, Esq., MR. TROY G. HOLDER to MISS CEABELL F. PACE - all of Twiggs county.

Jan. 22, 1851

    Married in Macon county, near Fort Valley, on Wednesday evening January 8th by the Rev. H. Powell, MR. WILLIAM FLOWERS to MISS JOSEPHENE, daughter of CAPT. JOHN LAMAR, both of Macon county.

Jan. 29, 1851

    Married in Fort Valley on the 15th inst. by the Rev. G.W. Persons, DR. WILLIAM A. MATHEWS to MRS. MARY BEAUFORT EVERETT.

    Married in Lee county on the 23d inst. by the Rev. J.D. Mathews, MAJ. JOHN H. POPE to MISS MARY FRANCES GILBERT.

Feb. 5, 1851

    Married on Tuesday evening 28th inst. by the Rev. W.H. Ellison, MR. HENRY E. BALL to MISS MARY VIRGINIA CLARKE, all of this city.

    Married in this city at the residence of, and by the Rev. John M. Field, on Thursday evening the 30th ult., HENRY G. ROSS, ESQ., Clerk of the Superior Court of Bibb County, to MISS AMELIA T. ROSS.

Feb. 12, 1851

   Married in Eufaula, Ala. on Wednesday 29th inst. by the Rev. W. Matthew, MAJ. SAMUEL D. IRVIN, of this city, to MISS JULIA A. CARGILE, of the former place.

   Married in Monroe county on the 14th inst. by Robert Mays, J.I.C., MR. LEVI W. MORRISON to MISS MATILDA A. HANSFORD, daughter of GEORGE W. HANSFORD, ESQ., of Monroe county.

Feb. 19, 1851

   Married on the morning of the 17th inst. by the Rev. Mr. Shanklin, MR. GEORGE B. CARHART, of New York, to MISS MARY E. ROSE, eldest daughter of MR. S. ROSE, of this city.

Mar. 5, 1851

   Married by the Rev. W.H. Ellison on the 4th inst. at the residence of her father, ROLAND BIVINS, ESQ., in Bibb county, MISS MARY F. BIVINS to JESSE C. JACKSON, ESQ., of Sumter county.

   Married on the morning of the 4th inst. by Rev. Mr. Evans, NELSON H. EDDY to MISS GEORGIANNA BEVERLY, daughter of R.B. WASHINGTON, ESQ., all of this city.

   Married in this city on the 25th February by the Rev. S. Landrum, MISS MARTHA D. MARTIN to COL. JOHN F. LAWSON, of Burke county.

   Married in Houston county on Thursday morning the 26th ult. by Rev. James E. Evans, DR. S.D. BRANTLY, of Washington, and MISS MARY E., daughter of SAMUEL DINKINS, ESQ., formerly of Macon.

Mar. 12, 1851

   Married near this city on the 10th inst. by Rev. S. Landrum, COL. MILO B. PARKER, of Ala., to MRS. SARAH ANN PERRY.

Apr. 23, 1851

   Married in this city on the morning of the 17th by the Rev. J.A. Shanklin, Rector of Christ's Church, MR. JAMES R. KING, of Roswell, to MISS ELIZABETH FRANCES, youngest daughter of the late OLIVER H. PRINCE.

May. 14, 1851

   Married at the Baptist Church in Starkeville, Lee county, by the Rev. E.W. Warren on the 1st day of May, MR. JARED IRWIN to MISS ANN TATE, both of Lee county.

May 28, 1851

   Married on the morning of the 26th inst. by the Rev. Mr. Evans, MR. T.A. GODWIN to MISS CORINTHIA A., daughter of the late LUKE J. MORGAN, all of this city.

June 4, 1851

   Married in Mobile on the 22d ult. by Rev. Mr. Melbourne, COL. JOHN J. RAWLS, of this city, to MISS M.S. DENT, first daughter of GEN. D. DENT, of Mobile.

   Married in Griffin on the 28th ult. by Rev. W.J. Keith, MR. JOSHUA CHERRY, of Macon, to MRS. SARAH McDONALD, of Griffin.

June 11, 1851

   Married in Leon county, Fla. on the 3d inst. by the Rev. Samuel Woodbury, MR. EDWIN SAULSBURY, of this city, to MISS ELMINA CHAIRS, daughter of GREEN H. CHAIRS.

June 11, 1851

　　Married in Pike county, Ala. on the 3d inst. at the residence of
　　Mr. Geo. A. Rodgers, by the Rev. James Mellard, DR. HENRY FARRIOR
　　to MISS SARAH ANN WANAMAKER.

June 18, 1851

　　Married on the 5th inst. by the Rev. Anderson Palee, COL. J.H.
　　WHALEY to MISS ELIZA, daughter of WILLIAM H. and DORCAS RAMSEY, all
　　of Thomas county, Georgia. (North Carolinian please copy)

　　Married on Thursday evening by Rev. Mr. Hooker, MR. WILLIAM BAILEY
　　of St. Marys, Ga., to MISS MARTHA J. HARDAWAY of this city.

June 25, 1851

　　Married on the 17th inst. by the Rev. James Harris, PHILIP TIMBERLAKE,
　　M.D. to MISS HENRIETTA E. LESTER, all of Culloden.

July 2, 1851

　　Married on the 26th inst. by Samuel Beall, J.I.C., MR. HARVEY M.
　　FREEMAN to MISS MISSOURI OCTAVO, daughter of HANSFORD DAVIS, ESQ.,
　　all of Wilkinson county. (Temperance Banner will please copy).

July 9, 1851

　　Married in Knoxville, Geo. on Sunday evening last by the Hon. Green
　　P. Culverhouse, MR. JOSHUA LOWE, of Nashville, Tennessee, to MISS
　　ELIZABETH SLATTER, second daughter of the late L.D. SLATTER of the
　　former place.

July 16, 1851

　　Married in Thomas county on the 24th of June by James T. Hays,
　　J.I.C., MR. JONATHAN HANCOCK to MISS SUSAN MUNSON, formerly of
　　East Macon.

July 30, 1851

　　Married on the evening of the 24th inst. by the Rev. Sam'l Henderson,
　　COL. ROBERT A. CRAWFORD, of Auburn, Ala., to MRS. JANE E. LYON,
　　of Harris county, Ga.

Aug. 20, 1851

　　Married in Macon on Tuesday morning August 5th by Rev. Richard
　　Hooker, MR. DAVIS SMITH, JR. to MISS JOSETTA A. HOLLINGSWORTH, all
　　of this city.

　　Married in Atlanta on the evening of the 24th ult. by the Rev. A.M.
　　Spaulding, MR. DAVID A. COOK, formerly of Macon, to MISS NANCY W.,
　　daughter of MERIL COLLIER, of the former place.

Sep. 17, 1851

　　Married on the 2d inst. by Rev. J.A. Shanklin, W.B. JOHNSTON, ESQ.
　　to MISS ANN C. TRACY, eldest of late JUDGE TRACY.

Oct. 8, 1851

　　Married on the evening of the 18th inst. at the residence of Wesley
　　Griggs in Putnam county, by the Rev. Wm. Arnold, DR. JAMES A. LONG,
　　of LaGrange, Troup county, Ga., to MISS SARAH C., eldest daughter
　　of WESLEY GRIGGS.

　　Married on the evening of 30th September by R.J.T. Little, Esq.,
　　MR. WILLIAM S.N. BISCOE to MISS NARCISSA H. NORTHRUP - all of West
　　Point, Ga.

Oct. 8, 1851

Married on the 25th ultimo by the Rev. Mr. Jabert, MR. AUGUSTUS McDANIELS to MISS MARY E. BLAYSINGAME, all of Crawford County.

Oct. 15, 1851

Married in Houston county on the 8th inst. by the Rev. Mr. Adam Holmes, EDWARD L. FELDER, ESQ., and MISS ADA J. THARPE.

Oct. 29, 1851

Married on Tuesday evening the 21st inst. at 4 o'clock, by the Rev. J.W. Twitty, COL. BENTON BYRD and MRS. MARY E. HORNE, all of Sumter county, Ga.

Nov. 5, 1851

Married on the 23d ultimo by the Rev. Mr. Speight of the Methodist Episcopal Church, DR. R.C. BRYAN to MISS ELIZA A. BROWN, daughter of CAPT. DEMPSEY BROWN, all of Houston county, Ga.

Married on the evening of the 7th ultimo by the Rev. Dr. Lewis, S.C. EDGEWORTH, M.D. of Houston county, to MRS MARY L. MICHAL, daughter of MAJ. JOHN S. ROWLAND, of Cass county.

Nov. 26, 1851

Married at the residence of Daniel McKlevain in Vienna, Dooly county, Ga. on the evening of 20th Nov. by the Rev. M.C. Smith, MR. THEOPHILUS J. JOHNSON, of Henry county, Ga., to MISS ELIZABETH A. McKLEVAIN, of Vienna, Ga.

Dec. 3, 1851

Married on the evening of 27th Nov. 1851 at the residence of Edward Broughton, by the Rev. C.D. Mallory, MR. JOHN B. LONG, of Troup county, Ga., to MISS FRANCES E. BROUGHTON.

Dec. 10, 1851

Married on the 30th ult. by the Rev. J.E. Evans, MR. ALEXANDER A. MENARD to MISS CAROLINE E. RICHARDS, both of this city.

Married at Hickory Grove on Sunday morning by the Rev. W.C. Cleveland MAJ. JOSEPH H. LONG to MISS MELISSA, daughter of JUDGE SIMMONS of this place.

Married in Eatonton on the 4th inst. MR. MARCELLUS TROUTMAN, of Crawford co., to MISS MARY BRANHAM, daughter of DR. H. BRANHAM.

Married on the 25th Nov. 1851 by D.H. Brown, Esq., MR. JACKSON W. WALKER and MISS SUSAN V. WEST, all of Sumpter Co., Ga.

Married in Lowndes County on the 26th ult., MR. BERRY A. FOLSOM to MISS SARAH E. WILSON.

Dec. 17, 1851

Married on the evening of the 4th of December by the Rev. Jesse Wood, MR. JAMES B. SHARP, of Forsyth, to MISS MARY H. WRIGHT, second daughter of MAJ. REUBEN WRIGHT, of Monroe county.

Married on the evening of the 2d inst. at the residence of Wm. Tinsley, by the Rev. E.C. Horniday, MR. S.G. PRYOR to MISS ADALINE TINSLEY, all of Sumter county.

Married in Macon county on the 2d inst. by Willis Beddingfield, MR. JAMES CHASTAIN, of Lee co., to MRS. USEBIA N. POWELL, of Macon county.

Dec. 17, 1851

Married on the 10th inst. in Clinton, Jones county, Ga., by Rev. Charles R. Jewitt, MR. WILEY A. GIBSON to MISS ANN MARIA, daughter of MR. JOHN PITTS, all of Clinton.

Married on the evening of the 18th Nov. at the residence of A. Tyson, by the Rev. E.C. Hornidy, MR. A.J. SCRUTCHIN, of Sumter county, to MISS MARY A. PORTER, of Dooly.

Dec. 24, 1851

Married at Fort Mitchell, Ala. on Wednesday evening the 10th inst. by the Rev. Charles King, JOS. C. WILKINS, ESQ., of Liberty county, to MISS SALLIE E. GORDON, daughter of the late CHAS. P. GORDON, of Columbus.

Married on the 21st inst. at his residence, by Joshua Tennison, Esq. THOS. D. HUMPHRIES, of Pike county, to MISS MARY A. BLOUNT, of Monroe county, Ga.

Dec. 31, 1851

Married on the 23d inst. in Monroe county, Ga. by the Rev. Charles R. Jewett, MR. JOSHUA S. GODDARD, to MISS MARY G. BUCKANAN, of Monroe county, Ga.

Married on Sunday the 21st inst. at the residence of her father, near Perry, Houston county, by the Rev. J.H. Luther, MR. A.K. LAMAR, of Augusta, Ga., to MISS KATE HILL, daughter of GREENE HILL, ESQ.

Jan. 7, 1852

Married on 25th Dec. by Rev. Mr. Lucky, MR. WM. C. BANDY, of this city, to MISS MARY H., daughter of PLINY SHEFFIELD, ESQ. of Thomas county.

Married on New Year's morning by George G. Miller, Esq., MR. COVINGTON MILLER to MISS LUCINDA TWILLEY, all of Bibb county.

Jan. 14, 1852

Married on the 11th inst. by Rev. S. Landrum, MR. CHAS. J. BEAVERS, of Crawford county, to MISS CAMELLA J. SHEFFIELD, of Bibb.

Jan. 21, 1852

Married on the 25th Dec. by the Rev. C.F. Patillo, MR. STEPHEN F. BROWN, of Houston county, to MISS JULIA A. SANDLIN, of Pulaski county, Ga.

Married also on the same evening, MR. J.W. HILL to MISS ELIZABETH BRYAN, all of Houston county.

Jan. 28, 1852

Married in Bibb county on the evening of the 15th, by R.A. Cain, MR. SAMUEL H. EVERETT, of Atlanta, to MISS ADRIAN SUSAN LOUISA, youngest daughter of MR. AUGUSTIN COOK.

Married at the residence of Mr. John Patillo, of Harris co., Ga. on Thursday evening the 8th inst., by the Rev. Mr. Willismaon, MR. HORTON S. TURNER, of Vienna, Ga., to MISS MARTHA PATILLO, of Harris county.

Married on the 22nd inst. by the Rev. J.B. Hanson, MR. THOMAS G. WILLIAMS to MISS LUCINDA A. ALLEN - all of Pike county, Ga.

Feb. 4, 1852

Married in Trinity Church, New Haven, Conn. on the 24th ult. by the Rev. Mr. Pitkin, ALBERT MIX, ESQ., of Macon, to MISS MARIA S. TOWNSEND, of the former city.

Feb. 11, 1852

Married in this city on the 5th inst. by Rev. S. Landrum, MR. PULASKI S. HOLT, JR. to MISS JULIA M. DAVIS.

Feb. 25, 1852

Married in Milledgeville on the 17th inst. by the Rev. John W. Baker, MR. JOSEPH H. NISBET to MISS EMILIE M. DeLAUNAY, the eldest daughter of the late F.V. DELAUNAY.

Married on the 8th inst. at the church of the Ascension, N.Y., by the Rev. Dr. Bedell, DR. J.W. BENSON, of this city, to MISS CAROLINE CORA, daughter of JOHN R. PETERS, ESQ., of New York.

Married in Macon county on the 19th inst., MR. D.W. ORR, of this city, to MISS LIZZIE SLAPPEY, daughter of URIAH SLAPPEY, of the above county.

Mar. 3, 1852

Married in Dooly county, Ga. by the Rev. Enos Young on the 15th inst., MR. MOSES J. BODIFORD to MISS NANCY PARKER, both of the same county.

Married in Athens on the 19th inst. by Rev. Dr. Hoyt, COL. PORTER KING, of Marion, Ala., to MISS CALLIE M. LUMPKIN, youngest daughter of HON. JOSEPH H. LUMPKIN.

Mar. 31, 1852

Married on the 10th inst. by the Rev. J.P. Dickerson, DR. R. HARWELL to MISS MARTHA H. DAY, all of Upson county.

Apr. 7, 1852

Married in Tallahassee on the 9th inst. at the residence of Hon. Thomas Beltzen by Rev. Mr. Hume, MR. GEORGE S. KING, of New Port, Florida, to MRS. JOANNA W. CLARK, daughter of REV. MIRON WINSLOW, Missionary to Madras, India.

Apr. 14, 1852

Married on the evening of the 30th ult. by the Rev. B.F. Sharp, REV. SYLVANUS LANDRUM, Pastor of the Baptist Church of this place, and MISS ELIZA JANE, daughter of GEN. ELI WARREN, of Houston county, Ga.

Apr. 21, 1852

Married in this city on the 4th inst. by the Rev. Samuel Anthony, MR. THOMAS SHINHOLSER to MISS MALINDA M., daughter of WM. B. GAMBLE, all of this city.

Apr. 28, 1852

Married in Irwin county on Tuesday evening the 13th of April by James Smith, J.P., COL. CLARK WILLCOX, of Telfair county, to MISS JANE E., youngest daughter of SAMUEL FULLER, ESQ., formerly of Bibb, now of Irwin county.

May 5, 1852

Married in Lee County on the 28th ult. by the Rev. Jesse Davis, MR. JOHN W. IHLY, of Savannah, to SARAH T., second daughter of GEO. S. OGLESBY, ESQ., of Lee County.

Married on the 15th inst. in Twiggs county by the Rev. David Roberts, REV. JAS. W. TRAWICK, of the Georgia Conference, to MISS PENELOPE A. BROWN, of Twiggs county.

Married near Sandersville on the 22nd inst. by the Rev. Jas. R. Smith, MR. W. ABNEY to MISS GRACY BAILEY.

May 12, 1852

Married on the 9th inst. by Wm. Herrington, Esq., at the residence of Wm. S. Moore, Esq., HENRY E. OLIVER, ESQ. to MISS SARAH MARSHALL SCARBOROUGH, all of Houston county.

May 19, 1852

Married in Milledgeville on Thursday evening 6th inst. by the Rev. Mr. Hinton, MR. JOHN W.W. SNEAD to MISS MARY A., eldest daughter of the late REV. JOHN DAVIES and grand-daughter of the late JUDGE DAVIES of Savannah.

Married on the 12th inst. by Rev. S. Landrum, MR. JOHN HOLTZENDORF to MISS ELIZA CASSIDY, all of this city.

Married in Christ's Church in this city on Wednesday evening the 12th inst. by the Rev. J.A. Shanklin, MR. JOHN S. HUTTON to MISS HARRIET, daughter of NATHAN MUNROE, ESQ., of Vineville.

May 26, 1852

Married near Drayton, Dooly county, on the 11th inst. by H.H. Bostick, Esq., MR. ALEXANDER HOLLIDAY to MISS MARGARET ROWELL, both of said county.

June 2, 1852

Married on the 25th ult. by Rev. James McCarter, MR. H. WARD MERRITT, of Monroe county, to MISS SUSAN M. WHITE, of Sumter.

Married at the residence of Mrs. Brooking, near Sparta, on the evening of the 20th instant, by the Rev. Wm. J. Hurley, DR. HENRY L. BATTLE, of Sparta, to MISS ANNA M. CHAMBLISS, of Brunswick county, Va.

June 9, 1852

Married on the 2d inst. by Rev. S. Landrum, MR. LEWIS B. WOOD to MISS MARTHA A. OLIVER - all of this city.

June 16, 1852

Married on the 10th inst. by the Rev. John P. Dickinson, MR. GEORGE W. FACKLER, of Upson county, to MISS MARTHA WILLIAMS, of Pike county, Ga.

Married in this county on Tuesday the 8th inst. by Rev. E.H. Myers, President of the Wesleyan Female College, DR. JOHN CALDERWOOD, of Monroe, La., to MISS LOUISA HUNTER, daughter of COL. SAMUEL B. HUNTER.

June 30, 1852

Married in Washington county on the 16th inst. by Rev. Mr. Shanklin, MR. O.H. PRINCE, of Macon, to MISS SARAH M.R. JACKSON, daughter of the late DR. HENRY JACKSON, of Athens, Ga.

Aug. 4, 1852

Married on the morning of the 26th ult. by the Rev. J.E. Sharp, of Twiggs county, MR. J.M. SHARP to MISS MARTHA W. SAUNDERS, both of Monroe county, Ga.

Aug. 11, 1852

Married on the 4th inst. by the Hon. Lott Warren, JOHN R. RESPESS, of Thomaston, to MISS ELIA RESPESS, of Albany, Ga.

Sep. 1, 1852

Married on Thursday evening last by Solomon R. Johnson, Esq., MR. HENRY G. ROSS, JR. to MISS FRANCES O., daughter of DR. T.B. GORMAN, all of Bibb county.

Sep. 8, 1852

Married in Newton county on the 24th ult. by the Rev. C.M. Irvin, MR. J.W. FEARS, of Madison, to MISS SARAH E. BLEDSOE, of the former place.

Married on Wednesday evening the 1st inst. by the Rev. Raleigh Greene, MR. WILLIAM W. HARTSFIELD, of Thomaston, to MISS S. PARMER TRAYLER, daughter of EDWARD TRAYLER, EDW., of Upson County, Ga.

Sep. 29, 1852

Married at the residence of Mrs. Laura Slappey on the 21st inst., by the Rev. Daniel F. Wade, MR. W.W. CARNES to MISS L.E.A. LAMAR, all of Macon county.

Oct. 6, 1852

Married on the 29th ult. by Rev. Mr. Birch, MR. WILLIAM NELSON to MISS JANE G., eldest daughter of WILLIAM SCOTT, ESQ., all of Houston county.

Married on the evening of the 23d ult. by the Rev. William Chambliss, JUDGE WILLIAM STROZIER to MRS. ELIZABETH MILBURN, all of Cusseta, Ala.

Oct. 20, 1852

Married in Washington, Wilkes county, 12th inst. by the Rev. Mr. Habersham, MR. TROUP BUTLER, of Lee county, to MISS A.C. ANDREWS, daughter of the HON. GARNET ANDREWS, of the former place.

Married on the evening of the 30th ult. by the Rev. Henry Bunn, MR. JAMES T. GLOVER to MISS GEORGIA ANN, daughter of JAMES BURNS, ESQ., all of Twiggs county.

Married on the evening of the 5th inst. by the Rev. Henry Bunn, DR. VIRGIL H. WALKER, of Harris county, to MISS ANTINETT, daughter of DAVID WALKER, of Pulaski county.

Oct. 27, 1852

Married on Monday evening 25th inst. by the Rev. E.H. Myers, DR. NATHAN BOZEMAN, of Montgomery, Ala., to MISS FRANCES M. LAMAR, of Vineville.

Married in Thomaston, Ga. on the 17th inst. by the Rev. John P. Dickinson, MR. THOMAS A. FLEWELLEN to MISS VICTORIA M. THWEATT.

Nov. 3, 1852

Married on the 18th inst. by the Rev. D. Smith, MR. THOMAS H. STEWART of Marion county, to MISS EMILY BOZEMAN, of Monroe county.

Nov. 10, 1852

    Married on Wednesday morning the 3d inst. at Fenn's Bridge, Jefferson county, by the Rev. Mr. Verduree, AUGUSTUS S. QUARTERMAN, ESQ., of Liberty county, to MISS ANNIE M., daughter of B.H. MOULTRIE, of the former place.

    Married on the 26th inst. by the Rev. G.W. Persons, DR. J.W. KEIGLER to MISS MARY E. TAYLOR, daughter of MR. N.J. TAYLOR, all of Macon county, Ga.

Nov. 17, 1852

    Married in Hayneville on Wednesday morning the 10th inst., by the Rev. E.P. Birch, MR. OLIVER R. PHELPS, of Forsyth, to MISS EUGENIA C. LANIER, of Hayneville.

Nov. 24, 1852

    Married in Forsyth on the morning of the 18th inst. by the Rev. Wm. C. Wilkes, Principal of Forsyth Female Colleigate Institute, MR. ALBERTIS H. WATTS, of Monroe County, to MISS SARAH A.J. THOMAS, daughter of JOHN H. THOMAS, of Forsyth.

Dec. 1, 1852

    Married at the residence of O. Morse, Esq. on the 24th inst., at Forsyth, by the Rev. Wm. C. Wilkes, Principal of Forsyth Female Collegiate Institutie, MR. DON CARLOS W. CHANDLER, of Irwinton, to MISS MARY E. BARLOW, of Forsyth, Ga.

    Married on the 25th ult. at Orangeburg, S.C. by the Rev. T.F. Montgomery, of LaGrange, Ga., MR. JAMES D. FREDERICK, of Marshalville, Ga., to MISS E.A. FELDER, of Orangeburg, S.C.

    Married in this County on the 23d inst. by the Rev. R.A. Cain, MR. RODERICK McLENAN, of Canada West, to MISS HARRIET REBECCA McARTHUR, of Bibb Co.

Dec. 8, 1852

    Married in Vineville on the evening of the 6th inst. by the Rev. E.H. Myers, MR. WILLIAM E. WALKER, of Burke county, to MISS CAROLINE M. RAWLS, of the former place.

    Married in Crawford county on the 9th ult. by Rev. George F. Pierce, J.C. LONGSTREET, ESQ. to MISS M.A. LAMAR, daughter of the late HON. L.Q.C. LAMAR.

    Married in Crawford county on the 28th ult. by John F. Taylor, Esq. MR. WILLIS W. TAYLOR to MISS FRANCES M. FOWLER, all of Crawford county, Ga.

    Married in this city on Monday morning last, by the Rev. Mr. Breck, MR. JOHN L. COPE, of Savannah, to MISS VIRGINIA SULLIVAN, of this city.

Dec. 15, 1852

    Married in Vineville on the 9th inst. by Rev. William Richards of S.C., MR. S.P. RICHARDS to MISS SARAH F. VANVALKENBURG.

    Married in Monroe county on the 1st of November by Rev. Seneca G. Bragg, L.M. DEMICK and MISS ELIZABETH ULTON, all of this city.

    Married on the 7th inst. by Judge Sturdevant, JOHN A.W. M'CANTS, ESQ., of Butler, Taylor county, Ga., Clerk of the Superior Court of Taylor county, to MISS MARTHA A. BATEMAN, of Marion county.

Dec. 15, 1852

Married on the 18th ult. at the house of Nathan Childers, in Crawford county, Ga., by Charl-s H. Walker, Esq., JOEL T. HANCOCK to ELIZABETH P. CHILDERS.

Married in Laurens county on the 9th inst. by the Rev. Mr. Parks, DR. JAMES E. BLACKSHAER, of Twiggs county, to MISS FANNIE MARIA, daughter of the late MAJOR JAMES BLACKSHEAR, of the former county.

Dec. 22, 1852

Married on the 19th inst. at the M.E. Church by Rev. G.H. Hancock, MR. OSCAR P. FITZGERALD to MISS SARAH E., daughter of B.F. GRIFFIN, ESQ., all of this city.

Married in Monroe county, Ga. on Tuesday evening 30th ult. by Rev. Mr. Atkinson, of Forsyth, DR. JOHN S. LESTEUR to MISS CAMILLA C., daughter of JOB and MARY TAYLOR, all of Monroe county.

Married in Monroe county on the 14th inst. by Rev. Wm. Hardy, WM. C. KING, of Talbot county, to MISS FANNY S. PERKINS, of Monroe county.

Dec. 29, 1852

Married on the morning of the 21st of December by the Rev. Wesley F. Smith, MR. A.G. ANDREWS to MRS. MARY W. GREEN, all of Crawford county.

Jan. 5, 1853

Married on Thursday evening 30th Dec. in Forsyth, by Rev. Samuel Anthony, JOSEPH R. BANKS, ESQ. to MISS CARRIE S. STEPHENS.

Jan. 12, 1853

Married in Oglethorpe county at the residence of Shelton Oliver, Esq. on Tuesday the 21st ult., by Rev. L.L Wittich, MARCUS A. PHARR, ESQ., of Madison, Ga., to MISS CAMILLA OLIVER of the former place.

Married in Raleigh, N.C. on the 16th December last, by Rev. T.W. Tobey, MR. R.P. ZIMMERMAN, of Madison, Ga., to MISS BETTIE, daughter of the late REV. DR. THOMAS MEREDITH, of the former place.

Married on the 5th of January in Pulaski county by the Hon. S.M. Manning, MR. JNO. H. BRANTLY, JR., of Houston county, to MISS EUOFAIR J. McGRIFF, of the former county.

Married at the residence of John McKay on Saturday 25th Dec. by H.M. Nixon, Esq., FRANCIS HILL, ESQ. to MISS M.E. POSTELL, all of Houston county.

Jan. 19, 1853

Married in Washington, Ga. on the 12th inst., by the Rev. P. McNeil Turner, WALLACE CUMMING, ESQ., of Savannah, to MISS HARRIET VIRGINIA, daughter of A.L. ALEXANDER.

Married on the 2nd of January 1853 by A.W. Asbell, Esq., MR. THOMAS THOMPSON to MISS MARGARET THOMPSON, all of Twiggs county, Ga.

Married on the 12th inst. by T.R. Denson, Esq., MR. JAMES ELLIS to MISS SENIA HAMMOCK, all of Twiggs county, Ga.

Jan. 26, 1853

Married on the 18th of January by Rev. C.W. Thomas, ROBERT C. BLACK, M.D., of Oglethorpe, to MISS G.A.J. BROOKS, of Stewart Co., Ga.

Jan. 26, 1853

   Married on the 20th inst. by Samuel N. Lasseter, Esq., WILLIAM LANE
   and SUSAN HILL - all of Dooly county, Ga.

Feb. 2, 1853

   Married on the 23d ult. by the Rev. Dr. Manson, DR. JAMES M.
   McDONALD, of Macon, Ga., and MISS MARTHA D. NALLY, daughter of
   DANIEL NALLY, of McDonough, Henry county, Ga.

   Married in this city on the 31st Jan. by Rev. S. Landrum, MR. W.W.
   RICHARDS to MISS FRANCIS WAGNON.

Feb. 9, 1853

   Married on Thursday the 13th of January by Rev. J.F. Weathersby,
   THADDEUS O. JACOB, ESQ., formerly of Northampton County, Virginia,
   to MISS MARTHA FRANCES, daughter of DANIEL PONDER, ESQ., of Monroe
   County, Ga.

Feb. 16, 1853

   Married on Sunday evening the 13th inst. by David Reid, Esq., at
   the residence of E.R. Haynes, MR. MELTON RYE to MISS SARAH GRAY,
   all of this city.

Feb. 23, 1853

   Married in Twiggs county on the 13th inst. at the residence of Mrs.
   F. Solomon, by the Rev. H. Bunn, MR. C.R. FAULK to MISS J.M.E.
   SOLOMON, daughter of MRS. F. SOLOMON, all of Twiggs county.
   (Chronicle & Sentinel please copy).

   Married in Vineville on the 17th inst. by the Rev. E.H. Myers,
   LUCIUS M. LAMAR, ESQ. to MISS MARY F., daughter of MRS. CAROLINA
   RAWLS.

Mar. 9, 1853

   Married at Baltimore Feb. 15th by the Rev. Dr. Atkinson, LIEUT.
   D.R. JONES, U.S. Army, to MISS REBECCA, daughter of COL. J.P.
   TAYLOR, U.S. Army.

Mar. 16, 1853

   Married on Wednesday evening 9th inst. by Rev. Enos Young, MR.
   JOHN M. CHESHORE to MISS MARY M. CALHOUN, all of Dooly Co., Ga.

   Married on the 13th inst. by the Rev. G.H. Hancock, MR. CHARLES H.
   ROGERS to MISS LAURA A., daughter of ALEXANDER RICHARDS, ESQ.,
   all of Macon.

Mar. 23, 1853

   Married on the 1st inst. by Rev. J.R. Danforth, MR. ROBERT R.
   WIMBERLY to MRS. PENELOPE BOYNTON, both of Jeffersonville, Twiggs
   co., Ga.

Mar. 30, 1853

   Married in Eatonton on the 15th inst. by Rev. Charles M. Irwin,
   DR. R.B. NISBET, of this city, to MRS. MARTHA A. GRIMES, of the
   former place.

   Married on the morning of the 17th inst. by the Rev. Wesley F.
   Smith, MR. RICHARDSON MONTFORD to MISS SARAH J. COLBERT, all of
   Crawford county.

Apr. 6, 1853

Married in Perry, Ga. on the 16th inst. by the Rev. E.P. Birch, MR. WM. M. ELDER, of Pike County, to MISS ANN T. JOBSON, of the former place.

Married on the 31st March by the Rev. G.H. Hancock, MR. JOSEPH H. SEYMOUR to MISS JULIA A.E. BOSTICK, daughter of H.H. BOSTICK, ESQ., all of Montezuma, Ga.

Apr. 13, 1853

Married in Lumpkin, Stewart county, on the 31st ult. by the Rev. Jno. J. Twiggs, COL. J.M. CLARK to MISS MARY M., daughter of MRS. L.A. WILLIAMS, all of Lumpkin.

Married on the 5th inst. by the Rev. N. Ousley, MR. HENRY M. BAILEY, of this city, to MISS MARY A. GATES, of this county.

Apr. 20, 1853

Married in this city on the 10th instant, by the Rev. Edward Quigley, MR. JOHN RODEN to MISS ELIZA TRACY.

Married on the 6th inst. at the Presbyterian Church by the Rev. R.L. Breck, MR. ROBT. CARVER to MISS MARY N. SHINHOLSER, all of this city.

Married on Thursday evening the 14th inst. by the Rev. J.A. Shanklin, MR. WALTER C. HODGKINS to MISS LEVINA MENARD, all of this city.

Married in the Presbyterian Church in Cuthbert, on Sunday night the 17th inst., by the Rev. J.H. Luther, MR. J.J. KIDDOO and MRS. A.C. CLARKE, daughter of the REV. J.W. WILSON.

Apr. 27, 1853

Married on the morning of the 19th inst. at the residence of Col. Parker Eason, in Henry county, by the Rev. Alfred Buckner, MR. ROBT. H. DIXON, of Talbot county, to MRS. ELIZA P. BROWN.

Married in Augusta on Wednesday evening the 20th inst. by the Rev. Mr. Rogers, COL. C. CAMPBELL, of Madison, Ga., to MISS E. BRYSON, daughter of H.C. BRYSON, of that city.

Married on Wednesday evening the 19th inst. in Christ Church, Savannah, by the Right Rev. Stephen Elliott, Bishop of Georgia, WM. P. CARMICHAEL, ESQ., of Augusta, to MISS ELIZABETH B. ELLIOTT, daughter of BISHOP ELLIOTT.

Married on the 20th inst. in Columbia co. by the Rev. Juriah Harris, W.H. TURPIN, JR., to EMILY M., eldest daughter of JAS. F. HAMILTON, ESQ.

May 4, 1853

Married on the 19th inst. by the Rev. R.L. Breck, JAMES N. KING, ESQ., to MISS SARAH A. KING, both of this county.

May 18, 1853

Married in Washington (Ga) on Tuesday, 28th of April 1853, by the Rev. George F. Pierce, D.D., WILLIAM F. ALEXANDER to MARY LOUISA, daughter of the HON. ROBERT TOOMBS.

Married in this city on Tuesday 10th inst. by the Rev. Robert L. Breck, SAMUEL E. BOYKIN, of Columbus, Ga., to LAURA J., eldest daughter of the HON. EUGENIUS A. NISBET.

May 18, 1853

　　Married in Vineville on Thursday the 12th inst. by the Rev. Mr. Spear, DR. JOSIAH A. FLOURNOY, of Baker county, to MISS ANNA, daughter of I. WINSHIP, ESQ., of this city.

　　Married in Houston county by the Rev. D.F. Wade on the 11th inst. DR. WM. HAFER, of Macon county, to MISS ARABELLA C. MURPH.

May 25, 1853

　　Married on the 17th inst. by the Rev. C.A. Tharp, MR. HUGH L. DENARD, of Houston co., Ga. to MRS. FRANCIS S.A. SOLOMON, of Twiggs co., Ga.

　　Married on the 17th inst. at the residence of Maj. Lewis Rumph in Houston county, by the Rev. G.W. Persons, DR. WILLIAM J. GREEN to MISS E.M. PLANT, both of Houston county.

June 1, 1853

　　Married on the 24th inst. by the Rev. J.T. Dickinson, MR. BENJAMIN BETHEL and MISS MARY K., daughter of MAJ. WM. A. COBB, of Upson county.

June 8, 1853

　　Married on the 2d inst. by the Rev. Richard A. Cain, of Bibb county, MR. JOHN J. ALLEN, of Macon, to MRS. SARAH W. REYNOLDS, of Houston county, Ga.

　　Married on the 24th inst. at Milledgeville, Ga. by the Rev. Geo. F. Pierce, D.D., HON. JAMES JACKSON and MISS ADA J., daughter of MR. WALTER H. MITCHELL.

　　Married in Sparta on Wednesday evening the 1st instant by the Rev. Wm. J. Sasnet, WM. HUDSON GREEN, M.D., and MISS R. FANNIE, eldest daughter of the late COL. RICHARD P. SASNETT.

June 15, 1853

　　Married on the 2d inst. by the Rev. Wm. J. Stephens, JOHN T. KNIGHT to MRS. LUCINDA McFARLIN, both of Houston county, Ga.

June 22, 1853

　　Married on the 9th of June by the Rev. Dr. E.T. McGehee, MR. CHARLES WEST to MISS MARENDA GRACE, all of Houston co'., Ga.

June 29, 1853

　　Married on the evening of the 21st inst. by John H. Harper, Esq., MR. GREEN B. GLOVER to MISS UNETTA COOK, of Sumter county, Ga.

July 6, 1853

　　Married in this city on the 30th ult. by Rev. S. Landrum, MR. N.B. COPE to MISS MARGARET D. SEYMOUR.

July 13, 1853

　　Married near Twiggsville, Twiggs county, Ga., by A.W. Asbel, Esq., MR. HENRY FLOYD to MISS ELIZABETH STOKES, all of Twiggs county.

　　Married on the 5th of July by the Rev. Cary Cox, MAJ. EDWIN HARRIS of Montezuma, Macon county, to MISS SARAH ELIZABETH, only daughter of D.R. ANDREWS, ESQ., of Stanfordville, Putnam county, Ga.

　　Married in Butler, Taylor Co. on the 10th inst., by the Rev. Royal Daniel, MR. GEORGE W. GREGORY to MISS MARY CARTER, all of Butler.

July 20, 1853

    Married in this city on Sunday morning the 17th inst. by the Hon. M.M. Mason, MR. AMBROSE CHAPMAN to MISS MARTHA ANN SEYMOUR.

Aug. 3, 1853

    Married at Marietta on the 25th July by the Rev. J.L. Rogers, DR. E.F. COLZEY, of Oglethorpe, to MISS MARY S. WALLIS, of Macon.

Aug. 10, 1853

    Married on the 10th inst. by the Rev. R.C. Smith, MR. GEORGE W. ROSS, of Baldwin, to MISS SAVANNAH CARTER, of Putnam county, Ga.

Sep. 7, 1853

    Married in Bibb county on the 28th ult. by the Hon. John H. Brantly, MR. ROBERT H. LODGE to MISS MARY E. WILLIAMS.

    Married in Americus on the 31st ult., DR. JOSEPH McDONALD, of this city, to MRS HARRIET A. FOSTER.

Sep. 14, 1853

    Married on the 17th of August by the Rev. Luke S. Nowel, MR. GREEN FOSTER to MISS M. ELIZABETH LAWSHE, all of Bi-b county.

    Married in Greensboro, Ga. on the 25th ult. at the house of Hon. Wm. C. Dawson, by Rev. Dr. Hoyt, MR. JOHN J. THOMAS, of Athens, to MISS CLAUDIA FISK McKINLEY, of the former place.

Sep. 21, 1853

    Married near twiggs ville on the 8th inst., by T.R. Denson, Esq., MR. WILLIAM DEFORE to MISS FRANCES C. HORNE, all of Twiggs county, Ga.

    Married in Macon county on the 14th inst. at the residence of Mr. David Gammage, by Joseph Johnson, Esq., COL. WILLIAM WEST, of Houston county, to MRS MARY GAMMAGE, of the former county.

Sep. 28, 1853

    Married on the 19th inst. by the Rev. Mr. Griffin, MR. W.C. BANDY, of the firm of Lightfoot, Flanders & Co., of this city, and MISS E.E. SHEFFIELD, of Thomas county.

Oct. 19, 1853

    Married at the Presbyterian Church in this city on the evening of the 13th inst., by the Rev. Robt. L. Breck, COL. CHARLES R. ARMSTRONG to MISS SARAH M. PRATT, all of Macon.

Nov. 2, 1853

    Married in Washington on Thursday evening 20th inst. by Rev. C.M. Irwin, ROBERT J. BACON, ESQ., of LaGrange, Ga., to MISS MARY ISABELLA WALTON, of the former place.

    Married on Tuesday morning the 25th of October by the Rev. Wm. C. Wilkes, Principal of Forsyth Female College, COL. WM. B. BOWEN, of Elbert county, to MISS MARY E. VARNER, of Monroe county.

Nov. 9, 1853

    Married in Americus, Sumter county, Ga. on Tuesday 1st inst. by Rev. James M. Miller, J.I.C., MR. LAMPSON D. YEOMANS to MRS. ELIZA J. KINCHIN, all of Americus, Geo.

Nov. 16, 1853

Married on the evening of the 10th of Nov. by Rev. Wm. C. Wilkes, Principal of the Forsyth Female College, MR. ARCHIBALD B. FLOYD, of Forsyth, to MISS JANE E., daughter of E.M. BUTLER, ESQ., of Monroe Co., Ga.

Nov. 23, 1853

Married on the 3rd inst. by the Rev. Charles M. Irwin, MR. GEORGE N. LESTER, ESQ., of Cumming, Ga., and MISS MARGARET A. IRWIN, daughter of the HON. DAVID IRWIN.

Married in Milledgeville on Thursday morning 10th inst. by the Rev. John W. Baker, JOHN MILLER, ESQ., of Thomasville, Ga., to MISS FRANCES, daughter of DR. C.J. PAINE, of the former place.

Married in Greensboro, Ga. on Tuesday 8th inst. by the Rev. E.L. Whatley, MR. THOMAS W. WHATLEY, of Beach Island, S.C., to MISS JULIA A., daughter of SAMUEL DAVIS, ESQ., of the former place. Also, MR. THOMAS S. MILLER, of Beach Island, S.C., to MISS MARY J., eldest daughter of J.E. JACKSON, ESQ., of Greensboro.

Nov. 30, 1853

Married on the evening of the 28th inst. at the residence of John H. Brantley, Esq., by the Rev. S. Landrum, MR. CHARLES TAYLOR, of Sacramento city, Cal., to MISS LILLY O. BRANTLEY, of Vineville.

Dec. 14, 1853

Married on the 29th of November by Rev. J.W. Ellis, Rev. A. ____? (illegible) SAMFORD to MISS ELIZABETH ATTAWAY, of Macon Co., Ala.

Dec. 21, 1853

Married in Americus on the 13th inst. at the residence of Col. Malone, by the Rev. Samuel Anthony, DAVID R. ADAMS to MRS. SARAH A. TRIPPE.

Married in this city on Thursday evening Dec. 8th by Rev. William Shanklin, MR. G.A. CHAINS, of Leyon Co., Florida, to MISS AMANDA C., daughter of DR. DAVID JAMESON, of this city.

Married on the 7th instant by the Rev. D.F. Wade, MR. AUGUSTIN L. PATTERSON, of Burke county, to MISS ELLEN A. EDGEWORTH, of Houston county, Ga.

Dec. 28, 1853

Married on the 5th inst. by the Rev. S. Anthony, ROBT. N. BAILEY, of Bibb county, and MISS LOUISA M., daughter of REV. THOS. BATTLE of Monroe county.

Married on Tuesday evening 20th inst. at the residence of her father, MR. GEO. B. TURPIN, of this city, and MISS ELIZABETH, daughter of GREEN G. GUNN, of Jones county.

Married in Columbus on the 25th inst. at 8 o'clock A.M. by the Rev. Dr. Woodruff, HENRY A. SCOTT, M.D., of Albany, Geo., to MISS V.A. LESTER, of Russell county, Ala.

Married in Athens on Wednesday evening the 21st inst. by the Rev. N. Hoyt, ROBERT T. McCAY, of Rome, to MISS SUSAN L. WILEY, of Athens.

Married on Thursday morning Dec. 1st by Rev. James Henderson, MR. WESLY GOOLSBY to MISS NANNIE R., daughter of EVAN H. POWELL, ESQ., all of Jasper county.

Dec. 28, 1853

   Married on the morning of the 15th inst. in Sparta, at the residence
   of her uncle, Dr. Wm. Terrell, by Bishop Elliott, MISS CORINNE
   AURELIA, daughter of the HON. JOEL CRAWFORD, of Early county, and
   DR. JEAN VERDIER, of Quincy, Florida.

Jan. 12, 1854

   Married in Bibb county on the 5th inst., by the Rev. S. Landrum,
   MR. WILLIAM G. HARRIS to MISS ELIZA A.E. BAILEY, daughter of JUDGE
   BAILEY.

Jan. 18, 1854

   Married in Sumter county on the 25th December, MR. HUGH CARMICHAEL,
   of Oglethorpe, to MISS LUCY A.E. BUCKNER, only daughter of REASON
   and ELIZABETH BUCKNER, of Sumter county. (Milledgeville papers
   copy).

   Married on Wednesday evening 11th inst. by Rev. John Marshal, MR.
   C.W. NIXON, of Marshallville, Ga., and MISS MARY Y., youngest
   daughter of SOLOMON FUDGE, ESQ., of Houston Co., Ga.

Jan. 25, 1854

   Married on the 18th inst. by the Rev. G.W. Persons, MAJ. JAMES H.
   McGARITY to MISS ANTOINETT LOCKETT, all of Crawford county.

   Married in Marshallville, Ga. on the 17th instant by the Rev. D.
   F. Wade, MR. S.R. MOORE to MISS SARAH E., daughter of MR. SEABORN
   C. and MRS. NANCY BRYAN, all of Macon co., Ga.

Feb. 8, 1854

   Married in Thomasville by the Rev. R.H. Luckey, at 10 o'clock on
   Sunday morning 29th ult., JUDGE CHARLES H. REMINGTON to MISS ELLEN
   P., daughter of REV. H.W. SHARP - all of that place.

Feb. 22, 1854

   Married on the evening of the 14th inst. by the Rev. Wm. Arnold,
   MR. FRANKLIN S. JENKINS to MISS CHARITY J. LAWRENCE, eldest daughter
   of JAMES J. LAWRENCE, of Putnam county.

Mar. 1, 1854

   Married in Lexington, Ga. on Thursday evening the 16th inst. by
   Rev. George Lumpkin, DR. WM. S. GREENE, of Sumter county, to MISS
   CALLIE LUMPKIN, of the former place.

Mar. 8, 1854

   Married on the 18th of February by the Rev. Thos. Jones, BENJAMIN
   LASSETER, 83 years of age, to MRS. ELMIRE EMBREE, 77 years of age -
   all of Campbell county, Ga.

Mar. 22, 1854

   Married near Montezuma on the 16th inst. at the residence of James
   G. Oliver, Esq., by Judge Carmichael, MR. JOHN R. DAVIS, of Macon
   county, to MISS MACY B. OLIVER, of Baker county, Ga.

Mar. 29, 1854

   Married on Wednesday 1st instant by the Rev. Jas. Hunter, REV.
   CARLISLE P.B. MARTIN, President of the Synodical Female College, at
   Griffin, and MISS ELIZA J. REES, daughter of JOHN REES, ESQ., of
   Meriwether county.

Mar. 29, 1854

Married on the 16th inst. in Sparta, by the Rev. C.W. Key, MR. BENJ. H. BIGHAM, of LaGrange, to MARY JANE, daughter of B.T. HARRIS, ESQ., of the former place.

Married in Watkinsville on the 7th inst. by Judge Woodson, MR. H.D. CALLAWAY, of LaGrange, to MISS S.H. POPE, of Athens.

Married in Talbotton on the 8th inst. by Wm. L. Walker, Esq., MR. JOHN W. BREWER to MISS MINDA TRIBBLE, both of Talbotton.

Married in Meriwether county on Thursday 22nd by Jas. M. Smith, Esq., MR. ROBERT McCURDY, of Talbot, to MISS MARY, daughter of RICHARD P. BONNER, of the former county.

Married on the 7th inst. by the Rev. Joel D. Trammel, MR. JOHN BUCHANAN, of Macon county, Ala., to MISS ELIZABETH C., daughter of COL. TOLIVER JONES, of Harris co., Ga.

Married in LaGrange on the 14th inst., MR. M.L. BRYAN, of Houston county, to MISS MADALINE V. JOURDAN, daughter of the late WARREN JOURDAN, of Jones co.

Married on the 18th inst. in Houston county by the Rev. D.F. Wade, DR. J.W. OSLIN to MISS A.E. EDGEWORTH.

Apr. 5, 1854

Married at Fort Gaines on the 28th ult. by the Rev. G.R. Wiggins, MR. JOHN F. TROUTMAN, of Crawford county, to MISS CORDELIA P. HOLMES, daughter of MAJOR JAMES HOLMES.

Apr. 26, 1854

Married in Columbia, S.C. on Tuesday evening 18th inst. by the Rev. S.J. Shand, D.D., HON. CHARLES J. JENKINS, of Georgia, and MISS EMILY GERTRUDE, daughter of the late JUDGE BARNES, of Philadelphia.

Married on the 10th inst. by Rev. Dr. Talmage, ELLIOTT R. CHAMBERLAIN and MISS MARY KATE, daughter of D.C. WATSON, ESQ., of Greene county.

May 3, 1854

Married in Vineville on the 27th ult. by the Rev. Mr. Spear, MR. WM. ELLISON GROCE to MISS LAURA BONE.

Married on the 26th inst. by the Rev. Stephen Castelaw, MR. ISAAC HAYDEN, of Atlanta, and MISS MARY E., daughter of STEPHEN WOODARD, ESQ., of Bibb county.

Married on the 18th inst. by the Rev. John L. Kirkpatrick, D.D., in Columbus, Ga., MR. GEORGE YOUNG BANKS and MISS SUSAN COOK MITCHELL, daughter of WM. H. MITCHELL.

May 10, 1854

Married on the morning of the 2d instant by the Rev. G.H. Hancock, OVID G. SPARKS, ESQ., and MISS JOSEPHINE BRAZEAL, all of this city.

Married on the 18th of April by Rev. B.F. Wells, COL. J.J. GRIFFIN, of Oxford, to MISS INDIANA E., second daughter of DR. H. BRANHAM, of Eatonton, Ga.

Married on the 18th of April by Rev. R.B. Lester, PAUL E. TARVER, of Baker co., Ga., to MISS CINDERELLA C. SOLOMON, of Houston co. Ga.

Married on 27th of April by the Rev. Michael Cullen, the HON. L.A. THOMPSON, late of Florida, and MISS JANE S. DeGRAFFENRIED, daughter of E.L. DeGRAFFENRIED, of Columbus.

May 17, 1854

    Married on the 7th inst. by E.A. Robinson, J.P., MR. R.L. OLIVER, to MISS MARY J. BROWN, all of Oglethorpe.

    Married on the 14th inst. by Rev. S. Landrum, MR. JOHN SMITH to MISS EMMA KILPATRICK, all of this city.

May 31, 1854

    Married on the 28th inst. by Rev. R.L. Breck, MR. JOHN GROSS, of Scriven county, to MISS M.C. DOUGLAS, of this place.

June 7, 1854

    Married in Augusta on the 15th inst. by the Rev. W.J. Hard, WILLIS A. HAWKINS, ESQ., of Americus, Ga., and MISS MARY E. FINN, of that city.

June 14, 1854

    Married on the 7th inst. by Rev. G.C. Clark, MISS MARY JANE PERRY, of Newton county, Geo., to MR GEORGE W. ADAIR, of the city of Atlanta.

June 21, 1854

    Married in Vineville on Wednesday morning the 31st May, CAPT. EZEKIEL WIMBERLY of Baker county, to MISS M.V. HOLT, daughter of the late DR. A.F. HOLT, of this city.

    Married on the 7th inst. by Judge C.H. Remington, MR. JAMES T. HALL and MISS FANNIE N., daughter of COL. RICHARD MITCHELL - all of Thomas county.

July 5, 1854

    Married at Judge Scarborough's in Fort Valley on the 27th June, by Rev. S. Landrum, MR. HORACE THOMPSON, of Pond Town, to MISS CARRIE SCARBOROUGH.

    Married by the Rev. Wesley F. Smith, June 20, in Crawford county, Ga., at the residence of Wm. Dickson, Esq., MR. JOHN R. COCHRAN, of Dublin, Laurens county, to MISS JULIA L. DICKSON, of the former place.

July 12, 1854

    Married on the 4th inst. by R.W. Sparrow, Esq., MR. WM. Q.W. JOHNSON to MISS CATHARINE LAREY, all of Bibb county.

July 19, 1854

    Married at Eatonton on Tuesday morning the 4th inst. by the Rev. Dr. Talmage, COL. THOMAS P. SAFFOLD, of Madison, to MISS SARAH E., only daughter of ANDREW REID, ESQ., of the former place.

    Married at Columbus on the evening of the 7th inst., at the residence of her brother-in-law, Joseph B. Hall, Esq., by the Rev. F. Bowman, D.D., MISS EMMA C., daughter of the HON. WM. C. DAWSON, and EDWARD W. SEABROOK, ESQ., of Edisto Island, South Carolina.

Aug. 16, 1854

    Married on Monday the 14th inst. by J.S. McCoy, Esq., MR. JOHN ARIGAL, of Atlanta, Ga., to MISS JANE A. WHITEHEAD, eldest daughter of BENNETT WHITEHEAD, ESQ., of Laurens co., Ga.

Aug. 23, 1854

Married on the 15th inst. in Pond Town by the Rev. J.Blakely Smith, MR. ABNER SMITH, of Jamestown, to MISS ANTOINETTE R. GREENE, daughter of DR. A.B. GREENE.

Married in this city on the 21st inst. by the Rev. Mr. O'Neal, MR. MICHAEL McNAMARA to MISS MARY LOUISA DOYLE, all of this city.

Aug. 30, 1854

Married in Christ Church, Macon, on Monday morning the 21st inst., by the Rev. J.A. Shanklin, LLOYD G. BOWERS, ESQ., to MISS SARAH T. BARTLETT, daughter of the late MYRON BARTLETT, of this city.

Sep. 20, 1854

Married in this county on the 8th inst. by A. Benton, Esq., MR. JOHN SMITH to MRS. SARAH ARTHUR; also on the 12th, MR. JAMES R. CALLEY to MISS NANCY M. MITCHELL, all of Bibb county.

Oct. 4, 1854

Married in Milledgeville on the 13th inst. by Rev. M.R. Foot, ROBT. J. MORGAN, ESQ., of LaGrange, and MISS M.F., daughter of DR. TOMLINSON FORT, of the former place.

Married in LaGrange on the 18th inst. by Rev. B.H. Overby, JOHN B. GORDON, ESQ., of Atlanta, and MISS FANNIE R., daughter of HON. HUGH A. HARALSON, of LaGrange.

Married in Meriwether co., Ga. on the 7th inst. by the Rev. Jesse Fallen, MR. JAMES HARDISON, of Houston co., to MISS LOUISA AMOSS, of Meriwether county.

Married on the 26th ult. by Rev. Dr. E.T. McGehee, MR. JAMES S. REDDICK to MISS ELVIRA C. LOMINAC, all of Houston county.

Oct. 25, 1854

Married in Atlanta on the 15th inst. by the Rev. J.E. Dubose, COL. R.H.D. SORREL, of Americus, to MRS. MARTHA E. BELL, of Texas.

Married on the evening of Oct. 19th by Rev. Wm. C. Wilkes, Principal of Forsyth Female Collegiate Institute, DR. LEANDER S. MORSE, of Forsyth, to MISS MARY H., daughter of E.M. BUTLER, ESQ., of Monroe Co.

Married at Columbus, Ga. on Thursday 19th inst. by the Rev. W.G. Connor, MR. ALFRED PRESCOTT, of Fort Gaines, Ga., and MISS EMMA J., daughter of the REV. THOMAS B. SLADE, of the former place.

Married on the 18th inst. by the Rev. Wm. Arnold, at the residence of Col. Wm. E. Adams, MR. A.W. MOSELEY, to MISS ANTOINETTE T. RUSSELL, all of Putnam County.

Married in Barnesville on the 19th inst., by the Rev. Sylvanus Landrum, of this city, CHAS. W. BROWN to MISS SALLIE, daughter of COL. FRYOR, all of the former place.

Married in Houston Co. on the morning of the 22nd inst., by the Rev. John Basset, MR. KINDRED KEMP to MISS ELIZA SIMMONS, all of Houston Co.

Married on the 17th inst. at the residence of Col. Henry Long, by Rev. Jno. E. Dawson, MR. WILLIAM A. PULLEN and MISS MARIETTA LONG, of LaGrange.

Married in Greensboro on the 11th inst. by the Rev. Joseph H. Echols, MR. W.D. SULLIVAN, Editor of the Madison Family Visitor, and MISS ANNIE GRESHAM, of Greensboro.

Nov. 1, 1854

Married on the 24th inst. at the house of her uncle, M.L. Greene, Fort Valley, by the Rev. G.W. Persons, LIEUT. JAMES P. LFEWELLEN, of U.S. Army, to MISS SARAH E. EVERETT, daughter of the late JAMES A. EVERETT.

Married in Marietta on Wednesday the 18th ult. by the Rev. Geo. H.W. Petrie, MR. JOHN I. DAVIS, of Washington, to MISS FANNIE D. PARK, of Greensboro.

Nov. 8, 1854

Married in Greene county on the 29th inst. by Bazzel Rowland, Esq., MR. JOHN O. DAVIES, Printer, of Milledgeville, to MISS MARY JANE EDEN.

Married on Thursday the 2d inst. by Rev. J.H. Corley, WILLIS J. CURREY, of Forsyth, to MISS EULIZA JANE MADDOX, of Butts county.

Married in Rome on the 31st ult. by the Rev. Mr. Cox, COL. A.W. REDDING, of Jamestown, Ga., to MRS. ELIZABETH SMITH, widow of the late HON. WM. SMITH.

Married in this city on Wednesday last by the Rev. Eustace Spear, COL. I.D.N. JOHNS, to MISS MARY C. HAMMOND, all of this city.

Nov. 15, 1854

Married in Knoxville on the 8th inst., MR. THOMAS CRUTCHFIELD, JR. to MISS S.E. OLIVER.

Married in Columbus, Ga. Nov. 7th by Rev. Mr. Dalzell, CAPT. JAS. M. BIVINS, of Macon, and MISS MARY FRANCES DRUMRIGHT, of the former place.

Married in Jasper county on Wednesday the 8th inst. by the Rev. Mr. Henderson, COL. GEORGE A. BROWN, of Americus, and MISS GEORGIA V., daughter of J. HOLLAND, ESQ., of that county.

Married in Upson county on the 9th inst. by the Rev. John M. Marshall, MR. FRANCIS A. PARKS to MISS VIRGINIA E. CUNNINGHAM.

Nov. 22, 1854

Married in Atlanta on the 13th inst. by the Rev. J.P. Duncan, MR. N.C. ROBERTSON, of Columbia, S.C., to MISS L.B. WINSHIP, daughter of ISAAC WINSHIP, ESQ., late of Vineville, Ga.

Married in this city on Wednesday evening last by the Rev. Mr. Spear, MR. D.B. WOODRUFF to MISS ADELIA SCATTERGOOD, all of this city.

Nov. 29, 1854

Married in Monroe county Nov. 1st by the Rev. Wesley F. Smith, THOMAS T. HOLLIS to MISS ALMIRA E. DAVIS, all of Monroe county.

Married in Culloden Nov. 8th by the Rev. Wesley F. Smith, WILLIAM W. MADDOCKS to MISS MARY C. FREEMAN, all of the former place.

Married in Crawford county Nov. 14th by the Rev. Wesley F. Smith, ROBERT A. FULLER, of Columbia County, Ga. to MISS WALKER F. DAINELLY, of the former place.

Married on Monday Nov. 13th by Rev. Thomas Jordan, MR. DAVIS SINGLETON, of Dahlonega, to MISS REBECCA L., daughter of ROBERT GRIGGS, of Putnam County.

Nov. 29, 1854

Married in Milledgeville on the 21st inst. by the Rev. Mr. Flinn, COL. W.L. MITCHELL, of Athens, Ga., to MISS L.L. BASS, of the former place.

Married in Lexington on the 23d November by Rev. S. Landrum of Macon, GEORGE T. LANDRUM, ESQ., to MISS SUSAN A. CLARK, daughter of Z.H. CLARK, ESQ., all of the former place.

Married at Perry, Houston county, Ga. on the 21st inst. by the Rev. Mr. Felder, CAPT. E.R. GOULDING, of Columbus, Ga., and MISS JENNIE E. BRYAN, only daughter of DAVID BRYAN, ESQ., of Talbott county, Ga.

Married in this city on the 27th inst. by the Rev. R.L. Breck, E.C. GRIER, ESQ., of Mecklenburg, N.C., to MISS FRANCES MATILDA, daughter of WASHINGTON POE, ESQ., of Macon.

Dec. 6, 1854

Married in Upson County on the 21st ult. by Rev. John M. Marshall, MR. JONATHAN T. WOODY, of Chambers County, Ala. to MISS MARTHA E. DUNCAN, daughter of JAMES DUNCAN, ESQ.

Married on the 23d ult. in Washington, Ga. by the Rev. Samuel Anthony, MR. THOMAS L. COOPER, of Atlanta, and MISS MARY S., daughter of ALEXANDER POPE, SR., ESQ., of the former place.

Dec. 13, 1854

Married on the 7th inst. in Vineville by Rev. S. Landrum, of Macon, DR. DAVID R.E. WINN, of Americus, to MISS FRANCES M. DEAN, daughter of COL. JAMES DEAN.

Dec. 20, 1854

Married in Vineville on the evening of the 14th inst. by Rev. G.H. Hancock, THOMAS W. BAXTER, ESQ., of Smith Co., Texas, to MISS ELLENORA F. SCOTT, of the former place.

Dec. 27, 1854

Married in Russel Co., Ala. on the morning of the 14th inst., at the country residence of Mrs. Boykin, by the Rev. John E. Dawson, MR. THADDEUS G. HOLT to MISS NARCISSA BOYKIN, all of Columbus, Ga.

Married in this city on the morning of the 21st inst. by Rev. Robt. L. Breck, WM. T. BROWN, of Americus, Ga., to MISS LUCIA M. TRAPP, of Macon, Ga.

Married on the evening of the 14th inst. by the Rev. O.C. Gibson, JOHN M. RIVEIRE, ESQ., of Barnesville, to MISS EUGENIA E. McCOY, eldest daughter of JAMES McCOY, of Upson county, Ga.

Married on the evening of the 19th inst. by the Rev. O.C. Gibson, COL. S.N. BRASWELL, of Barnesville, Ga., to MISS MARY A. ANDERSON, only daughter of DR. JAMES ANDERSON, of Upson County, Ga.

Married on the 13th inst. by Rev. C.W. Stevens, MR. CHARLES W. GAUSE, of Randolph co., to MISS GERTRUDE E. GONDER, of Hancock co.

Married in this city on the 17th inst. by Amos Benton, Esq., MR. ORREY ODOM to MISS FRANCES M. JORDAN - also on the 20th MR. G. JACKSON WILLIAMS to MISS ELPHANY SHERRY, all of this county.

Married at the residence of Samuel H. Caldwell, Esq. by S. Malone, Esq., COL. A.W. COZART, of Philadelphai, East Tenn., to MARTHA G., daughter of C.Y. CALDWELL, ESQ., late of Pike Co., Ga.

Dec. 27, 1854

Married on the evening of the 19th inst. by Rev. L. Solomon, WILLIAM S. KELLY, ESQ., of Twiggs county, to MRS. MARY A.E. CHAMPMAN, of the county of Bibb.

Married on the evening of the 21st inst. by Rev. L. Solomon, HENRY F. SOLOMON, ESQ., to MISS MARY E. FITZPATRICK, all of Twiggs county.

Jan. 3, 1855

Married in this city on the 28th Dec. 1854 by Rev. S. Landrum, MR. E.O. WHITTINGTON to MISS FANNIE E. RICHARDSON.

Married in this city on the evening of the 21st ult. by Rev. G.H. Hancock, MR. S.W. WALKER and MISS LAURA EVANS.

Married at her residence near Montezuma, Ga. on Wednesday evening 20th ult., by E.R. Young, Esq., MR. S.S. HATHAWAY to MRS. LEVINIA FELTON, all of Macon Co.

Married in this city on the 24th of Dec. by Amos Benton, Esq., MR. EDWARD K. GARVIN to MISS SUSAN SHERRY, all of this city.

Married in this city on the 17th inst. by Amos Benton, Esq., MR. ORREY ODOM to MISS FRANCES M. JORDAN - also on the 20th MR. G. JACKSON WILLIAMS to MISS ELPHANY SHERRY, all of this county.

Married in Savannah on the evening of the 28th ult. by the Rev. Mr. Connor, WM. F. PLANE, ESQ., of Columbus, Ga., to MISS C. HELEN JEMISON, of Tuscaloosa, Ala.

Jan. 10, 1855

Married at the house of Jonathan Dawson, Esq., in Upson county, on the morning of the 3d January, by Rev. W.F. Smith, DR. W.A. MATHEWS, of Fort Valley, to MISS TRYPHENA CRUTE, of Texas.

Married on the 20th Dec. in Crawford Co. by the Rev. W.F. Smith, DR. J.H.D. WORSHAM, of Bibb, to MISS MARGARET A.E. MURCHISON, of Crawford Co.

Married in this city on the 2d inst. by the Rev. S. Landrum, MR. FRIEDRICH SCHLUNZEN to MISS LOUISE KAUF, all of this city.

Jan. 17, 1855

Married in this city on the 15th inst. by Amos Benton, Esq., MR. JAMES MORRISY to MISS RACHAEL A. BEHANE.

Jan. 24, 1855

Married on the 10th inst. at the residence of D.F. Richardson, near Thomaston, by the Rev. O.C. Gibson, WM. H. PITTS, of Upshur county, Texas, to MRS. SARAH F. HARVEY, of Upson county, Ga.

Married in this city on the 23d inst. by Rev. S. Landrum, MR. ROBT. W. SCALES to MISS FANNIE MARTIN, all of Macon.

Married on the 17th inst. by the Rev. W. Keith, MR. JOB. E. TAYLER to MISS JULIA C. WINN, both of Monroe County.

Jan. 31, 1855

Married on the 25th inst. in this city by Rev. S. Landrum, MR. WM. O. HURT to MISS MARY SAGE.

Feb. 7, 1855

Married in this city on the 30th ult. by Judge Cook, MR. ISAAC B. PILGRIM to MISS MARY J. CASH, all of Atlanta. (Atlanta Republican copy)

Feb. 14, 1855

Married on the evening of the 8th inst. by the Rev. Wm. C. Wilkes, Principal of Forsyth Female Collegiate Institute, MR. THOS. S. SHARMAN to MISS SARAH DICKINSON, both of Upson Co., Ga.

Married at the same time and place by Rev. Wm. C. Wilkes, MR. ROWAN C. WARE, of Putnam Co., to MISS MARY ELIZA, daughter of THOS. S. SHARMAN, ESQ., of Upson Co., Ga.

Married in this city on Tuesday last by the Rev. R.L. Breck, MR. SAMUEL B. PALMER, of Savannah, to MISS MARY F. LEWIS, of Macon.

Feb. 21, 1855

Married on the evening of the 8th inst. by the Rev. E.P. Birch, MR. E.C. BUTLER to MISS FANNIE A., daughter of E. ETHERIDGE, ESQ., all of Monroe county.

Married in this city at the house of A.L. Audouin on the 20th of January last, by E.C. Granniss, Esq., MR. NATHAN GROSSMAYER to MISS SARAH BRINN, all of Macon.

Married in this city at the house of J.A. Sloan on the 18th inst. by E.C. Granniss, Esq., MR. JAMES HANLEY to MRS. LOUISA CLARK, all of Macon.

Mar. 7, 1855

Married in Columbus, Ga. on the 28th February, by the Rev. Mr. Speer, Minister of the Methodist Episcopal Church South, MAJ. WILLIAM A. COBB, Ordinary of Upson county, to MRS. MARIA R. HAMILL, of the former place.

Married on Monday evening March 5th, at the Methodist Episcopal Church, by Rev. Mr. Hinton, MR. WILLIAM H. BRAY to MISS MARY B. SIMS, both of this city.

Mar. 14, 1855

Married on the morning of the 8th inst. at Cuthbert, Randolph county, by the Rev. T.H. Foster, DR. JOHN R. BOON, of this city, to MISS ALLIE V. ALDEN, of the former place.

Married on Tuesday evening March 6th, by the Rev. E.W. Speer, of Columbus, MR. G.W. ATKINSON, of Columbus, to MISS LOUISA C. WASHINGTON, daughter of R.B. WASHINGTON, of this city.

Mar. 21, 1855

Married on Tuesday the 6th inst. by S.M. Manning, Esq., at the residence of Mrs. Jeannette Mitchell, MR. WARREN D. WOOD, of Macon, and MISS SARAH A.P. MITCHELL, of Hawkinsville, Georgia.

Apr. 4, 1855

Married on Tuesday morning the 13th inst. by the Hon. Isaac Mulkey, WM. J. HAMILTON, ESQ., of Butler, Ga., to MISS ELIZA N. CHRISTIE, of Crawford co.

Married on the evening of the 14th inst. by the Rev. W.W. Corbitt, DR. WALKER to MISS AUGUSTA R. SMEAD, daughter of E. SMEAD, ESQ., all of Butler.

Apr. 4, 1855

Married in Milledgeville on Wednesday evening 21st inst. by Rev. Mr. Flinn, DR. JAMES F. ALEXANDER, of Atlanta, to MISS GEORGIA JEAN, eldest daughter of R.M. ORME.

Apr. 11, 1855

Married in Athens, Ga. on the 2d inst. by the Rev. J.S. Key, REV. C.P. COOPER, of the Georgia Conference, to MISS HESSIE M. JACKSON.

Married on the 5th inst. by the Rev. R.L. Breck, of Macon, MINOR W. HARRIS, ESQ., to MISS CORNELIA RILEY, all of Houston county.

Apr. 18, 1855

Married in Columbus on the 10th inst. by the Hon. James N. Bethune, MR. W.S. REYNOLDS, (publisher of the "Corner Stone") and MISS SARAH B. FORD, all of that city.

Married on the 1st inst. MR. JOEL WILSON, aged 72 years, and MISS MARY E. EDWARDS, aged 16 - both of Troup.

May 2, 1855

Married in Albany, Ga. on Wednesday evening the 18th instant by the Rev. C.D. Mallary, MR. E.A. ROBERTS to MISS EMMA N. HINES, all of Albany.

Married in Russell county, Ala. on the 19th inst. by the Rev. John E. Dawson, MR. THOMAS J. WOOLFOLD, of Macon, to MISS S.P. CROMWELL, of Russell county.

Married in Houston county on the 26th of April, at the residence of Wm. Allen, by the Rev. G.W. Persons, REUBEN H. SLAPPEY, ESQ., of Sumter co., to MISS MARY A. KING, daughter of MR. DAVID KING, of Houston co.

May 9, 1855

Married in Cassville on Monday 30th ult. by Rev. John S. Wilson, D.D., MR. JOSEPH H. PITMAN, of Gordon county, Ga., to MISS LAURA C. WORD, of Cassville.

Married at the residence of Col. Lewis Tumlin, on the Etowah River, on Tuesday May 1st, by Rev. Geo. W. Tumlin, MR. SAMFORD ERWIN to MISS JOSEPHINE TIMLIN, all of Cass county.

Married on the 25th April by the Rev. J.Y. Alexander, MR. JOSEPH R. HOLLIDAY, of Baker county, to MISS MARY LUCY RAY, of Newnan, Ga.

Married on the 16th ult. by the Rev. John E. Dubose, COL. A.M. WALLACE, of Maryville, Tenn., to MISS FRANCES G. SINGLETON, of Dahlonega.

Married on the 26th ult. at the residence of Mr. Joseph Burch, THOS. L. TAYLOR, ESQ., to MISS MARY JANE PICKETT, all of Pulaski county.

May 16, 1855

Married at Wynnton, near Columbus, Ga. on the 10th inst., by Rev. Mr. Higgins, THOMAS U. CAMAK, ESQ., of Athens, Ga., and MISS LAURA A., daughter of THOMAS RAGLAND, of the <u>Columbus Enquirer</u>.

Married by the Rev. L.T. Doyal, D.D. DOYAL, ESQ., of Atlanta, to MRS. ELIZABETH BOYNTON, of Henry county.

June 6, 1855

Married in Vineville on Thursday evening the 31st ult. by Rev. Mr. Reese, Rector of Christ Church, CAPTAIN HUGH L. CLAY, of Huntsville, Ala., and MISS HARRIET CELESTIA, second daughter of MAJOR A. COMER.

Married on the 17th May by Rev. J.R. Horn, MR. THOS. S. COBB and MISS MARTHA A. TILL, all of Henderson, Houston Co., Ga.

Married in Goliad, Texas, at the residence of Judge Pryor Lea, on Monday morning the 7th ult. by the Rev. Mr. Cottingham, MR. M.A. WINGFIELD, of Madison, Ga., and MISS JULIA, daughter of JUDGE PRYOR LEA.

Married in Sumter county, Ga. by the Rev. P.A. Strobel, DR. B.J. HEAD, of Oglethorpe, Ga., and MRS. H.A. BURGE, of the former place.

June 13, 1855

Married on the 6th instant at the residence of Col. A. Reese, Madison, Ga., by Rev. C.M. Irwin, MISS FANNIE C. WALKER and MR. JOHN W. BURNEY, both of Morgan county.

June 20, 1855

Married in the Capitol, in Tallahassee, Florida, by the Rt. Rev. Bishop Rutledge, on the evening of the 6th inst., DR. ALFRED W. ALLEN, of New York City, to MISS ELIZA J. LOWCAY, of England.

June 27, 1855

Married in Athens on Thursday morning the 14th inst. by the Rev. Nathan Hoyt, D.D., MR. JOHN PHINIZY, of Rome, Ga., to MISS SUSAN SCOTT, daughter of WM. M. MORTON, of Athens.

Married in Athens on Thursday the 14th inst. by the Rev. W.T. Brantly D.D., MR. JOSIAH C. ORR to MISS ELIZABETH TOWNS, all of Athens.

Married in Athens on Tuesday morning the 19th inst. by the Rev. W.T. Brantly, D.D., COL. DAVID A. VASON, of Albany, Ga., to MISS MARY J. POPE, daughter of the late COL. HENRY POPE, of Athens.

Married in Columbus, Ga. on the 20th inst., MR. W.C. CLIFTON to MISS CLARA R. JONES, of Columbus.

July 4, 1855

Married at Fenn's bridge, on Wednesday morning the 13th ult., by the Rev. Mr. Verdaree, MR. ALEXANDER S. QUARTERMAN, of Liberty county, to MISS CAPLIE W., second daughter of MR. B.H. MOULTRIE.

Married on the 10th inst. in Brunswick county, Virginia, by the Rev. Mr. Mower, JESSE B. BATTLE, JR., of Sparta, Ga., and MISS MARY B. CHAMBLISS, of the former place.

July 11, 1855

Married on Sunday morning the 24th ult. by C.H. Walker, Esq., MR. JONATHAN COLBERT to MRS. NANCY HARRIS, all of Crawford county.

July 18, 1855

Married in Houston county on the 12th inst. by the Rev. B.F. Tharpe, COL. WILLIAM THARPE to MISS MARTHA A. FAGAN, all of said county.

Married in McDonough, Ga. on the eve of the 6th inst. by the Rev. Dr. F.E. Manson, COL. GEORGE M. NOLAN and MISS OPHELIA E.G. CAMBELL.

Married on the morning of the 10th inst. by the Rev. Mr. Conner, L.J. GARTRELL, of Atlanta, and MISS ANTOINETTE P. BURKE, of LaGrange.

July 18, 1855

Married at Oak Bowery, Ala. on the 10th inst. by the Rev. L.F. Dowdell, DR. AUGUSTIN O. STANLEY and MISS LILLIE R. DOWDELL.

July 25, 1855

Married near Eatonton on the 10th inst. by Rev. S.K. Talmage, D.D., MR. E.D. BROWN, of Milledgeville, to MISS SARAH TRIPPE, only daughter of JNO. B. TRIPPE, ESQ.

Married in Newton County on the 19th inst. at the residence of Iverson L. Graves, Esq., by the Rev. Bishop Pierce, MR. JAMES J. SLADE, of Columbus, and MISS ANN G. GRAHAM, of Newton.

Married in Jeffersonville, Ga. on the 12th inst. by Rev. G.R. McCall, MR. R.C. WALKER, of Longstreet, Ga., to MISS H.C. BREAZEAL, of the former place.

Married at the residence of Miles G. Harris, Esq., Hancock Co., on Tuesday evening 10th inst., by Rev. R.C. Smith, MISS ADA H. SEYMOUR to MR. JOHN C. CARMICHAEL, of Augusta.

Aug. 1, 1855

Married on the 10th ult. by the Rev. Mr. Hard, MR. C.M. KOLB to MISS M.P., second daughter of JOHN PHINZY, ESQ., all of Augusta, Ga.

Married in Sparta on the 18th ult. by the Rev. C.W. Key, COL. MARK JOHNSON, of Atlanta, to MISS ELIZABETH L. PENDERGRASS of the former place.

Married in Telfair county by the Rev. James Williamson, MR. JOHN K. WILLIAMSON to MISS MARIA E. MIZELL.

Married on the evening of the 22d ult. by the Hon. James H. Stark, COL. GILPIN J. GREEN to MRS. SARAH M. MAXWELL, all of Griffin.

Married on Thursday morning 19th inst. by the Rev. Thomas B. Slade, Esq., MR. WILLIAM C. BELLAMY and MISS FANNIE H. LINDSAY, all of Columbus.

Aug. 8, 1855

Married on Sunday evening July 29th, at the Roman Catholic Church, by the Rev. Dr. O'Neil, M.N. BARRY, ESQ., to MISS CATE LEONARD, all of this city.

Married on the 1st August by Rev. G.H. Hancock, MR. J.E. RYLANDER, of Sumter, to MISS A.E. MATHIS, of Marion County.

Married in Pulaski county, near Hawkinsville, on Thursday evening 26th July, by the Rev. Jesse R. Horne, MR. ELLIS W. JENKINS, of Montezuma, Ga., to MISS FRANCES R., only daughter of JOHN ANDERSON, ESQ., of the former place.

Married in Forsyth at the residence of Joseph R. Banks, on 23d ult., by the Rev. John H. Corley, JOHN T. STEPHENS to MISS MARY LOU BANKS.

Aug. 15, 1855

Married on the morning of the 2d inst. by Rev. Dr. Edward T. McGehee, of Houston Co., MR. J.W. BROWN and MRS. FANNIE A. SHINE, both of Dooly Co.

Married on the 9th inst. by the Rev. G.H. Hancock, ERASTUS H. LINK, ESQ., to MISS FRANCESCA R. GUTTENBERGER, all of Vineville.

Aug. 15, 1855

Married in Madison on the 8th inst. by the Rev. Jos. H. Echols, COL. WM. D. WOODSON, of Thomaston, Upson county, to MISS MARTHA REESE FLOYD, eldest daughter of the late STEWART FLOYD, dec'd, of this place.

Aug. 22, 1855

Married in Eatonton at the residence of R.T. Davis, Esq. on the morning of the 16th of August, by the Rev. Wm. C. Wilkes, President of Monroe Female University, GEN. E.H. BEALL, of Hamilton, to MRS. S.G. ASHURST, of the former place.

Aug. 29, 1855

Married on the 16th inst. by the Rev. Cary Cox, D.R. ANDREWS, ESQ., of Stanfordville, to MRS. MARY M. HOLT, all of Putnam co.

Married on the morning of the 26th of August by the Rev. L. Solomon, CHARLES P. REYNOLDS, ESQ., to MISS MARY A.E. RHODES, all of Twiggs county.

Sep. 5, 1855

Married at Col. Wilburn's near this city, on the 30th August, by the Rev. S. Landrum, MR. WILLIAM C. BANDY, of East Macon, to MISS MARTHA M. WILLET.

Sep. 12, 1855

Married on the 5th inst. by the Rev. E.W. Warren, of Cuthbert, COL. JAMES BUCHANAN to MISS LAURA J., daughter of COL. J.W. PERRY, all of Blakely, Ga.

Sep. 19, 1855

Married on the morning of the 11th inst. at Chalybeate Springs, in Meriwether county, by Rev. John M. Marshall, MR. JOSEPH J. ALLEN to MISS GEORGIA G. PATRICK, all of Talbot.

Sep. 26, 1855

Married on the 23d inst. by Rev. Jas. W. Hinton, MR. JOHN W. SWANSON, of Macon, to MISS MARTHA A.S. CALHOUN, of Houston co.

Married in this city at the residence of Judge Holt, on the 19th inst. by the Rev. S. Landrum, MR. JAMES A. HILL, of Houston county, to MISS MARIAH HOLT, daughter of the late DR. FOWLER HOLT, of Perry, Ga.

Married in Hamilton, Ga., MR. WM. D. KING, of Perry, Houston co., to MISS MARY C. PARR, daughter of MR. D.W. PARR, of Russell co., Alabama.

Oct. 3, 1855

Married in Musco-ee county on the 25th inst. by the Rev. J.T. Myers, MR. BENJ. P. JENKINS to MISS MARY E. FERGUSON.

Married on Thursday the 20th of September, in Baltimore, Md., MR. GEO. H. EVANS and MISS M.A. COWLES, eldest daughter of LOYAL COWLES, formerly of this city.

Oct. 24, 1855

Married on the morning of the 18th by Rev. Wm. C. Wilkes, President of Monroe Female University, DR. JOSEPH W. STEPHENSON, of Talbot county, to MISS LOUISA V., daughter of AQUILLA CHENY, ESQ., of Monroe county.

Oct. 31, 1855

Married on Wednesday morning the 17th inst. by Rev. Phinazee, MR. JAMES S. PHINAZEE to MRS. MARY BALDWIN, daughter of A. JOINER, ESQ., all of Monroe Co.

Married in Monroe Co. on the 18th inst. by Elder Wm. C. Wilkes, President of Monroe Female University, MR. JONATHAN A. McAFEE, of Pike Co., to MISS FRANCES M. SMARR.

Married in Marietta at the residence of John E. Ward, Esq., on the evening of Tuesday 23d inst. by the Rev. R. Elliott Habersham, MR. ROBERT E. ALLEN, of Savannah, to MISS GEORGIA A., daughter of the late WILLIAM WARD, ESQ., of Liberty county.

Nov. 7, 1855

Married on the 24th ult. by Rev. J.R. Danforth, MR. DAVID S. WALKER to MISS ANN ALICE, daughter of REV. E.D. LOWRY, all of Twiggs County, Ga.

Nov. 14, 1855

Married in Savannah on the 10th inst., at St. John's Church, by the Rev. George Clark, MR. THOMAS B. CLARK, of Knoxville, Tenn., to MISS ELIZA JESSE CRISP, eldest daughter of MR. WM. H. CRISP.

Married at Ravenswood, Richmond county, on the evening of Thursday 8th inst. by the Rev. Alfred Mann, MR. EDWARD W. HULL, of Athens, to MISS CORNELIA M., daughter of ROBT. A. ALLEN, ESQ., of Savannah.

Nov. 21, 1855

Married near Macon on the 14th inst. by the Rev. P.N. Maddox, MR. AUGUSTUS C. PRINGLE, of Barnesville, to MISS LOUISA C. KILPATRICK, daughter of MR. WM. KILPATRICK, of Bibb co.

Married on the 12th inst. at the residence of P.L. Fryer, near Barnesville, by the Rev. W.C. Wilkes, COL. WM. H.C. PERRY, of Burke county, to MISS MARY P. FRYER.

Married in Twiggs county on the 1st inst. by Warren S. McCoy, Esq., at the residence of John Gallmore, MR. LEWIS NOBLES to MISS ABIGAIL VEAL, daughter of the late BURREL VEAL.

Married on the 13th inst. at the residence of Dr. J.R. Cook by the Rev. W.H. Hollingshead, MR. EVANS S. CROCKER to MISS ANN E. HARMAN, all of Macon co., Ga.

Married in Albany, Ga. on the 30th ult. at the residence of R.K. Hines, Esq., by the Rev. Mr. Mallory, MR. L.P.D. WARREN to MISS BENNIE HINES, all of the above place.

Married in Pike county on the 12th inst. by Elder Wm. C. Wilkes, President of Monroe Female University, MR. WM. H.C. PERRY, of Burke county, to MISS MARY P. FRYER, daughter of Z.L. FRYER, ESQ.

Nov. 28, 1855

Married at the Laurens Hill Church, Laurens county, on the 18th inst. by Rev. James Williamson, MR. WM. J. GALIMORE, of Twiggs county, to MISS HANNAH E. SLADE, of Laurens county.

Married on the 20th inst. by the Rev. H. Phinazee, MR. SIMEON M. MABRY to MISS EMILY OGLETREE, daughter of JOHN B. OGLETREE, ESQ., all of Monroe county.

Married at Fort Valley on the 22d inst. by Rev. W.H. Hollinshead, M.D., REV. PETER M. RYBURN to MISS M. ANTOINETTE LUMPKIN, both of Fort Valley.

Dec. 5, 1855

   Married on Thursday evening the 22nd inst. by Rev. Wesley F. Smith, DR. CYRUS S. SNEED to MISS MARY E. STROTHER, all of Culloden, Ga.

Dec. 12, 1855

   Married on Tuesday morning the 4th inst. by Rev. Alfred Mann, MR. A.L. WOODWARD, of Monroe county, to MISS ANTOINETTE HAMMOND, daughter of DR. HAMMOND, of this city.

   Married in Pike Co. on the 29th of Nov. by Elder Wm. C. Wilkes, DR. GEO. M. McDOWELL, of Barnesville, to MISS SOPHRONIA L. MAYS.

   Married in Dooly Co. on Tuesday morning 4th inst. by Rev. E.T. McGehee, MR. T.W.T. WESTBROOK, of Houston Co., to MISS SARAH J. LEARY, of the former county.

Dec. 19, 1855

   Married in Monroe county Dec. 4th by Elder Wm. C. Wilkes, MR. JAS. W.H. PONDER to MISS ABI R. BOWDOIN.

   Married in the same county Dec. 12th by the same, MR. R.W. MILNER, of Pike county, to MISS SARAH E.S. RAVENS.

Dec. 26, 1855

   Married in Milledgeville on the 12th inst. by Rev. J. Knowles, J.A. HEADEN, ESQ., member of the House from Hall county, Ga., to MISS LOUISA E., daughter of COL. PETER FAIR, of that city.

   Married on the 13th inst. by the Rev. W.W. Robinson, MR. JAMES SIMMS, of Chambers county, Al., and MISS LUCRETIA CROSS, of Columbus, Ga.

   Married on the 6th inst. by Elder William L. Crawford, MR. AUGUSTUS M. HOLLIMAN (formerly of Columbia co., Ga.) and MISS ELIZA G., daughter of MR. JOHN RAINS, of Randolph co., Ga.

   Married in Wynnton on the 12th instant by the Rev. W.R. Branham, JOHN J. JONES, ESQ., of Burke county, Ga., and MISS EVA F. TOOMBS, of the former place.

   Married by the Rev. Thomas Muse on the 25th Nov., MR. JOHN WARD, of Stewart county, and MISS VIRGINIA W. MITCHELL, of Randolph county.

Jan. 9, 1856

   Married at Bel Air on the 20th ult. by the Rev. D. Ford, JAMES M. SAVAGE, ESQ., and MISS CAROLINE C. DENT, daughter of the late DR. JOHN DENT.

   Married at the residence of the father of the bride, in Savannah, on the evening of the 3d inst., by Rev. Wm. H. Crumley, of Augusta, ISAAC S. CLARK, ESQ., associate editor of the Savannah Daily Journal, to JULIA GOODALL, daughter of SEABORN GOODALL, ESQ. (NOTE: bride's name should read JULIA DOOGALL DOON.)

Jan. 16, 1856

   Married in Vineville, at the residence of P. Solomon, Esq., on Wednesday evening the 9th inst., by the Rev. H.R. Reese, MR. EMMET R. JOHNSON to MISS GERALDINE GRIFFIN, daughter of the late LARKIN GRIFFIN, ESQ.

   Married on the evening of the 25th ult. at the residence of Mrs. Taylor, by Henning D. Murden, Esq., MR. A.S. PINKSTON, of Stewart county, and MISS LIZZIE COLCLOUGH, of Taliaferro county, Ga.

Jan. 23, 1856

Married on the 15th Jan. by Rev. S.F. Montgomery, MR. JAMES M. HALL, of Scottsboro, to MISS MARY E. HAVIS, eldest daughter of COL. JESSE D. HAVIS, of Perry, Ga.

Married in Lawrenceville, Ga. on Tuesday the 8th inst., MR. F.T. PENTECOST, of Rome, to MISS MARY MOLTBIE, of the former place.

Jan. 30, 1856

Married on the 26th inst. by the Rev. J. Basset, MR. FRANK P. GAREY, of Macon, to MISS CHARLOTTE F., daughter of JAS. GAREY, ESQ., of Houston county.

Married on the 2d inst. at the residence of A. McAllum, Esq., in Twiggs county, MR. ALEXANDER DAWSON, of Houston county, to MISS ADDIE McCALLUM, of Twiggs co.

Feb. 6, 1856

Married on the 29th ult. by the Rev. Thomas Trice, at the residence of her father in Pike county, Ga., MISS SALLIA A., daughter of HENRY JONES, ESQ., to JUDGE W.E. MILLER, Editor of the Associate of the South Buena Vista, Ga.

Feb. 13, 1856

Married on Thursday Jan. 31st, 1856, by Rev. J.R. Horne, MR. JOHN W. SANDLIN and MISS SARAH F. TILL, all of Henderson, Houston county.

Married in Pike county, Ga. January 28th by Elder W.C. Wilkes, MR. LAZARUS B. PARKES, of Autauga county, Ala., to MISS BONETA M. MILNER, daughter of WILLIS MILNER, ESQ.

Married on the 17th ult. in Marnego county, Ala., at the residence of the Rev. Edward Baptist, CAPT. EDW. YOUNG HILL, JR., of LaGrange, Ga., and Editor of the Reporter, to MISS MAGGIE L. BAPTIST, of the former place.

Married in Milledgeville on Wednesday evening 6th inst. by the Rev. Wm. Flinn, DR. HANSELL HALL, of Thomasville, to MISS SARAH, third daughter of MAJ. I.L. HARRIS.

Feb. 20, 1856

Married on Monday the 11th inst. by Rev. Wm. Smith, C.L. BARBOUR, ESQ., Junior Editor of the Atlanta Examiner, and SALLIE C. MORGAN, of LaGrange.

Married in Barnesville Feb. 7th, at the residence of Geo. James, Esq. by Elder Wm. C. Wilkes, President of Monroe Female University, MR. WM. R. PIXLEY to MISS NANCY C. WALDRUSS.

Feb. 27, 1856

Married in Columbus, Ga. on Wednesday last by the Rev. Mr. Speer, the REV. D.D. COX, of the Georgia Conference, to MISS E. LUCKIE.

Mar. 5, 1856

Married in Huntsville, Ala. on the 19th ult. by the Rev. Dr. Ross, EDWARD D. TRACY, ESQ., of this city, and MISS ELLEN E. STEELE, daughter of the late CAPT. GEO. STEELE, of Huntsville.

Married by the Rev. R.L. Breck on the 21st ult., J.H. ANDREWS, ESQ., of South Carolina, to MISS LIZZIE S. DEAN, daughter of COL. JAMES DEAN, of Vineville.

Mar. 5, 1856

Married in Crawford co., Ga. on Sunday 24th ult. by C.H. Walker, J.P., ZACHARIAH LEWIS to ELIZABETH SANDERS.

Married on the 20th inst. at the residence of Col. R.W. Alston, near Thomasville, by the Rev. Wm. E. Hamilton, MR. E.L. ANDERSON, late of South Carolina, to MISS SUE WILLIS ALSTON, granddaughter of COL. ALSTON, of Thomas county.

Mar. 12, 1856

Married in this city on the 4th inst. by Rev. S. Landrum, MR. DANIEL L. DRIGGARS to MISS ANN M. CLARK.

Married on Thursday evening 28th Feb'y at the residence of Mrs. Clarissa Key, by the Rev. Folten K. Lewis, MR. WILLIAM L. GRAHAM to MISS SAMANTHA KEY, all of Dooly county, Ga.

Married at the residence of Dan'l McElvane in Baker Co., on Thursday morning the 28th Feb. by the Rev. Mr. Pincheron, MR. PETER ADAMS, of Vienna, to MISS MARY McELVANE, of the former place.

Married the evening of the 4th inst. at the Independent Presbyterian Church, in Savannah, by the Rev. Dr. Preston, MR. R. McALLISTER ORME, of Milledgeville, and MISS LAULA SMETS, daughter of A.A. SMETS of Savannah.

Mar. 26, 1856

Married in this city on the 20th inst. by the Rev. S. Landrum, MR. JAMES M. ARMOR to MISS SARAH J. WILLIAMS.

Married March 18th by the Rev. J.W. Hinton, MR. LEONIDAS N. RAINS, of Marion county, Ga., to MISS NANCY WRIGHT, of Lee county, Ga.

Married on the 18th inst. by the Rev. Charles R. Jewett, MR. M.E. GARDNER to MISS MARTHA E., daughter of MR. WM. C. LAWSHE, all of Atlanta, Ga.

Apr. 2, 1856

Married in this city at Brown's Hotel on Sunday the 23d inst., by the Rev. John H. Harris, of Columbus, Ga., ALBINUS P.B. HARRIS, ESQ. to MISS REBECCA A., daughter of B.F. DENSE, ESQ., both of this city.

Married on Thursday last, 27th inst., by the Rev. J.E. Evans, COL. SEYMOUR R. BONNER, of Columbus, to MRS. B.A. FORT, of this city.

Married in Milledgeville by the Rev. Geo. Macauley on the 13th inst., DR. JOHN W. DOWSING, of Mississippi, to MISS CATHARINE L. LEWIS, second daughter of MR. FIELDING and MRS. ELIZABETH LEWIS, of the above city.

Apr. 9, 1856

Married at Butler, Taylor Co. on the 3rd inst. by Rev. J.T. May, ROBERT SCANDRETT, ESQ., to MRS. SUSAN C. HARRIS, formerly of Columbus, Ga.

Married on the 26th ult. by the Rev. Mr. Clarke, at St. John's Church, Savannah, JAMES M. BALL, ESQ., of New York, to MISS SALLIE AUSTIN, youngest daughter of the late GEORGE HENDREE, of Richmond, Va.

Apr. 16, 1856

Married in this city on the 13th inst. by Rev. S. Landrum, MR. JOHN BROMLEY to MISS MARTHA J. JONES, all of Macon.

Apr. 16, 1856

Married in Savannah on Monday morning, April 7th, by the Rev. Joseph S. Key, REV. THOMAS H. JORDAN and MISS SARAH H. SAUSSEY, eldest daughter of the late DR. JOACHIM SAUSSY, all of this city.

Apr. 23, 1856

Married on the 17th ult. by Rev. E.W. Speer, DR. J. DICKINSON SMITH, of Forsyth, Ga., to MISS CARRIE V., daughter of J.B. ROSS, ESQ., of this city.

Married in Savannah, Ga. on the morning of the 15th by the Rev. Dr. Preston, MR. P.H. OLIVER, of Americus, to MISS HETTIE E. PATTEN, daughter of GEO. PATTEN, ESQ., of Savannah.

May 14, 1856

Married on the 1st inst. by Rev. F.K. Lewis, R.F. HERRINGTON, ESQ., to MISS JANE, eldest daughter of COL. WILLIAM SLADE, all of Dooly county, Ga.

Married on the 1st inst. by the Rev. Mr. Mulckly, DR. SPAN REGAN to MISS JULIA L., daughter of REV. THOMAS SPEIGHT, of Lee county.

Married at Midway, near Milledgeville, on Wednesday evening the 7th inst. by the Rev. Mr. Pryse, of Savannah, MR. J. PALMER GRAVES, of Waterford, Ireland, and MISS SARAH MARGIE FISH, of the former place.

Married at Hootensville, Upson county, on the 25th ult. by Rev. Wesley F. Smith, COL. JAMES H. BIVINS of Pond Town, Sumter county, to MISS MARY C. WALKER, of the former place.

Married on the 1st inst. in Tallapoosa county, Ala., by the Rev. F.H. Wardlaw, of the Ala. Conference, MR. O.P. NORMAN, of Forsyth, Ga., to MISS MARY M. TINSLEY, of the former place.

May 21, 1856

Married on the 15th inst. by the Rev. James E. Evans, MR. SAMUEL S. DUNLAP to MISS MARY ANN E. BURGE, all of Macon.

Married in Randolph county on Wednesday evening the 7th inst. by Charles T.F. Cardin, Esq., MR. THOMAS Y. BERRY and MISS NANCY J. HENIER.

Married on Thursday evening the 8th inst. by Charles T.F. Cardin, Esq., MR. ANDREW J. BERRY and MISS SARAH SMITH, all of Randolph county.

Married at Hootenville April 29th by Rev. Wesley Smith, MR. JAMES H. BIVINS, of Marion county, and MISS MARY C. WALKER, of the former place.

May 28, 1856

Married in this city on the 25th inst. by Rev. O.L. Smith, MR. P.F. CASON and MISS M.A. COUSINS.

Married at 9 o'clock on Sunday morning the 18th May, by the Rev. Wesley F. Smith, JAMES F. WARREN and MARY J. JOHN, all of Houston county, Ga.

Married at the residence of J.A. Pintock in Marietta on the 20th inst. by the Rev. T.R. Jasper, CAPT. H.J. BARRON, of Clinton, Ga. to MISS OPHELIA D. PINTOCK, of the former place.

June 4, 1856

   Married on the 28th May at the residence of Capt. Hardeman in
   Vineville, by the Rev. Sylvanus Landrum, JAMES W. GRIFFIN, ESQ.,
   to MISS ADELIA LUMSDEN.

June 11, 1856

   Married at New London, Ark. on 18th ult. by the Rev. Geo. Averett,
   MR. FRANCIS M. DURHAM to MISS MARY B. NORMAN, daughter of WM. S.
   NORMAN, ESQ., late of Forsyth, Ga.

   Married Thursday evening 29th ult. by Rev. Mr. Cowdry, JAMES
   HAMILTON, ESQ., of Columbus, Ga., to MISS MARY E., daughter of
   JAS. SHACKELFORD, ESQ., of Early county, Ga.

   Married at the residence of Mr. Abner Knight on the 28th ult. by
   Alfred White, Esq., MR. THOMAS HENRY and MISS MATILDA KNIGHT, all
   of Sumter county.

   Married in Sparta, Ga., at the residence of the bride's mother, on
   the 4th inst. by Rev. Samuel K. Talmage, D.D., EDGAR G. DAWSON,
   ESQ., of Columbus, Ga., and MISS LUCIE, only daughter of the late
   HON. WM. TERRELL, M.D.

June 18, 1856

   Married in this city on Thursday evening last, MR. W. SPAULDING
   to MISS MARIA MAULSBY, both of this city.

   Married on the 10th inst. by the Rev. G.R. McCall, MR. WILLIAM
   CHAPPELL to MISS MARY McALLUM, all of Twiggs county.

   Married in Atlanta on Tuesday the 10th inst. by the Rev. J.E.
   DuBose, MR. A.M. EDDLEMAN, Junior Editor of the Republican, and
   MISS TITE WALKER, of Madison, Ga.

   Married in Augusta on the 5th inst. by the Rev. Mr. Ryerson, DR.
   JAS. S. FISH, of Americus, and MISS LUCIA A., daughter of B.F.
   CHEW, ESQ., of the former place.

   Married in the city of Americus June 5th, 1856, by the Rev. W.P.
   Shea, JOHN M. GREER, ESQR., to MISS MARY F. McGLORHAM, all of
   Oglethorpe, Ga.

June 25, 1856

   Married at the Methodist Church in Buena Vista, Ga. on the morning
   of the 17th inst. by Rev. Smith Davenport, REV. P.L.J. MAY, of
   Salem, Ala., to MRS. EMILY E. CLARK, of the former place.

   Married near Hillsboro on the morning of the 12th June, by Dr.
   Cornwell, WILLIAM A. LANE, ESQ., of Clinton, to MRS. JOSEPHINE
   JACKSON, of Jasper county.

July 9, 1856

   Married in this city on the 6th inst. by Rev. S. Landrum, MR.
   CHARLES B. GARWOOD, of Alabama, to MISS MARY KENT, of Macon.

   Married on the 25th ult. in Oxford, MR. JOHN R. WIMBERLY, of Twiggs
   county, to MISS CAROLINE E., daughter of ROBERT BIRDSONG.

   Married in Tuskaloosa, Ala. on the 1st inst., MR. JOHN B. RUDULPH,
   of Lowndes county, Ala., to MISS VIRGINIA BLOUNT, of Jones county,
   Ga.

July 16, 1856

Married on the 3rd inst. by Rev. T.R. Stewart, MR. G.F. BERRY to MISS MARY E. BACHELOR, all of Randolph County, Ga.

Married on the evening of the 8th inst. by the Rev. Blakely Smith, MR. HENRY J. KING, of Augusta, Ga., and MISS JOSEPHINE B. FORSYTH, of this city.

Married on the evening of the 9th inst., in Vineville, by the Rev. S. Landrum, MR. EDWARD H. GILMER, of Monrgomery, Ala., and MISS GERALDINE LAMAR, of Vineville, Ga.

July 23, 1856

Married in Houston county on the 17th inst. by Rev. Josiah L. Warren, JACOB L. RILEY, ESQ., to MISS ELIZABETH D. BROWN, daughter of DAVID M. BROWN, ESQ.

Aug. 20, 1856

Married on Thursday evening the 7th August at the residence of Mr. Edmond Turner in Dooly county, by Abraham B. Paul, Esq., MR. EASON HIGHTOWER to MISS NARCISSA BROWN.

Aug. 27, 1856

Married on the evening of the 12th instant by the Rev. W.R. Foote, at the residence of the bride's mother, COL. JAMES D. LESTER, of Dooly county, and MRS. M.A. REBECCA DEVEREAUX, of Hancock county.

Sep. 10, 1856

Married on the 28th August by the Rev. Jacob King, JAMES B. TORBERT, ESQ., of Meriwether County, and MISS ELIZABETH A. DUKES, of Upson.

Married in Augusta, Ga. on the evening of the 4th inst. by the Rev. A.T. Mann, MAJ. A.G. NAGEL, of Edgefield District, S.C., and MRS. L.E. HALL, of Macon, Georgia.

Married at the house of Samuel W. Vissage by C.H. Walker, J.P., on Thursday 28th ult., JOHN L. WILLIAMS and MISS SARAH JANE MILLS, all of Crawford county, Ga.

Married on the evening of the 31st August by James Evins, Esq., ALFRED MIDDLEBROOKS, ESQ., and MISS NANCY C. WOOTEN, daughter of the REV. JOHN WOOTON, all of Monroe county.

Sep. 17, 1856

Married at Hootenville, Upson County, Ga. August 28th by Rev. Wesley F. Smith, MR. JOHN L. WOODWARD, JR., of Culloden, Monroe County, to MISS LAURA WALKER, of the former place.

Sep. 24, 1856

Married on the 8th inst. by James H. Evans, Esq., MR. THOMAS M. TYLER to MISS ALMIRA E., daughter of GEORGE HARRISON, all of Monroe county.

Oct. 1, 1856

Married on the 27th of August last by the Rev. John T. Everett, MR. THOMAS H. NORMAN and MISS KATE A., daughter of DR. E.R. THOMPSON, all of New London, Arkansas.

Married on the 14th inst. by Rev. James Cox, of Harris county, MR. A.C. BARRON and MISS MARY A.C. WYNN, both of Upson county.

Oct. 8, 1856

   Married on the 2d inst. by Rev. Sylvanus Landrum, at his residence, MR. JOHN G. MARTIN, JR. and MISS FANNIE GAMBLE, all of this city.

Oct. 15, 1856

   Married on Tuesday evening 7th inst. by the Rev. Dr. Foster in Trinity M.E. Church, MR. EDWARD P. CARTER, of this city, and MARY AUGUSTA, daughter of THOMAS M. FERGUSON, ESQ., of New York.

   Married on Sunday last by Rev. J.E. Evans, MR. W.J. VANVORST, to MISS JOANNA SULLIVAN, of this city.

   Married on Wednesday Oct. 1st by Rev. William D. Shea, COL. AARON A. LOWE, of Oglethorpe, Ga., and MISS BETTIE, eldest daughter of HON. BEN. J. HARRIS, of Macon county, Ga.

   Married in London, East Tennessee, by the Rev. J. Stringfield on the 7th inst., M.S. BENSON, ESQ., of Monroe county, Ga., to MISS LOU EMMA BAKER, of the former place.

   Married on Sunday morning the 5th inst. at the residence of Mrs. Lucinda Pearce, in Twiggs county, near Marion, by the Rev. Lewis Solomon, WILLIAM H. BECKOM, ESQ., to MISS GERALDINE C. SOLOMON, daughter of COL. HENRY SOLOMON, late of said county.

   Married in this city on the 8th inst. by the Rev. J.E. Evans, MR. G.W. STRICKLAND, of Pennsylvania, to MISS LAURA J. TAYLOR, of this city.

Oct. 22, 1856

   Married in Talbotton, Ga. on the 16th inst. by the Rev. R.B. Lester, COL. WILLIAM B. SPAIN and MISS FANNIE D. CALLIER.

   Married in Christ Church, Macon, on Wednesday evening Oct. 15th by Rev. Henry K. Rees, LIEUT. JOHN McINTOSH KELL, U.S.N., and MISS JULIA BLANCHE, daughter of N.C. MUNROE, ESQ., of Vineville.

   Married at the residence of Mr. John B. Hawkins, on the evening of the 4th Sept. by the Rev. Wm. Crawford, MR. BEN. W. JOHNSON, of Magnolia, Ark., and MISS NANNIE H. HAWKINS, of Columbia county, Ark.

Oct. 29, 1856

   Married at the residence of her father in Talbot county on the 14th inst. by J.N. Carter, Esq., MR. D.T. PULLIAM, of Upson county, to MISS FANNIE E. SAUNDERS, of the former place.

Nov. 12, 1856

   Married in Fort Valley, Houston county, Ga. Nov. 6th by the Rev. Wesley F. Smith, MR. ROBERT H. WRIGHT, of Knoxville, and MRS. SARAH S. HOLLINSHEAD, of the former place.

Nov. 19, 1856

   Married at the Baptist Church in Columbus by Rev. Mr. DeVotie on the 6th inst., MR. PETER PREER and MISS MATTIE A. JONES, all of that place.

   Married on the 5th inst. by Rev. M.W. Arnold, at Judge D.E. Blount's, MR. SAMUEL F. ANDERSON and MISS E.R. PITTS. Also, at the same time and place, COL. ISAAC HARDEMAN and MISS MARIETTA T. PITTS, all of Clinton, Ga.

Nov. 19, 1856

Married on the 6th inst. at Monticello, Ga. by the Rev. Dr. Talmage, MR. I.N. HARVEY, of Montgomery, Ala., to MISS REBECCA M. REESE, daughter of HON. D.A. REESE, of the former place.

Married at the residence of James Gachet, near Enon, Ala. on Tuesday the 4th inst. by Rev. Dr. Ellison, F.L. DeLAUNAY, ESQ., of Milledgeville, to MISS ANNE M. GACHET.

Married on Sunday the 2d inst. by the Hon. John W. Yopp, MR. JAMES F. ROBINSON and MISS ELLEN O'NEAL, eldest daughter of CULLEN O'NEAL, all of Laurens county.

Married in Gordon county on the 12th inst. by Rev. J. Knowles, MR. JOSEPH G. BLOUNT, of Alabama, and MISS MARIA L., daughter of MAJOR JAMES FREEMAN.

Married at the residence of Mrs. E.L. Lowther in Polk county, Ga. on the 13th inst. by Rev. Jesse Wood, R.A. STANLEY, ESQ., of Irwinton, Ga., to MISS M.R. LOWTHER.

At the same time and place and by the same minister, MR. W.M. OTTERSON, of Polk county, and MISS F.O. LOWTHER.

Married in this city by Rev. R.L. Breck on the 6th inst., HENRY C. BILLUPS, M.D., to MISS EMMA V. CONNALLY, of Burke county.

Married in Thomaston on Tuesday evening the 11th inst. by the Rev. John J. Groves, MR. BENJAMIN H. LOWE, of Harris Co., to MISS EMMA R., daughter of JUDGE WILLIAM LOWE, of the former place.

Nov. 26, 1856

Married in this city on the 18th inst. by the Rev. Mr. Breck, MR. WM. A. REID, of Eatonton, to MISS OPHELIA E., daughter of the HON. E.A. NISBET, of Macon.

Married in this city on the 19th inst. by the Rev. James E. Evans, PETER CORBIN, ESQ., of Crawford county, to MRS. PARTHENIA RAINES.

Married in Savannah on the 20th inst. by Rev. Sylvanus Landrum, of Macon, REV. JOSIAH L. WARREN, of Perry, Ga., and MISS ANNA ELIZA RYAN, of Savannah.

Married in Milledgeville on the 11th inst. by the Rev. Wm. Flinn, MR. BENJAMIN M. POLHILL, of Macon, to MISS EMMIE H. NISBET; also, MR. ALEXANDER MOFFETT, of Charleston, S.C., to MISS SARAH A. NISBET, daughters of A.M. NISBET, ESQ., of Milledgeville.

Married in Putnam county on the 28th ult. by Rev. Mr. Cloud, WM. T. GARRARD to MISS ELIZA H. WALLER, of Putnam Co.

Married on Tuesday 6th inst. by Rev. Edward M. Ford, D.D., MR. WILLIAM W. ALEXANDER and MISS MARY AUGUSTA, daughter of the HON. JAMES B. BISHOP, all of Augusta.

Married in Athens on Wednesday the 12th inst. by the Rev. S.M. Wynn, JOHN G. THOMAS, ESQ. of Americus, and MISS SUSAN A. CARR, of the former place.

Married on Tuesday the 4th inst. at Madison, Ga. by the Rev. Thomas F. Pierce, MISS MAT F. PORTER and MR. GEORGE W. WILLIAMS, of Charleston, S.C., also MISS SALLIE F. PORTER and MR. AZARIAH GRAVES, of Augusta - both daughters of JOHN W. PORTER, of the former place.

Married at Fort Gaines on the 11th inst., ELDER E.A. WARREN, of Cuthbert, to MISS MALVINA PRESCOTT.

Dec. 3, 1856

   Married in Macon County, Ga. on Sunday morning Nov. 24th by Rev. W.D. Shea, MR. THOS. H.B. FLEMMING and MRS. CAROLINE M. TEMPLETON.

   Married in Pulaski County, Ga. on Thursday evening Nov. 20th by John Ryals, Esq., DR. JAMES HUMPHREYS to MISS REBECCA S., daughter of MR. JOHN M. DANIELS. (Savannah Georgian and Journal please copy)

   Married in this city on 30th Nov. by Rev. S. Landrum, MR. NATHANIEL GLASON to MISS NANCY JOURDAN.

   Married on the 27th inst. at the residence of J.A. Sperry, of Houston county, Ga., by the Rev. James A. Roquemore, MR. WM. T. ALGER to MISS MARY C. PARMALEE, all of Houston co.

Dec. 10, 1856

   Married in Monroe County, Ga. Nov. 30th by the Rev. Wesley F. Smith, MR. JOHN H. BANKS, of Culloden, to MISS ELIZA ANN JONES, of the former place.

   Married in Monroe county Dec. 4th by Rev. C.A. Fulwood, MR. JAS. A.C. GOODRUM to MISS GEORGIA ANN OGLETREE, daughter of DAVID OGLETREE, ESQ.

Dec. 17, 1856

   Married on the 10th ult. by Rev. Geo. T. McCauley, MR. BENJ. BECK to MRS. ANGELINE R. STUBBS, all of this city.

   Married in Milledgeville on the 9th inst. by the Rev. Dr. Talmage, CHARLTON HINES WAY, of Savannah, to FANNIE MALONE, second daughter of the late P.J. WILLIAMS, of Milledgeville.

   Married in Houston County on the evening of the 8th inst. by Rev. J.L. Warren, MR. CALEB R. BARRETT and MISS ELIZA RATLIFF, all of said county.

   Married on the 29th of Nov. by the Rev. H. Phinazee, MR. URBAND C. FAMBROUGH to MISS SALLIE J. PYE, daughter of BERNIER PYE, ESQ., all of Monroe county.

   Married on the 11th instant by the Rev. H. Phinazee, MR. H.D. PEURIFOY to MISS MARTHA E. PHINAZEE, daughter of JOHN H. PHINAZEE, ESQ., all of Monroe county.

   Married on the 27th inst. by the Rev. Mr. Thigpen, MR. JOHN W. FINNEY to MISS FRANCES GODDARD, daughter of JUDGE JAMES GODDARD, all of Jones county.

   Married on the morning of the 9th inst., on Sapelo Island, by the Rev. S.J. Pinketon, DR. CHARLES HENRY HALL, of Milledgeville, Ga. and MISS AURIE DENAN, of the former place.

Dec. 24, 1856

   Married in Eatonton, Ga. on the 18th inst. by Rev. Dr. S.K. Talmage, JAMES T. NISBET, ESQ., of Macon (late Editor of this paper) and MISS MARY SEYMOUR, eldest daughter of JUNIUS WINGFIELD, ESQ., of the former place.

   Married on the 18th inst. by Rev. S. Landrum, MR. DAVID M. SMITH, of Americus, to MISS ANN E. BAGBY, of Bibb co.

   Married in this city on the 18th inst. by the Rev. Mr. Reese, MR. STEPHEN J. CLARK to MISS GEORGIA A. EVANS.

Dec. 24, 1856

Married in Milledgeville on the 16th inst., by Rev. Mr. Flinn, MR. J. BULOW CAMPBELL, of Houston county, and MISS VIRGINIA M., daughter of R.M. ORME, ESQ., of the former place.

Married on the 16th of December by Rev. H. Phinazee, MR. WM. J. PHINAZEE, to MISS SALINA C. HAM, daughter of REV. JOHN HAM, all of Monroe county.

Dec. 31, 1856

Married on Dec. 23 by Rev. Alex M. Thigpen, MR. LEVI W. JARREL, of Jones county, to MISS MARY C., daughter of REV. ISAAC C. HARRIS, of Fort Valley, Ga.

Married on the morning of the 30th inst. by Rev. Reddick Pierce, REV. GEO. G.N. MacDONNELL, of the Georgia Conference, to MISS MAGGIE R., eldest daughter of COL. ROBT. D. WALKER, of Savannah, Ga.

Married on the 25th inst. by Rev. S. Landrum, MR. ANDREW J. SCOTT to MISS VIRGINIA V. FOWLER, all of this city.

Married in Forsyth on the 16th inst., at the residence of Col. Z.E. Harman, by the Rev. W.C. Wilkes, MR. GEO. A. CABANISS, of Athens, Ga., to MISS JULIET H. McKAY, of the former place.

Jan. 7, 1857

Married on the 4th inst. by Rev. S. Landrum, MR. WM. H. SHAW, of Americus, to MISS MARGARET A. WAGNON, of this city.

Married on the 5th inst. by Rev. O.L. Smith, MR. D.N. HIGHTOWER, of Upson county, to MISS FRANCES MIMS, of Houston county, Ga.

Jan. 14, 1857

Married on the 12th inst. at the residence of E.A. Allen, Esq., COL. CHAS. E. NISBET, of Cuthbert, Ga., to MISS FANNIE L. EVANS, of Burke county.

Married in Wilmington, N.C. on the 6th inst. by the Rev. Mr. Drane, DR. JAMES ARRINGTON MILLER, of Oglethorpe, Ga., and MISS ANN ELIZA, daughter of the HON. WM. S. ASHE, of the former place.

Married in Americus on the 1st inst. by the Rev. J.W. Hinton, COL. GEO. KIMBROUGH, of Starkville, to MISS HENRIETTA McBAIN, of Americus.

Jan. 21, 1857

Married in this city on the 18th inst. by the Rev. R.L. Breck, CHARLES J. HARRIS, ESQ., of Thomasville, to MISS MARY O. WILEY.

Also on the 13th by the same, HON. CLIFFORD ANDERSON to MISS ANNA C. LeCONTE.

Married in Athens on the 14th inst. by Rev. Nathan Hoyt, D.D., MR. THOMAS F. GOULDING, of Columbus, Miss., to MISS ROSA, daughter of MAJ. JOHN CRAWFORD, of the former place.

Married in Cahaba, Ala. on Wednesday evening the 7th inst. by the Rev. George F. Cushman, MR. JOHN M. TUCKER, of Milledgeville, to MISS MARY E., daughter of EDMOND M. PERINE, of the former place.

Married on Wednesday the 14th inst. at the residence of Dr. Tomlinson Fort, Milledgeville, by the Rev. Dr. S.K. Talmage, J.W. DUNCAN, ESQ., of Atlanta, to MISS MARY ELIZABETH FORT.

Jan. 21, 1857

Married on the evening of the 24th Dec. in Twiggs county, near Tarversville, by Rev. Henry Bunn, MR. S.C. MARCHMAN and MISS MARY J. COLEY, daughter of MR. WM. COLEY.

Married in Monroe county on the 14th by J.H. Evans, Esq., MR. GEO. HARRISON to MRS. MARTHA BURGAY, all of Monroe Co.

Jan. 28, 1857

Married in Macon on the 20th inst. at the house of Asa Holt, Esq., by Rev. O.L. Smith, GEO. W. ROBERTSON, of Louisville, Ga. and MISS ELIZA A. HOLT, niece and adopted daughter of ASA HOLT, ESQ.

Married in Milledgeville, Ga. on the 20th inst. by Rev. C. Lane, COL. R.B. DeGRAFFENRIED and MISS SARAH WALKER, of Milledgeville.

Married on the 20th inst. at the residence of Hon. A.H. Chappell, by the Rev. J.E. Evans, COL. WM. POLK, of La., and MISS REBECCA E. LAMAR, of this city.

Feb. 4, 1857

Married in this city on the 3d inst. by Rev. R.L. Breck, MR. WM. H. SMITH, of Milwaukee, Wis., to MISS MARY C. THOMAS, daughter of WILLIAM D. THOMAS, of this county.

Married in this city on the 2d inst. at the Baptist Church, by the Rev. Mr. Landrum, MR. JOEL T. CALLAWAY to MISS LOUISA ELLIS.

Feb. 11, 1857

Married in Americus, Ga. on the 5th of February by Rev. O.L. Smith, FRANCIS A. HILL, ESQ., of Houston county, to MISS C.J. STONE, of Stewart county, Ga.

Married in Americus on Thursday evening the 29th January by Rev. James W. Hinton, REV. JOHN P. DUNCAN, of the Georgia Methodist Conference, and MRS. SARAH H. DANIEL, of Americus.

Feb. 18, 1857

Married in Savannah on Tuesday the 10th inst. by the Rev. C.A. Fulwood, MR. JOHN W. LAKE, of Forsyth, Monroe co., Ga., to MISS MARTHA G. GODFREY, of Savannah.

Feb. 25, 1857

Married in Crawford County at the residence of Col. John Foster on Thursday the 19th inst. by the Rev. Joseph W. Chissman, MR. PETER RANDALL, of Monroe County, to MISS ELIZA A. FOSTER, of Crawford co.

Mar. 4, 1857

Married on the 27th ult. by Rev. J.D. Pitts, DR. A.W. DENNING, of Drayton, Dooly county, to MISS LOUISA L. CURD, of this city.

Married in this city on the 27th ult. by Rev. S. Landrum, DR. JAS. J. PARK, of Albany, and MISS MARY J. STEWART, of this city.

Married on the morning of the 22nd inst. by Rev. L. Solomon, TROY G. HOLDER, ESQ., to MISS MARY A.T. BARTON, all of Twiggs County, Ga.

Mar. 11, 1857

Married on Wednesday evening March 4th by Rev. O.L. Smith, MR. HENRY K. DANIELS, of Americus, Ga., and MISS MARY E. MYRICK, daughter of GEN. S.P. MYRICK, of Midway, Ga.

Mar. 11, 1857

Married in the city of Baltimore on the 25th of February by the Rev. Dr. Backus, COL. LUCILIUS H. BRISCOE, Secretary of the Executive Department of Georgia, and MISS ARRAIANA, youngest daughter of COL. JAMES POLK, of Baltimore.

Mar. 18, 1857

Married in Vineville on the 10th inst. by the Rev. Mr. Evans, P. TRACY, ESQ., (former editor of the Telegraph) and CAROLINE M. WALKER, daughter of the late JOHN RAWLS.

Married on the 12th inst. by the Rev. R.L. Breck, DR. JOHN A. COMER to MISS HATTIE W. TOWNS, daughter of the late GOV. GEORGE W. TOWNS, all of this city.

Married on the evening of the 5th inst. by Rev. Asa Chandler, MR. WM. P. EDMONDSON, of Green county, and MISS SARAH E. BIRDSONG, of Oglethorpe county.

Married on the 10th inst. by the Rev. Dr. Church, JOHN E. GLENN, ESQ., and MISS ANNA R., daughter of the HON. TURNER H. TRIPPE, all of Cass county, Ga.

Mar. 25, 1857

Married in this city on the 23d inst. by the Rev. S. Landrum, CAPT. EDWARD P. DENNIS, of Brooklyn, N.Y., to MISS HERMIONE J. ROSE, daughter of the Senior Editor of this paper.

Married in Houston county on the 19th inst. by Rev. B.F. Tharp, CHARLES T. GOODE, of Thomaston, and MISS CORNELIA WARREN, daughter of GEN. E. WARREN.

Apr. 1, 1857

Married by the Rev. Mr. Dorman on Wednesday 25th inst., TENNENT LOMAX, ESQ., of Columbus, and editor of the Times & Sentinel, and MISS CAROLINE BILLINGSLEA SHORTER, of Montgomery, Ala.

Married in Forsyth on the 26th inst. by the Rev. S.M. Smith, W.G. McCOOK and MISS MARTHA H., daughter of C. BRITTINGHAM, of the former place.

Apr. 8, 1857

Married on the 31st ult., GEORGE B. DOUGLAS, M.D. and MRS. ROSA LIVINGSTON, daughter of R.T. LAWTON, all of Albany, Ga.

Married by Rev. S.B. Burnett on the 31st of March, MR. JOHN J. RILEY and MISS SARAH A. NEEL, of Bibb county.

Married on the 25th of March at Wyoming, near Sparta, Hancock county, Ga., by Bishop Geo. F. Pierce, MR. CHARLIE W. CARY, of Macon county, Ala., and MISS HELEN G., daughter of JOS. T. SIMMONS, ESQ., of the former place.

Apr. 15, 1857

Married in this city on the 6th inst. by Jas. C.C. Burnett, Esq., MR. EZEKIEL J. STEWART to MISS SARAH E. LANIER, all of this city.

Apr. 22, 1857

Married in Americus on the 15th inst. by Rev. H.C. Hornaday, MR. D.H. HILL and MISS MARY J. BARLOW, all of Americus.

Apr. 22, 1857

Married in Milledgeville on the 6th inst. by the Rev. Erasmus D. Eldrige, REV. C.W. LANE, of Oglethorpe University, to MISS MARY A., daughter of REV. E.D. ELDRIDGE.

Apr. 29, 1857

Married in LaGrange, Ga. on the 23d by Rev. Mr. Wynn, of this city, DR. CHARLES A. WARD to MISS JULIA M., eldest daughter of REV. JESSE BORING, of the Georgia Conference.

Married in Twiggs Co. by the Rev. C.A. Tharp on the evening of the 21st of April 1857, MR. ACTON E. NASH to MISS ROXEY ANN CHAPPELL, daughter of T.S. CHAPPELL, all of the above county.

Married on Tuesday the 21st inst. at 11 o'clock by Richard Hutcherson Esq., MR. THEOPHILUS J. HARISON, of Houston county, Ga., and MISS MARTHA C. MAULDIN, of Upson county, Ga.

May 6, 1857

Married on the morning of the 3d inst. by Rev. Lewis Solomon, DR. D.J. CANNON to MISS ELIZABETH R. BLACKSHEAR, all of Twiggs county, Ga.

May 13, 1857

Married in Salem, N.C. on Thursday morning the 7th inst. by Rev. Geo. F. Bahuson, MR. ARCHIBALD McCALLUM, of Twiggs county, Ga., and MISS EMILY E. BANNER, second daughter of C.L. BANNER, ESQ., of Salem, N.C.

May 20, 1857

Married in Forsyth on the 12th inst., at the residence of C. Sharp, Esq. by the Rev. Ira C. Patterson, MR. E.K. BOZEMAN, of Lumpkin, to MISS AUGUSTA SHARP, of the former place.

Married near Oglethorpe, Macon Co., Ga. May 13th, 1857 by the Rev. Wm. D. Shea, MR. GEO. WILLIAMS, JR., to MISS NANCY JANE REYNOLDS, all of Macon county.

Married on the 6th inst. by the Rev. W.J. Cotter, W.J. COLLINS, ESQ., of Oglethorpe, Ga. and MISS A.S. LEWIS, of Burke county, Ga.

Married by the Rev. W.F. Smith at the house of Mrs. Mary W. Andrews, in Knoxville, May 17th, WM. A. MACON, ESQ., of Smithville, to MISS F. ANNIE PERKINS, of Knoxville.

May 27, 1857

Married in Madison, Ga. on the 20th inst. by the Rev. Jas. L. Pierce, MR. J. KNOWLES, one of the Editors of this paper, to MISS SALLIE E. ROBERTS.

Married on the 20th inst. at the residence of Rev. Wm. Horne, by Rev. G.R. McCall, COL. E.A. WIMBERLY to MISS LOUISA A. HORNE, all of Twiggs co., Ga.

Married in Greensboro on the 17th inst. by E.H. Wingfield, Esq., MR. JAS. W. WALKER, of Madison, to MISS MARY ANN, daughter of MRS. W.S. WRIGHT, of Morgan County.

June 3, 1857

Married in Eatonton May 26th by Rev. E.P. Burch, REV. ALEX. THIGPEN to MISS JANE M., daughter of G.R. THOMAS, ESQ.

June 10, 1857

Married at Seymour's Point, East Florida, on Wednesday, 10th May, by Rev. R.M. Tydings, REV. WILLIAM DAVIS, of Georgia, and HENRIETTA L., eldest daughter of F.L. ROUX, of Charleston, S.C.

Married in Hayneville, Hourton co., Ga. on the 3rd of June 1857, by the Rev. John M. Bright, REV. WILLIAM D. SHEA, of the Georgia Conference, and MRS. SALLIE H. COALSON, daughter of the late DR. CHAS. F. PATTILLO.

Married on the 13th of May by Thos. S. Cobb, MR. WM. A. BARRON to MISS MARTHA A. GRIFFIN, all of Houston county.

June 17, 1857

Married at Decatur on the evening of the 9th inst. by Rev. John S. Wilson, COL. MILTON A. CANDLER, Editor of the Cassville Standard, and MISS ELIZA C., daughter of HON. CHARLES MURPHY.

July 8, 1857

Married on the evening of the 5th inst. by Rev. Lewis Solomon, MR. ROMALDO R. WHITEHEAD to MRS. SUSAN BULLARD, all of Twiggs county, Ga.

July 15, 1857

Married near Richland on the morning of the 5th inst. by Rev. W.G. Parks, COL. ROBERT WHITE, of Sumter, and MRS. R.L. STONE, of Stewart.

Married on the 2d inst. by Rev. J.R. Danforth, MR. CHARLES G. McLENDON, of Thomasville, Ga., to MISS ELIZA JANE, daughter of REV. F.D. LOWRY, of Twiggs county, Ga.

Married in Columbus on the 2d inst. by Rev. J.H. DeVotie, MR. ROSWELL ELLIS, Junior Editor of the Times & Sentinel, to MISS ANNA L., daughter of REV. THOMAS B. SLADE.

July 22, 1857

Married in this city on Sunday 19th inst. by E.C. Granniss, Esq., MR. WILLIAM H. HANCOCK to ANN A. McGUIRE, all of this city.

Married in Thomaston on Thursday morning the 9th inst. by the Rev. O.C. Gibson, MR. W.S. JACKSON, of Tuskegee, Alabama, and MISS ETHELIA JANE COBB, daughter of MAJ. WM. A. COBB.

July 29, 1857

Married in Oglethorpe, Ga. July 23d, 1857, by the Rev. Wm. D. Shea, MR. JOHN W. WILSON and MISS CELESTIA LUMPKIN, all of Oglethorpe.

Aug. 12, 1857

Married near this city on the 5th inst. by Rev. R.L. Breck, MR. JOHN CHAPMAN, of Twiggs county, to MISS ANNIE M. CARLETON.

Sep. 9, 1857

Married on the 23d ult. in Twiggs county by Rev. Henry Bunn, MR. WILLIAM A. DENSON and MISS E.N. ASBELL, daughter of BRYAN ASBELL, ESQ.

Sep. 16, 1857

Married on the 3d of September by the Rev. Dr. Hoyt, at the residence of Mordecai Edwards, MR. THOMAS J. PERRY, of Rome, Ga., and MISS MARY E. FULTON, of Oglethorpe county.

Sep. 16, 1857

　Married at Brunswick, Ga. on the 3d inst. by the Rev. E.P. Brown, COL. A.R. WRIGHT, of Jefferson county, and MISS CARRIE C. HAZLEHURST, of the former place.

Sep. 23, 1857

　Married in Americus on the evening of the 15th inst. at the M.E. Church, by the Rev. A.A. Robinson, MR. ROBERT HUBERT to MISS VIRGINIA A., eldest daughter of the REV. J.P. DUNCAN, of the Georgia Conference.

Oct. 14, 1857

　Married at Penfield on the evening of the 1st inst. by Prof. Wm. Williams, JOHN H. SEALS, editor of the Temperance Crusader, to MISS MARY E., daughter of the REV. B.M. SANDERS, all of Penfield.

Oct. 21, 1857

　Married on the 29th September at the residence of Jesse Stephens, by the Rev. E.W. Reynolds, DR. J.O. HOLLOWAY and MISS M.J. POWELL, both of Upson county.

Oct. 28, 1857

　Married in this city on Monday evening Oct. 12th by Rev. James E. Evans, JOHN LEMEN, of Buena Vista, to MISS A. AUGUSTA COMBS of Macon.

　Married by the Rev. Dr. Smith on the evening of the 19th instant, MR. GREENE HILL, of Houston county, and MRS. M.E. SNELLING, of Richland, Stewart county, Ga.

　Married in Griffin on Tuesday the 20th inst., at the residence of Judge J.B. Reid, by Rev. C.P.B. Martin, EMORY WINSHIP, ESQ., of this city, to MISS LIZZIE ALEXANDER, of the former place.

　Married on the 22d inst. by the Rev. James Beller of Barnesville, MR. FRANCIS L. MATTHEWS, to MRS. ANN ELIZABETH WEST, all of Upson county, Ga.

Nov. 4, 1857

　Married in this county on the 28th ult. by Rev. J. Knowles, DR. JAS. S. BUTTS, of Baldwin county, to MISS SALLIE C., daughter of ARTHUR FOSTER, ESQ., of Bibb.

Nov. 25, 1857

　Married in this city on the morning of the 24th inst. by Rev. James E. Evans, MR. HENRY S. GARFIELD, formerly of Bradford, N.H., and MISS LAURA B. WILLINGHAM, of this city.

　Married in Crawford county on the 5th inst. by Rev. R.M. Owen, MR. MARCELLUS A. MYRICK to MISS FRANCES W. STROUD.

　Married on the evening of the 17th inst. by Rev. Lewis Solomon, at the house of Dr. R.A. Nash, JOSEPH U. BURKITT, ESQ. and MISS ELIZABETH S. THARP, all of Twiggs County, Ga.

Dec. 2, 1857

　Married on the 19th inst. by Rev. W.H. Crane, MR. ALEXANDER G. CROMARTIE, of Leon Co., Florida, to MISS CLAUDIA REYNOLDS, daughter of COL. WM. REYNOLDS, of Thomas county, Ga.

Dec. 2, 1857

Married on Sabbath Evening 15th inst. at Washington, Wilkes county, by Rev. Mr. Boggs, GEN. G.W. GORDON, of Whitfield county, and MRS. MARY RANDOLPH, of the former place.

Married on the 25th inst. at the residence of Dr. H.V.M. Miller of Floyd county, by Rev. Mr. Evans, THOS. W. ALEXANDER, ESQ., of Rome, and MISS SALLIE J., daughter of JUDGE HOOPER, of Cass county.

Married by Rev. Lewis Solomon on the morning of the 22d inst., HENRY M. LOYLESS, ESQ., to MISS MARTHA LAND, daughter of HENRY LAND, all of Twiggs co., Ga.

Married on the 4th inst. at the house of Mr. Brown, by Rev. G.R. McCall, MR. JOHN G. CARSWELL to MISS MARY J. BROWN, all of Wilkinson co., Ga.

Married by the same on the evening of the 19th inst., MR. E.T. NAPPIER, of Macon, Ga., to MISS JENNIE CARSWELL, of Wilkinson Co., Ga.

Dec. 9, 1857

Married on the 25th November by Rev. S.W. Bendenbaugh, MR. HENRY F. TARRER and MISS JULIA F. JACKSON, all of Macon county.

Married in Sumter county on the 25th ult. by the Rev. D. Williams, MR. JAMES R. STEWART and MISS MARY E., eldest daughter of the REV. MATTHEW E. RYLANDER - all of Sumter.

Married on Tuesday evening Dec. 1 at the residence of the bride's father, by Rev. H.C. Hornaday, DR. JOHN D. WADE, of Winchester, Ga., and MISS AUGUSTA J., daughter of HON. J.J. SCARBOROUGH, of Americus, Ga.

Married in Monroe County on the 24th ult., in the morning, at the residence of Mrs. Hollis, by the Rev. Davis Smith, COL. K.L. WORTHY, of Hickory Grove, Crawford county, to MISS LIZZIE BOZEMAN.

Also at the same time and place, THOS. J. SIMMONS, ESQ., of Knoxville Ga., to MISS PENNIE HOLLIS.

Dec. 23, 1857

Married at the residence of Mrs. Sewell, by the Rev. J.E. Evans, on Sunday 20th inst., MR. LEWIS B. RHODES and MISS MARY ANN F. SEWELL, both of Macon.

Married in this city on the 15th inst. by Rev. J. Knowles, REV. WILLIAM F. COOK, of the Georgia Conference, to MISS LOU J., daughter of ALEXANDER RICHARDS, ESQ.

Married on the evening of the 25th ult. by the Rev. J.H. Echols, at the residence of T.M. Hunt, Esq., MR. T.M. MERRIT, of Monroe county, to MISS ANNA LEWIS, of "Lewisanna," Hancock county.

Married on Thursday Dec. 10th by Rev. Wm. H. Ellison, MR. JOSEPH M. ELLISON, of Talbot county, Ga., and MISS CAMILLA KEY, of Macon county, Ala.

Dec. 30, 1857

Married in the M.E. Church of this city on Wednesday evening Dec. 23d by Rev. O.L. Smith, D.D., SANFORD W. GLASS, ESQ., of Covington, Ga., to MISS MARY A.E.K. EVANS, eldest daughter of REV. JAS. E. EVANS, of the Georgia Conference.

Jan. 6, 1858

   Married in Jonesville, McIntosh county, on the 29th ult. by Rev. S.S.L. Harwell, REV. JAMES M. AUSTIN, of the Georgia Conference, and MISS O.S. QUARTERMAN, daughter of MR. EDWARD QUARTERMAN.

   Married on the 1st inst., WILLIAM WEBB, of Dooly county, and MISS MARY Q. COX, daughter of CULLEN COX, of Macon county.

   Married in Sparta, Ga. on the 22d ult., at the residence of W.W. Simpson, Esq., MR. G.A. DURE, of Macon, Ga., and MISS JULIA KENDRICK, of the former place.

   Married in Culloden on the 17th ult. by Rev. Wesley F. Smith, MR. BENJAMIN F. JORDAN and MISS MARY JANE ALSTON, all of Culloden, Ga.

   Married in Monroe county on the 22d ult. by the same, at the residence of Richard Wootten, MR. SEABORN F. MAYS and MISS P. PARKE, all of Monroe county.

Jan. 13, 1858

   Married in Athens, Ga. on the 22d ult. by Rev. H.H. Parks, MR. JAMES L. CALDWELL, of Tuskegee Ala., and MISS LAURA J. WHITMAN, of the former place.

   Married on the 5th inst. at the residence of Mrs. E. Dewberry, by Rev. A. Smith, COL. W.L. GORDON, of DeSoto Parish, La. and MISS FRANCES E. ANDERSON, of Monroe County, Ga.

Jan. 20, 1858

   Married in this city on the 12th inst. by the Rev. S. Landrum, MR. WM. H. POPE, of Albany, and MRS. A.M. SHAW, of this city.

   Married in this city on the 12th inst. by Rev. H.C. Hornady, COL. S.K. TAYLOR, of Americus, and MISS HARRIET L. Van VALKENBURGH, eldest daughter of JAMES VanVALKENBURGH of this city.

   Married in this city on the morning of the 14th inst. by Rev. S. Landrum, ALBERT JAMES MACARTHY, ESQ. and MISS VIRGINIA VICTORIA GORMAN, daughter of the late DR. GORMAN.

Jan. 27, 1858

   Married in this city on the 20th inst. by Rev. S. Landrum, COL. M.J. CLAY, of Clear Point, Arkansas, and MISS H.E. THOMPSON, of this city.

   Married on the 13th inst. at Glennville, Ala., MR. E.M. WALKER, of this city, to MISS SALLY DANIEL, of the former place.

   Married in Marshallville on the 13th inst., MR. ELISHA P. COLLINS, of this city, to MISS SUSAN E. COLLINS, of the former place.

   Married on the 19th inst. by Prof. G.W.W. Stone at the residence of the bride's father, MR. GEORGE W. JOHNSON, of Fort Valley, Ga. and MISS VICTORIA A., second daughter of REV. A. MEANS, D.D., of Oxford, Ga.

   Married in Milledgeville, Ga. on the 19th inst. by Rev. Dr. Talmage, REV. ROBERT W. BIGHAM, of Stockton, California (formerly of the Georgia Conference) and MISS CHARLOTTE E. DAVIES, of the former place.

   Married on the 6th inst. by Rev. A.M. Clontz, MR. SAMUEL M. SUBERS, of this city, to MISS ISA G. ARNSTOFF, of the former place.

   Married in Crawford county, Ga. on the 19th inst. by the Rev. Wesley F. Smith, MR. JOHN F. PASSMORE, of Harris county, and MISS SARAH E. DANIELY.

Feb. 3, 1858

Married on the 20th ult., MR. SAMUEL F. GOVE, of this city, and MISS G.A. SINGLETON, of Jones county.

Married at Eatonton on the 13th ult. by the Rev. Dr. Talmage, MR. DENNIS L. RYAN, of Sparta, Ga., and MISS ELLA S. MERIWETHER, daughter of the late HON. JAS. A. MERIWETHER.

Married in Putnam county on the 16th ult. by the Rev. William D. Shea, MR. JOHN A. REID and MISS MARY P. GRIGGS.

Married on the 18th ult. by the Rev. J.E. Ryerson, MR. ROBERT F. CONNELLY, of Burke county, and MISS ELIZA LAMAR, eldest daughter of DR. T.W. BATTEY, of Augusta.

Married on the 27th ult. by the Rev. B.F. Tharp, Sen., MR. A. THARP, of Houston Co., and MISS MARIA, daughter of S.P. CORBIN, ESQ., of Taylor Co., Ga.

Feb. 10, 1858

Married on Wednesday evening the 3rd inst. by Rev. O.L. Smith, D.D., MR. JOHN H. DUNLAP, of this city, and MISS EUGENIA CALLEN, of Houston county.

Married on the 3rd inst. by the Rev. Smith Davenport, WILLIAM H. FICKLING, of Taylor county, and MISS CAROLINE E. WALKER, of Crawford county.

Feb. 24, 1858

Married in Laurens county, Ga., on the 11th inst. by the Rev. Mr. Flinn, FRANCIS P. STUBBS, ESQ., of Monroe La., to MISS GEORGIA A., daughter of DR. NATHAN TUCKER.

Married in Jeffersonville, Ga. on the 11th inst. by the Rev. G.R. McCall, MR. M.J. CARSWELL, of Wilkinson county, to MISS ELLEN H. DUPREE, of Twiggs county.

Mar. 10, 1858

Married on the 4th inst. in this city by Rev. S. Landrum, REV. HENRY BUNN, of Twiggs county, and MRS. CATHERINE A. STEPHENS, of this city.

Married on the evening of the 2d inst. by Rev. T.A. Spaulding, MR. J.M. PONDER, of Forsyth, and MISS MARY E. HARRIS, of Morgan county, Ga.

Married on the evening of March 3rd by Rev. Arminius Wright, MR. JAMES FORD and MISS FRANCIS SWITZER, all of Forsyth.

Mar. 24, 1858

Married in Butler, Taylor county, Ga. on the 22nd inst. by the Rev. James T. May, COL. JENKINS M. HOLMES, of Savannah, Ga. to MISS LAURA WRIGHT, of the former place.

Mar. 31, 1858

Married on Tuesday the 18th inst. by the Rev. J.H. Harris, MR. TROUP PERRYMAN and MISS LEONORA WARD, all of Tandolph county, Ga.

Married in Putnam county, Ga. on the 23d inst. by the Rev. Wm. Arnold, MR. MARK A. HUBERT, of Americus, and MISS REBECCA A. MARSHALL, of the former county.

Apr. 7, 1858

Married in this city on the 6th inst. by Rev. S. Landrum, MR. CLEMMONS MASTERSON and MISS ELLEN TRACY, all of this city.

Apr. 14, 1858

Married in Monroe county on the 8th ult. by the Rev. Jas. P. Lyon, GREEN M. MIDDLEBROOKS, of Jones county, and MISS NANCY HARTSFIELD, of Monroe county.

Apr. 21, 1858

Married in Jones county on the 13th inst. by Rev. James L. Pierce, MR. A.M. PRICHETT, of Monticello, and MISS DRUSILLA LOWE.

Married on Thursday the 15th inst. at Smithville, Lee county, by W.S. Cox, Esq., DR. G.F. SMITH and MRS. N.E.A. RAINES.

Married in Americus on the 15th inst. at the residence of Mrs. Hampton, HON. JOSEPH DAY, of Houston county, and MISS MARY HAMPTON, of Americus.

Married in Knoxville on Sunday evening the 18th inst. by Wm. E. Mathews, J.P., JAMES J. RAY, ESQ. and MISS MARTHA G. WRIGHT, both of the above place.

Apr. 28, 1858

Married on the 15th inst. at the residence of the bride's father, in Washington City, by the Rev. Bishop Pierce, DUDLEY M. DuBOSE, ESQ., of Memphis, Tenn., and MISS SALLIE TOOMBS, only daughter of the HON. R. TOOMBS.

Married in Rome, Ga. on the 15th inst. by the Rev. J.C. Simmons, MR. THOMAS H. HOLLEYMAN and MISS MARY A. CRUMLEY, daughter of REV. WM. M. CRUMLEY.

Married in this city by Rev. R.L. Breck on Thursday evening 22d inst., MR. WM. M. TOWNSEND and MISS MATTIE A., daughter of ELIJAH BOND, ESQ., all of Macon.

May 5, 1858

Married on the 24th ult. by Rev. R.E. Mills, MR. THOMAS J. HORN and MISS M.J.C.H. DARSY, all of Pulaski county, Ga. (Georgia Citizen and Federal Union will please copy).

May 12, 1858

Married by the Rev. Alex. M. Thigpen on the 6th inst., MR. JOHN GLOVER and MISS MARY A. BENNETT, all of Twiggs county, Georgia.

Married on 5th May by Rev. Mr. Breck, GEORGE H. HAZLEHURST, Chief Engineer of the New Orleans and Jackson Rail Road, and MISS IRENE WINGFIELD, daughter of JAS. A. NISBET, ESQ., of this city.

Married on the 6th inst. at the residence of Mr. R.T. Turner, by the Rev. G.R. Clark, ZIBEON B. WHEELER, of Macon, Ga., and MISS ELIZABETH C. BRADLEY, of Savannah.

Married on Monday evening 3d inst. in Henry County, Ga. by Rev. L.T. Doyal, MR. JOHN A. BECK, of Spaulding County, and MISS JOSEPHINE HARDEN, of Henry County.

May 19, 1858

Married on the 6th inst. by Thomas S. Cobb, J.P., MR. THOMAS CARAWAY and MISS MARY TAYLOR, all of Houston county, Ga.

May 26, 1858

    Married on the evening of the 11th inst. at Chalybeate Springs, Meriwether county, by Rev. B.L. Ross, MR. JAMES L. ROCKMORE and MISS ANN ELIZA, eldest daughter of DR. JOHN L. CHENEY.

    Married on the 19th inst. by Rev. O.L. Smith, ROBERT J. REDDING, ESQ., of Pondtown, and MISS MARY E. BIVINS, of Americus.

June 2, 1858

    Married on the 24th May 1858, near Pond Town, by Rev. Jesse Stallings, MR. ICHABOD DAVIS, of Macon county, and MRS. MARY SMITH, of Schley county, Ga.

June 9, 1858

    Married in this city on the 1st inst. by Rev. S. Landrum, MR. JAMES SMITH and MISS GEORGIA S. CLARKE, all of Macon.

June 16, 1858

    Married in Bibb county on the 3rd inst. by Rev. Mr. Moncrief, MR. WILLIAM G. MOSELEY and MISS MARY A. WILLIAMS, all of this county.

    Married on the 10th inst. by Rev. E.T. McGehee, MR. JOHN MARSHALL and MISS ANN E., daughter of COL. W. LAIDLER, all of Houston County.

    Married near Tallahassee, Fla. on the 9th inst. by Rev. Bishop Rutledge, COL. ROBERT H. GAMBLE and MISS MARTHA CHAIRES, daughter of the late BEN CHAIRES. On the 25th ult., MR. LOUIS P. HOLLIDAY and MISS LETITIA B., daughter of COL. ROBT. GAMBLE.

July 7, 1858

    Married on the 29th June by Rev. Rufus Felder, THADDEUS G. HOLT, JR., ESQ., to MISS FLORINE, daughter of B.T. RUSSEL, ESQ., of Perry, Ga.

    Married in Vineville on the 30th inst. by the Rev. Dr. Jesse Boring, DR. WM. F. HOLT, of Houston county, Ga., to MISS MATTIE C., daughter of SKELTON NAPIER, ESQ.

    Married on the 24th inst. at the Methodist Church in this city by Rev. Dr. Jesse Boring, MR. JOHN D. NEELY, of Savannah, to MISS A.F., daughter of J.B. ROSS, ESQ., of Macon, Ga.

July 21, 1858

    Married on the 18th inst. by the Rev. Mr. Lane, of Oglethorpe University, the REV. WM. MATHEWS, of Decatur, Ga., to MISS MARTHA A. SHIVERS, second daughter of COL. WM. SHIVERS, JR., at his residence near the city.

July 28, 1858

    Married on the evening of the 22nd inst. by Rev. Lewis Solomon, WILLIAM L. SOLOMON, ESQ., and MISS AVARILA FITZPATRICK, daughter of COL. JOHN FITZPATRICK, all of the county of Twiggs, Ga.

Aug. 4, 1858

    Married on the 27th ult. by Thos. S. Cobb, J.P., MR. STANSEL BARWICK, of Sumter Co., and MISS NANCY W. BRIDGES, of Houston Co.

Aug. 11, 1858

    Married in this city on the 9th inst. by the Rev. R.L. Breck, ARTHUR DICKINSON, ESQ. to MISS MARGARET A. TOWNS, second daughter of the late GOV. TOWNS.

Aug. 11, 1858

Married on the 3rd inst. at Richland by Rev. J. Laurence King, MR. ANDREW F. HILL, of Houston county, to MISS JANIE V. SNELLING, of Stewart county, Ga.

Aug. 18, 1858

Married in Bainbridge on the 3rd inst. by Rev. Joel Johnson, Esq., JESSE M. DAVIS, of Dawson, Terrell County, and MRS. MARTHA L. McGOLDRICK, of the former place.

Sep. 8, 1858

Married in Griffin, on the 2d inst. by the Rev. J.H. Campbell, COL. L.T. DOYAL, of McDonough, and MRS. E.P. DIXON, of the former place.

Sep. 15, 1858

Married on Sunday evening 12th inst. at the residence of Mrs. A. Gorman, by the Rev. Sylvanus Landrum, DR. JOHN BROUGHTON, of Savannah, Ga. and MISS MATTIE A. GORMAN, of this city.

Married on the morning of the 5th inst. by Rev. Lewis Solomon, JOHN H. FITZPATRICK, ESQ., to MISS CLIFFORD WIGGINS, all of Twiggs co., Ga.

Married on the 31st of August at the residence of Dr. E.C. Jones, by Rev. James McBryde, B.H. MOULTRIE, ESQ., of Macon county, Ala., to MRS. M.J. REED, of Madison, Ga.

Sep. 29, 1858

Married in New Haven, Conn. on the 15th inst. by Rev. A.N. Littlejohn, WM. T. FITCH (one of the firm of H.T. Fitch & Co., of this city) to EMILY, daughter of the late H.W. BRINTNALL, all of New Haven, Conn.

Oct. 6, 1858

Married at the Baptist Church in this city on the 29th of Sept. by Rev. S. Landrum, the REV. J.B. HARTWELL, Missionary to Shanghai, China, and MISS ELIZA H. JEWETT, of this city.

Married at Peekskill, N.Y. Sep. 22nd by the Rev. Geo. G. Ferguson, MR. G.L. DENMAN, of Macon, Ga., of the firm of Denman and Waterman, to MISS AMIE A. ARNOLD, of Peekskill.

Married in Knoxville, Crawford Co. Sept. 28th by the Rev. Wesley F. Smith, MR. J.B. IVEY of Augusta, Ga., and MRS. M.A. LIZZIE BEELAND, of the former place.

Oct. 13, 1858

Married in this city on the 6th inst. by the Rev. Dr. Boring, at the residence of Thomas A. Harris, Esq., COL. JAMES W. GEARY (late of California) of Orange Spring, Marion county, East Florida, to MISS MARY E. HINES, daughter of JUDGE HINES, of Marion county, East Florida.

Married in Early county, Georgia on Wednesday the 15th of September, the REV. P.D. SMITH, of Appalachicola, Florida, to MISS MARY JANE ROBINSON.

Oct. 20, 1858

Married in Thomasville, Ga. on the 12th inst., AENEAS ARMSTRONG, U.S. Navy, to MISS HENRIETTA E. VICKERS, only daughter of the late JAMES M. VICKERS, ESQ.

Oct. 27, 1858

Married in Decatur county on the 18th inst., MR. DAVID L. PITTS, of Pulaski county, to MISS JANE E. BRASWELL.

Nov. 3, 1858

Married in Vineville on the morning of the 28th ult. by the Rev. Dr. Boring, WM. F. ANDERSON, ESQ., and MISS FRANCES ADA, daughter of THOS. HARDEMAN, SR., ESQ.

Married on the 19th ult. by Rev. W.H. Hollinshead, MR. JOHN J. TOMLINSON, of Lee county, to MISS VICTORIA E. CROCKER, of Macon co., Ga.

Married in Meriwether co. on the 26th inst. by Rev. Charles R. Jewett, MR. JOSIAH W. FREEMAN, of Griffin, and MISS MARY, daughter of MR. B.P. BUSSEY, of Meriwether.

Married in Griffin on the 28th inst. by Rev. Charles R. Jewett, MR. THOMAS S. McKEE, of LaGrange, Ga., and MISS LIZZIE D., daughter of MR. HENRY G. HOLCOMBE, of Griffin.

Nov. 10, 1858

Married in this city Thursday evening 4th inst., at the residence of Mrs. J.P. Evans, by Rev. Mr. Reese, MR. SAMUEL A. TOWNSLEY, of Americus, and MISS FRANCES C. EVANS, of this city.

Married in this city on the 3d inst. by Rev. S. Landrum, MR. FRANCIS LAKE and MISS LAURA M. HOLLINGSWORTH, all of this city.

Married in Greensboro, Ga. on the 3rd inst. by Rev. Dr. Talmage, MR. O.P. DANIEL and MISS JANE VICTORIA, only daughter of HON. F.H. CONE.

Married in Oglethorpe on the 4th inst., at the residence of George W. Fish, Esq., by the Rev. J.P. Duncan, MR. J.H. GRAYBILL, of Savannah, and MISS MARY FISH, of Midway, Ga.

Nov. 24, 1858

Married in Vineville on the 11th inst. by Rev. Mr. Reese, MR. T. McGLOHON, of Macon, Ga., to MISS MARY A., deG., daughter of COL. S.T. BAILEY, of Vineville.

Married at Berne, near St. Mary's Ga. by Rev. W.L. Murphy, DR. U. VAN GIESEN, of Macon, to MISS EUPHESNIA T., daughter of MAJ. ALEXANDER HOLZENDORF, of Camden Co.

Married in Vienna, Ga. on the 4th inst. by the Rev. E. Young, MR. W.G.B. BRITT to MISS SARAH A. NORRIS, all of Vienna.

Dec. 1, 1858

Married in Bibb county on the 28th November by the Rev. R.A. Cain, MR. HENRY A. WHITE to MISS HARRIET E. BOND.

Married in this county on the 10th day of November by the Rev. R. A. Cain, MR. HEZEKIAH McKINNIE to MISS SIDNEY ANN HARDIE - all of this county.

Dec. 8, 1858

Married in this city on the 30th ult. by the Rev. A.M. Wynn, of Columbus, the REV. THOS. H. STEWART, of the Georgia Conference, and MISS ELLA C., daughter of the REV. DR. BORING, of this city.

Dec. 8, 1858

Married on the evening of the 24th inst. by R.E. Wimberly, Esq., MR. WILLIAM METHVIN to MISS CORNELIA A., daughter of REV. WILLIAM D. HORNE, all of Twiggs county.

Married on 30th November by Rev. A.M. Thigpen, DR. T.F. WALKER, of Longstreet, to MISS N.W. BROWN, daughter of DEMPSEY BROWN, ESQ., of Houston county, Ga.

Married in Columbia county on the morning of the 23d ult., by Rev. W.H. Price, DR. G.L.L. RICE, of Houston county, to MISS OPHELIA E., daughter of JUDGE RAMSEY.

Married on the 25th ult. by Fulton R. Lewis, Esq., MR. PATRICK H.D. HARGROVE, of Jackson Parish, Louisiana, to MISS MARTHA BUTTS, of Dooly county, Ga.

Dec. 15, 1858

Married on the evening of the 30th ult. by Rev. Charles M. Irwin, MR. ANDREW DUNN, of Forsyth, to MISS LAURA COPE DEWS, near Albany, Geo.

Married at Oxford, Ga., on the 7th inst. by the Rev. Dr. Thomas, the REV. T.B. RUSSELL to MRS. FANNIE A. LANE.

Married at the Church of the Holy Trinity, N.Y., on Wednesday Dec. 1st by the Rev. Dr. W.H. Lewis, MR. EDGAR P. STRONG, of this city, and MISS HATTIE S., daughter of JOHN B. STOW, ESQ., of Brooklyn.

Married on the 24th Nov. by the Rev. T.B. Russell, W.A. WIGGINS, of Houston County, and MISS LIZZIE J. SANFORD, daughter of STERLING SANFORD, ESQ., of Talbot County.

Dec. 22, 1858

Married in this city on the 16th inst. by Rev. Sylvanus Landrum, JOSEPH H. DUPONT, ESQ., of Florida, and MISS MARY E. ATKINSON, of Macon.

Married in Houston county on the 14th inst. by Rev. W.H. Rice, MR. JOHN B. LEWIS, of Burke county, and MISS MARY JANE, daughter of SYLVANUS BRIEN, ESQ.

Dec. 29, 1858

Married in Bladwin on the morning of the 21st inst. by Rev. Wm. Flinn, MR. BENJ. T. HUNTER, of S.C., to MISS SUE DELAUNAY.

Married in Midway on Tuesday 21st by the Rev. Arthur Small, DR. WM. H. HARRIS, of Palatka, Fla., to MISS EUGINIA L. STUBBS, daughter of B.P. STUBBS, ESQ.

Married in Dublin, Ga. on the 15th inst. by the Rev. W.J. Baker, MR. W.S. RAMSEY to MISS MATTIE J. GUYTON, eldest daughter of MRS. E.L. and the late CAPT. GUYTON - all of Laurens County.

Also on the same evening by the same minister, at Vienna, at the residence of LOAM BROWN, SR., MR. WALTER P. DAVIES and MISS MARY J. BROWN.

Married on the 23d inst. by Laurence Jones, Esq., MR. FRANKLIN HOLLINGSWORTH and MISS E. GREEN, all of Bibb county.

Married at Oxford, Ga. on Thursday evening Dec. 2nd by Rev. Geo. W. Stone, ROBERT U. HARDEMAN, of Macon, Ga., and MISS EUGENIA MURRELL, of Oxford, Georgia.

Dec. 29, 1858

Married in Savannah on the 15th inst. at the residence of Dr. J.B. Fish, by the Rev. David H. Porter, JAMES W. WILLIAMS, ESQ., of Macon county, and MISS FANNIE FISH.

Jan. 5, 1859

Married in Thomaston on the 9th inst. by the Rev. W.G. Parks, DR. JOHN GOODE and MISS LIZZIE J. CAVEN.

Married in Elbert county, Ga. on the 23d ult. by the Rev. L.W. Stephens, HON. THOMAS W. THOMAS and MISS SALLIE E. CADE, daughter of D.B. CADE.

Jan. 12, 1859

Married in Sparta, Hancock county, on the 27th ult. by the Rev. John H. Caldwell, JAMES R. HOOD, Publisher of this Paper, to MISS LIZZIE BUFORD, of Augusta, Ga. (Upson Pilot).

Married on the 16th ult. by Rev. Jacob King, JULIUS C. WILLIAMS, ESQ., to MISS SARAH J. WORTHY, daughter of ANDERSON WORTHY, ESQ., all of Upson county.

Jan. 19, 1859

Married on the 18th inst. by the Rev. Jacob R. Danforth, ALONZO W. JONES, ESQ., of Sumter co., and MISS SARAH TINLEY, daughter of JAMES TINLEY, ESQ., of Bibb co., Ga.

Married on the 30th ult. in Telfair county, MR. YOUNG A. HARRELL and MISS MARGARET A.J. WILLIAMSON, all of Telfair county.

Feb. 2, 1859

Married in Columbus on the 12th December, in the Baptist Church, by the Rev. J. DeVotie, JAMES J. SLADE, ESQ., and MISS LEILA B.B. BONNER.

Married on the 29th inst. by the Rev. G.W. Persons, MR. JAMES JACKSON, of Charleston, S.C., and MISS MARGARET E. POSTELL, daughter of JUDGE WM. POSTELL, of Fort Valley, Houston co., Ga.

Married on Thursday evening 27th inst. at the residence of ISAAC HORN, of Pulaski county, by the Rev. R.E. Mills, MR. J.N. JONES, of Fort Valley, and MISS N.L. HORN. (Citizen and Index please copy).

Married at Talbotton on Tuesday the 18th inst. by the Rev. A.M. Wynn, MAJ. W.L. MITCHELL, of Athens, and MISS ANNA W. JONES, of the former place.

Married on the 23d inst. by Justice W.N. Hutchins, MR. DUNCAN SMITH, of Montgomery, Ala., and MISS SALLIE J. CLARK, of Columbus, Ga.

Feb. 9, 1859

Married in this city on the 6th inst. by the Rev. H.H. Parks, MR. THOMAS C. PARKER to MRS. M.A. McGREGOR, all of this city.

Feb. 16, 1859

Married near this city by Rev. H.H. Parks on the 6th inst., COL. JESSE D. HAVIS and MRS. MARTHA E. BLUNT, both of Houston county, Ga.

Married in Sumter county on the 2d inst. by Rev. R.M. Owen, MR. SAMUEL T. FEAGIN, of Crawford county, and MISS MARY A. DOUGLASS, of the former place. (Augusta Chronicle & Sentinel please copy).

Feb. 23, 1859

    Married in Houston county, Ga. on the 15th instant by the Rev. Edward T. McGhee, MR. EZEKIEL H. WIMBERLY to MISS FANNIE E. BYRD, all of Houston county.

Mar. 2, 1859

    Married on the 24th ult. in Mobile, Ala. by the Rev. Dr. Hamilton, MR. W.H. ROSS, of Macon, Ga. to MISS NETTIE S. SMITH, daughter of H.S. SMITH, ESQ. of Mobile.

Mar. 30, 1859

    Married in this city on the 23d inst. by Rev. S. Landrum, MR. JAMES A. WHITESIDES, of Columbus, and MISS ELIZABETH ANN DRIGGERS, of Macon.

    Married on the 15th inst. at the residence of the bride's father, in Sandersville, Ga., by the Rev. W.D. Cotter, DR. MATT R. FREEMAN, of Macon, and MISS FANNIE E. CULLEN, daughter of DR. A.A. CULLEN.

    Married in Telfair county on the evening of the 6th inst. at the residence of the bride's father, MR. JAMES W. WILLIAMSON and MISS ELIZABETH PARKER, all of Telfair county.

    Married on Wednesday morning the 16th by Rev. A.A. Robinson, COL. WILLIAM A. MAXWELL, of Lee, and MRS. S.L. GIBSON, of Americus.

    Married on the 3d inst. in Talbotton, Ga. by Rev. A.M. Wynn, MR. JAS. J. TOOKE, of Bienville Parish, La., and MISS MARIA F. JONES, of Talbotton, Ga.

Apr. 27, 1859

    Married on the 19th inst. in the Baptist Church of this city by Rev. S. Landrum, MR. RUFUS W. EVANS, of Savannah, and MISS MARY E. VAN VALKENBURG, of Bibb county.

    Married on the 13th inst. at the residence of the bride's father, by Judge B.F. DeLamar, MR. WM. BEMBRY and MISS MARY J. ALLEN, all of Pulaski county.

May 4, 1859

    Married on Thursday evening April 28th in the city of Macon, at Brown's Hotel, M.B. PETERS, of New York, and MISS ANNIE M. BROWN.

    Married on Tues. 26th inst. by the Rev. M. Ainsworth, MR. A.W. MARTIN, of Terrel, and MISS MOLLIE CUNNINGHAM, of Forsyth county, Ga.

May 11, 1859

    Married on the 4th inst. at the residence of the bride's father in Meriwether county by the Rev. Wm. D. Martin, MR. W.R. PHILLIPS, of Macon, and MISS MORGIANNA E. JONES, daughter of MR. JOHN JONES.

May 18, 1859

    Married in this city on the 5th inst. by the Rev. Dr. Hardenburg, DR. EDWARD FITZGERALD and MISS LOUISA M. WEED, daughter of the late E.B. WEED.

May 25, 1859

    Married on Thursday evening the 12th inst. by the Rev. Mr. Evans, MR. CHARLES E. CARNES to MISS JULIA A. HODGES, daughter of MR. JOSEPH J. HODGES, all of this city.

May 25, 1859

    Married at the Catholic Church on the 18th inst. by the Rev. J.F. O'Neal, MISS ELLEN DEMPSEY, of this city, to MR. J.T. WILKINSON, of Talbot county.

    Married in Pulaski county at the residence of Mathew Grace, Esq., on Thursday the 14th ult., MR. JOHN FAIL and MISS NANCY GRACE.

    Married in Griffin, Ga. on the 17th inst. by Rev. Charles R. Jewett, MR. WILLIAM REEVES and MISS EMILY A. LOKETT, all of Griffin.

June 1, 1859

    Married on the 25th by the Rev. Dr. Higgins, DR. THOMAS W. DAWSON and MISS ANNA E., daughter of C.C. CODY, ESQ., all of Columbus.

    Married in Columbus on the 24th by the Rev. A. March, MR. A.H. WARD, of Georgia, and MISS M.E. MOORE, daughter of ALEXANDER J. MOORE, of Arkansas.

June 8, 1859

    Married in this city on the 25th ult., at Christ Church, by the Rev. Mr. Reese, MR. ALFRED J. TYLER and MISS ANNA E. SCOTT, (daughter of ISAAC SCOTT, ESQ.), all of this city.

    Married in this city on the 1st inst. by Rev. S. Landrum, MR. GEORGE BURDICK and MISS ALICE T. PERCIVAL, all of Macon.

    Married on the 5th inst. by Rev. S. Landrum, MR. JOHN RUFF and MISS MARTHA E. AVANT, all of this city.

    Married in Oglethorpe, Ga. on the 29th May, by the Rev. W.S. Turner, JAMES D. GREENE, ESQ., of Columbia county, Ga., and MRS. EMILY BRIDGES, of Oglethorpe.

June 29, 1859

    Married in Eatonton, Putnam county, Ga. on the 21st inst. by Rev. C.W. Key, MR. GEO. W. LIVELY, of New York, and MRS. SUSAN W. HARWELL, of the former place.

June 20, 1859

    Married in this city on the 10th inst. by the Rev. Mr. O'Reilly, MR. R.J. COCHRANE, of Augusta, Ga., and MRS. B.A. BONNER, of the former place.

    Married in Gordon county on the 30th June by the Rev. James E. Evans, COL. O.A. LOCHRANE, of this city, and MISS JOSEPHINE FREEMAN, daughter of JAMES FREEMAN, ESQ.

    Married in Baldwin county on Thursday the 7th inst. by Rev. A.E. Cloud, MR. GEORGE J. COX, of this city, and MISS SARAH E., daughter of MRS. S.J. BAGLEY, of the former place.

    Married on the 28th ult. by L.S. Henderson, Esq., MAJ. COGDIL HAMILTON and MISS SARAH HENDERSON, all of Macon county, Ga.

Aug. 10, 1859

    Married in Columbus on the 2d inst. by the Rev. Mr. Devotie, MR. GRIGSBY E. THOMAS, of Tennessee, and MISS MARTHA B. SLADE, daughter of REV. THOS. B. SLADE.

Aug. 17, 1859

    Married in Macon on the 10th inst. by the Rev. Jacob Rosenfield, J.G. COHEN, ESQ., of Savannah, and REBECCA, ELDEST DAUGHTER OF A. DESSAU, ESQ.

Sep. 14, 1859

Married at Reynolds, Ga. Sept. 3rd by Rev. J.T. May, JOHN W. JAMES, and MISS VICTORIA A. MORRIS.

Married on the 8th inst. by James J. Locke, Esq., MR. ROBT. R. WALLACE, of Hawkinsville, and MISS AMANDA BOATRIGHT, daughter of ROLLY BOATRIGHT, of Dooly county.

Sep. 21, 1859

Married on the evening of the 14th inst. at the residence of Mr. H.T. Hall, in Aiken, South Carolina, by the Rev. J.H. Carroll, COL. A.A. GAULDING, of Atlanta, Ga., and MRS. SARAH G. BLUE, of the former place.

Sep. 28, 1859

Married on 8th Sept. by Rev. E.T. McGehee, MR. JOSEPH C. ELLIS and MRS. SARAH BACON, both of Houston county.

Married on the 22nd Sept. by Rev. E.T. McGehee, MR. HUMPHREY MARSHALL and MRS. SARAH A. LAIDLER, both of Houston county.

Married in Monroe co. on the 20th inst. by Rev. Wm. C. Wilkes, COL. L.T. DOYAL, of Griffin, and MRS. SETTIE BATTLE, of the former place.

Oct. 5, 1859

Married at the residence of Mr. Haywood Hughes, of Twiggs co., Ga., on the 22d inst. by Rev. Wm. R. Steely, MR. WM. ALLEN JR., of Pulaski county, and MISS ANNIE E. WYNNE, of Twiggs county.

Oct. 12, 1859

Married on the 6th inst. by Rev. S. Landrum, MR. NATHANIEL COATES, and MRS. SUSAN G. COOK, all of Macon, Ga.

Married on the 5th inst. by Rev. S. Landrum, MR. ACHILLES AUDOIN and MISS SARAH McMANUS, all of this city.

Oct. 19, 1859

Married on the 18th inst. at the house of the Rev. Jacob Kleckly, by the Rev. S.W. Bedenbaugh, JAMES W. SMITH and MISS CATHERINE KLECKLY, all of Macon county.

Oct. 26, 1859

Married on the 18th inst. at the residence of Charles H. McCalls in Macon county, by the Rev. James Terryman, L.M. FELTON, of Macon county, to MISS MARY J. LOVE.

Nov. 2, 1859

Married at Reynolds Oct. 20th by the Rev. J.T. May, W.H.C. GOODWIN, ESQ., to MISS JOSEPHINE E. HICKS.

Married on the 18th inst. at the residence of Judge James H. McCall, Marion County, by the Rev. James Perryman, HON. L.M. FELTON, of Macon county, to MISS MARY J. LOWE.

Married on the 26th of October at the residence of the bride's father, COL. DEMPSEY BROWN, by the Rev. Edward T. McGehee, MR. JOHN R. WIMBERLY to MISS EUGENIA M. BROWN, all of Houston county, Ga.

Nov. 2, 1859

Married on the 25th inst. by the Rev. G.W. Persons, GEORGE B. PLANT, to MISS L.E. McGEHEE, daughter of the HON. F.J. McGEHEE, all of Houston county.

Married at Midway on Thursday evening 27th ult. by Rev. J.M. Curtis, ARTHUR P. WRIGHT, ESQ., of Thomasville, Ga., to MISS ELIZA, second daughter of CAPT. J.S. THOMAS.

Nov. 9, 1859

Married in this city on Tuesday night Nov. 1st by the Rev. H.H. Parks, MR. WILLIAM E. DENSE and MISS MOLLIE CROSBIE, all of this city.

Married at the Meth. Church in this city by the Rev. Mr. Evans on the 25th ult., E.C. GRIER, ESQ. to MRS. E.T. DORSEY.

Married at Mrs. Harsley's in Milledgeville on 4th August last by the Rev. Mr. Flinn, MR. CHARLES M. LAMPRY, of Hampton, New Hampshire, to MISS KATE BACHLOTT, of Scottsboro, Ga. (Savannah Republican please copy).

Nov. 23, 1859

Married in this city on the 15th inst. by Rev. S. Landrum, GEN. WM. L. GORDON, of Griffin, and MRS. U.T. LAMAR, of Macon.

Married in Crawford county by Judge Culverhouse, JOHN W. DENT to MISS JANE JENKINS, all of Crawford county.

Married in this city on the 16th inst. by David Reid, Esq., MR. H. CHRISTOPHER to MISS GEORGIA CANDLER, all of this city.

Mar-ied on the 17th inst. by the Rev. E.M. Irwin, DR. R.H. NISBET, of Macon, to MISS MATTIE N. DENNIS, of Eatonton.

Married in this city on the 15th inst. by the Rev. H.H. Parks, the REV. G.H. PATTILLO, of the Georgia Conference, to MISS LUCY M., daughter of the REV. J.E. EVANS, of this city.

Nov. 30, 1859

Married in this city on the 27th inst. by Rev. John W. Burke, MR. F.T. PEALE and MISS MARTHA JACOBS.

Dec. 21, 1859

Married in this city on the 15th inst. by the Rev. Mr. Lane, MR. FRANK H. STONE and MISS OPHELIA LeCONTE.

Dec. 28, 1859

Married by the Rev. Wm. W. Oslin Dec. 18th in Bibb county, ELIJAH ROOKS and MISS RHODA BARTLETT.

Married on the 20th December by the Rev. W.F. Cook, MR. W.T. MORGAN, to MISS ANNIE E. NEWTON, both of this city.

Married in this city on the 22d inst. by Rev. George N. McDonald, WM. R. ROGERS, of Savannah, and MISS DELLIE B. CARVER, daughter of ROBERT CARVER, ESQ., of Oglethorpe.

Married in Montgomery, Ala. on the evening of the 20th inst. by the Rev. Mr. Mitchell, Rector of St. John's Church, MR. E.A. BANKS, Junior Editor of the Montgomery Confederation, to MISS ELIZA W. PICKETT, daughter of the late COL. ALBERT J. PICKETT of that city.

Dec. 28, 1859

Married in Montgomery, at the Baptist Church on Tuesday afternoon 20th inst. by the Rev. I.T. Tichenor, MR. HENRY F. COYNE, of the Montgomery Mail, to MRS. LOUISA C. MACON, all of that city.

Married on the evening of the 20th inst. by Rev. Lewis Solomon, DR. L.L. RICHARDSON and MISS SUSAN A.F. RADFORD, all of Twiggs county, Ga.

Jan. 11, 1860

Married in this city on the 8th instant by Rev. H.H. Parks, MR. THOS. A. WINBUSH, of Schley county, Ga. and MRS. CYNTHIA C. TAYLOR, of this city.

Married in Lee county on the 3d instant by the Rev. Mr. Irwin, MR. ROBERT COLEMAN, of this city, and MISS ANNE E. NEWSOM, daughter of JUDGE NEWSOM of the aforesaid co.

Feb. 1, 1860

Married Jan. 31st by Rev. H.H. Parks in East Macon, CAPT. THOS. HUNT, of Jones co., to MRS. EMILY J. DENTON, of the former place.

Married Jan. 30 by Rev. F. Foster, MR. S.G. WOOD to MISS EMMA C. CLARKE, all of this city.

Feb. 8, 1860

Married at the residence of Judge Floyd (Covington) on the evening of the 25th instant by the Rev. A. Means, DR. WM. A. SHELBY, of Atlanta, to MISS LOU FLOYD, of the former place.

Feb. 15, 1860

Married at the residence of Mrs. Lucretia Edmondson, in Putnam county, Ga. on the 13th inst. by Rev. C.W. Key, MISS ELIZABETH M. EDMONDSON and JOHN W. HUDSON, ESQ., of Eatonton, Ga.

Feb. 22, 1860

Married on the morning of the 19th inst. by the Rev. H. Camp, MR. J.R. HOLSENSAKE to MISS SALLIE V. JONES, all of Oglethorpe, Ga.

Married in Bossier Parish, La. Feb. 2nd, 1860 by Rev. J.F. Ford, GEN. JOHN L. HODGES to MISS J.V. HAMILTON.

Married by Dr. D.L. White on Thursday evening the 9th instant, ISAAC R. HARRIS to MRS. MARY C. SIBLEY, all of Quincy.

Married in this city on the 19th inst. by Rev. J.W. Burke, MR. WILEY SIKES to MISS MARTHA SHIDE, all of Macon, Ga.

Married in Bienville Parish, La. on the 25th of January by Rev. W.D. Shea, MR. GEO. E. WALKER, of Crawford county, Ga., to MISS MARY JOSEPHINE, daughter of JAS. J. TOOKE, formerly of Talbotton, Ga.

Feb. 29, 1860

Married in this city on the 23d inst., at the residence of Mrs. E. Blake, by Rev. Dr. Talmage, MR. C.C. SIMS and MISS ELEANOR HARRIS, all of this city.

Married in Atlanta on the evening of the 22d instant by Rev. Lewis Lawshe, MR. WM. G. WHIDBY, Grand Worthy Patriarch Sons of Temperance of the State of Georgia, and MISS MARY E., daughter of WM. H. JONES, ESQ., all of that city.

Mar. 28, 1860

Married at the residence of the bride's father on the evening of the 7th inst. by the Rev. Mr. Mitchell of St. John's Church, COL. JOHN W.A. SANFORD to MISS SALLIE, second daughter of COL. WM. HENRY TAYLOR, all of Montgomery, Ala.

Married on the 17th of January last by E.J. Blackshear, J.I.C., MR. NATHANIEL B. BOSTICK to MISS LAVINIA V. LINDER, all of Laurens county.

Married on the 29th of January last by E.J. Blackshear, J.I.C., MR. NATHAN T. MADDUX to MISS MARY E. HOLMES, all of Laurens county.

Married on the 23d of February last by E.J. Blackshear, J.I.C., MR. JOHN T. DAVIS to MISS MARY A. WALKER, all of Laurens county.

Apr. 11, 1860

Married at the residence of the bride's father in Dallas county, Alabama on Thursday evening the 29th inst. by Rev. Mr. Bunn, MR. F.D. WIMBERLY, of Tarversville, Ga. and MISS R. ISLINE MINTER, daughter of COL. W.T. MINTER, of Dallas county.

Apr. 25, 1860

Married on the 19th inst. in the Presbyterian Church by the Rev. David Wills, FREDERICK L. VILLEPIGUE, ESQ., of Tallahassee, Fla., and MISS MARGARET WATSON, eldest daughter of GEN. JAMES W. ARMSTRONG of this city.

Married on Tuesday morning 17th inst. by Rev. Thos. B. Langley, of Fort Valley, at the residence of E.S. Crocker, Esq., DR. E.H. RAWLS and MISS FANNIE HARMAN, all of Macon county, Ga.

May 2, 1860

Married on the evening of the 25th March by the Rev. H.H. Parks, DR. F.G. CASTLEN and MISS EFFIE M., daughter of P.E. BOWDRE, ESQ., of this city.

May 9, 1860

Married in Early county on the 1st inst. by the Rev. Mr. Bartlett, MR. JAMES F. ROBINSON, of Laurens county, and MISS FANNIE M. STOKES, of the former place.

May 16, 1860

Married in Dougherty county on the 1st inst. by the Rev. E. Warren of Macon, MR. CHARLES F. BEMIS, of Fort Gaines, and MISS EMMA ROBERT, of that county.

Married at the residence of D.W. Orr, Esq., of Macon county, on the evening of the 9th inst., by Rev. W.H. Rice, MR. CALVIN W. MIXON and MISS MARY ELIZABETH ORR.

June 6, 1860

Married at the Methodist E. Church on the 29th of May by Rev. H.H. Parks, DR. J.P. HINELE, of Montgomery, Ala., and MISS LAURA E. BUTTS, daughter of A.G. BUTTS, ESQ.

Married in the Presbyterian Church on the 31st of May by Rev. Dr. Wills, MR. W.A. HUFF and MISS MATTIE E. VIRGIN, all of this city.

Married in this city on the 24th inst. by Rev. David Wills, MR. THOMAS J. REDDING, of Thomaston, and MISS EMMA O. CAMPBELL, of this city.

June 13, 1860

Married in Twiggs county on the evening of the 6th inst. by R.R. Wimberly, Esq., COL. ORLAND BURKETTE, of Sumter Dist., S. Carolina, and MISS BETTIE KILPATRICK, of the former place.

June 20, 1860

Married on the morning of the 12th inst. at the residence of Danl. G. Hughes, by R.R. Wimberly, Esq., MR. WM. METHVIN and MISS SAMANTHA MIMMS, all of Twiggs county.

June 27, 1860

Married on the 21st instant by the Rev. David Wills, MR. JOHN C. SMART, of Barnwell, S.C., and MISS DELIA COLDING, of this city.

Married on the 20th of June at the residence of Judge Jolley, in Macon county, Ga., by the Rev. John Howell, MR. JOHN W. PARKS and MISS FANNIE JOLLEY.

July 4, 1860

Married in Raleigh, N.C. on the 27th ultimo by the Rev. Mr. Wathal, W.H. SAVAGE, ESQ., of Macon, Ga., and MISS JOSEPHINE, eldest daughter of CAPT. J.H. KIRKHAM.

July 25, 1860

Married at the residence of David Flanders, Esq. on the 17th inst., by the Rev. Mr. Evans, MR. JESSE M. HURT, of Jones county, to MISS M.E. CARVER, of this city.

Aug. 1, 1860

Married in Culloden, Ga. on Tuesday morning last by the Rev. W.F. Cook, MR. R.P. McEVOY, of this city, and MISS JENNIE M. COOK, daughter of the REV. FRANCIS COOK.

Married on Thursday July 26th by Rev. R.C. S-ith, JAS. AUGUSTINE HALL and ADIE E., daughter of DR. THOS. F. GREEN, all of Midway.

Married at Brighton, near Darien, Ga., by Rev. Joseph S. Key, MR. CHESLEY B. HOWARD, of Columbus, and MISS CARRIE E. SHACKELFORD, of the former place.

Aug. 15, 1860

Married on the morning of the 8th inst. by the Rev. Thos. T. Christian, COL. FRANK S. JOHNSON and MISS CORDELIA MORGAN, all of Clinton, Ga.

Aug. 22, 1860

Married in this city on the 7th inst. by E.C. Granniss, Esq., MR. GEORGE R. WAGNON and MISS MARGARET E. LAWRENCE.

Married in Jones county on the 16th inst. by Thos. Benden, Esq., MR. THOS. J. CHAMPION, of this county, and MISS MARY JANE KITCHENS.

Aug. 29, 1860

Married on the morning of the 23rd inst. at the residence of the bride, near Fort Valley, Ga., by the Rev. Geo. C. Clarke, CAPT. JOEL R. GRIFFIN, of Macon, Ga., and MRS. MARY A.E. SLAPPY.

Sep. 19, 1860

Married on the 30th ult. in the city of Macon by Rev. E.W. Warren, MR. LEONIDAS STEWART and LUCINDA WORTHINGTON.

Sep. 26, 1860

Married in the Episcopal Church in Atlanta on the 13th inst., by Rev. Mr. Freeman, DR. G. McDONALD, of Macon, Ga., and MRS. S.M. LAROCHE, of Aiken, S.C.

Married at the residence of the bride's father, in Dadeville, Tallapoosa county, Ala. on the evening of the 6th inst., MR. FRANCIS A. JOBSON, of Perry, Houston co., Ga. and MISS FIDELIA E. HIGGINS.

Oct. 3, 1860

Married in Memphis, Tenn. on the 20th ult. by the Rt. Rev. Bishop Otley, MR. GEORGE W. TROUTMAN, of Macon, Ga., and MISS ALICE, daughter of COL. J.M. WILLIAMSON, of Memphis.

Oct. 10, 1860

Married in New York on Thursday September 27th by the Rev. Robert G. Dickson, MR. R.L. WOOD, of Macon, Ga., to MISS JANE, only daughter of the late WM. LEARY, ESQ.

Oct. 17, 1860

Married in Tallapoosa county, Ala., at the residence of Col. John Rowe, on the evening of the 2d instant, by Judge Robert Dougherty, MR. OLIVER P. NORMAN, of Union co., Ark. to MRS. S.A. McLEMORE, of the former place.

Oct. 24, 1860

Married in Bibb co. Oct. 18th by Rev. W.W. Oslin, MR. GEORGE M. MONCRIEF and MISS ARTEMESIA R. DRAWHORN.

Nov. 7, 1860

Married on the evening of the 24th Oct. by the Rev. Geo. W. Persons, MR. B.W. SANFORD to MISS LIZZIE EVERETT, daughter of the late J.A. EVERETT of Fort Valley, Ga.

Married in Houston County on the 30th October by the Rev. Mr. Allen, DR. W.L. JONES and MISS MARY OPRY.

Dec. 5, 1860

Married in this city on the 27th ult. by Rev. Mr. Reese, MR. ADDISON P. CHERRY and MISS KATE M. CASTLEN.

Dec. 19, 1860

Married in Twiggs county on the 13th inst. by J.A. Clements, Esq., GEORGE R. ASBELL to MISS E.J. VAUGHAN, all of Twiggs.

Dec. 26, 1860

Married in Americus on the 4th inst., MR. GEORGE A. BIVINS, of Macon, Ga., and MISS JOANNA L., eldest daughter of DR. JARED TOMLINSON, of Americus.

Jan. 2, 1861

Married in the city of Macon on the 23d ult. by Rev. H.C. Hornaday, DAVID H. HILL and MISS WINNIE S. BARLOW, both of Americus.

Jan. 2, 1861

   Married on Thursday evening 27th ult. by Rev. Park Pledger, MR. B.F.
   HENRY, of Murray county, Ga., and MISS S.F. SMITH, of this city.

Jan. 9, 1861

   Married in this city on Tuesday January 1st by Rev. David Wills,
   of the Presbyterian Church, COL. B.B. LEWIS, of Mobile, Ala. and
   MISS JULIET R. COLLINS, daughter of DR. ROBERT COLLINS.

Jan. 16, 1861

   Married in Taylor county on the 27th ult., MR. WM. J. POLLARD, of
   Augusta, to MISS ISABELLA C. CORBIN.

   Married in Fort Valley on the 9th inst., MR. JOSEPH J. DASHER to
   MISS SARAH E. HARRIS.

Jan. 23, 1861

   Married on the 9th inst. by the Rt. Rev. Stephen Elliott, GEORGE
   W. ANDERSON, JR. and MISS KATHARINE H. BERRIEN, all of Savannah.

Jan. 30, 1861

   Married in Bibb county on the 23d inst. by Rev. Charles P.B. Martin,
   MR. N.B. POWERS - eldest son of the late JUDGE POWERS - and MISS
   JOSEPHINE H. FOSTER - youngest daughter of CAPT. ARTHUR FOSTER.

   Married on the 15th inst. in Eatonton, Ga. by Rev. A.M. Wynn, DR.
   G.W. ANDREWS and MISS ELLEN G. HARWELL.

   Married on the 13th inst. at the residence of the bride's father,
   by Elder Jacob King, MR. JNO. A. COCHRAN and MISS MARTHA STEPHENS,
   all of Upson county, Ga.

Feb. 6, 1861

   Married on the evening of the 29th ult. at the residence of the
   bride in Bibb county, by the Rev. N.B. Ousley of the Georgia Conference, ROBT. F. OUSLEY, ESQ., of Macon, to MRS. JULIA E. HOLT.

Feb. 13, 1861

   Married in the city of Macon on the 6th inst. by Rev. R.B. Lester,
   MR. JAMES W. LESTER, of Cobb county, and MISS HATTIE E. SMITH, of
   Warrenton, Ga. (Christian Index please copy).

   Married on Thursday 24th January 1861 at the residence of Wm. A.
   Blanton, Esq., in Spalding county, Ga., by the Rev. Wm. A. Rogers,
   MR. DANIEL S. REDDING, of Monroe county, Ga. and MISS CLARA P.
   BLANTON, of the former place.

   Married in Spalding county on the 29th ult. by Rev. L.T. Doyal, MR.
   JOSEPH G. DOYAL and MISS JOSEPHINE VICTORIA LESTER.

   Married at Montpelier, Ga. on the 9th ult. by Rev. Carlisle P.
   Beeman, D.D., COL. A.Z. BAILEY, of Florida, and MISS LAURA CLYDE
   MARTIN, daughter of REV. CARLISLE P.B. MARTIN, of Montpelier.

   Married in Milledgeville on Wednesday evening 6th inst. by the Rev.
   Wm. Flinn, PETERSON THWEATT, ESQ., Comptroller General and MRS.
   ANNA E. HAWLEY, daughter of COL. D.C. CAMPBELL, of Milledgeville.

   Married February 7th by Rev. G.C. Clarke, MR. WM. T. ALFORD, of
   Macon, and MISS LAURA N. McARTHUR, of Bibb co., Ga.

   Married on the 5th inst. by Rev. F.W. Warren, MR. E. CASON COX and
   MISS MARY J. FINDLAY, both of the city of Macon.

Feb. 27, 1861

Married on the 14th inst. at the residence of Mr. John Dailey in Henry Co., Ga., by Rev. F.E. Manson, COL. O.C. GIBSON, of Griffin, Ga. and MISS RACHEL DAILEY, of Henry co., Ga.

Married in Spalding county on the 10th instant by Rev. B.R. Searcy, MR. H.P. FREEMAN, of Upson county, and MISS M.L. BOSTWICK, of Spalding.

Mar. 6, 1861

Married at the residence of the bride's father on the evening of the 26th ult., by the Rev. Walter R. Branham, MR. ISHAM H. BRANHAM, of Floyd county, and MISS MOLLIE A.H. MATHEWS, daughter of DR. W.A. MATHEWS, of Fort Valley, Ga.

Mar. 13, 1861

Married in this city on the evening of the 7th by Rev. David Willis, MR. AMBROSE GAINES and MISS MARY WINSTON, daughter of the late GOV. TOWNS, all of Macon.

Mar. 20, 1861

Married on the 12th inst. at the residence of Mrs. Dr. Terrell in Sparta, Ga., by the Rev. Dr. Talmage, JAS. T. FLEWELLEN, ESQ. and MISS MAGGIE D. CRAWFORD, daughter of the late HON. JOEL CRAWFORD.

Married on Thursday 7th inst. at the home of the bride's mother, by the Rev. S.G. Daniel, COL. F.H. DeGRAFFENREID and MISS MARY E. COLLIER, all of Albany.

Married at the residence of the bride's father, WM. WALLACE, in Dougherty county on the 10th inst., by Eld. W.N. Chaudion, CAPT. T.T. BUTTRELL and MISS MARY ANN WALLACE.

Mar. 27, 1861

Married on the 12th inst. by the Rev. Arminius Wright, MR. JAS. T. REDDING, of La., to MISS MARTHA BIBB HARDAWAY, daughter of MAJ. R.S. HARDAWAY, of this city.

Apr. 3, 1861

Married on the 5th ult. at the residence of the bride's father in Drew county, Arkansas, by the Rev. L. Julian, MR. I.H.B. ROSS, of Bradley county, to MISS AMANDA M. EMMERSON, of the former place.

Married on the 28th March by Rev. E.T. McGehee, MR. S.T. LOFLEY to MISS T.M. HARVEY, all of Houston county, Georgia.

Apr. 17, 1861

Married at Christ Church on the 12th instant, by the Rt. Rev. Stephen Elliott, MISS ANNE E. COLE, daughter of JUDGE C.B. COLE, of Macon, and MR. FRANCIS J. CHAMPION, of Savannah.

Apr. 24, 1861

Married on the evening of the 20th inst. in Rome, Ga. by the Rev. Mr. Hinton, JOEL BRANHAM JR., ESQ., of Macon, Ga. and MISS GEORGIA C. CUYLER, of Rome.

Married at the residence of the bride's father by the Rev. David Wills, MR. CHARLES V. WOOD and MISS CATHERINE M. STRONG, all of this city.

Apr. 24, 1861

    Married on March 7th at the residence of the bride's father, by Rev. Pharley Sweat, MR. LEROY A. MURPHEY, of Burke co., and MISS MAGGIE V. CLOUD, of Chatham county, Ga.

May 1, 1861

    Married in this city on Monday evening 22d ult. by Rev. David Wills, MR. JAMES H. BLOUNT and MISS EUGENIA WILEY, daughter of DR. J.B. WILEY, all of Macon.

    Married at Brown's Hotel on the morning of the 29th by the Rev. David Wills, ROBERT H. JOHNSON, of Floyd county, and MRS. B.A. DICKENS, of Marianna, Fla.

May 29, 1861

    Married on Thursday evening, May 23d, 1861, by the Rev. H.K. Reese, MISS MARY E. ARTOPE and MR. JOHN C. HODGKINS, all of this city.

    Married at High Shoals, Clark co., Ga. on the 23rd inst. by the Rev. J.M. Stilwell, of Morgan co., J.H. WOODWARD, ESQ. to MISS CARRIE M., youngest daughter of B.S. CHEATS, ESQ. of the former place.

June 19, 1861

    Married in Fort Valley on Tuesday morning June 12th by Rev. Wm. H. Hollingshead, MR. GRENVILLE WOOD and MISS MARY O. LEGG.

June 26, 1861

    Married in Monroe county on the 20th inst. by the Rev. Mr. Moncrief, MR. JOSEPH E. HUDGENS, of this city, and MISS EMMA J. NORRIS.

    Married near Knoxville, Crawford county, June 20th, 1861, by Rev. Wesley F. Smith, WM. A. WALKER, ESQ., of Thomaston, and MISS DIZZIE LOWE, daughter of MR. JACOB LOWE, of the former place.

July 10, 1861

    Married on the 25th June by Rev. W.H. Clarke, DR. H.D. HUDSON and MISS MOLLIE LOU NORRIS, all of Baker county.

    Married on the 4th inst. by Rev. David Wills, DR. GEORGE G. GRIFFIN and MISS JULIET R. BEALL, all of this city.

July 17, 1861

    Married on Sunday afternoon July 14th in Jeffersonville, Twiggs county, Ga., by the Rev. M.R. Steeley, MR. N.A. MEGRATH, of this city, and MISS ROBA, daughter of WILLIAM BRYAN, ESQ., of the former place.

Aug. 7, 1861

    Married in Athens July 23rd by the Rev. J.S. Key, MR. JEFFERSON M. LAMAR, of Covington, and MISS MARY ANN, only daughter of the late ANDREW J. LAMAR.

    Married in Athens July 29th by Rev. J.S. Key, MR. LAMAR COBB, of Macon, and MISS ANN OLIVIA, daughter of MR. JOHN H. NEWTON.

Aug. 14, 1861

    Married in Savannah on the 29th ult. by the Rt. Rev. Bishop Elliott, LIEUT. WM. W. PAINE, of the Georgia Regulars, to CORNELIA, daughter of A.A. SMETS, ESQ., of Savannah.

Aug. 14, 1861

Married in Albany on the 30th ult. by Rev. S.G. Daniel, COL. JESSE S. BEALL and MISS EUGENIA A. COLEY, all of that city.

Sep. 4, 1861

Married on the morning of the 25th ult. by the Rev. John T. Clark, NATHANIEL PATCH and MISS MARY E. WHIDBY, all of Atlanta, Ga.

Married at Stribling Springs, Augusta county, Va. by the Rev. Mr. Sparrow, MR. H.B. DAVIS, of Perry, Houston county, Ga. and MRS. M.J. SUMMERHAYS, of Rome, Ga.

Married on the 27th ult. by Rev. F.M. Haygood, MR. J. JOSEPH HODGES and MISS JANE R., eldest daughter of MR. E.C. BULKLY, all of this city.

Sep. 18, 1861

Married on the morning of the 8th by Wm. S. Ogletree, Esq., JAMES M. SIMMONS to MISS MARY E.T. SEYMOUR - all of Crawford county.

Oct. 23, 1861

Married in Augusta, Ga. on the evening of the 17th inst. by the Rev. Mr. Huntington, JAS. NATHAN ELLS, of the Southern Field and Fireside, to MARY ELIZA GARMANY.

Oct. 30, 1861

Married in this city on the 24th inst. by the Rev. A.T. Mann, D.D., MR. BURTON W. BELLAMY, of Fla., and MISS ELLEN CLAYTON, only daughter of COL. J.H.R. WASHINGTON.

Married in Milledgeville on the 24th instant, by Rev. S.E. Brooks, GEORGE DUNLAYP, ESQ., of Macon, to MISS KATIE D. HAYGOOD, daughter of J.E. HAYGOOD, ESQ., of the former city.

Nov. 6, 1861

Married on Thursday evening Oct. 31st in Christ Church, Macon, by Rt. Rev. Stephen Elliott, J.W. BLACKSHEAR and MARIAN, daughter of the late DR. AMBROSE BABER, both of this city.

Dec. 11, 1861

Married at Christ Church, Savannah, on Tuesday the 3d inst. by Rt. Rev. Bishop Elliot, CAPT. T.A. BURKE and MISS ELIZA BATTEY, eldest daughter of L.N. FALLIGANT, ESQ., - all of Savannah.

Married on the 4th inst. at the residence of Dr. N. Tucker in Laurens county, by the Rev. David Wills, HON. A.E. COCHRAN, of Glynn county, to MISS EUGENIA TUCKER.

Dec. 18, 1861

Married at the residence of Judge Cason, near Macon, on the 12th inst. by Rev. E.W. Warren, JUDGE WILLIAM A. GORLEY, of Putnam county, to MRS. ELIZABETH E. SANDERS.

Dec. 25, 1861

Married in this city at Christ Church on the 19th inst. by the Rev. Mr. Reese, MR. ROBT. B. FINDLAY to MISS MARY A. BENTON, eldest daughter of AMOS BENTON, ESQ.

Married in Americus on the 19th inst. by Rev. E.W. Warren, JAMES SEYMOUR, of the firm of Ross & Seymour of this city, to MISS REBECCA HILL, of the former place.

Dec. 25, 1861

    Married in Sandersville, Ga. on the 17th inst. by the Rev. Dr. Talmage, MR. JOHN W. KENDRICK, of Macon county, Ala., to MISS SARAH F. LANGMADE, daughter of E.S. LANGMADE, ESQ., of the former place.

    Married in Houston County on the 18th instant by Rev. George C. Clarke, LIEUT. JAMES A. EVERETT to MISS JOSIE C., daughter of LEWIS RUMPH, ESQ.

Jan. 22, 1862

    Married in this city on the 17th inst. by Rev. J. Knowles, HENRY M. MALSBY, of the Independent Volunteers, to MISS MATTIE A. GARDNER, all of this city.

Jan. 29, 1862

    Married at Yorktown, Va. on the 25th of December by the Rev. Burton Jones, of Crawford county, Va., Private GEORGE W. ELLIS, of the Beauregard Volunteers, of Houston county, Ga., and MISS HARRIET WILLIS, of Yorktown, Va.

Feb. 5, 1862

    Married in Fort Valley, Ga. on the night of the 22d inst. by the Rev. R.W. Johnson, MR. MARCUS W. JOHNSON to MISS LAVINIA P. HOLLINSHEAD, eldest daughter of DR. WM. HOLLINSHEAD.

Apr. 2, 1862

    Married in Oglethorpe county on the 25th ult. by the Rev. J.W. Burke, ASA HOLT, ESQ., of this city, to MISS NORA M. BURKE, formerly of Athens, Ga.

Apr. 23, 1862

    Married at the residence of the bride's father by the Rev. James Williamson, AUGUSTUS G. McPHAIL and MISS MARY E. TAYLOR, all of Hawkinsville.

June 4, 1862

    Married in Forsyth on the 27th ult., THOMAS M. BRANTLEY, of Macon, and MISS CARRIE C. LAND, of the former place.

    Married on the 28th inst. by Rev. Jas. E. Patterson, MR. E.B. TAYLOR and MISS SHATTIE S. WINN, daughter of DR. G.A. WINN, all of Monroe county, Ga.

July 23, 1862

    Taking the shine off. Married in the town of Thomasville, at the residence of the bride's father, (this apparently added to show that it was not a runaway affair) MR. JAMES N. WINN and MISS KATTIE A. SHINE.

Jan. 28, 1863

    Married in Houston county on Thursday the 15th inst. by the Rev. James Williamson, Lieutenant O.A.V. Rose, of the 49th Reg. Ga. Vols., and MISS MARTHA A. SHEPPARD.

Apr. 22, 1863

    Married on the 16th inst. in this city by Rev. J.W. Burke, LIEUT. MARSHALL DeGRAFFENREID, qst Reg. of Ga. Regulars, and MISS PARMELIA M., daughter of B.F. ROSS, all of this city.

Apr. 29, 1863

Married in Columbus on the 22d inst. by the Rev. J.H. DeVotie, MR. JOHN B. LINDSAY to MISS HELEN R. SLADE - daughter of the REV. THOS. B. SLADE.

May 6, 1863

Married in this city on the 29th ult. by His Honor Judge Lochrane, LIEUT. ROBERT H. ATKINSON, Adj't 1st Ga. Regulars and MISS CORDELIA DESSAU.

Married on Thursday morning by Rev. David Wills, MR. JAS. H. DOUGLAS and MISS MARY M.B. SLOAN, all of this city.

May 13, 1863

Married at the residence of the bride's father, COL. N. BASS, on the 7th inst., CAPT. WM. L. GORDON, of Huntsville, Ala., and MISS EMMA W. HURT, of this city.

July 1, 1863

Married in this city on the 23d inst. by Rev. David Wills, CAPT. C.D. FINDLAY and MISS ELLEN A. EDWARDS.

Married at Longstreet on the 24th inst. by the Rev. G.R. McCall, MR. SAMUEL H. WASHINGTON, of Macon, and MISS M. FANNIE PHILLIPS, of Pulaski county, Ga.

Married on the 23d inst. by the Rev. John F. Berry, MR. H.M. BROWN, of Butler, Ga. and MISS D.A. POPE, of Box Spring, Ga.

July 22, 1863

Married at the residence of the Rev. Thomas B. Slade on Thursday the 16th inst., by the Rev. J.H. DeVotie, MR. WILLIAM R. GIGNILLIAT to MISS JANET E. SLADE.

Aug. 19, 1863

Married in Milner, Pike county, Ga. on the 3d inst. by the Rev. T. B. Cooper, LIEUT. A.J. PUGSLEY, of Jefferson county, Ga. and MISS MOLLIE E. HOWE.

Nov. 18, 1863

Married on the evening of the 11th instant, at the residence of Dr. C.P. Hartwell, near Albany, Ga., by C.D. Mallory, D.D., REV. LEWIS SOLOMON and MRS. T.E. BATEMAN, both of Twiggs county, Ga.

Dec. 9, 1863

Married on Thursday evening 26th ultimo by the Rev. Eustace Speer, MR. JAMES M. THOMAS, of Forsyth, Ga., to MISS GIRTA HAMMOND, of this city.

Dec. 23, 1863

Married on the 15th inst. by the Rev. Albert Gray, MR. T.S. COLEMAN, of Macon, to MISS ALICE, daughter of DR. JOSIAH and MRS. J. HILSMAN, of Crawford county.

Dec. 30, 1863

Married on the evening of the 22d inst. at the residence of Peter Solomon, in Vineville, Ga., by the Rev. E.W. Speer, CAPT. SAMUEL HUNTER, H.A.C.S. and MISS CORA SOLOMON.

Jan. 27, 1864

Married on the 12th inst. by the Rev. P.M. Ryburn, MR. B.H. WRIGLEY to MISS M.M. KNOTT, daughter of JUDGE KNOTT, of this vicinity.

Feb. 10, 1864

Married at Marshallville on the 8th (?) inst. by the Rev. T.B. Russell, MR. LEWIS O. NILES, of Griffin, and MISS M. OPHELIA SPERRY, of the former place.

Married at the residence of the bride's father in Hawkinsville on the 4th inst., by the Rev. James Williamson, CAPTAIN R.W. ANDERSON (of Anderson's Battery, First Battalion, Artillery Reserve, A.T.) and MISS AGNES MERRITT, all of Pulaski county.

Mar. 9, 1864

Married in this city on the 7th instant by the Rev. H.K. Rees, MR. H.F. REES and MRS. E.S. THOMPSON, both of this place.

Apr. 6, 1864

Married at the residence of Col. J.T. Smith, Hancock county, by Rev. C.W. Stephens on the 23d inst., DR. J.E. CLARKE, of Hawkinsville, Ga., and MISS EMILY A. LATIMER, of Sparta, Ga.

June 1, 1864

Married on the 25th inst., COL. A.W. ANDERSON, Commandant of the post at Andersonville, to MISS SUSAN M. MALONE, daughter of COL. CHAS. J. MALONE, of Americus.

Nov. 16, 1864

Married on the 16th instant by E.C. Granniss, Esq., Justice of the Peace, DR. GEO. W. HUMPHRIES and MRS. MARCISNA SIMS.

Feb. 8, 1865

Married on the 7th inst. by E.J. Collins, Esq., at the residence of Mrs. Lamb, MR. HENRY HOWELL and MRS. E.A. LAMB, both of Twiggs county.

Married on the 9th inst. at the residence of Mrs. Burns, by E.J. Collins, Esq., J.P., MR. R.R. MANNING and MISS A.E. HARRELL, both of Twiggs county.

July 22, 1865 (daily)

Married in Houston County, Ga. on the 11th inst. by the Rev. J.R. Felder, MR. BEN C. KENDRICK and MISS MARTHA ADELLA CATER.

June 28, 1865 (daily)

Married at Fort Valley, Ga. on the 27th inst. by Rev. John M. Marshall, COL. ROBT. H. ROWLANDS, of Cass Co., to MISS CORNELIA A. HOLLINSHEAD (daughter of DR. W.H. HOLLINSHEAD).

Dec. 26, 1866

Married at the residence of the bride's father, JUDGE JERE PEARSALL, in Duplin county, N.C. on the 18th inst., MR. W. PITT BALDWIN, of Macon, Ga. and MISS F.C. PEARSALL, of the former place.

Married in Vineville on the 21st inst. at the residence of Thos. A. Brewer, by the Rev. David Wills, R.B. CLAYTON, ESQ., and MRS. ADALINE CORBIN.

Dec. 26, 1866

    Married at the residence of the bride's grandfather, BARTLY McCREARY, in Taylor county, on the 20th inst., by the Rev. Dr. Ross, MR. ELDRIDGE M. PERRY and MISS EMMA C. RENFROE.

Jan. 9, 1867

    Married on the 26th of November last by Elder Wm. C. Wilkes, MR. REUBEN WILLIAMS and MISS V.C., daughter of the late EDMUND CHAMBLISS, all of Monroe county, Ga.

    Married on the 20th of Dec. at her father's residence, by Elder Wm. C. Wilkes, PROF. HIRAM PERDUE, of Upson county, and MISS HELEN M., eldest daughter of JUDGE N.W. NEWMAN, of Forsyth, Ga.

Jan. 23, 1867

    Married on the 12th inst. at 39 Finsbury-square, London, England, by the Rev. D. Piza, assisted by the Rev. J. Piperno, MR. S. ISAACS (formerly of Macon, Georgia) to HANNAH, second daughter of the late JACOB HENRIQUES VALLENTINE, of 6 High-street, Shoreditch.

Mar. 27, 1867

    Married on the 20th inst. in Daugherty at the residence of the bride's father, HON. P.F. DUNCAN, MR. GEORGE C. BEAL, of Terrell co., to MISS MATTIE P. DUNCAN.

Feb. 5, 1868

    Married near Twiggsville, Twiggs county, on the 23d instant by Rev. E.H. Godwin, CAPT. D.W. SHINE to MRS. MARY SHINE, of Montezuma.

    Married by the same on the same evening, MR. C.A. VAUGHN, ESQ. to MISS VIRGINIA CAMPBELL, both of Twiggs county.

Dec. 8, 1868

    Married on the evening of the 1st inst. at the Presbyterian Church in this city, Rev. David Wills, D.D. officiating, CHAS. E. CAMPBELL to CARRIE A., youngest daughter of the late EDWIN B. WEED.

    Married in this city Dec. 3d by Mr. Burnett, J.P., MR. JOHN PLUNKETT to MISS MISSOURI SIMPSON.

    Married on the evening of November 25th, 1868 by the Rev. W.H. Clarke, at St. Paul's Church, Augusta, Ga., F.W. CLARKE, of Macon, to RUTH, youngest daughter of MR. E.W. DOUGHTY, of Augusta.

Dec. 15, 1868

    Married in Perry, Georgia at the Methodist Episcopal Church, on the evening of the 10th of December by Rev. W.C. Bass, GEORGE H. WHITE, ESQ., to EMMA C., youngest daughter of DR. P.B.D. CULIER, all of Perry, Ga.

Dec. 22, 1868

    Married on Thursday 17th December by Rev. H.K. Rees, Rector of Christ Church, MR. JAMES R. RICE to MISS MOLLIE P., daughter of WILLIAM MASSENBURG, ESQ., all of Macon.

Dec. 29, 1868

    Married on the 22d December at Americus, Ga. by Rev. J.N. Hall, MR. THOS. J. ANDERSON, of Macon, to MISS ANNIE E. SULLIVAN, of Americus.

Dec. 29, 1868

Married in St. Paul's Church, Baltimore, Md. on the 8th inst. by the Rev. Dr. Grammer, MR. THOMAS MAHOOL to MRS. AUGUSTA CLIFFE, both of Baltimore, Md.

Married in this city on the 23d inst. by the Rev. Jos. E. Key, MR. W.B. GOFF, of Houston county, and MISS LAURA A. SUBERS, of this city.

June 15, 1869

Married on the 26th of May at Rugly, the residence of the bride's father, A.J. BROWN, ESQ., by Rev. J.S. Hanckel, MR. GEORGE A. STALEY, of Savannah, Ga. to MISS SUSIE L. BROWN, of Albemarle co., Va.

Married in Hawkinsville, Ga. on the 3d instant by Rev. Chas. R. Jewett, MR. JNO. L. BOHANNON and MISS SALLIE E., daughter of JUDGE C.M. BOZEMAN - all of Pulaski county, Ga.

June 19, 1867

Married on Thursday evening June 6th at the Church of the Atonement in Augusta, Ga., by Rev. F. Marion McAllister, MR. HUGH H. COLQUITT, of Savannah, and MISS MEL G., daughter of D. REDMOND, of Augusta.

Jan. 15, 1868

Married by Judge E.W. Crocker, at the residence of Mrs. M.A. GRIFFIN, the bride's mother - on the 2d of January 1868 at 3 o'clock p.m., MR. A.F. BECKCOM and MRS. ELLA JOHNSON, all of Twiggs county.

Married in Christ Church by Rev. H.K. Rees on Thursday the 9th inst., N.C. MUNROE JR. to IOLA E., daughter of the late JUDGE HENRY G. LAMAR, all of this city.

Oct. 20, 1868

Married in Eufaula, Ala. at the residence of Mrs. J.T. Malone, by the Rev. Mr. Wharton, WILLIS S. COX to MISS HATTIE WINGATE.

Nov. 3, 1868

Married in this city on the 27th instant by Rev. Jos. S. Key, MR. O.D. EDWARDS and MISS E. ISADORE HOLLINGSWORTH.

Married in Vineville at the residence of the bride's father on the evening of the 28th inst. by the Rev. Warner Clisby, CAPT. B.A. WISE and MISS LOUISE CLISBY.

Married in Marshallville, Georgia on the 27th of October by Rev. E.H. McGehee, CAPT. THOMAS J. MASSEY to MISS MARY S. MASSEY.

Nov. 10, 1868

Married on the 5th of November 1868 in Griffin, Ga., by the Rev. Mr. Dow, MR. GEO. T. ROGERS JR., of Macon, to MISS MARY LOU SAULSBURY of Griffin.

Married on Saturday October 21st at the First Presbyterian Church, Brooklyn, N.Y. by Rev. R.S. Storrs, D.D., SAMUEL WESTON HASTINGS, of St. Louis, Mo., to FRANCES AUGUSTA, daughter of THOMAS WOOD, ESQ., of Macon, Ga.

Married at Covington, Ga. November 3d, 1868 by Rev. P.A. Heard, CAPT. GEO. S. JONES, of Macon, to MISS RUTH M., daughter of BENJAMIN F. CARR, of Covington.

Nov. 17, 1868

Married at the Mulberry Street Methodist Church in this city on Wednesday evening November 11 by Rev. W.C. Bass, MR. ANDREW W. REESE, editor of the Journal and Messenger, to MISS VIOLA, daughter of J.B. ROSS, ESQ.

Jan. 5, 1869

Married in this city on Thursday December 31st by the Rev. J.W. Burke, MR. BRIDGES W. SMITH to MISS ANNA S. WADE, both of Macon.

Married at the residence of Peter C. Sawyer, near Macon, on the night of the 30th December by the Rev. J.W. Burke, ORREN E. MASSEY to FANNIE E. HOLSTEEN, all of Bibb County.

Married in Atlanta on the 22d of December by the Rev. W.P. Harrison, GEO. W. BURR, of Macon, to NELLIE C., daughter of JOS. WINSHIP, of the former place.

Married at the residence of the bride's father in Twiggs County, Ga. on the evening of the 30th of December, by the Rev. W.D. Horn of the same county, THOS. A. WARD, of Twiggs County, to N.A., daughter of ELIAS JONES.

Jan. 12, 1869

Married on Tuesday evening December 31st, 1868 at the bride's residence, by Rev. E.M. Gilbert, HERMANN L. SCHREINER to MISS CASSIE GEMENDEN, all of this city. (Savannah Republican, 8th).

Married at the residence of the bride's mother, MRS. M.A. DAY, by Rev. E.W. Warren, MR. G.H. BROWNING, of Atlanta, to MISS E.J. HAMPTON, of Vineville.

Mar. 2, 1869

Married at the residence of the bride's father, MR. A.V. JACKSON, on the 23d of February 1869 by the Rev. W.T. Lowe, MR. A. JUDSON HAYGOOD, of Macon, Ga., and MISS L. BLANCHE JACKSON, of Clarke county, Ga.

May 18, 1869

Married on the 11th by the Rev. David Wills, MR. R.W. BASKIN, of Perry, and MRS. MARY IVES, of this city.

June 13, 1869

Married by Rev. W.C. Bass on the evening of the 8th instant, MR. JAMES W. HANCOCK and MISS _____, both of Bibb county, Ga. (Ed. Note: Paper torn - not legible).

Married on the 8th July in Bibb county by Rev. J. Blakely Smith, ALEXANDER S. McGREGOR and MISS FRANCES D. JONES.

Aug. 3, 1869

Married on the 29th ult. by the Rev. Mr. Langley, at the residence of Mr. John L. Holland, COL. S. WISE PARKER to MISS ELLA F. HUDNELL, all of Fort Gaines, Ga.

Married on the 27th ult. at the residence of Col. R.E. Kennon, by the Rev. W.L. Crawford, MR. M. TUCKER, of Fort Gaines, Ga. to MISS EMMA W. WHITE, of Clay county, Ga.

Married on the 27th ult. at the residence of the bride's father, by the Rev. W.L. Crawford, COL. R.A. TURNIPSEED, of Fort Gaines, Ga. to MISS SALLIE M. MARABLE, of Clay county, Ga.

Oct. 19, 1869

Married on the evening of the 12th inst. by W.S. Ogletree, J.P., at the residence of the bride's father, MISS JOSEPHINE B., daughter of HON. G.P. CULVERHOUSE to MR. JOHN W. LOWE, all of Crawford county, Ga.

Oct. 26, 1869

Married on the evening of the 21st instant at the Mulberry Street Church by Rev. W.C. Bass, JAMES H. CAMPBELL, ESQ. and MISS FANNIE, only daughter of MAJ. DAVID E. BLOUNT, all of this city.

Married in Wilkinson county, Ga., at Jos. N. Meadors', Esq. on the 24th of October by Rev. C.B. Anderson, REV. JESSE PEACOCK to MISS MARIETTA R. ANDERSON, of Forsyth county, N.C.

Index
Compiled by
Norma J. Norman Dunten
La Marque, Texas 77568

---, Dinah 312
    Edward 192
    Farrall 208
    George W. 408
    Hannah 36
    James Dwight 444
    James M. 436
    John M. B. 435
    Martha T. 444
    Mary M. 436
    Sarah 35
    Susan Amelia 435
    Wild Cat 216
ABBOTT, Franklin W. 308
    J. A. 375
    James O. 13
    Joel, Dr. 9
    Marian S. 432
ABERCROMBIE, Charles 261
    James 275
    John 6
    Martha Elizabeth 401
ABERNATHA, J. 364
ABERNATHEY, J. J. 375
ABERNATHY, Henry C. 394
    T. J. 368
ABLE, Dan 321
ABNEY, Baily 304
    W. 465
ABRAHAM, Morris 186
ACHORO (?), Lewis H. 84
ADAIR, George W. 476
ADAMS, 251
    Governor 276
    Ann Elizabeth 38
    Bennett 38
    C. 363
    Celia 456
    Daniel 111
    David R. 473
    E. B. J. 111
    E. H. 456
    Elizabeth 38, 111
    Ezekiel H. 285
    Frances 66
    George 225
    Henry P. 455
    James 66
    Jefferson 298
    John 7
    John Q. 231, 232
    Leonard A. 92
    Mrs. M. R. 261
    N. A. G. 375
    Peter 489
    Robert 261
    S. W. 364
    Stephen 213
    Susan V. 459
    W. 372
    Wm. 366
    Wm. E. 477
ADDISON, Andrew J. 159
    Eliza 404
    George B. 355
    James 355
ADGER, James 233
ADKINS, Chas. G. 74
    Joseph 348
AGILVY, J. D. 360
AIKEN, James 259
AINSLEY, Thomas J. 316
AINSWORTH, M. 511
AIRD, Geo. M. 244
ALBRIGHT, Wm. G. 362
ALBRITTON, Matthew J. 250
ALCOTT, Misses 306

ALDAY, -- 260
ALDEN, Allie V. 481
    Geo. W. 71
    Louisiana Susan 71
    Piety 71
ALDER, Wm. T. 495
ALDERMAN, Daniel 375
    Thos. 360
ALDRED, J. A. 384
ALDRICH, Latitia S. 437
    N. 438
    W. 437
ALDRIDGE, Thomas B. 121
ALEXANDER, A. L. 468
    Adam L. 178
    C. H. 306
    Catharine 69
    Collin W. 3
    Ebenezer 212
    Elam 293, 438
    H. L. 369
    Harriet Virginia 468
    J. Y. 482
    James Bolivar 97
    James F. 482
    Lizzie 501
    Mary Louisa 178
    Mary S. 455
    Peter 196
    Robert Attcherson 337
    Robert Mathew 3
    Robert R. 129
    Sarah H. 178
    Thos. W. 502
    Wm. F. 178, 470
    William W. 494
    Wlam 419
ALFORD, Collin 35
    George W. 35, 36
    Wm. T. 519
ALFRIEND, B. C. 282
    Laura Jane 282
ALISON, Matilda 409
    Paul 49
ALL, William 359
ALLBRITTON, Mathew J. 255
ALLEM, H. D. 375
ALLEN, Rev. Mr. 518
ALLEN, -- 222
    Alfred W. 483
    Alva 129
    Anna V. 164
    B. 24
    Benjamin 93
    Charles 143, 174
    Cornelia M. 486
    D. 375
    E. A. 496
    Eason 135
    Elijah P. 436
    Eliza 402
    E. W. 129
    Elizabeth 36
    Fariba 114
    Francis 70
    George 316
    Henry 98
    Hugh 114, 191
    J. M. 368
    Jas. P. 164
    John J. 471
    Joseph J. 485
    Lucinda A. 463
    M. A. 129
    Martha 174
    Mary E. 160
    Mary J. 511

ALLEN (cont.)
    Mary Jane 455
    N. B. 222
    Newton J. 191
    Robert A. 144, 486
    Robert E. 486
    Susanna 24
    Thomas 288, 455
    Velinda R. 114
    W. 278
    Walter C. 277
    W. H. 375
    Wm. 482
    Wm., Jr. 513
    William E. 428
    Willis 456
ALLEY, Mr. and Mrs. F. H. 318
ALLISON, -- 310
    J. H. 165
ALLMOND, B. W. 42
ALPHOUSE, Joseph 335
ALSTON, Col. 489
    -?- Iloclen 318
    Miss 400
    James 400, 416
    Margaret 395
    Mary Jane 503
    Philip H. 395
    R. W. 255, 489
    Robert W. 256
    Sue Willis 489
    Willis 396
ALTMAN, Richard 120
ALVERSON, C. P. 365
ALVESTON, A. H. 364
AMAR, Mrs. 334
AMASON, James H. 129
AMERSON, A. J. 383
AMMOND, J. N. 367
AMMONS, J. 373
    Jesse 165
AMOS, Adeline 442
    Henry 300
AMOSS, Loiusa 477
ANDERSON, A. W. 525
    Andrew T. 440
    Anna L. C. 274
    Annie 216
    C. B. 529
    Catherine 43
    Charles 326
    Clifford 274, 496
    E. L. 489
    Edward R. 208
    Elijah 397
    Eliza 232
    Frances E. 503
    Frances R. 484
    G. W. 291
    George H. 185
    George W., Jr. 519
    Henry 321
    Isaac 207
    J. 362
    J. L. 375
    J. M. 359, 375
    James 264, 279
    James L. 31
    John 95, 100, 484
    John I. 298
    John S. 132
    John T. 232
    L. 363
    Margaret 114, 415
    Maridley 132
    Marietta R. 529

ANDERSON (cont.)
  Mary A. 479
  Sarah M.
  R. W. 525
  Robert 431
  S. J. 364
  S. M. 448
  Samuel F. 493
  Samuel J. P. 435
  T. 361
  T. D. 383
  Thomas 357
  Thos. J. 526
  Tho. W. 43, 114, 185
  W. T. 375
  William 363
  Wm. F. 508
  William H. 122
  Wm. J. 446
  William LeConte 274
  Wm. Q. 249
  Wm. R. 31, 216
ANDRES, W. J. 365
ANDREW, Jas. O. 402
  Rev. Dr. 419
  A. C. 466
  A. G. 130, 468
  Bell 356
  Charlotte 429
  D. R. 471, 485
  Elizabeth 77
  G. W. 519
  Garnet 466
  Isaac 401
  J. B. 77
  J. H. 488
  Jas. 361, 422
  James W. 459
  Joanna S. 442
  John 318, 381
  L. F. W. 204
  Mary W. 499
  R. H. 365
  Robbins 408
  Robine 401
  Ruthy M. 408
  Sarah Elizabeth 471
  Sarah M. 130
  Tolcott B. 288
  W. 356
  W. J. 375
  W. O. 358
ANERCHACIM, Charles 311
ANGEL, Nathan 367
ANGLIN, Wm. 366
ANNESLY, Alexander 440
ANSLEY, Rev. Mr. 430
  Marlin 447
  Martin 447
  William 145
ANTHONY, Rev. Mr. 415,
    417, 434, 441, 442
  Jesse 224
  M. C. 383
  S. 439, 442, 473
  Samuel 410, 438, 464,
    468, 473, 479
APPLING, A. 380
ARANT, Christian 355
ARCHER, Hugh 223
  Williamston 415
ARGO, A. J. 375
ARGOLE, John W. 193
ARIGAL, John 476
ARMOR, James M. 489
ARMS, Elvira P. 418
  Lucius 47
ARMSTRONG, General 161
  Aaneas 507
  Charles Cray 190
  Chas. R. 190, 472
  J. J. 367
  J. W. 326
  James W. 516

ARMSTRONG (cont.)
  Sarah M. 190
  W. J. 373
ARNETT, Catharine 402
ARNOLD, Rev. Mr. 433
  Amie A. 507
  Francis 415
  Henry 366
  J. N. 326
  Luke 352
  M. W. 493
  Mary 137
  N. 316
  Narcissa 148
  Obadiah 177
  Peter 148
  Robert 352
  William 255, 461, 474,
    477, 504
  William W. 157
ARNOW, Miss 173
ARNSTOFF, Miss Isa G. 503
ARRINGTON, M. G. 363
  Temperance 425
  Thomas 15, 425
ARRISON, John 300
ARTHUR, Sarah 477
ARTIS, Alfred 175
  George 310
ARTOPE, J. B. 441
  Julia E. 341
  Mary E. 521
ASBELL, A. W. 468, 471
  Bryan 500
  Miss E. N. 500
  Elisha 455
  George R. 518
  Julia 455
ASHBURN, Geo. W. 338
  John C. 450
ASHE, Ann Eliza 496
  John S. 320
  Wm. S. 496
ASHLEY, Chester 111
  Hannah 392
  Jonathan 185
  Nat 333
ASHURST, S. G. 485
ASKEN, Jno. 361
ASPINWALL, James 122
ATCHISON, Hamilton 75
ATHERTON, Senator 147
  C. J. 157
  Charles H. 147
ATKINS, Hugh 260
  William T. 128
ATKINSON, Rev. Mr. 468,
    469
  E. A. 271
  Eliza A. 96
  G. W. 481
  J. T. 378
  Lewis 392
  Mary E. 509
  R. A. L. 96
  Robert H. 524
  William Albert 96
ATTANY, E. 370
ATTAWAY, Elizabeth 473
ATTIWAY, J. W. 444
ATWELL, Philo P. 391
AUDAS, H. W., Mrs. 240
  Henriette M. 234
  T. H. 240
  Thomas C. 234
  Tuttle H. 234
AUDOIN, Achilles 513
AUDOUIN, A. L. 481
AULDY, Wm. 370
AUSTIN, James M. 503
  Thos. A. 367
  Valentine 204
  W. W. 336

AVANT, Martha E. 512
  P. A. 365
AVERETT, Geo. 491
AWTREY, Newton 350
AYCOCK, W. C. 380
AYER, Dr. 349
  A. K. 229
  Benjamin 328
AYERS, C. L. 379
AYRES, B. B. 381
  Enos 397
  James B. 256
BABB, Pri 370
BABCOCK, Harriet A. 133
  J. W. 133
  John W. 436
  Lewis W. 145
BABER, Ambrose 26, 397,
    522
  Henry St. George 26
  Mary 26
BACHELOR, Mary E. 492
BACHLOTT, Kate 514
BACKLY, F. 378
BACKUS, Rev. Mr. 498
BACON, Jr. 173
  Miss 398
  Mr. 309
  Mrs. 19
  Francis E. 215
  John N. 27
  L. 207
  Robert J. 472
  Sarah 513
BAGBY, A. C. 135
  Ann E. 495
  Arthur P. 233
  Elizabeth 389
  Frances M. 407
  Martha G. 135
BAGGERLY, Rev. Mr. 450
  F. W. 448
BAGGETT, H. H. 375
BAGGS, W. A. 375
BAGLEY, J. M. 375
  Mrs. S. J. 512
  Sarah E. 512
  T. A. 363
BAGWELL, Wm. A. 277
BAHUSON, Geo. F. 499
BAILEY, Judge 429, 474
  A. Z. 519
  Amanda 349
  Caroline 406
  Eliza A. E. 474
  Eliza F. 150
  G. R. 384
  Gracy 465
  Henry M. 470
  J. O. 363
  James 432
  John 71, 281, 427
  Jonathan 358
  L. 363
  Martha C. 440
  Martha W. 103
  Mary 409
  Mary A. 508
  Milley 391
  R. M. 371
  Robert N. 381, 473
  S. T. 415, 508
  S. Armstrong 144
  Samuel T. 103, 150,
    397
  Theodorus, Gen. 14
  W. T. 361
  William 317, 461
BAILY, John 166, 413
  John B. 359
  Maria 400
BAIRD, Rev. Mr. 437
  Washington 452

BAISMORE, Monroe 431
BAKER, Rev. Mr. 419
  A. 384
  Benj. H. 23
  Daniel 222
  Edward 257
  John 323, 391
  John W. 414, 464, 473
  Jordan 414
  Lou Emma 493
  Martha 23
  Milton S. 415
  W. J. 509
  W. M. 375
  Wm. 199
BALBRIDGE, Ellen C. 194
  Joseph H. 194
BALDWIN, Henry 87
  John 170
  John S. M. 102
  L. H. 274
  Martha A. 423
  Mary 486
  Moses H. 429
  Robert P. 91
  W. Pitt 525
  Wm. W. 130
BALES, James 372
BALL, Henry E. 198, 216, 217, 459
  James M. 50, 489
  James Martin 198
  Joe 365
  Mary Virginia 198, 216, 217
  Nancy 50
  Wm. B. 390
BALLARD, Edward R. 29, 56
  Jack 319
  John P. 94
  Mary Ann S. 29
  Stephen 36
  Wm. M. 277
BALTON, Bryant 438
BALTZELL, Judge 234
  Thomas 234
BAMFORD, -- 334
BANCHUM, Thomas 358
BANDY, G. M. 383
  Mary H. 143
  W. C. 472
  William C. 143, 463, 485
BANE, Wm. 191
BANKS, Mr. 309
  E. A. 514
  G. H. 375
  George Young 475
  Harriet W. 133
  Jas. 133
  John H. 495
  Joseph R. 439, 468, 484
  Mary Lou 484
  P. E. 361
  Richard 196
  W. H. 133
BANNER, C. L. 499
  Emily E. 499
BANNKSTON, A. J. 375
BAPTIST, Edward 488
  Maggie L. 488
BARBEE, J. T. 363
BARBER, Henry 203
  James 368
  Jas. P. 371
BARBOUR, Col. 488
BARCLAY, -- 316
  J. C. 363
BARDWELL, E. J. 361
BAREFIELD, Wm. J. 367
BARER, Lawyer 350
BARFIELD, B. F. 343

BARFIELD (cont.)
  Ellen 343
BARKER, David 105
  John 349
  Joseph 105, 165
  Malissa 165
  Mary 165
  Mary Gardner 58, 59
  Nathaniel 58, 257
  W. H. H. 380
BARKSDALE, Jeffrey 27
BARLOW, Amanda 246
  George 71
  Mary E. 467
  Mary J. 498
  W. W. 246
  Winnie S. 518
BARNARD, Eliza A. E. 431
  Thomas A. 76
BARNEARD, D. G. 381
BARNER, Judge 181
BARNES, Judge 475
  Eliza J. 143
  Emily Gertrude 475
  J. 373
  Jackson 131, 434
  John 163
  Mary 131
  Moses D. 233, 235, 452
  Octavios Lafayette 163
  Patrick 367
  R. L. 397
  Thomas 368
  William 29
  William E. 143
BARNETT, N. C. 202
BARNEY, J. J. 370
  John 207
BARNS, Jas. H. 375
BARNUM, Wiley W. 316
BARR, Augustus P. 225
  Caroline A. 434
  Jas. 362
  John 102
  Margaret 401
  Samuel 321
BARRENTINE, J. M. 362
BARRETT, Caleb R. 495
BARRICK, J. R. 347
BARRIER, James 375
BARRINGER, John L. 172
BARRON, Bishop 170
  Rev. Mr. 436
  A. C. 492
  H. J. 490
  James 131
  James M. 446
  Thomas Greene 125
  Virginia C. 459
  W. T. 372
  William 404
  Wm. A. 500
BARROW, Harmon H. 424
  M. N. 484
  Mary 49
  Rebecca A. 49
  Susannah 421
  Warren 49, 421
BARRY, Geo. L. 343
  Osgood A. 343
  Wm. T. 39
BARSTOW, Wm. A. 303
BARTLETT, Rev. Mr. 516
  Charles Eugenius 133
  Cosam Emir 127
  Geo. T. 133
  J. E. 276
  Munroe 55
  Myron 28, 55, 108, 109, 401, 477
  Oglethorpe 28
  Rhoda 514
  Sarah T. 477

BARTLETT (cont.)
  Tabitha N. 108
  Virginia L. 133
BARTON, Benjamin 397
  Joshua 1
  Mary A. T. 497
  William 416
BARTOW, General 278
  F. S. 278
  Francis S. 205
  Theodosius 205
BARTREE, James R. 303
BARWICK, Stansel 506
  William 182
BASKIN, Alonzo P. 309
  H. P. 383
  Laura J. 309
  R. W. 528
BASON, William J. 354
BASS, Rev. Mr. 399
  Charles L. 414
  Jas. Aug. 181
  Miss L. L. 479
  N. 524
  W. C. 526, 528, 529
BASSETT, Catherine G. 442
BASSET, J. 488
  John 477
BASSETT, L. W. 458
BATCHELER, H. N. 190
BATCHELER, Mary D. 190
BATCHELOR, J. 361
BATEMAN, Bryan 419
  Martha A. 467
  Mary 419
  Bryant 349
  Simon 68
  Mrs. T. E. 524
  William 445
BATES, Agnes 345
  Anna D. 13
  Issachar 3
  John C. 218
  Rowell 279
  Martin W. 342
  Roxana K. 3
  Roxana Kendall 29
  Thomas G. 13, 29, 56, 393, 396
BATHROP, James J. 368
BATTEY, Eliza 522
  Eliza Lamar 504
  T. W. 504
BATTLE, Andrew 139
  Bertha 177
  Calvin W. 87, 439
  Caroline M. 139
  Henry L. 465
  H. L. 68
  H. N. 383
  J. 362
  Jesse B. 483
  Joseph 72, 222
  Jos. J. 418
  Louisa M. 473
  Martha Hightower 222
  Martha Jane 418
  Mary Ann 426
  Nicholas W. 443
  Rhoda 72
  R. T. 177
  Mrs. Settie 513
  Thos. 400, 403, 410, 426, 473
  William 48
  William W. 409
BAUGH, Alexander 345
BAXTER, James D. 366
  Margaret 16
  Mary E. 434
  Peter 314
  Robert 255
  Thos. W. 434, 479

BAYLISS, W. J. 365
BAYLY, Thomas H. 199
BAYNE, C. 398
BAYNES, R. 382
BAZEMORE, Jane 393
BEACH, Chauncy 67
   J. M. 362
BEACHNIAN, Mrs. 323
BEADLEN, Wm. 323
BEAL, Frances 431
   George C. 526
   James S. 236
   Mary Adaline 431
   Robert 390
BEALL, Judge 409
   Ann F. 405
   Antionette E. 428
   Caroline S. 417
   E. H. 485
   E. S. 370
   Eilliam E. 121
   Elias 75, 409, 435, 447
   Ellen A. 407
   Frederick 53
   J. 444
   Jesse S. 522
   John 326
   Josiah 398
   Julia Ann 409
   Juliet R. 521
   Margaret 420
   Mary 75
   Peggy 399
   Robert A. 28, 43, 395
   Samuel 218, 461
   Thos. 419, 422, 434
   Tho. N. 407
   William 326
BEALLE, Wm. F. 283
BEALLIE, James S. 236
BEARD, Edmund C. 389
   John W. 389
   Josephine 425
   Sarah 425
BEASLEY, Catharine 422
   Helen J. 443
   Jarrel 176
   John J. 389
BEAVERS, Charles G. 286
   Chas. J. 463
   Mary 286
   Richard M. 286
   Spencer M. 286
BECHUS, Thos. 367
BECK, Benj. 495
   F. R. 381
   John A. 505
BECKLEY, Wm. 373
BECKCOM, A. F. 527
   W. H. 338
BECKOM, Geraldine 338
   William H. 493
BECKUM, G. W. 375
BEDDINGFIELD, Lewis 83
   Robert 83
   Willis 462
BEDINGFILL, J. W. 383
BEDELL, Rev. Dr. 464
BEDENBAUGH, S. W. 513
BEE, Barnard E. 277
   Robt. M. 360
BEECHER, Samuel T. 401
BEEL, L. D. 143
BEELAND, M. A. Lizzie 507
BEEMAN, Carlisle P. 519
BEGGS, Andrew I. 379
BEHANE, Rachael A. 480
BELCHER, Mary E. 401
   W. T. 361
BELL, Admiral 338
   B. 372
   Clayton 205
   J. W. 361

BELL (cont.)
   James 213
   John 356
   John M. 372
   Lucinda B. 403
   Martha E. 477
   R. M. 369
   Sampson 205
   Samuel 213
   Sarah C. 189
   Thomas W. 189
BELLAMY, Alexander 405, 420
   Burton W. 522
   Val 221
   William C. 484
BELLER, James 501
BELLOW, J. 362
BELTZEN, Thomas 464
BELVIN, Major 227
BELWE, T. V. 363
BEMAN, Rev. Dr. 255
   Edward D. 255
   Kate 255
   W. C. 172
BEMBRY, Wm. 511
BEMETT, Rev. Mr. 425
BEMIS, Charles F. 516
BENARD, John J. 375
BENDEN, Thos. 517
BENDENBAUGH, S. W. 502
BENDER, Christiana 452
BENJAMIN, R. 368
BENNETT, J. A. R. 126
   J. C. 320
   J. M. 362
   Jas. W. 236
   James 336, 340
   Joel B. 46
   Joseph 147
BENSON, Joseph Wesley 117
BENNETT, Joseph Thomas 126
   L. S. 314
   Mary A. 126, 505
   R. 375
   Rev. Mr. 438
   S. W. 416
BENNEYFIELD, David 359
BENNING, Eliza Rowenna 402
   Sarah Amanda 59
BENSON, B. R. 380
   Caroline Elizabeth 117
   Richard A. 433
BENTON, Elizabeth 170
   J. G. 363
   J. W. 117, 464
   Jno. 367, 374
   N. E. 400
   M. S. 493
   Stephen Allen 300
BENTLY, Giddeon 223
   H. L. 375
BENTON, Col. 227
   A. 477
   Amos 286, 479, 522
   Archibald P. 396
   J. R. P. 382
   John 107, 117
   Mary A. 522
   Mordicai S. 428
   Sophiah 107
   Thos. H. 170, 336
BERAGLIE, -- 313
BERNER, Wm. R. 436
BERND, Joseph 261
BERRIEN, J. W. M. 245
BERRIEN, John 188
   John M. 401
   John Macpherson 188, 406
   Katherine H. 519

BERRIEN (cont.)
   Margaret 188
   Margaret L. M. 401
   Wm. Macpherson 188
BERRY, Andrew J. 490
   G. F. 492
   John F. 524
   M. P. 380
   Thomas Y. 490
BERTINE, John M. 179
BETHEL, Benjamin 471
BETHUNE, B. T. 123
   Benjamin T. 192
   Elizabeth 123
   James N. 404, 482
   John 282
   Marlor 192
BETLAY, B. F. 368
BETTON, Lucinda 24
   Solomon 24, 27
BETTS, -- 315
   Margaret 300
BEVERLY, Georgianna 460
BIBB, Martha 250
   Mary 197
   Wm. W. 197
BICKFORD, Geo. A. 348
BIDDLE, Judge 2
   Marks John 2
   Nicholas 86
BIEHLER, Peter 320
BIGHAM, Benj. H. 475
   Robert W. 503
BILLETTE, C. H. 383
BILLINGSLEA, Caroline 45
   James 18
   James Augustus 198
BILLINGSLEY, Mary W. 68
BILLUPS, E. A. 92
   Henry C. 494
   Thomas A. 13
BINDER, Jacob 207
BINNEY, James Ronaldson 54
BINWIDDLE, A. A. 363
BIRCH, Rev. Mr. 466
   E. P. 467, 481
   John L. 352
BIRD, Benj. 372
   Miss C. Dalton 437
   E. P. 470
   Frances 186
   Lucinda 412
   M. 359
   Newel 433
   T. 393
   Thompson 389
   W. H. 360
   William 186, 325
BIRDSONG, Caroline E. 491
   George E. F. 332
   George L. F. 424
   Louisa Pleasant 46
   Marcellus Stoval 23
   Mary 46
   Mary Anna Elizabeth 29
   Mary H. 29, 337
   Robert 23, 29, 46, 321, 491
   Sarah E. 498
BISCOE, William S. N. 461
BISHOP, Brinkly 128
   G. W. 138
   J. W. 457
   James B. 494
   James H. 98, 429
   James Herbert 98
   Laura A. 98
   Mary Augusta 494
BISSELL, E. E. 395
   Edwin E. 394
BISSEY, Amey 238
BIVENS, Samuel 69

BLIVINS, Ann Eliza 418
  Caroline L. 406
  Carrie 449
  Eliza W. 98
  Emeline C. 430
  George A. 518
  George W. 421
  James 167, 430
  James H. 490
  Jas. M. 478
  James S. 122
  Martha 268
  Mary 398
  Mary E. 506
  Mary F. 460
  Nancy 37
  Roland 191, 268, 279, 460
  Rolin 122, 215
  Mrs. Rolin 215
  Rollen 418
  Rowland 37
  Stephen 237
  Thomas 198, 200
  William 98, 125
  Wm. Thomas Clayton 37
  W. R. 375
BLACK, Alice 172
  Edward J. 119
  J. A. 361, 378
  Jane E. 172
  R. C. 285
  Robert C. 127, 468
  Sarah J. 127
  Thomas M. 226
  William 267
  W. W. 58
  Wm. A. 172
BLACKBURN, Harman 306
  John I. 199
BLACKFORD, Benjamin 184
  Wm. 184
BLACKLEY, Joseph 395
BLACKMAN, L. 363
BLACKSHEAR, Mrs. 322
  Ann 270
  Mrs. C. L. 285
  David 46, 185
  E. J. 211, 455, 516
  Edward Jefferson 141
  Elizabeth R. 499
  Fannie Maria 468
  Isabella S. 285
  J. W. 522
  James 468
  James David 211
  James E. 468
  Jas. Hamilton 285
  Marian 522
  Mary Jane 141
  Sallie Baines 185
  Susan 185
  Thos. 315
BLACKWELL, James 384
  John O. 359
  William 334
BLAIR, W. T. 385
BLAKE, Mrs. 347
  Clifton 453
  E. D. 53
  Mrs. E. 515
  E. Clifton 120
  Edmund 419
  Eleanor 268
  Eliza 102
  Green J. 102, 443
  James M. 122
  Luther 393
  Mary Adaline 89, 103
  Samuel R. 89, 103, 431, 448
  Zephaniah Edmund 89
BLAKEY, Dr. 261

BLAKELY, J. B. 365
BLAKEY, Mr. 261
BLANFORD, Clark 106
BLANTON, Clara P. 519
  James 28, 399
  James A. 46
  Wm. A. 519
BLATCHFORD, T. A. 373
BLAYSINGAMES, Mary E. 462
BLEDSOE, Robert 151
  Sarah E. 466
BLENNERHASSETT, Harman 171
  Jos. L. 171
BLISS, Col. 153
  James N. 20
BLITH, James 371
BLODGETT, Phineas U. 239
BLOIS, Theodore 340
BLOOD, E. B. 425
BLOOM, Eliza M. 426
  Franklin S. 285
  T. R. 458
BLOOMFIELD, William 301
BLOUNT, D. E. 493
  David E. 529
  Elizabeth 31
  Fannie 529
  James 31
  James H. 521
  Joseph G. 494
  Lavinia E. H. 395
  Mark Donald 120
  Mary A. 463
  Mary Ann 139
  Sarah A. R. 103
  Sarah R. 120
  Thomas H. 103, 120, 414
  Virginia 491
BLOW, Richard 427
BLUE, D. M. 383
  Sarah G. 513
BLUNT, Ann G. 391
  Martha E. 510
  Thomas 391, 397
BOAL, W. J. 374
BOARDMAN, Elijah 2
  George Maynard 198
  J. M. 173, 174, 198
  Maria T. 105
  Maria Therese 174
  Millie Pierpont 174
  Therese 173
BOATRIGHT, Amanda 513
  Rolly 513
BOATWRIGHT, James 213
BODIFORD, Moses J. 464
BOGGART, Wilhemus 354
BOGGESS, A. J. 279
  Ahaz J. 279
BOGGS, Rev. Mr. 502
  Joseph M. 143
BOHANNON, Jno. L. 527
BOIFEUILLET, Geo. A. 253
BOLTON, Wade 331
BOND, Elijah 505
  Harriet E. 508
  Henry 223
  Joseph 241
  Mary Louisa 409
  Mattie A. 505
BONE, Laura 475
BONNER, Mrs. B. A. 512
  B. F. 448
  E. L. 151, 152
  Hamilton 90
  John 397
  Mary 475
  Richard P. 475
  Lelila B. B. 510
  R. W. 151, 152
  Seymour C. 204

BONNER (cont.)
  Seymour R. 444, 489
  Walter 151, 152
BOOKER, J. C. 383
BOOKMAN, David 381
BOOKOUT, T. J. 375
BOON, Mrs. 131
  J. R. 131
  John R. 481
BOOTH, David S. 51, 390
  John M. 113
  John P. 24
  Permelia S. 390
  Teresa Margaret 24
  Wm. 228
BOOTHE, Sarah E. 451
  Theophilus D. 113, 451
BOREN, Emily P. 404
  M. P. 44
  Wm. E. 398, 416
BORIN, Louisa 393
  Mary 173
BORING, Rev. Mr. 447, 507, 508
  Ella C. 508
  Isaac 124
  Jesse 401, 499, 506
  Julia M. 499
BOROUGHS, Benjamin 169
  Joseph 169
BOSEMAN, Margaret 393
BOSTICK, Albert G. 187
  Aurelia 187
  H. H. 250, 465, 470
  Julia A. E. 470
  Nathaniel B. 516
  Robert Atkinson 187
BOSTON, John 297
BOSTWICK, A. G. 214
  C. C. 182
  Jas. B. 222
  Miss M. L. 520
  Margaret R. H. 409
  Robert 182
BOTTS, John M. 343
BOUCHE, M. 238
BOUDEL, Charles 318
BOUGHTON, S. H. 278
  Wm. P. 278
BOUM, B. 375
BOUYER, Adelaid Julia 431
BOWDEN, Frances 442
BOWDOIN, Abi R. 487
BOWDRE, Amelia 206
  Amelia M. F. 448
  Drusilla 403
  Effie M. 516
  Hays 203
  James 399
  P. E. 206, 448, 516
  Samuel 145
BOWEN, 250
  C. J. 223
  Francis M. 173
  Horatio 268
  J. E. 365
  James 255
  W. N. 280
  William B. 472
  Wm. P. 252
BOWERS, Charles L. 67
  Enoch T. 389
  Lloyd G. 477
BOWLEGS, Billy 244
BOWLES, J. W. 732
BOWMAN, Rev. Mr. 448
  F. 476
  John 187
  Sarah Jane 455
BOYD, John T. 146
  Linn 254
  Wm. 382

BOYDE, Lucy 111
    Richard 111
BOYDSTON, M. V. 362
BOYKIN, Ann C. 410
    James 410
    John T. 327
    Narcissa 479
    Samuel 111
    Samuel E. 470
BOYNTON, -- 397
    Elizabeth 482
    Hinton B. 174
    Joseph J. 432
    Moses 50
    Penelope 469
    Roba 174
    Roby 149
    Tabitha 50
    Willard 149, 174
    Willard B. 149
BOYT, James 201
BOZEMAN, C. M. 527
    E. K. 499
    Eli W. 50
    Emily 466
    Fanny M. 273
    John 402
    Lizzie 502
    Mary Jane 455
    Nathan 273, 466
    Sallie E. 527
BRABHAM, Agnes 305
    Hattie 305
BRACKBILL, Henry 6
BRADDY, H. S. 285
BRADEN, R. 362
    R. N. 311
BRADLEY, Elijah A. 445
    Eliza Jane 431
    Elizabeth C. 505
    John C. 442
BRADLY, Ann, Mrs. 426
BRADSHAW, Lott 368
BRADY, Alfred 399
    J. W. 384
    James T. 345
    William 220
    Wm. M. 206
BRAGG, Rev. Mr. 408, 409,
    410, 415, 417, 423,
    426, 427, 429, 430,
    432, 440, 443
    S. G. 412, 413, 414,
    416, 419, 422, 423,
    424, 425, 430, 431,
    432, 433, 434, 435,
    436, 437, 441, 442,
    443, 445, 451, 452
    Samuel 106, 137
    Sarah E. 427
    Sarah L. 106
    Senaca G. 270, 410,
    417, 431, 467
    Silas 312
BRAINARD, John G. C. 15
BRAKE, B. 172
BRALEY, Jas. 320
BRAME, Harriet P. 400
    Samuel C. 20
BRANAN, Jake 381
BRANCH, John L. 278
BRANCY, G. W. 359
BRANDON, Jas. A. 368
BRANDT, Henry C. 320
BRANHAM, Rev. Mr. 457
    Emily 298
    H. 132, 462, 475
    Henry 217, 218
    Indiana E. 475
    Isham H. 520
    J. R. 448
    Joel 263, 298, 520
    Mary 462

BRANHAM (cont.)
    Philip A. 362
    Valinda 132
    W. B. 449
    W. R. 450, 456, 487
    Walter 449, 453
    Walter H. 455
    Walter R. 453, 520
BRANSBY, Wm. 438
BRANTLEY, Benjamin 76
BRANTLEY, Benjamin 76
    Benjamin T. 240
    G. J. 361
    Jeptha 41
    Lilly O. 473
    Thadeus W. 425
    Thomas M. 523
    Zachariah 244
BRANTLY, Mrs. 196
    Rev. Mr. 418
    Benjamin 220, 415
    Chas. E. S. 181
    J. P. 369
    John 193
    Jno. H. 468, 472, 473
    John W. 196
    Macon Crawford 220
    Mark 274
    S. D. 460
    Sophronia E. 193
    Susan A. 181
    Susan F. 220
    W. T. 843
    Wm. S. 181
BRASWELL, Duke W. 417
    Jane E. 508
    S. N. 479
BRAXTON, W. J. 375
    W. Welch 368
BRAY, Catherine E. 275
    Clifford Willis 275
    Nathan M. 275
    Rufus 381
    Sarah A. E. 116
    Sarah Sims 125
    William H. 116, 125,
    450, 481
BRAZEAL, Josephine 475
BRAZIL, Marion 368
BREAZEAL, Miss H. C. 484
    Willis S. 403, 447
BRECK, Rev. Mr. 467, 498,
    500
    Martha R. 302
    R. L. 470, 476, 479,
    481, 482, 488, 494,
    496, 497, 505, 506
    Robert L. 302, 470, 472,
    479
BRECKENRIDGE, Robert J.
    313
BREDING, J. L. 359
BREEDLOVE, Martha F. W.
    396
BREITHAUPT, Col. 415
    Anna E. 410
    Christian 410
    Sarah L. 415
BRELAND, C. A. 361
BREMER, Caroline 312
BRENT, S. A. 431
    Wm. L. 431
BREWER, Catherine E. 433
    John W. 475
    Mary F. 198
    Mary G. Georgia 198
    T. A. 134
    Thomas A. 198, 433, 525
BREWSTER, Mrs. 335
BREWTON, A. M. 361
BRIANT, Wm. J. 367
BRICE, Geo. 185
BRICKHOUSE, C. P. 259

BRICKMAN, Frederick 325
BRIDGEFORD, -- 334
BRIDGER, Bartlett 159
BRIDGES, Mrs. Emily 512
    J. 375
    Nancy W. 506
    Susan 411
    W. H. 375
BRIDGEWATER, Captain 313
BRIDWEL, -- 310
BRIEN, John S. 336
    Mary Jane 509
    Sylvanus 509
BRIEVE, Miller 406
BRIGGS, Mrs. 173
BRIGHT, A. 366
    John M. 500
BRINKLEY, Augustus 257
BRINN, Sarah 481
BRINTNALL, Emily 507
    H. W. 507
BRISCOE, Lucilius H. 498
BRISTON, J. A. 358
BRITT, I. 356
    John 326
    W. 356
    W. G. B. 508
BRITTINGHAM, C. 498
    Martha H. 498
BRITTINHAM, Narcissa 405
BRITTON, Wm. 351
BROACH, George 93
    Rachel 93
BROAD, Mr. 300
BROADNAX, Frances A. 410
BROADWELL, H. M. 383
    W. A. 345
BROBERG, William 314
BROCK, A. J. 372
    T. W. 373
BROCKENBOROUGH, John 423
BRODDUS, Edward A. 133
BROMLEY, John 489
BROMWELL, Francis B. 273
BRONLY, M. 366
BRONSON, H. W. 422
    Mary B. 439
    Silas 316
BROOK, J. D. 375
BROOKIN, Maj. 147
BROOKING, Mrs. 465
    Frances V L. 389
BROOKS, Lt. T18
    Alfred 75
    Cephelonia Covington
    154
    Covington 154
    G. A. J. 468
    Iverson L. 400
    John 339
    Jno. P. 365
    Joseph D. 342
    Louisa C. 446
    Mary 448
    Micajah 268
    Preston S. 207
    S. E. 522
    Simeon 79, 422
    William H. 444, 450
BROOME, Gov. 175
    John Scott 175
BROUGHTON, E. 263
    Edward 462
    Frances E. 462
    John 507
BROWN, -- 234, 313
    A. 92, 400
    Major 429
    Rev. Dr. 395, 406, 418
    Aaron V. 241
    A. J. 376, 527
    Alexander D. 12, 390
    Allison Saxon 195

BROWN (cont.)
  Alonzo 107
  Annie M. 511
  Barbara Frank 411
  C. 375
  C. A. 431
  C. N. 277
  Catharine 438
  Chas. A. 419
  Chas. W. 477
  Crawford W. 223
  D. H. 453, 454, 457, 462
  David 282
  David M. 492
  Dempsey 462, 509, 513
  E. A. 92
  E. D. 484
  E. E. 291, 370, 425
  E. P. 501
  E. R. 203
  Edward G. 69
  Eliphalet E. 436
  Eliza A. 434, 462
  Eliza Ann 81
  Eliza P. 470
  Emily C. 12
  Elizabeth D. 181, 492
  Eppes 11
  Ethalina U. 430
  Eugenia M. 513
  Fenner 103
  George 138, 442
  George A. 401, 402, 409, 478
  Green 235
  H. M. 524
  Hardy 31, 455
  Israel 33
  J. 373
  J. A. 375
  J. W. 484
  J. Y. 375
  Jacob 13
  James 1
  James G. 375
  Joel 360
  John 203, 375
  John Dempsey 160
  John M. 298
  John R. 199
  John S. 382
  John T. 231, 342, 421
  Joseph E. 291
  Joseph Morgan 92
  Julia 138
  Laura P. 401
  Loam 509
  Louisa H. 455
  Lucia M. 228
  M. V. 375
  Maria L. 33
  Mary 14, 409, 453
  Mary A. 231
  Mary C. 195
  Mary J. 476, 502, 509
  Mitchell 434
  N. 358, 367
  N. B. 382
  Miss N. W. 509
  Narcissa 492
  O. V. 448
  Owen 14
  Penelope A. 465
  Rebecca 108
  Robert 108, 322, 430
  Robert C. 78
  S. T. 384
  Sallie C. 231
  Samuel 384
  Sarah C. 421
  Stephen 195
  Stephen F. 463

BROWN (cont.)
  Susie L. 527
  Thomas 458
  Thos. A. 81
  Virginia L. 458
  W. D. 294
  William 86, 367
  Wm. G. 408
  Wm. M. 453, 454
  Wm. Spencer 181
  William F. 12, 17
  William T. 228, 479
  Zenobia Palmyra 81
BROWNING, G. H. 528
  Philo 426
BRUCE, A. D. 316
  Doctor 442
  Archibald 328
  Augustus C. 94
  John M.
BRUNER, Lewis 438
BRUNSON, Wm. O. 341
BRUTON, -- 312
BRYAN, A. B. 385
  Benjamin 140, 146, 173, 182, 281, 397, 432
  Benjamin B. 249
  Benjamin W. 140
  Blackshear 78, 98, 146
  Catherine 157
  Catherine H. 272
  David 157, 479
  Elizabeth 289, 389, 463
  Ellen A. 449
  G. W. 363
  Hardy B. 444
  James A. 102, 272
  James C. 393
  Jennie E. 479
  Jno. 289
  John D. 187
  Joseph M. 146
  M. L. 475
  Nancy 126, 140, 281, 474
  Needham R. 69
  Penelope 432
  R. C. 462
  Roba 521
  Ruby 397
  Sarah 393
  Sarah A. 187
  Sarah E. 474
  Samuel 341
  Seaborn C. 474
  T. A. 372
  Temperance 78, 146
  William 521
  Wm. T. 157
BRYANT, David 340
  G. W. 371
  J. D. 380
  J. R. 375
  Jas. L. 369
  Jno. 365
  O. L. 340
  W. D. 382
  W. J. 374
BRYCE, James E. 243
BRYNE, Richard 331
BRYSON, Miss E. 470
  H. C. 470
  Harper C. 163
BUCHANAN, Ex-Pres. 319
  Rev. Mr. 392, 393
  B. B. 404
  D. 399
  James 485
  John 475
  Martha 437
BUCHANON, W. W. 370
BUCK, W. E. 350

BUCKANAN, Mary G. 463
BUCKLEY, Edward C. 404
  Francis H. 76
BUCKNER, Alfred 470
  Elizabeth 474
  Justice M. 415
  Lucy A. E. 474
  Reason 474
BUDD, Richard F. 192
BUELL, Wm. P. 443
BUEN, Henry 393
BUFORD, Lizzie 510
  Simeon 134
BUGG, Elizabeth W. 400
BUKER, Edwin W. 296
BULKEY, Anna 278
BULKLEY, Edward C. 72, 87, 298
  Harriet J. 72
  Seneca Bragg 298
BUCKLY, E. C. 522
BULKLY, Jane R. 522
BULL, J. B. 198
  O. A. 338
BULLARD, Rev. 436
  Stephen 36
  Susan 500
BULLION, Hardy J. 375
BULLOCH, Archibald 137
  William B. 137
BULLOCK, Amaretta S. 427
  Charles 19, 20, 24, 93, 394
  Daniel 93
  Eliza A. 24
  Elizabeth W. 392
  Evelina 425
  George C. 157
  Irwin 157, 158, 427
  James S. 115
  Mary Ann 412
  Uriah B. 158
  Uriah Irwin 163
  Uriah J. 424
  Mrs. W. B. 319
BUNCE, William J. 221
BUNN, Rev. Mr. 516
  H. 469
  Harriet M. 407
  Henry 393, 407, 466, 497, 500, 504
  Marcus H. 433
BUNYARDS, J. 362
BURBANK, J. 118
  Jacob A. 448
  Jacon 118
BURCH, Mrs. 270
  Edward A. 135, 140
  E. P. 499
  Joseph 482
  Mary Ann 135
  Mary C. 439
  Mary Edith 140
  Morton N. 286
BURCHARD, Samuel B. 440
BURDELL, J. R. 372
BURDICK, George 512
  Benjamin 197
  Mary A. 197
  Mary Alice 197
BURDINE, John M. 416
BURDON, -- 437
BURDSALL, William R. 242
BURDSHAW, J. D. 359
BURFORD, Mrs. 231
BURGAMY, Wm. 368
BURGAY, Martha, Mrs. 497
  William 326
BURGE, -- 120
  Elizabeth 265
  H. A. 483
  J. L. 265
  Mary Ann E. 490

BURGEVINE, Henry 304
BURK, W. H. 371
BURKE, Antoinette P. 483
  C. A., Mrs. 261
  Daniel 134
  Elliott Chase 261
  Henry F. 446
  J. W. 261, 515, 523,
    528
  John W. 514
  Nora M. 523
  Richard E. 287
  T. A. 522
BURKETTE, Orland 517
BURKETT, Mrs. 364
BURKHALTER, D. N. 453
BURKITT, Joseph U. 501
BURNAM, William 296
BURNAP, L. 33
BURNET, John W. 299
BURNETT, C. C. 498
  Jeremiah 119
  Rachel 402
  S. B. 498
  Sam'l 432
BURNEY, John W. 483
  S. F. 125
BURNHAM, Wm. C. 155
BURNS, Cornelia 119
  Georgia Ann 466
  J. W. 375
  James 296, 466
  James C. 119
  Mary Ann 119
BURR, A. P. 301
  Augustus 422
  Geo. W. 528
BURRELL, C. 371
  Otto 310
BURROUGHS, Alethia 172
  Berrien 172
  Reuben 27
BURT, Gov. 173
  Armistead 347
  Martha Calhoun 347
BURTON, G. W. 380
  Jno. 363
  John W. 436
BURWELL, Thomas N. 343
BUSEY, James 444
BUSH, B. J. 362
  J. H. 279
  W. S. 354
BUSHING, O. H. 365
BUSSEY, B. P. 508
  W. D. 438
BUSTAIN, Ed. 319
BUTLER, Mrs. 53, 400
  A. J. 281
  Andrew P. 213
  B. F. 235
  Champion 100, 443
  David B. 76
  E. C. 481
  E. M. 473, 477
  Elizabeth C. 443
  Elizur 210
  G. M. 278
  Gersham 74
  H. J. 366
  Jane E. 473
  John 251
  Louisa 100
  Mary H. 477
  R. J. 307
  Thomas 122
  Troup 466
BUTTERWORTH, S. A. 381
BUTTREEE, John 400
BUTTREILL, Britton 207
BUTTRELL, T. T. 520
BUTTRILL, William 207
BUTTS, A. G. 516

BUTTS (cont.)
  C. 370
  Elijah 272
  Henry 422
  James R. 331, 429
  Jas. S. 501
  Laura E. 516
  Louisa C. 422
  Martha 509
  S. 242
BYERS, James 372
BYINGTON, A. F. 293
  Charles A. 293
  James L. 345
BYRD, Abraham C. 399
  Benton 462
  Fannie E. 511
  J. C. 326
  Wm. J. 369
BYRES, W. 365
BYRON, Ann 183
CABANISS, Mrs. Judge 273
  E. G. 443, 457
  Eliza J. 457
  Geo. A. 496
  Harrison 435
  Mary 443
  Sarah 435
  Sarah H. 435
CABELL, Governor 147
  E. C. 147
CADE, D. B. 510
  Jack 248
  R. D. 364, 373
  Sallie E. 510
CADISH, Benj. 361
CADWELL, A. T. 376
CAGLE, Benjamin 405
CAIN, Phillip 201
  R. A. 463, 467, 508
  Richard A. 451, 456,
    471
CALDEN, Albert A. 309
CALDER, E. E., Mrs. 352
CALDERWOOD, John 465
CALDWELL, Mr. 190
  C. Y. 446, 479
  Charles 46
  Charles Y. 155, 169,
    237, 443
  Elizabeth 419
  George W. 46
  H. 173
  James L. 503
  John H. 510
  Julia A. E. 446
  Martha G. 443, 479
  Mary 46
  Samuel 439
  Samuel H. 479
  Wm. 458
  Wm. T. 359
CALHOUN, A. T. 425
  E. 19
  Elbert 72, 200, 399,
    421
  Elizabeth S. 421
  John C. 123, 145, 183,
    233
  Levi 193
  Lucy B. 145
  Margaret Jane 19
  Martha A. S. 485
  Martha Cornelia 213
  Mary M. 469
  R. H. 382
  Susan 450
  Thomas 171
  Wm. H. 402
CALL, J. O. 382
CALLAHAN, John 317
CALLAWAY, Rev. Mr. 418
  A. C. 286

CALLAWAY (cont.)
  Edward 435
  H. D. 475
  Henrietta A. 435
  Joel T. 497
  Wm. A. 414
CALLEN, Eugenia 504
CALLEY, James R. 477
  J. T. 383
CALLOWAY, Caroline 406
  Edward 406
  J. 391
  John W. 168
  Joshua S. 397
CALLIER, Fannie D. 493
CALLY, J. T. 384
CALTS, A. H. 369
CAMAK, Jas. 104
  Thomas U. 482
CAMBELL, Ophelia E. G.
    483
CAMILLA, Laura 397
CAMP, G. H. 337
  H. 515
  W. E. 366
  William 337
CAMPBELL, Miss 53
  Rev. Mr. 400, 448
  Col. 53
  A. J. 366
  Archibald M. 403
  C. 470
  Catherine 49
  Charles 255
  Chas. E. 526
  Charter 163
  Colin C. 262
  D. C. 519
  David C. 287
  Duncan G. 14
  Edward F. 282
  Emily S. 411
  Emma O. 516
  Flora A. 449
  Frances 420
  Frances A. M. 394
  H. T. 358
  J. 382
  James 274
  James A. 29, 409
  James H. 529
  James P. 29
  Jane 50
  J. Bulow 496
  Jehu 49, 405, 413,
    421, 426
  Jesse 433
  Jesse H. 432, 447, 450
  J. H. 421, 433, 436,
    507
  J. R. 443
  John 211, 310
  John G. 166
  John W. 122
  Margaret 91
  Mary Jane 409
  Rebecca Caroline 410
  Susan 396
  Thomas 32
  Virginia 526
  Walter L. 165
  Wm. 91, 262
CANDLER, Georgia 514
  Henry A. 94
  John 107
  John R. 421
  Milton A. 500
CANNON, D. J. 499
  Mary 315
  William 289
CAPERS, Ann S. 31
  Carolina Calhoun 31
  G. 402

CAPERS (cont.)
  Gabriel 31
  Mary 402
  Thomas Humphries 405
  William 177
CAPHS, J. A. 285
CAPPS, Hamilton 223
CARACTER, J. 370
CARAWAY, Thomas 505
CARD, Adam 229
  Mary 146
CARDEN, Catherine 433
  Charles, Capt. 21
  J. A. A. S. 380
CARDIN, Charles F. 206
  Charles T. F. 490
  Thomas M. 249
CARDRY, D. 363
CARDWELL, J. 359
CAREY, -- 374
  M. A. 163
  Matthew 59
CARGILE, Julia A. 460
CARHART, James D. 444
  George B. 460
CARLES, Wm. P. 36
CARLETON, Annie M. 500
  I. M. H. 130
CARLISLE, James B. 296
  V. 370
CARMICHAEL, Judge 474
  Geo. B. 277
  Gilbert C. 438
  Hugh 474
  John C. 484
  Wm. P. 470
CARNALD, William 290
CARNELL, W. C. 373
CARNES, Charles E. 511
  Peter J. 411
  Wm. E. 40
  W. W. 466
CAROLINUS, -- 321
CARPENTER, W. 364
CARR, Benjamin 260
  Benjamin F. 527
  H. 391
  Ruth M. 527
  Susan A. 494
  William 316, 370, 390
  Wm. A. 259
CARRAWAY, Samuel 148, 150
CARRELL, T. 363
CARRINGTON, -- 306
  T. B. 192
CARROLL, Alex. 201
  J. H. 513
  Susan 53
  Thos. W. 53, 420
  Turner 376
  William 87
CARRUTHERS, Richard C.
  214
CARRY, M. C. 374
CARSON, Bersheba 390
  Jas. P. 366
CARSWELL, Jennie 502
  John G. 502
  M. J. 504
  W. C. 368
CARTER, Mrs. Dr. 335
  Rev. Mr. 428
  B. B. 299
  Benjamin F. 192
  Caroline Eulalia 85
  Charles 319
  Edward P. 493
  Emily 114
  F. 192
  Farish 275, 409
  Henry K. 85
  J. 360, 414
  J. M. 384

CARTER (cont.)
  J. N. 493
  James 432
  John E. 48
  M. M. 361
  Margaret E. 303
  Mary 471
  Nancy 317
  P. H. 368
  R. P. 359
  Richard 118
  Robert 352
  Savannah 472
  W. Y. 369
  Wm. 369
  Wm. W. 447
  Willie 352
CARTFIELD, M. 372
CARTHY, Henry M. 368
CARUTHERS, J. W. 278
CARVENOUGH, Jas. 336
CARVER, Dellie B. 514
  Ann Eliza 128
  Miss M. E. 517
  Robert 128, 470, 514
CARY, Charles W. 498
  George 82
  Scott 124
CASEY, Mr. 327
CASH, G. W. 371
  Mary J. 481
  Steward 368
CASHON, T. 371
CASON, Margaret 74
  P. F. 490
  Samuel 74
  Seth 74, 450
CASS, General 149
  Mrs. 149
CASSELS, Rev. Mr. 414,
    416, 426
  R. K. 376
  S. G. 420
  S. J. 151, 416, 419,
    420, 423, 424
  Samuel J. 418, 419, 425
  Sarah Ann 68
CASSIDY, Eliza 465
CASTELLOW, Rev. Mr. 441
CASTELAW, Stephen 475
CASTENS, Ann 130
  James W. 130, 436
CASTLEN, F. G. 516
  John 439
  Kate M. 518
  Sarah E. 439
CASTTIN, John 256
CASWELL, General 25
  William 398
CATER, A. E. 215
  J. E. 184
  Lucia Johnson 184
  Martha Adelia 525
  T. J. 184, 215
  Thomas J. 433
  Thomas Wimberly 215
CAUBLE, Franklin 358
CAUSEY, D. M. 449
  David M. 113
  Wm. J. 450
CAVEN, Lizzie J. 510
CAVENRY, Michael 153
CAVR, N. J. 380
CECIL, Eliza 406
CH----ING, Wm. A. 381
CHAFFIN, John 368
CHAIN, Elizabeth 113
  Irene C. 113
  John 398, 399, 401,
    403
CHAINE, Mrs. E. A. 448
CHAINS, G. A. 473
CHAIRES, Ben 506

CHAIRES (cont.)
  Benjamin 440
  Martha 506
CHAIRS, Ben 251
  Emmina 460
  Green H. 460
CHAMBERLAIN, B. F. 191
  Elliott R. 475
  Remembrance 191
  Theophilus M. 10
CHAMBERS, James M. 204
  John L. 204
  Martha J. 204
  S. J. 384
  T. J. 371
  Thos. J. 363
CHAMBLESS, Edmond 428
  Jackson 442
  Zachariah 343
CHAMBLISS, Anna M. 465
  Edmund 526
  Mary B. 483
  Miss V. C. 526
  William 466
CHAMPION, Francis J. 520
  Henry 37
  Martha Ann Camilla 37
  Murphey 12
  Thos. J. 517
CHAMPLAIN, Guy 36
CHAMPLIN, G. 400
CHAMPMAN, Mary A. E. 480
CHANCY, J. B. 372
CHANDION, W. N. 520
CHANDLER, A. J. 380
  Asa 498
  C. P. 302
  Don Carlos W. 467
  T. M. 367, 374
CHANGE, Stimpson 49
CHAPLIN, John 347
CHAPMAN, A. W. 445
  Ambrose 52, 73, 426,
    472
  Asa W. 106
  Augustus B. 177
  Bradford T. 426
  Caroline M. 84
  Elizabeth 73
  Elizabeth A. 426
  Henry J. 52
  Henry Jefferson 84
  Isaiah 67
  John 500
  John T. 167
  Lydia 17
  Nathaniel 152
  Sarah W. 106
  Stephen D. 428
  W. W. 250
  William W. 84, 426
CHAPPEL, Rev. Mr. 410
  John 15
  Thomas S. 106
CHAPPELL, A. H. 497
  Benjamin T. 47
  Henry 137
  Roxey Ann 499
  T. S. 499
  Wm. 240, 491
CHARES, Geo. 318
CHARLES, Edwin 352
CHARLTON, John Fulton 246
  John K. M. 13
  Mary Theresa 246
  Robert M. 160
  T. U. P. 40
  Wm. Oscar 246
CHASE, Albon 312
CHASTAIN, James 462
  John M. 412
  Wm. 278
CHATHAM, Dr. 262

CHEATS, B. S. 521
  Carrie M. 521
CHEEK, Walter 320
  Wm. P. 366
CHENEY, Ann Eliza 506
  Aquila 329
  Bobbie 208
  Mrs. E. B. 208
  J. L. 208
  John L. 506
CHENY, Aquilla 485
  Louisa V. 485
CHERRY, Addison P. 518
  Hilliard J. 449
  Joel T. 414
  Joshua 460
  Thompson 211
  William A. 442
  William M. 140
CHEVES, Judge 181
  Francis H. 325
  Langdon 215
CHEW, B. F. 491
  Lucia A. 491
CHEWING, J. S. 359
CHILDENS, John S. 245
CHILDERS, Elizabeth P. 468
  John S. 333
  Malinda 409
  Martha J. 424
  Nathan 468
  Sarah E. 439
  Y. B. 375
CHILDRESS, A. A. 371
CHILDS, Benjamin D. 284
CHILES, Joseph 423
CHILTON, Joshua 292
CHIPMAN, Father 273
  Rev. Mr. 430
CHISHOLM, John 191
CHISSMAN, Joseph W. 497
CHITTY, L. M. 248
CHOAT, Jacob J. 453
  Julia Anne 453
CHOATE, Rufus 247
CHOATES, Leslie L. 141
CHOICE, W. A. 237
CHOTARD, John Alexander 46
CHRISTIAN, Rev. Mr. 411
  Gabriel 427
  Henry P. 427
  Isaac, Jr. 165
  Thos. T. 517
CHRISTIE, Eliza N. 481
CHRISTOPHER, H. 514
CHRYSTIE (CLARYSTIE), Mr. 14
CHURCH, Mr. 214
  Mrs. 271
  Rev. Dr. 271, 498
  A. 410
  Alonzo 430
  Calven 358
  M. E. 42
  Mary 451
  Maria N. 60
  Nathan 132
  R. E. 42, 60
  Rodman E. 61
  Robert L. 3
  Rollin Leonidas 42
CHURCHILL, Wm. L. 342
CISNEY, Theophilus 310
CLACK, James 405
  Wm. F. 408
CLAIBORNE, J. F. H. 356
  John 161
  Willis H. 356
CLANTON, N. H. 187
CLAPP, John Milton 221
CLARK, -- 229
  Governor 38
  A. F. 384

CLARK (cont.)
  Adeline 439
  Anna Beverige 216
  Ann M. 489
  B. H. 193
  Benj. W. 118
  Chas. A. 309
  Chauncey 3
  D. F. 76
  Daniel F. 412
  Edward C. 130
  Edward Henry 76
  Eliza 412
  Elizabeth 443
  Eloisa 76
  Emily E. 491
  Ezekiel D. 198
  G. C. 476
  G. R. 505
  George 94, 439, 486
  Isaac S. 487
  J. B. 278
  J. G. 376
  J. M. 470
  Jeremiah 118, 443
  Joanna W. 464
  John C. F. 414
  John T. 522
  Joseph 7
  Joseph Hill 39
  Julius 50
  L. M. 381
  Levinia 401
  Louisa 481
  Lucy 261
  Mark D. 103
  Michael N. 232
  Mosely 342
  Nancy M. 103
  Noel 39
  Col. and Mrs. R. H. 216
  R. W. 38
  S. D. 234
  Sallie J. 510
  Stephen J. 495
  Susan A. 479
  Thomas B. 486
  W. F. 376
  Wiley D. 276
  William F. 406, 429
  Z. H. 479
CLARKE, Rev. Mr. 489
  Mrs. A. C. 470
  Emma C. 515
  F. W. 526
  G. C. 519
  Geo. C. 517, 523
  Georgia A. 229
  Georgia S. 506
  Henry 419
  Isabella 76, 77
  J. E. 525
  Jack D. 15
  James 58
  Mark D. 126, 217
  Martha-Ann 15
  Mary Virginia 459
  Nancy M. 217
  S. P. 229
  Sarah R. 414
  W. H. 521, 526
CLAY, C. C. 362
  Henry 141
  Hugh L. 483
  M. J. 503
CLAYTON, A. S. 19
  Augustine C. 56
  Augustin Smith, Jr. 19
  Carrie 234
  Charles Augustus 30
  D., Dr. 20
  Delamar 45

CLAYTON (cont.)
  Eliza D. 212
  Eliza Mildred 30
  Elizabeth A. 30
  Elizabeth W. 212
  Geo. R. 65, 160, 418, 421
  Leonora Valerea 30
  Mary B. 246
  P. A. 234
  Philip A. 30
  Philip Augustus 395
  Philip P. 454
  R. B. 525
  Richard 149
  Robert B. 390
  Susannah 20
  William 212
CLEGG, F. 359
CLEMENCE, Charles P. 14
CLEMENS, U. J. 376
CLEMENTS, Henry 333
  J. A. 518
  James 258
  John A. 455
  Lucy 409
  Ralph 258
CLENDINEN, Araminta Jane 68
CLEVELAND, A. C. 152
  Absalom C. 406
  Allen 349
  Daniel R. 45
  Early 402
  James 88
  Jesse F. 88
  Mary F. 88
  Nancy 141
  W. 376
  W. C. 141, 280, 462
  W. C., Jr. 280
  Washington C. 454
  William 459
CLEWELL, F. C. 311
CLIFFE, Augusta, Mrs. 527
CLIFTON, W. C. 483
CLINCH, Gen. 431
  Eliza Bayard 431
CLINTHERALL, Alexander B. 345
CLINTON, De Witt 13, 182
  R. A. 367
CLISBY, Louise 527
  Warner 527
CLONTZ, A. M. 503
CLOPTON, Ann G. 411
  David 117
  J. W. 384
CLOUD, Rev. Mr. 494
  A. E. 512
  A. H. 383
  George 315
  Maggie V. 521
  N. M. 358
CLOWER, James M. 454
  Lurany 240
  Peter 106, 134
  Stephen 106
CLUAR, W. T. 373
CLUKE, R. S. 297
COALSON, Andrew J. 458
  Sallie H. 500
  William S. 116
COALTER, Miss 262
  David 262
COATES, Charles 91
  Elizabeth Rea 91
  Elizabeth W. 91
  Nathaniel 459
  Henry 223
  John G. 399
  William H. 223
COBB, Gen. 323

COBB (cont.)
  A. 376, 380
  Ethelia Jane 500
  Howell 61, 147, 187,
    275, 341, 426
  Mrs. Howell 145, 354
  Jane 159
  John, Jr. 234, 246
  John A. 187
  Lamar 521
  Mary Ann 61
  Mary K. 471
  Mary S. 426
  Peyton B. 164
  Rebecca 275
  Thomas 27
  Thomas R. 187
  Thos. S. 483, 500, 505,
    506
  Wm. A. 159, 164, 471,
    481, 500
  Zacharian Lamar 61
COBBS, Laura Rootes 145
COCHRAN, John 198
  Jno. A. 519
  John R. 476
  Mary Jane 198
  M. W. 375
COCHRANE, A. E. 230, 522
  Rebecca M. 230
  R. J. 512
  W. F. 364
COCKERELL, T. 371
CODY, Anna E. 512
  C. C. 512
  Terence 425
COFFEE, Gen. 229
  Rev. Mr. 438
  J. M. 368
  John 43
COFFIN, Patrick 153
  Robert S. 10
COGART, Abram W. 446
COGGIN, J. N. 358
  Wm. 268
COGGINS, James 232
COHAN, J. G. 512
COHN, Leopold 171
COHORN, James 20
COHRAN, Jasper 197
  Jesse 197
COLBERT, Frances A. 424
  Jonathan 483
  O. M. 106
  Sarah J. 469
  Thomas 241
COLBY, John 429
COLCLOUGH, Lizzie 487
COLDING, Delia 517
COLDWELL, A. C. 408
COLE, Anne E. 520
  C. B. 520
  John J. 371
COLEMAN, D. S. 380
  Elizabeth 59
  J. H. 373
  Judith S. 6
  Mary J. 113
  Richard 282
  Robert 6, 65, 393, 515
  T. S. 524
  W. R. 375
  William R. 256
COLEY, Eliza E. 452
  Eugenia A. 522
  J. A. L. 180
  John A. D. 452
  Mary J. 497
  Wm. 497
COLQUITT, F. 370
  Hugh H. 527
COLLIER, Clarence 354
  Isaac C. 62

COLLIER (cont.)
  J. 376
  James 372
  M. 361
  Mary E. 520
  Meril 461
  Nancy 439
  N. W. 417
  Nancy W. 461
  Robert 121, 394
  Sarah 394
COLLIN, B. F. 370
COLLINGS, E. P. 299
COLLINS, Dr. 3, 271
  Judge 411
  Mrs. 53
  Bell 300
  E. J. 525
  Chalkeey B. 47
  Charles 33, 53, 81,
    206, 299
  Mrs. E. 218
  Elisha P. 503
  Elizabeth 439
  Harriet 33
  Hamilton Stephen 81
  H. G. 381
  Harriet E. 32
  J. A. 212
  Judy 60
  Juliet R. 519
  Louis 133
  Louisa E. 133
  Mattie 218
  P. A. 359
  Patrick 336
  Robert 32, 156, 218,
    519
  Sarah Sophia 206
  Sophia F. 206
  Stephen 133
  Susan E. 503
  Thomas 60, 73, 336,
    439
  W. J. 499
COLLUM, Erasmus 360
COLQUITT, A. H. 180
  Alphia 67
  Dolly 180
  Walter T. 67, 180,
    184, 430
COLSON, Hope H. 350
  Martha A. 350
COLTART, John G. 339
COLTON, Calvin 209
COLVARD, Alpheus 194
  Alpheus C. 446
COLWELL, James S. 459
COLZEY, E. F. 472
COLZY, E. F. 187
  Mary Seline 187
COMAS, Jno. 362
COMBS, A. Augusta 501
  Geo. D. 425
  John 123
COMER, A. 455, 483
  Alfred A. 398
  C. Victoria 455
  Harriet Clestia 483
  John A. 498
  W. W. 376
COMFORT, R. 363
COMICO, B. T. 373
COMPTON, Jordan 143
  M. 379
CONE, Edwin 22
  F. H. 508
  Jane Victoria 508
  Jesse W. 292
  O. 72
  Peter 304
  W. G. 294
CONGER, Stephen H. 457

CONGLETON, A. 448
  Burton A. 252
CONLEY, J. H. 373
CONN, Jos. 369
CONNALLY, Charles Turner
    81
  Emma V. 494
  James 81, 108
  Mary S. 453
  Patrick B. 453
  Sarah C. 81
CONNELLY, Mrs. 166
  P. B. 150
  Robert F. 504
CONNER, Rev. Mr. 483
  J. C. 376
  John 431
  T. B. 376
  Zephaniah T. 407
CONNOLLY, Patrick 336
CONNOR, Miss 322
  Rev. Mr. 480
  Edward 348
  F. 376
  John 368
  Margaret 171
  W. G. 477
CONRAD, Robert T. 229
CONROY, Michael 369
CONSTADT, Jacques 324
CONVERSE, Rev. Mr. 397
CONY, Captain Joseph S.
    309
CONYNGHAM, Mr. and Mrs.
    355
COODE, R. 363
COOK, -- 310, 384
  Judge 481
  Rev. Mr. 431
  A. M. 312
  Adrian Susan Louisa
    463
  Asa B. 397
  Augustin 217, 463
  Caroline 396
  David A. 461
  Elizabeth 59
  Elizabeth Ann 58, 60
  Emily H. 312
  Francis 517
  George W. 426
  H. L. 60, 92
  Henry L. 58, 109, 427
  Jennie M. 517
  Joel 360
  J. R. 486
  J. (?) R. 450
  John R. 138
  Julia A. 436
  Keelin 455
  Lavinia A. 138
  Martha 398
  Martha A. P. 394
  Nancy 25
  Philip 25, 71, 208,
    257, 394, 432
  Sarah G. 257
  Susan J. 217
  Thomas 336
  Unetta 471
  W. F. 514, 517
  William F. 502
COOKE, Mr. 408
  Susan W. 408
COOMBS, D. H. 459
  Jas. R. 451
COOPER, Mr. 232
  Rev. Mr. 439
  Alexander A. 92
  Amanda M. 452
  Ann E. 92
  C. P. 482
  Camilla 104

COOPER (cont.)
  Ellen C. 62, 63
  George F. 450
  Geo. P. 62, 63, 414
  I. E. 365
  J. A. 368
  J. J. 373
  Jas. 363
  James F. 357
  Jesse 455
  John 335
  Jno. D. 367
  John W. 124
  Joseph 62
  Josephine 63
  Mark A. 104
  Martin 366
  Stiles 173
  T. B. 524
  Thomas L. 479
  Thomas W. 258
  Wm. J. 359
COPE, John L. 467
  N. B. 166, 471
COPELAND, Mathew 182
  Richard 295
  T. 376
  Thos. 360
COPENHAVER, Gideon 169
CORBETT, John 395
CORBILL, Jas. M. 371
CORBIN, Adaline 525
  Caroline M. 131, 153
  Damuel, Jr. 142
  Isabella C. 519
  Louisa C. 131
  Maria 504
  Peter 494
  Riley 339
  S. P. 504
  Samuel P. 131, 153
  W. B. 134
CORBITT, Samuel D. 125
  W. W. 481
  Wm. A. 260
CORLAND, Wm. 369
CORLEY, J. H. 478
  Jno. 364
  John H. 484
  W. A. 385
CORN, W. R. 367
CORNAN, Lewis 368
CORNOCHAN, Harriet Frances 204
CORNWALLIS, Lord 10
CORNWELL, Dr. 491
  Nathaniel 12
CORTURIET, Louis 365
COSGROVE, Chas. 242
COTTEN, Caroline E. 433
  Emeline E. 433
  Joseph 21
  Mrs. Mary 433
COTTER, Miss N. A. 436
  W. D. 511
  W. J. 499
COTTING, John R. 192
  Mary M. 192
COTTINGHAM, Rev. Mr. 483
COTTLE, Cullen H. 449
COTTON, Charles 50, 86, 138, 182, 186, 392
  Elijah 42, 400
  Eliza W. 182, 186
  Elizabeth 400
  Elizabeth W. 50
  Henry S. 430
  Joseph J. 192
  Maria Annette 86
  Mary 192
  W. 372
COUNCIL, A. J. 363
COUNCTZ, Jordan T. 401

COURSON, Samuel W. 401
COURTNEY, L. 373
COUSINS, Miss M. A. 490
COVINGTON, Judge 515
COWAN, -- 158
COWART, Zacharian 95
COWDRY, Rev. Mr. 491
COWLES, J. 58
  James Hamilton 63
  Jerry 63, 253, 396
  John Randolph 58
  Joseph Loyal 216
  Loyal 216, 485
  Miss M. A. 485
  William 253
COX, Mr. 184
  Eliza Jesse 486
  Rev. Mr. 478
  Andrew 166
  C. T. 373
  Cary 471, 485
  Cullen 503
  D. D. 488
  David 6
  E. Cason 519
  George J. 512
  James 160, 492
  Mary Q. 503
  P. A. 166
  Sarah S. 424
  Sidney R. 372
  W. S. 505
  Wade C. 447
  Wm. 362
  Willis S. 527
COXE, J. T. 123
  Louisa E. 123
COXWELL, Mitchell 207
COYNE, Henry F. 515
COZART, A. W. 169, 479
  Julia 169
CRAFT, George W. 425
  William 163
CRAFTON, Samuel B. 159
CRAFTS, William 8
CRAIG, Col. 142
  J. B. 366
  John C. 367
  Louisa G. 420
CRAIN, -- 177
CRANCH, Judge 184
CRANCH, Judge 184
  Elijah 189
  J. G. 330
  Jacob 353
  W. H. 278, 331, 501
CRAWFORD, -- 261
  Alley 118
  Anne Elizabeth 149
  Charles 393
  Corinne Aurelia 474
  Emily 390
  George 227
  George W. 149
  Hardy 56, 209, 427
  J. A. 363
  Jane M. 396
  Joel 226, 474, 520
  John 43, 496
  Joseph B. 220
  Louisa V. 204
  M. J. 209
  Maggie D. 520
  Mary Virginia 455
  Mathias 358
  Minerva D. 427
  Peter 22, 45, 396
  Robert A. 461
  Rosa 496
  Susan 327
  Thomas 118
  W. L. 528
  William 446, 493
  William H. 35, 187, 327

CRAWFORD (cont.)
  William L. 487
CRAWLY, Joaish 362
CRAY, Mary L. 267
  Scott 267
CREAGH, John G. 417
CRELE, Joseph 304
CREMER, J. W. 384
CRENSHAW, Geo. P. 375
  W. 361
CRENTON, James 320
CRESSWELL, Chas. 355
  J. D. 355
CRICHTON, William 186
CRISP, Mr. 337
  Eliza Jesse 486
  Wm. H. 486
CRISSON, E. A. 376
CRITTENDEN, J. T. 364
CROCEER, William 38
CROCKER, E. E. 153, 314
  E. S. 516
  E. W. 527
  Edward 319
  Elijah E. 32
  Evans S. 486
  Geo. F. 116
  John W. 457
  Louisa Jane Henrietta 96
  Mary 406
  Mary V. 456
  Mary Wimberly 32
  Victoria E. 508
  William N. L. 96, 261, 456
CROCKET, John W. 146
CROCKETT, Davy 258
  Elizabeth 258
  Radford 227
  Radford J. 246
  W. N. L. 449
CROFT, Thomas 254
CROMARTIE, Alexander G. 501
CROMWELL, Miss S. P. 482
CRON, Wm. M. 359
CRONE, G. T. 362
CROOK, Elizabeth 209
  O. 209
CROOM, Mary Ann 450
CROSBIE, Mollie 514
CROSBY, Henry 362
  J. J. 366
  W. 376
CROSS, Joseph 314
  Joseph S. 224
  Lucretia 487
  W. 376
CROW, -- 50
CROWDER, Adline A. E. 396
  Frederick 147
  Frederic L. 131
  Phoebe 131, 147
  Waidll 131
CROWELL, Henry 333, 403
  John 99
  Martha W. 403
CROWNINGSHIELD, B. W. 128
CRUMLEY, Mary A. 505
  W. H. 446
  Wm. M. 447, 453, 457, 487, 505
  Rev. Mr. 445, 446
  Wm. M. 451
CRUMP, J. L. 372
  John 370
CRUTCHFIELD, Thomas 478
  Ulysses 135
CRUTE, Samuel E. 459
  Tryphena 480
CRYMES, T. T. 376
CULIER, Emma C. 526

CULIER (cont.)
  P. B. D. 526
CULLAN, James 359
CULLEN, A. A. 511
  Fannie E. 511
  Michael 475
CULLENS, Frederic 220
CULLER, P. B. D. H. 426
CULLIN, John 303
CULLODEN, William 20
CULPEPPER, Mariner 52
  J. F. 366
  Lucinda C. 445
CULVERHOUSE, G. P. 529
  Green P. 461
  Josephine B. 529
CUMBY, Martha 407
CUMMING, Augusta M. 442
  David E. 324
  Joseph 102
  Wallace 468
  Wm. 87, 292, 415
CUMMINGS, Gray 430
  Wm. 53
CUMMINS, Malinda S. 440
CUNNIAN, Michael 140
CUNNINGHAM, Mrs. 356
  A. S. 285
  Cornelia Paranella 285
  Cynthia 399
  Eliza 400
  Eliza Clara 187
  Frances M. 442
  J. S. 364
  John 442
  Mary 356
  Mollie 511
  Owen 191
  P. 417
  Patrick 181
  Philip 411
  Robert 325, 400
  Robert B. 271
  Shira 259
  Thos. 369
  Virginia E. 478
  W. W. 285
  Wm. R. 187
CURBOW, Isabella M. 419
  Mary Ann 402
CURD, Edward 268
  Louisa L. 497
  Martha E. 434
  Sarah A. 444
CURETON, John 56
CURLISS, Timothy 113
CURRAN, John 336
CURREN, James 295
CURREY, Willis J. 478
CURRY, B. M. 376
  Wiley 229
CURTIS, J. C. 219
  John 114, 338
  Peter A. 261
CURTIS, Rev. Dr. 427
  J. M. 514
  Thomas 239
CUSHING, Isaac T. 101
CUSHMAN, C. T. 343
  George F. 496
CUTCHING, W. T. 358
CUTHBERT, John A. 83,
    118, 260
  Louisa 118
  Louise Eugenia 260
CUTTER, Anna 47
  Catharine H. 445
  Henry S. 41, 47, 89
  Joseph Palmer 47
CUTTING, James 334
CUTTS, H. H. 376
CUYLER, Georgia C. 520
  Geo. W. 333

CUYLER (cont.)
  T. 152
CYPHERS, Aaron 359
D----, John A. 376
DABBS, W. 371
DABNEY, Catharine M. 411
  George 95, 411
DACY, John 179
DAILEY, John 520
  Rachel 520
  S. R. 376
DAILY, John 376
DAINELLY, Miss Walker F.
    478
DALE, Rev. Dr. 234
  John 305
DALTON, D. F. 368
  John 31
  Michael 153
DALZELL, Rev. Mr. 478
DAME, John B. 92
DAMOUR, J. H. 82, 87
  Louisa Ann 87
  John H. 288
  Pauline Mary Elizabeth
    82
DAMPLER, J. 383
DANE, George 7
DANELLY, Capt. 13
  Ann Eliza 404
  Helen H. 443
  Maria 398
  Wm. J. 23, 394
DANFORD, Elizabeth 269
  J. 456
  Joseph C. 394
  William 269
DANFORTH, J. R. 469, 486,
    500
  Jacob R. 510
  Mary 399
DANIEL, Mr. 208
  Amariah 408
  Aug. 278
  J. N. 376
  James 241
  James R. 424
  John C. 424
  Josiah 407
  Mary 40
  Mary Drusilla 26
  Moses 280, 376
  O. P. 508
  Royal 471
  S. G. 520, 522
  Sally 530
  Sarah H. 497
  W. R. 376
  William 26, 270
  Zadock J. 405
DANIELL, Martha 32
  W. C. 32
DANIELLY, Jim 215
DANIELS, Henry 445
  Henry K. 497
  John D. 186
  John M. 495
  Rebecca S. 495
  S. 360
  Susan A. 213
  W. B. 213
  W. H. 373
DANIELY, Sarah E. 503
DANNELLY, William J. 105
D'ANTIGNAC, Wm. 281
DARBY, William 172
DARDEN, Daniel P. 370
DARGAN, John A. 308
DARKIN, Rev. Mr. 418
DARLEY, Rev. Mr. 392,
    394, 397
  Thomas, Rev. 25, 389
DARNEL, M. V. 359

DARNELL, W. W. 369
DARRAGH, Archibald 41
DARSEY, Harriet Bowdre
    163
DARSY, M. J. C. H. 505
DASHER, Joseph J. 519
DAUGHERTY, J. 382
DAUGHTRY, Allen 362
DAVENPORT, Frank 316
  Smith 491, 504
  W. A. 376
DAVIDSON, Mrs. 326
  Samuel W. 234
DAVIES, Judge 465
  Charlotte E. 503
  Henrietta L. 224
  John 465
  John O. 478
  Mary A. 465
  Rebecca S. 414
  Walter P. 509
  William 17, 224, 452
DAVIS, Captain 2, 285
  Judge 453
  Miss 262
  Almira E. 478
  Amanda M. 457
  America Ann 447
  Archibald 457
  Baldwin 239
  Benjamin 97
  Caroline E. 97
  Clarisa Amanda 453
  D. B. 370
  David J. 407
  Dolphin 174, 448
  Duncan J. 220
  E. A. 360
  Elisha 408
  H. B. 522
  H. Winter 303
  Hansford 461
  Harman 414
  Henry 353, 361
  Ichabod 221, 407, 409,
    447, 453, 459, 506
  J. M. 360
  J. P. 365
  J. W. 442
  James 110, 262, 428
  James M. 434
  Jesse 465
  Jesse M. 507
  John 6, 298
  John I. 478
  John R. 474
  John T. 516
  Jonathan 417
  Julia A. 473
  Julia M. 464
  Mary Ann 221
  Mike 227
  Morgan W. 446
  Moses 317
  R. L. 362
  R. T. 485
  Samuel 473
  Stephen 124
  T. L. 363
  T. W. 337
  W. 285
  W. E. 370
  Warren W. 458
  William 500
  William R. 404
DAWSON, Mrs. 123
  Alexander 488
  Edgar G. 491
  Emma C. 476
  H. H. 250
  J. E. 268
  Jacintha E. 396
  Jno. E. 452, 477, 479,

DAWSON (cont.)
    Jno. E. (cont.) 482
    Jonathan 480
    Martha B. 7
    Thomas W. 251, 512
    W. C. 123
    William C. 53, 251,
        472, 476
    William Crosby 195
    William R. 53
    Wm. W. 7
DAVIS, W. A. S. 383
DAY, Carolina 285
    Charles 51, 53, 406
    Charles B. 231
    Charlotte M. 285
    H. G. 242
    Jane 210
    Joseph 210, 454, 505
    Mrs. M. A. 528
    Martha H. 464
    Mary 51
    Mary J. 231
    Nancy 393
DEAN, -- 337
    Arabella O. 451
    Arthur 19
    Elizabeth 23
    Frances M. 479
    Henry G. 315
    J. C. H. 376
    James 23, 264, 403,
        451, 479, 488
    James, Jr. 264
    Lizzie S. 488
    Rufus 361
    S. 235
    William A. 175
DEANALL, Henrietta J. 439
    James 439
DEAR, J. B. L. 384
DEARBORN, Henry, Gen. 19
DEARING, William 151
DEAVORS, George A. 221
DECATUR, Stephen 264
    Susan 264
DEERING, Christopher 305
DEERSON, G. W. 360
DEES, Sarah 391
DEFORE, William 472
DEGNAN, Mary 434
    Michael 89
DE GRAFFENREID, F. H. 520
    Marshall 523
DE GRAFFENRIED, E. L. 475
    Jane S. 475, 497
DEGRASSE, Madame Silvie
    176
DELAHANNTY, W. H. 385
DE LAMAR, B. F. 511
DE LA MOTTA, Emanuel 52
DE LAUNAY, Emilie M. 464
    F. L. 494
    F. V. 464
    Sue 509
DE LAUNEY, J. L. 429
DELF, J. R. 380
DELINE, Lewis 149
DE LOACHE, Francis Wright
    173
    George Wilcoxsen 173
    Jackson 173
    Ryland Kendrick 173
DEMICK, L. M. 467
DEMMING, Jacob 169
DEMPSEY, Dermot 232
    Dermot Alden 227
    Ellen 512
    G. T. 364
    Maria L. 227
    Thomas C. 227
DENAN, Aurie 495
DENARD, Hugh L. 471

DENBY, E. 376
DENHAM, Nathaniel 234
    Thomas P. 458
DENISON, H. M. 233
DENMAN, G. L. 507
DENNING, A. W. 497
DENNIS, Dr. 298
    Mrs. 154, 308
    Edward P. 498
    Harriet R. 154
    J. P. 298
    J. Y. 384
    M. 154
    Mattie N. 514
    Michael 154
    R. G. 190
    Wm., Jr. 172
DENNY, A. W. 274
    Andrew W. 272
DENSE, B. F. 228, 489
    Jacob 228
    James B. 157
    Rebecca A. 489
    William E. 514
DENSON, E. Y. 376
    Elizabeth 134
    Joel 116, 153
    John H. 134
    N. Amelia 452
    T. R. 468, 472
    Tillman R. 425
    William A. 500
DENT, Caroline C. 487
    D. 460
    Elizabeth 241
    John 487
    John W. 241, 514
    Miss M. S. 460
    W. B. W. 184
DENTON, Emily J. 515
    James 219, 413, 424,
        426, 431
    James W. 110, 112
    Joel 398
    Martha M. 110, 112
DE PAU, Alexandrine 176
DE PAUL, Mr. 176
DERACKIN, Emily 429
DERCE, George 293
    John 293
DESHAZO, Richard 148
DESSAU, A. 512
    Cordelia 524
    Rebecca 512
DEUTCH, Adolf 336
DEVEAUX, William 115
DEVEREAUX, M. A. Rebecca
    492
    A. C. 177
DE VOTIE, Rev. Mr. 493,
    512
DEBOTIE, J. 510
    J. H. 500, 524
    Noble 270
DEWBERRY, Mrs. E. 503
DEWS, Laura Cope 509
DICKENS, Dr. 331
    Mrs. B. A. 521
DICKERSON, G. W. 370
    J. P. 464
DICKINSON, J. T. 471
    John P. 420
    M. 421
DICKEY, J. L. 366
DICKLY, E. C. 373
DICKINSON, Rev. Mr. 422,
    423, 446
    Arthur 506
    Henry 355
    John P. 458, 465, 466
    Sarah 481
    Timothy 145
DICKISON, Rev. Mr. 457

DICKS, Maria A. 416
DICKSON, Caroline T. 398
    James S. 29
    Julia L. 476
    Mary J. 431
    Robert G. 518
    Samuel F. 408
    Wm. 476
DIEDRICK, John 428
DIGGS, Wm. R. 358
DILL, D. 180
DILLARD, -- 344
    Hansell 155
DILLERY, Armand 368
DILLINGHAM, George W. 34,
    404
DINKINS, Louis Williamson
    112
    Martha E. 112
    Mary E. 460
    Paul S. 112
    Samuel 237, 460
DIRGHAM, John 153
DISCOL, T. C. 373
DISHMAN, Robt. L. 383
DISHROON, -- 306
DIXON, Mrs. E. P. 507
    J. 381
    Josiah 68
    Martha Hines 458
    Mary 68
    Robert 42, 458
    Robert Emmett 293
    Robert H. 204, 470
DOBARTY, E. 384
DOBBIN, James C. 355
DODD, -- 59
DODGE, Charles S. 54
    Thomas A. 152
DOEST, Newton 376
DOLES, Goerge P. 298
    W. 400
DOMINGUES, Peter A. 366
DOMINY, H. E. T. 367
DOMONY, Albert 368
DONALD, Pat 367
DONEGAN, A. 248
DONELSON, A. S. 249
DONN, M. T. 370
DONNELLY, -- 351
DONOHO, Archimedes 11
DONOHOE, John 280
DONOLD, P. 374
DOOLIE, Adam 347
DOOLY, E. 365
DOON, Julia Doogall 487
DORMAN, Rev. Mr. 498
    Allen 24
    T. W. 353
DORR, Jona. 77
    Thomas W. 176
DORSEY, Mrs. E. T. 514
    Harry 170
    John 11
DOSWELL, Virginia 171
DOUGHERTY, Alexander H.
    407
    Charles 158
    Daniel 179
    Robert 518
    Thomas 272, 458
    Wm. 337
COUGHTRY, Charles T. 214
    M. E. 214
    T. 214
DOUGHTY, E. W. 526
    Ruth 526
DOUGLAS, Andrew D. 10
    George B. 498
    Jas. H. 524
    Logan 438
    M. C. 476
    Stephen A. 274

DOUGLASS, C. H. 457
　Charles G. 429
　George 402
　George L. 178
　John W. 168
　Joseph 82
　Mary A. 510
　S. J. 163
　Thomas 184
DOUGLAST, Daniel E. 359
DOW, Rev. Mr. 527
　Lorenzo 31
DOWDELL, L. F. 484
　Lillie R. 484
DOWDY, Wm. H. 358
DOWLING, A. S. 374
　E. 374
DOWNES, Robert 173
DOWNS, Ex-Senator 169
　John 302
　M. F. 360
　S. U. 168
DOWSING, John W. 489
DOYAL, Joseph G. 519
　L. T. 248, 482, 505,
　　507, 513, 519
　Leonard T. 229
　Mrs. Matilda 229
　D. D. 482
DOYLE, -- 170
　Drury 203
　James 345, 409
　Mary Loiusa 477
　Wm. 203
　Wm. P. 203
DOZIER, Rev. Dr. 451
　A. F. 113
　J. A. 384
　Lucy H. 113
　Mary A. E. 446
　R. 448
　Richard 409
DRAKE, John C. 420
　John W. W. 449
　Louisa A. 421
DRANE, Rev. Mr. 496
DRAPER, James M. 183
　Johnnie 322
　Joshua 183
　Moses R. 183
　Mrs. S. A. 322
DRAWHAN, R. F. 374
DRAWHORN, Artemesia R. 518
　James 282
　Thomas 282
DREUX, Charles D. 275
DRIGGARS, Daniel L. 489
　Daniel T. 63, 161
　Elizabeth Ann 511
　Frances 63, 161
　William Henry 63
DRINKARD, -- 385
DRISCOLL, Thomas M. 26
　W. M. 368
DRIVER, Giles 415
　W. C. 383
DRUMRIGHT, Mary Frances
　　478
DUANE, William 301
DUBBS, D. C. 367
DUBOSE, Dudley M. 505
　J. E. 477, 491
　John E. 482
　Maria A. 422
DUCK, L. B. 330
DUDLEY, Edward B. 186
　George M. 201
　George M., Jr. 201
　J. J. 373
　James A. 136
DUEFEY, Samuel 210
DUELL, Zachariah 393
DUER, John 231

DUER (cont.)
　Wm. 231
DUETT, Ann 413
DUFFEY, Daniel 51
　Jas. 336
DUFFIE, Daniel 399
DUFOUE, Eliza R. 55
　John J. 55
　Laura Beatrice 55
DUGAN, Bridget 34
DUGGER, John L. 130
DUGGON, J. A. 376
　R. 376
DUKE, J. H. 380
　J. W. 367
　Mary 114
　T. F. 376
DUKES, Elizabeth A. 492
　W. 383
DUMAS, J. J. 289
　Jeanette 289
　O. F. 369
　Susannah 346
DUN, J. H. 376
DUNBAR, D. 132
DUNCAN, Capt. 144
　A. B. 449
　A. H. 380
　Mrs. A. H. 190
　Catharine 244
　J. P. 190, 265, 453,
　　455, 457, 478, 501,
　　508
　J. T. 278
　J. W. 496
　James 268, 479
　James E. 132, 244
　John P. 497
　John T. 269
　Joseph 247
　Lenora 450
　Martha E. 479
　Mattie P. 526
　Noah 359
　P. F. 526
　Virginia A. 501
　W. 373
DUNHAM, -- 382
DUNEAN (?), Alexander B.
　　417
DUNHAM, E. J. 384
DUNLAP, John H. 504
　L. D. 385
　Mary 245
　Samuel 245
　Samuel S. 490
DUNLAYP, George 522
DUNN, Superintendent 210
　A. P. 379
　Andrew 509
　Ann 210
　Ann E. C. 423
　Josee 87
　Nehemiah 210
　Wm. 379
DUNNING, Dilbert 374
　S. C. 226
DUNSON, Wm. C. 284
DUNWOODY, Rev. Mr. 412
DUPONT, Chas. J. 344
　Joseph H. 271, 509
　Mary A. 271
　Virgil P. 418
DUPREE, Ellen H. 504
　Ira E. 152, 156, 328,
　　346
DUPRESS, Ira. E., Jr. 156
　Sarah T. 152
DURE, G. A. 503
DURHAM, Caroline C. 407
　Francis M. 491
　Hardy 264, 407
　Mary F. 437

DURHAM (cont.)
　S. W. 422, 447
　Thomas 217
DURRETT, David M. 267
　Elizabeth L. 267
　Engerton 92
　L. B., Mrs. 109
　Rice 109
　S. G. 427
DURYEA, James M. 356
DUVAL, Gov. 162
DWYER, Matt. 340
DYER, Anthony 157
　J. L. 374
DYKES, A. M. 458
　Warren 289
DYSON, Elizabeth Bolton
　　219
　Thomas 108, 219
　Thomas J. 294
EANES, Antoinette V. 432
　John 135
EARL, Chauncey P. 301
EARLY, J. I. 412
EARNEST, Asa E. 287
　Martha 425
EASON, Parker 470
　S. F. 376
　Thos. D. 452
EASTMAN, E. G. 252
　Mr. 343
EATON, Charles R. 93
　J. 374
　Joel 367
　John H. 204
　Sarah G. 451
EBERLEIN, George 334
ECCLESTON, Samuel 131
ECHOLS, J. H. 502
　Joseph H. 477, 485
　Miller 194
　Philip Henry 401
　R. M. 200
ECKLEY, Charles Levi 28
　George 266
　Julia Eleanor Virginia
　　34
　Levi 22, 28, 34, 53,
　　436
　M. T. C. 436
　Thomas Ketler 22
EDDLEMAN, A. M. 491
EDDY, Nelson H. 460
EDEN, Mary Jane 478
　Melinda H. 215
　Olivia Melinda 215
　Thomas M. 215
EDGEWORTH, Mr. 131
　Mrs. 131
　A. S. 230
　Ellen A. 473
　S. C. 462
EDGWORTH, Anna Maria 444
EDMONDSON, Elizabeth M.
　　515
　Lauranah 256
　Lucretia 515
　Wm. P. 498
EDMONSON, Jas., Mrs. 308
EDWARDS, Ambrose 393
　Dick 335
　Ellen A. 524
　George 430
　J. C. 376
　J. P. 375
　James C. 273, 422
　Jesse 330
　John 212, 359
　Joseph 450
　Lafayette 92
　Martha F. 450
　Mary E. 482
　Mary Louisa 444

EDWARDS (cont.)
    O. D. 527
    P. H. 370
    R. H. 362
    S. H. 374
    Sterling 444
    Thos. 354
    W. O. 366
EELLS, Nathaniel 117
ELDER, Ann T. 215
    David 454
    Sarah Ann 454
    William M. 215, 470
    William Newman 215
ELDRIDGE, E. D. 499
    Erasmus D. 499
    Mary A. 499
ELKINS, --- 173
    Samuel 124
ELLIOT, -- 208
    G. I. 376
    James M. 381
ELLIOTT, Bishop 451, 470,
    474, 521
    Daniel 230
    Elizabeth B. 470
    J. W. 361
    John 11
    Stephen 307, 470, 519,
    520, 522
ELLIS, Mr. 37
    Anne L. 224
    George W. 523
    J. T. 367
    J. W. 473
    James 468
    James Monroe 412
    Jane 398
    John 411
    John H. 276
    John M. 332
    John W. 275
    Joseph C. 513
    Louisa 497
    Louisa C. 458
    Martha 47
    Mary Ann B. 400
    Richard W. 145
    Robt. A. 384
    Roswell 224, 500
    Sarah Ann 411
    T. B. 281
    Thomas M. 252, 393, 400
    Vespasian 241
    William 244
    William S. 47, 443
ELLISON, Lieut. 369
    Rev. Mr. 423, 424, 431,
    440, 443, 448, 454,
    455, 456, 494
    Joseph M. 502
    W. H. 423, 439, 446,
    451, 455, 459, 460
    W. M. 368
    Wm. H. 158, 412, 425,
    426, 432, 433, 436,
    437, 441, 444, 450,
    452, 453, 457, 502
ELLS, Jas. Nathan 522
ELLSWORTH, Col. 273
    Ann 48
    Henry L. 238
    John 48
    Mary 414
ELMORE, Franklin H. 124
ELY, Allen E. 238
EMANUEL, Benj. T. 162
    Elizabeth 397
EMBREE, Elmire 474
EMERSON, -- 315
    A. J. 368
EMLINGER, Lucretia 303
EMMERSON, Amanda M. 520

EMMET, Thomas Adam 13
EMPINGER, John W. 426
EMPIRE, Rev. Dr. 423
ENGLAND, W. 367
ENGLISH, Edwin 222
    Florence 258
    John H. 258
    Tallulah F. 258
ENGRAM, -- 159
EPPES, John W. 2
ERMBERT, Caleb W. 138
    Jane G. 138
ERNIS, G. M. 376
ERWIN, Mrs. 27
    Archibald H. 297
    E. T. 376
    Leander A. 27
    Samford 482
ESKEW, Isaac Q. 422
ESLINGER, J. 376
ESTER, J. T. 376
ESTIS, -- 381
ETHERIDGE, -- 325, 389
    E. 481
    Fannie A. 481
ETHRIDGE, J. H. 288
EUBANKS, Edward 96
    Elizabeth D. 96
EUSTIS, George 237
EVANS, Captain 4
    Rev. Mr. 460, 498,
    502, 511, 514, 517
    A. E. K. 502
    B. P. 364
    Benjamin C. H. 103
    Elizabeth 26
    Ezekiel 165
    Fannie L. 496
    Frances C. 508
    Geo. A. 35
    Geo. H. 485
    Georgia A. 495
    Isaac P. 37
    J. 179
    J. E. 462, 489, 497,
    502, 514
    J. H. 497
    Mrs. J. P. 508
    James E. 409, 460,
    490, 494, 501, 502,
    512
    James H. 492
    James Loyless 280
    Jno. B. 369
    John P. 99, 103, 229,
    254
    Joseph M. 424
    Joseph N. 99
    Josiah 205
    Josiah J. 228
    Laura 480
    Lucius G. 436
    Lucy Clary Ann 88
    Lucy M. 514
    M. E. 76
    Mrs. R. A. 229, 254
    Robert 165
    Rufus K. 88
    Rufus W. 511
    Susan C. 436
    Thomas C. 228
EVE, John P. 320
    Louisa 131
    Oswell B. 280
    Paul F. 131
EVERETT, A. 379
    D. Porter 435
    J. A. 518
    James A. 112, 478, 523
    John T. 492
    Lizzie 518
    Mary Beaufort 459
    Samuel H. 463

EVERETT (cont.)
    Sarah E. 478
EVERITT, Rev. Mr. 409
    Jas. S. 315
EVERS, Ephram 358
EVINS, James 492
EWING, J. C. P. 225
EXPERIENCE, John E. 121
EXUM, Mathew 78
EZELL, John 455
    Levi 74
    Sarah G. 74
FACKLER, G. W. 167
    George W. 465
    Martha 167
    Sarah Victoria 167
FAGAN, Martha A. 483
FAIL, John 512
FAIR, Louisa E. 487
    Peter 487
    R. C. 383
FAIRCHILD, Benj. 430
    David Sherman 97
    Susan A. 430
FAIRCLOTH, T. 358
FAIRFIELD, Senator 108
FALLEN, Jesse 477
FALLIGANT, L. N. 522
FAMBROUGH, Urband C. 495
FAREWELL, Levi 302
FARLEY, Rev. Mr. 432
    Alice 327
FARMER, S. T. 383
FARNHAM, Ralph 269
FARRAR, Jesse 232
FARRELL, Michael 311
FARRIER, Hugh 440
FARRIOR, Henry 461
FAUCETT, R. 358
FAUCHE, James 37
FAULINBERRY, D. 364
FAULK, C. R. 469
    Henry 255, 256
    Janet 432
    Lucretia 416
    Mark 323, 432
    Nancy 323
    William 447
FEAGAN, G. W. 344
    Richardson 133
FEAGIN, Samuel T. 510
FEARS, D. 370
    J. W. 466
FEDELIS, Mary 425
FELD, J. M. 413
FELDER, Rev. Mr. 479
    Miss E. A. 467
    Edward L. 462
    John R. 279
    Rufus 506
FELL, Frederick S. 25
FELT, Joseph 114, 118,
    270, 438
    Oliver Proctor 118
    Sarah A. F. 438
FELTON, Alfred 358
    John Latimer 300
    John R. 206
    L. M. 513
    Levinia 480
    Rebecca A. 300
    Richard 48
    Selina C. 48
    Shadrack R. 434
    Wm. 297
    Wm. H. 300, 456
FELTS, G. B. 132
FENDER, J. R. 525
FERETER, Geo. H. 369
FERGUSON, -- 335
    Mr. 331
    Geo. G. 507
    Green 399

FERGUSON (cont.)
　Malcom 38
　Mary Augusta 493
　Mary E. 485
　Thomas M. 493
FERRELL, J. A. 278
　Wiley 421
　Wm. 279
FERRILL, Officer 331
　William B. 430
FEW, I. 399, 404, 407
　Ignatius A. 96
FICKLIN, F. 349
FICKLING, Hester C. 442
　William H. 504
FIDDY, Wm. 365
FIELD, Anna W. 92
　John M. 459
　Samuel 92
　Thomas H. 357
FIELDING, Mr. 489
FIELDS, Elias D. 115
　John M. 448
　William 13
　Wm. E. 374
FILLMORE, Ex-President 167
　Mrs. 149
　Chas. 167
FINCH, Henry 8
　John 108
　Martha 448
　William 448
　William C. 209
FINDLAY, C. D. 524
　Mary J. 519
　Robert 253
　Robt. B. 522
FINERON, Thos. 59
FINIGAN, John 374
FINLISON, Amanda 239
　John 239
FINN, Mary E. 476
FINNEY, Benjamin 444
　Ezekiel 125
　Hezekiah 111
　John W. 495
　Martha J. 444
FISH, Fannie 510
　George W. 97, 508
　J. B. 510
　Jas. S. 491
　John Clarence 97
　Martha E. 97
　Mary 508
　Sarah Margie 490
FISHER, W. T. 364
FISK, Martha 72
FITCH, Harriet 63
　Horace 63
　Horace Kellogg 63
　Lewis 142, 391
　Louisa 142
　Rebecca H. 208
　Wm. T. 208, 507
FITZGERALD, Catherine 142
　Edward 511
　James 336
　Oscar P. 467
　Reuben 103
　W. I. 383
FITZPATRICK, Elizabeth 24
　Avarila 506
　John 506
　John H. 507
　Mary E. 480
　Rene 24
　Susannah 37
　Thirza Ann 402
　Wm. G. 37
FLAMUGAN, Jno. 367
FLANAGAN, Joel 9
FLANDERS, Henry 84
　James J. 425

FLANDERS (cont.)
　Mary Ann 418
　Sarah P. 456
FLANEGAN, Gamil 149
FLANNAGAN, Bernard 187
FLANNER, J. 195
FLEENIN, J. H. 359
FLEISCHMANN, Gertrude 434
FLEMING, Allen 445
　Benjamin F. 215
　Cynthia 428
　Eleanor 434
　Emily 245
　Francis 215
　QM. G. 250
　J. C. C. 215
　J. W. 373
　John 54, 95
　Martha 95
　Mary M. 16
　Nancy 396
　Robert 16
　Thursa L. 456
　Walter R. 169, 170
　William M. 245
FLEMMING, D. F. 376
　Thos. H. B. 495
FLETCHER, Capt. 349
　Miss 390
　John U. 216
　Richard H. 348
FLEURY, Patrick 232
FLEWELLEN, A. H. 61, 423
　Abner 245
　Abner H. 121, 128
　Alexander Holloway 128
　Caroline Elizabeth 167
　Elvira 128, 245
　James 20, 390
　Jas. T. 520
　Mary Ann 420
　Robert J. 449
　Robert T. 167
　Thomas A. 466
　William 39
FLINN, Rev. Mr. 479, 482,
　　496, 504, 514
　Wm. 309, 488, 494, 509,
　　519
FLINT, Cassandra M. 437
　Jane 49
　Lucinda 431
　Mary A. 446
　Matilda A. 97
　Thos. H. 97, 253, 437
FLITZ, F. I. C. 379
FLORENCE, T. W. 373
FLOURNEY, W. H. 376
FLOURNOY, Col. 330
　General 278
　Anne A. 192
　Josiah A. 192, 471
　Robert 32
　Samuel W. 211
　Sarah Lawton 192
　Thomas 239
　Wilson 349
FLOWERS, William 459
FLOYD, Gov. 295
　Archibald B. 473
　Dolphin 91
　H. 367
　Henry 471
　J. 173
　John J. 454
　Lou 515
　Martha Reese 485
　Stewart 154, 485
　Wm. 254
FLUKER, Miss 202
　Mrs. 449
　Anna E. 458
　Baldwin 16, 221

FLUKER (cont.)
　Rebecca Mary 456
　Sarah 456
　Sarah Q. 202, 221
FLUMAN, J. L. 374
FLYNN, Anna 207
FOARD, Wm. J. 81
　Wyatt 23
FOGARTY, Chas. 367
FOKES, Jas. M. 153
FOLDS, Edward 399
FOLEY, James B. 242
FOLSOM, Berry A. 462
　James M. 145
　Randal 133
　Sarah 133
FOOT, M. R. 477
FOOTE, Emerson 233
　Guy E. 404
　W. R. 492
FORBES, Catherine 437
FORCE, Adelia 171
FORD, -- 259
　Rev. Mr. 410
　D. 487
　Edward M. 494
　Garey G. 249
　J. F. 515
　J. R. 384
　James 504
　Julia 423
　Mary Ann 413
　Sarah B. 482
　William P. 219
FORDE, R. E. 293
FOREHAND, James H. 228
　Penelope Ellen 228
FORRESTER, Chas. A. 297
　Minnie E. 297
　Sarah C. 297
FORSTER, Altona H. 12
　Anthony, Rev. 12
FORSYTH, John 400
　Josephine B. 492
　Julia Frances 400
　Robert Brewer 180
　Robert C. 180
FORT, Adeline M. 75
　Mrs. B. A. 489
　Benjamin 154, 458
　Edwin 415
　I. E. 422
　Louisa Virginia 35
　Mary Elizabeth 496
　Margaret L. 243
　Owen C., Dr. 19
　Robert W. 35, 57, 75
　Susan E. 243
　Tomlinson 244, 401, 477
FOOT, Miss M. F. 477
FOSTER, Rev. Dr. 493
　Senator 278
　Alexander H. 413
　Arthur 448, 501, 519
　Eliza A. 497
　Eliza H. 448
　Ephriam H. 170
　F. 515
　Green 472
　Harriet A. 472
　J. B. 444
　John 497
　Josephine H. 519
　Kinchen 310
　Mose 310
　R. S. 310
　Sallie C. 501
　T. H. 481
FOWLER, Frances M. 467
　G. C. 376
　Isaac N. 331
　J. J. 376
　T. O. Mrs. 176

FOWLER (cont.)
    Virginia V. 496
    W. H. 335
    William 411
FOX, R. 330
    Mrs. Samuel W. 176
    Jacob 72
    Sarah 446
FOY, Frances 391
    Frederick 391
FRALEY, George 189
FRANCES, D. 373
FRANCHER, W. F. B. 373
FRANK, Ed. 366
FRANKLIN, Dr. 2, 53, 226
    Abednego 39
    B. L. 88
    M. S. 291
    Marcus Aurelius 409
    Mary L. 291
    William Temple 2
FRANKS, Delilah 139
    Robert Hardeman 139
    Wiley 139
FRASER, William Martin 139
FRAZER, Geo. R. 437
FRAZIER, G. 373
    Georgia V. 120
    R. B. 376
    Wim. M. 120
FREDRICK, Daniel 440
    Frances 448
    James D. 467
FREDRICK, Olivia R. 440
FREEDON, L. 364
FREEMAN, Judge 331
    Rev. Mr. 518
    A. R. 30, 432
    E. 380
    Eunice 423
    G. H. 376
    H. P. 520
    Harvey M. 461
    Henry C. 429
    Holman 197
    James 494, 512
    John R. 218, 455
    Joseph A. 30
    Josephine 512
    Josiah 397
    Josiah W. 508
    Lula Rebecca 218
    Maria L. 494
    Mary 197
    Mary C. 478
    Mary T. 218
    Matt R. 511
    Robert 189, 441
    Thomas 94
    Warren 438
    Williamson 403
FREENY, Julia Ann 401
FRENCH, Mrs. 15
    John 433
    L. M. 286
    Lewis, Dr. 3
    Rachel Elizabeth 433
FRIARSON, James S. 3
    Susan G. 3
FRIDAY, C. A. 361
FRIERSON, Adeline L. 433
    Ann Eliza 406
    James D. 409
    James S. 63, 401
    Sophia 401
FRIES, George 307
FRILL, John 59
FRY, -- 310
FRYER, Elizabeth 183
    John A. 183
    John Lathrop 183
    Mary P. 486
    P. L. 486
    Z. L. 486
FRY

FRYER (cont.)
    Z. L. 486
FRYOR, Col. 477
    Sallie 477
FUGE, Franics Jane 457
    Jacob 72
    Mary Y. 474
    Solomon 474
FULBRIGHT, A. C. 369
FULGHUM, J. M. 380
    W. 380
FULLER, Rev. Mr. 452
    Amelia E. 404
    Jane E. 464
    John M. 77
    Martha E. 427
    Martha Virginia 156
    Rebecca T. 442
    Robert A. 478
    Samuel 427, 464
    Samuel D. 156, 455
    Sarah 77
    Sarah Jane 156
    Wade H. 427
FULLINDER, Joseph 370
FULLWOOD, J. S. 193
    John 122, 452
    John Thomas 194
    Nancy J. 395
    Rebecca J. 194
    William 11
FULSOM, Mary G. 404
FULTON, F. M. 219
    Louisa 448
    Mary E. 500
    Robert 427
FULWOOD, C. A. 495, 497
    John 369
    Randall 311
FUMNIER, W. S. 373
FUNDERBANK, J. F. 376
FURGERSON, A. H. 365
FURLOW, Charlotte Mary 51, 53
    Harriett T. 41
    James W. 41, 95, 237, 416, 417, 419
    Louisa 95
    Margaret E. 80
    Martha Eliza 80
    Mary A. 237
    T. M. 80
    Timothy M. 51, 53, 423
    William Matthews 95
FUTCH, Matilda Elizabeth 350
    John A. 350
GAAR, Leonidas A. 449
GACHET, Anne M. 494
    James 494
GADBY, W. H. C. 278
GADSDEN, Rev. Dr. 430
    Christopher 141
    Christopher Edwards 141
    James 237
GAERON, Thomas 351
GAHAGIN, John R. 49
GAILLARD, John 6
GAINER, Cinderilla 45
    Joseph 45, 67, 410, 420
    Margaret 67
GAINES, Ambrose 520
    George M. 284
GAITHER, Mrs. J. C. 453
GALAGER, S. 366
GALES, Joseph 12, 69, 264
GALIMORE, Levi 456
    Wm. J. 486
GALLAGHER, Ellen B. 427
    Hugh 6
    S. 373
GALLATIN, Albert 118

GALLMORE, John 486
GAMBALL, Chas. A. 345
GAMBELE, J. 382
GAMBLE, Lt. 5
    Ann 397
    Fannie 493
    Letitia B. 506
    Martha Ann 446
    Malinda M. 464
    Robert 437, 506
    Robert H. 506
    Roger L. 108
    Sarah A. 437
    W. B. 240
    William B. 446, 464
    Wm. G. 35
GAMBRILL, A. A. 255
GAMMAGE, David 472
    Davis 125
    Mary 472
    Sarah Frances 125
GAMMELL, Elizabeth 250
GANAWAY, Henry 95
GANTT, -- 265
    Geo. 265
GARDEN, Reuben 379
GARDINER, Mrs. J. T. 171
    Dr. 161
    Rev. Mr. 392, 395, 397
    Anna 310
    B. R. 193
    Charles 161
    Ellen Corrinna 64
    G. W. 86
    H. B. 193
    J. F. 363
    James 86
    John 401, 428
    Julian 86
    M. A. 371
    M. E. 489
    Mary N. 428
    Mattie A. 523
    Nancy G. 240
    Thomas 396, 424
    Thomas R. 96
    Wm. 211
GAREY, CHarlotte F. 488
    F. P. 278, 310
    Fanny C. 310
    Frank P. 488
    Jas. 488
    John P. 310
    Wm. 278
GARFIELD, Henry S. 501
GARLAND, Henry 177
    Hugh A. 172
GARMANY, Hamilton 198
    Mary Eliza 522
GARNER, Abram 432
    Benjamin 64
    Catharine 64
    F. W. 368
GARNETT, Robert Selden 277
    W. B. 372
GARRARD, Wm. T. 494
GARRETT, J. L. 285
    J. M. 383
    M. B. 364
GARRISON, Elizabeth 412
GARTLAND, Francis Xavier 170
GARTRELL, Colonel 278
    Homer L. 240
    L. J. 483
GARVIN, Edward K. 480
GARWOOD, Charles B. 491
GAR-YAN-WAH-GAH, -- 41
GATES, Maj. 118
    Arnold 381
    James 85, 145
    Mary A. 470
    Thomas 78

GATES (cont.)
  Thomas R. 446
GATEWAY, P. 376
GATLIN, Martha W. 416
GAULDING, -- 260
  A. A. 233, 513
  Clementina 392
  Emeline J. 393
  F. A. 233
  James W. 453
  John 9
  Martha 9
GAUSE, Charles W. 479
GAVIN, J. P. 80
  Martin 130
GAY, Mr. 227
  M. 376
  Milly 389
GAYNE, H. C. 365
GEARY, James W. 507
GEGON, Jas. L. 372
GEMENDEN, Cassie 528
GENTRY, J. T. 385
GEORGE A. M. 198
  E. A. T. 198
  Frank 374
  J. A. 380
  J. H. 198
  J. S. 278
  James Ulla 198
  Mark A. 273
  Mary 273
  Wm. B. 234
GERRALD, Fred 353
GESNER, A. C. 358
GIBBERS, J. E. 363
GIBBS, Charles R. 417
  J. L. 365
  John M. 231
  R. A. 366
  Thomas F. 253
GIBSON, Miss 287
  Abner F. 393
  Benjamin 401
  Churchill 38, 54
  Elizabeth S. 414
  Emma C. 138
  Felix 169
  Frances 177
  Frances E. 416
  G. F. 373
  J. G. 138
  John 56
  Lizzie 224
  Mary 38
  Mary A. 428
  Mary M. 106
  O. C. 424, 428, 455, 479, 480, 500, 520
  Obediah 420, 428
  Obadiah C. 65
  Rebecca A. 424
  Mrs. S. L. 511
  Sarah Burk 65
  Tennessee 259
  Thomas 106, 170
  Wiley A. 463
  Wiley J. 56
  William 224
  William G. 281
GIDDENS, James H. 383
GIDDING, F. C. 378
GIDEON, W. H. 365
GIESE, Mr. 149
GIFFORD, Mr. 355
GIGNILLIAT, William R. 524
GILBERT, Miss 398
  A. G., Miss 425
  Amy G. 126
  E. M. 528
  Edmund 425
  Edmund 126, 144, 206, 219

GILBERT (cont.)
  Eliza 335
  Felix H. 178
  Henry 370
  J. E. 371
  M. L. 219
  M. T. 219
  Malcolm T. 100
  Margaret 405
  Mary Frances 459
  Randolphus M. 214
  S. A. F. 445
GILCHRIST, J. J. 228
GILES, Henry 353
  John 244
  John Mason 422
  Nora 353
GILLESPIE, Samuel 21
  W. A. 385
GILLIAM, Charles 370
GILLIN, James H. 299
GILLINS, James H. 449
GILLIS, Angus 395
  M. C., Mrs. 173
GILMAN, O. L. 305
  Samuel 223
GILMER, E. H. 247
  Edward H. 492
  G. E. 247
  George R. 252
  Henry Lamar 247
  James D. 445
  Mary 413
GILMORE, John A. 319
  P. 364
  S. G. 382
  William M. 159
GINN, A. 392
GIPSON, N. 358
GLASON, Nathaniel 495
GLASS, John 177
  Sanford W. 502
  Simeon 177
GLEN, Geo. 142
  Rob 370
GLENN, Clarissa W. 437
  J. N. 450
  John E. 498
  Mary S. 211
  Wm. 211
GLESE, Martin 302
GLINN, Clarissa L. 407
GLOVER, Anne Matthews 123
  Anna S. 123, 255
  E. F. 277
  Eli S. 128
  Elizabeth 147
  Green B. 471
  Henry 214
  Henry H. 458
  Henry S. 123, 255
  James T. 466
  John 299, 505
  Kelly 147
  Mary 398
  Rebecca M. 128
  Thos. 425, 455
GNECH, Eliza Maria 86
GODDARD, Judge 427
  Bailey 115, 395
  Catherine B. 35
  Catherine R. 115
  Emeline L. C. 115
  Frances 495
  James Edmond (Edward?) 29
  James 29, 61, 64, 101, 103, 495
  Joshua A. 463
  Sophronia 61, 64
  Wm. B. 213
GODFREY, F. H. 11, 21, 22,

GODFREY (cont.)
  F. H. (cont.) 39, 389
  Godfrey Virginia 440
  Martha G. 497
  Susan 394
  Wm. 267
GODREY, Nancy 21, 22
  William Morriss 21, 22
GODSEY, Susan Caroline 355
GODWIN, Dr. 312
  E. H. 526
  Louisa Ann 407
  T. A. 460
GOFF, W. B. 527
GOINS, Calvin 418
GOLD, Mrs. 166
GOLDEN, J. 373
  Joseph A. 233
GOLDING, Francis 170
GOLHARD, David 364
GONDER, Gertrude E. 479
GONNELL, A. J. 370
GOOCH, Elizabeth 117
  Wm. D. 117
GOODALL, Julia 487
  Seaborn 487
GOODARD, Bailey 24
GOODE, Amanda V. 213
  Charles T. 498
  Elizabeth 253
  George 359
  John 253, 510
  Thomas W. 213, 253
GOODMAN, J. L. 367
GOODRUM, Jas. A. C. 495
GOODSON, A. 278
GOODWILLIE, Wm. 348
GOODWIN, Joseph 366
  W. H. C. 513
GOODYEAR, Timothy 442
GOOLSBY, Wesly 473
GORDIN, Z. A. 410, 411
GORDON, Ann 441
  Chas. P. 463
  Elley H. 262
  G. W. 502
  J. D. 294
  John B. 477
  John D. 210
  John W. 157
  Martha C. 157
  Sallie E. 463
  Thomas B. 441
  W. J. 362
  W. L. 503
  W. P. H. 381
GORLEY, William A. 522
GORDON, Wm. L. 514, 524
  Wm. W. 73
GORMAN, Dr. 503
  Mrs. A. 507
  Amos 323
  Frances O. 466
  Mattie A. 507
  T. B. 466
  Thomas B. 176
  Virginia Victoria 503
GOUGH, James H. 346
GOULD, Judge 22
  James G. 171
  James R. 22
  W. T. 171
GOULDIN, Samuel 179
GOULDING, Mrs. 155
  Rev. Dr. 133
  E. R. 288, 479
  Eloise 118
  John C. 133
  T. 442
  Thomas 112, 396
  Thos. B. 118
  Thomas F. 496

GOVE, Mrs. 213
  Samuel F. 213, 438,
    504
GOWAN, Mr. and Mrs. 334
GRACE, Emily L. 212
  James 368
  Marenda 471
  Mathew 212
  Nancy 512
  Nancy M. 212
  Samuel 212
GRADY, Elizabeth 204
GRAEFF, Frederick 188
GRAHAM, -- 334
  Rev. Mr. 256
  Alexander 160
  Anderson 449
  Ann G. 484
  B. A. 375
  E. 365
  James 78, 79, 427
  Mary 160
  Robert M. 168
  W. 382
  W. A. 371
  W. H. 364
  William L. 489
GRAMMAGE, Charity Ann
    Delilah 132
    Davis 132
GRAMMER, Rev. Dr. 527
GRAN, John M. 119
GRANBERRY, George 1, 23,
    390, 427
  James M. 397
  James N. 405
  Jane Ann 1
  Sarah S. 23
GRANBURY, George 404
GRANDISON, Charles F. 17
GRANDLAND, Sam'l 264
GRANGIR, Alfred 382
GRANNISS, E. C. 459, 481,
    500, 517, 525
GRANT, James 345
  Joshua 368
GRANTHAM, Henry 303
GRANTHEM, -- 241
GRANTLAND, Catherine M. 95
  Eliza A. 394
  Fleming 406
  Fleming Tinsley 174
  Sarah C. 406
  Seaton 95, 174, 411
GRAVES, A. 231
  Azariah 494
  Edwin 110, 265
  Fanny R. 424
  Henrietta A. 110
  Iverson L. 484
  J. Palmer 490
  Matilda E. 405
  R. C. 366
  W. Y. 374
GRAY, A. A. 90
  Albert 524
  Alice 115, 327
  Ann A. 185
  Catherine Dangerfield
    391
  D. L. 384
  David 327
  Geo. 318
  Harriet E. 454
  J. D. 90
  J. F. 362
  James 367, 435
  James B. 327
  John B. 327
  John D. 90, 115, 185
  John O. 34
  M. 374
  Margaret 327

GRAY (cont.)
  Martha J. 443
  Nellie Jane 327
  Sarah 469
  Theodore H. 127
  Wm. 86, 127, 185, 443,
    454
GRAYBILL, J. H. 508
  Midas L. 137, 409
GRAYCORE, G. J. 368
GREEN, Rev. Mr. 416
  A. E. A. 258
  Adeline 420
  Adie E. 517
  Alston H. 104
  Ashbel 111
  Miss E. 509
  E. A. E. 262
  Elizabeth 219
  Ella Jane 104
  F. T. 365
  G. P. 365
  George W. 172
  Gilpin J. 484
  H. K. 104
  Henry Clay 292
  Henry K. 429
  John 448
  John S. 331
  Martha 448
  Mary W. 468
  Miles 406
  Miles L. 456
  Nancy B. 33
  Raleigh 219, 466
  S. M. 373
  Theodosia 104
  Thomas B. 420
  Thomas F. 258, 262,
    271, 396, 517
  W. G. 175
  Wm. 99
  Wm. A. 33, 250, 417
  Wm. E. 205
  Wm. Hudson 471
  William J. 471
  William Montgomery 148
GREENE, Major General 246
  A. B. 477
  Alexander B. 220
  Antoinette R. 477
  Burwell 292
  Henry Clay 292
  James D. 512
  James M. 148, 443
  M. L. 478
  Miles 220
  Nathaniel Ray 246
  Peter B. 42
  Wm. S. 474
GREENOUGH, Horatio 146
GREER, E. C. 217
  Elizabeth L. 402
  Fannie 265
  Frances M. 217, 441
  Henrietta 331, 351
  John Carlton 245
  John M. 245, 265, 491
  Mary F. 245, 265
  Thomas 402
GREESON, P. G. 154
GREGG, Maj. 243
GREGORY, Eph. 376
  George W. 471
  James L. 366
  Ossian 410
  Ovide 356
GREINER, William S. 161
GRESHAM, Annie 477
  Catharine B. 61
  Edmund Jones 99
  J. J. 61
  John J. 99, 423, 434

GRESHAM (cont.)
  Mary E. 99
  Robert 87
  Samuel 392
  William 454
GRESSOM, G. B. 371
GREY, John 369
  Simeon 66
GRIER, E. C. 479, 514
  James V. 318
  Phebe 318
  Robert 421
GRIEVE, Miller 273
  Sarah A. 423
GRIFFIN, Mr. 53
  Rev. Mr. 472
  B. F. 104, 468
  Benjamin F. 61
  Charles Joseph 104
  D. F. 61
  Daniel 69, 422, 451
  Edward 26
  Elizabeth 80, 390
  Elizabeth E. 65
  Etheldred 409
  George G. 521
  Geraldine 487
  J. J. 475
  James W. 273, 491
  Joel R. 517
  L. L. 80, 334
  Larkin 35, 97, 164,
    251, 421, 487
  Lucinda H. 35
  Mrs. M. A. 527
  Martha A. 500
  Matthew D. 258
  Narcissa 69
  Sarah E. 468
  Sarah L. 104
  W. 376
  William E. 318
GRIFFIT, Corpl 369
GRIFFITH, L. 363
  Thomas H. 90
  W. A. 359
GRIGGS, Mary P. 504
  Rebecca L. 478
  Robert 478
  Sarah C. 461
  Wesley 461
GRIGSBY, E. 380
GRIMES, David S. 427
  George 250
  J. W. 372
  M. J. 362
  Martha A. 469
  Mary 396
GRIMESLY, Wm. 368
GRIMKE, Thomas S. 36
GRINES, C. W. 383
GRISWOLD, Caroline
    Matilda 204
  E. C. 181
  Elisha 436
  Elisha C. 211
  Elizabeth H. 181
  J. C. 171
  John 98
  Louisa 243
  Lucia 408
  Samuel 242, 243, 314,
    408
  Wm. H. 204
GROCE, America 423
  Lewis J. 405
  John Thomas 43
  Lewis 43
  Lewis J. 130, 214
  Margaret 130, 214
  Ryland Judson 130
  Solomon 44, 92
  Wm. Ellison 475

GROOVER, J. H. 361
  John 242
GROSS, J. 371
  John 359, 476
GROSSMAYER, Nathan 481
GROVES, Rev. Mr. 409
GROVE, John J. 416, 494
GROW, C. W. M. 379
GUARDED, T. M. 371
GUE, Frank 322
  P. L. 322
GUERRY, Eliza 42
  James 23, 198
  Margaret 198
  Mary A. K. 394
  T. Legrand 414
  Theodore 42
GUIEU, P. C. 120
GUINGNARD, J. S. 204
GUNBY, Frances 404
  Gibhard 367
GUNISON, H. B. 417
GUNLY, J. H. 372
GUNN, Daniel 105, 121
  Elizabeth 473
  Green C. 246
  Green G. 473
  Virginia 105
GUNTER, Mr. 175
GURGANUS, Abraham 375
GUTHRIE, James 380
GUTTENBERGER, Francesca R. 484
GUY, Miss 238
GUYTON, Capt. 509
  C. B. 214
  Mrs. E. L. 509
  Eliza 389
  John 8
  Mattie J. 509
  Tabitha 389
GWYN, William L. 411
HABERSHAM, Rev. Mr. 466
  J. C. 186
  R. Elliott 486
  R. W. 78, 172
  Sarah E. 172
HABFIELD, D. M. 365
HACKEY, W. 304
HADEL, Dr. 188
HADLEY, W. D. 371
HAFER, Amanda M. 227
  John 227
  Wm. 471
HAGANS, J. T. 376
HAGLER, J. A. 358
HAILE, E. O. 356
HAILES, W. C. 365
HAINES, A. C. 381
HAIRSTONE, Moses B. 104
HALFIELD, D. H. 373
HALL, Adie E. 271
  Amanda 180
  Ann E. 425
  Caroline G. 447
  Charles Henry 495
  E. 429
  H. T. 513
  Hansell 488
  Henry 5
  J. G. 376
  J. M. 384
  J. N. 526
  J. P. 380
  J. S. 364
  J. W. 337
  James A. 271, 400
  Jas. Augustine 517
  James C. 233
  James M. 488
  James T. 476
  John 180
  Joseph B. 476

HALL (cont.)
  Joseph Y. 284
  Mrs. L. E. 492
  Marianna 429
  Martin 92
  Mary 92
  Ransley 310
  Richard 447
  Robert P. 174
  Salina P. 92
  Samuel 362
  Wm. 359
HALLAGHAM, Pat 171
HALPIN, Edward 355
  T. 372
HALPINE, Chas. G. 340
HALSTEAD, Wm. 431
HAM, John 496
  Salina C. 496
HAMBLETON, -- 173
HAMBRICK, J. E. 376
  Jas. 376
  Tarpley 290
HAMES, John, Sr. 268
  Luke P. 328
HAMILL, Miss 418
  Maria R. 481
  Thomas 390
HAMILTON, Rev. Dr. 511
  Alexander 174
  Charles 127
  Cogdil 512
  David B. 426
  Duke 397
  Elizabeth 174
  Emily M. 470
  Evalina 458
  Everard 102, 174
  Harriet S. 413
  Miss J. V. 515
  James 250, 581, 405, 491
  Jas. F. 470
  Jane Ann 405
  John 9, 157, 309
  John Wesley 40
  Joseph J. 44
  Mary B. 421
  Mary E. 250
  Mary Troup 455
  R. B. 278
  Richard Wayne 174
  Thomas 30, 152, 455
  Thomas Sydenham 30
  Wm. 421
  Wm. J. 481
HAMMACK, W. W. 225
  Wm. E. 452, 489
HAMMERSLEY, Alexander E. 172
HAMMIL, William S. 308, 446
HAMMOCK, A. J. 384
  A. W. 430
  Senia 468
  W. 430
HAMMOND, Dr. 217, 487
  Amos M. 62
  Amos. W., Jr. 193
  Antionette 487
  Bud 305, 310
  Eliza C. 62
  Ellen 423
  Girta 524
  H. B. 380
  Mary C. 478
  Thomas S. 459
  W. H. 363
HAMMONDS, H. 372
  J. G. 360
HAMMONRE, S. 367
HAMPTON, B. 364
  Miss E. J. 528
  Jacob 278

HAMPTON (cont.)
  John J. 189
  John W. 411
  Mary 505
  Wade 37
  Wm. 278
HANCKEL, J. S. 527
HANCOCK, -- 251
  Charles W. 216
  D. J. 367
  George H. 186
  G. H. 185, 468, 469, 470, 475, 479, 480, 484
  J. C. 363
  James 188
  James W. 528
  Joel T. 468
  Jonathan 461
  William H. 500
HAND, Rev. Mr. 397
HANDCOCK, John 369
HANHAM, James R. 303
HANLEITER, Cornelius R. 413
HANLEY, James 481
HANLY, D. P. 370
HANMOND, Amos W. 428
HANNEGAN, E. O. 144
HANNEY, D. J. 361
HAMMON, John 82
HANSELL, Julia S. 88
  Wm. Y. 88
HANSFORD, George W. 460
  Matilda A. 460
  Robt. B. 454
HANSON, F. T. 60
  J. B. 463
  Martha 60
HARALSON, Fannie R. 477
  Hugh A. 171, 235, 477
  Kinchen L. 235
  Paul A. 136
HARBAUM, John T. 434
  John Theodore 121
HARBRUM, Theodore 421
HARBUCK, James 132
  Sarah H. 132
HARCOURT, Dr. 336
HARD, Rev. Mr. 484
  W. J. 476
HARDAGE, J. M. 367
HARDAWAY, Georgia Logan 111
  Indiana 81
  James H. 81, 128, 265
  Martha Bibb 520
  Martha J. 461
  R. H. 420
  R. S. 250, 520
  Samuel 308
  Samuel G. 111
HARDEE, John 54
HARDEMAN, Elizabeth 436
  Frances Ada 508
  Garten Sparks 127
  Isaac 493
  J. J. 376
  Jane 127
  Pauline 457
  R. V. 443
  Robert U. 509
  Sarah 181
  Sarah Jane 455
  Thos. 64, 181, 279, 436, 455, 508
  Thomas, Jr. 127, 449
HARDEN, Ann B. 76
  A. T. 286
  Isaac 372
  James 76
  Josephine 505
  Martin L. 79, 423

HARDEN (cont.)
  Matilda 450
  Walter Scott 286
  Wm. 18
HARDENBURG, Rev. Dr. 511
HARDIE, Robert C. 292
  Sidney Ann 508
HARDIMAN, Sarah E. (?) 43
  Thomas 43
  Volumnia Jemison 43
HARDIN, E. J. 199
  John 102, 405
  Lodoiski 405
  W. S. 340
HARDING, Dr. 249
HARDINKESQ, John 415
  Matilda 415
HARDISON, James 477
  Thomas 148
HARDT, George 317
HARDWICK, G. 370
  George W. 121
HARDY, Rev. Mr. 394
  Charles 53, 395, 402, 403, 404, 405
  Thomas 359
  W. W. 442
  William 436, 440, 468
HARE, Willis 390
HARGRAVE, Almira 396
HARGROVE, A. H. L. 272
  D. C. 278
  Martha 272
  Patrick H. D. 509
HARISON, Theophilus J. 499
HARKNESS, James W. 111
  John 336
  Martha 111
HARLEY, Wm. J. 177
HARLOW, Southworth 27
HARMAN, Amanda 415
  Ann E. 486
  Elizabeth 126
  Fannie 516
  Henry A. 415
  John K. 441
  Jno. R. 126
  Miles K. 89, 424
  Z. E. 496
  Zachariah 89, 99
  Zachariah E. 291
HARMON, Elizabeth R. 452
  Lavinia A. 450
HARNEY, Mr. 344
HARNISS, Wm. F. 365
HARP, Dickson 411
  Elizabeth 411
  Lucinda D. 406
  R. D. 381
HARPER, Chancellor 107
  Jas. 278
  John H. 471
  John J. 393
  John S. 298
  Robert Goodloe 5
  William H. 236
HARRALD, Joshua 361
HARRALL, M. 362
HARRALSON, Col. 234
  Mrs. 226
  H. A. 226
  Hugh A. 234
  R. 366
HARRELL, Miss A. E. 525
  Hardy 47
  Holliday 366
  John 259
  L. N. 369
  Moses 263
  Young A. 510
HARRIL, J. E. 380
HARRIS, Dr. 298
  Albinus P. B. 489

HARRIS (cont.)
  Ann 407
  Ann D. 60
  B. T. 475
  Ben. J. 493
  Bettie 493
  Charles J. 496
  E. M. 380
  Ed 358
  Edward S. 199
  Edwin 471
  Eleanor 419, 515
  G. 372
  G. W. 376
  I. L. 488
  Isaac C. 496
  Isaac R. 515
  Iverson L. 329
  J. A. 363
  J. H. 368, 504
  J. M. 365
  James 461
  Jeptha 324
  Jeptha V. 199
  Jno. 367
  John H. 489
  John L. 272
  John S. 295
  Joshua 413
  Juriah 470
  Lucinda 389
  M. T. 331
  Martha H. 427
  Mary Ann 272
  Mary C. 496
  Mary E. 504
  Mary Jane 475
  Mary Winn 456
  Miles G. 484
  Minor W. 482
  Nancy 483
  Nat 185
  Raymond 456
  Richard 12
  Robt. H. 365
  Sampson W. 210
  Samuel H. 429
  Samuel W. 405
  Sarah 488
  Sarah E. 519
  Susan C. 489
  T. L. 235
  Thomas A. 441, 507
  Thomas Alston 303
  Thomas W. 163
  William G. 474
  Wm. H. 509
  Wm. L. 324
  Wm. T. 60, 294
HARRISON, Rev. Mr. 415
  Almira E. 492
  Aurelia M. 441
  Burrell K. 255
  C. 404
  C. A. 104
  Charles 416
  Daniel S. 290
  Daniel Shine 290
  G. 263
  Gabriel 293
  George 492, 497
  George A. 441
  J. B. 335
  James 359
  Jim 316
  John 32
  Jonathan Hughes 104
  Martha 414
  Mary 103
  Mary B. 425
  Simeon 256
  W. H. 384
  W. P. 528

HARRISON (cont.)
  Wm. 103
  Wm. B. 104
  William C. 185
HARRISS, Edward J. 38
  Lucy S. 38
  William 38
HARROLD, Thomas 412
HARROLL, S. B. 372
HARSHAW, A. 278
HART, Col. 164
  Judge 236
  Edwin 1
  John 363, 444
  Julia Emily 68
  Lucia R. 45
  M. J. 68
  S. 68
  Sarah Ann 444
  Seth 424
  Susan 1
  Truman 45
HARTFIELD, M. 366
HARTFORD, Henry 8
HARTLEY, Daniel 372
  Jas. 327
HARTMUS, Major 314
HARTSFIELD, Nancy 505
  W. A. 384
  W. W. 266
  William W. 466
HARTSON, Mary E. S. 129
HARTWELL, C. P. 524
  J. B. 507
HARVARD, V. A. 294
HARVEY, Ann 401
  I. N. 494
  Isaac, Jr. 30
  Isaac, Sr. 30, 52, 401
  J. C. 181, 215
  John 401
  John P. 297
  Richard 181
  Sarah F. 480
  Miss T. M. 520
HARWELL, Ellen G. 519
  James R. 392
  R. 464
  S. S. L. 503
  Samuel 428
  Susan W. 512
HASELTON, John 43
HASKELL, W. T. 241
HASKIE, John 185
HASLIP, George 208
HASTINGS, Samuel Weston 527
  Wm. 378
HATCH, James L. 232
HATCHER, Bethia 389
  Thomas 176
HATFIELD, James 394
  Richard 236
HATHAWAY, H. B. 53, 65
  Margaret Cornelia 65
  Maria E. 442
  S. S. 480
  William Henry 53
HATHOM, Eliza E. 417
  Hugh 417
  James 416
  Lucinda 416
  Lurena 416
HATHORN, Susan K. 427
  Thomas 427
  Thomas J. 284
HAUGABROOK, Ann Elizabeth 458
  Georgiana V. 458
  Harriet 459
  J. J. 458
  Mary 441
HAUOABOOK, John J. 113

HAVIS, Cornelia A. 199
  J. D. 116
  Jesse D. 488, 510
  M. W. 199
  Mary 110
  Mary E. 488
  Sophia C. 116
HAWES, Joel 333
HAWFIELD, Priscilla A.
    424
HAWKES, A. B. 452
HAWKINS, Gov. 10
  Mr. 161
  Benjamin 390
  Eugene A. 298
  H. C. 380
  I. B. 364
  John B. 493
  M. 380
  Margaret P. 194
  Nannie H. 493
  Nathan 194
  Strother Jones 314
  Terrinda F. 156
  Virginia 390
  W. A. 269
  Wm. 374
  Willis A. 156, 476
HAWLEY, Anna E. 519
  Charles F. 98
HAY, Mr. 53
HAYDEN, Isaac 475
  Samuel M. 452
  Susan E. 452
  W. H. 373
HAYES, Duke Hamilton 423
  F. 425
  John R. 101
  W. 374
HAYGOOD, A. Judson 528
  Benjamin 67
  F. M. 522
  J. E. 522
  Katie D. 522
HAYMAN, Fanny 335
HAYNE, Robert Y. 59, 292
HAYNES, Captain 354
  Chs. Easton 69
  E. R. 469
  Wm. P. 189
HAYNIE, Charles Richard
    69
  Francis 54
  Martha E. 54
HAYS, Duke 75
  Duke H. 159
  George Hamilton 75
  Jack 117
  James T. 461
  John 402
  Sarah 75
  W. A. 366
  Warren 349
  Wm. 367
HAYWOOD, -- 177
  Ebenezer 206
  John 13
HAZLEHURST, Carrie C. 501
  George H. 505
HEAD, B. J. 483
  Geo. 278
  Wm. J. 393
HEADEN, J. A. 487
HEADLEY, J. T. 234
HEADSPETH, Jane 418
HEARD, Carter 310
  Isaac 311
  John A., Maj. Gen. 16
  P. A. 527
  William J. 452
HEATH, Mrs. 59
  Adam Orsamus 55
  Elizabeth 55

HEATH (cont.)
  Elizabeth W. 441
  John 214
  John F. 436
  Maria A. 434
  Mary 413
  P. 434
  Pleasant 55, 441
HEBBARD, M. H. 271
  Meltiah 73
  W. H. 445
HEENEY, Cornelius 111
HEGGIE, James 231
HEIDELBERG, T. C. 365
HEIDT, Daniel 136
HEISS, John P. 300
HELATHER, Mrs. 311
HELMES, Joseph 348
  Matthew 359
HELVENSTEIN, F. B. 149
HELVINSTON, Alexander
    Humboldt 202
  Eugene 202
  J. C. 200, 202
  John C. 292
HENDERSON, Rev. Mr. 478
  Senator 228
  Elrich 384
  G. H. 381
  H. L. 308
  J. 370
  James 349, 473
  "Mage" 308
  Mary Ann 56
  Sam'l 461
  Sarah 56, 512
  Thos. 370
  W. 285
  Wm. 56, 364, 402
HENDREE, George 489
  Sallie Austin 489
HENDRICK, Elizabeth G.
    389
HENDRICKS, J. P. 208
  James 368
  John 199, 437
HENIER, Nancy J. 490
HENLEY, Robert, Commodore
    15
  Wm. 385
HENRY, Amelia 134
  B. F. 519
  James 356
  James A. 395
  Matthew 352
  Nathaniel 164
  Patrick 164, 262
  Patrick L. 364
  Thomas 491
  William J. 134, 452
  William P. 28
HENSHAW, David 145
HENTZ, Caroline Lee 190
HERBERK, Rev. Mr. 448
HERBERT, Mr. 196
HERMANN, Lucien 161
HERNDON, G. 376
HERRING, Mr. 135
  Mrs. 135
  Bright B. 290
  G. 365
  J. D. 383
  James 178
HERRINGTON, Jas. M. 372
  R. F. 490
  Wm. 465
HESS, William H. 314
HESTER, Mitchell G. 337
  R. 364
  S. C. 380
HEWELL, John 368
HEWITT, Nathan 309
HEWSTON, Jas. F. 360

HIBBETTS, Mike 259
HICKEY, Michael 221, 222
HICKIMBURG, Francis H.
    392
HICKLING, John 236
HICKS, Isham 118
  Josephine E. 513
  L. F. 447
  L. M. 379
  Oliver 371
  Samuel 139
  Sarah 441
HIGDON, C. F. 359
HIGGINS, Rev. Mr. 482,
    512
  C. A. 409, 419, 421,
    428, 431, 433
  Elizabeth A. 429
  Fidelia E. 518
  Palmer A. 418
HIGGS, Augustus B. 91
  William 359
HIGHTOWER, D. N. 496
  Daniel 154, 222, 418
  David 57
  Eason 492
  Garland 407
  James 57
  Louisa J. 83
  Wm. 53, 105, 318
HILEY, Jacob 454
HILL, Judge 268
  Mrs. 23
  Rev. Mr. 415
  Alfred 316
  Andrew F. 507
  Barnard 439, 454
  Charles 130
  Chester 65
  D. H. 498
  David H. 518
  E. A. 362
  Elbridge Greene 69
  F. A. 190
  Francis 468
  Francis A. 497
  Grace L. 391
  Green 130
  Greene 69, 463, 501
  H. B. 401, 412
  H. W. 325
  Harriet J. 404
  Henry 23, 87
  Henry B. 402, 404, 407,
    413
  Isaac 30, 34
  J. M. 361
  J. W. 463
  James A. 485
  John 185, 207
  John C. 322
  Joshua 182
  Kate 463
  Louisa M. 420
  Lucy 438
  M. E. 69
  Mary Augusta 454
  Mary Louisa 412
  Rebecca 522
  Sarah S. 390
  Slaughter 274
  Susan 469
  W. C. 34
  Whitman C. 270
  William 219
  Wm. S. 190
  Young 488
HILLIARD, H. W. 429
  Roltha 392
HILLSBOROUGH, J. C. 373
HILLYER, Rev. Mr. 429
  S. T. 432
HILSMAN, Alice 524

HILSMAN (cont.)
  James 175
  Josiah 524
HINDMAN, J. B. 379
HINDS, Powell 319
HINE, Treat 413
HINELE, J. P. 516
HINES, Judge 507
  Bennie 486
  Bessie 209
  Emily O. 103
  Emma N. 482
  George 303
  John Bolling 202
  Martha 441
  Mary A. 507
  Mary M. 390
  R. K. 279, 486
  Richard K. 103, 137
  Richard Kennon 136
HINTON, Rev. Mr. 465, 481, 496, 520
  J. W. 489
  Jas. W. 485, 497
HITCH, J. W. 165
HIX, J. 381
HOBBS, Alvah H. 355
  Amanda 279
  Berry 148
  G. A. 358
  Jas. A. 360
  James Augustus 148
  Martha Elizabeth 449
  Richard 279
HOBBY, Alfred M. 61, 116, 404
  Ann E. 61
  Felix McKenne 61
HOBER, Jacob 171
HOBSON, William H. 304
HODGE, Lucy 33
  S. B. 359
HODGES, Rev. Mr. 395, 396
  Debora 127
  Edmund 79
  H. A. 127
  J. O. 445
  J. Joseph 272, 522
  John 348
  John L. 164, 421, 515
  John T. 156
  Joseph J. 511
  Josiah 127
  Julia A. 511
  Julia Ann 272
  Mary 455
  Mary B. 164
  Matthew 417
  William 187, 404
HODGKINS, Jane 36
  John C. 521
  Walter C. 470
HOEFER, -- 345
HOFFMAN, Wiley 150
HOGAN, Eliza B. 429
  Sarah N. 444
  T. A. 362
  William (Wilson?) 29
  Wm. 444
HOGE, Caroline E. 449
  Cassandra Olivia 47
  D. B. 416
  John G. 193
  John S. 433
  Mary Ann 407
  Solomon 17, 47, 392
  J. W. 289
HOGUE, J. Anson 155
HOLCOMBE, Henry G. 508
  James B. 140
HOLD, Eva 116
  Hines 116
  Sarah A. C. 116

HOLDER, A. 83
  Julia Laura 83
  Troy G. 459, 497
  Wiley F. D. 104
HOLDERNESS, James 389
HOLLAND, Mr. 276
  G. W. 431
  Georgia V. 478
  J. 478
  John H. 331
  John L. 528
  Sarah Ann 453
  W. H. 364
HOLLEMAN, Anne 117
  Joseph J. 408
  Martha Louisa 117
  Zachariah 117
HOLLEMONS, J. 53
HOLLENBEK, Rev. Mr. 396
HOLLEYMAN, Thomas H. 505
HOLLIDAY, Alexander 465
  Joseph R. 482
  Louis P. 506
HOLLIMAN, Augustus M. 487
HOLLINGSHEAD, W. H. 486, 508
  Wm. H. 521
HOLLINGSWORTH, Aaron H. 372
  Andrew J. 34, 438
  E. Isadore 527
  Elizabeth 62
  Franklin 509
  J. A. 371
  J. B. 368
  James 62, 104, 134
  John 53
  John, Jr. 435
  Josetta A. 461
  Laura M. 508
  Malvina 420
  Thomas J. 62
  W. T. 446
HOLLINSHEAD, Cornelia A. 525
  James S. 217
HOLLINSHED, Lavinia A. 424
HOLLINSHEAD, Lavinia P. 523
  Rebecca C. 446
  Sarah S. 493
  W. H. 486, 525
  William 73, 523
HOLLIS, Pennie 502
  Susan 459
  Thomas T. 478
HOLLMAN, W. H. 171
HOLLOMAN, Eaton 24
  Sarah 24
  Z. 391
HOLLOMON, John 370
HOLLOWAY, Achsah (?) 422
  Edward 125, 422
  J. O. 501
HOLLY, Polly 36
  W. Y. 369
HOLM, Thos. Wolsten 316
HOLMAN, Rev. Mr. 425
  J. B. 358
HOLMES, Dr. 192
  Rev. Mr. 411, 412, 413, 426
  A. T. 408, 414, 424, 427, 442, 444, 450
  Adam 409, 462
  Adam T. 412, 413, 415
  Caroline E. 455
  Chas. L. 418
  Cordelia P. 475
  David M. 175
  Edward L. 64
  George N. 344

HOLMES (cont.)
  Isaac 53, 102, 103, 344, 413
  J. 290
  J. E. 282
  James 95, 453, 475
  James P. 120, 130, 197, 450
  James Randolph 53
  Jenkins M. 504
  John 39, 406
  John B. 110
  John S. 415
  Lucretia 399
  Martha 130
  Mary 95
  Mary E. 516
  Richard 449, 450
  Victoria J. 450
HOLSEY, Hopkins 242, 390
HOLSONBAKE, Elizzie
  Ellen 295
  J. R. 295, 515
  S. V. 295
HOLSTEAD, E. P. 299
HOLSTEEN, Fannie E. 528
HOLSTON, A. P. 364
HOLT, Judge 485
  Rev. Mr. 402, 406, 407, 434
  A. F. 75, 94, 176
  Abner 217, 234
  Abner F. 113, 404
  Ann Lane 407
  Asa 269, 497, 523
  Daniel 149
  David I. 71
  E. 94, 403, 405
  Eliza 75
  Eliza A. 497
  Ella Lane 94
  Fowler 180, 485
  Grimes T. 212
  Henry D. 295
  Hines 75, 115
  J. G. 376
  Julia E. 519
  Julia M. 212
  Leroy 281
  Lucinda 208
  Miss M. V. 476
  Margaret Ella 423
  Mariah 485
  Martha Sarah 430
  Mary D. 115
  Mary H. 406
  Mary M. 485
  Parthanai R. 217
  Peyton 128, 208
  Peyton C. 212, 214
  Philip Thurmond 74
  Pulaski S. 212
  Pulaski S., Jr. 237, 464
  R. A. 383
  Richard 137
  Robt. S. 211
  Simon 119
  Stephen 406
  T. G. 397
  Tarpley 62, 407, 423
  Thaddeus G. 396, 479, 506
  Wm. 219
  Wm. F. 506
  Wm. S. 439
HOLTON, Abel 85, 421
  Rachel Jane 85
  Warren Abel 85
HOLYOKE, Edward Qugustus, Dr. 17
HOLZENDORF, Mrs. 173
  Alexander 268, 508

HOLZENDORF (cont.)
    Eliza B. 124
    Euphesnia T. 508
    John 124, 465
HONNELL, Wm. 366
HOOBERRY, -- 336
HOOD, James R. 510
HOOK, H. J. 330
    Patrick 238
HOOKER, Rev. Mr. 443, 445,
    446, 449, 452, 461
    Margaret A. 435
    R. 222, 456, 458
    R. M. 447
    Richard 444, 461
HOOKS, J. R. 383
HOOPER, Judge 502
    J. B. 362
    Thomas 325
HOOTEN, James B. 407
HOPKINS, B. B. 150
    Benjamin B. 129, 144
    Elizabeth 129
    Wm. P. 27
HOPPER, Charles 303
HORMON, Thos. 379
HORN, Ferdinand 108
    Isaac 510
    J. R. 483
    Miss L. N. 510
    Thomas J. 505
    W. D. 528
HORNADAY, H. C. 498, 502,
    503, 518
HORNE, A. J. C. 119
    Cornelia A. 509
    Ferdinand 441
    Frances C. 472
    Henry 322
    J. C. 313
    J. R. 488
    Jesse R. 484
    Louisa A. 499
    Mary E. 462
    Whitmill 254
    Wm. 499
    William D. 509
HORNER, Wm. E. 149
HORNIDAY, E. C. 462, 463
HORREL, Sergt. 365
HORSLEY, James 83
    Valentine 83
HORTMAN, Ernana M. 341
HORTON, -- 311
    Daniel 326
    Emily Jane 68
    G. W. 370
    Hosea 235
    Joseph 392
    Josiah 68
    S. 362
HOUGH, B. C. 73
HOUGHTON, R. B. 441
HOUSE, James 54
    Jno. 364
HOUSTON, Adlais O. 258
    Mary E. 258
HOWARD, Capt. 282
    Rev. Mr. 406
    Augustus 32, 76, 400
    Aurelius John Benjamin
        36
    C. W. 278
    Caroline 436
    Caroline E. Susan 231
    Chesley B. 517
    Daniel 448
    David 221, 416
    Eleanor 43
    Elenor A. 416
    Elizabeth Sarah 396
    H. John 404
    Henrietta 36

HOWARD (cont.)
    J. L. 359
    John 42, 191, 209,
        231, 371, 396, 402,
        404, 411, 428, 447
    John A. 221
    John H. 200, 329
    Joseph 43
    Louisa 416
    Mary Ann 428
    Martha 76, 428
    Mary A. 447
    Mary Jane 32
    N. 436
    Samuel S. 43
    Susan 221, 404
    Thacker 329
    Thomas 36, 58, 400,
        416
    Thomas C. 429, 453
    Troup 200
HOWE, Daniel 299
    Joseph 179
    Mollie E. 524
    S., Mrs. 116
    Samuel 224
HOWELL, Emma 206
    H. C. 262
    Henry 525
    John 244, 517
    T. S. 276
HOWLAND, Edward 356
HOXEY, A. B. 94
    John J. B. 433
    Thomas 200
HOY, James A. 244
    T. M. 380
HOYT, Rev. Dr. 431, 439,
    464, 472, 473, 500
    Nathan 483, 496
HUBBARD, A. D. 367
    Elizabeth C. 443
    Samuel D. 185
HUBBERS, W. B. 360
HUBER, Mrs. 171
HUBERT, M. D. 376
    Mark A. 504
    Matthew A. 108
    Robert 265, 501
    Virginia 265
HUCKABY, Felix 442
    J. C. 366
    Jane 442
    W. J. 376
HUDGENS, Joseph E. 521
    Josiah 100
HUDGINS, J. W. 368
    James 95
HUDNELL, Ella F. 528
HUDSON, David 366
    H. D. 521
    Irby 416
    James 117, 421, 433
    Jane A. 416
    John W. 515
    Jonathan A. 83, 401
    Leander M. 135
    M. J. 364
HUEY, Wm. F. J. 51
HUFF, Mr. 33
    Isaac B. 458
    W. A. 516
HUFFMAN, Baloffe 305
HUGER, Benjamin 178
    Francis Kinloch 178
HUGHER, Daniel E. 168
HUGHES, -- 209, 334
    Miss 308
    Daniel G. 357, 517
    Hayden 357, 456
    Haywood 513
    Henry B. 439
    Lucy Ann 412

HUGHES (cont.)
    Michael 175
    Sarah 152
    William Henry 357
    Willis H. 407
HUGHS, John 409
HUGUENIN, E. D. 292, 296
    Julia E. 296
HUINGTON, T. M. 383
HULL, Edward W. 486
    George, Rev. 19
HUME, Rev. Mr. 464
    David 208
HUMPHREYS, Alexander 328
    Jas. 151, 267, 495
    Sarah P. 151
HUMPHRIES, Geo. W. 525
    Hillory B. 353
    Jehu 422
    John 9, 440
    John P. 185
    Martin 358
    Nancy 148
    Peter S. 262, 263
    Solomon 183
    Thomas 401
    Thos. D. 463
    Thomas S. 148
HUNNICUTT, Young 315
HUNT, Adeline S. 419
    Alexander J. 147
    Della 84
    Elizabeth 129
    Elizabeth G. 422
    Ellen Augusta 422
    Jenkins 84
    John 189
    Joseph C. 431
    L. W. 415
    T. M. 502
    Thos. 515
    Thomas S. 406
    Turner 84, 415
    Virginia 144
    Wilkins 416
    Wm. L. 418
HUNTER, -- 334
    Annie A. 335
    Benj. T. 509
    Charles 134
    Fannie 329
    George R. 296
    J. P. 361
    James 398, 406, 474
    John 101, 174
    John W. 72
    Louisa 465
    R. L. 329
    Richard L. 97
    Samuel 524
    Samuel B. 450, 465
    Sarah Jane 97
    Thos. T. 335
    Wm. 426
    William P. 347
HUNTINGTON, Rev. Mr. 522
HUNTON, Corbin L. 111
HURLBUT, Caroline 405
    Geo. R. 73
    Lemuel 405
    Richard W. 441
HURLEY, Wm. J. 465
HURMONDS, Ann 132
    William 132
HURST, -- 435
    Elizabeth M. 435
    Isaac 255
HURT, Benjamin 431
    Charles S. 197
    Elizabeth 435
    Emma W. 524
    G. W. 88
    James Monroe 89

HURT (cont.)
  Jesse M. 517
  Joel 435
  Priscilla 431
  Sarah 197
  William D. 89
  Wm. O. 88, 158, 480
HUSKQITH, Joe 298
HUSON, Charles R. 162
  Frances 143
  Thomas Robinson 173
HUTCHERSON, Richard 499
HUTCHINS, Charles 432
  W. N. 510
HUTCHINSON, Jacob W. 366
  John W. 351
HUTTON, John S. 465
HYSMITH, S. 376
IHLY, John W. 465
INGERSOLD, Dr. 206
INGERSOLL, Charles J. 257, 288
  Charles Jared 338
  Joseph R. 338
INGLES, Rev. Mr. 432
  John 382
INGRAHAM, Ellen 95
  John S. 95, 434, 446
INGRAM, Charles 128, 389, 399
  Creed A. 202
  Margaret Ann 202
  O. R. 385
  W. T. 227
IRVIN, C. M. 466
  I. T. 266
  James 110
  James, Jr. 110
  John 153
  Samuel D. 460
  Washington 253
IRWIN, Gov. 193
  Mr. 296
  Rev. Mr. 515
  C. M. 472, 483
  Chas. M. 454, 469, 473, 509
  David 473
  E. M. 514
  Jane 193
  Jared 460
  Margaret A. 473
ISAAC, Sarah 36
ISAACS, Emanuel 443
  S. 526
ISEY, L. C. 363
ISLER, Sarah Ann Caroline 389
  Wm. 364
ISOM, J. T. 366
IVERSON, Mrs. 283
  Alfred 21, 283, 400, 448
  Caroline 21
  Eliza L. 399
  Julia Maria 448
IVES, Edwin 196
  Emma 196
  Mrs. Mary 528
IVEY, Curtiss W. 459
  Elizabeth W. 397
  J. B. 507
  Robert 397
JABERT, Rev. Mr. 462
JACKET, Red 20
JACKSON, General 16
  Miss 398
  Mr. 273
  Mrs. 171
  Rev. Mr. 338
  A. E. 382
  A. V. 528
  A. W. 328

JACKSON (cont.)
  Alexander 443
  Ann 405
  Caroline E. 428
  Drury 124
  E. H. 272
  Eliza 22
  Green W. 182
  Hatwell 119
  Henry 465
  Henry R. 152
  Hessie M. 482
  J. A. 365
  J. E. 473
  James 210, 471, 510
  Jesse C. 460
  Joe 325
  John 432, 458
  John Wyche 134
  Joseph W. 171
  Josephine 491
  Julia F. 502
  L. Blanche 528
  Louisa M. 399
  Lucinda 414
  Malvina C. 437
  Maria 239
  Martha A. 433
  Mary A. 119, 134, 139
  Mary J. 473
  N. P. 283
  R. W. 377
  Rachel 16
  Robert 405
  Robert M. 403
  Sallie 458
  Samuel W. 405
  Sarah M. R. 465
  Stonewell 293
  Thos. 378
  Thos. G. 191
  Thomas J. 293
  W. J. 382
  W. S. 500
  Warner 379
  Warren 239
  Wilkins W. 459
  Wm. A. 322
  William F. 22, 399
  Z. 134
  Zadok 119, 139
JACOB, Thaddeus O. 469
JACOBS, Eliza 52
  J. J. 287
  Mariah L. 417
  Martha 514
  R. 362
JAMES, Absalom 411
  Allen 402
  Geo. 488
  John W. 327, 513
  Nancy 402
JAMESON, Dr. 253
  Amanda C. 473
  Ann 413
  D. 413
  David 104, 436, 473
  Elizabeth 104
  Sarah 436
JAMIESON, T. S. T. 457
JAMISON, David 271
JANERETT, James M. 437
JANES, Austin, Dr. 20
  David H. 200
  Felix W. 157
  William 169
JAPPIE, Ann 182
  Mary Ann 124
JAQUES, Abraham 440
  Eliza 440
JAQUORS, A. J. 381
JARED, A. S. 367
JARRATT, Eliza M. 124

JARRATT (cont.)
  W. A. 124
  William A. 440
  William D. 66
JARREL, Levi W. 496
JARVIS, Eliza Ann 446
  Elizabeth 64
  George 64
  James 154
JASPER, T. R. 490
JAY, John 18
JEFFERS, John E. 112, 372
JEFFERSON, Thomas, Pres. 7
JEFFRES, Charles 211
  J. M. 360
JEMISON, C. Helen 480
JENKINS, Mr. 229
  Rev. Mr. 415
  Benj. P. 485
  Charles 192
  Charles J. 475
  Eli 205
  Ellis W. 484
  Frances R. 205
  Franklin S. 433, 474
  G. W. 375
  James 37
  Jane 514
  John 14, 105
  Jno. J. 404
  Levi 323
  Mary Ann 398
  Samuel 422
  Susan 404
  Wm. 209
JENNINGS, L. C. 375
  Robert 48
JEPSON, John 78
JERMAINE, Elizabeth 58
JERMANY, Sarah E. 59
JERNIGAN, L. A. 272
  W. G. 322
  W. H. 322
JESSOP, Mary Jane 392
JESSUP, Thomas S. 263
JETER, Andrew, Capt. 13
  Ezekiel 231
JEWETT, Charles R. 463, 489, 508, 512, 527
  Eliza 55
  Eliza H. 507
  George 10, 55, 58, 63, 115, 389, 423
  Henry Cossett 93
  Henry L. 93, 210, 428
  Jane M. 85
  Jonathan 179
  Joshua R. 317
  Judith Harriet 10
  Martha J. 93, 210
  Mary Tabitha 58, 59
  Sallie Louise 210
  William Pettibone 63
JEWITT, Charles R. 463
  George 96
  George Frederick 96
JIROGG, D. 366
JOACHIM, King 391
JOBSON, Ann T. 470
  Elizabeth 202
  Fidelia 341
  Francis A. 341, 518
  Irene Elizabeth 202
  Joseph Higgins 341
  Joseph S. 202
JOHN, Mary J. 490
JOHNS, B. M. 193
  Henry V. D. 243
  I. D. N. 217
  John L. 226
  Mary E. 217
JOHNSIN, Sam 330

JOHNSON, -- 159, 269, 304
  A. L. 361
  Abraham 451
  Adeline J. 410
  Anna S. 412
  Anna T. 197
  B. F. 384
  B. L. 383
  Ben W. 493
  Benjamin J. 277
  Cyrus 176
  D. 380
  Daniel Dupree 353
  E. C. 363
  E. J.
  E. R. 251
  Edmund J. 165
  Edward William 316
  Mrs. Ella 527
  Emmet R. 487
  F. S. 243, 408
  Flora 165, 166
  Francis S. 151
  Frank S. 517
  George W. 288, 503
  Geraldine E. 251
  H. 371
  H. A. 359
  H. V. 251
  H. W. 365
  Harriet J. 405
  J. 326, 366, 376
  J. L. 373
  J. M. 365
  J. R. 364
  Jacob 416
  James 379, 407
  Jeremiah 392
  Job 288
  Joel 507
  John 310
  John Calvin 450
  John J. 366
  John R. 190
  Joseph 167, 472
  Joseph E. 316
  Joseph Gales 52
  L. H. 364
  Lawrence 261
  Lucia 151, 243
  M. H. 377
  Marcus A. 437
  Marcus W. 523
  Margaret A. 316
  Marion 332
  Mark 484
  Mary 71
  Mildred H. 435
  Prince 338
  R. 310
  R. W. 523
  Richard M. 127, 410
  Robert . 521
  Samuel 38, 405
  Solomon R. 421, 466
  Susan 399
  Susan Mary 197
  Theophilus J. 462
  W. 365, 366
  W. J. 363
  W. L. 396
  W. S. 383
  Wm. 35, 282, 416
  Wm. B. 197
  Wm. J. 371
  Wm. Q. W. 476
  Wm. W. 432
JOHNSTON, Ann M. 446
  Arnold 114
  E. J. 166
  Edward J. 449
  Eliza 408
  Felix 446

JOHNSTON (cont.)
  Jacob 71
  James 453
  John 139
  John W. 419
  Margaret J. 453
  Robert R. 10
  T. J. 144
  Thomas Cater 151
  Vashti 421
  W. B. 461
  W. Cost 261
  William 53, 408, 421
  William B. 406
  William K. 412
  Young 95
JOINER, A. 486
  J. 372
  Lawrence 398
  Mary 146
  Meredith 146
  Winford A. M. 459
JOLLEY, Fannie 517
  Georgia Ann 430
  Manson 355
  W. 380
JONES, Co. 403
  Miss 401
  Alonzo W. 510
  Amanda F. 411
  Amos 366
  Anna E. W. 444
  Anna W. 510
  Arabella 185
  Artemesia E. 146
  Burton 523
  Charles A. 32
  Clara R. 483
  Cooper 397
  D. C. 374
  D. R. 469
  Dabney P. 243
  David 53
  Donald B. 157
  Dudley S. 441
  E. C. 507
  E. E. 135, 261
  Eliah 446
  Elias 528
  Eliza Ann 495
  Elizabeth C. 475
  Ellen 269
  Frances D. 528
  Frances Jeanett 408
  G. W. 134
  Gabriel 246, 251
  Geo. S. 527
  George W. 420
  H. 374
  Harriet E. 403
  Henry 367, 488
  Henry P. 156
  Henry W. 137
  Isaac 25
  J. 381
  J. A. 376, 385
  J. B. 377, 430
  J. N. 510
  J. W. 383
  James 402
  James C. 251
  James M. 146, 300
  James Randal 410
  James V. 435
  James W. 256
  James William 146
  Jarrett J. 371
  John 93, 212, 217,
    338, 511
  John E. 185, 451
  Jno. H. 377
  John J. 252, 487
  John Lewis 399

JONES (cont.)
  John W. 368
  John Winston 109
  Judson 364
  Laurence 509
  Letty 426
  Lot 391
  Lum 306
  Mary Ann 416
  Mary E. 515
  Mattie A. 493
  Melvin 243
  Melvina 134
  Morgianna E. 511
  Miss N. A. 528
  Paul 377
  R. 362
  Roger 142
  S. M. 368
  S. W. 383
  Sallia A. 488
  Sallie V. 515
  Sam 238
  Sam'l F. 444
  Samuel P. 434
  Seaborn H. 252
  Stephen 115, 411
  Susan 446
  Syman Hall 137
  T. C. 370
  Thomas, Sr. 346, 474
  Toliver 475
  Valeria B. 457
  Virginia E. 454
  W. B. 362
  W. L. 518
  W. T. 363
  Wiley 191
  Wiley E. 457
  Wm. B. 269
  Mahala 440
  Malcolm D. 357
  Martha E. 217
  Martha F. 511
  Martha J. 489
  Mary 53, 338
  Wm. C. 22
  William Carey 227, 336
  Wm. Drayton 269
  Wm. H. 515
  Wm. M. 278
  Wm. W. 277
  Zeno Alvoreno 22
JOHNS, I. D. N. 478
  J. J. 380
JORDAN, Mr. 143
  Absalom 413
  Ann T. 435
  Aron 85
  Benjamin F. 503
  Benj. S. 203
  Elias 61
  Enoch 121
  Frances M. 479, 480
  Green H. 177
  J. G. 427
  J. J. 437
  Josiah G. 85
  K. 358
  Lewis J. 65
  Martha E. 430
  Matthew G. 408
  Nancy 413
  Nancy J. 435
  Thomas 478
  Thomas H. 490
  W. M. 363
  Wallace 281
  Wm. W. 430
JORDIN, John R. 442
JOURDAN, Isaac G. 452
  Madaline V. 475
  Nancy 495

JOURDAN, Tabitha 390
   Warren 475
JOURDON, T. 382
JUDGE, Philip 308
JUDSON, P. M. 174
JULIAN, L. 520
JULORT, Wm. 370
JUMPER, John 244
JUNG, Charles 169
JUSTICE, Dempsey 15
   Eliza 15
   Rebecca 452
JUSTISS, Martha Ann 413
KABLE, Magdolena 305
KAMEN, F. M. 360
KAPPEL, J., Sr. 97
KAUF, Louise 480
KAUGH, M. 360
KEAN, -- 125
KEATING, -- 196
KEATZ, Louis Jefferson
   Williamson 37
KEEBLER, Capt. 246
KEENE, Ann T. 140
KEENEY, E. 390
KEENIM, W. J. 381
KEIGLER, J. W. 467
KEITER, Capt. 283
KEITH, W. 480
   W. J. 460
KEITT, L. M. 258
   W. J. 258
KELL, John McIntosh 493
KELLAM, Rossel 392
   Joseph O. 333
KELLEY, Jackson 365
KELLUM, Elizabeth 453
KELLY, B. A. 362
   David 438
   Henry 398
   Hugh 220
   John W. 288
   William S. 480
KELSEY, Caroline W. 427
   Chloe N. 220
   D. 446
   Daniel 72, 113, 448
   Elizabeth 113
   Joel 336
   Mercy 72
   Noah 220
KELTON, Lucinda 55
   Robert 55, 412
KEMP, Kindred 477
KENAN, John 194
   Michael J. 403
   Owen H. 182, 193, 194, 257
   Uriah T. 417
KENDALL, Capt. 110
   Amos 354
   David 263
KENDRICK, Rev. Mr. 434, 439
   Allen 370
   Ben C. 525
   Ephraim 404
   J. R. 124, 433, 434, 435, 436, 438, 439, 440, 442, 443, 445
   James R. 435
   Jno. B. 445
   John W. 523
   Judson A. 141, 435
   Julia 503
   L. 259
   Martin 280, 434
   Mary Angelina 141
   Wm. 378
KENNEDY, E. B. 87
   E. B., Mrs. 185
   Ellen B. 75
   Frances J. 87

KENNEDY (cont.)
   James 171
   Jesse J. 418
   W. C. 87
   Wm. C. 75, 185, 427
   William T. 75
KENNON, R. E. 528
KENNY, Jemmin 322
KENT, Mary 491
KERCE, James H. 311
   William C. 311
KERLEN, W. J. 377
KERLER, V. H. W. 370
KERR, E. 368
   S. F. 372
KEY, Rev. Mr. 449
   Adeline 418
   B. P. 284
   Camilla 502
   Clarissa 489
   C. W. 82, 181, 411, 418, 420, 439, 475, 484, 512, 515
   Eliza Virginia 458
   Elizabeth 82
   Francis S. 79, 245
   J. C. G. 445
   J. S. 482, 521
   Joseph 279
   Jos. E. 527
   Joseph P. 418
   Joseph S. 490, 517, 527
   Joshua 397
   Mary Ann D. 418
   Mary E. 438
   Mary Taylor 245
   P. Barton 245
   Philip Barton 240
   Pleasant Wimberly 82
   Rebecca 181
   Samantha 489
   T. W. 418
   Tandy W. 63
   Temperance 284
KIBBEE, Mary 249
   Wm. 192
KICKENSON, Rev. Mr. 419
KIDDOO, J. J. 470
KILLINGSWORTH, A. G. 439
KILLPATRICK, Mary S. W. 353
   William 353
KILPATRICK, Bettie 517
   Emma 517
   Frances W. 203
   J. A. 365
   J. J. 372
   Louisa C. 486
   T. S. 263
   Wm. 205, 486
   William G. 203
KIMBERLY, Anson 401
   Edward Augustus 86
   Eliza A. 418
   Louisa Jones 86
   Geo. A. 87
KIMBLE, Mary Ann 392
KIMBRO, Mrs. Jane 433
   Rebecca Ann 431
   W. B. 384
KIMBROUGH, C. M. 377
   Geo. 496
KINBROUGH, Martha W. 448
   O. S. 208
KINCHIN, Eliza J. 472
KINCHLEY, Edward F. 316
KING, A. J. 384
   A. M. B. 412
   Anderson 266
   Angus M. 155
   Butler 399
   C. 359

KING (cont.)
   Charles 463
   David 247, 482
   George 424
   George S. 450, 464
   Harvey 333
   Henry J. 492
   Hiram 359
   Hugh M. D. 267
   Isabella Catherine 7
   J. Laurence 507
   J. T. 372
   Jackson S. 367
   Jacob 411, 492, 510, 519
   James Lawrence 434
   James N. 183, 470
   James R. 460
   John 123
   John A. 313
   M. 362, 363
   Mary A. 482
   Miles 39
   Nancy 456
   Porter 464
   Ralph 7
   Rufus, Hon. 10
   Sarah A. 470
   Sarah Ann 183
   Susan 212
   Thomas 157
   Thomas Butler 297
   Thomas Clarence 183
   Thomas D. 162
   W. S. 138
   Wesley 266
   William 182, 333
   William Augustus, Dr. 21
   Wm. C. 468
   Wm. D. 485
   William Skelton 150
   Yelverton P. 321
KINGDOM, Thomas 248
KINGMAN, Asbury 443
KINKINS, Samuel 200
KINNEY, Choice 135
KIRBY, Rev. Mr. 445
KIRCHOFF, Charles 311
KIRK, Thomas 277
KIRKHAM, J. H. 517
   Josephine 517
KIRKPATRICK, John 122
   John L. 475
KIRKSEY, James 125
KIRTLAND, Erastus 453
KITCHEN, Thomas W. 360
KITCHENS, Boaz 269
   Mrs. Mary H. 269
   Mary Jane 517
KLECKLEY, Dan'l 202
KLECKLY, Catherine 513
   Jacob 513
KNAPP, Samuel 4
KNICKERBACKER, Harman 178
KNIGHT, Judge 525
   Abner 491
   Eliza R. 19
   Elizabeth 230
   George 219
   James A. 90, 429, 451
   John 230
   John T. 471
   Mary 307
   Matilda 491
   Paranella 230
   Tabitha L. 90
   Walter T. 19
KNOTT, J. W. 116
   Miss M. M. 525
   Marie Helen Cook 116
KNOWLES, J. 487, 494, 499, 501, 502, 523

KNOWLES (cont.)
  J. P. 364
  James Sheridan 267
  Joseph E. 421
  Joshua 441
  Thos. 455
KNOX, H. 27
  Susan P. 27
  Wm. 329
KNOYLE, John 359
KOELER, Fred 314
KOLB, Mrs. 330
  C. M. 484
KOLLINGSWORTH, Anderson G.
  273
KUH, Philipina 433
KUNZE, John M. 180
KYLE, H. C. 361
  John 200
LADD, Daniel 457
LAFAYETTE, Gen. 10
LAGGETT, Jordan 377
LAHAY, W. 366
LAIDLER, Ann E. 506
  John 280
  Sarah A. 513
  W. 506
LAKE, Francis 508
  John W. 497
  W. A. 283
LALLEMAND, Henry, Gen. 2
LAMAR, A. 440
  A. K. 463
  Anderson 249
  Andrew J. 521
  Ann 446
  Ann H. 230
  B. B., Mrs. 147, 273
  Benjamin 47
  Benj. B. 41
  Benjamin Jones 132
  Clementius Davis 98
  Eliza W. 128
  Eliza W. W. 412
  Ellen 193
  Frances M. 466
  Francis 70
  G. B. 75
  Gazaway Basil 106
  Geraldine 492
  H. G. 47, 94, 95, 98,
    220, 245, 277, 280,
    440
  H. J. 132
  Henry C. 280
  Henry G. 86, 246, 249,
    395, 527
  Henry G., Jr. 220
  Henry J. 457
  Iola E. 527
  Jack 354
  James 40, 47, 200, 412
  Jefferson J. 53, 66,
    395
  Jefferson M. 521
  Jenny 354
  John 70, 77, 82, 93,
    245, 246, 250, 412,
    459
  John B. 291, 354
  John T. 75, 391, 417,
    440
  John Y. 230
  Josephene 459
  Miss L. E. A. 466
  L. Q. C. 33, 447, 467
  Lafayette 284
  Leonidas 277, 278
  Lucius M. 469
  M. A. 98, 467
  M. B. 57
  Martha A. 106
  Mary 40

LAMAR (cont.)
  Mary Ann 521
  Mary Frances 82
  Mirabeau B. 21, 82,
    254, 389
  Nancy 27
  Rebecca 57, 82, 395
  Rebecca A. 53
  Rebecca E. 497
  Savannah 191
  Tabitha B. 21
  Thomas 200
  Thomas A. 147
  Thomas B. J. 148
  Thomas C. 292
  Thos. R. 27, 128, 227,
    395, 412
  Mrs. U. T. 514
  V. B. 132
  Virginia 86
  Zach 408
  Zachariah 36, 106, 158
LAMB, Mrs. E. A. 525
  G. W. 353
  Leonidas Beattie 353
LAMEMI, J. 373
LAMKIN, John L. 218
LAMPRY, Charles M. 514
LANCASTER, H. H. 377
  Joseph B. 205
LAND, Calvin 366
  Carrie C. 523
  Constantine H. 111
  Henry 239
  Isaac 382
  James 416
LANDERS, D. 373
LANDRUM, -- 246
  Rev. Mr. 497
  George T. 231, 479
  Naomi 129
  S. 231, 459, 460, 463,
    464, 465, 469, 471,
    473, 474, 476, 479,
    480, 485, 489, 491,
    492, 495, 496, 497,
    498, 503, 504, 505,
    506, 508, 511, 512,
    513
  Samuel 227, 234
  Sylvanus 129, 456, 457,
    464, 477, 491, 493,
    494, 507, 509
  Wm. T. 231
LANE, Mr. 306
  Rev. Mr. 506, 514
  B. F. 390
  Bryan F. 398
  C. 497
  C. W. 499
  David 197
  Fannie A. 509
  Fannie H. 197
  Florida H. 240
  Henry 502
  James 305
  James S. 240
  Jim 229
  Martha 502
  Penelope 408
  R. J. 359
  William 469
  William A. 491
LANERY, A. 374
LANEY, Noah 412
  W. P. 285
LANG, W. 377
  Wm. 316
LANGLEY, Rev. Mr. 528
  Isaiah 406, 435
  Thos. B. 516
LANGMADE, E. S. 523
  Sarah F. 523

LANGSTON, John 370
LANIER, Cynthia 453
  Eugenia C. 467
  Mary 453
  Sampson Massey 447
  Sarah E. 498
  Sterling 452
  Thos. 373
  Wilhelmina L. 452
LANSON, Andrew 445
LAPSEY, -- 351
LAREY, Catharine 476
LARK, W. J. 373
LARMER, Author D. 373
LAROCHE, Mrs. S. M. 518
LARY, Wilson 189
LASSETER, Amos 452
  Benjamin 474
  Samuel N. 469
LATHAM, Henry T. 146
LATHROP, Frank 278
LATIMER, Anderson J. 416
  Emily A. 525
LATIMORE, Edward 416
LATTIMORE, D. B. 380
LAURIMORE, Newton 371
LAVIALLE, Bishop 312
LAW, Benjamin Virginius
  28
  Isiah 65
  J. S. 456
  John A. 297
  John S. B. 28
  Margaret E. 297
  Sarah 297
LAWER, John 358
LAWHON, Allen 214
LAWRENCE, Amanda 418
  Amos 147
  Charity J. 474
  James J. 474
  Margaret E. 517
  R. 377
  Sherrod A. 170
  T. B. 346
LAWSHE, Elizabeth 472
  Lewis 515
  Martha E. 489
  Wm. C. 489
LAWSON, Elizabeth 392
  Hugh 196, 393, 453
  James 354
  John F. 460
  Lucinda 389
  N. A. 361
  P. A. 84
  Thomas Hardin 84
LAWTON, A. 371
  Albert S. 155
  Louisa H. 154
  R. T. 498
  T. T. 372
LAYTON, Lowther 395
LEA, Pryor 483
LEACH, James 306
  James H. C. 307
LEAK, Jane 66
  Jeremiah 437
  Samuel 66
LEAKE, Jeremiah 96
LEARY, Calvin 153
  Hepsey 153
  Jeremiah 153
  Sarah J. 487
  Wm. 518
LEAVANS, F. W. 360
LE CONTE, Anna C. 496
  Ophelia 514
  Sarah A. 450
LEDBETTER, A. 364
LEDDEN, M. E. 445
LEDLOW, B. 370
LEE, -- 349

LEE (cont.)
  A. W. 354, 371
  D. C. 208
  Greene B. 188
  John 348, 454
  Lewis 219
  Louisa 452
  R. E. 331
  Richard Henry 152
  S. S. 331
LEECH, Joseph 171
LEFEVER, William 85
LEFEVRE, Bishop 346
LEFILS, Armand 254
  Carrie Alabama 254
  John Armand 254
LEFTAN, Philip 318
LEGARE, Hugh S. 80
LEGG, Mary O. 521
LEGGITT, Jas. 290
LEIGHTNER, T. R. 359
LELIS, H. H. 358
LEMEN, John 501
LEML, Andrew 370
LEMON, Jane 407
LENAR, James D. 379
LENGEL, Herr 322
LENORE, W. J. 374
LENTZ, Otto 171
LEONARD, Cate 484
  John S. 93
  Roderick 72
  Susan 409
LEQUEX, Peter, Captain
    12
LESDERNIER, Emily P.,
    Mrs. 240
LE SEUR, Meade, Sr. 283
LESLIE, Eliza 222
  James 16
  R. 373
LESSES, Benjamin 171
LESTER, -- 242
  Benjamin L. 111
  Camilla S. 454
  Caroline M. 426
  Caswell 10
  D. 362
  George N. 473
  Henrietta E. 461
  James D. 426, 492
  James W. 519
  John 179
  John E. 454
  Josephine Victoria 519
  R. B. 263, 475, 493,
    519
  Robert B. 454
  Sarah L. 438
  Sarah P. 167
  Miss V. A. 473
  W. 360
  Wade H. 263
LESTEUR, John S. 468
LESUEUR, Camilla 190
  John 190
  Stephen 414
  Susan 439
LEVERETT, R. Manning 453
  Thomas, Rev. 7
LEVERETTE, Thomas 238
LEVI, Marcus 1
LEVY, Ann Louisa 190
  Benj. 256
  Chas. P. 190
  Lyon J. 307
LEWELLEN, James T. 48
LEWIS, Mr. 344
  Rev. Mr. 462
  Miss A. S. 499
  Adkin B. 351
  Alvin 325
  Anna 502

LEWIS (cont.)
  Anna C. 88
  Archibald 97
  B. B. 519
  Benj. 361
  Catharine L. 489
  Charles S. 392
  Curtis 87, 283
  Elizabeth 489
  F. F. 232
  F. K. 490
  Folten K. 489
  Frederick F. 403
  Fulton R. 509
  J. S. 383
  Jane 283
  John 249
  John B. 509
  John L. 88
  John Langdon 406
  Joseph 377
  L. T. 373
  Mary F. 481
  Morgan 87
  Nathan 358
  Nathan G. 158
  Noland 452
  Robt. 361
  Sarah A. 430
  W. H. 509
  Wash 325
  Zachariah 489
LFEWELLEN, James P. 478
LIBBY, William 346
LIDDEN, Catherine 428
LIDDON, Benjamin G. 154
  Cora Eliza 154
  Susan E. 154
LIGHT, H. B. 383
LIGHTFOOT, -- 91
  John B. 274
  John William 169
  Josephine 91, 274
  Thomas 118
  W. S. 263, 451
  Walter 274
  Wm. S. 169
LILES, J. McDuffie 252
LILLIBRIDGE, Gardner L.
    439
LINCH, D. H. 384
  Mary Ann 411
LINDER, Lavinia V. 516
LINDLEY, J. T. 377
LINDSAY, Fannie H. 484
  G. B. 377
  H. M. 446
  John 379
  John B. 524
  John M. 358
  Moses 377
LINDSLEY, Joel 306
LINGERS, L. 370
LINGO, Wm. S. 288
LINK, Erastus H. 484
LINTEPOWDER, Miss 171
LIPPITT, Mary Ann 45
  Samuel C. 186
LIPSHUT, Jacob 382
LIPSCOMBE, Nathan 340
LISTER, J. 377
LITTLE, Charles C. 355
  Frank 319
  K. J. T. 431
  R. J. T. 461
LITTLEJOHN, A. N. 507
  T. L. 365
LIVELY, Geo. W. 512
LIVINGSTON, Elizabeth Ann
    149
  H. A. 224
  Jno. S. 149
  Mrs. Mortimer 176

LIVINGSTON (cont.)
  Philo Emma 149
  Rosa 498
LLEARY, John A. 116
LLOCKETT, Benj. G. 256
  Sarah 256
LLOYD, Levi A. 267
  Louisiana B. 402
LOBDELL, Charles 317
LOCHRANE, Judge 524
  O. A. 512
LOCKE, James J. 513
LOCKET, Cullen 106
  Sarah W. 445
LOCKETT, Antoinett 474
  Emily A. 512
  Susan A. 424
  Wm. G. 242, 243
LOCKHART, Henry 286
  Martha 400
LODGE, Robert H. 472
LOFLEY, S. T. 520
LOFTIN, Joel 104
  Nancy 104
LOGAN, Geo. M. 150, 457
  John M. 149
LOGSDON, -- 324
LOMAX, Tennent 498
LOMINAC, Elvira C. 477
LONE, S. 381
LONG, David 372
  Elias 116
  Ellis 177
  English 369
  Evans 80
  Gabriel, Maj. 10
  Mr. and Mrs. Geo. M.
    246
  Henry 306, 477
  James A. 461
  John 58, 353
  John B. 462
  John J. 125
  John Pendleton 116
  Joseph H. 462
  Louisa 80
  Maria L. 177
  Mariah L. 116
  Marietta 477
  Mary Ann R. 197
  R. H. 235
  Robert Hardeman 246
  S. 364
  Thomas T. 197
  William 432
  William H. 235
LONGSTREET, J. C. 467
  James B. 230
  Virginia L. 447
LOOMIS, Harris 48
  I. N. 452
LOPER, Elizabeth C. 100
  M. J. 443
  N. J. 100
  Susannah 438
  W. W. 383
LORD, Frances Anna 432
  Frederick 198
  Helen L. 36
  John P. 418
  Joseph L. 36, 432
  Sylvester S. 182
LORING, Charles 168
  Joseph S. 5
LOUDON, Robert 64
LOVE, Mary J. 513
LOVELL, G. 363
LOVETT, J. 361
  Martha 81
  Robert 369
LOVING, J. 47
  John 49
  Nancy 49

LOW, Obedeance H. 403
LOWCAY, Eliza J. 483
  Aaron A. 493
  Benjamin H. 494
  Caroline A. 446
  Dizzie 521
  Drusilla 505
  Eliza A. 44
  Emma R. 494
  Geo. Y. 420
  Jacob 348, 521
  John W. 145, 529
  Joshua 461
  Kizziah 348
  Mary J. 513
  Patience Z. 446
  Thomas 44, 83, 420
  W. T. 528
  Wm. 290, 494
  Wm. H. 446
LOWELL, W. W. 361
LOWERY, James 407
  James R. 411
LOWNDES, William 233
LOWREY, Rev. Mr. 405
LOWRY, Ann Alice 486
  Davis 432
  E. D. 486
  Eliza Jane 500
  F. D. 414, 432, 500
  John 278
  Laura W. 429
LOWTHER, Mrs. E. L. 494
  Miss F. O. 494
  John 141
  Miss M. R. 494
  Samuel 51
  William 414
LOYD, James V. 221
  R. L. 385
LOYLESS, Henry M. 502
LUBLIN, E. 368
LUCAS, Alah 421
  C. M. 130
  D. 372
  Henry E., Jr. 346
  L. B. 427
  Leonora C. 427
  William 340
LUCE, Allen L. 83, 431
LUCKEY, James 84
  John 84
  R. H. 474
LUCKIE, Miss E. 488
LUCKY, Rev. Mr. 463
LUDLOW, Charles D. 237
LUDWIG, Jacob 433
LUGG, Arnon 377
LUKE, -- 321
  Daniel 340
  James 340
  William 340
LUMPKIN, Alice Marion 192
  Callie 474
  Callie M. 464
  Celestia 500
  George 222, 474
  H. H. 81, 410
  Helen 81
  Henry H. 257
  Henry H., Jr. 135, 435
  Henry Hopson 201
  Jack 129
  John B. 396
  John H. 218, 263, 413
  John Henry 52
  John T. 192, 201
  Joseph H. 201, 464
  Joseph Henry 332
  Joseph Henry, Jr. 167
  Lucy 257
  M. Antoinette 486
  Marion M. 410

LUMPKIN (cont.)
  Martha Antionette 52
  Sarah G. 432
LUMSDEN, Adelia 49
LUNDAY, Julia A. 253
LUNDY, Abner A. 90
  James Tharp 253
  Jane 396
  John W. 257
  Lucy L. 393
  Luracy (Mrs.) 69
  Robert 282
  Thomas 9, 22, 393
  William 253, 440
LUNSFORD, Bazil Lamar 134
  Enoch 122
  George J. 134, 421
  James 429
LUSK, -- 304
  Wm. 365
LUTHER, J. H. 463, 470
LUTIER, Joseph 208
LUTS, F. 363
LYLES, J. B. 374
  R. B. 337
LYNCH, William F. 301
LYNCHBURGER, F. M. 362
LYNN, Asa 80
  Phillips 377
  Sterling P. 80
LYON, General 279
  Frank 345
  Jas. P. 505
  Jane E. 461
  John 120
  Rebecca 120
  T. L. 345
LYTLE, Thomas T. 330
MAAS, Mr. 323
MABERY, Thomas 403
  Woodford 432
MABREY, Wm. R. 363
MABRY, --- Ford 299
  John --- Ford 299
  Laura 299
  Simeon M. 486
MACARTHY, Arabella 439
  Roger 439
MACAULEY, Geo. 489
MAC DONNELL, Geo. G. N. 496
MACK, J. M. 377
MACKEY, Thomas 4
MACKIE, James D. 174
MACON, Charity D. 180
  Louisa C. 515
  Maria W. 97
  Martha S. 431
  Nathaniel 46
  Sarah E. 423
  Wm. A. 499
  Wm. G. 97, 109, 180, 431
MADDOCKS, William W. 478
MADDOX, Rev. Mr. 428
  Eliza 392
  Euliza Jane 478
  George W. 101
  John J. 267
  Lewis 392
  P. N. 443, 486
MADDUX, H. A. 384
  P. N. 407
  Nathan T. 516
MADEN, J. A. 362
MADISON, Mrs. D. 117
  Eleanor 17
  James 117
MADRAY, J. L. 359
MADREY, F. 278
MAFFIT, Francis A. 247
MAFFITT, John Newland 247
MAFFORD, Thomas 399

MAGEE, H. W. 362
MAGILLIS, -- 173
MAGRATH, -- 314
MAGRUDER, Henry C. 301
MAGUIRE, Thomas 352
MAHER, Michael 171
MAHOOL, Thomas 527
MAIRS, Juliet Ann 438
MAJORS, Mrs. 286
MALDEN, Caleb 185, 208
MALLARY, C. D. 400, 462, 482
  Susan 417
MALLORY, Rev. Mr. 440, 486
  C. D. 427, 524
  George W. 404
  Sarah 241
MALLRY, Charles 274
MALONE, Col. 473
  Chas. J. 416, 525
  Henry A. 37
  Mrs. J. T. 527
  Lucinda J. 453
  Matthew 153
  S. 479
  Susan M. 525
  Thomas F. 453
MALSBY, Henry M. 523
  John 267
  Lott 197, 263
  M. E. 263
  Mariah 267
  Thomas 197
MALUS, Florian 161
MAMS, T. M. 358
MANARD, A. A. 181
  C. E. 181
  Carrie Alida 181
MANDAL, A. 392
MANGHAM, Ann J. 158
  James H. 232
  John C. 158
  Wm. D. 50
MANGUM, Sysigambis 142
MANLY, Rev. Mr. 399
  K. H. 185
MANN, Rev. Mr. 429
  A. T. 492, 522
  A. V. 452
  Alfred 486, 487
  Alfred T. 430
  Alice 301
  Asa V. 414
  Hector
  Henrietta Ann 218
  J. D. 408, 411
  John H. 218
  Louisa A. T. 443
  Stephen A. 443
  Thomas M. 98
MANNING, John 367
  R. R. 525
  S. M. 468, 481
MANSE, F. G. 380
MANSON, Rev. Mr. 418, 469
  F. E. 483, 520
  Thomas 440
MARABLE, Sallie M. 528
MARBLE, A. G. 385
MARCELLIN, Richard 34
MARCH, A. 512
  C. W. 171
MARCHMAN, S. C. 497
MARCY, Wm. L. 215
MARION, Gen. 18
MARKS, Cornelia 442
  James R. 368
  R. T. 435, 442
  Richard T. 316, 396
MARR, -- 329
  John Q. 274
  R. H. 329

MARS, H. 384
MARSH, Chas. 170
  John 205
  Mulford 190
  Sarah 205
MARSHAL, J. H. 359
  William 343
MARSHALL, -- 351
  Alexander 226
  Humphrey 513
  J. B. 364
  John 38, 474, 506
  John M. 459, 478, 479, 485, 525
  Rebecca A. 504
MARSON, John 37
MARSTON, Carlos, Mrs. 300
  R. M. 344
MARTIN, Captain 336
  A. W. 205, 406, 511
  Absalom 112
  B. Y. 268
  C. P. B. 272, 501
  Carlisle P. B. 474, 519
  Catharine 35
  Charles P. B. 519
  Eliza J. 272
  Eliza M. 440
  Elizabeth C. 445
  Elizabeth J. 189
  Exer A. 205
  Fannie 480
  G. G. 278
  Gabriel 327, 342
  J. 361
  J. A. 381
  Jacob 152
  James 179
  John 74, 189
  John G., Jr. 493
  Laura Clyde 519
  Martha D. 460
  Riley 305
  Robert 296, 372
  Robert E. 254
  W. 362
  W. J. 367, 473
  Wm. 181, 299, 339
  William D. 511
  Wm. J. 181
  William M. 410
MASH, J. T. 377
MASKILL, P. W. S. 369
MASON, C. T. 383
  D. H. 377
  Rev. Gideon 398
  Lizzie 156, 330
  M. M. 156, 157, 165, 166, 472
  R. B. 125
  W. F. 331
MASSENBURG, Mollie P. 526
  William 526
MASSETT, John 292
MASSEY, Abram 126
  J. J. 367
  Mary S. 527
  Nathan M. 456
  Orren E. 528
  Thomas J. 527
MASTERSON, Clemmons 505
MASTIAN, J. L. 35
MASTICK, Jacob 170
MATHER, E. C. 104
  Emeline C. 168
  J. C. 104, 450
  Jane I. 435
  John C. 168, 443
  Roselle 168
MATHESON, Daniel 391
MATHEW, J. 381
MATHEWS, A. J. 377

MATHEWS (cont.)
  Friar 428
  G. M. 367
  J. D. 459
  James 349
  John C. 193
  Mary Beaufort 136
  Mollie A. H. 520
  Moses 29
  W. A. 136, 480, 519
  Wm. 506
  William A. 459
  Wm. E. 505
MATHIS, Miss A. E. 484
  Charles 346
MATHISON, Hattie 305
MATTHEW, W. 460
MATTHEWS, A. M. 324
  Elizabeth 297
  Emeline L. 416
  Francis L. 501
  Francis S. 297
  James 126
  Maria 421
  Mary D. 297
  Morris 51
  Nancy 349
  Romulus W. 454
  W. D. 417
  Wm. A. 422
MATTISON, Spencer 426
MAUK, Francis, Mrs. 249
  Matthias 249
MAULDIN, J. N. 384
MAULDING, Martha C. 499
MAULSBY, Maria 491
MAURY, John W. 177
MAUSSENET, Delie 293
MAXWELL, Elizabeth F. 104
  J. 363
  J. E. 168
  Manfredonia 74
  Mary Ann 104
  Sarah M. 484
  Wm. A. 104, 511
  William L. 74
MAY, J. T. 489, 513
  James T. 504
  Nelson H. 303
  P. L. J. 491
MAYFIELD, R. E. 381
MAYNARD, Sanford F. 451
MAYO, John 323
MAYOE, H. L. 381
MAYS, G. W. 377
  Robert 454, 458, 460
  Seaborn F. 503
  Sophronia L. 487
MC ABEE, J. E. 364
MC ADEE, M. 380
MC AFEE, Effie 228
  John 382
  Jonathan A. 486
  Mary 228
  W. M. 228
MC ALHANNON, -- 377
MC ALISTER, Mr. 344
MC ALLISTER, F. Marion 527
MC ALLUM, A. 488
  Archibald 110
  Mary 491
MC ALPIN, Amelia 206
  Joseph 206, 448
MC ALPIR, Alex 369
M'CANTS, John A. W. 467
MC ARTHUR, C. W. 384
  D. R. 305
  Harriet Rebecca 467
  Laura N. 519
  Mary J. 305
  Samuel 432
  Sarah Elizabeth 305

MC ARTHY, K. 206
MC BAIN, Col. 217
  Henrietta 496
  Newman 216
MC BEE, -- 377
  A. H. 365
MC BRIDE, John H. 290
MC BRYDE, James 399, 507
MC CAIN, Alexander 197
  J. B. 364
MC CALL, Eleazar 148, 393
  G. R. 484, 491, 499, 502, 504, 524
  James D. 317
  James H. 513
  Lucas 89, 426
  Roger 90, 436
  Sarah Georgianna 394
  Thomas 394
MC CALLS, Charles H. 513
MC CALLUM, Addie 488
  Angus 70
  Archibald 499
  Catharine 409
  John 444
  Margaret 24
  Mary 415
  Patrick 65
  Sarah 415
  Susan 414
MC CANTERY, Wm. 379
MC CANTS, Mrs. A. B. 60
  John 60
MC CARDLE, John M. 262
  Josephine 262
MC CAREY, J. F. 370
MC CARROLL, T. 373
MC CARTER, James 465
  James R. 209, 451
  John 57
  John H. 399
MC CARTHY, Albert James 503
  Chas. 284
  Dan 368
  Roger 45, 100
MC CAULEY, Rev. Dr. 422
  Geo. T. 495
MC CAULY, M. A. 372
MC CAWLEY, Rev. Dr. 438
MC CAY, Robert T. 463
MC CLELLAN, -- 315
MC CLENDON, Edna 349
MC CLOUD, A. 374
  D. H. 374
MC CLUNG, Col. 179
MC CLURE, E. 367, 380
  John 82
MC COLL, John 402
MC COMB, Mary C. 195
  Mathew B. 181
  R. 195
MC COMBS, Robert 21, 210
  Sarah W. 21
MC CONNELL, Capt. 272
MC COOK, Mary 92
  W. G. 498
MC COOL, Susan A. 201, 436
MC CORD, D. J. 180
MC CORKLE, A. 362
MC CORMACK, Mathew 288
MC CORMICK, James 336
MC COY, Abner 392
  Burwel 290
  Edward 416
  Eugenia E. 479
  H. E., Mrs. 225
  Henry 225
  J. 364
  J. S. 476
  James 479
  Martha 392

MC COY (cont.)
  Warren S. 486
MC CRANEY, J. J. 368
MC CRARY, J. B. 265
  Mary A. 265
MC CRAW, Emily Milledge
  56
MC CRAW, Miller W. 56,
  428
MC CREADY, P. B. 414
MC CREARY, Bartly 526
MC CULLERS, Isabella L.
  29
  Matthew 29
  Penelope 29
MC CULLOCH, F. 380
MC CUNE, Elizabeth A. 454
  James A. 110
  Oliver J. 454
  R. J. 110
  Rufus W. 455
  William A. 454
MC CURDY, Robert 475
MC DANIEL, C. 290
  Jas. 377
MC DANIELS, Augustus 462
MC DILL, Margaret 198
MC DOE, Jno. 110
MC DONALD, Sr. 173
  Judge 393
  Ann 39
  Catherine 258
  Charlotte J. 318
  Chas. J. 39, 260, 269,
    390, 423
  Eliza 260
  G. 425, 517
  Geo. 369
  George N. 514
  J. T. 377
  J. W. 370
  James M. 469
  Joseph 284, 472
  Joshua 164
  Sarah 460
MC DOUGLAD, Alex. 199
MC DOWELL, Geo. M. 487
MC DOWN, Ann 140
MC DUFFIE, Ann Eliza 144
  George 130
  George W. 144, 203
  John 124
  Laura 203
  Sarah Ann 144, 203
  V. J. 374
MC EACHIN, J. Wesley 200
MC ELROY, R. B. 374
  W. 457
MC ELVANE, Dan'l 489
  Mary 489
MC EVOY, R. P. 517
MC EWEN, Abel 266
MC FARLIN, James M. 134
  Lucinda 471
MC FERSON, Arthur 389
MC GARITY, James H. 474
MC GEE, Mary 390
  O. W. 363
MC GEHEE, Rev. Dr. 450
  E. H. 527
  E. T. 477, 506, 513,
    520
  Edmund 220
  Edward T. 398, 445,
    484, 487, 511, 513
  F. J. 514
  John Samuel 220
  Miss L. E. 514
MC GETRICK, Michael 153
MC GHEE, E. T. 458, 471
MC GILL, W. W. 381
MC GINNIS, Jewett 320
  R. J. 368

MC GINTRY, R. C. 377
MC GLOHON, T. 508
MC GLORHAM, Mary F. 491
MC GOLDRICK, Martha L.
  507
  R. H. 159
  Richard 410
MC GRADY, J. T. 366
MC GRATH, A. 365
MC GRAW, Catherine
  Rebecca 160
  Elizabeth 160, 414
  Hezekiah 160, 162
  J. F. 360
MC GREAL, Catharine 457
MC GREGOR, Alexander 202
  Alexander S. 528
  John A. 453
  Mrs. M. A. 510
MC GRIFF, Euofair J. 468
  J. A. 458
MC GUIRE, -- 351
  Dr. 234
  Absolam B. 414
  Ann A. 500
  C. 364
MC HENRY, Thomas 382
MC HUGH, J. W. 384
MC ILHANE, N. 364
MC ILHENY, D. W. 362
MC INTOSH, Col. 107
  Rev. Mr. 435
  James M. 266
  M. 374
  Spaulding 291
MC INVALS, W. B. 372
MC KASKILL, Murdock 420
MC KAY, Mr. 195
  Daniel 5, 48
  John 468
  Juliet 48
  Juliet H. 496
  William 195
MC KEE, Mr. 53
  Rev. Mr. 349
  Thomas S. 508
MC KEEN, Robert W. 399
MC KENDREE, Bishop 37
MC KENZIE, John 134
  Kenneth 166
  Milton S. 447
MC KINLEY, Mrs. 215
  Claudia Fisk 472
  John 142
MC KINNIE, -- 171
  Hezekiah 508
MC KINNON, John B. 339
MC KLEVAIN, Daniel 462
  Elizabeth A. 462
MC KNETT, -- 250
MC KNIGHT, J. 371
  R. J. 364
  Robert 333
MC LANE, D. N. 383
MC LAUGHLIN, A. K. 219
  Alexander 400
  A. Louisa 219
  E. W. 219
MC MULLIN, George 148
MC NAB, Jane 350
  John 350
MC NAIR, -- 373
  D. S. 374
  Elizabeth 456
  Wm. 456
MC NAMARA, Michael 477
MC NEAL, Frederic B. 407
  Martha 430
MC NEAR, M. C. 374
MC NEELY, J. P. 384
MC NEER, W. T. 360
MC NEILL, Daniel D. 135
  George C. 67

MC NEIL, J. T. 164
MC NEILL, Mary S. 67
MC NELL, Elizabeth 439
MC NELTY, Capt. 135
MC NIEL, Elizabeth 179
  Hugh 7
  John 179
MC NULTY, Caleb J. 99
MC NUTT, Ex-Governor 114
MC PEEK, B. 361
MC PHAIL, Augustus G. 523
MC PHERSON, Ennels 283
MC PHURES, Benj. 370
MC QUEEN, Wm. 454
MC RAE, Philip 129
  T. W. 377
MC SWAIN, McGilbert 170
MC SWAYNE, Dav. 377
MC WHORTER, Geo. C. 205
  Moses E 354
  Sidney 338
MC WILLIAMS, S. G. I. 377
M'DONALD, Alex 99
M'DUFFIE, George 397
MEAD, Mr. 309
MEADORS, A. 427
  Jos. N. 529
MEADOW, Sarah E. 436
MEADOWS, Allen 359
  Edward S. 413
MEAGHER, Francis 277
  T. F. 164
MEALD, William Gregg 308
MEALY, Stephen A. 415
MEANS, A. 447, 503, 515
  Francis M. 130
  James 130
  Mary Ann 130
  Victoria A. 503
MEARA, Daniel Milford 212
  Jas. 212
MEASLES, Louisa 12
  William 12
MEDLIN, T. W. 377
MEEK, A. B. 302
MEEKIN, O. F. 366
MEEKS, E. 383
  Jno. 371
MEGARITY, L. W. 377
MEGRATH, N. A. 521
MELBOURNE, Rev. Mr. 460
MELL, P. H., Mrs. 276
MELLARD, James 461
MELLSON, Rev. Mr. 411
MELROSE, Alexander 425
  Wm. 173
MELTON, David 42
  Louisa 427
  Wm. 392
MELVILLE, Herman 314
MEMMINGER, G. G. 287
MENARD, Alexander A. 462
  Augustus Mitchell 103
  Catherine Virginia 85
  Emily 424
  Francis Alexander 147
  Levina 470
  M. B. 456
  Mich'l B. 202
  Stephen 46, 85, 103
MERCER, Ann Maria 417
  Charles Fenton 24, 228
  J. H. 372
  J. M. 383
  Jacob 188
  Jesse 70, 134
  Joshua 417
  L. B. 253
  Matthew 354
MEREDITH, -- 173
  John 358
  Thomas 468
MERITS, Wm. 358

MERITT, Eliza Ann 459
MERIWETHER, Ella S. 504
  James A. 139, 199, 201, 504
MERRIAM, Isaac S. 425
MERRILL, Eliza B. 17
  Lemuel 17
MERRIT, T. M. 502
MERRITT, Agnes 525
  H. Ward 465
  J. 370
  W. B. 455
MESSER, Gilla Elizabeth 451
  J. A. 362
MESSIER, Joseph 336, 451
METCALFE, Thomas 184
METHVIN, William 509, 517
MEUILLOT, Alfred 308
MEYER, B. H. 274
MICHAEL, W. H. 385
MICHAL, Mary L. 462
MICKLEJOHN, Elizabeth 26
  George 26
MIDDLEBROOKS, Alfred 492
  Green M. 505
MIDDLETON, Hugh 368
  James 322
MILBURN, Elizabeth 466
MILES, Bishop 257
  J. T. 362
  John 6
  S. 360
MILIRONS, A. J. 277
MILLEGE, Gov. 258
  Mrs. 258
MILLEN, Mr. 352
  Isaac A. 358
MILLER, -- 175, 188
  A. J. 189
  Andrew J. 190
  Beth S. 153
  Coote 318
  Covington 463
  D. W. 444
  Daniel W. 337, 439
  Elbert 413
  Elizabeth 429
  Elois M. 395
  Ethamea 84
  F. 434
  George G. 463
  H. V. M. 502
  Harriet Thomas 265
  Henry 238
  James A. 422
  James Arrington 496
  James M. 472
  John 473
  John G. 196
  John J. 83, 430
  Martha H. 153
  Mary A. 421
  Mary Ann 422
  Stephen F. 265
  Tho. 166
  Thomas S. 473
  W. E. 488
  William 121
  Wm. H. 265
  Wm. M. 265
MILLING, Mariah 399
MILLS, B. F. 384
  David 457
  G. W. 380
  J. G. W. 456
  Julia Ann 457
  Lucinda 395
  Matilda J. 424
  R. E. 505, 510
  Sarah Jane 492
  Thomas 312
  Thomas K. 423

MILLS (cont.)
  Timothy 424
  W. W. 363
MILNER, Boneta M. 488
  John 409, 422
  Jonathan J. 422
  Mireum M. 422
  Pitt 57
  R. W. 487
  Willis 488
MIMMS, Samantha 517
  Williamson 295
MIMS, Elias 445
  Frances 496
  James L. 452
  Julius E. 218
  Mary Frances 205
  Robert L. 205, 445
  Robert S. 218
  Sarah A. F. 205
MINCHEW, Mortimer 326
MINER, Madison 358
  Riley 377
  Samuel Wright 221
  William 221
MINS, Drury Y. 63
MINSHEW, J. 377
MINTER, Miss R. Isline 516
  Wm. T. 516
M'INTOSH, John, Major Gen. 9
M'INTYRE, Archibald C. 393
MISSROON, John S. 301
MITCHEL, W. F. 366
MITCHELL, -- 329, 406
  Dr. 265
  Mr. 248
  Rev. Mr. 406, 514, 516
  A. H. 429
  Ada J. 471
  Cadwell 11
  D. B. 45
  Daniel R. 347
  Mrs. Daniel R. 347
  Elizabeth 390, 452
  Elizabeth W. 159
  Fannie N. 476
  Henry 56
  Hugh N. 159
  Jas. 379, 390
  Jeannette 481
  John 250
  John C. 298
  John V. 173
  L. G. 372
  L. N. 146
  Lewis 146
  Margaret E. 452
  Margrette Virginia 448
  Martha J. 390
  Nancy 208
  Nancy M. 477
  Nathaniel 420
  Nathaniel R. 438
  Peter C. 146
  Richard 191, 476
  Robert 197
  Sarah A. P. 481
  Susan Cook 475
  Thos. 208
  Thomas G. 270, 452
  Virginia W. 487
  Volicia V. A. 449
  W. F. 374
  W. L. 479, 510
  W. Letcher 265
  Walter H. 471
  William 320
  Wm. H. 475
MIX, Albert 464
  Timothy 4
  Wm. T. 179

MIZELL, Maria E. 484
  Wm. 406, 407
MIXON, Calvin W. 516
M'LANE, Allen, Capt. 18
M'LAUGHLIN, Gerald 397
MOBLEY, Capt. 337
  Abner 185
  T. S. 278
  Wm. 401
MOCK, J. D. 373
  Jno. D. 367
MOFFETT, Alexander 494
MOLTBIE, Mary 488
MONCRIEF, Rev. Mr. 506, 521
  George M. 518
MONGHER, Thomas Francis 289
MONK, Susan T. 136
MONROE, James, Pres. 23
  Joseph Jones 4
  Nathan C. 47
  Victoria 47
MONTEZ, Lola 335
MONTFORD, John 422
  Richardson 469
MONTFORT, Theodorick L. 276
MONTGOMERY, Rev. Mr. 436
  Bartly 353
  Benjamin R. 159
  D. 380
  James 192
  S. F. 488
  Stiles 353
  T. F. 436, 437, 467
MONUK, Susan Adeline 428
  Winneford Hamilton 428
MOODY, Margaret 389
MOON, Charles 370
MOONEY, Rev. Mr. 424
  Geo. W. 379
MOORE, -- 304
  Mr. 279
  Mrs. 177
  Rev. Dr. 436
  A. H. 353
  Alexander J. 512
  Amasa R. 402
  Ann 393
  Chas. 213
  Dora A. 454
  George 177
  George W. 96, 295
  H. C. 377
  Henry 369
  Hetty 44
  J. H. 61
  J. W. 247
  Jacob W. 221
  John G. 325
  John M. 44
  John R. 413, 423
  Joshua G. 86, 92
  Lee 367
  Lucy G. 33
  Miss M. E. 512
  Margaret Jane 414
  Martha 452
  Matilda J. 447
  Newton L. 362
  P. E. 377
  S. R. 474
  Samuel 33
  Tabitha E. 47
  Thomas 92, 414
  Wm. S. 465
MORAN, Caroline G. 436
  Thomas 153
MORAND, John 349
MORDY, T. S. 382
MOREHEAD, Gov. 155
  Chas. D. 155

MOREHOUSE, A. C. 118,
    434
  Alfred C. 145
  Mary Elizabeth 118
  Rebecca L. 118
MOREL, B. 278
  John H. 33
MORELAND, Mr. 241
  Amrtha 432
  Isaac H. 88, 91, 431,
    444
  Isaac T. 101
  James Dickson 88
  Mary J. 91
  Robert O. 435
  Wm. H. 265
MORGAN, Capt. 381
  Gen. 53
  Maj. 6
  Mr. 52
  A. 363
  Arthur A. 82
  Charles W. 147
  Cordelia 517
  Corinthia A. 460
  Elizabeth 333, 391
  J. R. 373
  John H. 339
  John Henry 137
  Joseph 6
  Jos. K. 367
  Luke J. 18, 67, 408,
    460
  Mary Ann 408
  Mary Hawkins 139
  Perthena 449
  R. H. 362
  Rebecca 434
  Robert J. 139, 477
  Sallie C. 488
  W. T. 514
MORMON, Thomas 379
MORRELL, Eliza 443
  Isaac 338
  Jonathan B. 88
MORRIS, A. G. 375
  Ann 341
  Elizabeth 122
  G. J. 361
  Hardy 205
  J. H. 367
  James 365
  John G. 98, 112, 403
  Lucinda R. 98
  Martha D. 203
  T. 358
  Thomas 341
  Victoria A. 513
  W. 377
MORRISON, Rev. Mr. 456
  J. W. 380
  Levi W. 460
MORRISY, James 480
MORROW, E. M. 110
  H. E. 110
  Jane Henrietta 110
MORSE, Jedidiah, Rev. 7
  John K. 458
  Leander S. 477
  Mary Olivia 144
  O., Mr. 144, 467
  O., Mrs. 144
MORTON, John 198
  Sarah 14
  Wm. J. 184
  Wm. M. 198, 199, 410,
    483
MORVAN, J. R. 381
MOSELEY, A. W. 477
  W. H. 412
  William G. 506
MOSELY, E. 238
  J. 179

MOSELY (cont.)
  John W. 251
  Roger 179
  William 405
MOSES, R. J. 328
MOSS, A. J. 375
  Alec 378
MOST, L. L. 373
MOTBY, M. 361
MOTES, T. A. 361
MOTHERHEAD, J. A. 373
  W. J. 372
MOTT, Elenora 30
  Eliphalet 304
  Louisa J. 413
  Mary A. 161
  Randolph L. 30, 102
  Wm. A. 161
MOUGHON, Thomas 105
MOUGHOUN, Camilla M. 236
  Thos. H. 236
MOULTON, Eliza 414
  Julia A. 152
  Thos. 152
MOULTRIE, Gen. 350
  Anne M. 467
  B. H. 467, 483, 507
  Briggs H. 195
  Caplie W. 483
  J. 416
  James 350
  Joseph 420
  Joseph L. 403
  Mary Ann 195
  Thomas 172
MOUNT, Joseph H. 431
  Wm. 322
MOWER, Rev. Mr. 483
MOWMAN, Rebecca 455
MOWRY, F. 358
MOZELEY, W. D. 377
MUCE, M. L. 371
MULCARE, Thomas 336
MULCKLY, Rev. Mr. 490
MULFORD, Thomas S. 51
MULHOLLAND, Adaline S. 186
  C. 186
  Collin 419
MULKEY, Isaac 481
  J. B. 385
MULLAN, Thomas 335
MULLANY, John 299
  Mary 299
MULLINS, Thos. 369, 377
MUNNERLYN, Charles, Sr.
    220
MUNROE, Harriet 465
  Julia Blanche 493
  Mary Josephine 39
  N. C. 122, 493, 527
  Nathan 180, 465
  Nathan C. 39, 180, 231
  Rowena 122
  Tabitha E. 39, 231
MUNSON, Martha L. 410
  Mary B. 415
  Sarah Ann 423
  Susan 461
  Theodosia 426
MURAT, Achille 391
MURCHISON, Calvin 448
  Colin 2
  Isabella E. 480
MURDEN, Henning D. 487
MURDOCH, Katy 164
MURDOCK, Francis H. 299
MURPH, Arabella C. 471
  Sarah C. 438
MURPHEY, Calista Matilda
    247
  Elizabeth 247
  Leory A. 521
  Solomon D. 247

MURPHY, Rev. Mr. 434
  Chas. 269, 500
  Eliza C. 500
  J. W. 371
  John 291
  M. 368
  Thos. 370
  W. L. 508
MURRAY, Rev. Mr. 458
  Ezekiel 134
  J. B. 369
  James 455
  Robert 149
  Thomas W. 26
  W. M. 362
MURRELL, Eugenia 509
  Joseph A. 340
  Joseph H. 454
MUSE, Thomas 487
MUSGROVE, Robert H. 39
  Wm. St. Leger 79
MUSSEY, W. M. 204
MYERS, Dr. 174
  Lieut. 335
  Rev. Prof. 455
  E. H. 465, 466, 467,
    469
  J. T. 485
  Sarah Jane 400
  Thomas 143
  W. P. 371
MYRICK, Benjamin 315
  Evans 50
  Frances E. A. 417
  Marcellus A. 501
  Mary E. 497
  S. P. 497
NABERS, Beatie 304
NAGEL, A. G. 492
NALAR, J. P. 372
NALL, Archibald 412
NALLY, Daniel 469
  Martha D. 469
NANCE, John 315
NAPIER, Mrs. 55
  Caroline 450
  Anna Josephine 253
  Eliza B. 113
  Fanny C. 251, 253
  John T. 251, 253
  Joseph A. 186
  Leroy 165, 186, 450
  M. L. 186
  Mattie C. 506
  Sarah C. 429
  Skelton 249, 506
  T. T. 53
  Tabitha 401
  Thomas 53, 55
  Thomas A. 249
  Thos. T. 74, 429
  William T. W. 430
NAPPER, Robert 331
NAPPIER, E. T. 502
NARERI, H. M. 371
NARVIS, Ralf 372
NASH, -- 175
  Acton E. 499
  Hezekiah A. 442
  R. A. 501
NATION, Amos 382
NEAL, John 409, 454
  Jonathan 432
  Mary Ann 454
  Matilda 432
  Rev. Mr. 410
  S. H. 415
  S. R. 363
  William 278
NEEL, J. 391
  John H. 212
  Jonathan 425, 434
  Sarah A. 498

NEELEY, H. J. 438
NEELY, John D. 506
NEEVES, Jno. 369
NEGEL, A. G. 332
NEIGHBORS, J. E. 359
NEIL, William 457
NEISBER, Hugh 439
   Susan H. 439
NEISLER, Hugh 286
NELMS, L. A. 282
NELSON, -- 321
   Lieut. 273
   J. B. 154
   James B. 178
   Jno. 364
   John A. 444
   Mary J. 154, 178
   Rebecca G. 415
   Robert 443
   W. D. 367
   William 466
   Wm. G. 246
   William H. B. 154
NESBET, Thos. 373
NESBIT, George F. 347
NESBITT, Robert 140
NESMITH, C. M. 377
NETHERLAND, Mr. 53
NETHVIN, Emily Minnie 341
   William 341
NEUFVILLE, Rev. Mr. 397
   Edward 128
NEWBERRY, Isaac J. 157, 427
   Martha C. 157
NEWBURY, Walter L. 343
NEWCOMB, Lemuel 36, 394
   Martha G. 416
NEWELL, Harriet 422
NEWHALL, Isaac 417
   Satah L. 417
NEWMAN, A. 119
   David 180
   Helen M. 526
   Jas. 327
   James A. 442
   L. C. 371
   N. W. 526
MEWNAN, E. L. 377
NEWSOM, Judge 515
   Anne E. 515
   Anthony 271
   Caroline 448
NEWSOME, Belfield 319
NEWSON, Andrew 322
NEWSTON, Ann Olivia 521
NEWTON, Rev. Dr. 253
   Annie E. 514
   George M. 238
   Isaac D. 47, 402
   J. 431
   John H. 521
   Julia Ann 3
   L. F. 365
   Louisa B. 47
   Sarah 431
   Sarah Dubois 47
   Thomas F. 143
   Thomas J. 411
   Thomas M. 280
NICHOLL, Judge 33
NICOLL, Francis Edward 120
NICHOLL, John C. 296
NICHOLS, -- 334
   Henrietta 355
   J. T. 372
   M. V 361
   Morgianah 412
   Roxana 195
   S. W. 195
   T. 380
   Wm. N. 195
NICHOLSON, John 268

NICHOLSON (cont.)
   Julia E. 410
NIGHT, J. D. 377
NILES, Lewis O. 525
NIMO, W. D. 380
NISBET, A. M. 494
   A. M. F. 120
   Bessie 175
   C. E. 175
   Charles E. 135, 454, 496
   E. A. 68, 120, 273, 494
   Eliza Clay 206
   Ella Amanda 68
   Emmie H. 494
   Eugenia A. 273, 470
   James 103, 136, 301
   Jas. A. 505
   James T. 495
   Joseph H. 464
   Laura J. 470
   Lemle Duncan 131
   Mary C. 206
   Ophelia E. 494
   R. B. 469
   R. H. 263, 514
   Robert 131, 432
   Sarah A. 494
   Thomas C. 206
   Thomas Cosper 206
   Virginia E. 135
NIX, Thomas 356
NIXON, Mrs. 81
   C. W. 474
   Eliza Ann 420
   Elizabeth C. 434
   F. L. 453
   H. M. 468
   M. A. 371
   Mary Ella 419
   Wm. 62. 420, 434
NOBLE, Mr. and Mrs. 239
   Christopher 214
NOBLES, Major 250
   Clarinda 247
   J. A. 371
   Lewis 486
NOITE, Andrew 309
NOLAN, George M. 483
   T. 377
NOLINS, Lt. 372
NORMAN, -- 334
   Augusta Adelaide 58
   G. G. 312
   Geo. W. 209
   Marth 58
   Mary B. 491
   Mary M. 240
   O. P. 490
   Oliver P. 240, 518
   Salina S. 398
   Sarah 187
   Sarah Ann 391
   Thomas H. 492
   William S. 58, 491
   Wm. Shepherd 392
NORRALL, John B. 455
   Rachael Ann 455
   Henrietta 459
   James N. 186
   John B. 459
NORRIS, Mr. 176
   Emma J. 521
   Isaac 408
   Mollie Lou 521
   Sarah A. 508
   Thomas 377, 417
NORTH, Harriet A. 425
   Marcus A. 277
NORTHCUT, Elijah 454
   Thos. 373
NORTHEY, L. M. 232

NORTHRUP, Narcissa H. 461
NORTON, C. B. 278
NORWELL, Arnold 367
NORWOOD, Jane 416
NOTHCUT, J. 364
NOTTALL, Ann 418
NOTTINGHAM, Custis B. 433
NOWEL, Luke S. 472
NOWELL, Rev. Mr. 444
   Luke J. 442
NUNN, Francis 392
   Hawkins H. 257
   Medora 257
NUTT, F. 364
NUTTING, Chs. A. 143
   Emily C. 143
OATES, Thos. J. 327
O'BAIL, Henry 41
OBARR, T. 362
OBEAR, George S. 454
   Josiah H. 269
OBREGON, Don Pablo 14
O'BRIEN, Major 123
O'CALLAHAN, -- 344
O'CONNELL, Mr. 345
O'CONNER, William E. 260
OCTAVO, Missouri 461
O'DANIEL, Daniel 321
ODOM, E. A. 433
   John H. 379
   Jordan 53
   Orrey 479, 480
   S. 95
   Sarah Elizabeth 95
ODUM, S. 366
   Saberd 90
   William Thomas 90
OFERRELL, -- 164
OFF, -- 313
OGDEN, Francis J. 441
OGILVIE, Alfred 301
OGLESBY, Geo. S. 465
   John H. 67
   Sarah T. 465
OGLETREE, Rev. Mr. 390, 418
   A. 441, 459
   David 495
   Emily 486
   Georgia Ann 495
   J. L. 363
   James 392
   John B. 486
   W. S. 529
   Wm. S. 522
OHARA, Thos. 360
O'KEEFE, John 146
OLCOTT, D. G. 345
OLDEN, W. 377
OLDERSHAW, J. H. 242
   James C. 40
OLIPHANT, Jos. 449
   Nancy J. 449
OLIVER, Ann V. 436
   Camilla 468
   Catharine 269
   E. Pluribusunum 269
   Henry E. 465
   James 31, 436
   James G. 474
   James M. 341
   James Stiles 32
   John 32, 75
   John T. 269
   Macy B. 474
   Martha A. 465
   Mary A. 341
   McCarty 438
   Nancy 32
   P. H. 490
   R. L. 476
   Miss S. E. 478
   Samuel C. 111

OLIVER (cont.)
　Shelton 468
　W. 377
ONDAYKA, -- 60
ONDERDONK, Bishop 236
O'NEAL, Rev. Mr. 477
　Cullen 494
　Ellen 494
　J. F. 512
　Jeremiah F., Jr. 342
　R. 379
　Rev. Dr. 484
OPPELT, F. W. 380
OPRY, Mary 518
O'REAILLY, Rev. Mr. 512
ORGAN, John 344
ORME, Georgia Jean 482
　Jean Moncure 55
　R. M. 482, 496
　R. McAllister 489
　Richard M. 55, 390
　Virginia M. 496
ORR, A. M. 278
　Andrew J. 436
　D. W. 464, 516
　J. J. 183
　Josiah C. 483
　Mary Elizabeth 516
　Susan A. 201
ORRA, A. J. 264
ORTES, Elizabeth 303
ORWOOD, David 358
OSBORN, George 426
　Samantha N. 426
　Selleck 8
OSBORNE, John H. 181
　Maria Foissin 181
OSGOOD, Harrison M. 409
OSLIN, J. W. 152
　Mary N. J. 152
　W. W. 518
　Wm. W. 514
OSTEEN, W. D. 377
OTEY, Bishop 274
　Mrs. 274
OTLEY, Rev. Bishop 518
OTTERSON, W. M. 494
OTTO, F. W. 364
OUSLEY, Rev. Mr. 442, 446
　E. C. 134
　Joseph A. 134
　Mary Ann 421
　N. 439, 443, 444, 457, 458, 470
　N. B. 519
　R. Y. 419
　Robert C. 288
　Robert F. 134, 237, 519
　Thomas D. 440
OVERBY, Rev. Mr. 457
　B. H. 253, 477
OVERSTREET, Elizabeth A. 457
OWEN, Alexander F. 437
　Allen P. 416
　Elizabeth E. 423
　G. W. 191
　Jesse L. 429
　John B. 257
　O. A. 236
　R. M. 501, 510
　Thomas 368
　W. J. 377
OWENS, Mrs. 53
　Abraham 333
　B. 365
　Benjamin F. 28, 396
　Clara A. 398
　Dennis N. 37
　Elijah S. 404
　James N. 35, 410
　John J. 398

OWENS (cont.)
　Matilda R. 35
　W. H. 359
　Wash 318
OWINS, W. 373
OXENDINE, Archibald 331
OXFORD, James 330
PACE, Ceabell F. 459
　Mary 410
　Nathaniel 9
　Rebecca 399
　Richard 238
　Sarah Elizabeth 113
　Thomas, Major 3, 9, 113
　Thomas I. 3
PACKER, W. M. 379
PADDOCK, James 277
PAGE, Adam 309
　L. H. 383
PAIGE, Eldridge F. 255
PAINE, C. J. 239, 473
　Edward 18
　William Henry 18
　Wm. W. 521
PALEE, Anderson 461
PALMER, Mary L. 232
　Sam'l B. 232, 481
　Susan 411
　W. R. 255
　Wm. M. 381
PALMORE, Jas. 278
PALUCIE, J. 308
PARDLY, S. M. 373
PARHAM, Jerusha Ann (Howard) 43
　Robert 394
　Stith 43
PARISH, H. J. 379
　H. W. 373
　Jonathan 276
　Nathan 393
PARK, Columbus M. 329
　Ellsworth Foster 121
　Ezekiel M. 329
　Fannie D. 478
　Henry H. 156
　James 394
　James J. 497
　John G. 121
PARKE, Miss P. 503
PARKER, Amanda Symmantha 34
　B. 382
　Barwell 413
　Christopher 398
　Eldecia 411
　Elizabeth 511
　Gabriel 18
　George Summerfield 33
　J. S. 383
　Jackson 34
　Jacob 259
　John 408
　Kader 433
　Margaret Bell 294
　Mazy G. 408
　Milo B. 460
　Nancy 464
　S. Wise 528
　Theodore 294
　Theodosia 429
　Thomas C. 510
　Virginia 294
　Wm. B. 53
　William C. 33, 34, 407, 411
PARKHAM, Wm. S. 381
PARKES, Lazarus B. 488
PARKILL, Capt. 222
PARKMAN, David 381
　Julia 399
PARKS, Rev. Mr. 468

PARKS (cont.)
　Francis A. 478
　H. 370
　H. H. 503, 510, 514, 515, 516
　Isaac C. 426
　James K. 290
　John W. 294, 517
　Levi 426
　M. P. 431
　Mary 2
　Sarah D. 395
　W. G. 500, 510
　William G. 456
PARKYN, H. H. 274
PARMALEE, J. C. 380
　Loretta Jane 440
　Mary C. 495
PARMELEE, A. C. 54, 409, 442
　Catherine 54
PARMENTO, J. S. 382
PARR, D. W. 485
　Mary C. 485
PARRISH, -- 311
　Capt. 278
　Nancy 278
PARSHALL, -- 327
PARSON, Henry P. 107
PARSONS, Dr. 338
　J. M. 273, 427
　John A. 85
　Julia Virginia 108
　M. V. 107, 108
　T. A. 107, 108
PARTIN, A. D. 366
　David 353
PARTRIDGE, E. Peuribus 289
PASS, John 259
PASSMORE, John G. 503
PATCH, Nathaniel 522
PATE, Mrs. E. V. 323
　John A. 369
　John Watkins 323
　R. H. 323
　Wm. H. 371
PATEN, W. S. 379
PATERSON, R. 403
PATILLO, C. F. 463
　Charles F. 196
　John 463
　Leroy 138
　Martha 463
PATRICK, Abraham P. 101
　Georgia G. 485
　James Dr. 56
PATTEN, Electa 92
　George 63, 92, 109, 490
　Grace 109
　Harry 109
　John M. 109
　Jonathan 92
　Mary 63
　Mary L. 109
　William 63
PATTERSON, Col. 131
　Mrs. 131
　Rev. Mr. 395, 398, 399, 402
　Augustin L. 473
　Charles B. 124
　Daniel T. 59
　George 326
　Ira C. 499
　J. A. 383
　James C. 398
　Jas. E. 523
　John T. 188
　R. M. 372
　Susannah B. 124
　Tellulah 124

PATTERSON (cont.)
   William Augustine 131
   William J. 444
PATTILLO, Charles F. 438,
   439, 500
   Elizabeth Ann 438
   G. H. 514
   Leroy 248
   Sarah H. 458
PATTILO, James W. 168
PATTON, Miss 393
   Alexander E. 85
   H. 362
   Henry 371
   James H. 393
   Martha 426
   R. C. 380
   Robert 390
   Robert S. 220, 399
   Samuel C. 368
   Sarah M. 445
PAUL, Abraham B. 492
   Charles 432
   Robert 375
   Sallie 230
   William 398
PAULDING, James Kirke 260
PAULETT, Harriet 211
   J. C. 211
PAULK, -- 188
PAXTON, Frank 293
PAYN, A. L. 368
PAYNE, Mr. 408
   Rev. Mr. 437
   C. J. 358
   Charles J. 120
   Edwin 456
   George 437
   James B. 438
   Josiah 364
   June M. 390
   Mary 119, 408
   Sarah E. 456
PEABODY, Augustus 436
PEACOCK, D. W. L. 300
   Jesse 529
   John H. 281
PEAK, D. 308
   G. A. 308
PEAKE, John Samuel 354
PEALE, F. T. 514
PEARCE, Elias 220, 450
   Lida 456
   Lucinda 220, 493
   Theophilus 10, 230
PEARSALL, Miss F. C. 525
   Jere 525
PEARSON, A. J. 361
   George F. 333
   James 125, 168, 459
   John W. 168
   Martha A. 447
PEASE, Albert Henry 117
   E. R. 434
   Edward R. 117
   G. A. 272
   Harriet 272
   Martha E. 117
   Peter 10
PECK, Charles 398
   Marietta 162
   Nathan, Jr. 162
PEEL, Matt 244
PEELER, Barry 356
PEEPLES, Cincinnatus 457
   Wm. J. 243
PEIRSON, T. A. 374
PEMBERTON, James C. 441
   Mary Jane 441
PENDERGRASS, Elizabeth L.
   484
PENDERGAST, Johnny 356
PENDIN, L. T. 372

PENDLETON, P. C. 430
   Phillip C. 352
PENDLY, S. M. 365
PENLETON, Judge 429
PENN, J. W. 243
PENNERGAST, Nicholas 230
PENNINGTON, L. J. 377
PENNY, Hampton 353
   Wm. J. 358
PENTECOST, F. T. 488
PERCELL, Duncan 358
PERCIVAL, Alice T. 512
   James G. 195
PERDUE, Hiram 526
PERINE, Edmond M. 496
PERKINS, Adeline 419
   Alex 419
   Archibald 90
   B. H. 204
   F. Annie 499
   Fanny S. 468
   Wm. H. 401
PERRIMAN, Matilda T. 142
PERRY, Commodore 225
   Dow 452
   Eldridge M. 526
   Fannie Eller 200
   J. R. 421
   J. W. 485
   James R. 94
   Laura J. 485
   Lavinia C. 425
   Mary A. 138
   Mary Jane 476
   Robert 325
   Sarah Ann 460
   T. J. 138
   Thomas J. 200, 500
   Wm. 76
   Wm. H. C. 486
PERRYMAN, Rev. Mr. 430,
   442
   James 416, 513
   Troup 504
   W. 420
PERSONS, Ann E. 456
   Augustus A. 457
   G. W. 514
   George W. 426, 456,
      457, 459, 467, 471,
      474, 478, 482, 510,
      518
   Nicholas W. 405
   T. H. 353
PESMETER, Wright 379
PESSENDEN, William Pitt
   356
PETERS, Caroline Cora 464
   John R. 464
   M. B. 511
   R. L. 322
PETRIE, H. W. 478
PETTES, Wm. R. 443
PETTICOLAS, Arthur E. 323
PETTIGREW, J. 363
PETTIGRU, James L. 292
PETTIS, Moses 389
PETTIT, Waren 313
PETTUS, Harriet Helen 105
   John 105
   William Richard 105
PEURIFOY, Rev. Mr. 452
   H. D. P. 495
PHARR, Marcus A. 468
PHELPS, Anson G. 158
   Henry 207
   James M. 84
   Jonathan C. 43
   Joshua 450
   Oliver R. 467
PHILBROOK, Samuel 176
PHILIP, Ansley 449
   Robert 419

PHILIPS, Caroline A. 15
   Dawson 413
   Emily J. 413
   M., Col. 15
PHILLIPS, -- 308
   Augustus C. 238
   Benjamin 59
   Benjamin J. 30
   Dawson 91
   H. A. 362
   Henrietta 30
   J. T. 377
   James 258
   John 57, 77, 363
   M. Fannie 524
   Margaret Gorham 57
   Marie 30
   Mary Ann 258
   Matthew 398
   Nimrod 117
   Phetis A. 344
   Sarah Ann 77
   Susan 238
   W. R. 511
   William 238
   Zachariah 25
PHINAZEE, Rev. 486
   H. 486, 495, 496
   James S. 486
   John H. 495
   Martha E. 495
   Wm. J. 496
PHINIZY, John 483, 484
PHINZY, Miss M. P. 484
PHIPPS, J. T. 361
   Jackson 320
PICETT, Richard 420
PICK, Henry 426
PICKARD, Henry H. 51
   Nancy 51
PICKENS, Ex-Gov. 344
   Alexander 426
   Elizabeth J. 426
PICKERING, Timothy 16
PICKETT, Alfred 349
   Albert J. 514
   Eliza W. 514
   J. 122
   Mary Jane 482
PICKNEY, William 248
PIERCE, Bishop 505
   Rev. Dr. 398, 414, 447,
      450, 484
   Alfred 283
   Everett H. 209
   Franklin 357
   G. F. 423
   George F. 422, 423,
      424, 427, 428, 430,
      431, 432, 433, 467,
      470, 471, 498
   H. R. 240
   Hamilton R. 239
   Jas. L. 499, 505
   L. 264
   Lovick 239, 240, 396
   Reddick 264, 496
   Thomas F. 494
PIERPONT, F. P. 343
PIERSON, Elizabeth
   Caroline 408
   James 392, 408
   Jeremiah 411
   Mary 411
   Washington 351
PIGOTT, Arthur J. 170
PIKE, Albert 237
   Philips 417
PILAN, Jas. 358
PILGRIM, Isaac B. 481
PILKENTON, James 288
PILOJEAN, J. 363
PINCHERON, Rev. Mr. 489

PINCKARD, J. S. 295
  Mrs. J. S. 295
  John 344
  Thomas C. 419
PINCKNEY, Thos. 15
PINES, James 202
  Sarah Ann 202
PINKETON, S. J. 495
PINKSTON, A. S. 487
PINTOCK, J. A. 490
  Ophelia D. 490
PIPERNO, J. 526
PITKIN, Rev. Mr. 464
PITMAN, James J. 141
  Joseph H. 482
  Martha 141
PITTMAN, Daniel N. 201
  John 402
  Reuben 201
PITTS, Ann Maria 463
  David L. 508
  Drusilla 393
  E. R. 493
  Elizabeth M. 216
  Isaac 393
  J. D. 497
  J. W. 377
  John 463
  Marietta T. 493
  Wm. H. 480
PIXLEY, Wm. R. 488
PIZA, D. 526
PLANE, Wm. F. 480
PLANT, Eddie McGehee 341
  E. M., Miss 471
  G. B. 341
  George H. 514
  I. C. 435
  Mrs. L. F. 341
PLATT, Benj. W. 52
  Henry 119
PLAUE, Helen 256
  Rebecca 256
  Wm. F. 256
PLEASONTON, Stephen 177
PLEDGER, Park 519
PLUNKETT, Officer 331
  John 526
POE, Edgar A. 120
  Francis Matilda 479
  George Robert 96
  Robert F. 173
  Salina 194
  Salina S. 96
  Selina Shirley 194
  Washington 96, 194,
    217, 398, 479
  William 186
POINDEXTER, George 155
POLHILL, B. M. 246
  Benjamin M. 494
  J. G. 451
  John 246
  John G. 429
  Joseph 236, 423
  Louisa M. 429
  Thomas G. 452
POLK, Arraiana 498
  F. J. 362
  James 498
  James K. 116
  Patty 306
POLLARD, B. L. 361
  H. Rives 324
  Rives 345
  Wm. 411
  Wm. J. 519
POLLOCK, Casander 451
POMEROY, Robert H. 315
POND, Charles 272
  Charles H. 272
PONDER, Amos 129
  Daniel 469

PONDER (cont.)
  Dulane F. 284
  J. M. 504
  Jas. W. H. 487
  John G. 120
  Martha Frances 469
  Mildred 394
POOL, James Jackson
    Scarbourgh 215
  John Hillsman 209
  Jonathan H. 215
  Josiah 209
  Martha 209
  Mary A. E. 215
  Sarah F. 449
POPE, Rev. Mr. 400, 401,
    402, 403, 404
  A. B., Dr. 19
  Alexander 479
  Benjamin 40, 401
  Burwell 62
  Caroline 393
  Miss D. A. 524
  Henrietta J. 407
  Henry 166, 483
  James 289, 292
  John H. 459
  Gideon 292
  Martha H. 417
  Mary Ann 428
  Mary J. 483
  Mary S. 479
  Owen Clinton 281
  Miss S. H. 475
  Solomon L. 420
  Thomas L. 428
  Urania 166
  Wiley 417
  Wm. H. 503
POPLEAN, J. C. 370
PORTER, A. 377
  David H. 510
  Miss E. W. 395
  John W. 494
  Mary A. 463
  Miss Mat F. 494
  R. G. 310
  R. K. 354
  Richard J. H. 424
  Sallie F. 494
  Thomas 395
  Urania 62
  William T. 230
PORTRESS, Major 392
  Mary E. 392
POSEY, Gen. 296
POST, Reuben 233
POSTELL, --- C. 436
  Rev. Mr. 441
  Caroline Emma 436
  J. C. 434, 453, 454,
    458
  Jas. C. 438
  M. E., Miss 468
  Margaret E. 510
  Wm. 510
POTTER, Charles 309
  Charles M. 11
  Washington 328
POTTS, Lewis 379
  Wm. 384
POU, Edwin W. 230
POUND, Hannon B. 389
  John E. 456
POWEL, Elizabeth 397
  J. W. 379
POWELL, A. D. 114
  Absalom D. 428
  Alexander 355
  E. P. 182
  Emily 455
  Evan 455
  Evan H. 473

POWELL (cont.)
  George L. 358
  H. 427, 459
  Hugh T. 237
  J. 361
  J. A. 374
  James 366, 414
  James E. 360
  Julia L. 225
  Miss M. J. 501
  Mary A. F. 451
  Mary Elizabeth 114
  Mary William Spencer
    225
  Nannie R. 473
  O. J. 193
  Richard 2
  Samuel S. 433
  Thomas S. 225
  Usebia N. 462
  Wade H. 109
  William 77, 143
POWERS, Judge 519
  Mrs. 184
  Rev. Dr. 418
  A. P. 250
  Abner P. 264, 431
  Ann E. 242
  Anna G. 242
  Charles West 128
  Clifford S. 128
  Edward E. 182
  J. H. 128
  John 69, 116, 166,
    421, 451
  John H. 449
  John W. 413
  Julia A. 232
  Mary Elizabeth 451
  Michal 116
  N. B. 519
  Narcissa 422
  Virgil 204, 242
POWLEDGE, Gideon 394
  John M. 391
  Lucy V. 11
  Philip 11
PRATT, -- 214
  Rev. Mr. 401
  Addison 67
  Daniel 393
  Ellen 119
  Lucretia 417
  Matilda 392
  Sarah M. 472
  Wm. O. 105
PREER, Peter 493
PRENTISS, Angeline 139
  Angelina G. 139
  George A. 318
  William 139
PRESBY, J. A. 359
PRESCOTT, Alfred 477
  Malvina 494
  William H. 239
PRESTON, Rev. Mr. 406,
    489, 490
  Francis 262
  John S. 262
  Willard 194
  Wm. C. 110
  William Campbell 262
PREVAT, -- 173
PRICE, A. W. 284
  Elihu 423
  Elizabeth 54
  George W. 54, 284, 427
  J. V. 178
  Jas. A. 209
  James L. 337
  John T. 456
  L. B. 370
  L. M. 284

PRICE (cont.)
  Martha Jane 178
  Thos. J., Sr. 325
  W. H. 509
PRICHARD, Mary 439
  Piety 408
PRICHETT, A. M. 505
PRIDE, R. T. 328
PRINCE, E. C. 352
  Elizabeth Frances 460
  J. E. 352
  Mary R. 48
  O. H. 465
  Oliver H. 48, 443, 460
  Sarah Virginia 443
PRINGLE, Augustus C. 486
  Barton 337
  Gatsey Ann 104
  James Adger 104
PRITCHARD, -- 314
PROCTOR, Miss 173
PROVINCE, Hiram 326, 350
PRUETT, Elizabeth 447
PRY, Hugh 377
PRYOR, Julia 483
  Mary Ann 457
  Robert 457
  S. G. 462
PRYSE, Rev. Mr. 490
PSALTER, A. J. 426
PUCKETT, John A. 277
  Rice 313
PUGSLEY, A. J. 524
PULLEN, William A. 477
PULLIAM, D. T. 493
  L. B. 383
PULLINE, Jas. 377
PULLION, R. T. 378
PULLMAN, Wm. 314
PUREFOY, Rev. Dr. 436
PURSE, Edward J. 415
  Thos., Jr. 278
PURYEAR, D. O. 382
PUSHMAN, Wm. 329
PUTNAM, Clark S. 443
  Rufus 3, 4
PYE, A. 263
  Andrew 264
  Bernier 400, 495
  Freeman 377
  Sallie J. 495
  Susan 330
PYTAS, Abraham 262
QUARTERMAN, Alexander S. 483
  Augustus S. 467
  Edward 503
  Miss O. S. 503
QUIGLEY, Edward 470
  Francis 73
  Mary B. 457
QUIGLY, James 385
QUINCY, John W. 350
QUINN, B. J. 334
  John 185
  Terry 247
QUINTARD, Bayard Hand 126
  C. T. 126
QUITMAN, Gen. 313
  John A. 230
  Ruth 313
RABUN, Wm. 184
RADFORD, Robert W. 452
  Susan A. F. 515
RADIFORD, J. 361
RADWAY, R. R. 366
RAGAN, G. P. 363
RAGIN, Col. 243
RAGLAND, Laura A. 482
  Sarah Ann 263
  Thomas 263, 444, 482
RAIFORD, H. C. M. 446
  Hamilton 187

RAIFORD (cont.)
  Robert 212
RAINES, Allen 360
  Cadwell W. 189
  Edward 227
  Eugenia A. 457
  John G. 87
  Lucian H. 242
  Mary Jane 87
  Mary S. 87
  N. E. A. 505
  Nathaniel H. 138
  Parthenia 494
  Rebecca W. 138
  Robert H. 420
RAINEY, Andrew 100
  Ephraim 200
  James Signal 160
  Signal 160
RAINS, Eliza G. 487
  Isaac 280
  John 487
  Leonidas N. 489
RAINY, Philip Bethea 95, 98
  Rebecca T. 95, 98
  Wm. D. 95, 98, 429
RALEIGH, Bathsheba F. 323
  Richmond 323
RALEY, C. C. 385
  Jas. 360, 385
  Talbot 235
RALSTON, A. R. 53
  Anna V. 41
  James A. 440
  Laura Virginia 452
  Rosetta B. 412
  William 161
RAMEY, J. 363
  J. J. 369
RAMSEY, Dr. 201
  Judge 509
  Dorcas 461
  Eliza 461
  Isaac 255
  J. H. 380
  Ophelia E. 509
  W. S. 509
  William H. 461
RANDALL, Peter 329, 497
RANDLE, Arabella M. 435
  Eliza Ann 435
  John S. 124
  Mary Angelina 443
  Peter 140, 443
  Thos. G. 428
RANDOLPH, Eliza B. 457
  Eliza M. 121
  Mary 502
  R. H. 93, 121, 457
  Richard Henry 105
RANSOM, Marcella 394
RANSOME, Corinne 192
  U. A., Mr. and Mrs. 192
RANTOUL, Robert 142
RAPE, E. J. 369
RATHMORE, Wm. 373
RATLIFF, Eliza 495
RAVENS, Sarah E. S. 487
RAWLINS, John A. 356
RAWLS, Ann E. 454
  Mrs. Carolina 469
  Caroline M. 467
  E. H. 516
  J. 377
  John 85, 225, 498
  John J. 460
  Mary F. 469
RAY, B. A. 358
  James C. 116
  James J. 505
  Jencey Ellen 459

RAY (cont.)
  John W. 216
  Mary Lucy 482
  Nancy 116
  Samuel 147
  William 336
RAYFORD, Rev. Mr. 405
RAYMUR, Alexander J. 431
RAYNFROUGH, Campbell 410
REA, Daniel 44
  Daniel T. 420
  Elizabeth L. 44
  James 280
READ, Mr. 230
  James 290
READING, Arthur 419
  Lucintha Jane 419
REAGAN, W. J. 370
REAVES, J. A. 368
RED, C. A. 295
REDD, -- 381
  Thomas 62
REDDICK, James S. 477
REDDING, --- Rowland 436
  A. E. 156
  A. W. 124, 294, 478
  Abner F. 156
  Anderson 79
  Arthur 133, 410
  Cinderilla 410
  Clarissa 23
  Daniel S. 519
  Elizabeth 294
  Elizabeth A. 436
  H. P. 424
  Harriet G. 439
  J. M. 377
  Jas. T. 520
  John 93
  John A. 265
  Martha L. 440
  Mary 458
  Mary Ann 419
  Nancy 109
  Parrisade 109
  Robert C. 133, 164
  Robt. Campbell 403
  Robert G. 23, 109
  Robert J. 506
  Roland 265
  Susan R. 124
  Thomas J. 516
  W. C. 222, 440
  Wm. A. 156
  Wm. C. 419
RED JACKET, -- 41
REDMOND, D. 527
  Miss Mel G. 527
REED, Miss 147
  A. L. 372
  D. B. 361
  J. S. 381
  John B. 455
  M. J. 507
REEDY, F. 361
REES, Albert 95
  Eliza J. 474
  H. F. 525
  H. K. 526, 527
  Henry K. 493
  John 474
  Jordan 272
  S. S. 95
REESE, Mr. 170
  Rev. Mr. 251, 483, 495, 508, 512, 518, 522
  A. 483
  Amarintha 191
  Andrew W. 528
  Augustus 191
  Columbus 354
  Cuthbert 187

REESE (cont.)
  D. A. 494
  Donald A. 255
  Elisha 119
  H. K. 521, 525
  H. R. 487
  James H. 287
  M. 373
  Martha J. 191
  Mary G. 123
  Matthew 359
  Rebecca M. 494
  Susan A. 211
  Thos. S. 211
  William J. 453
REEVES, Francis M. 397
  Louisa F. 454
  N. 377
  W. L. 377
  William 512
REGISTER, Samuel 330
  Wm. 383
REICH, Owen 258
REID, Lieut. 338
  Andrew 476
  David 418, 440, 469, 514
  Elizabeth 399
  J. B. 501
  J. W. 412
  John A. 504
  John B. 261
  Sarah E. 476
  Wm. A. 494
  Wm. S. C. 57
REINHART, A. 201
REIVES, Priscilla 200
  Timothy 200
REMBERT, Caleb W. 138
  J. G. 456
  Jane G. 138
  Martha Anna W. 138
REMINGTON, C. H. 476
  Charles H. 474
RENBERT, Elizabeth M. 451
RENEN, Ward 358
RENFROE, Emma C. 526
  John 25
RENNER, Jacob 313
RENNO, Nathan 370
RENO, Frank 326
  Simeon 326
RENTS, Erbanna 305
RENTZ, Geo. 361
  Mary Julia 445
RENWICK, Professor 2
RESPESS, Elia 466
  Richard 55
  John R. 466
REUSSAM, J. J. 371
REVEL, James 225, 251
REW, Beverly 41
REYNOLDS, Chas. J. 430
  Charles P. 165, 485
  Claudia 501
  E. W. 501
  Emily 395
  Georgia Ann 165
  Ignatius Aloysius 178
  J. J. 365
  J. R. 358
  John 66
  L. O. 183
  Larkin 420
  Nancy 420
  Nancy Jane 499
  Sarah W. 471
  Thomas 86
  W. G. 363
  W. S. 482
  William 278, 501
  William H. 270
RHEA, Andrew 11

RHEA (cont.)
  Rebecca Frances 11
RHIND, James 171
  Jas. H. 171
RHINEHART, James 254
RHODES, Lewis B. 502
  Mary A. E. 485
  Robert 34
  Wm. W. 447
RICE, Colo. 453
  Anderson 90
  Celina 273
  Charles H. 122
  Cora 334
  G. L. L. 509
  Georgia A. R. 445
  James R. 526
  Martha 146
  Martha A. 408
  O. B. 146
  S. E. 453
  U. A. 273
  W. H. 509, 516
RICH, J. T. 377
  T. 374
RICHARDS, Alex. 188, 469, 502
  Alex. Few 188
  Blanche 150
  Caroline E. 462
  Cornelia H. B. 178
  Edith Manners 178
  J. J. 150
  John 239
  Laura A. 469
  Lou J. 502
  Mary E. 451
  S. M. H. 150
  S. P. 467
  Sarah Ann 411
  T. J. 362
  Thomas 434
  W. C. 150
  W. H. 380
  W. W. 469
  William 467
  Wm. C. 178
RICHARDSON, -- 349
  Caroline A. D. 157
  D. F. 480
  David 374
  Edmund 83, 431
  Eliza Jane 83
  Fannie E. 480
  George 83
  James 155, 265
  James S. 1
  L. L. 515
  Lydia 155
  M. 157
  Omer 252
  T. J. 371
RICHARDSONE, Cosmo P. 136
RICHBOURG, R. 363
RICKETTS, Mary 397
RICKS, -- 384
  George E. 289
RIDDELL, J. L. 302
RIDGWAY, John I. 194
RIDLEY, J. B. 169
  Louisa J. 169
RIGGINS, Stephen E. 453
  William 30
RIGGS, Chester 9
RIJELL, A. L. 384
  Jason 384
RILEY, Mr. 25
  Cornelia 482
  David F. 189
  George S. 195, 199, 459
  Jacob 199, 220
  Jacob L. 492

RILEY (cont.)
  John 361
  John J. 498
  Mary 319
  Spencer 252
  Wm. 419
RION, J. H. 183
RISE, N. G. 193
RITCHIE, Thomas 166
  Thomas, Jr. 166
RIVEIRE, John M. 479
RIVER, G. W. 377
RIVERS, Caroline Virginia 403
  Mary R. 398
  Thomas 398
RIVES, James T. 139
  John G. 54
  Mary Elizabeth 54
  Wm. C. 339
ROANE, Judge 260
  Spencer 423
  Wm. H. 260
ROATH, David L. 336
ROBARTS, John W. 390
ROBB, Frances L. 410
ROBERDS, A. M. 383
ROBERSON, John 371
  W. W. 433
ROBERT, Emma 516
ROBERTS, Augustus 260
  B. 72
  David 437, 455, 465
  E. A. 482
  Geo. B. 91
  Green 93
  J. 361
  Jackson 260
  Jane M. 171
  John 294
  Lewis 367
  M. A. 91
  Martha Ann 432
  Mary Ann 93
  Mary Elizabeth Felyn 91
  O. D. T. 382
  R. 377
  Reuben 132
  S. T. 368
  Sallie E. 499
  T. J. 361
ROBERTSON, -- 53, 389, 391
  Deputy Sheriff 176
  A. 363
  Adam 133
  Allen J. 359
  George 119
  Geo. W. 497
  J. A. 366
  Jabez 366
  John 171
  John M. 189
  John W. 411
  Laura Ellen 189
  Matthew 207
  N. C. 478
  Nathan C. 189
  William 3, 160, 406
ROBIND, W. M. 377
ROBINS, S. E. 364
ROBINSON, A. A. 501, 511
  Alexander Mark 161
  Ann 430
  Cuzziah 400
  E. A. 476
  Ebenezer 442
  Eliza A. M. 406
  Frances Eliza 419
  Geo. 102, 103
  J. C. 107
  J. J. 366

ROBINSON (cont.)
  John 313
  Martha 392
  Mary Jane 507
  Philip 397
  Robert P. 136, 408
  W. D. 371
  W. J. 365
  W. W. 442, 444, 487
ROBISON, J. 372
ROCKMORE, James L. 506
ROCKWELL, -- 334
  Cynthia Y. 436
  Peter P. 29
  Riley 16
  Samuel 69
  William S. 414
RODDEY, Robert L. 423
RODEN, John 470
RODGERS, Chas. M. 343
  D. R. 447
  Eveline L. 438
  George A. 461
  J. C. 369
  J. W. 360
  James E. 58
  James G. 450
  John C. 438
  Julia A. 458
ROFF, A. A. 160
  Cornelia J. T. 160
ROGERS, Rev. Mr. 470
  Britain F. 436
  Charles H. 469
  E. S. 457
  Elizabeth L. 247
  Frances Amanda 424
  Geo. A. 417
  George T. 247, 331, 527
  Henry Fuller 247
  J. L. 472
  Jas. G. 59
  Jane M. 409
  Job 200
  John C. 228
  Lucy A. M. 391
  M. R. 445
  Mary 200
  Osborn 428
  Sarah 150
  Simeon 150
  W. 364
  Wm. A. 519
  William B. 28
  Wm. R. 514
  Z. 365
ROLAND, E. C. 284
  Jas. 377
  Simeon A. 454
ROLIND, W. 377
ROLLIN, A. H. 357
ROLLINS, Mrs. 306
  Amos 362
ROMAIN, Rev. Mr. 397
RONALDSON, James H. 64
RONALSON, William J. 156
ROND, P. 358
ROOKS, Elijah 514
ROONEY, Charles 150
ROOT, Julia Ann 416
ROQUEMORE, Jas. A. 291, 495
ROSE, Augustus Beall 41
  Carolina Georgia 30
  David C. 437
  Hermione J. 498
  John 101
  John Bennett 407
  Juvenia 437
  Levi 142
  Marion P. 275
  Marion Preston 275

ROSE (cont.)
  Mary E. 460
  O. A. V. 523
  Philo Z. 111
  S. 28, 30, 41, 460
  Simri 275, 328, 346, 347, 395
  Virginia Caroline 28
ROSENFIELD, Jacob 512
ROSENTHUM, A. 380
ROSS, Rev. Dr. 488, 526
  Miss A. F. 506
  Amelia T. 459
  Ann L. 90
  B. L. 506
  Carrie V. 490
  Geo. W. 295, 472
  Harriet M. 430
  Henry G. 115, 206, 427, 459, 466
  I. H. B. 520
  J. B. 222, 490, 506, 528
  John 53, 168, 390
  John B. 90, 184, 440
  Luke 90, 96, 430
  Marina 389
  Martha 52, 390
  Martha L. 222
  Mary Grimes 96
  Mary M. 289
  Mary S. 427
  Nora 184
  Parmelia M. 523
  Sarah 115
  Sarah Elizabeth 52
  Thomas 53
  Thomas L. 52, 291
  Viola 528
  W. H. 360, 511
  William 168, 180
  William A. 276, 419
  Willie C. 360
ROSSER, F. A. 377
ROSSETER, Appleton 65, 66
  Elizabeth 421
  Mary B. 390
ROSSIN, B. 321
ROSTON, H. 385
ROUL, G. B. 370
ROULHAC, John G. 229
  Joseph B. 458
  P. G. 31
ROUNDTREE, Sarah E. 444
ROUNTREE, B. F. 380
  Caesar 333
  Moses 78
  William 406
ROUSE, W. C. 361
ROUSSEAU, General 343
ROUSTAN, L. A. 385
ROUX, D. L. 500
  Francis L. 224
  Henrietta L. 500
  Margaret S. 224
ROWAN, Wm. 385
ROWE, H. 414
  John 518
ROWELL, Margaret 465
ROWLAND, Bazzel 478
  E. F. T. 456
  Frances Alexander McKenzie 78
  Isaac B. 78, 394
  J. B. 456
  John S. 295, 462
  John T. 11
  Mary Henrietta 11
  Robt. H. 525
  Samuel T. 94
ROY, J. S. 370
  Wm. 365
ROYAL, Isaac H. 439

ROYAL (cont.)
  Wm. 358
  William H. 446
ROYNE, Noah 359
ROYSTON, G. D. 452
ROZIER, Amanda A. 454
RUBLEAN, Emilie 360
RUDULPH, John B. 491
RUFF, D. 374
  John 512
RUFFIN, Eliza 423
  Robert R., Col. 21
RUMLEY, W. L. 385
RUMPH, Charles E. 127
  David Howard 137
  Elizabeth C. 127
  Eugene Eugene Vastine 251
  Jacob 60
  Jacob V. 132, 451
  Josie C. 523
  Lewis 132, 137, 290, 471, 523
  Maria 137
  Samuel L. 139
  Sarah A. 60
RUNNELLS, Marshall M. 93
RUSH, Benjamin 248
  Richard 248
RUSHIN, Joel, Esq. 12
  John 79
  Rachael 79
  Rachel Jane 421
  William 421
RUSK, Gen. 216
  Mrs. 196
  Benj. Cleveland 196
RUSSEL, B. T. 506
  Florine 506
  J. J. 381
  J. P. 383
RUSSELL, Professor 211
  A. 51, 52
  Alexander 53
  Antoinette T. 477
  Benjamin 235
  Burwell 227
  Claudia A. 211
  D. Chester 446
  Edmund 40, 418
  Elizabeth 235
  F. 51, 52
  J. 363
  J. F. 377
  James A. 227
  M. 367
  Martha 227
  Mary E. 40
  S. T. 382
  Sarah Ann R. C. 51
  Stoddard 394
  T. B. 509, 525
RUST, James 22
RUSTIN, J. R. 361
RUTH, Eldridge S. 407
RUTHERFORD, Mrs. 172
  Anne L. 1
  B. H. 105, 440
  Elizabeth 1, 232
  H. T. V. 105
  James 1
  James A. S. 95
  John 359
  John, Jr. 405
  John H. 427, 448
  Martha Elizabeth 440
  Samuel 232
  William 95, 125
RUTHERS, J. W. 382
RUTLAND, Reddin 29
RUTLEDGE, Rt. Rev. Bishop 483, 506
  F. H. 458

RYALDS, W. R. 368
RYALS, Jas. 364
　John 495
RYAN, Anna Eliza 494
　Dennis L. 504
　John 309
　Victor 366
RYAR, M. 374
RYBURN, P. M. 525
　Peter M. 486
RYE, Nelton 469
RYERSON, Rev. Mr. 491
　J. E. 504
RYHMES, Elizabeth 187
　William 187
RYLAND, Eliza M. 426
RYLANDER, E. 51
　J. E. 298, 484
　John C. 79
　M. E. 421
　Mary E. 502
　Matthew E. 397, 502
RYNINGER, Herr 129
S-------, Frederick 38
S-------, John Bullock 38
S-------, Susan 38
SACKTON, G. 382
SACRAE, Frances P. A. 433
SAFFOLD, Isham H. 92
　Patience 92
　S. J. 245
　Thomas P. 476
SAGE, Mary 480
　Oliver 24, 38
　Oliver F., Jr. 24
　Willis T. 51, 52, 413
SAGERS, Solomon 361
SA-GU-YU-WHA-HAH, Seneca
　Chief 20
ST. CLAIR, Augusta 344
ST. JOHN, Charles G. 97
SALE, Jos. C. 426
SALFNER, John M. 79
SALIE, Aurelius 149
SALTAR, John D. 141
SAMFORD, A. -- 473
　Thomas 405
SAMUELS, Green B. 238
SANDERS, Ailie L. 199
　Ann G. 435
　B. M. 433, 501
　Elizabeth 46, 489
　Elizabeth E. 522
　Emily 392
　Geo. 433
　Henry 244
　J. J. 361
　Miss J. V. 444
　Louisa 410
　M. A. 212
　Martha E. E. 212
　Robt. 410
　Susan A. M. 419
　T. J. 212
　William 46, 199
SANDERSON, Richardson 429
SANDIFORD, Joseph J. 280
SANDLIN, John W. 488
　Julia A. 463
SANFORD, Rev. Mr. 410
　B. W. 518
　D. 420
　Daniel 409, 423, 424
　Frederick H. 228
　John W. A. 516
　Lizzie J. 509
　Sterling 509
　Wm. 368
SAPP, Lein 359
　Riley 378
SARELL, P. R. 369
SASNETT, R. Fannie 471
　Richard P. 471

SASNET, Wm. J. 471
SATTERWHITE, John Thomas
　204
SATTLINGS, Octavus 348
SAUCER, Stephen 176
SAULSBURY, Mr. and Mrs.
　272
　Ann 194
　Edwin 160
　Mary Lou 527
　Nina Clopton 272
SAULBURY, Thomas J. 68
SAUNDERS, B. M. 162
　D. 365
　Fannie E. 493
　Gabrilla E. A. 447
　Henry 244
　J. S. 367
　John H. 193
　Martha W. 466
　R. 376
　Rebecca T. E. 404
　Remembrance Chamberlin
　　63
　Seaborn J. 166
　Wm. 168, 421, 447
SAURIN, Mr. 317
SAUSSEY, Sarah H. 490
SAUSSY, Joachim 490
SAVAGE, J. H. 382
　J. P. K. 237
　James M. 487
　W. H. 517
SAWYER, Floyd 325
　G. B. 378
　Peter C. 528
　W. 374
SAYERS, W. P. 378
SAYLOR, David S. 132
　Esaias 132
SAYRE, Nathan C. 148
SCALES, John 301
　Robt. W. 480
SCANDRETT, Robert 489
SCARBOROUGH, -- 236
　Augusta J. 502
　Carrie 476
　Enos 457
　J. A. 278
　J. J. 502
　J. S. W. 368
　James J. 449
　Sarah Marshall 449
SCATTERGOOD, Adelia 478
SCHEONMAKER, Ann R. S.
　429
SCHLEY, Dr. 169
　Freeman 169
　Philip T. 290, 389
　William 235, 336
SCHNIERIE, John 327
SCHOLFIELD, J. W. 375
SCHULER, Ettiene 225
SCHLUNZEN, Freidrich 480
SCHREINER, Hermann L. 528
SCHUYLER, Philip S. 174
SCHWARTZ, Henry 313
SCORGGINS, J. F. 363
SCOTT, Bishop 313
　Mr. 271
　Alexander 93, 98, 151,
　　424
　Andrew J. 496
　Anna E. 512
　Antoinette 407
　Dred 233
　Elizabeth M. 138
　Ellenora F. 479
　Francis 139
　H. H. 373
　Harriette A. 441
　Henry A. 138, 451, 473
　Isaac 512

SCOTT (cont.)
　J. E. 364
　J. T. 364
　Jane G. 466
　John 280, 456
　Margaret 93, 98
　McDaniel 413
　O. P. 383
　Susan 483
　Thos. W. 410
　William 129, 441, 466
　William F. 101
　Wm. H. 365, 431
SCRANTON, Loyal 159
SCREVEN, James P. 247
　John 32
SCRUTCHEN, Josiah 454
　Sarah Jane 454
SCHRUTCHIN, A. J. 463
SEABORN, James 281
SEABROOK, Edward W. 476
　Elizabeth 455
　Smilie 455
SEABURY, Jane Amelia 457
SEAL, Alfred 367
SEALS, John H. 501
　Mary E. 501
SEARCY, B. 421
　B. R. 520
SEARS, Alfred 243
　Eli 456
　Wm. 400
SEATON, P. P. 380
SEAY, Thomas 164
SEDGWICK, Theodore 254
SEE, John 380
SEIGLER, L. M. 378
SELLECK, Clarence H. 313
　Sarah A. 451
SELLERS, W. R. 359
SENTER, J. R. 378
SETLER, Geo. 373
SETTLES, Charlott 413
SEWARD, Joseph J. 367
SEWELL, Mary Ann F. 502
　Washington 435
SEXTON, Wm. 366, 368
SEYMORE, Israel 132
SEYMOUR, Ada H. 484
　Mrs. C. E. 148
　Caroline Eulalia 34
　Mrs. Caroline E. 228
　Catherine E. 447
　Gurdon I. 76
　Henry G. 20
　Isaac C. 34
　Isaac G. 21, 76, 148,
　　228, 396
　James 522
　Joseph H. 470
　Kate 148
　Margaret D. 471
　Martha Ann 472
　Mary 282
　Mary E. T. 522
　Richard H. 105
SHACKELFORD, Carrie E. 517
　Fr. R. 66, 426
　J. W. 364
　James 491
　Jane 66
　Mary E. 491
　Samuel 168
　William 168, 328
SHAD, Eliza B. 242
　John R. 242
SHADD, J. F. 370
SHAHAM, L. 364
SHAND, S. J. 475
SHANKLIN, Rev. Mr. 449,
　　450, 461, 465, 470,
　　477
　Joseph A. 448

SHANKLIN (cont.)
    William 473
SHANNON, James 242, 354
    Peter 107
    Rufus 327
    Wm. 203
SHARMAN, Mary Eliza 481
    Thomas S. 257, 481
SHARP, Augusta 499
    B. F. 464
    C. 499
    Ellen P. 474
    H. W. 474
    J. E. 466
    J. M. 466
    James B. 462
    John M. 312
    Mordaunt 312
    Peyton 312
    Wm. Henry 426
SHARPE, J. E. 458
SHARPMAN, Louisa F. 257
SHAVER, W. L. 361
SHAW, Mrs. A. M. 503
    Chandler Holt 123
    Harvey W. 216, 442
    J. 380, 383
    J. W. 360
    James 123
    John 2
    Joseph 391
    Lemuel 271
    Margaret D. 123
    Orrin 9
    W. 171
    William 216
    William H. 496
SHEA, W. D. 495, 515
    W. P. 491
    William D. 493, 499, 500, 504
SHEALEY, A. E. 202
    Geo. 202
    John 202
    M. L. 202
    Martha 330
    Wm. 202
SHEALY, Andrew 200, 202
SHEDAMN, S. B. 372
SHEELT, Wm. 429
SHEFFIELD, Camelia J. 463
    Miss E. E. 472
    Edward O. 240
    John C. 413
    Jonathan 323
    Mary H. 463
    Pliney 143, 463
SHEFTALL, Delamotta 189
    Mordecai 197
    Sheftall 106
SHEHAN, Bartholomew 153
SHEHANE, C. F. R. 213
SHELBY, John L. 45
    Mary Ann 428
    Wm. A. 515
SHELFER, Elijah E. 358
SHELL, James 150
SHELLMAN, T. P. C. 416
SHELLY, James 370
SHELMAN, John M. 30
    Thomas 412
SHELTERFIELD, M. 381
SHELTON, Bascom 368
    E. L. 136, 440
    John 381
    Joseph T. 458
    Malinda 136
SHEPARD, Geo. I. 438
    Lorenzo B. 203
    W. 384
SHEPHERD, -- 315
    W. R. 378
    William 164

SHEPPARD, Martha A. 523
SHERIDAN, James 437
SHERMAN, Rev. Mr. 429
    Charles Henry 95
    D. 459
    H. 374
SHERRARD, Martha 449
    Wright 449
SHERRY, Elphany 479, 480
    Susan 480
SHERWOOD, Rev. Mr. 409
    A. E. 288
    A. F. 425
    Lottie 313
    Sabin 347
SHIDE, Martha 515
SHIELDS, James 209
SHINE, D. W. 437, 526
    Daniel W. 25, 324, 341
    Fannie A. 484
    John 25
    Kattie A. 523
    Mrs. Mary 526
SHINHOLSTER, Martha Ann 61
SHINHOLSER, Mary N. 470
    Thomas 464
    Thos. J. 61
SHIP, Wm. L. 359
SHIPIRINE, Wm. 392
SHIRLEY, J. 371
    William T. 435
SHIVER, John M. 353
    Susan F. 184
SHIVERS, Martha A. 506
    Sarah M. D. 422
    Wm., Jr. 129, 184, 506
SHOCKLEY, John 44
    Winfrey 412
SHOCKLY, Sarah 415
SHOEMAKER, J. H. 385
SHOPE, D. N. 234
SHORES, Caroline 128
    J. B. 128
    J. W. 378
SHORT, Elizabeth 77
    John W. 285
    M. 366
SHORTER, Judge 389
    Caroline Billingslea 498
    Reuben C. 450
SHOTWELL, Anna F. K. 441
    Harvey 109, 441
    Jacob 417
    Mary E. W. 445
SHOVERLAND, Margaret 171
SHROPSHIRE, Henry Clay 281
SHUPTRINE, Joshua 405
SHY, -- 356
SIBLEY, Amory 117
    Mary C. 515
    Sam'l S. 235
SIGOURNEY, Mrs. 176
    Charles 176
SIKES, Arthur 423
    Reuben 322
    Wiley 515
SIMMONDS, W. 378
SIMMONS, -- 280
    Judge 462
    A. 374
    Allen G. 239
    Ann 55
    Carry 305
    D. W. 457
    Daniel 97
    Eliza 477
    Elizabeth 265
    G. W. 368

SIMMONS (cont.)
    H. J. 366
    Helen G. 498
    J. C. 505
    J. H. 382
    James M. 522
    John 165, 265
    Jos. T. 498
    Martin 37
    Melissa 462
    N. 364
    P. E. 372
    Stern 155
    Thos. 366
    Thos. J. 502
    W. H. 364
    William 389
    Wm. M. 211
SIMMS, James 487
    L. 378
    Robert B. 394
SIMON, P. 171
SIMONTON, E. 130
    Isabella 453
    Joel R. 214, 436
    N. A., Mrs. 214
    Sallie Powers 214
SIMPSON, Aiden 376
    Amanda E. 415
    Edward 377
    J. W. 378
    L. C. 266
    Miss Missouri 526
    W. W. 503
    Wm. 209
    Wm. E. 277
SIMS, Benjamin 397
    C. C. 515
    Catharine Fay 246
    Catharine M. 232, 428
    Ed. Mitchell 38
    Eliza 51, 57, 81, 453
    Eliza Ellen 51
    Emily H. 437
    F. 428
    F. W. 246
    Frederick 93, 112, 116, 133, 134, 404, 414, 437
    Frederick W. 232
    John H. 57, 81, 403
    John M. 51
    Marcisna, Mrs. 525
    Mary 397
    Mary B. 481
    Sarah 450
    Susan 134
    Thomas J. 175
    Zachariah 38, 41
SINBRIS, Elmore 305
SINCLAIR, Rev. Mr. 408, 410, 411, 413, 417
    Albert E. 423
    E. 418, 420, 421
    Elijah 73, 97, 414, 418, 421
    James R. 43
    Martha A. E. 431
SINGLETON, Mrs. 270
    Davis 478
    Frances G. 482
    Miss G. A. 504
    Henry 346
    John 144
    Joseph J. 163, 440
    Mary E. 440
    Mary Rebecca 397
    Richard 397
    W. R. 448
    Wyatt R. 426, 449
SINS, Catharine M. 196
    Frederick Wm. 196
    Mary 196

SKELTON, Eugene 251
  Green 276
SKINNER, J. R. 380
  Mattie 325
  T. T. 325
  Thomas M. 325
  Eli 378
  Joel 223
SLACK, Wm. E. 367
SLADE, Ann Eliza 394
  Annie G. 195
  Annie Graham 198
  Ann L. 500
  Emma J. 477
  Hannah E. 486
  Helen R. 524
  James J. 195, 198, 484,
    510
  Jane 490
  Janet E. 524
  Marmaduke J. 216, 391
  Martha B. 512
  Mary L. 291
  T. B. 36
  Thomas B. 31, 56, 224,
    291, 458, 477, 484,
    500, 512, 524
  William 490
SLAPPEY, Mrs. 20
  Henry J. 322
  J. Thomas 248
  Jacob 248
  Joanna 394
  Laura 466
  Lizzie 464
  Martha J. 182
  Mary A. E. 517
  R. R. 182
  Reuben H. 482
  Uriah 143, 464
SLAPPY, Elizabeth 248
  Matilda 174
  Reuben H. 174
  S. 74
SLATER, William D. 343
SLATOR, J. M. 371
SLATTER, Elizabeth 461
  James E. 115
  L. D. 461
  Wm. -- 395
  William C. 112
SLAUGHTER, Rev. Mr. 419,
    420, 421
  George 205
  Hope A. 155
  James S. 624
  Martin G. 210
  N. G. 153, 421, 428
  Shadrach 276
SLEDGE, Isham D. 201, 434
SLOAN, J. A. 481
  Mary M. B. 524
SLOPER, Harrison 317
SMALL, Arthur 509
SMALLEN, John 123
SMALLWOOD, J. K. P. 362
SMARR, Frances M. 486
SMART, John C. 517
SMASH, Pompey 336
SMEAD, Augusta R. 481
  E. 481
  H. P. 431
SMELL, Henry C. 368
SMETS, A. A. 489, 521
  Cornelia 521
  Laula 489
SMITH, Major 365
  Mrs. 173, 238
  Rev. Mr. 395, 417,
    420, 453, 501
  A. 503
  A. G. 361
  A. J. 371

SMITH (cont.)
  A. L. 362
  A. P. 328
  Abner 477
  Alex'r 189
  Alfred 369
  Algenon Gaillard 195
  Amanda N. 195
  Andrew 367
  Ann Gilman 32
  Anthony G. 33
  B. F. 277
  B. Franklin 415
  B. M. 439
  B. Q. 165
  Ben 300
  Benjamin 125, 307
  Benjamin B. 215
  Benjamin T. 259
  Blakely 492
  Bridges W. 528
  C. C. 370
  Caroline 395
  Caroline A. 342
  Catharine A. 131
  Cephas 66
  D. 363, 466
  D. N. 242
  David 442, 451, 456
  David M. 495
  David O. 439
  David Washington 14
  Davis 68, 459, 502
  Davis, Jr. 461
  Duncan 510
  E. A. 290
  Mrs. E. E. 322
  Eliza 403
  Elizabeth 478
  Elliot I. 152
  Exer Ann 406
  Ezekiel 152, 398
  G. C. 41
  G. F. 505
  G. G. 85
  Garrett 156
  Geo. A. 153, 333
  George G. 404
  Gideon 193
  Griffin 269
  H. C. 273
  H. H. 307
  H. S. 322, 511
  Harriet J. 430
  Hartwell P. 439
  Hattie E. 519
  Henderson 316
  Henry C. 273
  Henry W. 448
  Hugh 391, 397, 399,
    435
  Isaac 404
  Isaac H. 32
  Isaac Newton 85
  J. 359, 449
  J. C. 367
  J. F. 364
  J. H. 365
  J. M. 382
  J. O. 359
  J. P. 402
  J. S. 383
  J. T. 457, 525
  J. Blakely 477, 528
  J. Dickinson 263, 490
  James 139, 152, 257,
    360, 361, 392, 396,
    464, 506
  Jas. M. 475
  James R. 404, 465
  James S. 94
  James W. 513
  Jane 32

SMITH (cont.)
  Jeremiah 14, 84, 391
  Joel E. J. 153
  John 26, 267, 368, 373,
    411, 475, 477
  John A. 428
  John E. 302
  John P. 23
  John Patterson 71
  John S. 152
  John T. 452
  John W. 438
  Joseph 50, 71, 81, 179
  L. L. 383
  L. V. 375
  Levi B. 290
  Louisa C. 23
  Lucretia 392
  M. C. 462
  Magor 319
  Malinda 407
  Maria Jane 26
  Martha C. 406
  Mary 50, 165, 506
  Mary A. 417
  Mary Ann 223
  Mary J. 153
  Mary S. 242
  Milly 84
  N. N. 342
  Nancy 439
  Nathan, M. D. 16
  Needham 165
  Nettie S. 511
  Nicholas W. 155
  O. A. 359
  O. L. 194, 490, 496,
    497, 504, 505
  P. D. 507
  Persifer F. 228
  Peyton T. 140
  R. C. 472, 484
  R. P. 362
  Ralph 68
  Renry 374
  Richard 395
  Robert A. 131, 289
  Robert Daniel 35
  Miss S. F. 519
  S. M. 498
  S. R. 374
  Samuel 153, 360
  Sarah 490
  Seaborn A. 420
  Silas P. 367
  Sumner J. 329
  T. F. 380
  Theodrick L. 60, 410
  Thomas 5, 175
  Thomas K. 417
  Turner 128, 433
  W. A. 385
  W. B. 372
  W. F. 480, 499
  W. G. 361
  W. L. 372
  W. M. 346
  W. T. 381
  Wesley 490
  Wesley, F. 459, 468,
    469, 478, 487, 490,
    492, 493, 495, 503,
    507, 521
  Wm. 478, 488
  Wm. E. 342
  Wm. G. 100, 223
  Wm. H. 497
  William R. D. 153
  William T. 281
SMITHWICK, Eliza 432
SMYER, Jacob 225
SNEAD, C. S. 240
  John 126

SNEAD (cont.)
    John W. W. 269, 465
    Julia Pope 240
    Mary A. 269
    Mary E. 240
    Philip B. 367
    W. F. 151
SNEED, Cyrus S. 487
    James R. 321
    Nora C. 321
    Nora Cohen 321
    Zachariah 425
SNEER, John M. 371
SNELGROVE, Charlotte 391
SNELL, Wm. H. 238
SNELLING, Janie V. 507
    Mrs. M. E. 501
SNIDER, Benjamin 138
SNODDY, Dr. 414
SNOW, Martha 394
SNOWDEN, Lieut. 283
SNYDER, Martin 70
SOLOMON, Cinderella C. 475
    Cora 524
    Cynthia 108
    Mrs. F. 469
    Francis S. A., Mrs. 471
    Geraldine C. 493
    H. L. 378
    Hardy 108, 427
    Henry 102, 220, 416, 447, 493
    Henry F. 480
    J. M. E. 369
    James 73, 398
    L. 480, 485, 497
    Lewis 493, 499, 500, 501, 502, 507, 506, 515, 524
    Louisa 99
    Lucinda 450
    Malone 99
    Martha 49
    Mary Ann 416
    Nathan Monroe 357
    Owen F. 251
    P. 487
    Peter 49, 99, 524
    Virginia A. 447
    William L. 266
SOLOMONS, Wm. 35
SOMERS, J. B. 359
SORREL, R. H. D. 477
SORRELLS, Thomas 214
SORRILL, Thos. 190
SOUTHALL, Mary 396
    William L. 400
SOWELL, Leighton 412
SPAIN, A. C. 455
    Drury, Dr. 8
    William B. 493
SPALDING, Catharine A. 403
    Charles 128
    Thomas 128
SPANN, Abram 333
SPANRREGAN, Dr. 490
SPARKS, Benjamin W. 64
    Jared 305
    Ovid G. 475
    Thos. 64
SPARROW, Rev. Mr. 522
    R. W. 476
SPAULDING, A. M. 461
    T. A. 504
    W. 491
SPEAR, Rev. Mr. 471, 475, 478
    A. 439
    Eustace 478
    James 372

SPEER, -- 287
    Rev. Mr. 481, 488
    A. M. 426
    A. S. 218
    Alex M. 196
    Alexander 194
    E. W. 481, 490, 524
    Eustace 524
    M. 445
    Mary A. 196
    Walker R. 196
SPEERY, J. A. 495
SPEIGHT, Rev. Mr. 419, 462
    Julia L. 490
    Thomas 243, 456, 490
SPEIR, John R. 287
SPELLERS, Henry 244
SPELSSEGER, Samuel 315
SPENCE, Robert Trail 8
    William 179
SPENCER, Capt. 369
    Ambrose 110
    David 407
    Joseph 149
    Robert 170, 350
SPERRY, Anson McCollum 283
    Jno. A. 283, 415
    Mary B. 283
    John A. 214
    M. Ophelia 525
SPEIR, William C. 186
SPIER, Washington 164
SPINKS, J. M. 365
    Mary T.
SPIVEY, E. B. W. 394
    James A. 458
    Littleton 412
    Sophia 412
SPRADLEY, L. J. 378
    Wm. 368
SPRAGINS, Mr. 5
SPRAGUE, Rev. Mr. 429
SPRAWLS, J. C. 384
SPRING, Rev. Dr. 406
SPRINGER, John 69
    Thos. 126
    William G. 62, 69
SPYKER, V. D. 362
SQUIRE, Harvey H. 25
STAFF, -- 310
STAFFORD, -- 371
    James 28, 404
    Mary Ann 424
    Wm. 424
STALEY, George A. 527
STALLINGS, Jesse 455, 506
    Sarah 404
    William 390
STALWORTH, J. P. 371
STAMPER, Rev. Mr. 448
    Lucretia 169
    Martin W. 169
STANFORD, Eliza 405
    Thomas 405
STANLEY, Augustin O. 484
    H. B. 383
    Ira 226
    R. A. 494
    W. C. 319
STANLY, Edward 176
    Julia 176
STANSELL, Levi 349
STANTON, J. 363
STAPLER, John 61, 96
    Polly N. 106
    Polly Virginia 96
STAPLES, John R. 436
    Sophos 7
STAPLETON, Rev. Mr. 449
STARK, James H. 484
    Mr. 53

STARKS (cont.)
    William S. 433
STARR, Mrs. 326
    Caroline 403
    Henry 308
    J. H. 405
STAUNTON, T. L. 372
STEADMAN, -- 276, 381
    Gen. 354
    John 276
STEAGALL, Sarah M. 405
STEEL, A. D. 419
STEELE, Ellen E. 488
    Geo. 81, 488
    George A. 203
STEELEY, M. R. 521
STELL, Rev. Mr. 427
STELLY, Wm. R. 513
STEMBRIDGE, John 217
STENSON, J. W. 359
STEPHENS, A. R. 38
    C. W. 525
    Carrie S. 468
    Catherine A. 504
    Charles 115
    E. 359
    Emeline 207
    J. D. 441
    James A. 359
    Jesse 501
    John T. 484
    L. W. 510
    Linton 207
    Lucy Ann 432
    Martha 519
    Miles G. 437
    Noah 38
    Simeon L. 160
    Solomon 161
    W. J. 446
    Wm. J. 471
STEPHENSON, Joseph W. 485
STERLING, Lady Catherine 231
    Lord 231
    William H. 434
STEVEN, Hooker 322
STEVENS, Adeline 414
    C. W. 479
    J. T. 335
    Mary 308
    Mollie 353
    R. B. 369
    Reuben 268
    Mrs. S. A. E. 353
    S. L. 414
    Seth C. 245
    Wm. 362
    William B. 307, 451
STEWARD, Bug 356
    Edward 413
    Thomas 8
    Wm. 105
STEWART, A. 371
    C. A. 370
    C. H. 360
    Charles 178, 305
    Charles H. 182
    Charles L. 339
    Charles W. 174
    Daniel 18
    Ezekiel J. 498
    Henry Jasper 136
    J. 358, 372
    James 137
    James R. 502
    Jas. S. 368
    Julia 323
    Julius W. 204
    Leonidas 518
    Margaret 137
    Marion Franklin 136
    Mary J. 497

STEWART (cont.)
 Naomi J. 12
 Polly H. 136
 T. R. 492
 Thomas H. 466, 508
 Thomas Jefferson 444
 Thomas W. 136
 William B. 359
 Wm. D. 130
 William N. 454
STILES, -- 391
 Rev. Mr. 394
 Amanda 432
 Benj. E. 179
 Carey W. 247
 J. C. 394
 Joseph 224, 432, 437, 450
 Joseph C. 391
 Sarah W. 73
STILL, A. J. 366
STILWELL, Elizabeth 341
 J. M. 521
 John 418
STINSON, James W. 398
STITH, -- 245
STITTLER, Rev. Mr. 205
STITT, A. A. 266
STOCKBURG, G. W. 367
STOCKING, Ashbel L. 80
 Harvey 80
STOCKTON, Edward D. 210
STODDARD, John 347
STOFER, Mr. 229
STOKES, -- 260, 274
 Cordy D. 116
 Elizabeth 471
 Fannie M. 516
 John 131
 Joseph H. 109
STOLTER, D. F. 381
STONE, Ann G. 419
 C. J. 497
 Frank H. 514
 G. W. W. 503
 Geo. W. 509
 J. S. 233
 Jeremy 44
 Martha 425
 Mrs. R. L. 500
 S. M. 419
 Sheppard A. 458
 Sumner 390
 Susannah 422
 Thomas 422
STONEY, W. J. 371
STORRE, Oliver A. 22
STORRS, Richard Henry 273
 R. S. 527
STORY, Harriet 417
STOVALL, Adelaide E. 432
 G. T. 278
 George T. 279
 J. B. 378
 Joseph 432
 Mary H. 391
STOW, Anthony 418
 Catherine W. 133
 E. J. 260
 Geo. W. 430
 Hattie S. 509
 John B. 133, 428, 509
STRANGE, H. 369
 Robert 161
STRATON, J. A. 362
STRATTON, Rev. Mr. 393
 Robert 312
STRAUNTON, P. 329
STREET, G. W. 366
 Sarah Ann 401
STRICKLAND, Mr. 329
 G. W. 493
 Lydia 418

STRICKLER, W. 378
STRICKLIN, S. 378
STRINGFIELD, J. 493
STRIPLING, Martha Ann 437
STRIPPLING, James W. 370
STROBEL, Mr. 317
 Arthur Davis 151
 Benjamin B. 119
 Eliza M. 151
 P. A. 119, 151, 453, 483
 Sarah J. 119
STROBHART, George W. 347
STROHECKER, E. L. 165, 166
 Lewis Charles 165
STROMAN, J. B. 365
STRONG, Judge 25, 168
 Mrs. 25
 Blake B. 168
 C. B. 71, 397
 Catherine M. 520
 Charles A. 432
 Christopher B. 47, 103, 131, 441
 Edgar P. 509
 Eliza Virginia 81
 Lucy Ann 71
 Martha D. 397
 Rebecca Marinda 25
 S. M. 81
 Sarah Taylor 441
 Virginia Woodson 47
STROTHER, George H. D. 158
 Harriett A. 158
 John W. 72, 158
 Mary E. 487
STROUD, Frances W. 501
 James 351
 Levi 50
 Nancy 351
 Sarah 398
STROZIER, William 466
STUART, Catharine C. 229
 James Jackson 229
 John W. 229
 Mary A. 441
STUBBS, Lieut. 282
 Abner P. 224, 441
 Angeline R. 495
 B. B. 403
 B. P. 509
 Catharine M. 433
 Caroline S. M. 418
 Edward 439
 Euginia L. 509
 Francis 196
 Francis P. 504
 J. M. 282
 J. W. 286
 James 264
 James A. 445
 Joel G. 286
 John James 196
 Mary Ella 88
 Peter 163, 224, 434
 Rebecca 88
 Sarah Ann 434
 T. P. 88
 Thomas P. 44, 248
STURAT, W. W. 378
STURDEVANT, Judge 467
STURGES, Benjamin H. 2
 Daniel 2
 J. R. 319
STURGIS, C. F. 435, 437
 Eliza J. 140
 John R. 140
 Joseph 163
 Laura Winship 140
STWO, John B. 264

SUBERS, Elam Alexander 88
 Laura A. 527
 Samuel M. 503
SUDKINS, Josiah 360
SUFFOLK, Lady 179
SULLIVAN, Annie E. 526
 Eugene 311
 Harriet 445
 J. W. 361
 James 210, 254
 Joanna 493
 M. 232
 Mark 143
 Virginia 467
 W. D. 477
 W. J. 378
SUMERS, Elizabeth 437
 Nicoles 437
SUMMERFORD, Jno. H. 369
 Wm. H. H. 287
SUMMERHAYS, Mrs. M. J. 522
SUMMERLIN, C. D. 202
SUMMING, Thomas 32
SUMNER, Wellington 41
SUMPTER, Gen. 18
SUTTLEMORE, E. K. 372
SUTTON, C. Amanda 275
 James N. 99
 Jerry 322
 John 357
 Mary W. 99
 Sarah Amme 275
 Thomas W. 275
 Warren 226
SWAIN, Augusta 182
 J. D. 359
 J. W. 165
 William M. 337
SWAN, W. G. 347
SWANNER, Jesse I. 441
SWANSON, John W. 485
SWEARENGEN, Mary Ann 421
 Thos. 421
SWEARINGEN, Oliver P. 439
 Thomas A. 457
SWEAT, Pharley 521
SWEENEY, Mark 151
 Thomas 89
SWEET, Geo. C. 397
 Mary E. 397
SWETT, SAmuel 307
SWIFE, Thos. 41
SWIFT, Alexander H. K. 222
 Clarissa 394
 Henry A. 346
 Joseph G. 300
 Mary T. 437
SWINEY, J. W. 360
SWINNEY, E. B. 205
SWITZER, Francis, Miss 504
SYKES, Daniel 179
SYKER, P. A. 372
SYMMES, John Cleves 18
SYNG, Philip 49
TAIT, Charles 40
TALBERT, -- 309
TALBOT, Matthew, Capt. 12
TALKINBERRY, D. 371
TALLEY, Jos. T. 445
TALLINGS, S. 384
TALLMAGE, Rev. Mr. 397
TALLY, D. E. 382
 John Henry 22
 John R. 22
 John W. 411, 412
 Susan H. 22
TALMAGE, Rev. Mr. 396, 447, 475, 476, 494, 495, 503, 504, 508, 515, 520, 523

TALMAGE (cont.)
　Jehiel 172
　P. S. 172
　S. K. 423, 484, 496
　Samuel K. 491
TANGLE, Henry 371
TANNER, David W. 366
　James M. 127
TAPLY, Mary 442
TARASH, David 392
TARRER, Henry F. 502
TARVER, Dr. 20
　Allevia Ann Elizabeth 438
　Benj. S. 438
　Frederick R. 144
　Hartwell H. 230
　Joanna R. 70
　John Randolph 20
　Maria D. 397
　Mary R. 20
　Paul E. 230, 475
　R. 280
　Wm. M. 70, 394
TARVIN, George 31
TATE, Ann 460
　David 371
　L. O. 374
TATNALL, Josiah 154
TATUM, James A. 213
TAYLOR, Capt. 259
　General 143, 153
　Rev. Dr. 391, 412
　B. 371
　Barnabas 362
　Benj. F. 437
　Camilla C. 468
　Charles 473
　Charles E. 151
　Chas. H. 368
　Cynthia C. 515
　E. B. 523
　E. R. 369
　George 161
　Geo. W. 292, 294
　Giles B. 401
　H. W. 369
　Hugh 8
　Ira H. 311, 453
　J. B. 193
　J. P. 469
　James 114, 161
　Jefferson 259
　Job 190, 191, 423, 468
　Job E. 480
　John 4, 59, 330
　John F. 467
　Jones M. 227
　Josiah S. 369
　Laura J. 493
　Mary 468, 505
　Mary B. 393
　Mary E. 467, 523
　Meredith 456
　Moses 309
　N. J. 467
　Nicholas 251
　Paul 333, 334, 335
　S. K. 503
　Sallie 516
　Samuel Benton 59
　Sarah M. 432
　Sol. R. 367
　T. L. 356
　Thomas 406
　Thos. L. 482
　W. A. 364
　W. B. 371
　William 146, 147, 193
　William A. 328
　Wm. Henry 516
　William J. 295
　William W. 428

TAYLOR (cont.)
　Willis W. 467
　Zachary 124, 153
TEAGLE, Geo. 329
　U. R. 363
　A. J. 362
TEAT, John 100
TEBEAU, Catherine M. 430
　F. E. 430
TEEL, A. J. 435
TEFT, C. E. 151
　J. I. 151
TEMPLETON, Caroline M. 495
TENNELL, B. 373
TENNANS, Elizabeth 379
TENNISON, Joshua 463
TERREL, James R. 360
TERRELL, Henry, Maj. 10
　Lucie 491
　William 182, 474, 491
TERRY, J. J. 370
　Martha 421
TERRYMAN, James 513
TERVIN, Clara Jane 399
　George 399
　Martha 60
　Wm. M. 50
THACKSON, J. M. 378
THARP, Rev. Mr. 389, 408
　A. 504
　B. F. 433, 498, 504
　C. A. 396, 408, 420, 427, 448, 455, 471, 499
　Mrs. Elizabeth 216
　Elizabeth S. 501
　Ellen 420
　Jeremiah 420
　Julia A. D. 440
　Lucinda 420
　Obedience A. 434
　Sarah A. 25
　V. A. 389
　Vincent A., Rev. 6, 25
　William A. 70, 440
THARPE, Ada J. 462
　B. F. 483
　William 483
THAXTON, Thomas 352
THESTON, A. 382
THEUS, B. T. 236
THIGPEN, Rev. Mr. 495
　A. M. 509
　Alex 499
　Alex M. 496, 505
THOMAS, -- 373
　Rev. Dr. 509
　A. L. 364
　C. W. 468
　Celia 399
　Charles S. 432
　David 54
　E. 367, 374
　Eliza 514
　G. R. 499
　Grigsby E. 300, 512
　Isaiah 23
　J. H. 360, 372
　J. Q. 361
　J. S. 514
　J. W. 353
　Jackson 315
　James 192, 454
　James M. 524
　Jas. R. 423
　Jane M. 499
　John 63, 399
　John G. 259, 494
　John H. 229, 467
　John J. 472
　John S. 192
　Joseph W. 240

THOMAS (cont.)
　Julia Ann 403
　Mary C. 497
　Micajah 174
　Richard 369
　Sarah A. J. 467
　Susan A. 259
　Theresa 453
　Thomas 224
　Thomas W. 297, 510
　W. 361, 380
　Wm. B. 163
　William D. 497
　William J. 300
THOMPKINS, W. P. 378
THOMPSON, A. J. 363
　Anthony M. 148
　B. D., Dr. 18
　Charles 4, 166
　Charles B. 27
　Charles Ernest 197
　D. 374
　David 43
　E. R. 492
　Mrs. E. S. 525
　Elizabeth 156
　Mr. 336
　Ellen 35
　Franklin 333
　George 379
　George W. 44
　Miss H. E. 503
　Henry A. 288
　Hester 186
　Hezekiah 186
　Horace 476
　Hugh 114
　J. E. 378
　J. Egbert 443
　J. L. 367
　J. W. 368
　Jack 350
　James 156, 389, 404
　James Egbert 140
　Jesse M. 371
　Joseph S. 44
　Kate A. 492
　L. A. 475
　Laura J. 197
　M. S. 288
　Margaret 468
　Mary Angelina 140
　Mary C. 166
　Mary Jane 156
　N. M. 370
　Norman C. 197
　Penelope 60
　R. L. 378
　S. H. 367
　Samuel M. 235
　Thomas 468
　William 327, 350
TAYLOR, Elizabeth 417
THOMSON, Eli C. 451
　Hezekiah 64, 433
　Mary Emma 64
　Rebecca Frances 433
THORNTON, Charles F. 340
　Dozier 262
　Emmaline H. 285
　H. A. 242
　J. 371
　J. C. 285
　Middleton 347
　T. T. 378
THORTON, V. R. 193
THORWEGAN, W. H. 321
THRAP, Wm. A. 78
THRIFT, J. 378
THROOP, Orramel H. 159
THURMAN, Philip 68
THURSTON, -- 88
THWEATT, Eliza Ann 58

THWEATT (cont.)
  Elizabeth P. 403
  Jas. 22, 402
  John 270
  Julia D. 270
  Kinchen P. 403
  Owen Thomas 314
  Peterson 519
  Susan F. 424
  Thacker Adolphus 270
  Thomas 424
  Victoria M. 466
TICHENOR, I. T. 515
TICKNER, Esther 393
  John 56
  Orray 404
TICKNOR, George C. 141
TIDWELL, -- 332
  J. 363
TIFT, Nelson 417
TIGNER, H. H. 45
TILDEN, B. G. 318
TILFORD, James McCown 55, 108
TILL, Martha A. 483
  Sarah F. 488
TILLINGHAST, Paris J. 323
TILLMAN, Daniel 154
  Henry 144
  William J. 447
TILTER, J. M. 372
TIMBERLAKE, Philip 461
TIMLIN, Josephine 482
TIMONY, E. McBarom 349
TINDALL, Henry W. 129
TINGEY, Thomas, Commodore 17
TINLEY, James 510
  Sarah 510
TINSLEY, Mrs. 240
  Adaline 462
  James 260
  James W. 78, 240
  Jane E. 454
  Mary M. 490
  Samuel G. 408
  Wm. 454, 462
TISSEREAU, Bertrand 430
  Josephine 445
TISSEROT, B. 49
  Mary 49
TITUS, Col. 213
TOBEY, T. W. 468
TOBIN, Ann 425
  Joana 438
TODD, Eley W. 438
  Henry M. 140
  Jacob I. 155
  T. F. 379
  Wm. 277
TOLEDANO, Christoval 161
TOLEFREE, William 113
TOMLINSON, Dr. 243, 296
  Ada V. 285
  Elizabeth Fort 61
  J. J. 261
  Jared 61, 518
  Joanna L. 518
  John 285
  John J. 508
  Reuben 318
  Victoria E. 261
TOMPKINS, Daniel D. 6
  Eber 8
  Francis 149
  Martha 449
  Samuel 113
TONEY, James 209
TONTON, A. 363
TONYBEE, Joseph 306
TOOK, Joseph 100, 184
TOOKE, J. J. 343
  Jas. J. 511, 515

TOOKE (cont.)
  John A. 231
  Joseph 270
  Kittie 270
  Mary Jane 184, 444
  Mary Josephine 515
  Sterling 125
  Susan E. 184
  Thos. B. 423
  William Burt 343
TOOL, Martha 82
TOOLES, Jas. A. 378
TOOMBS, Eva F. 487
  Mary Louisa 470
  R. 505
  Robert 178, 470
  Sallie 505
TOOMEY, Thomas 37
TORBERT, James B. 492
TORCHEN, Colonel 281
TORRANCE, Jane M. 45
  Mansfield 175
  Wm. H. 45, 396
TOUNSLEY, Sarah 113
TOURTELOTT, S. 66
TOWLES, John 182
TOWNS, Gov. 341, 506, 520
  Elizabeth 483
  George W. 341, 498
  Hattie W. 498
  Margaret A. 506
  Mary W. 341
TOWNSEND, Eliza 401
  Maria S. 464
  Wm. M. 505
TOWNSLEY, Samuel A. 508
TOWSON, Nathan 167
TRACEY, Judge 461
  E. D. 114
TRACY, Gen. 293
  Albert H. 249
  Alberta 114
  Ann C. 461
  Caroline 91, 114, 225
  Caroline 91, 114, 225
  Carolos 11
  Edward D. 35, 91, 115, 396, 410, 488
  Eliza 470
  Ellen 505
  Margaret Corinne 91
  P. 498
  Phil 293
  Philemon 225
  Susan C. 35
TRAMMEL, Joel D. 475
TRANUM, Lemuel 422
TRAP, Mrs. Eliza 228
TRAPP, Benjamin 40, 446
  Charles Cekley 40
  Eliza 40
  Elodia B. 446
  Lucia M. 479
TRAVIS, Eldocia R. 45
  John S. 45, 411
TRAWICK, Jas. W. 465
TRAYLER, Edward 266, 466
TRAYLOR, George H. 327
  John 419
  Miss S. Parmer 466
TREADWELL, H. B. 256
  Mary 256
TREZEVANT, Octavus W. 302
TRIBBLE, Minda 475
TRICE, James 221
  Nancy H. 221
  Thomas 488
TRIFLE, James 34
TRIPLETT, Dora 163
TRIPP, A. J. 94
TRIPPE, Anna R. 498
  Jno. B. 484
  Mary A. 137

TRIPPE (cont.)
  Richard A. 137
  Sarah 484
  Sarah A. 473
  Turner H. 137, 498
  William W. 418
TRITT, Ira 168
TROOST, Gerard 125
TROUP, Gov. 223
  George M. 194
TROUTMAN, Barsora 42
  George W. 518
  H. A. 339
  Joanna E. 420
  John F. 120, 450, 475
  Marcellus 462
  Victoria J. 120
TROXELL, Wm. J. 360
TROY, A. 380
TRULOCK, N. R. 451
  Norrel R. 446
TRULUCK, William S. 452
TRUSSELL, C. 433
  Mollie 308
TUCKER, Albert G. 408
  Anna M. 113
  Benjamin 113
  Charles 301
  Eli 211
  Eliza 13
  Elizabeth 66
  Eugenia 522
  G. M. 380
  George R. 231
  Georgia A. 504
  H. H. 444
  Harper 169, 231, 398
  Henry R. 366
  Jas. J. 371
  Joel T. 66, 430
  John A. 113, 220, 237
  John M. 496
  John W. 159
  Julia E. 430
  M. 528
  Mary M. 169
  N. 282, 522
  Nathan 13, 392, 504
  Nathan S. 122
  O. D. 216
  Orin D. 223, 224
  Rebecca Marshall 66
  Thomas Tudor 14
  Wm. L. 458
TUFTS, Francis 117
TUGET, R. 359
TUGGLE, Orry Cox 59
  Peyton Smith 59
  William L. 59
TULLER, W. J. 372
TULLIS, J. M. 371
TUMBLIN, David 366
TUMLIN, Geo. W. 482
  Lewis 482
TUOMEY, Professor 210
TUPPER, C. A. 374
TURNER, Mr. 225
  Mrs. 225
  Rev. Mr. 450
  Charles G. 192
  David M. 359
  E. J. 378
  Edmond 492
  Elisha P. 228
  Farmilla M. 304
  Geo. 379
  Henry 259
  Horton S. 463
  Icy A. 458
  J. B. 378
  J. W. 373
  Jackson P. 167
  John 399

TURNER (cont.)
  John T. B. 399
  John W. 449
  Levi C. 309
  Mary Francis 275, 446
  Menon N. 418
  P. M. 275
  P. McNeal 468
  R. T. 505
  Reuben 25
  S. L. 275
  Samuel 213
  Samuel L. 304
  T. O. 375
  Thomas H. 253
  Thomas M. 403
  W. S. 253, 512
TURNHILL, W. 371
TURPIN, Geo. B. 473
  John A. 202
  W. H., Jr. 470
TURNIPSEED, R. A. 528
TURRENTINE, James 436
TUTTLE, Mary C. 395
TWIGGS, Col. 307
  David 150
  George L. 131, 150
  John 150
  Jno. J. 470
TWILLEY, Lucinda 463
TWITCHELL, -- 347
TWITTY, J. W. 462
TYDINGS, R. M. 500
TYLER, Alfred J. 512
  Caroline Susan 91
  John 233, 286
  Thomas M. 492
  Wm. P. 91
TYNER, Barnard B. 238
  K. 195, 238
  Martha 195
TYSON, A. 463
  Abner 156
  Geo. W. 358
  Job R. 229
  L. D. 334
ULTON, Elizabeth 467
UNDERWOOD, Benj. F. 372
  Jerry 359
  William H. 248
UPCHURCH, B. 363
UPSHAW, J. C. 383
UPSON, Stephen 4
USHER, Catharine 395
  Rob't G. 244
  Robert O. 424
  Sarah A. 137
USSERY, G. G. 380
  J. T. 385
VADEN, James 371
VALENTINE, Mrs. 173
VALLENTINE, Hannah 526
  Jacob Henriques 526
VAN BIBBER, Henry 65
  Louisa Jane 65
VAN BUREN, Lawrence 321
VANCE, E. D. 372
VANCLEAVE, S. M. 364
VANDERSKEE, J. 380
VAN DORN, Gen. 293
VAN EPPS, A. C. 436
VAN GIESEN, E. T. 268
  U. 268, 508
VANMETER, W. H. 380
VANN, C. 358
VAN RENSSALEAR, John J. 15
VAN SOLEN, George L. 336
VAN VALKENBURGH, Harriet L. 503
  Jas. 132, 503
  Mary E. 130, 132, 511
  Sarah F. 467
VANVORST, W. J. 493

VAN WICKE, Dr. 285
VARNADO, Jas. B. 363
VARNER, H. 414
  Mary E. 472
VASON, C. A. 166
  David A. 166, 483
VAUGHAN, Miss E. J. 518
  W. J. 362
VAUGHN, Ann 431
  C. A. 526
  W. W. 378
VEAL, Abigail 486
  Burrel 486
VEALE, G. H. 379
VENABLE, Wm. E. 219
VERDAREE, Rev. Mr. 483
VERDERY, John P. 337
VERDIER, Jean 474
VERDUREE, Rev. Mr. 467
VERNOY, James 170
VICK, John F. 366
  M. G. 245
VICKERS, Henrietta E. 507
  J. F. 362
  James M. 507
  J. W. 364
  R. 383
VICKORY, Wm. 360
VICTORY, Elizabeth 410
VICKS, J. F. 374
VIELSTICH, Henry 230
VIGAL, George 129
  Georgia A. 447
  Lucy 128
VIGNES, A. 364
VINCENT, Isaac S. 282
  M. 378
VINSIN, H. N. 374
VINSON, Elvira 394
  Geo. W. 419
  R. H. 373
VIRGIN, Marcus A. Franklin 93
  Mattie E. 516
  S. D. 53
  Samuel 93
  Samuel S. 55, 411
  Sarah Ann 93
  Thomas 55
VISSAGE, Samuel W. 492
VISSCHER, Betty 318
  Frederick 318
  Kate Easton 318
VONDELKIN, H. 248
WADDEL, Moses 63, 179, 292, 312
WADDELL, James P. 179, 312
WADE, Rev. Mr. 417
  Anna S. 528
  B. F. 444
  Caroline C. 459
  D. F. 456, 471, 473, 474, 475
  D. L. 380
  Daniel F. 223, 459, 466
  Elijah, Jr. 163
  Elizabeth 64, 74, 163
  F. D. 448
  John D. 502
  R. M. 368
  Thomas S. 53
  William S. 74
  William Sutton 52
  Z. B. 74, 433
  Zachariah 64
WADSWORTH, Daniel 101, 121
  Eliza Ann 413
  Elizabeth 101
  Elizabeth McDonald 101
  James 60
  Wm. 70
WAGNER, Amanda B. 426
  Cordelia S. 412

WAGNER (cont.)
  Nicholas 412
WAGNON, Aurella Penice 41
  Charles Vaughan 257
  Francis 469
  George McDuffie 87
  George P. 41, 84, 86, 87, 342
  George R. 517
  Louisa B. 41, 84
  Margaret A. 496
  Mary V. 257
  Sarah Eliza 86
  W. W. 257, 455
  Wiley V. 148
  Wm. Henry Harrison 84
WAGONER, H. F. 385
WAINRIGHT, J. 53
WAKEMAN, James 275
WALCH, J. 370
  Jessie M. 372
WALDEN, O. 369
  Wm. 322
WALDRUSS, Nancy C. 488
WALES, S. A. 233
WALKER, -- 199
  Dr. 481
  Gov. 318
  Mr. 225, 306, 351
  Mrs. 351
  Ann 129
  Antinett 466
  Benjamin 413
  C. H. 298, 483, 489, 492
  Caroline E. 504
  Caroline M. 498
  Charles 134, 449
  Charles H. 468
  Charles S. 206
  D. F. 442
  Daniel 399
  David 466
  David S. 486
  E. M. 503
  Elizabeth 448
  Emma Florence 253
  Emma Lucinda 217
  Fannie C. 483
  Freeman 12
  George 21, 77, 112, 301, 448
  Geo. E. 515
  George T. 114, 129
  H. W. 360
  Henry K. 356
  Isham 369
  J. A. 378
  J. W. 217
  Jackson W. 462
  Jas. W. 499
  Joel 358
  John 257, 359- 432
  John D. 18, 291
  John S. 234
  John W. 445
  Joseph 222
  Laura 492
  Laura M. 254
  Lucinda 217
  M. J. 262
  Maggie R. 496
  Martha Ann 114
  Mary 442
  Mary A. 516
  Mary Ann 253, 413
  Mary Annie Brassey 325
  Mary C. 490
  Nathaniel F. 411
  Petronia 325
  R. C. 484
  R. D. 206
  Richard G. 334

WALKER (cont.)
  Richard S. 75
  Robert 5
  Robert B. 253
  Robert D. 496
  S. W. 480
  Samuel W. 254
  Sarah 497
  Simeon Artemus 129
  T. F. 509
  Miss Tite 491
  Valentine 44
  Virgil H. 466
  W. H. T. 291, 342
  Mrs. W. H. T. 342
  Wm. A. 521
  William E. 467
  Wm. H. 417
  Wm. L. 475
WALL, Clabern 423
  F. M. 370
  James G. 326
  M. N. 384
WALLACE, A. M. 482
  F. B. 378
  Mary Ann 520
  Mary T. 452
  Robt. R. 513
  W. 373
  Wm. 520
  William S. 446
WALLEN, J. C. 370
WALLER, Eliza H. 494
WALLIS, Alberto Fielding 393
  Mary S. 472
  Mortimer R. 26, 391
  Sarah Ann 419
WALLON, Fannie W. 170
WALLOR, J. 384
WALLS, Henry 367
WALSH, Dr. 402
  Ann P. 402
WALSON, E. S. 362
WALSTON, J. B. 301
WALTINGHAM, Jesse 143
WALTON, Anderson 307
  Anthony 306
  Aurelius A. 197
  Mary Isabella 472
WANNAMAKER, Mary Ann 417
WANAMAKER, Sarah Ann 461
WARD, -- 187
  Mrs. 251
  A. H. 512
  C. C. 363
  Chas. A. 233, 499
  Daniel 315
  Geo. T. 251
  Georgia A. 486
  James N. 237
  Jane M. 72
  John 487
  John E. 486
  Leonora 504
  Matt 282
  Nancy V. 415
  P. 373
  R. H. 430
  Sallie 346
  Seth, Dr. 16
  (?), Shadrach 437
  Thos. A. 528
  Thomas B. 409
  W. O. 380
  Wm. 2, 71, 486
WARDLAW, Jane 398
  John 320
WARDLOW, Amanda Louisa 32
  F. H. 490
  George B. 32, 256, 389
  Marita 32
WARDY, J. H. 382

WARE, A. G. 292
  Britton S. 288
  Edward 284
  J. B. 378
  James 110, 185, 199, 398
  Mary 110, 185, 398
  Nicholas 5
  Robert J. 315
  Rowan C. 481
  Sarah McAllum 110
  (?), Shadrach 437
  Thomas 162
WARFIELD, Joe 316
WARKER, L. D. 359
WARNER, Benjamin H. 150
  Benjamin R. 81, 99, 100, 402
  Carolina Capers 100
  Frances A. 443
  Hiram 444
  Joseph 354
  Mary M. 99
  Mary S. 100
  Mary Singletary 99
  Nathan, Col. 13
  Thomas Capers 81
WARNOCK, A. 278
WARR, Abel 384
WARREN, Cornelia 498
  E. 498, 516
  E. A. 494
  E. W. 485, 518, 522, 528
  Eli 464
  Eliza Jane 464
  F. W. 519
  Frederick 315
  J. L. 495
  James F. 490
  Josiah L. 492, 494
  Kittrell 49
  L. P. D. 209, 486
  L. W. 460
  Lott 275, 466
  M. D. L. 378
  Sarah Elizabeth 209
  T. J. 383
  Wm. 418
WARRICK, John 225
WART, Wm. J. 358
WARTHEN, Ann K. 447
  E. M. 154
WASHBURN, Joseph 46
  Mary Ann 46
WASHINGTON, Annie Tefft 242
  Elizabeth 83
  Ellen Clayton 522
  George 330
  George H. 83
  J. H. R. 242, 522
  James H. R. 196
  James William 62
  John A. 281
  L. M. H. 213
  Louisa C. 481
  Mary Ann 196, 242
  Mary Elizabeth 196
  R. B. 62, 411, 412, 460, 481
  Robert B. 425
  Samuel H. 524
  William 53
WATERER, William 453
WATERMAN, Caroline 341
  Joseph 341
WATERS, C. 362
  F. F. 305
  G. W. 380
  H. H. 305
WATHAL, Rev. Mr. 517
WATKINS, E. P. 320

WATKINS (cont.)
  Gilam 67
  Henry P. 423
  Jesse 349
  John D. 422
WATLEY, Ed. J. 365
WATSON, -- 259
  A. M., Dr. 17
  D. C. 475
  Douglas P. 298
  Ellen 427
  Fredonia C. 197
  J. 358
  J. D. 139
  Jacob 122
  Jas. C. 80
  John H. 39
  Jones 259
  Jos. 362
  K. D. 369
  Margaret 516
  Martha F. 420
  Mary F. 412
  Mary Kate 475
  Michael 392, 420
  William C., Col. 15
  Willis M. 122
WATTERS, John C. 162
WATTS, -- 381
  A. S. 176
  Adelaide 209
  Adilade 66
  Albertis H. 467
  Elenora H. 445
  Elizabeth A. T. 416
  John 366
  M. L. 338
  Martha Adeline 392
  Mary H. 395
  Naomi 289
  Parasade H. 403
  S. W. 338
  W. B. 210
  Wm. B. 66, 445
WAUGH, Beverly 224
WAY, Charlton Hines 495
WAYNE, Richard 229
WEATHERSBY, J. F. 469
WEATHERSPOON, W. A. 368
WEAVER, Francis A. D. 396
  J. A. 361
WEBB, -- 173
  Amelia 446
  Benjamin 444, 446
  Calvin 237
  Ewell 199, 447
  G. P. 371
  Isaac 448
  J. B. 70
  J. J. 366
  John 349
  Mrs. John 349
  T. A. 370
  T. M. 378
  William 503
WEBSTER, C. S. 290
WEDGEWORTH, T. P. 371
WEED, Mr. 53
  Carrie A. 526
  E. B. 97, 141, 511
  Edwin B. 158, 450, 526
  Elizabeth A. 229
  H. D. 141
  J. D. 363
  Joseph D. 52, 53
  Nathan 229
  Nathaniel B. 141
  Louisa M. 97, 511
  Thownsend S. 229
  W. W. 380
WEEK, E. B. 194
  Henry M. 194
WEEKS, Chas. U. 166

WEEKS (cont.)
  Jas. S. 24
  Leonard 62
  Robert I. 281
WEEMS, Thomas D. 208
WELCH, Geo. W. 54, 394, 403
  Isaac 20, 395
  J. 374
  James 367
  Mary T. 427
WELDON, J. W. 354
WELLBORN, Alfred 198
  Oliver H. P. 165
WELLINGTON, G. 365
WELLS, B. F. 475
  C. C. 73
  Franklin 281
  Harriet 302
  J. E. 73
  Robert M. 309
  S. A. 385
  Susan 404
  Virginia 73
  Wash 333
WELLSMAN, Mrs. 166
WELMAN, Francis H. 276
WELSMAN, Caroline Matilda 165
  James T. 165, 167, 450
WENTWORTH, Cyrus K. 107, 435
  Charles Edgar 119
  Jane L. 119
WEST, Major 309
  Ann Elizabeth 501
  Charles 184, 444, 449, 471
  Chas. W. 262
  Miss Clifford Stiles 449
  Frederick 455
  Isaac C. 293
  James P. 454
  Luke 164
  Mary E. 444
  Nancy Ann 405
  Pleasant N. 9
  R. S. 380
  Sam 190, 214
  Susan V. 462
  Wm. 326, 472
WESTBROOK, Parsilla C. 409
  T. W. T. 487
WESTCOTT, H. P. 441
WESTMORELAND, Mark 449
WESTON, S. 368
WESTWOOD, Zeb 316
WHALEN, Michael 336
WHALEY, J. H. 461
  John 100
  Rebecca 100
  Thomas 100
WHARTON, Rev. Mr. 527
  Samuel 336
WHATLEY, -- 369
  Amanda J. 426
  Daniel 218
  E. L. 473
  James 201
  J. B. 426
  James G. 259
  Thomas W. 473
WHEAT, -- 335
  A. W. 342
WHEATON, Henry 110
  Isaac T. 392
  Joseph 100
WHEELER, Charles T. 314
  Henry 319
  J. B. 361
  Zibeon B. 505
WHIDBY, Mary E. 522

WHIDBY (cont.)
  Wm. G. 515
WHIDDON, Edwd. 378
WHITAKER, Burton 151
  Henrietta 173
  R. W. 285
  Samuel D. 173
  Van Leonard 173
  Wm. H. 277
WHITE, Lt. and Judge 10
  A. J. 107
  Alfred 491
  C. F. 374
  Charles 356
  Charlotte 391
  D. L. 515
  Edward J. 192
  Elizabeth R. A. 438
  Emma W. 528
  George H. 526
  Henry A. 508
  J. A. 90
  James 133, 383
  Jas. P. 421
  James T. 433
  John F. 277
  John G. 112, 309
  Joseph 5
  Joseph A. 89, 423
  Joseph J. 192
  Lucinda 112
  Mahala 392
  Martha A. 90
  Martha Ann 89
  Peter 438
  R. J. 384
  Reuben H. 107
  Robert 500
  Robert S. 112
  Speight 90
  Susan M. 465
  T. C. 373
  William N. 313
WHITEHEAD, Bennett 476
  Cassandra 123
  Isaac P. 171
  Jas. 378
  Jane A. 476
  Romaldo R. 500
  Sarah L. 123
  W. L. 378
  Z. O. 123
  Zachariah O. 437
WHITEHURST, Charles 50
WHITESIDE, A. Jas. 267
  Jonathan 267
  W. B. 267
WHITESDIES, James A. 511
WHITFIELD, Benjamin 126
WHITFORD, J. F. 225
WHITING, Charles 163
WHITLOCK, Eulalia 396
  Henry 396
WHITLY, Emily 418
WHITMAN, A. C. 370
  George 400
  Hesperia D. 211
  J. T. 211
  Laura J. 503
WHITNEY, Eli 5
WHITTINGTON, E. O. 133, 480
  John W. W. 133
  Martha E. 133
WHITTLE, Conway Fortescue 137
  L. N. 131, 137
  Mrs. L. N. 131, 137
  Lewis N. 104
  Lewis Neale 131
  Narcissa Griffin 104
  Sarah H. 104
WHITTLESEY, A. B. 64

WHITTON, Horace 359
  Moses 362
WHITUS, Robt. 323
WHYTE, Robert A. 165
WICK, Elizabeth 390
WIECKING, Frederick 359
WIGGIN, John I. 309
WIGGINS, Miss Clifford 507
  G. R. 475
  John E. 233
  Lemuel G. R. 435
  Robert D. 97
  Samuel B. 332
  W. A. 509
  Wm. W. 416
WILBON, M. B. 365
WILBRECHT, -- 345
WILBUR, Elbert 339
WILBURN, William F. 457
  William H. 379
WILCHER, Jourdan 217
WILCOX, J. W. 171
  M. K. 374
WILDER, Lucy B. 402
  Martha E. 442
  Nahum 402
  Ward 76
WILDMAN, P. H. 169
WILEY, Dr. 53
  Eugenia 521
  J. B. 411, 521
  John B. 275
  Laird H. 143
  Leroy M. 339
  Mary O. 496
  Sarah Ann 402
  Susan L. 473
WILHELMINA, Lucy 250
WILKERSON, J. M. 371
  R. B. 378
  Thomas 328
WILKES, Henry 453
  J. D. 459
  W. C. 488, 496
  Wm. C. 467, 472, 473, 477, 481, 485, 486, 487, 488, 513, 526
WILKIES, L. 179
WILKIN, Andrew A. 132
  Loiusa 132
WILKINS, Dr. 195
  J. H. 463
  Jos. C. 463
WILKINSON, Allen 203
  Elizabeth 193
  Homer Burton 193
  J. R. 634
  J. T. 512
  J. W. 363
  John Hill 193
  Robert 193
  Robt. T. 192
WILLBANK, James 415
WILLCOX, Clark 464
  Martha 185
  Woodson 185
WILLEPIGUE, Frederick L. 516
WILLET, Benj. F. 157
  Martha M. 485
WILLETT, A. A. 438
  Frances I. 457
  Joseph 81, 126, 450
  Marietta 81
  Marinus, Col. 22
WILLIAMS, -- 159, 321
  Col. 344
  Rev. Mr. 447, 463
  A. J. 446
  Adeline 412
  Agnes 169, 211
  Alfred 328
  Ann R. 283

WILLIAMS (cont.)
  B. F. 285
  Catharine 68, 78, 84, 244
  Catharine Arnett 84
  Charles J. 447
  D. 502
  Dorcas 429
  Drury 98
  E. D. 414, 424
  Elizabeth 444
  Ellen E. 423
  Erasmus Darwin 285
  Fannie Malone 495
  G. E. 380
  G. Jackson 479, 480
  Geo., Jr. 499
  George W. 494
  Gilbert 358
  H. F. 81
  J. D. 453
  J. L. 381
  J. S. 380
  J. W. 62, 381, 383
  James 68, 78, 84, 244, 402
  James Edward 244
  James W. 510
  Jane 334
  Jethro 415
  John 57, 58, 283, 316
  John L. 83, 492
  John M. 1, 3
  Joseph 17
  Joseph B. 259
  Joseph T. 76
  Joshua 340
  Julius C. 510
  Mrs. L. A. 470
  Louisa 53
  Margaret 424
  Martha 465
  Martha T. 144
  Mary A. 506
  Mary B. 83
  Mary E. 472
  Mary Jane 78
  Mary M. 470
  Mathew E. 266
  N. B. 410
  P. J. 495
  Peter J. 162, 297
  Reuben 144, 342, 526
  Reuben S. 382
  S. F. 425
  Sarah C. 396
  Sarah J. 489
  Sarah Mason 68
  T. J. 331
  Thomas G. 169, 463
  W. F. 169, 211
  W. M. 383
  Wiley 390
  William 211, 501
  William T. 16
WILLIAMSON, Alice 518
  Ann H. 397
  Basi., Mrs. 341
  Caroline American 405
  Charles 15, 33, 402, 405
  Chas. H. 441
  E. C. 234
  Elizabeth 395
  Harriet A. R. 421
  J. 381
  J. M. 518
  J. N. 96
  James 452, 484, 486, 523, 525
  James W. 511
  John K. 484
  John N. 212, 213

WILLIAMSON (cont.)
  Lorena 96
  Margaret A. J. 510
  Mary 200
  Mathew 179
  Samuel 179
  Sterling 237
  Sterling C. 70, 200, 420
  Walker 358
  Zachariah 9
WILLIFORD, Sarah A. F. 114
  William S. 114, 225, 226, 438
WILLINGHAM, Elizabeth 442
  James W. 203
  Laura B. 501
WILLIS, A. G., Mrs. 235
  Byrd C. 391
  C. C. 447
  Caroline M. 456
  David 520
  Ellen C. 414
  Harriet 523
  Joel S. 117
  Mary W. 403
  N. Parker 308
  Owen J. 270
  Samuel 151
WILLISFORD, W. S. 455
WILLS, Rev. Dr. 516
  David 516, 517, 518, 520, 521, 522, 524, 525, 526, 528
  Irrena 428
WILLSHIESE, Jas. A. 367
WILLSHIRE, -- 373
WILLSON, Robert 366
WILSON, -- 328
  Dr. 251
  Catharine 393
  Charles 349
  Charley 322
  David 40
  David F. 19, 26
  Edward G. 322
  G. A. 366, 372
  Gabriel 353
  George 1
  Isabelle G. 435
  J. S. 366, 446
  J. W. 470
  James 371
  James H. 88
  Jerome 308
  Joel 482
  John 365
  John S. 443, 482, 500
  John W. 190, 259, 500
  Joseph 12, 20
  Joseph W. 418
  Larkin 414
  Lucy K. 414
  Mary 19
  Nathaniel 435
  Samuel 411
  Sarah E. 462
  Thomas E. 346
  Vincent 375
  William 165
  William S. 410
WIMBERLEY, Frederick D. 64, 407
WIMBERLY, -- 269
  General E. 400
  Abner 231
  Amelia Elizabeth 433
  Ann E. 153
  C. F. 94
  Caroline 243
  Dollie Ann 243
  E. 256

WIMBERLY (cont.)
  E. A. 153, 499
  Elizabeth 418
  Ezekiel 80, 112, 234, 276
  Ezekiel H. 511
  F. D. 516
  George H. 25
  Henry 25
  Henry Clay 94
  Henry E. 112, 448
  Henry S. 243, 407
  James 65, 231, 418
  James B. 393
  John J. 427
  John R. 491, 513
  Joshua R. 403
  Julia 157
  Laura P. M. 422
  Lewis 157, 257
  Martha 400
  Mary 393
  Mary E. 94
  Mary Victoria 234
  Nancy 25
  R. E. 509
  R. R. 517
  Rebecca C. 65
  Robert R. 469
  Wm. 257
WINANS, William 217
WINBUSH, Martha 411
  Thos. A. 515
WINCEY, E. W. 383
WINDER, Wm. H., Gen. 3
WINDSOR, M. M. 438
WING, Laura M. 432
WINGATE, Hattie 527
WINGFIELD, Alfred 442
  Augustin S. 222
  E. H. 499
  Irene 505
  Isaac 312
  John 209
  Junius 495
  M. A. 483
  Marcus A. 286
  Mark A. 287
  Mary Seymour 495
  Montgomery P. 440
WINN, Rev. Mr. 449
  David R. E. 479
  Elizabeth 125, 348
  G. A. 523
  Geo. A. 291
  George Augustus 49
  J. S. 68
  James N. 523
  John 252, 423
  John D. 49, 86, 98
  Julia C. 480
  Ker Boyce 86
  M. M. 68
  Mary M. 86, 98
  Mary W. 49
  Rachel 68
  Richard 125
  Shattie S. 523
  Thomas B. 125, 254
WINSHIP, Anna 471
  Emory 321, 501
  Mrs. Emory 321
  I. 471
  Isaac 167, 189, 260, 394, 478
  Mrs. Isaac 167
  Isaac P. 167
  Jos. 528
  Miss L. B. 478
  Nellie C. 528
WINSLETT, Jas. 364
  Thos. 367
WINSLOW, Chas. 103

WINSLOW (cont.)
  Miron 464
  Nancy 413
WINSTON, Mary 520
WINTERS, Isaac 151
WINTER, Francis 110
  James F. 455
  John G. 303
WISE, A. N. 365
  B. A. 527
  Henry A., Jr. 345
  U. W. 452
WISEMAN, John 311
WISON, Elizabeth 26
WITCHER, -- 222
  Vincent 258
WITHERALL, Robt. A. 366
WITHERS, J. D. 358
  T. J. 380
WITHERSBY, Vincent A. 401
WITTICH, L. L. 468
  Lucius L. 162
WODDARD, Martha 394
WOFFARD, W. B. 229
WOLFE, John W. 201
  Thos. 363
WOMACK, P. P. 364
WOMBLE, E. W. 434
  Mary A. M. 434
WOOD, Antoinette Virginia
    260
  C. C. 380
  Charles V. 520
  D. 383
  E. N. 107
  Frances Augusta 527
  Frances Biddle, Mrs. 2
  George 105, 455
  Granville 99, 260, 432
  Grenville 521
  Henry 303, 451
  J. 213
  J. H. 374
  J. M. 441
  Jacob 101
  James 26, 91, 102
  James Henry 99
  Jesse 462, 494
  John 191, 336
  Lewis B. 156, 465
  M. A. 359
  Matilda E. 60
  Nahum H. 249
  R. A. 108
  R. L. 518
  Rosa Irena 260
  S. G. 515
  Samuel 2
  Thos. 60, 108, 405,
    527
  Thomas Erastus 108
  Thomas G. 444
  Warren D. 481
  Wm. P. 416
WOODALL, Hiram 122
WOODARD, Martha Ann 441
  Mary E. 475
  Stephen 441, 475
WOODBURY, Samuel 460
WOODFORD, R. 361
  W. H. 364
WOODRUFF, Rev. Dr. 473
  Adelia 196
  D. B. 478
  Daniel 196
  George W. S. 196
  James 332
  John E. 277
WOODS, Ellen M. 65
  Joseph 423
WOODSON, Judge 475
  Creed Taylor 208
  Ephata C. 145

WOODSON (cont.)
  John G. 449
  William D. 145, 485
WOODWARD, Mr. 7
  A. L. 487
  A. P. 331
  J. H. 521
  John I. 55, 332, 442,
    492
  Sarah 55
  Thos. S. 257
WOODWORTH, Eleanor 423
WOODY, Jonathan T. 479
WOOLDRIDGE, Thomas F. 192
WOOLFOLD, Thomas J. 482
WOOLFOLK, Thomas 294
WOOTEN, John 415
  Nancy C. 492
WOOTON, John 492
WOOTTEN, Richard 503
WORCESTER, Joseph 302
WORD, J. J. 216
  Laura C. 482
WORK, Joseph 315
WORNUM, Charles P. 243
WORRELL, John R. 431
WORSHAM, Archer 244
  Augustus Franklin 21
  D. G. 157
  Daniel B. 39, 44
  David 305
  David G. 8, 21, 216
  G. A. 384
  J. H. D. 480
  James 216
  John 42
  John Archer 8
  Sarah 44, 216
  Virginia A. 244
WORTHEM, Henry C. 246
WORTHEN, -- 334
WORTHINGTON, Lucinda 518
WORTHY, Anderson 510
  K. L. 502
  Mary 453
  Williamson 410
WRAY, Joseph 379
  Louisa Virginia 391
  T. I. 397
  Thomas I. 391
  Wm. 361
WRIGHT, Mr. and Mrs. A. R.
    241, 457, 501
  Arminius 504, 520
  Arthur P. 514
  C. G. 383
  Carrie H. 241
  David 161, 176
  David L. 296
  E. M. 384
  Edmund Booker 75
  Edward W. 18, 333, 391,
    403
  Elizabeth 18
  Francis M. 208
  J. B. 458
  J. H. 372
  James 127, 246
  James H. 450
  Jessee B. 250
  John 453
  John H. 96
  Julia 250
  Laura 504
  Louisa G. 449
  M. O. 250
  Martha G. 505
  Mary Ann 447, 499
  Mary H. 167, 462
  Nancy 331, 351, 489
  Reuben 224, 272, 462
  Richard Henry 106
  Robert H. 493

WRIGHT (cont.)
  S. S. 447
  Sarah E. 450
  Shady Ann 390
  Silas 106
  U. I. 411
  Miss W. 449
  W. G. 455
  W. M. 380
  W. S., Mrs. 499
  Wm. 179, 382
  William D. 390
WRIGLEY, B. H. 525
  Caroline Plant 137
  Fordyce 100, 137
WRIGLY, F. 85
  Mary Elizabeth 85
WYATT, Rev. Mr. 439
  Frances P. 448
  Wm. 175
  Wm. U. 359
WYCHE, Ainsley H. 445
  Elizabeth Virginia 42
  Jeremiah 42
  Mary Louisa 42
  Rebecca 408
  Rebecca A. S. 429
  Thomas T. 420
WYLEY, W. 373
WYNN, Rev. Mr. 499
  A. M. 508, 510, 511,
    519
  Frances E. A. 399
  J. H. 378
  Mary A. C. 492
  S. M. 494
  W. L. 320
WYNNE, Annie E. 513
YANCEY, James 452
  Wm. L. 294
YARBROUGH, C. C. 374
  James C. 290
  L. 278
  R. F. 361
YATES, Cornelia B. 415
  J. D. 378
  J. H. 360
YEARY, -- 177
YEOMANS, Lampson D. 472
YERBY, Homer 369
YERGER, E. M. 330
YERTZ, Henry 369
YONGE, Henry 36
  Wm. P. 396, 398
YOPP, Jeremish H. 128, 141
  John W. 494
  Margaret S. 128
YOUNG, Rev. Mr. 439
  Ann F. 59
  E. 508
  E. R. 263, 480
  Edward B. 59, 401, 403
  Elizabeth C. 212
  Ellen Louisa 59
  Enos 397, 436, 441,
    464, 469
  G. L. 378
  Guilford D. 226
  Hosea 212
  John 406, 434
  Julia P. 226
  L. F. 363
  Lavinia 434
  M. 366
  Mary P. 406
  Miller A. 366
  Thomas 378
  Wilson Graham 212
  Wm. H. 407
YOUNGBLOOD, Caroline 411
  J. D. 381
ZACHARY, Lewis 258
  Sallie 258

ZACHARY (cont.)
  William T. 448
ZACHRY, Mary E. 120
ZEIGLER, William 181
ZIMMERMAN, G. 74
  Gotlip 77
  Gottleb 428
  R. P. 468
  Winnifred Hamilton 74

www.ingramcontent.com/pod-product-compliance
Lightning Source LLC
Chambersburg PA
CBHW020631300426
44112CB00007B/79